TRACE MODEL
RESEARCH AND MATERIAL
EVIDENCE AUTHENTICATION:
YUAN DYNASTY
UNDERGLAZE
BLUE PORCELAIN

元青花迹型研究与物证鉴定

周勇　周强　著

南方日报出版社
NANFANG DAILY PRESS
中国·广州

图书在版编目（CIP）数据

元青花迹型研究与物证鉴定 / 周勇，周强著. —广州 ： 南方日报出版社，2014.1
ISBN 978-7-5491-0995-1

Ⅰ. ①元… Ⅱ. ①周… ②周… Ⅲ. ①青花瓷（考古）－鉴定－中国－元代 Ⅳ. ①K876.34

中国版本图书馆 CIP 数据核字(2013)第 277470 号

YUANQINGHUA JIXING YANJIU YU WUZHENG JIANDING
元青花迹型研究与物证鉴定 周勇 周强 著

出版发行：南方日报出版社
地　　址：广州市广州大道中 289 号
电　　话：（020）83000502
经　　销：全国新华书店
印　　刷：广东信源彩色印务有限公司
开　　本：889mm×1194mm　1/8
印　　张：64.25
字　　数：800 千字
版　　次：2014 年 1 月第 1 版
印　　次：2014 年 1 月第 1 次印刷
定　　价：200.00 元

投稿热线：（020）83000503　读者热线：（020）83000502

网址：http://www.nfdailypress.com/

陶瓷迹型研究系列丛书

《陶瓷迹型学概论》

2013年出版

《元青花迹型研究与物证鉴定》

2014年出版

《清代康熙瓷器迹型研究与物证鉴定》
《汉代陶瓷迹型研究与物证鉴定》

计划2014年出版

《唐三彩迹型研究与物证鉴定》
《明代永乐、宣德青花迹型研究与物证鉴定》
《宋代越窑瓷器迹型研究与物证鉴定》

计划2015年出版

《宋代耀州窑瓷器迹型研究与物证鉴定》
《明代成化瓷器迹型研究与物证鉴定》

计划2016年出版

《宋代龙泉窑瓷器迹型研究与物证鉴定》
《宋代湖田窑瓷器迹型研究与物证鉴定》

计划2017年出版

《宋代吉州窑瓷器迹型研究与物证鉴定》
《宋代建窑瓷器迹型研究与物证鉴定》

计划2018年出版

The Ceramics Trace Model Study Series

Survey of Ceramics Trace Model Study
Published: 2013

Trace Model Research and Material Evidence Authentication: Yuan Dynasty Underglaze Blue Porcelain
Published: 2014

Trace Model Research and Material Evidence Authentication: Qing Dynasty Kangxi Porcelain
Trace Model Research and Material Evidence Authentication: Han Dynasty Ceramics
Planned Date of Publishing: 2014

Trace Model Research and Material Evidence Authentication: Tang Dynasty Three Color Ceramics
Trace Model Research and Material Evidence Authentication: Ming Dynasty Yongle and Xuande Underglaze Blue Porcelain
Trace Model Research and Material Evidence Authentication: Song Dynasty Yue Kiln Porcelain
Planned Date of Publishing: 2015

Trace Model Research and Material Evidence Authentication: Song Dynasty Yaozhou Kiln Porcelain
Trace Model Research and Material Evidence Authentication: Ming Dynasty Chenghua Porcelain
Planned Date of Publishing: 2016

Trace Model Research and Material Evidence Authentication: Song Dynasty Longquan Kiln Porcelain
Trace Model Research and Material Evidence Authentication: Song Dynasty Hutian Kiln Porcelain
Planned Date of Publishing: 2017

Trace Model Research and Material Evidence Authentication: Song Dynasty Jizhou Kiln Porcelain
Trace Model Research and Material Evidence Authentication: Song Dynasty Jian Kiln Porcelain
Planned Date of Publishing: 2018

陶瓷迹型学系列丛书编辑委员会

作者：

周勇（哲学学士，广州大学艺术系原讲师，现任广州东方博物馆馆长）
周强（化工硕士，高级工程师，曾任职广州市化学工业研究所，现任广州东方博物馆副馆长）

翻译：

周筱慧　马士宁（Matthew Bunney）　戴灵（Debby Bunney）

The Ceramics Trace Model Study Series Editing Committee

Chief Editor:

Hu Guohua, Guangdong Provincial Party Committee Propaganda Department, Assistant Minister of Operations

Vice Editors:

He Suihong, Guangzhou Panyu District Culture, Broadcast, and News Department, Department Head
Feng Songlin, Institute of High Energy Physics – Chinese Academy of Science, Research Fellow
Jiang Jianxin, Jingdezhen Ceramics Archeology Research Institute, Vice Director and Research Fellow
Xiao Qialong, Guangdong Cultural Relic Authentication Station, Station Director and Research Fellow
He Bin, Guangdong Provincial Cultural Relics and Archeology Research Institute, Director and Research Fellow
Liu Chengji, Guangdong Provincial Cultural Relics and Archeology Research Institute, Vice Director and Research Fellow

Chief Consultants:

Xu Shangwu, 10th CPPCC Guangdong Vice Chairman

Consultants:

Qi Shaoguang, Xu Jianlin, Pan Minggao, Li Sui, Su Huiqin

Editing Staff:

Chen Shaoxiang, Zeng Zhaoming, Zhao Guohua, Zhou Yong, Yang Yingzhi, Yin Chunlei, Zhang Haibin, Xiao Hua, Liu Zhiguang, Annabelle Bunney, Matthew Bunney, Zhou Meng, Zhou Qiang, Wen Jianhua, Xu Yiwei, Zheng Yang, Wang Can

Authors:

Zhou Yong, B.A. Philosophy, Former Professor of Aesthetics Guangzhou University, Current Director of Guangzhou Oriental Museum
Zhou Qiang, MA.Chemical Engineering, Senior Engineer, Former Research Fellow at Guangzhou Chemical Industry Research Institute, Current Vice Director of Guangzhou Oriental Museum

Translation:

Annabelle Bunney (Zhou Xiaohui), Matthew Bunney, Debby Bunney

科研项目牵头单位与合作单位
Sponsors and Partners

牵头单位：

广州番禺博物馆
广州东方博物馆
广东省收藏家协会
东方陶瓷迹型物证研究中心

Primary Research Project Sponsors

Guangzhou Panyu Museum
Guangzhou Oriental Museum
Guangdong Collectors Association
The Oriental Ceramic Trace Material Evidence Research Center

合作单位：

景德镇陶瓷考古研究所
中国科学院高能物理研究所
广东省文物鉴定站
广东省文物考古研究所
内蒙古包头博物馆
内蒙古明博草原文化博物馆
鄂尔多斯青铜器博物馆
鄂尔多斯农耕游牧博物馆
台湾鸿禧美术馆
金乐轩
泰国曼谷大学东南亚陶瓷博物馆
印度尼西亚国立博物馆
美国洁蕊堂
美国波士顿艺术博物馆
美国旧金山亚洲艺术博物馆
美国德克萨斯州金贝尔艺术博物馆
广州大学美术与设计学院
华南师范大学公共管理学院
景德镇景德陶瓷集团有限公司

Research Project Partners

Jingdezhen Ceramics Archeology Research Institute
Institute of High Energy Physics – Chinese Academy of Science
Guangdong Cultural Relics Authentication Station
Guangdong Provincial Cultural Relics and Archeology Research Institute
Inner Mongolia Baotou Museum
Inner Mongolia Mingbo Grasslands Culture Museum
Inner Mongolia Ordos Bronze Ware Museum
Inner Mongolia Ordos Farming and Nomadic Museum
The Chang Foundation, Taiwan
Jinlexuan Collection
Southeast Asian Ceramics Museum, Bangkok University
National Museum of Indonesia
Jie Rui Tang Collection
Museum of Fine Arts, Boston
Asian Art Museum of San Francisco
Kimbell Art Museum, Fort Worth
Guangzhou University, School of Art and Design
South China Normal University, School of Public Administration
Jingdezhen Jingde China Group Co., Ltd.

广州番禺博物馆简介
Guangzhou Panyu Museum

广州番禺博物馆坐落于广州市番禺区银平路龟岗东麓，于1997年11月落成开放，是国家二级博物馆，番禺八大美景之一。馆区所占面积240亩，分为多功能陈列大楼、番禺文博园、东汉古墓群景区等三部分。博物馆展览面积8000平方米，内容丰富，形式多样，表现出鲜明的地方特色；番禺文博园占地面积约30亩，古民居、石桥、牌坊、里弄、古炮、传统作坊等遗迹与田园水乡融于一体，景观宜人。墓葬景区规模宏大，并进行原貌展示，独具特色。

广州番禺博物馆是国家文物局首批展示与服务提升项目的试点单位之一。一楼设冼星海纪念馆；二楼设有“番禺古代文明”的3个展厅和多功能临展展厅；三楼设有“馆藏文物”“名家书画”“尹积昌雕塑艺术”等多个展厅，陈列独具匠心，融思想性、知识性、艺术性于一体，充分地展示了番禺灿烂的古代文明和今天的辉煌成就。

Panyu Museum is located in Guangzhou City, Panyu District along the Eastern edge of the Turtle Hill Reserve. Established in November 1997, it is a National Level 2 Museum and one of the '8 Scenic Locales of Panyu'. Sitting on 40 acres, the complex is divided into 3 main sections: The Main Multi-Purpose Building, Cultural Garden, and Han Dynasty Burial Grounds. The Main Building consists of 8000 square meters of Display Area with a multifaceted and abundant array of cultural relics from the local area. The Cultural Garden consists of 4 acres and includes: Ancient Peasant Buildings, Stone Bridge, Relic Cannons, and traditional Chinese garden fixtures.

Panyu Museum is one of the first National Cultural Bureau's experimental projects for an elevated level of Display and Service. The First floor is dedicated for the Memorial Hall for Musical Composer Xian Xinghai, a Chinese hero and musical legend. The second floor is divided in to three 'Panyu Ancient Culture' exhibitions as well as one multi-purpose hall. The third floor is allocated to housing Museum Relics, Special Exhibitions, and the Yi Zhichang Sculpture Hall. This Museum is dedicated to showing the wonderful ancient culture of Panyu as well as the modern accomplishments that this fine area boasts.

广州东方博物馆简介
Guangzhou Oriental Museum

广州东方博物馆占地30亩，总建筑面积约8000平方米，由中国建筑设计研究院设计，建筑群体简而不陋、素而不苍，姿横捭阖、藏风纳气。

博物馆按主题展览、专题展览和临时展览之形式分设七个展厅——钟表铜器厅、百砚厅、艺术品交流厅、两个书画厅、两个陶瓷展厅以及四个展廊。

博物馆未来的发展方向：科学研究、去伪存真，联合国内权威瓷器研究机构和大专院校，深入展开对陶瓷的量化研究，有效保护、传播、传承中华民族的文化薪火！

Guangzhou Oriental Museum, sitting on nearly 5 acres of land, includes a usable construction area of 8000 ㎡. Designed by China Architecture Design and Research Group (CAG), the entire construction is simple but not meek; plain but not dull; and appears open and expansive but still catches the wind.

The museum is comprised of main exhibitions, themed exhibitions, and special exhibitions spread across seven halls: Bronze Ware Hall, Hundred Ink Stone Hall, Collectors Exchange, two Calligraphy and Painting Halls, and two Ceramics Halls; these halls are linked by four Special Exhibition Corridors.

Guangzhou Oriental Museum's main developmental direction is anchored on: Scientific study, the elimination of bogus pieces and holding on to true relics, partnering with international ceramics studies organizations and major universities, thoroughly developing the quantification research of ceramics, and creating a ceramics research group to take in hand, protect, and pass on the torch of Chinese cultural study!

前言

世界上任何一个民族，都有自己的独特文化。这种独特的文化现象，就是这个民族的灵魂。如果一个民族失去了自己的文化，那么，这个民族就不复存在了。

人类许多文化现象，都是多个民族的文化在继承、融合、发展中所表现出的。一个民族只有不断地摒弃民族文化中的糟粕，传承民族优秀文化，吸收外来优秀文化，才能在世界民族之林中彰显民族的生存价值和意义，赢得世界的尊重。

民族的文化，同时也是世界文化的一部分，它当属人类共同文化、共同遗产。各民族文化异而不同，和谐共生。人类只有彼此认同，彼此尊重不同民族的文化，世界才会和谐发展，人类才能和平共处。

瓷器是中华民族的发明与创造，研究瓷器文化是为了更好地传承、弘扬瓷器文化。瓷器文化，是中华民族文明进程中重要的文化现象，它已经成为世界文化的一部分，属于人类的共同文化遗产。这一点，我们在元青花研究的过程中感受尤深。

伊朗国家博物馆是全世界元青花收藏最多的博物馆，当受邀到伊朗国家博物馆研究元青花时，广州东方博物馆美籍研究人员Mr. Bunney怕遇到签证麻烦，伊朗国家博物馆馆长Asadollah Mohammadpour说："没问题，我来帮你办签证。"可见瓷器文化研究已超越了信仰、国界、政治、种族，因为它属于全人类。

美国波士顿美术博物馆的人员也对我们十分友好，他们尽心为我们的科研服务，尽量去满足我们的科研需要。他们对瓷器文化研究，不分彼此，无论国界，境界之高，让人感慨。

在泰国东南亚陶瓷博物馆做研究时，馆长Pariwat Thammapreechakorn 亲自下厨款待我们，令人备感宾至如归。

文物收藏、文物研究本来的要义是解读器物所承载的历史文化信息，了解当时的社会状况，享受文化遗存的物件所带来的审美愉悦。如今，瓷器收藏已经普及到大众，只有鉴别出它们的真假，才能有效解读历史文化信息，真正享受到文物所带来的审美愉悦。如果收藏不分真假，如果只关注文物的经济效益，而不注重提高真假识别能力和文化研究水平，除了经济损失，最终更将挫伤收藏者的文化自信、文化爱心。

如何让更多的人识真断假，将文物真品、文物精品保护传承下去，就是陶瓷迹型科研项目要解决的主要问题。

陶瓷迹型研究属于物证研究。在陶瓷迹型研究的过程中，从来就不缺乏陶瓷迹型的客观物证，缺的是发现迹型物证的眼光。作为一门新学科，创建的过程，艰难而枯燥，但执着的追求和坚定的付出，让我们终有成效。

在科学研究过程中，我们得到了国内外众多博物馆、研究机构的支持与合作，获得了众多专家、学者、友人的帮助和支持，在本书出版之际，一并衷心感谢。

广州番禺博物馆馆长　曾昭明
广州东方博物馆馆长　周　勇
广东省收藏家协会主席　陈少湘

Foreword

Regardless of which nation on earth, all have their own distinct culture; it is the soul of the nation. If this culture is somehow lost, this nation ceases to exist.

All of humankind's various cultures have come about through a phenomenon of inheritance, merging, and development of each nation's culture. It is only through the continual cultural distillation (passing on the nation's beneficial culture, and absorbing benefits from foreign cultures) that a nation can stand out among the forest of other world cultures. Only then can they show the world the value and meaning of their existence, and earn the respect of other nations.

National culture, at the same time, is also just a part of a conglomerated World culture, which is the harmonization of every nation's different cultures. Only as we recognize differences and esteem other national cultures, can we, as humankind, converge towards harmony and peaceful coexistence.

Porcelain was the invention of the Chinese people, and through this research we hope to better pass down and even enhance porcelain culture. Even though porcelain culture is an integral facet in the progression of Chinese civilization, it is already considered more than that; a jointly shared product of mankind, a part of World culture. It was through our research of Yuan Dynasty Underglaze Blue (Blue and White) Porcelain that this fact resonated deeply.

The National Museum of Iran houses arguably one of the most important collections of Yuan Underglaze Blue Porcelain. When Matthew Bunney, a member of our research team from the United States, received an invitation from the National Museum of Iran to go and conduct research, he was apprehensive about the trouble in acquiring a visa for the visit. However, Mr. Asadollah Mohammadpour, the museum's director, assured him: "It's no problem, I will help you get the visa." Through this experience, we could see that porcelain cultural research belongs to all mankind, and is already going beyond religion and borders, extending outside politics and nationality.

The Museum of Fine Arts in Boston, offered us their entire collection for scientific research. When greeted by a staff that was accommodating and friendly, which went above and beyond simple hospitality to make us feel welcome, we deeply felt their heart for furthering the research of porcelain culture.

At Bangkok University's Southeast Asian Ceramics Museum in Thailand, the museum director, Mr. Pariwat Thammapreechakron, displayed amazing kindness by not only receiving us but also offering his own cooking services to give us a heartfelt welcome that we will hold with us.

Originally the priority of cultural relic collection and research was to explain and pass on the cultural information offered by a specific piece in order to enjoy the aesthetics of that culture that were carried through time by that ware. However now, as ceramic collection has already entered in to the realm of the general public, if priority is not shifted towards the authentication of such pieces, then the true beauty and information of past cultures will be lost. If collection is done without authentication, only focusing on economic gain rather than placing value on validation and cultural research; then not only will there be economic losses, but the collectors' trust and love of culture will be damaged.

How to allow more individuals to enter in to authentication and thus encourage the preservation of more genuine and fine wares is the one of the main problems that Ceramics Trace Model Study seeks to resolve.

As this is in fact a type of material evidence research, there has never been a lack of the objective material evidence that ceramic traces offer; only a lack of the collective insights to discover them.

The emergence of any new field of study, although a trailblazing scientific work, is arduous and at times tedious. After several years of perseverance, outcomes have finally come to fruition.

During the course of scientific research, we received the support and cooperation of museums and research institutions both domestically and abroad. Additionally, we received much participation and help from experts, academics, and friends. The research of porcelain culture truly belongs to everyone.

With the publication of this book, we would like to take time to thank all the organizations, colleagues and friends that have followed, supported and participated in this research.

Guangzhou Panyu Museum Director: Zeng Zhaoming

Guangzhou Oriental Museum Director: Zhou Yong

Guangdong Collectors Association Chairman: Chen Shaoxiang

序

在陶瓷迹型研究系列丛书中，《陶瓷迹型学概论》已率先出版。陶瓷迹型学的创立，意味着陶瓷鉴定从目前经验性为主的人证阶段，走向了科学的物证阶段。也就是说，陶瓷鉴定从过去主要讲感觉的经验性人证鉴定，进入到讲证据的科学物证鉴定阶段。

该著作的研究成果——改变了陶瓷鉴定证据。

鉴定不是审美，审美讲的是主观感觉，鉴定要讲客观证据。人类的司法证明，经历了从神证、人证到物证的过程，说明了人类社会的进步与文明。鉴定证据从主观到客观，从陶瓷的标型证据到陶瓷的迹型证据，说明了人类研究事物的方法在不断发展。

该著作的研究成果——改变了陶瓷鉴定的判断性质。

讲感觉的经验性人证得出的鉴定判断在逻辑上是或然性的，即“应该是、可能是”；讲科学的物证得出的鉴定判断在逻辑上是实然性的，即“它就是”或“它就不是”。

该著作的研究成果——改变了陶瓷鉴定的知识传承方法。

千百年来，陶瓷鉴定知识一直都是师傅带徒弟的传承方式。陶瓷迹型学提出了一些新概念，研究了概念之间的关系，总结出一系列规律，建立了新的知识体系，可以通过学制式教育进行传承。

该著作的研究成果——改变了陶瓷鉴定的神秘性。

过去的鉴定是神秘的，经常听到大师说：“有些东西，只可意会，不可言传。”科学的迹型物证鉴定是透明的、客观的，强调眼见为实。人人都可以借助迹型标准图谱，亲自参与比对。迹型物证鉴定有民生效应，易于普及。陶瓷鉴定只有专家没有大师，因为科学不相信大师。

因此，陶瓷迹型学这门学科的建立，发展、优化、升级了传统的陶瓷鉴定方法，开拓了陶瓷鉴定的新领域。

《元青花迹型研究与物证鉴定》一书，是在新创学科——陶瓷迹型学原理的指导下，用于元代青花瓷器物证鉴定实践的工具书，也是一本以元青花显微迹型作为客观物证，证明元青花真伪的学术专著。

Preface

From the Ceramics Trace Model Study Series, the first book *Survey of Ceramics Trace Model Study* has already been published. The emergence of Ceramics Trace Model Study marks the progression of ceramics authentication from an experience-based, human witness period; into a proof-based scientific material evidence period. Which is to say, we are moving ceramics authentication from the former basis of primarily perception and personal experience, into a realm reliant on scientific data and material evidence verification.

This publication marks a change in the authentication evidence system.

Authentication is not looking at aesthetics, aesthetics is based on a subjective feeling, whereas authentication needs objective proof. The progression of the human legal system from divine proof, to human witness, to material evidence is a reflection of society's development and civilization. The move of authentication from subjectivity to objectivity – that is, from ceramic typology to ceramic micro trace evidence – echoes the devleopment of society's method to study things.

This publication marks a change in the nature of authentication judgment:

From a logical standpoint, using personal impressions and experience in authentication judgment can only offer probability: i.e. "it likely is" or "it is quite possible". Whereas scientific material evidence offers authentication judgment with inevitability: i.e. "It is" or "It is not".

This publication marks a change in how authentication knowledge is passed on:

For hundreds of years, authentication knowledge has been propagated through the Master-Apprentice Method. Ceramics Trace Model Study has introduced new concepts, researched the relationships between these concepts, extracted a series of laws, and constructed a new knowledge system that can be propagated through the higher education system.

This publication marks the end of authentication inexplicableness:

In the past, authentication had a certain mystery to it; it was often heard: " This stuff… it's perceptual, hard to explain". Scientific trace model material evidence authentication is transparent, objective, and stresses visual proof. Anyone can utilize the Trace Atlas Model and personally take part in comparison, making it very laymen friendly. This is a huge step forward in the general availability of ceramic authentication, as science does not require a 'master' to determine truth.

Because of this, Ceramics Trace Model Study, as a new scientific field, is the development, improvement, and upgrade of traditional authentication and opens a new realm in ceramic research.

Trace Model Research and Material Evidence Authentication: Yuan Underglaze Blue Porcelain is a new field of study: Under the direction of the Ceramics Trace Model Study principles, this text is the practical and applicable tool used in the authentication of Yuan Dynasty Underglaze Blue Porcelain (here after referred to as YUB). It is also an academic text outlining the research of the microscopic traces and material evidences used in the authentication of YUB.

Translation Note

Translation from any language into another is quite a formidable task, as nuances and expressions are often simply unable to be translated across languages. Translations done word for word can often carry a certain rigidity that hinders the readability of the text, but a rough transliteration can lead to an understatement of the original meaning. Thus, very different translations of the same text can arise; for example: the Bible has roughly 900 different English translations and paraphrases alone.

As this is a very technical text, this is a relatively literal translation of the original Chinese; while still trying to retain a certain amount of interest and readability. There are certain expressions or idioms that were used that have been converted or paralleled into English in a way that should be more understandable for the reader, but still retain the general meaning of what is trying to be expressed. Throughout the text, conformity to international translating standards was adhered to as much as possible, but in some instances an internationally accepted or consistent version of a certain term or word has not yet been established, so translator discretion was used. As an example: The simplified term 元青花 (yuan qing hua) is the Chinese term for Yuan Dynasty Underglaze Blue Porcelain, which has taken on several other names in the West including Yuan Blue and White, Under the Glaze Cobalt-blue, and so forth. This text utilizes the former and often simplifies this as Yuan Underglaze Blue, or just simply YUB.

Additionally, there were also terms or expressions used that have no specific English translation, or the English is simply the pinyin (or Romanized) version of the Chinese word or phrase. These include certain materials or colors used within the Chinese ceramics vocabulary. As an example: 青 qing, which is a color that can take on a whole variety of forms from green, to blue, to clear, and so forth has even offered confusion for Chinese writers throughout history (we will discuss this more within the text). Also, commonly interchangeable terms such as: Silica, Silica Glass, Silicate, Silicone Dioxide, and so forth can all refer to the material with the chemical representation SiO_2, and are similarly used as such according to original context.

In the case of titles of books which do not have the title or text translated into English, the original pinyin is used for reference and ease of use in catalogue recall. Quotes from Chinese texts and sources have been independently translated for this publication, and any other translations that currently do exist, if any, were not consulted. In the case that a quotation in the Chinese text was translated originally from an English source, then the original text was used in the English translation and cited as such. Chinese authors' names utilize Chinese pinyin citation; whereas non-Chinese names retain Western spelling.

Additionally, due to the relatively trail-blazing nature of this research, many new terms and vocabulary were literally invented for the purpose of this text and further research. Specifically, the term 'Ceramics Trace Model Study' had to be invented in both Chinese and English in order to capture the essence of this groundbreaking research. Fortunately, many of the new terms are names and descriptions of appearances and characteristics encountered throughout the use of YUB Trace Model Research and Material Evidence Authentication. As such, English translations have followed as closely to the original Chinese as possible, straying only in an attempt to more vividly represent said characteristics. In the case of newly introduced Chinese terms, all care was taken to retain consistency in translation. However, any discrepancy should be conceded to the original Chinese text.

Similar to the nature of *Trace Model Research and Material Evidence Authentication: Yuan Underglaze Blue Porcelain*, this translation is also open and ongoing. We welcome academics, researchers, and other readers to actively participate in the continual improvement of its content for the betterment of human knowledge! Thank you for your understanding and continued involvement in our research.

Guangzhou Oriental Museum Research Fellow: Zhou Xiaohui
Guangzhou Oriental Museum Deputy Director: Matthew M. Bunney

目 录

CONTENTS

第一章

青花瓷起源与发展

阅读提示：

本章阐述了青花瓷的定义、起源及发展，论述了元代青花瓷器烧制成熟的条件及原因。

主要论述问题：

1. 什么叫青花瓷？
2. 青花瓷起源于哪个朝代？
3. 青花瓷在宋代沉寂的原因是什么？
4. 青花瓷为什么会在元代如此迅速地发展？

Chapter 1

The Origin and Development of Underglaze Blue Porcelain

Text Note:

This chapter covers the definition, emergence, and development of Underglaze Blue Porcelain. It also discusses the prerequisites and conditions that led to the matured firing of Yuan Dynasty Underglaze Blue Porcelain.

第一节
青花瓷定义

千百年来，青花瓷以呈色稳定、明净素雅的艺术魅力受到世界各地人民的广泛喜爱。但什么是青花瓷，它有哪些特点，它的起源和发展如何，又走过了怎样的研究历程，这是探索元青花瓷器迹型之前首先应该了解和关注的。

关于"青花瓷"，人们认识的角度和标准不同，其表述方式也不尽一致：

清代龚轼在他的《陶歌》中对青花瓷称赞有加，他对青花瓷文学性的描述可视为对它的定性表达："白釉青花一火成，花从釉里透分明。可参造化先天妙，无极由来太极生。"[1]

《中国陶瓷史》从较专业的角度给"青花瓷"做了如下定义："'青花'是指用钴料在瓷胎上绘画，然后上透明釉在高温下一次烧成，呈现蓝色花纹的釉下彩瓷器。"[2]

《中国陶瓷》做出的定义则更进一步："'青花瓷'是指一种在瓷胎上用钴料着色，然后施透明釉，以1300℃左右高温一次烧成的釉下彩瓷器。釉下钴料在高温烧成后，呈现出蓝色，习惯上称'青花'"。作者主张釉中彩不属于青花瓷[3]。

故宫博物院研究员李辉柄先生在《青花瓷器鉴定》一书中是这样给"青花"定义的："以钴料在白瓷素胎坯上描绘纹饰，再罩以透明釉，于高温下一次烧成的釉下彩瓷器。"[4]

百度搜索网站面向大众，给青花瓷的定义是："青花瓷，又称白地青花瓷，简称青花，是中国瓷器的主流品种之一，属釉下彩瓷。青花是用含氧化钴的钴矿为原料，在陶瓷坯体上描绘纹饰，再罩上一层透明釉，经高温还原焰一次烧成。钴料烧成后呈蓝色，具有着色力强、发色鲜艳、烧成率高、呈色稳定的特点。"[5]

上述定义从不同角度说明了青花瓷的共性，这些共性结合了如下要素：

第一，青花瓷的胎体为素色生胎；

第二，着色原料为钴料；

第三，着色方法为直接在素色生胎上描绘纹饰；

第四，在绘好的纹饰上罩透明釉；

第五，高温一次烧成。烧成温度在1200℃—1300℃。

这五个要素缺一不可，它涵括了青花瓷器的生产原料及烧制工艺等多个层面。科学的青花瓷定义一定是"五要素"的完整体现。因此，不管定义如何表述，同时满足上述五个要素的瓷器即为青花瓷。

Section 1：

Underglaze Blue Porcelain Defined

For centuries, Underglaze Blue Porcelain has held a steady color; bright and clean, with simple but elegant artistic charm; and has gained the broad-spread favor of individuals throughout the world. But what is Underglaze Blue Porcelain? What are its characteristics? What were its origins and developments? What kind of research advancements has it experienced? These are the questions that must be answered before exploring deeper into Yuan Dynasty Underglaze Blue Porcelain traces.

"Underglaze Blue" has often been seen from different perspectives and with different standards. Even its definition is widely varied depending on the source.

The Qing Dynasty book *Tao Ge* (Ceramics Anthem) by Gong Shi, takes a more literary approach in lauding praises on and further defining Underglaze Blue as such: "White glaze, blue pattern, once fired; with the pattern presenting from within the transparent glaze. Auspicious and innately refined; it is forever the Supreme and Ultimate." [1]

The book *Zhong Guo Tao Ci Shi* (History of Chinese Ceramics) takes a more professional perspective and offers Underglaze Blue Porcelain the following definition: "Underglaze Blue is the application of cobalt blue dye pattern directly to the porcelain body/biscuit. Then a clear glaze is applied, and the piece is completed in one high temperature firing. The result is an under the glaze, blue color pattern porcelain." [2]

The book *Zhong Guo Tao Ci* (Chinese Ceramics) goes one step further: "Underglaze Blue Porcelain points to porcelain with a cobalt blue dying agent on porcelain body/biscuit, then covered with clear glaze, and finally once fired at approximately 1300 ℃. The cobalt blue dye beneath the glaze surface becomes blue during the firing process, thus often called 'underglaze blue'. The writer specifically delineates mid-glaze coloration as not belonging to Underglaze Blue Porcelain [3].

Mr. Li Hui Bing, a researcher at the Palace Museum, writes in his book *Qing Hua Ci Qi Jian Ding* (Underglaze Blue Porcelain Authentication), "A cobalt blue dye pattern applied to a plain white porcelain body/biscuit, covered in transparent glaze, high temperature once fired, to create an under the glaze colored porcelain." [4]

The definition given to the general public by the online search engine, Baidu, states: "Underglaze Blue Porcelain, also called white ground blue pattern porcelain (Underglaze Blue for short), is one of the popular varieties of Chinese ceramics, belonging to under the glaze colored porcelain. Underglaze Blue uses cobalt mineral material with cobalt oxide as its coloring agent applied directly on to a porcelain body/biscuit, covered with a transparent glaze, and is completed in a single high temperature firing. Upon firing, the cobalt dye becomes blue, with high distinction and bright color; it is characterized by a high successful firing rate and stable coloration." [5]

According to the above definitions, the following parameters for Underglaze Blue Porcelain can be attained:

1. Underglaze Blue Porcelain body uses a plain color raw biscuit.

2. The coloring agent is a cobalt dye.

3. The coloring method is the application of the pattern directly on to the raw porcelain biscuit.

4. Transparent glaze is applied over the top of the painted pattern.

5. The firing is a single high temperature firing of approximately 1200-1300 ℃.

These five parameters are essential. They include the raw materials and the technique used in the creation of Underglaze Blue Porcelain. A scientific definition of Underglaze Blue

Porcelain is the conglomeration of these "Five Parameters". As such, regardless of the approach used to describe it, as long as these five parameters are met, a piece can be considered as Underglaze Blue Porcelain.

第二节
青花瓷起源与发展

一、青花瓷起源观点的演变

关于青花瓷的起源，学术界的认识是一个逐步深入的过程。

20世纪20年代以前，流行“青花始于永宣”一说。在英国学者和美国学者对元代青花瓷进行系统研究之前，持这种观点的人占绝大多数，因为文本资料的匮乏和考古实物的稀缺，青花瓷创烧于明代永乐、宣德年间这种认知左右了青花起源的相关研究。

随着20世纪20年代英国学者霍布逊《明代以前的青花瓷》一文的发表，40年代末美国两位学者沙瑞和考克斯首次分离出一批元青花瓷器，到50年代波普出版的对元代青花瓷比对研究的成果，“青花瓷始于元代”说占据了统治地位。

至20世纪70年代，由于扬州唐代青花瓷片的出土研究，青花瓷滥觞于唐代、延续于宋代、成熟在元代的观念逐渐成为主流并为学术界所接受，是谓“青花始于唐”说。

二、青花瓷起源

青花瓷作为陶瓷划时代的品种，自元代成熟以来，历经八百年而不衰，有其产生、发展和成熟的轨迹。但元青花给人们造成的印象是：它一出现就很成熟，好像没有发展的轨迹。不过，成熟的景德镇元青花还是有其孩提时代的，只是在过去很长的时间里，我们没有发现它的成长轨迹罢了。

目前主流观念认为，青花瓷起源于唐代。当今世界上已发现的完整的“唐青花”，让我们能依稀看到青花瓷童年的身影。它们包括：香港大学冯平山博物馆收藏的唐青花白釉蓝彩三足炉、丹麦哥本哈根装饰艺术博物馆收藏的巩县窑白釉蓝彩鱼藻纹罐、美国波士顿艺术博物馆收藏的唐青花碗、瑞典斯德哥尔摩远东古物博物馆收藏的唐青花注子；1998年在印尼海域的一艘唐代“黑石”号沉船上发现了三件完整的唐青花瓷盘。

1975年在扬州师范学院基建的唐代地层中出土的一片青花瓷枕残片，被视为青花瓷始于唐代的“铁证”。中国科学院上海硅酸盐研究所通过光学显微镜观察，使用扫描电子探针测试其胎、釉及青料中的元素分布情况，发现该青花残片使用的是低锰、低铁、低铜的钴料，烧造温度在1170—1210℃之间，属于釉下彩瓷器（这不排除那时也有釉中彩和釉上彩），年代为唐代中晚期[6]。在窑口的判定上，在对唐代巩县窑的物质和技术条件进行了分析后，初步判断唐青花的产地是河南巩县窑[7]。

通过中国科学院上海硅酸盐研究所对扬州师范学院出土的青花瓷片的分析结果我们可以推断：原始青花瓷始于唐代。

经过对唐青花的深入研究得知，唐青花釉料经历了由灰白色、土黄色半透明釉到白色乳浊釉、无色透明釉的变化历程；釉与彩的变化则经历了由初唐的单纯釉上彩过渡到中唐的釉上彩和釉下彩并存，再到晚唐的纯粹釉下彩的发展过程；钴蓝施彩技法经历了洒彩、点彩、条彩到描绘彩的过程，并使其钴蓝彩的形态由抽象图案发展为具象图案[8]。

通过唐青花釉料、钴料、图案、工艺及其相互之间的关系演变，我们能清楚地看到唐青花逐步发展的轨迹。这为青花瓷在元代最终成熟奠定了必要的基础。

三、青花瓷发展受阻

但是，青花瓷经过唐青花的初创期以后，在宋代并没有迅速发展起来，而是走向沉寂了。

有少量文献记述了宋代青花瓷的烧制：

吴仁敬的《中国陶瓷史》称“美丽绝伦之青花，其法起于宋代，何年不能考，但大观、政和时确已有此种作品之制造”[9]。

我国考古学家夏鼐同志也提到：“青花瓷是一种利用氧化钴显色的釉下彩，可能开始于南宋晚期”[10]。

Section 2:

The Origin and Development of Underglaze Blue Porcelain

1. The Development of the Underglaze Blue Porcelain Origin Viewpoint

In regards to the origins of Underglaze Blue Porcelain, academia is in an ongoing process of deeper understanding.

Up until the 1920s, Underglaze Blue was said to have originated during the Yongle and Xuande reign periods of the Ming Dynasty. Before the systematic research of Yuan Dynasty Underglaze Blue Porcelain (hence forth reffered to as YUB) carried out by British and American scholars, majority of academics held this viewpoint. Thus, as there were limited publications and few archeological samples, the predominantly held consensus was that Underglaze Blue originated during roughly the Yongle and Xuande periods of the Ming Dynasty.

In accordance with R. L. Hobson's article in the 20s: *Blue and White Before the Ming Dynasty*; Shinzo Shirae and Warren Cox's work in the 40s: *China's Earliest Blue and White Porcelain* and J. A. Pope's comparative research on YUB, the mainstream viewpoint on Underglaze Blue Porcelain origin shifted to the Yuan Dynasty.

In the 1970s, because of the research on Tang Dynasty Underglaze Blue Porcelain excavated in Yangzhou, an understanding was gained that Underglaze Blue Porcelain actually originated in the Tang Dynasty, lulled during the Song Dynasty, and fully matured during the Yuan Dynasty. Thus, academics now accept that Underglaze Blue Porcelain originated during the Tang Dynasty.

2. The Origin of Underglaze Blue Porcelain

Underglaze Blue Porcelain is an epoch-making variety of ceramics. From its maturity during the Yuan Dynasty, it has enjoyed eight hundred years of unending natural development and maturity. The impression that YUB gives people is that it was mature upon emergence, without any sort of developmental history. However, we now know that mature Jingdezhen YUB had its infancy, we had just, for quite some time, missed the path of its growth.

Currently, popular opinion is that Underglaze Blue Porcelain had its beginnings in the Tang Dynasty. We now have complete pieces of Tang Underglaze Blue, allowing us to catch a glimpse of the "childhood" of Underglaze Blue Porcelain. They include: Hong Kong University Museum, Tang Blue and White Tripod Censor; Museum of Decorative Arts Copenhagen, Tang Blue and White Fish Pattern Jar; Museum of Fine Arts Boston, Tang Blue and White Bowl; Museum of Far Eastern Antiques Stockholm, Tang Blue and White Ewer; and the three complete Tang Blue and White Porcelain plates found at the 'Black Rock' shipwreck in Indonesia in 1998.

In 1975, at Yangzhou Teachers College within the Tang Dynasty excavation site, there was discovered a shard of Underglaze Blue Porcelain. This cemented the view that Underglaze Blue actually started in the Tang Dynasty. The Shanghai Institute of Ceramics, Chinese Academy of Sciences, using microscopic analysis and electron probing technology tested the body, dye and glaze to conclude that said shard used a low Mn, low Fe, low Cu Cobalt dye; was fired at a temperature between 1170-1210℃; is an under the glaze color ware (that period did also have mid-glaze, and over the glaze color wares); and is from the Tang Dynasty [6]. As for determining the kiln site: According to the analysis done on the materials and technological practices of the Tang Dynasty Gong Kiln site, preliminary research indicates that Tang Underglaze Blue originated at the Gong County Kiln in

但从目前出土的宋代青花实物来看，迄今为止，我们能见到的宋代青花瓷只有1957年在浙江龙泉金沙塔塔基和1970年从浙江绍兴环翠塔塔基遗址出土的十余片青花瓷片[11]，还有民间一些缺乏考古信息的器物。

缺少更多实证的宋代青花瓷就像一个叛逆的少年，被人们忽略了。

为什么青花瓷的发展会在宋代拐弯，导致其少年发育缓慢，与陶瓷品种成长轨迹的一般性规律悖逆？答案是，条件不成熟！

事物的发展壮大，需要诸多条件形成的合力推动。一个瓷器新品种的诞生和成熟，尤其是要成为市场主导和大量生产的品种，应该具备如下条件：第一，政治支持；第二，市场需求；第三，材料充分；第四，技术允许。这四个条件以政治支持最为重要，它是其他条件的基础与核心。

从事物发展逻辑上看，既然唐代就出现了以钴料为呈色剂的青花瓷，说明在宋代也应该具备生产青花瓷的材料和技术条件。青花瓷之所以在宋代没有发展，主要是因为不具备最为重要的政治支持条件。

宋代君王好素瓷，喜欢“类玉”的单色釉，厌恶当时只在明器上使用的蓝色颜料。

中原汉文化对玉的崇尚有着渊源的历史。东汉时期，许慎在《说文解字·玉部》中总结了春秋时期延续下来的儒家“玉德”思想，提出了玉之“五德”说，并提出了玉乃“石之美者”，指出玉不仅有“玉德”，而且是“美”的，这使玉逐渐从皇室权贵走向世俗，为之后的瓷器代玉以及瓷器“尚玉”提供了理论前提[12]。

东汉发明的青瓷就曾被喻为“青玉”；越窑青瓷则被陆羽比喻为“越瓷如玉”（陆羽《茶经》）；宋代景德镇青白瓷“颜色比琼玖”（洪迈《容斋随笔》）；宋代词人李清照把宋代所产青白瓷枕称之为“玉枕”（李清照《醉花荫》）；蒋祈称宋代景德镇所产青白瓷为“饶玉”（蒋祈《陶记》）[13]。

宋代君王的这种审美观，注定了宫廷不需要大规模生产青花瓷器进贡君王。正所谓“上有所喜，下必好之”。臣子、百官、文人墨客、黎民百姓及各大窑口都以君王的审美为自己的审美观，因此，柴、汝、官、哥、定等以生产素色瓷为主的窑口在宋代发展迅猛，走向巅峰。

综上所述，宋代君王对瓷器的审美喜好以及其对臣民的影响，使青花瓷在宋代的继续发展缺少了政治支持和市场需求这两个至关重要的条件，就算具备了材料和技术条件，青花瓷的发展在宋代拐弯也成为必然。

四、青花瓷的成熟

成熟的青花瓷器在元代的景德镇大批量生产，而且一露头角就显得十分完美，主要有以下几点原因：

（一）政治支持

1. 统治阶级的审美意识

元代“国俗尚白，以白为吉”[14]，且“祭器尚纯”[15]。

元代祭祀的建筑，都强调有白色的装饰：

“世祖至元七年（公元1270年），以帝师八思巴之言，于大明殿御座上置白伞盖一……为镇伏邪魔护安国刹。自后每岁二月十五日，于大（明）殿启建白伞盖佛事，用诸色仪仗社直，迎引伞盖，周游皇城内外，云与众生祓除不祥，导迎福祉”[16]。

“兴圣殿七间，东西一百尺，深九十七尺……中设扆屏榻，张白盖……覆以白磁瓦。延华阁五间，方七十九二寸，重阿，十字脊白琉璃瓦覆”[17]。

元人尚白还见于当时的文物[18]：

（1）元世祖至元八年（公元1271年）由尼泊尔工艺家阿尼哥设计的喇嘛塔，塔身纯白，至今仍称“白塔”。

（2）元代画家绘制的成吉思汗遗像，其头戴白色皮冠。

（3）在景德镇或元大都出土的元代军事机关使用的印有“枢府”铭文的瓷器几乎全是白色。

（4）故宫博物院收藏的元代皇帝祖宗影堂中的供器——印花八宝龙纹盘，通体洁白。

此外，元代统治阶级对蓝色也情有独钟。蒙古族信奉萨满教的天命论，而天是蓝色的，他们便称自己为蓝色蒙古人。

《蒙古秘史·总译》卷一记载：“当初，元朝的人祖，是天生一个苍色的狼与一个惨白色的鹿相配了，……产生了一个人，名字叫巴塔赤罕。”“苍色”是蓝色，这样“苍狼白鹿”的蓝色和白色成为蒙古人心中的吉祥色。其次，蒙古人作为游牧民族的生活方式也有影响，自古以来，他们生活在辽阔的大草原上，视觉不离蓝天白云[19]。这造就了元人根深蒂固的“崇蓝尚白”的审美意识，构成了

Henan Province [7].

It is through the research carried out on the Yangzhou shards by the Shanghai Institute of Ceramics, Chinese Academy of Sciences that we can put forth that Underglaze Blue originated in the Tang Dynasty.

Upon further research of Tang Dynasty Underglaze Blue, we can assert that the glaze used for Tang Underglaze Blue experienced a transition from greyish-white, to partially transparent soil yellow, to milky white, to finally a clear transparent. Glaze and coloration changes included the early Tang period of all over the glaze color, to the mid Tang period of over and under the glaze coloration both present, to the late Tang period of all under the glaze color ceramics. Cobalt blue dye application experienced a transition from splashing, to dripping, to striping, and finally to pattern painting; and as such a development from abstract shapes to full embodiment patterns [8].

By looking at the evolution of the glazes, dyes, patterns, techniques, and their relationships to one another; we can clearly see the path of maturity upon which Tang Underglaze Blue Porcelain traveled. This progression was the essential foundation upon which the fully ripened Underglaze Blue Porcelain of the Yuan Dynasty was firmly planted.

3. Obstruction of Underglaze Blue Porcelain Development

However, after the early development enjoyed during the Tang Dynasty, Underglaze Blue Porcelain, under the Song Dynasty, didn't experience the same rapid development, but instead came to a stall. In fact, there is very minimal literature even referencing the firing of Song Dynasty Underglaze Blue:

The 1937 copy of Wu Ren Jing's *Zhong Guo Tao Ci Shi* (History of Chinese Ceramics) states: "The beautiful and unsurpassed Blue and White has its origins in the Song Dynasty, what year is unspecifiable, but before the time of Daguan and Zhenghe, this type of production was most assuredly present." [9]

Chinese archeologist, Xia Ding, mentioned: "Underglaze Blue Porcelain is a type of ceramic that uses cobalt oxide color under the glaze, it probably started around the period of the Southern Song Dynasty." [10]

Yet, currently the only samples of Song Dynasty Underglaze Blue are limited to the ten shards found in the 1957 excavation of the Zhejiang, Longquan Jinsha Pagoda foundation and the 1970 excavation Zhejiang, Shaoxing Huancui Pagoda foundation sites [11]. There are also some pieces in private collections, but they lack archeological record.

This lack of more Song Underglaze Blue pieces is like a rebellious youth, most people just overlook it.

Why during the Song Dynasty did Underglaze Blue take such a turn, slow its adolescent development and rebel against the normal course of progression seen in other types of ceramics? The answer is this: The conditions were not yet ripe for maturity.

Any object's developmental expansion needs several factors to join together for its push forward. Any new type of ceramic's emergence and maturity, specifically if it is to become a major market commodity item, should have the following conditions met: Political Support, Market Demand, Abundant Raw Material, and Technical Capability. The most important of these is political support, making it the foundational nucleus of the other three conditions.

From an object development logic standpoint, since the Tang Dynasty already had under the glaze blue coloration, the Song Dynasty should have also had the material and technology necessary. As such, the lack of progression to Underglaze Blue during the Song Dynasty most likely rests in a lack of political support.

The Song monarchy favored simple porcelain, preferring 'jade-like' single color (monochrome) glazes, and abhorred the use of blue on any funerary objects. Central Plain Han culture's advocacy of jade has deep roots in history. *Shuo Wen Jie Zi* (The original Han Dynasty Dictionary) has a section specifically dedicated to the praise of Jade. It is said that the "Jade Virtues" were passed down by Confucian ideology from the Spring and Autumn Period, and talks about the "Five Virtues" of jade as well as lauding it as the "Beauty among stones". This gradually brought jade from within the courts of the royal intellects into the hearts of all the Chinese people. It is specifically these premise principles that directed the

青花瓷的政治支持。

西亚、中东地区国家的伊斯兰民族自八九世纪就开始烧制一种白底蓝彩陶器，数量巨大，品种丰富，装饰方法多样，是最主要的陶瓷产品之一[20]。元蒙政权在征服西亚及中东部分地区后将这种伊斯兰民族特有的陶瓷工艺及原料带进了中原，与中原地区发达的制瓷技术结合，必然能创造出更完美的产品。

2. 政府的鼓励及保护措施

蒙古军队重视有手艺的工匠，在战争中奉行“惟匠得免”的政策[21]。

建立政权后，元王朝实施了一系列措施来保证景德镇瓷业的发展与创新，最典型的就是“从将作院到总管府再到浮梁瓷局，形成了朝廷对景德镇瓷业的垂直管理体制”[22]。

（二）市场需求

元代政府重视海外贸易。至元二十一年（公元1284年），元政府实行“官本船”制度，官方出资投入船只建造，海外贸易获得的利润七成归政府，三成归私人。至治三年（公元1323年）开始，元政府还放开了私人海外贸易[23]。这一系列的鼓励政策，都是为了扩大国家对外的商业活动。

西亚及中东部分地区已经有了对元青花审美喜好的基础，伊斯兰艺术文化与元王朝的蒙古文化及中原汉文化融合，影响了中原区域的审美观念，构成了从西亚到中原甚至到东南亚对青花瓷广泛的市场需求。

（三）材料充分

青花钴料的长期供应和高岭土的开采及应用，满足了青花瓷大量生产的材料支持条件。

陈尧成等人对元代青花瓷所用色料的组分做了较系统的分析研究，同时查阅了各种钴矿的组成及在世界各国的分布资料，并与元代历史相印证，最后得出的结论是：元青花钴料的矿物所在地很可能为中亚、欧洲或与中亚统一地质构造的我国甘肃、新疆地区[24]。当中大部分区域均属元代领土，所以原料提供应该不成问题。

其次，瓷胎制作引进高岭土的方法（即瓷石加高岭土的制胎法，俗称“二元配方”），挽救了景德镇南宋以来制瓷业出现的原料危机，也是元代瓷业生产高度发达的前提。

（四）技术允许

1. 景德镇优质白瓷

景德镇在宋代就以生产优质白瓷及青白瓷出名。这为青花纹饰绘制提供了理想的载体[25]。

在制备瓷胎时于瓷石中加入高岭土能减少变形，从而提高成品率，而且改善了瓷器的物理性能，使景德镇瓷器从低火度的软质瓷（烧成温度约1150℃±20℃）逐渐变成高火度的硬质瓷[26]。

2. 具备工匠人才

一统中原的蒙古统治者采取的保护手工业从业人员的政策，客观上促进了陶瓷生产的南北交融，大批工匠包括西亚工匠及人才涌聚景德镇，为青花瓷生产提供了技术支持和人才准备。

据文献记载，当蒙古军队横扫欧亚时，掠夺的财物人口中明确记载其中有中东地区的陶艺工匠，他们娴熟的青花绘制及烧造技术无疑会贡献在元青花的生产中[27]。

另一方面，刘新园先生通过比较发现元代景德镇窑与磁州窑的装烧工艺、绘画风格高度相似，加上元代景德镇窑址出现磁州窑残器及瓷片，以及文献上记载的大批人口由中原迁往江南的记录等一系列证据，他认为参与烧制元代景德镇青花瓷器的一部分工匠很有可能来自磁州窑[28]。

（五）小结

及至元代，青花瓷作为陶瓷主流品种而大量生产的四个条件全部成熟，元青花在元代惊艳登场就成为顺理成章的事了。

上述满足青花瓷成熟的四个条件中，最核心的还是统治阶层的政治支持。在中国封建社会，政治支持从来就是其他条件的基础与根本。有了政治支持，就会衍生出市场需求，技术与原料的供应就会有保障，这既是青花瓷诞生、发展与成熟的关键，也是中国陶瓷官窑一直超越民窑的根本原因。

成熟的元青花瓷器完全符合青花瓷定义的五个要素，也为之后明代的永宣青花瓷攀上艺术巅峰打下了基础。

上承唐宋，下启明清的元代青花瓷，开辟了由素瓷向彩瓷过渡的新时代，其富丽雄浑、画风豪放、

development of ceramics to become 'Jade-esque' [12].

For example: The ceramics developed under the Eastern Han Dynasty specifically were made to look like green jade; Yue Kiln Qing Porcelain being analogized as "Yue Porcelain As Jade" (Lu Yu's *Chajing*); Song Dynasty white glaze porcelain has "Color comparative to jade" (Hong Mai's *Rong Zhai Sui Bi*); Song Dynasty poet Li Qing Zhao aptly named Song Dynasty white pillows as "Jade Pillows" (*Zui Hua Yin*); and Jiang Qi lauded the Song Dynasty Jingdezhen produced white glaze porcelain as "Rao (Rao stands for Jingdezhen) Jade" (*Tao Ji*) [13].

The aesthetic preferences of the Song court deprived the lubrication needed for large scale Underglaze Blue production. This type of occurrence was referred to as "What delights the court, the masses must enjoy". The kilns used by officials, literati, and the common people had their aesthetics directly impacted by that of the royal family. Because of this; Cai, Ru, Guan, Ge, Ding, and so forth kilns that produced plain monochrome glaze wares enjoy a period of rapid development and reached their peak during the Song Dynasty.

To summarize, the aesthetic preferences of the Song emperors towards their ceramics directly impacted everyone that was under the feudal rule. This robbed Underglaze Blue of the much-needed prerequisites for continued development: Political support and market demand. Even though the materials and technology for production was available, the sharp down turn in Underglaze Blue development during the Song Dynasty was inevitable.

4. The Maturing of Underglaze Blue Porcelain

During the Yuan Dynasty matured Underglaze Blue Porcelain was produced in mass quantities at Jingdezhen, and as soon as it budded it reached near perfection. This is due large in part to the following factors:

A. Political Support

I. Aesthetic Awakening of the Ruling Class

The Yuan Dynasty, ushered in by the Mongols, had a prevailing custom of favoring white; in which white was considered lucky [14], and purity was sought after for all ritualistic wares [15].

Structures used for sacrifices during the Yuan Dynasty had a strict requisite to hold true to white decoration:

"The Seventh Year of the Kublai Khan reign (1270 AD), according to the words of a religious leader named Ba Si Ba, the royal throne within the Ming Temple must be covered with a white awning... for the protection of the nation from evil spirits. From now on, every year on the 25th day of the 2nd month, the white awning of the Ming Temple, adorned with the royal insignia, must be paraded around the city in order to dispel evil spirits and usher in blessings". [16]

"Build seven holy temples, stretching 100 chi (ancient measurement, close to 33cm) from east to west, with a depth of 97 chi... Place a white awning in the temple... use white ceramic tiles...cover the crossing spine with white glazed tiles". [17]

The high esteem held for white by the people of the Yuan Dynasty can also be seen in the following relics from that period: [18]

a. From the 8th year of the Kublai Khan reign (1271 AD), the tower body of the Lama Pagoda designed by Anige, a Nepalese designer, is pure white. It is still referred to today as the 'White Pagoda'.

b. A Yuan Dynasty portrait painting of Genghis Khan, in which he is wearing a white leather crown.

c. The excavated relics from Jingdezhen and the Yuan Dadu (Capital City) that are marked with the characters "Shu Fu" are almost all covered with white glaze.

d. The Eight Treasures and Dragon Impressed Pattern Plate from the Beijing Palace Museum lauded as an altar item specifically made for the Yuan imperial family, is pure white.

Aside from white, the ruling class of the Yuan Dynasty also held a special affinity towards the color blue. Mongolians originally believed in the shamanistic mandate of heaven, and as heaven is blue, they often referred to themselves as the blue Mongols.

In the first section of The Secret History of the Mongols it is recoded: "In the beginning, the father of the Yuan Dynasty was born to an ashen wolf and pale deer... They

层次繁多的绘画风格尽管与前代王朝的审美情趣大相径庭，但充分说明了中华民族文化，就是在不断地与外来文化元素交融渗透中发展壮大的，元青花的成熟不仅使其成为中国陶瓷史上的一朵奇葩，同时也使其生产地景德镇一跃成为中世纪世界制瓷业的中心。

gave birth to a man named Batachi-qan." This 'ashen' color was in fact referred to as blue, and in this way the "Ashen Wolf, Pale Deer" combination became the blue and white symbolism that was sealed within the hearts of the Mongolian people. In addition, its origins are rooted in the lifestyles of pastoral peoples. Since ancient times, they have made their homes amongst the vast grasslands of central Asia; their visual senses unable to escape the blue sky and white clouds of the plains [19]. This deeply ingrained within the Mongolian sense of beauty a "worship blue and esteem white" consciousness. This aesthetic attraction bolstered the political support gained by Underglaze Blue Porcelain.

In the 8th and 9th centuries, the Islamic cultures of Western Asia and the Middle East had already begun firing mass quantities of all different sorts of white ground and blue pattern potteries. These blue and white wares, of innumerable pattern styles, were one of the main ceramic outputs during that period [20]. After the Mongolian hoards had conquered most of Central Asia and the Middle East, they brought with them back towards China the techniques and materials used in firing these blue and white ceramic wares. They infused these techniques and materials into the already well-established ceramics industry within China, inevitably creating an even more perfect product.

II. Government Encouragement and Protective Measures

The Mongolian armies highly valued skilled artisans and craftsmen, and in wartimes pursued a policy of "Only spare the craftsmen". [21]

After establishing their political state, the Yuan imperial court put into effect a series of policies meant to ensure the development and creativity of the porcelain industry in Jingdezhen. This is best seen in the vertical management system put in place by imperial court to effectively run the porcelain industry in Jingdezhen [22].

B. Market Demand

The Yuan government highly regarded international trade. In the 21st year of Kublai Khan (1284 AD), the Yuan government implemented the "Official Use" ship building policy. The government would put forth the capital to build the ships; of the profits gained from international trade, 70% belonged to the government, and the private operator kept the remaining 30%. Then, beginning in the 3rd year of Zhizhi (1323 AD), the Yuan government completely deregulated the shipping industry [23]. These series of supportive policies all helped to improve the livelihood of the country's international production.

Based upon the attraction that Western Asia and Middle East countries and territories had already established towards the artistic qualities of YUB, there was a conglomeration of Islamic, Mongolian, and Chinese cultures that impacted and influenced the spread of Chinese aesthetics; thus creating a market demand for YUB that stretched from far Western Asia into China Southeast Asia, and beyond.

C. Abundance of Raw Materials

Both the long term supply of Underglaze Blue cobalt dye and the discovery and associated use of Kaolin clay thoroughly met the need of abundance of raw materials for the large scale production of YUB.

According to the systematic research and analysis of the coloring agent used in YUB done by Chen Yao Cheng et al, as well as detailed inspection of multiple cobalt ore mines and information from around the globe, in accordance with Yuan Dynasty historical records; the consensus is: The ore used in YUB cobalt dye would most likely be found in Central Asia, Europe, or in areas of similar geological composition such as China's Gansu and Xinjiang Provinces [24]. The majority of these areas were under the governance of the Yuan Dynasty; and as such the availability of cobalt dye supplies was most likely not an issue of concern.

D. Technical Capability

I. High-Grade Porcelain of Jingdezhen

During the Song Dynasty, Jingdezhen had already made a name for itself as a premier producer of high-grade white and bluish-white porcelain. This offered the perfect body on which Underglaze Blue could be founded [25].

The addition of Kaolin clay during the preparation process, which lowered the likelihood of a piece changing shape when fired, increased the percentage of successfully fired pieces, and improved the physical characteristics of the porcelain. It helped to gradually progress the porcelain fired at Jingdezhen from a low-temperature soft-paste clay (firing temperature around 1150℃) to a high-temperature hard-paste porcelain [26].

II. Talented Craftsmen

Once the Mongolian rulers had unified China and established policies that favored artisans and craftsmen, there was an objectively supported mingling of Northern and Southern craftsmen. Huge numbers of artisans (including West Asian artisans) made their way to Jingdezhen, offering the technical support and talented hands needed to carry out the production of Underglaze Blue Porcelain.

Records show that during the Mongolian sweep of Eurasia, amongst the plunder accumulated, there were clearly recorded to be many ceramic artisans and craftsmen from the Middle East. Their adept blue and white design work as well as firing techniques undoubtedly impacted the production of YUB [27].

On the other hand, research done by Liu Xin Yuan on the similarities between the firing techniques and patterns of Jingdezhen and Cizhou Kiln porcelain, the presence of Cizhou Kiln shards at Jingdezhen, and records that indicate that there was a mass migration of artisans from the central plains down to the Southern China region during the time of early Yuan Dynasty all indicate that it is highly likely that there were also artisans present in Jingdezhen that brought their craft with them from the Cizhou Kiln [28].

E. Summary

As it was during the Yuan Dynasty that the four criteria for commoditization and large-scale production were finally met, it is only logical that during this time Underglaze Blue Porcelain flourished abundantly.

During the maturity of the aforementioned criteria, the most important was still the political support given by the ruling class. In Chinese feudalist society, political support has always been the footing on which the other criteria can be founded. It is through government interest that the market demand and technology as well as raw material supply can achieve sustained levels. This is the central factor in the emergence, development, and maturity of Underglaze Blue, as well as the underlying factor that has kept official kilns vastly ahead of common kilns in ceramic production.

Mature YUB fully meets the five parameters that define Underglaze Blue Porcelain, and is the essential foundation on which the following Yongle and Xuande Underglaze Blue of the Ming Dynasty was firmly planted.

With the Tang and Song before and the Ming and Qing Dynasties after, YUB marked the beginning of a new age in porcelain making marked by a move from plain colored monochrome into the epoch of colorful porcelain. Its beauty is powerful, adornments forceful and free, with an abundance of layers. The painting style ignores the restrictive nature dictated by the reserved aesthetics of its predecessors, but still fully expresses that Chinese culture is developed through absorbing and adapting foreign elements into its story of maturation; the fully developed YUB stands out as an exotic bloom amongst the history of Chinese ceramics. At the same time, its production helped to establish Jingdezhen as the global center of the ceramics industry and foremost producer of porcelain throughout the recent centuries.

第二章

元青花生产情况及研究意义

阅读提示：

本章讨论了元青花的生产与流向，并阐明了研究元青花的意义。

主要论述问题：

1. 青花瓷在元代的生产规模如何？
2. 元青花流向了哪些国家和地区？
3. 研究元青花的意义是什么？

Chapter 2

The Production of Yuan Underglaze Blue and the Significance of Yuan Underglaze Blue Research

Text Note:

This chapter discusses the production and flow of Yuan Underglaze Blue, and expounds upon the significance of Yuan Underglaze Blue research.

第一节
元青花的生产

要全面认识元青花，需要了解它的生产状况。要了解元青花的生产状况，就必须搞清楚它的生产年代、生产阶段、生产规模、需求对象等诸多要素。这些要素以时间为纵轴，空间为横轴，形成了元青花生产与需求的坐标，凭借这个坐标，我们对元青花将会有更清晰的认识。

一、元青花的始烧年代

至元十五年（公元1278年），忽必烈在景德镇设置浮梁瓷局。至正十二年（公元1352年），元政权在浮梁地区势力瓦解，浮梁瓷局关闭。浮梁瓷局在元代统治期间领导组织景德镇的瓷业生产总共74年[29]。

学术界之前广泛认可的最早期的“元代延祐时期”的青花瓷，以在湖北黄梅县西池窑厂出土的“延祐六年（公元1319年）”牡丹纹塔式盖瓶为代表。但现已被证实其并非是使用钴料上彩的瓷器，而是以铁氧化物上彩，属釉下褐（黑）彩产品[30]。所以元青花生产不晚于1319年的说法并不可靠。

刘新园先生根据清・乾隆四十八年（公元1783年）《浮梁县志・食货・户口》中的浮梁县的人口记载得出了这样结论：

明洪武二十四年（公元1391年），即朱元璋灭元以后二十四年，由于残酷的战争，浮梁人口与至元二十七年（公元1290年）相比减少了八万余人；而至元二十七年，即蒙古大军灭南宋后的第十一个年头，浮梁人口与宋咸淳五年（公元1269年）相比，不但没有减少，反而增加了五万五千余人，这样的增长速度，与当时元代政府北人南迁、北匠南调的政策有很大关系。由于瓷局官匠大增，青花瓷很有可能创烧于这段时期[31]。

我们也可以在已发现的元青花瓷器的相关信息中推断元青花创烧的年代：

被认为大约是在元至顺二年（公元1331年）遇难的南韩新安沉船，有一万余件出水文物，主要为龙泉系青瓷（占总数近60%），其次为景德镇系青白瓷、白瓷（近30%），还包括少量景德镇出产的釉下黑彩瓷器，说明新安沉船上的中国瓷器数量之多，品种之全面。然而船上并未发现典型的元代青花瓷器，说明14世纪30年代元青花瓷器还未在海外流行[32]。

2009年景德镇红卫影院出土了一批元青花瓷器标本。从考古地层学等角度分析，这些标本的时代可以追溯到1323—1336年[33]。

2011年在西安曲江发掘的保存完好的张达夫及其夫人墓中（墓志铭记录为至元五年，也就是公元1339年）发现的仅有的一件青花人物图匜证明，在14世纪30年代景德镇已经开始生产青花瓷器了[34]。

由此可推断，元代很有可能在14世纪20至30年代（不迟于公元1339年）开始烧制青花瓷器。

二、元青花的生产阶段

由于实施了诸如“保护匠人”、设置浮梁瓷局等系列措施，元代的瓷器生产如火如荼，使之成为中国陶瓷史上承前启后的重要时期。

如果我们不讨论其他元代青花的生产状况（如云南玉溪窑、浙江江山窑等），只以景德镇窑作为研究的重点，那么，在时间的纵轴上，国祚不到百年的元代，官方在青花瓷的生产阶段上主要有两段时期：元蒙统治阶段和起义军占领阶段。

（一）元蒙统治阶段

元蒙统治下的青花瓷生产阶段，是从青花瓷始烧年代（大约在14世纪20或30年代）到元至正十二年（公元1352年）。

在此阶段，青花瓷的生产主要以元蒙统治阶级的喜好及需要为主，纹饰风格深受蒙古文化及伊斯兰文化影响。

Section 1:

Yuan Underglaze Blue Production

To fully understand YUB, it is important to first understand its production conditions. In order to grasp these conditions it is necessary to first clarify the following key elements: Production period, production stages, scale of production, and target demand. These key elements, based upon axis of time and space, become the coordinates of YUB production and demand. Founded on this chart of knowledge, we can gain a more distinct understanding of YUB.

1. The Beginning of YUB Firing

In the 15th year of Kublai Khan's reign (1278 AD), Kublai established the Fuliang Porcelain Bureau in Jingdezhen. In the 12th year of the Zhizheng reign (1352 AD), the Yuan government lost control of the Fuliang area, and the porcelain bureau came to a halt. All said and done, the Fuliang Porcelain Bureau, under the direction of the Yuan rule, oversaw the porcelain industry for 74 years [29].

In the past, academia had widely accepted that the earliest representation of YUB was a Pagoda Style Lidded Vase with Peony Pattern, marked in the 6th year of Yanyou reign (1319 AD), that was excavated in Hubei's Huangmei County Xichi Kiln. However, research has now shown that this piece did not in fact use cobalt dye as its coloring agent, but rather iron oxide, and as such belongs to the underglaze brown (black) production [30].

Mr. Liu Xin Yuan has since then, by looking through the Fuliang County Public Record written in the 48th year of the Qing Dynasty Qianlong reign, put forth the following observation:

Due to rigorous warring, the population of Fuliang county in the 24th year of the Ming Hongwu reign (1391 AD, 24 years after the fall of the Yuan Dynasty) was eighty-thousand less than during the 27th year of Kublai Khan's reign (1290 AD). Additionally, the population during the 27th year of Kublai Khan (11 years after the fall of the Song Dynasty) was in fact fifty-five thousand higher, not lower, than that of the Song Dynasty Xianchun Reign (1269 AD) . This is in part due to the Northern tradesmen moving south in concurrence to the Yuan Dynasty North to South migration policy. Due to the large influx to the Official Porcelain Bureau resources, it is highly likely that the creation of YUB occurred during this time [31].

Utilizing the evidence offered us by the discovery of YUB pieces, we can also put forth certain assertions about YUB induction:

According to the findings of the South Korean Xin'an shipwreck, pinned at about the 2nd year of the Zhishun reign (1331 AD), with over ten thousand artifacts found (60% Longquan Kiln celadon glaze, 30% Jingdezhen bluish-white and white glaze, and the remainder Jingdezhen underglaze brown) we can see that there was a large scale and variety of Chinese ceramics at that time. Additionally, the fact that on the entire ship there was found to be no YUB, we can assert that up until the 1330s YUB had not yet caught on in the overseas markets [32].

In the 2009 excavation of the Jingdezhen Hongwei Theater, a portion of YUB samples was unearthed. Through archeological layer research, these samples can be placed at approximately 1323-1336 AD [33].

In 2011 at Qujiang in Xi'an, the excavation of Zhang Dafu and his wife's tomb (tomb dated to 1339 AD) produced record of a YUB pouring vessel with figures. This lets us know that Jingdezhen had started producing YUB in the 1330s at the latest [34].

Because of this finding, we can assert that there is a high probability that the firing of YUB started during 20s or early

上文提及的在景德镇红卫影院出土的一批元青花瓷器标本，经上海博物馆文物保护与考古科学实验室测试，其青花料中铁的含量较高而锰的含量较低，属于典型的进口钴料[35]。这其中有七件瓷器上有用青花书写的波斯文字。从文字书写的流畅程度、书法水准及使用的工具可推断，这些器物的文字都出自波斯陶工之手。这证明元代政府与西亚在早期的元青花瓷器制作上有着紧密的合作关系[36]。

乾隆四十八年（公元1783年）《浮梁县志·陶政》谓："元更景德镇税课局监镇为提领。泰定后本路总管监陶，皆有命则供，否则止"。据此推测，原属将作院管辖的浮梁瓷局，至1324年后，已属本路——饶州路管辖(当时总管为段廷硅，秩正三品)[37]。这说明政府对景德镇瓷器生产的重视。

"有命则供，否则止"说明，过去只能生产贡品的官匠，至此时亦可生产商品了。国内外出土与传世的绝大多数精美的青花瓷器，极有可能为1324年之后的官匠们在朝廷无命的情况下所制。英国大维德中国艺术基金会藏的"至正十一年"(公元1351年)铭青花云龙纹象耳瓶，应该就是元代景德镇出品的青花瓷器。

（二）起义军占领阶段

浮梁瓷局所在地区在至正十二年（公元1352年）以前由元代政府统治。至正十二年三月起一直属于元政府与起义军之间的拉锯地区，战火频繁。到至正二十一年以后完全被朱元璋军队占有[38]。因此将至正十二年（公元1352年）到明代建国（公元1368年）之前这段时间的青花瓷生产称为起义军占领阶段。

这个阶段的青花瓷出现了纹饰风格的转变，增加了戏曲人物故事题材，如三顾茅庐、尉迟恭单鞭救主、昭君出塞等。这些历史人物故事宣扬了华夏民族的忠君忠义思想。元青花上戏曲人物故事图的出现，体现了起义军统治阶级的政治意识和审美观的改变，以及对本民族文化属性的强化。

元蒙政权是少数民族政权，加上伊斯兰宗教文化不崇尚瓷器上出现人物，所以照常理推测，元蒙统治阶级应该不会将此类题材绘在瓷器上。在起义军刚刚夺取政权，政权未稳的情况下宣传民族的忠君忠义思想，借古喻今，在这样关键的时期以此来引导臣民，有助于稳固政权。所以，这类纹饰题材的青花瓷应该是起义军政权初期的作品[39]。

至正二十一年，朱元璋军队攻克浮梁县，景德镇成为朱元璋的领地。朱元璋随即委派李庸任浮梁县知，"辟田野，通贸易"，采取一系列措施抓紧恢复窑业生产，此时完全有条件生产高品质的青花瓷。所以目前我们见到的具有中原汉文化忠义故事情节的人物图青花瓷，应该是至正十二年，尤其是至正二十一年朱元璋势力控制住了景德镇后烧制的[40]。

我们也可以从发掘的实物中来推断。首先，在明初汉人及民间出土的瓷器中，都发现了绘有戏曲人物故事图的青花瓷，如明初汉人将领沐英墓葬中出土的青花萧何追韩信图梅瓶，以及甘肃武威凉州区南大街民间窖藏出土的青花昭君出塞图高足杯。

其次，与元代官方有往来的国家及地区的收藏以及主要遗址、墓葬、窖藏、沉船出土、出水的元青花中均不见戏曲人物故事图瓷器。如伊朗国家博物馆馆藏、土耳其托普卡比宫博物馆馆藏、印度德里图格鲁克宫殿遗址出土、红海沉船出水、元大都遗址、新疆伊犁哈萨克自治州霍城县古城遗址出土等的元青花瓷器。经统计后发现，没有一件青花瓷绘有戏曲人物故事图[41]。

现在看到的元青花存在题材反差强烈的现象，就是因为其经历了不同民族统治下的生产过程，这些过程体现了不同民族之间的文化差异和相互交融，正是这种差异和交融使元青花的纹饰具有强烈的时代风貌和特色。

三、元青花的生产规模

在青花瓷的生产数量上，这一时期虽然没有确凿的数据，但我们可从三个方面来研究认识元青花的生产规模。

（一）从宋、元瓷税比较看

在宋代，景德镇一年上缴国家的税收，据《宋会要辑稿》载："景德镇，三千三百三十七贯九百五十文"。而这相当于宋代定窑的"曲阳县，八百三十一贯九十一文"的四倍多[42]。定窑是当时中国北方陶瓷生产的名窑，宋代五大窑口之一，由此可衡量出景德镇当时的生产能力和生产规模。

进入元代，根据《元典章校补》的记载："额办课税处

30s of the 14th century, and no later than 1339 AD.

2. YUB Production Stages

Because of the importance placed on the artisans and the creation of the Fuliang Porcelain Bureau, the Yuan Dynasty ceramics industry spread like wildfire, and became an important turning point in Chinese Ceramics History.

If for a moment we put aside the other kilns that fired YUB, i.e. Yunnan Yuxi Kiln, Zhejiang Jiangshan Kiln, and so forth; but instead focus our research directly on the production timeline of YUB solely at Jingdezhen, then we can see that there is less than a century time span of production, and this can be broken into two main periods of kiln activity: YUB Production Under the Monglolian Rule and YUB Production During the Transitional Period.

A. YUB Production Under the Mongolian Rule

The period of YUB production under the Mongolian Rule lasted from the emergence of YUB (appx 1320s or 1330s) until the 12th year of the Zhizheng reign (1352 AD).

During this period, the production of YUB was greatly impacted by the aesthetic and utility preferences of the Mongolian ruling class. The patterns and styles were predominantly dictated by the culture and tastes of the Mongolian and Islamic rulers of the day.

The aforementioned YUB samples gathered at the Hongwei Theater location (dated from around 1323-1326 AD) have gone through testing at the Relic Restoration and Archeological Research Center at the Shanghai Museum. The blue dye used in these pieces was found to have a relatively high amount of iron and relatively low amount of manganese, making it characteristic of imported cobalt dye [35]. Of these samples, seven contain Persian script written in under the glaze blue. According to the fluency, style, and tools used to write this script, it is evident that it was a Persian craftsman who penned them. This goes to further prove that in the very earliest stages of YUB production, the Yuan government and Western Asia had a very close cooperative relationship [36].

According to the Fuliang County Public Record written during the 48th year of the Qing Dynasty Qianlong reign: During the Taiding reign (1276—1328 AD) the rank of the Fuliang Porcelain Bureau Director was elevated from the level of local official, to the level of provincial authority. This shows the added importance that was placed on the porcelain industry [37].

Additionally mentioned in the record: A decree was given from the bureau to the artisans of Jingdezhen to only fire according to the order of the bureau. Of the domestic and foreign excavated samples and handed down pieces of YUB masterpieces, it is most probable that they were all made under this official artisan policy instated in 1324. The David Vases (Marked as made in the 11th year of the Zhizheng reign 1351 AD) are very likely to have been made in Jingdezhen.

B. YUB Production During the Tansitional Period

The area directed by the Fuliang Porcelain Bureau was under the control of the Yuan government until the 12th year of the Zhizheng reign (1352 AD). From the 3rd month of the 12th year onward, it became an area of seesaw struggle between the Yuan government and the uprising armies, often touched by the flames of war all the way until the 21st year of the Zhizheng reign (1361 AD). Then, it became the sole tenure of Zhu Yuan Zhang's (established the Ming Dynasty as the Hongwu Emperor) military forces [38]. Because of this, the period from Zhizheng year 12 until the establishment of the Ming Dynasty (1368 AD) has become known as the transitional period of YUB production.

It was during this period that the YUB pattern stylization began to change, and the addition of images from classical Chinese dramas began to take stage; i.e. San Gu Mao Lu (Three visits to the thatched cottage) and so forth. The occurrence of these historical images invoked notions of the monarchal ideologies of loyalty and integrity of the Chinese people. They also reflected the adjustment in political policy and aesthetics that came about under the direction of revolutionary armies, and strengthened the cultural influence of the people (the Han Chinese).

所：五百锭以上……浮梁县景德镇”。[43]换算后可知，景德镇一年要上缴国家的税额至少在两万五千贯。由此可见，元代上缴给国家的瓷业税收是宋代景德镇的七倍多。

由元末明初著名学者叶子奇对元朝“……轻刑薄赋、兵革罕用、生者有养、死者有葬……”[44]的评论可知，元代入主中原成为新的统治阶层，与前朝末代统治一般采用的高税制不同，元蒙统治采用的是低税制，对手工业、商业等采取鼓励政策。即使如此，景德镇瓷业年缴税依然高出宋代如此之多，元代景德镇生产瓷器的规模可见一斑。

（二）从国内及世界各地元青花出土范围看

在全国范围内，目前至少在16个省、市、自治区内发现了元青花[45]。

在全球范围内，目前已发现元青花的国家及地区包括：日本、韩国、柬埔寨、马来西亚、印尼、文莱、菲律宾、泰国、印度、巴林、阿联酋、伊朗、土耳其、马其顿、叙利亚、黎巴嫩、蒙古、乌兹别克斯坦、埃及、苏丹、阿曼、也门、红海、肯尼亚、坦桑尼亚等[46]。

出土范围广，意味着输出多；输出多，代表了产量多；而产量多，则生产规模大矣。

（三）从历史记载看

我们还可从古人的记载描述中一窥当时的生产、销售盛况：“窑火既歇，商争取售，而上者择焉，谓之捡窑。交易之际，牙侩主之……运器入河，肩夫执券，次第件具，以凭商筹，谓之非子。”[47]

此外，在浮梁瓷局初成立时的瓷局大使，秩仅九品，只能管匠户一百。但到公元1295年以后，就可管辖四百余匠户了。这个数字约为元初的四倍，也超过了明、清御器厂官匠“三百余”的规模[48]。

四、元青花的产品流向

研究青花瓷的产品流向，必须知道青花瓷的烧制用途。从国内及世界各地发现的元青花使用性质来看，其烧制用途主要有：

1. 封赏的载体，用它作为赏品赏给皇亲国戚、文武百官及外国使节等；

2. 外贸的交流，用它赚取钱财和交易其他物资；

3. 供器或明器。

与烧制用途对应，几十年来在国内外出土的元青花整器、残器及瓷片等都反映出元青花产品的三大流向。

（一）产品流向国内

在全国范围内，目前至少在16个省、市、自治区通过墓葬出土、窖藏出土、遗址出土或沉船、水域遗迹等方式发现了元青花[49]。

元代墓葬资料不是很多，其中出土元青花的更少。还有些明初墓葬中也出土有元青花。下面列举一些国内发现元青花瓷器的基本情况：

江苏省丹徒县共出土窖藏瓷器26件，其中有元青花高足杯6件[50]。

江苏金坛县一处元代窖藏出土1件青花云龙纹大罐[51]。

江苏句容市一处元代瓷器窖藏出土青花云龙盖罐1件，青花云龙梅瓶2件[52]。

江苏淮安市成化六年（公元1470年）墓出土青花盖罐1件[53]。

江苏南京市南郊明永乐八年（公元1410年）墓出土青花梅瓶1件[54]。

江苏南京市江宁县明沐英墓出土1件青花梅瓶[55]。

江苏南京市明墓出土青花大碗1件[56]。

江苏南京市明汪兴祖墓出土青花高足碗1件[57]。

河北保定市共出土元代窖藏瓷器11件，其中6件元青花，分别是青花釉里红开光镂花大罐2件、青花海水龙纹带盖八棱梅瓶2件、青花八棱玉壶春小瓶1件、青花八棱执壶1件[58]。

河北定兴县一处元代窖藏出土了1件青花凤纹高足碗和1件青花梅月纹高足碗[59]。

北京旧鼓楼大街出土窖藏瓷器青花瓷器10件[60]。

北京德胜门外元墓出土青花钵1件[61]。

内蒙古林西县一处元代窖藏共出土瓷器12件，其中青花7件，包括青花缠枝莲纹扁壶1件、青花鸳鸯纹盘2件、青花龙纹盘1件、青花菊纹高足杯1件、青花龙纹高足杯1件、青花凤纹高足杯1件[62]。

内蒙古自治区赤峰县一处元代窖藏出土青花龙纹高足杯5件[63]。

内蒙古呼和浩特东郊保合少乡一处元代瓷器窖藏，出土瓷器40余件，其中有一件青花梅草纹高足杯[64]。

内蒙古集宁路古城遗址窖藏

The Mongolian minority-led Yuan Dynasty, in addition to the infusion of Islamic culture, did not approve of the use of images of people on ceramics. Therefore, it is likely that these types of patterns and imagery would not have been found on YUB that was produced during the period of Mongol governance. However, during the burgeoning stages of the revolutionary armies' authority, it was important to propagate to their followers the ideologies of monarchal loyalty and integrity, borrowing from the past to model the present. The leadership and the stabilization of their power was hinged upon these frameworks. As such, it is most likely that pieces containing these types of images as decoration were produced during the foundational stages of the revolutionary armies' campaign [39].

In the 21st year of Zhizheng (1361 AD) Zhu Yuan Zhang's forces captured Fuliang County, and Jingdezhen became part of his domain. He immediately thereafter put Li Yong in charge of operations in Fuliang County instructing him to "break ground in the fields, and establish trade", and as such putting into place a series of measures to rehabilitate the deprived kiln industry. At this time, all the conditions for the production of high quality Underglaze Blue were in order. Currently we can infer that any pieces that include images of Chinese culture and stories of righteousness were fired after the 12th year (1352 AD) of Zhizheng, and were in fact most likely produced after the 21st year (1361 AD) in which Zhu Yuan Zhang took control of the ceramics industry [40].

We can also make inferences based on excavation records. First, we see that excavated pieces from the very early Ming Dynasty already included images of people. These include the excavation of the high-ranking official Mu Ying's grave, which produced the Xiao He Chasing Han Xin Pattern Underglaze Blue Meiping Vase, and Zhao Jun's Journey Pattern Underglaze Blue Stem Cup discovered in Gansu Province.

In addition, YUB found in territories and countries that were in cooperation with the Yuan rule, as well as major Yuan sites, graves, hoards, shipwrecks and excavations, have no recorded discoveries to date of pieces that include images from these historical stories and operas. For example, none of the pieces from the National Museum of Iran, Turkey's Topkapi Museum, India's palaces and other excavations sites, the Red Sea shipwreck, the Yuan Dadu excavation site, the ancient Huocheng excavation site in Xinjiang, and so forth locations are recorded as having Chinese operatic themes [41].

The stark contrast between production periods having and not having these images is due to the differences in societal groups at the helms of the Nation, as well as the cultural distinctions and amalgamations of those respective peoples. It is specifically these distinctions and amalgamations that give YUB its drastically unique decorative characteristics.

3. YUB Production Scale

In reference to the total number of YUB produced, even though there are no clear records of manufacturing scale during the Yuan Dynasty of YUB, we can take two different approaches when researching YUB production scale.

A. Song vs.Yuan Porcelain Taxes Perspective

During the Song Dynasty, Jingdezhen had to pay national duties and taxes once per year. It is recorded: "Jingdezhen, 3,337 guan and 950 wen" be paid. When we compare this to that of the Ding Kiln: "Qu Yang County, 831 guan and 91 wen"; we can see that it was around four times more [42]. At the time, the Ding Kiln was one of the most famous of Northern China, and one of the five famous kilns of the Song Dynasty. From this we can get a feeling for the massive scale at which Jingdezhen was producing ceramics.

As for the Yuan Dynasty, it is recorded: "Taxes Collected: Over 500 Ding...Fuliang County, Jingdezhen" [43]. If this is converted, it comes out to be more than 25,000 guan in national duties and taxes. From this we can see that the taxes collected each year from Jingdezhen during the Yuan Dynasty were around seven times that of the Song Dynasty.

From the perspective of a famous scholar in the late Yuan and early Ming era, Ye Zi Qi : "The Yuan give light sentences for crimes, require low tax and levees, and have relaxed military drafting policy; thus there is abundance for all in life and in death" [44]. We can see when the Mongols entered into China, they brought with them a certain political

出土了瓷器50件，其中有8件元青花，包括1件小盏、云龙纹高足杯2件、云凤纹高足杯3件、缠枝菊花纹高足杯1件、梨形壶1件[65]。

新疆伊犁地区霍城县出土一批瓷器，其中有1件青花双凤纹高足碗。其余多残破，大部分无法复原[66]。

江西九江高安一处元代窖藏共出土瓷器239件，有19件元青花，包括高足杯10件、云龙纹盖罐1件、云龙纹荷叶盖罐2件、云龙纹带盖梅瓶3件、缠枝牡丹如意云肩纹梅瓶2件、蕉叶纹花觚1件[67]。

江西萍乡市一处元代窖藏出土瓷器29件，其中有青花瓷器10件，包括菊花纹双耳带座香炉1件、梅花纹带座香炉2件、奔兔纹匜1件、飞凤纹高足杯1件、花卉纹碗5件[68]。

江西波阳县元墓出土青花带座梅瓶2件[69]。

江西上饶市元墓出土青花玉壶春瓶2件[70]。

江西九江至正十一年（公元1351年）元墓出土青花双耳连座香炉1件[71]。

安徽歙县一处元代窖藏出土54件瓷器，有1件青花云龙纹高足杯[72]。

安徽蚌埠市明汤和墓出土青花罐1件[73]。

浙江省杭州市一座瓷器窖藏共出土瓷器54件，其中青花笔架水盂1件[74]。

四川三台市一处元代窖藏共出土瓷器11件，其中有青花瓷器3件，包括折枝菊纹象耳瓶2件、缠枝牡丹纹双耳炉1件[75]。

湖南常德县元墓出土青花盘2件[76]。

由于青花瓷在元代才普遍生产，是带有异族统治阶级审美角度的艺术创作，从民间出土数量及青花瓷品种来看，在汉人百姓中无论从审美角度还是实用程度而言，应该都尚未普及到日常生活中。这从国内发现的青花瓷器器型种类就可看出，日用瓷种类还是占少数。

（二）产品流向西亚诸国

在元青花空间范围的坐标横轴上，伊朗、土耳其、叙利亚等西亚国家，占据了十分重要的位置。其中土耳其和伊朗，是目前世界上馆藏元青花最多的国家。

西亚诸国出土或传世的元青花，对应了当时特殊的烧制用途，即朝廷政治层面的赉赏、互馈和国家文化层面的沟通与交流。

伊朗在元代属伊儿汗国（Ilkhanate，公元1256—1335年）领地，“伊儿”一词的蒙古语意思是“从属”，即承认是大汗的属民[77]。史料记载，中国元代和波斯蒙古汗朝伊尔汗国始终都保持密切的藩属关系。伊儿汗国是元代开国皇帝忽必烈的亲兄弟——旭烈兀建立的蒙古四大汗国之一，双方使节往来非常频繁。元贞二年（公元1296年），元成宗遣拜住出使伊儿汗国。元贞四年（公元1298年），伊儿汗国的合赞汗遣使来中国，献大珠、宝石等珍物。皇庆二年（公元1313年），元仁宗派使臣拜住去伊儿汗国与完者都汗议事。完者都汗也派遣使臣来元朝进贡。泰定元年（公元1324年），不赛因遣使朝贺，并为其权臣出班请官，泰定帝派臣去伊朗，授出班以“开府仪同三司翌国公”头衔，赐银印、金符。这是元朝皇帝第二次直接给伊儿汗国大臣授官。不赛因不断地派使臣到中国来“朝贡”，献珠、玉、药物、马驼虎豹等，也从元朝领取大量的回赐。伊朗阿德比尔寺流传下来的精美的元青花应该是通过这种朝贡、回赐的方式抵达伊儿汗国的“赐赉瓷”[78]。

除伊朗以外，《岛夷志略》还记载了其他在元代时期输入中国瓷器的地区。元代输入中国“青白花瓷”“青白花器”等瓷器（陈万里先生认为这里指的就是青花瓷器）的港口包括波斯地区的“加里那”（今波斯湾东北岸部希尔东南的哈利勒角，为当时东西方海上交通的港口之一）、“甘埋里”（今伊朗东部，当波斯湾要冲，是东西方通商的重要口岸）、“天堂”（今麦加，穆斯林朝拜中心）等地[79]。

（三）产品流向世界其他国家及地区

除国内和前文提到的西亚诸国外，非洲、东亚、东南亚、南亚等国家及地区均有发现元青花。

1225年，赵汝适记载了中国与苏门答腊、爪哇和婆罗洲的贸易。1349年，汪大渊记录了1330年和1337—1339年的两次航海旅程，经过东南亚和印度洋，甚至远至东非。他列出了99个国家，其中超过一半的国家都进口中国瓷器[80]。

《岛夷志略》记载了古时印度及孟加拉等国及地区从中国输入的商品，其中就有青花瓷器；摩洛哥旅行家伊本·白图泰在自己的中国游记中也提到，14世纪40年代有大量中国青花瓷器出口到印度。印

structure. Different from the high tax system of the earlier dynasties, the Yuan government adopted a policy of low taxes in order to encourage crafts, production, and trade. This fact, in addition to the shear amount of tax paid by Jingdezhen, further solidifies that the production scale during the Yuan Dynasty was enormous.

B. Domestic and International Excavation Perspective

Domestically, there are at least 16 provinces, cities, or regions in which YUB has been excavated [45].

Internationally, the following countries and regions have recorded discoveries of YUB: Japan, Korea, Cambodia, Malaysia, Indonesia, Brunei, Philippines, Thailand, India, Bahrain, United Arab Emirates, Iran, Turkey, Macedonia, Syria, Lebanon, Mongolia, Uzbekistan, Egypt, Sudan, Oman, Yemen, Red Sea, Kenya, Tanzania, and so forth [46].

Broad excavation area points to a large distribution, large distribution is usually indicative of an elevated level of commodities, and as such points to large scale production.

C. Historical Records Perspective

It is also possible to see a few examples of records from the time period about the ceramics industry, in regards to production and sale: "As soon as the kiln cooled, customers rushed in to buy... The best wares were gobbled up... full ship set sail with porcelain cargo." [47].

Additionally, the Great Record of the Fuliang Porcelain Bureau indicates that the amount of artisan management at the beginning of the Yuan Dynasty was at a level of 100 artisan households. However, by 1295 AD, the numbers of artisan households increased to 400, four times that of the beginning of the Yuan. It was also higher than that of the 300 artisan households of official kilns managed during the following Ming and Qing Dynasties [48].

4. YUB Product Flow

In researching the production flow of YUB, it is important to first understand for what uses these products were being fired. Looking at the qualities of the domestic and international discoveries of YUB, we can see that the primary uses of such goods were as follows:

1. Royal Bestowments: Used as gifts to the royal family, civil and military officials, and foreign diplomats.

2. Foreign Trade: Used in trade for other foreign goods, or in direct exchange for silver bullion.

3. Altar or Funerary Use

As reflected in the primary uses, and in conjunction with the complete wares, broken pieces, and shards of YUB found domestically and internationally over the past few decades; production flow reflect these three aforementioned categories.

A. Domestic Flow

Domestically, YUB has been excavated from graves, hoards, sites, and shipwrecks in at least 16 provinces, cities and areas [49]. The following are just a few representative examples of YUB excavations from Yuan as well as Early Ming sites:

Jiangsu Province: 6 Stem Cups, 3 Large Jars, 4 Meiping Vases, 1 Large Bowl [50]-[57];

Hebei Province: 2 Stem Cups; 2 Meiping Vases, 1 Yuhuchun Vase, 1 ewer, 2 Stem Bowls [58][59];

Beijing: 11 Misc. pieces, 1 Bowl [60][61];

Inner Mongolia: 1 Flask, 1 Pear-shaped Ewer , 3 Plates, 15 Stem Cups, 1 Small Cup [62]-[65];

Xinjiang Region: 1 Stem Cup, large number of shards of indeterminable shape [66];

Jiangxi Province: 11 Stem Cups, 3 Large Jars, 5 Meiping Vases, 4 altar items, 1 Pouring Vessel, 5 Bowls, 2 Yuhuchun Vases, 1 Beaker [67]-[71];

Anhui Province: 1 Stem Cup, 1 Large Jar [72][73];

Zhejiang Province: 1 Brush Holder and Washer [74];

Sichuan Province: 2 Elephant Ear Vases, 1 Censor [75];

Hunan Province: 2 Plates [76].

Since the widespread production of YUB started during the Yuan Dynasty under the direct artistic and creative influence of a foreign nationality, whether from an aesthetic or practicality perspective, we can see from the domestic

度德里图格鲁克宫遗址发现的元青花瓷器，及在寇特拉·鲁菲兹城堡（印度德里图格鲁克皇宫遗址以北15公里处）发现的一批14世纪中国景德镇生产的青花瓷器残片（纹饰和造型与伊朗和土耳其的14世纪青花瓷器基本一致），都为元代青花瓷器的流向提供了新的证据[81]。

《岛夷志略》中也记录了在菲律宾和印尼青花瓷器贸易的情况[82]。菲律宾、印尼等东南亚地区发现的元青花可以分为两类；一类是大型器物，基本特点与西亚伊朗、土耳其收藏的一致，有大盘、大罐、梅瓶、玉壶春瓶等；另一类是简笔绘彩的小型器物，有瓶、盘、执壶、军持、小葫芦瓶、多棱小瓶、方形小罐等。其中军持、多棱小瓶、方形小罐等为东南亚所特有，在中国国内及西亚等地区都没有发现[83]。从器型大小、青料发色、纹饰主题方面来看有很大的差异，许多小型器物的"胎、釉、料、艺"表现出"粗、灰、暗、简"的特征。这类器物应该是专门为当地定制的。

14世纪以前，中国与东南亚诸岛国已有数百年的贸易往来。印尼的麻喏巴歇国在14世纪非常强盛，曾遣使节前来中国朝贡十来次。印尼现存的大件元青花精品可能源于那时官方之间的交易。同时，民间的贸易也进行得如火如荼。元代有许多商人前往爪哇与当地人贸易，印尼的商船也频繁往返于两国之间[84]。

在印尼所出土的青花瓷无论品质和数量都相当可观，其中大盘、大罐、梅瓶的总数还要超出土耳其和伊朗两个最负盛名的收藏[85]。广州东方博物馆研究人员赴印尼国立博物馆考察学习时也发现，其传世品中有的可与土耳其及伊朗的藏品媲美。

菲律宾群岛的北、中、南部三大岛都出土过元青花瓷。据统计，小件器物多出土于北部的吕宋岛，中型器物一般来自未沙亚岛，大件器物则大部分来自于南部的棉兰老岛北部的蒲端与东北部的苏里高。蒲端因盛产黄金，属于富裕地区，宋元时代曾多次派遣使节到中国朝贡，并获得朝廷的礼遇，《宋史》和《元史》都有记载。大件器物很有可能是入贡时所得。菲律宾早期的中国外销瓷居多出土于蒲端，可见当地两国民间的贸易很早就已非常活跃[86]。

（四）小结

元代青花瓷通过陆地和海上两条丝绸之路被运往世界多地。景德镇生产的元青花源源不断地流向国内外，将中国瓷业的辉煌传播到世界各地。景德镇也一跃成为世界制瓷业的中心，为明清两代的持续辉煌夯实了基础。

excavation sites that YUB had yet to find its way into the everyday lives of the Chinese people. The above listed domestic finds include very little daily use items for the common Chinese household.

B. Flow to Western Asia

Within the distribution chain of YUB, Western Asian territories (modern day Iran, Turkey, Syria, etc.) held the utmost importance. Of these, modern day Iran and Turkey currently house the largest known collections of YUB.

YUB discoveries of Western Asia specifically reflect particular uses of YUB during the Yuan Dynasty and suggest the cultural levels of diplomatic and trade relationships between these regions.

At the time of the Yuan Dynasty, Iran was part of a region called the Ilkhanate (1256-1335 AD). "Il-" was from the Mongolian language meaning "under", as in under the Great Khanate (Kublai's Yuan Dynasty Empire) [77]. History tells us that the Ilkhanate and the Great Khan Empire of the Yuan Dynasty retained a very close relationship after their induction. The Ilkhanate was in fact founded by the brother of Kublai, and was one of the Four Great Khanates established after the death of Genghis Khan. It retained frequent diplomatic relationship with the Great Khan Empire. In the 2nd year of Yuanzhen (1296 AD), an envoy accompanying Baizhu, a diplomat, was sent on a mission to the Ilkhanate, and in the 4th year of Yuanzhen (1298 AD), the reciprocal Khanate respect was dispatched to China from the Ilkhanate with pearls, jewels, and other great treasures. In the 2nd year of Huangqing (1313 AD), Baizhu again was sent to the Ilkhanate to discuss official business, and a return visit was paid. Again in 1324 AD, the emperor of the Yuan Dynasty sent his respected diplomatic bestowals to the ruler of the time in Iran. The Ilkhanate lord in turn continued to send gifts of precious stones, jewels, gold, and so forth. It is likely during these times of bestowal and reciprocation that gifts of the very finest YUB, as represented in the Ardebil Shrine of Iran, made their way across Central Asia and into Western Asia [78].

It is recorded that the "Blue and White Porcelain", "Blue and White Wares", etc. (Now suspected to be YUB) would have made its way to several important ports throughout Western Asia including: eHalileh (North East corner of the Persian Gulf), Karmān (Eastern Iran, important Persian Port), Heaven (Modern Mecca, center of the Muslim Culture) and so forth [79].

C. Flow to Other Countries and Territories

Currently, aside from the aforementioned domestic and Western Asia discoveries and collections of YUB, other important discoveries have been made in Africa, East Asia, Southeast Asia, South Asia, and so forth regions.

In 1225, Zhao Ru Shi recorded that China opened trade relations with Sumatra, Java, and Borneo. In 1349 AD, there were two ship voyages recorded in 1330 AD and 1337-1339 AD that sailed South through Southeast Asia and across the Indian Ocean, as far as East Africa. The voyages landed in 99 different countries, and over half of these countries imported a portion of Chinese porcelain [80].

In several different records and voyage journals there is clear record of YUB entering India, Bangladesh and surrounding areas. The journals of a famous Morrocan traveler recorded that a large portion of Chinese blue and white porcelain made its way into India during the 1340s. At the palace and other various excavation sites in India, large proportions of 14th century Jingdezhen YUB shards have been discovered (decorations and shapes similar to that of pieces found in Iran and Turkey). They have all offered new evidence of the YUB product flow during the Yuan Dynasty [81].

Similar records of the Underglaze Blue trade to the Philippines and Indonesia have also come to the surface [82]. The Philippines, Indonesia, and so forth Southeast Asian areas have discoveries of YUB that fall primarily into two categories: The first are the large pieces (Large plates, Large Jars, Meiping, Yuhuchun Vase, etc.) similar to that of Iran or Turkey; the second category are relatively simply decorated small wares including vases, plates, kettles, kendi, double-gourd vases, lobed plates, cube jars, and so forth. Of these, the kendis, lobed plates, cube jars, and so forth are specific to Southeast Asia, and have yet to be discovered domestically or in Western Asia collections [83]. From the size, coloration, and decoration, we can see quite specific differences in the "clay, glaze, dye, décor" combination; with the smaller pieces having a tendency towards "coarse, grey, light, simple" respectively. This category was most likely made specifically for the local market.

Before the 14th century, China and the island countries of Southeast Asia had already enjoyed hundreds of year of trade relationship. The Indonesian kingdom of Madjapahit was exceedingly powerful during the 14th century and came on at least ten different occasions to pay homage to the Yuan Dynasty. The large, high quality pieces that are currently held in or attributed to Indonesian discoveries were likely gained in trade during these official diplomatic visits. At the same time, regular trade between the peoples and business of each country was commonplace. Indonesian ships often made the trip between their ports and those of the Yuan Dynasty [84].

Specifically speaking of Indonesia, regardless of reference to quality or shear volume, the discoveries of YUB there, specifically the large plates, jars, and meiping vases, have exceeded that of the famous Western Asian collections [85]. A Guangzhou Oriental Museum researcher, on a research trip to the Nacional Museum of Indonesia, experienced first-hand that a few of the pieces there were on par quality and aesthetics wise with those of Iran and Turkey.

From a statistical perspective of the pieces excavated in the Philippines, the majority of the small wares were discovered on the northern islands of Luzon; whereas medium sized pieces were primarily discovered within the Visayas Island group. Large pieces primarily come from the southern island group of Mindanao, specifically the northern area of Butuan and north eastern area of Surigao. It was in Butuan that vast deposits of gold were found, allowing it the affluence required to enter into reciprocal diplomacy with China's Song and Yuan Dynasties, as recorded in the histories of each. It is very likely that during these diplomatic exchanges, YUB made its way in to the Philippine markets. The earliest Chinese wares made specifically for foreign markets were also discovered in Butuan, further illustrating the highly active trade relations between these two nations [86].

D. Summary

Traveling via the Silk Road and Maritime Silk Road, YUB made its way throughout the World. As the primary producer of Underglaze Blue, Jingdezhen quickly became the center of the World's ceramic industry and firmly planted itself as the foundation on which Ming and Qing Dynasty porcelain could root its development.

第二节
元青花的研究

20世纪20年代，英国的霍布逊以《明代之前的青花瓷器》一文开元青花研究之先河。之后，对元青花的研究缓慢进行，根据历年来研究元青花的书籍和论文的研究内容，可将元青花研究历史分为四个阶段。

一、1920年以前，空白研究阶段

20世纪20年代之前，人们对于元青花的认识极为浅薄。文献中也仅有少数几条语焉不详的记载。

二、1920—1950年，启蒙研究阶段

1920—1950年，是元青花研究的启蒙阶段，代表著作及重要论文是：

1929年，霍布逊在杂志《老家具》上发表《明代以前的青花瓷器》一文；

1931年，霍布逊又出版《私人收藏的中国陶瓷》一书；

1949年，沙瑞和考克思在《远东陶瓷通讯》第7期上发表《中国最早的青花瓷器》一文；

1952年，波普出版《14世纪青花瓷器：伊斯坦布尔托布卡普·撒莱宫所藏一组中国瓷器》一书；

1956年，波普出版《阿德比尔神殿收藏的中国瓷器》一书。

由此可见，在启蒙研究阶段，关于元青花的著作及论文屈指可数。元青花尚未受到广泛关注，但已经出现了先行者和开路人。

三、1950—1980年，附带研究阶段

1950—1980年，因为英国及美国学者的启蒙，国内陶瓷领域开始关注元青花瓷器。但由于资料欠缺、重视不够，加上十年动乱的影响，元青花研究并未作为独立的课题开展研究，只是作为陶瓷研究整体的一个部分加以涉及，因此对元青花的相关研究只是附带进行。同样，此阶段的研究成果著述及期刊论文较少。

四、1980—2012年，系统研究阶段

1980—2012年，是元青花的系统研究阶段，此时的研究已作为一个专门的领域从陶瓷研究整体中剥离出来。

这段时间出现的研究书籍和论文等研究成果呈现井喷状态，研究的内容涵括了青花起源、器型纹饰、制作工艺以及仪器分析、鉴定辨伪等综合内容，研究向更系统完善的方向发展。但在这一阶段，元青花仿制造假手段愈发高超，专家学者及行家里手在与造假者的博弈中并不占优势，制假猖獗，仿品泛滥当道，专家学者对元青花鉴定的公信力下降。

上述四个阶段的划分反映了元青花的研究历史。由于目前元青花制假的水平借助科技的力量水涨船高，因此未来的研究任重道远，研究的课题和重点将走出人证的局限，向发掘元青花的物证系统倾斜，这要求研究者拿出更有说服力的证据，为元青花鉴定提供物证支撑。只有分清真假，才能有效保护传承元代瓷器的文化。我们深信2013年之后，中国对元代瓷器的研究将走进一个新的物证时代！

Section 2:

Yuan Underglaze Blue Research

In the 1920s article, the British scholar Hobson's *Blue and White before the Ming Dynasty* opened the door for YUB research. After this, the history of YUB research slowly progressed, and according to the books and other publications we now have before us, we can divide the research of YUB into four major periods.

1. Pre 1920, The Empty Period

Before the 1920s, the research of YUB was, practically speaking, non-existent; and no elaborate description had been written. Even the mention of YUB in historical records is incredibly difficult to come by.

2. 1920-1950, The Rudimentary Research Period

The 1920-1950 period marks the beginning of rudimentary research of YUB. The primary works from the period include:

1929, in the magazine *Antique Furniture,* Hobson's article *Blue and White Porcelain before the Ming Dynasty*;

1931, Hobson's *Chinese Ceramics in Private Collections*;

1949, Shinzo Shirae and Warren Cox's article *China's Earliest Blue and White Porcelain* in the 7th Volume of Far Eastern Ceramics Bulletin;

1952, Pope's *14th Century Blue and White Porcelain: Chinese Ceramics from the Turkey Topkapi Palace Collection*;

1956, Pope's *Chinese Ceramics from the Ardebil Shrine*;

These few articles and publications represent the fundamental stages of YUB research. Before the widespread acceptance of YUB, these men were the trailblazers in this groundbreaking field of research.

3. 1950-1980, The Supplementary Research Period

Founded on the pioneering efforts of the British and American scholars, early interest in YUB by Chinese researchers quietly began. However, due to a lack of existent information, no assigned importance, and the general calamity of the day; the research of YUB could only be carried out as a supplementary portion of the general Chinese Ceramics field, and did not gain independence as its own specified area of study. Because of this, the amount of exploration carried out was minimal at best, and as such published results were few and far between.

4. 1980-2012, Systematic Research Period

From the 1980s until the present day has marked a period of systematic YUB research, in which YUB has been extracted out from general ceramic research and gained its own focal point of learning.

An explosion of research dissertations, publications, symposiums, and so forth characterizes this period. Areas researched include: YUB origins, shapes, decorations, techniques, scientific instrument analysis, as well as authentication, to name a few. Research is developing towards more systematic and comprehensive approaches. However, this period has also been marked by the foremost prowess of the forgery market, as copies now flood the streets. Scholars and experts have become entangled in an epic chess match with modern forgers, and no clear dominance has been asserted. In fact, the general public's trust in YUB authentication has taken a large hit because of this.

The aforementioned four periods of research reflect the history of YUB study. All boats rise with the tide, and modern technology has allowed for increasingly precise relic forgery. Because of this, the burden is heavy and the road is long for YUB researchers, and the problems and emphasis of research must move away from the confinements of human witness. There is now a need for researchers to have an inclination towards systematic material evidence-based study of YUB excavations, in order to strengthen the persuasiveness of their proofs and offer much needed support to the struggling ceramics authentication realm. It is only when we have a clear delineation between what is real and what is fake that we can truly protect the culture of Yuan Dynasty Porcelain. We are firmly convinced that 2013 will be marked as the emergence of a material-evidence stage in YUB research which will bring us in to a new age of understanding.

第三节
研究元青花的意义

一、历史的责任

元代青花瓷的兴起，逐步奠定了中国景德镇在世界上的“瓷都”地位。元代在瓷器制作上的创新，是历朝历代无法比拟的。元青花的崛起改变了中国人数千年来对瓷器色泽的审美观。青花瓷经800年而不衰，如今更被誉为国瓷，至今仍是人们艺术审美的追求。

元青花的故乡在中国。然而，元代瓷器的研究却在20世纪20年代的英国开始，50年代在美国发展。我国开始重视对元代瓷器的研究，已经是21世纪以后了。时至今日，我们这一代，应该肩负起对元代瓷器突破性研究的责任。

二、元青花是当代造假贩假的重灾区

元代瓷器较之明清瓷器更为罕见，价格更为高昂。2005年，元青花鬼谷下山人物图大罐，以2.3亿元人民币刷新了中国古瓷器单价的世界纪录。于是，大量欺世造假的元青花开始疯狂地涌入市场。

瓷器仿古历代均有，但明清仿古，是崇尚前朝，仿品中有明显的本朝标志，尤其是乾隆仿古，有的直接在底款上写明“仿古”两字，告知世人。前朝仿古而不欺世。而今的仿古，是欺世的，是追求暴利的商业欺诈。

乱象丛生的造假是对文化遗产的玷污，是对社会诚信的摧毁，久而久之，将会挫伤国人传承保护民族文化的爱心，将会导致国人文化的沉沦与文化自信的丧失，将会使世界对中国陶瓷市场失去信心。

《元青花迹型研究与物证鉴定》将是识别真假的“鹰眼”，是物证的裁判，它的客观公正，将重塑我们对文化保护与文化传承的信心！

三、有助于解决专家与藏家的对立

近年来学术界、收藏界对元代瓷器，尤其是对元青花看法的对立情绪不断高涨，多次出现以专家为主的否定派和以藏家为主的肯定派争执的场面，每次都争执不下，莫衷一是。主要原因在于，双方都是人证之争，缺乏有效的物证。

《元青花迹型研究与物证鉴定》联合了多家国内外的国家研究机构和民间研究机构，经过近十年的研究与探索，在观察了大量的元青花标本之后，选取具有明确发掘时间、发掘地点和年代依据或有明确传世记载的元青花整器、瓷片的标本，提炼建构了元青花迹型标准图谱模型。该模型属于物证系统，用之比对鉴定，并辅之迹型形成本质的逻辑论证，鉴定方法类似人类基因图谱的亲子鉴定，可有效识别出元青花真品。

这样，就可使专家与藏家在科学的旗帜下达成共识，使不同的争执融汇于真理的统一之中。

四、容易取得鉴定的突破口

不少文献著作表明：由于明清两代对元代文化的忽视与轻视，上至故宫没有收藏元代瓷器，下至市场没有买卖元代瓷器。在中国传统文化中，没有皇家喜好的上行，就没有百官庶民的下效，没有百官庶民的下效，就没有收藏市场，没有收藏市场就没有买卖市场。因此，1980年以前，基本没有仿造元代瓷器的动机与动力。直至在20世纪80年代以后，由于国家外贸的需求，仿品才出现。因此，在对元代瓷器的鉴定实践中，只要断定器物非80年代以后所仿，就基本上可以判断是到代的器物了。

中国掘墓现象，历朝历代一直未中断，不排除个别窑口对挖出的元代瓷器出于好奇也仿造过，但这种仿造是没有官仿的，只有民仿。但由于没有买卖市场，即使仿造也是属于历史的偶然现象，可忽略不计，不影响对元代瓷器鉴定的主流判断。再说，50年代以前的盗墓，是以盗金银、玉器、铜器为主，盗

Section 3:
The Significance of Yuan Underglaze Blue Research

1. Historical Responsibility

The rise of YUB, step by step, established Jingdezhen as the World's 'center of ceramics'. The creativity expressed by Yuan porcelain is unparalleled throughout Chinese history, and YUB's abrupt rise to prominence changed millenniums of Chinese ceramic's color palate and aesthetic standards. Underglaze Blue is now lauded as "China's China", and for over eight hundred years has not fallen out of favor of the public's artistic pursuits.

YUB's birthplace was China, yet it was in the 1920s in England and the 1950s in the U.S.A. that its research first took flight. It is now, in this new millenium, that [China] has finally placed importance on YUB research. In this late hour, our generation has the responsibility to shoulder the breakthrough exploration of YUB study.

2. The YUB Counterfeit Market is a Disaster Area

YUB is rarer than the porcelain of the Ming and Qing Dynasties, and as such its price can be much more exorbitant. In 2005, the YUB "Gui Gu Zi Coming Down from the Mountain" Large Jar was auctioned for 230 million RMB, establishing a new price record for Chinese antique ceramics. Due largely in part to this, the YUB forgery market was thrown into frenzy.

Copying ancient antiques is not new to this age, but during the Ming and Qing Dynasties, for example, copies were meant as a way of advocating past generations, and would commonly have a clear marking of the dynasty in which it was made. Specifically speaking, during the Qianlong reign of the Qing Dynasty, it was common for pieces to be marked as "Relic Copies" in order to offer public understanding, and not attempt to fool. However, modern forgers are out for blood, and only seek to make copies that can cheat the market.

The chaotic outbreak of forgeries is a blotch on cultural heritage that is destroying society's trust, and over the course of time will lead to cultural depravity as well as a loss of confidence in one's own culture. This in turn will deplete integrity within the ceramics market and destroy the public's trust.

Trace Model Research and Material Evidence Authentication: *Yuan Dynasty Underglaze Blue Porcelain* seeks to offer a "Hawkeye" view in authentication, establishing a material evidence referee. Its objective impartiality seeks to restore faith back into the protection and passing on of culture!

3. Helping to Resolve the Expert vs. Collector Opposition

In recent years, the YUB collectors' world, specifically on the topic of how to look at YUB, has come to a stalemate with authentication experts. There have been several occasions of heated debate between the two sides of primarily exclusive experts and primarily inclusive collectors, but no resolution has been made. This lack of resolution is mainly because both sides are relying on human witness, and there is a lack of resolute evidence.

After nearly ten years of deep study and observation of a numerous amount of sample pieces, *Trace Model Research and Material Evidence Authentication: Yuan Dynasty Underglaze Blue Porcelain* has unified a large number of domestic and international research organizations and private research institutions in YUB research. The samples

墓者对瓷器是不屑一顾的。例如：南京博物馆最著名的馆藏元青花萧何月下追韩信图梅瓶，就是从明朝开国皇帝朱元璋的养子，死后被追封为黔甯王的沐英墓中出土的。但沐英墓盗扰严重，此梅瓶是盗墓者光顾后留下的东西[87]。由此可见，盗墓者都不要的东西，仿造它的可能性就更小了。

used are of established excavation record or possess clearly dated provenance. Using these samples, a YUB Standard Trace Atlas Model was constructed; establishing a material-evidence system, supported by logical proofs of essential trace nature, which can be used in comparative authentication. This authentication method is similar to that of the Human DNA model for paternity testing, offering an effective method for determining authentic YUB.

In this way, the impasse between collectors and experts can finally reach a mutually acceptable resolution based upon scientific proof.

4. Easily Spanning the Authentication Gap

Several articles have stated : Due to the fact that the Ming and Qing Dynasties did not respect or revere the Yuan culture, the Palace did not collect and the markets did not carry Yuan Dynasty Porcelain. In traditional Chinese Culture, if the emperor is not fond of an item, there is no favor found amongst the court for it; if there is no favor in the court, there is no collection market for it; if there is no collection market, no one will buy and sell it. Because of this, before the 1980s, there was no push in the market for forged Yuan Porcelain. It was only during the 80s, due to the demand of the international market, that the forgery market for Yuan wares slowly began to roll. This offers a rare phenomenon for Yuan Porcelain authentication. If we are able to establish that a Yuan piece is not a copy made since the 1980s, we can rather assuredly assert that it is a relic of the period it is proposed to be.

Tomb raiding within China has always existed throughout history, and regardless of kiln, there is a possibility that out of curiosity some Yuan porcelain was faked. These fakes would have, however, been only done in small folk kilns, and would not have been carried out by the official kilns. A lack of sales market for these items would have stifled any desire to continue forgery, and any presence of these items can be considered as a chance appearance that will not affect the mainstream authentication of Yuan Porcelain. Additionally, before the 1950s, tomb raiders were primarily interested in gold, silver, jade, and bronze; ceramics would not spare a glance from them. For example: The Xiao He Chasing Han Xin Meiping Vase of Nanjing Museum was found in the tomb of Mu Ying, the adopted son to the establisher of the Ming Dynasty Zhu Yuan Zhang (the Hongwu Emperor). Mu Ying's tomb had undergone harsh robberies and vandalism, and the Meiping was left over after the visits of the grave robbers, it had not attracted their attention enough to even take it with them [87]. There is a very low likelihood that there would be a forgery market for items that even tomb raiders could not be bothered to carry out.

第三章

元青花标型特征

阅读提示：

本章从肉眼观察的角度，从元青花的器形、纹饰、发色、款识、胎釉特征和制作工艺六个方面，分析并阐明元青花的标型特征。

主要论述问题：

1. 元青花主要有哪些器形？
2. 元青花的纹饰特征是什么？
3. 元青花的发色有什么特征？
4. 元青花的款识特征是什么？
5. 元青花的胎和釉各有什么特征？
6. 元青花的制作工艺是怎么样的？

Chapter 3

Typical Yuan Underglaze Blue Characteristics

Text Note:

This chapter takes a look at the six main facets of YUB that are observable to the naked eye: Shape, decoration, coloration, markings, glaze and body characteristics, and techniques; to analyze and depict the typical characteristics of YUB.

第一节
元青花器形

一、元青花器形类别

元青花器形主要可分为七大类别：罐、瓶、壶、盘、碗、盒及其他类别。

图3-1-2
元青花凤凰缠枝牡丹纹铺兽耳大罐
金乐轩藏

二、元青花器形类别表

器形类别	罐	瓶	壶	盘	碗	盒	其他
器形种类	兽钮盖罐	（八棱）梅瓶	梨式壶	圆口盘	高足碗	盖盒	塑像
	荷叶盖罐	（八棱）玉壶春瓶	（八棱）执壶	花口盘	花口碗	套盒	炉 觚
	（八棱）铺首耳罐	（八棱）葫芦瓶	四系扁壶	菱口盘	敞口碗	砚盒	匜 水盂
	鼓式盖罐	六棱瓶	凤流扁壶	葵口盘	敛口碗		鸟食罐
	（八棱）无盖罐	蒜头瓶	扁执壶	莲瓣形盘	折腰碗		鼎
	筒式盖罐	象耳瓶					器座
	（八棱）双系罐	戟耳瓶					蒙古包
		连座瓶					船形水注

图3-1-3
元青花行龙纹盖罐
江西景德镇市陶瓷考古研究所藏

三、元青花器形类别图集

（一）罐类

见图3-1-1—图3-1-5。

图3-1-1
元青花云龙纹荷叶盖罐
高安市博物馆藏

图3-1-4
元青花云龙纹带盖筒罐
江西景德镇市陶瓷考古研究所藏

Section 1:
Yuan Underglaze Blue Shapes

1. YUB Shape Categories

YUB shapes can be broken into seven major categories: Jars, Vases, Kettles, Plates, Bowls, Cases, and Other Miscellaneous Shapes.

2. YUB Shape Table

Category	Jar	Vase	Kettle	Plate	Bowl	Case	Other
Types	Beast Lidded Jar	(8 Sided) Meiping Vase	Pear Shaped Kettle	Round Mouth Plate	Stem Bowl	Lidded Case	Statue
	Lotus Leaf Lidded Jar	(8 Sided) Yuhuchun Vase	(8 Sided) Ewer	Flower Mouth Plate	Flower Mouth Bowl	Layered Case	Lu (Incense Burner)
	(8 Sided) Jar with Handles	(8 Sided) Hulu (Double-Gourd) Vase	Flask with Four Rings	Foliate Mouth Plate	Open Mouth Bowl	Inkstone Case	Gu (Beaker)
	Drum Style Lidded Jar	6 Sided Vase	Phoenix Flask	Hibiscus Mouth Plate	Inward Turning Mouth Bowl		Yi (Pouring Vessel)
	(8 Sided) Lidless Jar	Garlic Head Vase	Ewer Flask	Lotus Petal Plate	Bowing Bowl		Water Pot
	Lidded Cylinder	Elephant Handle Vase					Bird Feeder
	(8 Sided) Jar with Double Ringlets	Flanged Vase					Ding (Footed Vessel)
		Vase with Attached Stand					Vessel Stand
							Mongolian Yurt
							Boat Shaped Pouring Vessel

图3-1-5
元青花花卉纹双系小罐
广州东方博物馆藏

（二）瓶类

见图3-1-6[88]—图3-1-13。

图3-1-6
元青花人物图梅瓶
美国波士顿艺术博物馆藏

图3-1-7
元青花海水白花龙纹八棱梅瓶
北京故宫博物院藏

图3-1-8
元青花开光花鸟水禽纹六棱瓶
英国剑桥大学费兹威廉博物馆藏

图3-1-9
元青花卉纹八棱玉壶春瓶
金乐轩藏

图3-1-10
元青花开光花卉纹八棱葫芦瓶
土耳其托普卡比宫博物馆藏

图3-1-11
元“至正十一年”铭青花云龙纹象耳瓶
英国大维德中国艺术基金会藏

图3-1-12
元青花莲池鸳鸯纹戟耳瓶
台湾鸿禧美术馆藏

图3-1-13
元青花缠枝菊纹连座瓶
金乐轩藏

3. YUB Shape Category Atlas

A. Jars

See pictures 3-1-1—3-1-5.

B. Vases

See pictures 3-1-6 [88]—3-1-13.

C. Kettles

See pictures 3-1-14—3-1-17.

D. Plates

See pictures 3-1-18—3-1-22.

E. Bowls

See pictures 3-1-23—3-1-26.

F. Boxes

See pictures 3-1-27—3-1-29.

G. Others

See pictures 3-1-30—3-1-36.

4. YUB Shape Styles

Ceramic shape styles reflect mankind's aesthetic pursuits and understanding through the creation of ceramics.

Each dynasty's style is built on the foundation of the prior dynasty, but also incorporates new influences from the contemporary culture. Thus, any particular dynasty's ceramic style represents the creativity and developments added to elements of prior periods.

A. YUB Shape Comprehensive Style Analysis

Comprehensively speaking, the contrast of sizes in shapes seen in the Yuan Dynasty is much starker than that of the prior period — Song Dynasty. From giant milling plates to tiny fist-sized jars, and bodies as delicate as Chenghua Porcelain to the thickness of ceiling tiles; the styles were wildly diverse.

The differences in shape styles between Song and Yuan Dynasties were due largely to the dissimilarities of cultural background between the two dynasties. Song was a dynasty governed by Confucian scholars and literati. Their artistic preferences were refrained, and they pursued jade as the ultimate expression of subtle beauty. Because of this, the articles made during the Song Dynasty were fine and elegant.

The Yuan Dynasty was built on the culture of the nomadic Mongolian people. A horseback nation, they were naturally vigorous with only simple demands for their livelihood. In addition to this, the new skills added to the ceramics industry under the Yuan rule allowed for a higher efficiency in firing large pieces; thus large jars, large plates, large bowls, and so forth became more common place in porcelain production.

B. YUB Primary Representative Style Analysis

I. Traditional Shapes

A traditional shape is one that has continued to develop change based on the elementary foundation of shapes that were present in dynasties prior to it.

a. Large Jars

The jar, ever since the beginning of ceramic making, has been a staple storage vessel shape that has continually developed along with the advancements made in ceramic techniques [89].

YUB large jars often have a straight mouth, short neck, broad shoulders, a tapered belly, short foot ring, and the base is usually unglazed. Large jars can also be made as 8 sided,

（三）壶类

见图3-1-14—图3-1-17。

图3-1-14
元青花凤首流扁执壶
新疆伊犁哈萨克自治州博物馆藏

图3-1-15
元青花云肩双龙戏珠纹四系扁方壶
日本出光美术馆藏

图3-1-16
元青花龙纹梨式壶（盖已失）
金乐轩藏

图3-1-17
元青花花卉纹葫芦形执壶
印度尼西亚国家博物馆藏

（四）盘类

见图3-1-18—图3-1-22。

图3-1-20
元青花凤穿花纹菱花口盘
广州东方博物馆藏

图3-1-18
元青花如意云纹花口盘
印度尼西亚国家博物馆藏

图3-1-21
元青花莲池杂宝纹莲瓣形盘
上海博物馆藏

图3-1-19
元青花莲池鸳鸯纹盘
泰国曼谷大学东南亚陶瓷博物馆藏

图3-1-22
元青花瓜果纹葵口盘
金乐轩藏

and the majority of the YUB large jars known in existence do not have accompanying lids. It is inferred that most jars were created to have accompanying lids, but most of them have become lost or broken (see pictures 3-1-37 and 3-1-38).

The Mongolian people loved a good festival, and when they were on the road, they tended to bring large amounts of alcohol to be used at any time. Large jars would have been used as alcohol containers, and some had rigged necks that were most likely used for tying with a rope and taking it in tow [90] (see picture 3-1-39).

The inventiveness of the YUB large jars comes in their use of double handle decoration. Current discoveries include beast (see picture 3-1-40) and dragon handles (see picture 3-1-41). The beast handles usually have an opening at the mouth in order to allow for the fastening of a ring. The YUB lidded jar with double beast handles of the Gao'an Museum collection, in fact, still has fully intact metal rings within the mouth of the beast handles (see picture 3-1-39).

b. Meiping Vases (Plum Vase)

Meiping, or plum vase, is a type of vessel created during the Northern Song Dynasty. It has a small mouth, short neck, broad shoulders, and gained its name because "the mouth is so narrow, it can only fit a plum branch" [91].

Compared to the slender elegant shape of the Northern Song, the Yuan Dynasty Meiping is seen to be more full of power, with full round shoulders and a broadening at the foot and base (see pictures 3-1-42 and 3-1-43 [92]).

The necks of Yuan Meipings are divided into two types. The first is straight neck with a vertical drop to the shoulders which are generally broader (see picture 3-1-44). The second type has a trapezoid shaped neck and slightly more rounded shoulders (see picture 3-1-43).

Yuan Dynasty Meiping vases were primarily used for the storage of alcohol, and had an accompanying lid. On the Gao'an Museum YUB Lidded Meiping, the interior of the lid is affixed with a short tube that would fit directly in the mouth of the vase. This would work to better seal the vase, helping to lessen evaporation and prevent contaminants from entering into the spirits [93] (see pictures 3-1-45 and 3-1-46).

c. Yuhuchun Vases

The Yuhuchun vase was also first created during the Northern Song Dynasty [94]. It has a trumpeted mouth, narrow neck, peach or pear shaped belly, and round foot ring. Yuhuchun vases were multi-purpose vessels used in the storage of alcohol, as flower vases, in sacrificial rituals, and so forth [95].

The Yuan Dynasty saw the standardization of the Yuhuchun shape. The mouth was broader, neck longer, and body more rotund than that of the earlier periods, offering an all in all more balanced and dignified shape than that of its predecessors (see pictures 3-1-47 [96] and 3-1-48). The Underglaze Blue Yuhuchun Vase was popular from the middle of the Yuan Dynasty all the way until its conclusion.

d. Hulu (Double-Gourd) Vases

The Hulu (double-gourd) vase takes it shape from the Chinese Hulu (Double or Bottle Gourd), one of the representative objects of Taoism. From the Tang Dynasty onward, due to its homophony with "Fu Lu" (Blessing and Fortune), it became a traditional shape in Chinese crafts [97].

During the Yuan Dynasty both the Jingdezhen and the Longquan Kilns were firing Hulu shaped vases. The Longquan Kiln predominantly made a large lower, small upper double globular Hulu vase; whereas in Jingdezhen the eight sided Hulu was in vogue (see picture 3-1-49). The Hulu vase of Turkey's Topkapi Museum is of the large lower, small upper double globular variety, and is very rare for the Jingdezhen Kiln. It is also twice the height of the average Hulu vase from the Longquan Kiln [98] (see picture 3-1-50).

There are also smaller kettles whose body is similar to that of the Hulu vase (see picture 3-1-51).

II. Metal Ware Inspired Shapes

A metal ware inspired ceramic shape is any vessel that draws inspiration from, or copies the shape of, an earlier or contemporary metal ware. Often the ceramic shapes of any given period are the creative development based upon the foundation laid by metal wares.

a. Yi (Pouring Vessels)

The bronze ware Yi was first seen during the Western

（五）碗类

见图3-1-23—图3-1-26。

图3-1-23
元青花云凤纹高足碗
新疆维吾尔自治区博物馆藏

图3-1-24
元青地白花孔雀牡丹纹敛口碗
伊朗国家博物馆藏

图3-1-25
元青花缠枝莲纹撇口碗
金乐轩藏

图3-1-26
元青花缠枝菊纹折腰碗
金乐轩藏

（六）盒类

见图3-1-27—图3-1-29。

图3-1-27
元青花人物杂宝纹六棱形盖盒
英国大英博物馆藏

图3-1-28
元青花莲池鸳鸯纹套盒
上海博物馆藏

图3-1-29
元青花云龙纹砚盒
江西景德镇市陶瓷考古研究所藏

Zhou Dynasty, and became popular during the Warring States Period. Similar to a ladle, it has a spout attached to a well or plate, and sometimes has a foot.

The YUB Yi was inspired by its bronze counterpart, and was most likely used as a vessel for washing the hands and face. The majority of these vessels are flat bottomed without a foot ring (see picture 3-1-53). Some have attached circular ringlets under the pouring spout attaching it to the body (see picture 3-1-54).

b. Ding (Footed Vessels)

The bronze ware Ding was a matured shape seen within the Erlitou Culture (2000-1600 BC). It has two erected handles, a drum or rectangular shaped body, and three or four feet; and was used as a cooking vessel (see picture 3-1-55).

The YUB Ding inspired by this early bronze ware shape is very rare (see picture 3-1-56).

c. Gu (Beakers)

The bronze ware Gu appeared during the early Shang Dynasty, and has a trumpeted mouth, slender waist, tall body, and flat base (see picture 3-1-57).

The epigraphy of the Song Dynasty brought rise to the Gu as an item of class for intellects to collect and ponder; it was often used as a decoration piece or as a flower vase. It was under this influence that the Gu entered into the fold of ceramic shapes [99].

As of now, the YUB Gu Beakers that have been found do not offer much change to the first ceramic wares of their type: trumpet mouth, slender body, round foot ring, and occasionally flanged (resembling axe blades) handles attached as decoration to the mid-section (see picture 3-1-58).

d. Lotus Leaf Lidded Jars

The Lotus Leaf Lidded Jar was first seen during the Tang Dynasty. The silver Suspended Fish Lid excavated from a cellar full of gold and silver in Jiangsu Province is in the shape of a lotus leaf. Its leaf stalk curls to form a handle, the leaf ridges spread out to form wavy edges of the lid, and suspended between each ridge is a small fish [100].

Currently, the two examples of YUB Lotus Leaf lids come from the Gao'an Museum collection and the Idemitsu Museum of Japan (see pictures 3-1-59 and 3-1-60). The lid of the Gao'an museum jar has a centrally located knob, a spiraling leaf vein pattern, and is divided into a four sided underwater scene with a carp, crab, catfish, and Mandarin fish design (see picture 3-1-61).

e. Incense Burners

Incense Burners, or simply Censers, are often seen in conjunction with a pair of vases as a common combination used for altar wares during the Yuan Dynasty, as seen in the three representative pieces excavated in Jiangxi and Hunan Provinces.

Bronze ware Dings, aside from cooking, were also used as sacrificial wares and were seen as a symbol of hierarchy during the Western Zhou Dynasty. Ding-style censers were used as altar wares and are also seen as a representative sacrificial ware with essentially the same cultural background as the Ding.

The YUB censer shapes are similar to that of their bronze ware counterparts; they have two erected handles and three feet. The newly added feature is the attached base and a knobbed lid (see picture 3-1-62).

III. Foreign Inspired Shapes

Foreign shapes are those shapes that have evoked reciprocal inspiration from minorities and nations of a non-Han Chinese culture.

a. Flasks

During their years of nomadic lifestyle, the Khitan people of ancient China carried with them leather pouches for storing water, which we now refer to as "Pi Nang", or leather flasks. Once they settled down as the Liao Nation, they used ceramics to commemorate the leather vessels in making the cockscomb flask (see picture 3-1-63).

Similarly, the Mongol people took from their nomadic culture in creating vessels of use. As an example, the four-handled flask has a flared mouth, a flattened body, and four rings positioned on the shoulder to add to its ease of mobility; this is characteristic of a vessel inspired by

（七）其他类

见图3-1-30—图3-1-36。

图3-1-30
元青花缠枝莲花杂宝纹蒙古包
俄罗斯艾尔米塔什博物馆藏

图3-1-31
元青花缠枝花卉纹器座
青海省博物馆藏

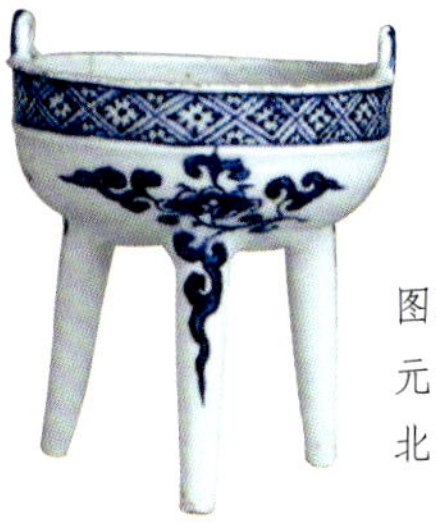
图3-1-32
元青花卉纹三足鼎
北京故宫博物院藏

图3-1-33
青花菊花蕉叶纹出戟觚
首都博物馆藏

图3-1-34
元青花天鹅戏水纹匜
广州东方博物馆藏

图3-1-35
元青花缠枝花卉纹盏和盏托
首都博物馆藏

图3-1-36
元青花菊花纹水盂
金乐轩藏

nomadic lifestyle [101] (see picture 3-1-64).

b. Stem Cups

Stem Cups likely rose to meet the need for drinking alcohol on horseback, a tradition commonly practiced by the Mongols, with the stem of the cup allowing for ease of grasping (see pictures 3-1-65 and 3-1-66). Some of the cup stems have a ridged surface, to further enhance its capacity to be grasped and prevent slipping (see picture 3-1-65).

c. Large Plates (Chargers)

Large Plates or Chargers, are shapes inherited from Islamic and Mongol culture. The Ming Dynasty writer, Ma Huan, writes: "The Persians take a plate full of rice, soak it with some soup, and feed themselves with their hands." We can also see from Islamic paintings that the eating style was characterized by a group of individuals all sitting around a large common dish, usually blue and white, and communally sharing from the center dish [102] (see picture 3-1-67 [103]).

In collections housed in Iran, Turkey, India, Thailand, Indonesia, and so forth; we see a large array of these large communal eating chargers. Their diameter is usually around 30 centimeters, but can reach up to 50-60 centimeters in diameter.

d. Small Jars (Jarlettes)

This type of small jar is usually only 5-8 centimeters tall with simplistic decoration and a greyish color. They primarily are adorned with floral scrolls painted in a very freehand style. Their shapes vary from squared, to round, to lobed; and can have a varying number of ringlets attached near the mouth [104] (see pictures 3-1-68 and 3-1-69).

These small jars are most likely burial items used by the Southeast Asian kingdoms of that time, as corroborated by the tomb excavation on Luzon Island in the Philippines. There are also some scholars that believe that these small ringlet jars, when accompanied with wood or metal lids, could have been used for incense and medicine storage [105].

四、元青花器形风格

陶瓷的器形风格反映了人类在进行陶瓷创作时的审美感受与认知。

陶瓷风格的形成既有对先代前朝文脉的继承，又会受到当代社会文化的影响。所以每个时代的陶瓷器形风格都在先代前朝文化要素的继承中有所创新与发展。

（一）元青花器形整体风格分析

元青花造型从整体上看，大小之间的比例较之宋代更为悬殊：既有硕大如碾台的盘，又有精巧如拳的罐，既有薄如成化瓷的碗，又有胎厚如瓦的瓶，可谓精粗兼备，丰富多姿。

宋、元两代的器形风格有较大差异，这与两代的文化背景有很大关系。宋代文人治国，追求儒学，在艺术审美方面以文人情怀至上，追求玉质的自然美、朴素美。因此，宋瓷造型精巧，清秀素雅。

而元代是由游牧民族蒙古族建立的。马背上的民族，生性豪放，生活要求简单，加上元代在制瓷工艺上的进步，烧制大器成功率大大提高，所以大罐、大盘、大碗等器物更常见。

（二）元青花器形风格主要代表分析

1. 传统文化器形

传统文化器形是指某个时代的某种陶瓷造型延续了先代前朝已有的器形风格。通常该时代的器形会在前朝的基础上有所创新发展。

（1）大罐

罐，作为盛储容器，自陶器出现就已经作为一种代表器形出现。随着陶瓷烧制技术的提高，罐的形制也在不断变化[89]。

元青花大罐多直口，短颈，丰肩，腹以下渐收，有矮圈足，底足一般无釉。大罐也有八方造型。现存的元青花大罐，大部分无盖。估计烧制时大部分都有盖相配套，但至今盖大都已破损丢失（见图3-1-37、图3-1-38）。

元蒙民族喜好宴饮，出游时总会携带大量美酒，随时饮用。大罐就是储酒用的器皿，在有些罐的颈部还有一道凸棱，可能是加固绳索捆绑之用[90]（见图3-1-39）。

元青花大罐的创新之处在于装饰于肩部的一对耳。目前发现的有兽首形（见图3-1-40）和回首龙形（见图3-1-41）。兽首状耳（也可称为铺首耳），兽口部为空，可放置衔环。高安市博物馆藏的元青花云龙缠枝牡丹纹兽耳盖罐，兽耳口中还完整保存着金属衔环（见图3-1-39）。

图3-1-37
元青花孔雀穿花纹大罐
伊朗国家博物馆藏

图3-1-38
元青花缠枝牡丹龙纹铺首耳大罐
金乐轩藏

图3-1-39
元青花云龙缠枝牡丹纹兽耳盖罐
高安市博物馆藏

图3-1-40
元青花缠枝牡丹龙纹铺首耳大罐
金乐轩藏

图3-1-41
元青花缠枝牡丹瑞兽纹双耳罐
伊朗国家博物馆藏

（2）梅瓶

梅瓶是北宋创烧的一种瓶式。小口、短颈、丰肩，因“口径之小仅与梅之瘦骨相称”而得名[91]。

相对于宋代梅瓶的修长秀美，元代梅瓶更为雄壮，肩部更丰满，胫部和底足也更宽（见图3-1-42、图3-1-43[92]）。

梅瓶颈部有两种形状，一是直颈，上下粗细均等，这类梅瓶通常肩部也更宽（见图3-1-44）；二是上窄下宽的梯形，这类梅瓶稍稍溜肩（见图3-1-43）。

图3-1-44
元青花缠枝牡丹纹云肩纹梅瓶
上海博物馆藏

元代时梅瓶大多作为储酒器使用，配有盖，高安市博物馆藏的元青花云龙纹带盖梅瓶，盖内有管状拴，是子母口的盖，增强了密封性，减少酒液挥发，同时避免灰尘进入污染酒液[93]（见图3-1-45、图3-1-46）。

（3）玉壶春瓶

玉壶春瓶是北宋时创烧的一种瓶式[94]。撇口、细弧颈，桃形或梨形腹、圈足。玉壶春瓶具有酒器、插花、祭祀等多个功能[95]。

元代是玉壶春瓶形制标准化时期，相对于前代，元代玉壶春瓶口部更大，颈部更细长，腹部更突出，整体比例更加协调端庄（见图3-1-47[96]、图3-1-48）。青花玉壶春瓶从元代中期到元代晚期一直流行。

图3-1-42
宋磁州窑梅瓶
北京故宫博物院藏

图3-1-47
宋定窑刻划花玉壶春瓶

图3-1-45
元青花云龙纹带盖梅瓶
高安市博物馆藏

图3-1-43
元青花人物图梅瓶
美国波士顿艺术博物馆藏

图3-1-46
元青花云龙纹带盖梅瓶——子母口盖
高安市博物馆藏

图3-1-48
元青花花卉纹八棱玉壶春瓶
金乐轩藏

（4）葫芦瓶

葫芦瓶形似葫芦，是道教的灵物之一，唐以来因谐音似“福禄”，逐渐成为传统器形[97]。

元代时，景德镇窑和龙泉窑都烧制葫芦瓶。龙泉窑多为上小下大双圆葫芦瓶，而景德镇窑则盛行八方造型（见图3-1-49）。土耳其托普卡比宫博物馆所藏的青花缠枝牡丹纹葫芦瓶，呈上小下大的束腰双圆葫芦式，在景德镇窑中不多见，也比龙泉窑的同类制品高出一倍[98]（见图3-1-50）。

有的小型执壶，壶身也为葫芦形制（见图3-1-51）。

图3-1-49
元青花八棱开光花卉纹葫芦瓶
土耳其托普卡比宫博物馆藏

图3-1-50
元青花缠枝牡丹纹葫芦瓶
土耳其托普卡比宫博物馆藏

图3-1-51
元青花花卉纹葫芦形执壶
印度尼西亚国家博物馆藏

2. 仿金属器造型器形

（1）匜

仿金属器造型器形是指某个时代的某种陶瓷造型模仿先代前朝或当代的某种金属器造型。通常该时代的陶瓷器形会在金属器造型的基础上有所创新发展。

青铜器匜于西周晚期开始出现，在战国流行。器身似瓢，前有流，后有鋬，有的有足（见图3-5-52）。

元青花匜仿青铜器造型，做盥洗用具。多为平底，没有足（见图3-1-53），有的在流的下部有圆环形小系（见图3-1-54）。

图3-1-52
齐侯匜
上海博物馆藏

图3-1-53
元青花天鹅戏水纹匜
广州东方博物馆藏

图3-1-54
元青花双凤纹匜
甘肃临洮县博物馆藏

（2）鼎

铜器鼎在二里头文化中已经有成熟的造型，有两立耳，垂鼓或者方形腹部，底有三足或四足，用作煮食器（见图3-1-55）。

仿铜器鼎造型的元青花陶瓷鼎较少见（见图3-1-56）。

图3-1-55
兽面扁足纹鼎
北京故宫博物院藏

图3-1-56
元青花花卉纹鼎
北京故宫博物院藏

（3）觚

青铜觚出现于商代早期，有喇叭口，细腰，高身，平底（见图3-1-57）。

宋代金石学兴起，青铜觚成为文人雅士鉴赏与把玩的雅物，被用作陈设品和插花器。在这种风气影响下，陶瓷中开始出现觚造型[99]。

目前发现的元青花觚，在整体造型上没有太大变化：敞口、细身、圈足，中部有时装饰出戟（见图3-1-58）。

图3-1-57
葵觚
北京故宫博物院藏

图3-1-58
元青花蕉叶纹出戟觚
首都博物馆藏

（4）荷叶盖罐

荷叶盖罐的器形最早见于唐代，江苏丹徒丁卯桥金银器窖藏中出土一荷叶形悬鱼银器盖，盖面呈荷叶状，叶柄蜷曲为钮，叶缘呈五曲起伏，曲凹下缘悬小鱼[100]。

目前发现的元青花大罐，存留有荷叶形盖子的有高安市博物馆藏的云龙纹大罐和日本出光美术馆藏的昭君出塞大罐。（见图3-1-59、图3-1-60）高安市博物馆的云龙纹大罐，罐盖呈荷叶形，盖面以钮为中心绘螺旋状散射的叶脉纹，四面分别绘青鱼、螃蟹、鲶鱼、鳜鱼，模拟水中状态（见图3-1-61）。

图3-1-59
元青花云龙纹荷叶盖罐
高安市博物馆藏

图3-1-60
元青花昭君出塞图荷叶盖罐
日本出光美术馆藏

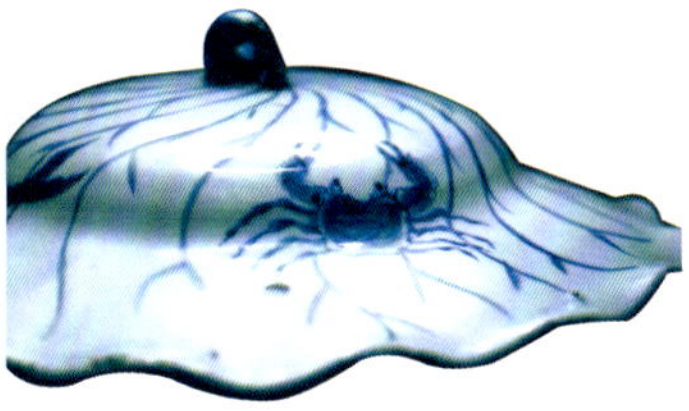

图3-1-61
元青花云龙纹荷叶盖罐盖子
高安市博物馆藏

（5）香炉

香炉常与花瓶配套使用，是元代供品的常规组合。以江西萍乡和湖南常德出土的瓷器三供为其典型代表。

铜器鼎除作为煮食器外，西周时还作为礼器成为等级制度的象征。鼎式香炉做供器用，也是“礼制”的象征，与铜器鼎有着相同的文化因素。

元青花香炉在形制上与铜器鼎相似，有对称两耳，三足。其创新之处在于相连的底座及配套的兽钮盖。（见图3 1 62）

图3-1-62
元青花菊花纹连座香炉
江西萍乡市博物馆

3. 外来文化器形

外来文化器形是指陶瓷的造型本身在中原文化中不曾有，是融合了少数民族文化或者其他国家文化而产生的器形。

（1）扁壶

契丹族在游牧时用一种皮革缝制的皮囊作为盛水用具，也就是我们现在所说的皮囊壶。契丹族建立辽政权之后，烧制了仿皮囊壶器形的陶瓷鸡冠壶（见图3-1-63）。

同为游牧民族的蒙古族，在文化上与契丹族有一些相通之处。元青花四系扁壶，唇口外翻，腹部垂直，肩部有四个系，方便携带，是具有游牧民族特色的器物[101]（见图3-1-64）。

图3-1-63
辽酱黄釉鸡冠壶

图3-1-64
元青花云肩双龙戏珠纹四系方扁壶
日本出光美术馆藏

（2）高足杯

高足杯应是适应蒙古人马上饮酒的习惯，高足易于抓握（见图3-1-65、图3-1-66）。一些圈足上凸棱的设置，也能增大摩擦力，防止滑落（见图3-1-65）。

图3-1-65
元青花龙纹高足杯
金乐轩藏

图3-1-66
元青花梅花纹高足杯
金乐轩藏

（3）大盘

大盘是在伊斯兰文化及蒙古游牧文化影响下形成的器形。

明代马欢著的《瀛涯胜览》中说道：“波斯人用盘满盛其饭，浇酥油汤汁，以手摄入口中而食。”从伊斯兰细密画中也可看出，当地的饮食习惯是，众人围坐一圈，中间放置白地蓝画的大盘盛放食物[102]（见图3-1-67[103]）。

在伊朗国家博物馆、土耳其托普卡比宫博物馆、印度尼西亚、泰国等地也发现众多此种类型的大盘，直径多在30厘米左右，大的可达50—60厘米。

图3-1-67
伊斯兰细密画用餐图

（4）小罐

此类小罐器高一般为5—8厘米，纹饰简练，发色偏灰。纹样多为缠枝和折枝花卉，绘画手法随性率性。造型有敛口四系方形、唇口双系扁腹式、唇口双系瓜棱形等[104]（见图3-1-68、图3-1-69）。

这些小罐很有可能是当时东南亚国家用于陪葬的器物，菲律宾吕宋岛出土的墓葬材料也证实了这一观点。也有一些研究者认为这些双系小罐配以木质或金属材质的盖子，可以用来存放香料和药物[105]。

图3-1-68
元青花唇口双系扁腹式小罐
广州东方博物馆藏

图3-1-69
元青花唇口双系瓜棱形小罐
美国旧金山亚洲艺术博物馆藏

第二节
元青花纹饰

一、纹饰的作用及意义

纹饰是器物上装饰图案的总称，是几千年来人类在创作活动中思想情感的一种表达方式，体现了人们对生活的期望、寄托和追求，具有鲜明的历史时代气息。

纹饰对人类生活的涵盖面非常广泛，可运用在建筑、家具、服饰、纺织、陶瓷等不同的类别上。

在陶瓷鉴定领域，陶瓷的纹饰具有时代延续性和发展创新性的历史特征。因此，在古陶瓷鉴定中，掌握纹饰在不同历史时期的固有特点，了解纹饰之间继承与发展的关系，有助于鉴定器物的年代。

二、元青花纹饰概念

元青花纹饰是指在元青花瓷器成型的素胎上用钴为着色剂并按一定的技法所绘制的各种图案的组合。

三、元青花纹饰类别

在纹饰题材上，元青花瓷器和当时的刺绣题材十分相似，在形式处理上也受刺绣影响[106]。根据绘制题材在图案组合中的作用，元青花纹饰可分为主题纹饰及辅助纹饰。元青花主题纹饰可分为植物题材、动物题材、人物题材三大类别（见表3-2-1）。

表3-2-1

纹饰题材类别	植物	动物	人物
纹饰题材种类	牡丹纹	龙纹	历史、戏曲人物故事情节
	莲花纹	凤纹	神话人物或文人高士形象
	菊花纹	麒麟纹	
	松竹梅纹	鱼纹	
	芭蕉纹	孔雀纹	
	瓜果纹	鸳鸯纹	
		白鹭纹	
		芦雁纹	
		天鹅纹	

（一）元青花主题纹饰

1. 植物纹

（1）牡丹纹

牡丹纹常以缠枝牡丹形式出现（见图3-2-1—图3-2-8），偶见折枝牡丹（见图3-2-9）。

缠枝牡丹大多作为元青花的主题纹饰绘于梅瓶、罐等琢器的腹部或碗、盘等圆器的中心位置；也有作为辅助纹饰装饰在琢器的颈部、肩部或圆器的内外壁；有时也与动物图案结合，如凤穿牡丹等纹饰题材。（参见本章本节动物纹部分）

缠枝牡丹广泛绘制于大型器物上，特征为花大叶大。部分缠枝牡丹纹是先描画或刻画花蕊、叶脉，然后涂青料。牡丹花朵不填满色，瓣边沿留白或涂淡色（见图3-2-1—图3-2-6）；也有拔白牡丹纹（见图3-2-7、图3-2-8）。

宋代的牡丹仅见正、侧两种姿态，而元代的牡丹有俯、仰、正、侧、向、背等多种姿态变化，同一器物上出现的牡丹花纹形态多不相同，有正面牡丹、侧面牡丹以及背面牡丹等（见图3-2-1—图3-2-6）。从出土实物来看，元青花瓷器上的牡丹与元代刺绣上的牡丹非常相似[107]。

正面牡丹花瓣分布均匀，外层花瓣数量通常为七瓣，也有八瓣的，末端呈鸡冠花状（见图3-2-1—图3-2-3）。

侧面牡丹纹样大致有两种形式：

第一种花朵下方展开着七片

Section 2:
Yuan Underglaze Blue Decorative Patterns

1. The Use and Meaning of Decorative Patterns

Decorative Pattern is the term used to describe the conglomeration of all enhancing images adorning a ware. For thousands of years decoration has been a way of expressing human thought and emotion in the process of cultivating and living. It goes to show hopes, curiosities, and pursuits in life, and offers a clear picture of each period in history.

Decoration touches a very broad part of human life and can be experienced through all types of lives as seen in architecture, furniture, clothing, ceramics, and so forth.

In the realm of ceramic authentication, ceramic decorative patterns have historical characteristics of era-to-era continuity as well as reflecting new developments. Because of this, fully grasping the specific characteristics of different historical periods and understanding the connected and developmental relationships between decorative motifs is very useful when determining the age of a piece.

2. YUB Decorative Patterns Defined

YUB decorative patterns refer to all types of images and compositions of cobalt coloring agent applied to the plain surface of the porcelain body using specified techniques.

3. YUB Decorative Pattern Categories

According to the subject matter and differences in composition importance, YUB decorative motifs can be divided into two main categories: Theme Decorations and Supplementary Patterns. Decorative subject matter on YUB took direct impact from its contemporary embroidery patterns; form processing was also directly reflected in the embroidery of the day [106].

YUB Theme Decorations can be further split into three main types: Flora, Fauna, and Personage (see Table 3-2-1).

Table 3-2-1

Theme Category	Flora	Fauna	Personage
Decoration Type	Peonies	Dragon	Historical and Opera Scenes
	Lotuses	Phoenix	Mythical, Scholarly, and Noble Idealized Figures
	Chrysanthemums	Qilin (Mythical Creature)	
	Pine, Bamboo, Plum	Fish	
	Banana (Bajiao)	Peacock	
	Melon and Fruit	Mandarin Ducks	
		Egret	
		Wild Goose	
		Swan	

A. YUB Theme Decoration

I. Flora Patterns

a. Peony Pattern

Commonly occurring as peony scrolls (see pictures 3-2-1—3-2-8), they are only occasionally seen as a peony spray (see picture 3-2-9).

Peony scrolls usually occur on YUB as a theme decoration on the body portion of closed pieces such as meiping vases and jars; and in the center of open pieces such as bowls and plates; or

（或六片）花瓣，形状为长条形，花瓣不重叠，根部细，至末端渐粗，末端呈鸡冠花状，颜色稍淡（见图3-2-4）。

第二种花朵下方展开着四片（或六片）花瓣，形状短而阔，花瓣不重叠，两侧微微合起，末梢涂淡或留白，更有立体感（见图3-2-5）。

牡丹花叶子形状多呈葫芦状，有一至五个尖瓣，中间的尖瓣细长，其余四片分别左右对称分布（见图3-2-1—图3-2-9）。

图3-2-1

图3-2-2

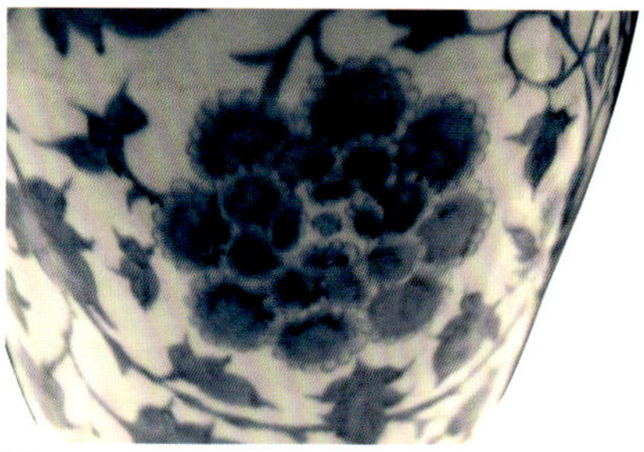
图3-2-3

图3-2-4

图3-2-5

图3-2-6

图3-2-7

图3-2-8

图3-2-9
元青花折枝牡丹纹执壶
内蒙古自治区文物考古研究所藏

can act as supplementary patterns on the neck and shoulders of closed pieces; or the internal and external walls of open pieces. They also can occasionally be seen as a theme decoration in conjunction with other fauna themes such as phoenix amongst peonies (see Fauna Pattern Heading of this section).

Peony scrolls are widely used on larger YUB wares, and have characteristically large flowers and leaves. Portions of peony scrolls are applied by first tracing or carving the floral stamen and veins and then filling in with cobalt dye. The peony blooms are not usually overflowing with color; often the edges remain uncolored or are filled with a light dye (see pictures 3-2-1—3-2-6). There is also occasion when peonies are done in white against a blue background (see pictures 3-2-7 and 3-2-8).

Song Dynasty peonies only presented with two postures, whilst the Yuan Dynasty saw a change to include bowing, raised head, face forward, side, upright, backside, and so forth postures. It is also common to have several postures, i.e. face, side, back, etc., all on one piece (see pictures 3-2-1—3-2-6). From excavated YUB samples we can see that the peony scrolls on porcelain very closely reflect those that were seen on contemporary Yuan embroidery works [107].

Face forward peony petals are evenly distributed and the outermost ring often has seven or eight petals; their edges ruffled like a cockscomb (see pictures 3-2-1—3-2-3).

Side view peonies are primarily presented in two different ways:

The first, six or seven elongated petals extend, without touching, down from around the bottom of the bloom; their bases thin and fanning out to a cockscomb edge that is lightly colored (see picture 3-2-4).

The second, four or six stout petals extend out from the bottom of the bloom, almost touching; their colors become progressively lighter, giving it more dimension (see picture 3-2-5).

The peony leaves are mainly in the general shape of the Hulu gourd, having one to five pointed tips. The central apex tip is elongated with the other four tips situated in pairs on either side (see pictures 3-2-1—3-2-9).

b. Lotus Pattern

Lotus patterns include lotus scrolls (see pictures 3-2-10—3-2-18), lotus bouquets (see pictures 3-2-19 and 3-2-20), and lotus ponds (see pictures 3-2-21 and 3-2-22).

Lotus scrolls are primarily seen as supplementary patterns on the neck and shoulders of closed pieces and around the walls of open pieces. Lotus bouquets are commonly theme decorations on YUB bowls and plates, and as such occur in the center of the piece. Lotus ponds are often used in conjunction with fauna themes such as Mandarin ducks or egrets (see Fauna Patterns Heading of this section).

Majority of lotus petals are first outlined; then are filled, but not completely with color: Petal centers are filled, but both or one side is left uncolored (see pictures 3-2-14 and 3-2-15); or the petal front is filled in, and the back half is white [108] (see picture 3-2-19).

Lotus leaves are predominantly split into two styles [109]:

The first is scissor style: The base points of the leaf curl back towards the stem creating a scissor handle effect, while two thin middle portions of the leaf extends out into an elongated Hulu shape (see pictures 3-2-10 and 3-2-11). Occasionally the central portions meld together into one (see pictures 3-2-12 and 3-2-13).

The second is the classic scroll style: The leaf shape develops off the foundational shape of the original, but becomes more simplified and formalized (see pictures 3-2-14—3-2-17). This style of leaf is most likely to have appeared later than the scissor style.

Lotus patterns are images arisen under the influence of Buddhism. The Southern Dynasties Celadon wares were the first to see lotus patterns, and it was under the Tang and Song Dynasties that lotuses became a widespread theme pattern [110]. In the Yuan Dynasty, the lotus continued to hold an important position. The Buddhist religion holds the lotus in high esteem and commonly uses the lotus as Buddha's seat or uses lotus petals for decoration to represent Buddha and thus receive his protection [111].

c. Chrysanthemum Pattern

Chrysanthemum decorations include two types: Scrolls (see pictures 3-2-23, 3-2-25, and 3-2-26) and Sprays (see pictures 3-2-27 and 3-2-28).

Similarly, chrysanthemums utilize a "trace first then fill in" color application method, with one side of each petal remaining white or being filled in with light color (see pictures 3-2-23—3-2-25); sometimes they are only outlined without filling in color

（2）莲花纹

莲花纹主要包括缠枝莲纹（见图3-2-10—图3-2-18）、把莲纹（见图3-2-19、图3-2-20）及莲池纹（见图3-2-21、图3-2-22）。

缠枝莲纹多作为辅助纹饰装饰在琢器的颈部、肩部或圆器的口沿、内外壁；把莲纹多作为元青花的主题纹饰绘于碗、盘等圆器的中心位置；有时莲池纹也与动物图案结合，如莲池鸳鸯纹及莲池白鹭纹等纹饰题材。（参见本章本节动物纹部分）

莲瓣大都先描边，后填青料，青料不填满：仅填花瓣中间，两边或一侧留白（见图3-2-14、图3-2-15）；或填花瓣前端，后半留白[108]（见图3-2-19）。

莲花的叶子主要有两种形式[109]：

一是呈剪刀形，根部左右两片尖瓣呈卷曲状，像剪刀的把柄，中间部分左右各两片尖瓣细长，末端呈葫芦状，延展较长（见图3-2-10、图3-2-11）；有时中间部分的两片细长尖瓣消失（见图3-2-12、图3-2-13）。

二是呈卷草纹式，叶子在原有的形状基础上更简单、形式化（见图3-2-14—图3-2-17）。这种叶子形式出现的时间应该晚于上述的剪刀形。

莲花纹是受佛教影响产生的图案。南朝青瓷上的莲瓣纹是最早的实例。唐宋时期以莲花作为主题的纹饰被广泛应用[110]。到了元代，莲花纹继续占重要地位。佛教信仰认为莲花出淤泥而不染，濯清涟而不妖，象征着西方净土，所以佛多以莲花为座，以莲花莲瓣为装饰并以此代替佛，有受佛庇护的吉意[111]。

图3-2-10

图3-2-11

图3-2-12

图3-2-13

图3-2-14

图3-2-15

图3-2-16

图3-2-17

图3-2-18

(see pictures 3-2-26—3-2-28). The flower bloom has one to three levels of petals, and sometimes each level of petal can present with a light-dark color gradation (see pictures 3-2-23—3-2-26).

Chrysanthemum leaves basically have two different styles:

The first is similar to that of the lotus leaf scissor style. Often the leaf has one point on either side (see picture 3-2-24) or three points (see pictures 3-2-25 and 3-2-26), and they generally assume a Hulu-gourd-like shape.

The second is a more simplified leaf style. The number of points varies and is not always clearly delineated (see pictures 3-2-23, 3-2-27, and 3-2-28).

d. Pine, Bamboo, Plum Pattern

The Pine, Bamboo, and Plum pattern is also called the "three friends of winter". The three friends of winter were often praised in Chinese literature for not withering in the cold weather. The three friends of winter's unwillingness to wilt in the cold, personified Han people's unwillingness to give in to the minority rule. It henceforth became a symbol of unrelenting character and unswerving loyalty [112].

This pattern is applied as a grouped set. The pine trunk and branches are first traced out, and the details are then added. The pine needles are tightly grouped into a bunch or fan shape; the bamboo shoot and leaves are all applied in single brush strokes; the plum blossom is first outlined and color is filled in, leaving a slight white edge (see pictures 3-2-29 and 3-2-30).

e. Banana Pattern

Banana plants were often accompanied by rocks.

The banana leaves would be filled with color on both edges, leaving a long strip of white as the leaf stalk (see pictures 3-2-31 and 3-2-32), and the leaves often present with sporadic cracks along both edges (see picture 3-2-31).

f. Melon and Fruit Pattern

Melon and fruit patterns used as a theme decoration started in the Tang Dynasty. YUB saw the application of melons and fruit as a symbol of autumn harvest, and would usually include in the decoration grouping things like grapes, pumpkins, bananas, and rocks to complete a harvest motif [113] (see pictures 3-2-33—3-2-35).

II. Fauna Patterns

a. Dragon Pattern

Dragons, although they are mythical creatures, have been the symbol of the Chinese people. Over the 5000 years of recorded Chinese history, the presence of the dragon has prevailed, although its depiction and features have changed throughout. Dragons painted onto YUB include heads facing forward (see pictures 3-2-36—3-2-41), and heads facing backwards (see pictures 3-2-42—3-2-45).

Most dragons have thin necks, slanted upward horns, parallel eyes, open mouths, and visible saw and canine teeth (see pictures 3-2-36—3-2-45). Some dragon heads have hairs or hair strands on the tops of their heads and beards (see pictures 3-2-36—3-2-45).

Dragon scales usually consist of sketched scales (see picture 3-2-46), cross-hatched scales (see picture 3-2-47), and outline-filled scales [114] (see picture 3-2-48).

There is a long fin running along the length of the dragon spine, and it is also possible for the underbelly and neck of the dragon to be adorned with neat symmetrical bands or ringlets of white running the length of the body (see pictures 3-2-36, 3-2-40, 3-2-42, and 3-2-43).

The legs of the dragon are noticeably muscular with bands of hair, sparse or concentrated, flowing freely from the elbow. The dragon claws are powerful and usually consist of three or four talons (see pictures 3-2-49—3-2-54).

The dragon tail is thinner than the body, and can taper to a finned point (see pictures 3-2-55—3-2-57).

From the 3rd year of Zhiyuan onward (1337 AD), five clawed (five talons per hand) dragons were reserved for exclusive use on wares to be used by the emperor [115].

b. Phoenix Pattern

The phoenix has the head of a fowl, the beak of an eagle, a scaled body, and fanning plumage. Phoenixes are often depicted amongst flowers, and can be seen on the same ware as dragons or even qilin (mythical creature, see following heading) (see pictures 3-2-58—3-2-61).

(3) 菊花纹

图3-2-19

菊花纹包括缠枝菊花纹（见图3-2-23、图3-2-25、图3-2-26）和折枝菊花纹（见图3-2-27、图3-2-28）两种表现形式。

菊花先勾边后涂青料，花瓣一侧留白或涂淡（见图3-2-23—图3-2-25），有时花瓣仅勾边不填色（见图3-2-26—图3-2-28），有时花朵可有一层到三层花瓣，有时每层花瓣有色阶深浅变化（见图3-2-23—图3-2-26）。

菊花纹的叶子大致也分两种：

一种为类似莲花叶子的剪刀形，左右通常有一对（见图3-2-24）或三对（见图3-2-25、图3-2-26）对称叶瓣，末端为葫芦形。

一种为较简易的叶子，叶子形状各异，尖瓣数量不定，也不明显（见图3-2-23、图3-2-27、图3-2-28）。

图3-2-25

图3-2-20

图3-2-26

图3-2-21

图3-2-23

图3-2-27

图3-2-22

图3-2-24

图3-2-28

c. Qilin (Mythical Creature) Pattern

The Qilin is a mythical creature composed of elements from several animals. It usually consists of a deer head, ox hooves, and horse tail; but it can also have a tiger head, horse head, and include lion claws [116] (see picture 3-2-62).

d. Fish Pattern

Fish include various types of carp, crucian, catfish, Mandarin fish and so forth. Fish normally appear amongst lotus or sea grass underwater scenes.

The fish are usually painted quite realistically, and the Mandarin fish is distinguished by its spotted body, spiny dorsal fin, and intimidating demeanor [117]. The sea grass is long and flowing, narrow at the root and flaring out at the leaf (see pictures 3-2-63—3-3-66).

e. Peacock Pattern

The peacock is depicted with a long beak, high crest, full body plumage, and long delicate legs. The peacocks are most often depicted as standing with wings spread or flying, and are commonly seen amongst peony sprays (see pictures 3-2-67—3-2-69).

f. Mandarin Ducks Pattern

Mandarin ducks were viewed by ancient Chinese as a symbol of love. As such, they are always seen in pairs, and often floating on a lotus pond [118]. Mandarin ducks have been depicted with lines along the water under them, thus giving a feeling of floating movement [119]. Mandarin ducks are always depicted facing one another, and even if their bodies are facing the same direction, their eyes will still retain a fixed gaze. The feathers of the ducks slightly rise upward [120] (see pictures 3-2-70—3-2-72).

g. Egret Pattern

The Egret pattern owes its beginnings to embroidery [121]. The white egret is often depicted amongst a lotus pond. At times the egret is depicted standing on both feet, and other times it uses only one foot with the other raised (see pictures 3-2-73—3-2-76).

h. Wild Goose Pattern

The wild goose was a popular design during the Song Dynasty, but during the Yuan Dynasty it slightly changed to include a reed in the flying goose's mouth, which was a decoration motif borrowed from officers' uniforms of the Mongol ranks [122] (see picture 3-2-77).

i. Swan Pattern

The Swan pattern is not very common, but often appears in conjunction with the lotus pond. Swans with upward facing gazes, and slightly raised plumage resemble that of the Mandarin duck (see picture 3-2-78).

III. Personages

In regards to the first appearance of personages (historical figures and other mythical characters), we can refer back to the detailed discussion in Chapter 2 Section 1.

Currently, there is a very small amount of complete YUB samples with personage decoration. However, those in existence are almost all of exquisite quality and appearance.

The character depiction method utilized a vertical brush stroke with ink wash technique; allowing for a series of dark and light colors to add detail and depth to characters' clothing [123] (see pictures 3-2-79—3-2-82)

According to the content of the images, personage decorations can be divided into two main categories:

a. History and Opera Scenes

The images of historical and traditional opera characters were painted with the following characteristics [124]:

i. Using specific clothing, certain characters are easily recognizable, and the mood of the story is set. The style of clothing was modeled after the actual apparel of the day. The Yuan Dynasty was a multi-religion and multi-culture nation; thus the characters gracing the surfaces of YUB were a reflection of the actual conglomerated customs of the day. For example, the clothes worn by Zhao Jun were actually articles of clothing an affluent Chinese woman would have worn during the Yuan Dynasty, and not something Zhao Jun would normally have worn. Additionally, the supporting characters were dressed in Mongol garb, not what their minority group would have worn at the time of the story.

ii. Using facial features, different nationalities could be

（4）松竹梅纹

松竹梅纹也叫岁寒三友图。“岁寒三友”之称滥觞于《论语·子罕》，“岁寒然后知松柏之后凋也”之句，至迟在元代已用岁寒代称松竹梅了。松竹梅不畏严寒的特征与当时不甘外族统治的汉族文人的心态是相吻合的，因而这一特征日渐人格化，直至成为忠贞不渝品格的象征[112]。

松竹梅纹的松树先描绘树干后点染细节，松针密茂，呈团状或扇状；竹干、竹叶一笔画成；梅花则先勾出花瓣轮廓，中心涂青，留有白边。（见图3-2-29、图3-2-30）

图3-2-29

图3-2-30

（5）芭蕉纹

芭蕉纹多与山石入画构成蕉石图。

芭蕉叶勾勒填青，中茎留白（见图3-2-31、图3-2-32），有的叶子两侧有不对称开裂现象（见图3-2-31）。

图3-2-31

图3-2-32

（6）瓜果纹

瓜果纹是以一些植物果实为母题的纹饰，始见于唐代。元代青花瓷器常以瓜果纹组成秋实画面，如大盘上多绘葡萄、南瓜、芭蕉、山石与花草组成的秋实图案[113]（见图3-2-33—图3-2-35）。

图3-2-33

图3-2-34

图3-2-35

2. 动物纹

（1）龙纹

龙是虚构的动物形象，也是中华民族的标志与象征。在中国上下五千年的文明进程中，龙的形象不断地演变。

元青花瓷器上的龙大都威武凶猛。有的头部面向前方（见图3-2-36—图3-2-41），有的回首（见图3-2-42—图3-2-45）。

龙大部分都是细颈，发角斜向上，两眼平正，龙嘴张开，可见锯齿及犬齿。有的龙头顶及下巴有须状或带状毛发。（见图3-2-36—图3-2-45）

龙鳞画法主要有素描鳞（见图3-2-46）、斜方鳞（见图3-2-47）以及勾边实填鳞[114]（见图3-2-48）。全身背部都有鳍，有时在颈部及腹部可见白描的排列整齐

emphasized, personalities could be given to the characters, and the mood of the story set.

iii. YUB historical and opera figures all had very clearly specific characteristics, different from that of the vagueness seen in the earlier Song and Jin Dynasties.

Known examples include: Xiao He Chasing Han Xin, Gui Gu Zi Coming Down From the Mountain, Yu Chi Gong Rescues His Master, Zhou Ya Fu's Encampment, Romance of the Western Chamber, Zhao Jun Disembarks, and The Three Visits to the Thatched Cottage (see pictures 3-2-79—3-2-81).

b. Mythical, Scholarly, and Noble Idealized Figures

This category of decoration usually only has personified characters, but not specific stories attached. For example, the YUB Yi of the Xi'an Relic Protection and Archeological Research Academy collection: Some believe the figure to be Lin He Jing (famous for his love of the plum and crane), others believe it to be the official Zhao Bian who entered the city with only "An instrument and a crane", still others believe it to be one of the eight immortals Cao Guo Jiu or Lan Cai He [125]. Often these figures' clothing does not make them immediately recognizable, and there are no accompanying words to help identify them [126] (see picture 3-2-82).

YUB character painting methods differed from that of the prior eras. There was a notable inventiveness in taking ink painting techniques and applying them to porcelain. This was rarely seen in the earlier Song and Jin Dynasties, and greatly influenced the decoration styles of the later Ming and Qing Dynasties [127].

B. YUB Supplementary Patterns

YUB Supplementary Patterns primarily include: Stylized Lotus Petal Design, Cape Jasmine Pattern, Lingzhi Pattern, Waves Pattern, Key Fret Scroll, Classic Scroll, Diamond Scroll, Banana Leaf Pattern, Cloud Collar, Coin Scroll, Miscellaneous Treasures, and the Eight Buddhist Emblems.

I. Stylized Lotus Petal Design

Stylized lotus petal designs often present on the external wall of bowls, plates, vases, jars or on the shoulder or foot of vases and jars. The interior of each lotus petal contains further supplemental designs including flowers, clouds, flames, miscellaneous treasures, and so forth. The lotus petal outlines consist of one thick and one thin parallel line with a certain space left between each petal (see pictures 3-2-83—3-2-85).

II. Cape Jasmine Pattern

The Cape Jasmine pattern most often presents on the mouth or outside wall of plates and bowls, or can act as a partition pattern between motifs on jars and vases. The flower petals are in collections of six, arranged in an even star pattern around a slightly separated stamen (see pictures 3-3-86—3-2-88).

III. Lingzhi (Auspicious Fungus) Pattern

The Lingzhi pattern is most commonly found in the center of a bowl, or along the outside wall of a bowl (see pictures 3-2-89—3-2-91).

IV. Wave Pattern

Wave patterns are usually found along the mouth of large plates, around the necks of jars, or as a partition pattern, but are not seen on small wares [129]. Waves are first painted with a thick outline then are filled with meticulous curved lines. The head of the wave is large, and the space between waves is often filled with wave foam or whirlpools (see pictures 3-2-92—3-2-94).

V. Key Fret Scroll

Key Fret Scrolls first appeared on the bronze wares of the Shang Dynasty. It is a geometric pattern constructed of interlocking lines looking similar to "key frets". The pattern is often started at the top left and follows a counter clockwise direction. They usually occur in two opposing frames, but single frames also present (see pictures 3-2-95 and 3-2-96).

VI. Juan Cao (Grass Curls) or Classic Scroll

Classic Scrolls often occur at the mouth, bottom or foot ring section of a piece, or act as partition patterns. The Classic Scroll is a series of "S" shaped lines in alternating and interlocking continuation around the circumference of the piece, but it is also possible to see 'two up, one down' or 'two down, one up' portions

的圆片（见图3-2-36、图3-2-40、图3-2-42、图3-2-43）。

龙的腿部肌肉明显，肘部有飘逸的带状毛发，毛发有稀疏有密集，爪刚劲有力，以三爪、四爪居多（见图3-2-49—图3-2-54）。

龙尾较龙身细，上方有鳍（见图3-2-55—图3-2-57）。

从至元三年（公元1337年）开始，五爪龙纹仅可出现在皇帝及皇族使用的器物上面[115]。

图3-2-40

图3-2-45

图3-2-41

图3-2-46

图3-2-36

图3-2-42

图3-2-47

图3-2-37

图3-2-38

图3-2-43

图3-2-48

图3-2-39

图3-2-44

图3-2-49

of the scroll where sections meet. The style of the scroll is very free flowing and unrestrained (see pictures 3-2-97—3-2-99).

VII. Diamond Scroll

Diamond Scroll is located across the mouth of a piece or used as a partition pattern. Each Diamond consists of a double outline, and the four center edges as well as center of the diamond are adorned with small dots creating a blossom effect (see pictures 3-2-100—3-2-102). It is very common to see diamond scroll around the mouth of large plates (see pictures 3-2-100 and 3-2-101).

VIII. Banana (Plantain) Leaf Pattern

Banana leaf patterns commonly occur on the neck of vases and on the lower and foot portions of pieces. The leaf stalk extends through the middle of the leaf to the tip, and is painted in one stroke or too strokes then filled in. The leaf edge is first outlined and either filled or left blank. Thin parallel lines make up the veins of the leaf and fill the entire interior (see pictures 3-2-103 and 3-2-104).

IX. Cloud Collar Pattern

Cloud Collars are often added to the shoulder of jars, vases, and flasks; or to the interior wall of large plates. The edge consists of three parallel lines, with the one central line thicker than the two surrounding. The cloud interior is filled with supplementary patterns of flora, waves, or even fauna (see pictures 3-2-105—3-2-107).

Cloud collars first appeared on Yuan Dynasty Porcelain, and they imitate the 'cloud collar' often seen on Yuan Dynasty apparel [130].

X. Coin Scroll

Coin Scrolls are often seen on the mouth or foot of wares or act as partition patterns. They are composed of a series of interlocking circles resulting in bronze coin-like scrolls (see pictures 3-2-108 and 3-2-109).

XI. Miscellaneous Treasures or Eight Buddhist Emblems

Miscellaneous treasures include: Double Horn, Silver Ignot, Rhinoceros Horn, Flame, Flaming Pearl, Conch, Coral, Flame Wheel, Double Coin, and so forth (see pictures 3-2-110 and 3-2-111). These are items that were adapted from Yuan Dynasty clothing and shawls, and are often found on the shoulder or around the foot of wares. They often made up the content of stylized lotus petals. Because there was no set pattern to the items, it was common to see repetition, and they gained the name miscellaneous treasures [131].

The Eight Buddhist Emblems are an adaptation of the offerings given in Tibetan Buddhism, they often include: The Eternal Wheel, The Conch, The Parasol, The Banner, The Lotus, The Treasure Vase, The Goldfish, and The Endless Knot [132].

XII. Words or Script

It is very uncommon for YUB to have words or script, and the content includes words such as "Shou" (Longevity), poems, and so forth (see pictures 3-2-112 and 3-2-113).

4. Characteristics of YUB Decoration Manifestation

YUB decoration can be divided into two categories: White Ground Blue Pattern and Blue Ground White Pattern.

White Ground Blue Pattern: This is the most common decoration style seen on YUB. It refers to the direct application of blue dye to the surface of the plain body in specific designs, then the application of clear glaze over the top (see picture 3-2-114).

Blue Ground White Pattern: This refers to the process of creating a decorative pattern with blue dye outlines and then filling in blue dye everywhere but inside the patterns, creating a blue background and leaving white patterns (see picture 3-2-115).

It is also possible to see the combination of the two styles on one ware.

5. Characteristics of YUB Decoration Painting Technique

YUB decoration application utilized a highly elastic, pointy, and absorbent brush being dipped into water to mix with the colored dye; this was then applied to a relatively absorbent clay body in the desired shapes and patterns [133]. It is very similar to

图3-2-50

图3-2-51

图3-2-52

图3-2-53

图3-2-54

图3-2-55

图3-2-56

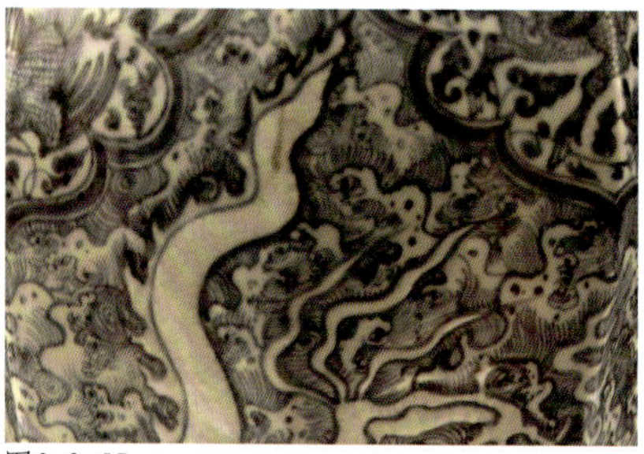
图3-2-57

（2）凤纹

凤纹表现为鸡头、鹰嘴、鳞身、花尾。凤纹多与花卉入画，有时也与龙、麒麟出现在同一器物上（见图3-2-58—图3-2-61）。

图3-2-58

图3-2-59

图3-2-60

图3-2-61

（3）麒麟纹

麒麟是虚构的动物形象。有鹿头、牛蹄、马尾，也有画成虎头、马头或带鬃狮爪的[116]（见图3-2-62）。

图3-2-62

（4）鱼纹

鱼纹包括鲤、鲇、鳜、鲫，多与莲花、水藻构成莲池鱼藻图。

鱼纹画法写实逼真，鳜鱼身上斑点一一点出，背脊尖利透明，神态凶猛[117]；水藻纹根细叶粗，排列有序（见图3-2-63—图3-2-66）。

the watercolor and ink wash painting techniques.

The first inkling of ink wash painting appeared in the Sui Dynasty; Zhan Zi Qian's "Spring Travels". Through the Tang, Song, and Five Dynasties periods, the techniques developed, and many famous artists emerged. During the Yuan Dynasty, the YUB artisans often studied the techniques of the ink painters, and the application of these techniques to the porcelain bodies was a natural transition [134].

YUB painting techniques primarily employ delineating, dotting, tracing, and dabbing [135].

Dotting is utilized on bamboo, lotuses, rocks, flowers, and other delicate locations. Delineating is primarily used on white ground YUB to create thick and thin outlines of objects and patterns (see picture 3-2-116). Some decorative items first utilize a thick delineation and they are touched up with thick and thin lines to complete the pattern. On the mouth of plates or the mouth and foot of jars, vases, and so forth, rings are applied with a more delicate tracing technique (see picture 3-2-117). Small pieces often will only utilize a single style of tracing to complete the entire pattern [136] (see picture 3-2-118). Dabbing is primarily used to add texture to natural objects such as rocks. The use of "Axe-Blade" dabbing, where the tip of the brush is placed along the delineated border and pulled at an oblique angle away; offered a clear, dark to light gradation and gave the appearance of texture [137] (see picture 3-2-119).

Under the inspiration of ink wash painting, Underglaze Blue porcelain first introduced the use of the water separation painting technique in the middle of the Yuan Dynasty. During the painting process, first using a relatively wet cockscomb goat hair brush then dipping it into diluted dye, they were able to utilize varying degrees of dye concentration in one filling brush stroke within the image outline; further giving them the ability to add color disparity to a single image [138].

Due to the differences presented by the dissimilar mediums of paper and clay, not all the techniques utilized in ink wash painting were able to be applied to the ceramic decoration process. Only the various layering techniques were achievable, but even still the likelihood of using them was quite low [139].

6. Characteristics of YUB Decoration Composition

YUB decoration composition can be divided into two types: Full and Sparse.

A. Full Decoration

Full composition decoration is characterized by highly concentrated patterns and motifs. The majority of the piece is covered, and the amount of clear white space is minimal (see pictures 3-2-120 and 3-2-121).

B. Sparse Decoration

Sparse composition decoration, compared to that of the full variety, is characterized by large amounts of free white space and lower amount of patterns and motifs (see picture 3-2-122).

YUB closed pieces such as vases and jars utilized a decoration technique of layered horizontal banding, and the open wares such as bowls and plates used a concentric layer decoration technique [140]. Each layer had its own characteristics, and the use of supplementary patterns was employed to partition separate decoration layers. Wares predominantly present with three to eleven layers, with only small wares presenting with a single layer (see picture 3-2-123). According to Islamic tradition, the layers were usually only occurring in odd numbers.

图3-2-63

图3-2-64

（5）孔雀纹

孔雀长喙、高冠，身躯上布满羽毛，腿高而且较细长。孔雀纹多见孔雀站立或展翅飞翔，常与缠枝牡丹一同出现（见图3-2-67—图3-2-69）。

（6）鸳鸯纹

古人视鸳鸯为爱情的象征，所以鸳鸯都成双成对出现，而且多与莲池相配[118]。鸳鸯、水藻下部都带有几笔水纹，仿佛水在流动[119]。鸳鸯表现形态为两只鸳鸯身体和头相对，有的虽然身体一前一后，但两只鸳鸯的两目都相对而视。鸳鸯的羽毛均呈现为上翘形状[120]（见图3-2-70—图3-2-72）。

图3-2-69

图3-2-70

图3-2-65

图3-2-67

图3-2-71

图3-2-66

图3-2-68

图3-2-72

（7）白鹭纹

白鹭纹来源于刺绣[121]，常与莲池相配入画。白鹭有的双腿直立，有的单腿直立，另一只迈开（见图3-2-73—图3-2-76）。

图3-2-73

图3-2-74

图3-2-75

图3-2-76

（8）芦雁纹

芦雁纹在宋代也流行，但到元代则演变成一飞雁衔着芦苇，这是对元代军官服装胸背花纹的临摹[122]（见图3-2-77）。

图3-2-77

（9）天鹅纹

天鹅纹不多见，天鹅与莲池一同入画，天鹅头扬起，羽毛与鸳鸯羽毛类似，呈上翘状（见图3-2-78）。

图3-2-78

3. 人物图

关于元青花瓷器上人物图案的出现时期，在第二章第一节中有详细的讨论。

目前已发现的完整的绘有人物图案的元青花瓷器存世量较少，但大多数瓷器上的人物绘制都十分精妙，形象生动传神。

人物着色方法多用竖笔上下渲染，有的留出空白衣纹，有的则是在浓笔处施以淡色[123]（见图3-2-79—图3-2-82）。

根据图案的内容，主要可以分为两大类：

（1）历史、戏曲人物故事情节

元青花上的历史、戏曲人物故事图案的表现手法具有如下几个特征[124]：

第一，通过特定的服饰特征来表现人物的不同身份，烘托故事情节。但图案中人物服饰的灵感来源却是当时的现实社会。元代时我国是一个有着不同宗教信仰的多民族国家，元青花上人物的不同装束实际上是当时现实生活的反映：比如昭君出塞图中的匈奴人所穿的其实是蒙古服，并非秦汉时期匈奴人所穿的衣服；昭君的穿戴也不是汉朝时期的风格，而是元代汉族贵妇的打扮。

第二，通过面部特征的细节表现不同民族、不同性格的特定人物，从而突出故事情节。

第三，元青花上的人物有明显的人物特征，能够表现故事情节，这点与宋金以前瓷器上人物图案的泛泛性不同。

目前在元青花上已有的故事题材包括：萧何月下追韩信、鬼谷子下山、尉迟恭单骑救主、周亚夫屯兵细柳营、西厢记、昭君出塞、三顾茅庐等（见图3-2-79—图3-2-81）。

（2）神话人物或文人高士形象

这类图案一般只有人物形象，没有明显的故事情节。比如西安市文物保护考古研究院藏的元青花人物图匾，有人认为图中人物为林和靖，他以爱梅花仙鹤出名；也有人认为构图布景与铁面御史赵抃“一琴一鹤，匹马入蜀”的故事相符；还有学者认为图中人物是八仙中的曹国舅或蓝采和[125]。这类图案中一般人物穿着打扮的辨识度不高，也没有文字标志[126]。（见图3-2-82）

元青花上的人物图案与以往的瓷器相比，在表现手法和构图上有明显的创新。它是将绘画艺术移植到瓷器装饰的开端。这种装饰手法在宋金以前很少见，对明清以后瓷器的纹饰风格产生了极大的影响[127]。

图3-2-79
萧何月下追韩信截图

图3-2-80
昭君出塞截图（局部一）

图3-2-81
昭君出塞截图（局部二）

图3-2-82
青花人物图匾截图

（二）元青花辅助纹饰

元青花辅助纹饰主要有：变形莲瓣纹、栀子花纹、灵芝纹、海水纹、回纹、卷草纹、菱形纹、蕉叶纹、如意云肩纹、钱纹、杂宝纹、八吉祥纹等。

1. 变形莲瓣纹

变形莲瓣纹俗称“八大码”[128]，常绘于碗、盘、瓶、罐外壁或瓶、罐的肩部、胫部等。在每个花瓣内常常会加绘多种花纹，包括朵花、朵云、火焰、杂宝等等。莲瓣纹用一道粗线和一道细线平行勾勒出轮廓线，每片花瓣间不相连，留有一定空隙（见图3-2-83—图3-2-85）。

图3-2-83

图3-2-84

图3-2-85

2. 栀子花纹

栀子花纹常常出现在碗、盘的口沿，碗的外壁或作为瓶、罐上纹饰间的间隔带出现。六片花瓣均匀分布，有时花蕊与花瓣间留有少许空隙（见图3-2-86—图3-2-88）。

图3-2-86

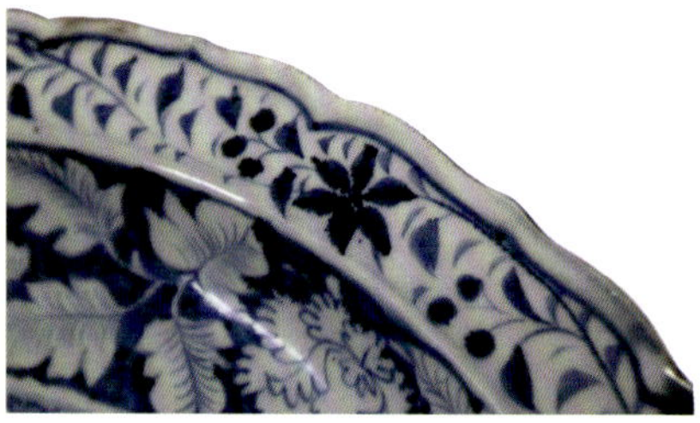

图3-2-87

图3-2-88

3. 灵芝纹

灵芝纹常见于碗内底部或碗外壁上（见图3-2-89—图3-2-91）。

图3-2-89

图3-2-90

图3-2-91

4. 海水纹

海水纹多绘于大盘口沿、大罐颈部或作为纹饰间的间隔带出现，在小件器物中不见[129]。海水纹以粗线勾画波涛外沿，然后在粗线上绘细密的曲线。浪头大，间有浪花和漩涡（见图3-2-92—图3-2-94）。

图3-2-92

图3-2-93

图3-2-94

5. 回纹

回纹最早出现在商周的青铜器上。线条呈方形卷折，形似“回”字。纹路一般从左上方起逆时针走笔，从外到内一般为套叠两框，也见单框（见图3-2-95、图3-2-96）。

图3-2-95

图3-2-96

6. 卷草纹

卷草纹多绘于器物的口沿、胫部或圈足上，或作为纹饰间的隔离带出现。卷草纹是独立绘制的“S”形波浪线条，一正一反相接。也有的二上一下或一上二下相接，笔画随意流畅（见图3-2-97—图3-2-99）。

图3-2-97

图3-2-98

图3-2-99

7. 菱形纹

菱形纹多绘于器物的口沿或作为纹饰的间隔带出现。每一单体为两个菱形套叠，内菱形中心和四边各有一点（见图3-2-100—图3-2-102）。大盘常用菱形纹装饰边沿（见图3-2-100、图3-2-101）。

图3-2-100

图3-2-101

图3-2-102

8. 蕉叶纹

蕉叶纹多饰于瓶的颈部、下腹部和胫部。蕉叶的中茎画至叶尖，一笔或两笔画成后填色。叶脉用细线勾勒，叶的边沿用细线勾勒后填色或留白（见图3-2-103、图3-2-104）。

图3-2-103

图3-2-104

9. 如意云肩纹

如意云肩纹多饰于瓶、罐、扁壶的肩部，在大盘中心也可见。云肩纹由中间粗、两边细的三条线画成，如意云头内满绘纹饰，有花卉纹、海水纹等，也有动物纹（见图3-2-105—图3-2-107）。

云肩纹首次出现在元代瓷器上，是临摹元代服饰上的“衬甲”或“云肩”[130]。

图3-2-105

图3-2-106

图3-2-107

10. 钱纹

钱纹多出现于器物口沿、足部，或作为隔离带绘于纹饰间，外圆内方（见图3-2-108、图3-2-109）。

图3-2-108

图3-2-109

11. 杂宝纹、八吉祥纹

杂宝纹为双角、银锭、犀角、火焰、火珠、法螺、珊瑚、火轮和双钱等（见图3-2-110、图3-2-111），由元代服饰披肩演变而来，多饰于肩、胫部的变形莲瓣纹内。因无固定形式，也有重复出现，故称“杂宝”[131]。

八吉祥纹原是藏密佛前的供品，由法轮、法螺、宝伞、白盖、莲花、宝瓶、金鱼、盘长结八种吉祥物组成[132]。

图3-2-110

图3-2-111

12. 文字

元青花瓷器上文字装饰出现内容包括“寿”字以及诗句等。文字装饰较少见（见图3-2-112、图3-2-113）。

图3-2-112

图3-2-113

四、元青花纹饰表现特征

元青花纹饰表现可分为白地青花和青地白花两种。

白地青花：元青花纹饰中多见的表现形式。指用青料在素胎上直接绘制纹饰，再施以透明釉覆盖（图3-2-114）。

青地白花：也称“青花留白”或“蓝地拔白”，是以青料描绘纹饰轮廓，轮廓以外填涂青料作为背景色，而留白处则呈现纹饰类别（图3-2-115）。

青地白花有时会和白地青花结合使用于同一器物上。

图3-2-114

图3-2-115

五、元青花纹饰绘画技法特征

元青花绘画是用弹性好、笔锋尖、吸收青料多的毛笔蘸取水调色料，在吸水性较强的胎体上绘制纹饰[133]。这与在宣纸上用笔蘸水和墨绘画的水墨画相似。

水墨画从隋代展子虔《游春图》就已经初露端倪，经过唐宋五代发展，名家辈出，技法更加成熟。元代时，青花绘画工匠学习与借鉴水墨画法，用于青花瓷的绘制也是自然而然的事[134]。

我们在元青花的绘画上，能够看到“勾、点、描、皴”等画法[135]。

“点”用于竹节、莲花、山石、花卉等细小处。“勾”主要是在白地青花上用各种粗细不等的线条勾勒轮廓（见图3-2-116），有些元青花上先用细线画出大体轮廓再用粗细不等的线条完成造型，最后加以修饰。在盘的边沿，瓶的口、底等处，辅助纹饰大多一次线描画成（见图3-2-117）。有些小件器物纹饰简约，则全部采用单一的白描方法[136]（见图3-2-118）。“皴”主要是在山石形态和质感的表现。采用“大斧劈”皴法，以中锋勾勒外形及大体结构，再用侧锋直扫，水墨俱下，轻重分明，见棱见角[137]（见图3-2-119）。

在水墨画的启迪之下，青花瓷最早在元代中期创新出分水的画法。绘制时先用能较大含水的鸡头形羊毫笔，蘸上稀释浓度不同的青料，染在线形构成的轮廓里，形成深浅不一的水色，增强了描绘对象在色度上的表现力[138]。

由于绘画对象的材质以及使用着色剂的不同，水墨画中大量的墨法，如积墨法、泼墨法、破墨法都不见于瓷器绘画之中，仅能见到透叠法和差叠法，而且运用的概率也不高[139]。

图3-2-116

图3-2-117

图3-2-118

图3-2-119

六、元青花纹饰构图特征

元青花纹饰在构图上可分为饱满型和疏朗型两种。

（一）饱满型纹饰

饱满型纹饰构图密集，纹饰覆盖元青花瓷器大部分面积，少有空白部分（见图3-2-120、图3-2-121）。

图3-2-120

图3-2-121

（二）疏朗型纹饰

与饱满型纹饰相比，疏朗型纹饰以少量的青花纹饰为装饰内容，纹饰构图疏朗，器身留有部分空白区域（见图3-2-122）。

元青花在瓶、罐等琢器上采用多层次的横向带状分区形式装饰，在碗、盘等圆器上采用同心圆分区的方式多层次进行装饰[140]。每层纹饰都各具特点，用辅助纹饰间隔带隔开。纹饰层数主要从三层到十一层不等，有的小件器物仅一层纹饰（见图3-2-123）。按照伊斯兰习惯，都是单数层。

图3-2-122
元青花云龙纹荷叶盖罐
高安市博物馆藏

图3-2-123
元青花唇口双系扁腹式小罐
广州东方博物馆藏

第三节 元青花青料及发色特征

一、元青花青料

（一）青料来源

元青花瓷器使用的青料主要来源于钴土矿。

钴土矿一般为结核状、块状或碎片状，呈铁锈色、褐黑或亮黑色。大多数钴土矿的钴含量在2%以下，最高也只有9%（比较少见），因此钴土矿必须经过一定的处理才能用于装饰瓷器，否则着色效果会比较差[141]。

元青花瓷器使用的青料可以分成国产料和西域料两种。

国产料在国内分布很广，一般产于浙江的绍兴、金华、东阳和江山，云南的宣威、富源、嵩明、宜良、会泽和榕峰，江西的上高、庐陵、永丰和玉山等地方[142]。

西域料主要分布在西亚，如伊拉克、伊朗，包括新疆等地。景德镇元青花所用钴料的组分特征与一种名为钴毒砂的硫砷钴矿最为相似[143]。

（二）青料主要化学成分

组成青料的化学元素主要有铁、锰及钴等等。

国产料以含高锰低铁为特征；西域料以高铁低锰，并含硫和砷，基本无镍和铜为特征。

从国内出土物看，也有些器物使用国产青料，青花色调与西域料的浓艳显然不同，极少黑斑。云南元青花所用青料与云南钴土矿原矿成分相似，可以推断云南元青花的青料是使用当地的钴土矿原矿[144]。

中国科学院上海硅酸盐研究所对景德镇湖田窑及元大都出土的三片元青花所做的物理和化学分析表明：这些元青花瓷器使用的青料与目前为止所分析的任何一种国产钴土矿成分都不一致，而是属于含锰极低，含铁量较高的钴土矿，且含硫、砷，应该属于西域料[145]。

（三）影响青料发色因素

元青花青料中的钴（Co）、铁（Fe）、锰（Mn）都是着色元素，青花呈现出的蓝色主要是由于Co元素的存在。Co的着色能力最强，烧成气氛对它影响较小，只要引入0.1%就能呈显蓝色；Fe的着色能力中等，受气氛影响较大，如果青料含Fe较多，对青花发色会有较大影响；Mn的着色能力较弱，在还原气氛中被还原成Mn^{2+}，在硅酸盐釉中基本无色，但在冷却过程中会受到二次氧化变成Mn^{3+}或Mn^{4+}，使青花的色调青中略带淡紫红色。西域料中含锰量低，所以对青花发色及釉色都无明显影响，但国产料锰含量较高，对青花发色和釉色的影响较明显[146]。

影响元青花发色的主要因素如下：

1. 青料中Co、Fe及Mn元素的含量和比例

西域料发色艳丽，常见褐黑色斑，MnO/CoO在0.01—0.06之间，Fe_2O_3/CoO在2.21—3.02之间；国产料蓝中带灰，MnO/CoO在3.74—16.19之间，Fe_2O_3/CoO在0.11—3.74之间[147]。

MnO与CoO形成的尖晶石结构呈蓝中带紫红的色调，MnO含量高会加深紫色[148]。

2. 青料中Al_2O_3的含量

由于Co^{2+}离子在釉层玻璃相中扩散比较容易，在黏度较小的釉中易随釉流动，因此在釉层中形成晕散的现象[149]。有研究表明，当青料中Al_2O_3的含量在18%-20%时，青料附近就会有钙长石、莫来石等晶体析出，使青料在烧制过程中不易流散[150]。

3. 烧制工艺

景德镇窑烧成气氛通常都是还原焰，在还原焰中，釉中的Fe^{2+}浓度不太高的情况下，使釉着色成绿色，如果局部聚集浓度高了则会变成褐色甚至黑色，即形成Fe^{3+}的着

Section 3:
Yuan Underglaze Blue Dye and Coloration Characteristics

1. YUB Blue Dye

A. Dye Origins

The blue dye adorning YUB mainly comes from cobalt ore mines.

Cobalt ore most commonly comes in clump, granule, or chip shapes; and is rusty, brown, or shiny black. Most cobalt ores contains less than 2% cobalt (very rarely reaching 9% at the highest) and as such must undergo a certain amount of processing before it can be used as a coloring agent on ceramics, less the resultant color be flawed [141].

The dyes used on YUB can be divided by general mine location into two categories: Domestic and Western.

Domestic dye mine locations are broadly spread throughout China and are known to be found in Zhejiang, Yunnan, and Jiangxi Provinces [142].

Western dyes were found through most of Western Asia in areas such as Iraq, Iran, Xinjiang and so forth. The ore used at Jingdezhen for the majority of YUB wares most closely resembles this Cobalt Arsenopyrite Ore (Cobalt, Sulfur, and Arsenic) [143].

B. Primary Chemical Composition of the Dye

The primary chemical components of YUB dye are Iron, Manganese, and Cobalt.

Domestic dyes are characteristically high in Manganese and low in Iron; while Western dyes are characteristically low in Manganese and high in Iron with trace amounts of Sulfur and Arsenic and little or no Copper or Nickel.

Domestic excavations of YUB have shown that some wares did in fact use domestic dyes. Their colors are less bright and vibrant than their Western counterpart, and there is a lack of black spotting present. The dyes used on YUB made in Yunnan Province have characteristics similar to the dyes found around that province, and it can be asserted that the wares made in Yunnan utilized dyes that were local to production [144].

The Shanghai Ceramics Institute, Chinese Academy of Sciences did physical chemical composition analysis on excavated pieces of Jingdezhen Hutian Kiln YUB and came up with the following conclusion: Dyes used in the production of YUB are not consistent with any domestically produced dyes. Their composition is comparitively low in Manganese and high in Iron and contains trace amounts of Sulfur and Arsenic. The dyes used were from Western origin [145].

C. Elements that Effect YUB Dye Coloration

In the YUB dyes, Co, Fe, and Mn all have coloring agent properties, but the blue coloration comes predominantly from the presence of Co. The coloring ability of Co is relatively high, and the impact received from firing gasses is relatively low. There only needs to be .1% Co present in order to achieve a blue color. The coloring ability of Fe is within the mid-range, and it is highly impacted by firing gasses. Only if the Fe content in the dye is relatively high, will it have an impact on the coloration. The coloring effect of Mn is particularly weak. Under the influence of the reducing atmosphere, Mn^{2+} is created and within the silicate glaze, it is without color. However, during the cooling process, the Mn can receive second stage oxidation creating Mn^{3+} or Mn^{4+}, which creates a slight purplish tinge within the blue dye. As Western dyes have a relatively low amount of Mn, the felt effect on the coloration is minimal; as the domestic dyes contain elevated

色或Fe^{2+}、Fe^{3+}的复合着色，在蓝色着色区内形成褐黑色斑点，在釉表面会有下沉的表现。表3-3-1展示了青花青料在不同温度下烧成后的颜色[151]。

元青花的青花发色有三种情况：一是正烧，发色青翠沉着；二是过烧（即温度过高），发色靛青泛紫，由于青料在釉中扩散加剧可加重晕散；三是欠烧（即温度过低），发色青蓝偏灰，由于青料未能在釉中充分扩散熔解，通常呈现带灰的蓝色[152]。

表3-3-1 青花青料在不同温度下烧成后的颜色

编号	1280℃	1350℃
213	深蓝	蓝带黑
214	深蓝	蓝带微黑
215	深蓝微紫	蓝带微黑
216	深蓝	蓝带黑
217	深蓝微紫	黑蓝
I	深蓝	蓝微紫
II	深蓝	蓝微黑紫

4. 釉层厚度

釉层过厚，通常青花发色偏淡发灰；釉层过薄，则青花发色偏黑。

二、元青花颜色色标

（一）传统描述方法

釉的发色是陶瓷“外衣”的颜色，不同的颜色会带来不同的视觉效果和美感。在文人墨客及里手玩家之间，多以物比色，即用所熟知实物的颜色比喻瓷器的颜色。例如：形容青色有天青、梅子青、豆青、灰青、粉青等。这里以梅子、豆等植物的颜色形容青色，而灰青和粉青则是以颜色的调和来描述。类似描述瓷器颜色的词语还有很多，描述红色的有豇豆红、胭脂红、绛红、铜红、霁红、珊瑚红、粉红、枣红、牛血红等，描述黄色的有鳝鱼黄、鸡油黄、姜黄、柠檬黄、米黄等。以上均为以比喻方法描述陶瓷的颜色，由于个人的视觉感受及审美经验有差异，因此颜色的指向在传播过程中是宽泛模糊的。

我们之所以不能直观且精确地表述颜色，根本原因在于不能将颜色的描述量化。

（二）创新描述方法

笔者认为，可以尝试采用色彩表达模式来表述元青花瓷器的青花发色。

色彩表达模式是一种在数字化设备上表达色彩的方式。采用数字化形式来描述色彩更加精确明晰。计算机表达色彩的方式有多种，每一种表达方式都有自己的特点和适用范围：如RGB模式、CMYK模式、Lab模式、HSB模式等等[153]。

用色彩表达模式数值来描述元青花瓷器青花的颜色，旨在量化颜色认知，创新一种描述瓷器颜色的新方法。

（三）元青花颜色色值

目前较精确、科学地确定颜色的方法为：使用颜色探测器，在一定的环境下对准被测物，读出其颜色数值。

在科学量化表述瓷器青花发色方面，我们尚处初级阶段，由于研究标本的限制和科学仪器的缺乏，我们无法现场测量现存的每一件元青花的颜色数值。

为让读者更好地理解这一创新的颜色表述方法，我们以CMYK模式的表述方式为例，对个别元青花标本的颜色进行了现场目测，在比对国家标准色谱后得出它们的CMYK数值（见表3-3-2）：

注：CMYK是印刷色彩模型，C代表青色（Cyan），M代表洋红色（Magenta），Y代表黄色（Yellow），K代表黑色比例（Black Ratio）。C、M、Y、K的不同数值代表了印刷色油墨颜色相应的百分比[154]。这里CMYK值为参考值，瓷器实际的颜色受测量时的灯光、温度及个人等因素影响。

levels of Mn, they have a more evident effect on the coloration of the ware [146].

The following key factors have an impact on the coloration of YUB:

I. Amounts and Ratios of Co, Fe, and Mn

Western dyes have a bright and beautiful coloration, often presenting with brown or black spots (Heaping and Piling). The MnO/CoO ratio is between .01 and .06, and the Fe_2O_3/CoO ratio is between 2.21 and 3.02. Domestic dyes, with a MnO/CoO ratio of 3.74-16.19 and Fe_2O_3/CoO ratio of .11-3.74, present with a greyish blue coloration [147].

The crystals structure formed by MnO and CoO creates a purple hue in the blue dye, and a high content of MnO brings about a deep purple coloration [148].

II. Aluminum Oxide in the Dye

Co^{2+} within the glaze level is easily dispersed, and glaze with relatively low viscosity allows for easier movement within the glaze level, allowing for the resulting coloration to present with runs [149]. Research has shown that when a dye's Al_2O_3 content reaches 18-20%, the dye will form Anorthite, Mullite, and so forth crystallizations, which help to stabilize the movement of the glaze during the firing process and prevents runs [150].

III. Firing Technique

The Jingdezhen kilns were often able to reach reducing atmosphere. In a reducing atmosphere, if the amount of Fe^{2+} is relatively low, the glaze can present with a slight greenish coloration. If a portion of Iron is able to pool together, it creates brown or black spots, which are the primary coloration of Fe^{3+} and the composite color of the Fe^{2+} and Fe^{3+}. Within the blue coloration areas, these pools can create brown or black spots, and these spots sink down into the glaze. Table 3-3-1 shows us the different coloration of certain blue dyes fired under different temperatures [151].

Table 3-3-1 Coloration of Underglaze Blue Dyes Under Varied Temperatures

Sample	1280℃	1350℃
213	Dark Blue	Blackish Blue
214	Dark Blue	Blue with a Tinge of Black
215	Purplish Dark Blue	Blue with a Tinge of Black
216	Dark Blue	Blackish Blue
217	Purplish Dark Blue	Bluish Black
I	Dark Blue	Purplish Blue
II	Dark Blue	Blue with Blackish Purple

YUB coloration has three types of outcomes [152]:

1. Firing temperature within range, coloration fresh and steady
2. Firing temperature too high, coloration becomes purplish, and because of the viscosity of the glaze, blurriness and color runs are present.
3. Firing temperature too low, coloration has greyish tinge because the blue dye is not able to achieve full diffusion into the glaze and only a greyish blue is achieved.

IV. Glaze Thickness

If the glaze is too thick, the coloration has a tendency towards grey, and if the glaze is too thin, the coloration has a tendency towards black.

2. YUB Coloration Standard

A. Traditional Description Method

A ceramic's glaze is its 'Outer Garment', and its color brings about different visual and aesthetic results. Between scholars and collectors, there is a standard use of common objects to offer color reference. Metaphoric comparisons to known objects help lend a hand in the oral depiction of ceramic colors. For example, of blue: Sky Blue, Plum Blue, Bean Blue, Ashen Blue, Powder Blue and so forth. Using

表3-3-2 元青花瓷器典型颜色CMYK数值表

Table 3-3-2 CMYK Values of YUB Colors

名称 Name	图片 Picture	CMYK色谱值 CMYK Value
“至正十一年”云龙纹象耳瓶 英国大维德中国艺术基金会藏		C=100 M=40 Y=0 K=10
青花昭君出塞盖罐 日本出光美术馆藏		C=100 M=50 Y=0 K=10
青花鬼谷子下山图大罐 英国Eskenazi Ltd.藏		C=90 M=50 Y=0 K=40
蓝地拔白缠枝牡丹纹菱口盘 日本大阪市立东洋陶瓷美术馆藏		C=80 M=20 Y=0 K=10
青花波涛龙纹盘 伊朗国家博物馆藏		C=80 M=30 Y=0 K=20
青地百花凤凰穿花纹菱口盘 伊朗国家博物馆藏		C=80 M=20 Y=0 K=10
青花云龙纹罐 镇江市博物馆藏		C=60 M=10 Y=0 K=20
元青花云龙纹荷叶盖罐 高安市博物馆藏		C=70 M=10 Y=0 K=10
青花菊花纹堆塑螭龙水盂 金乐轩藏		C=70 M=20 Y=0 K=40
青花缠枝花卉纹葫芦形执壶 印度尼西亚国立博物馆藏		C=60 M=10 Y=0 K=30

plums, beans and flora of the like, or palettes of ash and powder, allow for more accurate descriptions of said colors. Similar descriptive words to describe ceramic glazes are in abundance. Of red: Red Bean Red, Carmine, Magneta, Copper, Bright Red, Coral, Rose, Crimson, Ox Blood and so on. Of yellow: Eel, Chicken Oil, Ginger, Lemon, Rice, and so forth. All of the above are oral descriptions of ceramic glaze colors, but because of perspective and ideas of beauty being different, there becomes a broadened confusion in the transmission of the ceramic color palette.

Our inability to clearly and objectively assign an easily spreadable color description is primarily due to the fact that there is no quantitative standard in its description.

B. Innovative Description Method

It is possible to utilize a standard color palette to state the coloration of YUB.

Standard color palettes are used to express color on digital devices. There are many ways to describe color in digital forms, i.e. there are many types of standard color palettes, such as RGB Palette, CMYK Palette, Lab Palette and HSB Palette. Each of which has its own characteristics and range of application [153].

The use of a standard colorpalette value in the explanation of YUB coloration allows for an understandable quantitative description, and is an innovative new step in accounting for the color of YUB.

C. YUB Color Value

Currently, the most clear and quantitative way to describe the coloration of YUB is to employ a more scientific method for color measurement. Using a color detection device, once a standard color panel has been established, the instrument will allow for an accurate value for the porcelain coloration.

From a quantitative scientific color measurement stand point, we are still in the early stages. This is a due to a lack in sample pieces, apparatus limitations, and an inability to take measurements at all locations in which YUB is stored (i.e. taking measurements through glass and under certain display lights will produce distorted values).

In an effort to better explain our method, using the CMYK color palette as our standard, we carried out field research on the observable color of YUB samples. In comparison to the National Color Standard, we were able to attain the following approximate CMYK readings (see Table 3-3-2).

Note: The CMYK scale is used in printing, CMYK stands for Cyan (Blue), Magenta (Red), Yellow, and Key (Black Ratio). Printers use this scale to adjust the ratio of each ink to be used in relation to black (key) [154]. These are manually observed CMYK values; key factors including the impact of the light brightness and temperature, as well as the operator discrepancy may have impacted the results.

Using Standard Color Palettes to describe the coloration of YUB is one type of quantitative color description method that is both more accurate and more easily propagated. However, due to sample and apparatus limitations, we are not able to put forth a Standard Color Palette for YUB in this publication.

3. Characteristics of YUB Dye Coloration

YUB coloration is not entirely the same across all pieces and has multiple characteristics. According to these characteristics, YUB colorations can be divided into three main coloration categories: Over Glaze Dark Spots, Underglaze Dark Spots, and Coloration Runs.

A. Over Glaze Dark Spots

I. Over Glaze Dark Spots Defined

Often generally called Heaping and Piling, Over Glaze Dark Spots occur on the surface of YUB in areas of darkest dye concentration. Composed primarily of Oxidized Iron and Manganese, the appearance is an irregularly shaped crystallization of dark brown-black color.

These dark spots, observed under refracted light, appear to be floating on the top of the reflective glaze surface.

II. Formation of Over Glaze Dark Spots

During the firing of YUB, cobalt-blue dye and glaze

用色彩表达模式来表述元青花瓷器青花的颜色，是一种量化表述颜色的方法，可以使青花的颜色表述更加精确，更易传播。但由于标本限制及仪器缺乏，本书尚未能给出精确的色彩模式数值。

三、元青花青料发色特征

元青花的青料发色是不均匀而且多样的，根据其发色的多样性特征，可以分成以下三种类型：釉上浓黑处、釉下浓黑处和晕散现象。

（一）釉上浓黑处

1. 釉上浓黑处概念

釉上浓黑处是处于元青花瓷器釉表面青料处，以铁氧化物及锰氧化物为主，形貌不规则的深褐色析晶。

釉上浓黑处的深褐色晶体在折光时观察，表现为浮于釉表面的反光部位。

2. 釉上浓黑处形成

元青花瓷器在高温烧制时，青料及釉料会逐渐熔化成熔融态，在浮力、表面张力及气泡搅动的作用下，釉料以及青料中的铁氧化物及锰氧化物易在气泡边缘积聚，部分会随气泡升至釉表面，顺着凹凸不平的釉表面向四周扩散，流动铺展，并结晶析出，也可能产生分相。当温度下降时，会有更多结晶析出。根据它们的成分、密度、表面张力不同，在釉表面形成形貌、颜色不一的晶体，就是釉上浓黑处。

3. 釉上浓黑处分类

釉上浓黑处可分为流淌型和凝固型。它们分布随机，颜色主要为深褐色，有金属质感。

（1）流淌型

流淌型釉上浓黑处的形成与以下几个因素有关：

① 元青花釉料的黏度。釉料黏度越小，釉料越易于流动，易形成流淌型釉上浓黑处。

② 烧造时所处位置。处于垂直位置的青料更易形成流淌型釉上浓黑处。

流淌型釉上浓黑处通常表现为斑块状，斑块整体有下垂流淌感，大都超出纹饰区域(见图3-3-1—图3-3-3)。

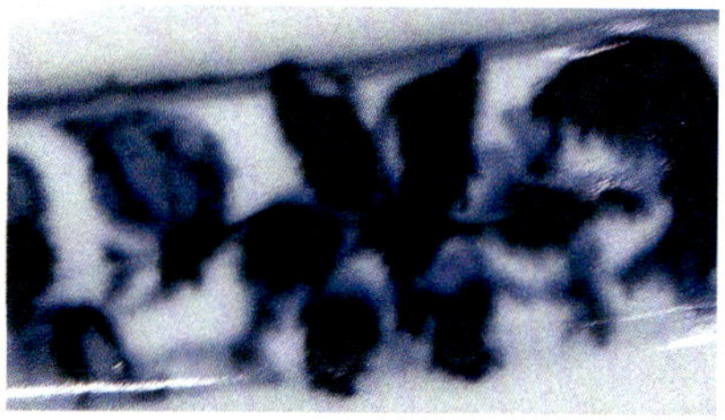

图3-3-1

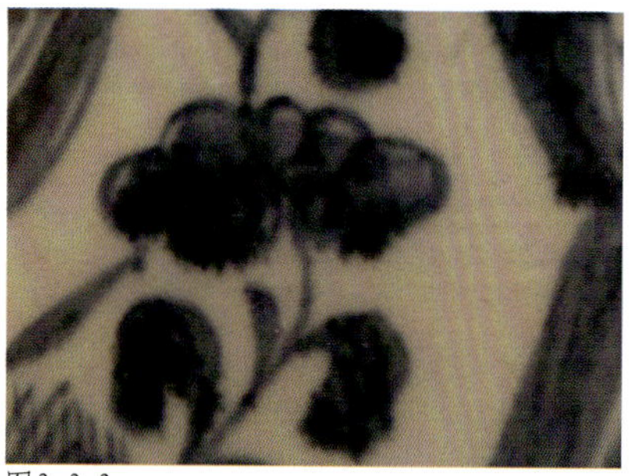

图3-3-2

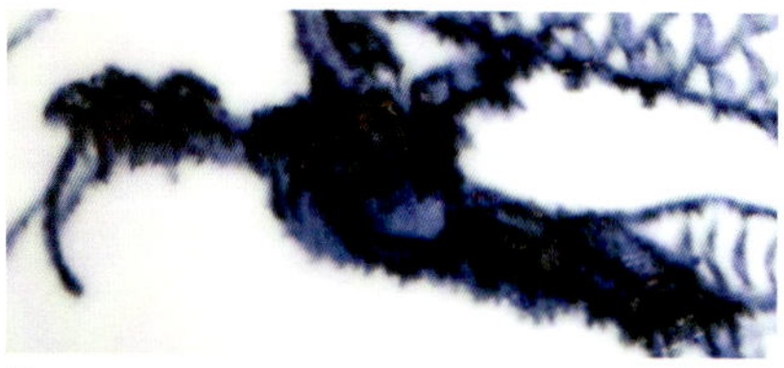

图3-3-3

（2）凝固型

凝固型釉上浓黑处的形成与以下几个因素有关：

① 元青花瓷器釉料的黏度。釉料黏度越大，釉料越难以流动，易形成凝固型釉上浓黑处。

② 烧造时所处位置。处于水平位置的青料更易形成凝固型釉上浓黑处，如盘或碗的内底。

凝固型釉上浓黑处通常表现为斑状或线状，没有下垂流淌感。部分情况下超出纹饰区域（见图3-3-4—图3-3-6）。

图3-3-4

图3-3-5

图3-3-6

gradually transition into a molten state. Due to the buoyancy, surface tension and movement of the air bubbles within the glaze level, the Oxidized Iron and Manganese within the glaze and dye collects around the edges of gaseous bodies within the glaze, and rise with these bubbles to the surface of the glaze.

According to the uneven topography of the surface, these compounds diffuse and flow across the glaze surface and crystallize, some producing split phases. When the temperature drops, more crystallization occurs. According to differences in composition, density, and surface tension, these compounds pool together, creating appearances of different crystallizations and colors. These are the Over Glaze Dark Spots.

III. Types of Over Glaze Dark Spots

Over Glaze Dark Spots can be divided into two types: Flowing and Congealed. Their distribution is situation dependent, color is predominantly dark brown, and has a metallic texture.

a. Flowing Type

Flowing Over Glaze Dark Spots are formed in accordance with the following key factors:

1. YUB Glaze Viscosity: The less viscous the glaze, the more easily it can diffuse, allowing for the formation of flowing dark spots.

2. Location During Firing: Dyes that are on vertical surfaces during the firing process more easily present with flowing characteristics.

Flowing Over Glaze Dark Spots often appear in blotch-like shapes with a downward flowing feel. The flow usually extends beyond the edge of intended decoration (see pictures 3-3-1—3-3-3).

b. Congealed Type

Congealed Over Glaze Dark Spots are formed in accordance with following key factors:

1. YUB Glaze Viscosity: The more viscous the glaze, the more difficult it is to diffuse, allowing for the formation of congealed dark spots.

2. Location During Firing: Dyes that are on horizontal surfaces during the firing process more easily present with congealed characteristics, i.e. bowl and plate centers.

Congealed Over Glaze Dark Spots often appear in blotch and stripe-like shapes without any specific flowing feel. They sometimes extend beyond the boundary of the intended decoration (see pictures 3-3-4—3-3-6).

Majority of congealed spots are slightly depressed below the glaze level. Some appear with reflective needlepoints or flakes of silver across their surface (see pictures 3-3-7 and 3-3-8).

c. Summary

Over Glaze Dark Spots commonly occur on YUB, and are at the surface level of the glaze without any glaze coverage. Under microscopic observation, they are characterized as flowing mottles, radiating mottles, or the combination of the two.

B. Underglaze Dark Spots

I. Underglaze Dark Spots Defined

Underglaze Dark Spots occur under the surface of YUB in areas of dark dye concentration. Composed primarily of Oxidized Iron and Manganese, the appearance is an irregularly shaped crystallization of dark brown color.

II. Formation of Underglaze Dark Spots

During the firing of YUB, cobalt-blue dye and glaze gradually transition into a molten state. Due to the buoyancy, surface tension and movement of the air bubbles within the glaze level, the Oxidized Iron and Manganese within the glaze and dye collects around the edges of gaseous bodies within the glaze, and rise with these bubbles to the surface of the glaze.

According to the uneven topography of the surface, these compounds diffuse and flow across the glaze surface and crystallize, some producing split phases. When the temperature drops, more crystallization occurs. The Oxidized Iron and Manganese that were not carried to the glaze surface remain covered by a small layer of glaze, and create Underglaze Dark Spots.

大部分凝固型釉上浓黑处都呈下凹状，有的表面还可见针眼状或片状银斑（见图3-3-7、图3-3-8）。

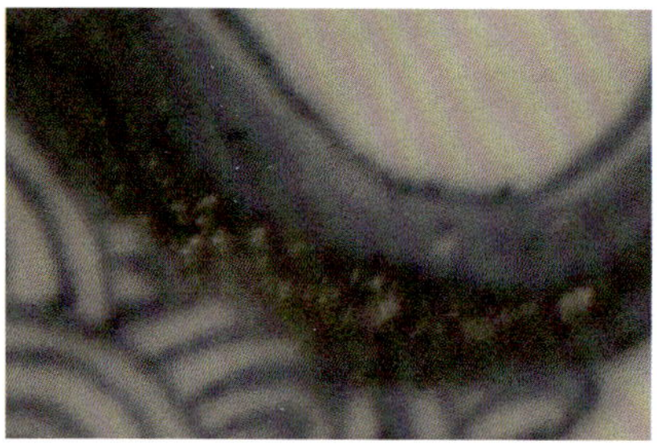

图3-3-7

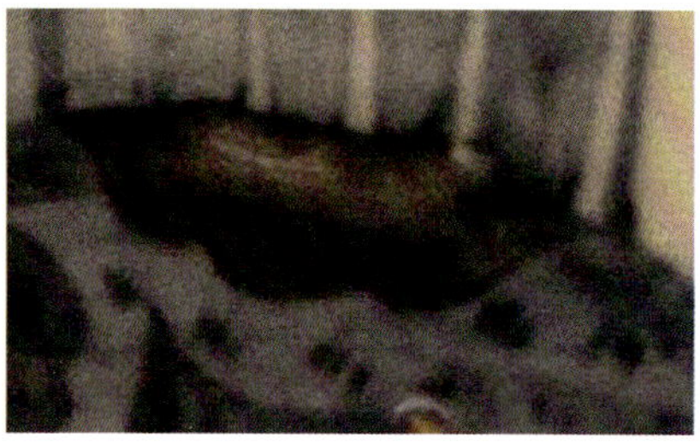

图3-3-8

（3）小结

釉上浓黑处是元青花瓷器上常见的现象，釉上浓黑处的表面基本无釉覆盖。它在显微摄像头下可以表现为釉表面的流淌斑、放射斑或二者的组合。

（二）釉下浓黑处

1. 釉下浓黑处概念

釉下浓黑处是位于元青花瓷器釉层中青料浓处，以铁氧化物及锰氧化物为主，形貌不规则的深褐色析晶。

2. 釉下浓黑处形成

元青花瓷器在高温烧制时，青料及釉料会逐渐熔化成熔融态，在浮力、表面张力及气泡搅动的作用下，釉料以及青料中的铁氧化物及锰氧化物易在气泡边缘积聚，部分会随气泡升至釉表面，顺着凹凸不平的釉表面向四周扩散，流动铺展，并结晶析出，也可能产生分相。当温度下降时，会有更多结晶析出。而未随气泡升至釉表面的铁氧化物及锰氧化物则在釉层中形成釉下浓黑处。

3. 釉下浓黑处分类

釉下浓黑处可分为斑状、线状及点状，分布随机。

（1）斑状

斑状釉下浓黑处通常出现在纹饰的起笔、落笔或笔尖重叠处，因此也可称为“起落斑”（见图3-3-9、图3-3-10）。

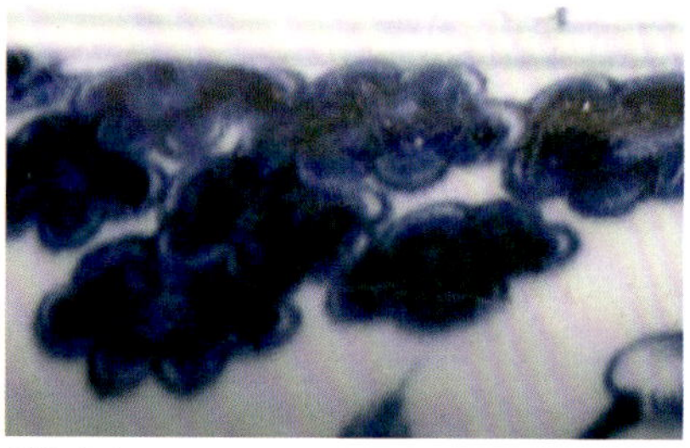

图3-3-9

图3-3-10

（2）线状

线状釉下浓黑处呈直线或曲线状，也可称为“笔势线”。

浓黑的笔势线都一定程度地下凹，较淡的笔势线下凹不明显。笔势线通常分布在花瓣、叶脉上（见图3-3-11、图3-3-12），有可能是刻意模仿刺绣上以丝线绣出的花瓣和叶子的效果[155]；有的则是填色时随机分布的黑色线条（见图3-3-13—图3-3-15）。

图3-3-11

图3-3-12

图3-3-13

III. Types of Underglaze Dark Spots

Underglaze Dark Spots can appear as Blotches, Stripes, and Dots; their distribution is situation dependent.

a. Blotches

Underglaze Dark Blotches often occur in areas where the brushwork began, stopped, or was overlapping. As such, they are often called "Start-Stop Blotches" (see pictures 3-3-9 and 3-3-10).

b. Stripes

Underglaze Dark Stripes occur in straight and curved lines, and are often called "Brushwork Stripes".

Dark brushwork stripes all create a certain indention on the glaze, and lighter brushwork stripes have a less pronounced indention. Brushwork stripes most often occur in areas of flora, such as flowers and leaves (see pictures 3-3-11 and 3-3-12). There is a possibility that some were intentionally created to mimic the effect of flora texture created by embroidery [155], but others dark stripes occur randomly across areas of broadened brushstrokes (see pictures 3-3-13—3-3-15).

c. Dots

According to the distribution of Underglaze Dark Dots across the dye, we can divide them into two types.

i. Dotted Lines

Dotted lines are the distribution of darks spots along blue decoration lines. Dotted lines usually occur on the thin decoration lines of waves, classic scrolls, and so forth (see picture 3-3-16).

ii. Dotted Surfaces

Dotted surfaces refer to dark speckling across larger surface areas of blue decoration (see pictures 3-3-17 and 3-3-18).

C. Coloration Runs

Similar to the coloration runs (sometimes called bleeding) seen in ink wash painting or calligraphy, YUB too can present with coloration runs. Coloration runs occur primarily because of the ability of colors to easily diffuse into the viscous melted glaze. Low viscosity glazes have an increased likelihood of flowing, and it is flowing that causes coloration to run. Coloration runs usually occur under the glaze in areas of particularly dense dye, but can also occur in areas of less intense color.

In actuality, coloration runs on YUB would have been considered an imperfection in the firing process, and it is quite likely that the artisans would have known about this firing imperfection and would have taken preventative measure to improve their techniques. Because of this, it is not all YUB wares that present with coloration runs, and of the most exquisite pieces have very insignificant running.

According to the characteristics of the coloration runs, they can be classified into Whiskers, Icicles, and Cloudy style runs.

I. Whiskers

Whiskers are small filament-like coloration runs on the outer edges YUB decorations (see pictures 3-3-19 and 3-3-20).

II. Icicle

Icicles are larger dagger-like coloration runs on the outer edges YUB decorations (see pictures 3-3-21 and 3-3-22).

III. Cloudy

Cloudy runsare blotch-like coloration runs on the outer edges YUB decorations. They usually appear in areas of less intense color (see pictures 3-3-23 and 3-3-24).

图3-3-14

图3-3-15

（3）点状

根据点状釉下浓黑处在青料纹饰上的分布位置，我们可将其分为以下两类：

① 线上点

线上点是元青花瓷器上青料纹饰线条上的黑点。线上点大多出现在海水纹或卷草纹等较细的纹饰线条上（见图3-3-16）。

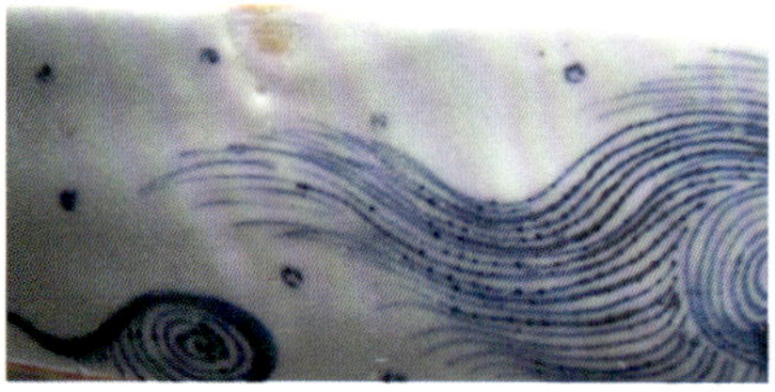
图3-3-16

② 面上点

面上点是元青花瓷器上较大面积的纹饰上出现的黑点（见图3-3-17、图3-3-18）。

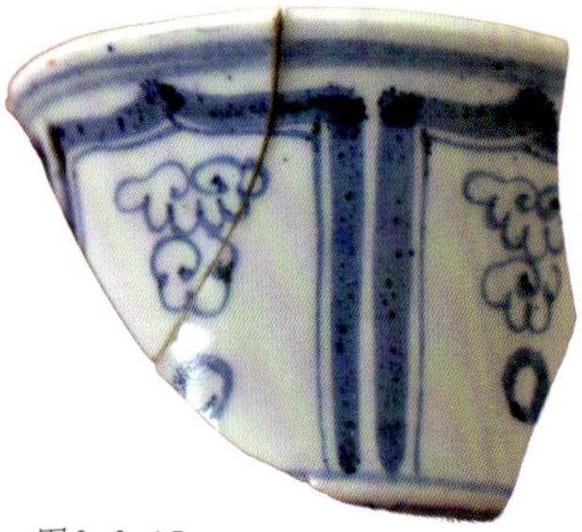
图3-3-17

图3-3-18

（三）晕散现象

部分元青花瓷器上会出现青料晕散现象，如同在宣纸上写毛笔字，墨水在纸上有不同程度的晕散。青料晕散现象主要是由于钴离子在熔融的玻璃相中易于扩散，在黏度较小的釉中易于随着釉的流动而流动形成的。晕散现象主要出现在釉下浓黑处，有时在青花颜色较淡处也会出现。

元青花的晕散现象其实是当时烧制工艺上的一种缺陷，元代工匠们很可能已经认识到这种缺陷，并采取一定的措施去改进工艺。所以，并不是所有元青花青料都有晕散现象，很多元青花精品上的晕散现象都不明显。

根据青料晕散的形态可将其分为毛刺晕散、冰挂晕散及云状晕散。

1. 毛刺晕散

毛刺晕散是元青花瓷器的青花纹饰边沿呈毛刺状的晕散现象（见图3-3-19、图3-3-20）。

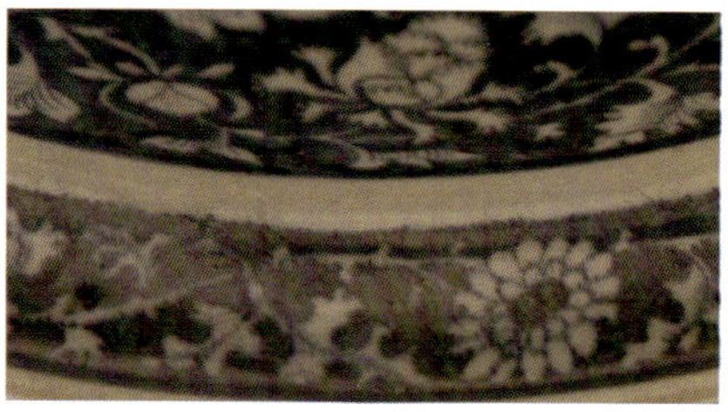
图3-3-19

图3-3-20

2. 冰挂晕散

冰挂晕散是元青花瓷器的青花纹饰边沿呈冰挂状的晕散现象（见图3-3-21、图3-3-22）。

图3-3-21

图3-3-22

3. 云状晕散

云状晕散是元青花瓷器的青花纹饰呈云朵状的晕散现象，通常出现在青花较淡处（见图3-3-23、图3-3-24）。

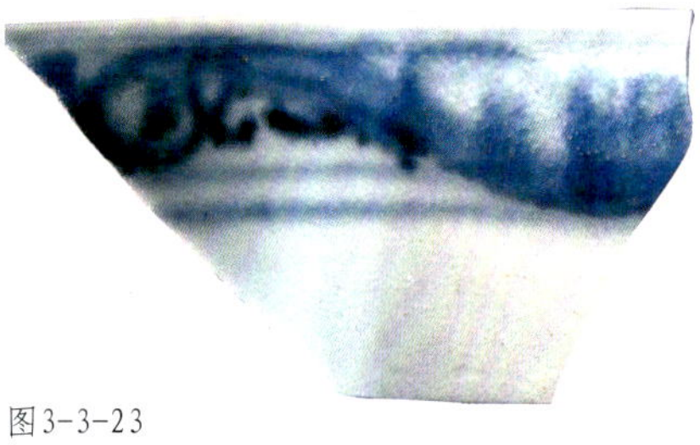
图3-3-23

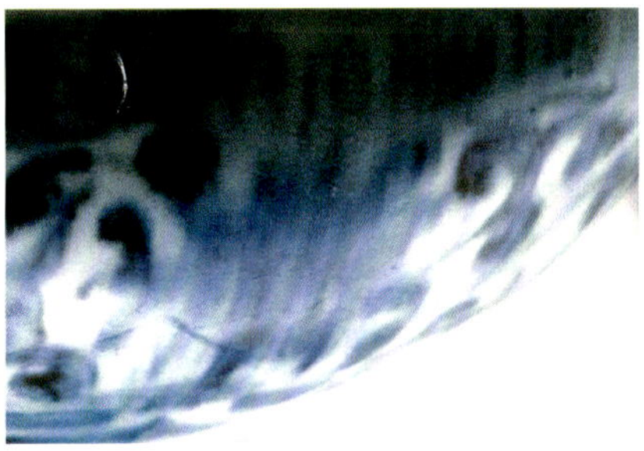
图3-3-24

第四节
元青花款识

一、纪年款

目前为止在元青花上还未见到帝王款，仅是纪年纪事款，且数量也不多。比如：蓝料直书“至正七年置”五字楷款的青白釉盖罐（见图3-4-1）、“至正十一年”铭文的青花云龙象耳瓶一对（见图3-4-2）等等。

二、红料款

在伊朗馆藏的一部分元青花瓷器的胫部、底部、盘外壁，或梅瓶肩部上有阿拉伯文标志，呈长方形。有的是由钻刻的小圆坑组成，有的则是直接刻上去，颜色为红色（见图3-4-3）。

这类款识是在瓷器到达伊朗后刻上去的，其中大部分都是古代波斯的阿巴斯王捐赠给阿德比尔寺的标记。阿巴斯王在位时间为公元1587年到1629年，他捐赠了许多瓷器给阿德比尔寺。这些款识很有可能是当时一位阿德比尔寺的管理人员（名为Maulana Muhammad Husain Hakka Khurasani）所刻。其内容包括较简短的“阿巴斯王捐赠”或者较详细的“阿巴斯，圣洁之王的奴仆，谨以此献给萨菲王国的神寺”，其中以后者更常见[156]。

图3-4-1
“至正七年置”铭双系盖罐
雅安市博物馆藏

图3-4-2
“至正十一年”铭文

图3-4-3

Section 4:
Yuan Underglaze Blue Markings

1. Date Markings

Currently there are no known YUB wares with Imperial Reign markings, and only a very small number of pieces with date markings, they include: A small white jar with the five words "Zhi Zheng Qi Nian Zhi" written in blue dye (made in the 7th year of Zhi Zheng Reign; see picture 3-4-1); The pair of David Vases marked "Zhi Zheng Shi Yi Nian" (11th year of Zhi Zheng; see picture 3-4-2).

2. Red Markings

A large portion of the pieces in the Iran National Museum collection have red colored markings on the foot, bottom, outside wall (large plate) or shoulder (meiping vase). They are Persian scripts written, drilled, bored, or affixed to the surface of the ware (see picture 3-4-3).

Most of the inscriptions include the name of the owner of the piece, commonly Shah 'Abbas (Persian Ruler) who gave many gifts to the Ardebil Shrine. The markings were not made by the Shah himself, but by someone at the Shrine on his behalf, probably Maulana Muhammad Husain Hakka Khurasani. It is a form of 'waqf'(bestowment) inscription, which essentially means that the piece was given as a gift to the religious building (as is the custom in Islamic culture). The marks are written in Persian and either have just the simplified: "Gift of Shah 'Abbas", or the full inscription: "Abbas, slave of the king of saintliness (Ali) made endowment of this to the threshold of Shah Safi". The most common on the YUB was the full inscription [156].

第五节
元青花胎和釉

一、元青花瓷胎

（一）元青花瓷胎用料

中国科学院上海硅酸盐研究所的吴隽和李家治先生对元代青花瓷胎进行了多元统计分析，元青花瓷胎的化学组成见表3-5-1[157]：

从这些数据来看，其Al_2O_3含量在20%左右，Na_2O也在1.22%—2.76%，该类氧化物均普遍高于该地元以前的瓷胎。

刘新园先生认为，元代瓷胎中较高的Al_2O_3应该是从引进新的原料获得，而在景德镇地区含铝量较高、质地纯净的黏土，仅有高岭土。如做模拟实验，只要将25%的高岭土加上75%的下层瓷石，便能配成和元代瓷胎的化学组分相近的原料。据此，高岭土在元代已经引入瓷胎，明清时代使用的瓷石加高岭土的所谓二元配方制胎法亦始创于元代[158]。

元代陶工在制备瓷胎时于瓷石中加入高岭土[159]：

1. 提高了瓷胎的耐火度，使过去无法利用的蕴藏量巨大的中下层瓷石得以使用；

2. 能提高瓷胎中Al_2O_3的含量，使制品的烧成范围增宽，减少变形，从而提高了成品率；

3. 因高岭土为土质原料，仅需淘洗即可使用，因而降低了瓷器的成本；

4. 使瓷胎中的玻璃相减少，莫来石增加，瓷器的热稳定性也随之提高。

表3-5-1 景德镇历代青花瓷胎的化学组成（wt%）

Table 3-5-1 Chemical Composition of Jingdezhen Underglaze Blue Porcelain Clays Throughout History （wt%）

编号 #	朝代 Period	SiO_2	Al_2O_3	Fe_2O_3	TiO_2	CaO	MgO	K_2O	Na_2O	MnO	P_2O_5	合计 Total
Y2	元 Yuan	72.64	21.08	0.97	0.00	0.20	0.18	2.69	1.52	0.080	0.090	99.45
Y5	元 Yuan	71.95	20.75	0.84	0.12	0.15	0.16	2.73	2.76	0.090	0.050	99.60
Y-8	元 Yuan	74.91	19.47	0.16	0.07	0.90	0.08	3.03	2.39	0.000	0.000	101.01
Y-11	元 Yuan	74.58	19.53	0.81	0.00	0.04	0.17	2.72	2.34	0.020	0.000	100.21
YG1	元 Yuan	74.42	18.83	1.14	0.11	0.15	0.24	3.11	2.06	0.030	0.000	100.09
YG	元 Yuan	74.18	19.94	1.30	0.22	0.13	0.30	3.50	1.22	0.033	0.000	100.82

Section 5:
Yuan Underglaze Blue Clay and Glaze

1. YUB Clay

A. Raw Material of YUB Clay

Wu Jun and Li Jia Zhi of the Shanghai Ceramics Research Institute, Chinese Science Academy have conducted multivariable statistical analysis of YUB clay. The chemical composition of YUB clay is as shown in Table 3-5-1 [157]:

Survey shows that Al_2O_3 is above 20%, and Na_2O is between 1.22-2.76%, thus these oxides in Yuan Dynasty clay was higher than that of earlier periods.

As such, Mr. Liu Xin Yuan has asserted that Yuan Dynasty clay was not composed simply of porcelain clay. This type of high Aluminum Oxide clay must have incorporated a new material, and the only pure loam in the Jingdezhen area to have such high amounts of Aluminum was Kaolin clay. His experiments have shown that by utilizing 25% Kaolin and 75% porcelain clay, it is possible to achieve the chemical compositions that are present in Yuan Dynasty porcelain raw materials. Thus, it was during the Yuan Dynasty that Kaolin clay was introduced to porcelain bodies, and the double material mixture of porcelain and Kaolin clay accredited to the Ming and Qing Dynasties actually started during the Yuan [158].

Yuan Dynasty Ceramic body manufacturing included the mixture of porcelain and Kaolin clay which [159]:

I. Increased the refractory of the body, allowing for the use of the huge, previously unusable, reserves of middle and low-middle strata porcelain clay.

II. Increased the Aluminum Oxide level of the body, broadening the firing temperature range, alleviating morphing, and as such increasing the successful firing rate.

III. Due to the quality of the Kaolin clay, only washing was needed, thus bringing down the overhead cost of ceramic production.

IV. As the silicates in the clay decreased and mullite increased, its thermo stability congruently increased.

B. Characteristics of YUB Clay

See pictures 3-5-1—3-5-4.

I. Majority of YUB clay bodies were thicker and more robust than that of the earlier Song or late Ming and Qing, but there are also pieces with a very thin body.

II. The color of the clay is usually an ashen grey.

III. The large majority of YUB clay has a certain amount of small pockets and cavities within the body. This is because the clay was not ground evenly, and during the drying process air and moisture pockets could form due to the decomposition of organic matter. Additionally, during the firing process certain minerals also broke down, and resulting gasses were unable to escape. In general, the thicker the body, the more cavities there are within the clay.

IV. In areas of exposed clay, there is a common phenomenon: reddish-orange appearance on the clay body; often called "Huo Shi Hong" or "Flint Red". Flint red can appear at any point on the ware in which the body is exposed, usually including: The interior, mouth, bottom, foot ring, and any point where the glaze meets the clay (see pictures 3-5-5—3-5-9). Flint red coloration occurs with a light to dark gradation, and most often follows the general line of the glaze-body meeting point. The color extends from the glaze, dark to light with a natural dwindling, until it disappears. It is possible for large areas of exposed glaze to lack even color gradation. Flint red coloration comes from the Iron and dissolvable salts collected on the exposed clay during the drying process. After firing, while the piece cools, second stage oxidation of the Iron

（二）元青花瓷胎特征

见图3-5-1—图3-5-4。

1. 大部分元青花瓷胎较前朝宋代及后朝明代的瓷胎要厚重、坚致。偶尔也有胎薄者。

2. 瓷胎颜色大多为灰白色。

3. 大部分元青花瓷胎都或多或少含有孔洞（较厚的胎体较多孔洞）。那是因为当时胎泥搅拌不够均匀，瓷胎在干燥过程中有机物质分解，以及在烧制过程中矿物质发生分解，产生的气体及水分未能逸出，从而形成孔洞。

图3-5-4

图3-5-6

4. 在元青花瓷器露胎部位呈现橘红色或橙色，俗称“火石红”。火石红一般在露胎处可见，可以分布在器物口沿、底部、圈足上，以及器物任意一处胎釉结合的地方（见图3-5-5—图3-5-9）。

胎釉结合处的火石红通常有颜色的浓淡过渡，通常从胎釉结合线向露胎的方向，颜色由浓到淡，自然过渡，直到消失；大面积露胎处有时不见明显的浓淡过渡。火石红是由于胎中的铁质和可溶盐类在干燥过程中在露胎处富集，在烧窑结束后的冷却过程中由于二次氧化出现的色调，是Fe^{2+}被氧化成Fe^{3+}的呈色结果[160]。

图3-5-1

图3-5-7

图3-5-2

图3-5-8

图3-5-3

图3-5-5

图3-5-9

occurs, changing Fe^{2+} into Fe^{3+}, resulting in coloration [160].

2. YUB Glaze

A. Characteristics of YUB Glaze

I. Scale of Glaze Reflectivity

According to the general sheen or reflectivity of YUB glaze, it can be divided into: Matte, Moist, and Sheen.

a. Matte

Matte glaze, for the most part, has lost all of its reflective properties, and has a slightly matted texture, with some pieces even gaining a slightly cloudy appearance (see pictures 3-5-10 and 3-5-11).

b. Moist

Moist glazes have a soft reflective quality, and appear to be wet to the touch (see pictures 3-5-12 and 3-5-13).

c. Sheen

Sheen glazes have a highly reflective quality, and the surface of the glaze appears to be glossy smooth (see pictures 3-5-14 and 3-5-15).

II. YUB Glaze Color

YUB glaze belongs to the clear glaze category, but most has a very slight "shrimp" bluish tinge (see pictures 3-5-16 and 3-5-17).

III. Glaze Humps

Slight humps randomly distributed on the surface of YUB glaze can present (see pictures 3-5-18 and 3-5-19).

IV. Glaze Crawling

Glaze crawling is a phenomenon cause by the receding of the glaze, and exposing the body beneath (see pictures 3-5-20 and 3-5-21).

Glaze crawling is formed when the glaze is too thin to cover the body of the glaze in certain areas, and may be caused by the surface tension of the glaze, moisture on the surface of the clay, viscosity of the glaze being too high, and so forth, which causes the glaze's inability to cover the body [161].

V. Glaze Flaking

Glaze flaking is caused by the breakdown of YUB glaze, and is most often seen at the mouth of the porcelain (see pictures 3-5-22 and 3-5-23).

VI. Bristle Pitting

Also called "pin-holes", are small hair follicle-like holes in the surface of the glaze that were caused during the firing process (see Chapter 6 Section 4).

Bristle Pits are observable holes in the glaze, however the porcelain body is not visible to the naked eye (see pictures 3-5-24 and 3-5-25).

VII. Glaze Cracks

Also called crazing, glaze cracks are all of the straight, curved, and sporadic fissures that are disbursed across the glaze formed during the firing process or under the influence of the post-firing environment (see Chapter 6 Section 2 Glaze Cracks Heading).

Glaze cracks on YUB are not considered to be intentionally created for aesthetic purposes, have a relatively low occurrence rate, and are considered to be glaze flaws.

Cracks can occur at certain portions on the surface of a piece (see picture 3-5-26), or occur across the entire glazed surface (see pictures 3-5-28 and 3-5-29). Crazing on aged pieces often has associated color change (see pictures 3-5-26—3-5-29).

VIII. Scratches

Scratches are the imperfections on YUB glaze that present as lines on the glaze surface that were left by the abrasive force of a solid external object.

Scratches can occur across the entire glaze surface, and varying severities of scratches can coexist or overlap. Scratches can be wide or narrow, long or short, deep or shallow, and can include colorations of yellow, soil, brown, and so forth (see pictures 3-5-30—3-5-32).

二、元青花瓷釉

（一）元青花瓷釉特征

1. 元青花瓷釉光亮特征

元青花瓷釉的光亮特征可分为三种：哑光、润光、亮光。

（1）哑光

哑光瓷釉整体有涩感，有的瓷釉部分整体泛白，多见于海捞瓷（见图3-5-10、图3-5-11）。

图3-5-10

图3-5-11

（2）润光

润光瓷釉整体泛柔光，给人以莹润之感（见图3-5-12、图3-5-13）。

图3-5-12

图3-5-13

（3）亮光

亮光瓷釉整体透亮，瓷釉显得光滑（见图3-5-14、图3-5-15）。

图3-5-14

图3-5-15

2. 元青花瓷釉颜色

元青花瓷釉属于透明釉。在釉厚处有时会呈现出浅浅的虾青色，主要是Fe^{2+}的呈色（见图3-5-16、图3-5-17）。

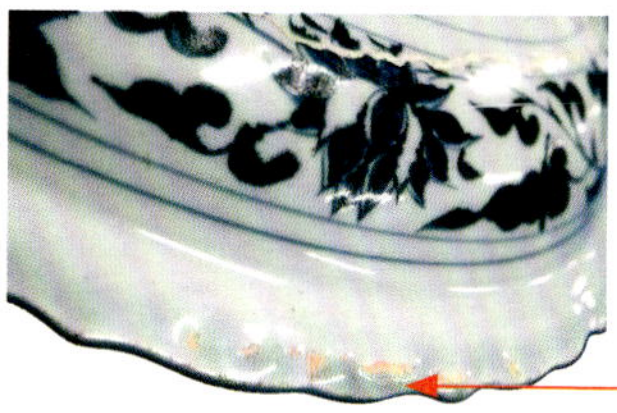

图3-5-16

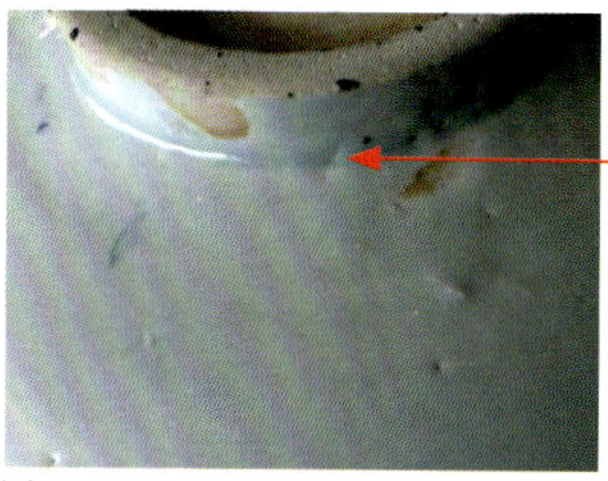

图3-5-17

3. 釉凸

有的元青花瓷器釉表面随机分布凸起的疙瘩（见图3-5-18、图3-5-19）。

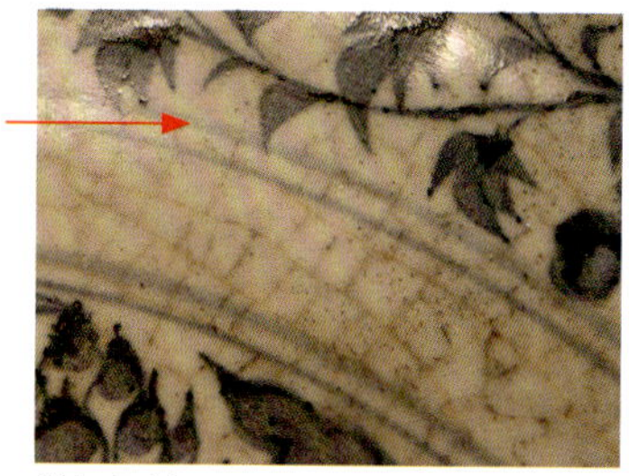

图3-5-18

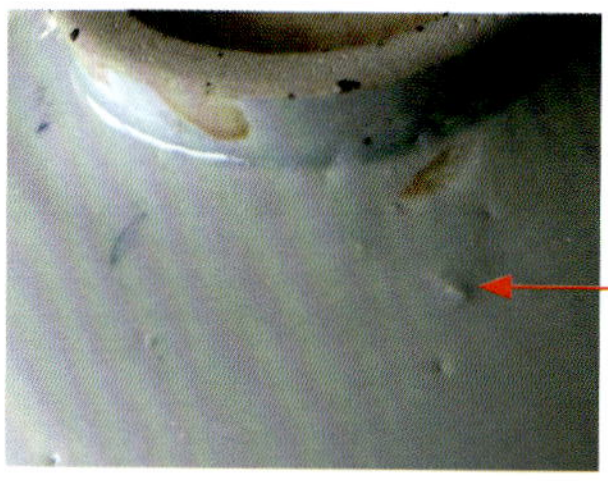

图3-5-19

IX. Speckling

Speckling refers to the presence of fine dots of dark coloration on the surface of the glaze (see picture 3-5-33).

X. Individual Iron Spots

On occasion, small individual brown iron spots appear on the glaze surface (see pictures 3-5-34 and 3-5-35).

4. 缩釉

缩釉是元青花瓷器釉表面向周边滚缩，形成中间缺釉露出胎体（见图3-5-20、图3-5-21）。

造成缩釉的原因有很多，如釉表面张力的作用、坯胎潮湿、釉的黏度过大，都可能会造成缩釉[161]。

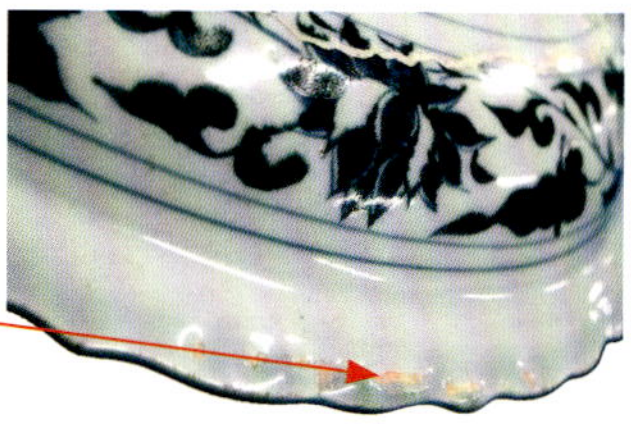

图3-5-20

图3-5-21

5. 剥釉

剥釉是元青花瓷器釉层脱落的现象。剥釉现象常见于瓷器口沿处（见图3-5-22、图3-5-23）。

图3-5-22

图3-5-23

6. 鬃眼

鬃眼是在元青花瓷器烧制过程中形成的釉层小孔(参见第六章第四节)。

鬃眼是瓷器釉表面的缺陷，凭肉眼可见，但用肉眼通过小孔观察不到胎体（见图3-5-24、图3-5-25）。

图3-5-24

图3-5-25

7. 釉裂纹

釉裂纹是元青花瓷器在烧制过程中和在后天环境影响下形成的，以直线、曲线等不规则线条形貌分布在釉表面的开裂纹路(参见第六章第二节釉裂纹部分)。

元青花瓷器上的釉裂纹不属于因审美要求而刻意造成的，而且很少出现，如果有釉裂现象，都属于瓷器缺陷。

釉裂纹既可以局部存在（见图3-5-26），也可以遍布全器（见图3-5-28、图3-5-29）。

通常有一定年份的釉裂纹都会有变色现象（见图3-5-26—图3-5-29）。

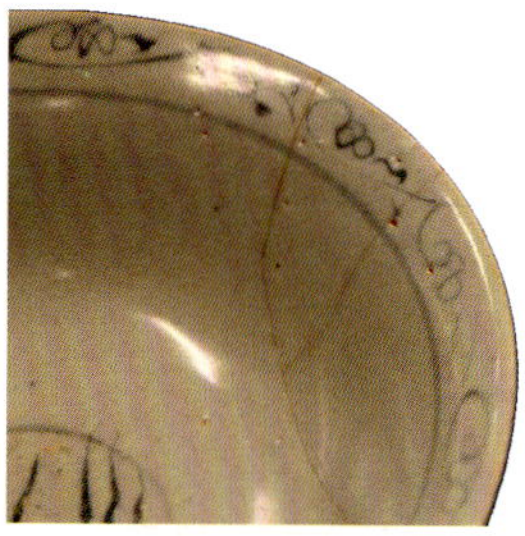

图3-5-26

图3-5-27

图3-5-28

图3-5-29

8. 划痕

划痕是元青花瓷器釉表面与硬物碰划留下的破坏性纹路。

划痕通常随机无序地分布在釉表面，深浅交织共存，有粗有细，有长有短，颜色有无色、黄色、褐色等（见图3-5-30—图3-5-32）。

9. 麻点

麻点是元青花瓷器釉表面以针眼形式成片分布的黑色或褐色斑点（见图3-5-33）。

10. 独立铁斑

有时元青花瓷釉上会随机出现个别褐色的独立铁斑（图3-5-34、图3-5-35）。

图3-5-30

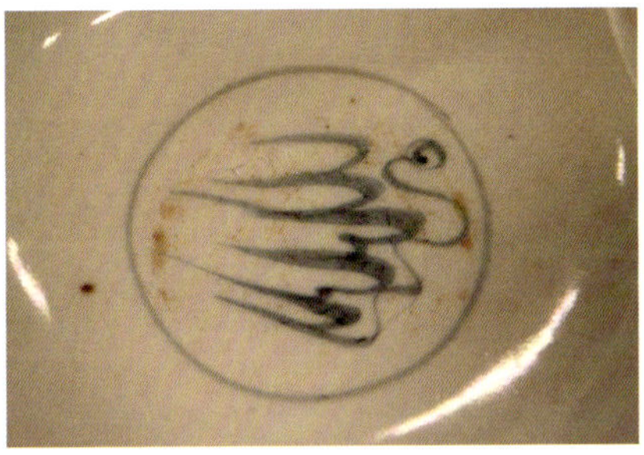
图3-5-31

图3-5-32

图3-5-33

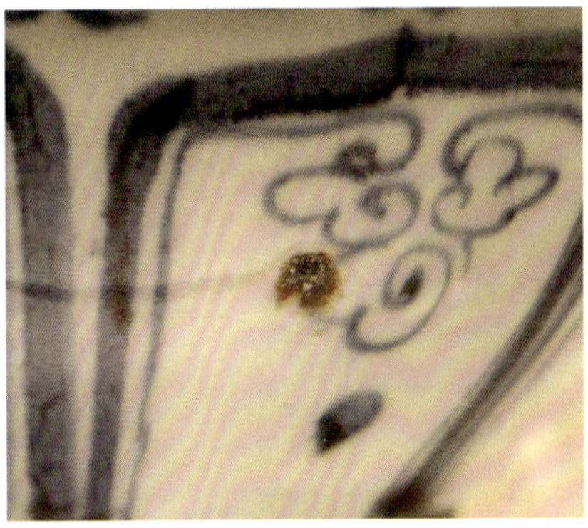
图3-5-34

图3-5-35

第六节
元青花制作工艺

一、元青花成型工艺

元青花的成型工艺是指将胎泥制成一定形状及规格坯体的过程。按照不同器形的成型方法大致可分为琢器成型及圆器成型两种。

（一）琢器成型工艺

琢器是指不能仅靠陶车一次拉坯成型，而需要多种工序加工成型的器物[162]。一般包括瓶、罐、觚、炉、壶之类的“立件”。

琢器一般用阴模印多个节坯然后拼接节坯而成型。阴模是指工作面内凹，用于形成器物外表面的模具[163]（见图3-6-1[164]）。

图3-6-1
阴模模具

（二）琢器成型过程

1. 印节坯

元青花琢器多由几个节坯拼接而成。将坯泥搓成粗条状环置于阴模内，接着挤压坯泥使泥均匀铺开紧贴模内壁，然后抹平内壁，保证节坯的平整和厚薄均匀[165]。

2. 脱模

待节坯与模有所分离时，就可将节坯从模内取出[166]。

3. 挖足

脱模后，用铁刀将印好的底挖足[167]。

4. 接节坯

各个节坯按一定顺序用泥接正、接固[168]。

5. 接圈足

玉壶春瓶、双耳瓶、蒜头瓶、执壶等高圈足的一类器物，圈足都是另外接上[169]。

6. 梅瓶接口

在梅瓶的接口处留有约1厘米高的“止口”，瓶口拌上接头泥与止口相卡接合。这种接法，接头接触面大，比较牢固[170]。

（三）琢器成型特征

1. 器物表面多不平整，特别是较大的器形，用手摸有高低起伏感。用手可感触到梅瓶口内壁上的接头痕。

2. 大罐内壁可见不规则旋纹（见图3-6-2、图3-6-3）。

图3-6-2

图3-6-3

3. 梅瓶、罐的底部多为浅挖足，底足足端大都不平、足壁厚、内壁外斜，底部可见深浅、疏密不一的旋削纹（见图3-6-4、图3-6-5）。

图3-6-4

Section 6:

Yuan Underglaze Blue Manufacturing Techniques

1. YUB Shaping Techniques

Shaping refers to the process of forming raw clay into a ceramic body of specified shape. According to the general shapes of YUB ceramics, the shaping techniques can be divided into two main categories: Closed Shaping and Open Shaping.

A. Closed Shaping Technique

Closed shaping refers to the technique of shaping pieces that are unable to be formed in one throw on the potter's wheel, but need to utilize two or more shaping processes [162]. Included are most vases, jars, beakers, censers, kettles, and so forth "standing pieces".

Many closed shapes are formed by joining two or more pieces of clay body that are formed using cavity molds. Cavity molds are premade molding tools that form the shape of a piece in its internal cavity [163] (see picture 3-6-1 [164]).

B. The Closed Shaping Process

I. Mold Pressing

YUB closed shape pieces consist of the connection of several clay forms. After wedging the clay, strips of clay are evenly pressed against the internal mold cavity walls, and the interior is pressed flat to ensure the face of the clay is smooth and the thickness uniform [165].

II. Mold Separation

The process of extracting the clay body from within the interior of the mold is called mold separation [166].

III. Digging

After the mold is removed, an iron tool is used to dig out the bottom of the piece, forming the indented base [167].

IV. Attaching

The molded clay bodies are attached to one another using porcelain slip (mixture of porcelain clay and water) to solidify the piece [168].

V. Attaching the Foot Ring

On vases and kettle varieties that have an attached foot ring, the foot ring is attached separately to the base of the piece [169].

VI. Attaching the Mouth (Meiping Vases)

On Meiping vases, a small one-centimeter slat encircles the base of the mouthpiece. The molded meiping mouth slat is then pressed inside the shoulder opening and slip is added. This added connection joint allows for a more stable linking point [170].

C. Characteristics of Closed Pieces

I. The external surface of most closed pieces is topographically uneven; particularly the larger wares, and the bumpiness can be detected by running one's hand across the surface. The internal connection joint of the meiping vase mouth can also be felt.

II. Irregular spiral lines can clearly be seen on the interior wall of large jars (see pictures 3-6-2 and 3-6-3).

III. Meiping and jar bases are usually shallowly dug out. The base surface is uneven, the foot rim thick, with an

图3-6-5

4.小件瓶、罐、壶、水注、鸟食罐等都是平沙底（见图3-6-6、图3-6-7）。

图3-6-6

图3-6-7

5.玉壶春瓶的圈足通常是外撇或垂直，圈足多为不正圆，圈足底平切处理（见图3-6-8、图3-6-9）。

图3-6-8

图3-6-9

6.有的琢器外壁上节坯泥接痕经刮平后表现不明显，而内壁接痕则比较明显（见图3-6-10、图3-6-11）。

图3-6-10

图3-6-11

（四）圆器成型工艺

圆器是指能够直接在陶车上拉坯或用陶模成型的器物[171]。一般包括碗、盘、杯、碟、盏等圆形的日用器皿。这类器物大部分是先经过拉坯，后用阳模定型的。阳模是指工作面凸起，用于形成器物内表面的模型[172]（见图3-6-12[173]）。

小盘、匜、盒等平底器物由阴

图3-6-12
阳模模具

1. 碗、盘类成型过程

（1）印坯：将坯泥置于阳模上，挤压拍打，按一定的厚度均匀地抚平坯泥[174]。

（2）修坯：待坯稍干将坯置于辘轳车上，用刀修平外壁，并挖出高圈足[175]。

（3）脱模：待坯与模有所分离时，将坯取出。

2. 碗、盘类成型特征

（1）元代的碗大部分是底部和腹部较厚，而口沿较薄（见图3-6-13）。碗的圈足外撇或垂直，圈足小但深，足壁厚。圈足内墙及器底有时可见挖足时留下的旋削纹，旋削纹有浅有深，有疏有密（见图3-6-14、图3-6-15）。

图3-6-13

图3-6-14

outward slanting inner foot wall, and there are visible spiraling scratch lines of varying thickness on the base (see pictures 3-6-4 and 3-6-5).

IV. Small wares, vases, jars, kettles, and so forth all have flat bottoms (see pictures 3-6-6 and 3-6-7).

V. The foot ring on Yuhuchun vases are usually slanted outward or vertical, and the circular shape is rarely even. The base of the foot ring is flattened (see pictures 3-6-8 and 3-6-9).

VI. Some of the connection joints on closed pieces are scraped smooth on the outside, and become barely noticeable, while the interior joint is left untouched (see pictures 3-6-10 and 3-6-11).

D. Open Shaping Technique

Open shaping refers to the process of creating a piece by throwing it once on the potter wheel or using only one mold to complete the shape [171]. Shapes often include bowls, plates, cups, saucers, and so forth circular daily use utensils. The majority of these shapes are first thrown, and then standardized with a force mold. Force molds are the opposite of cavity molds in that the clay is pressed over the mold rather than forced into it [172]. (see picture 3-6-12 [173]).

Small plates, yi, cases, and so forth; flat bottom clay bodies are all formed using force molds.

I. Bowl, Plate Shaping Process

Step 1 Molding the body: Placing the clay onto the force mold, the hands are used to press and form the body into a uniform thickness [174].

Step 2 Trimming the body: The semi-dry pressed mold is placed on a pulley driven wheel and a knife is used to trim the edges and carve out the raised foot of the ware [175].

Step3 Mold Separation: Once the piece begins to dry, the mold can be separated from the body.

II. Bowl, Plate Shaping Characteristics

a. Yuan dynasty bowls are characterized by a relatively thick foot and belly, and thin mouth (see picture 3-6-13). The bowl foot ring is slightly slanted outward or straight, the ring interior is small but deep, and the foot ring wall is thick. Sometimes visible spiral carving marks from the foot trimming are left on the interior of the foot ring and on the base; they can be deep or shallow as well as sparse or dense (see pictures 3-6-14 and 3-6-15).

b. Similar to bowls, plate foot rings can be slightly outwards slanting or straight in an inverted trapezoid shape (see picture 3-6-16) or dorsal fin shape (see picture 3-6-17). The foot is small but deep and not as thick as bowl foot rings. The foot ring and base can present with spiral or radiating trimming marks (see pictures 3-6-18—3-6-20).

III. Stem Bowls, Cups Shaping Process

Stem bowls and cups are almost always formed using force molds, but the stem feet are formed in cavity molds and attached later [176].

IV. Stem Bowls, Cups Shaping Characteristics

Stem wares have flat trimmed foot rings (see picture 3-6-21). The center of the stem has a small mound of clay at the connection point (see pictures 3-6-21—3-6-23).

2. YUB Glazing Techniques

In general, glaze on YUB wares is relatively thick.

A. Large Closed Pieces

On large mouthed closed wares such as jars and vases, the glazed is poured on the outside and smeared on the inside.

Exterior Glaze Pouring: Covering the piece's mouth, the glaze is poured over the shoulder and neck areas of the ware until the entire piece is covered, and glaze spills over onto the foot [177].

Interior Glaze Smearing: Using a large brush dipped in glaze; the interior of the vessel is nonchalantly brushed over [178], and most of the interior is covered (see pictures 3-6-24—3-6-26). Sometimes the glaze is applied relatively thin and uneven, and there are areas of visible brushstrokes where the porcelain body is still visible. Brushstrokes are often accompanied by flint red (see pictures 3-6-25 and

图3-6-15

（2）盘类圈足外撇或垂直，呈倒梯形（见图3-6-16）或鲫鱼背形（见图3-6-17）。圈足小但较深，足壁不及碗类的厚。圈足内墙及器底可见挖足时留下的旋削纹或放射状的跳刀痕（见图3-6-18—图3-6-20）。

图3-6-16

图3-6-17

图3-6-18

图3-6-19

图3-6-20

3. 高足碗、杯成型过程

高足碗、杯的上半部采用阳模印坯制成，而高足部分则由阴模制成[176]。

4. 高足碗、杯成型特征

高足为平切底，高足内接头中心处有凸起小泥团（见图3-6-21—图3-6-23）。

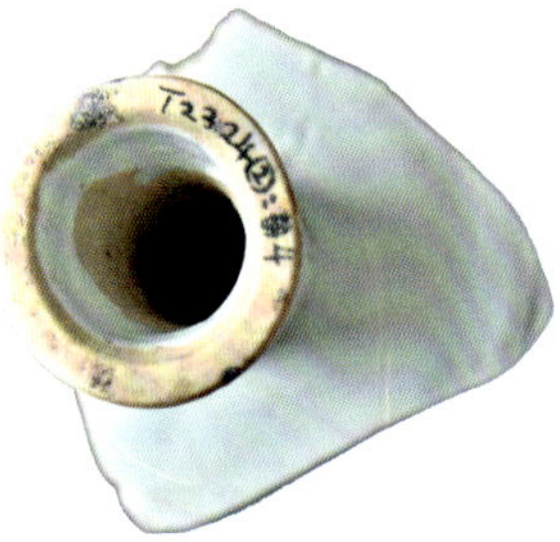

图3-6-21

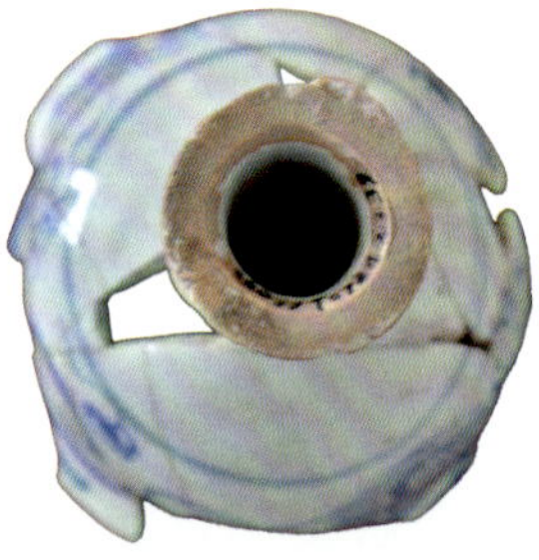

图3-6-22

图3-6-23

二、元青花施釉工艺

一般说来，元青花瓷器施釉较厚。

（一）大件琢器

大口的罐、瓶等器外用浇釉，器内用涂釉。

器外浇釉：把大件琢器口部盖住，然后将釉同时往颈、肩部浇去，釉便往下流满全器，并有一部分流到器底部[177]。

器内涂釉：用大笔沾釉涂抹器内壁，操作随意[178]。罐内大部分满釉（见图3-6-24—图3-6-26）。有时施釉较薄且不均匀，会有漏笔现象，漏笔处可见胎，有时呈火石红（见图3-6-25、图3-6-26），有时呈牙黄色（见图3-6-27）。

图3-6-24

3-6-26) or ivory yellow markings (see picture 3-6-27).

The base of large jars and vases are generally not glazed, but may have glaze drips and blotches present (see pictures 3-6-28 and 3-6-29).

B. Small Closed Pieces

Small closed pieces utilize a "Zhan" (dipping) glazing technique in which the foot of the piece is grasped in the hand, and the piece is submerged into the glaze (not passing the foot rim). After a moment, the piece is lifted out [179]. Therefore, often the base of the glaze is uneven around the bottom at roughly the location of the 3-4-finger grip on the body (see picture 3-6-30). The bases of closed pieces do not usually have glaze, save for the Yuhuchun vase foot ring interiors, of which most are entirely glazed, with occasionally a partial sandy base presenting (see pictures 3-6-31 and 3-6-32).

Small closed piece interiors are rarely fully glazed, but do have a 1-3 centimeter glaze layer extending down into the mouth, and sometimes glaze drip marks are present (see picture 3-6-33).

Vase type wares have a layer of glaze on the interior portion of the mouth and neck (see picture 3-6-34).

Stem wares have a small ring of glaze around the interior of the foot (see picture 3-6-35).

C. Large Open Pieces

Large bowls and plates all utilized a glaze covering technique called glaze throwing.

Interior Wall Throwing: Affixing the piece to a spinning wheel, the glaze is poured in the center of the ware, and thrown outward along with the centrifugal force of the spinning ware until the interior is uniformly covered [180].

Exterior Wall Throwing: Affixing the piece upside down on the spinning wheel, the ware is spun and the glaze is applied nearest the foot ring and thrown downward along with the centrifugal force of the spinning ware until the entire exterior of the ware is uniformly covered in glaze [181]. At the mouth of some open pieces, due to being double glazed during throwing, thicker portions of glaze can appear, causing a "shrimp" blue hue after firing.

Large open ware bases do not undergo glazing.

D. Medium and Small Open Pieces

Medium and small open pieces such as bowls, saucers and cases utilize glaze pouring on the interior, and glaze dipping or pouring on the exterior [182].

At times glaze accumulates at the mouth portion of these wares (see picture 3-6-36).

Small bowl foot rings are trimmed after glazing is complete. This is to say, they must be fully glazed first, then the foot is dug out; thus all small bowls should not have glazed bases [183] (see picture 3-6-37).

3. YUB Firing Techniques

YUB wares were all outfitted with saggars (protective firing cases), and then fired. The firing process is as follows:

A. Glaze Trimming

Before a piece could be fitted with a saggar, in order to scale back the occurrence of the foot ring sticking to the kiln, the glaze (usually on the outside of the foot) would be trimmed away with a blade, simply called "Glaze Trimming" [184]. The marks left by the scraping could be either thick or thin, and have regular spiraling or relatively nonchalant irregular scratches (see pictures 3-6-38—3-6-45).

B. Placing Bedding Sediments or Risers

Bedding sediments consisted of a mixture of rice husk, saggar sediments, and Kaolin clay sediments. Risers were made from various fireproof minerals.

As the bottoms of saggars were uneven, it was necessary to first place a bedding of sediments across the bottom to even it out. Large plates would have had their foot ring placed directly onto the sediments, and a riser placed under the center to prevent it from sagging during firing [185]. The use of this

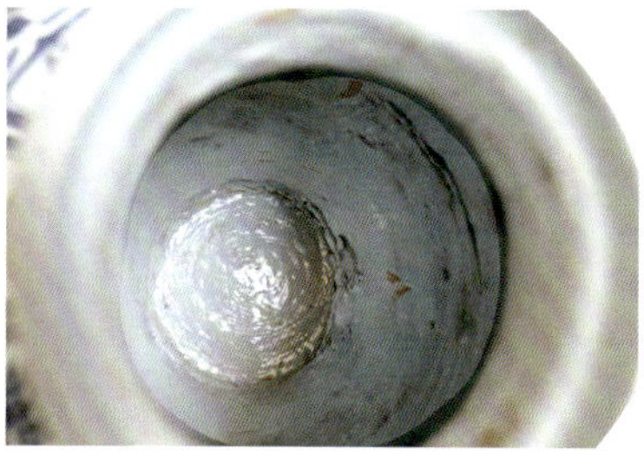
图3-6-25

图3-6-26

图3-6-27

大件瓶、罐等器底基本不施釉，有时可见随机分布的釉斑（见图3-6-28、图3-6-29）。

图3-6-28

图3-6-29

（二）小件琢器

小件琢器如小罐、小瓶等，器外均采用蘸釉法，即用手指抓住器足，浸入釉料中（不超过足沿），片刻后提起[179]。所以足沿常有一圈不规则的露胎——大概有3—4个指头抓坯的痕迹（见图3-6-30）。琢器的足底一般不施釉，但玉壶春瓶足底普遍都满釉，有时可见小部分砂底（见图3-6-31、图3-6-32）。

图3-6-30

图3-6-31

图3-6-32

小件琢器器内一般不施满釉，仅在口沿处施有1—3厘米的釉，有时可见釉水流淌痕迹（见图3-6-33）。

图3-6-33

瓶类如玉壶春瓶等在口颈内施上一节釉（见图3-6-34）。

高足器物的圈足内靠底部有一圈釉斑（见图3-6-35）。

图3-6-34

图3-6-35

firing technique often left bedding sediments on the base and foot ring of YUB wares. On large jars and vases, sediments are often seen on the base of the ware; and on footed pieces, they are seen on the inside, outside, and bottom of the foot ring (see pictures 3-6-46, 3-6-47, and 3-6-50—3-6-53).

With large jars and vases, in order to prevent the collapse of the base, a fireproof stone riser (cake or ring) would be placed under its center as a fulcrum point [186]. This would often leave a ring marking on the base of such wares (see pictures 3-6-46 and 3-6-47).

On unglazed, small, deep-footed wares such as bowls, there can often be seen a small convex mark that resembles the navel of a gong, and as such is called a "Gong Navel" mark [187] (see pictures 3-6-48 and 3-6-49).

Aside from sediments, YUB foot rings and bases often have sand granules sticking to them, called "Stuck Sand" [188]. Stuck sand can be seen across the base, on the foot, and even up to the edge of the glaze on large wares. On wares with foot rings, sand can become stuck to the interior, exterior, and bottom of the foot ring (see pictures 3-5-54—3-6-57).

C. Saggar Outfitting

Large pieces would be fired one piece per saggar, while smaller wares could have as many as ten pieces in one saggar. It was also possible in large saggars to place smaller pieces around the foot of the saggar, under the large ware [189].

D. Firing

Once outfitted, the saggars would be placed in a certain order into the kiln. Once loaded, the kiln was fired using firewood as fuel [190].

（三）大件圆器

大盘、大碗内外施釉均采用甩釉方法。

内壁施釉：把大件圆器仰置于辘轳车上快速旋转，在离心力的作用下，倒入的釉水顺着内壁流动并甩出，使器内壁均匀地被釉覆盖[180]。

外壁施釉：将大件圆器覆置于辘轳车上快速旋转，将釉淋在靠近圈足的外壁上，通过离心力和釉的流动性，使外壁均匀地挂满釉[181]。有的器物口沿会因两次施釉而出现釉层较厚的现象，呈现虾青色。

大件圆器如碗、盘类底部不施釉。

（四）中小件圆器

中小件圆器如碗、碟、盒等，器内采用浇釉法，器外用蘸釉或浇釉法[182]。

有时外壁口沿处可见积釉（见图3-6-36）。

小件碗类的圈足，在利坯时留下的实心高足。待施釉完全后再挖足，所以碗类圈足内均无釉[183]（见图3-6-37）。

图3-6-36

图3-6-37

三、元青花装烧工艺

元代青花瓷多采用匣钵装坯，然后入窑烧制。装烧过程如下：

（一）取釉

胎体在装匣之前，为防止足端出现大面积窑粘，必须将足端上（多在外墙部分）的釉用刀刮去，俗称“取釉”[184]。取釉留下的旋削纹有粗有细，有的旋削纹利索规整，也有的不规整较随意（见图3-6-38—图3-6-45）。

图3-6-38

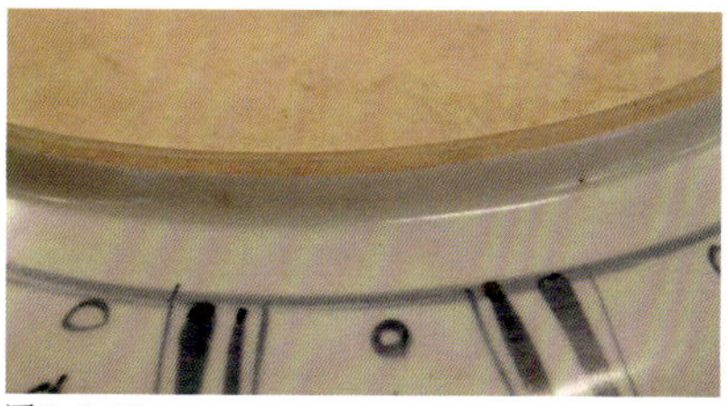

图3-6-39

图3-6-40

图3-6-41

图3-6-42

图3-6-43

图3-6-44

图3-6-45

（二）铺垫渣或垫饼

垫渣是用早稻谷壳灰拌的匣土渣或高岭土渣制成，垫饼用耐火土制成。

装元青花的匣钵由于底不平，会在匣底铺一层垫渣。大盘通常都直接置于垫渣之上，底内铺垫渣并顶住盘子上底，防止盘子底下沉[185]。因为这种垫烧工艺，元青花足端和底部常常粘有垫渣，在罐类、瓶类的底部露胎处可见；在有圈足的器物上，圈足内外及圈足上也可见（见图3-6-46、图3-6-47、图3-6-50—图3-6-53）。

在烧制瓶、罐等大型器物时，为防止塌底，需在底部中心或稍偏处放一个用耐火土做成的圆饼或圆圈做支点[186]，这会在瓷器底部留下一个近似圆点的痕迹（见图3-6-46、图3-6-47）。

在胎体较厚、圈足较小、圈足内无釉、器形较小的碗等器物上，可见呈乳钉凸起的痕迹，如同铜锣之脐，可称其为“脐底”[187]（见图2-5-48、图2-5-49）。

除此以外，元青花瓷器足端和底部还会粘有砂粒，简称“粘砂”[188]。粘砂在罐类、瓶类的底部露胎处或底部胎釉结合处的釉表面上都可见；在有圈足的器物上，圈足内外及圈足上也可见（见图3-6-54—图3-6-57）。

（三）装匣

大件器物一匣装一个，小件器物十余件装一匣，也有的一匣装一大件，下部插装一些小件器物[189]。

（四）装烧

装好的匣入窑，并按一定的顺序叠起，以木柴为燃料烧制[190]。

图3-6-46

图3-6-47

图3-6-48

图3-6-49

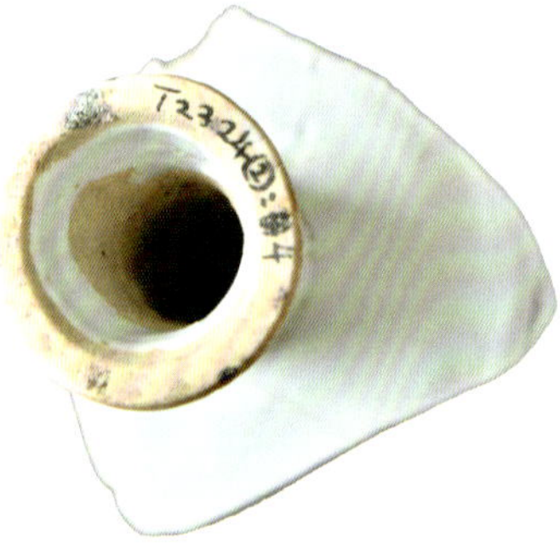
图3-6-50

图3-6-51

图3-6-52

图3-6-53

图3-6-54

图3-6-55

图3-6-56

图3-6-57

第四章

元青花釉层的化学成分、性质与形貌

阅读提示：

本章将对元青花瓷釉的化学成分、性质与形貌做理论性论述与阐明。

主要论述问题：

1. 元青花釉层的化学成分有哪些？它们各自的作用是什么？
2. 元青花釉层为什么会风化？
3. 元青花釉层的形貌是怎样的？

Chapter 4

Chemical Composition, Nature, and Appearance of Yuan Underglaze Blue Glaze

Text Note:

This chapter theorizes the chemical composition, nature and appearance of YUB in order to fully discuss and depict its characteristics.

第一节
元青花瓷釉化学成分

一、元青花瓷釉的概念

元青花瓷釉是施于元青花瓷器坯体表面，利用天然矿物原料按比例配合，在高温作用下熔融而覆盖在坯体表面的玻璃质层[191]。

二、元青花瓷釉的构成

元青花瓷釉主要由网络形成剂、助熔剂和着色剂组成。

（一）网络形成剂

玻璃相是元青花釉层的主相，形成玻璃相的主要氧化物是二氧化硅（SiO_2），它在釉层中以四面体的形式相互结合成不规则网络，所以SiO_2又称为网络形成剂[192]。

（二）助熔剂

在元青花釉料熔化过程中，助熔剂能促进高温分解反应，加速高熔点晶体（如SiO_2）化学键的断裂和生成低共熔物。助熔剂还起着调整釉层物理化学性质（如力学性质、膨胀系数、黏度、化学稳定性等）的作用[193]。

常用的助熔剂化合物有氧化钠（Na_2O）、氧化钾（K_2O）、氧化钙（CaO）等。

（三）着色剂

着色剂是在陶瓷的胎、釉中起呈色作用的物质[194]。着色剂包括氧化亚铁（FeO）、三氧化二铁（Fe_2O_3）、氧化钴（CoO）和氧化锰（MnO）等氧化物。

元青花瓷釉属于透明釉，有的元青花釉色呈青色，那是Fe^{2+}在釉中所呈现的颜色。

（四）其他成分

元青花瓷釉中还含有三氧化二铝（Al_2O_3）和其他成分。Al_2O_3是一种重要成分，适量的Al_2O_3能与SiO_2形成网络，可增强釉层的强度及化学稳定性。

三、元青花瓷釉化学成分

元青花是在1150℃以上的温度烧成的，属高温釉瓷器。

陈尧成等人对各时期典型青花釉的化学构成做了分析，表4-1-1为部分景德镇地区元青花标本的瓷釉构成数据[195]。

中国科学院上海硅酸盐研究所对元大都出土的青花瓷片的瓷釉化学构成做了分析，表4-1-2为部分数据[196]。

由以上研究结果可得出，元青花瓷釉的化学成分主要有：SiO_2、Al_2O_3、Fe_2O_3、TiO_2、CaO、MgO、K_2O、Na_2O、MnO、P_2O_5等。

为了方便描述，我们将元青花瓷釉中影响其釉层结构的主要成分归纳成一个系统，所以元青花瓷釉可归于$Na_2O-K_2O-CaO-MgO-Al_2O_3-SiO_2$系统。

四、元青花瓷釉的配方

元青花瓷釉的配方主要由瓷石加草木灰或釉灰配制而成[197]。

元青花瓷釉中的CaO主要由草木灰或釉灰提供。用草木灰的釉式统计值作为参照标准，可以将以CaO为主要助熔剂的釉（钙系釉）划分为钙釉、钙碱釉和碱钙釉。元代景德镇窑的青花多数属于钙碱釉，少数属于碱钙釉[198]。

Section 1:

Chemical Composition of Yuan Underglaze Blue Glaze

1. The Definition of YUB Glaze

A specifically mixed set of natural and mineral raw materials for application to the surface of YUB clay body that when fired, melts and then cools to become a glass phase layer over the body [191].

2. The Components of YUB Glaze

YUB Glaze primarily consists of: Networking Agents, Flux, and Coloring Agents.

A. Networking Agents

Glass is the main phase of the YUB glaze level; composed primarily of Silicone Dioxide (SiO_2) in tetrahedron shapes, mutually interlocking to create an irregular network; thus being slated as networking agents [192].

B. Flux

During the melting of YUB glaze, these solvents promote high temperature split reactions and accelerate the splitting of high-melting-point crystals (such as SiO_2) into eutectic solutions. Fluxes also bring rise to changes in the physical chemical properties of the glaze (Such as mechanics, coefficient of expansion, viscosity, and chemical stability) [193].

Commonly used fluxes are: Sodium Oxide (Na_2O), Potassium Oxide (K_2O), Calcium Oxide (CaO), and so forth.

C. Coloring Agents

Coloring Agents are substances between the clay body and glaze that act to add color to a ceramic piece [194]. They include: Iron Oxide (FeO), Ferric Oxide (Fe_2O_3), Cobaltous Oxide (CoO), Manganese Oxide (MnO), and so forth various metal oxides.

YUB glaze is considered to be of the clear glaze variety. However, it can present with slight shades of blue. This blue coloration is due to the presence of Fe^{2+} ions in the glaze level.

D. Other Components

YUB Glaze also contains Aluminum Oxide (Al_2O_3) and other elements. Aluminum Oxide is a more instrumental component in that, with the proper quantities, it can network with Silicone Dioxide to increase the strength and chemical stability of the glaze level.

3. The Chemical Composition of YUB Glaze

YUB glazes are formed in temperatures over 1150°C, and are considered High-Temperature Glazes.

Chen Yao Cheng et al undertook analytical research of the characteristic compositions of underglaze blue wares. Table 4-1-1 outlines the chemical compositions of Jingdezhen area YUB [195].

The Shanghai Institute of Ceramics, Chinese Academy of Sciences, also undertook a similar endeavor, analyzing the compositions of the YUB shards excavated from the Yuan Dadu (Capital City). Table 4-1-2 outlines a portion of the results [196].

From the above we can see the primary chemical components of YUB glazes are: SiO_2, Al_2O_3, Fe_2O_3, TiO_2, CaO, MgO, K_2O, Na_2O, MnO, and P_2O_5.

表4-1-1 元青花瓷釉化学成分

Table 4-1-1 Yuan Underglaze Blue Glaze Chemical Composition

品名 Article Name	氧化物含量 Wt（%） Amount of Oxidized Materials Wt(%)											
	SiO_2	Al_2O_3	TiO_2	CaO	Fe_2O_3	MgO	MnO	CoO	K_2O	Na_2O	P_2O_5	总数 Total
景德镇元青花大盘碎片 Jingdezhen YUB Large Plate Shard	69.53	14.87	0.004	8.97	0.84	0.31	0.10	<0.01	2.70	3.12	0.12	100.56
景德镇元青花碎片 Jingdezhen YUB Shard	67.97	15.23	—	10.06	0.90	0.34	0.10	0.01	2.92	2.57	0.17	100.27
景德镇湖田窑元青花碎片 Jingdezhen Hutian Kiln YUB Shard	70.54	15.11	0.05	7.32	0.97	0.40	0.11	<0.01	3.09	3.14	—	100.73
景德镇元青花碎片 Jingdezhen YUB Shard	70.27	14.54	—	6.52	0.82	0.36	0.13	<0.01	2.82	3.14	0.16	98.76

表4-1-2 元大都出土青花瓷片瓷釉化学成分

Table 4-1-2 Yuan Underglaze Blue Glaze Chemical Composition

编号 #	SiO_2	Al_2O_3	Fe_2O_3	TiO_2	CaO	MgO	K_2O	Na_2O	MnO	P_2O_5	合计 Total
YM(74)IV-5	70.17	14.02	0.78	—	8.00	0.40	2.72	3.13	0.12	0.15	99.49
YK(70)IV-6	69.82	14.52	0.84	0.25	7.57	0.26	2.24	3.65	0.10	0.28	99.54
YK(70)IV-7	68.81	14.72	1.24	—	8.04	0.26	2.47	4.04	0.10	0.21	99.95

For ease of description, we systemize high-temperature glaze based upon the primary elements that are acting on the composition of the glaze level. Therefore, the system for categorizing the high-temperature glazes used in YUB is based on a chemical composition of the Na_2O-K_2O-CaO-MgO-Al_2O_3-SiO_2 system.

4. The Formulation of YUB Glaze

YUB glazes were primarily formulated using porcelain clay, and added plant ash or glaze ash [197].

The CaO found in YUB glaze comes primarily from plant ash or glaze ash. Using glazes that utilize plant ash as the sample selection, research showed that the primary flux was CaO (thus named Calcium Glazes). These Calcium Glazes can be further categorized in Calcium Glaze, Calcium Alkaline Glaze, and Alkaline Calcium Glaze. The majority of Jingdezhen kiln YUB glazes are Calcium Alkaline Glazes, while only a minority are Alkaline Calcium Glazes [198].

第二节
元青花瓷釉各化学成分的作用

从第一节我们了解到元青花釉层是各类氧化物在高温作用下被熔化，然后冷却形成的玻璃体。但并不是所有的氧化物都能形成玻璃体，只有在氧化物的分子结构能形成特定的网络结构时，才能形成玻璃体。

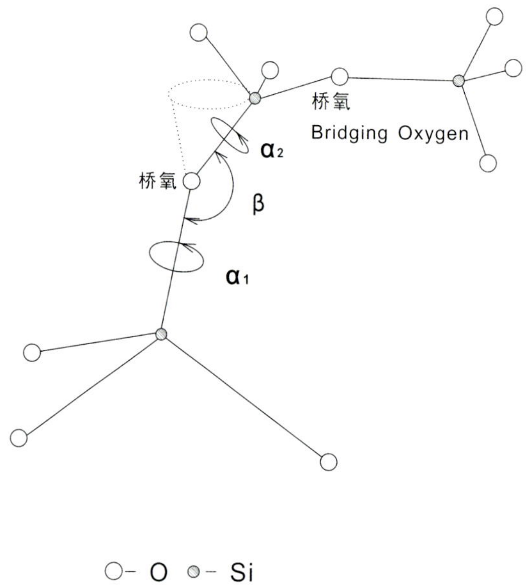

图4-2-2

一、网络形成剂作用

网络形成剂主要由SiO_2构成。SiO_2的基本结构是硅氧四面体（简写为[SiO_4]四面体），Si与O通过硅氧键（Si—O）相连，一个硅原子与四个氧原子相连接形成四面体（见图4-2-1）。为了便于书写，将其简化成≡Si—。

氧原子通过与两个硅原子相连将四面体连接起来，连接这四面体的氧原子称为桥氧。它们以顶角相连而构成连续的架状三维硅氧网络（见图4-2-2[199]）。

为了便于书写，将其简化成≡Si—O—Si≡（中间的O为桥氧）。≡Si—O—Si≡的连接角度是不定的，也就是说，图4-2-2中的$α_1$、$α_2$和β角的度数是可变化的，故就整体而言，形成的是不规则的硅氧网络。通过这样的连接形成的SiO_2三维网络（也就是玻璃体），是没有对称性和周期性的，它是最简单的单组份硅酸盐玻璃。

由于SiO_2是一种能相互连接形成三维空间网络的氧化物，我们称之为网络形成体氧化物。SiO_2是釉层的主要成分，机械强度及化学稳定性都比较好，所以釉层有保护瓷器的作用。

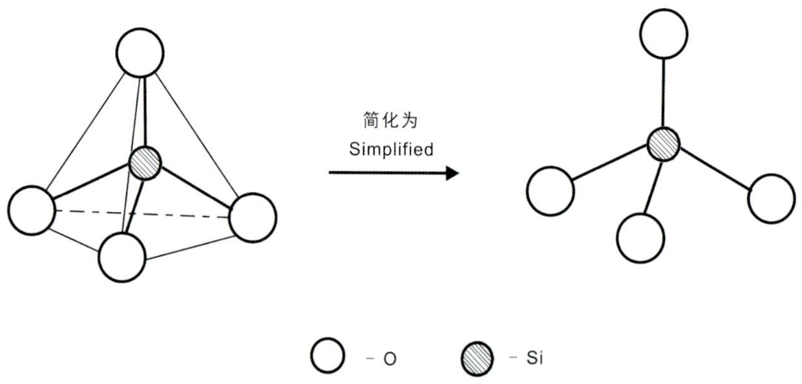

图4-2-1

二、助熔剂作用

元青花釉料配方中的石英熔点较高，达到1750℃，而当代瓷窑最高的烧成温度也不过1400℃。由第一节可知，碱金属氧化物Na_2O和K_2O以及碱土金属氧化物CaO、MgO都可在元青花瓷釉中充当助熔剂的角色，它们可以降低石英的熔点，从而降低元青花瓷器的烧结温度。

Section 2:
The Functions of Yuan Underglaze Blue Glaze Chemical Components

According to Section 1, YUB glaze is a fusion of certain oxidized components, melded under high temperatures, and cooled to form a glass-like coating. However, not all oxidized compounds have the ability to form glass; only those that have set networking construction are able to arrange as such.

1. The Function of Networking Agents

Networking agents are comprised primarily of Silica SiO_2. The foundational construction of SiO_2 is a Silicone and Oxygen tetrahedron (Simplified as $[SiO_4]$ tetrahedron) in which one Si atom is combined with four O atoms to form the shape illustrated in Picture 4-2-1. Hereafter to be simplified as ≡ Si —.

An Oxygen atom that links two Silicone atoms is called a 'bridging Oxygen'. They affix in static angles to form a three-dimensional silica network structure illustrated in 4-2-2 [199]. Hereafter to be simplified as ≡Si—O—Si≡ (the central O as the bridging Oxygen).

Because of the unfixed angle of attachment of the ≡Si—O—Si≡ we can see in Picture 4-2-2 that angles α_1, α_2 and β can vary. It is due to this that SiO_2 molecules fuse to form an irregularly shaped network structure that lacks symmetry and periodicity; this structure is generically called silicate glass. This irregular construction of SiO_2 is the main building block of YUB glaze. Because SiO_2 is able to interconnect and form a three-dimensional network structure, we call it a networking oxide. This glaze level geometric structure is relatively strong with a good chemical stability, creating an inherent functionality of protecting the porcelain body.

2. The Function of Flux

Quartz, used in YUB glaze, has a very high melting point, as high as 1750 °C; and currently the highest temperature used in firing ceramics is around 1400 °C. Because of this, alkaline metal oxides Na_2O and K_2O as well as alkaline earth metal oxides CaO and MgO are added to YUB glazes to act as a flux, effectively lowering the melting temperature of quartz and allowing for a lower firing temperature.

During the fusion of SiO_2, if alkaline metal oxides (R_2O, where R represents Na, K) or alkaline earth metal oxides (RO where R represents Ca, Mg) are added, the bond of the R—O is primary and much weaker than that of Si—O. This is to say that the Si—O Si^{4+} ions can attract the O^{2-} ions of the R—O creating a bond of ≡Si—O—R that has a ≡Si—O bond that is stronger than that of the ≡Si—O bond found in ≡Si—O—Si≡. The result is the breaking away of the bridging O (≡Si•••O—Si≡). Thus, the bridging Oxygen becomes a non-bridging Oxygen and a new ≡Si—O—R bond is formed. After the breakdown of ≡Si—O—Si≡, the ≡Si—O bond's strength, length, and angle all undergo change [200] (see picture 4-2-3).

Therefore, the network experiences several locations of breakdown where Si and O are no longer conjoined on both sides, but rather an O and R bond takes its place.

SiO_2 silicone dioxide has a Si:O ratio of 1:2. With the addition of R_2O or RO, this Si:O ratio can increase to 1:3 or 1:4, from which the three-dimensional $[SiO_4]$ tetrahedron network is split into stratified, chain, and toroidal structures until the entire network is spilt into island structured $[SiO_4]$ tetrahedrons. During the breaking down process, chains of SiO_4 come together to form low polymers, under the right circumstances these low polymers begin to interact and form

当在SiO_2熔体中加入碱金属（R_2O，R在此指Na、K）或碱土金属氧化物（RO，R在此指Ca、Mg）时，由于R—O是离子键为主，其键强比Si—O键弱得多，因此，Si—O键中的Si^{4+}能把R—O键上的O^{2-}吸引到自己的周围，使≡Si—O—R中的≡Si—O键比≡Si—O—Si≡中的≡Si—O键还要强，结果是使原来的桥氧键（≡Si…O—Si≡）从虚线处断开，桥氧成为非桥氧，同时形成新的≡Si—O—R键。≡Si—O—Si≡断裂后，Si—O键的键强、键长和键角都会发生变化[200]（见图4-2-3）。

这样，硅氧网络中许多地方会出现断点，即O不是与两个Si相连，而是其中一端与R相连。

SiO_2的硅氧比（Si/O）为1:2。随着Na_2O、K_2O、CaO的加入，Si/O可由原来的1:2上升到1:3或1:4，从而使$[SiO_4]$四面体的架状三维网络发生断裂，连接方式随着硅氧比的不同会由架状变为层状、链状、环状，直至最后桥氧全部断裂形成岛状的$[SiO_4]$四面体。在这个过程中，许多断裂的$[SiO_4]$四面体短链会聚集，形成低聚物。这种低聚物不断增多，在一定条件下会产生相互作用，形成高聚物，直至平衡。所以，釉层的结构会因Na_2O、K_2O、CaO、MgO的加入而发生变化。

这些碱金属氧化物（Na_2O、K_2O）和碱土金属氧化物（CaO、MgO）的加入，并没有参与到硅氧网络中去，而是使网络断裂，从而使其熔点降低。它们改变了硅氧网络的性质，我们称它们为网络外体氧化物。（注：MgO只有在碱金属氧化物较多而且不存在Al_2O_3及B_2O_3等氧化物时，才可进入硅氧网络）

三、其他成分作用

元青花瓷釉中除了网络形成剂、助熔剂、着色剂以外，还有其他成分，如三氧化二铝（Al_2O_3），这是一个重要成分。

在硅酸盐玻璃中，Al_2O_3中的Al^{3+}有4、6两种配位状态，即位于四面体或八面体中。当摩尔比$R_2O/Al_2O_3>1$时，Al^{3+}位于四面体中，以$[AlO_4]$四面体形式将一些$[SiO_4]$四面体的断点连接起来，与$[SiO_4]$组成统一的网络，使玻璃结构趋向紧密，对硅氧网络起补网作用，提高釉层结构的稳定性；当摩尔比$R_2O/Al_2O_3<1$时，碱金属离子不足以使Al^{3+}离子形成$[AlO_4]$四面体时的化合价平衡，超出的Al^{3+}离子只能在玻璃中以六配位的形式[201]，作为网络外体存在于八面体之中，从而使玻璃结构趋向于松散，使硅氧网络的紧密程度下降，化学稳定性也随之下降[202]。

Al_2O_3既可以与SiO_2形成网络，也可处于网络外，所以它是一种中间体氧化物。

四、元青花瓷釉的化学成分与釉层结构稳定性的关系

在元青花瓷釉中，由于$[SiO_4]$四面体间隙的存在，碱金属或碱土金属离子会均匀而无序地分布在某些$[SiO_4]$四面体之间的空隙中，以维持网络中局部的电中性。与Si—O连接较弱的原子、离子或原子团在釉层中可以移动，如H^+、Li^+、Na^+、K^+、Rb^+、Cs^+、Ag^+、Cu^+等一价离子可以不破坏釉层网络而进入釉层之中，即使在常温下，也较易在玻璃中移动；此外，H_2、H_2O等小分子也可以在釉层中通过[203]。由前述得知，碱金属氧化物的介入，打断了原有$[SiO_4]$四面体的网络连接；同时，碱金属离子的移动，使釉层易于与空气、水、酸、碱发生反应，从而釉层遭到腐蚀。所以碱金属氧化物含量越高，釉层抗腐蚀能力越差，机械强度也会越弱。

此外，中间体氧化物Al_2O_3的加入可使$[SiO_4]$网络加强，釉层化学稳定性提高；但如果Al_2O_3含量过高，反而会使网络紧密程度下降，化学稳定性也会下降[204]。

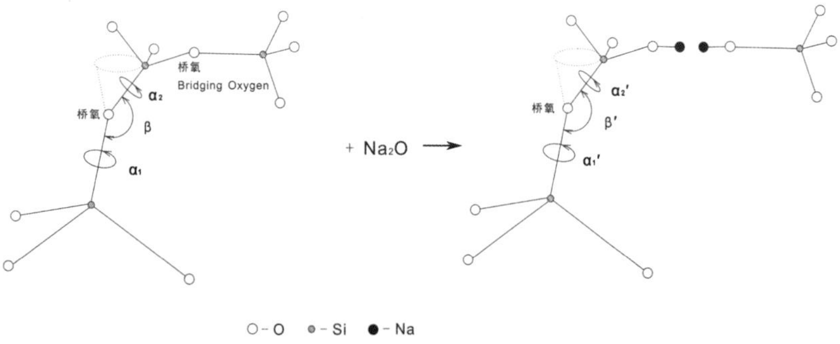

图4-2-3

high polymers until equilibrium is reached. Therefore because of the addition of Na_2O, K_2O, CaO, MgO, the structure of the glaze undergoes change.

These alkaline metal oxides and alkaline earth metal oxides do not enter into the silicate network, but only assist in the network breakdown and bringing down the melting point. As such, they only work to change the structural characteristics of the silicate network, so we call them external oxides (note: Without the presence of Al_2O_3, B_2O_3 or other Oxides, and with large amounts of alkaline metal oxides present, MgO can enter into the silica network).

3. The Function of Other Components

Apart from networking agents, flux, and coloring agents; YUB glaze contains a few other inclusions, such as Aluminum Oxide (Al_2O_3), which is a critical component.

Within silicate glass, positive Al^{3+} ions of Al_2O_3 has two types of coordinate pairs; 4 and 6 arranged into tetrahedron and hexahedron shapes respectively. When the Molar Ratio $R_2O/Al_2O_3>1$, Al^{3+} ions match to the $[SiO_4]$ tetrahedron as a $[AlO_4]$ tetrahedron network, this tightly woven network improves the stability of the silica glass. However, when the Molar Ratio $R_2O/Al_2O_3<1$ the amount of alkaline metal ions are less than the Al^{3+} ions, the Al^{3+} ions exceed chemical equilibrium and are pushed into hexahedron pairing with the silicate glass network rather than the tetrahedron shape [201]. This creates a more loosely woven network with lower density of silicate glass and thus a lower physical chemical stability [202].

Al_2O_3 can network together with SiO_2 as well as remain outside the glass network; because of this we call them intermediate oxides.

4. The Relationship Between Glaze Composition and Glaze Stability

In order to maintain ionic neutrality, alkaline metal ions and alkaline earth metal ions will disperse evenly but without order throughout the naturally occurring spaces within the silica tetrahedron network of YUB glaze. These ions and atoms that have weaker bonds with the Si—O can collect and move throughout the glaze level. For example: H^+, Li^+, Na^+, K^+, Rb^+, Cs^+, Ag^+, Cu^+, and other monovalent ions can network and enter into, without breakingdown the glaze level. Even under normal temperatures, they can continue to move within the silicate glass. Additionally, small molecules such as Hydrogen and water can also move throughout the glaze level [203]. According to the above stated, the introduction of alkaline metal oxides breaks down the tetrahedron $[SiO_4]$ network. At the same time, the presence of alkaline metal ions increases the likelihood of the glaze level receiving corrosion caused by reaction with air, water, acids, and bases. Therefore, the higher the concentration of alkaline metal oxides within the glaze, the lower the resistance the glaze has to weathering and decay, as well as having a weakened mechanical strength.

Moreover, the addition of Al_2O_3 into the $[SiO_4]$ network increases the strength and chemical stability of the glaze level. However, if the amount of Al_2O_3 becomes too high, the network density decreases and with it the strength and chemical stability [204].

5. Summary

YUB glaze level is in glass phase (Na_2O-K_2O-CaO-MgO-Al_2O_3-SiO_2), it is a non-crystalline solid formed on the foundation of a three-dimensional $[SiO_4]$ tetrahedron network.

The resistance to weathering of YUB glaze is related to the amount of alkaline metal and alkaline earth metal oxides within the glaze level, with the higher the amount of these oxides the lower the resistance. YUB glaze, with relatively lower Na_2O and K_2O, has a higher chemical stability and resistance to weathering.

五、小结

元青花瓷器釉层是玻璃体（Na_2O-K_2O-CaO-MgO-Al_2O_3-SiO_2），它是由[SiO_4]四面体为基础结构的三维空间网络所组成的非晶体固体。

元青花瓷器釉层的抗风化能力与碱金属、碱土金属氧化物含量有关，这些氧化物含量越高，釉层抗风化能力越差。元青花瓷釉中Na_2O、K_2O含量较低，所以釉层结构较为稳定，抗风化能力较好。

第三节 元青花瓷釉表面活性

一、元青花瓷釉表面活性概念

元青花瓷釉表面活性是元青花瓷器釉表面与外部环境中的物质发生反应的能力。

二、元青花瓷釉表面活性产生原因

元青花瓷釉表面具有活性的产生原因主要有：

1. 元青花釉料在高温熔融后形成玻璃体，由于高温与助熔剂的作用，玻璃熔体中会有很多断键，不完全配位。在釉料冷却时断键应该合拢，但由于釉表面冷却速度比内部快，断键来不及合拢，键角也不容易恢复，从而在釉表面存在着更多断键。因为釉表面的断键，釉表面会产生极性，从而会在大气中吸收羟基，这些羟基可以吸附水或与其他化合物反应。

2. 有研究指出：在玻璃熔体中，Al_2O_3挥发量为0.5%－5%，B_2O_3为1%－5%，Na_2O和K_2O的挥发量可达5%。釉表面成分的挥发会造成空位，这些空位迁移聚集，会在釉表面形成多个孔隙，使其具有多孔性[205]。

3. 釉裂纹的存在。

三、小结

元青花瓷器釉表面具有活性，易于吸附和积聚水分，从而便于釉表面的离子交换。这样的瓷器釉表面容易与酸、碱、盐溶液发生反应，造成釉表面的风化。

Section 3:
Active Nature of the Yuan Underglaze Blue Glaze Surface

1. The Active Nature of the YUB Glaze Surface Defined

This is the ability of the YUB glaze surface to undergo physical and chemical changes with materials within the external environment.

2. Causes of the Glaze Surface Activity

Causes of activity on the glaze surface are roughly split into three types:

A. After the high temperature firing of YUB glaze, it forms a molten glass. Due to high temperature and the presence of flux, the glass body has many broken bonds and is not completely coordinated evenly. During the cooling of the glaze, these broken bonds should join together; but because the surface of the glaze cools faster than the center of the glaze, not all broken bonds are able to join together and the bonding angles are difficult to repair. Because of this, the glaze surface presents with numerous bond separations. Glaze surface bond separations gives rise to chemical polarity, which absorbs hydroxyls from the surrounding atmosphere. These hydroxyls absorb water and react with other chemical compounds, leaving the face of the glaze chemically activated.

B. Research shows: Within molten glass, with a volatized Al_2O_3 quantity of 0.5-5% and B_2O_3 1-5%; volatized Na_2O and K_2O quantity can reach 5%. This volatized composition can create empty space, these empty spaces, in turn, migrate and assemble to create small holes which effectively bring about a porous glaze surface [205].

C. The presence of glaze cracks.

3. Summary

The glaze surface is active; prone to attracting and absorbing surrounding water that partakes in ion swapping across the face of the glaze. These characteristics make the surface of the glaze susceptible to weathering due to the ease of physical and chemical reactions with acids, bases, and salt solutions.

第四节
元青花釉层形貌

一、元青花釉层概念

元青花釉层是由玻璃相、气相、晶相及少量原料残留颗粒构成的覆盖在元青花瓷器坯体上的玻璃体[206]。

二、元青花釉层形貌

（一）元青花釉层形貌概念

元青花釉层形貌是元青花瓷器釉层在一定观察角度下的三维可视状况。

（二）元青花釉层形貌特征

用肉眼观察元青花釉表面，非常平滑，但它在显微成像下却凹凸不平，主要可分为两种特征：凸形特征及凹形特征。

1. 凸形特征

元青花釉层形貌大部分呈凸形特征，类似星球表面（见图4-4-1、图4-4-2[207]、图4-4-3[208]）。

凸形特征的形成原因参见本章本节玻璃相形成及特征部分及图4-4-9。

釉表面凸起处通常也是一些析晶存在的地方，如C形、O形纹（简称CO纹）。CO纹是存在于釉层的析晶或分相，它们与玻璃相结合处的组织结构稳定性较差，通常风化从这里开始。

2. 凹形特征

元青花釉层形貌的凹形特征如同弹坑（见图4-4-5箭头所指处）。凹形特征的形成原因参见本章本节玻璃相形成及特征部分及图4-4-8。

釉表面凹陷处易于集聚沉积外界物质，易于吸附水及空气。所以，风化往往先从凹陷处开始，如壁变泡的形成（见图4-4-4、图4-4-5，二者为同一器物同一位置图片，图4-4-4为二维图片，图4-4-5为三维图片）。

图4-4-1

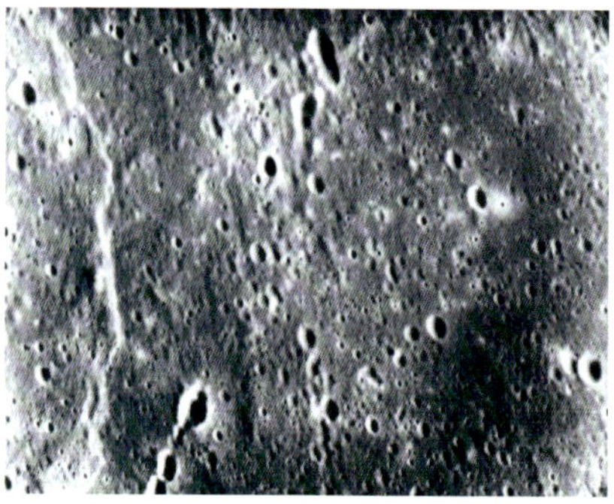
图4-4-2
美国国家航空航天局公布的水星表面照片
Photo taken by NASA of the surface of Mercury

图4-4-3
阿波罗11号飞船在1969年绕月飞行时拍摄的月球背面环形山
Picture taken in 1969 of the Moon by Apollo 11

Section 4:

Yuan Underglaze Blue Glaze Level Appearance

1. YUB Glaze Level Defined

The YUB glaze level is composed of glass, gas, crystals and trace amounts of other raw materials left over after forming into a vitreous body. Essentially, it is a layer of glass of varying thickness that covers all or a certain portion of the porcelain body [206].

2. YUB Glaze Level Appearance

A. YUB Glaze Level Appearance Defined

Describes the three-dimensional state of the glaze surface; including the micro-topography of the glaze.

B. YUB Glaze Level Appearance Characteristics

To the naked eye, glaze appears smooth and level; but under 500X microscopic magnification the surface appears uneven with humps and pits, and can be split into two primary types of glaze surface: Bumpy Surface and Pitted Surface.

I. Bumpy Surface Characteristics

The majority of YUB glaze surfaces present with bumpy characteristics, similar to that of celestial bodies (compare pictures 4-4-1, 4-4-2 [207], 4-4-3 [208]). For the causes of these characteristics please refer to the Glass Phase Formation and Characteristics of this chapter as well as picture 4-4-9.

The raised portions of the bumpy surface generally are areas in which crystallization exists, such as C and O striae. C and O striae occur at these points of crystallization or split phase within the glaze level because the connection point with the glass phase at these points is less structurally stable, thus weathering can first occur.

II. Pitted Surface Characteristics

The YUB pitted surface resembles that of a bullet crater (see the point indicated by the Arrow in picture 4-4-5). For the causes of these characteristics please refer to the Glass Phase Formation and Characteristics of this chapter as well as picture 4-4-8.

The pits on the surface of the glaze often collect foreign materials, as well as water and air from the surrounding environment. The effects of weathering present first at these pits. They include traces such as textured bubbles (see pictures 4-4-4 and 4-4-5, where 4-4-4 is the two-dimensional, and 4-4-5 is the three-dimensional image of the same spot).

C. YUB Glaze Appearance Types

I. Glass Phase

a. Glass Phase Defined

Refers to all the non-crystalline composite materials that emerged from a series of physical and chemical reactions during firing of YUB that solidify when cooled [209].

b. Glass Phase Formation and Characteristics

During the firing of YUB, gaseous bodies are formed (see Gas Phase Formation of this section). When the glaze is in a molten state, a portion of gasses from within the body or the glaze level escape, while the remainder remain within the glaze level. Due to the turbulent motion of the formation and movement of these air bubbles within the molten glaze level as well as the unevenness of the porcelain body, the post-firing glaze surface is topographically uneven. From illustration

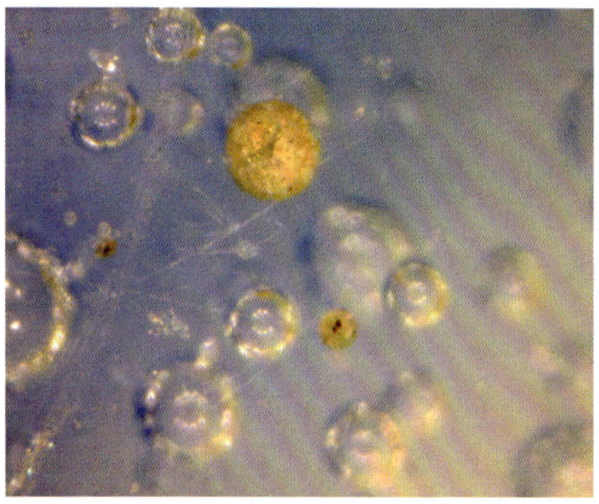

图4-4-4

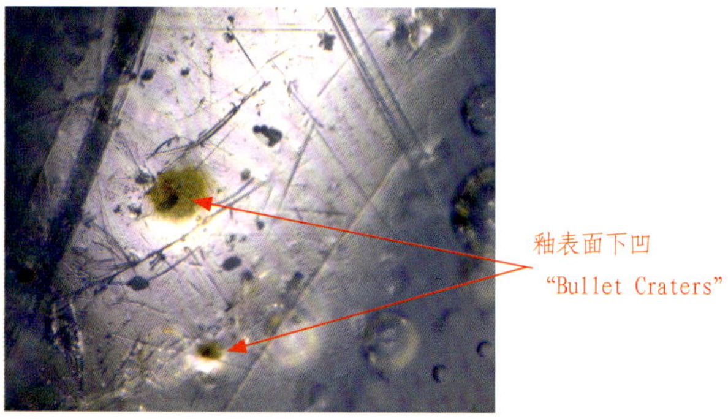

图4-4-5

（三）元青花釉层形貌分类

1．玻璃相

（1）玻璃相概念

玻璃相是元青花瓷器高温烧制时各组成物质产生一系列物理变化、化学反应后冷却凝固形成的一种非晶态物质[209]。

（2）玻璃相形成及特征

元青花瓷器在烧制过程中产生气体（参见本章本节气相形成部分），当釉料熔化时，一部分气体从胎面（胎釉结合处）或釉层中逸出，一部分则留在釉层中形成气泡。由于气泡在熔融釉层中的运动而产生的扰动效应及胎面不平，烧制好的瓷器釉表面会有凹凸不平的现象（见图4-4-6，图中箭头所指处为釉表面同一处在烧制过程中的变化）。

有些气孔由于降温较快或釉层黏度较大而没有闭合，从而使釉表面出现微小的孔洞。不过这些孔洞过于微小，用500倍显微镜一般是观察不到的（见图4-4-7，图中箭头所指处为釉表面同一处在烧制过程中的变化）。

当气泡接近釉表面，温度下降时，气体体积缩小，待釉表面冷却凝固后，气泡上方的釉表面就会形成凹坑（见图4-4-8，图中箭头所指处为釉表面同一处在烧制过程中的变化）。

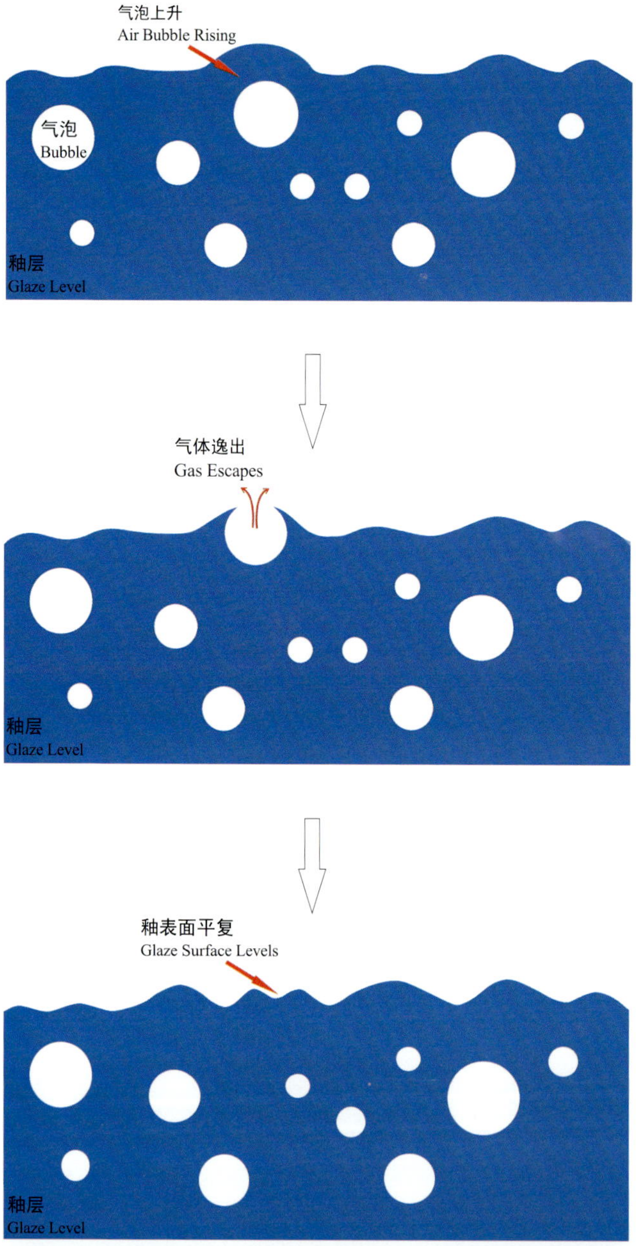

图4-4-6

4-4-6 we can see the progression of one point on the glaze surface as indicated by the red arrow.

There are some air holes, due to the rapid cooling or viscous nature of the glaze, that were unable to close and leave behind microscopic pits across the glaze surface (see picture 4-4-7). However, there are some pits that are microscopically invisible (while using a 500X magnification microscope, they are usually unobservable).

When air bubbles approach the surface, while the glaze is cooling, the gas within the bubble contracts; this creates a small depression on the surface of the glaze over the top of the air pocket once the glaze hardens (see picture 4-4-8) .

If an air bubble extrudes above the surface level while the glaze is cooling, the gas within the bubble still contracts; these bubbles create an extruding crater on the surface of the glaze (similar to that of moon craters, see picture 4-4-9). The area surrounding the air bubble is slightly lower, forming a trough.

II. Gas Phase

a. Gas Phase Defined

Gas phase is the gaseous materials left within the glaze level of fired YUB.

b. Gas Phase Formation

Gas phases are formed due to the following reasons [210]:

i. YUB Body-Glaze Reaction Formed Air Bubbles

a) The YUB body presents with open and closed air pockets, when temperatures increase, these gaseous bodies expand. Open air pockets eject air directly into the glaze level. Molten glaze also moistens the porcelain body; dissolving some of the clay and opening up closed air pockets, which allows gas to enter into the glaze.

b) YUB clay and glaze have trace amounts of CO_3^{2-}, SO_4^{2-}, NO^{3-}, Fe_2O_3, $CaCO_3$, Pb_3O_4, and so forth which under high temperatures react and form gasses that create air bubbles. Some of the above-mentioned reactions are listed below:

$CaCO_3 \rightarrow CaO + CO_2\uparrow$ (600 ℃ - 1050 ℃)

$MgCO_3 \rightarrow MgO + CO_2\uparrow$ (400 ℃ - 900 ℃)

$FeCO_3 \rightarrow FeO + CO_2\uparrow$ (>200 ℃)

$2Fe_2O_3 \rightarrow 4FeO + O_2\uparrow$ (1250 ℃ - 1370 ℃)

$Fe_2O_3 + CO \rightarrow 2FeO + CO_2\uparrow$ (1000 ℃ - 1100 ℃)

$CaSO_4 \rightarrow CaO + SO_3\uparrow$ (1250 ℃ - 1370 ℃)

$Na_2SO_4 \rightarrow Na_2O + SO_3\uparrow$ (1200 ℃ - 1370 ℃)

c) The minerals within the ceramic body and glaze, under high temperatures, discharge water of crystallization that can form air bubbles.

d) Water particles in the molten bodies, under high temperatures, create air bubbles.

ii. Carbon Formed Air Bubbles

During the firing process, CO undergoes decomposition, splitting to form C and CO_2. At the same time, Carbon deposits on the surface of the glaze oxidize to form CO_2, creating air bubbles.

iii. Air Bubbles Formed By Technical Influences

During the glazing process, a small portion of air can become trapped within the glaze level; these expand while firing to form air bubbles. Additionally, during the firing process, combustion products within the kiln furnace can also become dislodged into the glaze level and create air bubbles.

iv. Summary

During the firing of YUB, because of the aforementioned reasons, gasses can enter into the glaze level; some of which seep out of the glaze surface, some of which remain to create air bubbles. The possible gasses within air bubbles are: O_2, H_2, H_2O, N_2, CO, CO_2, and SO_2.

While air bubbles are moving throughout the molten glaze, some small bubbles converge with other bubbles to create larger bubbles. Additionally, the coarseness and refinement of the porcelain clay has a direct impact on the size of the bubbles within the glaze. The distribution and size of air bubbles are affected by the following: Firing heat distribution, forming techniques, body and glaze chemical composition,

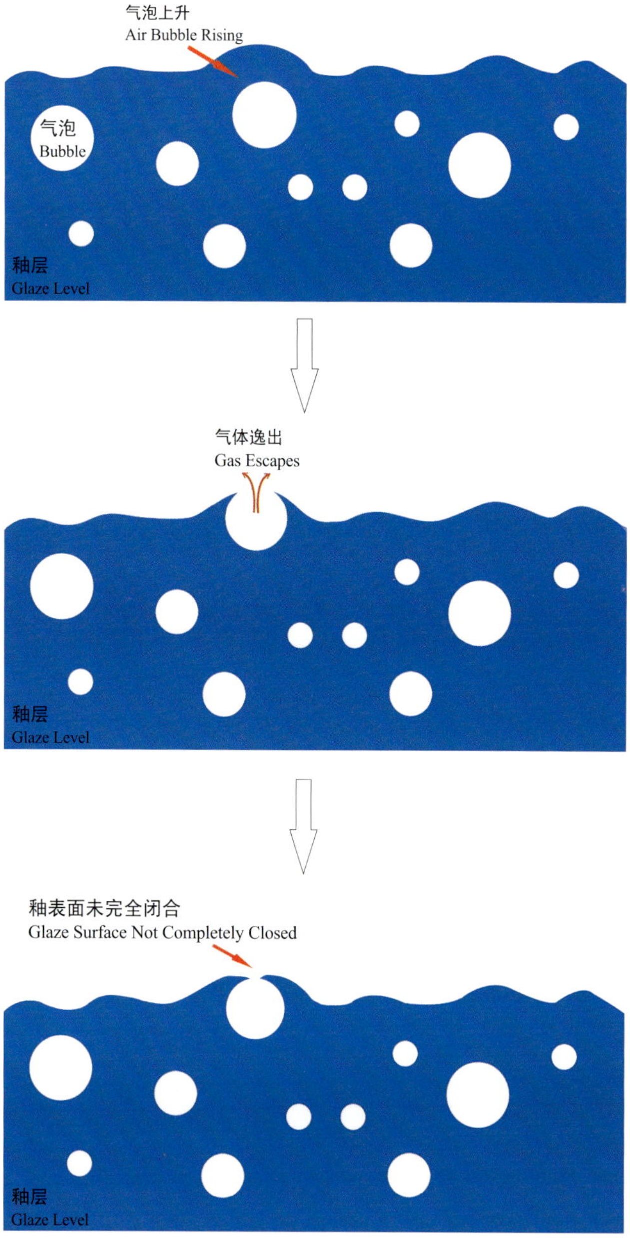
气泡上升
Air Bubble Rising
气泡
Bubble
釉层
Glaze Level
气体逸出
Gas Escapes
釉层
Glaze Level
釉表面未完全闭合
Glaze Surface Not Completely Closed
釉层
Glaze Level
图4-4-7

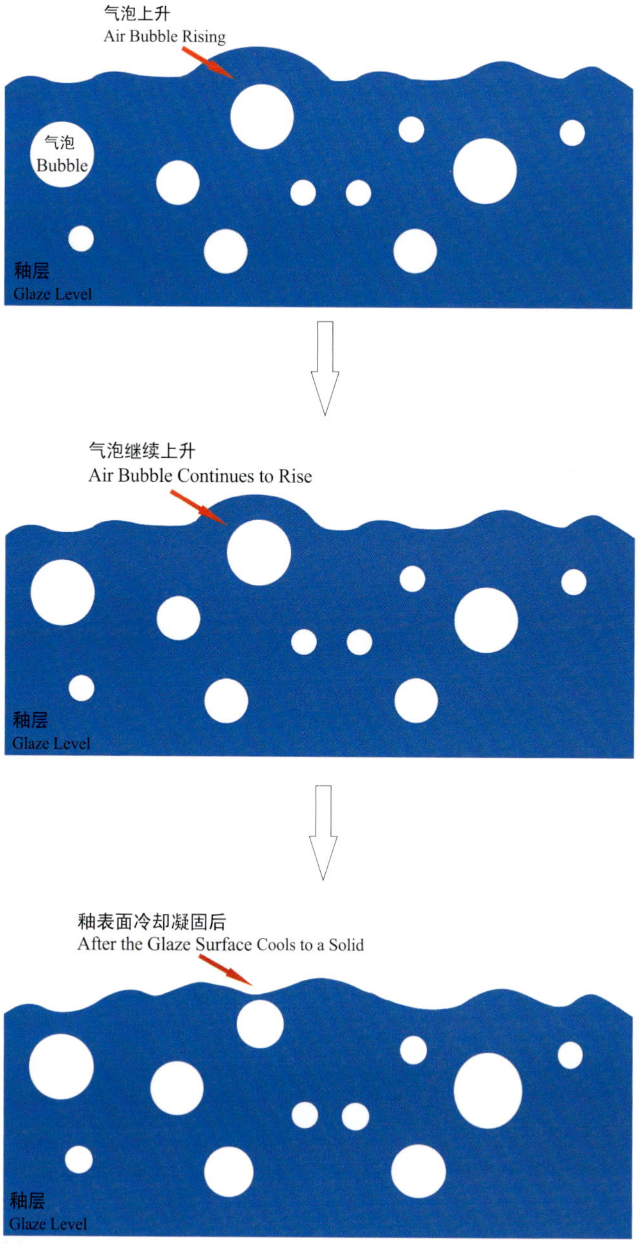
气泡上升
Air Bubble Rising
气泡
Bubble
釉层
Glaze Level
气泡继续上升
Air Bubble Continues to Rise
釉层
Glaze Level
釉表面冷却凝固后
After the Glaze Surface Cools to a Solid
釉层
Glaze Level
图4-4-8

glaze thickness, and so forth.

c. Gas Phase Characteristics

Most bubbles occur with sparse distribution (see picture 4-4-10); occasionally dense distribution presents (see picture 4-4-11); or random distribution with independent large bubbles (see picture 4-4-11). The bubble size disparity is much larger than that of Ming or Qing Dynasty Underglaze Blue (see pictures 4-4-12—4-4-15).

III. Crystal Phase

a. Crystal Phase Defined

Crystal phase refers to the crystallized formations, with certain shape and color, which have formed within the glaze level or on the glaze surface.

b. Crystal Phase Formation

From a thermodynamics perspective, when any specific state of matter cools (or heats) to a point of phase change, it will undergo phase change and a new phase is formed. This is precisely the process of crystal phase formation during the cooling of melted glaze.

Crystallization has two processes, first is nucleation into crystal nuclei and the second is crystal growth into mature crystallizations. However, it is not all crystal nuclei that can grow crystals, it is only nuclei that have achieved critical mass that can stabilize to form crystals.

Nucleation occurs in two different ways, homogeneously distributed and heterogeneously distributed nucleation. Homogeneously distributed nucleation occurs in well-dispersed base solvents, having nothing to do with structural flaws of the solution. It is brought on by the undulation caused by heat induction, and causes a change from the high Gibbs free energy state (i.e. liquid) into the low Gibbs free energy state (i.e. solid). Heterogeneously distributed nucleation occurs at the interface point of two phases, i.e. a liquid and its containing vessel, liquid and foreign material grains, or liquid and air interfaces. It also often occurs at points of structural flaw within the solution. As the required compiled energy needed for heterogeneously distributed nucleation is lower than that of homogeneously distributed, the vast majority of crystal nucleation is of the heterogeneously distributed variety.

During the firing of YUB, cobalt-blue dye and glaze gradually transition into a molten state. Due to the buoyancy, surface tension, and movement of the air bubbles within the glaze level, the Oxidized Iron and Manganese within the glaze and dye collects around the edges of gaseous bodies within the glaze and rise with these bubbles to the surface of the glaze, forming heterogeneously distributed nuclei crystallizations. As the glaze cools, more crystallization happens. Crystal types are dictated by the chemical composition of the dye: High Iron low Manganese dyes easily form Iron Oxide crystals of different valances, whereas low Iron high Manganese dyes more easily form Iron and Cobalt ion solid solutions of Manganese Oxide [211].

According to their composition, their density, and differences in surface tension of the glaze; these crystallizations present with different appearances, colors, and amounts of mottles (blotches) and striae (lines).

As the glaze cools to a solid, Iron and Cobalt ions (Primarily Fe^{3+}) dissolved within the glaze level form flowing mottles or flowing striae.

Other crystallization within the YUB glaze level could include unmelted quartz granules in the form of mullite and anorthite crystallizations formed during the cooling process. They can also occur on the glaze surface.

c. Crystal Phase Characteristics

Crystal phases within the glaze level of YUB primarily present as mottles and striae.

i. Mottles

Mottles include Flowing Mottles and Radiating Mottles (see Chapter 6 Flowing Mottles and Radiating Mottles sections).

Flowing mottles on the surface of the glaze have a relatively high ability to soak the surface of the glaze, allowing for an even distribution between the mottle and the surrounding glass phase (see pictures 4-4-12 and 4-4-13, where 4-4-12 is the two-dimensional, and 4-4-13 is the three-dimensional image of the same location).

如果气泡高出釉表面，温度下降时，气体体积缩小，高出釉表面的气泡上方会有凹坑出现，如同月球上的环形山，气泡周围较低的地方则形成沟壑（见图4-4-9，图中箭头所指处为釉表面同一处在烧制过程中的变化）。

2. 气相

（1）气相概念

气相是存在于烧制好的元青花瓷器釉层中的气体。

（2）气相形成

气相的形成有以下几个原因[210]：

① 元青花胎釉本身反应形成气泡

元青花瓷器胎体中存在开口气孔和闭口气孔。温度升高时，气体体积膨胀，经开口气孔进入釉层；熔融的釉层将坯体润湿，釉对坯体的溶解作用可以打开一些闭口气孔，使气体进入釉层。

元青花瓷器胎釉中含有CO_3^{2-}、SO_4^{2-}、NO^{3-}、Fe_2O_3、$CaCO_3$、Pb_3O_4等，它们在高温下发生化学反应，产生气体，形成气泡。部分反应方程式如下：

$CaCO_3 \rightarrow CaO + CO_2\uparrow$
（600℃—1050℃）

$MgCO_3 \rightarrow MgO + CO_2\uparrow$
（400℃—900℃）

$FeCO_3 \rightarrow FeO + CO_2\uparrow$
（>200℃）

$2Fe_2O_3 \rightarrow 4FeO + O_2\uparrow$
（1250℃—1370℃）

$Fe_2O_3 + CO \rightarrow 2FeO + CO_2\uparrow$
（1000℃—1100℃）

$CaSO_4 \rightarrow CaO + SO_3\uparrow$
（1250℃-1370℃）

$Na_2SO_4 \rightarrow Na_2O + SO_3\uparrow$
（1200℃—1370℃）

元青花胎釉中的矿物质在高温下排出结晶水，也会形成气泡被排出。

熔块中的水分在高温下形成气泡。

② 碳素形成气泡

在元青花瓷器烧制过程中，CO在高温下裂解产生CO_2和C，同时C沉积在釉表面，在高温下氧化生成CO_2，形成气泡。

③ 工艺影响形成气泡

在施釉时将一部分气体封闭在釉层中，烧制时膨胀形成气泡。在烧制时，窑炉中的燃烧产物会被夹带进入釉层形成气泡。

④ 小结

元青花瓷器烧制过程中，由上述原因生成的气体进入釉层，部分

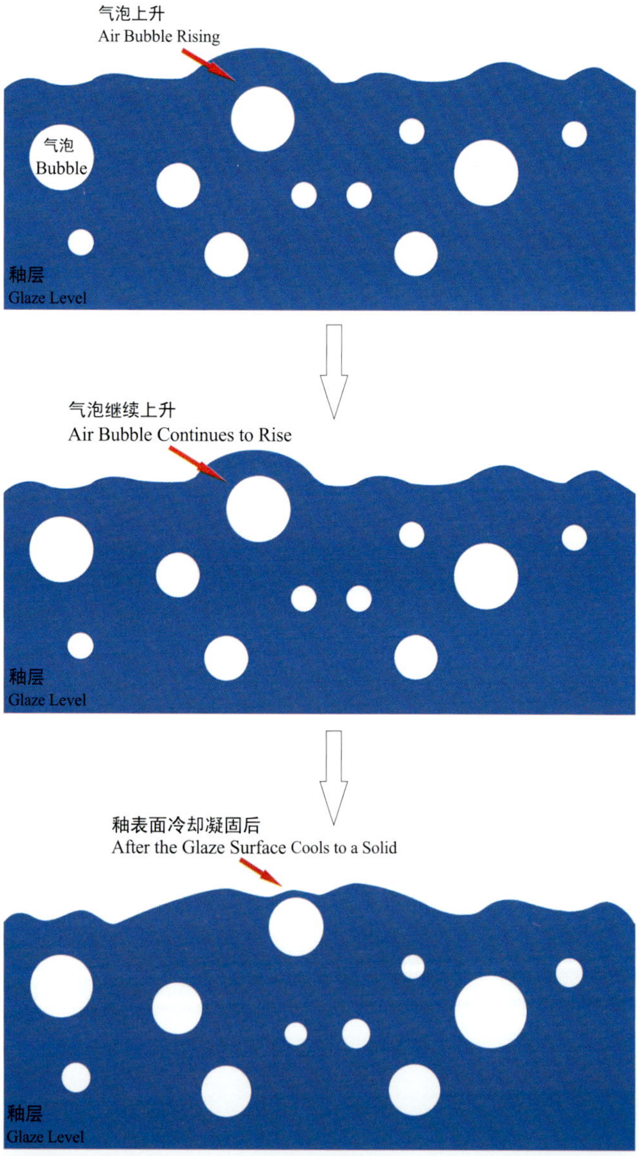

图4-4-9

When radiating mottle crystallizations form on the glaze surface during the firing of YUB, due to the continued rising of the firing temperature and the reduction of viscosity of the glaze, some crystallizations meld into the molten glass and can easily move and become covered by the glaze level. However, the composition of the glass above these radiating mottles has already achieved a different composition from than that of the primary glass surrounding the mottle. Thus the interface between the mottle and the surrounding glass phase becomes the border of the mottle (see pictures 4-4-14 and 4-4-15, where 4-4-14 is the two-dimensional, and 4-4-15 is the three-dimensional image of the same location).

At times, there is a possibility that the temperature is not high enough, or viscosity of the glaze is relatively high, and the mottle is unable to be submerged (see picture 4-4-16).

It is also possible for radiating mottles to go through a second split phase process and crystalize again (see pictures 4-4-17 and 4-4-18).

Radiating mottles can achieve red, orange, or yellow coloration in a maple leaf or irregular shape crystallization distributed along the glaze surface (see pictures 4-4-19 and 4-4-20).

ii. Striae

When crystallization amounts are relatively low, unable to form mottles, they will be forced into striae by the surrounding glass phase, creating flowing striae usually in areas of blue dye (see picture 4-4-21). When they are even lower in number, they can occur all across the glaze surface as C and O shaped striae (see picture 4-4-22).

d. Summary

The crystallization within the glaze level of YUB is directly impacted by the composition and compound ratios of the glaze and dye as well as the firing techniques (temperature and reduction control).

From a thermodynamics perspective, glaze cooling into a solid does not achieve perfect equilibrium, but remains in a metastable state in which crystallization has a tendency to still occur. However, from a kinetics perspective, as the molecules in the solidified glaze have difficulty in continued movement, crystallization has essentially stopped, and as such, a vitrified glaze level is in a relatively stable state.

气体逸出釉面，部分留在釉层中形成气泡。气泡中的气体可以是O_2、H_2、H_2O、N_2、CO、CO_2、SO_2等。

在气泡的运动过程中，一些小气泡会在熔融的釉层中相聚变成大气泡。另外，胎泥的粗与精，对气泡大小的生成有直接关系。烧制火力分布不均匀、工艺参数不同、胎釉的化学组成不同以及釉层的厚度不同等因素，都会影响釉层中气泡的分布和大小。

（3）气相特征

大部分气相即气泡分布舒朗（见图4-4-10）；偶见气泡密集分布；随机可见独立大气泡分布（见图4-4-11）。

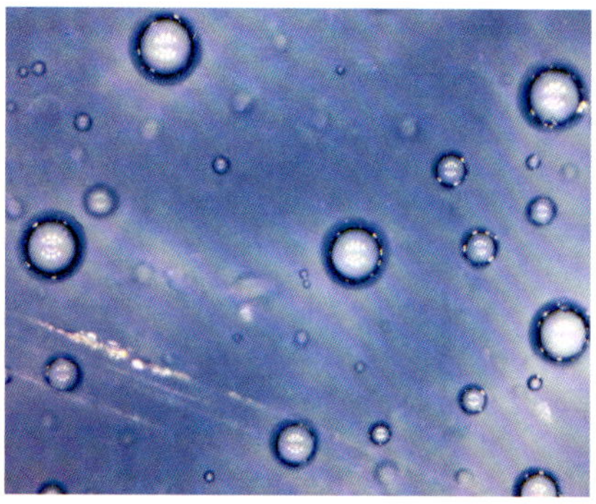
图4-4-10

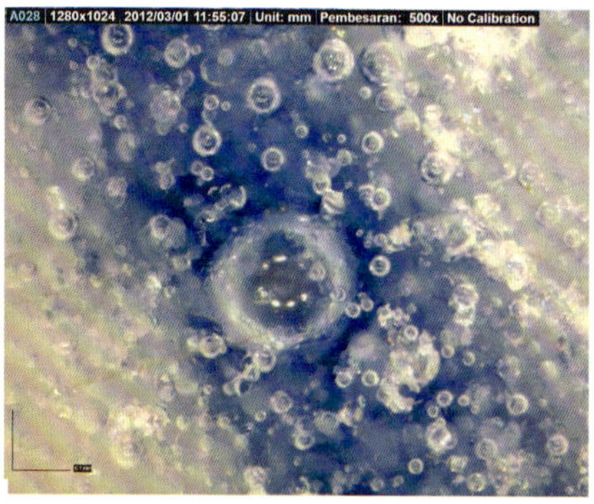

图4-4-11

3. 晶相

（1）晶相概念

晶相是元青花瓷器釉表面或釉层中析出的有一定形状和颜色的结晶体。

（2）晶相形成

从热力学的观点来看，将一定状态的物体冷却（或加热）到相变温度，就会发生相转变而产生新相。在熔融釉中晶体析出便是产生新相的过程。

析晶有两个过程，一是形成稳定晶核的成核过程，二是晶核成长为晶体的晶体长大过程。但并非所有的晶核都能长成晶体，只有超过临界尺寸的晶核才有可能稳定成长而形成晶体。

形成晶核的成核过程又分为均匀成核与非均匀成核两种。

均匀成核发生于均匀基质内部，与相界结构缺陷无关。它是由于热运动引起组织和结构上的起伏，使得部分质点从高的吉布斯自由能状态（如液相）转变为低的吉布斯自由能状态（如晶体）形成的。

非均匀成核，发生于系统中两相的界面处，如液相与容器的界面、液相与杂质颗粒的界面或液相与气相的界面，也常常发生在液体中结构缺陷处。由于非均匀成核所需克服的能垒比均匀成核所需克服的能垒要小，实际上大多数析晶相变的成核都属于非均匀成核。

元青花瓷器在高温烧制时，青料及釉料会逐渐熔化成熔融态，在浮力、表面张力及气泡搅动的作用下，釉料以及青料中的铁氧化物及锰氧化物易在气泡边缘积聚，也可能再形成分相，部分会随气泡升至釉表面，形成非均匀成核析晶。在降温过程中，会有更多的结晶在釉表面析出。结晶的种类取决于青料的化学组成：高铁低锰的青料易形成不同价态的铁氧化物晶体，而低铁高锰的青料则易形成固溶了铁离子、钴离子的锰氧化物晶体[211]。根据它们的成分、密度、表面张力不同，这些晶体表现为不同形貌、不同颜色和不同层次的斑块或纹路。

当釉层冷却凝固时，溶解在釉层中的铁离子、钴离子等（主要是Fe^{3+}）便在釉层中形成流淌斑或流淌纹。

元青花釉层中的晶相还可能是未熔的残留石英颗粒及其变体以及在冷却时析出的莫来石、钙长石等。它们也可以存在于釉表面。

（3）晶相特征

元青花釉层中的晶相主要以斑块及纹路两种形式出现。

① 斑块

斑块包括流淌斑及放射斑（见第六章第一节流淌斑及放射斑部分）。

位于釉表面的流淌斑，其析出的晶体能润湿釉表面，通常斑块与玻璃相之间过渡均匀（见图4-4-12、图4-4-13，二者为同一器物同一位置图片，图4-4-12为二维图片，图4-4-13为三维图片）。

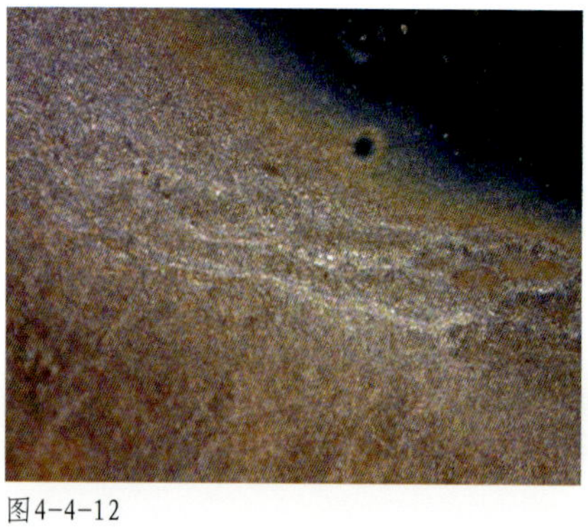
图4-4-12

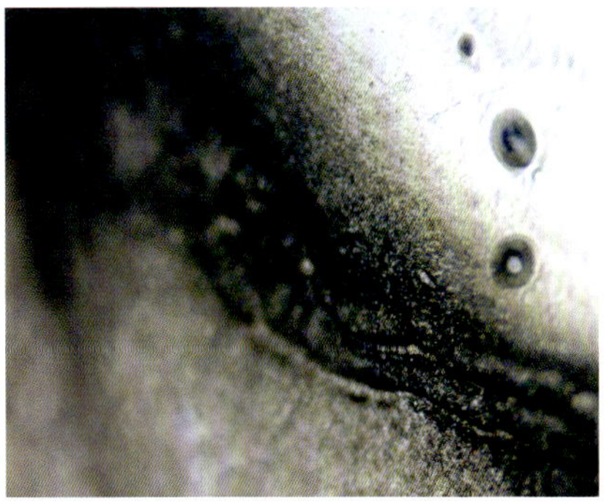

图4-4-13

在元青花瓷器的烧制过程中，当放射斑晶体在釉表面析出时，由于烧制温度继续升高，部分晶体又会被熔解在玻璃相中；同时釉的黏度降低，相对易流动，以至晶体又被玻璃相覆盖，但这时覆盖于放射斑上的玻璃相的成分已与主玻璃相有差异，所以这两相的界面就表现为放射斑的边线（见图4-4-14、图4-4-15，二者为同一器物同一位置图片，图4-4-14二维图片，图4-4-15为三维图片）。

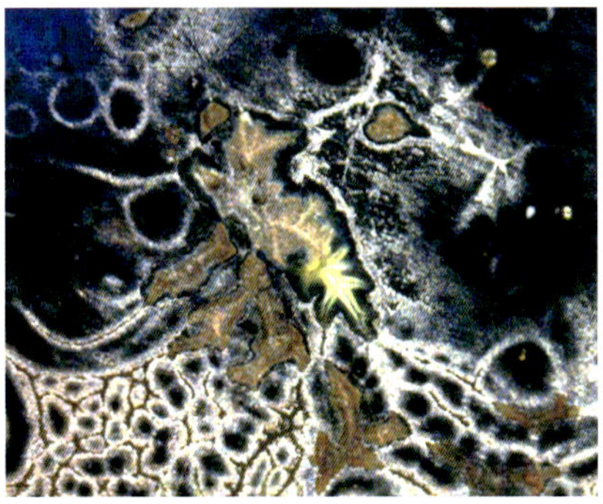

图4-4-14

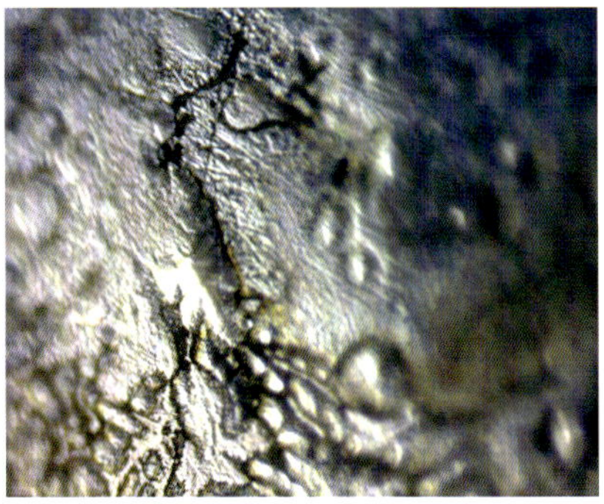

图4-4-15

有时也有可能因为温度不够高，或釉的黏度较大，玻璃相不能完全覆盖放射斑（图4-4-16）。

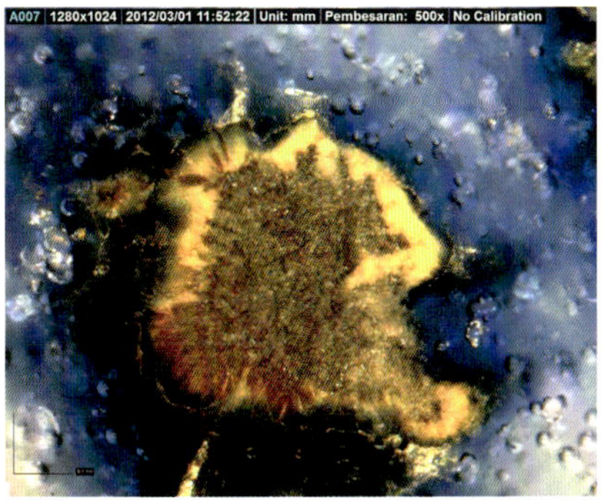

图4-4-16

放射斑还有可能发生二次分相，再次析晶（见图4-4-17、图4-4-18）。

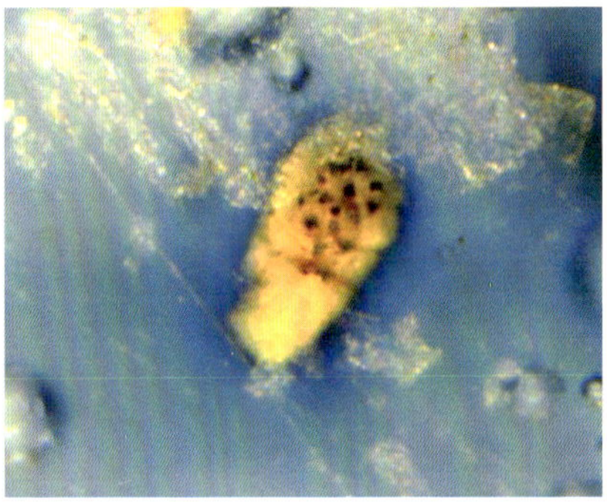

图4-4-17*

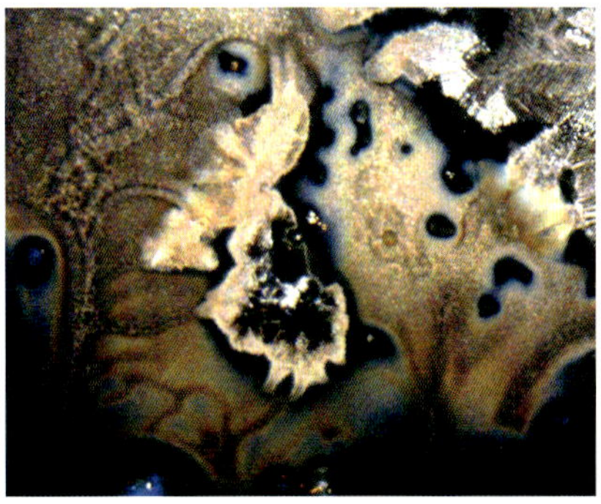

图4-4-18

放射斑还可以呈红色、橘黄色的枫叶形状或不规则形状分布在釉表面（见图4-4-19、图4-4-20）。

② 纹路

当析出的晶体数量较少，不足以形成斑块时，会被其周围的玻璃相排挤形成流淌纹，它们通常出现在青料处（图4-4-21）；数量更少的时候，在釉表面任何地方都可以形成C形、O形纹（图4-4-22）

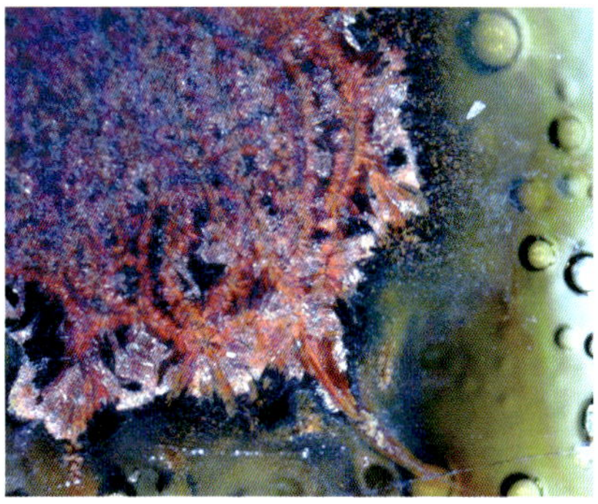

图4-4-19

图4-4-20

图4-4-21

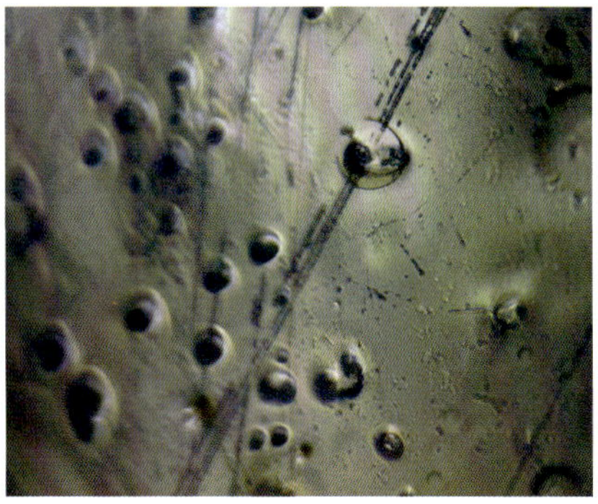

图4-4-22

*图片经过裁剪放大处理。
*Picture cropped and enlarged to show detail.

（4）小结

元青花釉层析晶与釉料、青料的成分及含量有关，而烧制工艺（温度控制、氧化和还原气氛控制等）也是重要的影响因素。

从热力学的观点来看，冷却凝固了的釉层并未达到平衡，处于介稳状态，仍有继续析出结晶的趋势。但从动力学的观点来看，由于釉层降温固化，分子运动较为困难，析晶几乎停止。所以，冷却凝固了的釉层应处于一个相对稳定的状态。

第五节 总结

元青花釉层的性质是由釉层的成分及其含量决定的。

釉层不同的成分，会形成不同结构的网络，形成釉层不同的性质；相同的釉层构成成分，但各成分含量的差异，也会造成釉层网络结构的差异，形成不同性质的釉层。

根据元青花瓷釉各成分含量的差异，可将其分为钙釉、钙碱釉及碱钙釉。

此外，工艺参数如烧制温度、烧制气氛等也会对元青花釉层的性质产生影响。

不同性质的釉层会有不同的先天迹型表现，继而在后天的环境中也会出现不同的风化迹型特征。

一般来说，元青花釉层的风化都从釉层结构稳定性较差（如釉层本身存在的一些裂纹、孔隙）或釉层成分物理化学性质相对较活跃的地方开始（如铁氧化物聚集暴露处）。元青花釉层在经过几百年的风化作用后产生的迹型特征是缓慢量变的结果。现代人为制假做旧，在短时间内以质变、突变的方式制造出的迹型特征，与长期自然风化的迹型特征有本质的区别。

元青花釉层性质的不同是先天性的。釉料配方、工艺参数的差异表现出不同的迹型特征，加上后天环境变化的差异，最终形成釉层迹型风化作用强度快慢的差异和风化强度高低的不同。这样就形成了迹型风化的多样性及复杂性。这是观察、认识和了解元青花的迹型变化现象以及迹型变化规律的理论基础。

Section 5:
Conclusion

The characteristics of YUB glaze are determined by the different chemical compositions and respective amounts of individual components.

The different compositions of glaze create different glaze network constructions, and thus different glaze characteristics. Even though the chemical components of two certain glazes are the same, differences in characteristics can arise from using different amounts of associated components.

According to the differences in YUB glaze composition, they can be divided into calcium glaze, calcium alkaline glaze, and alkaline calcium glaze.

Additionally, the technological parameters under which a piece is fired, such as the firing temperature and atmosphere, also have an impact on the characteristics of the glaze.

Different glaze qualities bring about varied inherent traces, which under the influences of the post firing environment, create different weathered trace characteristics.

Usually, weathering first takes place where defects in the glaze level are present; namely crazing and openings or areas in the glaze level with a relatively active nature (i.e. exposed Iron Oxide). Corrosion caused by external materials start at these defects. The trace characteristic changes within the YUB glaze level, after hundreds of years of weathering, are the result of slow quantitative changes. Modern methods of aging ceramics utilize a qualitative change over a very short period of time and create trace characteristics that are innately differentiated from natural weathering changes.

The differences in glaze characteristics are intrinsic, and these innate differences form unique traces. Additionally, various post-firing environments ultimately bring forth dissimilarities in weathering intensity, and as such, disparities in weathering severity. This brings about complexity and multiplicity in YUB trace weathering. This is the theoretical foundation for observing, recognizing, and understanding the appearance of trace changes and the laws that govern them.

第五章

元青花釉层变化

阅读提示：

本章主要阐述元青花釉层变化机理，论述釉层变化与环境的关系，并列举元青花釉层风化的迹型特征。

主要论述问题：

1. 元青花釉层在外界环境中会有哪些物理变化和化学反应？
2. 元青花釉层的变化与其所处环境有什么关系？
3. 元青花釉层迹型的风化特征是什么？

Chapter 5

Yuan Underglaze Blue Glaze Level Changes

Text Note:

This chapter explains the mechanics of YUB glaze level change, discusses the relationship between the post-firing environment and YUB glaze level change, and presents the characteristics of weathred YUB traces.

第一节 元青花釉层变化机理

一、元青花釉层与水的反应

由于元青花釉表面的活性，易于吸附水分子，会形成单羟基、双羟基团，单羟基之间会通过氢键键合形成闭合羟基团[212]，反应如下（氢键用虚线表示）：

$\equiv Si— + OH^- \rightarrow \equiv Si—OH$　单羟基

$\equiv Si—O^- + H_2O \rightarrow = Si(OH)_2$　双羟基团

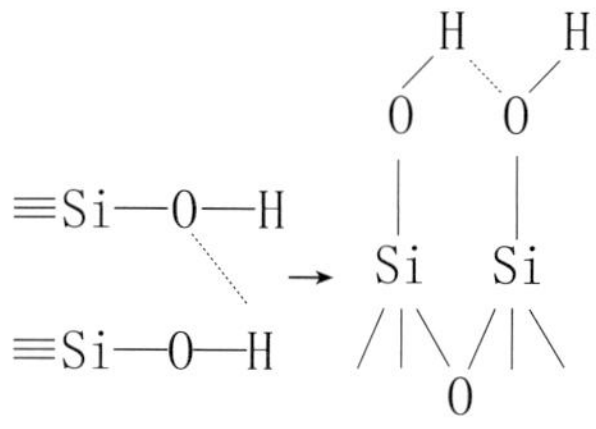

闭合羟基团

通过羟基的氢键再进一步物理吸附水分子，在釉层表面形成水膜。

对元青花瓷釉（Na_2O-K_2O-CaO-MgO-Al_2O_3-SiO_2系统）来说，釉层中的碱金属离子和碱土金属离子没有参加硅氧网络，均为网络外离子，具有较大的可迁移性。它们会和吸附在釉表面的水分子中的H^+进行离子交换，生成碱（ROH）（见反应①）。

$\equiv Si—O—R^+ + H^+OH^- \rightarrow \equiv Si—O—H + ROH$　①

接着又有下列反应：

$\equiv Si—O—H + \frac{3}{2}H_2O \rightarrow Si(OH)_4$　②

水分子（H_2O）也能与硅氧网络直接反应：

$\equiv Si—O—Si\equiv + H_2O \rightarrow 2[\equiv Si—O—H]$　③

随着反应③的继续，Si原子周围原有的4个桥氧全部变成—OH，形成$Si(OH)_4$，这是水对硅氧网络的直接破坏[213]。

以上反应的产物$Si(OH)_4$是一种极性分子，它能使周围的水分子极化，然后吸附在自己周围，成为$Si(OH)_4 \cdot nH_2O$，通常称为硅酸凝胶[214]。这种硅酸凝胶除了有一部分溶于水之外，大部分都会附着在釉表面，形成一层薄膜。它具有较强的抗水和抗酸能力。

反应①中，由于R^+比H^+要大，它们交换后，H^+代替R^+，使釉层产生空位，结构变疏松，稳定性下降，所以易受到风化侵蚀。

二、元青花釉层与碱的反应

碱的来源有两个方面：一是来自反应①，水与釉表面作用生成的，它取决于H^+和R^+交换的速度；二是外部环境提供的。

碱（ROH）可溶解硅酸凝胶$Si(OH)_4 \cdot nH_2O$（见反应④），使釉表面失去保护，风化得以继续进行。

$Si(OH)_4 + ROH \rightarrow [Si(OH)_3O]^- R^+ + H_2O$　④

ROH也可以直接与硅氧网络反应，使Si—O键断裂，网络解体，产生$\equiv Si—O^-$粒子群，使SiO_2溶于碱液中，因而破坏釉表面（见反应⑤）：

$\equiv Si—O—Si\equiv + OH^- \rightarrow \equiv Si—OH + \equiv Si—O^-$　⑤

而断裂一端的$\equiv Si—O^-$又能与H_2O反应：

$\equiv Si—O^- + H_2O \rightarrow \equiv Si—OH + OH^-$　⑥

反应⑥产生的碱可使反应⑤继续发生，从而溶解SiO_2。

对于元青花瓷釉（Na_2O-K_2O-CaO-MgO-Al_2O_3-SiO_2系统）而言，随着R^+（R在此指Na、K）的不断迁出，Ca^{2+}的含量相对增多，Ca^{2+}会对R^+产生“抑制效应”，使得H^+和R^+的离子交换变得缓慢，碱（ROH）的生成速度变慢（反应①速度变慢），从而反应⑤也变得缓慢。这样对釉层的侵蚀就变得非常

Section 1:

Mechanics of Yuan Underglaze Blue Glaze Level Change

1. YUB Glaze Level Reactions with Water

The active nature of the YUB glaze surface and its high absorption allows for the formation of single and double hydroxyls, as well as the hydrogen bonding between single hydroxyls forming closed hydroxyl groups [212]. The reactions are shown below (Hydrogen bonding is represented with a dotted line):

$\equiv Si— + OH^- \rightarrow \equiv Si—OH$ Single Hydroxyl

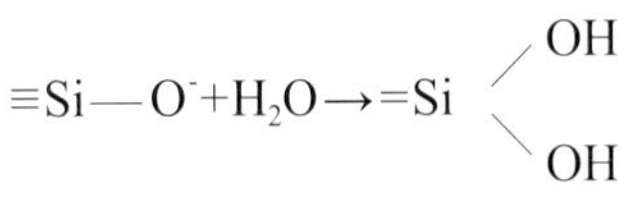

Double Hydroxyls

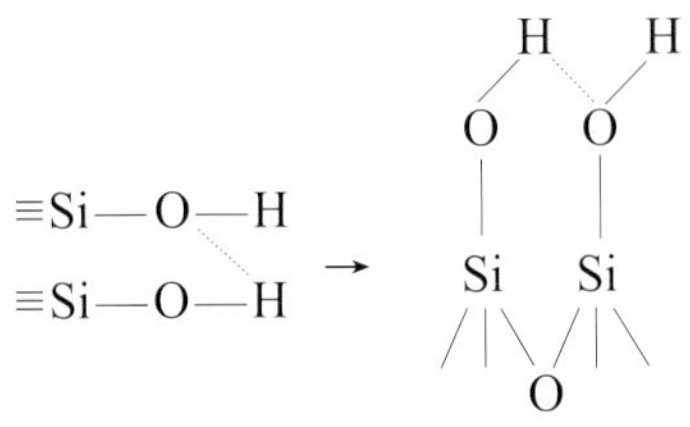

Hydroxyl Group

The Hydrogen bonds of these hydroxyls physically attract water molecules, forming a film of water over the surface of the glaze.

As the alkaline metal and alkaline earth metal ions in YUB (Na_2O-K_2O-CaO-MgO-Al_2O_3-SiO_2 System) glazes do not take part in the silica network, they retain a relatively high ability to migrate throughout the glaze level. This allows them to partake in ion exchange with the H^+ ion of the water that has been absorbed to the glaze surface, creating alkali (ROH) (see reaction ①).

$$\equiv Si—O—R^+ + H^+OH^- \rightarrow \equiv Si—O—H + ROH \qquad ①$$

Additionally there are the following reactions:

$$\equiv Si—O—H + \frac{3}{2}H_2O \rightarrow Si(OH)_4 \qquad ②$$

Water particles can also react directly with the silica network:

$$\equiv Si—O—Si\equiv + H_2O \rightarrow 2[\equiv Si—O—H] \qquad ③$$

The continuation of reaction ③ is the four bridging oxygen surrounding the Si atom becoming —OH particles, forming $Si(OH)_4$. This is the direct breakdown effect water has on the silica network [213].

The $Si(OH)_4$ created in the above reaction is a polarized molecule that can also polarize the surrounding water molecules, attracting them to itself creating $Si(OH)_4$•nH_2O, often called silicic acid gel [214]. Aside from a small portion that dissolves in water, this silicic acid gel can absorb to the glaze surface, forming a thin layer or film. This film, in turn, has a relatively high resistance to water and other acids.

In reaction ①, the location left by the R^+ ion, being larger than the H^+ ion with which they change places, leaves voids in the glaze level. This in turn, loosens the structure, decreases the stability, and increases the susceptibility to corrosion.

2. YUB Glaze Level Reactions with Alkali

The introduction of alkali occurs in two different ways: The first being the aforementioned reaction ① water-glaze reaction, depending on the speed of R^+ and H^+ ion exchange. The second is the introduction via external environment.

缓慢，甚至几乎停止了。但如果外部环境是碱性的，风化作用会继续进行。

由于碱（ROH）的作用，硅氧网络遭到破坏后（见反应⑤），以≡Si—O^-粒子群的形式溶解下来，和釉表面游离的R^+、R^{2+}等阳离子结合成硅酸盐。这些风化产物不断堆积，在釉表面形成一个壳层。当这一壳层达到一定厚度时，会令釉表面失去光泽，严重时呈不透明状。此壳层是疏松多孔的，吸水性也很强，它提供了一个有高浓度的碱性水溶液的环境，使釉表面无法形成保护膜，原有的硅酸凝胶薄膜也会遭到破坏。因此，这种壳层的形成会大大加剧外界对釉层的侵蚀[215]。

三、元青花釉层与酸的反应

元青花釉层与酸的反应跟其与水的反应相似，除氢氟酸外，一般的酸并不直接与釉发生反应，而是通过水起作用。

氢氟酸对玻璃的作用是直接破坏硅氧网络（见反应⑦）：

$$\equiv Si—O—Si\equiv + H^+F^- \rightarrow \equiv Si—O—H + \equiv Si—F \quad ⑦$$

对元青花瓷釉（Na_2O-K_2O-CaO-MgO-Al_2O_3-SiO_2系统）来说，酸溶液中的H^+浓度比水中的H^+浓度要大，所以H^+与R^+的离子交换速度在酸中比在水中快，即反应①有较快的速度，生成的碱（ROH）会侵蚀釉表面。如果R_2O含量低或有Ca^{2+}的“抑制效应”，反应①就会减缓速度或停止。

$Si(OH)_4$不溶于酸，在酸性溶液中溶解度减小，即减慢了④的反应速度，从而能够减缓釉表面的侵蚀。

在高碱釉中，R_2O含量较高时，R^+的浓度较高，反应①是主要的，有碱不断生成，侵蚀釉表面；在高硅釉中，SiO_2含量较高时，反应④的速度会变得缓慢，也就是说硅酸凝胶被溶解的速度减慢，风化得以减缓。所以，高碱釉的耐酸性小于耐水性，而高硅釉的耐酸性大于耐水性。

四、元青花釉层与CO_2的反应

CO_2会与釉表面的碱反应生成碳酸盐（Na_2CO_3或$NaHCO_3$）（见反应⑧、⑨）：

$$NaOH + CO_2 \rightarrow NaHCO_3 \quad ⑧$$

$$2NaOH + CO_2 \rightarrow Na_2CO_3 + H_2O \quad ⑨$$

它们在釉表面会进一步吸附水分子，形成随机分布的白色雾状斑点，属于可溶盐[216]。当水分蒸发后，这些盐便析出，它能稳定存在于空气中。由于CO_2与碱反应生成盐，降低了釉表面的R^+和OH^-的浓度，这更有利于反应①中的离子交换。而釉表面的碱被中和成盐，减缓了碱对釉层的直接侵蚀，有利于硅酸凝胶的形成与保持。

但是，当釉表面吸附水分子时，处于釉表面的碳酸盐结晶颗粒（Na_2CO_3或$NaHCO_3$）又会水解生成碱（ROH），ROH溶解硅酸凝胶（见反应④），侵蚀釉表面。

CO_2还会与析出到釉表面的游离Ca^{2+}等作用形成碳酸盐晶体，属于难溶盐（见反应⑩）：

$$Ca^{2+} + CO_3^{2-} \rightarrow CaCO_3\downarrow \quad ⑩$$

五、元青花釉层与盐溶液的反应

釉层中迁出的金属离子会与盐溶液的酸根（如CO_3^{2-}，SO_4^{2-}，SiO_3^{2-}，PO_4^{3-}）发生反应，生成可溶盐或难溶盐。部分反应如下：

$$Na^+ + CO_3^{2-} \rightarrow Na_2CO_3 \quad ⑪$$

$$Ca^{2+} + CO_3^{2-} \rightarrow CaCO_3\downarrow \quad ⑫$$

$$Pb^{2+} + SO_4^{2-} \rightarrow PbSO_4\downarrow \quad ⑬$$

$$Ca^{2+} + SO_4^{2-} \rightarrow CaSO_4\downarrow \quad ⑭$$

$$Pb^{2+} + CO_3^{2-} \rightarrow PbCO_3\downarrow \quad ⑮$$

在干湿交替的环境中，可溶盐如Na_2CO_3、$NaHCO_3$可能流失，也可能渗入釉裂纹中，当水分蒸发后便结晶析出。难溶盐会附着于釉表面或沉积于釉裂纹中。

六、小结

元青花釉层的风化过程是一个漫长、复杂的物理变化和化学反应的综合过程，上述的各种化学反应并非是一个单一过程，可能会有几种反应同时进行。如当H^+与R^+产生交换的同时，也有ROH与釉层的反应，ROH还可能同时与CO_2发生反应；同时也有物理变化发生，如盐溶液中的晶体析出，温度变化使釉层产生裂纹等。

由于元青花瓷器所存在的后天环境是复杂多样的，风化的产物也多种多样，所以，元青花的迹型也呈现出多样性。

Alkali (ROH) can dissolve silicic acid gel (see reaction ④); this destroys the glaze surface protection, and starts the weathering process.

$$Si(OH)_4 + ROH \rightarrow [Si(OH)_3O]^- R^+ + H_2O \quad ④$$

ROH can also react directly with the silica network, breaking down the Si—O bonds, creating Si—O⁻ grains, dissolving the SiO_2 in alkali solution, and breaking down the glaze surface (see reaction ⑤):

$$\equiv Si—O—Si\equiv + OH^- \rightarrow \equiv Si—OH + \equiv Si—O^- \quad ⑤$$

The other side of the ≡Si—O⁻split is able to react with water:

$$\equiv Si—O^- + H_2O \rightarrow \equiv Si—OH + OH^- \quad ⑥$$

The alkali formed in reaction ⑥ can facilitate the continuation of reaction ⑦, and break down the glaze surface.

In reference to the continuous migrating out of R^+ ions (where R represents Na and K) in YUB (Na_2O-K_2O-CaO-MgO-Al_2O_3-SiO_2 System), Ca^{2+} ions in relatively high numbers can act as reaction inhibitors; slowing the H^+ and R^+ ion exchange, slowing the creation of alkali (ROH) (reaction ① slows), and slowing the occurrence of reaction ⑤. This drastically reduces the speed at which the glaze surface corrodes, almost bringing it to a stop. However, if the external environment has an alkaline nature, weathering can proceed.

With the introduction of alkali (ROH), after the silica network encounters breakdown (see reaction ⑤), ≡Si—O⁻ grains dissolve down together with the free R^+ and R^{2+} ions on the surface and join to create silicate salts. This weathering causes continuous sedimentation, forming a sort of shell over the glaze level. As this shell reaches a certain thickness, it depletes the sheen of the glaze surface and decreases its translucency. This shell is loosely porous and highly water absorbent; creating a strong alkali solvent liquid covering, disallowing the glaze to form its protective film, and destroying the silicic acid gel film originally present. Because of this shell, the corrosion to the glaze surface by the external environment is drastically increased [215].

3. YUB Glaze Level Reactions with Acid

The YUB glaze level and acid reactions are very similar to that of reactions with water. Aside from hydrofluoric acid, normal acids don't directly react with the glaze surface, but rely on water to react.

The effect of hydrofluoric acid on glass is direct destruction to the silica network (see reaction ⑦).

$$\equiv Si—O—Si\equiv + H^+F^- \rightarrow \equiv Si—O—H + \equiv Si—F \quad ⑦$$

For YUB (Na_2O-K_2O-CaO-MgO-Al_2O_3-SiO_2 System) glazes, the amount of H^+ions in acid solutions is much higher than that of water, therefore the R^+ and H^+ ion exchange rate is much higher than that of water; accelerating reaction ① and creating glaze-corrosive alkali (ROH). If the amount of R_2O is low or the Ca^{2+} ion's inhibiting effect is present, and reaction ① slows or even stops.

$Si(OH)_4$ is not acid soluble, therefore its solubility in acid solution is very slow, which can slow reaction ④ and slow glaze surface corrosion.

In high alkaline glazes, R_2O is relatively high and R^+ions are abundant. Reaction ① is predominant, and the continuous formation of alkali corrodes the glaze surface. In high Silicone glazes, SiO_2 is relatively high. This slows reaction ④; which is to say the dissolving of the silicic acid gel slows, thus slowing the weathering process. Therefore, high alkaline glazes are more water-resistant than acid-resistant, and high Silicone glazes are more acid-resistant than water-resistant.

4. YUB Glaze Level Reaction with Carbon Dioxide

Carbon Dioxide can react with the alkali on the glaze surface creating carbonates (Na_2CO_3 or $NaHCO_3$) (see reactions ⑧ and ⑨).

$$NaOH + CO_2 \rightarrow NaHCO_3 \quad ⑧$$

$$2NaOH + CO_2 \rightarrow Na_2CO_3 + H_2O \quad ⑨$$

Carbonates act to absorb water on the glaze surface forming randomly distributed, foggy-white blotches, which are soluble salts that crystallize as the water evaporates and stabilize in open air [216]. As the Carbon Dioxide and alkali form salts, the amount of R^+ and OH^- ions decrease, fostering the ion exchange in reaction ①. The neutralization of alkali into salt on the glaze surface slows its ability to directly corrode the glaze surface, and promotes the formation of the protective silicic acid gel.

However, once the glaze surface absorbs water, surface level crystallized salts (Na_2CO_3 or $NaHCO_3$) again dissolve into alkali (ROH); which in turn dissolves the silicic acid gel (see reaction ④) and corrodes the glaze surface.

Carbon Dioxide can also join with surface level free ions such as Ca^{2+} and form carbonate crystals which are partially soluble salts (see reaction ⑩).

$$Ca^{2+} + CO_3^{2-} \rightarrow CaCO_3\downarrow \quad ⑩$$

5. YUB Glaze Level Reaction with Salt Solutions

The migrating metal ions on the glaze surface can react with the acid radicals (i.e. CO_3^{2-}, SO_4^{2-}, SiO_3^{2-}, PO_4^{3-}) in salt solutions to form soluble and partially soluble salts. Sample reactions:

$$Na+ + CO_3^{2-} \rightarrow Na_2CO_3 \quad ⑪$$

$$Ca^{2+} + CO_3^{2-} \rightarrow CaCO_3 \downarrow \quad ⑫$$

$$Pb^{2+} + SO_4^{2-} \rightarrow PbSO_4 \downarrow \quad ⑬$$

$$Ca^{2+} + SO_4^{2-} \rightarrow CaSO_4 \downarrow \quad ⑭$$

$$Pb^{2+} + CO_3^{2-} \rightarrow PbCO_3 \downarrow \quad ⑮$$

In environments of alternating moisture, soluble salts such as Na_2CO_3 and $NaHCO_3$ can dissolve away. It is also possible that they permeate into glaze cracks and crystallize when the water evaporates. Partially soluble salts can become absorbed by the glaze surface or deposit into glaze cracks.

6. Summary

YUB glaze level weathering is the accumulation of a lengthy, complicated physical change and chemical reaction processes. The above mentioned physical changes and chemical reactions are not entirely independent processes, but rather a series of simultaneously occurring events: For example, as the R^+ and H^+ ions exchange, the ROH and glaze level reaction is taking place; ROH could also be reacting with Carbon Dioxide. Meanwhile, physical changes can be occurring: For example the crystallization of salt solutions or temperature changes creating glaze cracks.

Due to the multi-faceted and complex characteristics of post-firing environments in which YUB wares pass time, the materialization of weathering is not limited to the aforementioned reactions, but can contain other byproducts. Therefore, YUB traces present with multiple variations.

第二节
元青花釉层变化与环境的关系

一、地上环境

（一）地上环境概念

地上环境是指元青花瓷器所处的自然大气情况。

（二）地上环境组成

大气的主要成分是氮N_2（78.08%）、氧O_2（20.95%）、氩Ar（0.934%）和CO_2（0.034%）。大气中也含有水，但水的含量是一个可变化的数值，在不同的时间、不同的地点及不同的气候条件下，水的含量是不一样的，其数值一般在1%－3%的范围内发生变化。此外，大气中还有很多痕量组分，如H_2、CH_4、CO、SO_2、NH_3、N_2O、NO_2、O_3[217]。地上环境中还有细小灰尘，它们会被吸附或沉积在釉表面上。

（三）地上环境的风化

元青花釉表面在地上环境中的风化实质是水、CO_2、SO_2等在釉表面作用的总和。釉表面灰尘积聚处易吸附大气中的水分，有利于风化的进行。

由第一节可知，元青花釉表面会吸附空气中的水分子，在釉表面形成水膜；通过H^+和R^+离子交换等一些反应，釉表面会产生硅酸凝胶薄膜（见反应①②③）。如果釉层的R_2O含量少，这种薄膜的形成及发展非常缓慢；如果R_2O含量较高，迁出的R^+则形成ROH（见反应①），ROH会溶解附在釉表面的硅酸凝胶薄膜（见反应④），接着直接与釉表面的硅氧网络反应，使网络解体（见反应⑤），破坏釉表面。

风化后，通常有雾状或颗粒状白斑，自然分布在釉表面或深入釉层中。

二、地下环境

（一）地下环境概念

地下环境是指元青花瓷器所处的土壤情况。

（二）地下环境组成

土壤是由固体、液体和气体三相共同组成的多相体系。固相是指矿物质和有机质，矿物质约占90%以上，有机质占1%－10%。液相是指土壤中的水分及其水溶物。气相是指充斥在土壤无数孔隙中的空气。

不同于在大气中，土壤中的水是具有一定酸碱性的。我国土壤的pH值大多在4.5－8.5范围内，并有由南向北pH值递增的规律性：如华南、西南地区大多为pH值4.5－5.5，有少数低至3.6－3.8；华中、华东地区为5.5－6.5；长江以北的土壤多为中性或碱性，如华北、西北的土壤大多含$CaCO_3$，pH值一般在7.5－8.5，少数强碱性土壤的pH值高达10.5[218]。

（三）地下环境的风化

1. 液相产生的风化作用

在土壤中由液相产生的风化作用是以水溶液的形式与釉表面进行的。风化作用可以是H^+与碱金属离子交换，其结果是釉层产生空位，结构变疏松（见反应①），也可以是碱直接破坏硅氧网络（见反应②），或者是生成难溶盐沉积在釉表面，或生成可溶盐流失。水溶液中的可溶盐可渗入釉裂纹、孔隙等釉层的疏松结构中，水分蒸发后，可溶盐结晶析出。在干湿交替的过程中，溶解、结晶反复进行，产生的应力会使釉表面开裂，甚至出现剥釉。

土壤中的及釉表面的阴阳离子（Ca^{2+}，Mg^{2+}，Fe^{3+}，Mn^{2+}，Pb^{4+}，CO_3^{2-}，SO_4^{2-}，OH^-，SiO_3^{2-}，PO_4^{3-}）会发生反应，形成不同颜色的难溶盐沉积物。难溶盐在沉积过程中还可胶结土壤颗粒，在釉表面形成坚硬的垢层。

Section 2:

Relationship Between Environment and YUB Glaze Level Change

1. Above Ground Environment

A. Above Ground Environment Defined

Above Ground Environment indicates a positioning situation in which a YUB piece is exposed to open air.

B. Above Ground Environmental Components

Atmosphere (or open air) consists of primarily N_2 (78.08%), O_2 (20.95%), Ar (0.934%), and CO_2 (0.034%). Open air also includes a certain amount of water, but to varying degrees. Due to humidity changing over time and different weather conditions, water usually compiles 1~3% of the atmosphere. In addition, open air often includes trace amounts of the following compounds: H_2, CH_4, CO, SO_2, NH_3, N_2O, NO_2, O_3[217]. The above ground environment also includes minute dust particles, which can be absorbed by or deposited into the glaze surface.

C. Above Ground Environment Weathering

Above ground weathering of YUB glaze is the accumulation of the interaction between the glaze level and water, CO_2, SO_2 and so forth. Glaze areas that have dust deposits tend to absorb water; creating a starting point for weathering.

From Section 1, we know that YUB glaze surfaces absorb water, creating a sort of wet film across the surface. Through H^+ and R^+ion exchange, the surface can present with a thin silicic acid gel covering (see reactions ①②③). If the amount of R_2O is relatively low, the formation of this film is extremely slow. If the amount of R_2O is relatively high, free R^+ ions separate out to form ROH (see reaction ①), which in turn dissolves the silicic acid gel film (see reaction ④). The result is direct contact between ROH and the silica network, and the breaking down and corrosion of the glaze surface (see reaction ⑤).

After weathering, it is common to see foggy-white and grainy-white mottles naturally occurring across the glaze surface, and entering in to the glaze level.

2. Underground Environment

A. Underground Environment Defined

Underground Environment indicates a positioning situation in which a YUB piece is under the surface of the earth.

B. Underground Environmental Components

Soil is a multi-phase body that consists of a conglomeration of gas, liquid, and solid phases. Solids consist of primarily +90% minerals and 1~10% organics. Liquids are a combination of water and hydrotropes. Gasses are comprised of a combination of any air components that exist in the numerous cavities within the soil.

Unlike open-air moisture, the water within soil has certain acidic or basic properties. Chinese soil, for example, primarily ranges from 4.5-8.5 pH, with the pH generally increasing as you move toward northern latitudes: Southern and Southwestern China soil primarily ranges between 4.5~5.5 pH, with a small portion between 3.6~3.8 pH; Central and Eastern China soil ranges from 5.5~5.6 pH; soil north of the Yangtze River is primarily neutral or basic, North and

水溶液侵蚀釉表面，从而使釉层变成疏松的多孔层，这时，如果有土壤细小颗粒进入釉层中，待水分蒸发时，便会形成土沁，颜色与周围土壤接近。

土壤中各种矿物质颗粒并非均匀分布，而由于土壤颗粒表面的吸附力和微细孔隙的毛细管作用，水分被保持在土壤中不流动，这使土壤中各处的水溶液成分及干湿程度有差异。所以，元青花釉表面各处被风化侵蚀的方式和程度就有所不同。

2. 气相产生的风化作用

土壤中的空气组成与大气基本相似，主要成分都是N_2、O_2、CO_2。其差异是：

（1）土壤空气存在于相互隔离的土壤孔隙中，是一个不连续的体系。

（2）在O_2和CO_2含量上有很大差别，土壤空气中的CO_2含量比大气中高得多，大气中CO_2含量仅为0.02%－0.03%，而土壤空气中CO_2含量一般在0.15%－0.65%，甚至高达5%，它主要是由生物呼吸作用和有机物分解产生；土壤中的氧气含量低于大气，而水蒸气的含量比大气中高得多；土壤空气中还含有少量还原性气体，如CH_4、H_2S、H_2、NH_3等[219]。

土壤中的CO_2和水的含量比大气中要高得多，存在于土壤中的陶瓷风化强度比大气中的要高很多。

需要注意的是有些墓室和窖藏环境密封较好，基本隔绝了其内部与外界的物质交换，使墓室和窖藏环境长期处于一个较稳定的状态。在这种保存情况下的元青花瓷器，其釉层的风化强度往往比较低，甚至比在大气环境中保存的还要好。

（四）小结

地下环境的复杂性及不均匀性，造成元青花釉表面风化的随机性：有的地方风化严重，有的地方保存相对完好。

潮湿的土壤比干燥的土壤腐蚀性强，干湿交替的土壤比湿度恒定的土壤腐蚀性强，酸性或碱性土壤比中性土壤腐蚀性强。与地上风化形貌最大的差异是，由于有难溶盐及土壤小颗粒的存在，地下环境的风化产物可以是黄色、褐色或其他颜色。

三、水中环境

（一）水中环境概念

水中环境是指元青花瓷器所处的水下情况。

（二）水中环境风化

当元青花瓷器处在水中时，釉层中的网络外的金属离子（如Na^+、K^+等）与H^+交换，生成碱。一般情况下，碱会被水稀释，因而不能进一步腐蚀釉表面。但如果R_2O含量较高，则R^+与H^+的交换会继续进行，使釉表面变得疏松多孔。当水偏碱性时，则会对釉表面进一步产生腐蚀作用，碱性增强时反应会加快。

（三）元青花釉层在水中环境不同覆盖物下的表现

当元青花瓷器在水下环境中时，其表面覆盖的沉积物大致可分为两种：致密的沉积物和疏松的沉积物。致密的沉积物通常为颗粒细小的黏土软泥，疏松的沉积物为砾石、沙、贝壳、珊瑚碎片等。由于致密的沉积物层隔断了陶瓷与外界的物质交换，水也难以渗透，所以釉表面的风化作用难以进行，在这种情况下，陶瓷保存得较好。而在疏松的沉积物下，由于水流涌动带动沙粒等与釉面不断发生摩擦，对釉表面造成损害，同时，水对釉层的腐蚀在不同程度下进行，使釉层孔隙扩大，向纵深发展，甚至致使釉层剥落。

例如，南海Ⅰ号沉船掩埋于珠江口海域一米以下的黏土质软泥中，该船所出瓷器光亮如新，而南海西沙和渤海湾中沉船的陶瓷，因其沉船遗址在粉砂以及砂与珊瑚碎屑交错的沉积物上，海水易渗透，加之海水涌动带动大量粉砂及珊瑚碎屑，与沉积层中的陶瓷不断发生摩擦，致使釉表面风化强度较高[220]。

（四）元青花釉层出水后的变化

元青花瓷器长期处于水下环境中，胎及釉的疏松部分均有水及可溶盐溶液渗入。当陶瓷出水后，原有的平衡被打破，析出的可溶盐结晶会对周围釉层产生压力，可能会导致釉表面发生开裂，甚至釉层剥落。

Northwestern China ranges from 7.5~8.5 pH and presents with high amounts of $CaCO_3$; the highest recorded PH reached as much as 10.5 [218].

C. Underground Environment Weathering

I. Weathering Caused By Liquids

Hydro-solutions reacting with the YUB glaze surface are the primary causes of liquid weathering within the soil. The forms of weathering include: The H+ and alkali metal ion exchange, producing voids and weakened glass structural integrity (see reaction ①); direct decomposition of the silica network by alkali bases (see reaction ②); or the deposit of partially soluble salts and dissolving of soluble salts.Water-soluble salts can enter into cracks, openings, and other glaze imperfections. As water evaporates, these salts crystallize. The repetitive dissolving and crystallization during the process of alternating moisture creates tension, and can crack the glaze, or even cause glaze erosion.

Both the soil and the YUB glaze level contain many positive and negative particles (Ca^{2+}, Mg^{2+}, Fe^{3+}, Mn^{2+}, Pb^{4+}, CO_3^{2-}, SO_4^{2-}, OH^-, SiO_3^{2-}, PO_4^{3-}), which can react with each other, creating varying colors of partially soluble salt deposits. It is possible for these partially soluble salts to become cemented to the surrounding soil, forming a hard dirt layer on the surface of the glaze.

Water solutions corrode the glaze surface, and develop a loosely porous geography across its face. At this time, if the surrounding soil particles enter into the glaze level, as the water evaporates, it leaves behind dirt deposits. The deposits' colors reflect the surrounding soil.

Due to the absorptive and porous capillary qualities of soil; water remains within the soil without flowing away. The mineral particles of soil are unevenly distributed, leading to different solutions and moisture in different areas. Therefore, a YUB piece can present with varying severities and types of weathering across the glaze.

II. Weathering Caused By Gasses

Air within soil is composed of essentially the same gasses as open air, with the main differences being:

a. Soil air exists in mutually isolated spaces within the soil; it is not a continuous system.

b. O_2 and CO^2 levels in soil are vastly different, with CO_2 being much higher than open air. Open air consists of 0.02~0.03%, whereas the amount in soil is 0.15-0.65% and as high as 5%. This is due primarily to the presence of organism respiration and the breakdown of organic materials. The amount of O_2 in soil is lower than that of open air, and moisture is much higher. Soil also contains trace amounts of reduced gasses such as: CH_4, H_2S, H_2, NH_3 and so forth [219].

Because of the heightened amounts of CO_2 and water in soil, associated weathering severity is drastically higher.

Special attention must be paid to the fact that some underground burial chambers and cellars are relatively well sealed; essentially isolating the internal content from the outside environment. Thus burial chambers and cellars represent a long-term stable environment. In most cases, YUB found in these types of locations have a lower glaze weathering severity, even lower than pieces stored in open air.

D. Summary

As the underground environment is complex and heterogeneous, glaze corrosion is randomly distributed, with areas of severe weathering and areas retaining relatively innate characteristics.

Moist soil corrodes more severely than dry soil. Soils of alternating moisture corrode more severely than soils of consistent moisture. Acidic and basic soils corrode more than soils of pH neutrality. Differing from open-air weathering, the presence of partially soluble salts and soil particles in underground weathering can materialize yellow, brown, black and so forth discolorations.

If a piece is present within a relatively sealed and dry underground environment the weathering severity is lower than that of pieces that come into direct contact with soil.

3. Underwater Environment

A. Underwater Environment Defined

Underwater Environment indicates a positioning situation in which a YUB piece becomes submerged in a body of water.

B. Underwater Environment Weathering

When a YUB piece becomes submerged in water, the metallic ions (i.e. Na^+, K^+, Pb^{2+}) that are outside of the silica network enter into H^+ ion exchange, however the alkali formed become diluted in the water and cannot further corrode the glaze surface. If R_2O is relatively high, ion exchange continues, therefore persistently increasing glaze surface porosity. Water with alkalinity can move forward in glaze surface corrosion, with higher alkalinity increasing reaction speed.

C. YUB Glaze Level Under Different Underwater Material Covering

The material deposits that present on underwater YUB wares can be divided into two main categories: Compact sediments and loose sediments. Compact sediments are clay and silt, while loose sediments are gravel, sand, shell fragments, and pieces of coral. Compact sediments can act as a partition, inhibiting exchange between the glaze and external elements, as well as water permeation; because of this, it is difficult for weathering to proceed, and under this type of situation, the glaze is protected from corrosion. Whereas, with loose sediments the continuous contact of sand and other hard particles with the glaze face can cause damage. Additionally, water can continue corrosion to a certain degree, broadening and deepening glaze openings, even causing glaze corrosion.

An example of this is Nanhai No. 1 shipwreck, which was buried under one meter of silt at the mouth of the Pearl River. The pieces excavated have a like-new sheen. Alternatively, in Xisha and Bohai Bay of the South China Sea, shipwreck pieces that were located among sand and coral debris, due to the contact with salt-water and constant friction caused by sand movement in underwater currents, presented with a much higher weathering severity [220].

D. Changes To Glaze Level After Water Excavation

Water and soluble salt solutions enter into the loosened glaze and body of YUB that have spent a long period of time underwater. After excavation, the original equilibrium is disturbed, soluble salts crystallize, and stress is placed on the surrounding glaze. This can possibly cause glaze cracks, leading to glaze corrosion.

第三节 元青花釉层迹型风化特征

陶瓷釉层主要是由玻璃相、气相和晶相构成的，在经历岁月风化后，陶瓷迹型类别会发生各自不同的变化（各迹型类别的详细风化特征描述参见第六章）。

一、玻璃相迹型风化特征

由于元青花釉层玻璃相先天的凹凸不平以及釉层结构稳定性的差异，釉层经风化后，会在釉表面及釉层中的玻璃相上形成斑块和纹路两大迹型类别。

（一）斑块

1. 针眼斑

针眼斑是大小较均匀、深浅大致相同、疏密不定的独立微孔，以聚集形式呈不规则形貌出现的斑块。它是元青花瓷器在后天环境影响下，在釉表面随机形成的。

2. 坑点斑

坑点斑是深浅不一、大小不一、形貌不一的不规则凹形斑块。它是元青花瓷器在后天环境影响下，在釉表面形成的。

3. 物盖斑

物盖斑是元青花瓷器在后天环境影响下，釉表面被外界物质覆盖而形成的斑块。

4. 泡根斑

泡根斑是元青花瓷器在后天环境影响下，由破口泡发展形成，内有沉积物的凹形斑块。

5. 絮状斑

絮状斑是以白色为主，呈无序状，具有流淌、渗透、漫延趋势的不规则斑块。它是元青花瓷器在后天环境影响下，在釉表面及釉层中，由可溶盐、难溶盐和灰尘等物质沉积形成的。

（二）纹路

1. 釉裂纹

釉裂纹是元青花瓷器在烧制过程中和在后天环境影响下形成的，以直线、曲线等不规则线条形貌分布在釉表面的开裂纹路。

2. 划痕

划痕是元青花瓷器釉表面与硬物碰划留下的破坏性纹路。

二、气相迹型风化特征

（一）色变泡

色变泡是元青花瓷器在后天环境影响下，釉层中透明气泡的颜色发生了变化，但仍具透影性的气泡。

（二）壁变泡

壁变泡是元青花瓷器在后天环境影响下，釉层中的气泡内壁质地发生了风化现象，被风化处失去了透影性的气泡。

三、晶相迹型风化特征

（一）针眼斑出现在流淌斑上

流淌斑含铁与锰较高，比较容易风化。瓷器烧制成后，流淌斑上无釉层保护的部分最先风化，形成针眼斑。有釉层保护的，在后天釉层受到侵蚀后也以针眼斑形式开始风化。

（二）针眼斑出现在放射斑上

放射斑含一定量的铁氧化物及锰氧化物，比较容易风化。瓷器烧制成后，无釉层保护的放射斑最先风化，形成针眼斑。有釉层保护的，在后天釉层受到侵蚀后也以针眼斑形式开始风化。

Section 3:

Characteristics of Weathered Yuan Underglaze Blue Glaze Level Traces

YUB glaze consists of glass, gas, and crystal phase components. After experiencing centuries of weathering, trace categories begin to experience different types of changes (for detailed characteristics of trace categories please see Chapter 6).

1. Characteristics of Weathered Glass Phase Traces

After weathering, due to the innate uneven topography of the YUB glaze level glass phase and differences in glaze level structural stability, the following two main categories: Mottles (Blotches) and Striae (Lines), can appear in the glass phase, across the glaze surface, or within the glaze level.

A. Mottles

I. Needlepoint Mottles

Needlepoint Mottles are acquired pits formed under post-firing surroundings with a limited variation of size and depth, either accumulated or independent, randomly dispersed on the YUB glaze surface.

II. Pit Mottles

Pit Mottles (also called Pitting) are the irregularly shaped small depressions or pits on YUB glaze, caused by external post-firing conditions, with non-uniform depth, size, and appearance.

III. Overlay Mottles

Overlay Mottles are acquired in the post-firing environment, and are the result of corrosion brought on by the coverage of YUB glaze by a foreign material.

IV. Bubble Roots

A Bubble Root (mottle) is depressed shaped mottle with internal sediments, formed by the progression of a broken mouth bubble on the surface of YUB glaze under the influences of post-firing factors.

V. Floccus Mottles

Floccus Mottles are primarily white colored appearances on the YUB glaze surface and within the glaze level brought about under post-firing conditions; with irregular, free flowing, and disorderly shapes that were formed by the depositing of soluble and partially soluble salts, dust particles, and so forth materials.

B. Striae

I. Glaze Cracks

Also called crazing, Glaze Cracks are any appearance of straight, round, or irregular lines splitting the glaze surface or glaze level of YUB, which was caused either during firing or under the influence of the post-firing environment.

II. Scratches

Scratches are the YUB glaze-damage lines, left on the glaze surface because of the abrasive forces of hardened external objects.

（三）针眼斑出现在流淌纹上

流淌纹含一定量的铁氧化物及锰氧化物，比较容易风化。瓷器烧制成后，没有被釉层保护的流淌纹以针眼斑形式开始风化，表现为针眼型阴纹。

（四）C形纹、O形纹

C形纹、O形纹是元青花瓷器在烧制过程中及后天环境影响下，以铁氧化物、锰氧化物等金属氧化物为主，以字母C、O形貌分布在釉表面的线形纹路。

C形纹、O形纹是元青花瓷器上的先天性迹型，但通常要经过风化后其二维成像才能用显微镜观察到。

2. Characteristics Of Weathered Gas Phase Traces

A. Color Change Bubbles

Color Change Bubbles are the appearance of air bubbles within the YUB glaze level that have undergone a coloration change under the influences of the post-firing environment, but have retained their original translucency.

B. Textured Bubbles

Textured Bubbles are the appearance of YUB glaze bubbles in which the interior has undergone weathering brought on by the post-firing environment; gaining texture and losing their inherent translucency.

3. Characteristics Of Weathered Crystallized Traces

A. Needlepoint Mottling On Flowing Mottles

Flowing mottles consist primarily of Iron Oxide, which exposed to air is easily weathered. After firing, the areas without glaze protection are the first to undergo weathering and form needlepoint mottles. Areas receiving protection from a thin glaze covering, when the glaze level encounters corrosion, can also present with needlepoint style weathering patterns.

B. Needlepoint Mottling On Radiating Mottles

Radiating mottles contain trace amounts of Iron Oxide, which exposed to air is easily weathered. After firing, the areas without glaze protection are the first to undergo weathering and form needlepoint mottles. Areas receiving protection from a thin glaze covering, when the glaze level encounters corrosion, can also present with needlepoint style weathering patterns.

C. Needlepoint Mottling On Flowing Striae

Flowing striae consist primarily of Iron Oxide, which exposed to air is easily weathered. After firing, the areas without glaze protection undergo weathering and form needlepoint mottling.

D. C and O Shaped Striae

C and O shaped lines in areas of structurally weakened YUB glaze, acquired under the influence of the post-firing environment.

YUB CO striae are formed during the firing process, but need to undergo weathering in order to be observable through two-dimensional microscopic imaging.

第四节
总结

元青花釉层的变化是釉层风化的结果，是釉层与多种物质发生物理变化、化学反应的综合结果。

在不同的存放环境中，无论是物理变化还是化学反应，其结果都会使元青花釉层迹型发生变化。元青花瓷器存放环境的变化，会使其釉层的风化作用强度产生快慢的差异，从而导致釉层迹型风化强度有高有低。

这些迹型现象从一定程度上能够帮助我们推断元青花瓷器在后天存放环境的简单性或复杂性。

在长时间的风化过程中，风化产物在釉层的物理堆积方式和釉层被溶蚀的形貌，一定与短时间人为的物理堆积和化学溶蚀结果有根本的区别。

Section 4:

Conclusion

YUB glaze level change is the total accumulated outcome of the physical changes and chemical reactions between the glaze level and various materials.

Regardless of physical change or chemical reaction, the results are glaze level trace changes with varying characteristics. These weathering trace changes are heterogeneous. Changes in the post-firing environment bring forth differences in the weathering intensity, thus the weathering severities experienced by the glaze level traces are similarly varied.

These trace change characteristics reflect the complexity of YUB post-firing environments.

The aforementioned glaze level byproducts of physical amassing and chemical corrosion created over a long period of time, have fundamental differences to those resulting from immediate man-made physical amassing and chemical corrosion of forged weathering.

第六章

元青花典型迹型类别

阅读提示：

元青花瓷器釉层在烧制过程中及后天环境影响下，会表现出各种迹型特征。这些不同的迹型特征主要是因不同的釉料配方、烧制工艺以及在不同环境中风化作用的差异造成的。通过观察与研究，可将纷繁多样的元青花迹型归纳总结出不同的类别。本章主要介绍元青花迹型中最典型的四大类别：斑块、纹路、气泡和鬃眼。

主要论述问题：

1. 元青花釉层中有哪些斑块种类？它们各自有什么特征？
2. 元青花釉层中有哪些纹路种类？它们各自有什么特征？
3. 元青花釉层中有哪些气泡种类？它们各自有什么特征？
4. 元青花鬃眼的主要特征是什么？

Chapter 6:

Yuan Underglaze Blue Typical Trace Categories

Text Note:

During the firing process and under the post-firing environment, YUB glazes present with several different varieties of traces. Due to differences in glaze recipes, craftsmanship, as well as the variances in weathering as caused by the post-firing environment, several typical trace categories become evident. Through observation and research, we have been able to surmise and classify the different categories of typical YUB traces. The purpose of this chapter is to introduce the four typical categories of YUB traces: Mottles, Striae, Air Bubbles, and Bristle Pits.

第一节 元青花斑块类别

一、元青花斑块概念

元青花斑块是元青花瓷器在烧制过程中和后天环境影响下形成的，以不规则形貌分布在釉表面及釉层中的迹型类别。

二、元青花斑块类型

如果将在烧制过程中形成的斑块称为先天性斑块，在后天环境影响下形成的斑块称为后天性斑块，那么元青花斑块就可以分成两大类型。

（一）先天性元青花斑块

1. 先天性元青花斑块概念

先天性元青花斑块是元青花瓷器在烧制过程中形成的，以不规则形貌分布在釉表面及釉层中的各类斑块。

2. 先天性元青花斑块种类

先天性元青花斑块按照其形貌特征可分成三个种类：流淌斑、放射斑和团状斑。

（1）流淌斑

① 流淌斑概念

流淌斑是含铁和锰为主，具有流淌感和不规则形貌的片状斑块。它是元青花瓷器在烧制过程中，在其釉表面及釉层中形成的。

流淌斑中的铁元素及锰元素主要来源于青料。

② 流淌斑形成

元青花瓷器在高温烧制时，青料及釉料会逐渐熔化成熔融态。在浮力、表面张力及气泡搅动的作用下，釉料以及青料中的铁氧化物和锰氧化物易在气泡边缘积聚，部分会随气泡升至釉表面，顺着凹凸不平的釉表面向四周扩散，流动铺展，并结晶析出，也可能产生分相。当温度下降时，会有更多结晶析出，这就是一个润湿过程。

由于结晶的成分、密度和表面张力不同，会在釉表面形成不同形貌、不同颜色的流淌斑。溶解在釉层中的铁离子（主要是Fe^{3+}），当釉层冷却凝固时在釉层中形成流淌斑。

③ 流淌斑分类

流淌斑可分为碘酒斑和沙滩斑两种。

A. 碘酒斑概念

碘酒斑是釉层中呈褐色的流淌斑。

B. 沙滩斑概念

沙滩斑是釉表面呈褐色的流淌斑。

④ 流淌斑分布

一般来说，流淌斑都出现在有青料的地方（见图6-1-1—图6-1-3，图6-1-5—图6-1-7，图6-1-9—图6-1-12），少数会出现在无青料处（见图6-1-4、图6-1-8）。

⑤ 流淌斑特征

A. 碘酒斑

碘酒斑二维特征

见图6-1-1—图6-1-4。

I. 碘酒斑颜色有深有浅。

II. 由于碘酒斑已经和玻璃相融为一体，较难受到侵蚀，所以基本保持刚烧制出来的原态。

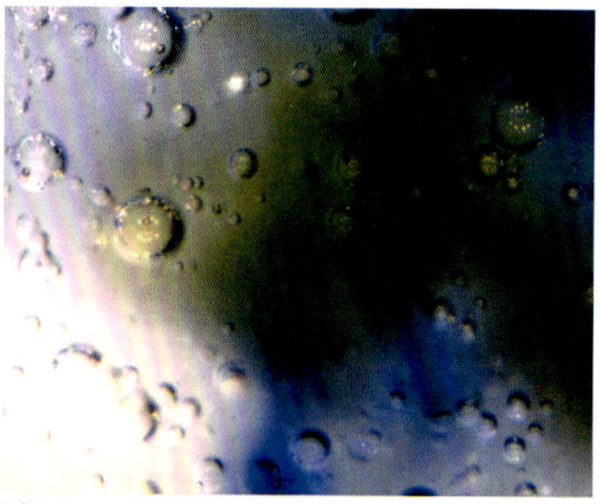

图6-1-1

Section 1:

The Yuan Underglaze Blue Mottle Category

1. YUB Mottles Defined

YUB Mottles (spots and blotches) are a category of irregularly shaped appearances, created during the firing process and acquired under the post-firing environment, that are unevenly disbursed across the glaze surface and within the glaze level of YUB.

2. YUB Mottle Classes

Mottles created during the firing process are called Innate Mottles. For those formed under the influences of the post-firing environment, the term Acquired Mottles is used. These are the two main classes of YUB Mottles.

A. Innate YUB Mottles

I. Innate YUB Mottles Defined

Innate YUB Mottles are mottles of irregular shape and distribution on the glaze surface and within the glaze level of YUB that were formed during the firing process.

II. Innate YUB Mottle Types

According to the appearance characteristics of Innate Mottles, they can be split into three types: Flowing Mottles, Radiating Mottles, and Blotch Mottles.

a. Flowing Mottle

i. Flowing Mottle Defined

Primarily consisting of Iron and Manganese, Flowing Mottles are the irregular blotch-shaped appearances across the glaze surface and within the glaze level which have a free flowing shape and were formed during the firing of YUB.

The elemental Iron and Manganese within Flowing Mottles comes primarily from the cobalt-blue dye.

ii. Formation of Flowing Mottles

During the firing of YUB, cobalt-blue dye and glaze gradually transition into a molten state. Due to the buoyancy, surface tension and movement of the air bubbles within the glaze level, the Iron and Manganese Oxides within the glaze and dye collect around the edges of gaseous bodies within the glaze, and rise with these bubbles to the surface of the glaze. According to the uneven topography of the surface, these compounds diffuse and flow across the glaze surface and crystallize, some producing split phases. When the temperature drops, more crystallization can occur. This flowing dispersion is a fluid process.

According to their composition, density, and surface tension differences, they present with alternate appearances and colors of flowing mottles across the surface of the glaze. When the glaze cools and solidifies, Iron ions (mainly Fe^{3+}) diffused within the glaze level form flowing mottles.

iii. Types of Flowing Mottles

There are two types of flowing mottles: Iodine Mottles and Beach Mottles.

(a) Iodine Mottle Defined

Iodine Mottles are brown colored flowing mottles that exist within the glaze level.

(b) Beach Mottle Defined

Beach Mottles are flowing mottles with brown coloration located on the surface of the glaze.

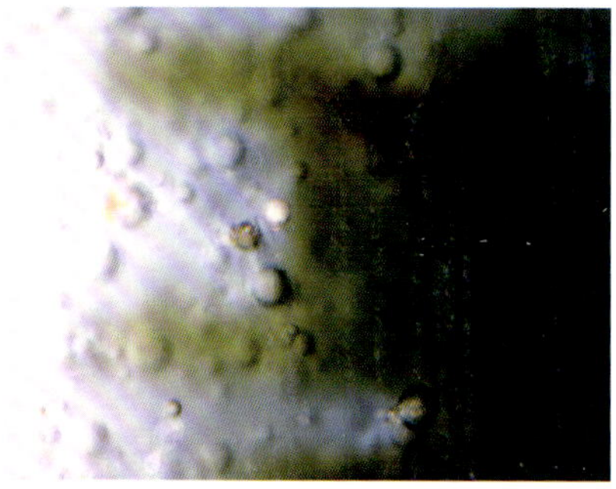
图6-1-2

图6-1-3

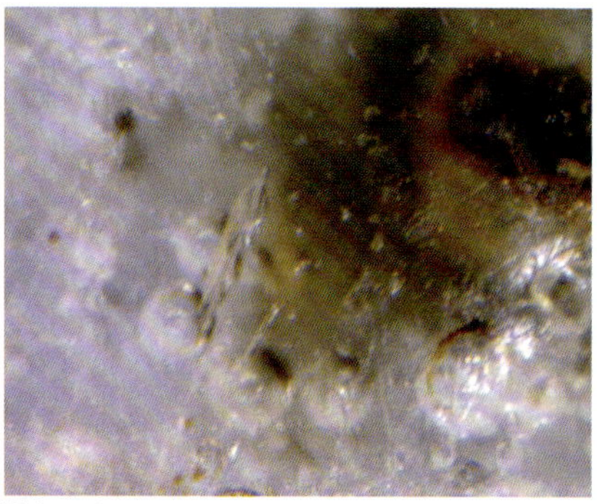
图6-1-4

B. 沙滩斑

a. 沙滩斑二维特征

I. 有的沙滩斑边沿呈火焰形，这种火焰形沙滩斑通常外围釉层中会延展出较明显的碘酒斑，这类沙滩斑是元青花瓷器上较典型的一种斑块（见图6-1-5—图6-1-8）。

II. 有的沙滩斑边沿呈荷叶形，这类斑块在流淌铺展时，表面张力比火焰形沙滩斑大（见图6-1-9—图6-1-12）。

III. 由于釉表面凹凸不平，沙滩斑在流淌润湿时无法完全覆盖釉表面，会造成沙滩斑上出现不规则圆孔的现象，圆孔分布如同筛网。一般来说，荷叶形沙滩斑上出现圆孔的概率要比火焰形沙滩斑高（见图6-1-7、图6-1-9—图6-1-12）。

IV. 由于受釉层保护程度较低，沙滩斑较易风化，大部分沙滩斑上会出现针眼斑。（参见本章本节针眼斑部分）

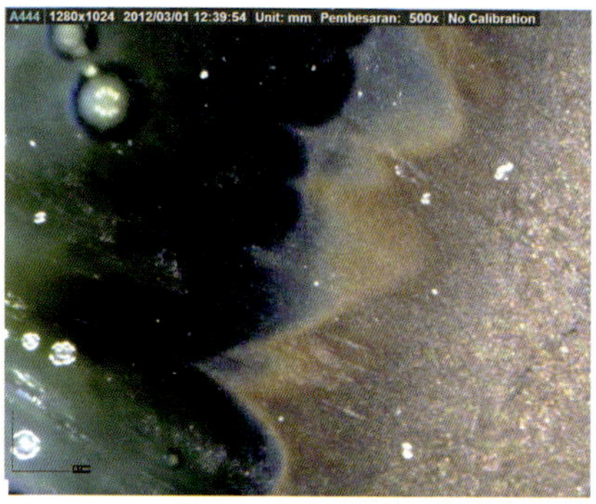

图6-1-5

图6-1-6

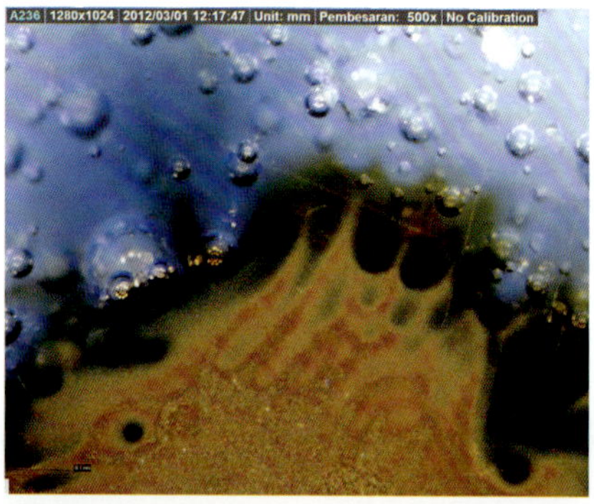

图6-1-7

图6-1-8

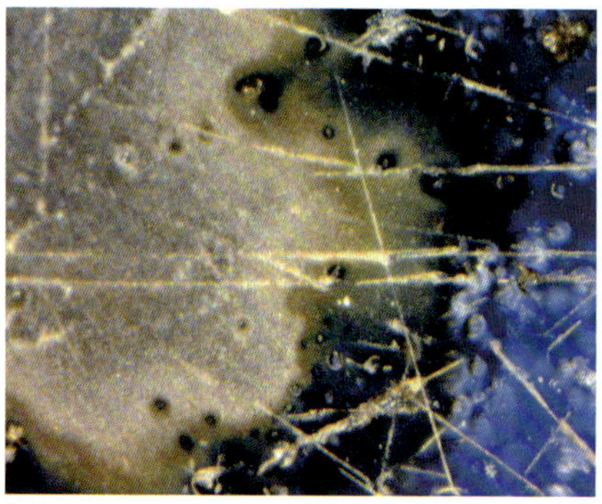
图6-1-9

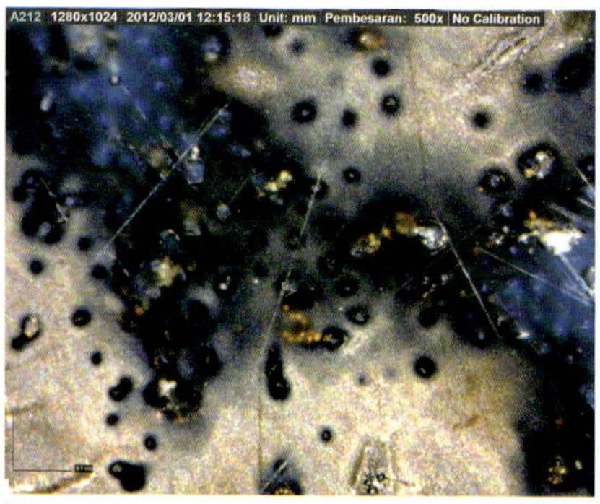

图6-1-10

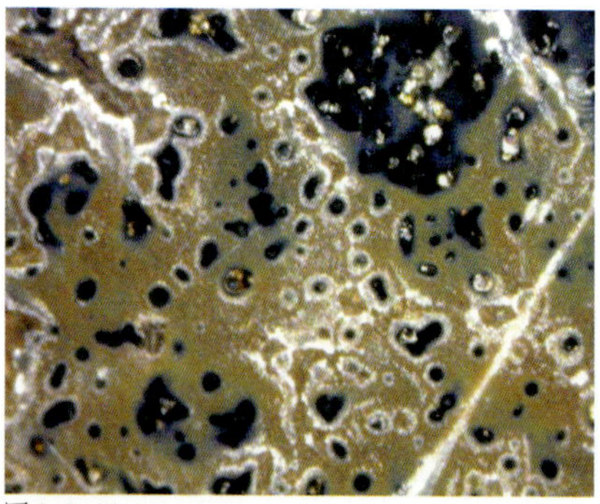
图6-1-11

iv. Distribution of Flowing Mottles

In general, flowing mottles occur in areas of cobalt dye (see pictures 6-1-1—6-1-3, 6-1-5—6-1-7, and 6-1-9—6-1-12), but occasionally can occur in areas without cobalt dye (see pictures 6-1-4 and 6-1-8).

v. Characteristics of Flowing Mottles

(a) Iodine Mottle

Two-dimensional Characteristics of Iodine Mottles

See pictures 6-1-1—6-1-4.

(1) Iodine mottles have dark and light coloration.

(2) As iodine mottles are diffused within the glaze, it is difficult for them to receive corrosion, thus they retain their original inherent characteristics.

(b) Beach Mottle

(i) Two-dimensional Characteristics of Beach Mottles

(1) Beach mottles can appear with flame-like edges. Often the outer edges of these flame shaped mottles have relatively evident iodine mottles within the glaze level surrounding them. This classification of beach mottle is a particularly typical type of mottle on YUB (see pictures 6-1-5—6-1-8).

(2) Beach mottles can also appear with lotus leaf-like edges. This classification of beach mottle occurs due to a higher surface tension during the mottle's flowing formation stage (see pictures 6-1-9—6-1-12).

(3) Due to the topographical unevenness of the glaze surface, during the fluid state of the mottle, the mottle is not able to completely cover the glaze surface, leaving irregularly shaped openings, resembling a sieve. In general, the probability that sieve-like openings will appear on lotus leaf edged mottles is higher than that of flame-edged mottles (see pictures 6-1-7 and 6-1-9—6-1-12).

(4) Due to the relatively low protection received from glaze, beach mottles are easily weathered, and as such the mottle surface presents with needlepoint mottling (see Needlepoint Mottle Heading of this section).

(ii) Three-dimensional Characteristics of Beach Mottles

(1) Some needlepoint mottling on beach mottles is not evident, and it retains a relatively smooth surface.

(2) Some needlepoint mottling on beach mottles is clearly evident, and presents as pin points. In general, the more congested the distribution of needlepoint mottling, the more evident its pitting and darker its coloration.

(3) The irregularly shaped openings in the beach mottle are glass phase, which is clearly higher than the surrounding beach mottle.

(4) The gradation between the mottle edge and the surrounding glass phase is uniform.

See pictures 6-1-13 and 6-1-14, where 6-1-13 is the two-dimensional and 6-1-14 is the three-dimensional image of the same location.

The brown beach mottle in picture 6-1-13 is the light colored area of 6-1-14. The portion indicated by Arrow A which has little or no needlepoint mottling, is relatively smooth and clean.

The white frosted needlepoint mottling in picture 6-1-13 is the dark colored area of 6-1-14. The needlepoint mottling indicated by Arrow B forms pin points of crowded distribution resembling cinder.

See pictures 6-1-15 and 6-1-16, where 6-1-15 is the two-dimensional and 6-1-16 is the three-dimensional image of the same location.

The brown beach mottle in picture 6-1-15 is the dark colored area of 6-1-16. The mottle edge is evident. The needlepoint mottle distribution is not clear, and there are no evident pin points. The surface of the mottle is relatively smooth, and the gradation from the edge of the mottle to the glass phase is uniform.

See pictures 6-1-17 and 6-1-18, where 6-1-17 is the two-dimensional and 6-1-18 is the three-dimensional image of the same location.

The dark glass phase opening in picture 6-1-17 is the light colored area of 6-1-18 indicated by Arrow C. It is higher than the surrounding mottle. As the weathering severity of the glass phase is less evident, the raised area C retains a clean and smooth surface. It has a clear delineation with the surrounding

图6-1-12

b. 沙滩斑三维特征

I. 有的沙滩斑上针眼斑不明显，沙滩斑较光滑。

II. 有的沙滩斑上有针眼斑，表现为独立的点状凹坑。一般来说，针眼斑分布越密集，凹坑越明显，颜色越深。

III. 沙滩斑中心的玻璃相圆孔高于沙滩斑，二者有明显的高度差。

IV. 沙滩斑边沿与玻璃相过渡平润。

见图6-1-13、图6-1-14，二者为同一器物同一位置图片，图6-1-13为二维图片，图6-1-14为三维图片。

图6-1-13中的褐色沙滩斑在图6-1-14中呈浅色，成像清晰。沙滩斑上无针眼斑或针眼斑较稀疏处显得干净细腻（见箭头A所指处）。

图6-1-13中的白色磨砂针眼斑在图6-1-14中呈深色，成像清晰。针眼斑呈独立的点状凹坑，分布密集处形貌如微小细碎的煤渣（见箭头B所指处）。

见图6-1-15、图6-1-16，二者为同一器物同一位置图片，图6-1-15为二维图片，图6-1-16为三维图片。

图6-1-15中的褐色沙滩斑在图6-1-16中呈深色，可见斑块轮廓。沙滩斑上针眼斑分布并不明显，不见针眼斑形成的点状凹坑，沙滩斑表面较光滑。沙滩斑边沿与玻璃相过渡平润。

见图6-1-17、图6-1-18，二者为同一器物同一位置图片，图6-1-17为二维图片，图6-1-18为三维图片。

图6-1-17中的深色玻璃相圆孔在图6-1-18中呈浅色，位置高出沙滩斑，成像清晰（见箭头C所指处）。玻璃相风化作用不明显，因此圆孔C表面光滑洁净，与周围沙滩斑界线分明。

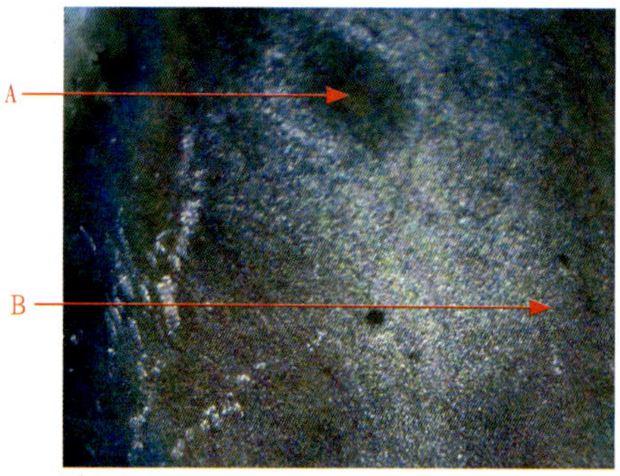

图6-1-13

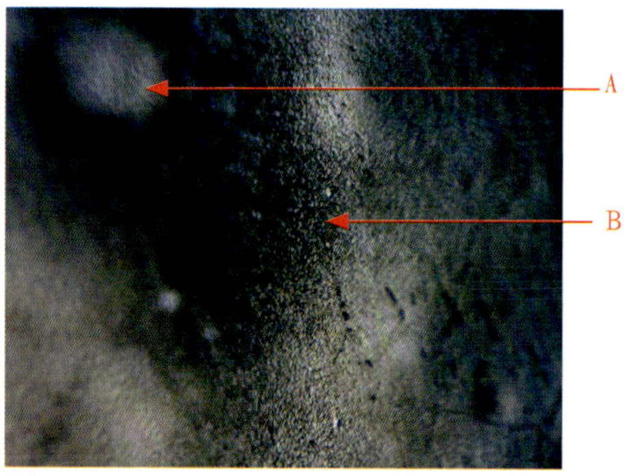

图6-1-14

图6-1-15

图6-1-16

beach mottle.

See pictures 6-1-19 and 6-1-20, where 6-1-19 is the two-dimensional and 6-1-20 is the three-dimensional image of the same location.

The dark glass phase opening in picture 6-1-19 is the light colored area of 6-1-20 indicated by Arrow D. The beach mottle surrounding glass phase opening D is a markedly lower depression, and the delineation between the two is evident.

After the Iron Oxide on beach mottles weathers, it is difficult for it to adhere to the glaze surface, and is easily corroded away. After a long period of weathering and corrosion, the beach mottle gradually forms a concave depression, lower than the surrounding glass phase.

b. Radiating Mottle

i. Radiating Mottle Defined

Formed during the firing of YUB, Radiating Mottles are the irregular shaped appearances across the glaze surface and within the glaze level, which have a crystallized, radiating form.

ii. Formation of Radiating Mottles

During the firing of YUB, cobalt-blue dye and glaze gradually transition into a molten state. Due to the buoyancy and movement of the air bubbles within the glaze level, the Iron and Manganese Oxides (or mullite, feldspar and so forth compounds) within the glaze and dye, under the effect of surface tension, accumulate together. A portion of these Oxides accumulate around air bubbles and is then carried to and dispersed across the uneven surface of the glaze, crystalize, and can form into spilt phases. As the temperature drops, more crystallization occurs throughout the glaze level.

According to their composition, density, and surface tension differences, they present with alternate appearances and colors of radiating mottles across the surface of the glaze or within the glaze level.

Additionally, the firing atmosphere within the kiln can also affect the composition of the radiating mottle. In a relatively strong reducing atmosphere, Iron Oxides form as Fe_3O_4 crystallizations, with black coloration. When there is a high amount of these crystallizations and their surface areas extends across the surface of the glaze, there is a gunmetal coloration observable by the naked eye. In an oxidation atmosphere or relatively weak reducing atmosphere environment, Iron Oxides crystallize as Fe_2O_3 and have a brown or yellow coloration.

iii. Types of Radiating Mottles

Radiating mottles can be divided into five color series: white series, red series, yellow series, brown series and black series.

Almost all radiating mottles have certain amounts of Iron and Manganese Oxides, white series being the exception with little or none. Due to the differences in Iron and Manganese valance, composition, and density, as well as the degree to which they receive glaze protection, these mottles present with various colors and appearances.

iv. Distribution of Radiating Mottles

In general, radiating mottles occur in areas of cobalt-blue dye; primarily areas of dense decoration (see pictures 6-1-21—6-1-24) or in conjunction with flowing mottles, and only vary rarely occur in areas without dye.

White series mottles most often appear within the glaze level. Red series often occur in association with flowing mottles and in areas of dense decoration. Yellow series often present in association with iodine mottles or areas of dense decoration within the glaze level. Brown series often occur across the surface of the glaze, and receive relatively low glaze level protection from weathering. Black series are distributed according to the following circumstances:

(1) Within an area of iodine mottle, receiving relatively high glaze level protection, and retaining its original post-firing inherent characteristics;

(2) On the surface of the glaze, in association with flowing mottles;

(3) On the surface of the glaze, over the top of yellow series radiating mottles;

(4) On the surface of the glaze, over the top of brown series radiating mottles.

v. Characteristics of Radiating Mottles

(a) White Series Radiating Mottles

White series radiating mottles have a primarily white coloration, and can be split into the two following groups:

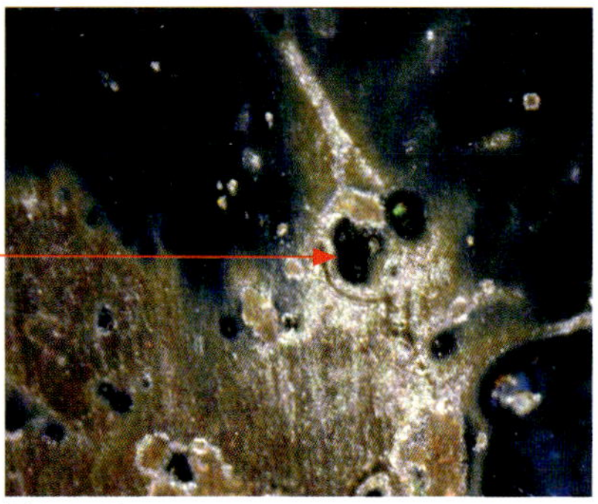

图6-1-17

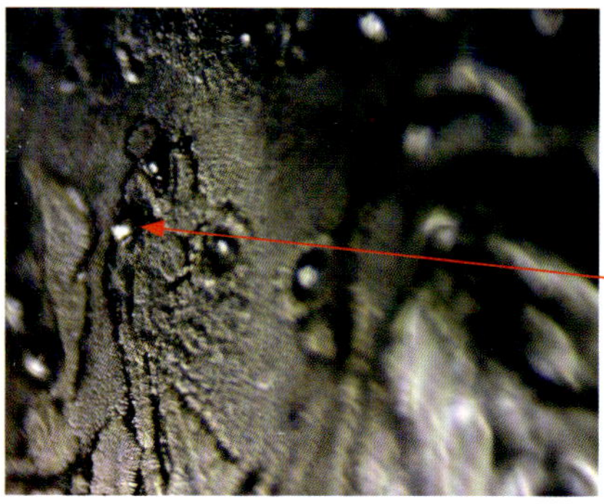

图6-1-18

见图6-1-19、图6-1-20，二者为同一器物同一位置图片，图6-1-19为二维图片，图6-1-20为三维图片。

图6-1-19中的深色玻璃相圆孔在图6-1-20中呈浅色，成像清晰（见箭头D所指处）。圆孔D周围的沙滩斑明显低于圆孔，呈凹陷状，二者之间界线分明。

沙滩斑上的铁氧化物风化后，不易附着在釉表面，较易脱落。在长时间的风化与脱落后，沙滩斑逐渐变成凹下去的“洼地”，低于周围玻璃相。

（2）放射斑

① 放射斑概念

放射斑是具有放射感的析晶斑块。它是元青花瓷器在烧制过程中，在其釉表面及釉层中形成的。

② 放射斑形成

元青花瓷器在高温烧制时，青料及釉料会逐渐熔化成熔融态，在浮力、表面张力及气泡搅动的作用下，釉料以及青料中的铁氧化物和锰氧化物（或莫来石、长石等物质）易在气泡边缘积聚，部分会随气泡升至釉表面，并结晶析出，也可能产生分相。当温度下降时，会有更多结晶析出。由于放射斑的成分、密度和表面张力不同，会在釉表面、釉层中形成不同形貌、不同颜色的放射斑。

此外，窑内的烧制气氛也会影响放射斑的成分。在较强的还原气氛下，铁氧化物大都会形成Fe_3O_4晶体，颜色为黑色，当析出的Fe_3O_4晶体较大，且晶面大多平行于釉表面时，用肉眼就可以看见锡光。在氧化气氛或弱还原气氛下，铁氧化物形成的晶体大都为Fe_2O_3晶体，颜色有褐色或黄色等。

③ 放射斑分类

放射斑可分成五大色系：白色系、红色系、黄色系、褐色系及黑色系。

除白色系放射斑不含或含极少铁氧化物和锰氧化物之外，大部分放射斑都一定程度地含有铁氧化物和锰氧化物。由于铁和锰的价位、结构及浓度的不同，加之受釉层保护程度不同，这些放射斑呈现颜色及形貌差异。

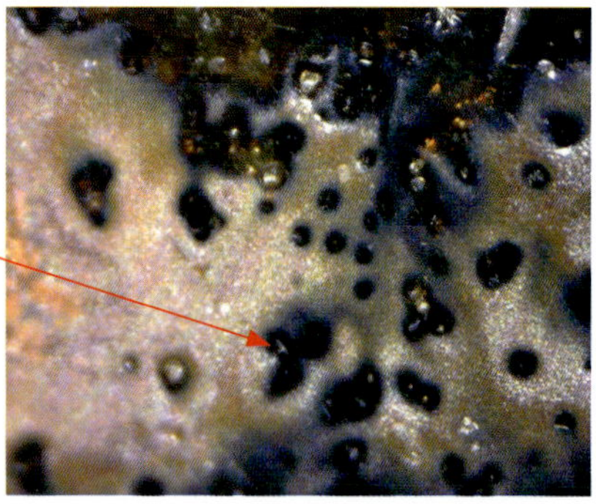

图6-1-19

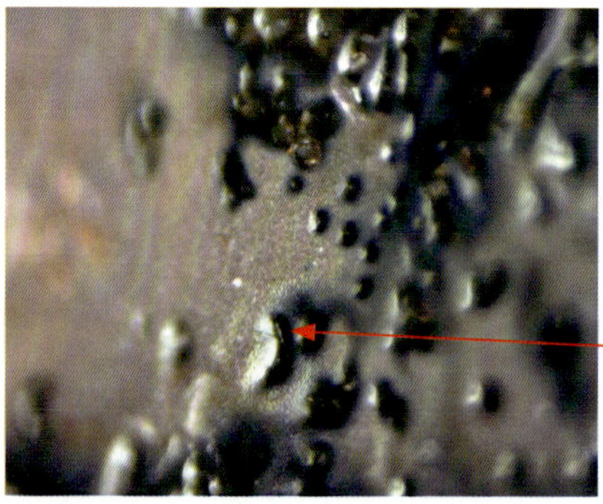

图6-1-20

Chrysanthemum Shape and Pine Needle Shape

(i) Two-dimensional Characteristics of Chrysanthemum Radiating Mottles

See pictures 6-1-21 and 6-1-22.

(1) Shape similar to that of a chrysanthemum flower, with a radiating feel.

(2) Mottle center muddled, with an overall blurred appearance.

(ii) Two-dimensional Characteristics of Pine Needle Radiating Mottles

The mottle's 'pine needle' widths are not consistent, and can intermingle and overlap (see pictures 6-1-23—6-1-26).

(b) Red Series Radiating Mottles

(i) Two-dimensional Characteristics of Red Series

(1) Colors primarily range within rust, blood orange, and tangerine (see pictures 6-1-27—6-1-30).

(2) Often seen in a maple leaf shape (see pictures 6-1-27 and 6-1-28), but can also assume an irregular shape (see pictures 6-1-29 and 6-1-30).

(3) Receiving a relatively low amount of glaze protection, they are relatively easily weathered allowing for needlepoint mottling over the mottle (see Needlepoint Mottle Heading of this section).

(ii) Three-dimensional Characteristics of Red Series

(1) Mottle borders clearly delineated.

(2) Some mottle surfaces present with fine texturized striations, some are smooth and reflective.

(3) Most of the radiating mottles are higher than that of the surrounding beach mottle, and there is a clearly delineated border between the two.

See pictures 6-1-31 and 6-1-32, where 6-1-31 is the two-dimensional and 6-1-32 is the three-dimensional image of the same location.

The tangerine-colored maple leaf shaped mottle in picture 6-1-31 is the clearly delineated light-colored leaf shape in picture 6-1-32 as indicated by Arrow A. Mottle A is higher than the surrounding beach mottle, and is clearly delineated from it.

See pictures 6-1-33 and 6-1-34, where 6-1-33 is the two-dimensional and 6-1-34 is the three-dimensional image of the same location.

The rust colored radiating mottle in picture 6-1-33 is the clearly delineated light colored shape in picture 6-1-34 as indicated by Arrow B. The mottle is reflective and slightly concave, with a smooth appearance.

(c) Yellow Series Radiating Mottles

(i) Two-dimensional Characteristics of Yellow Series

(1) Colorations fall within the bright to dark yellow spectrum.

(2) Some pine needle shaped (see picture 6-1-35), but most are of irregular shape and appearance (see pictures 6-1-36—6-1-41).

(3) Some mottle edge colorations gradually diffuse into semi-transparent, and lose their radiating character (see picture 6-1-37 and 6-1-39).

(4) The mottle edge often has a lined border. The borders are usually thin and delicate in appearance and rarely attain any relative thickness, but all retain clear distinction. The border retains a certain distance from the edge of the mottle and the glass phase can be seen between the mottle and its lined border (see pictures 6-1-36 and 6-1-37).

(5) They can present in conjunction with white (see picture 6-1-35) and or red series radiating mottles (see picture 6-1-40).

(6) These mottles receive a relatively high amount of glaze protection, and as such are not easily weathered and can retain their original post-firing characteristics. However, it is possible for the glass phase surrounding these mottles to present with needlepoint mottling (see Needlepoint Mottle Heading of this section).

(ii) Three-dimensional Characteristics of Yellow Series

(1) These mottles are present within the glaze level, receiving relatively high glaze protection. As such, their

④ 放射斑分布

一般来说，放射斑都出现在有青料处，这包括蓝色色浓处（图6-1-21—图6-1-24）或流淌斑处，极少数会出现在没有青料的地方。

白色系放射斑通常出现在釉层中；红色系放射斑通常与流淌斑同时出现，有时出现在蓝色色浓处；黄色系放射斑通常与碘酒斑同时出现在釉层中，有时出现在蓝色色浓处的釉层中；褐色系放射斑通常出现在釉表面，受到的釉层保护程度较低。

黑色系放射斑的分布有以下几种情况：

A. 位于釉层中碘酒斑处，受釉层保护程度较高，基本保持刚烧制出来的原态；

B. 位于釉表面，与流淌斑并存；

C. 位于釉表面，出现在黄色系放射斑上；

D. 位于釉表面，出现在褐色系放射斑上。

⑤ 放射斑特征

A. 白色系放射斑

白色系放射斑颜色主要为白色。白色系放射斑又可分为菊花形及松针形放射斑。

a. 菊花形放射斑二维特征

见图6-1-21、图6-1-22。

I. 菊花形放射斑形状像菊花，具有放射感。

II. 放射斑中心核模糊，整体呈绒状。

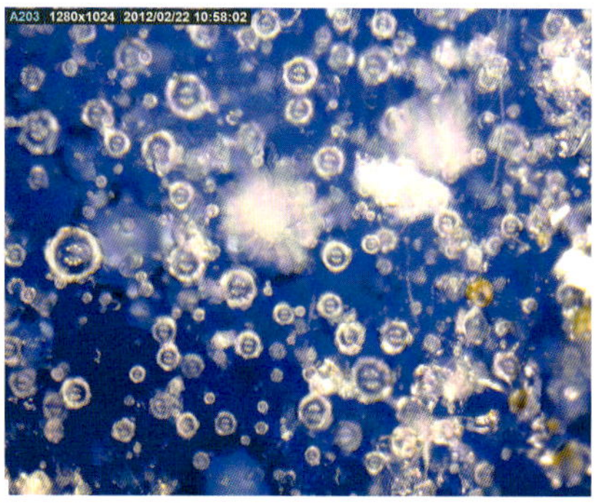

图6-1-21

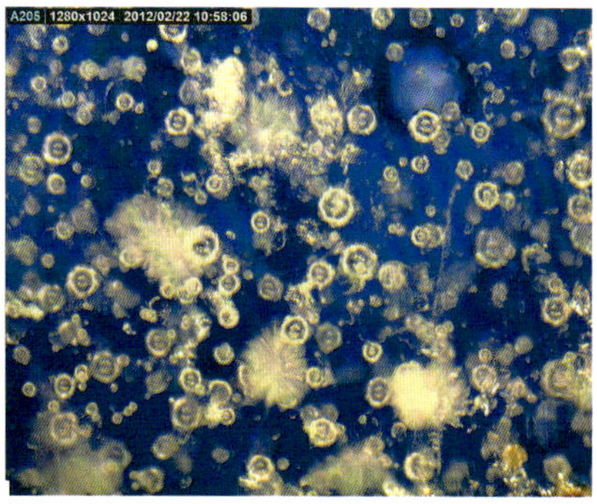

图6-1-22

b. 松针形放射斑二维特征

松针形放射斑的“松针”粗细不一，互叠交错（见图6-1-23—图6-1-26）。

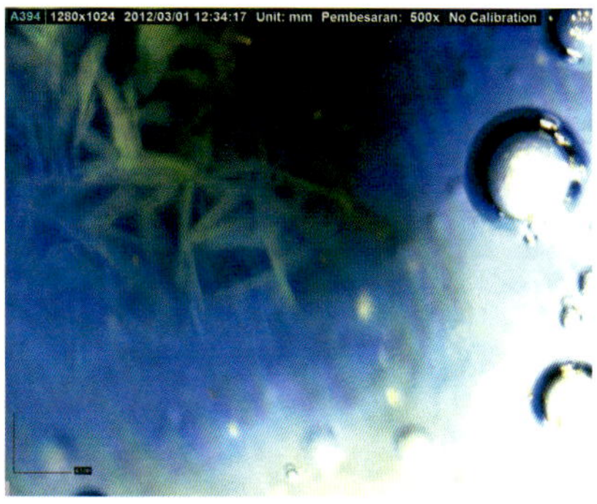

图6-1-23

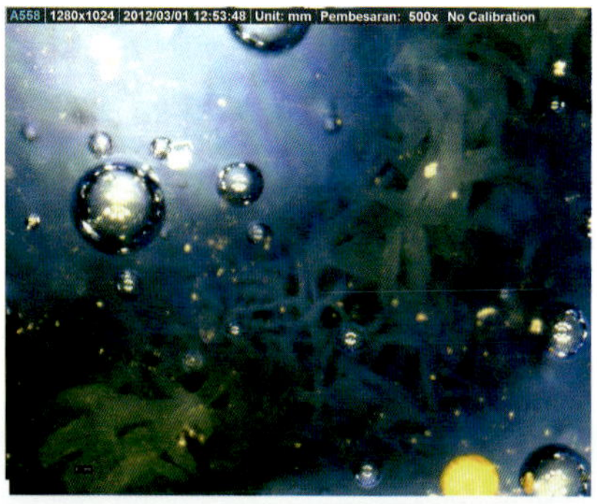

图6-1-24

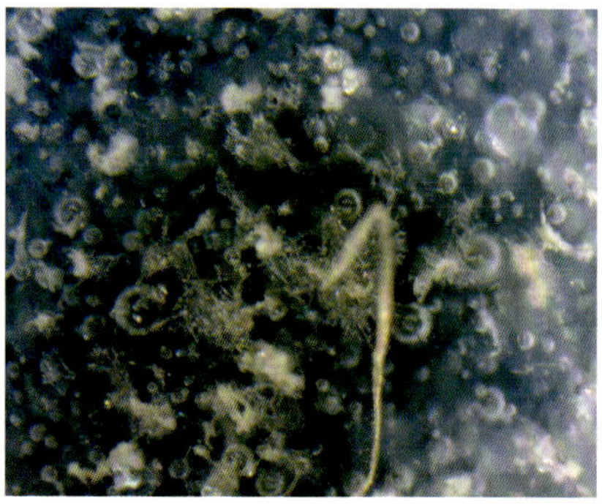
图6-1-25

图6-1-26

B. 红色系放射斑

a. 红色系放射斑二维特征

I. 红色系放射斑的颜色以铁红和橘红色为主，也有橘黄色（见图6-1-27—图6-1-30）。

II. 红色系放射斑常见有枫叶形（见图6-1-27、图6-1-28），也有其他不规则形状（见图6-1-29、图6-1-30）。

III. 受釉层保护程度较低的红色系放射斑较易风化，有的放射斑上会出现针眼斑。（参见本章本节针眼斑部分）

图6-1-27

surface is often smooth and clean.

(2) The mottles have a slightly convex shape and present with a topographical unevenness with the surrounding glaze. The borders are clearly delineated.

See pictures 6-1-42 and 6-1-43, where 6-1-42 is the two-dimensional and 6-1-43 is the three-dimensional image of the same location.

See pictures 6-1-44 and 6-1-45, where 6-1-44 is the two-dimensional and 6-1-45 is the three-dimensional image of the same location.

Mottles indicated by Arrows C and D in pictures 6-1-42 and 6-1-44 respectively, are of lighter color and are clearly visible with a smooth surface in pictures 6-1-43 and 6-1-45. Mottles C and D are both within the glaze level, but have a convex shape that is clearly higher and well delineated from the surrounding glaze surface.

(d) Brown Series Radiating Mottles

(i) Two-dimensional Characteristics of Brown Series

(1) Coloration primarily consists of a coffee-like color with an irregular shape.

(2) Some mottles do not have a lined border (see pictures 6-1-46, 6-1-53, and 6-1-54).

(3) Some mottles have a lined border. The border is usually thin and delicate in appearance and rarely attains any relative thickness, but retain clear distinction. The border often retains a certain distance from the edge of the mottle and the glass phase can be seen between the mottle and its lined border (see pictures 6-1-47—6-1-51), sometimes the glass phase is not visible (see picture 6-1-52).

(4) These mottles can rarely occur as a collective of relatively small and irregularly shaped mottles in conjunction with one another, rather than as an independent shape (see picture 6-1-53).

(5) Brown series mottles can occur in conjunction with yellow series (see pictures 6-1-50, 6-1-51, and 6-1-53), in conjunction with iodine and beach mottles (see pictures 6-1-50, 6-1-53, and 6-1-54), or in conjunction with just iodine mottles (see pictures 6-1-46—6-1-49, 6-1-51, and 6-1-52).

(6) Due to a relatively low amount of glaze protection, they are easily weathered and can present with needlepoint mottling on the mottle (see Needlepoint Mottle Heading of this section).

(ii) Three-dimensional Characteristics of Brown Series

(1) The surface of these mottles can present with fine striations, a clear radiation effect, or as granulated.

(2) In general, these mottles are higher than the surrounding glaze level or flowing mottles, and present with clearly delineated borders between them.

See pictures 6-1-55 and 6-1-56, where 6-1-55 is the two-dimensional and 6-1-56 is the three-dimensional image of the same location.

The brown series radiating mottle in picture 6-1-55 is the lighter colored mottle in picture 6-1-56. The mottle is clearly higher than the surrounding glaze and its surface is striated yet smooth and clear, and has a clearly delineated border with the surrounding glass phase.

See pictures 6-1-57 and 6-1-58, where 6-1-57 is the two-dimensional and 6-1-58 is the three-dimensional image of the same location.

The brown series radiating mottle in picture 6-1-57 is the lighter colored mottle with radiating effect in picture 6-1-58 as indicated Arrow E.

See pictures 6-1-59 and 6-1-60, where 6-1-59 is the two-dimensional and 6-1-60 is the three-dimensional image of the same location.

See pictures 6-1-61 and 6-1-62, where 6-1-61 is the two-dimensional and 6-1-62 is the three-dimensional image of the same location.

The brown series radiating mottles in pictures 6-1-59 and 6-1-61 are the lighter colored mottles in pictures 6-1-60 and 6-1-62. The mottles have a convex shape and their surfaces are striated yet smooth and clear, and have clearly delineated borders with the surrounding beach mottles.

See pictures 6-1-63 and 6-1-64, where 6-1-63 is the two-dimensional and 6-1-64 is the three-dimensional image of the same location.

The brown series radiating mottle in picture 6-1-63 is the lighter colored mottle in picture 6-1-64 as indicated by Arrow F. It appears as island cliffs rising up above the surrounding

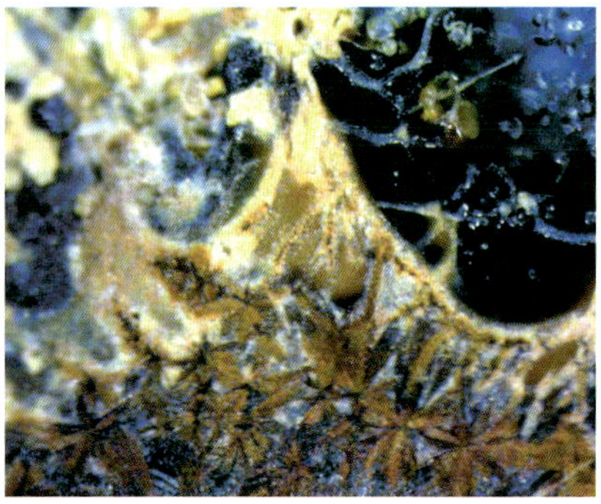
图6-1-28

图6-1-29

图6-1-30

b. 红色系放射斑三维特征

I. 红色系放射斑形状轮廓清晰。

II. 有的放射斑表面有细密纹路；有的较光滑，反光。

III. 放射斑大部分呈凸起状，与周围沙滩斑有高度差，界线分明。

见图6-1-31、图6-1-32，二者为同一器物同一位置图片，图6-1-31为二维图片，图6-1-32为三维图片。

图6-1-31中的橘黄色枫叶形放射斑在图6-1-32中呈浅色，枫叶形状清晰（见箭头A所指处）。斑块A整体凸起，并且与周围沙滩斑界线分明。

见图6-1-33、图6-1-34，二者为同一器物同一位置图片，图6-1-33为二维图片，图6-1-34为三维图片。

图6-1-33中的铁红色放射斑在图6-1-34中呈浅色，形状清晰（见箭头B所指处）。斑块B反光，略微下凹，显得平滑。

图6-1-31

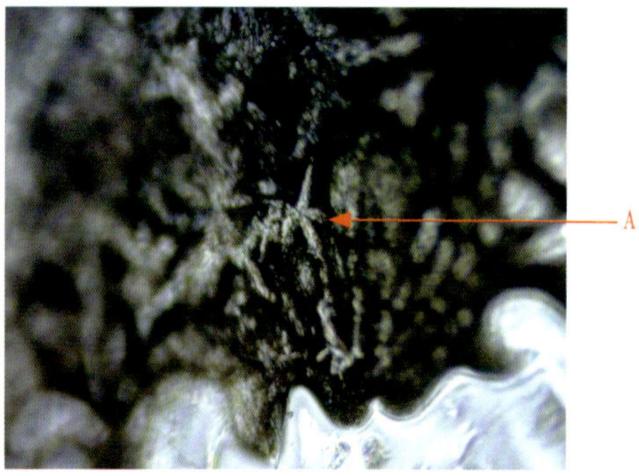

图6-1-32

图6-1-33

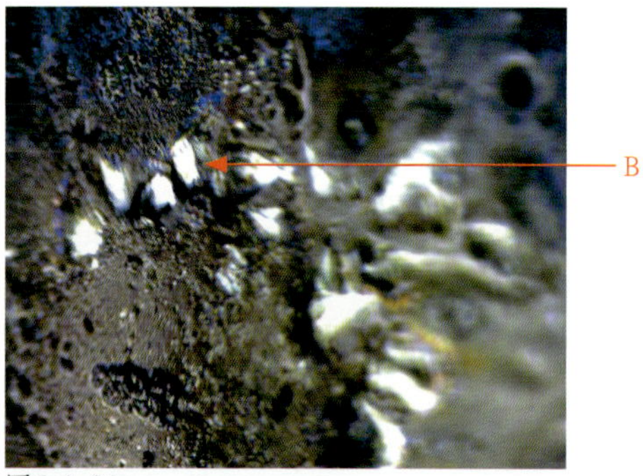

图6-1-34

glaze surface, and as such has a clearly delineated border.

(e) Black Series Radiating Mottles

(i) Two-dimensional Characteristics of Black Series

(1) Coloration is primarily black and the shape is irregular.

(2) Some black series mottles can have a granulated appearance with crowded (see pictures 6-1-65—6-1-67), or sparse granulation (see picture 6-1-69).

(3) Some mottles present with irregularly shaped elongated granules that can appear with surface striations of crowded distribution (see picture 6-1-73).

(4) Some mottles present irregularly shaped with jagged and radiating edges (see pictures 6-1-68, 6-1-70, and 6-1-72).

(5) Some mottles are at the surface of the glaze, receiving little glaze level protection, and are relatively easily weathered thus present with needlepoint mottling (see Needlepoint Mottle Heading of this section).

(ii) Three-dimensional Characteristics of Black Series

(1) Mottles within the glaze level are not clearly apparent under three-dimensional observation.

(2) Mottles presenting on the glaze surface present with a granulated texture; some with closely distributed accordion-like shapes, some with irregular shapes.

(3) Surface level mottles have a convex shape and are topographically uneven with the surrounding glaze.

See pictures 6-1-74 and 6-1-75, where 6-1-74 is the two-dimensional and 6-1-75 is the three-dimensional image of the same location.

The mottle indicated in picture 6-1-75 by Arrow G, is the convex wavy surface with smooth glaze covering. As such, weathering is not clearly evident.

See pictures 6-1-76 and 6-1-77, where 6-1-76 is the two-dimensional and 6-1-77 is the three-dimensional image of the same location.

The mottle indicated in picture 6-1-76 by Arrow H is the lighter colored individual convex granule in picture 6-1-77.

See pictures 6-1-78 and 6-1-79, where 6-1-78 is the two-dimensional and 6-1-79 is the three-dimensional image of the same location.

The black mottle in picture 6-1-78 is the lighter colored area in picture 6-1-79. The three-dimensional view of the mottle shows even more distinctly the clearly individual accordion-like striations on the surface of the mottle, which is higher than the surrounding glaze.

See pictures 6-1-80 and 6-1-81, where 6-1-80 is the two-dimensional and 6-1-81 is the three-dimensional image of the same location.

The black mottle in picture 6-1-80 is the raised light colored area in picture 6-1-81. The surface is distinct, and has some smooth and some rough portions.

c. Blotch Mottle

i. Blotch Mottle Defined

Formed during the firing of YUB, Blotch Mottles are those crystallized formations within the glaze level that have assembled into a clustered group but do not possess a radiating shape.

ii. Formation of Blotch Mottles

Blotch mottles are similar to the white series radiating mottles discussed earlier in that they are both formed by the crystallization of mullite (or feldspar and so forth compounds).

However, both white series and blotch mottles are rarely seen within YUB, due in part to the glaze recipes and techniques. Research by Chen Yao Cheng et al goes to show [221]: Only if the amount of Aluminum Oxide in the dye exceeds 18-20%, the fusion of dye and glaze can occur to create mullite or anorthite crystallizations. During high temperature firing, when utilizing Aluminum-rich blue dye to color underglaze blue porcelain, only a portion of the blue dye melts to create rich Aluminum blue coloration in the glass phase. During the cooling, at the dye-glaze fusion points, mullite and anorthite crystals can form. Because the majority of YUB samples do not have an Aluminum content exceeding 18%, these types of mottles are rarely seen; however, they become much more common on early Ming Dynasty pieces.

Additionally, since mullite crystallization is directly impacted by firing temperature, its presence indicates a firing

C. 黄色系放射斑

a. 黄色系放射斑二维特征

I. 黄色系放射斑包括淡黄、深黄等颜色。

II. 有的形如松针（见图6-1-35），其余大多数都属于不规则形貌一类（见图6-1-36—图6-1-41）。

III. 有的黄色系放射斑边沿颜色逐渐变浅，甚至呈半透明状，失去放射感（见图6-1-37、图6-1-39）。

IV. 放射斑边沿通常有一条包边，包边整体纤细、精致，少量的稍粗，但总体都是清晰的，与放射斑轮廓保持一致，放射斑与包边之间可见玻璃相（见图6-1-36、图6-1-37）。

V. 黄色系放射斑可以与白色系（见图6-1-35）或红色系放射斑同时存在（见图6-1-40）。

VI. 黄色系放射斑受釉层保护程度较高，不易风化，所以基本保持刚烧制出来的原态。但有时在黄色系放射斑所在处及周边的玻璃相上会出现针眼斑。（参见本章本节针眼斑部分）

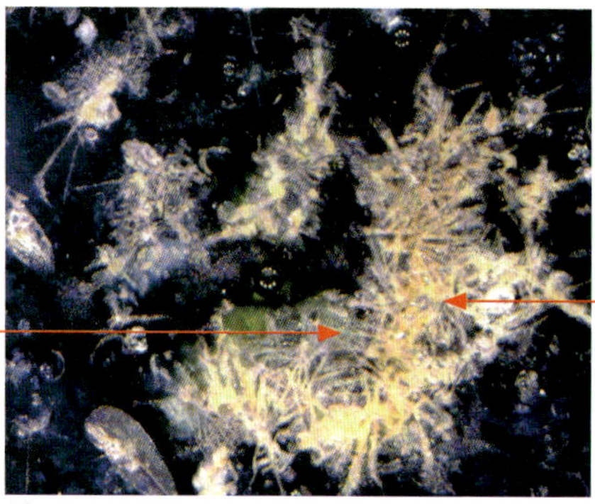

图6-1-35

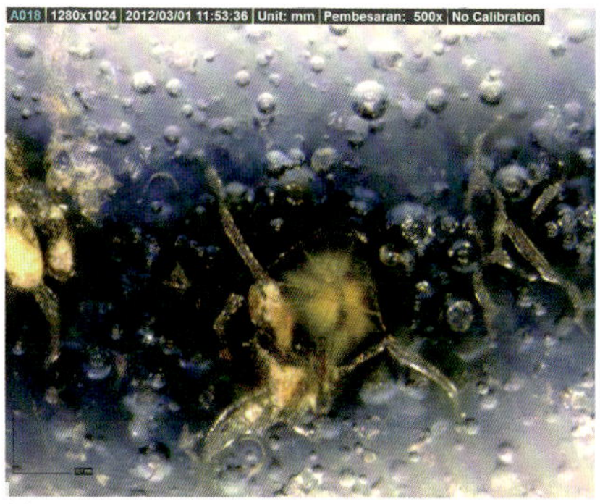

图6-1-36

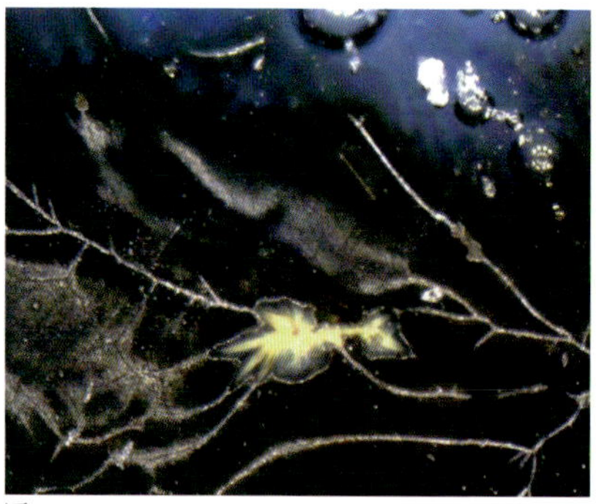
图6-1-37

图6-1-38

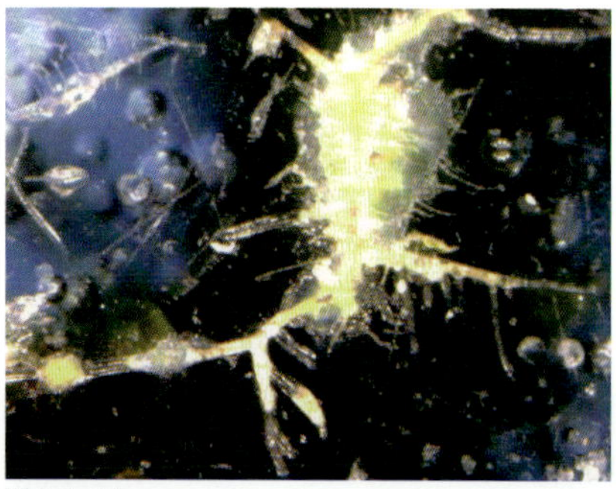
图6-1-39

图6-1-40

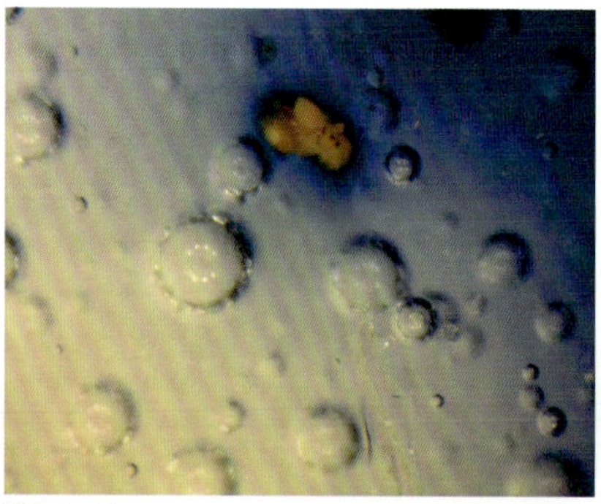
图6-1-41

temperature of over 1000℃ [222]. According to Chapter 3, Yuan artisans added Kaolin clay to the porcelain body mixture, which required an increase in firing temperature [223].

iii. Characteristics of Blotch Mottles

Two dimensional Characteristics of Blotch Mottles

See pictures 6-1-82 and 6-1-83.

(1) Blotch mottles appear in the shape of smooth stones, with white and yellow being the primary colors.

(2) Portions of mottles can present as translucent, while others are not translucent.

(3) Some blotch mottles present with a single color (see picture 6-1-82) while some present with a color spectrum (see picture 6-1-83).

(4) Blotch mottles receive relatively high glaze protection, and as such have low weathering severity and are able to generally retain their inherent qualities.

d. Summary

The YUB body and glaze both have certain amounts of elemental Iron and Manganese, but the amount of Iron and Manganese in the cobalt-blue dye is higher.

There are different types and appearances of crystallization mottles; some spilling over onto the glaze surface and some existing only within the glaze level. Most of them occur in areas of dense blue dye, with the majority containing a certain amount of Iron and Manganese Oxides.

The multiplicity of appearances and colorations of crystallizations within mottles are dependent on the viscosity and thickness of the glaze as well as the surface tension, density, and valence of elemental Iron and Manganese within crystallizations or split phase components.

Note: All microscopic pictures of innate characteristics on YUB samples have undergone weathering; all of the observable qualities of innate mottles have experienced approximately eight hundred years of history. Even the most protected pieces of porcelain have undergone certain amounts of weathering. As we do not have the capability of entering back into the unique YUB firing environment, we can only use the pictures gained through microscopic observation in addition to current scientific knowledge to postulate the appearance and characteristics of the original inherent qualities.

B. Acquired YUB Mottle

I. Acquired YUB Mottle Defined

Acquired YUB Mottles are mottles of irregular shape and distribution on the glaze surface and within the glaze level of YUB that were formed under the influences of the post-firing environment.

II. Acquired YUB Mottle Types

a. Needlepoint Mottle

i. Needlepoint Mottle Defined

Needlepoint Mottles are a collection of relatively unified variation of size and depth, either amassed or independent, and randomly dispersed pits on the YUB glaze surface, formed under post-firing environment.

Generally, needlepoint mottles are first formed in areas on crystallization mottles without glaze coverage, in areas of glaze defect, or areas covered by soil or sand.

ii. Types of Needlepoint Mottles

Needlepoint mottles occur with random distribution, and can occur anywhere on the glaze surface; they can be divided into three types of appearances: Foggy, Frosted, and Grainy.

(a) Foggy Needlepoint Mottle

Two-dimensional Characteristics of Foggy Needlepoint Mottles

See pictures 6-1-84—6-1-86.

(1) They present with a fine, white, and evenly distributed foggy appearance.

(2) They often have a clear density gradation, and occur on areas of transition from beach mottle to glass phase.

(b) Frosted Needlepoint Mottle

Frosted Needlepoint Mottles can be further divided into two types:

The first type is the progression from foggy needlepoint mottles, with a higher density and severity of weathering, but also presenting on areas of exposed Iron or Manganese Oxide.

b. 黄色系放射斑三维特征

I. 黄色系放射斑位于釉层中，受釉层保护程度较高，通常表面显得光滑细腻。

II. 放射斑凸起，与周围釉表面有高度差，界线分明。

见图6-1-42、图6-1-43，二者为同一器物同一位置图片，图6-1-42为二维图片，图6-1-43为三维图片。

见图6-1-44、图6-1-45，二者为同一器物同一位置图片，图6-1-44为二维图片，图6-1-45为三维图片。

图6-1-42箭头C及图6-1-44中箭头D所指的黄色系放射斑在图6-1-43及图6-1-45中分别呈浅色，形状清晰可见，表面光滑细腻。放射斑C及放射斑D均位于釉层中，呈凸起状，与周围釉表面有明显高度差，且界线分明。

D. 褐色系放射斑

a. 褐色系放射斑二维特征

I. 褐色系放射斑主要是咖啡色，属于不规则形貌一类。

II. 有的褐色系放射斑没有包边（见图6-1-46、图6-1-53、图6-1-54）。

III. 有的褐色系放射斑边沿有包边，包边整体纤细、精致，少量的稍粗，但总体都是清晰的，放射斑与包边之间大部分时候可见玻璃相（见图6-1-47—图6-1-51），有时不可见（见图6-1-52）。

IV. 少数褐色系放射斑不是一整片出现，而是以多个面积较小、形状不一的斑块聚集在一起的形式出现（见图6-1-53）。

V. 褐色系放射斑既可以和黄色系放射斑组合（见图6-1-50、图6-1-51、图6-1-53），也可以与碘酒斑、沙滩斑组合（见图6-1-50、图6-1-53、图6-1-54），还可以单独与碘酒斑组合（见图6-1-46—图6-1-49、图6-1-51、图6-1-52）。

VI. 由于受釉层保护程度较低，褐色系放射斑较易风化，褐色系放射斑上会出现针眼斑。（参见本章本节针眼斑部分）

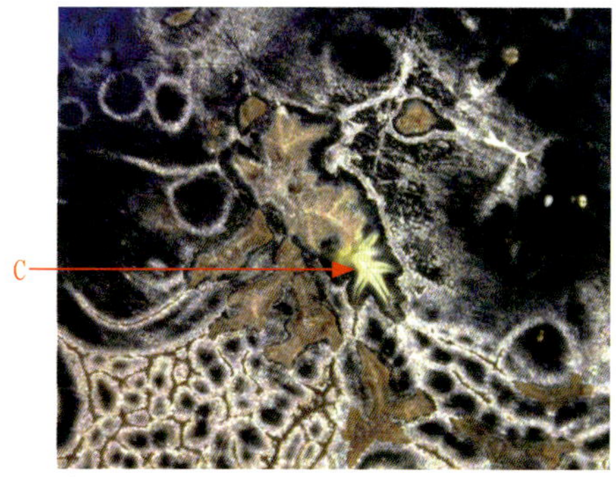

图6-1-42

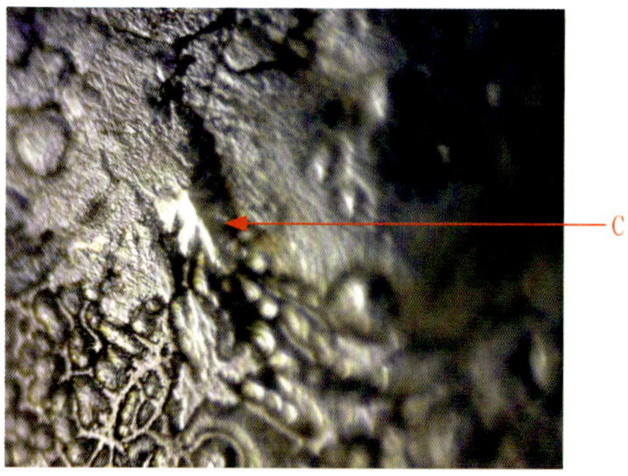

图6-1-43

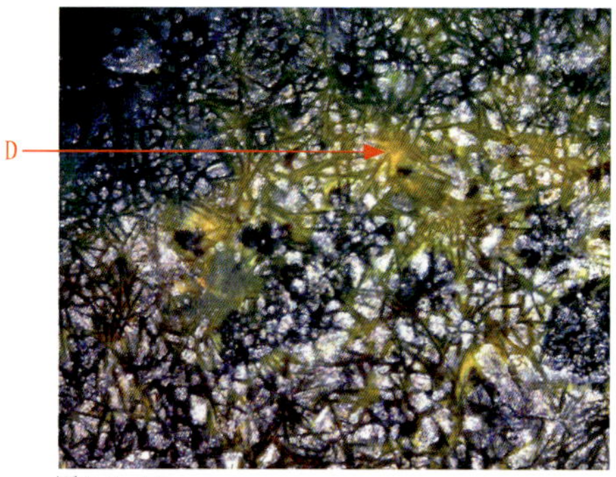

图6-1-44

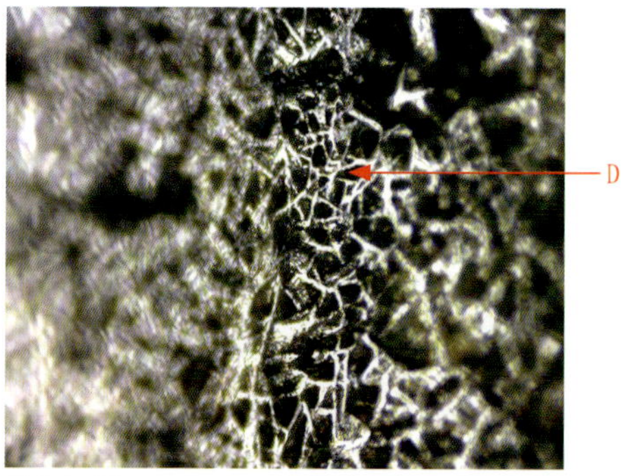

图6-1-45

The second type occurs in areas where Overlay Mottles have been cleaned away from the glaze surface, leaving frosted needlepoint mottles. For clarity sake, we refer to this type as overlay frosted needlepoint mottling.

Two-dimensional Characteristics of Frosted Needlepoint Mottles

(1) These mottles have a white coloration similar to sandblasted or frosted glass with pits larger than that of foggy needlepoint mottling. The weathering severity is higher than that of foggy needlepoint mottling, and in general, has a less dense to sparse gradation, but retains clear delineation (see pictures 6-1-87—6-1-90).

(2) Overlay mottles are also white and have random distribution and irregular shape. Normally not presenting with a density progression, they retain clearly delineated boundaries with the surrounding traces, similar to that of coastlines (see pictures 6-1-91 and 6-1-92).

(c) Grainy Needlepoint Mottle

Grainy Needlepoint Mottles can similarly be further divided into two types:

The first type also presents on exposed Iron or Manganese Oxidized areas with little or no glaze or in areas of glaze defect.

The second type occurs in areas where Overlay Mottles have been cleaned away from the glaze surface, leaving grainy needlepoint mottles. For clarity sake, we refer to this type as overlay grainy needlepoint mottling.

Two-dimensional Characteristics of Grainy Needlepoint Mottles

(1) Coloration is usually white or light yellow. Grainy needlepoint mottles are those with even deeper pits than that of foggy and frosted needlepoint mottles, large clearly delineated independent granules. The distribution density is usually lower than that of frosted and foggy needlepoint mottles (see pictures 6-1-93—6-1-98).

(2) Overlay grainy mottles present with similar coloration, occurring in relatively sparse or slightly denser distribution, but retaining independence and delineation from the surrounding traces (see picture 6-1-96).

(3) Some individual granules can present with a fine lined border. The interior granule is clear and independent with delineation from the surrounding traces (see pictures 6-1-97 and 6-1-98).

iii. Distribution of Needlepoint Mottling

(a) Needlepoint Mottling on Flowing Mottles

(i) Formation of Needlepoint Mottling on Flowing Mottles

Flowing mottles have a relatively high amount of Iron and Manganese, which are more susceptible to weathering change. After firing, the areas without any glaze covering are the first to undergo weathering change and form needlepoint mottles. Areas receiving protection from a thin glaze covering, when the glaze level encounters corrosion, can also present with needlepoint style weathering properties.

(ii) Two-dimensional Characteristics of Needlepoint Mottling on Beach Mottles

Needlepoint mottles appear white due to their refractive properties and are dispersed over beach mottles, with some areas dense and some areas sparse. In general, the needlepoint mottling does not extend past the boundaries of the flowing mottle, and needlepoint mottling generally does not present on sieve openings.

Generally, due to the fluid formation of beach mottles, the center of the mottle has a higher concentration of Iron and Manganese Oxides, and lower amount of glass phase. Whereas the edges of the mottles are the opposite, with higher glass phase and lower Iron and Manganese Oxide concentration. Needlepoint mottling distribution and density on beach mottles is directly impacted by the amount of glass phase protection. In the center portions of the mottle, where Iron and Manganese Oxide amounts are higher, the weathering severity is higher and mottling presents as the frosted needlepoint variety. Towards the edges of the mottle, as the glass phase proportion increases, weathering is less severe, thus mottling occurs as the foggy needlepoint variety.

This mottling regularity creates a three-to-four-color

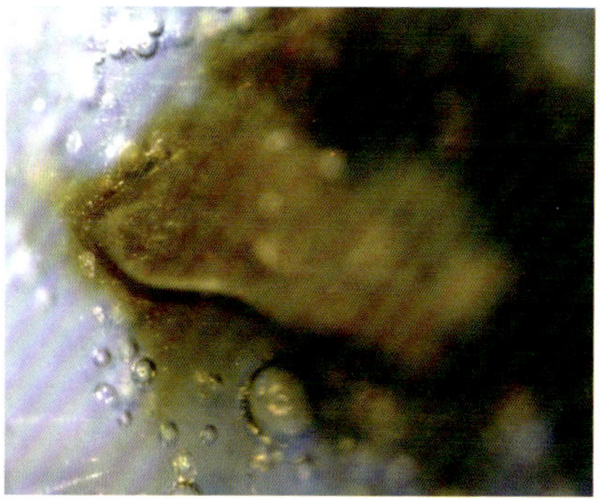
图6-1-46

图6-1-47

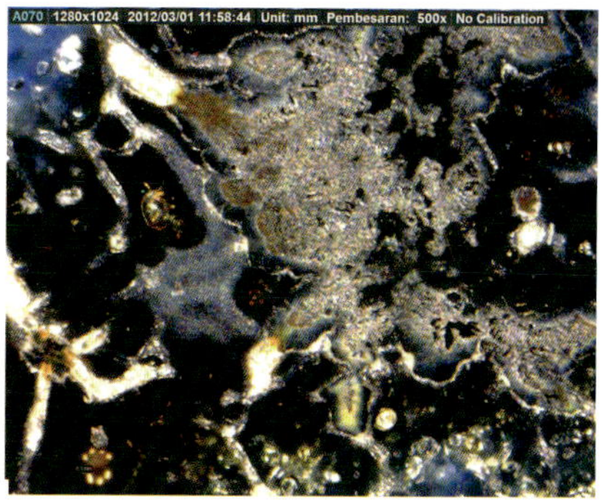

图6-1-48

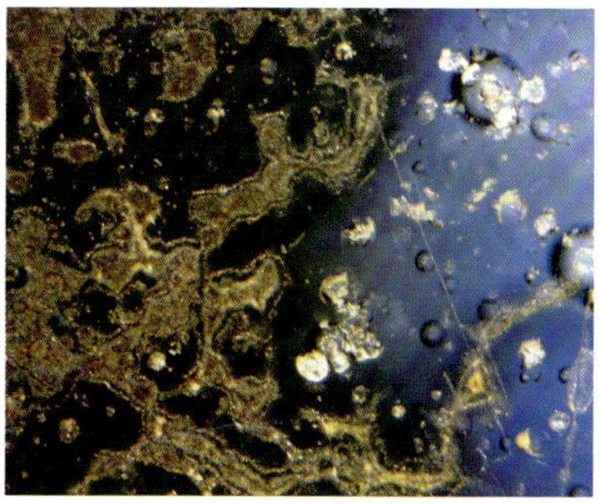
图6-1-49

图6-1-50

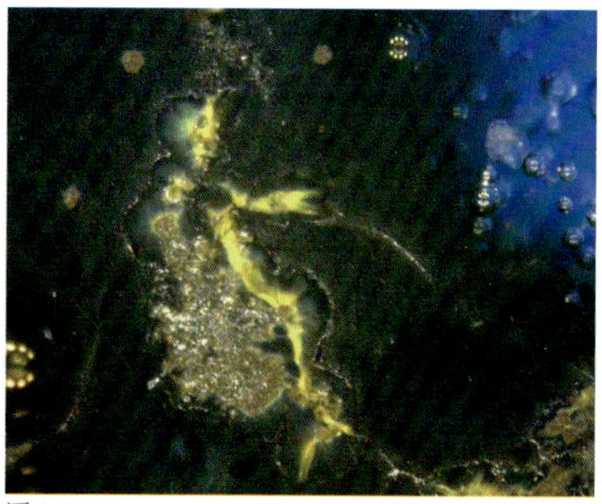
图6-1-51

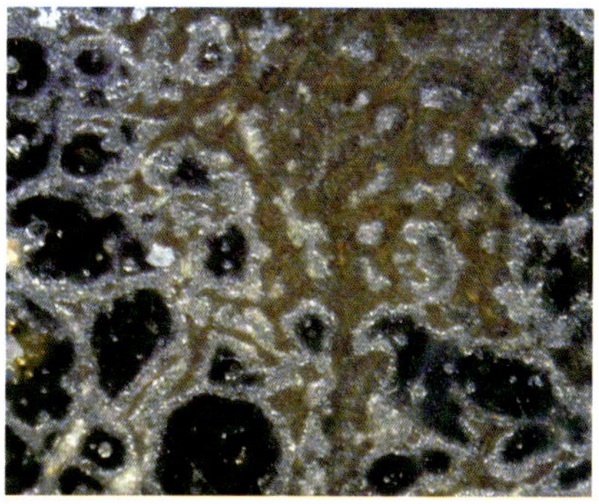
图6-1-52

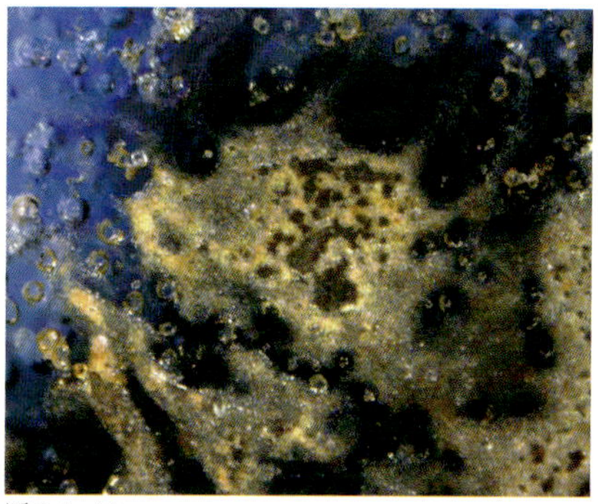
图6-1-53

图6-1-54

b. 褐色系放射斑三维特征

I. 有的褐色系放射斑表面有细密纹路，有的有明显放射感，有的呈颗粒状。

II. 一般来说，褐色系放射斑所处位置较周边玻璃相或流淌斑明显要高，彼此界线分明。

见图6-1-55、图6-1-56，二者为同一器物同一位置图片，图6-1-55为二维图片，图6-1-56为三维图片。

图6-1-55中的褐色系放射斑在图6-1-56中呈浅色，成像清晰。斑块明显高于釉表面，表面有细密纹路，但总体还是显得较平滑细腻，与周围玻璃相界线分明。

见图6-1-57、图6-1-58，二者为同一器物同一位置图片，图6-1-57为二维图片，图6-1-58为三维图片。

图6-1-57中的褐色系放射斑位于釉表面，在图6-1-58中呈浅色，可见放射形貌（见箭头E所指处）。

见图6-1-59、图6-1-60，二者为同一器物同一位置图片，图6-1-59为二维图片，图6-1-60为三维图片。

见图6-1-61、图6-1-62，二者为同一器物同一位置图片，图6-1-61为二维图片，图6-1-62为三维图片。

图6-1-59及图6-1-61中的褐色系放射斑在图6-1-60及图6-1-62中成像清晰，呈现浅色，表面有细密纹路，总体还是比较平滑细腻，斑块呈凸起状，高出周围沙滩斑，二者之间界线分明。

gradation on beach mottles from outside to inside: Dark Brown, Dark Blue, Light Brown, White (see pictures 6-1-99, 6-1-100, 6-1-102).

(1) Foggy Needlepoint Mottling

The fine misting distribution of foggy needlepoint mottling on the surface of the glaze resembles the spray of spray paint. The distribution more dense and coloration more white towards the center of the mottle, and distribution less dense and color lighter towards the edges, eventually fading to the coloration of the glass phase. Even though there is no clear delineation with the surrounding glass phase, there is a noticeablly uniform dense to sparse gradation (see pictures 6-1-99—6-1-102).

(2) Frosted Needlepoint Mottling

Frosted needlepoint mottling has a more dense coverage than that of foggy, and as such the coloration appears whiter. The mottling edge has a more defined border than that of the foggy variety, and in general has limited dense to sparse gradation. This mottling can present with very crowded density, or with widely sparse distribution, allowing visibility of the brown flowing mottle below (see pictures 6-1-99—6-1-106). Frosted needlepoint mottling can also occur on the outer edge of the underlying mottle (see pictures 6-1-105 and 6-1-106).

(3) Grainy Needlepoint Mottling

Grainy needlepoint mottling has a relatively low occurrence on beach mottles, and is much more sparsely distributed than foggy or frosted varieties, with clearly individual granules presenting (see picture 6-1-107).

(iii) Three-dimensional Characteristics of Needlepoint Mottling on Beach Mottles

(1) Foggy needlepoint mottling has a uniform gradation.

(2) In areas of sparse foggy mottling, characteristics are not highly visible; and areas of dense distribution are uniformly fine.

(3) Frosted mottling appears as dark colored pin points.

(4) Needlepoint mottle edges follow the general contours of the beach mottle, creating a border-like edge.

(5) The color gradation of beach mottles retains its clear and fine characteristics.

See pictures 6-1-108 and 6-1-109, where 6-1-108 is the two-dimensional and 6-1-109 is the three-dimensional image of the same location.

See pictures 6-1-110 and 6-1-111, where 6-1-110 is the two-dimensional and 6-1-111 is the three-dimensional image of the same location.

The foggy needlepoint mottling in pictures 6-1-109 and 6-1-111 both have even density gradation. Areas of sparse distribution (see Arrows A and D) have unobvious characteristics, and the surface retains its smooth qualities. Areas of denser distribution (see Arrows B and E) have uniform, fine, dense distribution.

The frosted needlepoint mottles with darker pin points indicated by Arrow C in picture 6-1-109 and Arrow F in 6-1-111 have a denser coverage and darker coloration than the foggy variety. The surface is notably more textured.

The edges of the mottling closely follow the general contour of the underlying beach mottle creating a coastline-like effect. The beach mottle as a whole is clean and clearly visible (see pictures 6-1-109 and 6-1-111).

The needlepoint mottling has regular distribution creating a color gradation from right to left, giving a layered effect (see picture 6-1-111).

See pictures 6-1-112 and 6-1-113, where 6-1-112 is the two-dimensional and 6-1-113 is the three-dimensional image of the same location.

The beach mottle in picture 6-1-112 is primarily covered with frosted needlepoint mottling; the white needlepoint mottling presents as clear darker colored pin points in picture 6-1-113.

The portion of the beach mottle in picture 6-1-112 that has not become covered by frosted needlepoint mottling is a lighter color in picture 6-1-113. This area has a lower weathering severity and retains its clean and smooth characteristics (see Arrow G).

The area of dark glass phase in picture 6-1-112 has light coloration in picture 6-1-113. It is higher than the neighboring beach mottle, as its weathering severity is lower, so its surface

褐色系放射斑
Brown Series Mottle

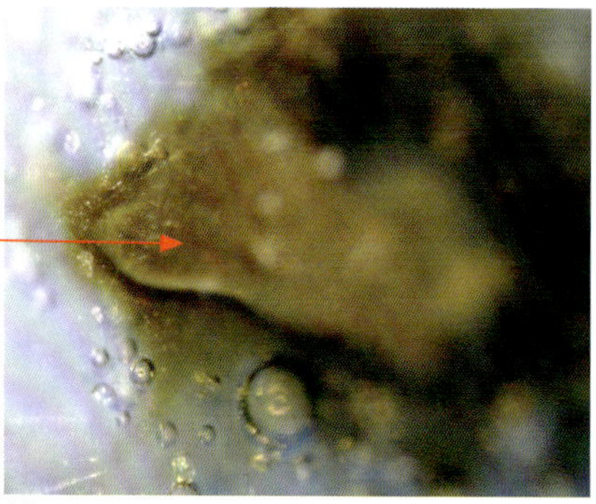

图6-1-55

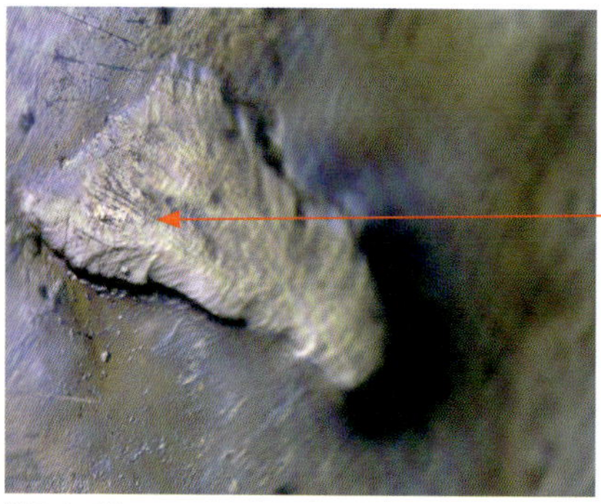

图6-1-56

褐色系放射斑表面有纹路，高出周围釉表面
Brown Series Mottle surface with fine crowded striations, higher than surrounding glaze surface

E

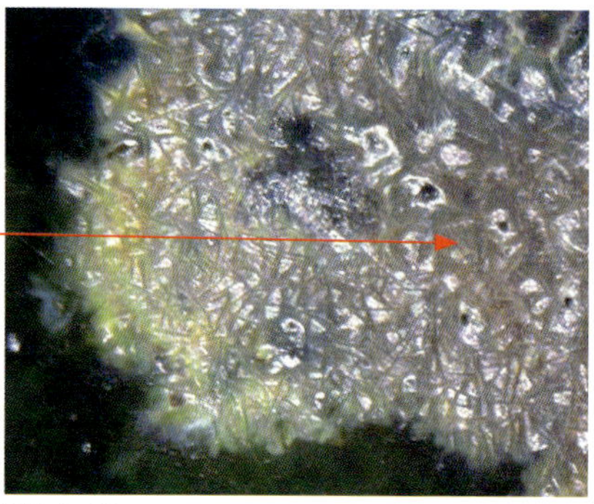

图6-1-57

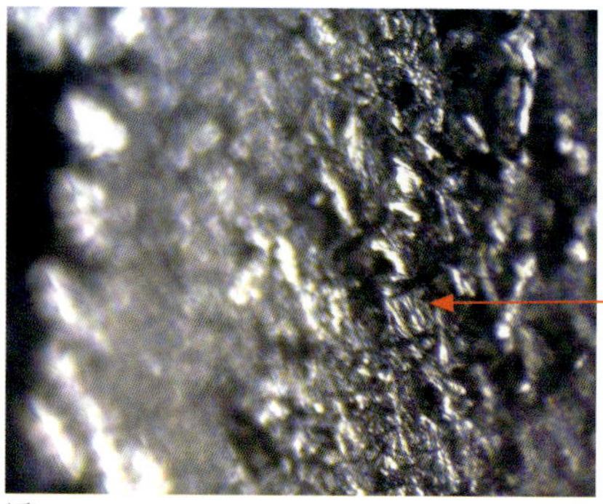

图6-1-58

E

褐色系放射斑
Brown Series Mottle

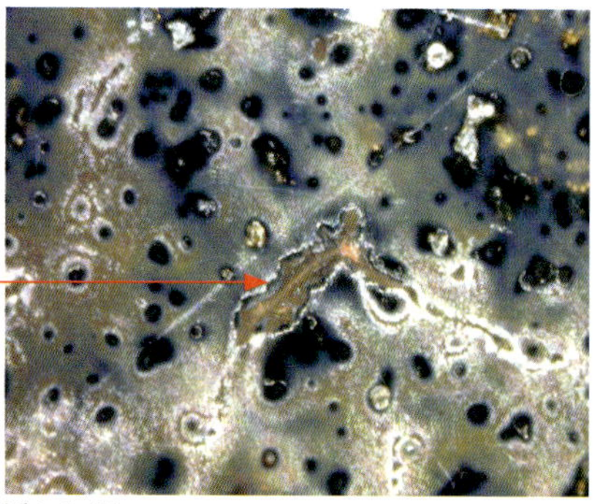

图6-1-59

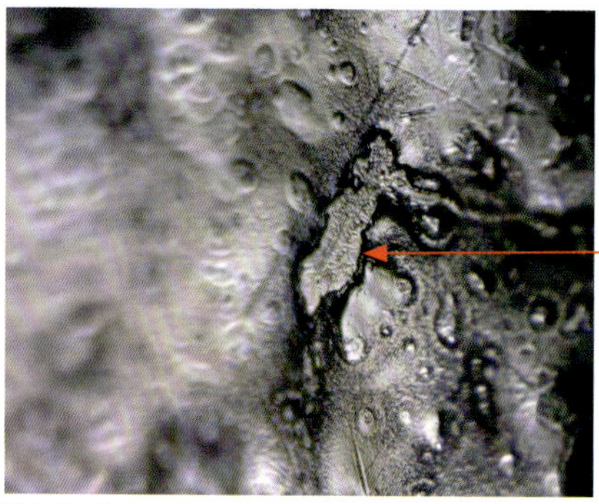

图6-1-60

褐色系放射斑表面有纹路，高出周围釉表面
Brown Series Mottle surface with fine crowded striations, higher than surrounding glaze surface

褐色系放射斑
Brown Series Mottle

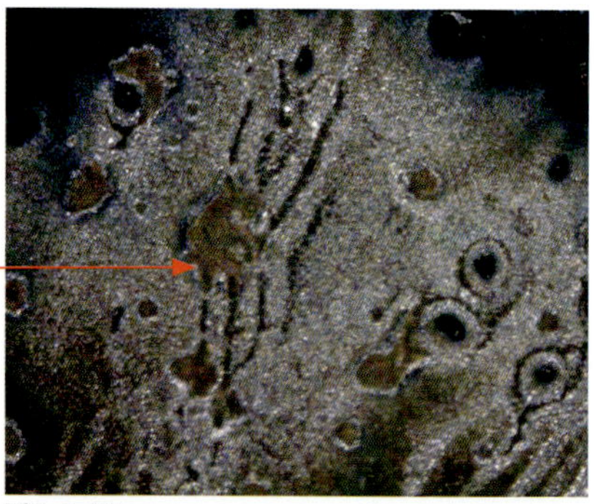

图6-1-61

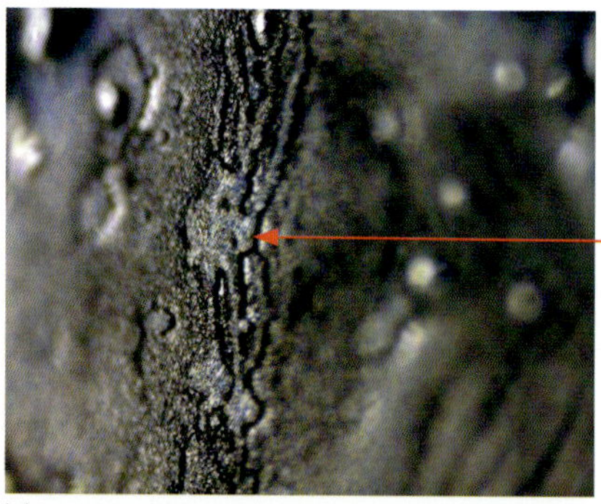

图6-1-62

褐色系放射斑表面有纹路，高出周围釉表面
Brown Series Mottle surface with fine crowded striations, higher than surrounding glaze surface

remains clean and smooth (see Arrow H).

(b) Needlepoint Mottling on Radiating Mottles

(i) Formation of Needlepoint Mottling on Radiating Mottles

Radiating mottles contain trace amounts of Iron and Manganese Oxide, which exposed, easily weathers. After firing, the areas of without any glaze covering are the easiest to undergo weathering and form needlepoint mottles. Areas receiving protection from a thin glaze covering, when the glaze level encounters corrosion, can also present with needlepoint style weathering properties.

(ii) Two-dimensional Characteristics of Needlepoint Mottling on Radiating Mottles

See pictures 6-1-114—6-1-116.

(1) Frosted needlepoint mottling has white coloration.

(2) Frosted needlepoint mottling lacks a density gradation.

(3) Frosted needlepoint mottling follows the shape of the radiating mottle crystallization, and generally does not exceed the edges of the radiating mottle.

(c) Needlepoint Mottling on Glass Phase

(i) Formation of Needlepoint Mottling on Glass Phase

Needlepoint Mottling on glass phase glaze occurs because of two main reasons:

First, areas on the glaze surface with exposed structural flaws; for example areas of split phasing are easily weathered and needlepoint mottling can occur.

Second, areas of the glaze surface that have undergone a long period of foreign material covering (i.e. dirt, soot, soil, etc.), when cleared away, often leave needlepoint mottling at the point of foreign material coverage. This type of needlepoint mottling is corrosion caused by the foreign material.

(ii) Two-dimensional Characteristics of Needlepoint Mottling on Glass Phase

(1) Grainy needlepoint mottling presents as white or with light yellow coloration, and mottles are independent and granule shaped. Granule pits are deeper and larger than that of the frosted variety, and distribution is generally sparser than that of frosted or foggy varieties (see pictures 6-1-117—6-1-124).

(2) Overlay frosted needlepoint mottles have white coloration, random distribution, and irregular shape. In general, they lack density gradation and present with an irregularly delineated border with the surrounding glass phase, similar to a coastline (see picture 6-1-122).

(3) Overlay grainy needlepoint mottles present with similar coloration, occurring in relatively sparse or slightly denser distribution, but retaining independence and delineation from the surrounding traces (see picture 6-1-123).

(4) Some individual granules can present with a fine lined border. The interior granule is clear and independent with delineation from the surrounding traces (see picture 6-1-124).

(iii) Three-dimensional Characteristics of Needlepoint Mottling on Glass Phase

(1) Granules are independent concave pits.

(2) Granules are delineated from the surrounding glass phase.

See pictures 6-1-125 and 6-1-126, where 6-1-125 is the two-dimensional and 6-1-126 is the three-dimensional image of the same location.

The white grainy needlepoint mottling in picture 6-1-125 is the clear points of dark coloration in picture 6-1-126. Granules are independent pin points, and are delineated from the surrounding glass phase.

b. Pit Mottle

i. Pit Mottle Defined

Pit Mottles (also called Pitting) are the irregularly shaped small depressions or pits on YUB glaze, caused by the post-firing environment, with non-uniform depth, size, and appearance.

ii. Formation of Pit Mottles

There are five main causes of Pit Mottles:

(a) The progression of 'C' and 'O' shaped striae: C and

见图6-1-63、图6-1-64，二者为同一器物同一位置图片，图6-1-63为二维图片，图6-1-64为三维图片。

图6-1-63中的褐色系放射斑在图6-1-64中呈浅色，独立清晰。像是凸起的岩石颗粒，高出周围釉表面，二者之间界线分明（见箭头F所指处）。

E. 黑色系放射斑

a. 黑色系放射斑二维特征

I. 黑色系放射斑中主要是黑色，属于不规则形貌一类。

II. 有的黑色系放射斑呈颗粒状，分布有密集（见图6-1-65—图6-1-67），有稀疏（见图6-1-69）。

III. 有的黑色系放射斑呈长条形，上面分布有密集的线条，在斑块上形成皱褶般的纹路（见图6-1-73）。

IV. 有的黑色系放射斑呈不规则形状，末端显尖锐，边沿有放射感（见图6-1-68、图6-1-70—图6-1-72）。

V. 黑色系放射斑大都位于釉表面，受釉层保护程度较低，较易风化，斑块上分布的针眼斑明显。（参见本章本节针眼斑部分）

b. 黑色系放射斑三维特征

I. 釉层中的黑色系放射斑三维特征不明显。

II. 釉表面的黑色系放射斑有的呈颗粒状、有的呈具有密集皱褶纹路的长条形、有的呈不规则形貌。

III. 釉表面的黑色系放射斑凸起，与周围釉表面有高度差。

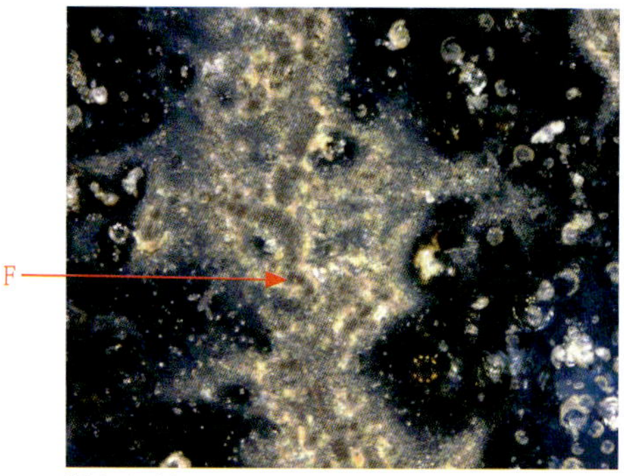

图6-1-63

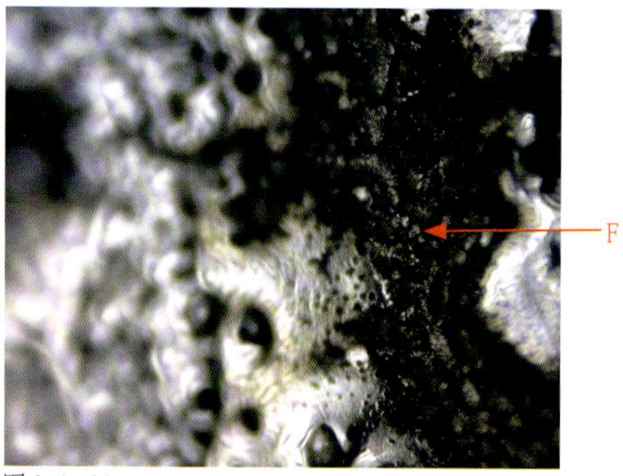

图6-1-64

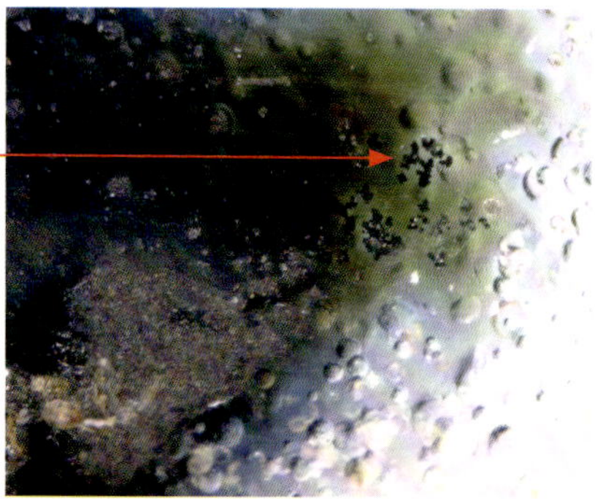

图6-1-65

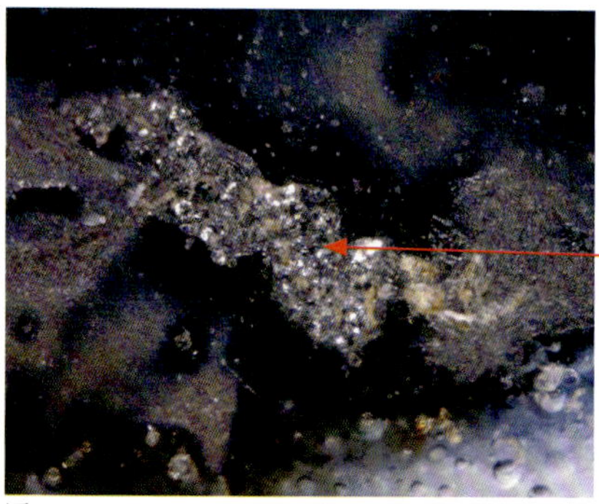

图6-1-66

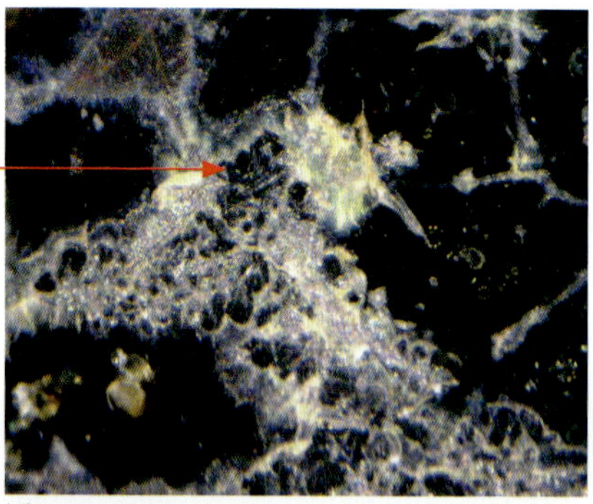

图6-1-67

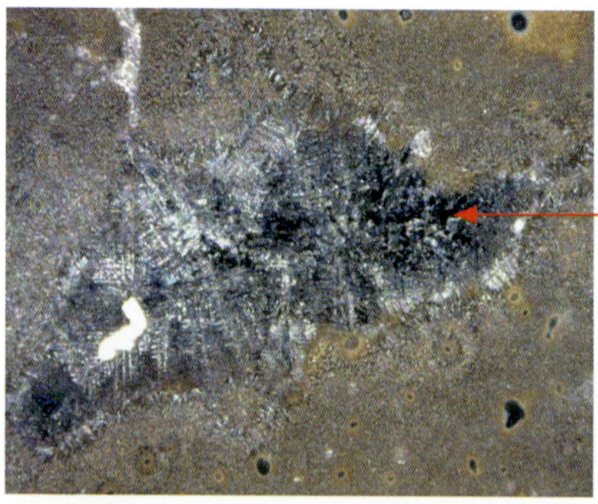

图6-1-68

O striae are crystallizations or split phases on the glaze surface, and their point of contact with the surrounding glass phase is structurally unstable; and as such, are easily weathered (see C and O Shaped Striae Heading of this section). As these C and O shaped striae continue to be weathered, they form pit mottles. These are referred to as CO Type Pit Mottles.

(b) The progression of needlepoint mottling: The further weathering of needlepoint mottles changes into pitting. These are referred to as Needlepoint Type Pit Mottles.

(c) Damage caused by external collision: This type of pitting is usually larger in surface area. These are referred to as Damage Type Pit Mottles.

(d) Overlay Material Corrosion: Once foreign materials are washed away, pitting can present. These are referred to as Overlay Type Pit Mottles.

(e) Long-term Underwater Submersion: Sustained underwater environments, such as shipwrecks, can cause glaze surface pitting. These are referred to as Underwater Type Pit Mottles.

Multiple types of pitting can occur simultaneously (see pictures 6-1-127—6-1-131).

iii. Characteristics of Pit Mottles

(a) CO type Pitting

(i) Two-dimensional Characteristics of CO Type Pitting

(1) Pits have alternating size, depth, and distance of separation from surrounding pits.

(2) C and O shaped striae are visible in conjunction with pits. These primarily appear in two forms: The first is in the close vicinity of C and O striae (see picture 6-1-132) mostly in a crescent form (see pictures 6-1-133—6-1-136) but also occurring in other shapes (see pictures 6-1-137 and 6-1-138), these shapes often retain clear delineation. The second is overlapping with C and O striae; both are clearly present, and sometimes the outline of the C and O striae are still observable (see pictures 6-1-139 and 6-1-140).

(3) Initially, these pits are independently distributed, but as weathering continues pits can become interlocked in a chain-like fashion. These spiraled pit chains often have an irregular shape (see pictures 6-1-141—6-1-143, 6-1-146, 6-1-147, 6-1-149).

(4) It is possible to observe C and O striae, individual pits, and pit groups concurrently in one unit image. Each trace is independent and retains clear delineation with the surrounding glass phase (see pictures 6-1-146—6-1-149).

(5) Coloration is primarily white or yellow. It is possible for the pits to have the same coloration as the C and O striae (see pictures 6-1-135, 6-1-137—6-1-140, 6-1-145—6-1-147), or different coloration (see pictures 6-1-133, 6-1-136, 6-1-148 and 6-1-149).

(6) It is possible for under the glaze floccus mottling to occur in conjunction with pits (see pictures 6-1-143, 6-1-144, 6-1-146 and Floccus Mottle Heading of this section).

(ii) Three-dimensional Characteristics of CO Type Pitting

(1) This type of pitting occurs primarily in areas of convex glaze surface.

(2) It is possible to only observe small, fine, reserved C and O striae on the glaze surface

(3) It is also possible to observe C and O striae as well as pit openings on the glaze surface with a smaller area than that of the two-dimensionally observable pit.

See pictures 6-1-150 and 6-1-151, where 6-1-150 is the two-dimensional and 6-1-151 is the three-dimensional image of the same location.

The pit indicated by the arrow in picture 6-1-150 is only observable as two C shaped striae in picture 6-1-151. The striae are fine and reserved, retaining independent delineation with the surrounding glass phase.

These pits are the result of weathering development of the C shaped striae, and extend down into the glaze level. Three-dimensional imaging is unable to observe the pit within the glaze level.

See pictures 6-1-152 and 6-1-153, where 6-1-152 is the two-dimensional and 6-1-153 is the three-dimensional image of the same location.

The pit indicated by the arrow in picture 6-1-152 is observable as a C shaped striation in picture 6-1-153. Additionally, two small dark pits, smaller than that of picture

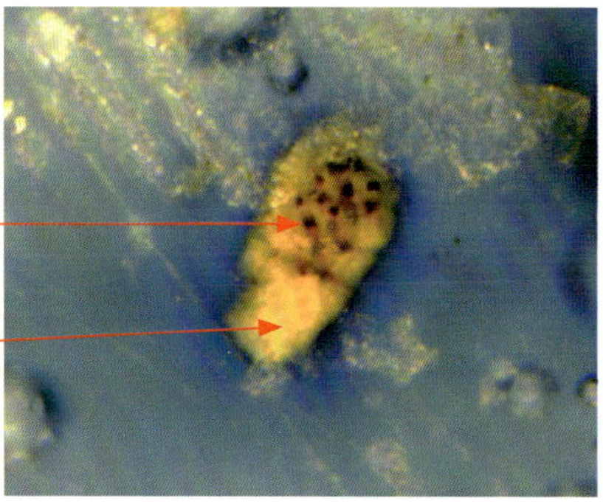

图6-1-69*

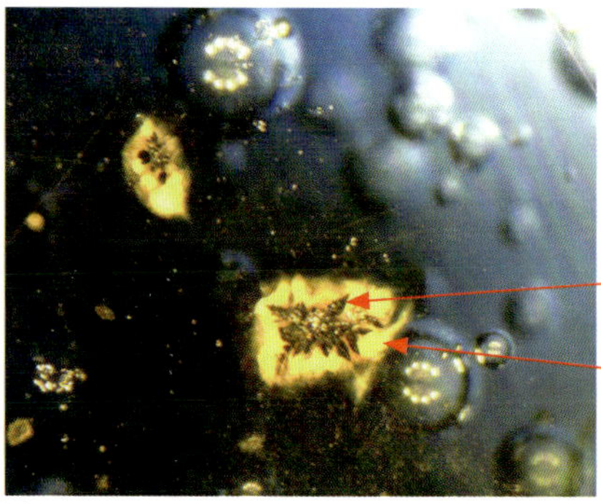

图6-1-70

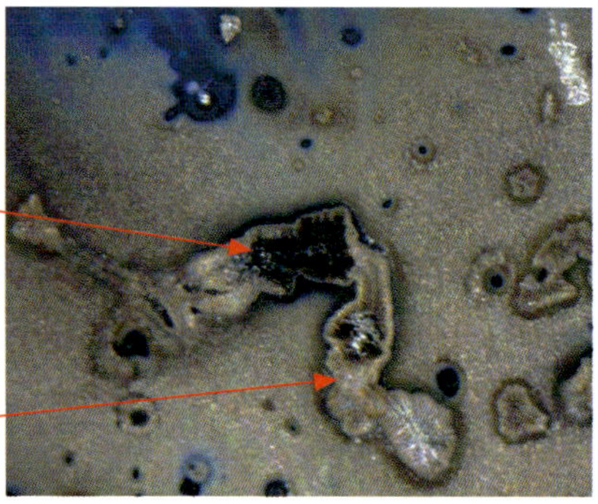

图6-1-71

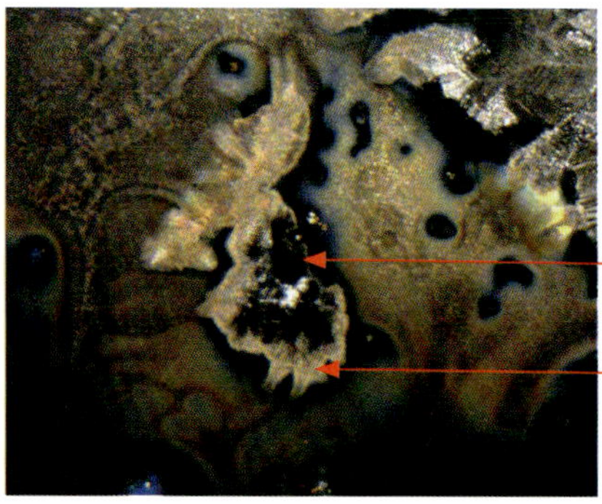

图6-1-72

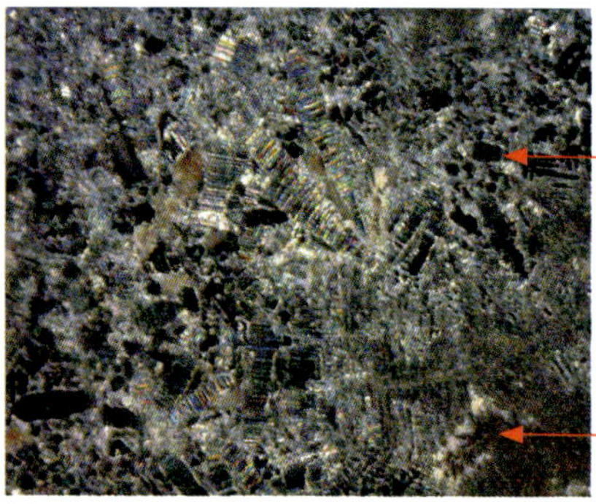

图6-1-73

见图6-1-74、图6-1-75，二者为同一器物同一位置图片，图6-1-74为二维图片，图6-1-75为三维图片。

图6-1-74中的黑色系放射斑，在图6-1-75中为凸起的颗粒状物质，被釉层覆盖，表面光滑，风化作用不明显（见箭头G所指处）。

见图6-1-76、图6-1-77，二者为同一器物同一位置图片，图6-1-76为二维图片，图6-1-77为三维图片。

图6-1-76中的黑色系放射斑，在图6-1-77中颜色稍浅，为一个个凸起的颗粒状物质，如同一颗颗石子，独立清晰（见箭头H所指处）。

见图6-1-78、图6-1-79，二者为同一器物同一位置图片，图6-1-73为二维图片，图6-1-74为三维图片。

图6-1-78中的黑色系放射斑，在图6-1-79中呈浅色，细长的形貌更清晰可见，斑块独立清晰，长条形的斑块上密集分布着凸起的线条，形成皱褶般的纹路，高出釉表面。

*图片经过裁剪放大处理。
*Picture cropped and enlarged to show detail.

6-1-152, are visible on the glaze surface (see Arrow A). The pits are clearly independent and delineated from the surrounding glass phase.

The pits indicated by Arrow A are the continued weathering of a C shaped striation. The continuation of weathering gradually extends the pit into the glaze level creating a CO type pit. Three-dimensional imaging does not allow for the observation of the pit below the glaze surface, and as such the observable opening is smaller than the size of the pit observable by two-dimensional imaging.

See pictures 6-1-154 and 6-1-155, where 6-1-154 is the two-dimensional and 6-1-155 is the three-dimensional image of the same location.

The two pits in picture 6-1-154 are the area of dark coloration in picture 6-1-155, and are both on convex portions of glaze as indicated by Arrow B. The pit indicated by Arrow C in picture 6-1-154 is the lighter area in picture 6-1-155, which is not evidently convex but presents as a split C shaped striation. The striae are clearly independent and retain delineation with the surrounding glass phase.

Generally, CO type pitting occurs on areas of convex glaze. The two-dimensionally observable pitting in picture 6-1-154 is directly correlated with the "small hills" observable with three-dimensional microscopic imaging in picture 6-1-155. Portions of the glaze without convex formations remain clean and smooth. As the areas of pitting are points of relatively unstable composition within the glass phase, weathering easily occurs. On the other hand, areas of smooth glass phase are relatively stable, and weathering severity is lower, thus it is able to retain a clean and smooth surface.

See pictures 6-1-156 and 6-1-157, where 6-1-156 is the two-dimensional and 6-1-157 is the three-dimensional image of the same location.

The white CO type pit in picture 6-1-156 is the darker area in picture 6-1-157 as indicated by Arrow D. The pit in the latter picture is clearly independent and retains delineation from the surrounding glass phase, and is observably smaller than in the earlier picture.

The darker pit as indicated by Arrow D in picture 6-1-157 is the continued weathering development of an O shaped striation. Weathering gradually extended the pit into the glaze level. Three-dimensional imaging does not allow for the observation of the pit below the glaze surface, and as such the observable opening is smaller than the size of the pit observable by two-dimensional imaging.

See pictures 6-1-158 and 6-1-159, where 6-1-158 is the two-dimensional and 6-1-159 is the three-dimensional image of the same location.

The chain-like pit group in picture 6-1-158 is the collection of interlocking C and O striae visible in picture 6-1-159 indicated by Arrow E. The striae are clearly independent and retain delineation with the surrounding glass phase.

This pit group is the progression of C and O striae within the glaze level, and the chain-like pit group under the glaze is not observable using three-dimension microscopic imaging.

(b) Needlepoint Type Pitting

(i) Two-dimensional Characteristics of Needlepoint Type Pitting

(1) Pits have white coloration, alternating size, and random distribution (see pictures 6-1-160—6-1-164).

(2) Pit edges have fine lined borders, and needlepoint distribution is evident within the pit (see pictures 6-1-160 and 6-1-161).

(3) Pit borders not evident, independent needlepoint mottling not visible within the pit (see picture 6-1-162).

(4) Needlepoint mottling within the pit has dense distribution, to the point that independent needlepoints are not observable (see pictures 6-1-163 and 6-1-164).

(ii) Three-dimensional Characteristics of Needlepoint Type Pitting

(1) Pits have clear independence with a concave shape.

(2) Clearly delineated border with the surrounding glass phase.

See pictures 6-1-165 and 6-1-166, where 6-1-165 is the two-dimensional and 6-1-166 is the three-dimensional image of the same location.

The white pitting in picture 6-1-165 presents clearly as dark coloration in picture 6-1-166. The pits are concave

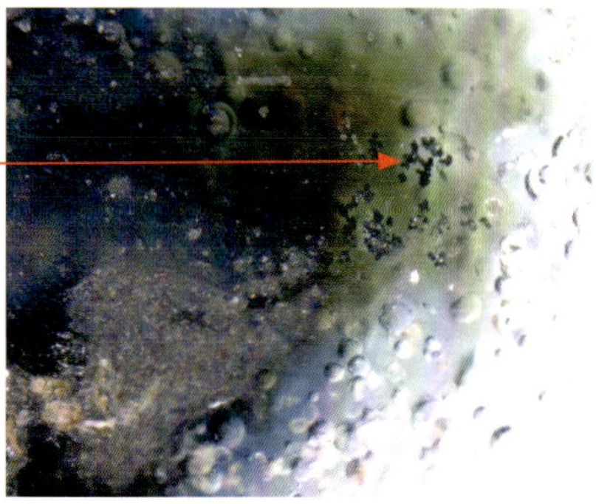

图6-1-74

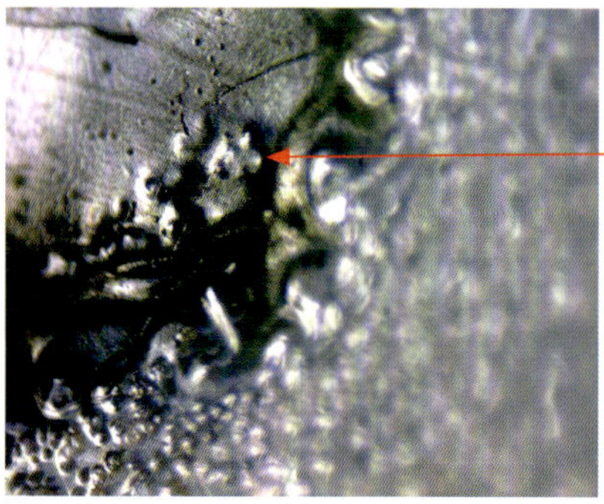

图6-1-75

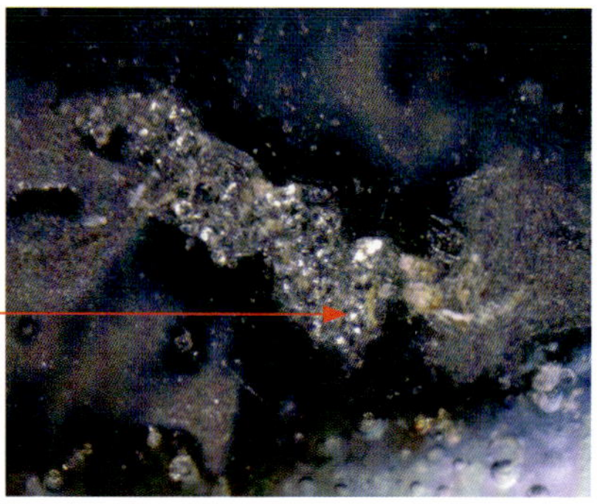

图6-1-76

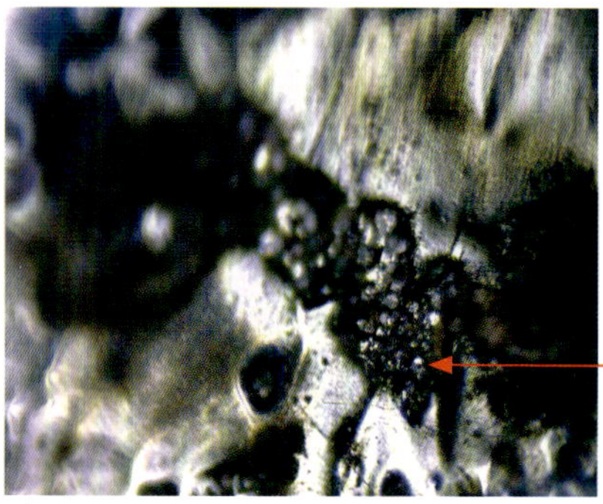

图6-1-77

图6-1-78

图6-1-79

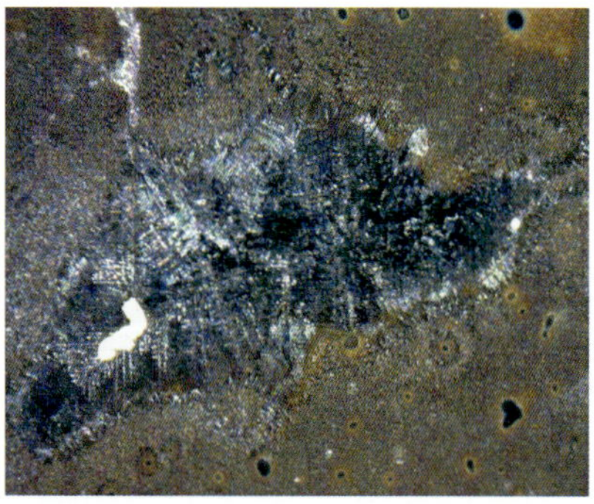
图6-1-80

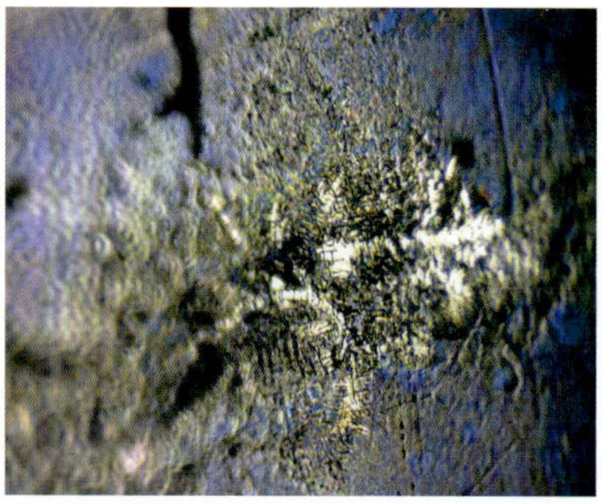
图6-1-81

openings on the surface of the glaze, with similarly observable size in both two and three-dimensional microscopic imaging, and have clear delineation with the surrounding glass phase.

(c) Damage Type Pitting

Two-dimensional Characteristics of Damage Type Pitting

(1) Pits present with irregular shapes and often present with coloration (see pictures 6-1-167—6-1-170).

(2) Pits with a larger area often present with needlepoint mottling or material deposits in the internal cavity of the pit (see pictures 6-1-167 and 6-1-168).

(3) Floccus mottling can occur in conjunction with these pits (see picture 6-1-169).

(d) Immersion Type Pitting

(i) Two-dimensional Characteristics of Immersion Type Pitting

(1) Pits can present at any location on the glaze with random distribution. Pit interior presents with frosted needlepoint mottling (see pictures 6-1-171—6-1-174).

(2) Some pits can present with disconnected semi-circles (see picture 6-1-175).

(3) Pits retain clear delineation with the surrounding glass phase (see pictures 6-1-171—6-1-175).

(ii) Three-dimensional Characteristics of Immersion Type Pitting

Three-dimensionally, immersion pits present as clear concave pits in the surface of the glaze as indicated by Arrow F in picture 6-1-176.

c. Overlay Mottle

i. Overlay Mottle Defined

Overlay Mottles are acquired under the effect of the post-firing environment, and are the result of coverage of a foreign material over YUB glaze.

ii. Formation of Overlay Mottles

Majority of YUB overlay mottles are formed by the coverage of dirt and other materials on the surface of the porcelain, as well as any man-made or foreign materials added to repair or restore the piece.

iii. Characteristics of Overlay Mottles

Two-dimensional Characteristics of Overlay Mottles

(i) The primary colors of overlay mottles are yellow, brown, or greyish-white (see pictures 6-1-177—6-1-184).

(ii) Mottles are clearly delineated from the surrounding glass phase and can have straight or irregular edges (see pictures 6-1-177—6-1-184).

(iii) Mottles can have distinct layers, presenting as flaky skin (see picture 6-1-177), or as tortoise shell, resembling dried mud (see picture 6-1-178).

(iv) It is common to see scratches across the mottle (see picture 6-1-179).

(v) Some mottles occur in conjunction with floccus mottling (see Floccus Mottle Heading of this section) (see pictures 6-1-180 and 6-1-181).

(vi) Due to the several different chemical components used in the restoration of ceramics, the characteristics of overlay mottles created by these materials can be widely varying. Looking at the sample pieces from Thailand, the materials used create a white, opaque film over the glaze surface (see picture 6-1-182); a small portion resembling needlepoint mottling. When reassembling pieces, trace amounts of dust and colored grains become trapped in said material (see picture 6-1-183). Looking at samples taken from Jingdezhen which utilized clear glue (see picture 6-1-184), it is very difficult to tell the difference between glue, natural overlay mottles, and needlepoint mottles, as such there is a need for naked-eye inspection to tell whether or not an observed item has undergone repair.

d. Bubble Root

i. Bubble Root Defined

A Bubble Root (mottle) is a concave mottle which is the progression of a broken mouth bubble on the surface of YUB glaze with internal sedimentation, formed by under the influences of the post-firing environment.

见图6-1-80、图6-1-81，二者为同一器物同一位置图片，图6-1-80为二维图片，图6-1-81为三维图片。

图6-1-80中的黑色系放射斑在图6-1-81中高出釉表面，呈浅色，成像清晰。斑块表面有的光滑，有的粗糙。

（3）团状斑

① 团状斑概念

团状斑是聚集成一团、没有放射感的析晶斑块。它是元青花瓷器在烧制过程中，在其釉层中形成的。

② 团状斑形成

团状斑与放射斑中的白色系放射斑类似，应是莫来石（或长石类）的析晶。

白色系放射斑与团状斑在元青花上都较少见，这与釉料配方变化及工艺改变有关。陈尧成等人的研究表明，如果青料中的氧化铝含量达到18%－20%，釉与青料结合处的成分才有可能析出钙长石或莫来石结晶。当用含高铝青料着色时，烧成的青花瓷器只有一部分青料被釉熔融形成富铝蓝色玻璃相，冷却时釉与青料结合处就会有钙长石或莫来石相析出。而大部分元青花标本的青料中氧化铝含量都不及18%，所以元青花瓷器上少有这类析晶斑，而在明早期青花瓷器上较常见[221]。

此外，莫来石结晶与烧造温度也有关。有莫来石结晶出现说明瓷器的烧结温度至少达1000℃[222]。由第三章可知，元代的工匠在制作元青花瓷器时，在瓷胎原料中加入了高岭土，提高了瓷器的烧结温度[223]。

③ 团状斑特征

团状斑二维特征

见图6-1-82、图6-1-83。

I. 团状斑形貌如石块，颜色主要以白色、黄色为主。

II. 部分斑块具备透影性，部分不具备透影性。

III. 部分斑块颜色单一（见图6-1-82），部分有色阶变化（见图6-1-83）。

IV. 团状斑通常受釉层保护较好，风化强度低，基本保持刚烧制出来的原态。

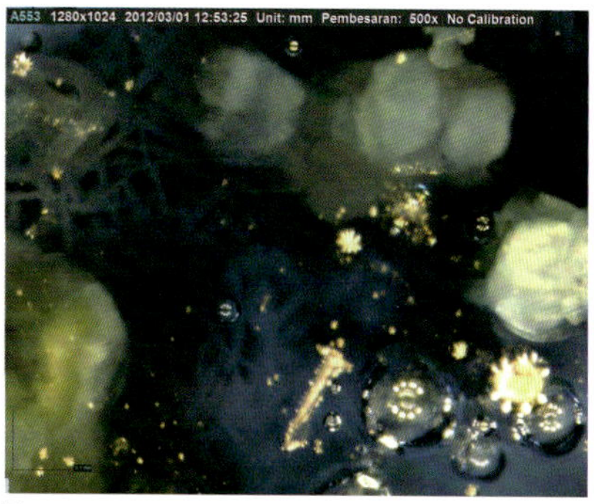

图6-1-82

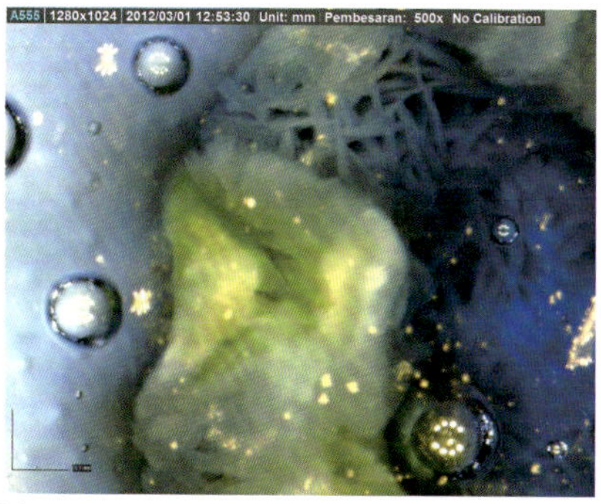

图6-1-83

（4）小结

元青花瓷器的胎和釉中均含有铁元素和锰元素，但青料中含铁和锰是最高的。

不同种类、不同形貌的析晶斑，有的溢出釉表面，有的存在于釉层中，它们大都出现在青料浓处，大部分都含一定量的铁氧化物和锰氧化物。

这些析晶斑形貌和颜色的多样性，与釉的黏度及厚度有关，与结晶或分相物质的张力、密度、铁元素和锰元素的价位都有关。

注：在现今采集的元青花标本的显微成像图片上，我们能看到所有的先天性斑块特征都已经过了800年左右时间的历练，即使是保存再好的瓷器也会有一定程度的风化。我们无法回到元代探索元青花瓷器先天斑块的原貌，只能在迹型风化的绝对时间内，根据图片情况，运用科学知识加以推理，想象元青花先天性斑块的本来面目。

ii. Formation of Bubble Roots

After YUB glaze undergoes corrosive weathering, small portions of bubbles within the glaze level become flayed, leaving a deep depressed pit on the glaze surface, also called a bubble root. Completely exposed to the elements, foreign materials are easily accumulated within the pit leaving deposited sediments on the internal wall, thus creating a bubble root mottle.

Generally, the mouth or rim portion of the porcelain piece presents with bubble roots. On shipwrecked pieces with normally more severe weathering, it is also common for bubble roots to present.

iii. Characteristics of Bubble Roots

Two-dimensional Characteristics of Bubble Roots

(i) The majority of bubble roots retain their inherent round shape, with a small portion also having ovular or irregular shape (see pictures 6-1-185—6-1-189).

(ii) Commonly seen colors in bubble roots are: White, yellow, brown, and black (see pictures 6-6-185—6-1-189).

(iii) Some bubble roots can present with multiple types of sedimentation and as such a spectrum of colors (see pictures 6-1-186 and 6-1-189).

(iv) Several different roots on the same piece can present with different colors (see pictures 6-1-187 and 6-1-189).

e. Floccus Mottle

i. Floccus Mottle Defined

Floccus Mottles are primarily white colored appearances within the YUB glaze level and on the glaze surface brought about by the post-firing environment; they have indistinct, free flowing, and irregular shapes that were formed by the depositing of soluble and partially soluble salts, dust particles, and other materials.

ii. Formation of Floccus Mottles

The fired YUB glaze surface has randomly distributed cracks and openings. Additionally, as soil contains acidic and alkaline solutions that corrode the glaze surface, small cracks and openings in the glaze surface can be further created. It is through these small cracks and openings that foreign material can enter into the glaze level, forming soluble and partially soluble salts.

When the water in the soil evaporates, the soluble salts crystalize. However, due to the solubility of these salts, surface level water can dissolve and wash them away. Therefore, the rate of floccus mottling is relatively low across the surface, but common within the glaze level.

In environments of alternating moisture, it is difficult for partially soluble salts to be dissolved away from the glaze level. Soluble salts dispersed within the glaze level crystalized after the evaporation of water and trap with them microscopic dust particles within the glaze level; these sedimentations form floccus mottles.

Soil and the glaze surface also contain positive and negative ions that, in reaction with each other, create partially soluble salt deposits of varying colors.

iii. Characteristics of Floccus Mottles

(a) Two-dimensional Characteristics of Floccus Mottles

(i) Floccus Mottles are primarily white in color. Within the glaze level, these mottles mainly assume irregular blotch and spot shapes, similar to wisps of clouds (see pictures 6-1-190—6-1-206).

(ii) Mottles occur in conjunction with areas of relatively instable glaze composition or glaze flaw. For example under pitting (see pictures 6-1-191—6-1-194), under overlay mottles (see pictures 6-1-199 and 6-1-200), under glaze cracks (see pictures 6-1-190, 6-1-195, and 6-1-196), under C and O striae (see pictures 6-1-197 and 6-1-198), under scrathes (see picture 6-1-201), around bristle pits (see pictures 6-1-202—6-1-205), and under areas of other glaze defect (see picture 6-1-206).

(iii) The mottle forms at the location of glaze flaw and permeates down into the glaze level. The center of the mottle is non-transparent and milky white, and the edges feather out like goose down.

(b) Three-dimensional Characteristics of Floccus Mottles

（二）后天性元青花斑块

1. 后天性元青花斑块概念

后天性元青花斑块是元青花瓷器在后天环境影响下形成的，以不规则形貌分布在釉表面及釉层中的各类斑块。

2. 后天性元青花斑块种类

（1）针眼斑

① 针眼斑概念

针眼斑是大小较均匀、深浅大致相同、疏密不定的独立微孔，以聚集形式呈不规则形貌出现的斑块。它是元青花瓷器在后天环境影响下，在釉表面随机形成的。

通常情况下，在元青花析晶斑无釉覆盖处、釉表面组织结构稳定性较差处，或曾有泥沙等异物覆盖处，会较先以针眼斑形式开始风化。

② 针眼斑分类

针眼斑的形貌主要分为三种：雾状针眼斑、磨砂针眼斑和颗粒针眼斑。

A. 雾状针眼斑

雾状针眼斑二维特征

见图6-1-84—图6-1-86。

I. 雾状针眼斑呈白色雾状，均匀细腻。

II. 雾状针眼斑一般有由浓到淡的清晰过渡，通常存在于沙滩斑与玻璃相过渡的区域。

B. 磨砂针眼斑

磨砂针眼斑的成因主要分为两种：

第一种磨砂针眼斑属于雾状针眼斑的发展，是风化强度更高的表现，分布密集，存在于无釉覆盖的铁氧化物及锰氧化物暴露处。

第二种磨砂针眼斑的主要成因为：物盖物侵蚀釉表面，清除物盖物后暴露出磨砂针眼斑。为了区别，我们称这一类为物盖磨砂针眼斑。

磨砂针眼斑二维特征

I. 磨砂针眼斑呈白色，有磨砂感，针眼较雾状针眼斑粗粝，风化强度大于雾状针眼斑，一般没有浓淡过渡，但边界感较强（见图6-1-87—图6-1-90）。

II. 物盖磨砂针眼斑一般也呈白色，分布随机，形状不规则，一般没有浓淡过渡，但有清晰的边界，界线呈不规则曲线，如同不规则的海岸线，与周围迹型界线分明（见图6-1-91、图6-1-92）。

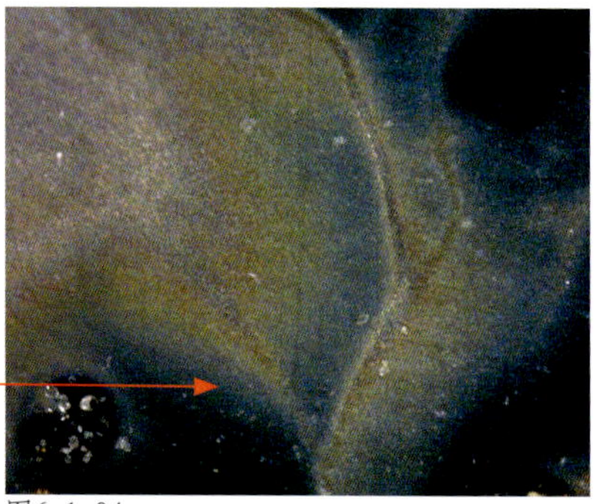

图6-1-84

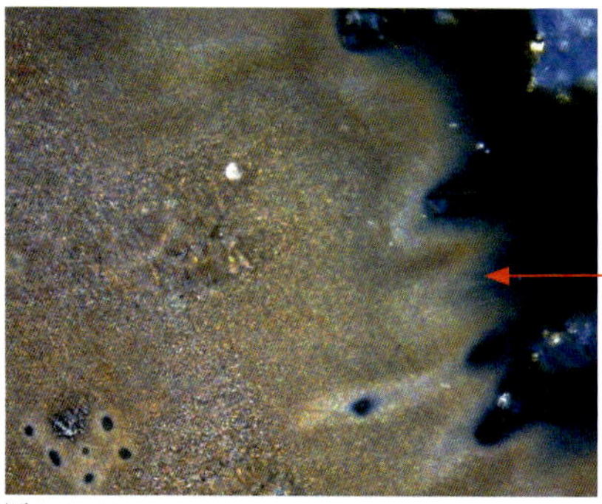

图6-1-85

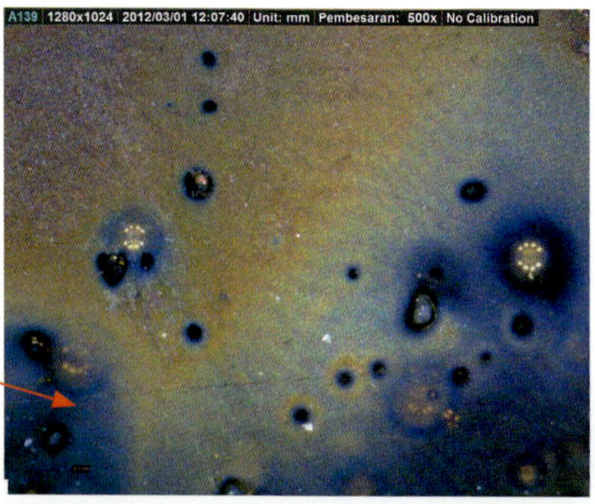

图6-1-86

(i) Under the glaze floccus mottling is not visible, and the glaze surface defect (i.e. pit, crack) is much smaller than the defect and floccus mottling observable through two-dimension microscopic imaging of the same location.

(ii) Aside from glaze defect, the glaze surface remains smooth without any other large area flaws.

See pictures 6-1-207 and 6-1-208, where 6-1-207 is the two-dimensional and 6-1-208 is the three-dimensional image of the same location.

The floccus mottle indicated by Arrow A in picture 6-1-207 is not visible in picture 6-1-208. It is only possible to observe small individual pits on the glaze surface, thus the floccus mottle is clearly beneath the surface of the glaze.

The floccus mottle indicated by Arrow B in picture 6-1-207 is also not visible in picture 6-1-208, and the glaze is smooth. There is a surface pit indicated by Arrow C that is near to but smaller than the floccus mottle indicated by Arrow B, demonstrating that a portion of the floccus mottle is present under the glaze surface. The pit indicated by Arrow C is most likely the glaze defect from which the floccus mottling entered into the glaze level.

See pictures 6-1-209 and 6-1-210, where 6-1-209 is the two-dimensional and 6-1-210 is the three-dimensional image of the same location.

The white floccus mottling indicated by Arrow D in picture 6-1-209 is faintly evident in picture 6-1-210. The glaze crack is the only evident glaze flaw without any large area glaze flaws in the vicinity, demonstrating that the floccus mottle is present under the glaze surface.

3. Summary

YUB Mottles can be divided into two categories: Innate and Acquired.

The multiplicity of YUB innate mottles is primarily due to differences in glaze, dye, and firing techniques; and as such, to some extent reflects the materials and techniques used in that day.

Acquired mottles are formed because of the post-firing environments and changes and differences in those environments. The multiplicity of acquired mottles reflects the corresponding relationship between the formation of YUB traces and their post-firing environments. The characteristics of these mottles are in accordance with the quantitative change and passage of time principles of ceramic traces, and embody the various laws that govern ceramic trace formation and change.

图6-1-87

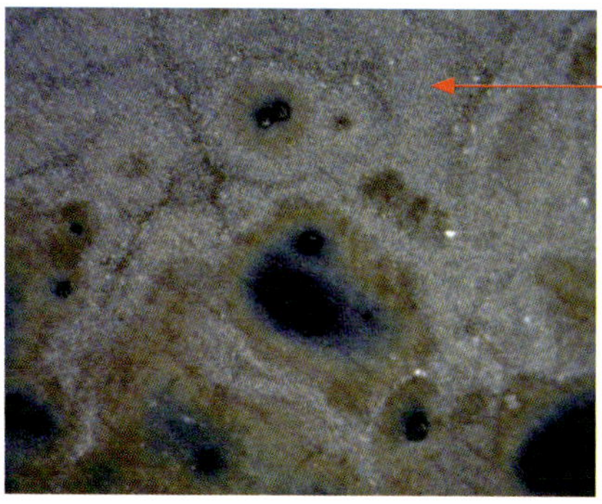

图6-1-88

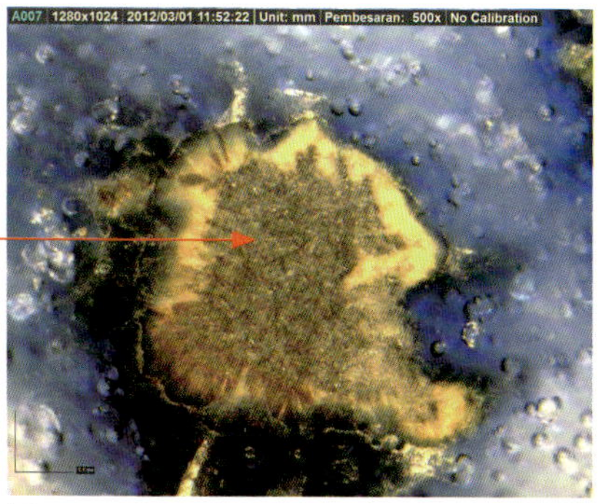

图6-1-89

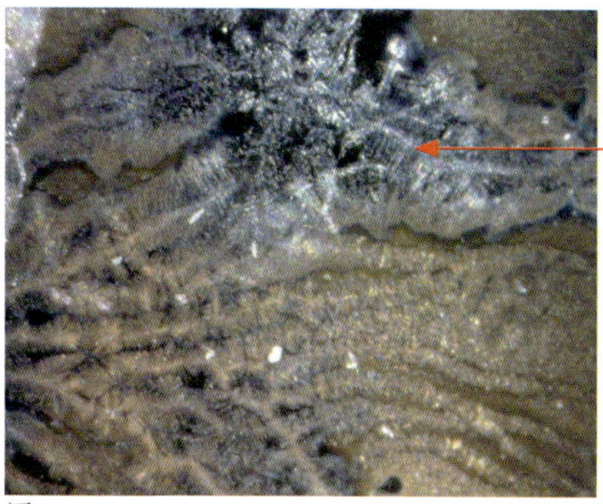

图6-1-90

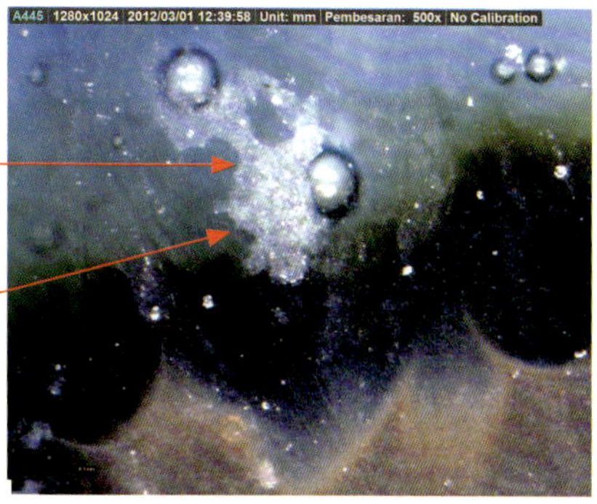

图6-1-91

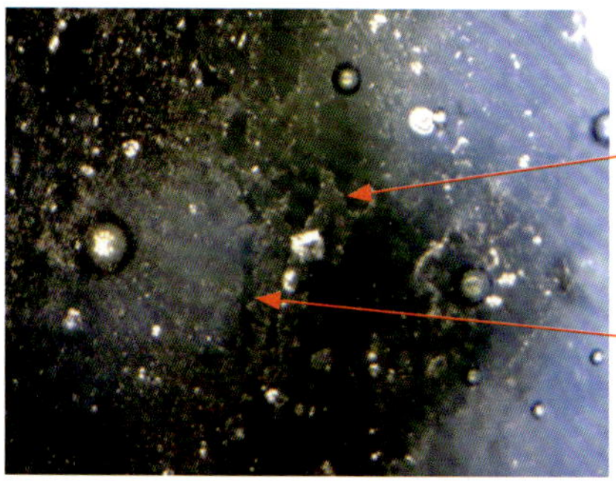

图6-1-92

C. 颗粒针眼斑

颗粒针眼斑的成因主要分为两种：

第一种颗粒针眼斑主要分布在无釉覆盖的铁氧化物及锰氧化物暴露处或釉层组织结构稳定性较差的地方。

第二种颗粒针眼斑的主要成因是：物盖物侵蚀釉表面，清除物盖物后，暴露出颗粒针眼斑。为了区别，我们称这一类为物盖颗粒针眼斑。

颗粒针眼斑二维特征

I. 颗粒针眼斑呈白色，有时呈浅黄色。针眼斑独立，呈颗粒状，较磨砂针眼斑更深更粗粝，通常分布的密集程度不及雾状及磨砂针眼斑（见图6-1-93—图6-1-98）。

II. 物盖颗粒针眼斑一般也呈白色，针眼独立清晰，有的分布较稀疏，有的分布较密集，与周围其他迹型界线分明（见图6-1-96）。

III. 有的物盖颗粒针眼斑外沿有一圈纤细的包边，圈内的颗粒针眼斑清晰独立，包边与周围其他迹型界线分明（见图6-1-97、图6-1-98）。

颗粒针眼斑
Grainy Needlepoint
Mottling

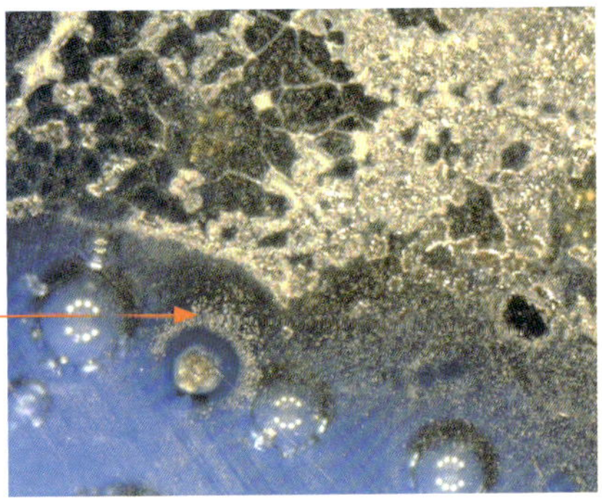

图6-1-93

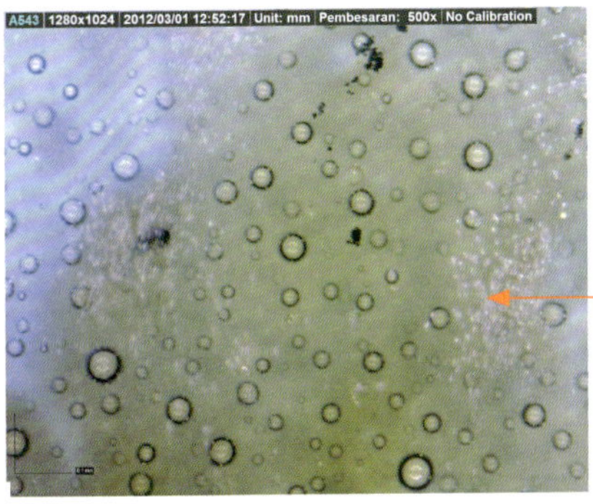

颗粒针眼斑
Grainy Needlepoint
Mottling

图6-1-94

颗粒针眼斑
Grainy Needlepoint
Mottling

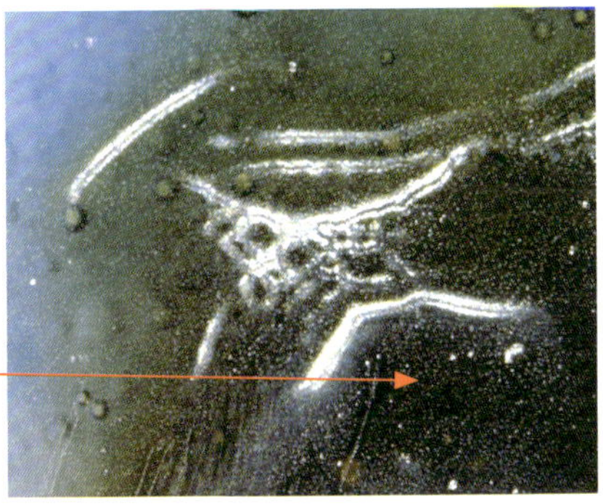

图6-1-95

物盖颗粒针眼斑
Overlay Grainy
Needlepoint Mottling

图6-1-96

有纤细包边的物盖颗粒针眼斑
Overlay Grainy Needlepoint Mottle with Fine Line Border

图6-1-97

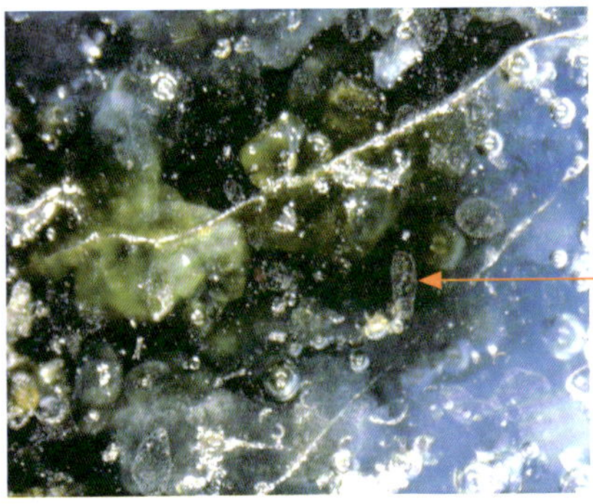

有纤细包边的物盖颗粒针眼斑
Overlay Grainy Needlepoint Mottle with Fine Line Border

图6-1-98

③ 针眼斑分布状况

A. 针眼斑在流淌斑上的状况

a. 针眼斑在流淌斑上的形成

流淌斑含铁与锰较高，比较容易风化。瓷器烧制成后，流淌斑上无釉层保护的部分最先风化，形成针眼斑。有釉层保护的，在后天釉层受到侵蚀后也以针眼斑形式开始风化。

b. 针眼斑在沙滩斑上的二维特征

针眼斑呈白色。在沙滩斑上的分布有的密集，有的稀疏。一般情况下，针眼斑风化的轨迹只在流淌斑形貌范围内，“筛网”式的圆孔上一般没有针眼斑。

通常来说，沙滩斑由于其润湿铺展的特性，斑块中间铁氧化物和锰氧化物较多，玻璃相成分较少；边沿铁氧化物和锰氧化物较少，玻璃相成分较多。针眼斑在沙滩斑上的形貌、疏密分布随着其受釉层的保护程度改变。沙滩斑中心铁氧化物和锰氧化物较多，风化强度更高，所以针眼斑表现为磨砂针眼斑；沙滩斑边沿铁氧化物或锰氧化物少，风化强度低，针眼斑表现为雾状针眼斑。

针眼斑这种分布规律使沙滩斑从外至内产生三到四种颜色变化：

深褐色、深青色、浅褐色、白色（见图6-1-99、图6-1-100、图6-1-102）。

I. 雾状针眼斑

雾状针眼斑像雾化的喷漆均匀地喷在釉表面，越往沙滩斑中心部分雾状针眼斑分布越密集，颜色越白；越往沙滩斑边沿处雾状针眼斑分布越稀疏，颜色越趋淡，呈玻璃相的颜色。尽管与玻璃相之间没有明显的边界线，但有一个从浓到淡的均匀过渡（见图6-1-99—图6-1-102）。

II. 磨砂针眼斑

磨砂针眼斑分布较雾状针眼斑更密集，所以颜色更显白。磨砂针眼斑边界感较强，一般没有浓淡过渡，有的地方分布密集，有的地方几乎没有，露出褐色的沙滩斑（见图6-1-99—图6-1-106）。也有磨砂针眼斑出现在沙滩斑外围的情况（见图6-1-105、图6-1-106）。

III. 颗粒针眼斑

颗粒针眼斑在沙滩斑上较少见，分布较雾状及磨砂针眼斑要稀疏，针眼之间独立分明（见图6-1-107）。

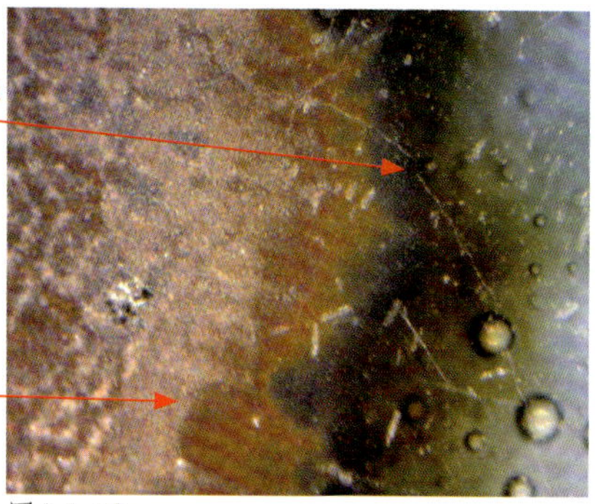

图6-1-99

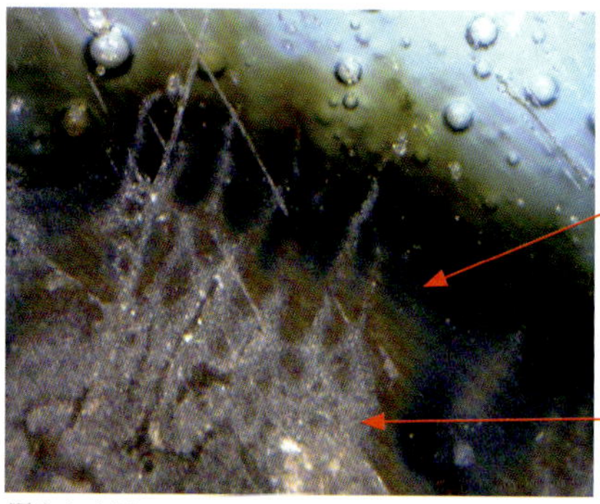

图6-1-100

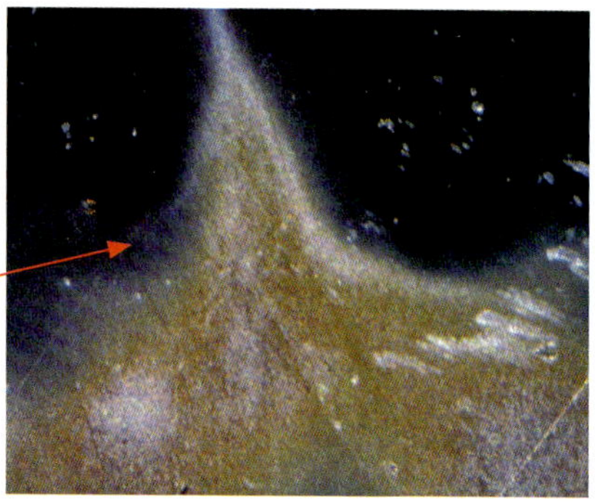

图6-1-101

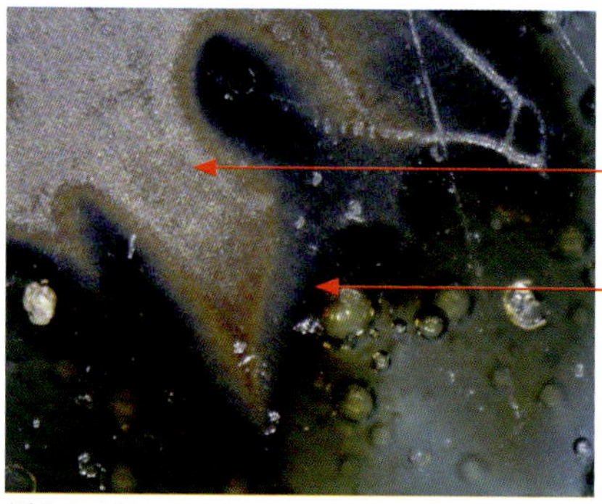

图6-1-102

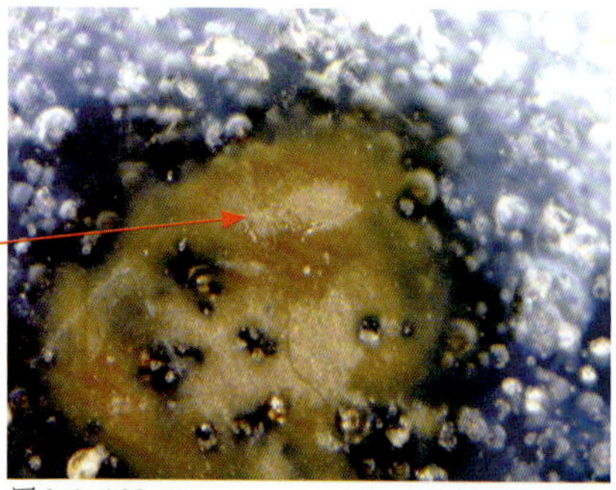

图6-1-103

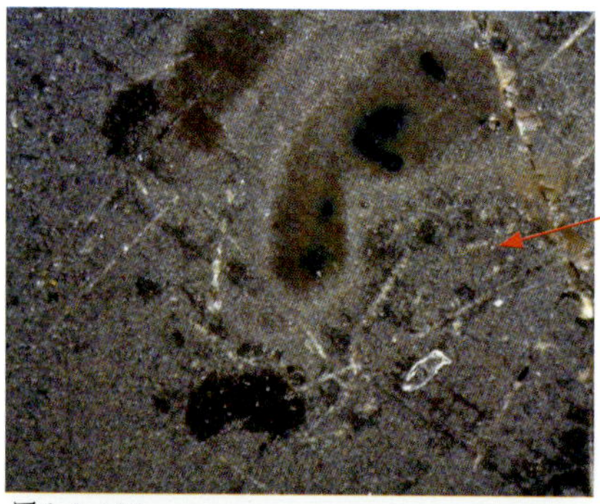

图6-1-104

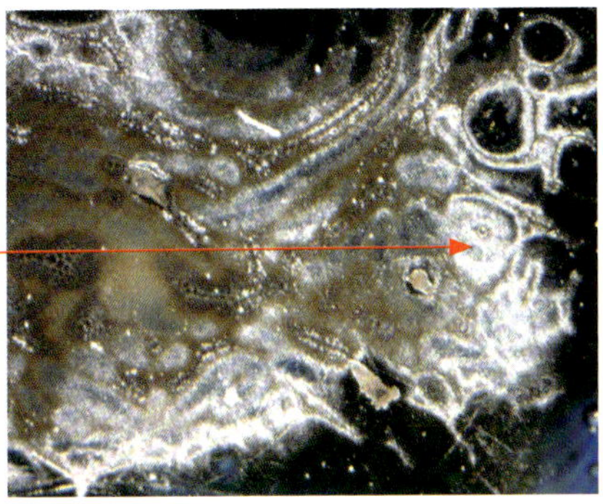

图6-1-105

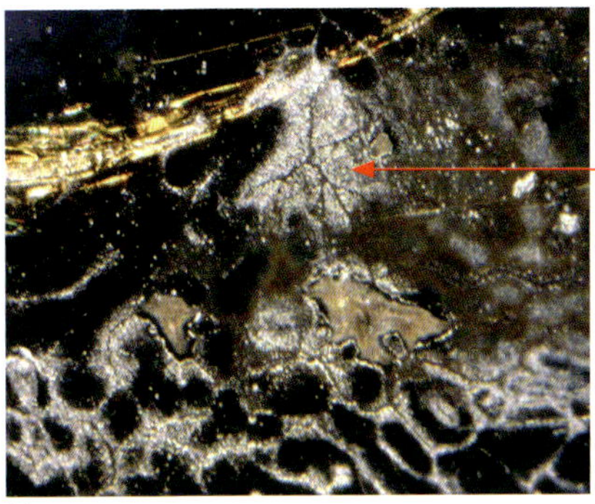

图6-1-106

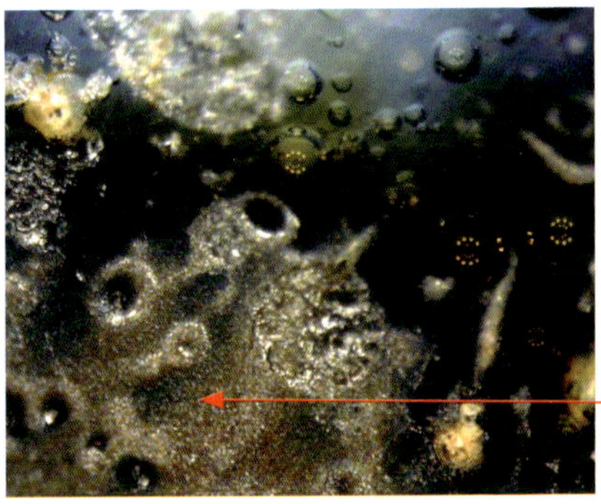

图6-1-107

c. 针眼斑在沙滩斑上的三维特征

I. 雾状针眼斑表现出均匀的过渡。

II. 雾状针眼斑分布稀疏处特征不明显；雾状针眼斑分布密集的地方如同均匀铺展的细沙。

III. 磨砂针眼斑表现为独立点状凹坑。

IV. 针眼斑的分布随着沙滩斑的轮廓走势，有较整齐的边界。

V. 沙滩斑有色阶变化，整体显得精致、细腻。

见图6-1-108、图6-1-109，二者为同一器物同一位置图片，图6-1-108为二维图片，图6-1-109为三维图片。

见图6-1-110、图6-1-111，二者为同一器物同一位置图片，图6-1-110为二维图片，图6-1-111为三维图片。

雾状针眼斑在图6-1-109及图6-1-111中均表现出均匀的过渡：雾状针眼斑分布稀疏处特征不明显，釉表面显得光滑洁净（见箭头A、箭头D所指处）；雾状针眼斑分布更密集的地方如同均匀铺展的细沙（见箭头B、箭头E所指处）。

图6-1-109中箭头C及图6-1-111中箭头F所指的磨砂针眼斑是分布较雾状针眼斑更加密集的深色点状凹坑，立体感较强，斑块整体呈现的颜色较雾状针眼斑更深。

针眼斑在沙滩斑上整体的分布基本随着沙滩斑的轮廓走势，有较整齐的边界，而不是杂乱无章地分布。沙滩斑整体显得细腻、精致（见图6-1-109、图6-1-111）。

针眼斑有规律地分布也使沙滩斑从右至左产生色阶变化，富有层次感（见图6-1-111）。

见图6-1-112、图6-1-113，二者为同一器物同一位置图片，图6-1-112为二维图片，图6-1-113为三维图片。

图6-1-112中的沙滩斑上主要分布着磨砂针眼斑，白色的磨砂针眼斑在图6-1-113中呈深色，成像清晰，表现为密集的点状凹坑。

图6-1-112中未被磨砂针眼斑覆盖的沙滩斑在图6-1-113中呈浅色。该处风化强度较其周围被针眼斑覆盖处要低，显得光滑洁净（见箭头G所指处）。

图6-1-112中的深色玻璃相在图6-1-113中呈浅色，高于周围沙滩斑，因其风化强度低，显得光滑洁净（见箭头H所指处）。

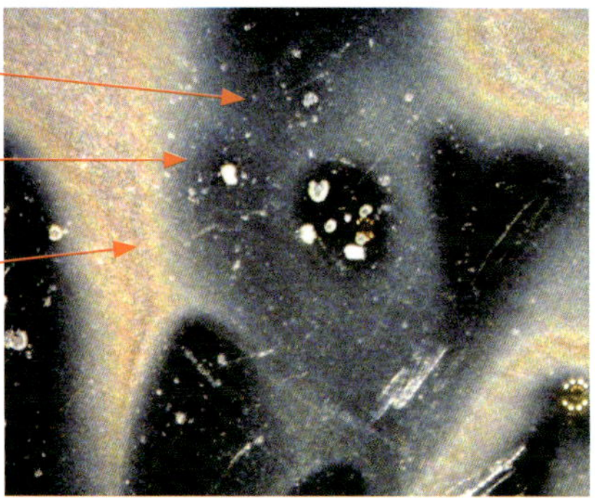

图6-1-108

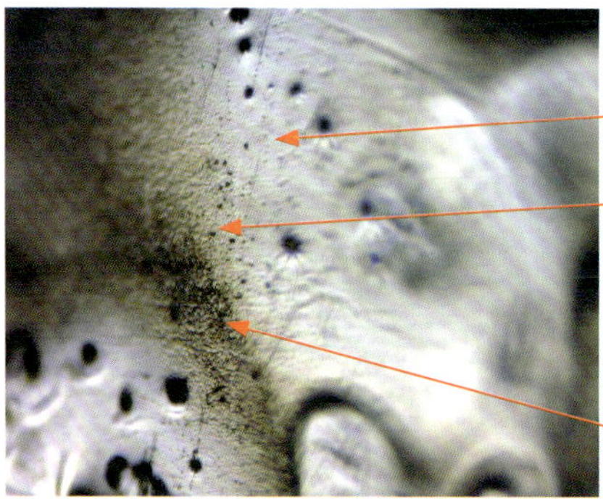

图6-1-109

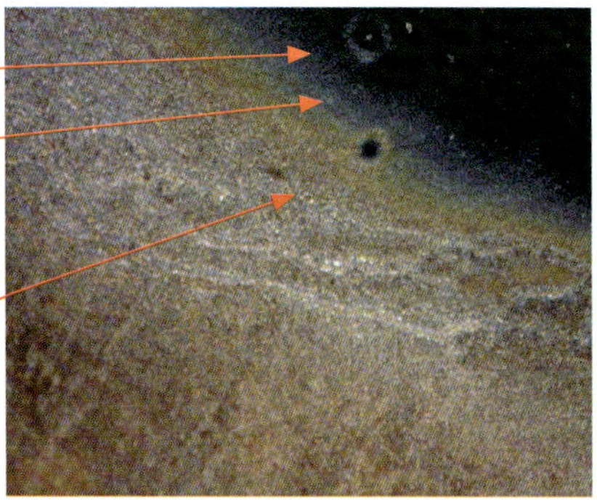

图6-1-110

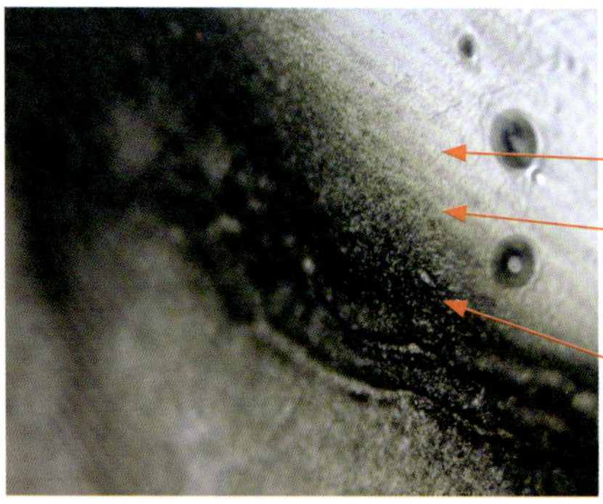

图6-1-111

图6-1-112

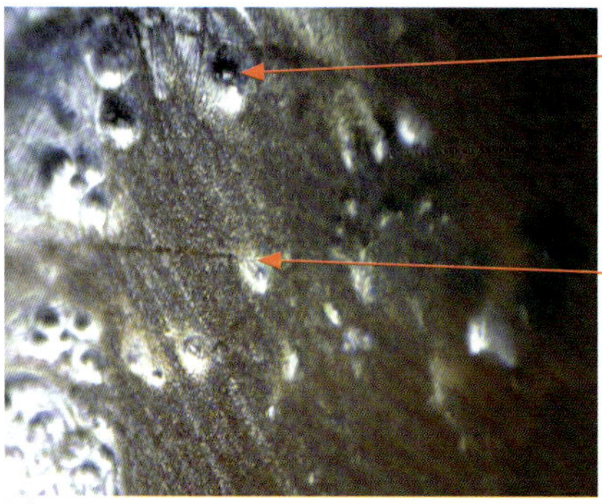

图6-1-113

B. 针眼斑在放射斑上的状况

a. 针眼斑在放射斑上的形成

放射斑含一定量的铁氧化物及锰氧化物，比较容易风化。瓷器烧制成后，无釉层保护的放射斑最先风化，形成针眼斑。有釉层保护的，在后天釉层受到侵蚀后也以针眼斑形式开始风化。

b. 针眼斑在放射斑上的二维特征

见图6-1-114—图6-1-116。

I. 磨砂针眼斑颜色呈白色。

II. 磨砂针眼斑没有浓淡过渡。

III. 磨砂针眼斑随放射斑的析晶形状密集分布，一般不超出放射斑的范围。

C. 针眼斑在玻璃相上的状况

a. 针眼斑在玻璃相上的形成

针眼斑在玻璃相上的形成主要有两个原因：

一是釉表面组织结构稳定性较差处的风化，比如分相结合处易风化形成针眼斑。

二是釉表面受到外界物质长期覆盖后，清除掉物盖物，会在物盖处的釉表面留下针眼斑，这类针眼斑是长期物盖侵蚀所致。

b. 针眼斑在玻璃相上的二维特征

I. 颗粒针眼斑呈白色，有时呈浅黄色。针眼斑独立，呈颗粒状，针眼较磨砂针眼斑更深更粗糙，通常分布的密集程度不及雾状及磨砂针眼斑（见图6-1-117—图6-1-124）。

II. 物盖磨砂针眼斑一般也呈白色，分布随机，形状不规则，一般没有浓淡过渡，但有清晰的边界，界线呈不规则曲线，如同不规则的海岸线，与周围玻璃相界线分明（见图6-1-122）。

III. 物盖颗粒针眼斑一般也呈白色，针眼独立清晰，有的分布较稀疏，有的分布较密集，与周围其他迹型界线分明（见图6-1-123）。

IV. 有的物盖颗粒针眼斑外沿有一圈纤细的包边，圈内的颗粒针眼斑清晰独立，包边与周围其他迹型界线分明（见图6-1-124）。

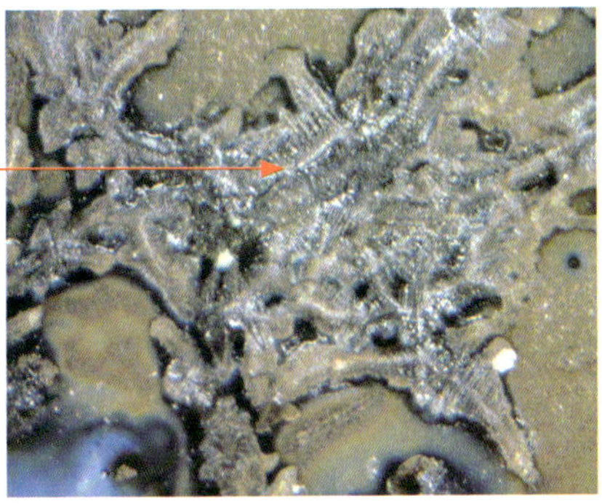

图6-1-114

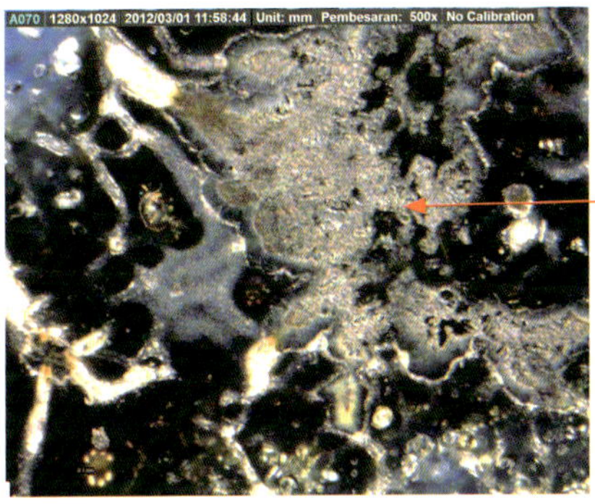

图6-1-115

图6-1-116

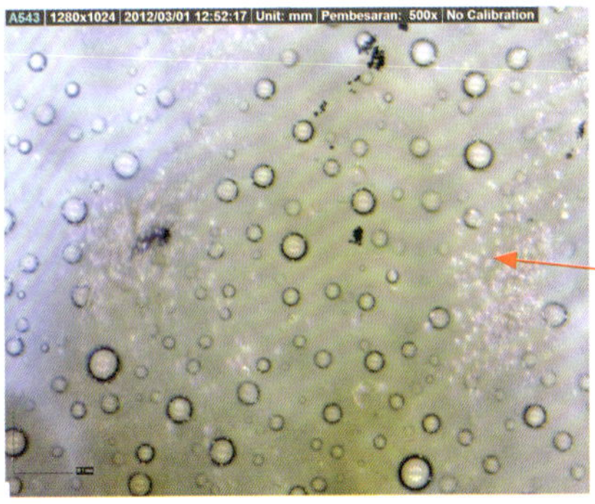

图6-1-117

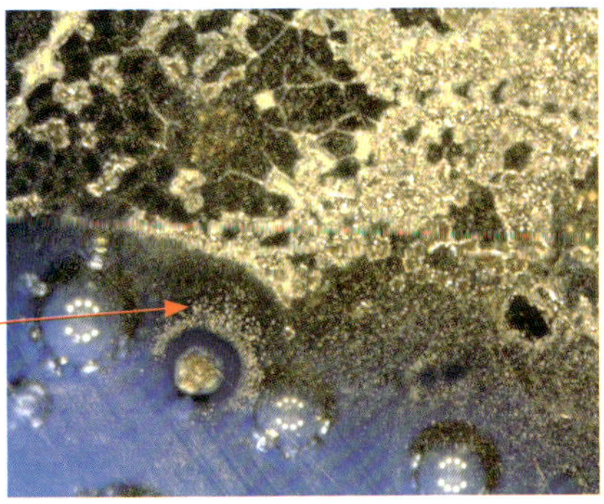

图6-1-118

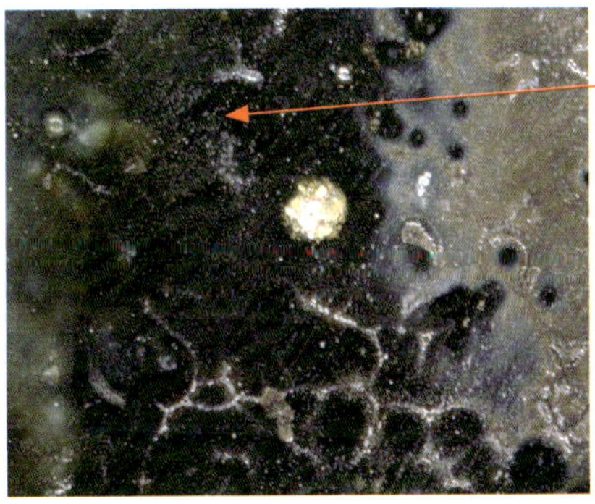

图6-1-119

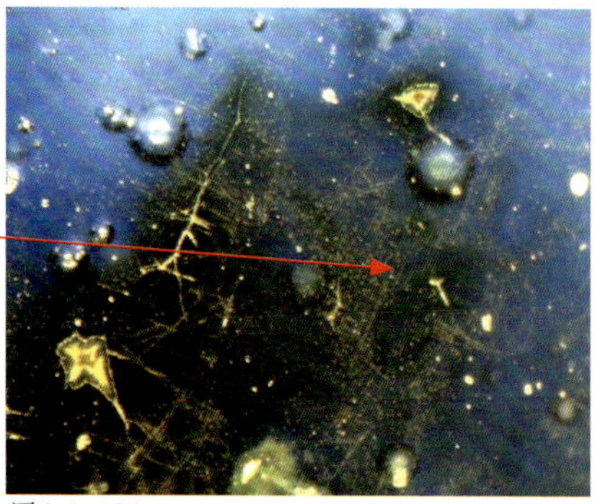

图6-1-120

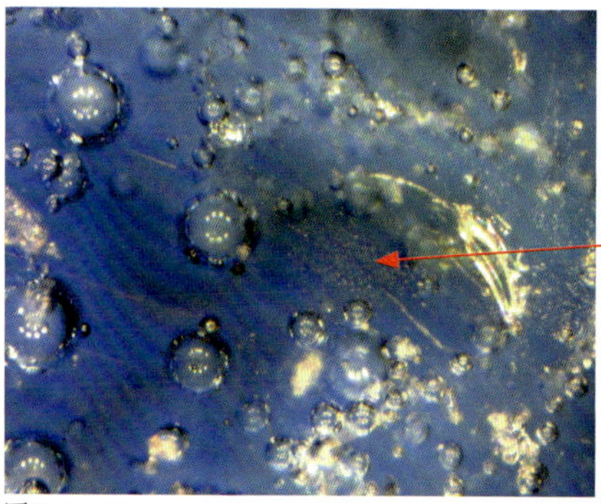

图6-1-121

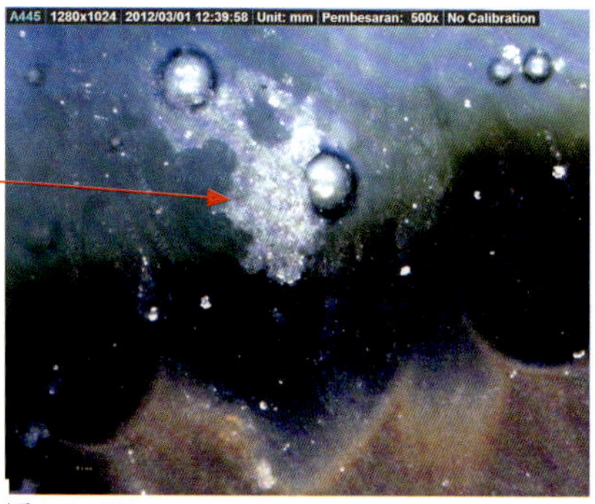

图6-1-122

图6-1-123

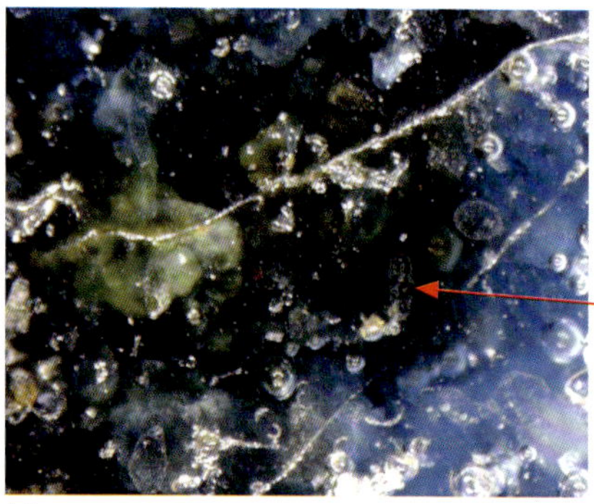

图6-1-124

c. 针眼斑在玻璃相上的三维特征

I. 颗粒针眼斑为独立点状凹坑。

II. 与周围玻璃相界线分明。

见图6-1-125、图6-1-126，二者为同一器物同一位置图片，图6-1-125为二维图片，图6-1-126为三维图片。

图6-1-125中的白色颗粒针眼斑在图6-1-126中呈深色，成像清晰。颗粒针眼斑为一个个独立的点状凹坑，与周围玻璃相界线分明。

（2）坑点斑

① 坑点斑概念

坑点斑是深浅不一、大小不一、形貌不一的不规则凹形斑块。它是元青花瓷器在后天环境影响下，在其釉表面形成的。

② 坑点斑形成

坑点斑的形成原因主要有五种：

A. 由C形、O形纹发展而成。C形、O形纹路（以下简称CO纹）是釉层的析晶或分相，它们与玻璃相结合处的组织结构稳定性较差，易风化。CO纹继续风化就会形成坑点斑。我们称这类坑点斑为CO型坑点斑。（参见本章第二节C形、O形纹部分）

B. 由针眼斑发展而成。针眼斑进一步风化后，形成坑点斑。我们称这类坑点斑为针眼型坑点斑。

C. 外界磕碰或磨损形成。釉

表面被磕碰或磨损后，形成坑点斑。我们称这类坑点斑为外伤型坑点斑。

D. 物盖物侵蚀釉表面，清除物盖物后，暴露出坑点斑。我们称这类坑点斑为物盖型坑点斑。

E. 由于长期浸泡在水中，釉表面风化形成坑点斑。这类坑点斑通常出现在海捞瓷上。我们称这类坑点斑为浸水型坑点斑。

不同成因的坑点斑可以共存（见图6-1-127—图6-1-131）。

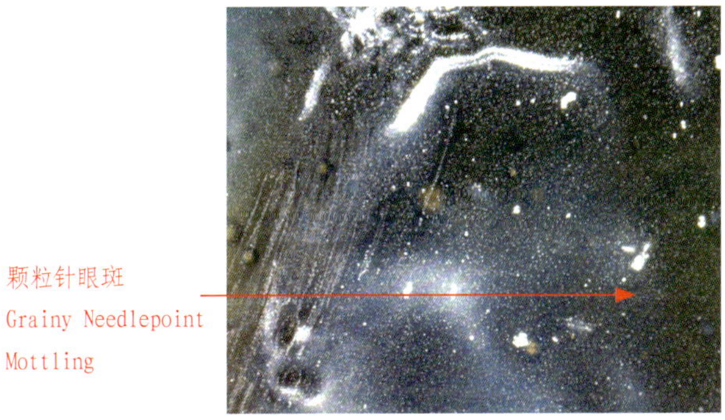

图6-1-125

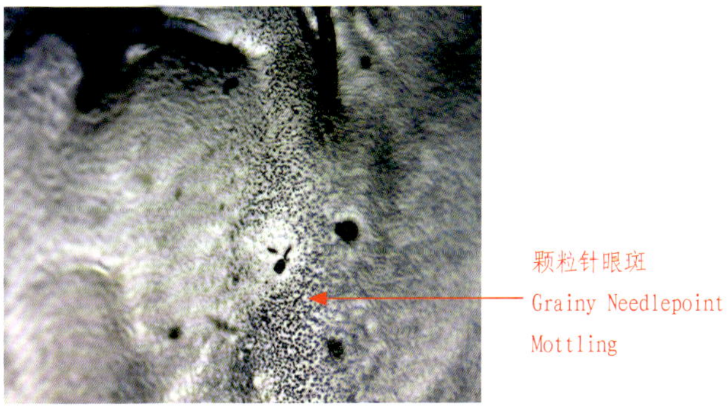

图6-1-126

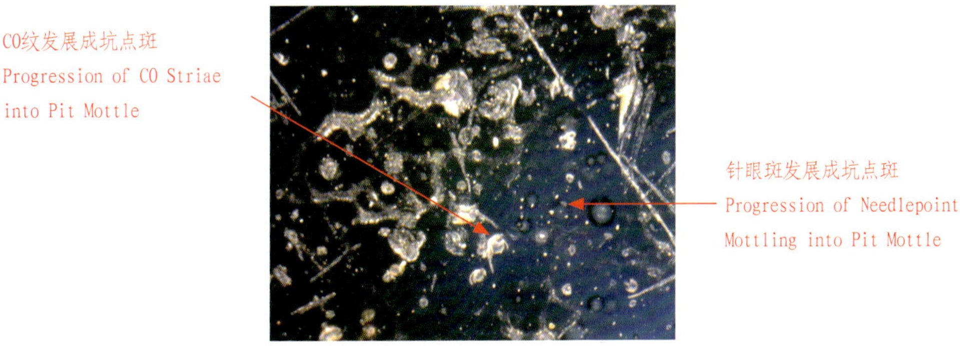

图6-1-127

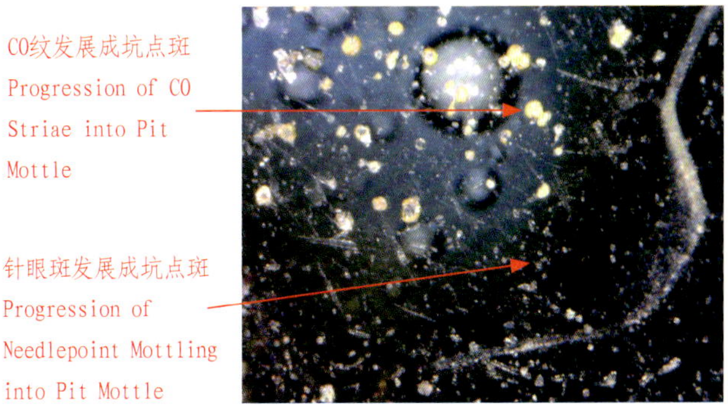

图6-1-128

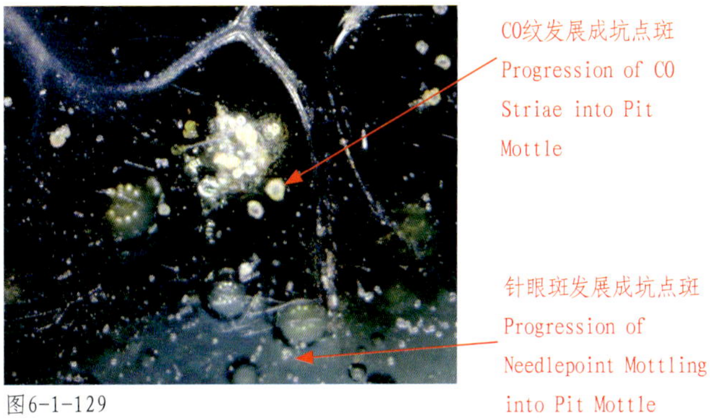

图6-1-129

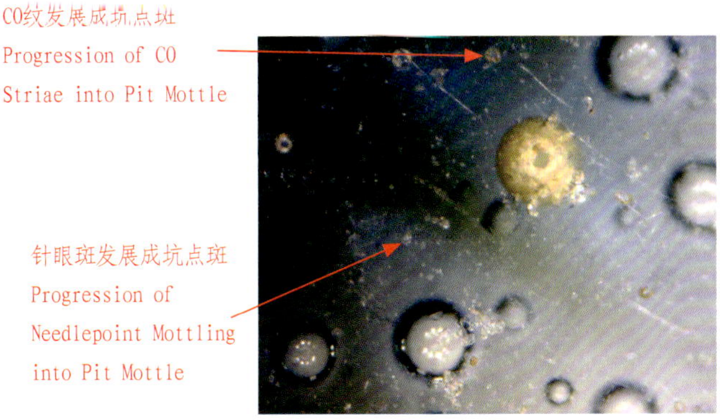

图6-1-130

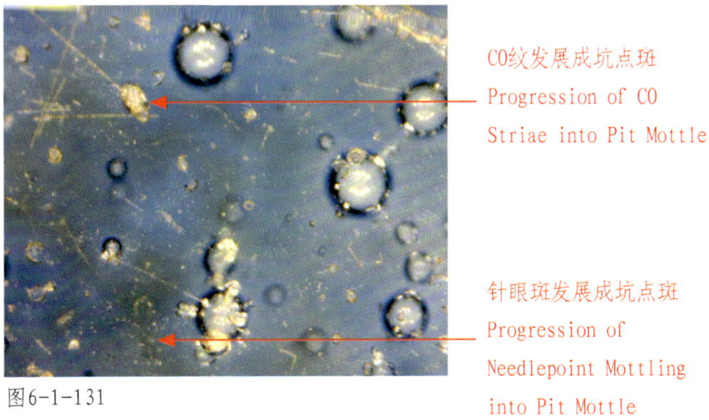

图6-1-131

③ 坑点斑特征

A. CO型坑点斑

a. CO型坑点斑二维特征

I. CO型坑点斑大小不一、深浅不一，各个坑点斑之间距离不等。

II. 坑点斑上能见CO纹，产生坑点斑与CO纹伴生的现象。主要有两种形式：一种是坑点斑与CO纹紧挨或邻近（见图6-1-132），大部分呈元宝形状（见图6-1-133—图6-1-136），也有其他形状（见图6-1-137、图6-1-138），通常二者界线清晰分明；一种是坑点斑与CO纹重叠，二者皆清晰，有时可见CO纹纹路轮廓（见图6-1-139、图6-1-140）。

III. 一开始CO型坑点斑独立零星分布，如果风化继续，坑点斑之间相连贯通，就变成连环状、有螺旋感的坑点斑群，通常呈不规则形状（见图6-1-141—图6-1-143、图6-1-146、图6-1-147、图6-1-149）。

IV. 单位图片中，有C形纹、O形纹、独立的CO型坑点斑以及坑点斑群共同存在，它们各自独立，并与周围玻璃相界线分明（见图6-1-146—图6-1-149）。

V. CO纹有时呈白色，有时呈黄色，伴生的CO型坑点斑大部分时候颜色与C形纹或O形纹一致（见图6-1-135、图6-1-137—图6-1-140、图6-1-145—图6-1-147），有时二者颜色不一致（见图6-1-133、图6-1-136、图6-1-148、图6-1-149）。

VI. CO型坑点斑所在处釉下有絮状斑（见图6-1-143、图6-1-144、图6-1-146）。（参见本章本节絮状斑部分）

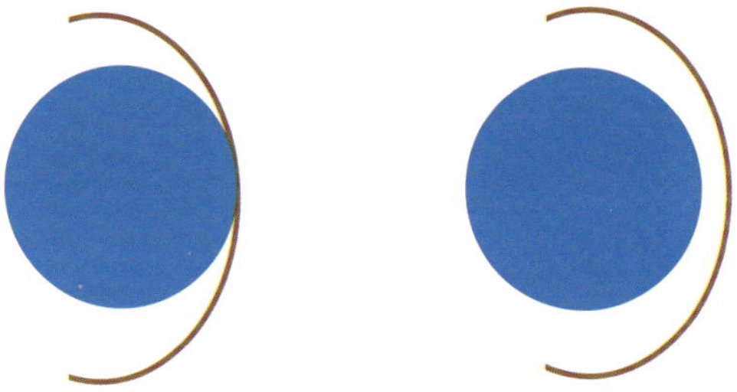

图6-1-132

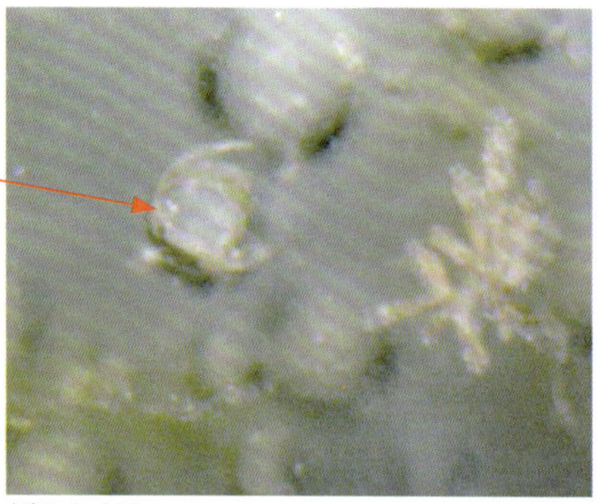

CO型坑点斑与C形纹紧挨
CO Type Pitting and C Shaped Striation in Close Vicinity

图6-1-133*

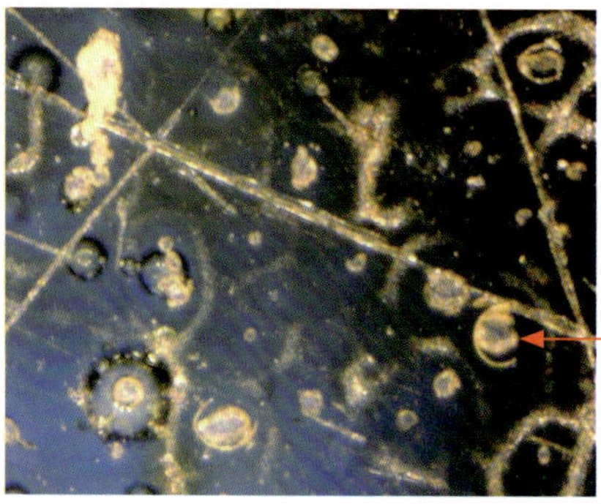

CO型坑点斑与C形纹紧挨
CO Type Pitting and C Shaped Striation in Close Vicinity

图6-1-134*

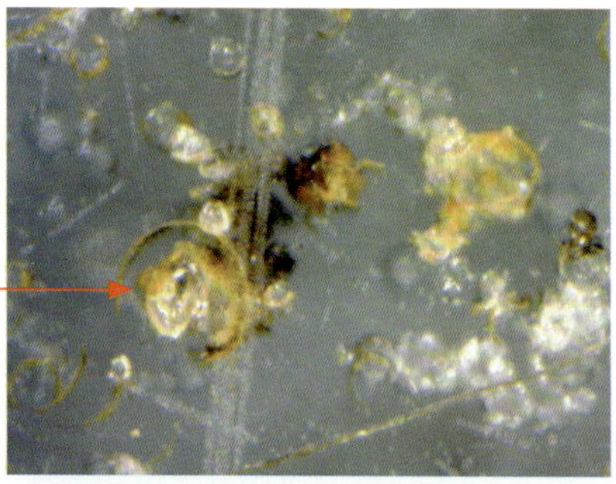

CO型坑点斑与C形纹邻近
CO Type Pitting and C Shaped Striation Occurring Congruently

图6-1-135*

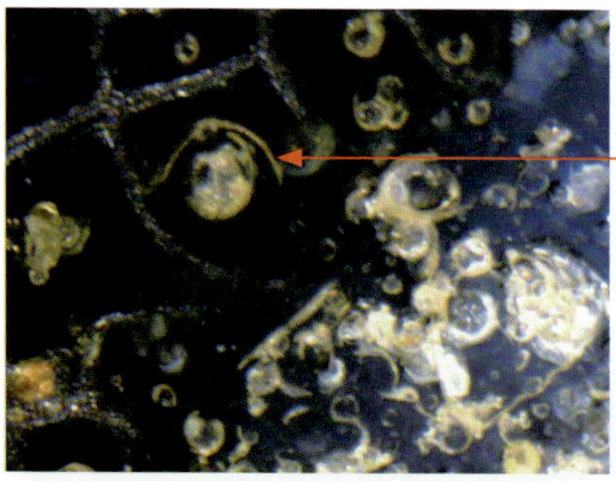

CO型坑点斑与C形纹邻近
CO Type Pitting and C Shaped Striation Occurring Congruently

图6-1-136*

*图片经过裁剪放大处理。

*Picture cropped and enlarged to show detail.

图6-1-137

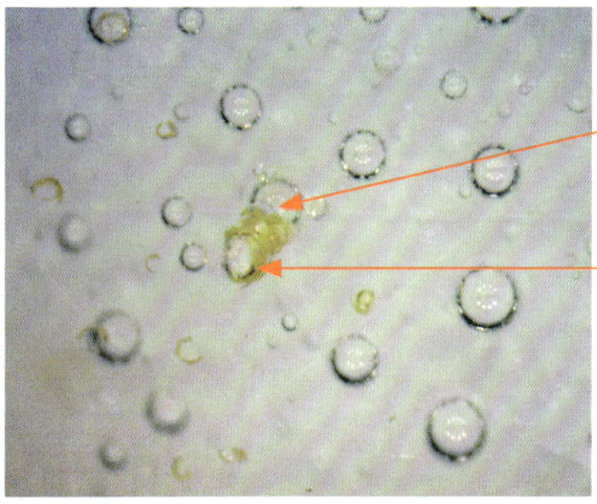

图6-1-138

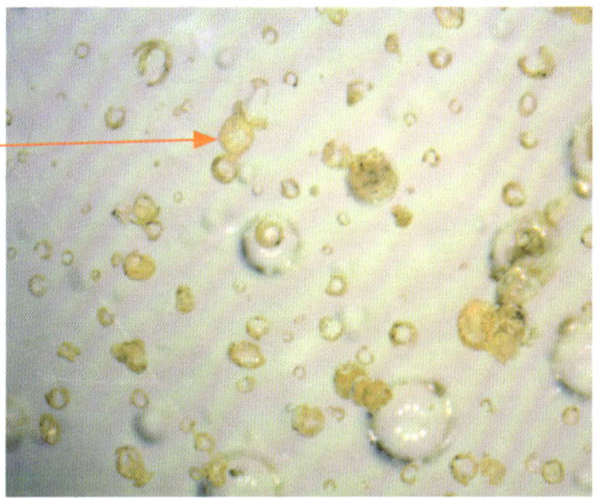

图6-1-139

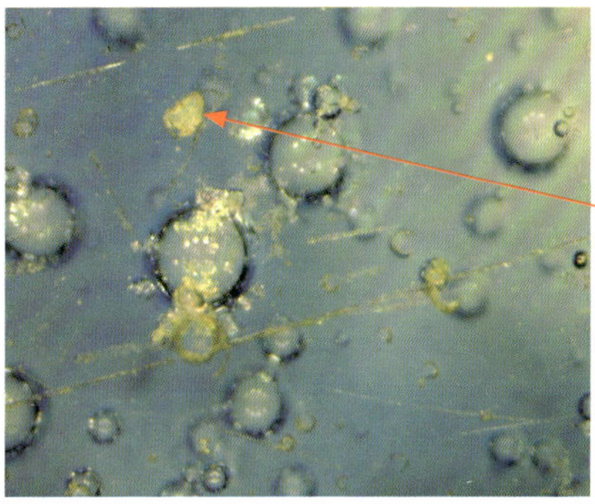

图6-1-140

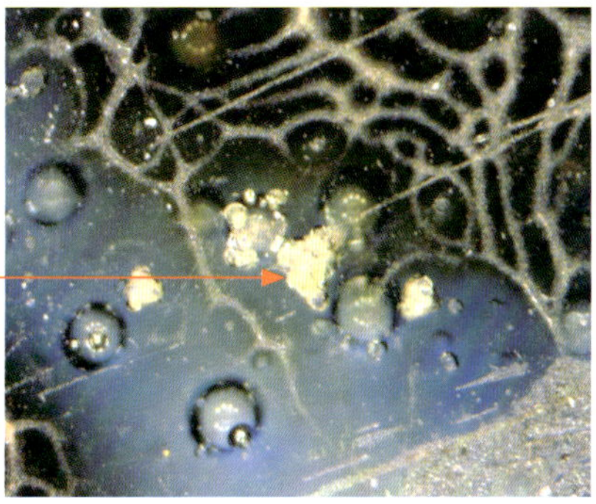

图6-1-141

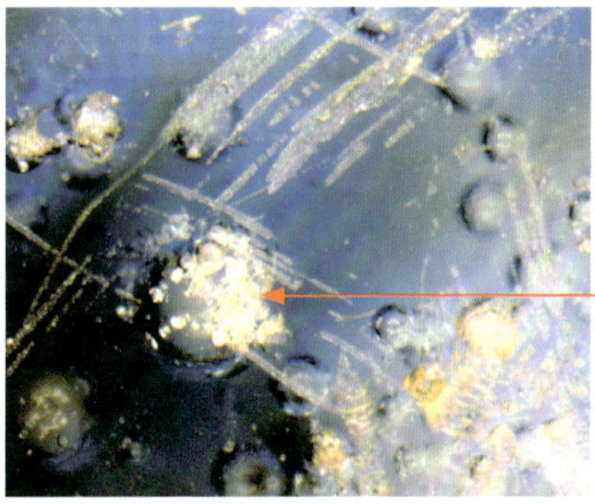

图6-1-142

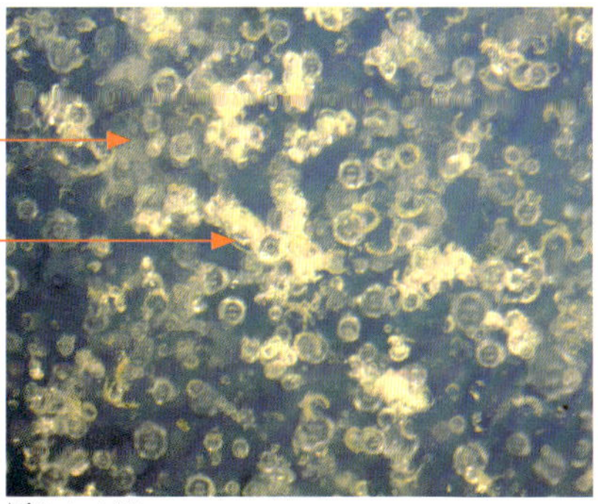

图6-1-143

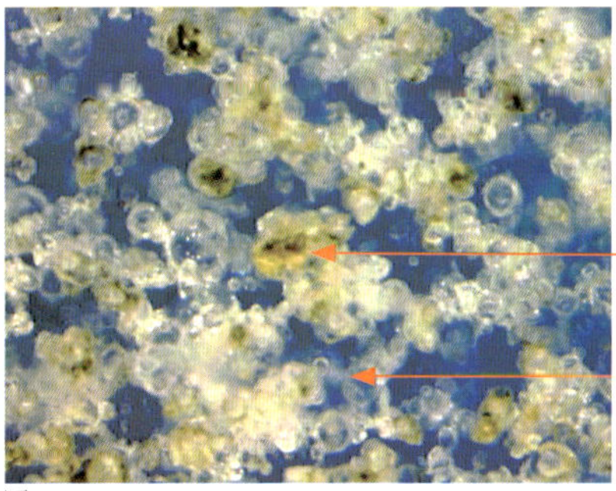

图6-1-144

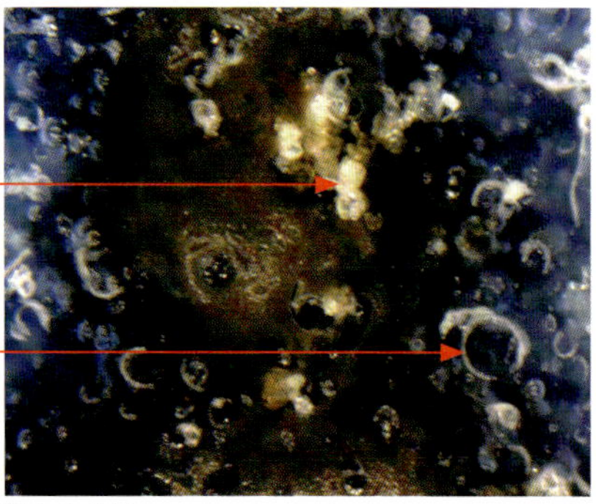

图6-1-145

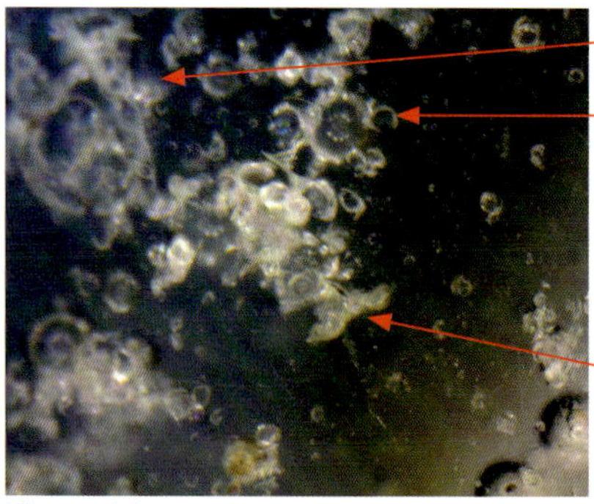

图6-1-146

图6-1-147

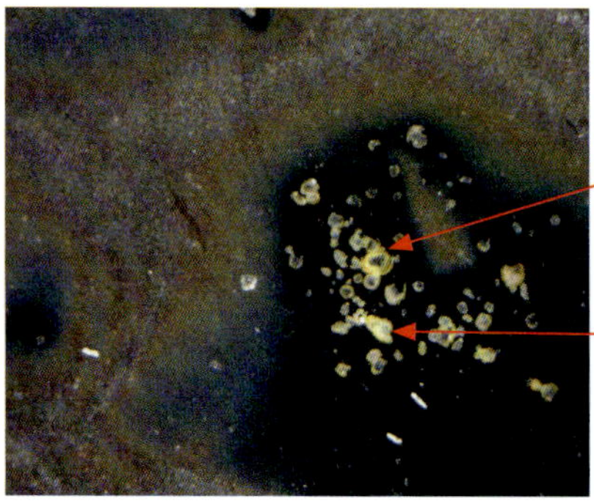

图6-1-148

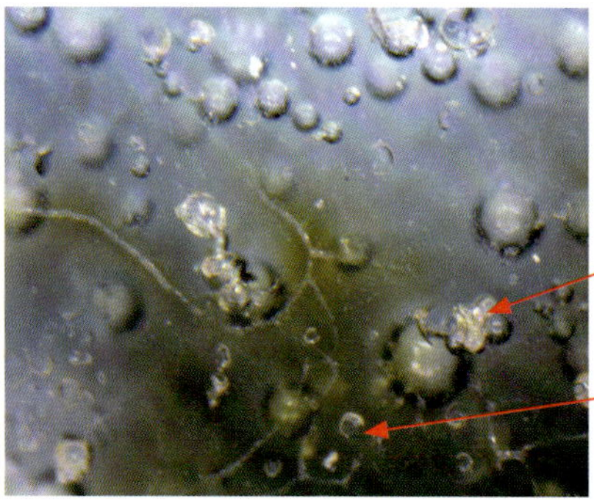

图6-1-149

b. CO型坑点斑三维特征

I. CO型坑点斑大都分布在釉表面凸起处。

II. 釉表面只见纤细收敛的C形纹或O形纹，清晰独立。

III. 釉表面只见纤细收敛的C形纹或O形纹以及面积小于坑点斑二维面积的风化斑块，彼此界线分明。

见图6-1-150、图6-1-151，二者为同一器物同一位置图片，图6-1-150为二维图片，图6-1-151为三维图片。

图6-1-150中箭头所指的CO型坑点斑在图6-1-151中只见两条C形纹。纹路纤细收敛，清晰独立，与周围玻璃相界线分明。

CO型坑点斑是C形纹纵向往釉层中发展的结果，坑点斑深入釉层，三维成像无法全面观察到深入釉层的坑点斑。

见图6-1-152、图6-1-153，二者为同一器物同一位置图片，图6-1-152为二维图片，图6-1-153为三维图片。

图6-1-152中箭头所指的CO型坑点斑在图6-1-153中只见C形纹，同时还有两处面积小于图6-1-152中CO型坑点斑的深色斑块（见箭头A所指处），斑块清晰独立，与玻璃相界线分明。

箭头A所指的深色斑块是由C形纹继续风化发展而形成的风化斑块，风化斑块继续向釉层中发展，就逐渐形成深入釉层的CO型坑点斑，三维成像无法全面观察到深入釉层的坑点斑，所以面积显得比二维成像要小。

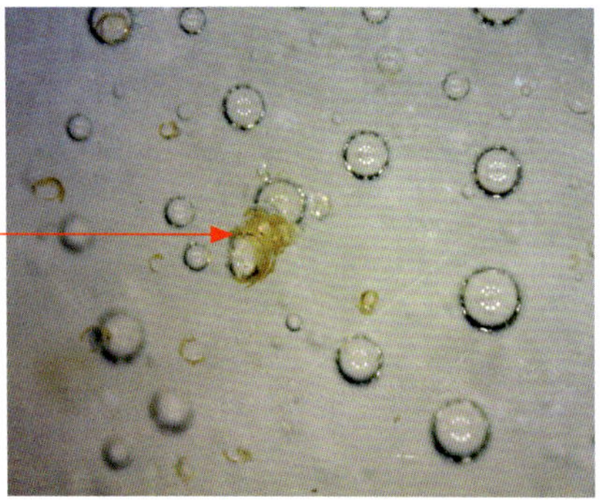

图6-1-150

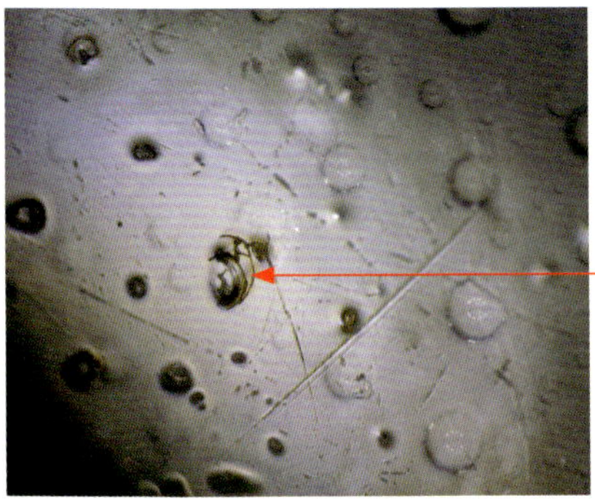

图6-1-151

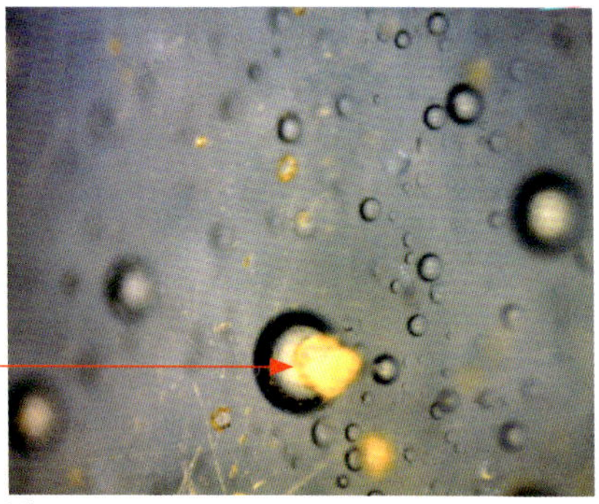

图6-1-152

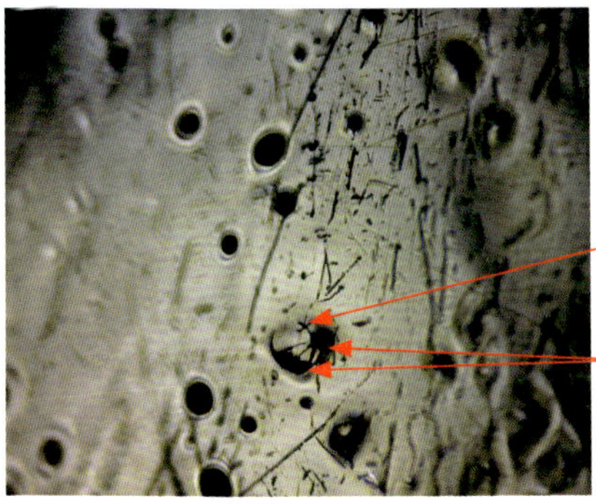

图6-1-153

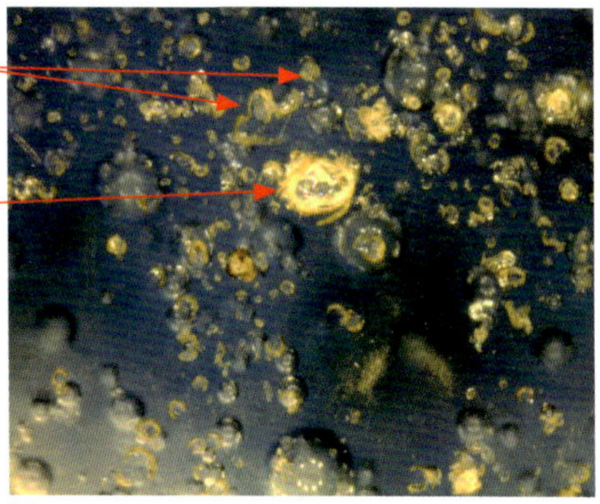

图6-1-154

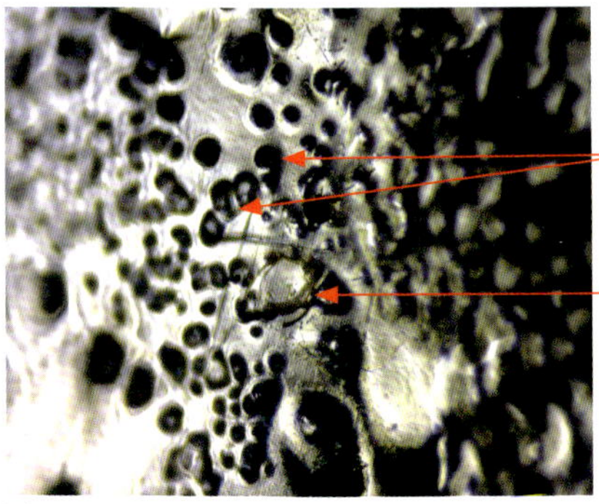

图6-1-155

见图6-1-154、图6-1-155，二者为同一器物同一位置图片，图6-1-154为二维图片，图6-1-155为三维图片。

图6-1-154中的两个CO型坑点斑在图6-1-155中呈深色，均存在于釉表面凸起处（见箭头B所指处）；图6-1-154中的CO型坑点斑在图6-1-155中呈浅色，所在处凸起不明显，可见一条末端有分叉的C形纹（见箭头C所指处），纹路纤细收敛，清晰独立，与周围玻璃相界线分明。

一般来说，CO型坑点斑大部分布在釉表面凸起处。在图6-1-154和图6-1-155中，二维成像的CO型坑点斑，与三维成像中一个个凸起的“小山包”一一对应，釉表面没有凸起的地方光滑洁净。这是由于CO型坑点斑与玻璃相结合处的组织结构稳定性较差，容易风化；釉表面较平滑处组织结构稳定性较好，风化强度低，表现光滑洁净。

见图6-1-156、图6-1-157，二者为同一器物同一位置图片，图6-1-156为二维图片，图6-1-157为三维图片。

图6-1-156中的白色CO型坑点斑在图6-1-157中呈深色，斑块清晰独立，与玻璃相界线分明，且面积明显比图6-1-157中要小（见箭头D所指处）。

图6-1-157中的深色斑块D是由O形纹继续风化发展而形成的风化斑块，风化斑块继续向釉层中发展，就逐渐形成深入釉层的CO型坑点斑，三维成像无法全面观察到深入釉层的坑点斑，所以面积显得比二维成像要小。

见图6-1-158、图6-1-159，二者为同一器物同一位置图片，图6-1-158为二维图片，图6-1-159为三维图片。

图6-1-158中的连环坑点斑群在图6-1-159中只见几条交错重叠C形纹及O形纹，纹路纤细收敛，清晰独立，与周围玻璃相界线分明（见箭头E所指处）。这是因为CO型坑点斑群是C形纹、O形纹纵向往釉层中发展的结果，三维成像无法全面观察到深入釉层的坑点斑群。

B. 针眼型坑点斑

a. 针眼型坑点斑二维特征

I. 针眼型坑点斑一般呈白色，大小不一，分布随机（见图6-1-160—图6-1-164）。

II. 针眼型坑点斑外沿有纤细的包边，斑内还可见针眼斑分布（见图6-1-160、图6-1-161）。

III. 针眼型坑点斑包边不明显，坑点斑内也不见独立针眼斑（见图6-1-162）。

IV. 针眼型坑点斑内针眼斑分布密集，密集处已看不见独立的针眼斑（见图6-1-163、图6-1-164）。

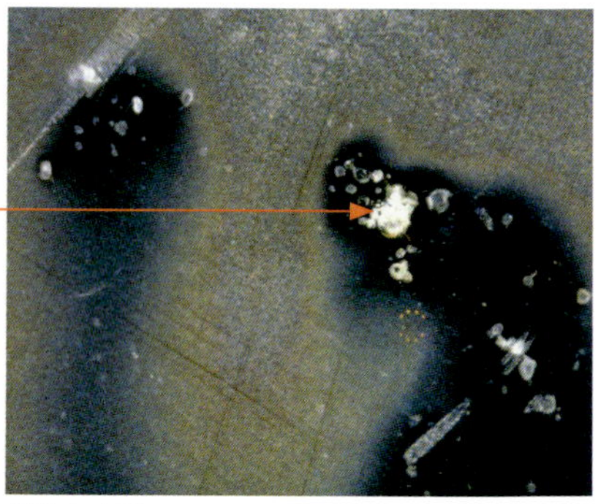

图6-1-156

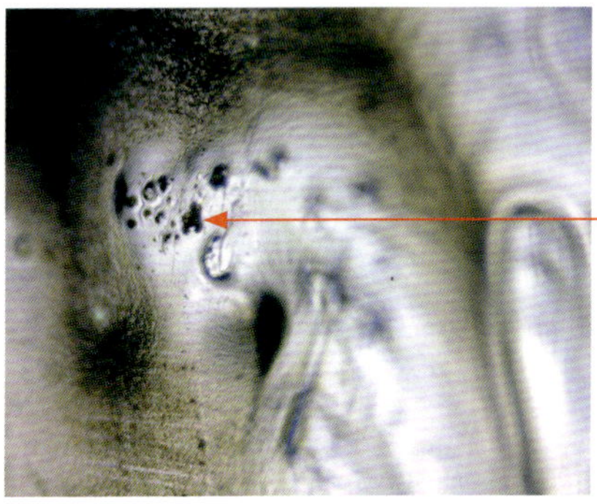

图6-1-157

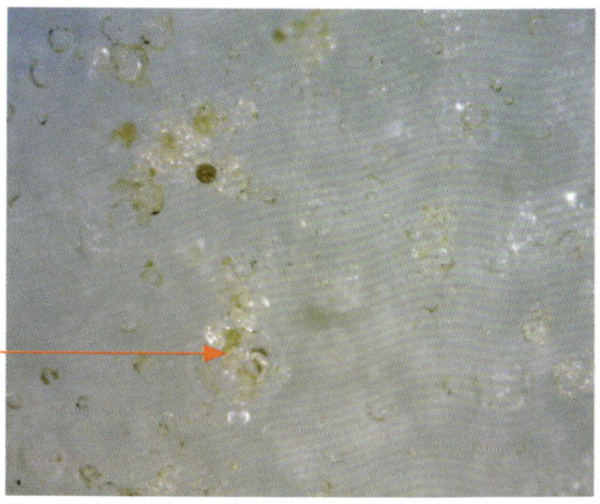

图6-1-158

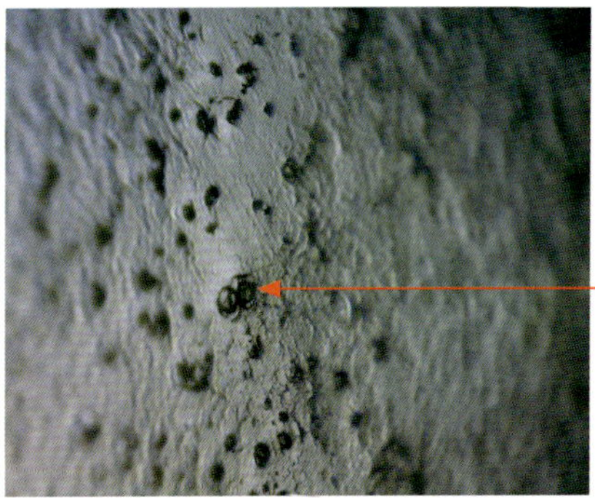

图6-1-159

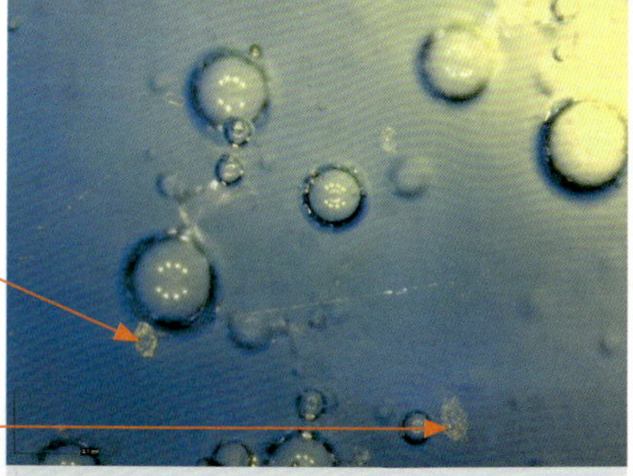

图6-1-160

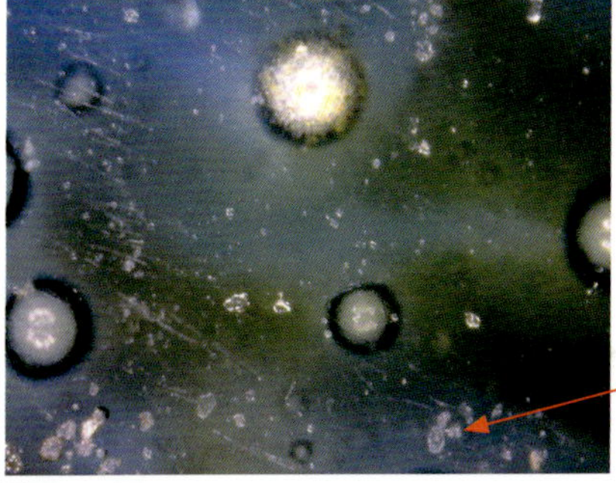

图6-1-161

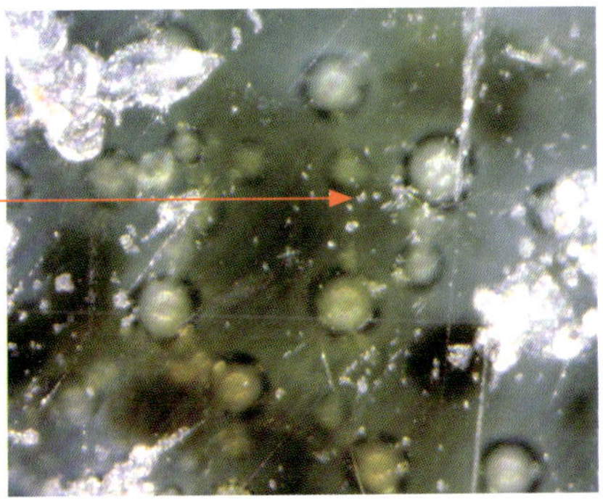

图6-1-162

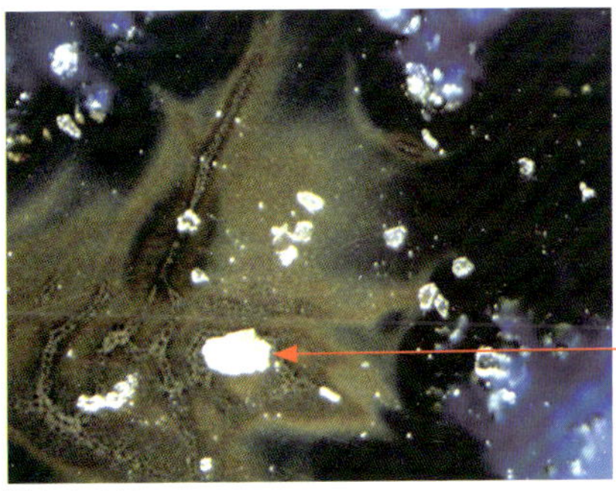

图6-1-163

b. 针眼型坑点斑三维特征

I. 针眼型坑点斑呈凹陷状，清晰独立。

II. 针眼型坑点斑与周围玻璃相界线分明。

见图6-1-165、图6-1-166，二者为同一器物同一位置图片，图6-1-165为二维图片，图6-1-166为三维图片。

图6-1-165中白色的针眼型坑点斑在图6-1-166中呈深色，成像清晰。坑点斑为釉表面上一凹坑，三维成像面积与二维成像面积相当，与周围玻璃相界线分明。

C. 外伤型坑点斑

外伤型坑点斑二维特征

I. 外伤型坑点斑通常形状不规则，大都有色阶变化（见图6-1-167—图6-1-170）。

II. 面积较大的坑点斑还能够观察到斑块内的针眼斑和沉积物（见图6-1-167、图6-1-168）。

III. 坑点斑所在处釉下有絮状斑（见图6-1-169）。

D. 浸水型坑点斑

a. 浸水型坑点斑二维特征

I. 浸水型坑点斑可以出现在釉表面任何地方，分布随机。坑点斑内分布有磨砂针眼斑（见图6-1-171—图6-1-174）。

II. 浸水型坑点斑呈不规则形状，有的由上下各一条弧线组成，形如未合拢的圆圈（见图6-1-175）。

III. 浸水型坑点斑与周围釉表面界线分明（见图6-1-171—图6-1-175）。

b. 浸水型坑点斑三维特征

浸水型坑点斑三维显微特征为明显凹陷的凹坑（见图6-1-176箭头F所指处）。

图6-1-164

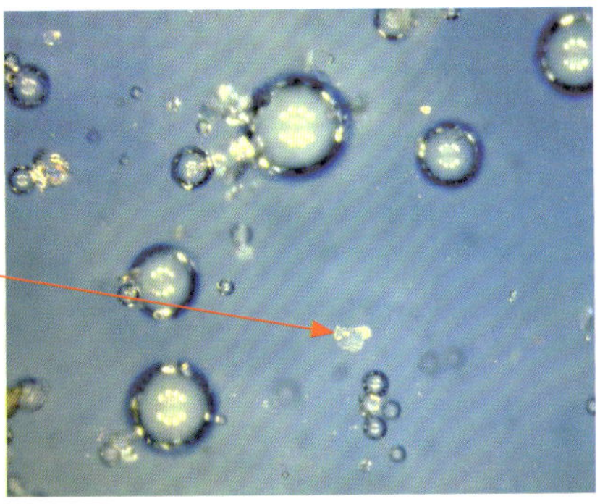

图6-1-165

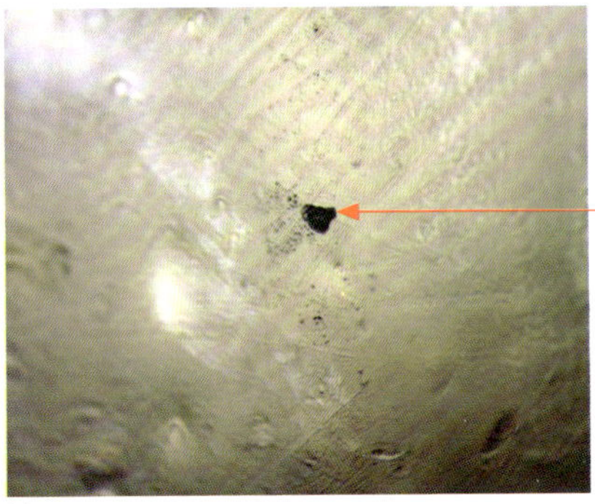

图6-1-166

坑点斑内沉积物、针眼斑，富有色阶变化
Sediments, Needlepoint Mottling within Pit Mottle, with Color Spectrum

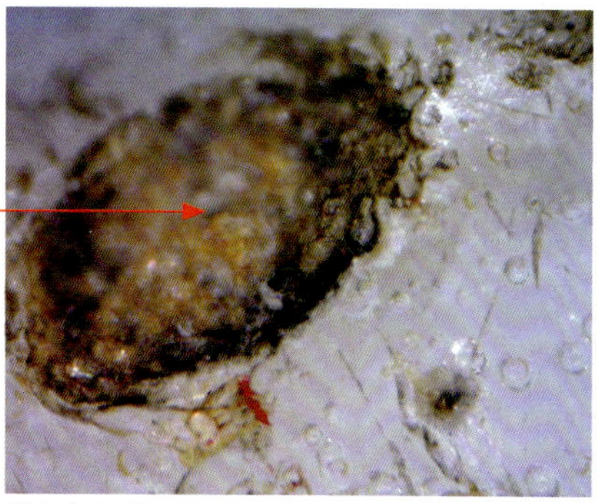

图6-1-167

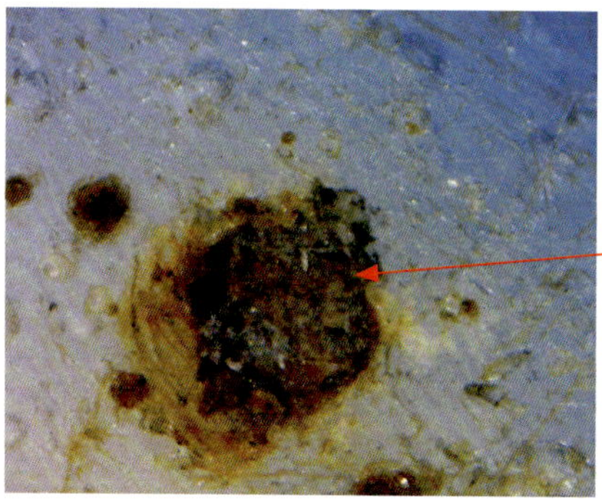

坑点斑内沉积物、针眼斑，富有色阶变化
Sediments, Needlepoint Mottling within Pit Mottle, with Color Spectrum

图6-1-168

絮状斑
Floccus Mottling

色阶变化
Color Spectrum

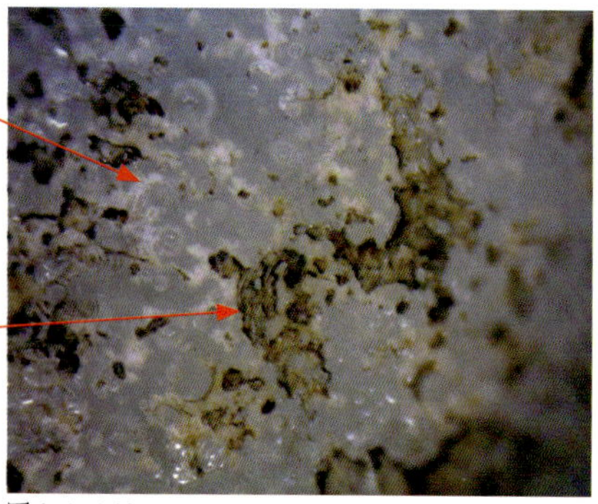

图6-1-169

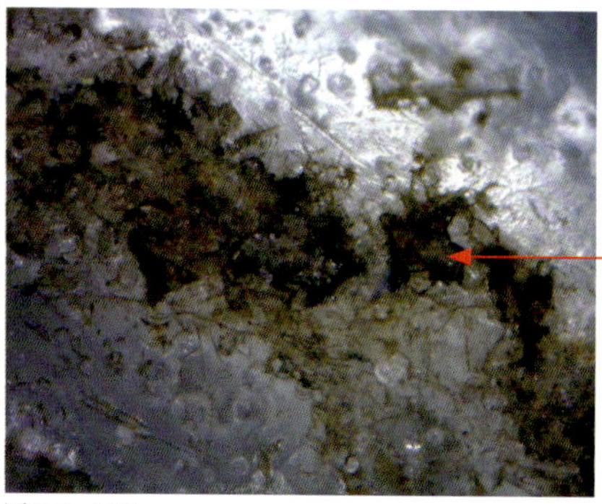

色阶变化
Color Spectrum

图6-1-170

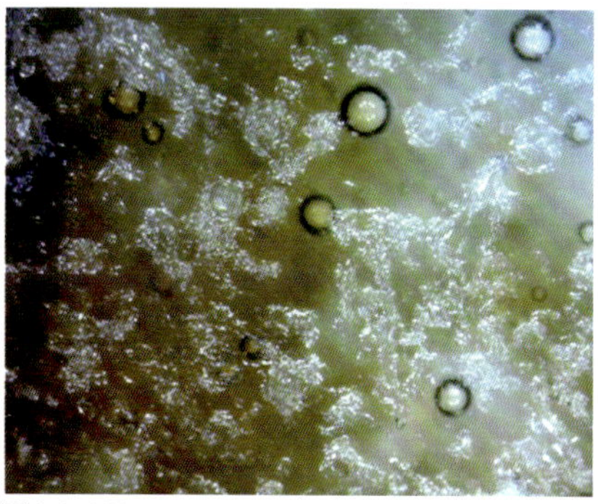

图6-1-171

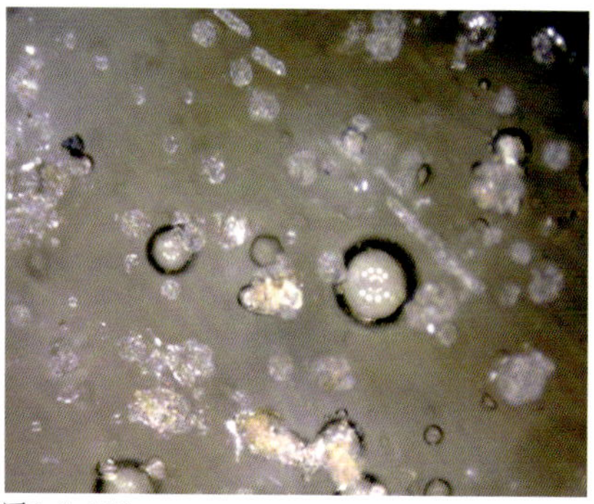

图6-1-172

图6-1-173

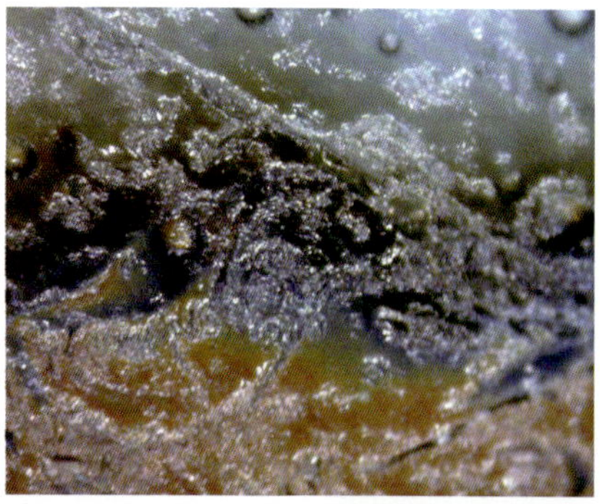

图6-1-174

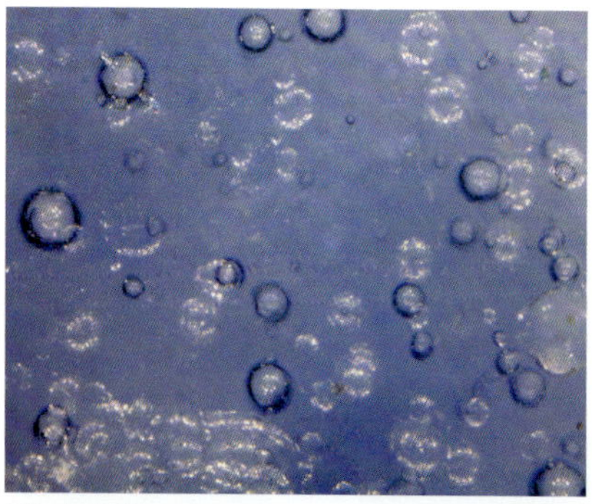

图6-1-175

F

图6-1-176

（3）物盖斑

①物盖斑概念

物盖斑是元青花瓷器在后天环境影响下，釉表面被外界物质覆盖而形成的斑块。

②物盖斑形成

元青花瓷器上的物盖斑大都是后天环境中的泥沙等物质长期覆盖在瓷器表面形成的，也有后来人们对瓷器修补时留下的黏合剂印记。

③物盖斑特征

物盖斑二维特征

a. 物盖斑颜色主要有黄色、褐色及灰白色（见图6-1-177—图6-1-184）。

b. 物盖斑与周围未被覆盖的底板界线是分明的，边界有直线、有曲线。（见图6-1-177—图6-1-184）

c. 物盖斑有层次，有的呈起皮状（见图6-1-177），有的有龟裂纹，像旱地（见图6-1-178）。

d. 有的物盖斑上有划痕（见图6-1-179）。

e. 物盖斑下存在絮状斑（见图6-1-180、图6-1-181）。（参见本章本节絮状斑部分）

f. 修补瓷器留下的印记根据其使用的化学用剂的不同，其物盖斑形貌也不同。如泰国标本的黏合剂，剂量多处呈白色，不透明（见图6-1-182），剂量少处形貌如针眼斑，掺杂着灰尘及其他有色颗粒（见图6-1-183）；部分景德镇标本的黏合剂呈透明状（见图6-1-184）。有时黏合剂形成的物盖斑与针眼斑形貌相近，难以区分，必要时需要结合肉眼来观察瓷器。

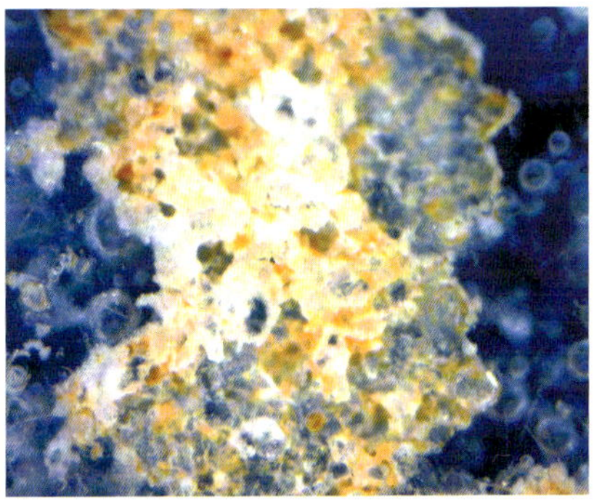

图6-1-177

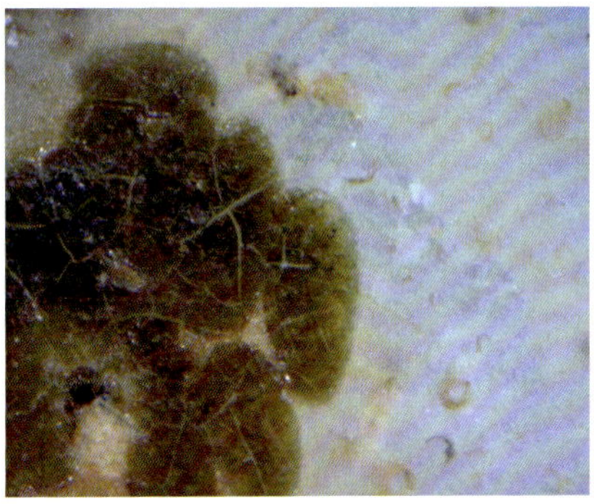

图6-1-178

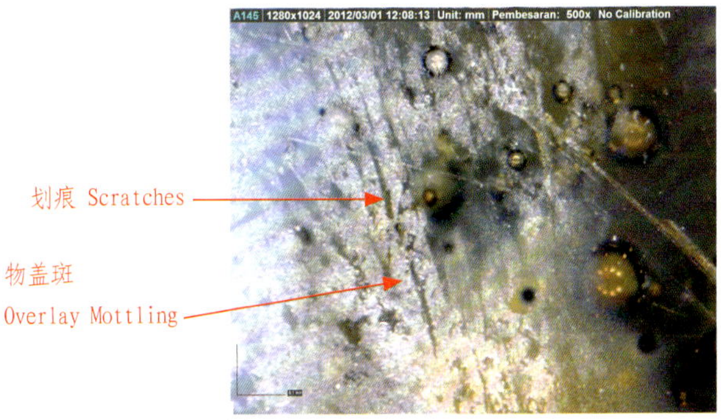

图6-1-179

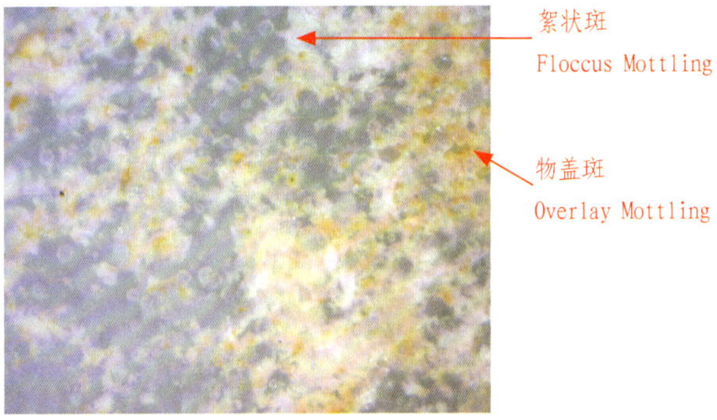

图6-1-180

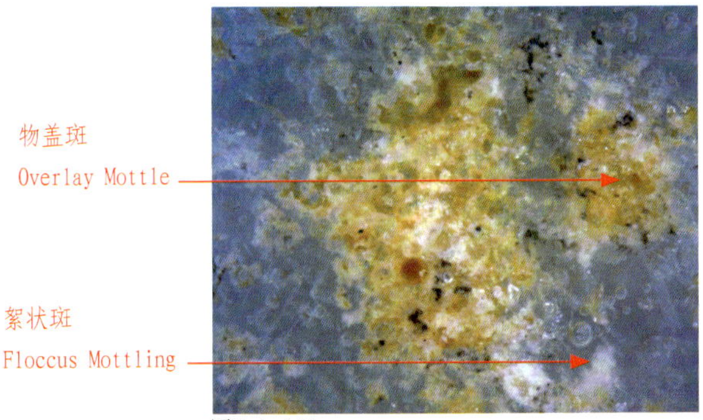

图6-1-181

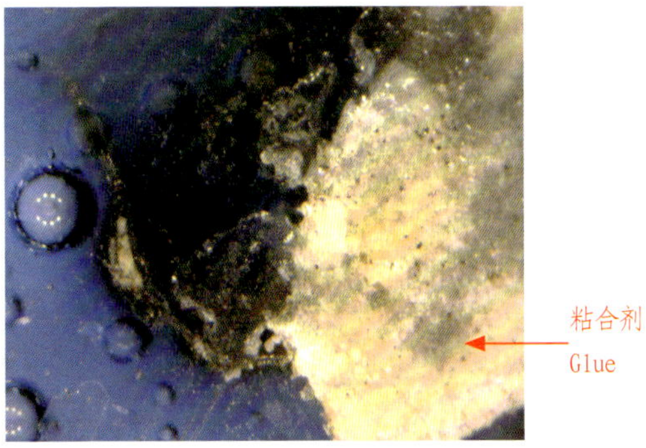

图6-1-182

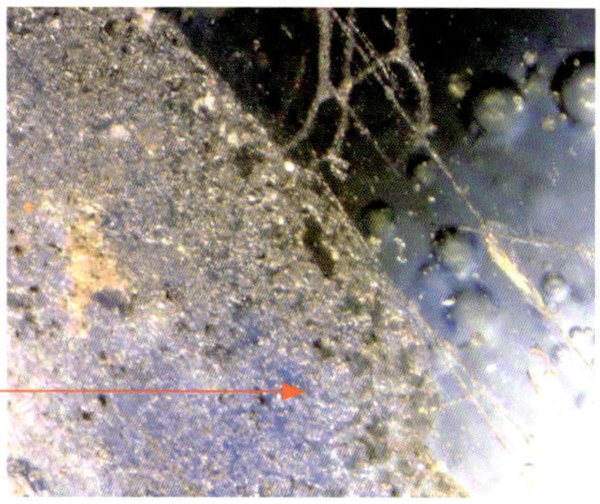

图6-1-183

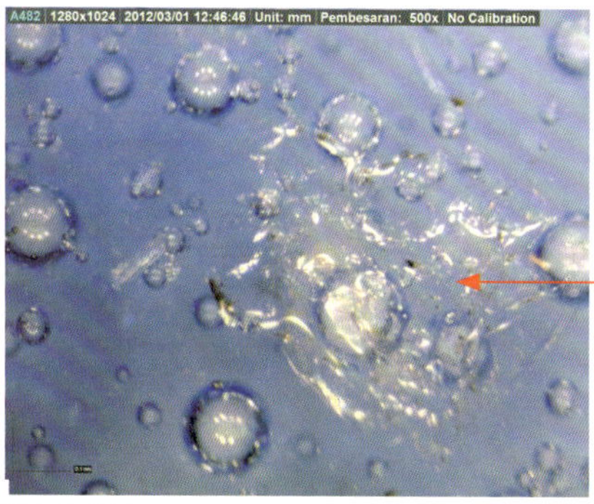

图6-1-184

（4）泡根斑

① 泡根斑概念

泡根斑是元青花瓷器在后天环境影响下，由破口泡发展形成，内有沉积物的凹形斑块。

② 泡根斑形成

元青花瓷器的釉表面被风化侵蚀或磨损后，存在于釉层中的部分气泡无釉层包裹，完全暴露在外界环境中，变成泡根，形成深浅不一的凹坑，外界物质长期在泡根内沉积形成泡根斑。

一般来说，瓷器的口沿处易形成泡根斑。在风化强度普遍比较高的海捞瓷上，泡根斑在瓷器上各处都可以出现。

③ 泡根斑特征

泡根斑二维特征

a. 泡根斑大部分是圆形，也有椭圆形和不规则形貌（见图6-1-185—图6-1-189）。

b. 泡根斑颜色有白色、黄色、褐色及黑色等（见图6-1-185—图6-1-189）。

c. 有的同一泡根斑内有多种沉积物，且有色阶变化（见图6-1-186、图6-1-189）。

d. 有的临近的几个泡根斑之间有色差（见图6-1-187、图6-1-189）。

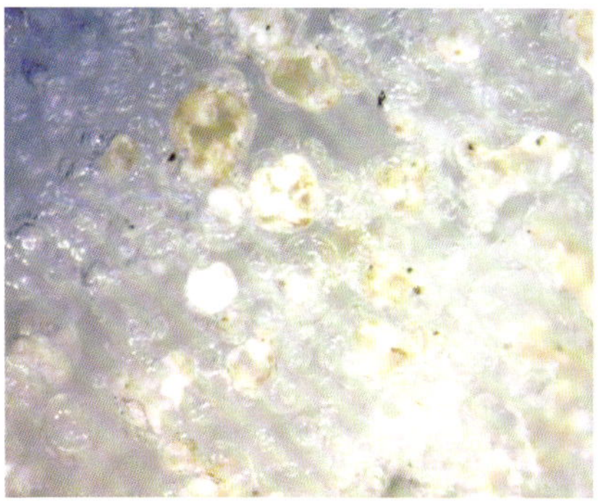
图6-1-185

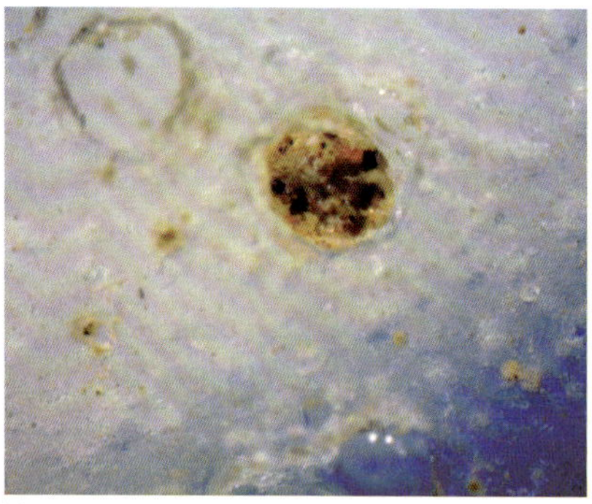
图6-1-186

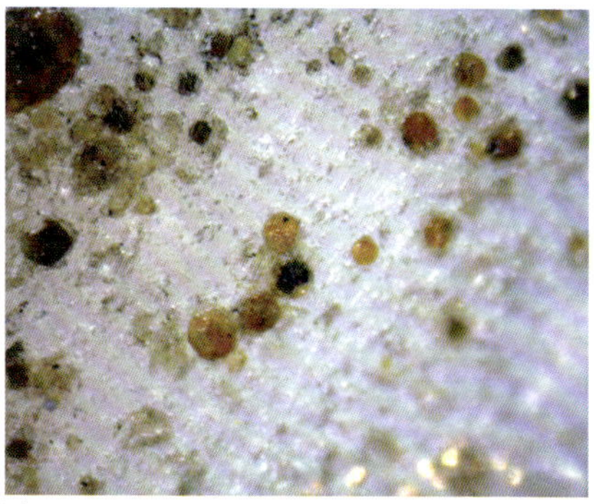
图6-1-187

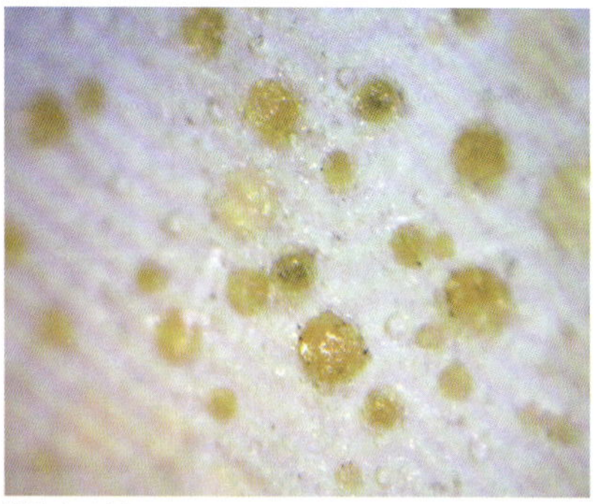
图6-1-188

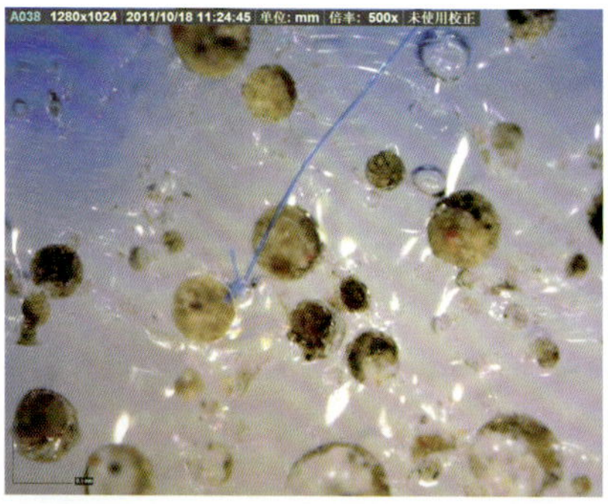
图6-1-189

（5）絮状斑

① 絮状斑概念

絮状斑是以白色为主，呈无序状，具有流淌、渗透、漫延趋势的不规则斑块。它是元青花瓷器在后天环境影响下，在其釉表面及釉层中，由可溶盐、难溶盐和灰尘等物质沉积形成的。

② 絮状斑形成

元青花瓷器釉表面随机分布有裂纹或孔隙。此外，大气及土壤中具有一定酸性或碱性的水溶液会侵蚀元青花瓷器釉表面，在釉表面形成新的裂纹或孔隙。外界物质通过这些裂纹和孔隙进入釉层，在釉层中形成可溶盐及难溶盐。

当土壤中水分蒸发，可溶盐在釉表面及釉层中析出。在釉表面的可溶盐易因溶于水而流失，难溶盐也易掉落，所以絮状斑在釉表面存在的概率较小，普遍存在于釉层中。

在干湿交替的环境中，渗入釉层中的难溶盐难以流失，可溶盐会在水分蒸发后的釉层中形成结晶，它们连同一些细小灰尘在釉层中叠加沉积形成絮状斑。

土壤中的及釉表面的阴阳离子会发生反应，形成不同颜色的难溶盐沉积物。

③ 絮状斑特征

A. 絮状斑二维特征

a. 絮状斑以白色为主，一般都以块状、片状等不规则形貌分布在釉层中（见图6-1-190—图6-1-206）。

b. 絮状斑一般在釉层组织结构稳定性较差处或破损处出现，如坑点斑下方（见图6-1-191—图6-1-194），物盖斑下方（见图6-1-199、图6-1-200），釉裂纹下方（见图6-1-190、图6-1-195、图6-1-196）C形、O形纹下方（见图6-1-197、图6-1-198），划痕下方（见图6-1-201），鬃眼下方（见图6-1-202—图6-1-205）和其他釉损处下方（见图6-1-206）等。

c. 絮状斑由釉损处呈梯度向周边的釉下扩散。斑块中心色白如牛奶，不透明；斑块边沿呈绒状，半透明，有向四周漫延的趋势（见图6-1-190—图6-1-206）。

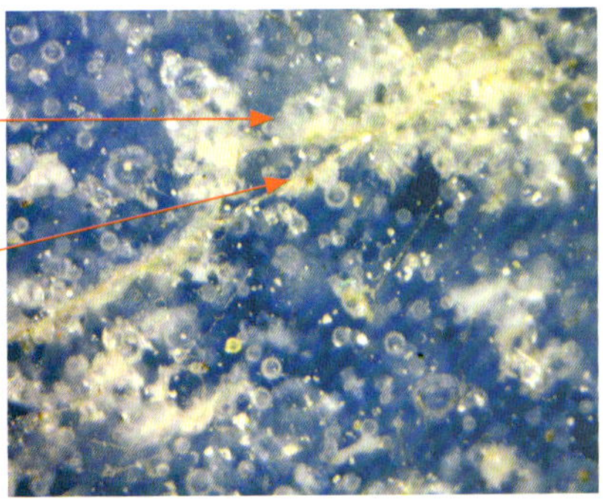

图6-1-190

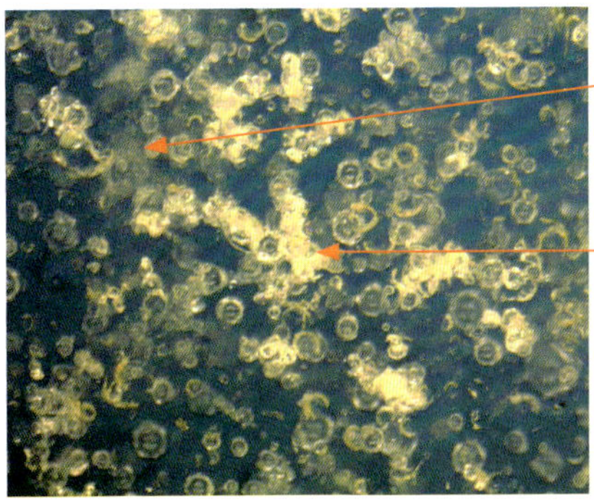

图6-1-191

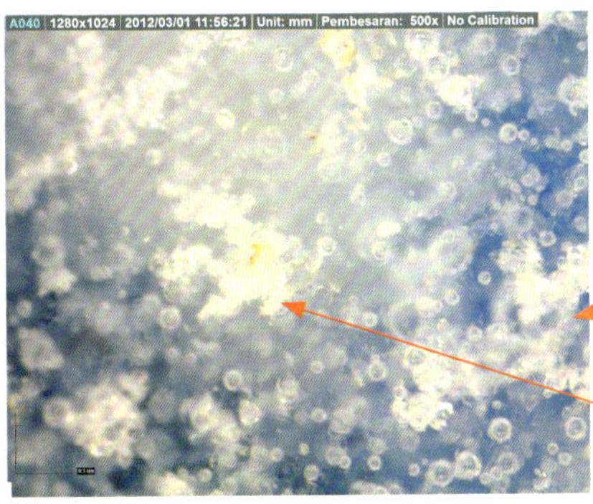

图6-1-192

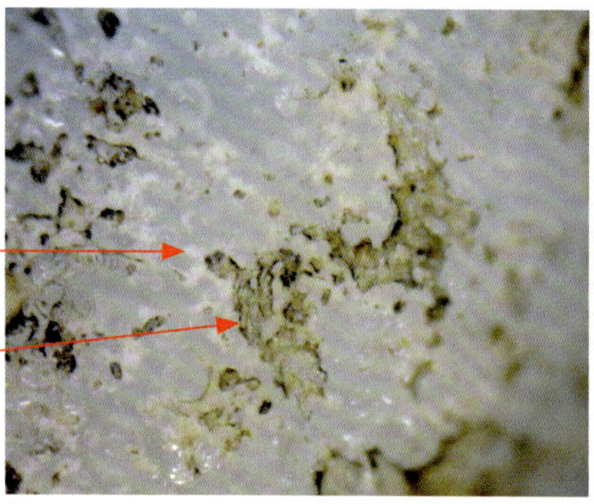

图6-1-193

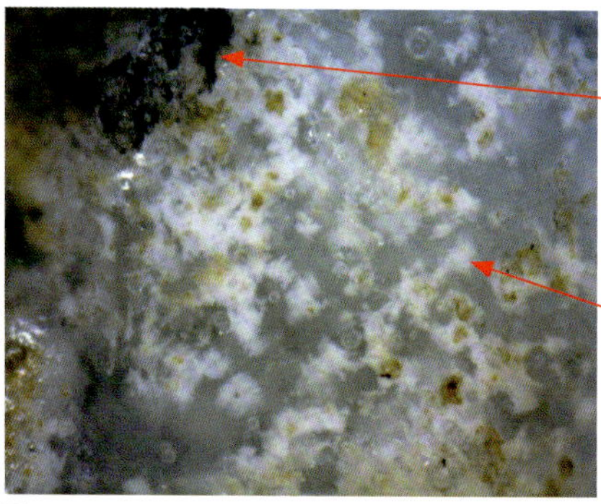

图6-1-194

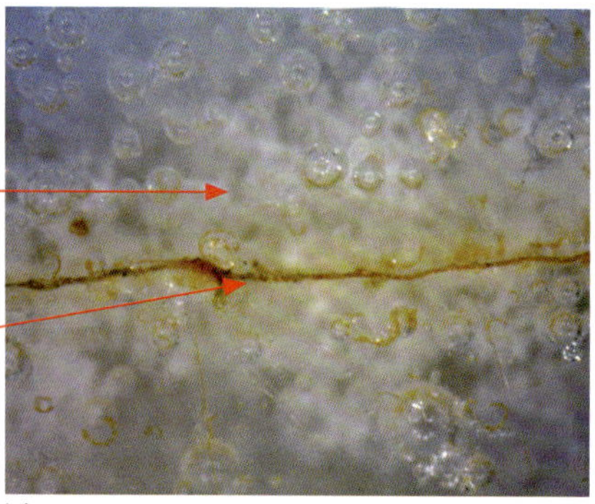

图6-1-195

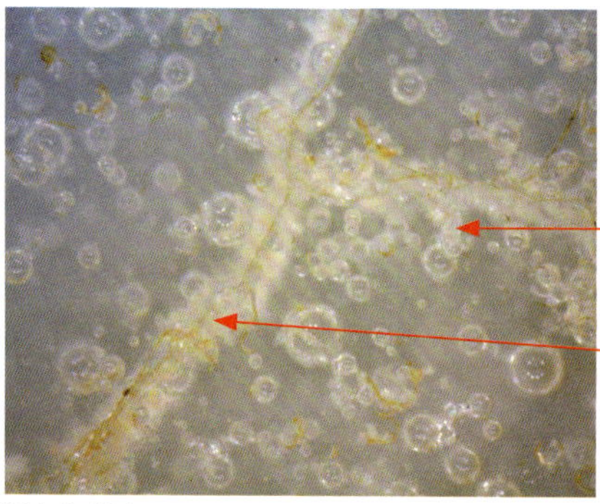

图6-1-196

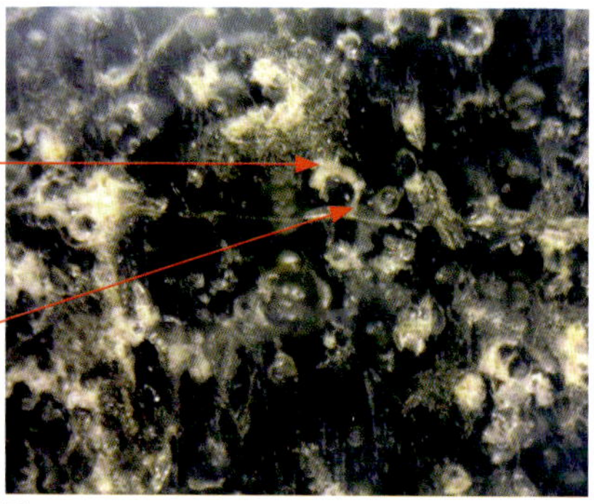

图6-1-197

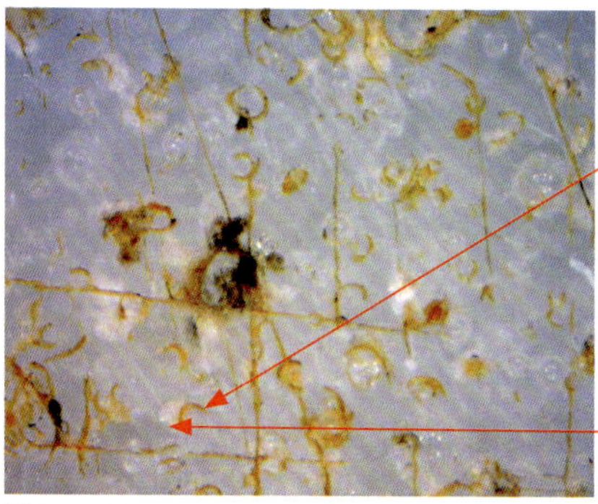

图6-1-198

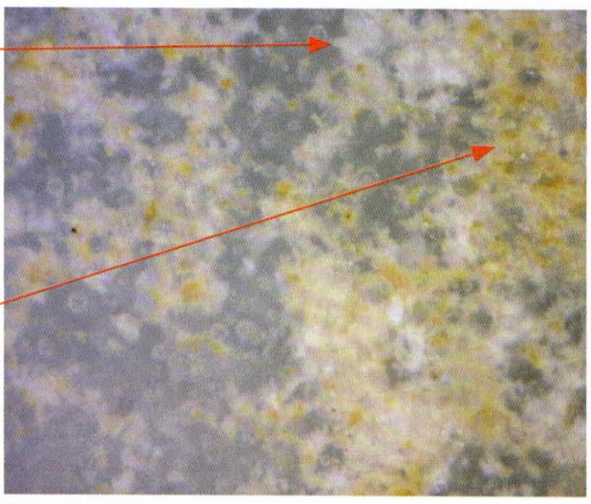

图6-1-199

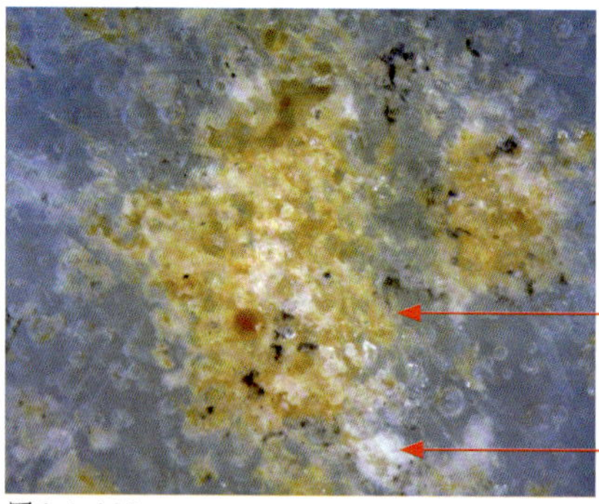

图6-1-200

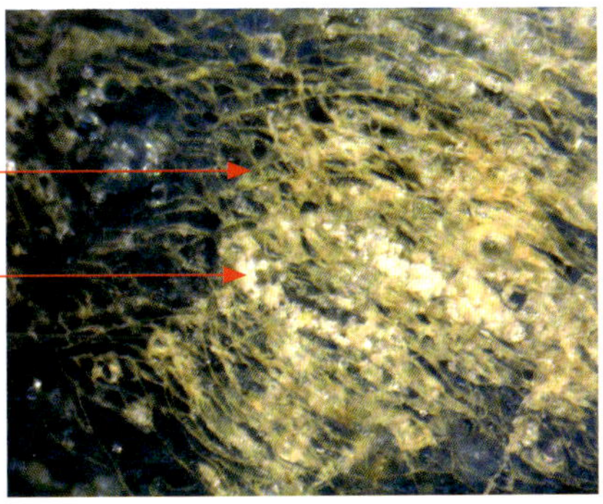

图6-1-201

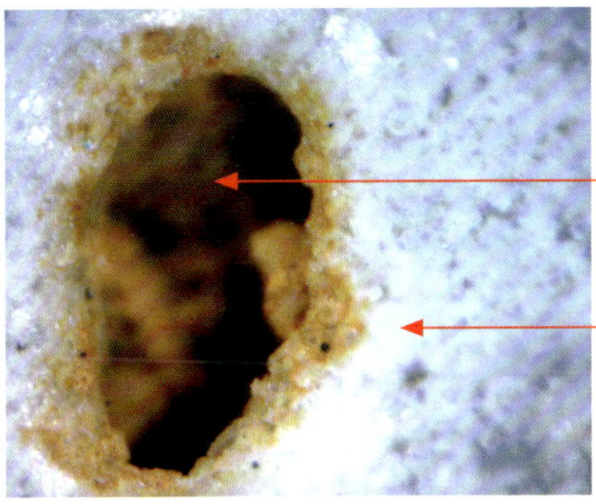

图6-1-202

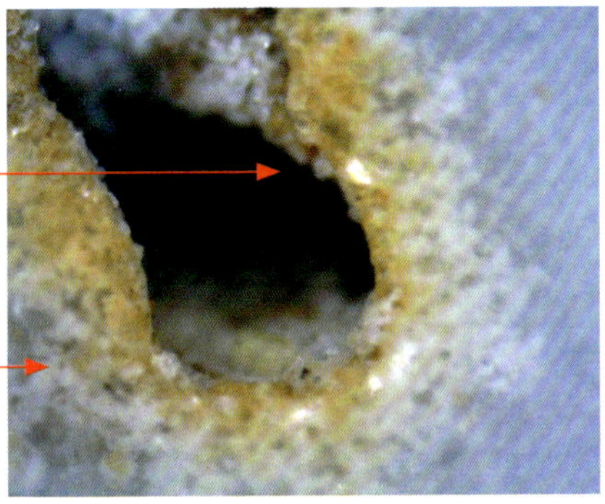

图6-1-203

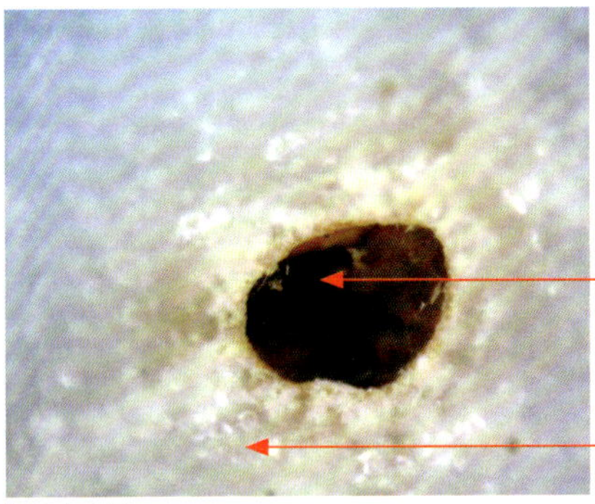

图6-1-204

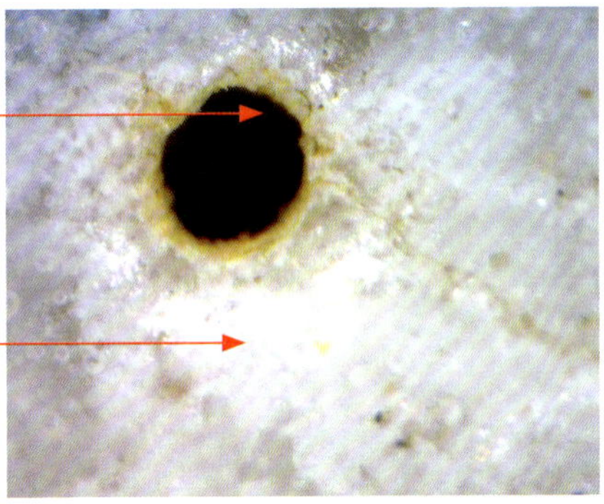

图6-1-205

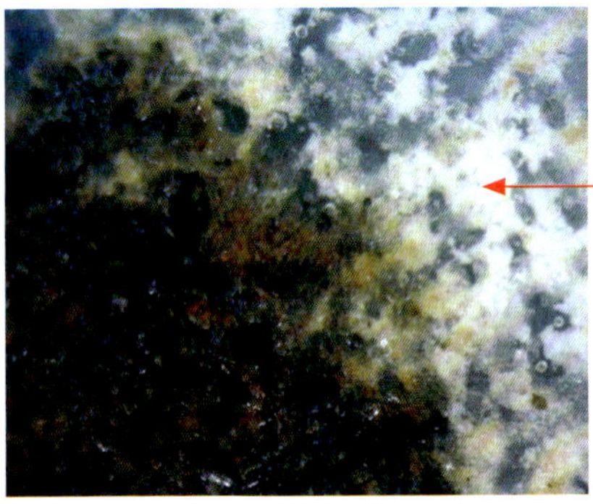

图6-1-206

B. 絮状斑三维特征

a. 絮状斑在釉表面不可见，釉表面釉损处（如坑点斑、釉裂纹）的面积远远小于釉损处与絮状斑二维成像面积的总和。

b. 釉表面釉损处以外的地方光滑洁净，无其他明显的大面积损伤。

见图6-1-207、图6-1-208，二者为同一器物同一位置图片，图6-1-207为二维图片，图6-1-208为三维图片。

图6-1-207中箭头A所指的白色絮状斑在图6-1-208中却不可见，釉表面只见零星几处坑点斑，说明絮状斑存在于釉层中。

图6-1-207中箭头B所指的絮状斑在图6-1-208中不可见，釉表面光滑洁净。箭头B邻近的釉表面可见一处面积小于絮状斑的坑点斑（见箭头C所指处），说明絮状斑有一部分存在于釉层中。箭头C所指的坑点斑属于釉表面破损处，应该是絮状斑形成的通道。

见图6-1-209、图6-1-210，二者为同一器物同一位置图片，图6-1-209为二维图片，图6-1-210为三维图片。

图6-1-209中的白色絮状斑在图6-1-210中难以观察到，釉表面只见釉裂纹，无其他明显损伤，说明絮状斑存在于釉层中（见箭头D所指处）。

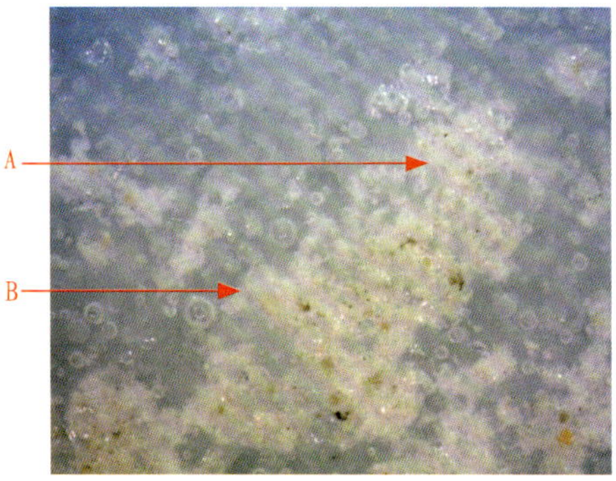

图6-1-207

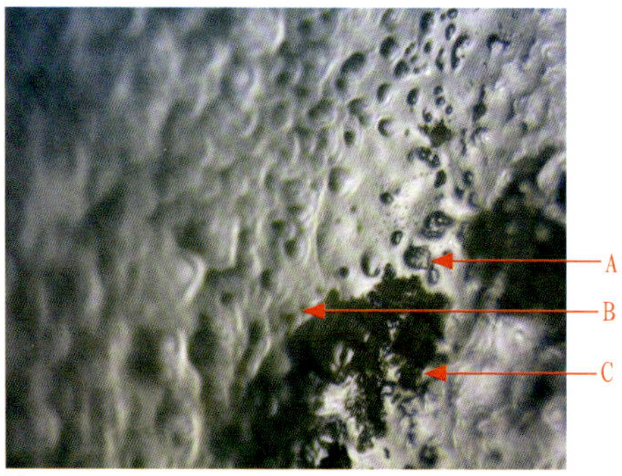

图6-1-208

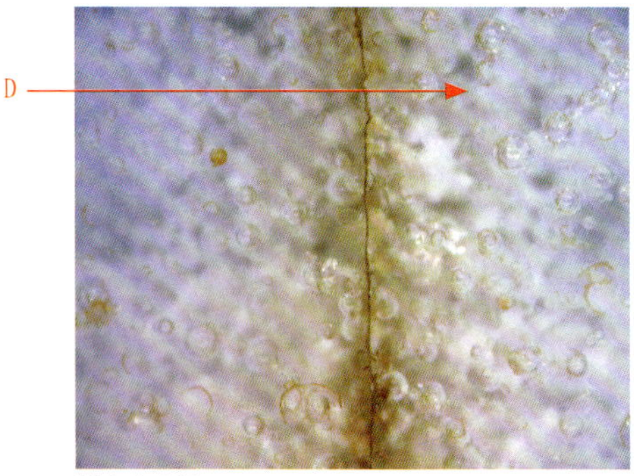

图6-1-209

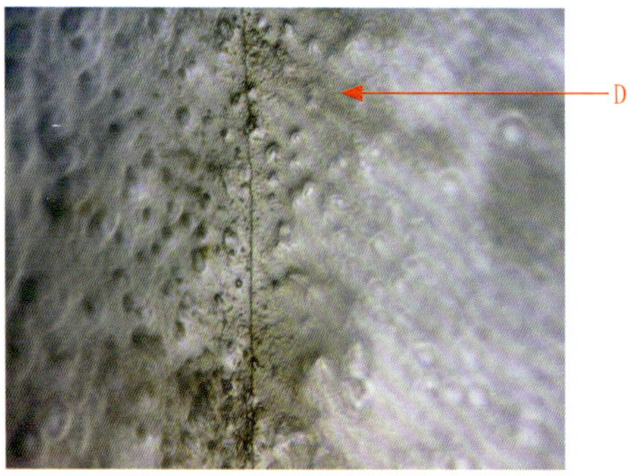

图6-1-210

三、总结

元青花斑块分为先天性斑块和后天性斑块两大类型。

元青花先天性斑块的多样性，主要是由釉料、青料及烧制工艺的不同所致。所以元青花先天性斑块从一定程度上能够反映当时制作元青花的用材及烧制工艺。

元青花后天性斑块，主要是由其后天的存放环境和环境变化的差异造成的。元青花瓷器上后天性斑块呈现出多样性，能够说明元青花瓷器的迹型生成与环境变化的相关性，它们的特征也符合陶瓷迹型变化的量变原理及时间过程性原理，也体现了陶瓷迹型形成与变化的诸规律。

第二节 元青花纹路类别

一、元青花纹路概念

元青花纹路是元青花瓷器在烧制过程中和后天环境影响下形成的，是以线状、条状、网状等形貌分布在釉表面和釉层中的迹型类别。

二、元青花纹路种类

（一）流淌纹

1．流淌纹概念

流淌纹是以线状、条状、网状等形貌分布在元青花瓷器釉表面和釉层中的纹路。它的主要成分有铁氧化物及锰氧化物等，是在元青花烧制过程中和后天环境影响下形成的。

2．流淌纹形成

元青花瓷器在高温烧制时，青料及釉料会逐渐熔化成熔融态。在浮力、表面张力及气泡搅动的作用下，釉料以及青料中的铁氧化物和锰氧化物易在气泡边缘积聚，部分会随气泡升至釉表面，顺着凹凸不平的釉表面向四周扩散，流动铺展，并结晶析出，也可能产生分相。当温度下降时，会有更多结晶析出，铁氧化物及锰氧化物数量多的形成斑块，铁氧化物及锰氧化物少的形成纹路，就是流淌纹。

釉层中未升至釉表面的铁离子在高温下熔融在釉料中，釉层冷却凝固时在釉层中形成碘酒纹。

位于釉表面，铁氧化物及锰氧化物含量较高的流淌纹形貌为凹槽，更易风化，就是阴纹。这些阴纹呈现不同形貌。

釉表面SiO_2含量较高的流淌纹相对凸起，不易被风化，为阳纹。

3．流淌纹分类

流淌纹可分为三类：碘酒纹、阴纹、阳纹。

（1）碘酒纹

①碘酒纹概念

碘酒纹是元青花瓷器在烧制过程中形成的，存在于釉层中的褐色流淌纹。

②碘酒纹特征

碘酒斑二维特征

见图6-2-1、图6-2-2。

a．碘酒纹呈溪流流淌状。

b．碘酒纹颜色呈褐色，颜色有深有浅。

（2）阴纹

①阴纹概念

阴纹是元青花瓷器在烧制过程中及后天环境影响下形成的凹形流淌纹。

②阴纹种类

阴纹可分成中空型阴纹及针眼型阴纹。

A．中空型阴纹概念

中空型阴纹是纹路未被针眼斑完全覆盖的阴纹。

B．针眼型阴纹概念

针眼型阴纹是纹路被针眼斑完全覆盖的阴纹。

③阴纹分布

阴纹主要出现在流淌斑或碘酒纹处，少数出现在蓝色青料处，一般不超它们的范围。

中空型阴纹通常不会出现在沙滩斑上，大都出现在铁氧化物含量较少的玻璃相上（碘酒斑处或蓝色青料处）。

针眼型阴纹主要出现在流淌斑上。

④阴纹特征

A．中空型阴纹特征

a．中空型阴纹二维特征

Ⅰ．中空型阴纹有粗有细，一般都有两条白色细边，细边夹住的中间部分主要成分为玻璃相，风化

Section 2:

Yuan Underglaze Blue Striae Category

1. YUB Striae Defined

YUB Striae are the category of line, stripe, and web shaped appearances, created during the firing process and acquired under the influences of the post-firing environment, that are disbursed across the glaze surface and within the glaze level of YUB.

2. Types of YUB Striae

A. Flowing Striae

I. Flowing Striae Defined

Flowing Striae are line, stripe, and web shaped appearances across the surface and within the glaze level of YUB, created during the firing process or acquired under the influences of the post-firing environment, that consist primarily of Iron and Manganese Oxide.

II. Formation of Flowing Striae

During the firing of YUB, cobalt-blue dye and glaze gradually transition into a molten state. Due to the buoyancy, surface tension and movement of the air bubbles within the glaze level, the Iron and Manganese Oxides of the glaze and dye collect around the edges of gaseous bodies within the glaze, and rise with these bubbles to the surface of the glaze. According to the uneven topography of the surface, these compounds diffuse and flow across the glaze surface and crystallize, some producing split phases. When the temperature drops, more crystallization can occur. Areas of higher Iron and Manganese amounts culminate to form mottles, and areas of lower amounts accumulate into channels, called flowing striae.

Iron ions that remained within the molten glaze level, when the glaze cools and solidifies can pull together to form iodine striae.

On the surface of the glaze, flowing striae with relatively high Iron and Manganese forms concave troughs, called depressed striae. These depressed striae can assume a variety of appearances.

Surface level flowing striae in which the amount of SiO_2 is relatively high, are not easily weathered and form convex furrows, called raised striae.

III. Types of Flowing Striae

As per above, there are three types of Flowing Striae: Iodine Striae, Depressed Striae and Raised Striae.

a. Iodine Striae

i. Iodine Striae Defined

Formed during the firing of YUB, these striae are present within the glaze level and are brown colored flowing striae.

ii. Characteristics of Iodine Striae

Two-dimensional Characteristics of Iodine Striae

See pictures 6-2-1 and 6-2-2.

(i) Presents with a flowing stream appearance.

(ii) Consist of a brownish color with varying degrees of color density.

b. Depressed Striae

i. Depressed Striae Defined

Concave flowing striae formed during the firing and

作用不明显，未完全被针眼斑覆盖，所以纹路内部像是“中空”的（见图6-2-3—图6-2-9）。

II.有的中空型阴纹有多条细边，边与边有的间断，有的错综，亮度也有差异，但都各自清晰分明（见图6-2-3—图6-2-6）。

III.中空型阴纹并未被针眼斑完全充满，与细边之间留有一定的空间。（见图6-2-7—图6-2-9）

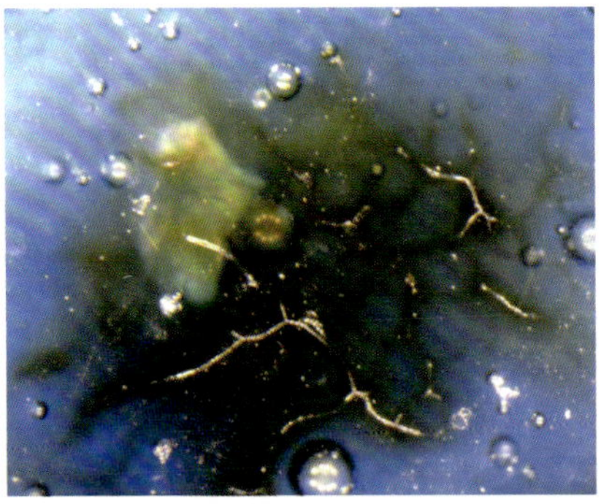
图6-2-1

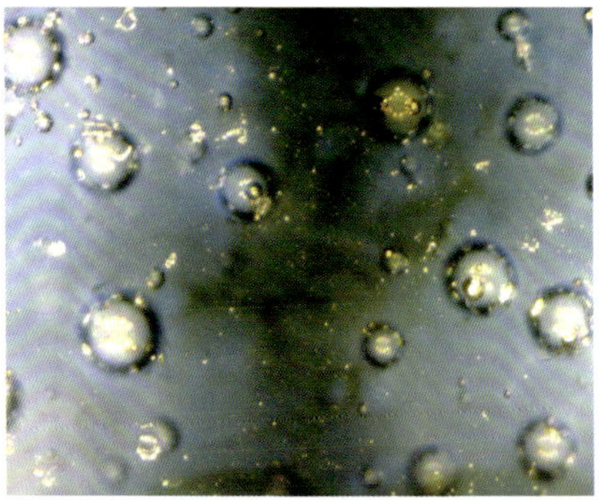
图6-2-2

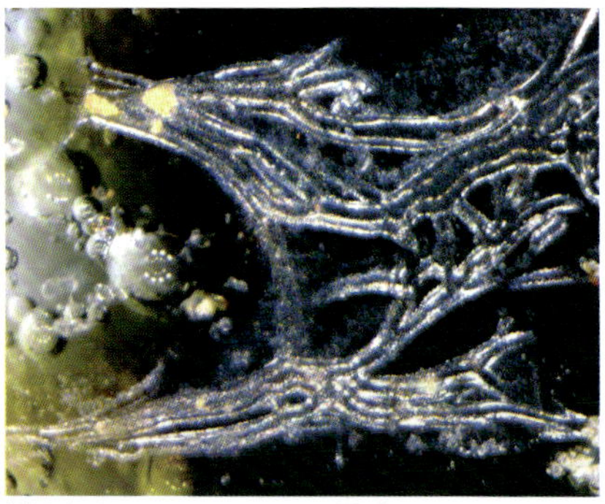
图6-2-3

图6-2-4

图6-2-5

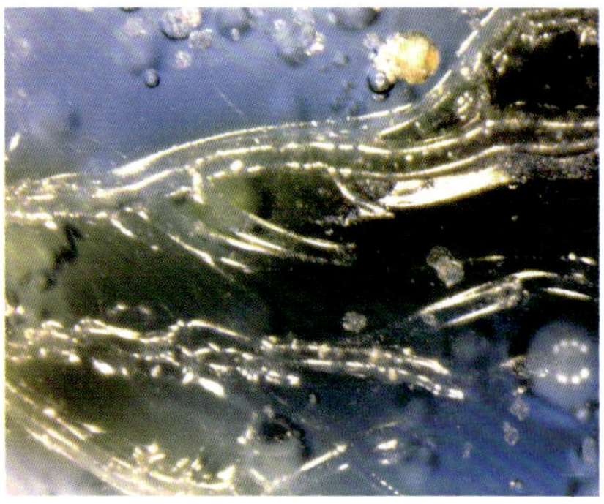
图6-2-6

图6-2-7

图6-2-8

图6-2-9

b. 中空型阴纹三维特征

I. 中空型阴纹纹路剖面一般都呈“W”形（见图6-2-14）。

II. 纹路脊部凸起，脊部有的光滑洁净，反光部分断断续续，不反光的部分有风化物质堆积。

III. 纹路与周边玻璃相界线分明。

见图6-2-10、图6-2-11，二者为同一器物同一位置图片，图6-2-10为二维图片，图6-2-11为三维图片。

图6-2-10中的白色纹路在图6-2-11中呈深色，成像清晰。纹路脊部凸起，光滑洁净，像水管（见箭头A所指处）。纹路与周边玻璃相界线分明。

见图6-2-12、图6-2-13，二者为同一器物同一位置图片，图6-2-12为二维图片，图6-2-13为三维图片。

图6-2-12中的白色纹路在图6-2-13中呈深色，成像清晰。纹路脊部凸起，脊部上反光的部分断断续续，不反光的部分有风化物质堆积（见箭头B所指处）。玻璃相被纹路以网状形式切割，一块块玻璃相凸起，像蒸笼里的馒头。纹路与周边玻璃相界线分明。

under the influences of the post-firing environment of YUB.

ii. Types of Depressed Striae

Empty Striae and Needlepoint Striae are the two types of Depressed Striae.

(a) Empty Striae Defined

Depressed Striae that have not become completely filled with needlepoint mottling.

(b) Needlepoint Striae Defined

Depressed striae that have become covered by needlepoint mottling.

iii. Distribution of Depressed Striae

Depressed striae primarily present on areas of flowing mottles or iodine striae with a few occurring on areas of just blue dye; they very rarely extend beyond the borders of said areas.

Empty striae do not occur over beach mottles, but rather areas of lower Iron Oxide to glass phase ratio, i.e. iodine mottles and areas with only blue dye.

Needlepoint striae generally occur in association with flowing mottles.

iv. Characteristics of Depressed Striae

(a) Characteristics of Empty Striae

(i) Two-dimensional Characteristics of Empty Striae

(1) Striae can be of varied width, usually occurring with two white outlines. The area between the outlines is primarily glass phase, thus resistant to weathering, allowing it to stay uncovered by needlepoint mottling, giving it an 'Empty' effect (see pictures 6-2-3—6-2-9).

(2) Some striae can occur with multiple lines. The individual lines may have brightness differences and intersect other lines, but they retain clearly delineated independence (see pictures 6-2-3—6-2-6).

(3) Striae do not become completely covered by needlepoint mottling, with a certain amount of empty space between the outlines (see pictures 6-2-7—6-2-9).

(ii) Three-dimensional Characteristics of Empty Striae

(1) Striae cross-section has an approximate "W" shape (see picture 6-2-14).

(2) Central section of striae is convex, retaining a smooth and reflective surface. Reflective surface may be intermittent, with non-reflective areas presenting with weathering or material deposits.

(3) Striae retain clear delineation with the surrounding glass phase.

See pictures 6-2-10 and 6-2-11, where 6-2-10 is the two-dimensional and 6-2-11 is the three-dimensional view of the same location.

The white striation in picture 6-2-10 is the clearly depicted darker area in picture 6-2-11. The central portion of the striation is convex and smooth, resembling a water pipe. The striation retains delineation with the surrounding glass phase (see Arrow A).

See pictures 6-2-12 and 6-2-13, where 6-2-12 is the two-dimensional and 6-2-13 is the three-dimensional view of the same location.

The white striation in picture 6-2-12 is the clearly depicted darker area in picture 6-2-13. The central portion of the striation is convex and intermittently reflective, non-reflective portions contain material deposits (indicated by Arrow B). Intersecting lines create humps of glass phase that resemble a batch of baking buns. Striae retain delineation with the surrounding glass phase.

(b) Characteristics of Needlepoint Striae

(i) Two-dimensional Characteristics of Needlepoint Striae

(1) Striae width can range from wide to thin (see pictures 6-2-15—6-2-22).

(2) Thin striae present as fine lines with clear yet reserved appearance (see pictures 6-2-15—6-2-18).

(3) Sometimes striae have clearly defined borders (see pictures 6-2-21 and 6-2-22).

(4) The transition area between the edge of the striae and glass phase can present with foggy needlepoint mottling. The ends of the striae narrowing to a tip, and the midsection of the

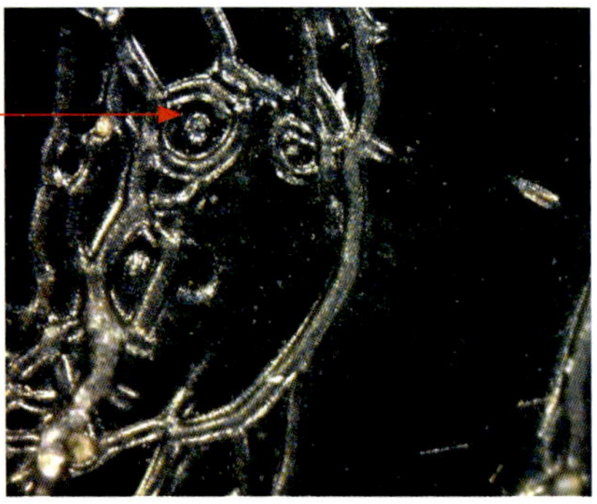

图6-2-10

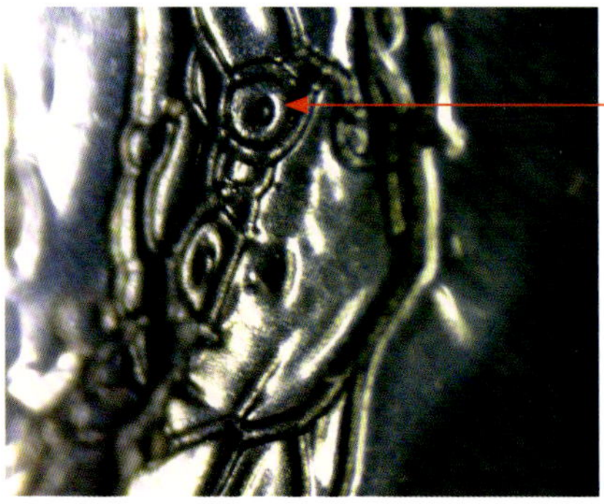

图6-2-11

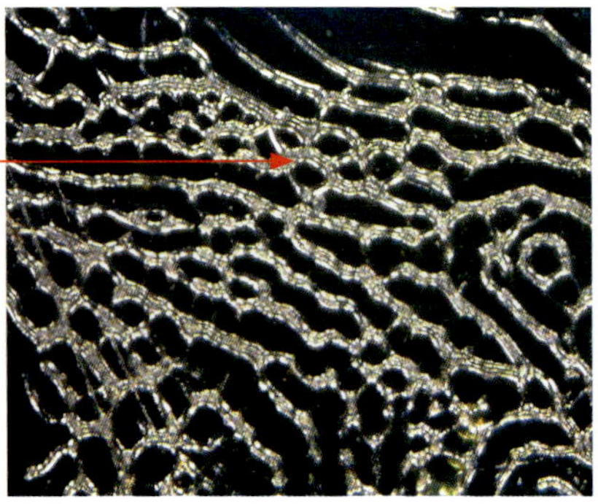

图6-2-12

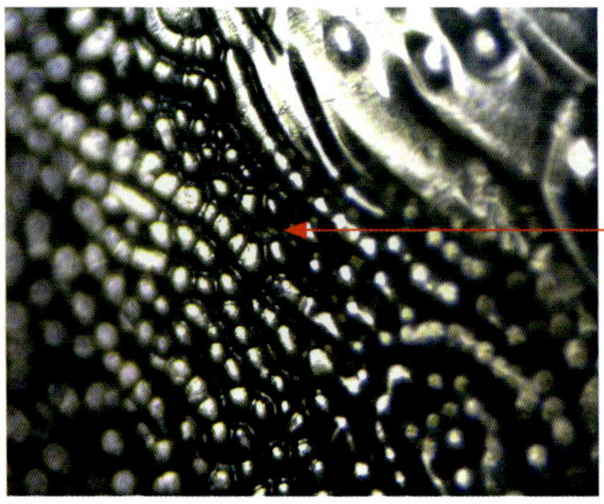

图6-2-13

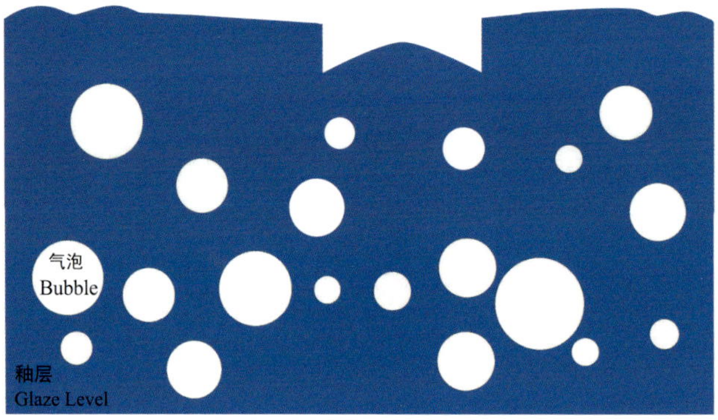

图6-2-14

B. 针眼型阴纹特征

a. 针眼型阴纹二维特征

I. 针眼型阴纹纹路有粗有细（见图6-2-15—图6-2-22）。

II. 较细的纹路形如细线，纹路清晰，紧致收敛（见图6-2-15—图6-2-18）。

III. 有时可清楚看见纹路的两条细边（见图6-2-21、图6-2-22）。

IV. 有的纹路与玻璃相的过渡区域分布有雾状针眼斑，这类纹路通常是两端较窄，越往纹路中部纹路越宽（见图6-2-19、图6-2-20）。

V. 纹路内的针眼斑大部分呈白色，有的呈橘黄色，有色阶变化（见图6-2-21）。

b. 针眼型阴纹三维特征

I. 针眼型阴纹剖面可以是“U”形，也可以是“V”形。

II. 剖面是“V”形的纹路上，针眼斑三维成像面积小于二维。

III. 剖面是“U”形的纹路上，较宽的纹路内可见颗粒物质、针眼斑及色阶变化。

IV. 纹路与周围玻璃相界线分明。

见图6-2-23、图6-2-24，二者为同一器物同一位置图片，图6-2-23为二维图片，图6-2-24为三维图片。

图6-2-23中的浅色纹路在图6-2-24中呈深色，成像清晰。纹路呈凹陷状，进入釉层一定深度，与周围玻璃相界线分明（见箭头C所指处）。

纹路C剖面呈“U”形（见图6-2-25）。

striae relatively broad (see pictures 6-2-19 and 6-2-20).

(5) Needlepoint mottling within the striae has color spectrum, which often presents as white or yellowish-orange (see picture 6-2-21).

(ii) Three-dimensional Characteristics of Needlepoint Striae

(1) Striae cross-sections have approximate "U" or "V" shapes.

(2) Striae have concave shapes.

(3) "V" shaped striae have a three-dimensionally observable needlepoint mottling surface area that is smaller than what is two-dimensionally observable.

(4) Within the broadened cavity of "U" shaped striae, granules, needlepoint mottling and coloration can present.

(5) There is delineation between the striae and the surrounding glass phase.

See pictures 6-2-23 and 6-2-24, where 6-2-23 is the two-dimensional and 6-2-24 is the three-dimensional view of the same location.

The light colored striation indicated by Arrow C in picture 6-2-23 is the clearly depicted darker area in picture 6-2-24. The striation is concave and extends a certain depth into the glaze level, but retains delineation from the surrounding glass phase.

Striation C has a "U" shaped cross-section (see picture 6-2-25).

See pictures 6-2-26 and 6-2-27, where 6-2-26 is the two-dimensional and 6-2-27 is the three-dimensional view of the same location.

The light colored striation indicated by Arrow D in picture 6-2-26 is the clearly depicted darker area in picture 6-2-27. The striation is concave and extends a certain depth into the glaze level, but retains delineation from the surrounding glass phase.

The striation in picture 6-2-26 appears wider than that of 6-2-27, because the foggy needlepoint mottling on the contact point between the striation and the glass phase is not observable from a three-dimensional perspective. As such, the foggy needlepoint mottling in picture 6-2-26 is wider than the darker area on the glass phase in picture 6-2-27 as indicated by Arrow E.

Striation D has a "V" shaped cross-section (see picture 6-2-28).

See pictures 6-2-29 and 6-2-30, where 6-2-29 is the two-dimensional and 6-2-30 is the three-dimensional view of the same location.

See pictures 6-2-31 and 6-2-32, where 6-2-31 is the two-dimensional and 6-2-32 is the three-dimensional view of the same location.

The light colored striae indicated by Arrow F in picture 6-2-29 and Arrow G in picture 6-2-30 are the clearly depicted darker areas in pictures 6-2-30 and 6-2-32 respectively. Both Striae F and G are relatively broad and have a concave shape that extends some depth into the glaze level, similar to a water slide. The internal cavities of the striae present with plainly evident granules and assume delineated borders with the surrounding glass phase.

Striation G has clear color spectrum (see picture 6-2-32).

Striae F and G are both "U" shaped (see picture 6-2-25).

See pictures 6-2-33 and 6-2-34, where 6-2-33 is the two-dimensional and 6-2-34 is the three-dimensional view of the same location.

See pictures 6-2-35 and 6-2-36, where 6-2-35 is the two-dimensional and 6-2-36 is the three-dimensional view of the same location.

The light colored striae indicated by Arrow H in picture 6-2-33 and Arrow I in picture 6-2-35 are the clearly depicted darker areas in pictures 6-2-34 and 6-2-36 respectively.

Striation H has a concave shape that extends some depth into the glaze level. Its edges are rounded, but it is delineated from the surrounding glass phase (see picture 6-2-34).

Striation I is relatively broad and has a concave shape that extends some depth into the glaze level, and its edges are rounded. The internal cavity of the striation presents with plainly evident granules and assumes delineated borders with the surrounding glass phase, and has clear color spectrum (see picture 6-2-36).

Striae H and I are both "U" shaped (see picture 6-2-25).

See pictures 6-2-37 and 6-2-38, where 6-2-37 is the two-dimensional and 6-2-38 is the three-dimensional view of the same location.

See pictures 6-2-39 and 6-2-40, where 6-2-39 is the two-

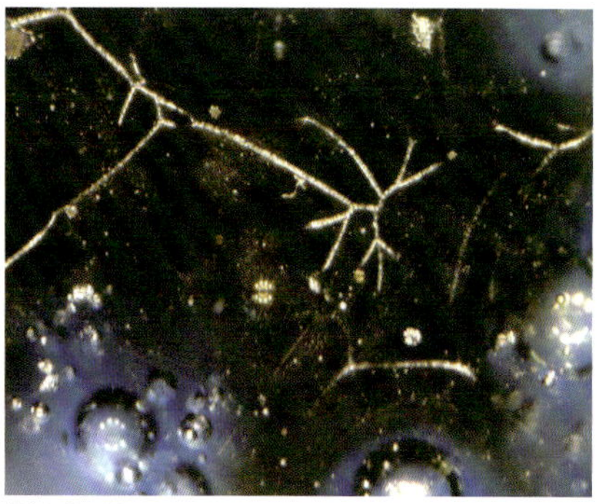
图6-2-15

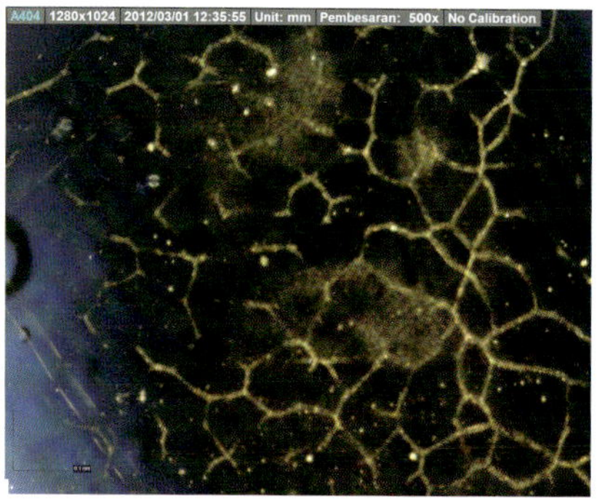

图6-2-16

图6-2-17

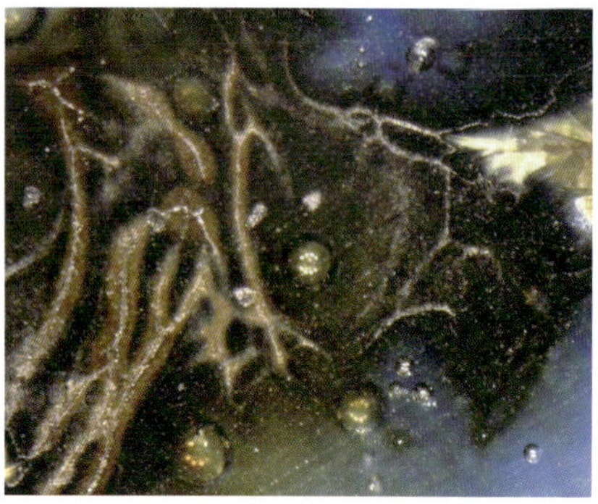
图6-2-18

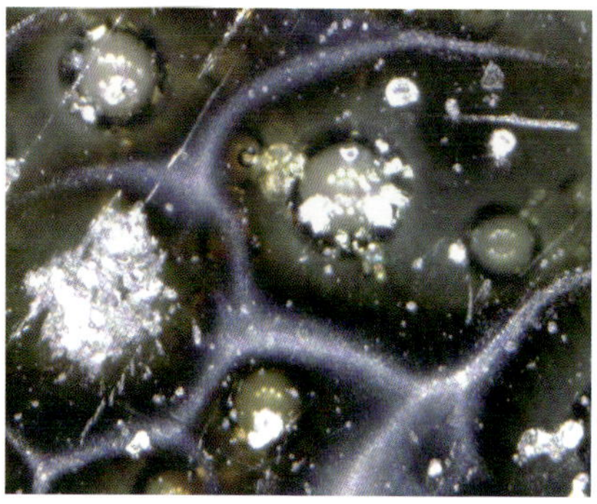
图6-2-19

图6-2-20

图6-2-21

图6-2-22

图6-2-23

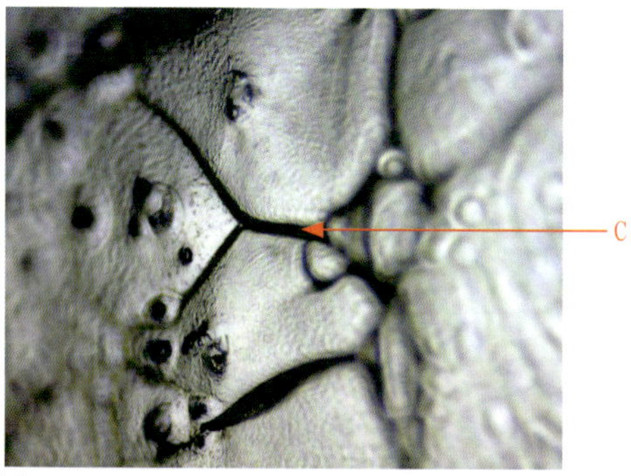

图6-2-24

dimensional and 6-2-40 is the three-dimensional view of the same location.

As we can see by the points indicated by Arrows J, K, L, and M there is evident color spectrum within the striae.

Striae J, K, L, and M are all relatively broad and have a concave shape that extends a certain depth into the glaze level (see pictures 6-2-38 and 6-2-40).

Both Striae, K and M, have evident color spectrum and retain clear delineation from the surrounding glass phase (see pictures 6-2-38 and 6-2-40).

All Striae J, K, L, and M have a "U" shaped cross-section (see picture 6-2-25).

See pictures 6-2-41 and 6-2-42, where 6-2-41 is the two-dimensional and 6-2-42 is the three-dimensional view of the same location.

The yellow colored striae indicated by Arrow N in picture 6-2-41 is also clearly depicted as yellow in picture 6-2-42. The striation is relatively broad with a concave shape that extends a certain depth into the glaze level. There is fine white needlepoint mottling evenly distributed throughout the striation, and it retains a clear delineation with the surrounding glass phase.

Striation N has a "U" shaped cross-section (see picture 6-2-25).

c. Raised Striae

i. Raised Striae Defined

The convex shaped flowing striae on YUB that were formed under the weathering influences of the post-firing environment.

ii. Distribution of Raised Striae

These striae occur primarily towards the center of beach mottles.

iii. Characteristics of Raised Striae

(a) Two-dimensional Characteristics of Raised Striae

See pictures 6-2-43—6-2-46.

(i) Coloration is brown.

(ii) Striae are full and evenly distributed.

(iii) Clear delineation with the surrounding beach mottles.

(b) Three-dimensional Characteristics of Raised Striae

(i) Wider striae can present with saw-like edges, while the surface retains smooth texture.

(ii) Striae are convex and higher than the surrounding beach mottle.

(iii) Clear delineation between the striae and surrounding mottle.

See pictures 6-2-47 and 6-2-48, where 6-2-47 is the two-dimensional and 6-2-48 is the three-dimensional view of the same location.

The brown colored striae indicated by Arrow A in picture 6-2-47 is clearly depicted as lighter color in picture 6-2-42. The striation is raised above the surrounding beach mottle, its edges saw-like, surface smooth, and it has clear delineation with the surrounding beach mottle.

d. Summary

Flowing striae can assume a wide variety of thickness, depth and coloration. A unit image can present with multiple flowing striae in conjunction with one another; with their appearance, color, and disbursement all having certain regularities.

The appearance, color, and disbursement regularities of striae depend on the composition and amount of glaze, amount of Iron and Manganese Oxide, and topography of the glaze surface.

Iodine Striae are essentially non-weathered, and thus retain their initial appearance.

On iodine mottles, due to the grooves in the glaze and higher glaze to Iron Oxide ratio, the most common types are thin and empty flowing striae, which assume a white coloration. As the glaze gradually becomes more weathered, flowing striae slowly transitions into the needlepoint variety and assumes a white or tangerine color.

In areas of beach mottling with high degrees of weathering, the areas of different composition from the beach mottle have lower weathering severity, thus form thick raised striae of a brown coloration that are three-dimensionally

图6-2-25

见图6-2-26、图6-2-27，二者为同一器物同一位置图片，图6-2-26为二维图片，图6-2-27为三维图片。

图6-2-26中的浅色纹路在图6-2-27中呈深色，成像清晰。纹路呈凹陷状，进入釉层一定深度，与周围玻璃相界线分明（见箭头D所指处）。

纹路D在图6-2-27中显得比图6-2-26中要窄，这是因为纹路与玻璃相结合处的雾状针眼斑三维成像并不明显。如图6-2-26中的雾状针眼斑，在图6-2-27中为玻璃相上的深色斑块，面积比图6-2-26中的要小（见箭头E所指处）。

纹路D剖面呈“V”形（见图6-2-28）。

见图6-2-29、图6-2-30，二者为同一器物同一位置图片，图6-2-29为二维图片，图6-2-30为三维图片。

见图6-2-31、图6-2-32，二者为同一器物同一位置图片，图6-2-31为二维图片，图6-2-32为三维图片。

图6-2-29中箭头F及图6-2-31中箭头G所指的浅色纹路在图6-2-30及图6-2-32中呈深色，成像清晰。纹路F及纹路G都比较宽，呈凹陷状，进入釉层一定深度，像游乐园的滑梯。纹路内部的颗粒物质明显，纹路与周围玻璃相界线分明。

纹路G内部色阶变化明显（见图6-2-32）。

纹路F及纹路G的剖面均呈“U”形（见图6-2-25）。

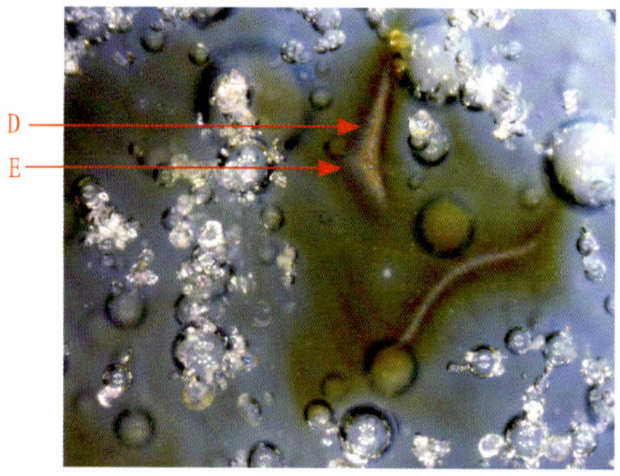

图6-2-26

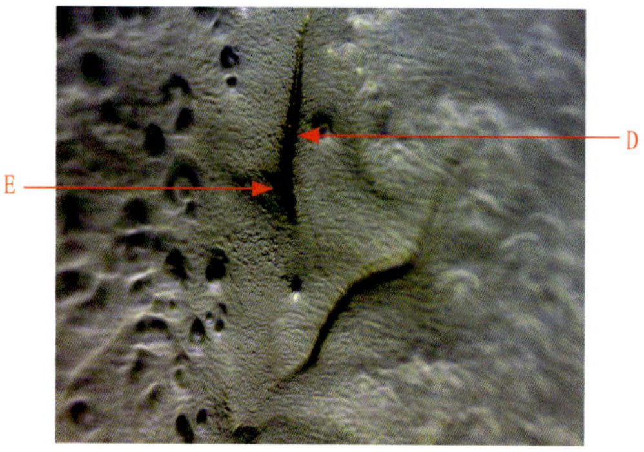

图6-2-27

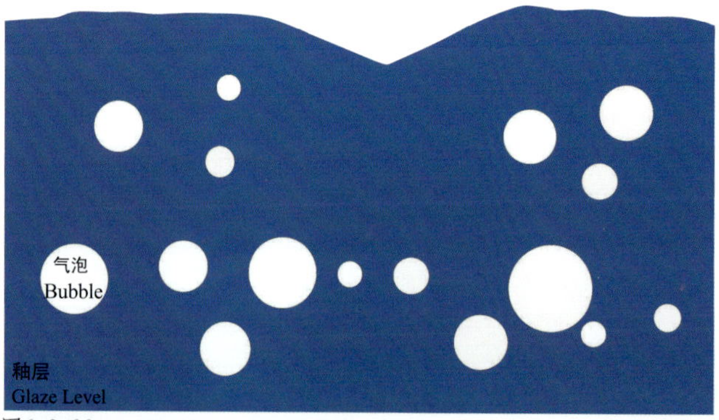

图6-2-28

convex (see pictures 6-2-49—6-2-54).

B. C and O Shaped Striae

I. C and O Shaped Striae Defined

C and O shaped lines consisting primarily of Iron, Manganese, and so forth metal Oxides; disbursed across the surface of YUB glaze; that are acquired during the firing process and under the influence of the post-firing environment (simplified as CO Striae).

II. Formation of C and O Shaped Striae

During the firing of YUB, the glaze and dye slowly transition into a molten state. Due to the buoyancy and movement of the air bubbles within the glaze level, Iron and Manganese Oxides within the glaze and dye easily collect around the edges of gaseous bodies within the glaze, and rise with these bubbles to the surface of the glaze. According to the uneven topography of the surface, these compounds diffuse and flow across the glaze surface and crystallize, some producing split phases. When the temperature drops, more crystallization can occur, under the influence of surface tension of the glaze, some crystallizations form ring shapes on the glaze surface and within the glaze level. In general, these deposits are less chemically stable than the surrounding glass phase, and the areas where these two phases meet have structural integrity flaws, thus allowing for easier weathering and as such form C and O shaped striae.

Additionally, during the firing of YUB, gaseous bodies that rise up and erupt upon the surface of the molten glaze can leave a circular trace on the glaze surface. Foreign materials are easily deposited within the grooves present across the glaze surface, and these areas weather to become C and O shaped striae.

III. Distribution of C and O Shaped Striae

These striae all occur on the glass phase. The majority occur on areas of raised glaze surface (see area indicated by Arrow A in pictures 6-2-55 and 6-2-56), but can also occur on areas of indistinct unevenness (see Arrow B in picture 6-2-57)

IV. Characteristics of C and O Shaped Striae

a. Two-dimensional Characteristics of C and O Shaped Striae

i. C and O shaped striae primarily occur in C and O shapes: C shaped striae are semi-circle lines, and O shaped striae are circular and ovular lines.

ii. Striae extend a certain depth into the glaze level with varying size and thickness, but retain clear delineation with the surrounding glass phase (see pictures 6-2-58—6-2-82).

iii. Striae can assume "L", "8", and "6" shaped appearances (see pictures 6-2-62—6-2-64), and it is common for striae to occur concentrically or in close proximity, forming a Y shaped fork (see pictures 6-2-65—6-3-69).

iv. Their colors include yellow, brown, and black (see pictures 6-2-58—6-2-82).

v. CO striae can present with color variation on a single porcelain piece, but rarely present with wide color variation within a unit image (see pictures 6-2-72 and 6-2-74). A single striae can present with color spectrum (see pictures 6-2-70—6-2-72).

vi. In general, striae present with the same coloration as their surrounding traces, such as scratches (see pictures 6-2-61, 6-2-64, 6-2-66, 6-2-74, and 6-2-75).

vii. On pieces with suitable weathering, it is possible for CO striae to have floccus mottling underneath (see pictures 6-2-76 and 6-2-77).

viii. As weathering continues, the striae gradually broaden (see pictures 6-2-78 and 6-2-79). The interior of the C arc or O ring becomes white and loses transparency. It gradually develops into a pit mottle, and finally presents as the aggregation of CO striae and pit mottles (see pictures 6-2-80—6-2-82).

b. Three-dimensional Characteristics of C and O Shaped Striae

i. Most CO striae occur at points of raised glaze surface.

ii. The striae are thin and reserved, markedly independent.

iii. Clear delineation between the striae and surrounding

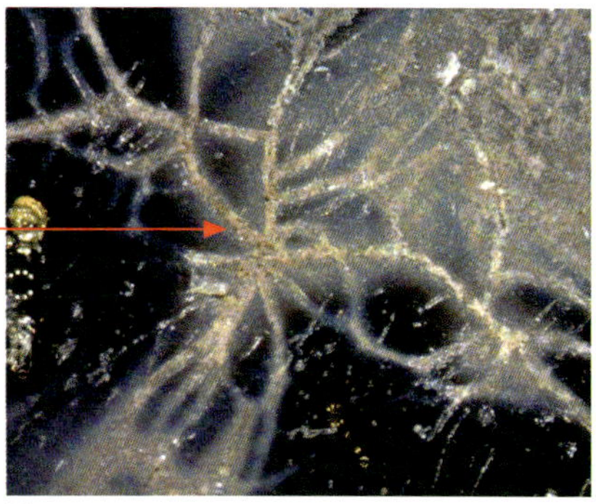

图6-2-29

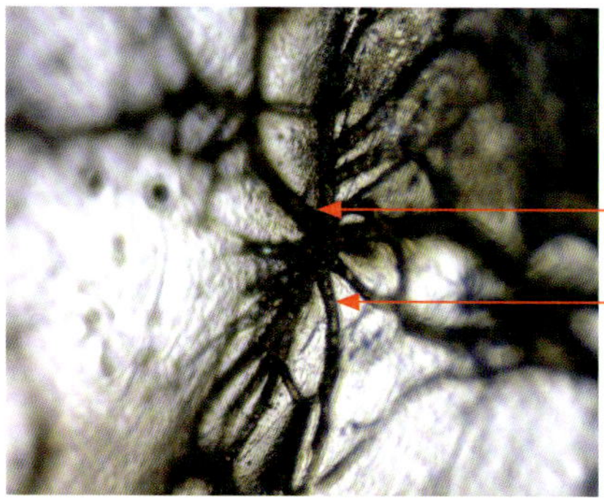

图6-2-30

图6-2-31

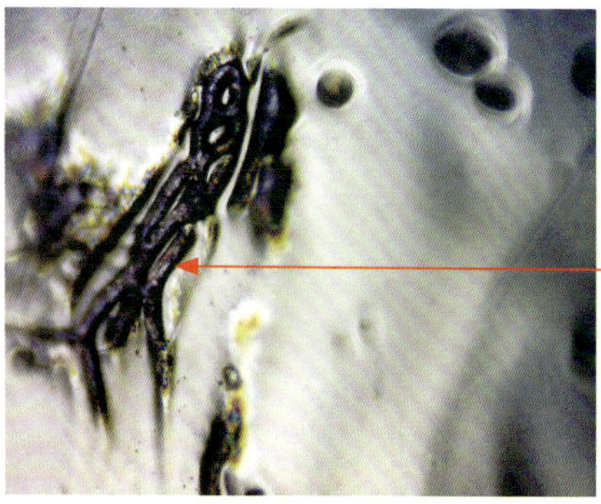

图6-2-32

见图6-2-33、图6-2-34，二者为同一器物同一位置图片，图6-2-33为二维图片，图6-2-34为三维图片。

见图6-2-35、图6-2-36，二者为同一器物同一位置图片，图6-2-35为二维图片，图6-2-36为三维图片。

图6-2-33中箭头H及图6-2-35箭头I中所指的浅色纹路在图6-2-34及图6-2-36中均呈深色，成像清晰。

纹路H呈凹陷状，进入釉层一定深度，边沿圆滑，纹路与周围玻璃相界线分明。（见图6-2-34）

纹路I较宽，呈凹陷状，进入釉层一定深度，边沿圆滑，内部有明显的微小颗粒，有色阶变化，纹路与周围玻璃相界线分明（见图6-2-36）。

纹路H和纹路I的剖面均呈“U”形（见图6-2-25）。

见图6-2-37、图6-2-38，二者为同一器物同一位置图片，图6-2-37为二维图片，图6-2-38为三维图片。

见图6-2-39、图6-2-40，二者为同一器物同一位置图片，图6-2-39为二维图片，图6-2-40为三维图片。

图6-2-37中箭头J及图6-2-39中箭头L所指的白色纹路在图6-2-38及图6-2-40中呈紫蓝色；图6-2-37中箭头K及图6-2-39中箭头M所指的白色纹路中掺杂着橘黄色，在图6-2-38及图6-2-40中的三维成像表现为紫蓝色中掺杂着橘黄色，成像清晰。

纹路J、纹路K、纹路L、纹路M都较宽，均呈凹陷状，进入釉层一定深度（见图6-2-38、图6-2-40）。

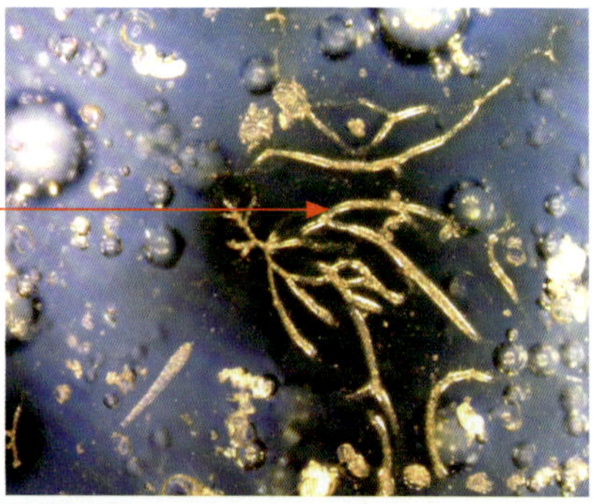

图6-2-33

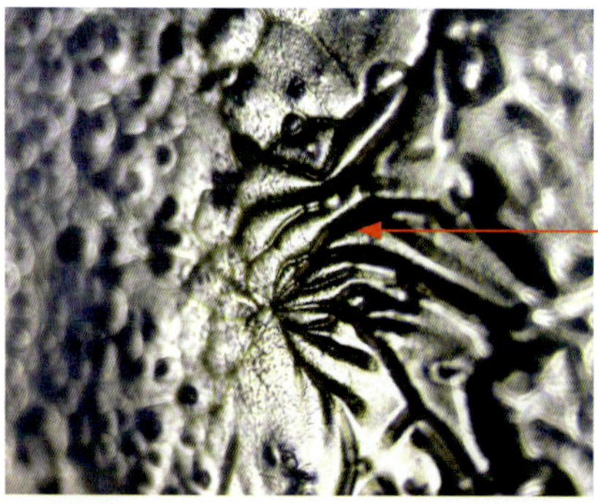

图6-2-34

glass phase.

See pictures 6-2-83 and 6-2-84, where 6-2-83 is the two-dimensional and 6-2-84 is the three-dimensional view of the same location.

See pictures 6-2-85 and 6-2-86, where 6-2-85 is the two-dimensional and 6-2-86 is the three-dimensional view of the same location.

The yellow C striae indicated by Arrow C in picture 6-2-83 and Arrow D in picture 6-2-85 are the clearly depicted darker areas on pictures 6-2-84 and 6-2-86 respectively. They both occur on areas of raised glaze, and both retain clear delineation with the surrounding glass phase.

The C striation indicated by Arrow C in picture 6-2-83 only presents as a dark colored mound in picture 6-2-84, and the striation is not easily observable.

See pictures 6-2-87 and 6-2-88, where 6-2-87 is the two-dimensional and 6-2-88 is the three-dimensional view of the same location.

The yellow C striation in picture 6-2-87 appears darker than in picture 6-2-88, but is even more thin and fine. The dark colored mottle indicated by Arrow E in picture 6-2-87 only presents as two fine forking lines in picture 6-2-88, and they have clear delineation with the surrounding glaze.

C. Glaze Crack

a. Glaze Crack Defined

Also called crazing, Glaze Cracks are any appearance of straight, curved, or irregular lines splitting the glaze surface of YUB that was caused either during firing or under the influence of the post-firing environment.

b. Formation of Glaze Cracks

Glaze cracks can be caused by any number of the following reasons:

i. During the firing process, the components of the glaze volatilize and create empty spaces. Due to the stress caused by the accumulation of these spaces into gaps, the glaze cracks.

ii. If the micro phases within the glaze expand at different rates, cracks in the glaze can occur.

iii. The stress tension caused by the R^+ and H^+ ion exchange of ≡Si—O—R, because of the H^+ ion being relatively smaller than the R^+ ion, can create glaze cracks [224].

iv. The composition of glaze and clay body being different, their expansion rates are also different. As the porcelain cools, stress is created, which the thicker glaze body can absorb, but the glaze reaches a breaking point at which it cracks.

v. Glaze lacks malleability. As such, when hard external forces collide with the glaze, the inability to absorb the blow can result in cracking.

Cracks are not necessarily a direct result of weathering; some are caused inherently during the firing process but some are indeed acquired under the influence of the post-firing environment. Additionally, not all cracks are visible under microscopic observation. If, after firing, the glaze encounters drastic temperature changes or the stress imposed by the crystallization of soluble salt or partially soluble salt deposits, the glaze cracks can become broadened.

There is a type of glaze crazing that is intentionally man-made, in the pursuit of aesthetic beauty, by utilizing the differences in body-glaze expansion rates. However, the crazing that presents on YUB was not intentionally created with this sort of artistic outcome in mind. Therefore, crazing that presents is considered to be a glaze flaw.

c. Characteristics of Glaze Cracks

Two-dimensional Characteristics of Glaze Cracks

(i) Cracks can occur as straight or curved lines.

(ii) Some cracks can occur with several cracks branching off of it (see picture 6-2-95).

(iii) Crack width spectrum have the following characteristics:

(1) No clear width spectrum (see pictures 6-2-89 and 6-2-90).

(2) Width spectrum (see picture 6-2-91).

(iv). Crack colorations have the following characteristics:

(1) No evident coloration (see picture 6-2-92).

(2) Complete coloration but not evident color spectrum

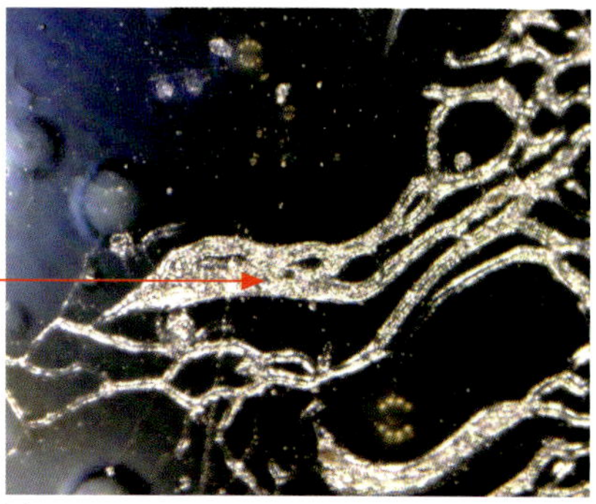

图6-2-35

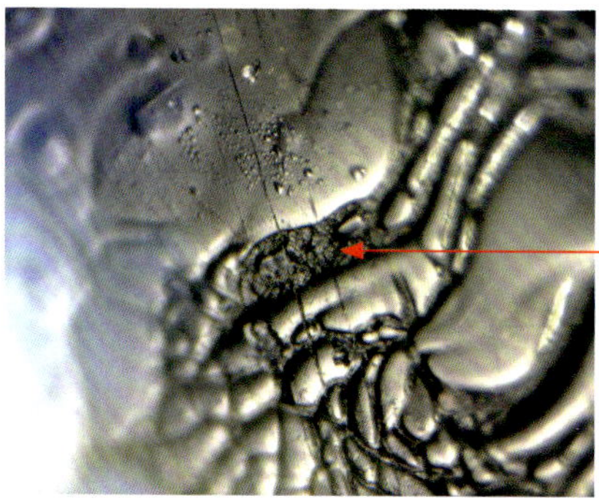

图6-2-36

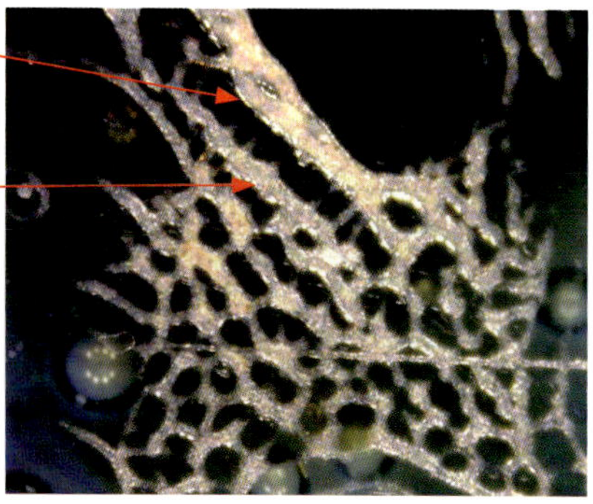

图6-2-37

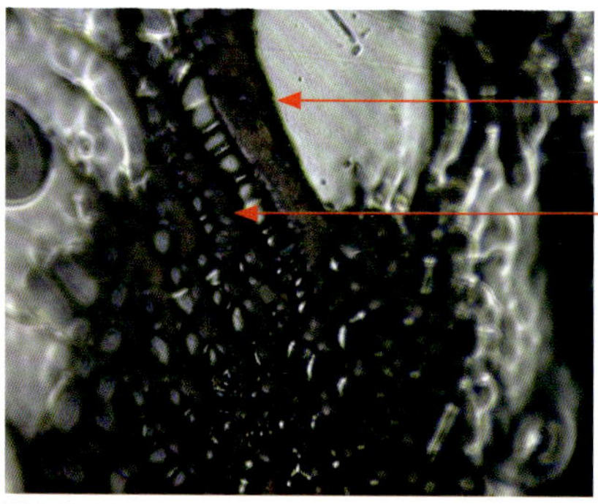

图6-2-38

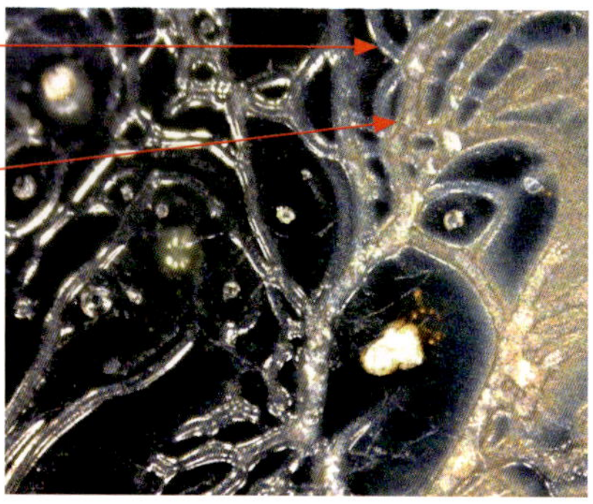

图6-2-39

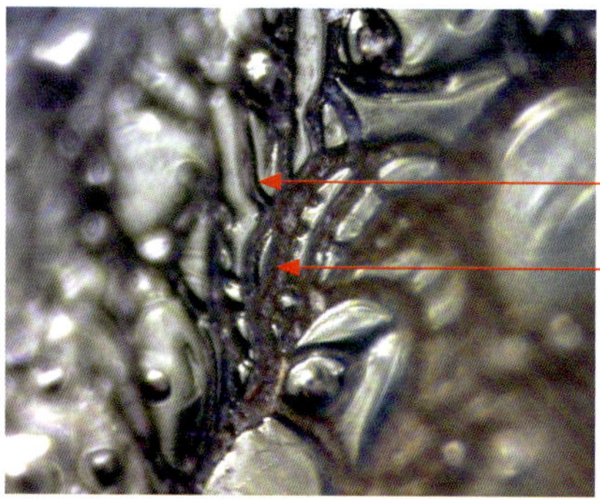

图6-2-40

纹路K及纹路M内部均有明显的色阶变化，纹路与周围玻璃相界线分明（见图6-2-38、图6-2-40）。

纹路J、纹路K、纹路L和纹路M的剖面均呈“U”形（见图6-2-25）。

见图6-2-41、图6-2-42，二者为同一器物同一位置图片，图6-2-41为二维图片，图6-2-42为三维图片。

图6-2-41中的黄色纹路在图6-2-42中也呈黄色，成像清晰，纹路较宽，呈凹陷状，进入釉层一定深度，纹路上可见细腻均匀的白色针眼斑，纹路与周围玻璃相界线分明（见箭头N所指处）。

纹路N的剖面呈“U”形（见图6-2-25）。

（3）阳纹

① 阳纹概念

阳纹是元青花瓷器在烧制过程中形成的凸形流淌纹。

② 阳纹分布

阳纹基本都出现在沙滩斑上。

③ 阳纹特征

A. 阳纹二维特征

见图6-2-43—图6-2-46。

a. 阳纹颜色呈褐色。

b. 纹路饱满均匀。

c. 通常与周围沙滩斑界线分明。

B. 阳纹三维特征

a. 较粗的阳纹边沿呈明显锯齿状，纹路表面较光滑。

b. 阳纹凸起，高出周围沙

(see picture 6-2-89).

(3) Color spectrum, colors include: White, yellow, brown, black and so forth (see pictures 6-2-90, 6-2-93, and 6-2-94).

(4) Partial coloration (see picture 6-2-94).

(v) Crack surroundings characteristics include:

(1) Appearance of color change or textured bubbles (see pictures 6-2-96 and 6-2-97).

(2) Under the glaze coloration (see pictures 6-2-98 and 6-2-99).

(3) Floccus mottling can occur in conjunction with cracks (see pictures 6-2-95 and 6-2-100).

D. Scratches

I. Scratches Defined

Scratches are the imperfections on YUB glaze that present as lines on the glaze surface that were left by the abrasive force of a solid external object.

II. Formation of Scratches

During post-firing use, and due to coming into contact with hard objects in the surrounding environment, the glaze surface can become scratched.

III. Characteristics of Scratches

a. Two-dimensional Characteristics of Scratches

i. Scratches can be broad or thin, long or short, deep or shallow, solid or intermittent, and straight or curved (see pictures 6-2-101—6-2-116).

ii. Some scratches have 'ox hair' features; short and thin with wild, directionless distribution (see pictures 6-2-101 and 6-2-102).

iii. Some scratches look like centipedes (see pictures 6-2-104—6-2-106).

iv. Some scratches have irregular shapes (see pictures 6-2-107—6-2-116).

v. Scratch colorations include white, yellow, brown and so forth (see pictures 6-2-101—6-2-116).

vi. Generally scratches occur randomly and without regularity. They can occur with several directions, depths, lengths, and colors in conjunction (see pictures 6-2-101, 6-2-104, 6-2-106, 6-2-110, and 6-2-112).

vii. Deep scratches have an evident concavity, over time they are easily filled with foreign material deposits and can weather to present with needlepoint mottling (see pictures 6-2-110—6-2-113).

viii. As scratches are an area of glaze flaw, they are commonly a location of floccus mottling (see pictures 6-2-114—6-2-116).

b. Three-dimensional Characteristics of Scratches

i. Scratches can appear as tiny evenly distributed pits, 'centipede feet', tiny directionless 'ox hair', larger concavities, and so forth.

ii. Pitting and needlepoint mottling occurring in conjunction with scratches are observably smaller three-dimensionally than they are two-dimensionally.

iii. The inner cavities of the scratches are coarse and the edges of the scratch are rounded.

iv. Scratches retain clear delineation with the surrounding glass phase.

See pictures 6-2-117 and 6-2-118, where 6-2-117 is the two-dimensional and 6-2-118 is the three-dimensional view of the same location.

The light colored scratch in picture 6-2-117 is the clearly depicted darker area in picture 6-2-118. It presents as an evenly distributed chain of small pits, and the pits retain clear delineation with the surrounding glass phase.

See pictures 6-2-119 and 6-2-120, where 6-2-119 is the two-dimensional and 6-2-120 is the three-dimensional view of the same location.

See pictures 6-2-121 and 6-2-122, where 6-2-121 is the two-dimensional and 6-2-122 is the three-dimensional view of the same location.

The light colored centipede scratches indicated by the Arrows in pictures 6-2-119 and 6-2-121 are the clearly depicted darker areas of 'centipede feet' in pictures 6-2-120 and 6-2-122. The 'centipede feet' are fine yet clearly visible, and have a certain observable separation in which the

滩斑。

c. 阳纹与周围沙滩斑界线分明。

见图6-2-47、图6-2-48，二者为同一器物同一位置图片，图6-2-47为二维图片，图6-2-48为三维图片。

图6-2-47中的褐色纹路在图6-2-48中呈浅色，成像清晰。阳纹凸起，高出周围沙滩斑，边沿呈锯齿状，纹路表面较光滑，与周围沙滩斑界线分明（见箭头A所指处）。

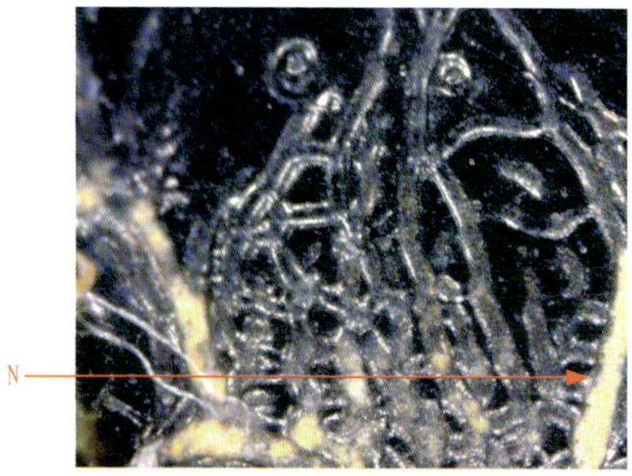

图6-2-41

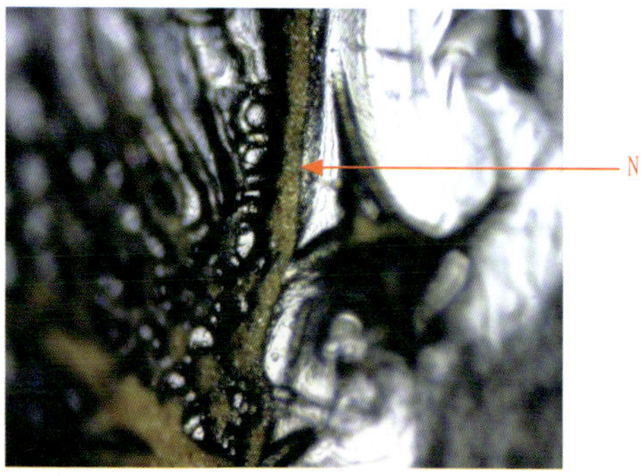

图6-2-42

图6-2-43

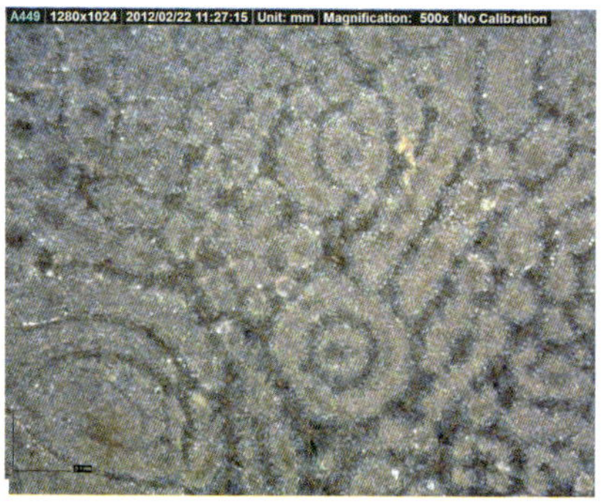

图6-2-44

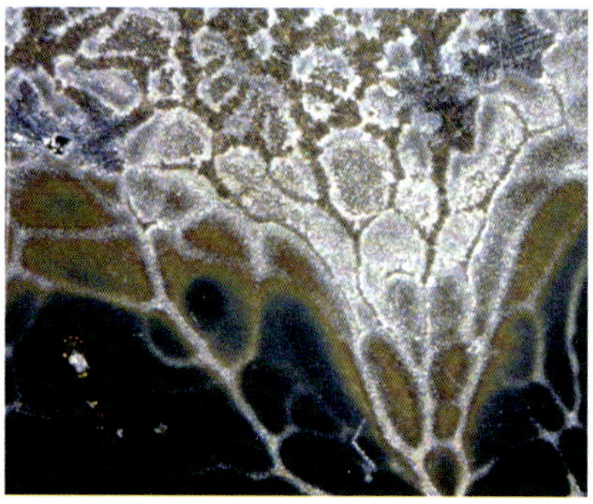
图6-2-45

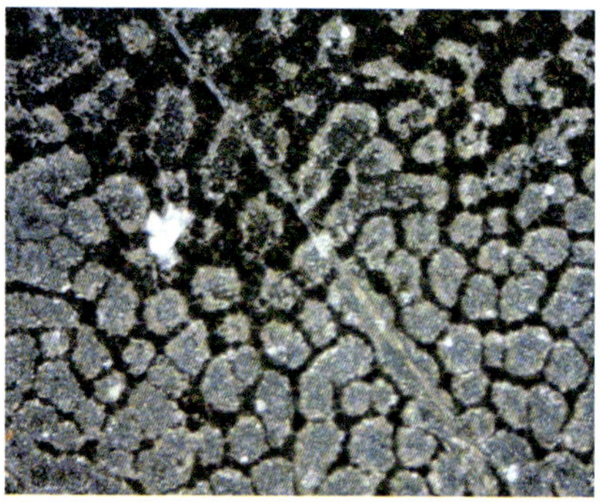
图6-2-46

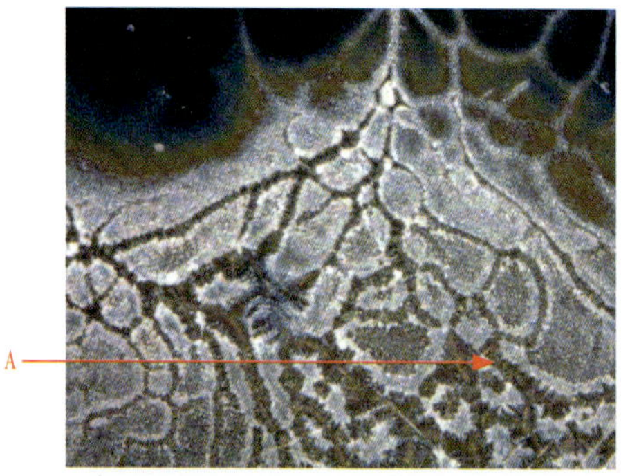

图6-2-47

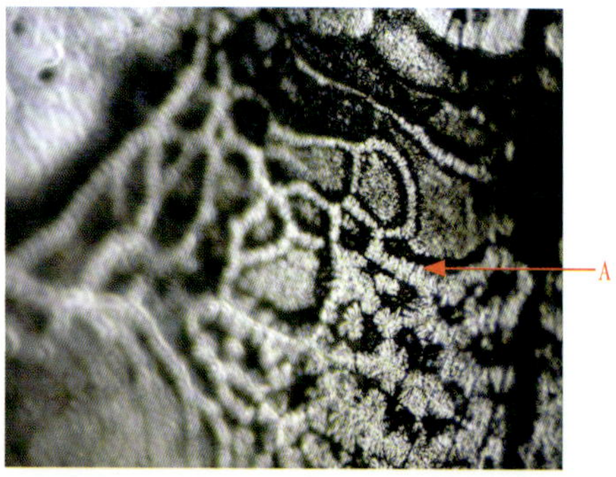

图6-2-48

glass phase is visible. As a whole, the scratches retain clear delineation with the surrounding glass phase.

See pictures 6-2-123 and 6-2-124, where 6-2-123 is the two-dimensional and 6-2-124 is the three-dimensional view of the same location.

The light colored scratch in picture 6-2-123 is the clearly depicted darker area in picture 6-2-124. The mottles that present in picture 6-2-123 all but disappears in picture 6-2-124, but the scratch still retains clear delineation with the surrounding glass phase as indicated by Arrow A. This is due to the fact that the pitting is a development from the scratch down into the glaze level, and three-dimensional observation does not allow for its full visibility.

See pictures 6-2-125 and 6-2-126, where 6-2-125 is the two-dimensional and 6-2-126 is the three-dimensional view of the same location.

The light colored scratch in picture 6-2-125 is the clearly depicted darker area in picture 6-2-126. The scratch is clearly concave, and the pit interior is coarse and uneven. The edge of the scratch is rounded, but still retains clear delineation with the surrounding glass phase.

'Ox hair' scratches have varied depth, length, direction and width. Deeper scratches present with rounded edges, and retain clear delineation with the surrounding glass phase (see picture 6-2-127).

E. Summary

YUB striae can be innate or acquired.

The formation of flowing striae occurs during the firing of YUB glaze, but many flowing striae require years of weathering in order to be observable through two-dimension microscopic imaging. The cross section of flowing striae can be divided as "W", "U", and "V" shaped. It is possible for the interior of striae to present with needlepoint mottling or granulation, the edges are reserved and rounded, and there is a clear delineation between the striae and the surrounding beach mottle or glass phase.

YUB CO striae are also formed during the firing process, but need to undergo weathering in order to be observable through two-dimensional microscopic imaging. Majority of CO striae occur on portions of raised glaze, and are finely minute under three-dimensional observation. CO striae can occur in conjunction with CO type pit mottles, but as a whole, the surface area under three-dimensional observation is smaller than that observable through two-dimensional microscopic imaging.

Scratches are all acquired damage striae that have come about in the post-firing environment. Scratch appearances are numerous. They can present with internal needlepoint mottling, and round edges can be observed through three-dimensional microscopic imaging.

Glaze cracks can be formed during the firing process or can be acquired, and are considered as a glaze structural flaw. Over time they allow for the gradual formation of other acquired traces such as color change bubbles, texturized bubbles, floccus mottles, and so forth.

These striae and the multiplicity of their appearances and characteristics reflect the quantitative change and passage of time principles of ceramic traces, and embody the various laws that govern ceramic trace formation and change.

（4）小结

流淌纹有粗、细、深、浅的形貌变化，也有颜色的变化。单位图片上可有上述多种流淌纹并存，它们的形貌、颜色及分布都有一定的规律。

流淌纹的形貌、颜色及分布规律与流淌纹所处区域釉的配方、含量、铁氧化物和锰氧化物的数量以及釉表面的凹凸情况有关。

碘酒纹基本未风化，呈先天性原貌。

在碘酒斑上出现的流淌纹，尽管该区域釉表面存在凹槽，但凹槽处SiO_2的含量较高，因此风化强度较低，流淌纹主要以细线型及中空型阴纹出现，颜色主要呈白色。

当釉表面逐渐被侵蚀，风化作用加深，流淌纹主要以针眼型阴纹出现，颜色有白色或橘黄色。

当逐渐进入几乎无釉覆盖的沙滩斑区域时，那里分布的流淌纹由于成分有别于沙滩斑，风化强度较沙滩斑轻，主要以阳纹出现，颜色呈褐色，三维成像为凸起部分（见图6-2-49—图6-2-54）。

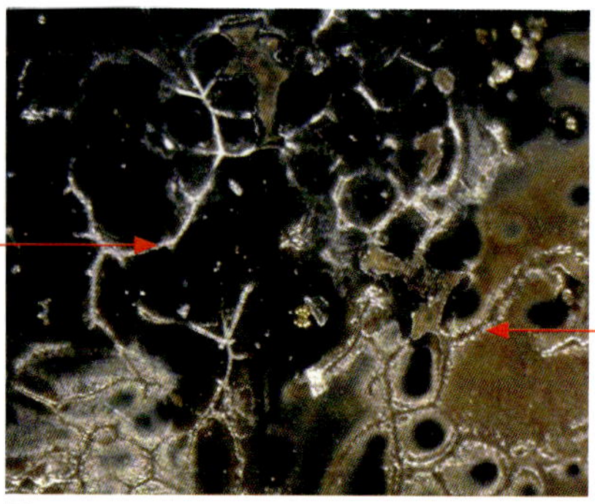

图6-2-49

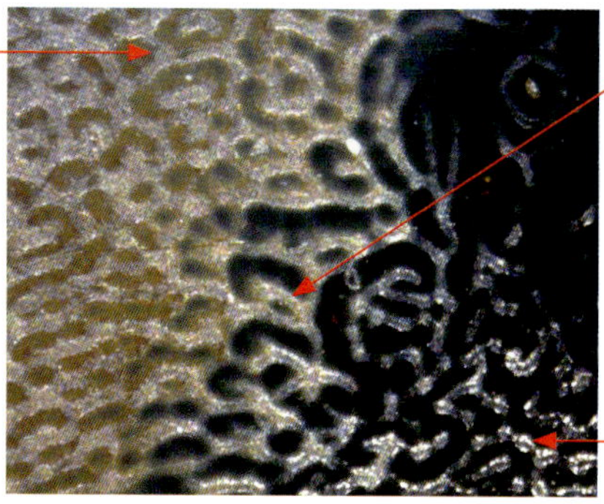

图6-2-50

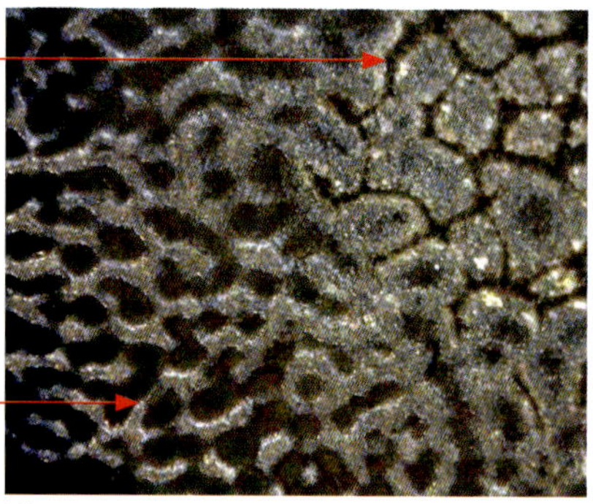

图6-2-51

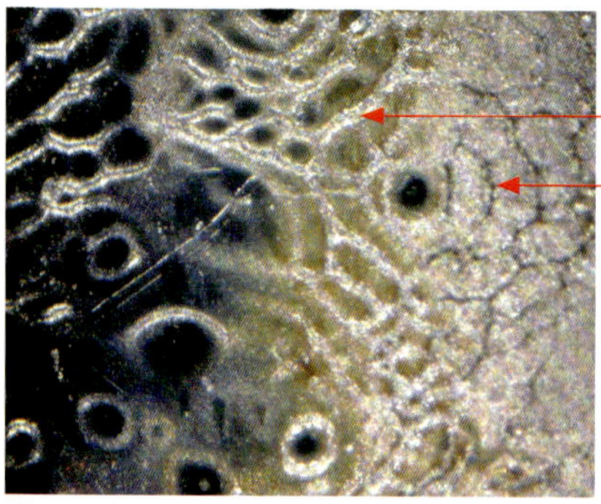

图6-2-52

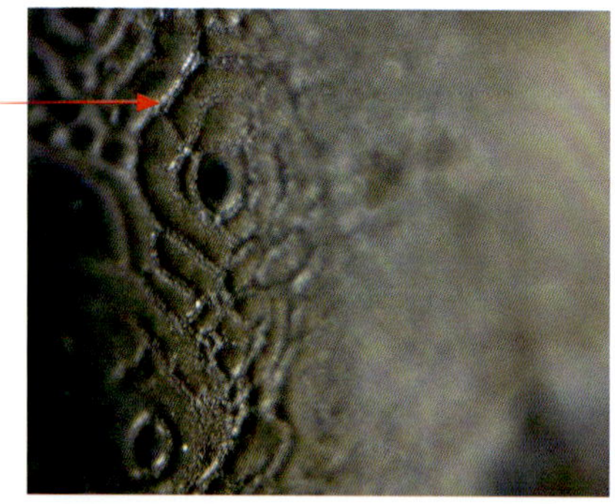

图6-2-53

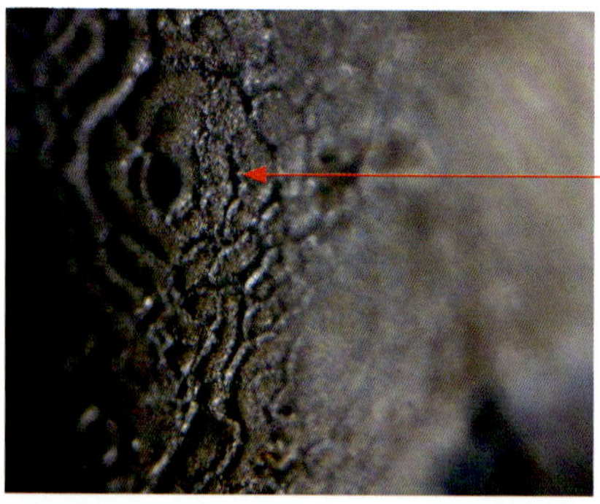

图6-2-54

（二）C形纹、O形纹

1. C形纹、O形纹概念

C形纹、O形纹是元青花瓷器在烧制过程中及后天环境影响下，以铁氧化物、锰氧化物等金属氧化物为主，以字母C、O形貌分布在釉表面的线形纹路。

2. C形纹、O形纹形成

元青花瓷器在高温烧制时，青料及釉料会逐渐熔化成熔融态。在浮力、表面张力及气泡搅动的作用下，釉料以及青料中的铁氧化物和锰氧化物易于在气泡边缘积聚，部分会随气泡升至釉表面，并结晶析出，也可能产生分相。当温度下降时，会有更多结晶析出，在表面张力的作用下，有的析晶主要以环状形式存在于釉表面及釉层中。一般情况下，它们的化学稳定性不及玻璃相，而且两相结合处组织结构有缺陷，易风化，从而逐渐形成可被观察到的C形纹、O形纹。

另一方面，高温烧制元青花瓷器时，产生的气泡在熔融的釉料中不断上升，有的冲出釉表面。当釉料冷却凝固下来时，气泡冲出釉表面时留下的环状凹槽便会留在釉表面上，外界物质容易在釉表面的这些环状凹槽处沉积，逐渐风化形成C形纹、O形纹。

3. C形纹、O形纹分布

C形纹、O形纹一般都出现在玻璃相上。大都出现在釉表面凸起处（见图6-2-55、图6-2-56箭头A所指处），也会在不明显凸起的地方出现（见图6-2-57箭头B所指处）。

4. C形纹、O形纹特征

（1）C形纹、O形纹二维特征

I. C形纹、O形纹的基本型以C形和O形为主：C形纹是半圆形貌的纹路，O形纹是圆形、椭圆形貌的纹路。（以下简称CO纹）

II. CO纹均进入釉层一定的深度，大小参差，粗细不一，与周围玻璃相界线清晰（见图6-2-58—图6-2-82）。

III. CO纹可以产生如“L”形、“8”形、“6”形等其他变体（见图6-2-62—图6-2-64）；还常见有两条紧挨或距离较近的C形纹，如同分杈的枝丫（见图6-2-65—图6-2-69）。

IV. CO纹的颜色以黄色和褐色居多，也可出现白色和黑灰色（见图6-2-58—图6-2-82）。

V. 对一件器物整体来说，CO纹一般会有色差，但在单位图片里，它们大都缺乏明显的色差变化，少数呈现明显色差变化（见图6-2-72、图6-2-74）。有时单项C形纹或O形纹也会有色阶变化（见图6-2-70—图6-2-72）。

VI. 通常CO纹的颜色与相邻的其他迹型如划痕等保持一致（见图6-2-61、图6-2-64、图6-2-66、图6-2-74、图6-2-75）。

VII. 有时CO纹下会出现絮状斑（见图6-2-76、图6-2-77）。

VIII. CO纹继续风化，纹路线条逐渐变粗（见图6-2-78、图6-2-79），C形弧线内或O形圈内变成白色，由透影发展至不透影，逐渐往坑点斑发展，最后形成CO纹与坑点斑共存的现象（见图6-2-80—图6-2-82）。

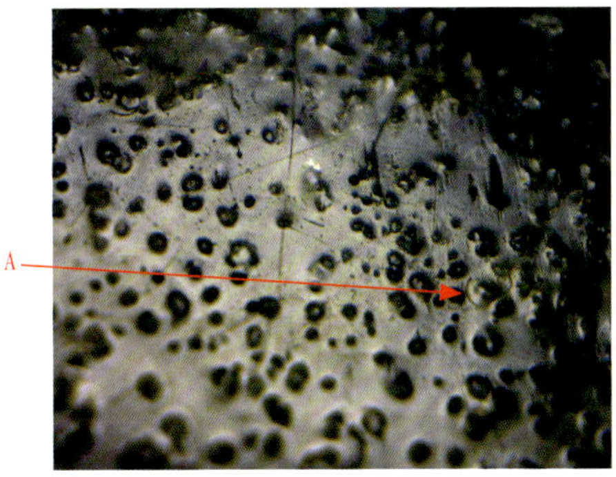

图6-2-55

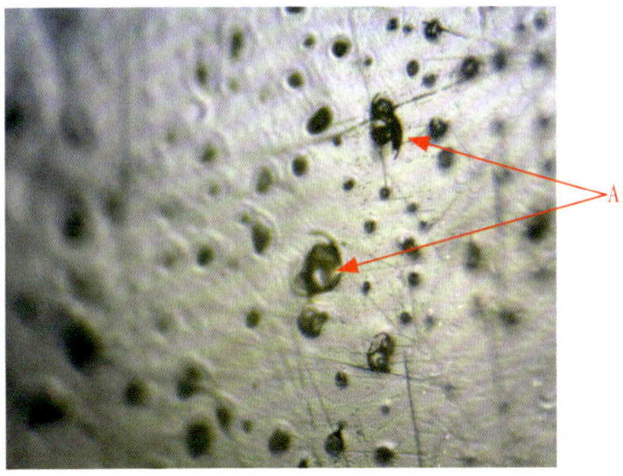

图6-2-56

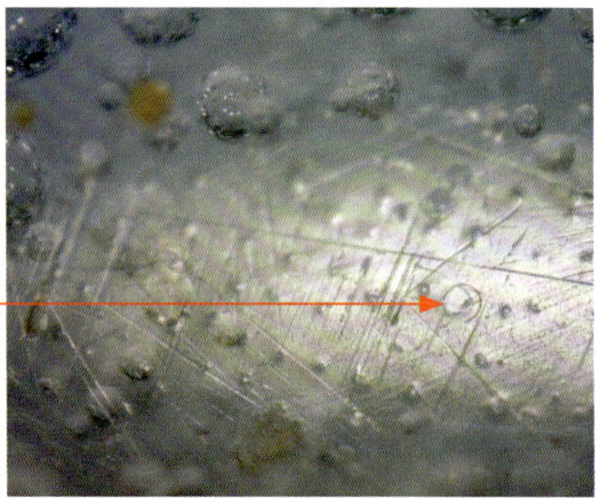

图6-2-57

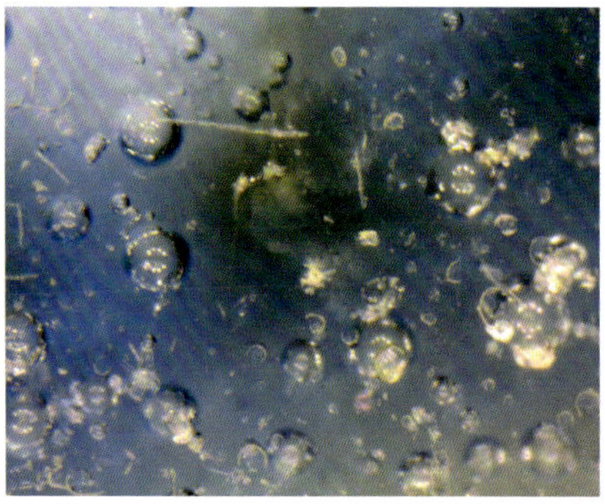

图6-2-58

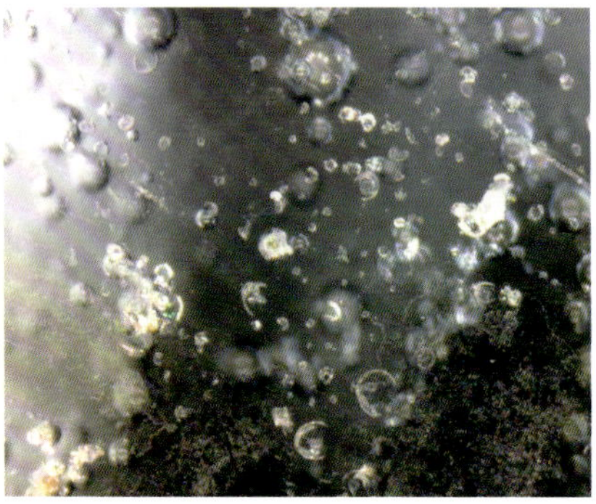

图6-2-59

图6-2-60

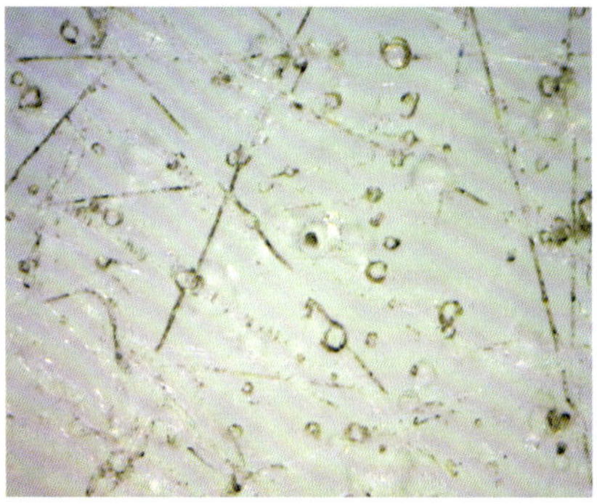

图6-2-61

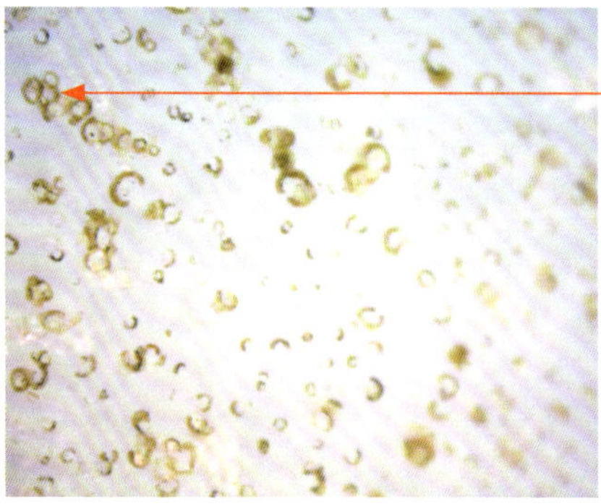

图6-2-62

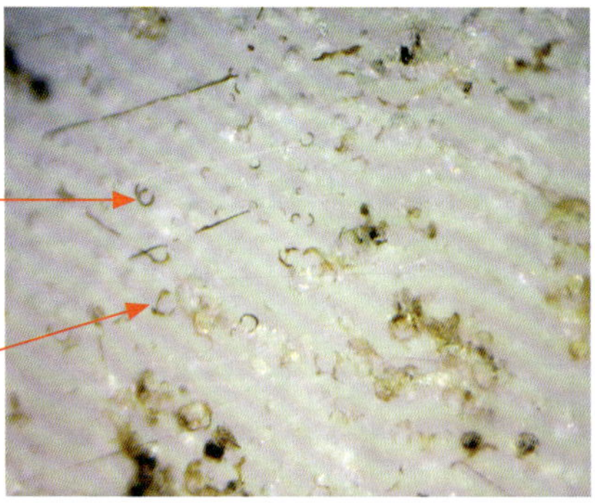

图6-2-63

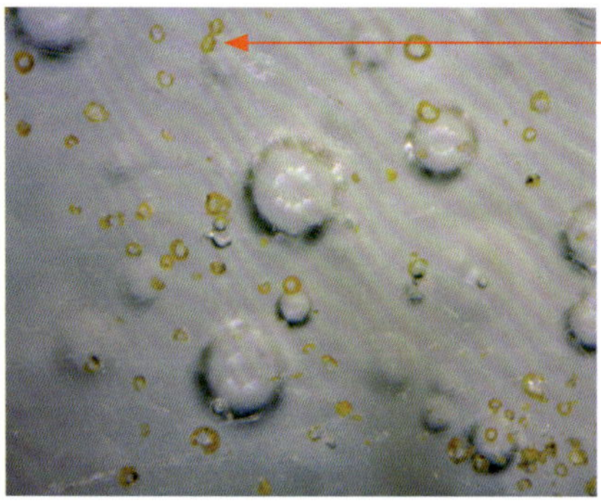

图6-2-64

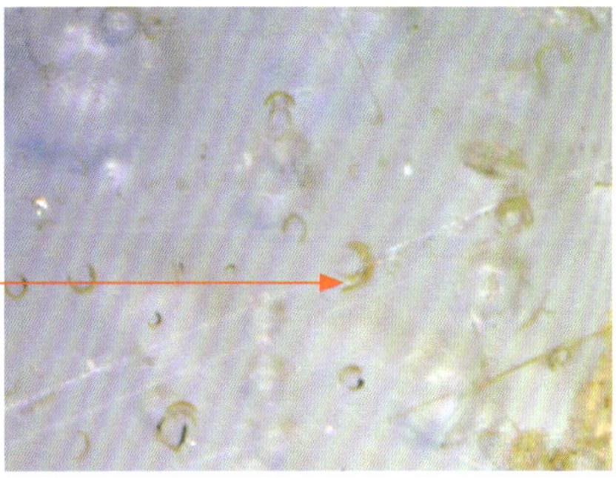

图6-2-65*

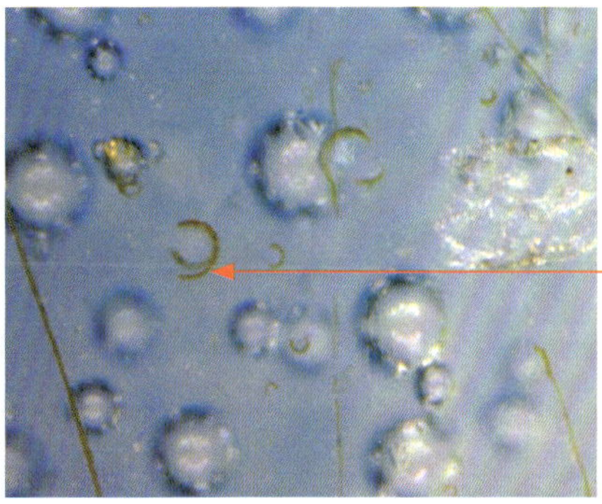

图6-2-66*

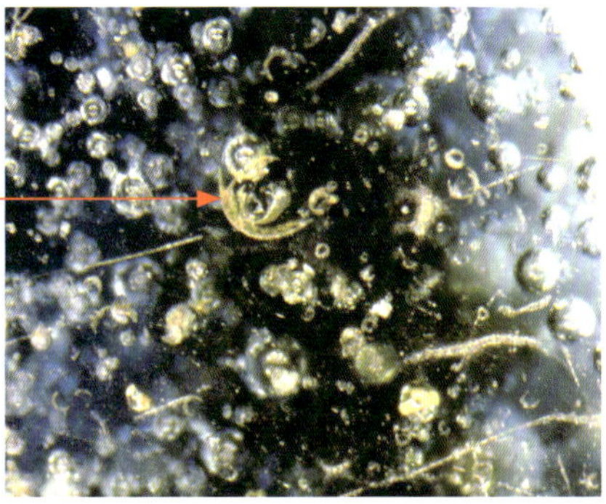

图6-2-67

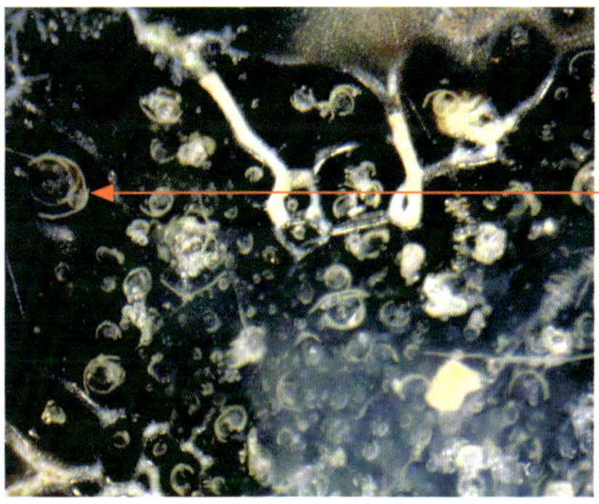

图6-2-68

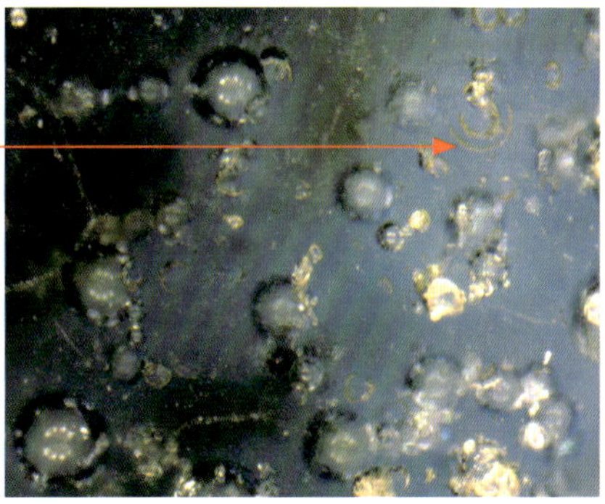

图6-2-69

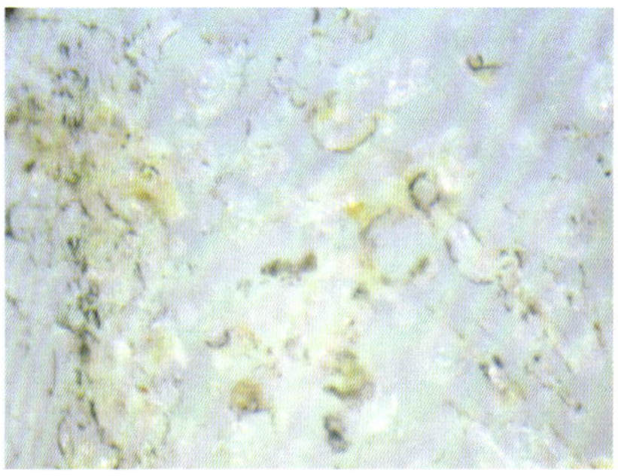
图6-2-70*

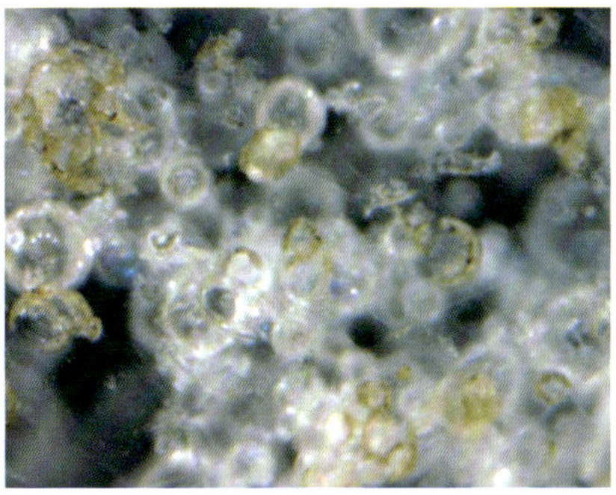
图6-2-71*

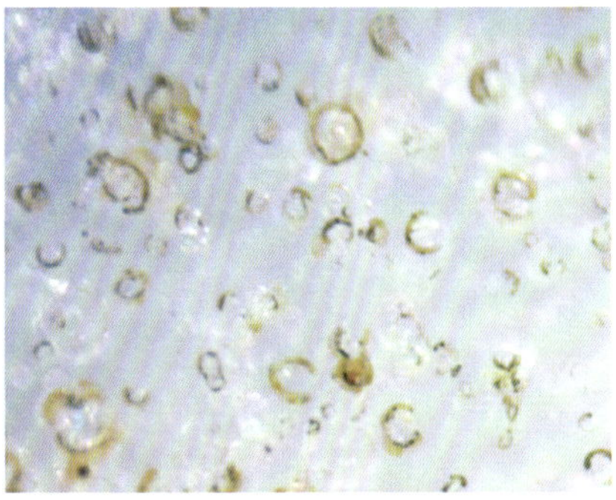
图6-2-72*

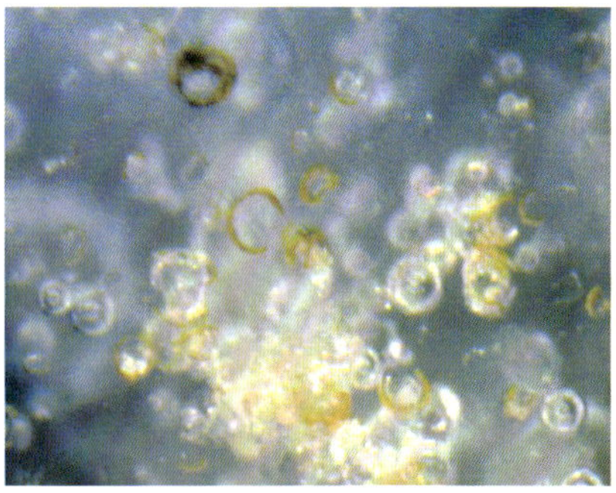
图6-2-73*

*图片经过裁剪放大处理。
*Picture cropped and enlarged to show detail.

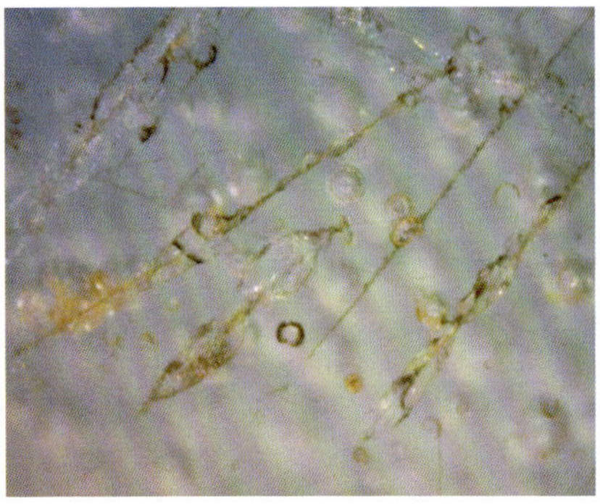
图6-2-74

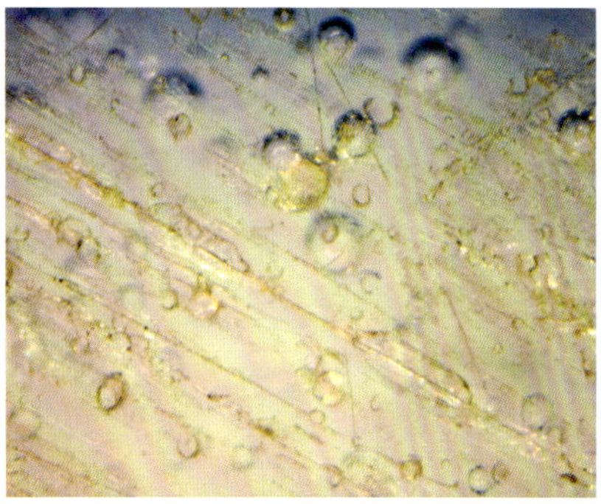
图6-2-75

图6-2-76

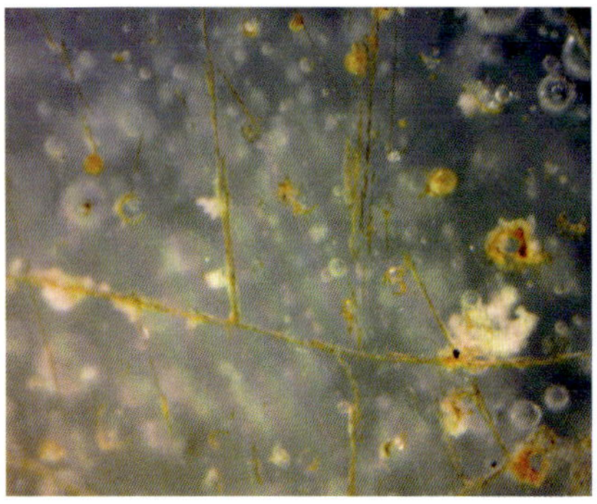
图6-2-77

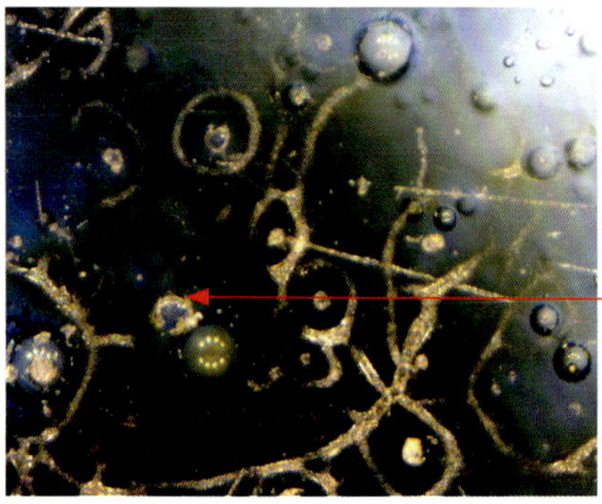
C形纹变粗
C Shaped Striation
Widens

图6-2-78

C形纹变粗
C Shaped Striation
Widens

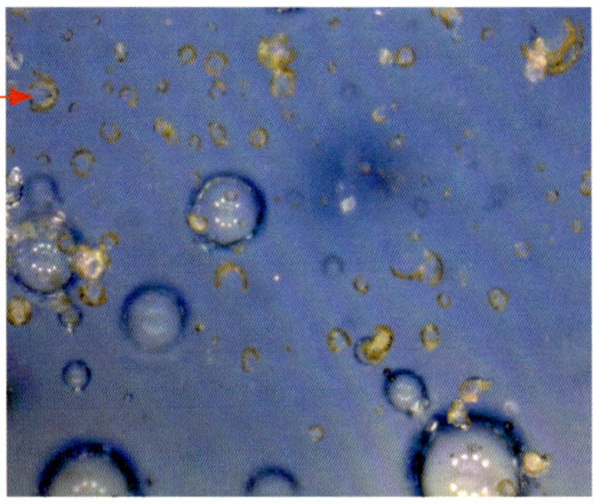
图6-2-79

C形纹内部变白
C Shaped Striation
with White Center

图6-2-80*

C形纹内部变白
C Shaped Striation
with White Center

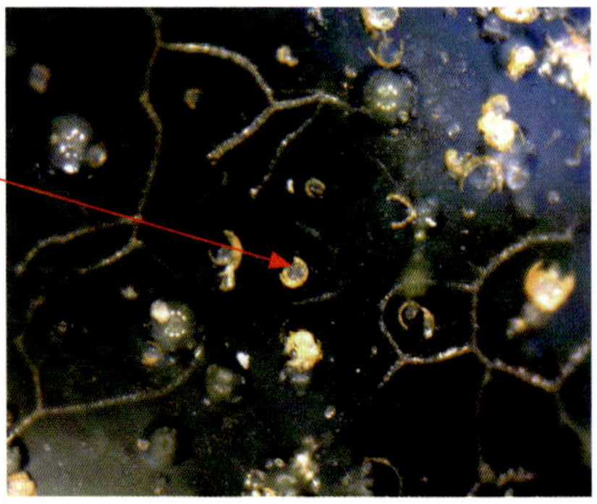
图6-2-81

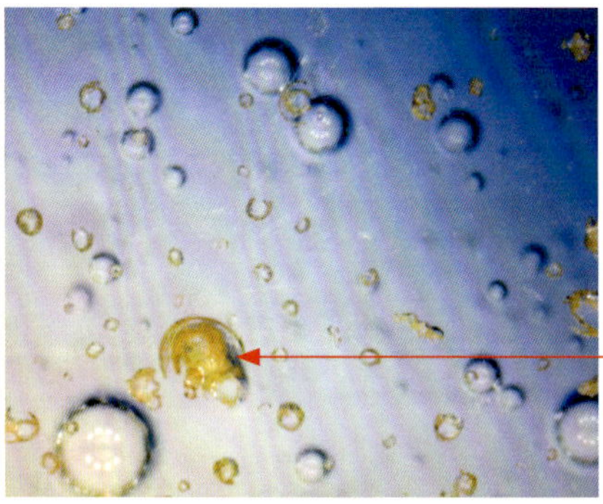
C形纹、坑点斑共存
C Shaped Striation
and CO Type Pit
Mottle Occurring
Congruently

图6-2-82

*图片经过裁剪放大处理。

*Picture cropped and enlarged to show detail.

（2）C形纹、O形纹三维特征

I. CO纹大都分布在釉表面凸起处。

II. CO纹纤细收敛，清晰独立。

III. CO纹与周围玻璃相界线分明。

见图6-2-83、图6-2-84，二者为同一器物同一位置图片，图6-2-83为二维图片，图6-2-84为三维图片。

见图6-2-85、图6-2-86，二者为同一器物同一位置图片，图6-2-85为二维图片，图6-2-86为三维图片。

图6-2-83中箭头C及图6-2-85中箭头D所指的黄色C形纹在图6-2-84和图6-2-86中均呈深色，成像清晰，它们都存在于釉表面凸起处，并与周边玻璃相界线分明。

图6-2-83中箭头C所指的C形纹在图6-2-84中只见于深色凸起处，难以观察到。

见图6-2-87、图6-2-88，二者为同一器物同一位置图片，图6-2-87为二维图片，图6-2-88为三维图片。

图6-2-87中黄色的C形纹在图6-2-88中颜色显得更深，但纹路比图6-2-87中的更细更紧致；图6-2-87中箭头E所指的深色斑块在图6-2-88中表现为两条纤细的分权纹路，纹路与周围玻璃相界线清晰。

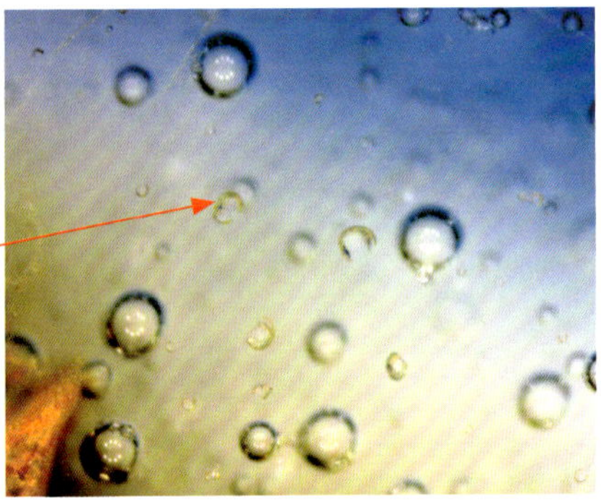

图6-2-83

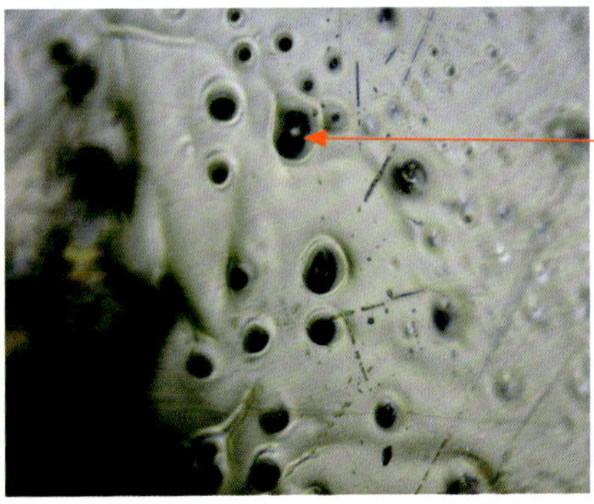

图6-2-84

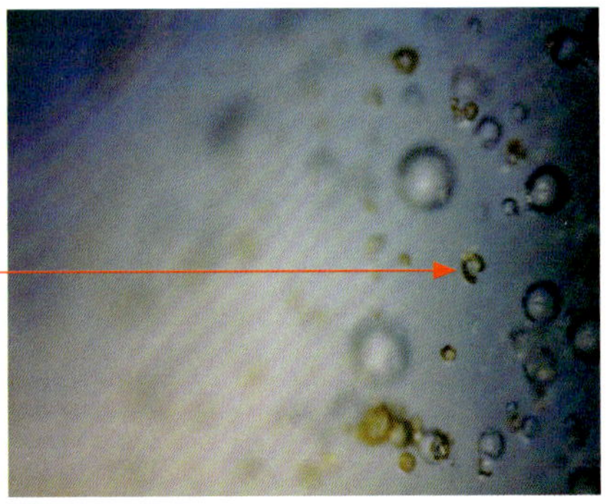

图6-2-85

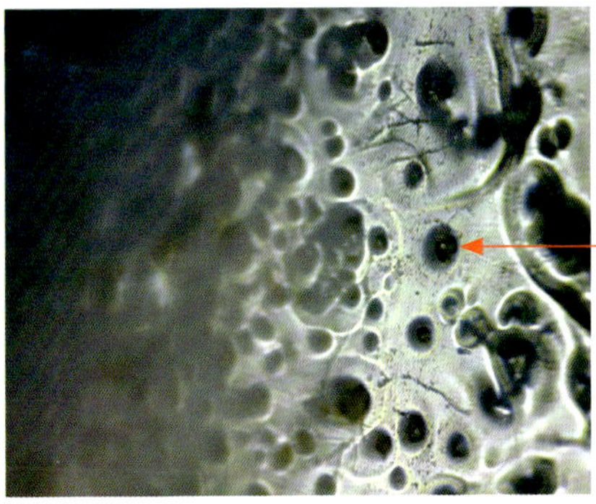

图6-2-86

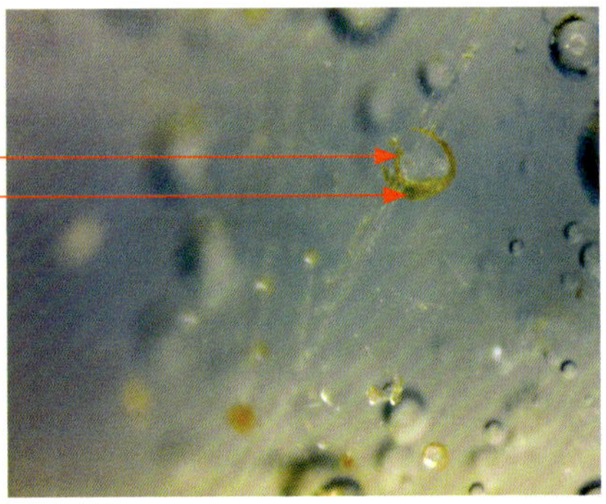

图6-2-87

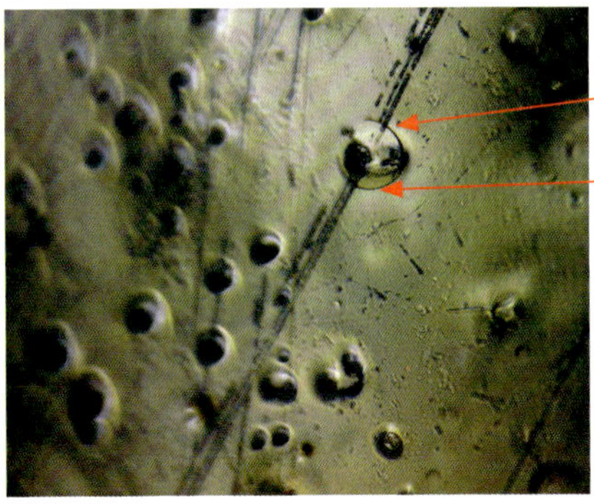

图6-2-88

（三）釉裂纹

1. 釉裂纹概念

釉裂纹是元青花瓷器在烧制过程中和在后天环境影响下形成的，以直线、曲线等不规则线条形貌分布在釉表面的开裂纹路。

2. 釉裂纹形成

釉裂纹的形成主要有以下几种原因：

（1）元青花瓷器在高温烧制时，釉表面的成分挥发会造成空位，这些空位集聚成为空隙，因应力形成釉裂纹。

（2）釉层与微相之间膨胀不一可形成釉裂纹。

（3）由于≡Si－O－R中R^+和H+的离子交换，H^+离子取代R^+位置，而H^+又比R^+小，因而产生应力，形成釉裂纹[224]。

（4）釉层与胎的膨胀系数不同，当温度变化时，胎釉之间会产生应力，由于胎较厚，承受应力的能力比釉层强，当应力大到一定程度时，釉层不能承受，便形成釉裂纹。

（5）釉层没有延展性，当外力打击超过其承受能力时，釉层便开裂形成釉裂纹。

釉裂纹未必与风化作用有直接的因果关系，有些釉裂纹是烧制过程中形成的，有的是后天环境影响下形成的。不是所有釉裂纹在显微成像下都能被观察到。

在后天环境中，当温度发生变化或有可溶盐或难溶盐渗入而又析出时，产生的应力会使釉裂纹逐渐扩大。

陶瓷的釉表面出现裂纹，有时是人们利用胎与釉膨胀系数的差异，刻意追求的艺术效果。元青花瓷器的釉裂现象不属于人们刻意追求的艺术效果，而且较少出现，如果有釉裂现象，都属于瓷器缺陷。

3. 釉裂纹特征

釉裂纹二维特征

① 釉裂纹有直线形貌，也有曲线形貌。

② 釉裂纹上会延伸出多条裂纹，像人参须一样（见图6-2-95）。

③ 釉裂纹的粗细变化特征有：

A. 粗细变化不明显的（见图6-2-89、图6-2-90）。

B. 粗细有变化的（见图6-2-91）。

④ 釉裂纹的颜色变化特征有：

A. 颜色没有明显变化的（见图6-2-92）。

B. 全部变色但无明显色阶变化（见图6-2-89）。

C. 有色阶变化，颜色有白色、黄色、褐色、黑色等（见图6-2-90、图6-2-93、图6-2-94）。

D. 部分变色（见图6-2-94）。

⑤ 釉裂纹周边的特征包括：

A. 色变泡或壁变泡的出现（见图6-2-96、图6-2-97）。

B. 釉下变色（见图6-2-98、图6-2-99）。

C. 釉下形成絮状斑（见图6-2-95、图6-2-100）。

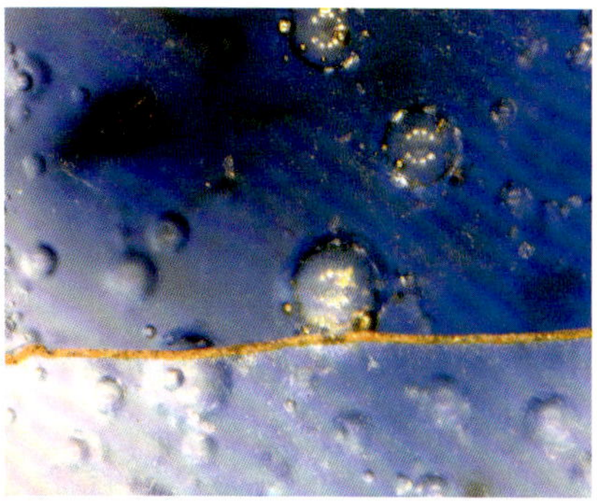
图6-2-89

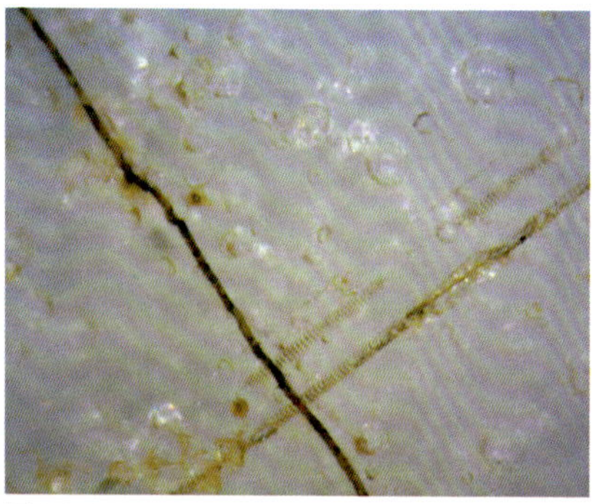
图6-2-90

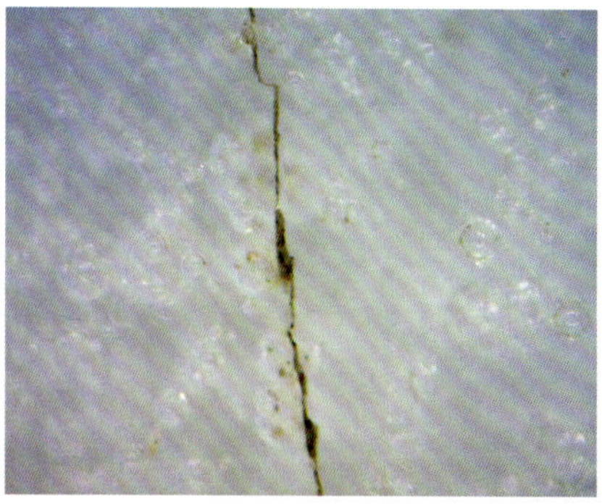
图6-2-91

图6-2-92

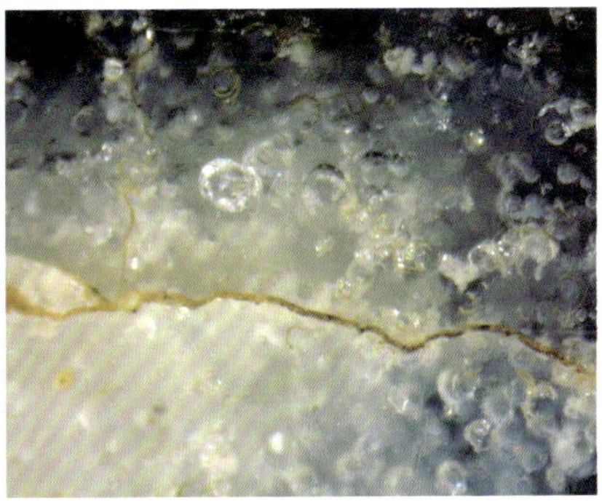

图6-2-93

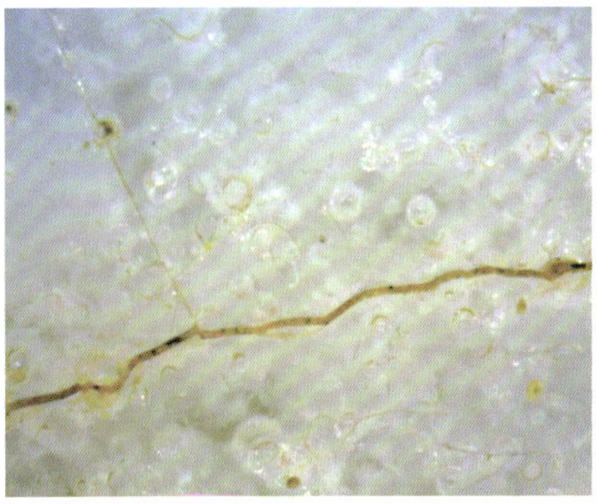

图6-2-94

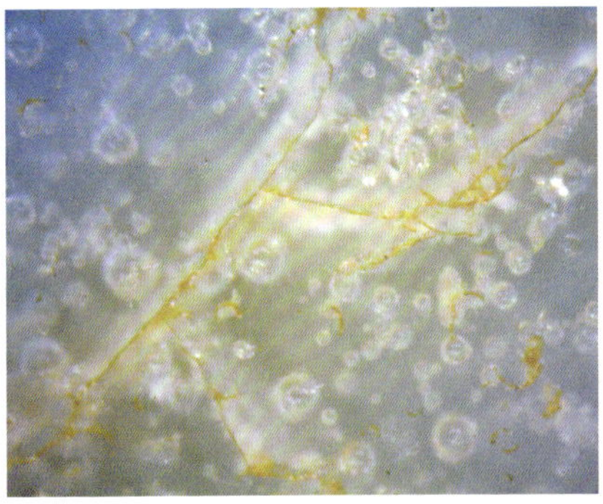

图6-2-95

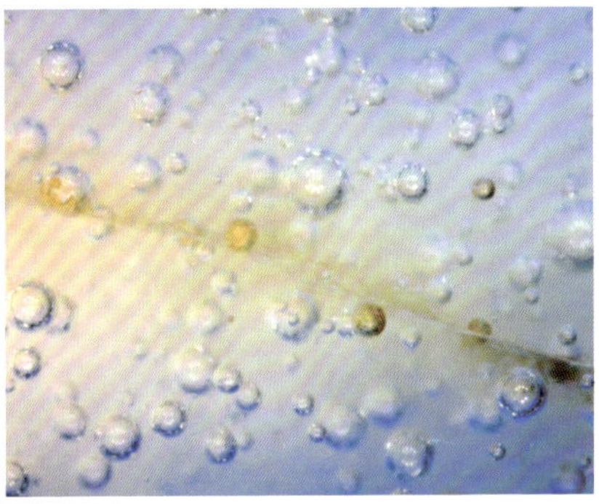

图6-2-96

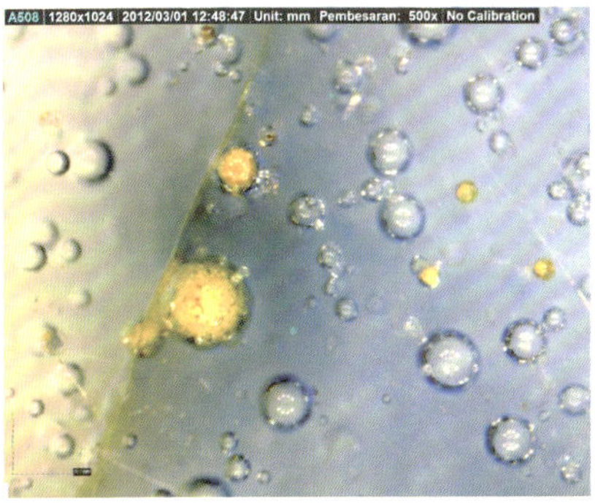

图6-2-97

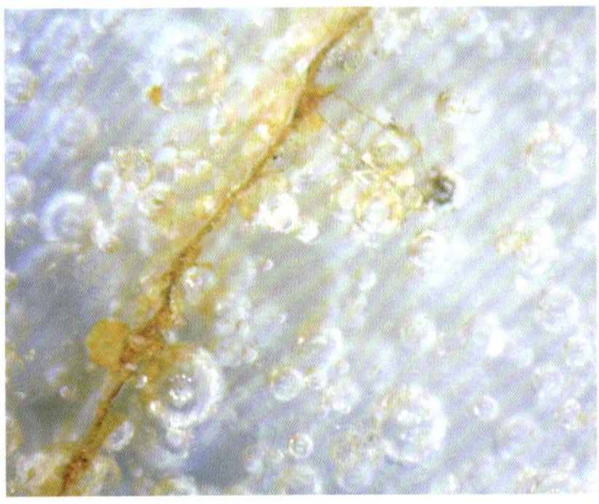

图6-2-98

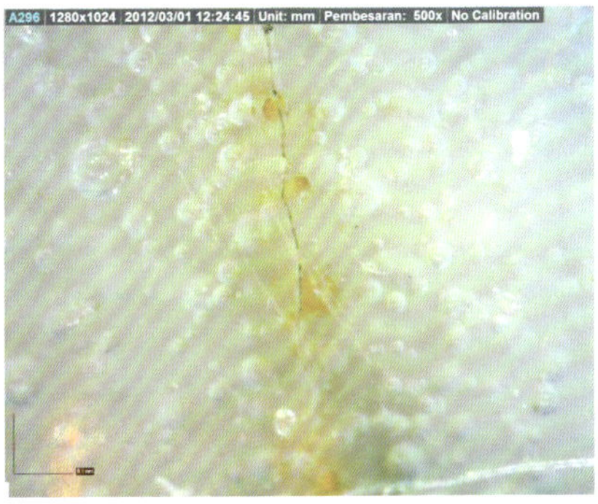

图6-2-99

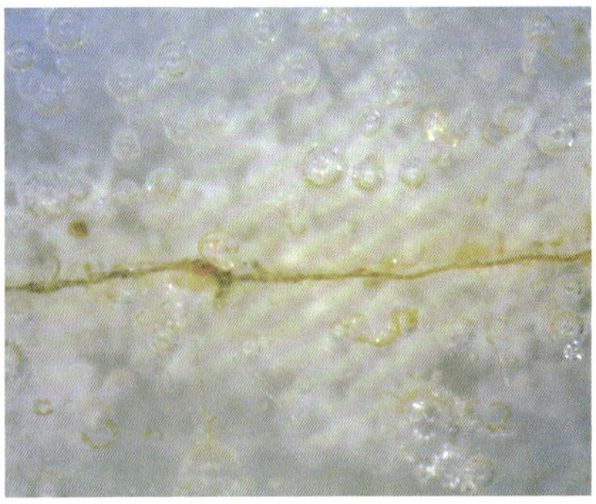

图6-2-100

（四）划痕

1. 划痕概念

划痕是元青花瓷器釉表面与硬物碰划留下的破坏性纹路。

2. 划痕形成

元青花瓷器在后天长期使用中或存在环境中与硬物碰划，在釉表面会留下划痕。

3. 划痕特征

（1）划痕二维特征

① 划痕有粗有细，有长有短，有深有浅，有连有断，有直线有曲线（见图6-2-101—图6-2-116）。

② 有的划痕如牛毛，细而短，杂乱无章地分布（见图6-2-101、图6-2-102）。

③ 有的划痕形如蜈蚣（见图6-2-104—图6-2-106）。

④ 有的划痕呈不规则形貌（见图6-2-107—图6-2-116）。

⑤ 划痕颜色有白色、黄色、褐色等（见图6-2-101—图6-2-116）。

⑥ 划痕通常随机无序地分布在釉表面，深浅交织共存。在同一张图片上可以同时存在不同形貌、不同颜色的划痕（见图6-2-101、图6-2-104、图6-2-106、图6-2-110、图6-2-112）。

⑦ 划痕入釉较深，形成一定的凹槽，长期易积聚外来物质风化形成针眼斑（见图6-2-110—图6-2-113）。

⑧ 由于划痕属于釉层结构缺陷，其所在处的釉下容易形成絮状斑（见图6-2-114—图6-2-116）。

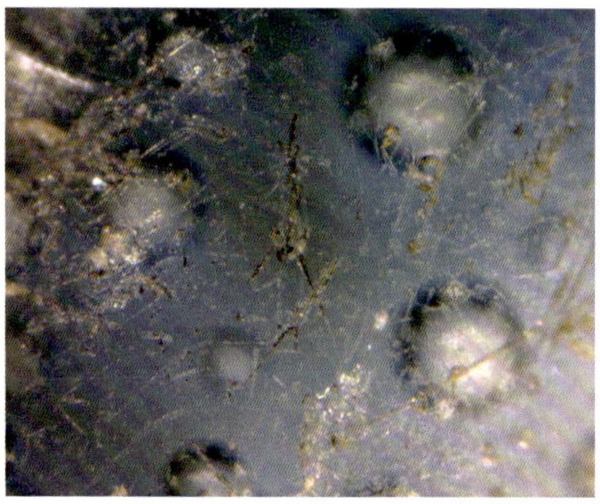
图6-2-101

图6-2-102

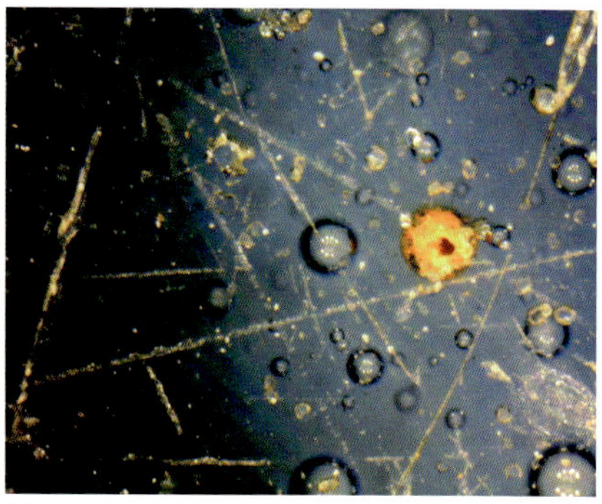
图6-2-103

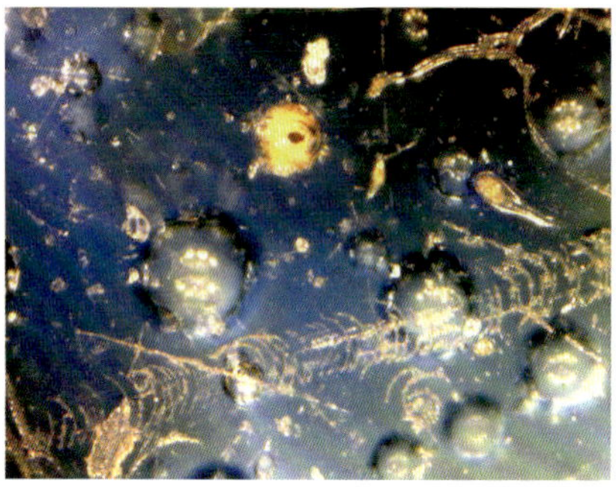
图6-2-104

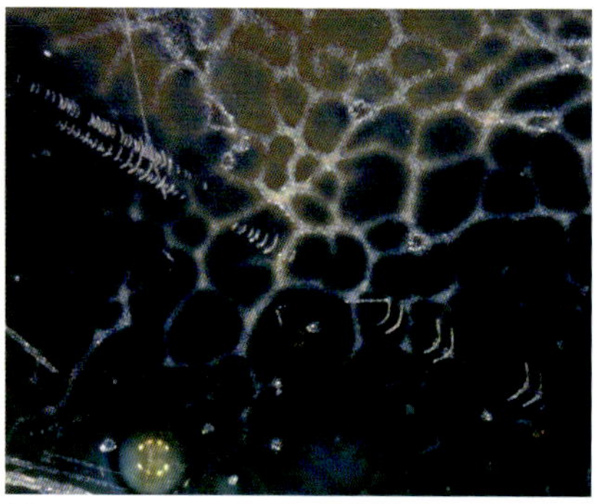
图6-2-105

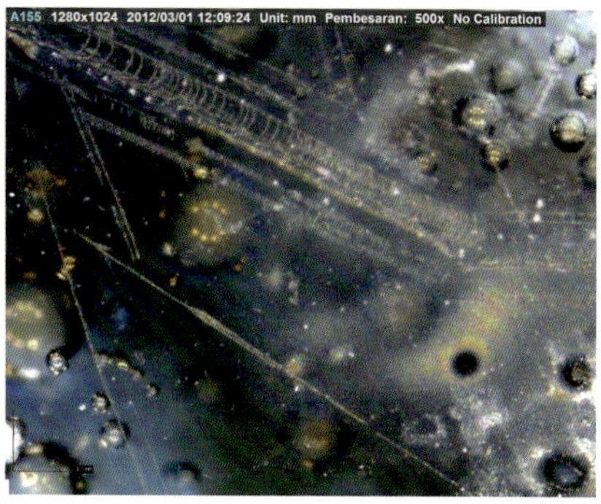

图6-2-106

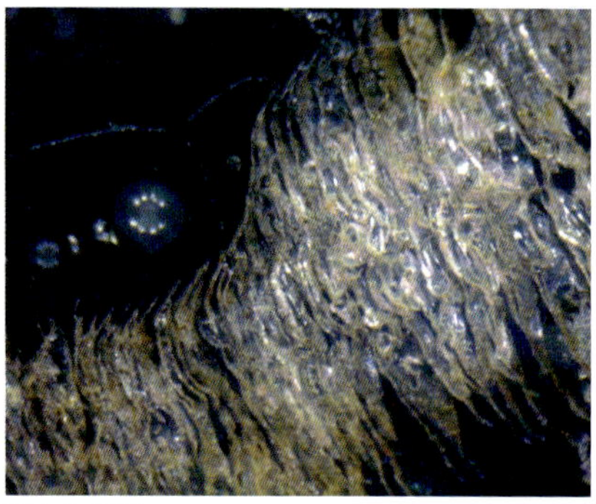
图6-2-107

图6-2-108

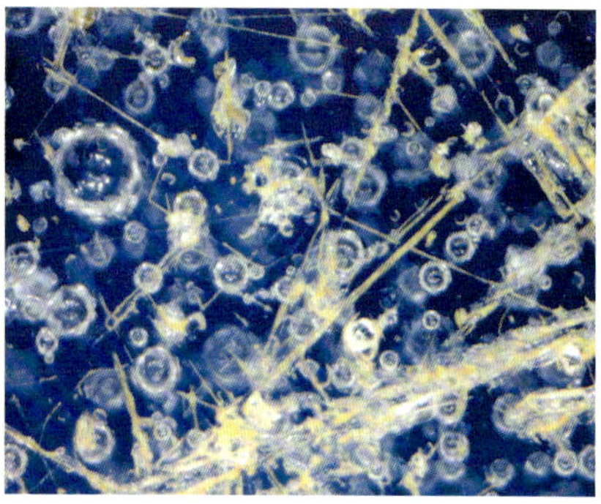
图6-2-109

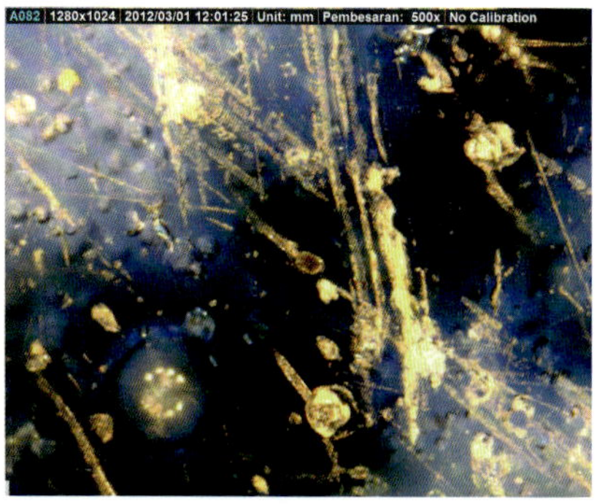

图6-2-110

图6-2-111

图6-2-112

图6-2-113

图6-2-114

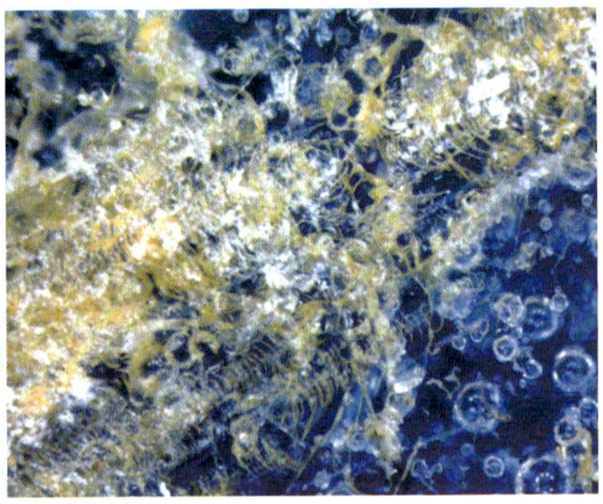
图6-2-115

图6-2-116

（2）划痕三维特征

① 划痕可以表现为间隔均匀的小凹坑、清晰的“蜈蚣脚”、细小且杂乱无章的牛毛划痕及面积较大的凹坑等。

② 划痕周围出现的针眼斑及坑点斑三维成像面积要小于二维。

③ 划痕的凹坑内粗糙不平，边沿圆滑。

④ 划痕与周围玻璃相界线分明。

见图6-2-117、图6-2-118，二者为同一器物同一位置图片，图6-2-117为二维图片，图6-2-118为三维图片。

图6-2-117中浅色的划痕在图6-2-118中呈深色，成像清晰，呈一个个间隔均匀的小凹坑，凹坑与周围玻璃相界线分明。

见图6-2-119、图6-2-120，二者为同一器物同一位置图片，图6-2-119为二维图片，图6-2-120为三维图片。

见图6-2-121、图6-2-122，二者为同一器物同一位置图片，图6-2-121为二维图片，图6-2-122为三维图片。

图6-2-119及图6-2-121中箭头所指的浅色蜈蚣形划痕在图6-2-120和图6-2-122中均呈深色，“蜈蚣脚”细微但清晰可见，“蜈蚣脚”之间的玻璃相也清晰可见，划痕整体与周围玻璃相界线分明。

见图6-2-123、图6-2-124，二者为同一器物同一位置图片，图6-2-123为二维图片，图6-2-124为三维图片。

图6-2-123中的划痕在图6-2-124中呈深色，成像清晰，图6-2-123中划痕上出现的白色风化斑块在图6-2-124中三维成像却消失不见，但划痕与周围玻璃相界线分明（见箭头A所指处）。这是因为斑块是划痕纵向往釉层中发展的结果，三维成像无法全面观察到深入釉层的斑块。

见图6-2-125、图6-2-126，二者为同一器物同一位置图片，图6-2-125为二维图片，图6-2-126为三维图片。

图6-2-125中浅色的划痕在图6-2-126中呈深色，成像清晰，划痕呈现凹坑状，内部粗糙不平，凹坑边缘圆滑，与周围玻璃相界线分明。

牛毛状划痕粗细、长短、方向不一，有深有浅，较深的划痕边沿圆滑，划痕与周围玻璃相界线分明（见图6-2-127）。

图6-2-117

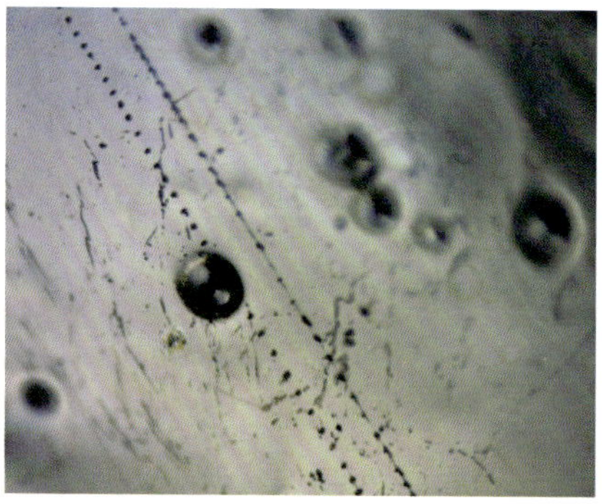

图6-2-118

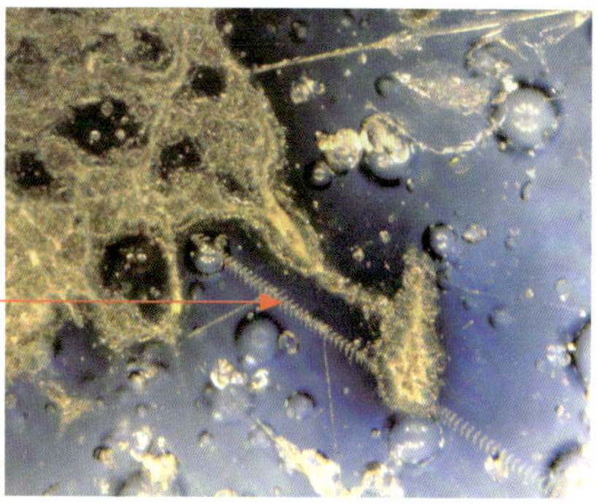

图6-2-119

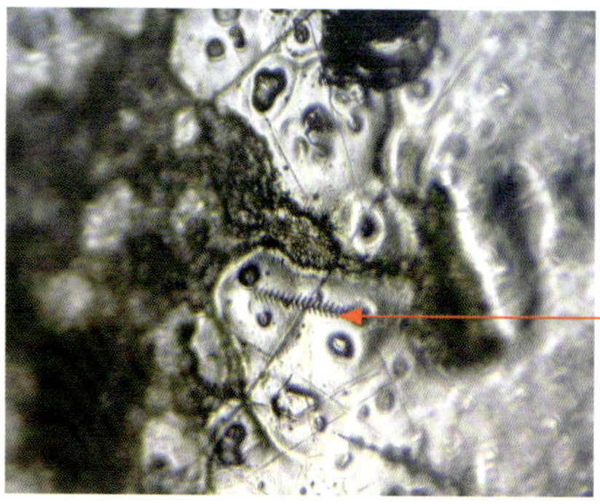

图6-2-120

图6-2-121

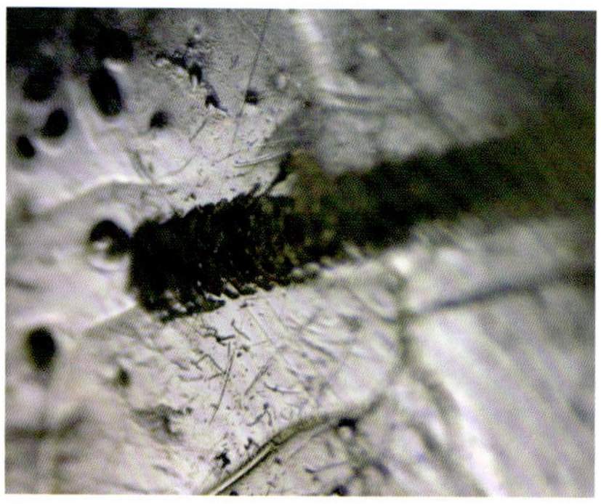

图6-2-122

图6-2-123

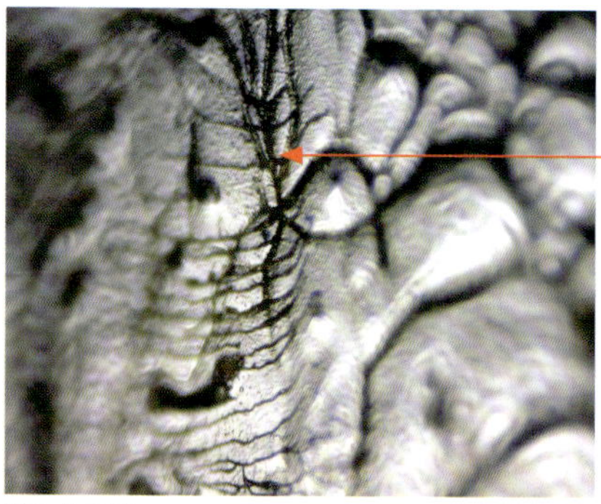

图6-2-124

图6-2-125

图6-2-126

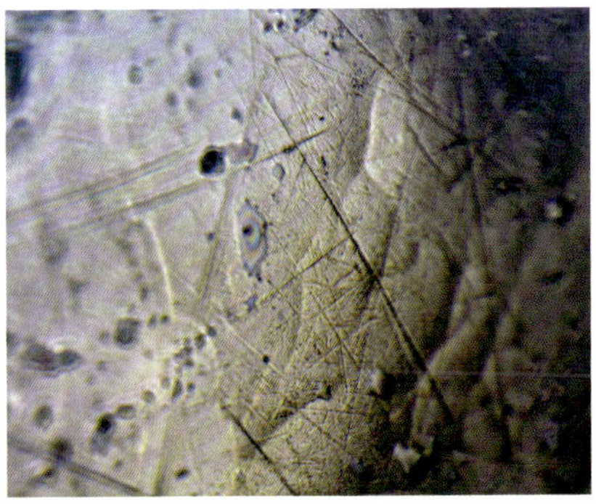
图6-2-127

（五）总结

元青花纹路也有先天形成与后天形成之分。

元青花流淌纹的形貌先天就已形成，但有的流淌纹往往要经历长久的风化后其二维成像才能在显微镜下被观察到。流淌纹剖面可以是“W”型、“U”型或“V”型。纹路内部有时可见针眼斑或颗粒，边沿收敛圆滑，与周围玻璃相和沙滩斑界线分明。

元青花CO纹的形貌也是先天形成的，但通常也是要经过风化后其二维成像才能用显微镜观察到。CO纹大都出现在釉表面凸起处，三维成像纤细紧致，有时CO纹与坑点斑伴生，但整体三维面积都要小于二维。

划痕属于在后天环境影响下形成的破坏性纹路，形貌多变，有时划痕内部可见针眼斑，三维成像边沿圆滑。

釉裂纹既可以是先天形成的也可以是后天形成的，它属于釉层结构的缺陷，长期存在会导致其周边逐渐形成一些后天性风化迹型，如色变泡、壁变泡及絮状斑等。

元青花瓷器上的这些纹路种类和特征能够反映陶瓷迹型变化的量变原理及时间过程原理，也能够体现陶瓷迹型形成及变化的诸规律。

第三节 元青花气泡类别

一、元青花气泡概念

元青花气泡是在元青花瓷器烧制过程中，在釉层中形成的气相迹型类别。

釉层中的气泡在烧制产生时，绝大多数都是透明无色的。

总体来说，元青花瓷器上气泡的大小及分布特征，与明清时期青花瓷器上的气泡不一样。元青花上要么气泡很大，要么气泡较小，中等大小的气泡较少，而且元青花较大的气泡往往是三两个一组，零零星星，随机分布，不会密集成群出现；明清时期青花瓷器上中等大小的气泡较多，分布密集（见图6-3-1—图6-3-6）。

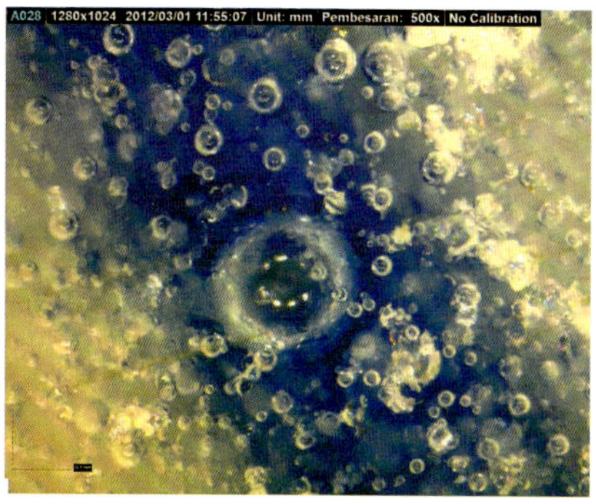

图6-3-1
元青花
YUB

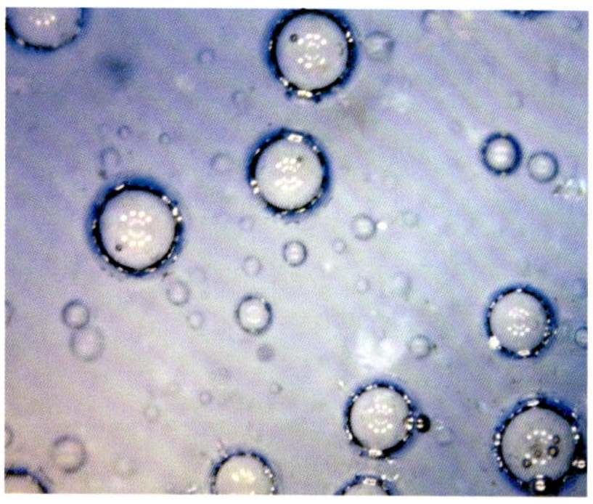
图6-3-2
元青花
YUB

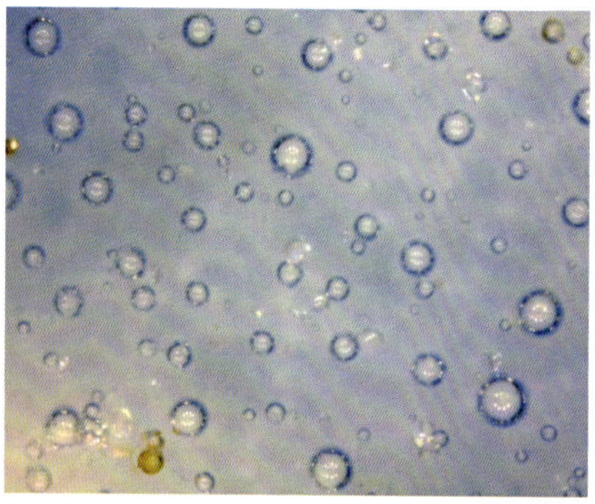
图6-3-3
明永乐青花
Ming Yongle

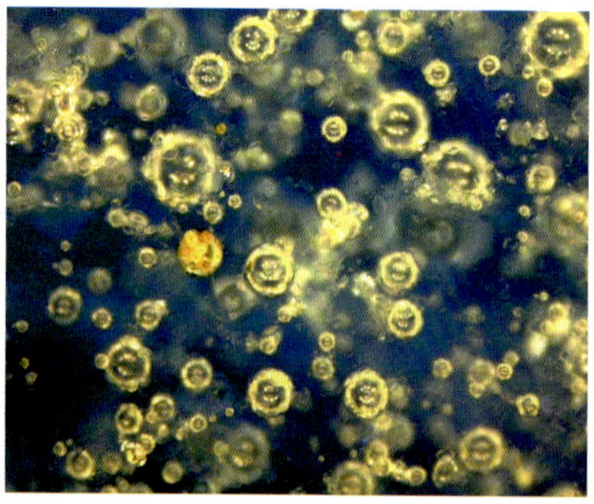
图6-3-4
明宣德青花
Ming Xuande

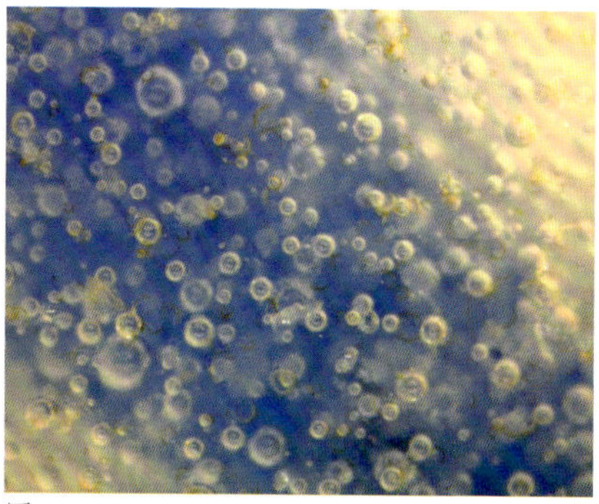
图6-3-5
清康熙青花
Qing Kangxi

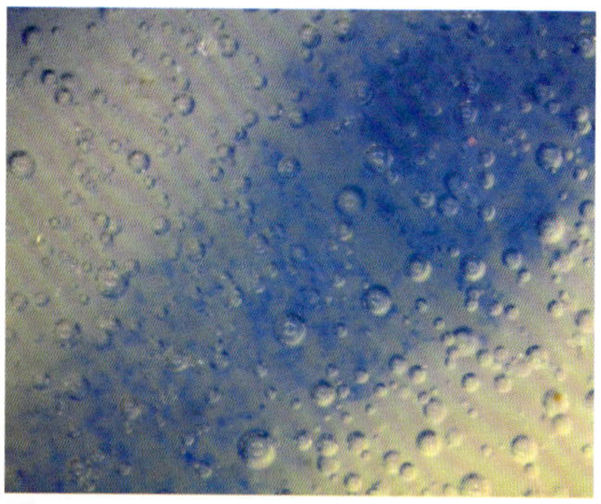
图6-3-6
清雍正青花
Qing Yongzheng

Section 3:
Yuan Underglaze Blue Air Bubble Category

1. YUB Air Bubble Defined

YUB Air Bubbles (also simplified as 'bubbles') are the trace category of gas phase appearances, formed during the firing process, within the glaze level of YUB.

Almost all bubbles formed during the firing process are clear and colorless.

The size, distribution, and properties of air bubbles within the glaze level of YUB are different from those found in later Ming and Qing Dynasty Underglaze Blue wares. The range in size from largest to smallest bubble in YUB is larger than that of later wares. Additionally, the distribution consists of primarily sparsely spread large and small bubbles, with medium size bubbles making up only a small minority. This is different from Early Ming Dynasty wares, which have a large portion of medium sized bubbles and a denser distribution in general (see pictures 6-3-1—6-3-6).

2. YUB Air Bubble Types

We use the color and internal texture changing properties of air bubbles to divide YUB air bubbles into two types: Color Change Bubble and Textured Bubble.

Note: Bubbles only have an interior, no exterior (see pictures 6-3-7 and 6-3-8).

A. Color Change Bubble

I. Color Change Bubble Defined

Color Change Bubbles are the appearance of air bubbles within the glaze level that have undergone a coloration change under the influences of the post-firing environment, but have retained their translucency.

II. Formation of Color Change Bubbles

For a bubble to change from clear transparency to having coloration, it must fulfill the following criterion:

a. Certain Amount of Iron

The change from a non-colored to colored bubble is primarily due to the reaction of Iron.

The vast majority of bubbles are clear directly after firing, and only a few of them—randomly distributed throughout the glaze level—contain trace amounts of elemental Iron. It is also possible, under the influence of the post-firing environment, for Iron to enter through channels into the glaze level and create colored bubbles.

b. Certain Amount of Water

Coloration is dependent on the presence of moisture. Not only can moisture help to carry foreign materials into the bubble, but it also aids in the reactions that cause coloration.

c. Contact with the Outside Surroundings

Channels through the glaze level into the bubble interior can be:

i. Formed during the firing process:

(a) When cooling from a molten state, the glaze is unable to fully recede over the mouth of an air bubble's escape passage, leaving a microscopic opening in the surface of the glaze. This opening acts as a channel between the bubble and the outside world.

(b) The Firing process creates glaze cracks that act as channels.

二、元青花气泡种类

按气泡颜色变化与气泡内壁质地变化的特征，可将元青花气泡分为色变泡与壁变泡两大种类。

注：气泡只有内壁，没有外壁（见图6-3-7、图6-3-8）。

（一）色变泡

1. 色变泡概念

色变泡是元青花瓷器在后天环境影响下，釉层中透明气泡的颜色发生了变化，但仍具透影性的气泡（即半透明状态）。

2. 色变泡形成

无色透明的气泡变成有色气泡需要以下条件：

（1）有一定量的铁元素

气泡从无色变成有色，是气泡内一定量的铁元素发生反应的结果。

刚烧制出来的元青花瓷器，釉层中的气泡绝大多数是无色透明的，在这些无色透明的气泡中，只有部分气泡内壁含有铁元素，这些气泡随机分布在釉层中。在后天环境的影响下，外界的铁元素也可经通道进入气泡内，使气泡变色。

（2）有一定量的水分

气泡从无色变成有色，离不开水的作用，水既可以是输送外界元素进入气泡的媒介，也可以参与反应使气泡变色。

（3）有连接外界环境的通道

釉层通往气泡内的通道可以有两种：

① 烧制过程中形成的

在烧制过程中形成的，有以下两种情况：

A. 元青花高温烧制时，在熔融釉层冷却平复的过程中，釉未能将气泡冲出釉表面时产生的破口完全填满，使釉表面留有微小孔隙，这些微小孔隙构成了连接气泡与外界环境的通道。

B. 元青花烧制时形成的釉裂纹成为通道。

② 后天环境影响下形成的

釉层长期风化受到侵蚀，形成新的裂纹或孔隙，成为通道。这些通道会随着时间的推移逐渐变大。

由于通道的存在，气泡与外界环境相通，外界环境中的各类物质可进入气泡内。

通道存在是气泡变色的关键因素，它可以使部分含铁元素的气泡变色，也可以让不含铁元素的气泡变色。

（4）经一定时间反应

气泡从无色变成有色的自然风化是一个较长的时间过程，因为通道极为细小。统计观察大量民国瓷器与“文革”瓷器的结果表明，部分存放在大气环境中的瓷器，至少经过40年的时间才有色变泡产生。40年之内的瓷器除了在烧制过程中产生的极个别灰泡之外，很少能观察到黄色、褐色等色变泡现象。

3. 色变泡种类

（1）非破口色变泡

① 非破口色变泡概念

非破口色变泡是用500倍显微镜观察到的完整无破口的色变泡。

② 非破口色变泡种类

A. 局变泡

a. 局变泡概念

局变泡是整个气泡仅部分发生了颜色改变的非破口色变泡。

b. 局变泡特征

Ⅰ. 局变泡二维特征

i. 通道明显的局变泡

气泡内壁局部发生色变，有的地方颜色浓重呈深褐色，有的部分还完全透明，色浓处应该就是通道所在处（见图6-3-9）。

ii. 通道不明显的局变泡

有的气泡仅仅是泡壁外延一圈改变了颜色，像土星光环围绕，气泡内颜色未变或部分变色。通常这类气泡都是泡壁外延一圈的颜色较浓，越往气泡中心方向的颜色越淡（见图6-3-10）。

有的局变泡通道不明显（见图6-3-11）。

iii. 界线分明的局变泡

气泡变色部分与未变色部分界线分明，没有渐变的形式。形成这种现象主要有两种原因：

一是气泡内壁出现裂纹，泡壁发生错位，形成气泡内壁风化的屏障。这是一种特殊的局变泡（见图6-3-12）。

二是气泡内壁是凹凸不平的，凹凸不平的表面会形成气泡内壁风化的屏障（见图6-3-13、图6-3-14）。

ii. Formed under the influences of the post-firing environment:

Over long periods of corrosive weathering, the glaze can present with new cracks and holes, these act as channels. Some channels can gradually become larger over time.

Due to the presence of channels, some air bubbles are in contact with the external elements. This allows for the entrance of foreign materials into the bubble interior.

The presence of these channels is necessary for the formation of color change bubbles; they allow for bubbles inherently containing Iron to change color, as well as allow external Iron to enter in and color the bubbles, post-firing.

d. Certain Amount of Reaction Time

The coloration of air bubbles through natural weathering is a relatively long process due to the minute size of the channels. Through several controlled observations, it has been found that pieces sitting in an open air environment take approximately forty years to naturally develop color change bubbles. On pieces less than forty years of age, it is extremely rare to find yellow, brown, and so forth colored bubbles appearing (except for a trace amount of ashen colored bubbles sometimes created during the firing process).

III. Color Change Bubble Types

a. Unbroken Mouth Color Change Bubbles

i. Unbroken Mouth Color Change Bubble Defined

Color change bubbles without an observable mouth under 500X magnification.

ii. Unbroken Mouth Color Change Bubble Types

(a) Semi-Changed Bubbles

(i) Semi-Changed Bubble Defined

An unbroken mouth color change bubble in which only a portion of the bubble has undergone coloration.

(ii) Characteristics of Semi-Changed Bubbles

(1) Two-dimensional Characteristics of Semi-Changed Bubbles

a) Semi-Changed Bubbles with Evident Channel

Partially colored interior with color density gradation, some portions completely transparent, area of darker coloration most likely the area of coloration channel (see picture 6-3-9)

b) Semi-Changed Bubbles with Non-Evident Channel

Often presenting with external coloration, resembling a halo, the interior of the bubble can also undergo partial coloration; Often the coloration is darker towards the outside of the bubble, and gradually grades to a lighter color in the center (see picture 6-3-10).

Some semi-changed bubbles do not have obvious channels (see picture 6-3-11).

c) Semi-Changed Bubbles with Clear Delineation

Clearly delineated border between the colored portion and uncolored portion, no gradation evident, primarily cause by two types of factors:

First, the interior wall of the bubble cracks, creating a displaced surface, blocking the progression of weathering along the bubble interior. This is an atypical type of semi-changed bubble (see picture 6-3-12).

Second, the interior of the bubble is topographically uneven, these concave and convex distortions act as barriers to weathering along the bubble interior (see pictures 6-3-13 and 6-3-14).

(2) Three-dimensional Characteristics of Semi-Changed Bubbles

a) Some bubbles have clearly visible coloration channels visible on the glaze surface.

b) The channel surface area is always much smaller than the underlying bubble.

c) The glaze surface surrounding the channel retains its smooth reflective nature.

d) Some bubbles do not present with visible channels, and the overlying glaze retains smooth reflective nature.

See pictures 6-3-15 and 6-3-16, where 6-3-15 is the two-

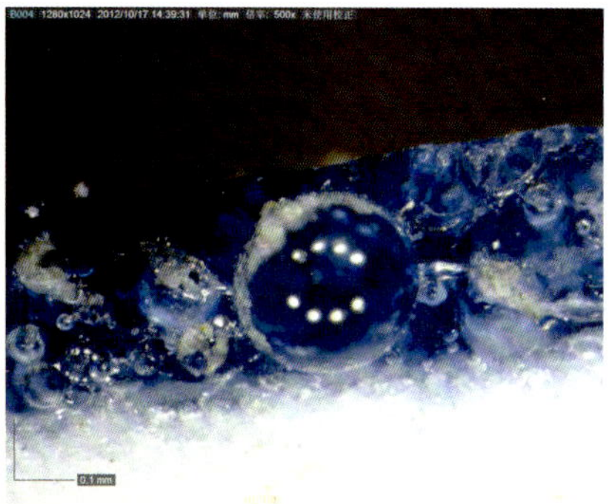

图6-3-7

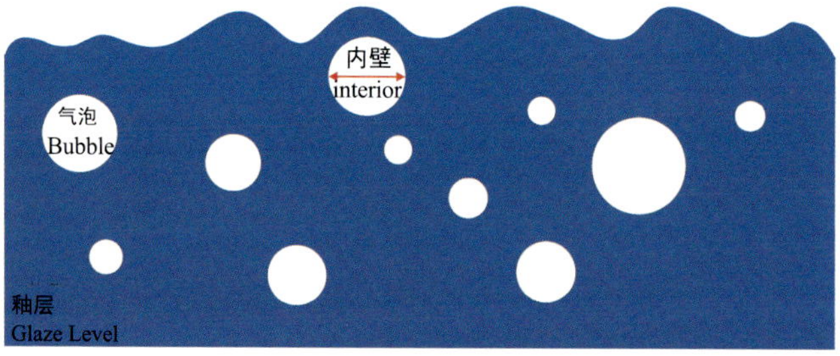

图6-3-8

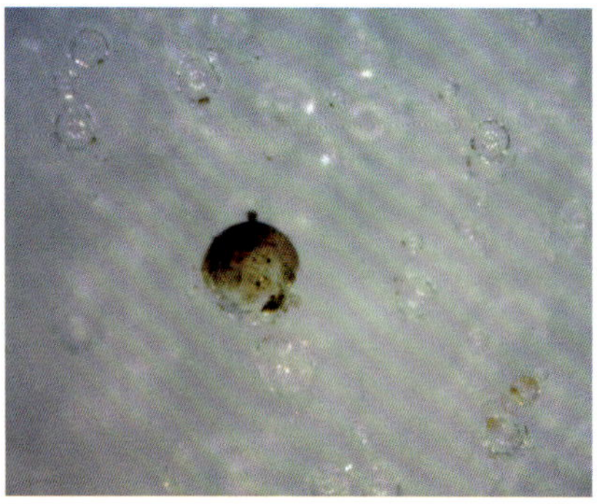

图6-3-9

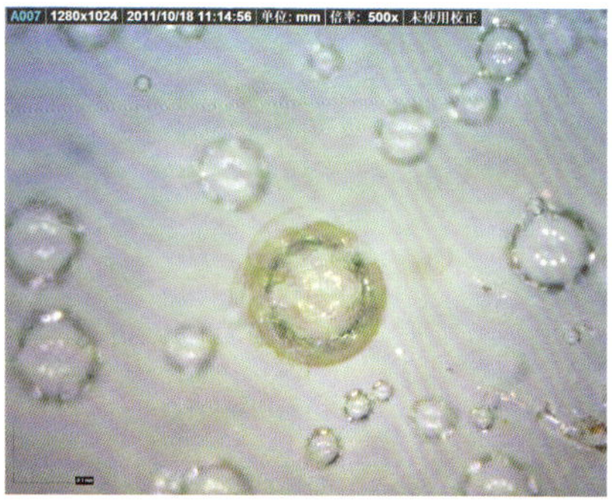

图6-3-10

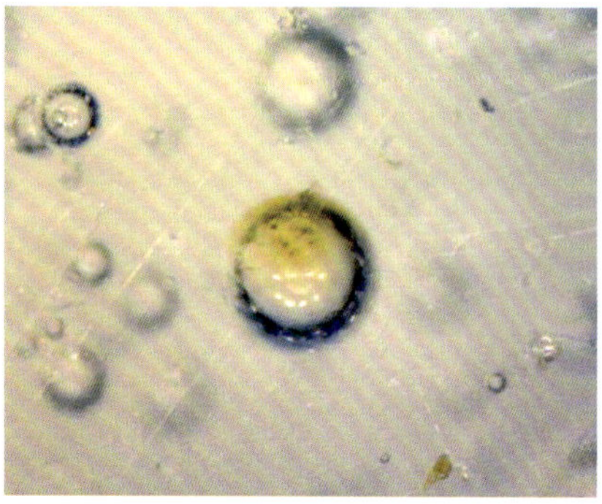

图6-3-11*

图6-3-12*

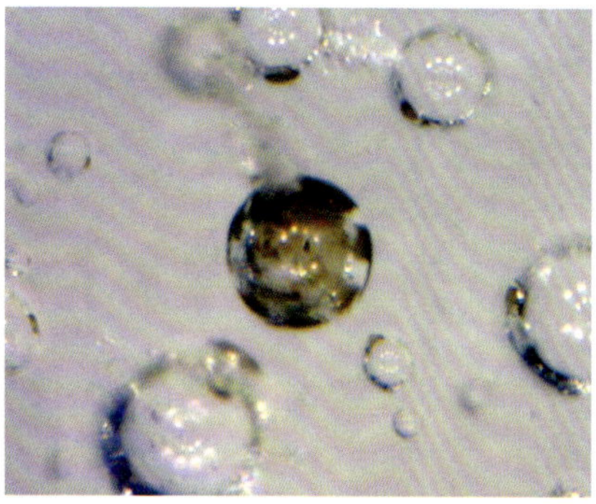

图6-3-13*

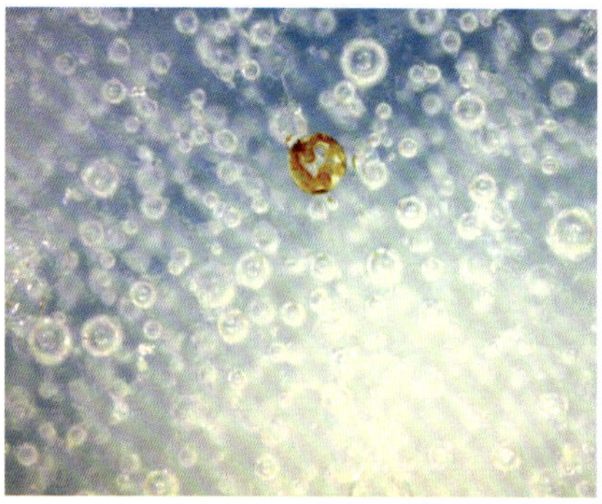

图6-3-14

II. 局变泡三维特征

i. 有的气泡所在处釉表面可见清晰独立的通道。

ii. 通道的面积远远小于气泡面积。

iii. 通道周围的釉表面保持光滑洁净。

iv. 有的气泡所在处釉表面不可见明显通道，釉表面光滑洁净。

见图6-3-15、图6-3-16，二者为同一器物同一位置图片，图6-3-15为二维图片，图6-3-16为三维图片。

图6-3-15中气泡A在图6-3-16中位于红圈釉下处，不可见。气泡A所在处的釉表面除箭头B所指一条较明显的划痕以外，还有较多微小划痕。划痕是釉表面遭到破坏的现象，这种破坏形成了外界连接气泡内的通道。

见图6-3-17、图6-3-18，二者为同一器物同一位置图片，图6-3-17为二维图片，图6-3-18为三维图片。

图6-3-17中气泡C在图6-3-18中位于红圈釉下处，隐约可见淡淡的轮廓，气泡C所在处的釉表面无明显划痕或损伤，但有一处颜色较浓（见箭头D所指处），这应该是外界连接气泡内的通道所在处。

见图6-3-19、图6-3-20，二者为同一器物同一位置图片，图6-3-19为二维图片，图6-3-20为三维图片。

图6-3-19中的气泡E，在图

*图片经过裁剪放大处理。
*Picture cropped and enlarged to show detail.

dimensional and 6-3-16 is the three-dimensional view of the same location.

Bubble A in picture 6-3-15 is not visible, but indicated by the red circle in picture 6-3-16. Bubble A is below the surface of the scratch indicated by Arrow B. Aside from this relatively large and clear scratch, there are also multiple smaller scratches on the surface. Scratches are areas of damage to the glaze, and can offer direct contact with the external environment, acting as the coloration channel with the underlying bubble.

See pictures 6-3-17 and 6-3-18, where 6-3-17 is the two-dimensional and 6-3-18 is the three-dimensional view of the same location.

Bubble C in picture 6-3-17 is faintly visible beneath the glaze surface in picture 6-3-18 as indicated by the red circle. There is no clear scratches or damage to the glaze surface above Bubble C, thus the area of darker coloration is most likely the area of coloration channel (see Arrow D).

See pictures 6-3-19 and 6-3-20, where 6-3-19 is the two-dimensional and 6-3-20 is the three-dimensional view of the same location.

Bubble E in picture 6-3-19 is not visible, but indicated by the red circle in picture 6-3-20. The overlying glaze surface is smooth and reflective, and no clear channel is evident. This is likely due to the minute size of the channel, and it is unable to be observed under 500X magnification.

Foreign materials are able to slowly pass through channels in the glaze surface and gradually create coloration within the bubbles, while the surface of the glaze is able to retain its smooth reflectivity.

(b) Fully-Changed Bubbles

(i) Fully-Changed Bubble Defined

Fully-Changed Bubbles are unbroken mouth color change bubbles in which the entirety of the air bubble has changed color.

(ii) Characteristics of Fully-Changed Bubbles

(1) Two-dimensional Characteristics of Fully-Changed Bubbles

a) Fully-changed bubbles primarily consist of yellow, brown, and black coloration

b) Majority of fully-changed bubbles present with a color spectrum (see pictures 6-3-21—6-3-24), while the remainder present with a single color (see picture 6-3-25).

c) Some bubbles can present with clearly visible coloration channels (Areas of darker coloration) (see pictures 6-3-23 and 6-3-24).

d) Some of the bubble interiors have crazing (see picture 6-3-26).

e) Bubbles within close proximity can present with different colorations (see pictures 6-3-27 and 6-3-28).

f) At times, when bubbles in close proximity change color, the glass phase between them also becomes discolored, creating a fully-changed bubble group (see pictures 6-3-29 and 6-3-30).

(2) Three-dimensional Characteristics of Fully-Changed Bubbles

See Three-dimensional Characteristics of Semi-Changed Bubbles.

See pictures 6-3-31 and 6-3-32, where 6-3-31 is the two-dimensional and 6-3-32 is the three-dimensional view of the same location.

See pictures 6-3-33 and 6-3-34, where 6-3-33 is the two-dimensional and 6-3-34 is the three-dimensional view of the same location.

Bubbles F, G, and H in pictures 6-3-31 and 6-3-33 are only faintly visible below the surface in pictures 6-3-32 and 6-3-34 as light colored spots. At the same time, there are scratches on the glaze surfaces that act as the channels between the bubbles and external environment.

See pictures 6-3-35 and 6-3-36, where 6-3-35 is the two-dimensional and 6-3-36 is the three-dimensional view of the same location.

See pictures 6-3-37 and 6-3-38, where 6-3-37 is the two-dimensional and 6-3-38 is the three-dimensional view of the same location.

Bubbles I and J in pictures 6-3-35 and 6-3-37 are faintly visible in pictures 6-3-36 and 6-3-38, and the multiple scratches presenting act as the coloration channels.

These channels allow for foreign materials to pass into the glaze level bubbles and coloration to occur, creating colored bubbles. The glaze surface around the channels

6-3-20中位于红圈釉下处，不可见。气泡E所在处的釉表面光滑洁净，通道不明显，可能是因为通道较小，用500倍显微镜难以观察到。

外界物质通过釉表面的这些通道进入釉层中的气泡内，使气泡变色，形成色变泡。通道周围的釉表面保持光滑洁净。

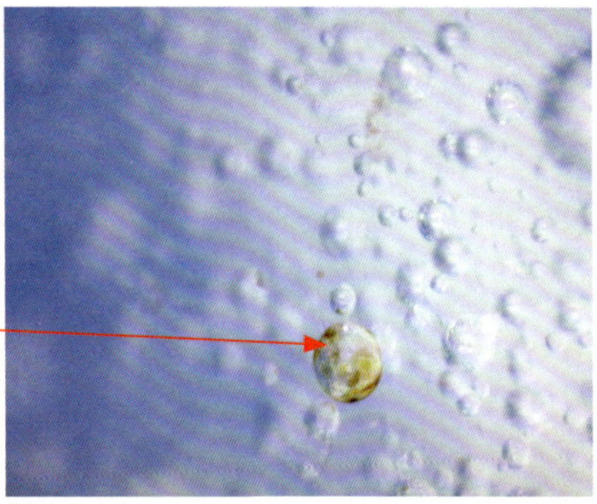

图6-3-15

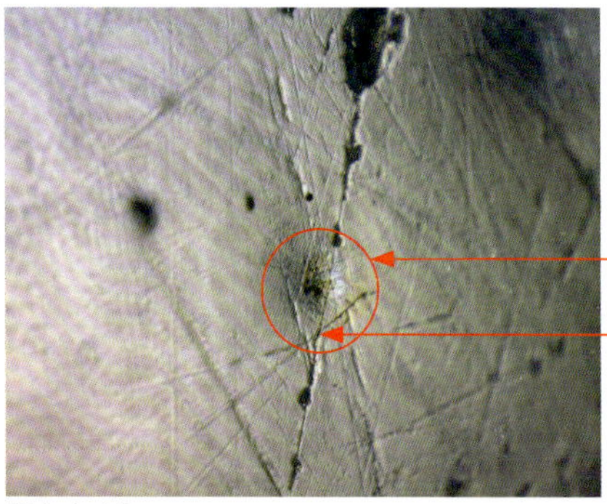

图6-3-16

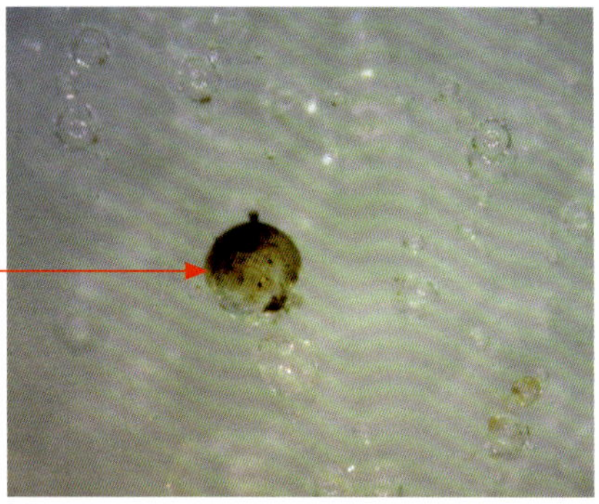

图6-3-17

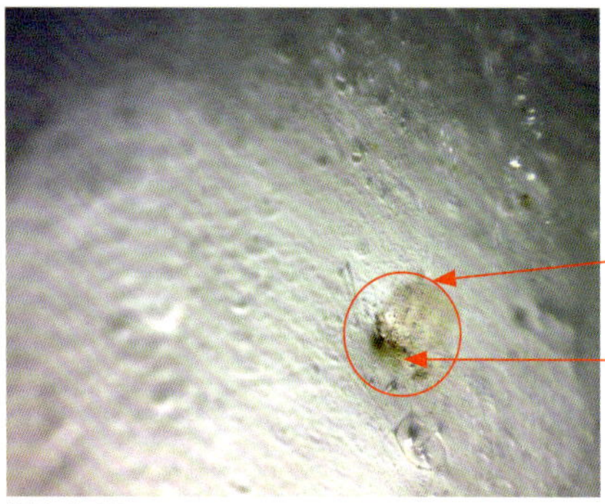

图6-3-18

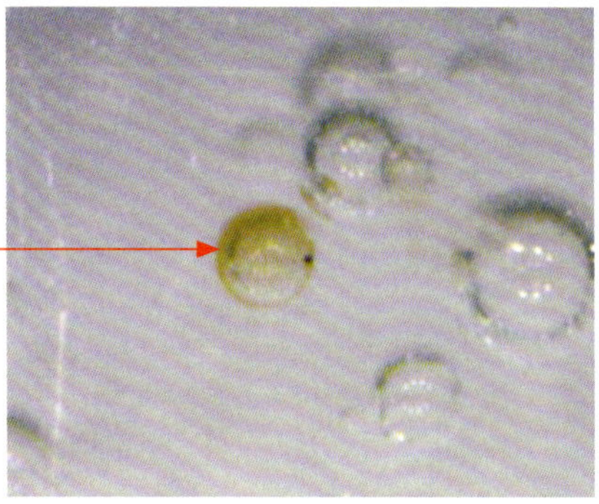

图6-3-19*

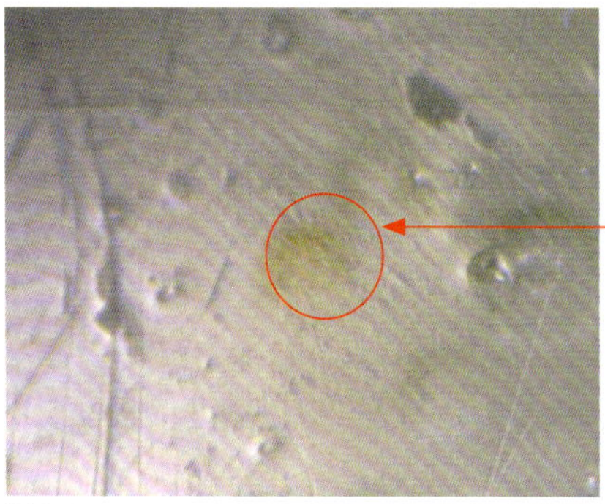

图6-3-20*

B. 全变泡

a. 全变泡概念

全变泡是整个气泡颜色都发生了改变的非破口色变泡。

b. 全变泡特征

I. 全变泡二维特征

i. 全变泡的颜色有黄色、褐色及黑色等。

ii. 大部分全变泡在同一气泡内都有色阶变化（见图6-3-21—图6-3-24），小部分气泡没有明显色阶变化（见图6-3-25）。

iii. 部分气泡上可观察到通道（即颜色浓重处，见图6-3-23、图6-3-24）。

iv. 部分气泡内有龟裂纹路（见图6-3-26）。

v. 距离较近的几个全变泡间有色差（见图6-3-27、图6-3-28）。

vi. 有时全变泡之间的玻璃相也会变色，形成连环全变泡（见图6-3-29、图6-3-30）。

II. 全变泡三维特征

参见本章本节局变泡三维特征部分。

---

*图片经过裁剪放大处理。

*Picture cropped and enlarged to show detail.

retains smooth reflectivity.

(c) Summary

A single piece of YUB can present with both semi and fully-changed colored bubbles.

Bubbles changing from colorless to colored, and from semi-changed to fully changed is a process of quantitative change, a bubble can present with a wide spectrum of color, and a variety of colors can present within different bubbles.

While semi and fully-changed bubbles can exist congruently, they must all retain translucency (see pictures 6-3-39 and 6-3-40).

The characteristics of bubble coloration show that coloration happens as a result of the corrosive weathering materials adhering to the interior wall of each bubble, an indication of gradual weathering accumulation, and is not a filling of the entire bubble cavity.

Sometimes coloration happens with density gradation, and the area of a bubble with the darkest coloration is an indication of a channel offering contact with the external environment. This entry point is often the first to undergo weathering, and thus has the deepest coloration within the bubble. At times, the channels are observable through three-dimension microscopic imaging (i.e. scratches, weathering mottles, etc.); other bubbles do not have clearly observable channels. The glaze above the bubbles retains smooth reflectivity.

b. Broken Mouth Color Change Bubbles

Broken Mouth Color Change Bubble Defined

Broken mouth bubbles have an opening diameter, observable under 500X magnification, which does not exceed the diameter of the bubble.

Currently on YUB samples, we have yet to discover Broken Mouth Color Change Bubbles (all are textured bubbles).

B. Textured Bubbles

I. Textured Bubble Defined

Textured Bubbles are the appearance of YUB bubbles in which the interior has undergone weathering under the influence of the post-firing environment; gaining texture and losing their inherent translucency.

The determining factor as to whether a bubble can be considered textured is whether or not it has lost its translucency. If the bubble has a portion that has lost translucency, it can be considered a textured bubble.

II. Types of Textured Bubbles

a. Unbroken Mouth Textured Bubbles

i. Unbroken Mouth Textured Bubble Defined

These are textured bubbles that do not have an opening observable under 500X magnification.

ii. Unbroken Mouth Textured Bubble Formation

Porcelain glazes present with a random distribution of cracks and openings. Additionally, acidic and alkaline solutions within soil can act to corrode the YUB glaze surface, creating new cracks and openings on the glaze surface.

Foreign materials are able to pass through these channels and enter into the glaze bubbles, forming soluble and partially soluble salts. In environments of changing moisture, it is difficult for these materials to dissolve away. When water evaporates, salts and other particles can adhere and accumulate on the bubble interior, creating a textured bubble.

Ions within the soil and the glaze level react to form colored partially soluble salt deposits, thus textured bubble can present with multiple colors.

Similar to the coloration patterns of colored bubbles, the area of darkest coloration indicates a channel to the external environment. These channel entry points are the first to experience weathering change, and coloration is most dense.

iii. Unbroken Mouth Textured Bubble Types

Unbroken mouth textured bubbles assume white, yellow, brown, and black coloration, with some bubble interiors undergoing full texture change and some only experiencing partial change.

According to the interior topography and multiplicity of weathering intensity, unbroken mouth textured bubbles can assume several different types of appearance. In accordance

见图6-3-31、图6-3-32，二者为同一器物同一位置图片，图6-3-31为二维图片，图6-3-32为三维图片。

见图6-3-33、图6-3-34，二者为同一器物同一位置图片，图6-3-33为二维图片，图6-3-34为三维图片。

图6-3-31中的气泡F、气泡G以及图6-3-33中的气泡H，在图6-3-32和图6-3-34中隐约只见淡淡的轮廓，气泡所在处的釉表面都各有颜色较浓的地方，同时也存在划痕，它们都应是外界连接气泡内的通道。

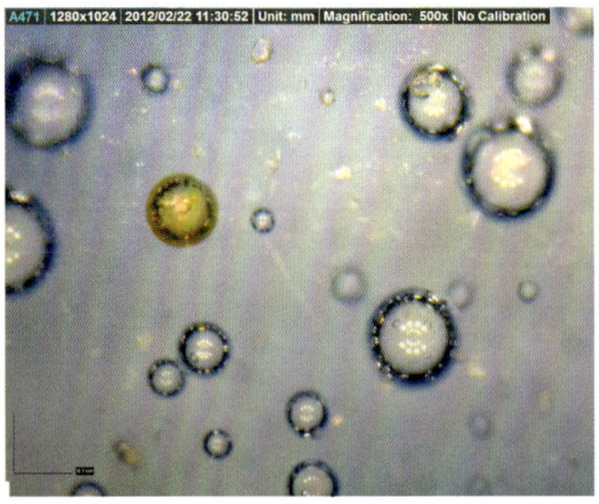

图6-3-21

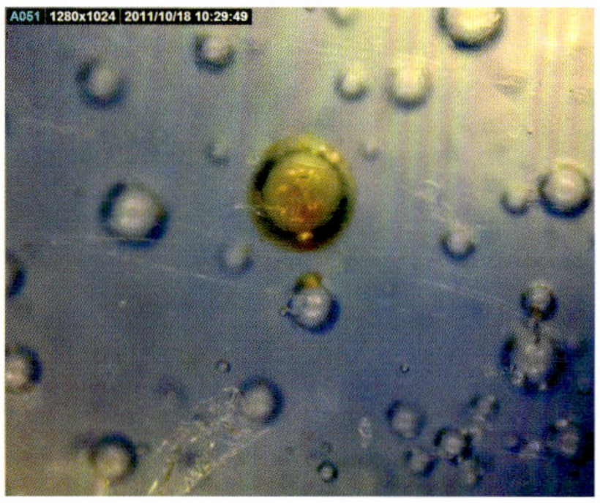

图6-3-22

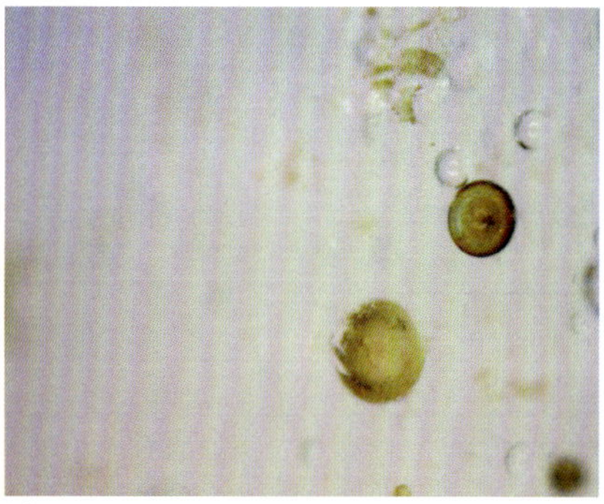
图6-3-23*

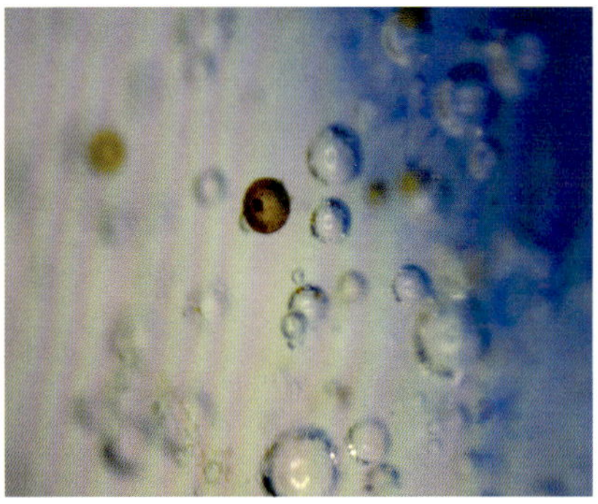
图6-3-24

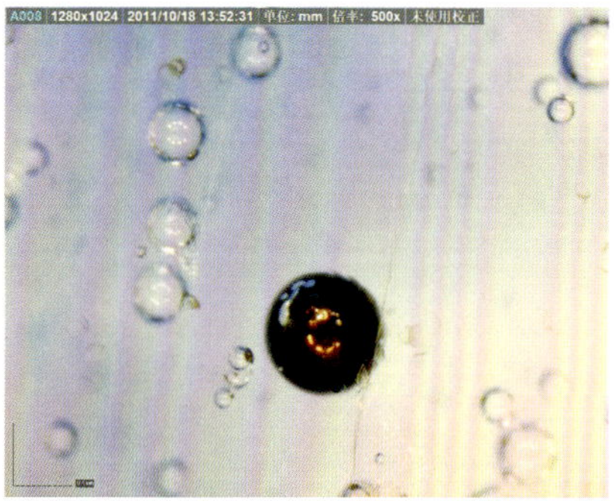

图6-3-25

图6-3-26*

图6-3-27

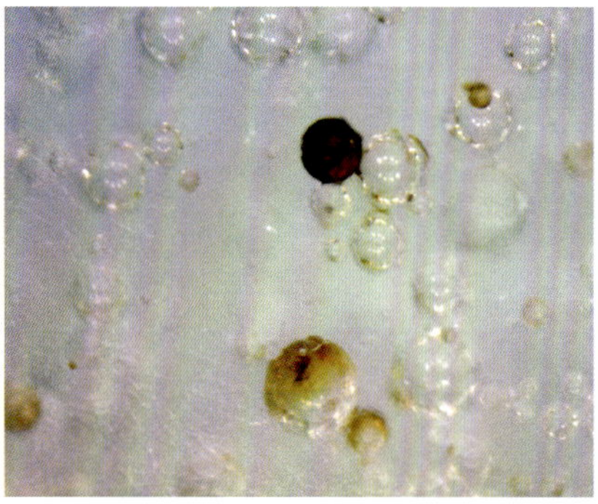
图6-3-28

图6-3-29

*图片经过裁剪放大处理。

*Picture cropped and enlarged to show detail.

with the variances in appearance, we can divide them into the following four types:

(a) Unusual Textured Bubbles

Two-dimensional Characteristics of Unusual Textured Bubbles

(1) Bubble interior weathers to form web-like striae, this type is very rare.

(2) Coloration is primarily yellow, no color spectrum.

From picture 6-3-41 we can see that this bubble occurs in an area of glaze cracks, which can be presumed to be the channel with the external environment. Due to the uneven topography of the bubble interior, and as weathering occurs across the interior, the areas of concavity easily collects deposits and form the web-like striae. As the bubble is located in an area of blue dye, and the dye contains trace amounts of Iron Oxides; these oxides weather to give a yellow coloration to the bubble.

(b) Foggy Needlepoint Textured Bubbles

(i) Two-dimensional Characteristics of Foggy Needlepoint Textured Bubbles

See pictures 6-3-42—6-3-44.

(1) The interior texture of the bubble has weathered into an even foggy needlepoint texture, most are fully textured.

(2) Even distribution of needlepoint mottling, glass phase no longer visible.

(3) Some appear with color variation, some are a single color.

(ii) Three-dimensional Characteristics of Foggy Needlepoint Textured Bubbles

(1) Clearly depicted independent channel evident over the bubble.

(2) The channel surface area is much smaller than the surface area of the bubble.

(3) Glass phase surrounding the channel retains smooth reflectivity.

See pictures 6-3-45 and 6-3-46, where 6-3-45 is the two-dimensional and 6-3-46 is the three-dimensional view of the same location.

Bubble A in picture 6-3-45 is not visible in picture 6-3-46, but is indicated by a red circle. Scratch B is clearly visible amongst the clearly smooth and reflective surrounding glass phase, and is most likely the channel between the bubble and the external environment.

(c) Frosted Needlepoint Texture Bubbles

(i) Two-dimensional Characteristics of Frosted Needlepoint Textured Bubbles

See pictures 6-3-47—6-3-50.

(1) The interior texture of the bubble has weathered into a frosted needlepoint texture; its needlepoints are more coarse than the foggy variety.

(2) A small portion of bubbles become only partially textured, and the vast majority are fully textured.

(3) There is even distribution of the needlepoint mottling, with the appearance of piling deposits, and in general the glass phase is no longer visible.

(4) Some appear with color spectrum, some are a single color.

(ii) Three-dimensional Characteristics of Frosted Needlepoint Textured Bubbles

See Three-dimensional Characteristics of Foggy Needlepoint Textured Bubbles.

See pictures 6-3-51 and 6-3-52, where 6-3-51 is the two-dimensional and 6-3-52 is the three-dimensional view of the same location.

The surface area of Bubble C in picture 6-3-52 is smaller than that of the two-dimensional depiction in picture 6-3-51, the darker area on Bubble C in picture 6-3-51 is most likely the channel between the bubble and the external environment.

See pictures 6-3-53 and 6-3-54, where 6-3-53 is the two-dimensional and 6-3-54 is the three-dimensional view of the same location.

Bubble D in picture 6-3-53 is faintly visible in picture 6-3-54, and is indicated with a red circle. The glaze surface surrounding Bubble D has multiple scratches which are most likely the channels between the bubble and the external

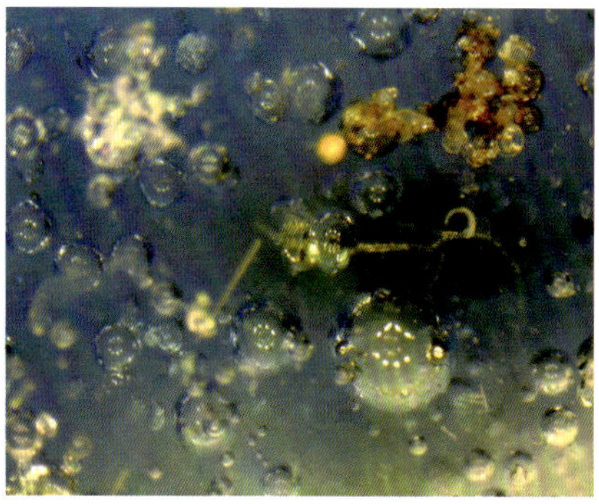

图6-3-30

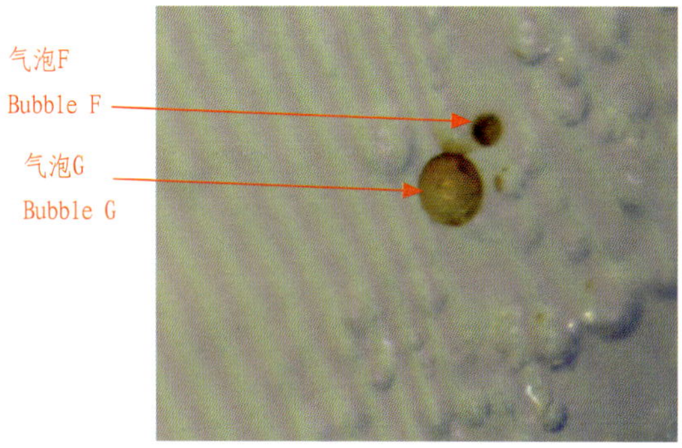

图6-3-31

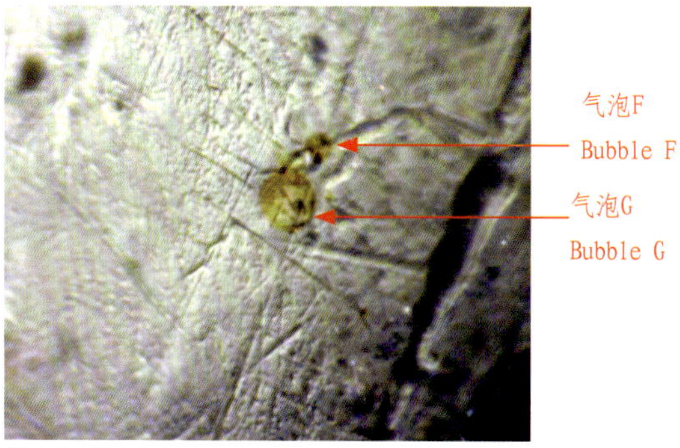

图6-3-32

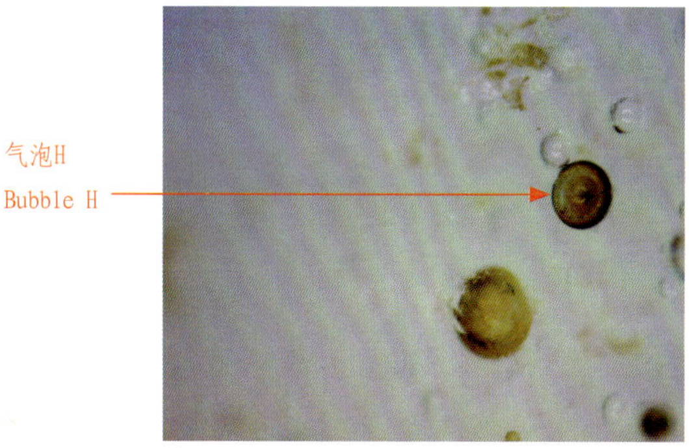

图6-3-33

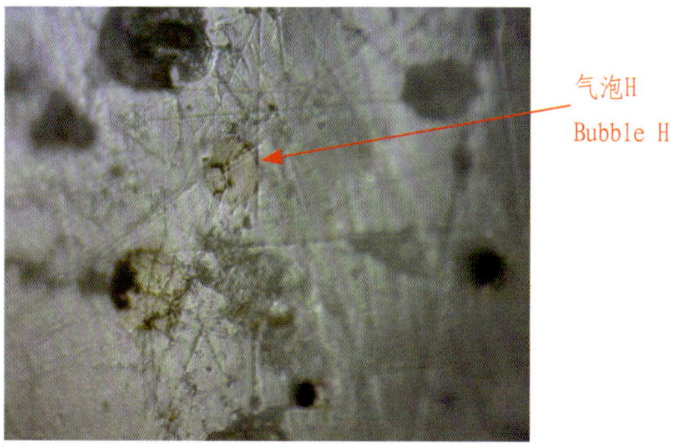

图6-3-34

见图6-3-35、图6-3-36，二者为同一器物同一位置图片，图6-3-35为二维图片，图6-3-36为三维图片。

见图6-3-37、图6-3-38，二者为同一器物同一位置图片，图6-3-37为二维图片，图6-3-38为三维图片。

图6-3-35中的气泡I及图6-3-37中的气泡J，在图6-3-36和图6-3-38中隐约只见淡淡的轮廓，气泡所在处的釉表面存在许多划痕，它们应该是外界连接气泡内的通道。

外界物质通过釉表面的这些通道进入釉层中的气泡内，使气泡变色，形成色变泡。通道周围的釉表面保持光滑洁净。

C. 小结

在同一元青花瓷器上，局变泡与全变泡可以同时存在。

气泡从无色泡变成色变泡、从局变泡变成全变泡是一个量变过程，这些气泡会有色阶浓淡变化，泡与泡之间也会有色差变化。

局变泡与全变泡可以同时存在，但它们均未失去透影性（见图6-3-39、图6-3-40）。

色变泡的风化特征表明，气泡内的风化过程是侵蚀物紧贴气泡的内壁，以积累的模式渐进风化，而不是弥漫在气泡内的空间风化。

有时色变泡上有颜色明显较浓的地方，这些地方往往是通道所在处，也是气泡最早开始变色的地方。三维成像有时可观察到清晰的通道（如划痕、风化斑块等）；有时通道不明显，釉表面光滑洁净。

environment.

The glass phase surrounding the channels retains clearly smooth reflectivity.

(d) Grainy Needlepoint Textured Bubbles

(i) Two-dimensional Characteristics of Grainy Needlepoint Textured Bubbles

See pictures 6-3-55—6-3-58.

(1) The interior texture of the bubble has weathered into a rough granulated texture; its granules have varied size.

(2) A small portion of bubbles become only partially textured, and the vast majority are fully textured.

(3) The granules are predominantly independent, and in general the glass phase is visible between granules.

(4) Some appear with color spectrum, some are a single color.

(ii) Three-dimensional Characteristics of Grainy Needlepoint Textured Bubbles

See Three-dimensional Characteristics of Foggy Needlepoint Textured Bubbles.

See pictures 6-3-59 and 6-3-60, where 6-3-59 is the two-dimensional and 6-3-60 is the three-dimensional view of the same location.

Bubble E in picture 6-3-59 is not visible in picture 6-3-60, but is indicated with a red circle. Mottle F in picture 6-3-59 is not visible in picture 6-3-60. The mottle on Bubble E indicated by Arrow G in picture 6-3-59 is also visible in picture 6-3-60.

Because of this, we can surmise that the mottle indicated by Arrow F is not on the glaze surface, but on the interior of Bubble E. Also, Mottle G is on the glaze surface, and is a weathered mottle on the surface of the glaze, and is most likely the channel between the bubble and the external environment. The glass phase surrounding the mottle retains clearly smooth reflectivity.

b. Broken Mouth Textured Bubbles

i. Broken Mouth Textured Bubble Defined

Broken mouth bubbles have an opening diameter, observable under 500X magnification, which does not exceed the largest diameter of the bubble.

Note: Conceptually, some bubble mouths are microscopically small, unobservable under 500X magnification. These are unobservable-broken-mouth 'broken mouth bubbles'. For the time being, these are classified as the unbroken mouth bubble type.

ii. Formation of Broken Mouth Textured Bubbles

The formation of broken mouth textured bubbles is similar to that of color change and unbroken mouth textured bubbles (See Formation of Color Change Bubbles and Formation of Unbroken Mouth Textured Bubbles Headings of this section).

The weathering occurring in the bubble interior corrodes the internal glaze level; additionally, the weathering occurring on the glaze surface can also work to corrode towards the bubble. Thus, the formation of broken mouth bubbles can be divided into two types:

(a) Single Direction

(i) During the firing of YUB, as molten glaze cools, if air bubbles come near to the surface of the glaze without breaking and the temperature cools relatively quickly, the air within the bubble contracts. This causes a small crater on the surface of the glaze, lower than the surrounding glaze surface (see picture 6-3-61), or higher than the surrounding glaze surface (see picture 6-3-62). This indention tends to collect sediments, which corrode the glaze.

(ii) During the firing of YUB, as molten glaze cools, if air bubbles burst through the surface of the glaze and the temperature drops relatively quickly or the glaze is relatively viscous, the mouth of the bubble is unable to close, and a tiny hole in the surface of the glaze forms. However, these openings are often unobservable under 500X magnification. Over a long period of weathering, the glaze surface corrodes, and the mouth of the bubble progressively enlarges (see picture 6-3-63).

Under the above stated two types of glaze surface corrosion, the final result is a break in the bubble apex; creating a broken mouth bubble. Once a bubble mouth has opened, materials from the external environment can enter even more easily and weather the bubble, forming a broken

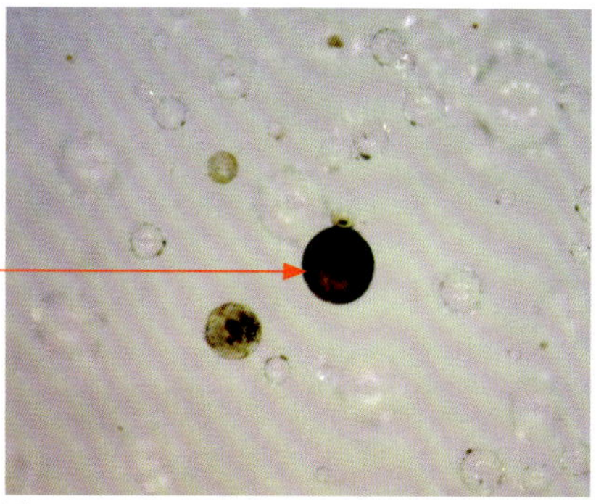

图6-3-35

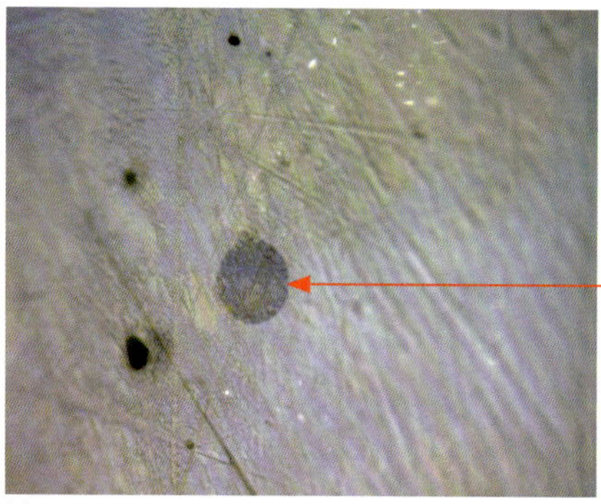

图6-3-36

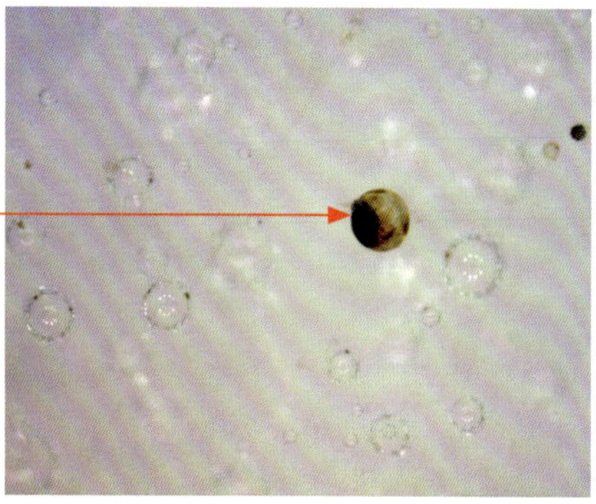

图6-3-37

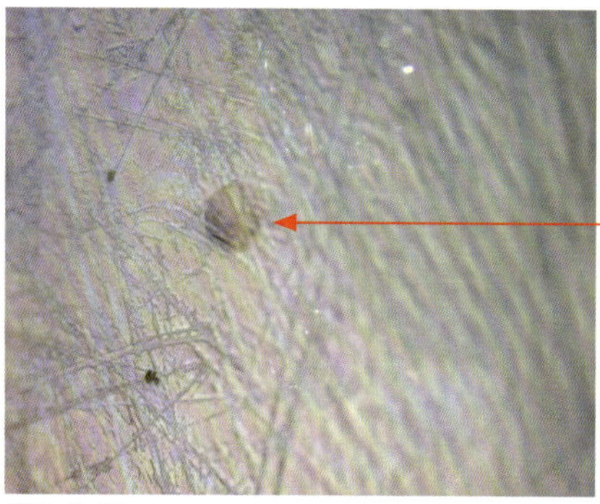

图6-3-38

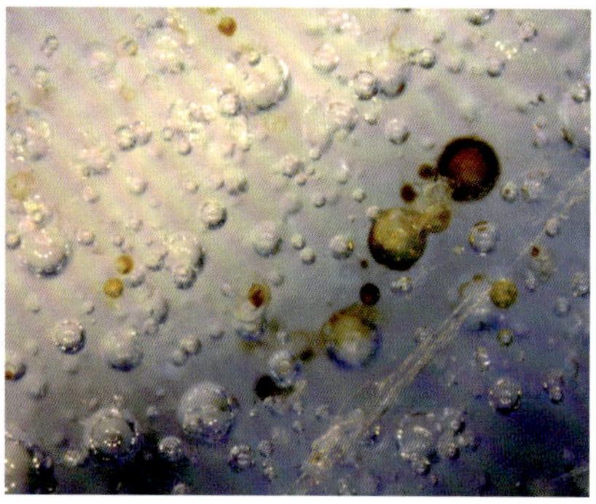
图6-3-39

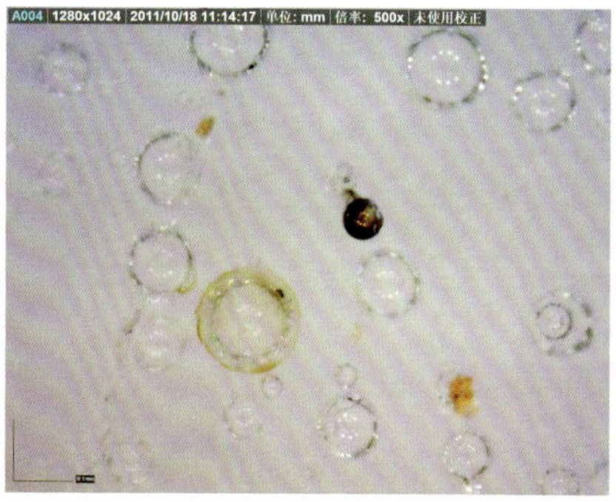

图6-3-40

（2）破口色变泡

破口色变泡概念

破口色变泡用500倍显微镜能观察得到，其破口直径小于气泡直径的色变泡。

目前在元青花标本上尚未发现破口色变泡（破口泡均为壁变泡）。

（二）壁变泡

1. 壁变泡概念

壁变泡是元青花瓷器在后天环境影响下，釉层中的气泡内壁质地发生风化现象，被风化处失去了透影性的气泡。

区分气泡内壁是否发生质变的依据就是气泡是否失去了透影性。如果气泡有部分风化处不具有透影性，气泡就属于壁变泡。

2. 壁变泡种类

（1）非破口壁变泡

① 非破口壁变泡概念

非破口壁变泡是用500倍显微镜能观察到的完整无破口的壁变泡。

② 非破口壁变泡形成

瓷器釉表面随机分布有裂纹或孔隙。此外，土壤中具有一定酸性或碱性的水溶液会侵蚀元青花瓷器釉表面，使釉表面形成新的裂纹或孔隙。

外界物质通过这些裂纹和孔隙进入气泡内，在气泡内生成可溶盐及难溶盐。在干湿交替的环境中，气泡中的难溶盐难以流失，可溶盐及一些细小灰尘在水蒸发后的气泡中形成结晶，它们在气泡内壁叠加

mouth textured bubble.

(b) Double Direction

Similar to single direction, while one of the two types of glaze surface level corrosion is occurring; simultaneously, because of alternate existing channels, internal weathering also occurs. Internal and external double directional corrosion thins the bubble wall and eventually creates a bubble mouth. At the same time, the interior of the bubble is undergoing textural changes; the result is a broken mouth textured bubble.

iii. Broken Mouth Textured Bubble Types

(a) Round Mouth Textured Bubbles

(i) Round Mouth Textured Bubble Defined

A broken mouth textured bubble with a general circular mouth opening.

(ii) Characteristics of Round Mouth Textured Bubble

(1) Two-dimensional Characteristics of Round Mouth Textured Bubbles

a) The mouth portion of the bubble has a general circular shape, the edges smooth (see pictures 6-3-64—6-3-69); sometimes materials are observable beneath the mouth opening (see pictures 6-3-65 and 6-3-66).

b) The internal texture is similar to that of unbroken mouth textured bubbles, some presenting with frosted needlepoint mottling (see pictures 6-3-64—6-3-67), some with grainy needlepoint mottling (see picture 6-3-68), and some with both frosted and grainy needlepoint mottling (see picture 6-3-69).

c) Some appear with color spectrum (see pictures 6-3-65—6-3-67), some are a single color (see pictures 6-3-64 and 6-3-68).

d) Some bubbles become fully textured (see pictures 6-3-64—6-3-66), and some become only partially textured, with the glass phase still visible (see pictures 6-3-67—6-3-69).

(2) Three-dimensional Characteristics of Round Mouth Textured Bubbles

a) The mouth edge is round and smooth.

b) It is possible to see other surface level channels other than the bubble mouth.

c) The channel surface area is smaller than that of the bubble.

d) The glass phase surrounding the channel retains clearly smooth reflectivity.

See pictures 6-3-70 and 6-3-71, where 6-3-70 is the two-dimensional and 6-3-71 is the three-dimensional view of the same location.

Bubble H in picture 6-3-70 is not visible in picture 6-3-71 and is indicated by the red circle. The mouth of Bubble H is clearly visible in picture 6-3-71; its edges round and smooth. Other than the pit mottle indicated by Arrow I and the scratches indicated by Arrow J, the glass phase surrounding the bubble mouth is clean and smooth. This shows that the majority of weathering is present on the interior of the bubble, and the bubble mouth, pit mottle and scratch are the channels between the bubble and the external environment.

See pictures 6-3-72 and 6-3-73, where 6-3-72 is the two-dimensional and 6-3-73 is the three-dimensional view of the same location.

Bubble K in picture 6-3-72 is not visible in picture 6-3-73 and is indicated by the red circle. The mouth of Bubble K is clearly visible in picture 6-3-73; its edges round and smooth. Other than the CO type pit mottles indicated by Arrow L, the glass phase surrounding the bubble mouth is clean and smooth. This shows that the majority of weathering is present on the interior of the bubble, and the bubble mouth and CO type pit mottles are the channels between the bubble and the external environment.

Foreign materials are able to pass through these channels into the underlying bubble, creating a change to the bubble, causing it to lose its translucency, becoming a textured bubble. Aside from these channels, the surrounding glass phase retains clearly smooth reflectivity.

(b) Irregular Mouth Textured Bubbles

(i) Irregular Mouth Textured Bubble Defined

A broken mouth textured bubble with an irregularly shaped mouth opening.

沉积，形成壁变泡。

土壤中的及釉层中的阴阳离子会在气泡内发生反应，形成不同颜色的难溶盐沉积物，所以壁变泡有多种颜色。

与色变泡颜色变化规律类似，通常壁变泡哪个部位颜色浓，说明哪个部位很可能有连接外界的通道存在。所以，通道在壁变泡内的出口处，一般就是颜色最早变化和颜色较浓的地方。

③ 非破口壁变泡分类

非破口壁变泡颜色有白色、黄色、褐色及黑色等，有的为全变，即整个内壁质地发生变化，有的为局变，仅局部发生变化。

由于气泡内壁的凹凸不平，风化作用多样，非破口壁变泡质地也呈现多种不同的形貌。根据非破口壁变泡内部的风化形貌，可将其分成四大类：特殊型、雾状针眼型、磨砂针眼型及颗粒针眼型。

A. 特殊型

特殊型二维特征

I. 气泡内壁的风化纹路以蜘蛛网纹形式呈现，这类壁变泡较罕见。

II. 颜色为黄色，无色阶变化。

由图6-3-41可见，气泡所处上方的釉表面存在釉裂纹，由此可推断釉裂纹为连接外界与气泡内部的通道。由于气泡内壁凹凸不平，风化作用紧贴气泡内壁进行，气泡内壁凹槽处风化物质堆积，从而形成如蜘蛛网般的纹路。由于气泡位于青料处，青料含铁氧化物，铁氧化物的风化使气泡颜色变为黄色。

B. 雾状针眼型

a. 雾状针眼型二维特征

见图6-3-42—图6-3-44。

I. 雾状针眼型非破口壁变泡内壁的风化以雾状针眼斑形式呈现，大部分属于全变壁变泡。

II. 气泡内壁上雾状针眼斑分布均匀，通常看不见玻璃相。

III. 气泡有的没有明显色阶变化，有的有色阶变化。

釉裂纹
Glaze Crack

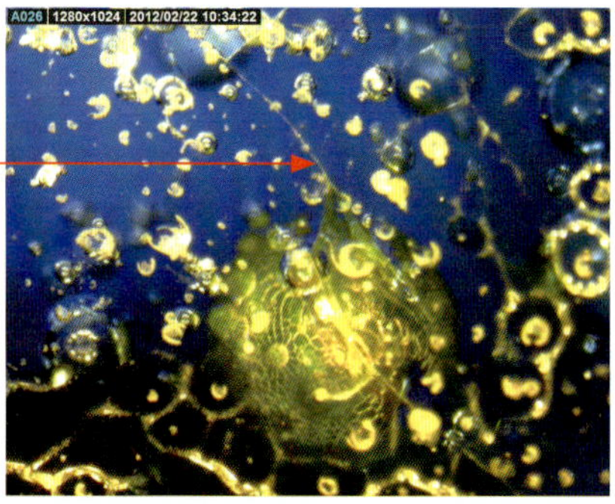

图6-3-41

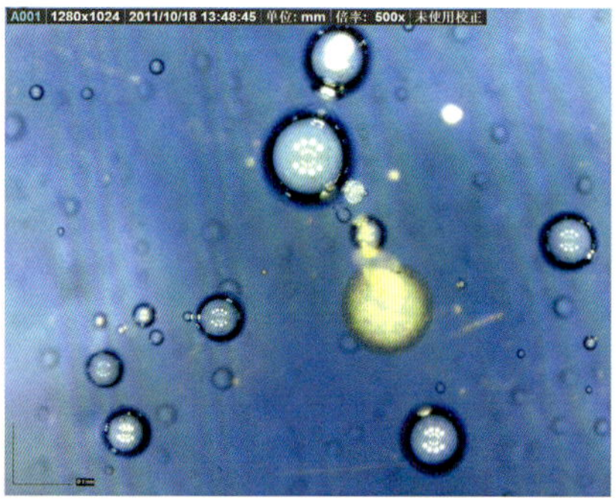

图6-3-42

图6-3-43

图6-3-44

(ii) Characteristics of Irregular Mouth Textured Bubbles

(1) Two-dimensional Characteristics of Irregular Mouth Textured Bubbles

a) The mouth portion of the bubble has an irregular shape, the edges smooth, and sometimes materials are observable beneath the mouth opening (see pictures 6-3-76—6-3-80, 6-3-85, and 6-3-86).

b) The internal texture is similar to that of unbroken mouth textured bubbles, some presenting with frosted needlepoint mottling (see pictures 6-3-74—6-3-80), some with grainy needlepoint mottling (see pictures 6-3-81—6-3-86).

c) Some appear with color spectrum (see pictures 6-3-74 and 6-3-82—6-3-86), some are a single color (see pictures 6-3-75—6-3-81).

d) Some bubbles become fully textured (see pictures 6-3-79, 6-3-80, and 6-3-84), and some become only partially textured, with the glass phase still visible (see pictures 6-3-74—6-3-78, 6-3-81—6-3-83, 6-3-85, and 6-3-86).

(2) Three-dimensional Characteristics of Irregular Mouth Textured Bubbles

See Three-dimensional Characteristics of Round Mouth Textured Bubbles.

See pictures 6-3-87 and 6-3-88, where 6-3-87 is the two-dimensional and 6-3-88 is the three-dimensional view of the same location.

Bubble M in picture 6-3-87 is not visible in picture 6-3-88 and is indicated by the red circle. The mouth of Bubble M is clearly visible in picture 6-3-88; its edges round and smooth. Other than the dark mottle indicated by Arrow N, the glass phase surrounding the bubble mouth is clean and smooth. This shows that the majority of weathering is present on the interior of the bubble, and the bubble mouth and mottle are the channels between the bubble and the external environment.

See pictures 6-3-89 and 6-3-90, where 6-3-89 is the two-dimensional and 6-3-90 is the three-dimensional view of the same location.

Bubble O in picture 6-3-89 is not visible in picture 6-3-89 and is indicated by the red circle. The mouth of Bubble O is clearly visible in picture 6-3-89; its edges round and smooth. Other than the bubble mouth, there are multiple scratches. The bubble mouth and surrounding scratches are the channels between the bubble and the external environment.

Foreign materials are able to pass through these channels into the underlying bubble, creating a change to the bubble, causing it to lose its translucency, becoming a textured bubble. Aside from these channels, the surrounding glass phase retains clearly smooth reflectivity.

(c) Summary

On a single piece of YUB, round and irregular mouth bubbles can present simultaneously. The majority of the mouth edges present with a certain smoothness; the higher percentage of smooth openings being a quantitative trace change characteristic.

The phenomenon of broken mouth bubble weathering is a gradual process of material accumulation on the internal bubble wall, and not the complete filling of the bubble cavity.

Coloration begins at the bubble mouth, where the coloration is darker. This is due to the fact that the open mouth is the channel to the external environment, and coloration begins at this point.

Aside from the bubble mouth, dark discolorations can also present over the bubble. These spots are the location of channels. Three-dimensional imaging can sometimes show clearly these channels (i.e. scratches, pit mottles, etc.), and sometimes these channels are not evident. The surrounding glaze surface is clean and smooth.

c. Summary

On a single piece of YUB, it is possible for there to be a congruent appearance of unbroken mouth and broken mouth textured bubbles. The weathering severity on the inside of unbroken mouth textured bubbles is usually less than that of broken mouth bubbles, which embodies the ceramic trace weathering passage of time principle.

C. Faux Textured Bubbles

I. Faux Textured Bubbles Defined

Faux Textured Bubbles are the appearance of

b. 雾状针眼型三维特征

I. 气泡所在处釉表面可见清晰独立的通道。

II. 通道的面积远远小于气泡面积。

III. 通道周围的釉表面保持光滑洁净。

见图6-3-45、图6-3-46，二者为同一器物同一位置图片，图6-3-45为二维图片，图6-3-46为三维图片。

图6-3-45中的气泡A，在图6-3-46中位于红圈釉下处，不可见。图6-3-46中的划痕B在光滑洁净的釉表面清晰可见，应是外界连接气泡内的通道。通道周围的釉表面保持光滑洁净。

C. 磨砂针眼型

a. 磨砂针眼型二维特征

见图6-3-47—图6-3-50。

I. 磨砂针眼型非破口壁变泡内壁的风化以磨砂针眼斑形式呈现，其针眼要比雾状型粗粝。

II. 这类气泡小部分是局变，大部分属于全变非破口壁变泡。

III. 气泡内风化物质质地较均匀，有堆积感，通常看不见玻璃相。

IV. 气泡有的没有明显色阶变化，有的有色阶变化。

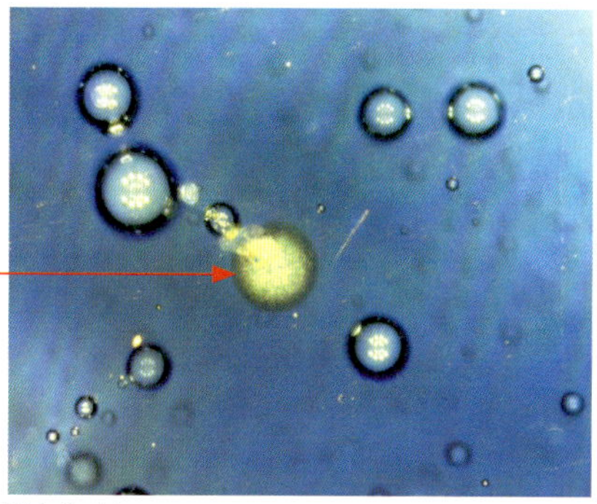

图6-3-45

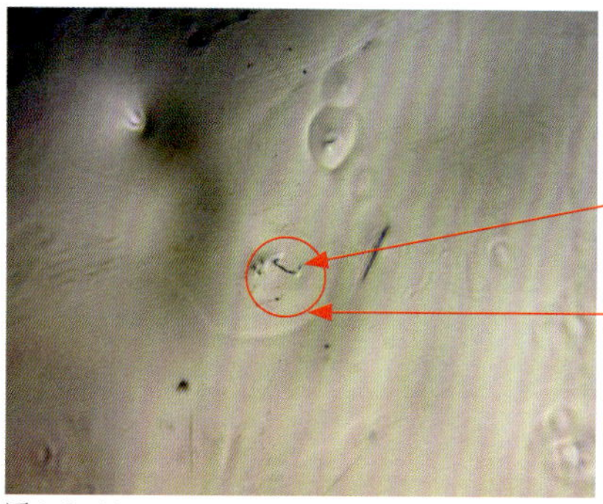

图6-3-46

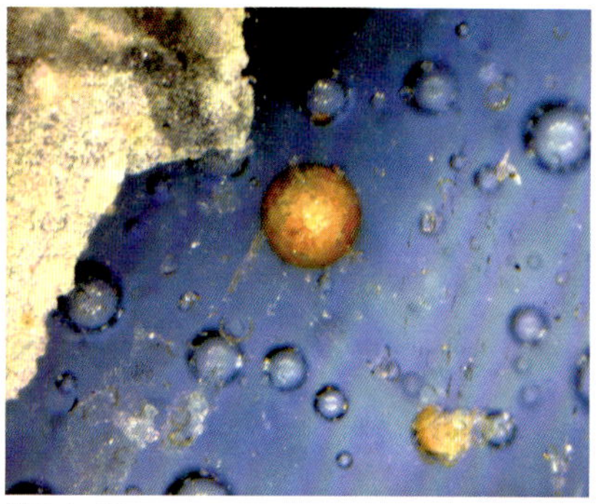
图6-3-47

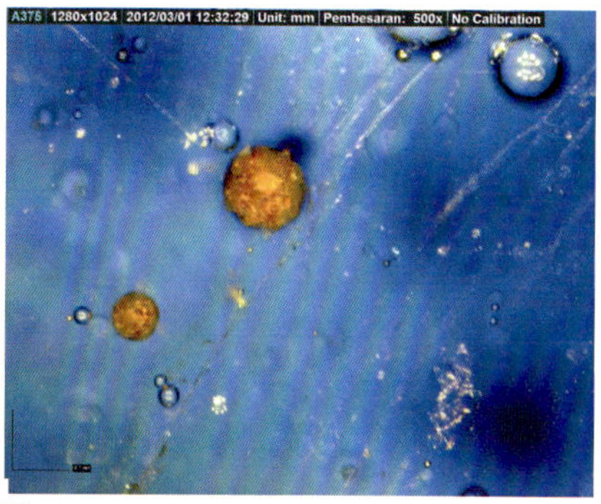

图6-3-48

图6-3-49

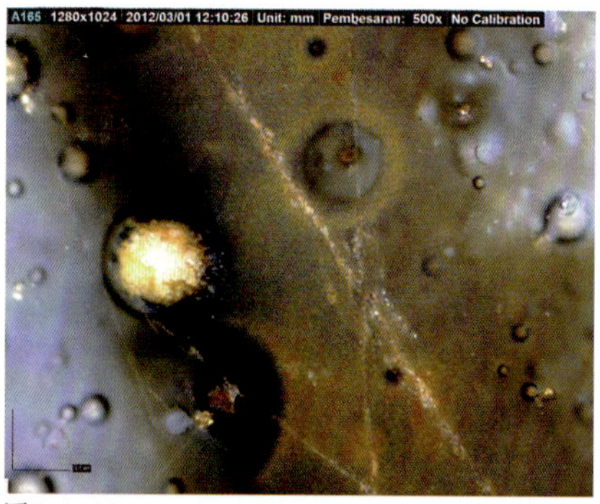

图6-3-50

needlepoint, pit, or overlay mottles, caused by natural weathering or man-made aging, presenting directly over an air bubble within the glaze level; they are easily misconstrued as a textured bubble.

II. Method for Determining Faux Textured Bubbles

There are three methods for distinguishing faux and real textured bubbles:

Diameter Comparison Method;

Focus Selection Method;

Bunney Imaging Method.

When the diameter of the mottle is larger than the diameter of the air bubble we can use the Diameter Comparison or Bunney Imaging Method to differentiate; when the diameter of the mottle is smaller than that of the air bubble we can use the Focus Selection Method or Bunney Imaging Method to differentiate.

a. Diameter of the Mottle Larger than the Bubble

Using the Diameter Comparison Method: When the diameter of the air bubble is smaller than that of the mottle, and the mottle completely covers the air bubble; we can directly distinguish this bubble as the faux textured bubble type (see picture 6-3-91 Bubble A).

If the diameter of the mottle is larger than the air bubble, but does not completely cover the bubble below; we must utilize the Bunney Imaging Method to further distinguish the true type of the bubble.

Look at pictures 6-3-92 and 6-3-93, where 6-3-92 is the two-dimensional and 6-3-93 is the three-dimensional view of the same location.

The textured Bubble B indicated in picture 6-3-92 is not visible in picture 6-3-93, but is actually present below the surface of the circle; whereas the dark colored mottle indicated by Arrow C in picture 6-3-92 is also visible in picture 6-3-93, with shape and size the same as picture 6-3-92.

Bubble B in picture 6-3-92 is a valid unbroken mouth textured bubble. This is because the texture is on the bubble interior and not on the glaze surface. The dark colored mottle indicated by Arrow C in both pictures is the same point on the pictured bubble. This indicates that the mottle indicated at point C is on the glaze surface, and actually a glaze flaw and a channel connecting the external environment with the bubble interior.

b. Diameter of the Mottle Smaller than the Bubble

When the mottle on the air bubble has a diameter that is smaller than that of the air bubble, we can utilize the Focus Selection Method to differentiate.

When an appropriate focus has been selected for clearly observing said mottling, we must notice what point of the observed object is most clear, any portions of the object that are on a different depth will gradually become blurred. If we observe one or more mottle points with clarity at different depths it tells us one of two things:

First: Part of the mottle is in the air bubble interior, and another part is on the surface level.

Second: Both points of the mottle are both within the air bubble, but at different depths.

Regardless of which of the two is true, this is a true textured bubble.

The Focus Selection Method is usually only suitable for air bubbles with a larger size. If the bubble is too small, it is difficult to differentiate clarity at different depths of the bubble. In this case, we can use the Bunney Imaging Method to help differentiate.

Due to the small size of the air bubble in question pictured in 6-3-94, it is too difficult to utilize the Focus Comparison Method, thus the Bunney Imaging Method must be used.

Look at pictures 6-3-94 and 6-3-95, where 6-3-94 is the two-dimensional and 6-3-95 is the three-dimensional view of the same location.

Mottle D in picture 6-3-94, is clearly visible on the glaze surface in picture 6-3-95. This is to say that the 'texture' of Mottle D is actually only present on the glaze surface and not the bubble interior. Therefore this bubble is classified as a faux textured bubble.

Look at pictures 6-3-96 and 6-3-97, where 6-3-96 is the two-dimensional and 6-3-97 is the three-dimensional view of the same location.

The textured Bubble E in picture 6-3-96 is not visible

b. 磨砂针眼型三维特征

参见本章本节雾状针眼型三维特征部分。

见图6-3-51、图6-3-52，二者为同一器物同一位置图片，图6-3-51为二维图片，图6-3-52为三维图片。

气泡C在图6-3-52中釉表面的三维可视面积小于在图6-3-51中的二维可视面积，气泡C在图6-3-52中颜色较浓的地方，应该是外界连接气泡内的通道。

见图6-3-53、图6-3-54，二者为同一器物同一位置图片，图6-3-53为二维图片，图6-3-54为三维图片。

图6-3-53中的气泡D在图6-3-54中隐约只见淡淡的轮廓，气泡所在处的釉表面存在许多划痕，应该是外界连接气泡内的通道。这些通道周围的釉表面还是保持光滑洁净。

D. 颗粒针眼型

a. 颗粒针眼型二维特征

见图6-3-55—图6-3-58。

I. 颗粒针眼型非破口壁变泡内壁的风化以颗粒针眼斑形式呈现，颗粒大小不一。

II. 气泡小部分是局变，大部分属于全变非破口壁变泡。

III. 颗粒针眼斑独立，通常能看见玻璃相。

IV. 气泡大多有色阶变化，小部分无色阶变化。

图6-3-51

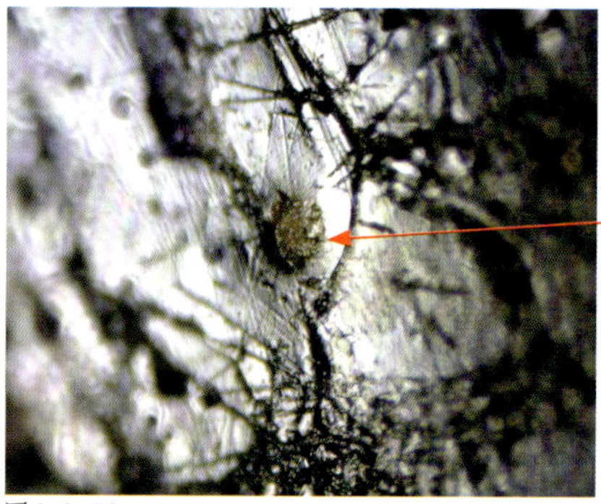

图6-3-52

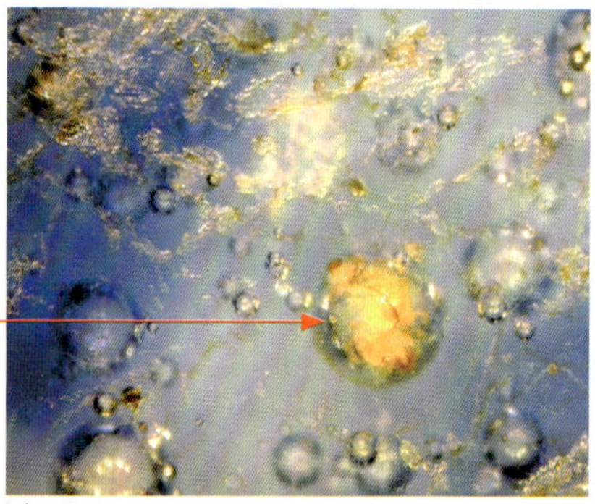

图6-3-53

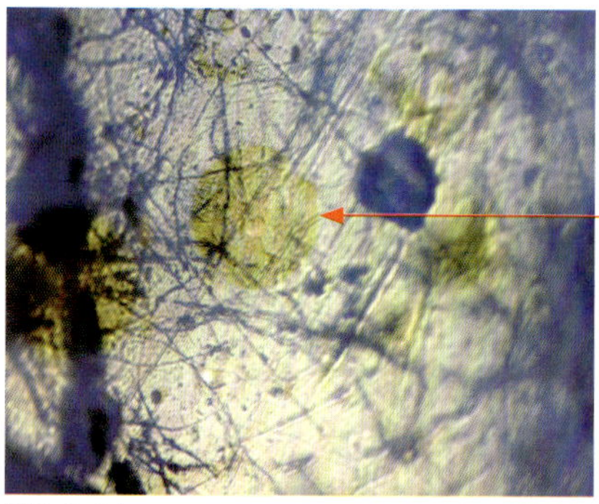

图6-3-54

图6-3-55

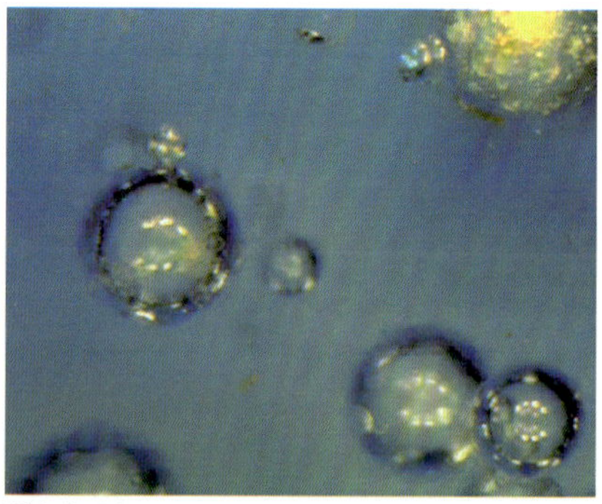
图6-3-56

in picture 6-3-97, but is actually present below glaze at the position marked with a circle. The dark colored mottle indicated by Arrow F on picture 6-3-96, becomes invisible on picture 6-3-97. Meanwhile the dark colored mottle indicated by Arrow G, is however visible on picture 6-3-97.

Mottle F is not on the glaze surface, but rather inside Bubble E; formed by weathering on the bubble interior. Mottle G is present on the surface of the glaze, and is a glaze flaw that was formed by weathering directly on the glaze surface. It is a channel between the external environment and the bubble interior, allowing for the passage of foreign materials into the bubble, and creating a textural change to the bubble interior; losing its translucency and becoming a textured bubble.

D. Summary

Directly after the firing of YUB, the air bubbles in the glaze are colorless and transparent, but under the influences of the post-firing environment, these bubbles can gradually weather to form colored and textured bubbles.

Some bubbles present with an even gradation of light to dark color spectrum.

Some bubbles can present with clearly darker areas of coloration that are the coloration channels, and represent the areas that first weathered. Through three-dimensional microscopic observation, some of these channels are visible (i.e. scratches, mottles, etc.) and some are not. The surrounding glaze surface retains clearly smooth reflectivity.

Color disparity between color change bubbles is also possible.

Textured bubbles include foggy, frosted, and grainy needlepoint mottling, which represent differences in weathering severity. Textured bubbles can present with color spectrum, as well as a color disparity between bubbles.

It is sometimes possible to observe areas that have a clearly darker coloration on textured bubbles, these spots are locations of channels. Through three-dimensional microscopic observation, some of these channels are visible (i.e. scratches, mottles, etc.) and some are not. The surrounding glaze retains clearly smooth reflectivity.

The large majority of broken mouth bubble mouths are rounded and smooth.

The weathering characteristics of the bubble category on YUB are consistent with the quantitative change and passage of time principles of ceramic traces, and embody the laws of ceramic trace formation and change.

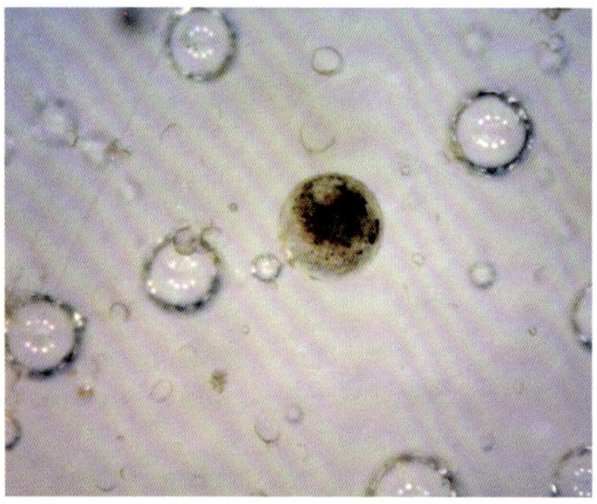
图6-3-57

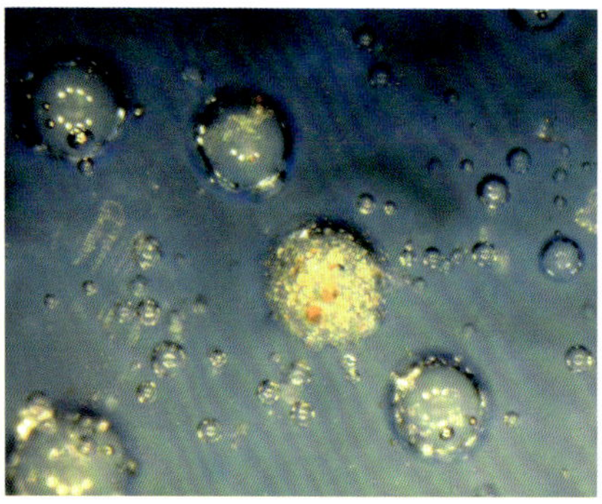
图6-3-58

b. 颗粒针眼型三维特征

参见本章本节雾状针眼型三维特征部分。

见图6-3-59、图6-3-60，二者为同一器物同一位置图片，图6-3-59为二维图片，图6-3-60为三维图片。

图6-3-59中的气泡E在图6-3-60中位于红圈釉下处，不可见。图6-3-59中箭头F所指斑块，在图6-3-60中却消失了。图6-3-59中箭头G所指斑块，在图6-3-60中也可见。

由此可推断，箭头F所指斑块不在釉表面，而在气泡E内壁，是内壁风化形成的斑块。箭头G所指斑块处于釉表面，是釉表面风化形成的斑块，也应是外界连接气泡内的通道所在处。通道周围的釉表面保持光滑洁净。

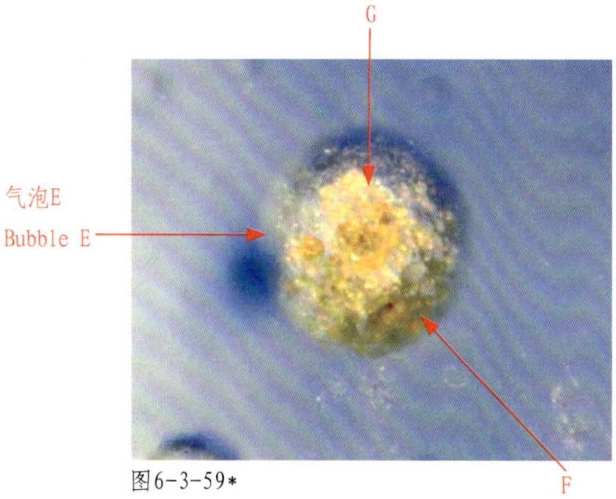

图6-3-59*

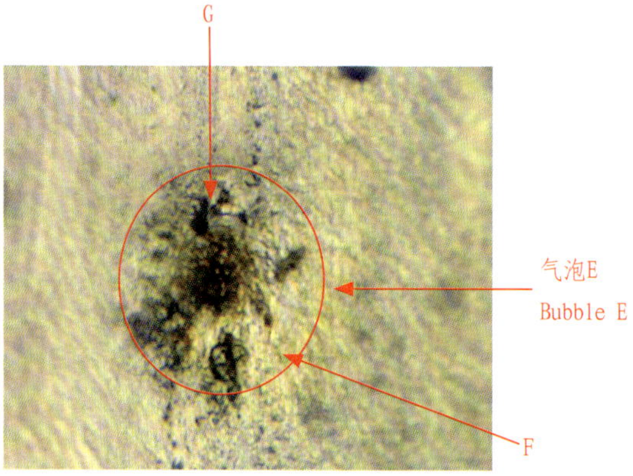

图6-3-60*

（2）破口壁变泡

① 破口壁变泡概念

破口壁变泡是用500倍显微镜能观察到的，其破口直径小于气泡直径的壁变泡。

注：从理论上分析，有的气泡破口极其微小，即使使用500倍显微镜也观察不到。我们将这些观察不到破口的“破口泡”，暂时都列入非破口泡种类。

② 破口壁变泡形成

破口壁变泡的形成原因与色变泡以及非破口壁变泡的形成原因相似（参见本章本节色变泡形成及非破口壁变泡形成）。

气泡内壁的风化会对气泡内壁的釉层造成侵蚀，而气泡所在处釉表面的风化也会对釉层造成侵蚀，所以我们可将破口壁变泡的形成分成两类：

A. 单向侵蚀

a. 元青花高温烧制时，在熔融釉层冷却平复的过程中，当气泡升至釉表面而又未冲破釉表面时，如果降温较快，气体体积缩小，气泡上方的釉表面会形成凹槽，或低于釉表面（见图6-3-61）或高出釉表面（见图6-3-62）。凹槽易长期积垢从而侵蚀釉表面。

b. 元青花高温烧制时，在熔融釉层冷却平复的过程中，有些升至釉表面的气泡，由于降温较快或釉层黏度较大而没有闭合，从而使釉表面出现微小的孔洞。不过这些孔洞过于微小，用500倍显微镜一般是观察不到的。长期的风化作用侵蚀釉表面，使孔洞逐渐变大（见图6-3-63）。

B．双向侵蚀

双向侵蚀，一方面同单向侵蚀的情况类似，另一方面，气泡内壁因通道存在也会产生风化作用。内外双向的风化作用会侵蚀气泡壁，从而产生破口；同时，气泡内壁的风化也使气泡内壁的质地发生改变，最终形成破口壁变泡。

③ 破口壁变泡种类

A．圆口破口壁变泡

a．圆口破口壁变泡概念

圆口破口壁变泡是破口为较规整圆形的壁变泡。

b．圆口破口壁变泡特征

I．圆口破口壁变泡二维特征

i．气泡破口呈较规整的圆形，边沿圆滑（见图6-3-64—图6-3-69），有时破口下方可见物质存在（见图6-3-65、图6-3-66）。

ii．圆口破口壁变泡内壁的风化形貌与非破口壁变泡的风化形貌类似（参见本章本节非破口壁变泡种类），有磨砂针眼型（见图6-3-64—图6-3-67）、颗粒针眼型（见图6-3-68），以及磨砂针眼与颗粒针眼并存的壁变形式（见图6-3-69）。

iii．有的气泡内壁有色阶变化（见图6-3-65—图6-3-67），有的没有明显色阶变化（见图6-3-64、图6-3-68）。

iv．有的气泡为全变破口壁变泡（见图6-3-64—图6-3-66），有的为局变，能见玻璃相（见图6-3-67—图6-3-69）。

两种形式的风化作用不断侵蚀釉表面，最终导致气泡上方的釉表面出现较大破口，形成破口泡，外界物质更易进入产生风化作用，形成破口壁变泡。

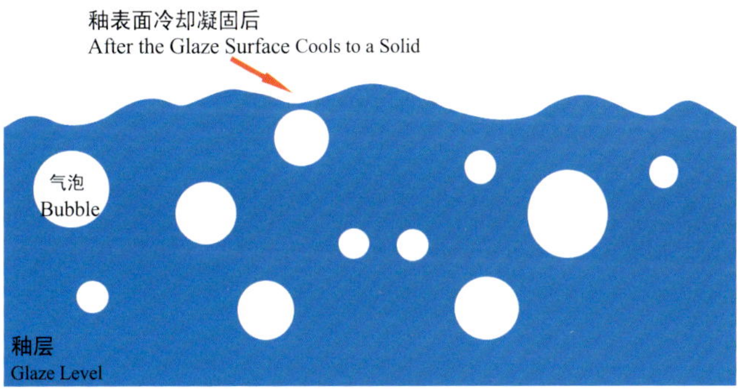

图6-3-61

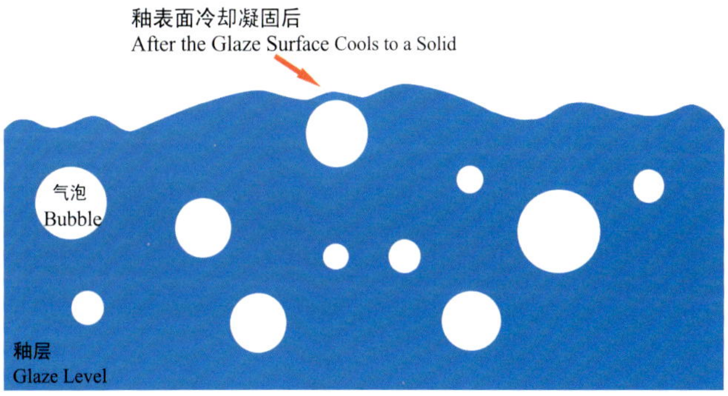

图6-3-62

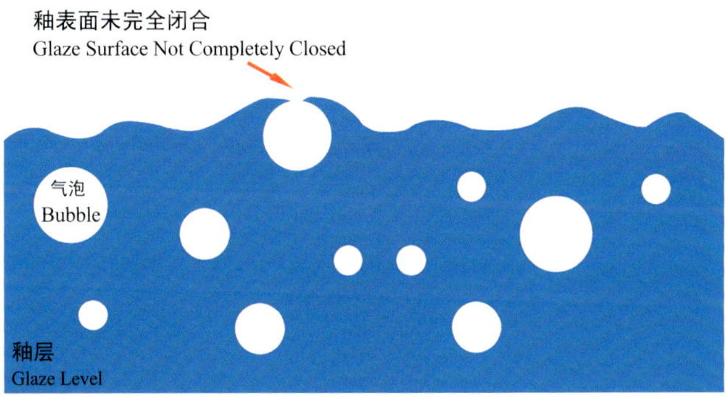

图6-3-63

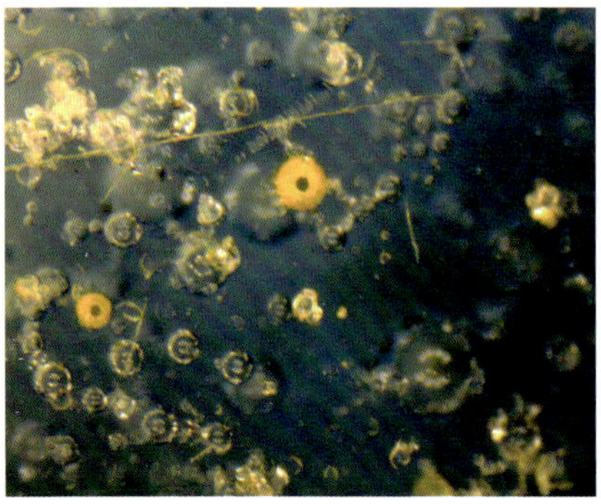

图6-3-64

图6-3-65

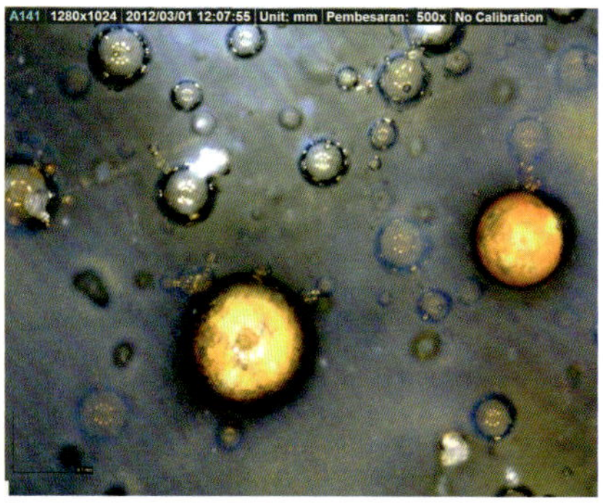

图6-3-66

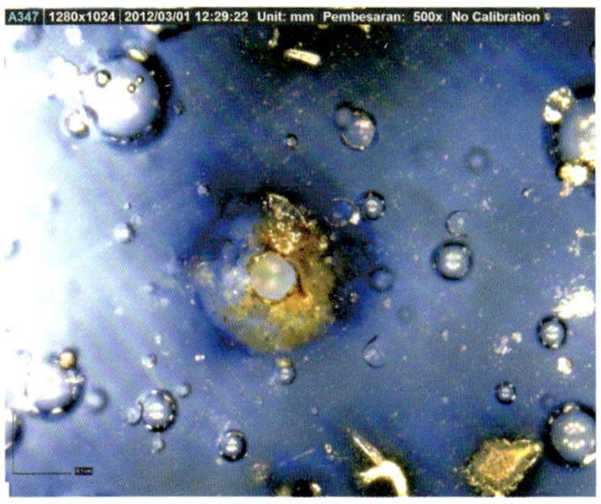

图6-3-67

图6-3-68

图6-3-69

II. 圆口破口壁变泡三维特征

i. 气泡破口边沿圆滑。

ii. 气泡所在处釉表面可见除破口以外的通道。

iii. 通道的面积小于气泡面积。

iv. 通道周围的釉表面保持光滑洁净。

见图6-3-70、图6-3-71，二者为同一器物同一位置图片，图6-3-70为二维图片，图6-3-71为三维图片。

图6-3-70中的气泡H在图6-3-71中位于红圈釉下处，不可见。气泡H的破口在图6-3-71中清晰可见，破口圆滑。破口周围有一处坑点斑（见箭头I所指处）和几处划痕（见箭头J所指处），除此以外釉表面光滑洁净。这说明图6-3-71中气泡H的风化斑块大部分都处于气泡内壁。坑点斑、划痕及破口都可以是外界连接气泡内的通道所在处。

见图6-3-72、图6-3-73，二者为同一器物同一位置图片，图6-3-72为二维图片，图6-3-73为三维图片。

图6-3-72中的气泡K在图6-3-73中位于红圈釉下处，不可见。气泡K的破口在图6-3-73中清晰可见，破口圆滑。破口周围有几处颜色较深的CO型坑点斑（见箭头L所指处），除此以外釉表面光滑洁净。这说明气泡K的风化斑块大部分都处于气泡内壁，破口以及破口周围的几处CO型坑点斑应该是外界连接气泡内的通道。

外界物质通过釉表面的这些通道进入釉层中的气泡内，使气泡内壁发生质地变化，失去了透影性，形成壁变泡。通道周围的釉表面保持光滑洁净。

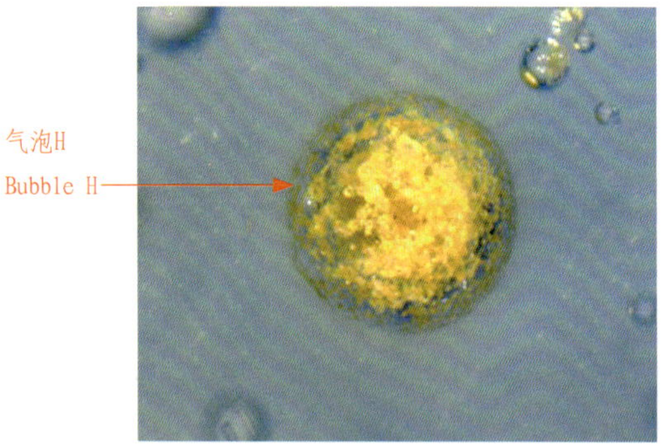

图6-3-70

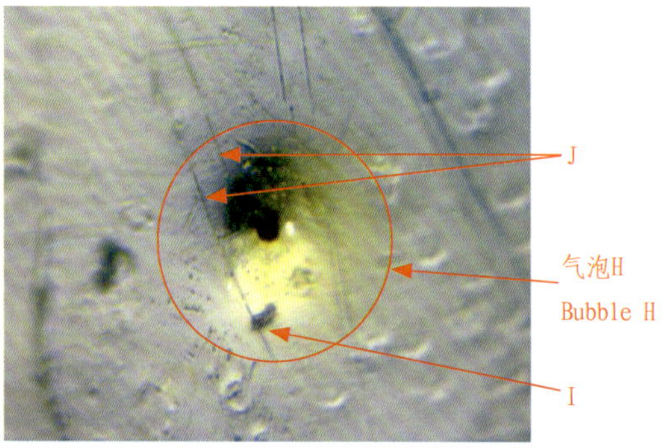

图6-3-71

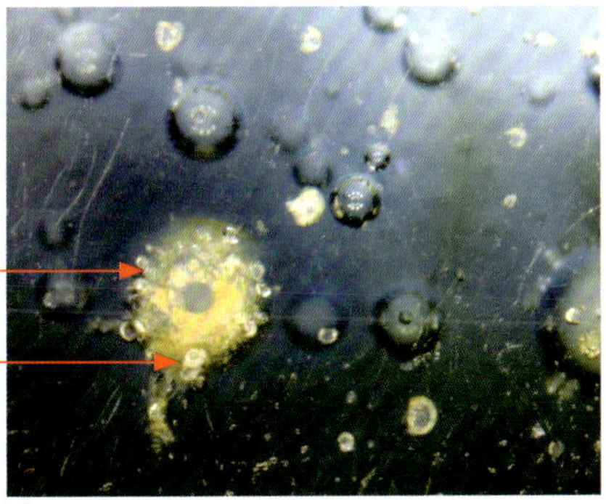

图6-3-72

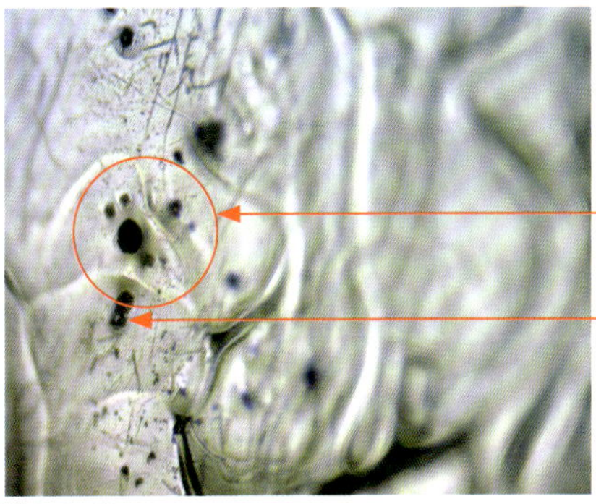

图6-3-73

B. 非圆口破口壁变泡

a. 非圆口破口壁变泡概念

非圆口破口壁变泡是破口为不规则形状的壁变泡。

b. 非圆口破口壁变泡特征

Ⅰ. 非圆口破口壁变泡二维特征

i. 气泡破口呈不规则形状，边沿圆滑，有时破口下方可见物质存在（见图6-3-76—图6-3-80、图6-3-85、图6-3-86）。

ii. 非圆口破口壁变泡内壁的风化形貌与非破口壁变泡风化形貌类似（参见本章本节非破口壁变泡种类），有磨砂针眼型（见图6-3-74—图6-3-80），也有颗粒针眼型（见图6-3-81—图6-3-86）。

iii. 有的气泡内壁有色阶变化（见图6-3-74、图6-3-82—图6-3-86），有的没有明显色阶变化（见图6-3-75—图6-3-81）。

iv. 有的气泡为全变破口壁变泡（见图6-3-79、图6-3-80、图6-3-84），有的为局变，能见玻璃相（见图6-3-74—图6-3-78、图6-3-81—图6-3-83、图6-3-85、图6-3-86）。

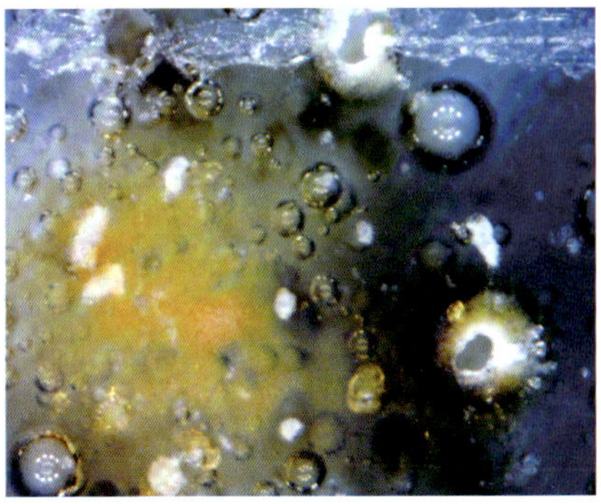
图6-3-74

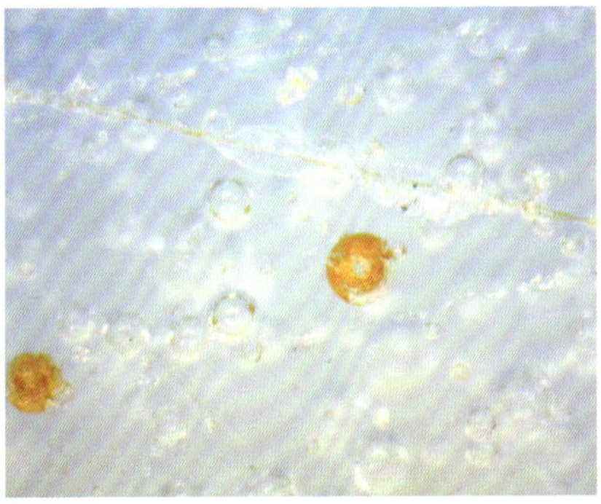
图6-3-75

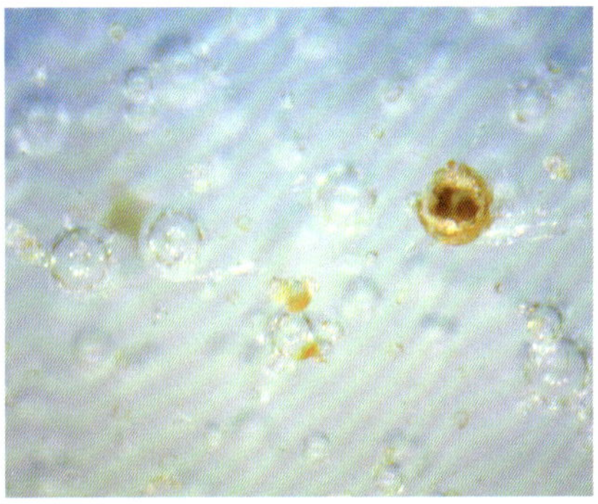
图6-3-76

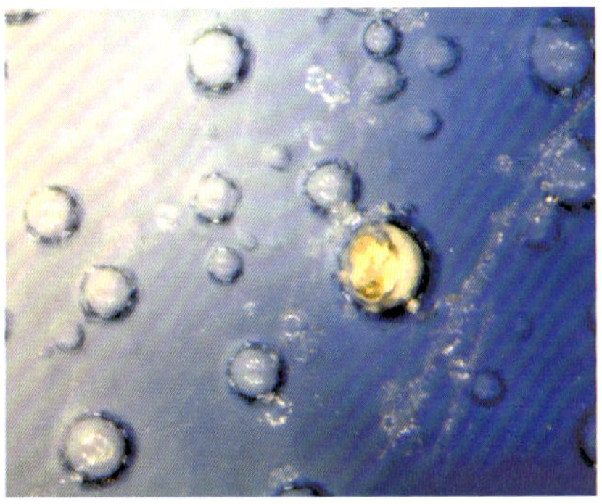
图6-3-77

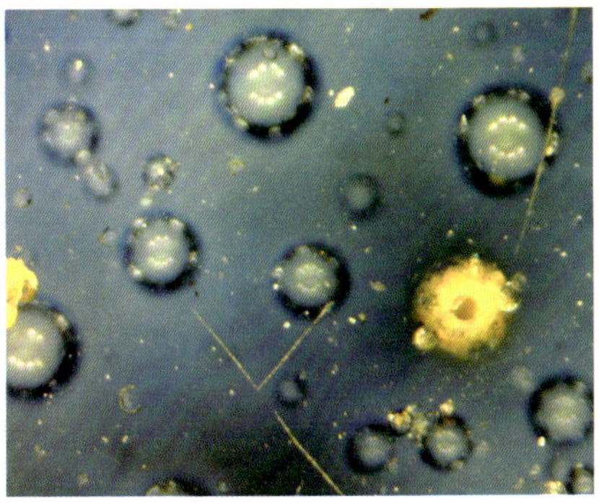
图6-3-78

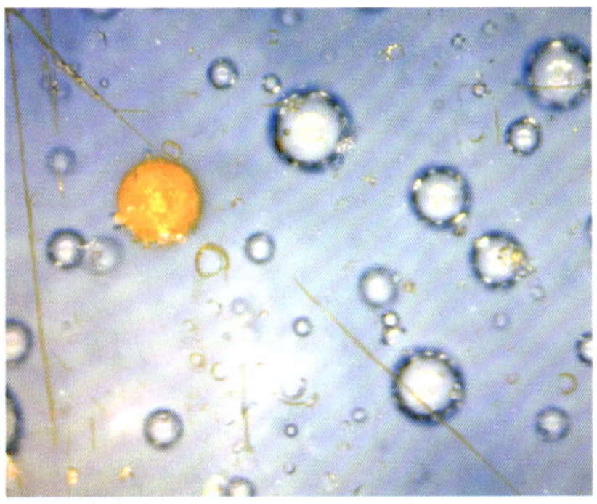
图6-3-79

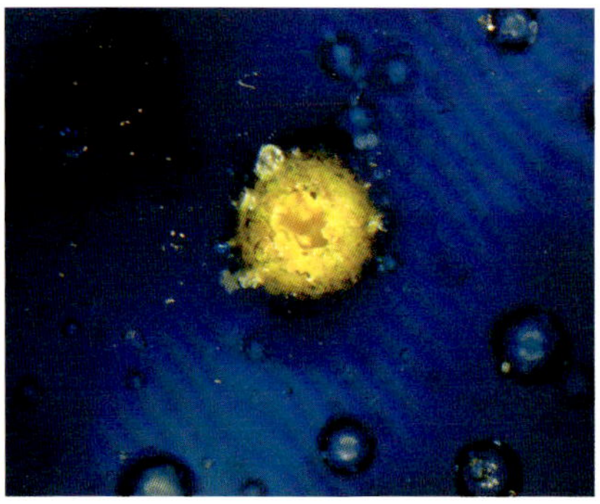

图6-3-80

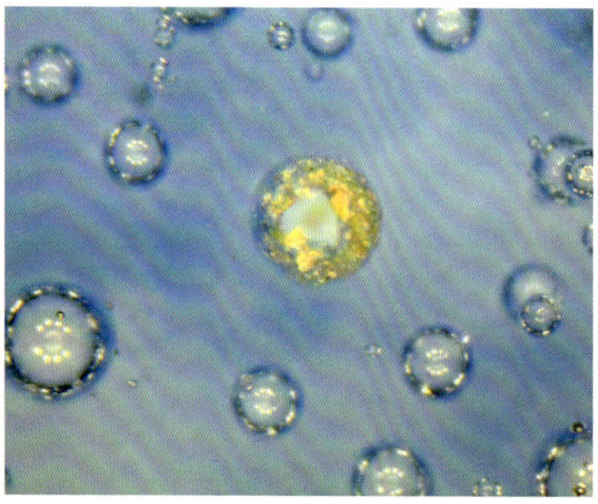

图6-3-81

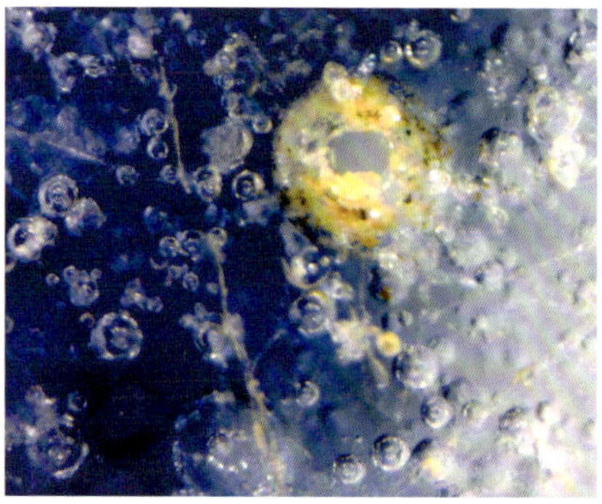

图6-3-82

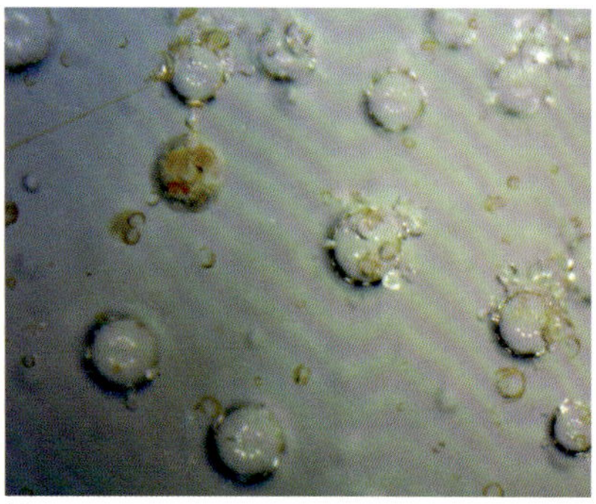

图6-3-83

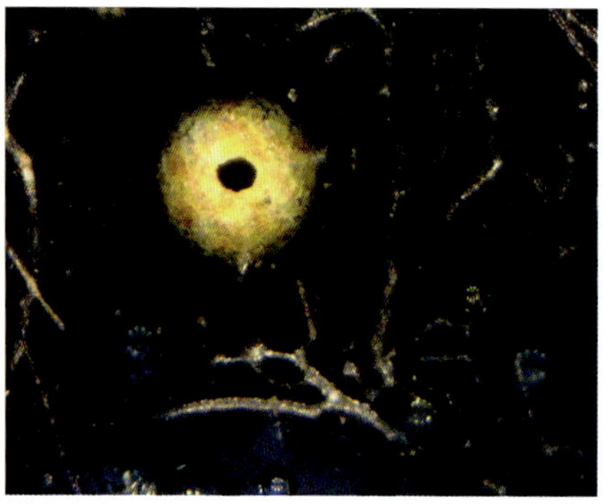

图6-3-84

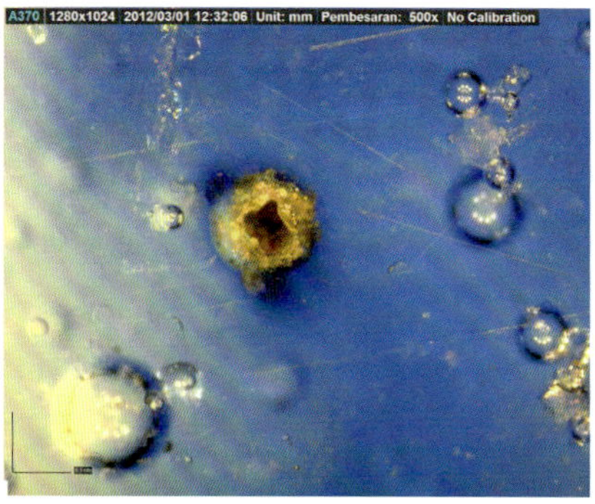

图6-3-85

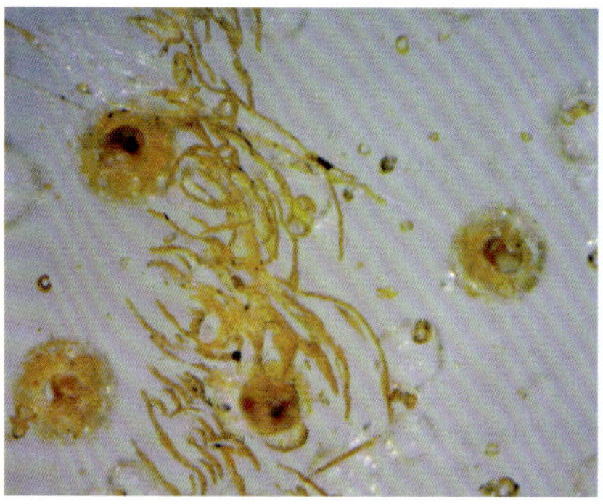

图6-3-86

II.非圆口破口壁变泡三维特征

参见本章本节圆口破口壁变泡三维特征部分。

见图6-3-87、图6-3-88，二者为同一器物同一位置图片，图6-3-87为二维图片，图6-3-88为三维图片。

图6-3-87中的气泡M在图6-3-88中位于红圈釉下处，不可见。气泡M的破口在图6-3-88中清晰可见，破口圆滑。破口周围有颜色较浓的斑块（如箭头N所指处），除此以外釉表面光滑洁净。这说明气泡M的风化斑块大部分都处于气泡内壁，斑块N及破口应该是外界连接气泡内的通道所在处。

见图6-3-89、图6-3-90，二者为同一器物同一位置图片，图6-3-89为二维图片，图6-3-90为三维图片。

图6-3-89中的气泡O在图6-3-90中位于红圈釉下处，不可见。气泡O的破口在图6-3-90中清晰可见，破口圆滑。除破口以外，气泡O所在处的釉表面还存在许多划痕，划痕及破口应该是外界连接气泡内的通道。

外界物质通过釉表面的这些通道进入釉层中的气泡内，使气泡内壁发生质地变化，失去了透影性，形成壁变泡。通道周围的釉表面保持光滑洁净。

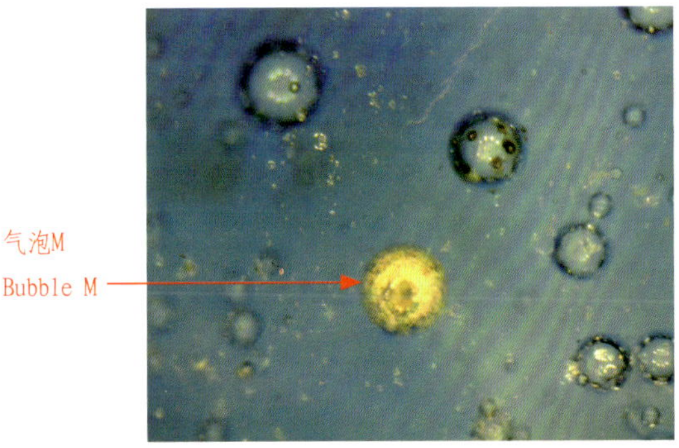

图6-3-87

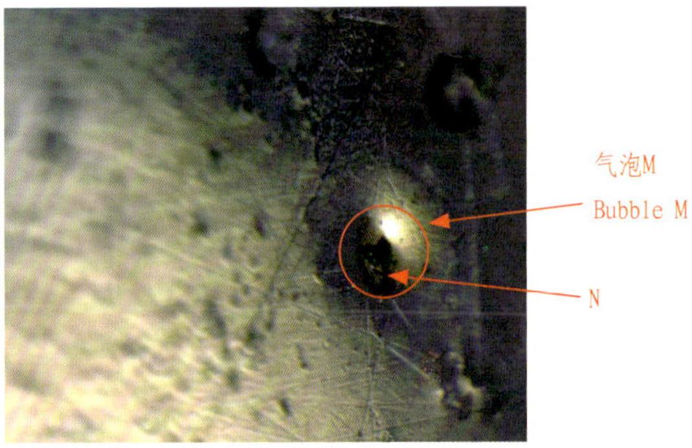

图6-3-88

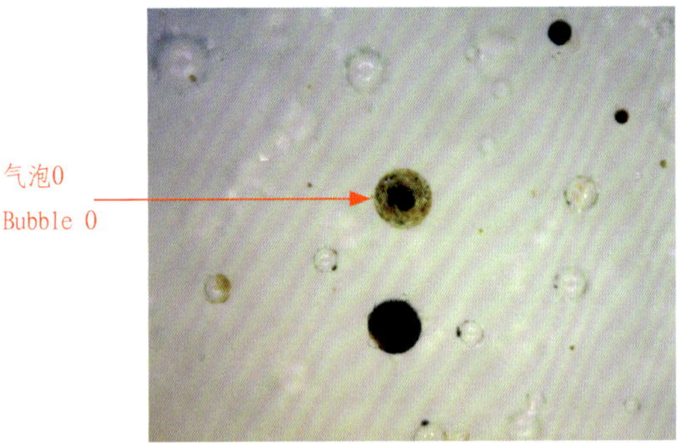

图6-3-89

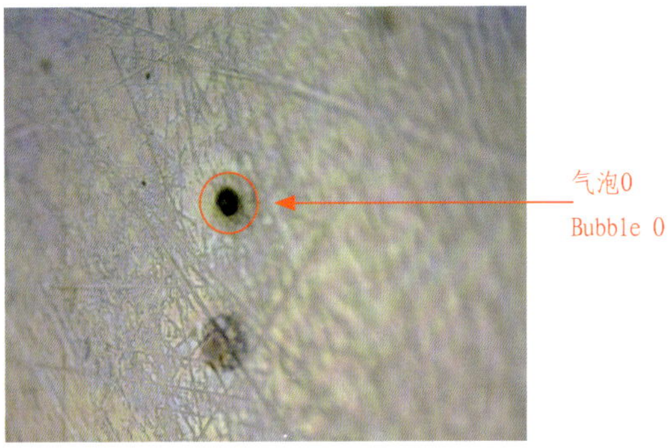

图6-3-90

C. 小结

在同一元青花瓷器上，圆口破口壁变泡与非圆口破口壁变泡可以同时存在。它们中绝大部分破口边沿是圆滑的。同一器物上，破口圆滑率越高越能体现迹型的量变特征。

破口壁变泡内的风化现象是侵蚀物紧贴气泡的内壁，以积累的模式渐进风化，而不是弥漫在空间风化。

气泡破口周围往往是颜色最早变化和颜色较浓的地方，因为破口是气泡连接外界的通道。

除破口以外，破口壁变泡上还会有其他颜色明显较浓的地方，这些地方往往就是通道所在处。三维成像有时可观察到清晰的通道（如划痕、风化斑块等）；有时通道不明显，釉表面光滑洁净。

（3）小结

在同一元青花瓷器上，非破口壁变泡与破口壁变泡可以同时存在。非破口泡内壁的风化程度一般要比破口壁变泡低，体现了陶瓷迹型风化的时间过程性原理。

（三）假象壁变泡

1. 假象壁变泡概念

假象壁变泡是釉表面由于自然风化，或人为做旧形成的针眼斑、坑点斑、物盖斑等，恰好处于釉层中某一气泡的正上方，观察时易被误认为是壁变泡的气泡。

2. 假象壁变泡辨别方法

辨别假象壁变泡的方法有三种，它们分别是：直径比较法、焦距调整法、马士宁成像法。

当位于气泡上方斑块的最大直径超出气泡最大直径时，我们可以运用直径比较法和马士宁成像法来辨别；当位于气泡上方斑块的最大直径小于气泡最大直径时，我们可以运用焦距调整法和马士宁成像法来辨别。

（1）当斑块最大直径大于气泡最大直径时

运用直径比较法，当位于气泡上方斑块的最大直径超出气泡最大直径，且斑块将气泡完全覆盖时，可以直接判定该气泡属于假象壁变泡（见图6-3-91中气泡A）。

当位于气泡上方斑块的最大直径大于气泡的最大直径，但又没有将其完全覆盖时，我们需要采用马士宁成像法进一步判断。

见图6-3-92、6-3-93，二者为同一器物同一位置图片，图6-3-92为二维图片，6-3-93为三维图片。

图6-3-92中的气泡B在图6-3-93中位于红圈釉下处，不可见；图6-3-92中箭头C所指的深色斑块，在图6-3-93中形状大小相当。

图6-3-92中的气泡B是真正的

壁变泡，因为气泡斑块的三维成像面积小于二维，说明斑块部分处于气泡内壁而非釉表面。两图中箭头C所指深色斑块是在同一气泡上的同一位置，且大小相当，说明箭头C所指斑块处于釉表面，属于釉表面风化形成的斑块，也应是外界连接气泡内的通道所在处。

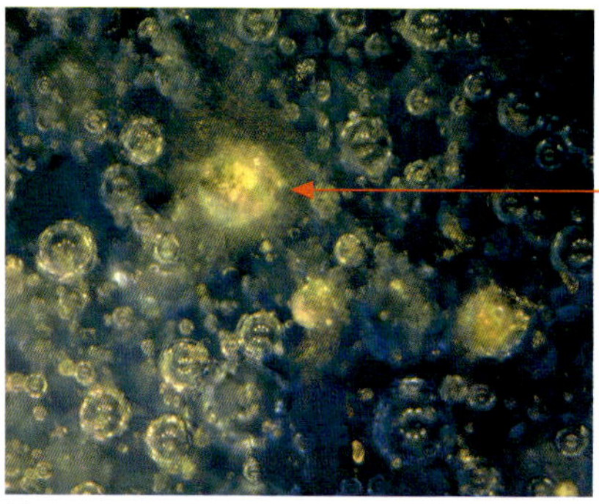

图6-3-91

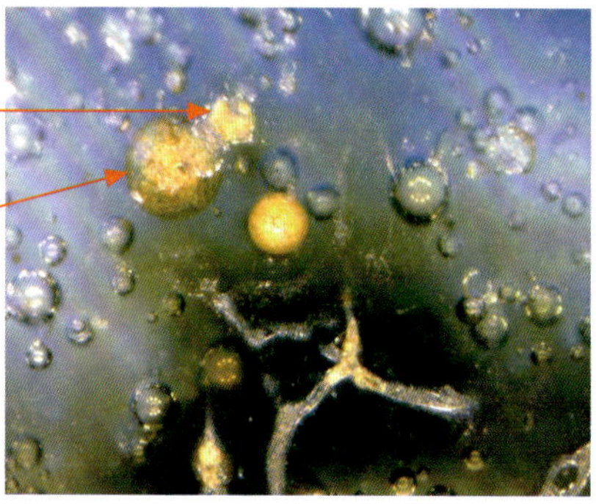

图6-3-92

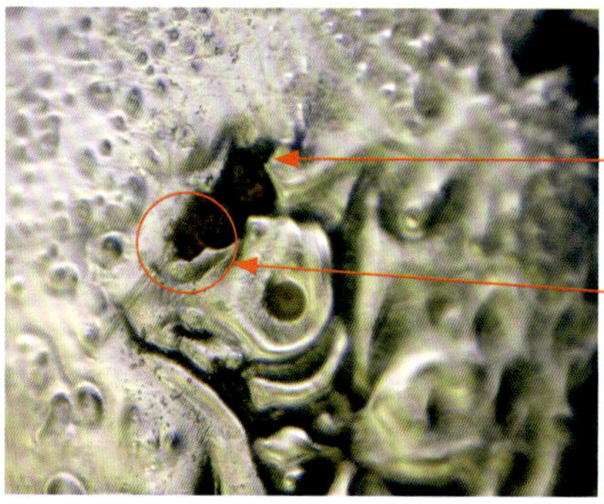

图6-3-93

（2）当斑块最大直径小于气泡最大直径时

当位于气泡上方斑块的最大直径小于气泡最大直径时，可以运用焦距调整法去判断。当摄像头调好焦距后，焦距对准的那一平面上的观察物都是最清晰的，凡不在同一平面上的其他物质成像都是模糊的。如果发现两个或多个斑块在调好焦距后观察仍有清晰与模糊的差别，说明有两种可能：

第一种，斑块一部分在泡内壁，一部分在釉表面；第二种，斑块都处于泡内壁，但不在同一平面上。无论是哪一种可能，该气泡都属于真正的壁变泡。

焦距调整法一般只适用于体积较大的气泡，如果气泡太小，很难分辨出焦距调整前后物像清晰度的区别。这时，我们可以采用马士宁成像法协助判断。

见图6-3-94，由于气泡体积较小，使用焦距调整法无法分辨，需要采用马士宁成像法。

见图6-3-94、图6-3-95，二者为同一器物同一位置图片，图6-3-94为二维图片，图6-3-95为三维图片。

图6-3-94中的斑块D，在图6-3-95中的釉表面清晰可见，二维面积与三维面积相当，也就是说，存在于釉表面的斑块D，造成了气泡“壁变”的假象，所以该气泡属于假象壁变泡。

见图6-3-96、图6-3-97，二者为同一器物同一位置图片，图6-3-96为二维图片，图6-3-97为三维图片。

图6-3-96中的气泡E，在图6-3-97中位于红圈釉下处，不可见。图6-3-96箭头F所指深色斑块，在图6-3-97中却消失了。图6-3-96中箭头G所指深色斑块，在图6-3-97中也可见。

由此可推断，箭头F所指斑块不在釉表面，而在气泡E内壁，是内壁风化形成的斑块。箭头G所指斑块处于釉表面，是釉表面风化形成的斑块，应是外界连接气泡内的通道所在处。所以气泡E应是真正的壁变泡。

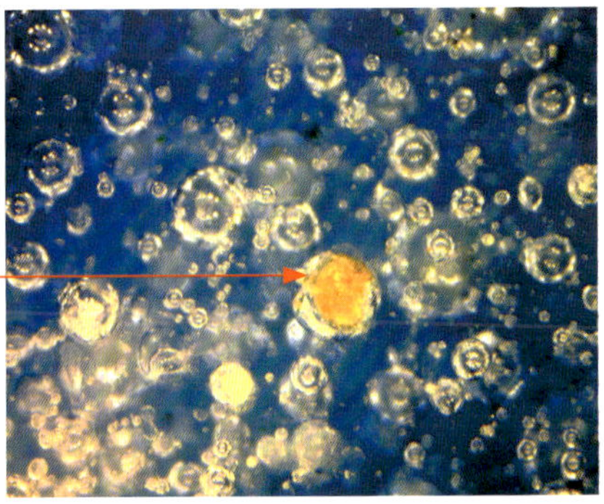

图6-3-94

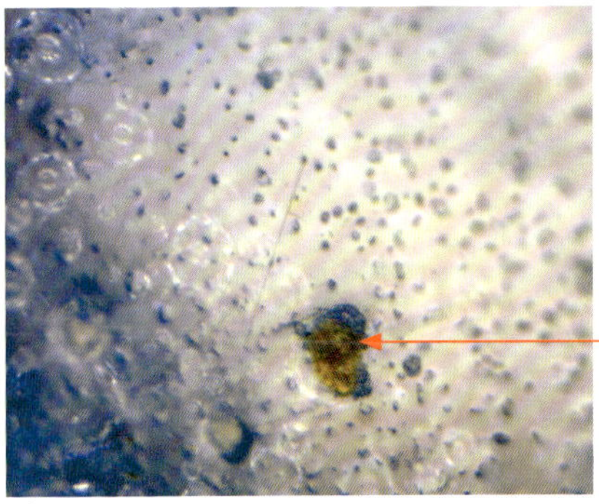

图6-3-95

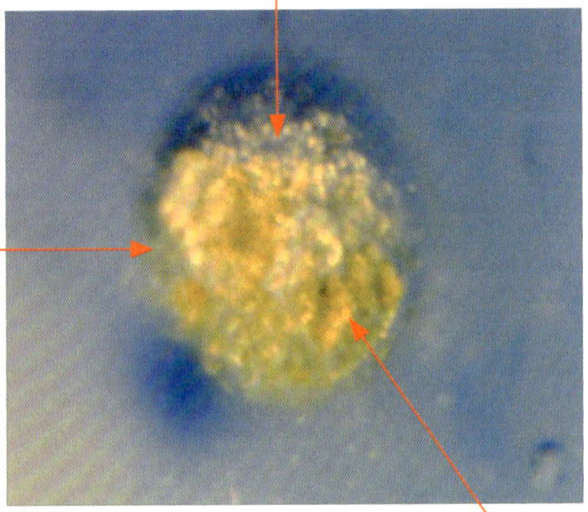

图6-3-96*

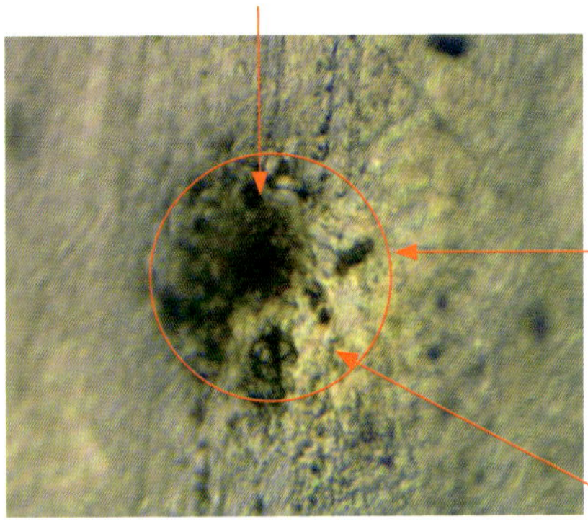

图6-3-97*

（四） 总结

元青花瓷器釉层中的气泡，在刚烧制出来时基本上都是无色透明的，在后天环境的影响下，部分无色气泡会逐渐风化成色变泡和壁变泡。

有时色变泡呈现具有色阶浓淡的均匀过渡。

有时在色变泡上可观察到颜色明显较浓的地方，这些地方往往就是通道所在处，也是气泡最早开始变色的地方。三维成像有时可观察到清晰的通道（如划痕、风化斑块等），有时通道不明显，釉表面光滑洁净。

色变泡之间也会有色差变化。

壁变泡包括雾状型、磨砂型、颗粒型等不同风化强度的表现。壁变泡内有时有色阶变化，壁变泡之间有色差变化。

有时在壁变泡上可观察到颜色明显较浓的地方，这些地方往往就是通道所在处，三维成像有时可观察到清晰的通道（如划痕、风化斑块等），有时通道不明显，釉表面光滑洁净。

壁变泡破口大都比较圆滑。

元青花瓷器上气泡类别的风化特征符合陶瓷迹型量变原理和时间过程原理，体现了陶瓷迹型形成及变化的诸规律。

---

*图片经过裁剪放大处理。

*Picture cropped and enlarged to show detail.

第四节 元青花鬃眼类别

一、元青花鬃眼概念

元青花鬃眼是在瓷器烧制过程中形成的釉层小孔。

鬃眼是瓷器釉表面的缺陷，凭肉眼可见，但用肉眼通过小孔观察不到胎体。

二、元青花鬃眼形成与分布

元青花瓷器高温烧制过程中产生气泡，产生的气泡冲出釉表面后，会在釉表面留下小孔。当釉的黏度较高时，流动性差，加上瓷器胎质疏松等缺陷，会导致胎中有较多气体排出。在熔融釉层恢复的过程中，有些小孔不能被釉层覆盖，成为鬃眼。鬃眼现象与瓷器坯胎质地有直接关系，与釉料配方及釉层厚薄也有关系。

鬃眼随机分布在瓷器有釉处，大都出现在瓷器上的白色部分（见图6-4-1、图6-4-2），也有的出现在蓝色青花纹饰处（见图6-4-3）及釉上黑斑处（见图6-4-4）。

三、元青花鬃眼特征

（一）鬃眼口部形状特征

1. 大多数鬃眼口部为不规则形状（见图6-4-5—图6-4-8），少数口部形状近似圆形或椭圆（见图6-4-9、图6-4-10）。

2. 有的鬃眼口部圆滑（见图6-4-5、图6-4-8—图6-4-10），有的呈锯齿状（见图6-4-6、图6-4-7）。

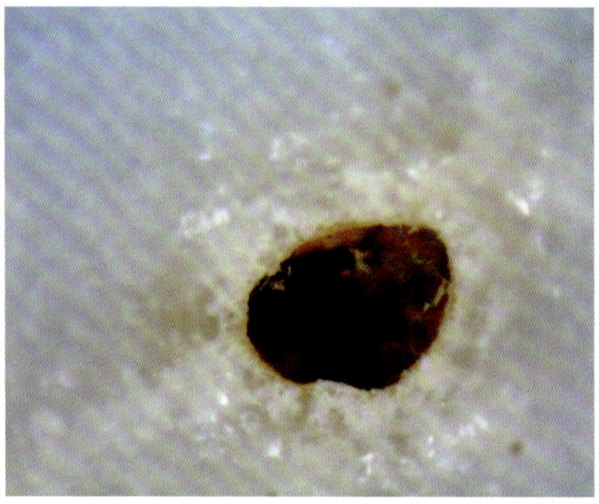
图6-4-1

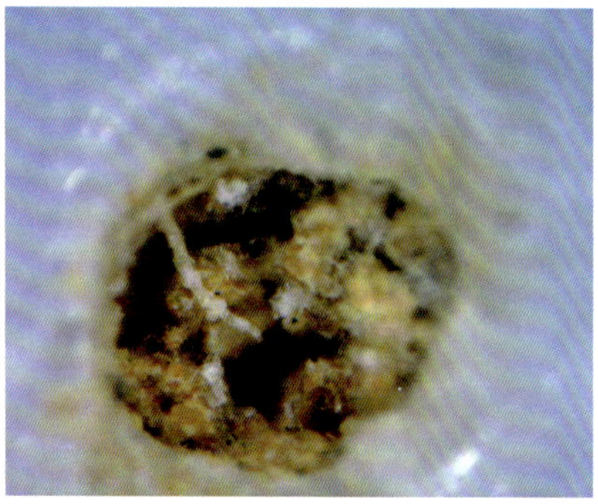
图6-4-2

图6-4-3

图6-4-4

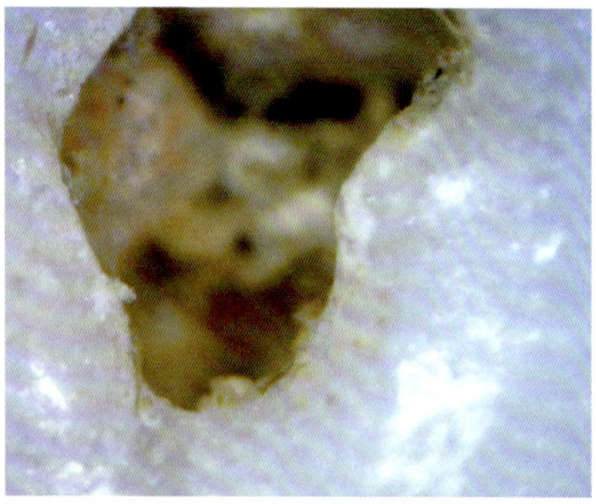
图6-4-5

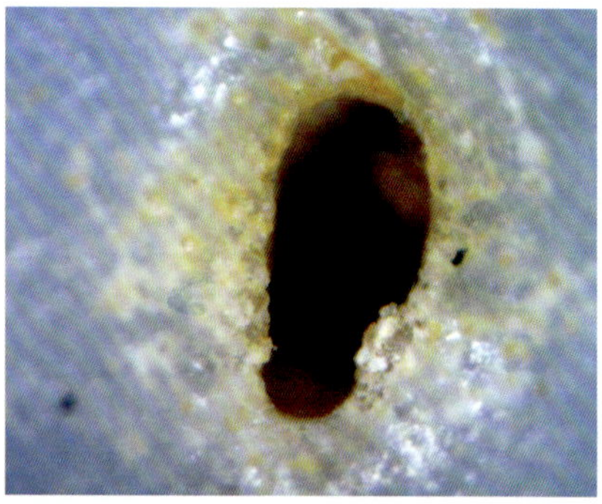
图6-4-6

Section 4:
Yuan Underglaze Blue Bristle Pit Category

1. YUB Bristle Pit Defined

Bristle Pits are the holes in the glaze level that were formed during the firing process of YUB.

Bristle Pits are glaze flaws visible to the naked eye, however the ceramic body is not observable by the naked eye.

2. YUB Bristle Pit Formation and Distribution

During the firing of YUB, air bubbles are formed that can burst through the glaze level leaving small openings in the glaze surface. When the viscosity of the glaze is relatively high, its fluidity low, in addition to the looseness or other flaws of the ceramic body, larger amounts of gaseous bodies are expelled from the body. There are some openings that are not able to be completely covered by the molten glaze, forming bristle pits. The bristle pit phenomenon has a direct relationship with the qualities of the ceramic clay as well as the recipe and thickness of the glaze.

Bristle pitting occurs randomly across the glaze of the porcelain, with the majority occurring on white glaze areas (see pictures 6-4-1 and 6-4-2), but some occur also on areas of blue dye (see picture 6-4-3) or on over glaze dark spots (see picture 6-4-4).

3. YUB Bristle Pit Characteristics

A. YUB Bristle Pit Mouth Shape Characteristics

I. The majority of bristle pits present with irregularly shaped mouth openings (see pictures 6-4-5—6-4-8), a portion can also present as circular or ovular (see pictures 6-4-9 and 6-4-10).

II. Bristle pits mouths can present as round and smooth (see pictures 6-4-5, 6-4-8—6-4-10), and can also present with saw-like teeth (see pictures 6-4-6 and 6-4-7).

B. YUB Bristle Pit Mouth Surroundings Characteristics

I. Coloration

Some bristle pit mouths can present with coloration, these include yellow, brown, black and so forth (see pictures 6-4-11—6-4-14).

II. Presence of Other Traces

a. Floccus mottling under the glaze surrounding the pit mouth (see pictures 6-4-15—6-4-17).

b. Glaze cracks can present around bristle pits, and floccus mottling can occur under these cracks (see pictures 6-4-18—6-4-20).

c. Colored bubbles can occur in conjunction with bristle pits (see pictures 6-4-21—6-4-23).

III. Presence of Other Materials

a. Bristle pit mouths can present with filaments, primarily white in color. They can be long or short, thick or thin, independent or networked (see pictures 6-4-24—6-4-29).

b. It is possible for granulated materials to become covered by glaze surrounding the bristle pit mouth, colors include yellow, brown, and so forth (see pictures 6-4-30—6-4-34).

图6-4-7

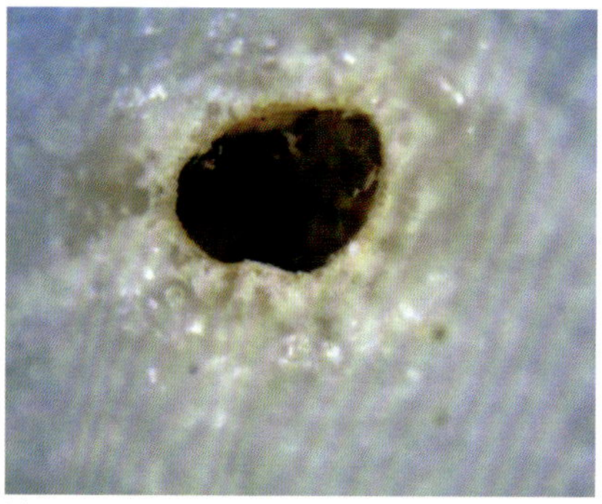

图6-4-8

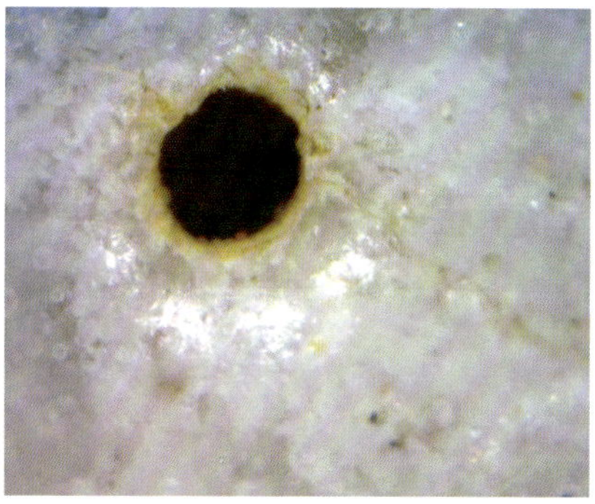

图6-4-9

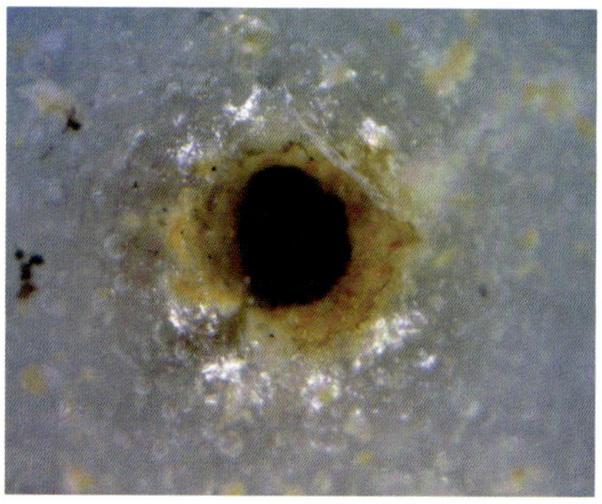

图6-4-10

（二）鬃眼口部周围特征

1. 颜色变化特征

部分鬃眼口部周围的釉表面会有颜色变化，包括黄色、褐色及黑色等（见图6-4-11—图6-4-14）。

2. 其他迹型出现特征

（1）鬃眼口部周围釉下出现絮状斑（见图6-4-15—图6-4-17）。

（2）鬃眼口部周围釉表面有时会出现釉裂纹，釉裂纹下方有时会出现絮状斑（见图6-4-18—图6-4-20）。

（3）鬃眼口部周围釉下存在色变泡（见图6-4-21—图6-4-23）。

3. 其他物质出现特征

（1）鬃眼口部周围釉表面上存在纤丝，主要是白色。纤丝有粗有细，有长有短，有的单一出现，有的错综出现（见图6-4-24—图6-4-29）。

（2）鬃眼口部周围釉表面存在颗粒物质，颜色包括黄色及褐色等，覆盖部分釉表面（见图6-4-30—图6-4-34）。

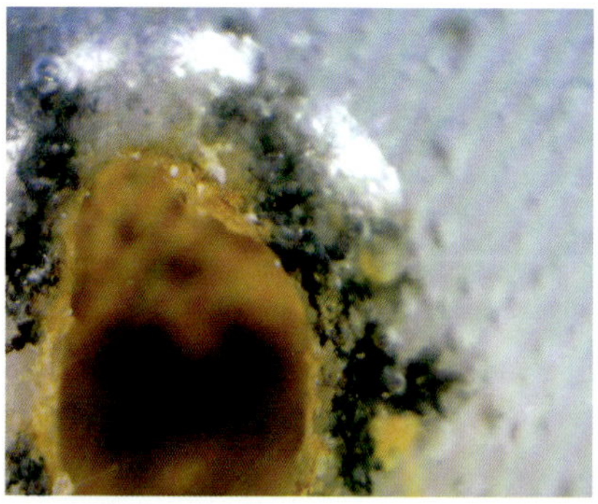

图6-4-11

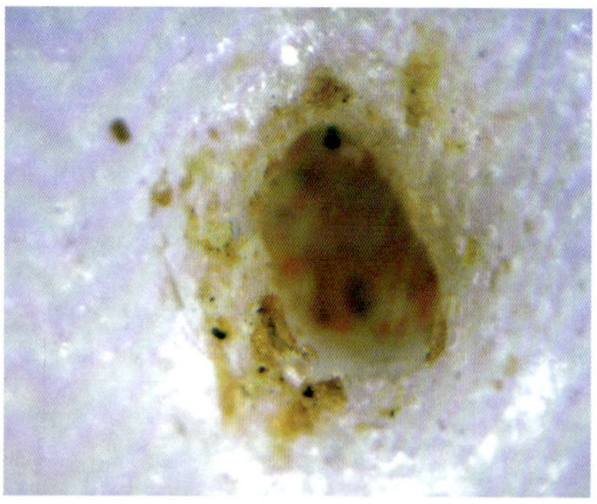

图6-4-12

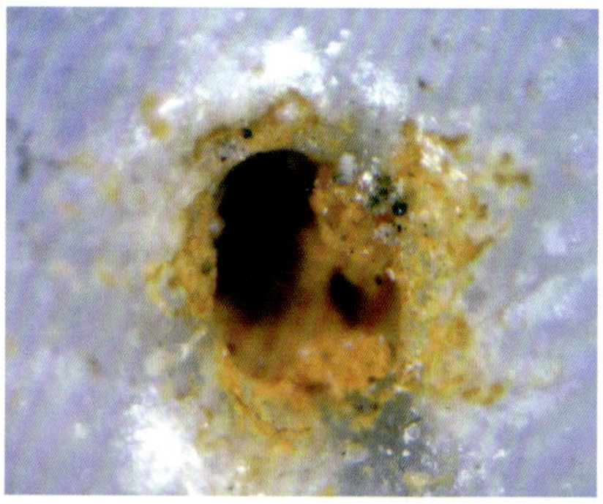

图6-4-13

C. YUB Bristle Pit Interior Characteristics

I. Coloration

Bristle pit interiors can undergo coloration, colors include yellow, brown, black and so forth (see pictures 6-5-35—6-4-38).

II. Presence of Other Materials

a. Bristle pit interiors can present with granulated material deposits. Granules can be large or small, independent or in clusters, and colors include white, yellow, brown, black, and so forth (see pictures 6-4-39—6-4-49).

b. Bristle pit interiors can also present with filaments, such characteristics are similar to those listed above (see pictures 6-4-50—6-4-60).

4. Summary

Bristle pits are a common appearance in the YUB glaze level. Pieces smaller in size or with relatively thin glaze rarely present with bristle pits.

The pit interior and mouth area often present with granule deposits and filaments. They can also present with color variation, and a portion of bristle pits present with floccus mottling or colored bubbles around the pit mouth.

Bristle pits reflect the glaze and clay composition as well as firing techniques characteristic to YUB. Their weathering characteristics are in conjunction with the quantitative change and passage of time principles of ceramic traces and embody the laws of ceramic trace formaiton and change.

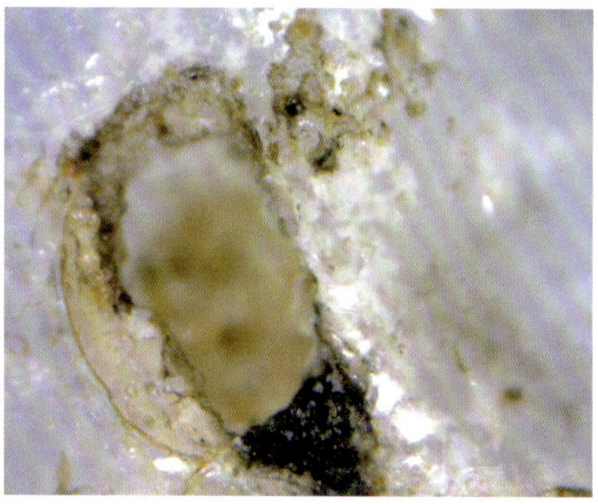
图6-4-14

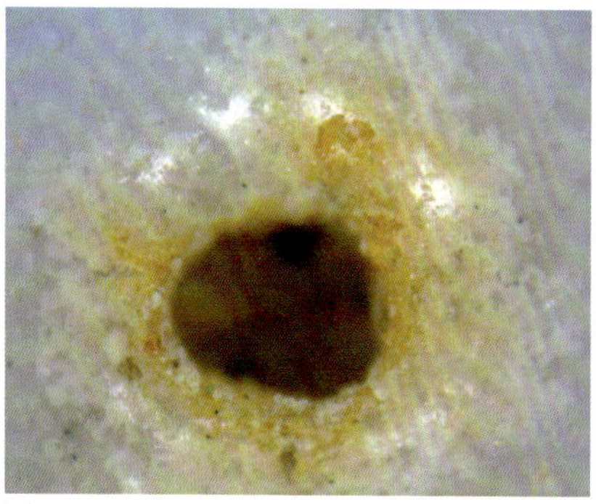
图6-4-15

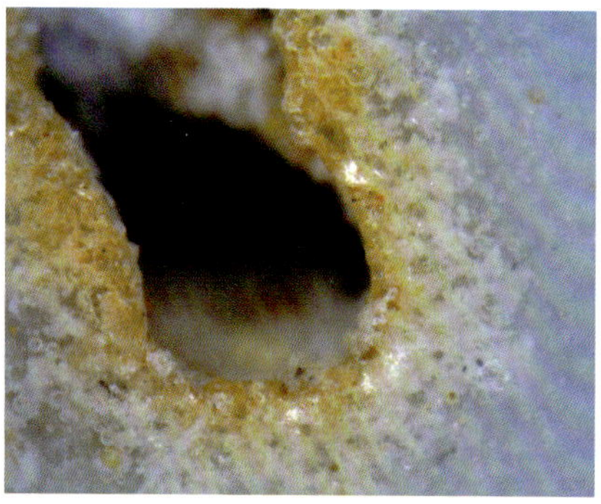
图6-4-16

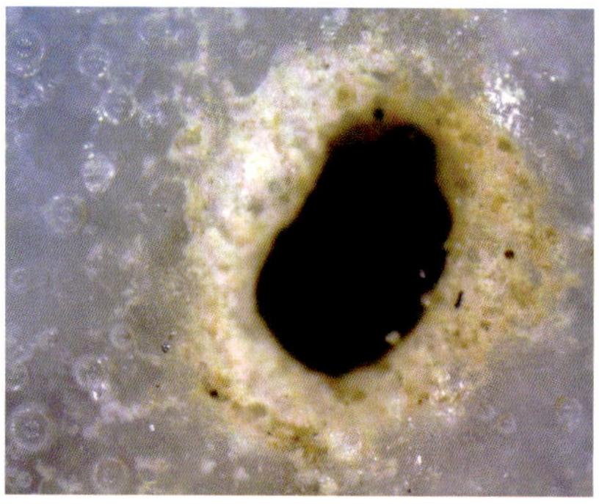
图6-4-17

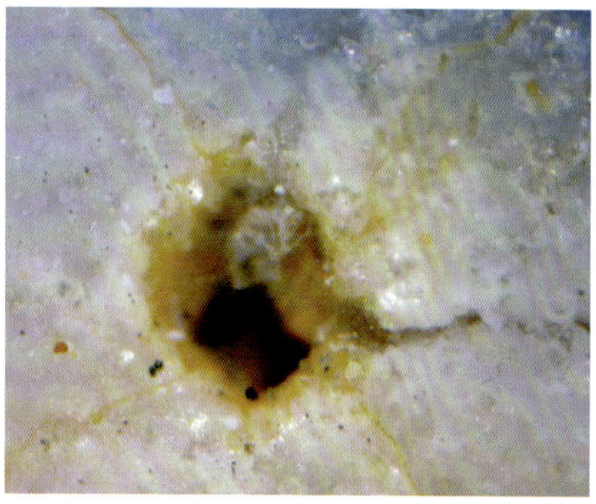
图6-4-18

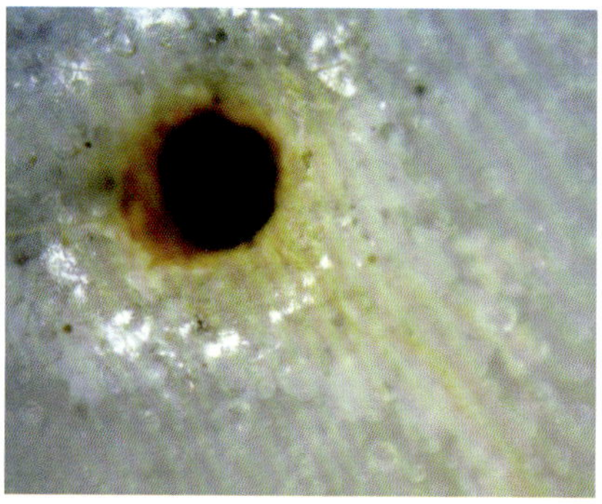
图6-4-19

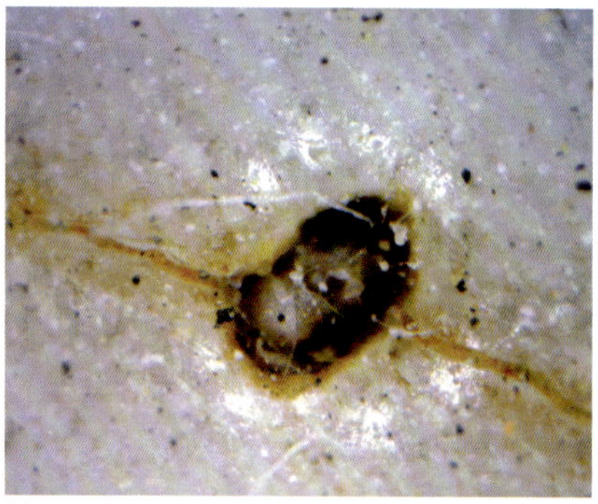
图6-4-20

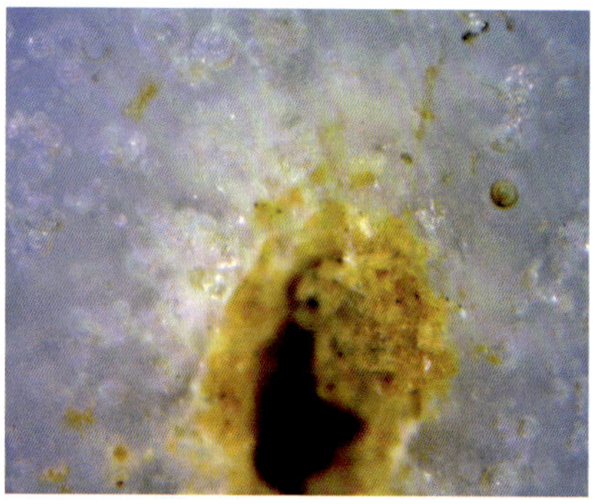
图6-4-21

图6-4-22

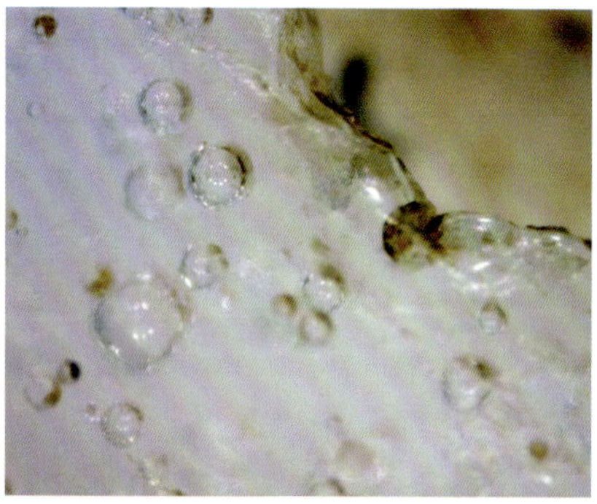
图6-4-23

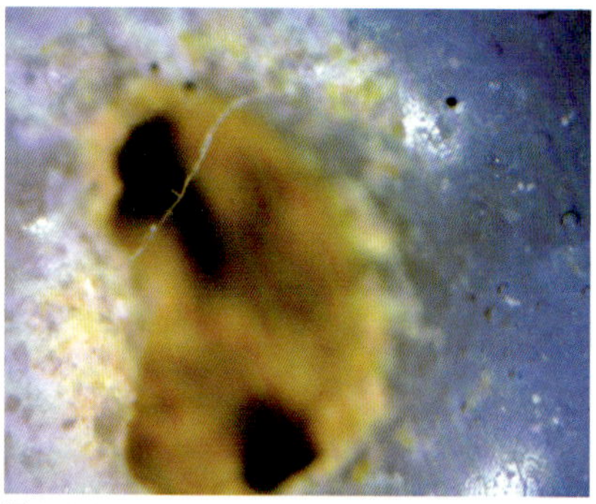
图6-4-24

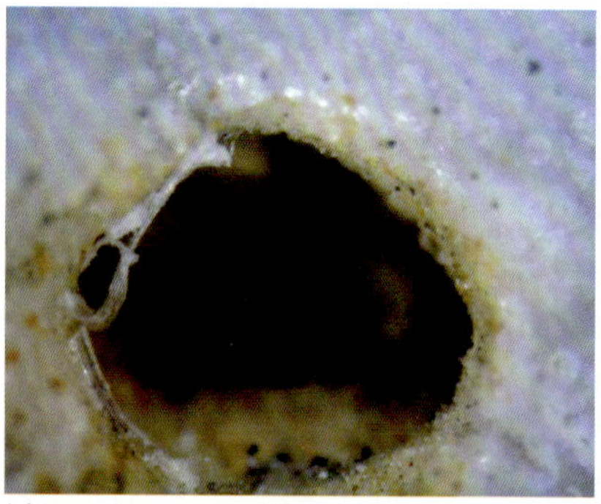
图6-4-25

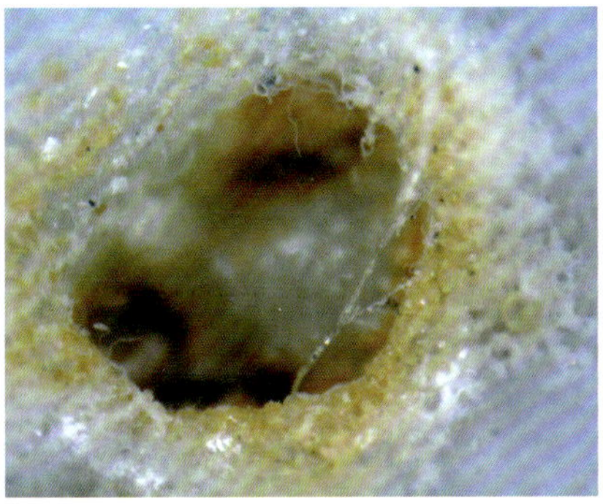
图6-4-26

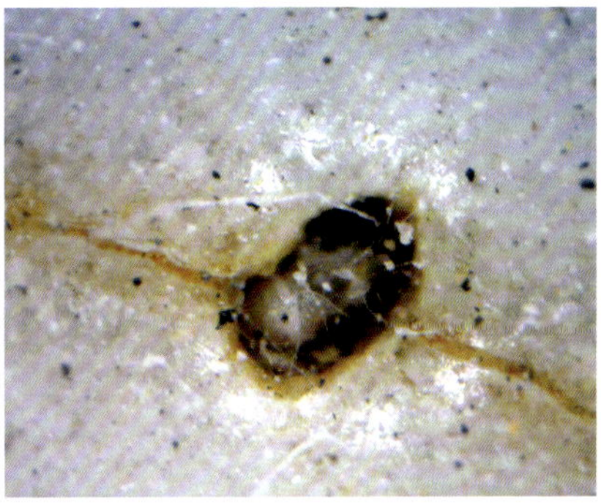
图6-4-27

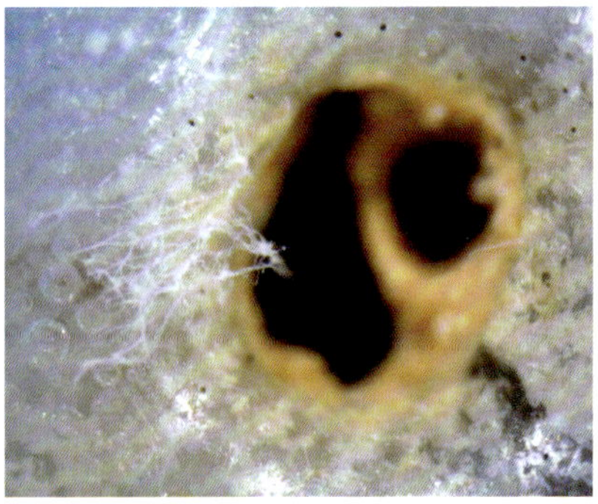
图6-4-28

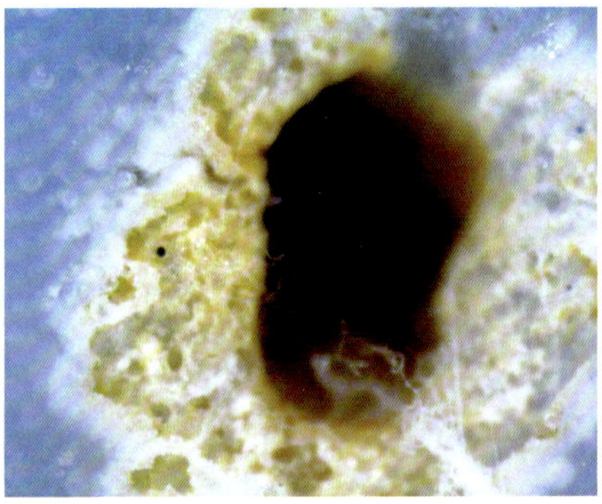
图6-4-29

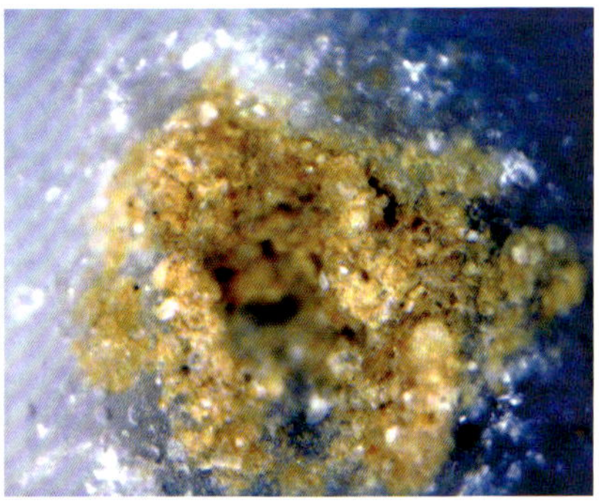
图6-4-30

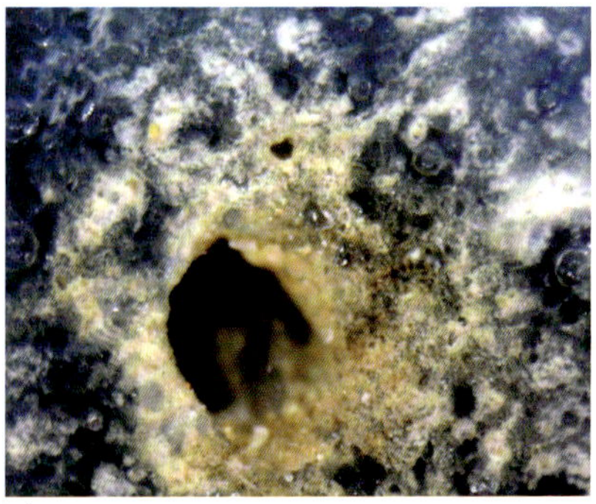
图6-4-31

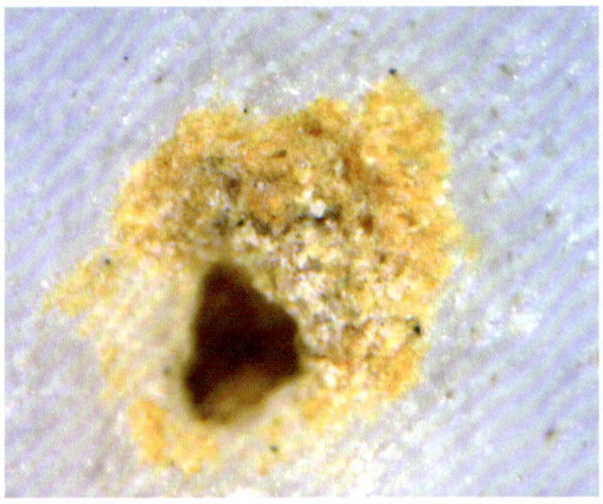
图6-4-32

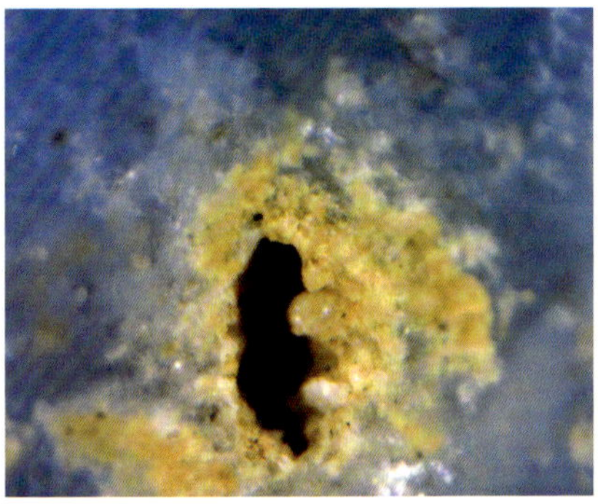
图6-4-33

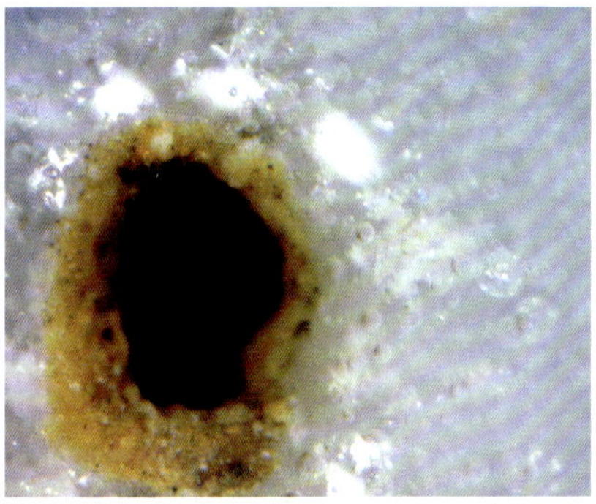
图6-4-34

（三）鬃眼内部特征

1. 颜色变化特征

有时鬃眼内部可见颜色变化，如黄色、褐色及黑色等（见图6-4-35—图6-4-38）。

2. 其他物质出现特征

（1）鬃眼内部有颗粒沉积，颗粒物有大有小，有的独立存在，有的以团簇形式存在，颜色包括白色、黄色、褐色及黑色（见图6-4-39—图6-4-49）。

（2）鬃眼内部有纤丝现象，纤丝有粗有细，有长有短，有细微颜色变化，包括白色、黄色等。纤丝有的单一出现，有的错综出现（见图6-4-50—图6-4-60）。

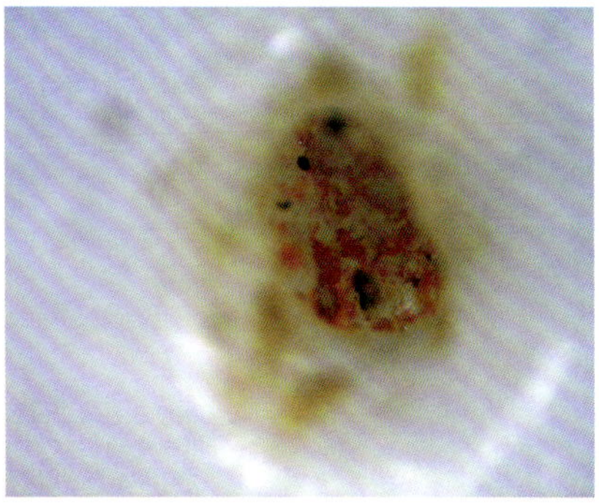
图6-4-35

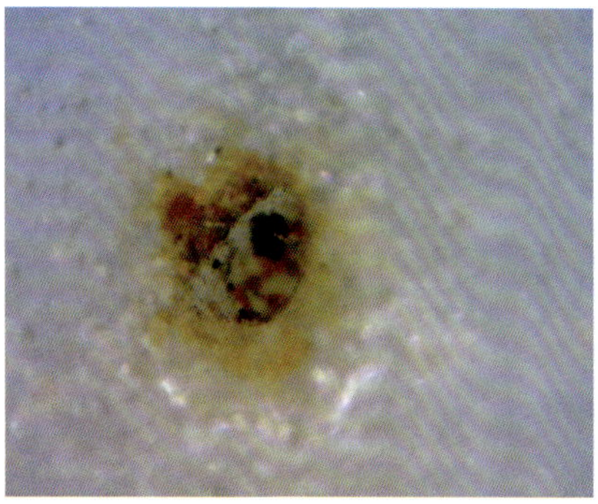
图6-4-36

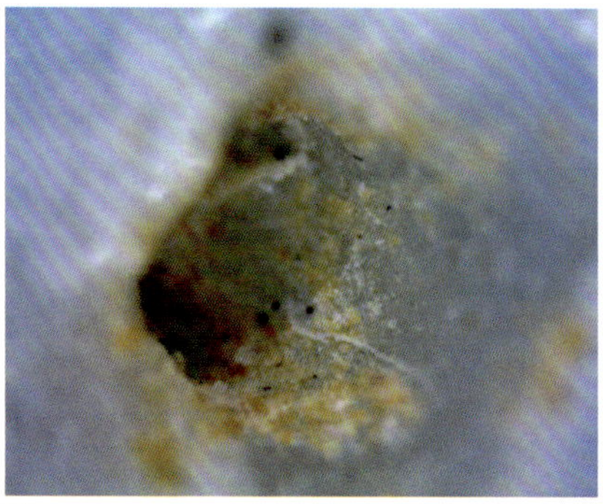
图6-4-37

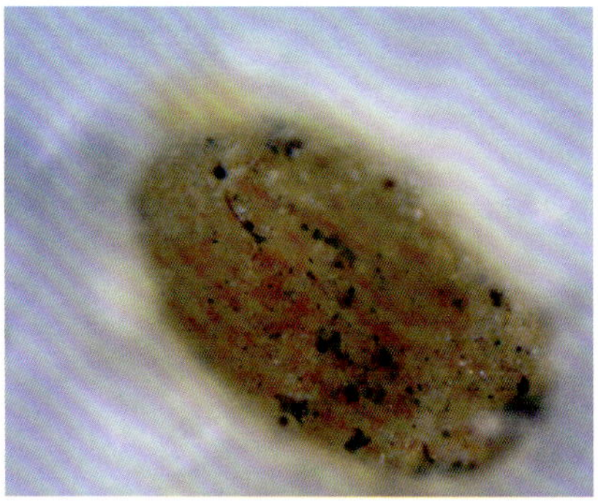
图6-4-38

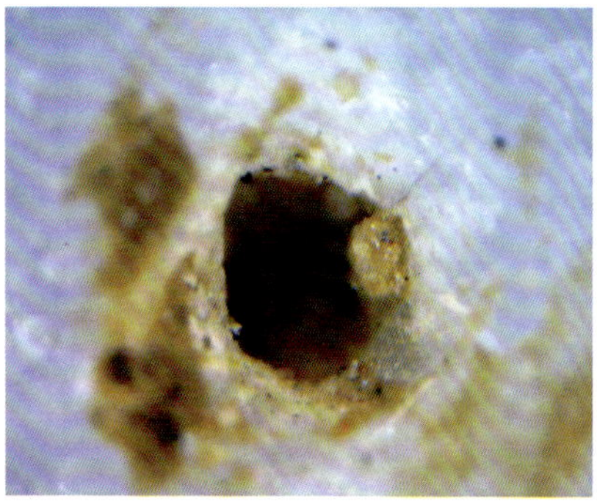
图6-4-39

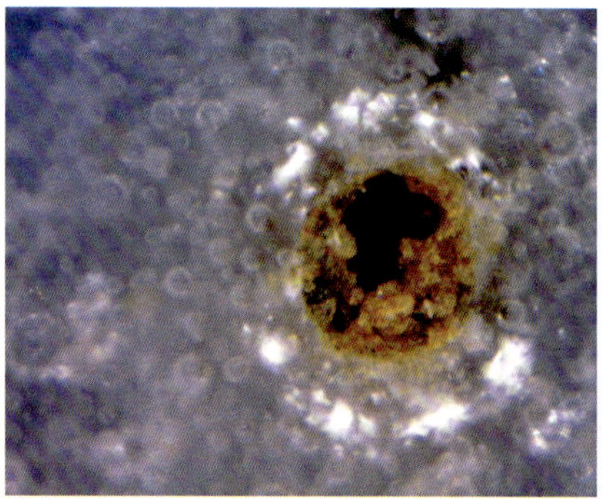
图6-4-40

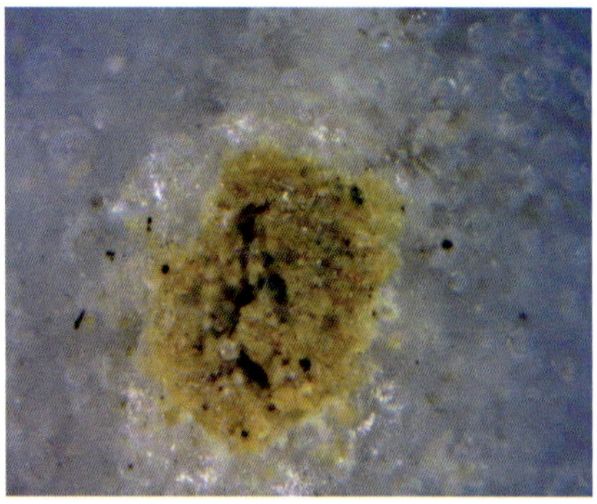
图6-4-41

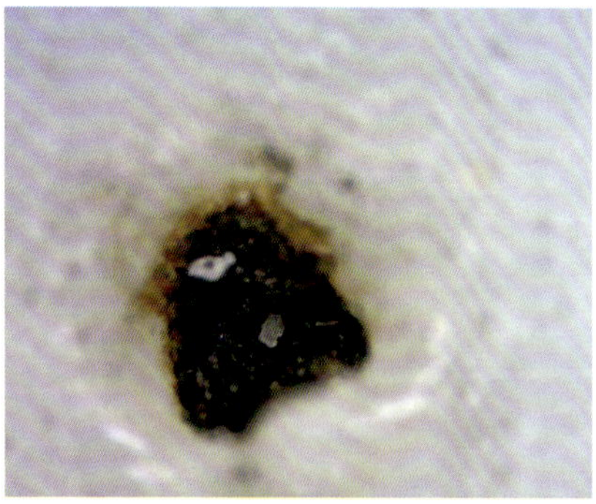
图6-4-42

图6-4-43

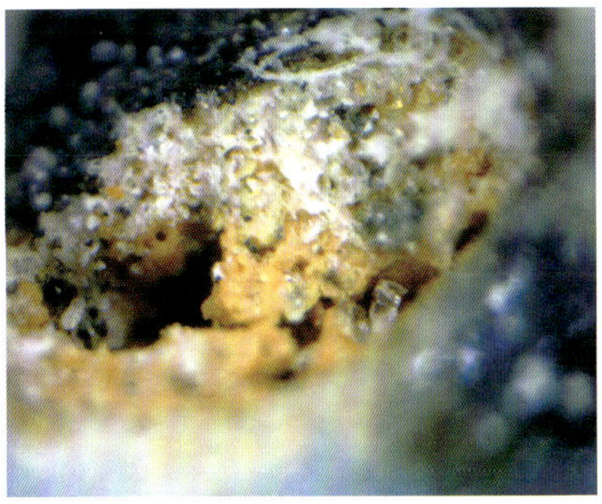
图6-4-44

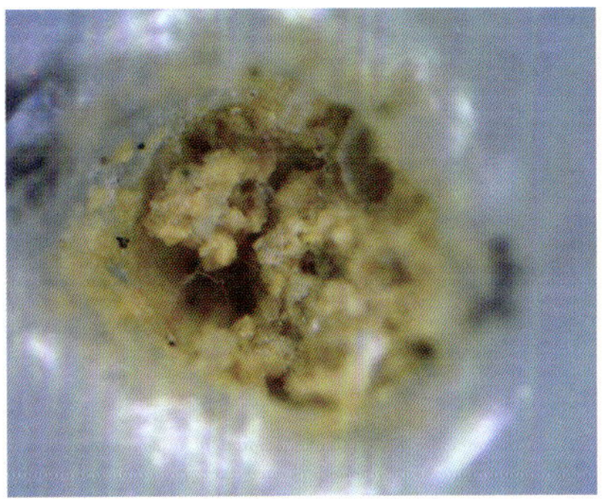
图6-4-45

图6-4-46

图6-4-47

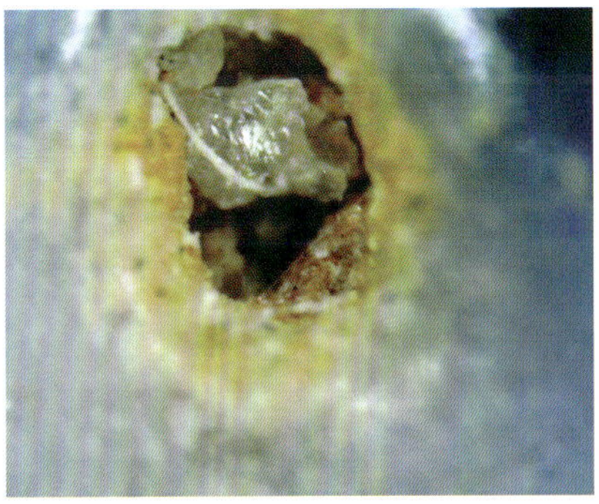
图6-4-48

图6-4-49

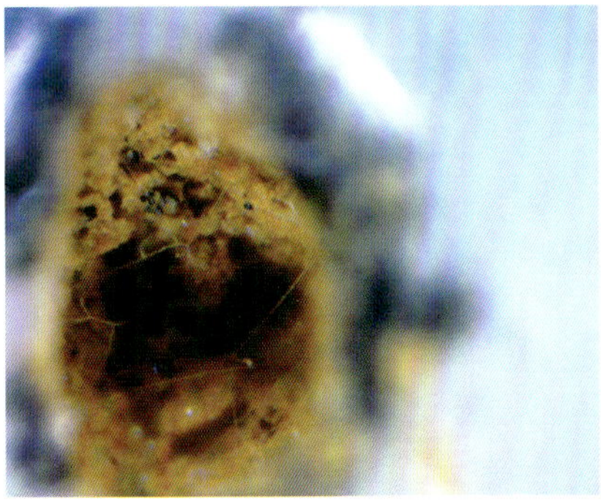
图6-4-50

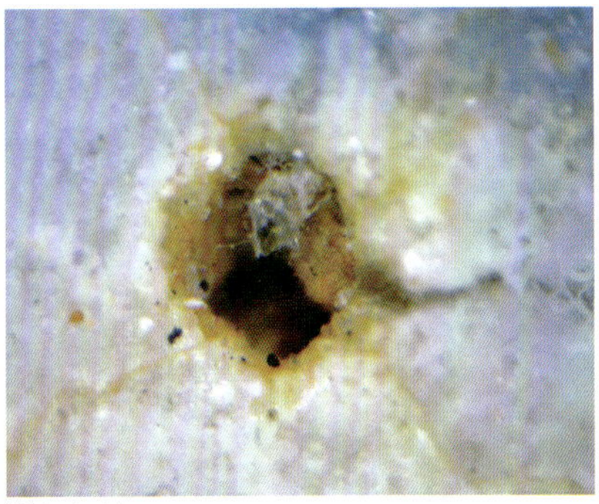
图6-4-51

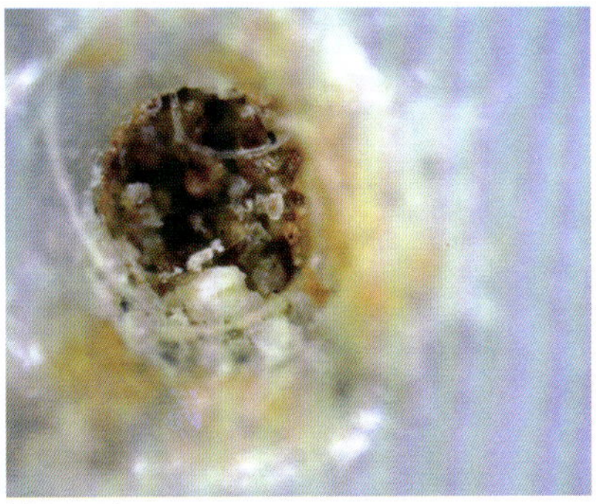
图6-4-52

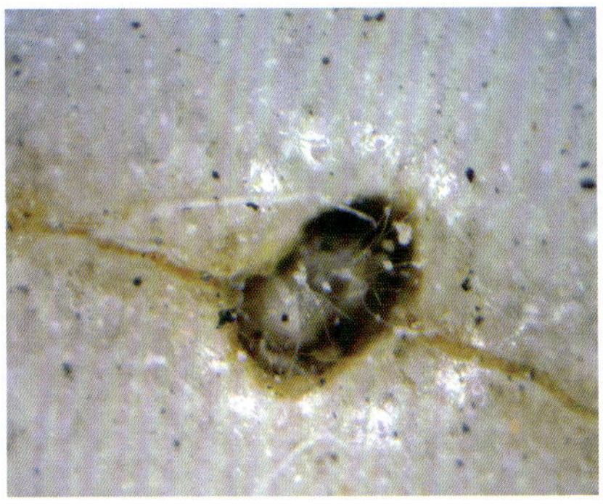
图6-4-53

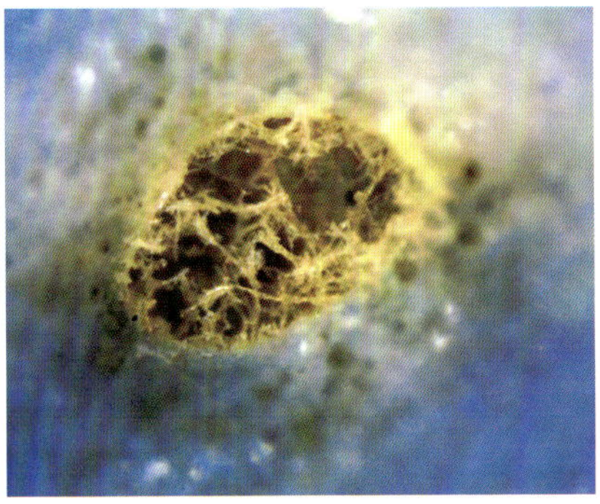
图6-4-54

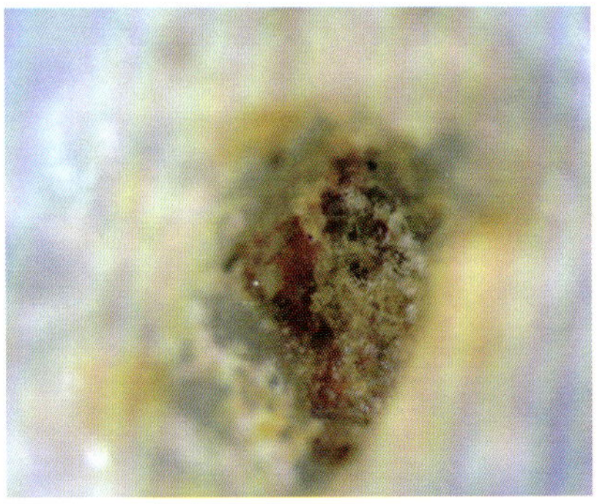
图6-4-55

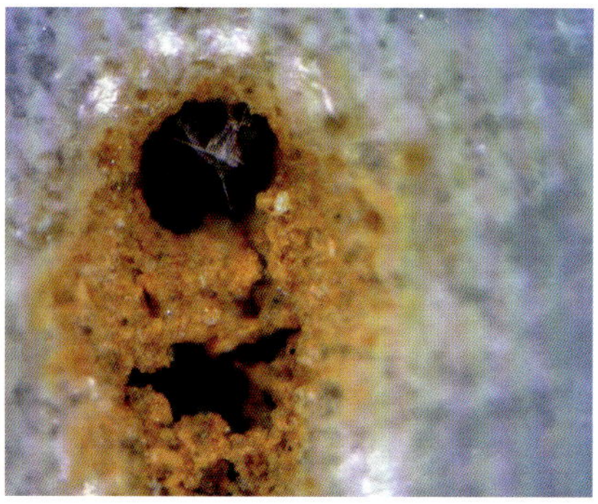
图6-4-56

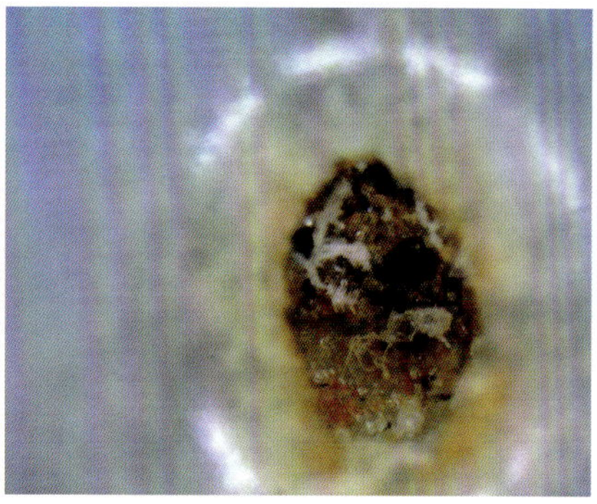
图6-4-57

图6-4-58

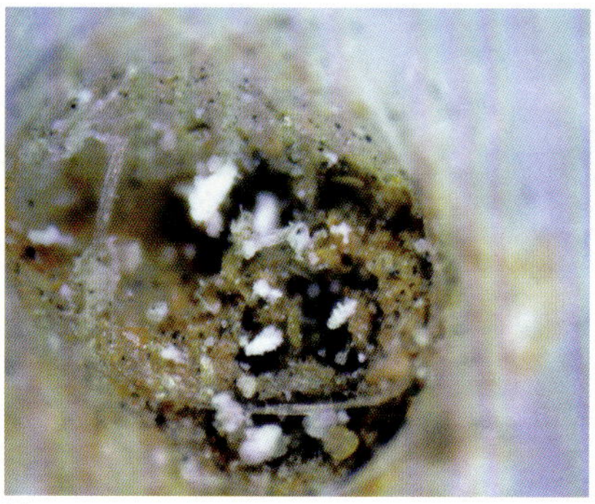
图6-4-59

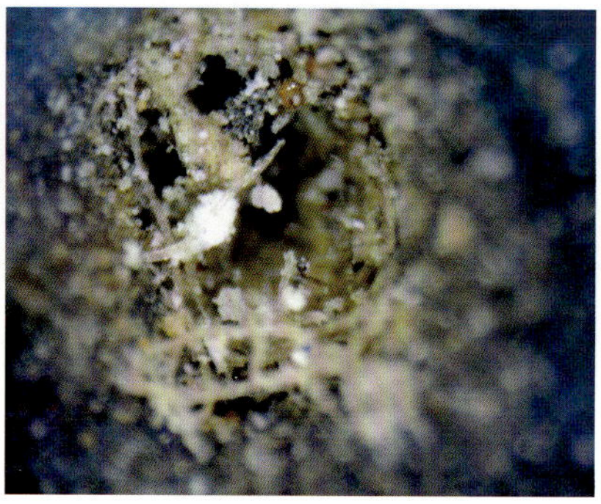
图6-4-60

四、总结

鬃眼是元青花釉层存在的普遍现象，在体积较小或釉层较薄的器物上一般比较少见。

鬃眼内部及口部周围的釉表面常会发现有颗粒物质及纤丝的存在，还会有颜色变化，部分鬃眼口部周围釉下会出现絮状斑或色变泡。

鬃眼现象反映了元青花的胎釉特征和烧制工艺特征，其风化特征符合陶瓷迹型的量变原理与时间过程性原理，也反映了陶瓷迹型形成及变化的诸规律。

第五节
元青花常见迹型组合

本章第一至第四节分别阐述了元青花瓷器的四个典型迹型类别。我们常常会发现，在元青花瓷器上，一些同一类别或不同类别的迹型种类常常在单位图片中同时出现，它们的组合出现有一定的规律可循。

一、流淌斑、放射斑及流淌纹组合

流淌斑、放射斑及流淌纹都属于含铁和锰较高的迹型种类。

元青花瓷器在烧制过程中，根据各处的成分、密度、表面张力的不同，会在釉表面及釉层中形成形貌各异的流淌斑、放射斑及流淌纹。它们之间可以两两组合出现，也可以三种同时出现。

（一）流淌斑与放射斑组合

1. 流淌斑与放射斑组合二维特征

（1）流淌斑与放射斑的组合主要是碘酒斑、沙滩斑与红色系、黄色系、褐色系、黑色系的放射斑为主的组合（见图6-5-1—图6-5-15）。

（2）也有碘酒斑、沙滩斑与红色系、黄色系的放射斑的组合（见图6-5-12）。

（3）还有碘酒斑与放射斑的组合（见图6-5-15）。

（4）在沙滩斑和放射斑的组合中，主要有“斑套斑”“斑上斑”等特征。

（5）“斑套斑”是指外围的沙滩斑环绕着中间的放射斑，两种斑块之间有玻璃相间隔（见图6-5-1、图6-5-6、图6-5-8）。

（6）“斑上斑”是指放射斑与沙滩斑组合，两种斑块之间不可见玻璃相（见图6-5-2—图6-5-4、图6-5-7、图6-5-9—图6-5-12）。

（7）也有“斑套斑”、“斑上斑”同时出现的现象（见图6-5-13、图6-5-14）。

（8）有时放射斑外沿会有一条包边（见图6-5-3—图6-5-5、图6-5-12、图6-5-13、图6-5-15）。

图6-5-1

图6-5-2

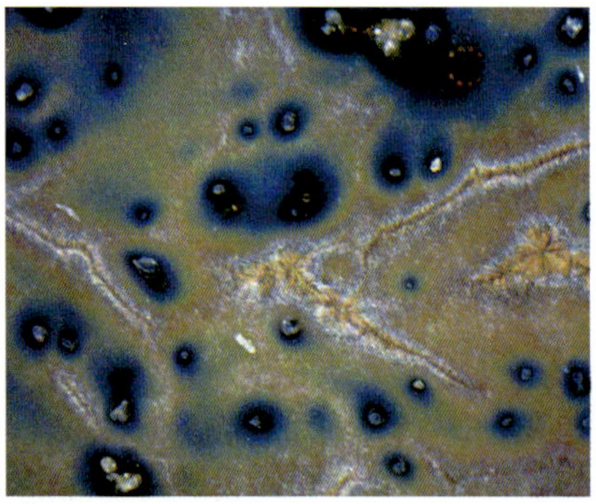
图6-5-3

图6-5-4

Section 5:

Commonly Seen Yuan Underglaze Blue Trace Combinations

Sections 1-4 of this chapter described the typical trace categories on YUB. We often discover that traces of the same or different categories often present in conjunction in one unit image. These combinations occur with certain regularity.

1. Flowing Mottle, Radiating Mottle, and Flowing Striae Combinations

Flowing Mottle, Radiating Mottle, and Flowing Striae are trace types with relatively high Iron and Manganese contents.

These mottles and striae are formed during the firing process according to differences in composition, density, and surface tensions. They can occur concurrently in pairs or all three simultaneously.

A. Flowing Mottle and Radiating Mottle Combinations

I. Two-dimensional Characteristics of Flowing Mottle and Radiating Mottle Combinations

a. Flowing Mottle and Radiating Mottle Combinations most commonly consist of combinations of iodine mottle, beach mottle, red series, yellow series, brown series, and black series (see pictures 6-5-1—6-5-15).

b. There is also a combination of iodine mottle, beach mottle, red series and yellow series radiating mottle (see picture 6-5-12).

c. There is also a combination of only iodine mottle and radiating mottle (see picture 6-5-15).

d. Beach and radiating mottle combinations are separated into two categories: 'Mottle within Mottle' and 'Mottle on Mottle'.

e. Mottle within Mottle: The surrounding beach mottle encompasses the radiating mottle with a glass phase border separating the two mottles (see pictures 6-5-1, 6-5-6 and 6-5-8).

f. Mottle on Mottle: Radiating and beach mottles overlap with no visible glass phase boundary (see pictures 6-5-2—6-5-4, 6-5-7, and 6-5-9—6-5-12).

g. It is also possible for 'mottle on mottle' and 'mottle within mottle' to occur simultaneously (see pictures 6-5-13 and 6-5-14).

h. The radiating mottle edge sometimes has a lined border (see pictures 6-5-3—6-5-5, 6-5-12, 6-5-13 and 6-5-15).

II. Three-dimensional Characteristics of Flowing Mottle and Radiating Mottle Combinations

a. Radiating mottle is higher than the beach mottle, with clear delineation.

b. If there is glass phase between beach mottle and radiating mottle, glass phase is smooth and clean.

See pictures 6-5-16 and 6-5-17, where 6-5-16 is the two-dimensional and 6-5-17 is the three-dimensional image of the same location.

The red series radiating mottle indicated by Arrow A in picture 6-5-16 is dark colored in 6-5-17, the color is lighter than surrounding beach mottle, and clearly delineated from the surrounding beach mottle with height discrepancy.

See pictures 6-5-18 and 6-5-19, where 6-5-18 is the two-dimensional and 6-5-19 is the three-dimensional images of the same location.

The brown series radiating mottle indicated by Arrow B in picture 6-5-18 is the lighter colored mottle in picture 6-5-19, and clearly delineated from the surrounding beach mottle with

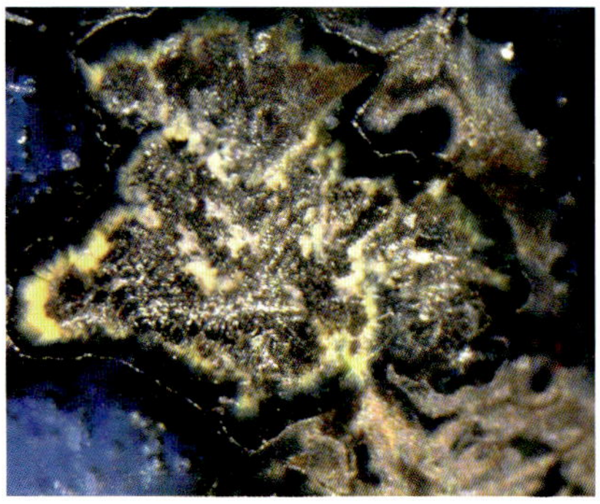
图6-5-5

图6-5-6

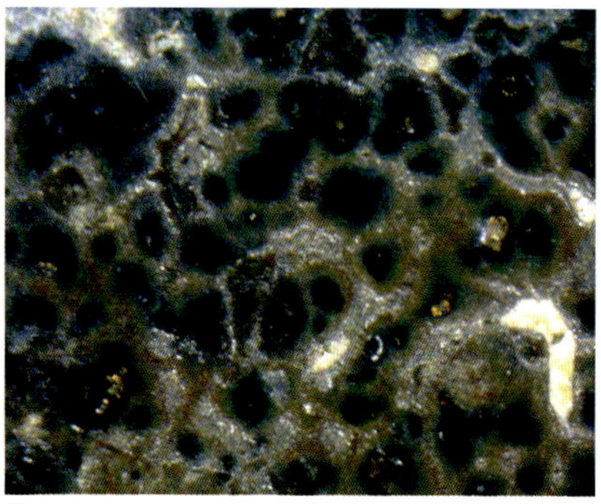
图6-5-7

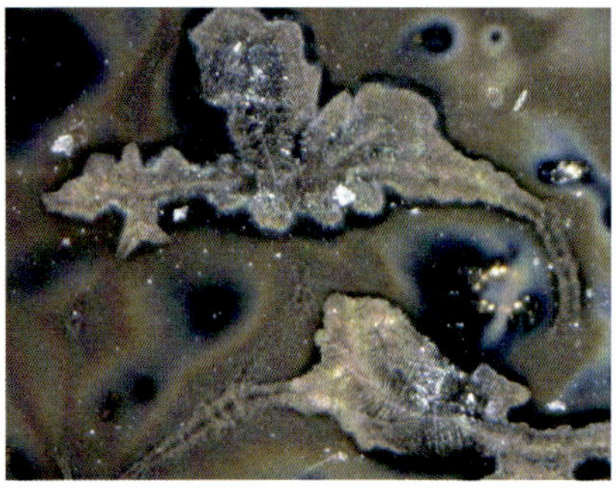
图6-5-8

图6-5-9

图6-5-10

图6-5-11

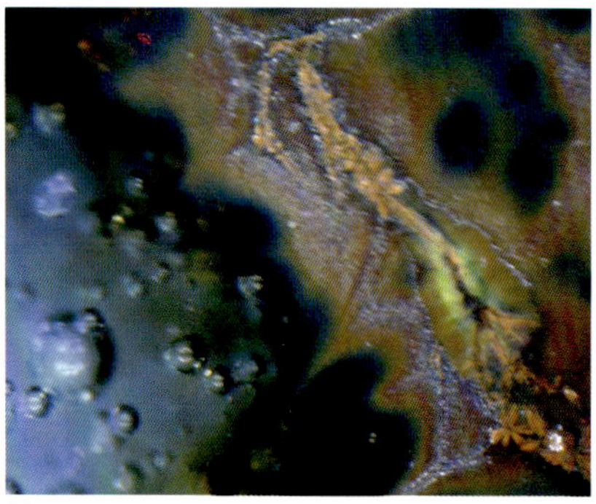
图6-5-12

图6-5-13

图6-5-14

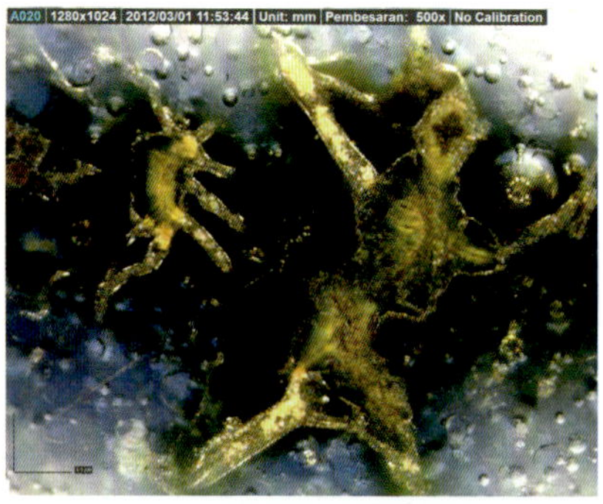

图6-5-15

height discrepancy.

See pictures 6-5-20 and 6-5-21, where 6-5-20 is the two-dimensional and 6-5-21 is the three-dimensional image of the same location.

The brown series radiating mottle indicated by Arrow C in picture 6-5-20 is the lighter colored mottle in picture 6-5-21, and clearly delineated from the surrounding beach mottle.

The dark glass phase area indicated by Arrow D in picture 6-5-20 is a lighter color in picture 6-5-21, the glaze surface is clearly depicted as smooth and clean.

See pictures 6-5-22 and 6-5-23, where 6-5-22 is the two-dimensional and 6-5-23 is the three-dimensional image of the same location.

The brown series radiating mottle indicated by Arrow E and beach mottle indicated by Arrow F in picture 6-5-22 are the lighter colored mottles in picture 6-5-23, Mottle E has a clearly depicted border with a relatively smooth surface and slight convexity. It is higher than the surrounding beach mottle and clearly delineated from it.

B. Flowing Mottle and Flowing Striae Combinations

I. Two-dimensional Characteristics of Flowing Mottle and Flowing Striae Combinations

a. Flowing shaped mottles often present with higher amounts of Iron and Manganese oxides towards the center of the mottle, and lower amounts towards the edges. According to these differences in levels of metal oxides, the flowing mottles often gradually transition into flowing striae at the edges. These striae are usually depressed striae (see pictures 6-5-24—6-5-27).

b. On some flowing mottles it is possible to observe flowing striae present as raised striae in the mottle center and depressed striae on the mottle edges (see pictures 6-5-28—6-5-30).

II. Three-dimensional Characteristics of Flowing Mottle and Flowing Striae Combinations

a. Depressed striae have a concave shape and extend lower into the glaze level than the surrounding beach mottle.

b. Raised striae have a convex shape and are higher than the surrounding beach mottle.

See pictures 6-5-31 and 6-5-32, where 6-5-31 is the two-dimensional and 6-5-32 is the three-dimensional image of the same location.

The light colored flowing striation indicated by Arrow A in picture 6-5-31 is the clearly depicted darker colored striation in picture 6-5-32. It is clearly delineated from the surrounding glaze surface and extends a certain depth in to the glaze level.

See pictures 6-5-33 and 6-5-34, where 6-5-33 is the two-dimensional and 6-5-34 is the three-dimensional image of the same location.

The dark colored flowing striation indicated by Arrow B in picture 6-5-33 is the clearly depicted lighter colored striation in picture 6-5-34. It has a convex shape, is clearly delineated, and has a distinct height discrepancy with the surrounding beach mottle.

C. Radiating Mottle and Flowing Striae Combinations

Two-dimensional Characteristics of Radiating Mottle and Flowing Striae Combinations

See pictures 6-5-35—6-5-42.

a. The edges of the radiating mottle (usually yellow or brown series) sometimes present with flowing striae.

b. Striae present as depressed type, and are most likely empty or needlepoint striae.

D. Flowing Mottle, Radiating Mottle, and Flowing Striae Combinations

Two-dimensional Characteristics of Flowing Mottle, Radiating Mottle, and Flowing Striae Combinations

a. Occurring with certain regularity: Beach mottle interiors can present with radiating mottles (red, brown, or black series) as well as raised and depressed striae, the edges gradually transform into depressed striae (see pictures

2. 流淌斑与放射斑组合三维特征

（1）放射斑所处位置较沙滩斑明显要高，彼此界线分明。

（2）沙滩斑与放射斑之间有玻璃相相隔，玻璃相光滑洁净。

见图6-5-16、图6-5-17，二者为同一器物同一位置图片，图6-5-16为二维图片，图6-5-17为三维图片。

图6-5-16中箭头A所指的红色系放射斑在图6-5-17中呈深色，成像清晰，颜色较周围沙滩斑浅，与周围沙滩斑有高度差。

见图6-5-18、图6-5-19，二者为同一器物同一位置图片，图6-5-18为二维图片，图6-5-19为三维图片。

图6-5-18中箭头B所指的褐色系放射斑在图6-5-19中呈浅色，成像清晰，与周围沙滩斑有高度差。

见图6-5-20、图6-5-21，二者为同一器物同一位置图片，图6-5-20为二维图片，图6-5-21为三维图片。

图6-5-20中箭头C所指的褐色系放射斑在图6-5-21中呈深色，可见清晰的轮廓，与周围玻璃相界线分明。图6-5-20中箭头D所指的黑色玻璃相在图6-5-21中呈浅色，成像清晰，表面光滑洁净。

见图6-5-22、图6-5-23，二者为同一器物同一位置图片，图6-5-22为二维图片，图6-5-23为三维图片。

图6-5-22中褐色系放射斑E及周围沙滩斑F在图6-5-23中均呈浅色。放射斑E轮廓清晰，表面较光滑，稍微凸起，高于周围沙滩斑，并与其界线分明。

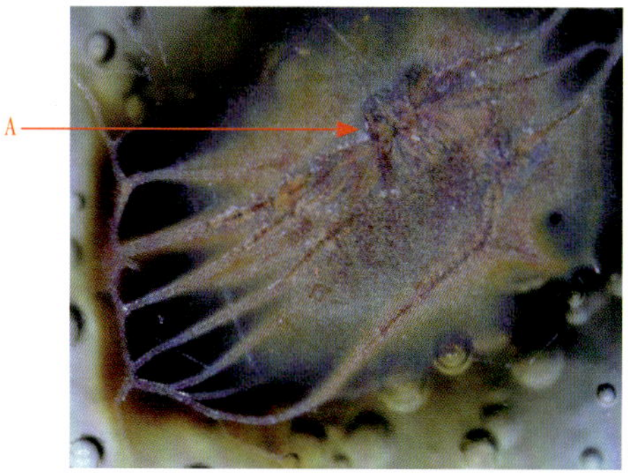

图6-5-16

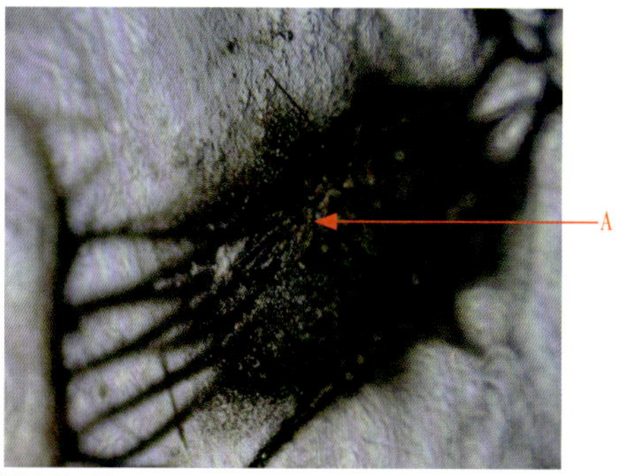

图6-5-17

图6-5-18

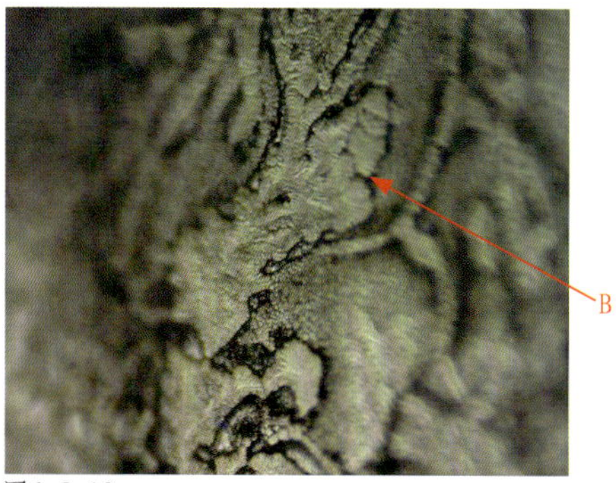

图6-5-19

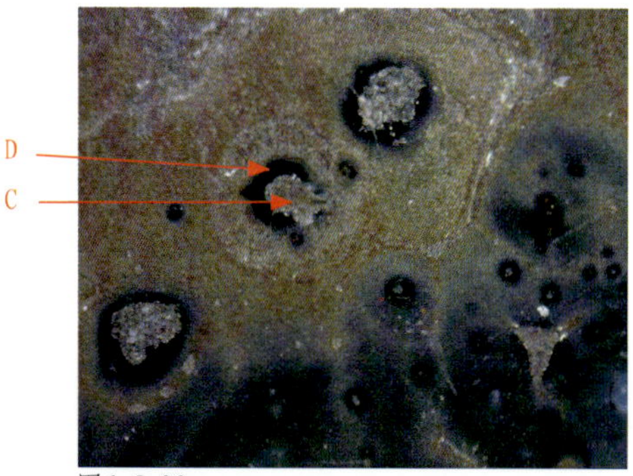

图6-5-20

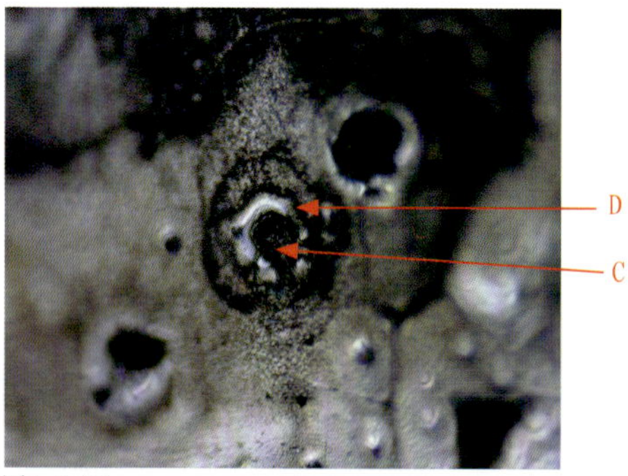

图6-5-21

6-5-43—6-5-46).

b. At times they present outside the constraints of regular distribution (see picture 6-5-49).

c. It is possible for the border of the radiating mottle or flowing striae to present with a thin lined border (see pictures 6-5-43, 6-5-44, 6-5-47, and 6-5-48).

2. Flowing Mottle and CO Striae or CO Type Pit Mottle Combinations

A. Flowing Mottle and CO Striae Combinations

I. Two-dimensional Characteristics of Flowing Mottle and CO Striae Combinations

See pictures 6-5-50 and 6-5-51.

a. CO striae often present among beach mottles in areas where the glass phase has not become covered by the beach mottle.

b. The striae are independent and clear and the surrounding beach mottle and glass phase are clearly delineated.

B. Flowing Mottle and CO Type Pit Mottle Combinations

Two-dimensional Characteristics of Flowing Mottle and CO Type Pit Mottle Combinations

a. CO type pit mottles or pit mottle groups often present among beach mottles in areas where the glass phase has not become covered by the beach mottle (see pictures 6-5-52, 6-5-53, 6-5-56, and 6-5-57).

b. Pit mottles present along the glass phase boundary edges of the beach mottle (see pictures 6-5-54—6-5-57).

c. Pit mottles retain clear delineation from the glass phase and the surrounding beach mottle (see pictures 6-5-52—6-5-57).

3. Flowing Mottle, Radiating Mottle, Flowing Striae, and Textured Bubble Combinations

Areas of flowing and radiating mottles and flowing striae have a higher tendency to present with textured bubbles. This is due to the higher amounts of Iron in the area and also because the mottle and glass phase transition area is a location of lowered structural stability. Additionally, areas surrounding bubbles have a tendency to collect Iron Oxides, and as Iron is chemically more active, it easily weathers, and textured bubbles more easily form in these areas.

A. Flowing Mottle and Textured Bubble Combinations

Two-dimensional Characteristics of Flowing Mottle and Textured Bubble Combinations

a. Combinations can present as an iodine mottle and textured bubble combination (see picture 6-5-58); or as an iodine mottle, beach mottle, and textured bubble combination (see pictures 6-5-59—6-5-61).

b. Bubbles can present as broken mouth (see pictures 6-5-58 and 6-5-60), or as unbroken mouth textured bubbles (see pictures 6-5-59 and 6-5-61).

B. Flowing Striae and Textured Bubble Combinations

Two-dimensional Characteristics of Flowing Striae and Textured Bubble Combinations

a. Most often present as depressed striae and textured bubble combination.

b. Bubbles can present as broken mouth (see pictures 6-5-62—6-5-66), or as unbroken mouth textured bubbles (see pictures 6-5-67 and 6-5-68).

c. Bubbles can occur in close proximity to (see pictures 6-5-62—6-5-64 and 6-5-68), or underneath the striae (see

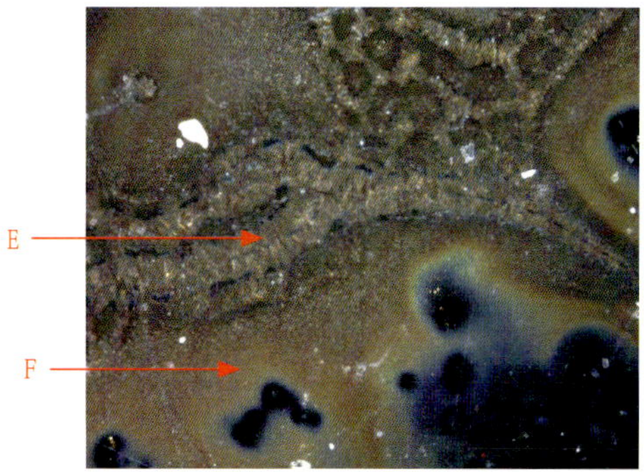

图6-5-22

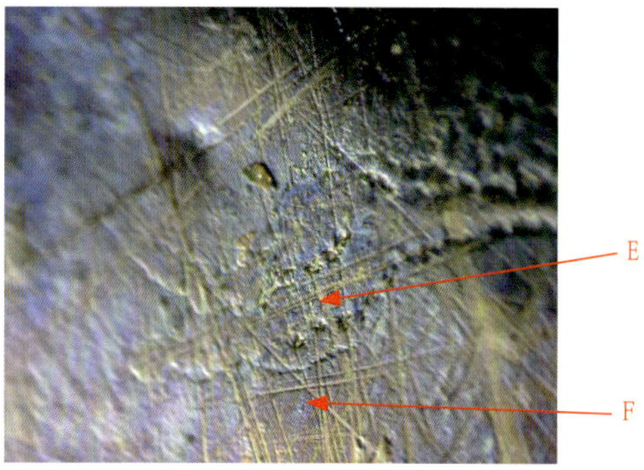

图6-5-23

（二）流淌斑与流淌纹组合

1. 流淌斑与流淌纹组合二维特征

（1）流淌铺展形成的沙滩斑，通常铁氧化物和锰氧化物的含量在斑块中间较高，边沿较低，随着这些金属氧化物含量的减少，沙滩斑边沿会逐渐过渡成为流淌纹，通常都以阴纹形式出现（见图6-5-24—图6-5-27）。

（2）有时沙滩斑上也会出现流淌纹、阴纹及阳纹形式（见图6-5-28—图6-5-30）。

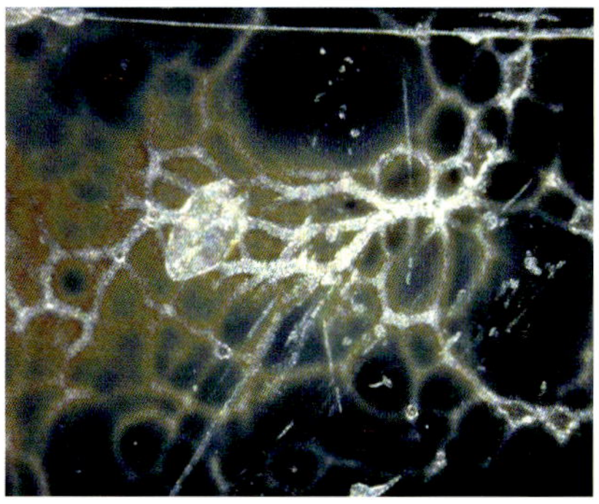

图6-5-24

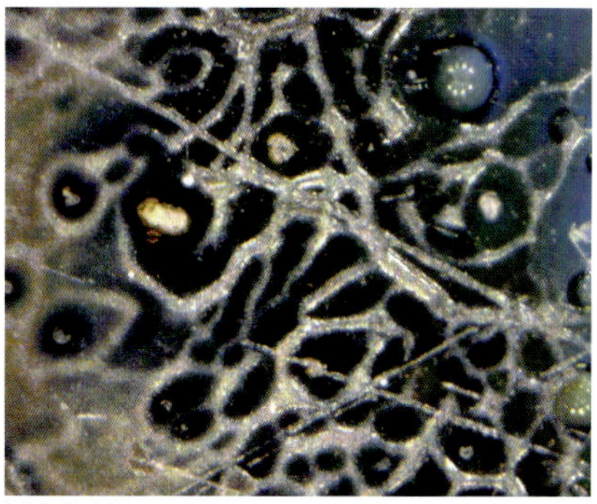

图6-5-25

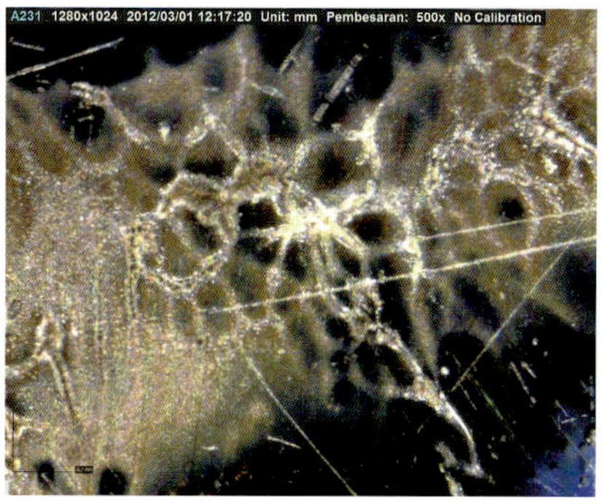

图6-5-26

图6-5-27

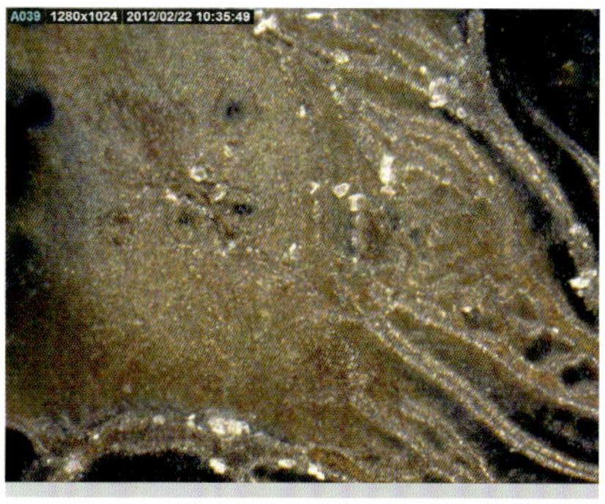

图6-5-28

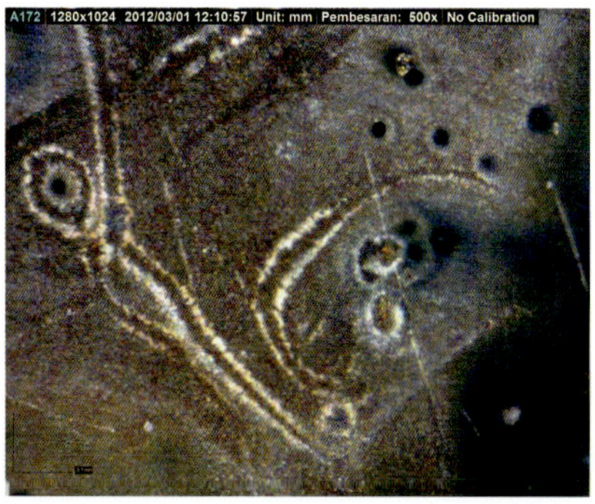

图6-5-29

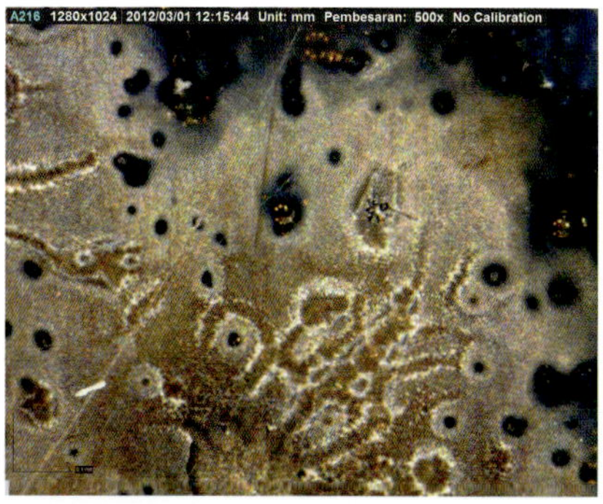

图6-5-30

pictures 6-5-65—6-5-67).

C. Flowing Mottle, Flowing Striae, and Textured Bubble Combinations

Two-dimensional Characteristics of Flowing Mottle, Flowing Striae and Textured Bubble Combinations

a. Most common combination is beach mottle, depressed or raised striae, and textured bubble.

b. Bubbles can present as broken mouth (see pictures 6-5-69—6-5-74), or as unbroken mouth textured bubbles (see picture 6-5-75).

c. Bubbles can occur in close proximity to (see pictures 6-5-69—6-5-71 and 6-5-73—6-5-75), or underneath the beach mottle and striae (see picture 6-5-72).

D. Flowing Mottle, Radiating Mottle, Flowing Striae and Textured Bubble Combinations

Two-dimensional Characteristics of Flowing Mottle, Radiating Mottle, Flowing Striae, and Textured Bubble Combinations

a. Most common combination is beach mottle, radiating mottle, depressed or raised striae, and textured bubble.

b. Bubbles can present as broken mouth (see pictures 6-5-76 and 6-5-77), or as unbroken mouth textured bubbles (see picture 6-5-78).

c. Bubbles can occur in close proximity to the beach mottle, radiating mottle and striae (see picture 6-5-78), or underneath the beach mottle (see pictures 6-5-76 and 6-5-77).

4. CO Striae, CO Type Pit Mottle, Color Change Bubble, and Textured Bubble Combinations

CO striae and CO type pit mottles occur in areas of relatively low stability on the glaze surface, and can cause channels between the glaze-level bubbles and the external environment. Foreign materials can pass through these channels into the bubbles and cause color or texture change within the bubbles.

A. CO Striae, CO Type Pit Mottle, and Color Change Bubble Combinations

Two-dimensional Characteristics of CO Striae, CO Type Pit Mottle, and Color Change Bubble Combinations

a. In areas where color change bubbles occur in conjunction with CO striae, CO type pit mottles, and pit mottle groups, the glaze surface traces (CO striae, pits, and pit groups) are clearly delineated and distinct.

b. Color change bubbles can present as semi-changed (see pictures 6-5-79—6-5-82), fully-changed (see picture 6-5-83), or in color change bubble groups (see picture 6-5-84).

c. At times the glaze level traces (CO striae, pits, and pit groups) present with coloration similar to the bubbles (see picture 6-5-79), dissimilar (see picture 6-5-82), and sometimes the coloration is not distinct (see pictures 6-5-80, 6-5-81, 6-5-83, and 6-5-84).

B. CO Striae, CO Type Pit Mottle, and Textured Bubble Combinations

I. Two-dimensional Characteristics of CO Striae, CO Type Pit Mottle, and Textured Bubble Combinations

a. In areas where textured bubbles occur in conjunction with CO striae, CO type pit mottles, and pit mottle groups, the glaze surface traces (CO striae, pits, and pit groups) are clearly delineated and distinct.

b. Textured bubbles can present as unbroken mouthed (see pictures 6-5-85—6-5-90), or as broken mouth textured bubbles (see pictures 6-5-91—6-5-95).

c. At times the glaze level traces (CO striae, pits, and pit groups) present with coloration similar to the bubbles (see pictures 6-5-86, 6-5-88, and 6-5-94), dissimilar (see picture 6-5-85), and sometimes the coloration is not distinct (see pictures 6-5-90, 6-5-91, and 6-5-95).

II. Three-dimensional Characteristics of CO Type Pit Mottle and Textured Bubble Combinations

a. CO type pit mottles are clear and independent.

2. 流淌斑与流淌纹组合三维特征

（1）阴纹呈明显凹槽，低于周围沙滩斑。

（2）阳纹明显凸起，高于周围沙滩斑。

见图6-5-31、图6-5-32，二者为同一器物同一位置图片，图6-5-31为二维图片，图6-5-33为三维图片。

图6-5-31中箭头A所指的浅色流淌纹在图6-5-32中呈深色，成像清晰，纹路呈凹陷状，进入釉层一定深度，与周围釉表面界线分明。

见图6-5-33、图6-5-34，二者为同一器物同一位置图片，图6-5-33为二维图片，图6-5-34为三维图片。

图6-5-33中箭头B所指的深色流淌纹在图6-5-34中呈浅色，成像清晰，纹路凸起，高于周围沙滩斑，纹路与周围沙滩斑界线分明。

（三）放射斑与流淌纹组合

放射斑与流淌纹组合二维特征

见图6-5-35—图6-5-42。

（1）放射斑（主要是黄色系与褐色系放射斑）边沿有时会出现流淌纹。

（2）流淌纹通常都以阴纹形式出现，既有中空型阴纹，也有针眼型阴纹。

图6-5-31

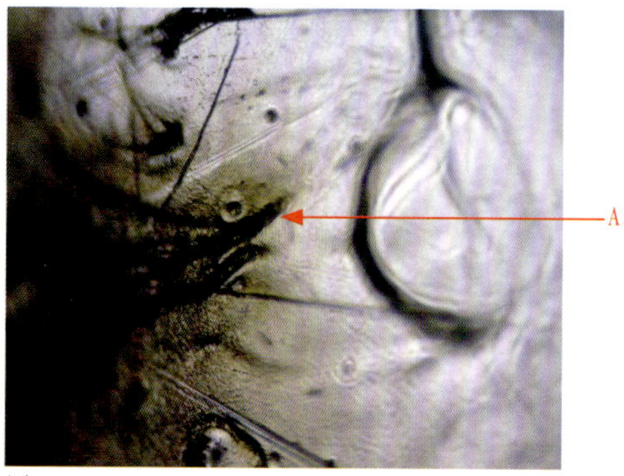

图6-5-32

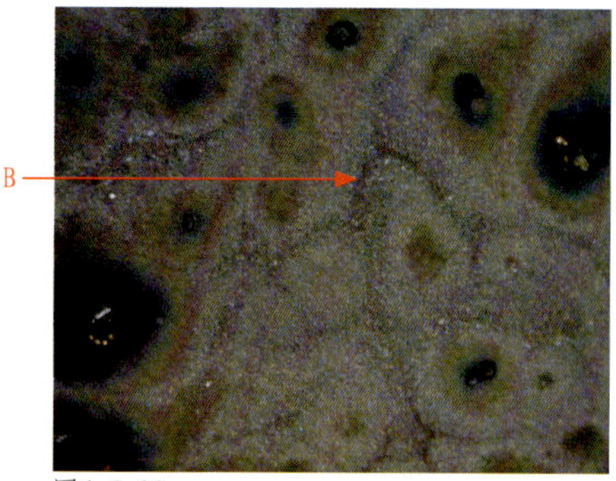

图6-5-33

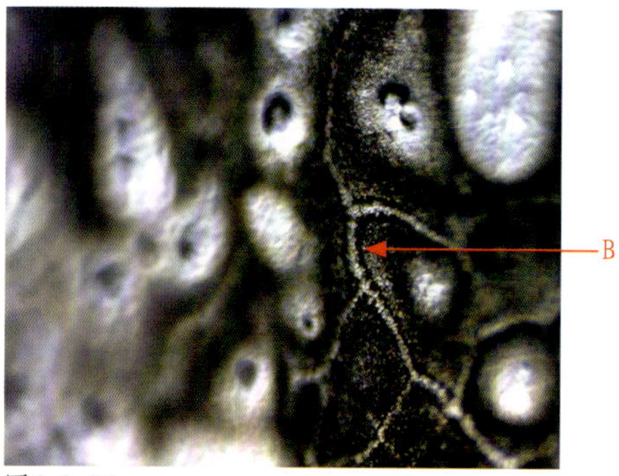

图6-5-34

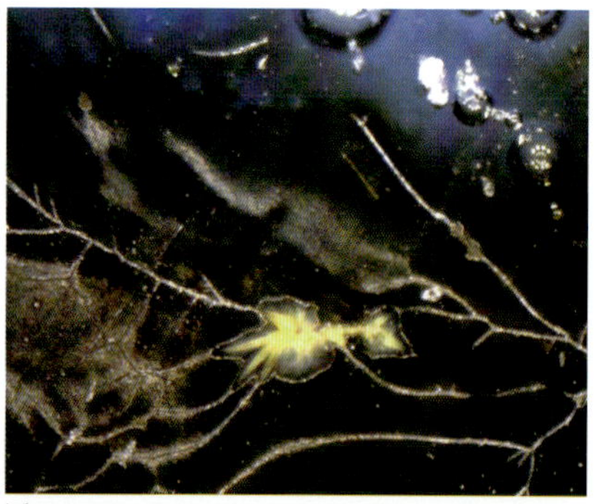
图6-5-35

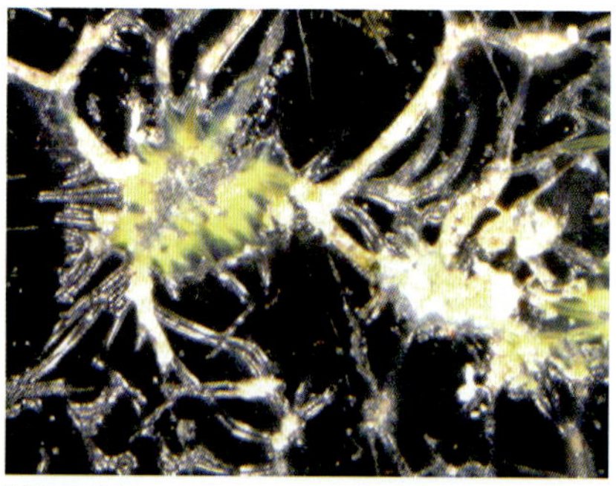
图6-5-36

b. The mouth of the bubbles, pits, and surrounding glass phase are clearly delineated.

See pictures 6-5-96 and 6-5-97, where 6-5-96 is the two-dimensional and 6-5-97 is the three-dimensional image of the same location.

The unbroken mouth textured bubble indicated by Arrow A in picture 6-5-96 is not visible but indicated by a red circle in picture 6-5-97.

The white pit mottle indicated by Arrow B in picture 6-5-96 is clearly depicted as a darker colored pit in picture 6-5-97. The pit mottle is independent and is clearly delineated form the surrounding glaze surface.

See pictures 6-5-98 and 6-5-99, where 6-5-98 is the two-dimensional and 6-5-99 is the three-dimensional image of the same location.

The broken mouth textured bubble indicated by ArrowC in picture 6-5-98 is not visible but indicated by a red circle in picture 6-5-99.

The bubble mouth indicated by Arrow D in picture 6-5-98 is clearly depicted as a rounded, smooth, and darker colored opening in picture 6-5-99.

The white pit mottle indicated by Arrow E in picture 6-5-98 is clearly depicted as a darker colored pit in picture 6-5-99. The pit mottle is independent and is clearly delineated form the surrounding glass phase and bubble mouth.

图6-5-37

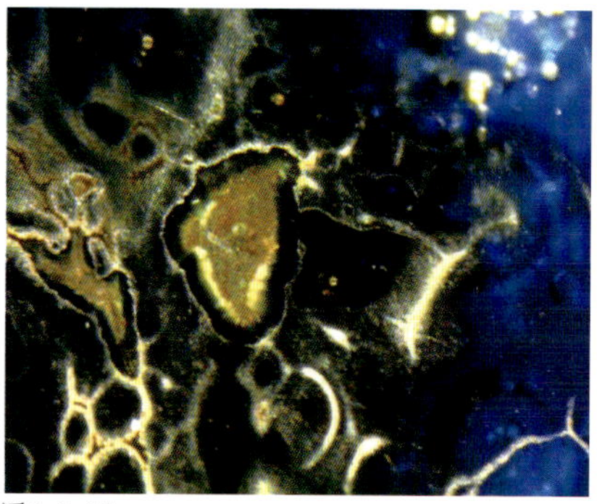

图6-5-38

图6-5-39

图6-5-40

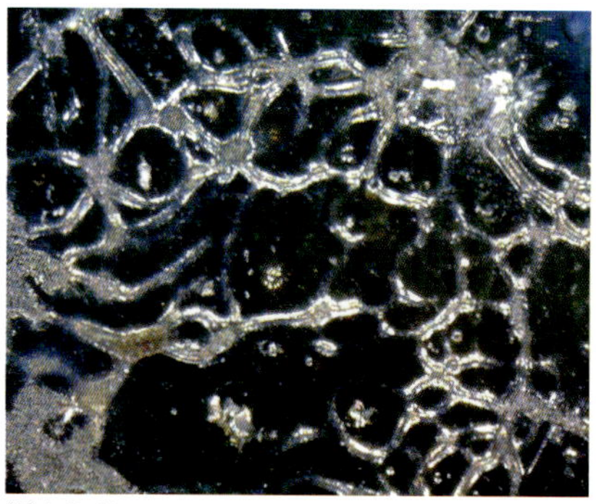

图6-5-41

图6-5-42

（四） 流淌斑、放射斑与流淌纹组合

流淌斑、放射斑与流淌纹组合二维特征

（1）流淌斑、放射斑与流淌纹三者之间分布有一定的规律：沙滩斑上分布有放射斑（主要有红色系、褐色系及黑色系）或阴纹、阳纹，到了沙滩斑边沿会逐渐过渡成为阴纹（见图6-5-43—图6-5-46）。

（2）有时组合中的各迹型分布不一定遵循此规律（见图6-5-49）。

（3）有时放射斑或流淌纹外沿会有一条包边（见图6-5-43、图6-5-44、图6-5-47、图6-5-48）。

二、流淌斑与C形、O形纹或CO型坑点斑组合

（一）流淌斑与C形、O形纹组合

流淌斑与C形、O形纹组合二维特征

见图6-5-50、图6-5-51。

（1）C形、O形纹通常出现在位于沙滩斑中心却又未被沙滩斑覆盖的玻璃相上。

（2）纹路独立清晰，与周围玻璃相与沙滩斑之间的界线都比较分明。

图6-5-43

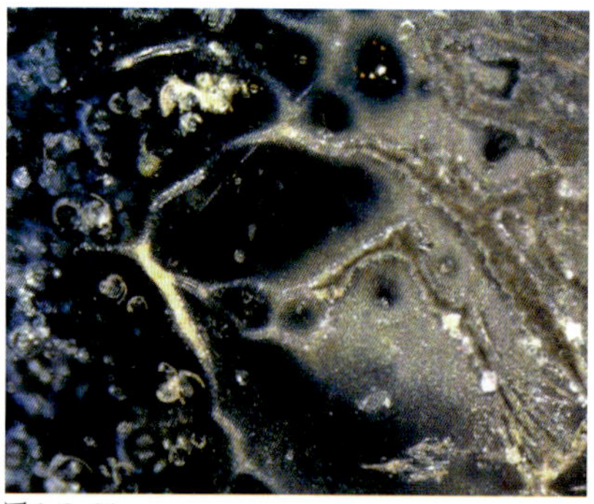

图6-5-44

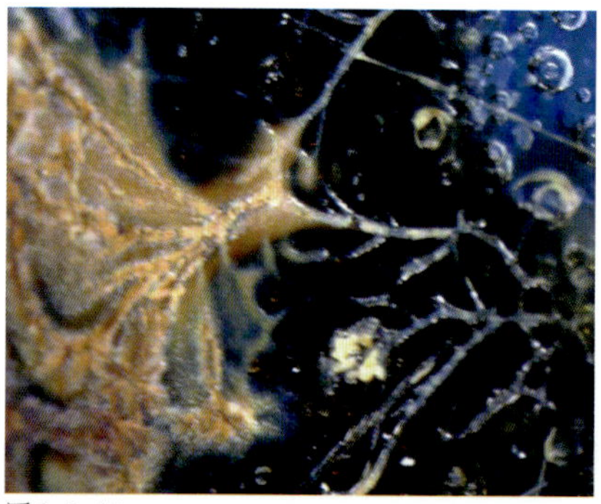

图6-5-45

图6-5-46

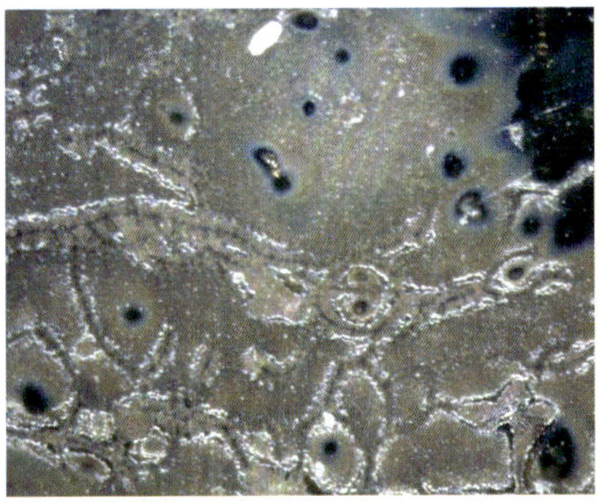
图6-5-47

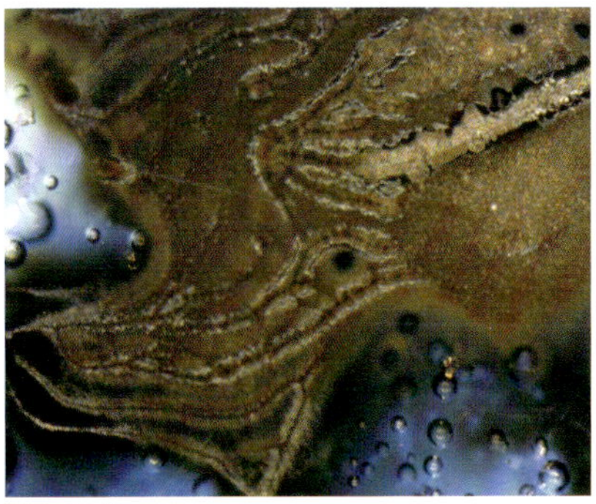
图6-5-48

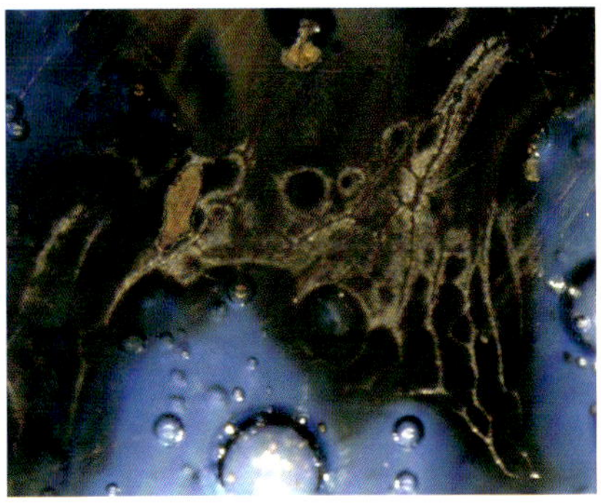
图6-5-49

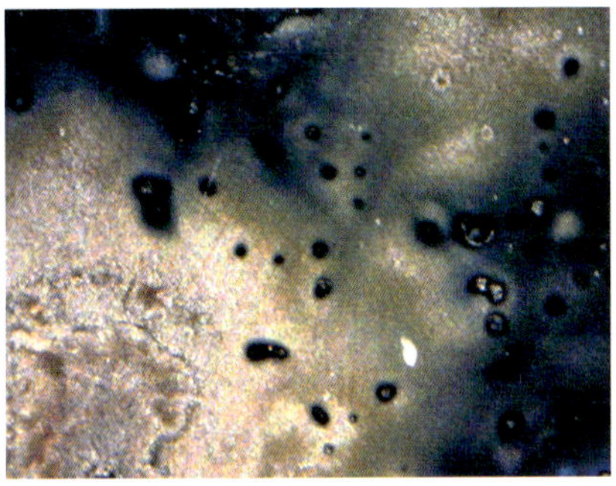
图6-5-50

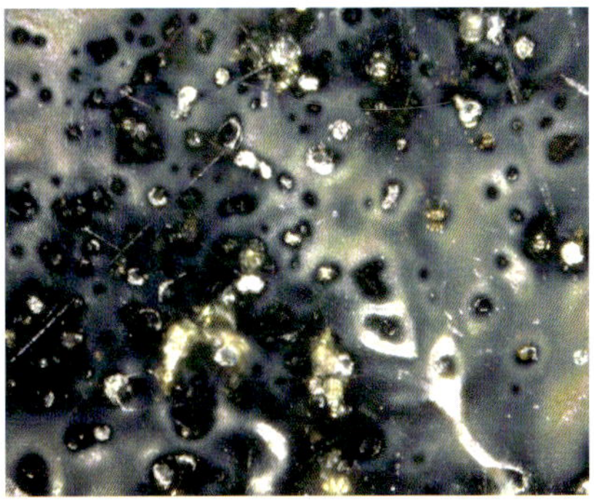
图6-5-51

（二）流淌斑与CO型坑点斑组合

流淌斑与CO型坑点斑组合二维特征

（1）CO型坑点斑或CO型坑点斑群通常出现在位于沙滩斑中心却又未被沙滩斑覆盖的玻璃相上（见图6-5-52、图6-5-53、图6-5-56、图6-5-57）。

（2）CO型坑点斑或CO型坑点斑群也会出现在沙滩斑邻近的玻璃相上（见图6-5-54—图6-5-57）。

（3）坑点斑与周围玻璃相与沙滩斑之间的界线分明（见图6-5-52—图6-5-57）。

三、流淌斑、放射斑、流淌纹与壁变泡组合

流淌斑、放射斑及流淌纹所在处附近出现壁变泡的概率较高，这是因为流淌斑所在处含铁较高，斑块与玻璃相结合处组织结构稳定性较差，气泡附近也易积聚铁氧化物，而铁元素的物理化学性质比较活跃，易于风化，所以易形成壁变泡。

（一）流淌斑与壁变泡组合

流淌斑与壁变泡组合二维特征

（1）流淌斑与壁变泡的组合可以是碘酒斑单独与壁变泡组合（见图6-5-58），也可以是碘酒斑、沙滩斑与壁变泡组合（见图6-5-59—图6-5-61）。

（2）出现的壁变泡有破口壁变泡（见图6-5-58、图6-5-60），也有非破口壁变泡（见图6-5-59、图6-5-61）。

图6-5-52

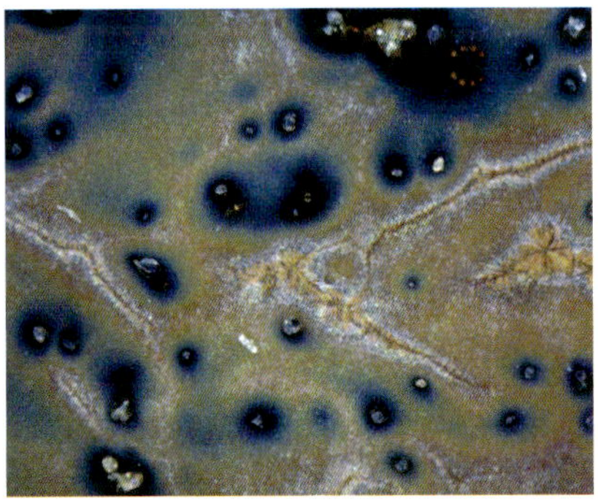
图6-5-53

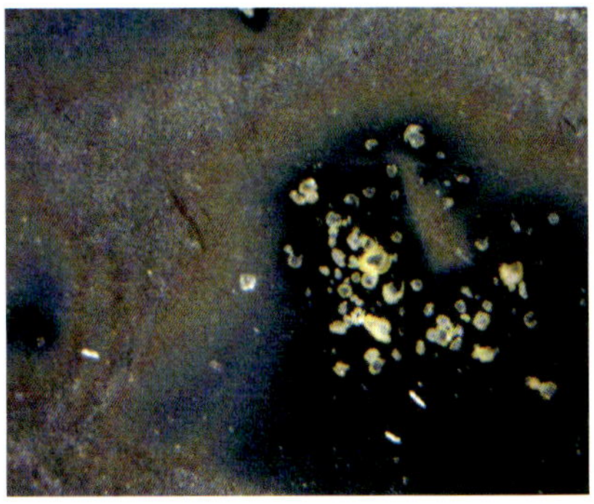
图6-5-54（T21）

图6-5-55（T34）

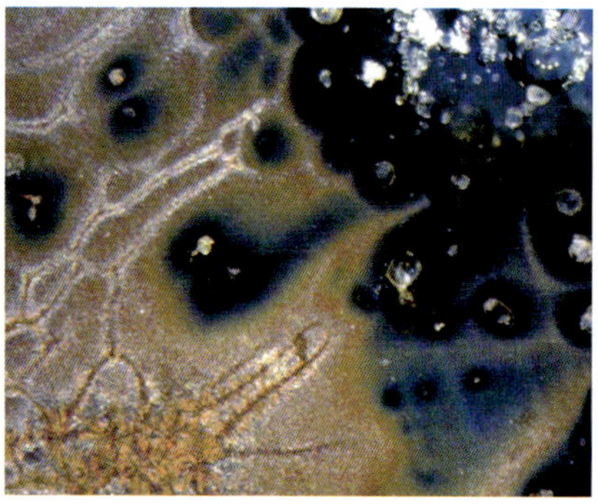
图6-5-56

图6-5-57

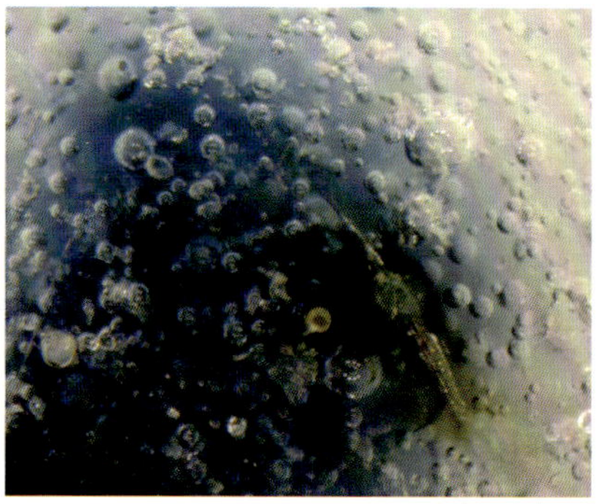
图6-5-58

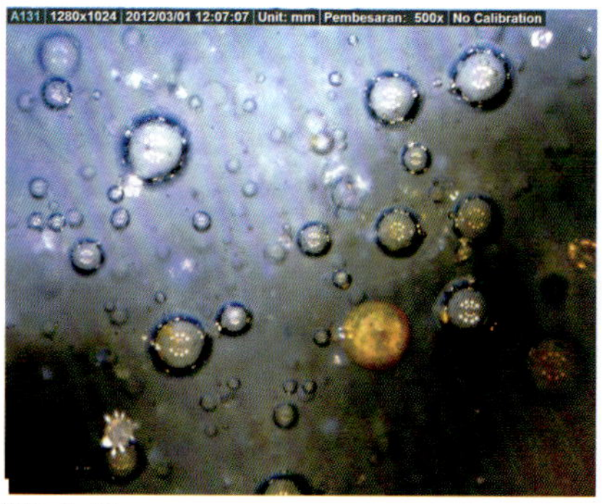

图6-5-59

图6-5-61

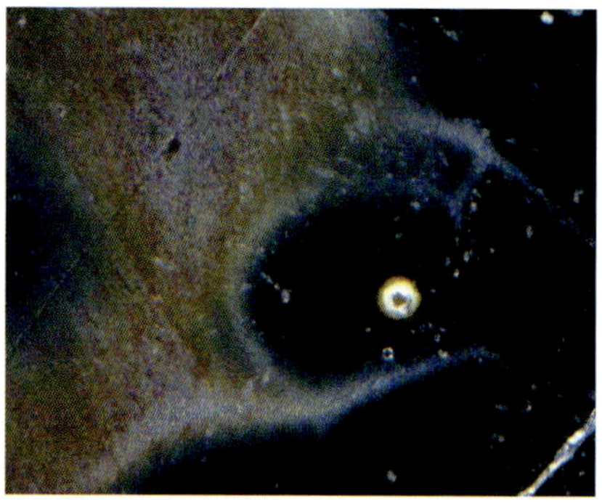
图6-5-60

（二）流淌纹与壁变泡组合

流淌纹与壁变泡组合二维特征

（1）流淌纹与壁变泡的组合主要是阴纹与壁变泡的组合。

（2）出现的壁变泡有破口壁变泡（见图6-5-62—图6-5-66），也有非破口壁变泡（见图6-5-67、图6-5-68）。

（3）壁变泡可以出现在纹路邻近的釉层中（见图6-5-62—图6-5-64、图6-5-68），也可以出现在纹路下方（见图6-5-65—图6-5-67）。

（三）流淌斑、流淌纹与壁变泡组合

流淌斑、流淌纹与壁变泡组合二维特征

（1）流淌斑、流淌纹与壁变泡的组合主要是沙滩斑、阴纹或阳纹与壁变泡的组合。

（2）出现的壁变泡有破口壁变泡（见图6-5-69—图6-5-74），也有非破口壁变泡（见图6-5-75）。

（3）壁变泡可以出现在沙滩斑、流淌纹邻近的釉层中（见图6-5-69—图6-5-71、图6-5-73—图6-5-75），也可以出现在沙滩斑下方（见图6-5-72）。

（四）流淌斑、放射斑、流淌纹与壁变泡组合

流淌斑、放射斑、流淌纹与壁变泡组合二维特征

（1）流淌斑、放射斑、流淌纹与壁变泡的组合主要是沙滩斑、放射斑、阴纹或阳纹与壁变泡的组合。

（2）出现的壁变泡有破口壁变泡（见图6-5-76、图6-5-77），也有非破口壁变泡（见图6-5-78）。

（3）壁变泡可以出现在沙滩斑、放射斑及流淌纹邻近的釉层中（见图6-5-78），也可以出现在沙滩斑下方（见图6-5-76、图6-5-77）。

图6-5-62

图6-5-63

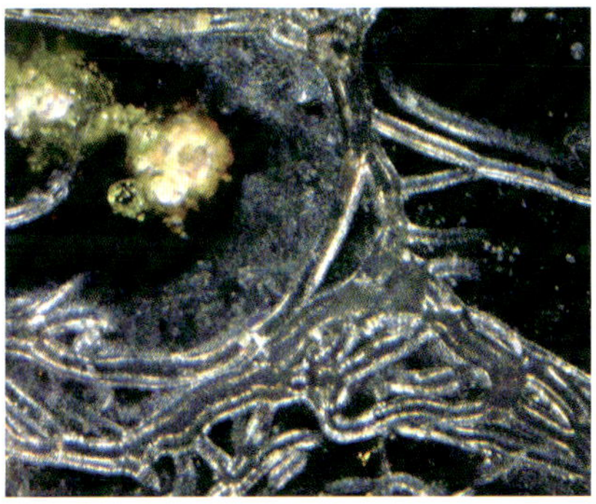
图6-5-64

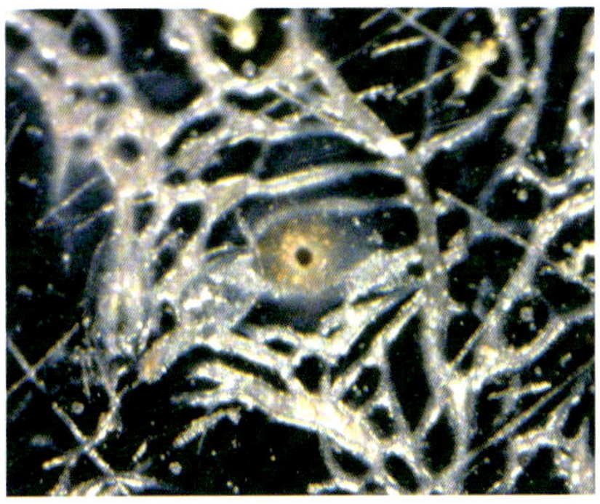
图6-5-65

图6-5-66

图6-5-67

图6-5-68

图6-5-69

图6-5-70

图6-5-71

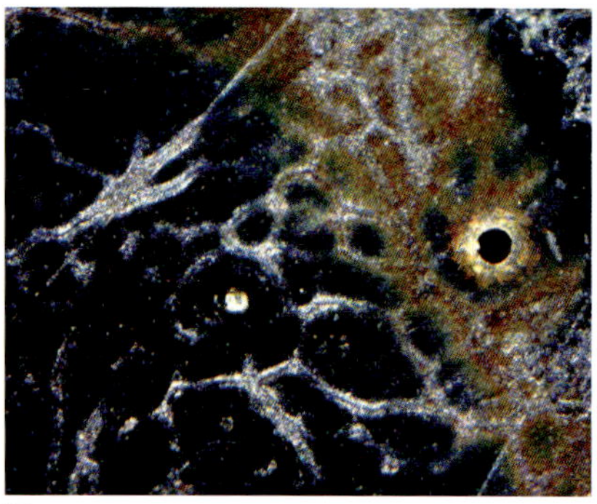
图6-5-72

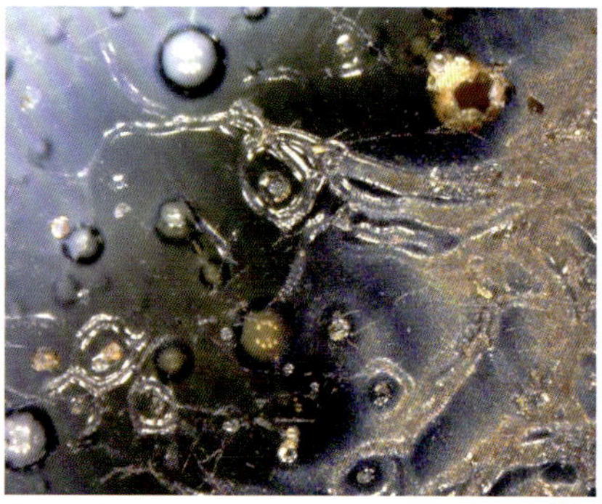
图6-5-73

图6-5-74

图6-5-75

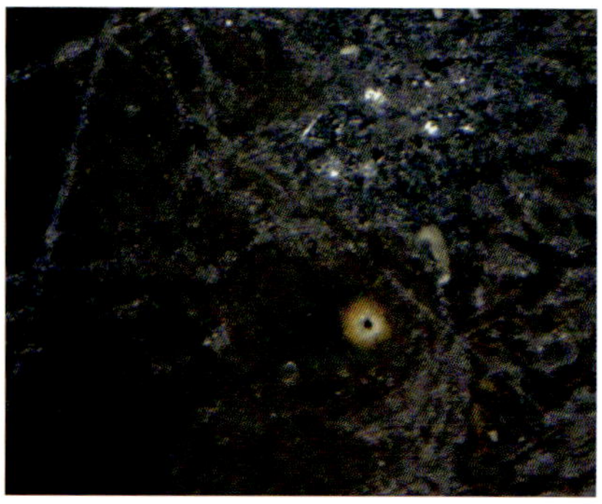
图6-5-76

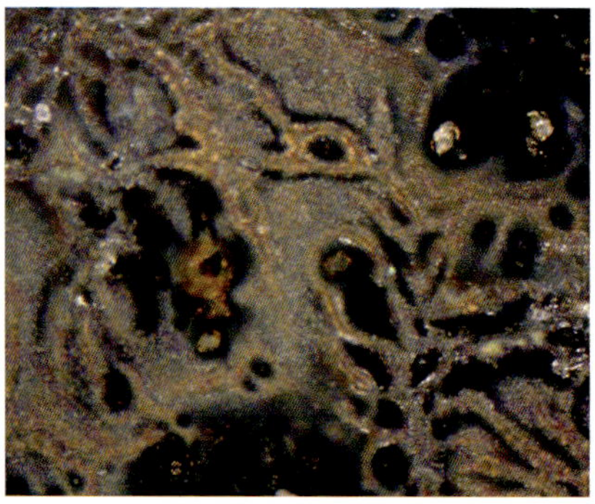
图6-5-77

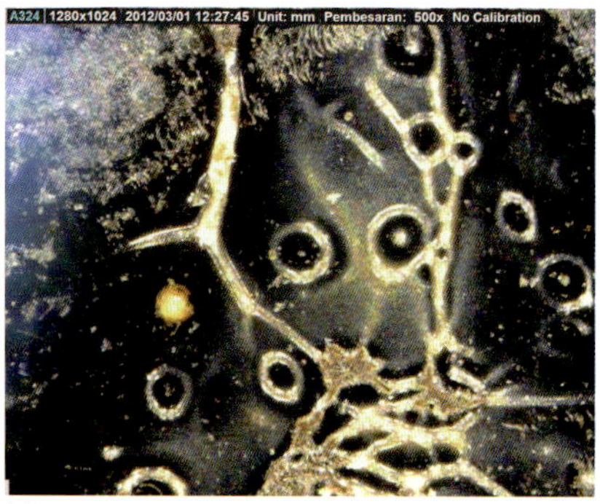

图6-5-78

四、C形、O形纹及CO型坑点斑与色变泡、壁变泡的组合

C形、O形纹及CO型坑点斑所在处组织结构稳定性较差，它们所处的釉表面会成为外界与釉层中气泡连接的通道，外界物质通过通道进入气泡，造成气泡颜色变化或质地变化。

（一） C形、O形纹及CO型坑点斑与色变泡组合

C形、O形纹及CO型坑点斑与色变泡组合二维特征

（1）C形、O形纹及CO型坑点斑所在处的釉层中出现色变泡，釉表面C形、O形纹及CO型坑点斑或CO型坑点斑群的轮廓还清晰可见。

（2）釉层中的色变泡既有局变泡（见图6-5-79—图6-5-82），也有全变泡（见图6-5-83），还有连环色变泡（见图6-5-84）。

（3）有时釉表面的C形、O形纹及CO型坑点斑或CO型坑点斑群也有颜色改变，颜色与色变泡颜色相近（见图6-5-79），也有的有色差（见图6-5-82），有时变色不明显（见图6-5-80、图6-5-81、图6-5-83、图6-5-84）。

（二）C形、O形纹及CO型坑点斑与壁变泡组合

1. C形、O形纹及CO型坑点斑与壁变泡组合二维特征

（1）C形、O形纹及CO型坑点斑所在处的釉层中出现壁变泡，釉表面C形、O形纹及CO型坑点斑或CO型坑点斑群的轮廓还清晰可见。

（2）釉层中的壁变泡既有非破口壁变泡（见图6-5-85—图6-5-90），也有破口壁变泡（见图6-5-91—图6-5-95）。

（3）有时釉表面的C形、O形纹及CO型坑点斑或CO型坑点斑群也有颜色改变，颜色与壁变泡颜色相近（见图6-5-86、图6-5-88、图6-5-94），也有的有色差（见图6-5-85），有时变色不明显（见图6-5-90、图6-5-91、图6-5-95）。

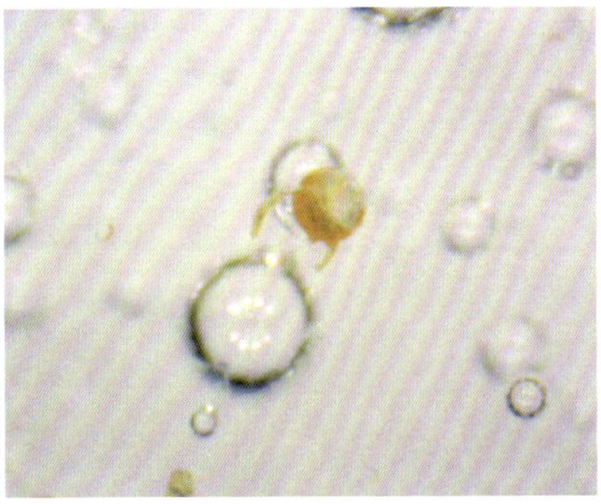

图6-5-79

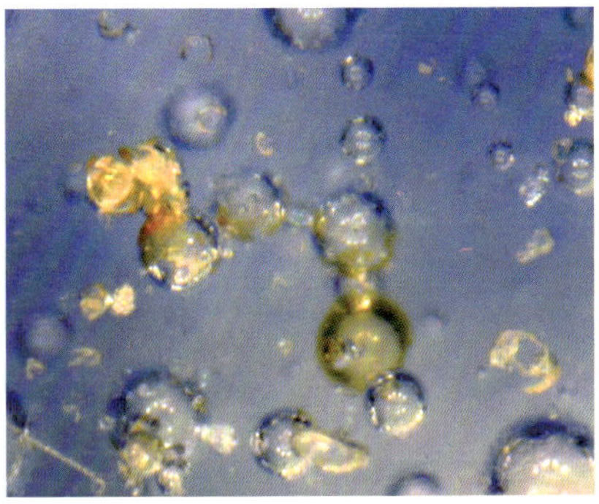

图6-5-80

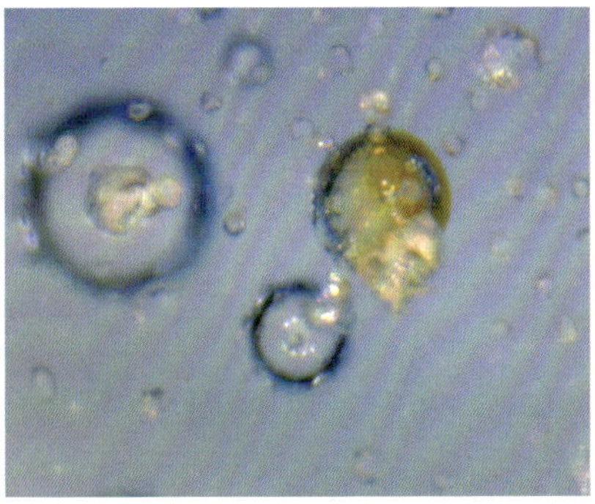

图6-5-81

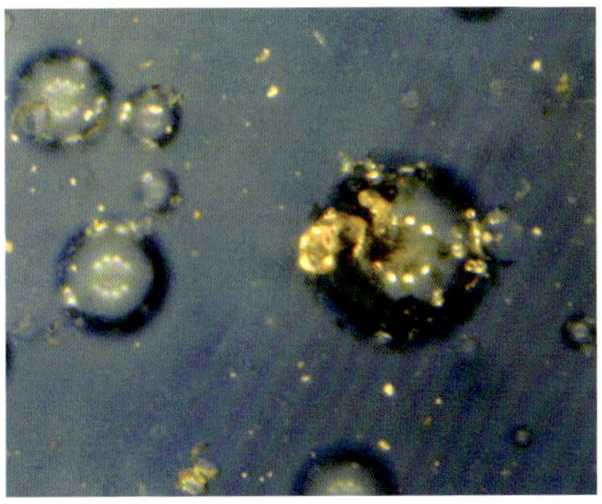

图6-5-82

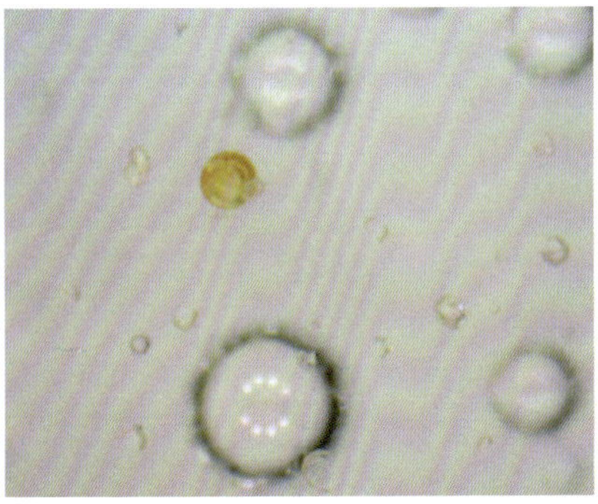

图6-5-83

图6-5-84

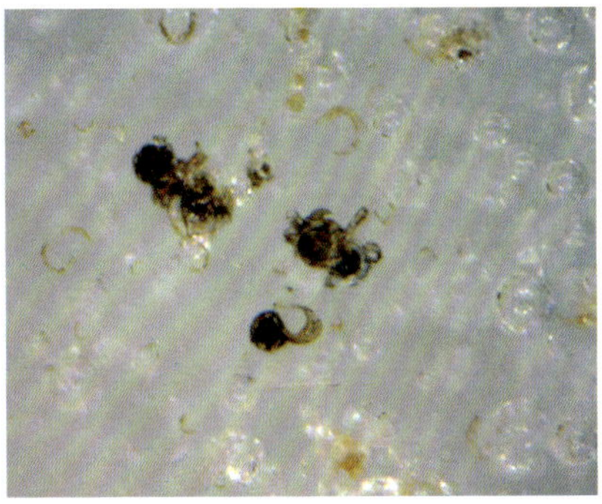

图6-5-85

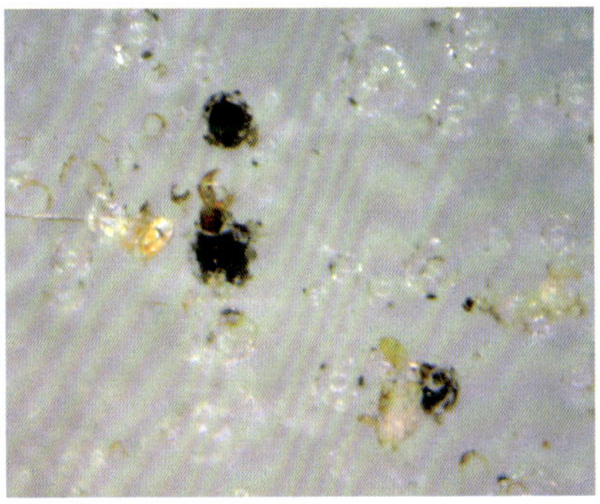

图6-5-86

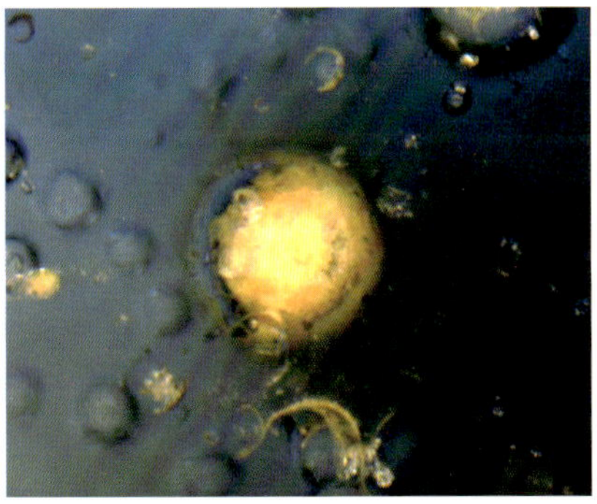

图6-5-87

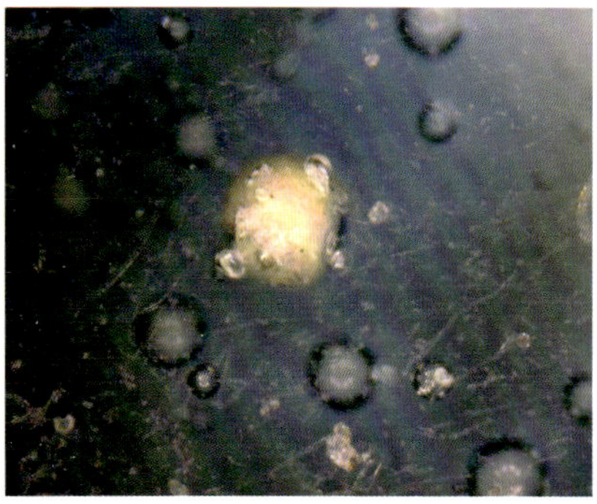
图6-5-88

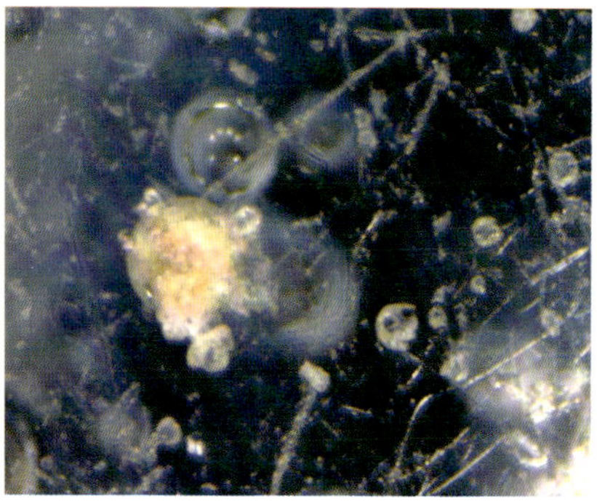
图6-5-89

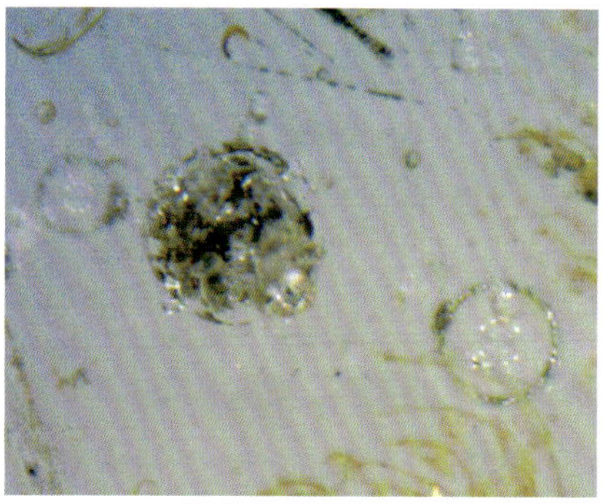
图6-5-90

图6-5-91

图6-5-92

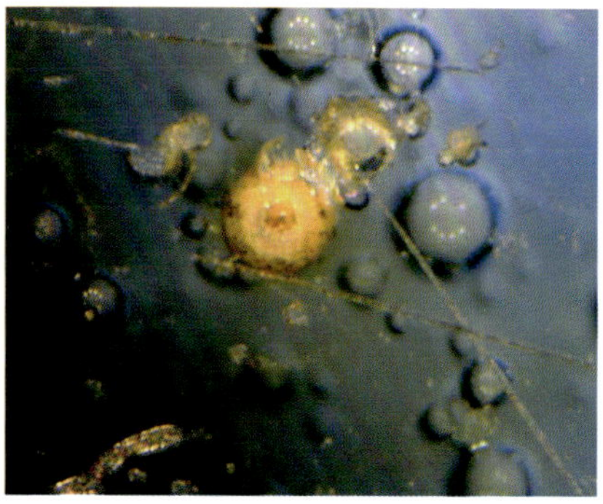
图6-5-93

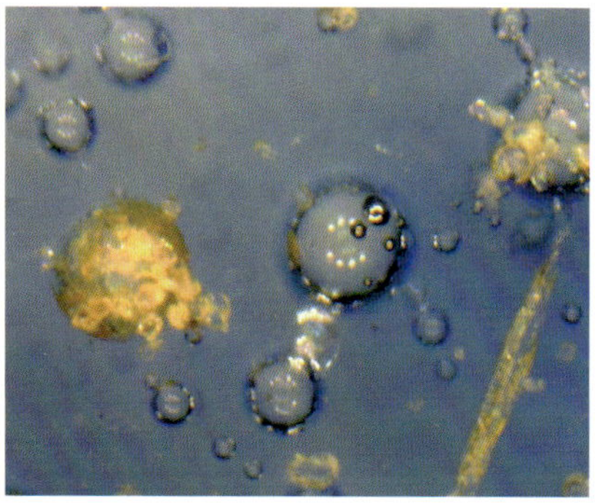
图6-5-94

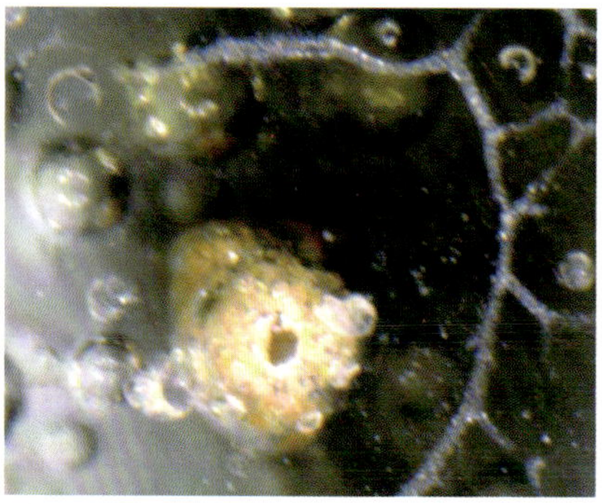
图6-5-95

2. CO型坑点斑与壁变泡组合三维特征

（1）CO型坑点斑独立清晰。

（2）壁变泡破口与坑点斑及周围玻璃相之间界线分明。

见图6-5-96、图6-5-97，二者为同一器物同一位置图片，图6-5-96为二维图片，图6-5-97为三维图片。

图6-5-96中的非破口壁变泡A在图6-5-97中位于红圈釉下处，不可见。图6-5-96中箭头B所指的白色坑点斑在图6-5-97中呈深色，成像清晰，坑点斑独立存在，与周围玻璃相界线分明。

见图6-5-98、图6-5-99，二者同一器物同一位置图片，图6-5-98为二维图片，图6-5-99为三维图片。

图6-5-98中破口壁变泡C在图6-5-99中位于红圈釉下处，不可见。图6-5-98中箭头D所指的破口在图6-5-99中呈深色，成像清晰，破口圆滑。图6-5-98中箭头E所指的白色坑点斑在图6-5-99中呈深色，独立存在，与气泡破口及周围玻璃相界线分明。

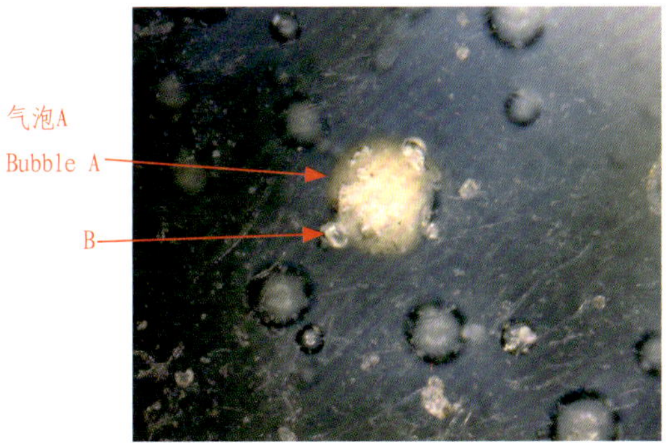

图6-5-96

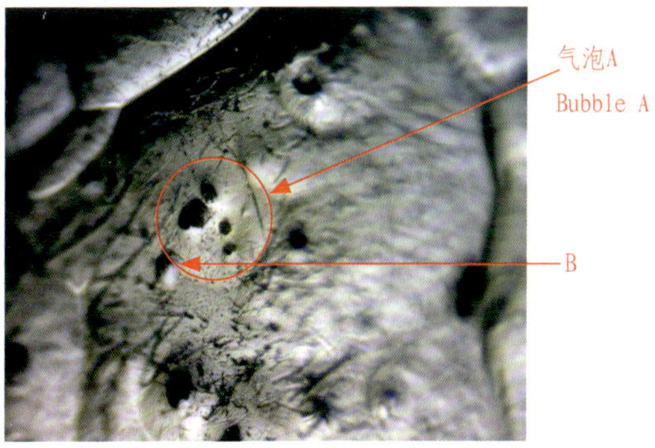

图6-5-97

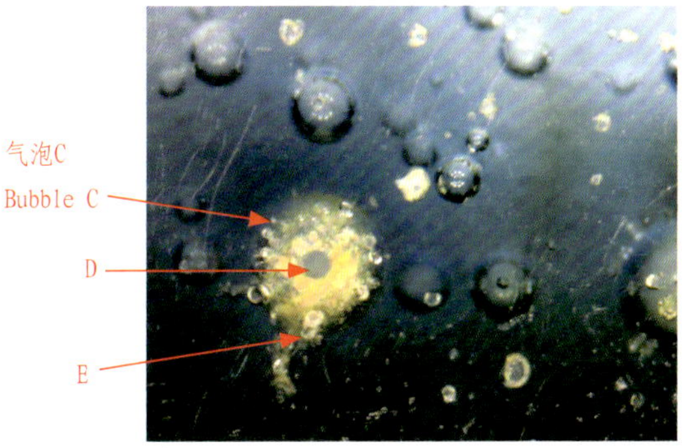

图6-5-98

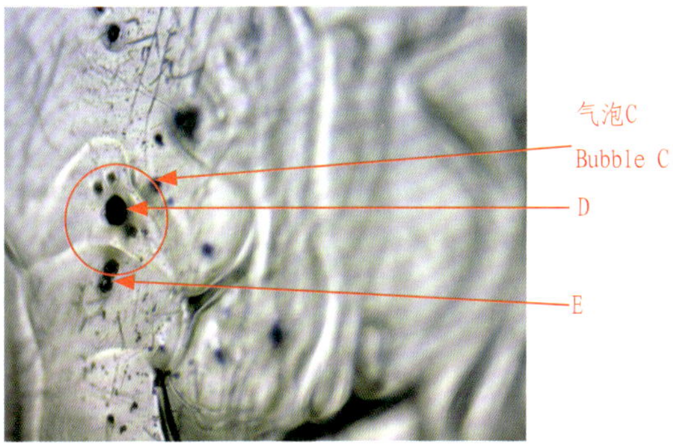

图6-5-99

第七章

陶瓷迹型原理及规律

阅读提示：

本章阐述了陶瓷迹型的两个基本原理、七大规律以及其出现位置的合理性和变化的同步性。

主要论述问题：

1. 陶瓷迹型的基本原理有哪两个？
2. 陶瓷迹型有哪七大规律？
3. 陶瓷迹型出现位置的合理性和变化的同步性是怎样的？

Chapter 7

Principles and Laws of Ceramic Traces

Text Note:

This chapter explains the two principles and seven laws of ceramic traces, as well as trace location rationality and change congruency.

第一节 陶瓷迹型基本原理

一、陶瓷迹型量变原理

陶瓷迹型的量变原理是：陶瓷迹型的风化强度是在绝对风化时间内，以缓慢、渐变的形式形成的（其中包含无数个在相对风化时间内形成的风化强度），具有细腻、精致、分明等特征。

量变原理的具体迹型表现见本章第二节陶瓷迹型量变规律部分。

二、陶瓷迹型时间过程性原理

陶瓷迹型的时间过程性原理是：在绝对风化时间内，陶瓷迹型特征反映了其生成、发展的时间过程。以下是元青花迹型反映陶瓷迹型时间过程性原理的举例说明：

（一）沙滩斑与周围玻璃相的高度差

单位图片中的沙滩斑呈凹陷状，与玻璃相圆孔有明显高度差。

（二）CO纹与CO型坑点斑伴生现象

单位图片中CO纹、CO型坑点斑及坑点斑群同时存在，彼此界线分明。

Section 1:

The Principles of Ceramic Traces

1. The Quantitative Change Principle

The Quantitative Change Principle states: The weathering severity of ceramic traces occurs within an absolute weathering time. It is a slow, gradual formation that is the accumulation of weathering severities formed during innumerable variable weathering time periods, it has minute, fine, and distinct characteristics.

For the specifics of the Quantitative Change Principle see Ceramic Trace Law of Quantitative Change in Section 2 of this Chapter.

2. The Passage of Time Principle

The Passage of Time Principle states: Throughout the absolute weathering time, the ceramic trace generation and transformation processes, within numerous variable weathering time periods, form the multiplicity and complexity of trace weathering severities throughout the ceramic glaze level. The following are two specific examples that illustrate the passage of time principle as see in YUB traces.

A. Beach Mottle and Surrounding Glass Phase Height Discrepancy

In a unit image, a beach mottle is concavely depressed; there is clear height discrepancy with the associated glaze surface.

B. CO Striae and CO Type Pits Accompaniment

There are clearly delineated CO striae, CO type pits, and pit groups all presenting within a unit image.

第二节 陶瓷迹型规律

元青花瓷器上的一系列迹型特征体现了陶瓷迹型形成及发展的七大规律。下面将选取一些典型的元青花迹型现象加以说明。

一、陶瓷迹型随机性规律

陶瓷迹型随机性规律是在烧制过程中和后天环境影响下形成的，分布在釉表面及釉层中的陶瓷迹型具有不可预测性、非人为设定性的现象。

（一）先天性迹型的随机性

元青花瓷器上的放射斑可以出现在任何一处青料上，比如在一件元青花盘的内壁和外壁都可以观察到随机出现的同一种类的放射斑。

（二）后天性迹型的随机性

元青花瓷器上的色变泡和壁变泡可以随机出现在瓷器釉层的任何一处。

二、陶瓷迹型色差规律

陶瓷迹型色差规律是在烧制过程中和后天环境影响下形成的，分布在釉表面及釉层中的同一陶瓷迹型种类表现出颜色差异的现象。

（一）色阶变化

1. 元青花瓷器上同一流淌斑上可观察到色阶变化。

2. 元青花瓷器上同一釉裂纹上可观察到色阶变化。

3. 元青花瓷器上同一色变泡上可观察到色阶变化。

（二）色差变化

1. 元青花瓷器上的CO纹路群中可观察到色差变化。

2. 元青花瓷器上的多个色变泡之间可观察到色差变化。

三、陶瓷迹型量变规律

陶瓷迹型量变规律是分布在陶瓷釉表面及釉层中的迹型在后天的风化过程中，有着缓慢性、渐变性、细腻性、精致性、分明性等特征的现象。

（一）曲线性特征

元青花瓷器上物盖斑及物盖针眼斑的边界，通常呈曲线状。

（二）细腻性特征

元青花瓷器上雾状针眼斑在沙滩斑上的分布，有从浓到淡的均匀过渡，显得细腻。

（三）内敛性特征

元青花瓷器上C形纹、O形纹的三维成像纤细、紧致且收敛，没有发散的毛边。

（四）精致性特征

元青花瓷器上放射斑周围的包边纤细精致。

四、陶瓷迹型层次性规律

陶瓷迹型层次性规律是陶瓷迹型不同类别之间和同一类别之间迹型风化强度的差异，通过它们在釉层（釉表面或釉层中）纵向垂直的位置表现出来的现象。

（一）就某一迹型单项而言

流淌斑分布于釉表面及釉层中，受釉层保护的程度不一，这使它们各处风化强度有差异。针眼斑在流淌斑上疏密不一的分布，就是

Section 2:

Ceramic Trace Laws

The series of trace characteristics on YUB embodies the seven laws of ceramic trace change and development. Below are a few typical examples of YUB trace phenomenon.

1. Ceramic Trace Law of Randomness

The Ceramic Trace Law of Randomness states: The distribution of trace appearances across the glaze surface and within the glaze level, created during firing and under the influence of the post-firing environment, is unpredictable and a non-human-controlled phenomenon.

A. Inherent Trace Randomness

Radiating mottles can appear at any point on the porcelain glaze that has blue dye, for example a plate interior or exterior can both present with the random distribution of the same type of radiating mottle.

B. Acquired Trace Randomness

Color change bubbles or textured bubbles can appear at any point on the porcelain glaze.

2. Ceramic Trace Law of Chromatic Aberration

The Ceramic Trace Law of Chromatic Aberration states: Within a single trace type, distributed across the glazc surface and within the glaze level, both innate and acquired, the phenomenon of chromatic aberration (differences in color) can be present.

A. Color Spectrum

I. A color spectrum presenting on a single flowing mottle.

II. A color spectrum presenting in a single glaze crack.

III. A color spectrum presenting in a single color change bubble.

B. Color Disparity

I. A color disparity presenting in a CO Striae group.

II. A color disparity presenting across several color change bubbles.

3. Ceramic Trace Law of Quantitative Change

The Ceramic Trace Law of Quantitative Change states: The innate and acquired trace appearances distributed across the glaze surface and within the glaze level, have all undergone slow, gradual, and minute processes and appear with fine and distinct characteristics.

A. Irregular Border Characteristics

For example: The border of overlay mottles or overlay type needlepoint mottles.

B. Minute Characteristics

For example: Foggy needlepoint mottling distribution on beach mottles, appear with a dark to light even progression.

流淌斑风化强度不一的表现。流淌斑的分布特征以及覆盖在上面的针眼斑分布特征使其有了层次感。

（二）就同一类别中相邻的两个或多个迹型单项而言

坑点斑形成后成为连接外界物质与釉层内部的通道之一，长期存放于干湿交替的环境中，釉下絮状斑会在坑点斑下的釉层中及坑点斑周围的釉层中逐渐形成，坑点斑与釉层中存在的絮状斑就有了层次关系。

（三）就不同类别中相邻的两个或多个迹型单项而言

由C形纹、O形纹发展而来的坑点斑，这两种不同类别之间的迹型种类也可表现出层次性。从存在于釉表面的C形纹、O形纹发展到深入釉层中的坑点斑，由浅到深，富有层次。

五、陶瓷迹型多样性规律

陶瓷迹型多样性规律是陶瓷在后天环境影响下，在釉表面及釉层中，因风化而形成的迹型，比其先天形成的迹型类别或种类数量增加的现象。

观察统计表明绝大多数元青花瓷器存在至少五种后天性风化迹型。

六、陶瓷迹型差异性规律

陶瓷迹型差异性规律是陶瓷迹型类别或迹型种类的风化强度，与其邻近的相同或不同迹型类别、迹型种类不一致的现象。

如破口壁变泡周围是干净清晰的玻璃相，螺旋叠加的坑点斑周围是干净清晰的玻璃相。

七、陶瓷迹型分明性规律

陶瓷迹型分明性规律是陶瓷在后天环境影响下形成的，分布在釉表面及釉层中的迹型类别或种类之间保持界线清晰，各自独立的现象。

如针眼型阴纹与周围玻璃相的界线清晰分明，放射斑与其周围的流淌斑之间界线清晰分明，伴生的C形纹与坑点斑之间界线清晰分明。

注：关于陶瓷迹型规律更详细的论述，请参阅《陶瓷迹型学概论》。

C. Restrained Characteristics

C and O shaped striae edges are tightly constrained instead of roughly dispersed.

D. Fine Characteristics

For example: The finely exquisite thin border of radiating mottles.

4. Ceramic Trace Law of Gradation

The Ceramic Trace Law of Gradation (Layering) states: The weathering severity, whether inter or intra-trace category has variation; a phenomenon resulting due to their positioning throughout the glaze level (across the glaze surface or within the glaze level).

A. In reference to a single trace

Flowing mottles are located above and below the surface of the glaze and receive different degrees of glaze protection allowing a range of weathering severity. Therefore, the differences in density of needlepoint mottling are a direct result of differences in weathering severity. The characteristics of flowing mottles and associated overlaid needlepoint mottling appear with a feeling of layers or gradation.

B. In reference to two or more adjacent individual traces (belonging to the same category)

After the formation of pit mottles, these mottles act as channels between the external environment and the glaze level. After a long period of time in an environment of alternating moisture, floccus mottling can present under the overlaid pit mottle and disperse down into the glaze level. The pit mottle and floccus mottling have a layered relationship.

C. In reference to two or more adjacent individual traces (belonging to different categories)

The progression from C and O shaped striae into pit mottles represents the layered relationship between different trace categories. The temporal process ofprogression from C to O shaped striae, then to pit mottles gives varying depths and a feeling of gradation.

5. Ceramic Trace Law of Variegation

The Ceramic Trace Law of Variegation describes the phenomenon of an increase in appearances of trace categories and types distributed across the glaze surface and throughout the glaze level due to weathering incurred in the post-firing environment.

Statistical observation has shown that the vast majority of YUB samples present with at least five types of acquired traces.

6. Ceramic Trace Law of Disparity

The Ceramic Trace Law of Disparity describes the phenomenon of two similar or dissimilar ceramic trace categories or types within the same vicinity appearing with differences in weathering severity.

For example:

The clean and clear glass phase surrounding a broken mouthed textured bubble;

The clean and clear glass phase surrounding a CO pit group.

7. Ceramic Trace Law of Distinction

The Ceramic Trace Law of Distinction describes the phenomenon of trace categories and types distributed across the glaze surface and within the glaze level, formed within the post-firing environment, retaining clear delineation and respective independence from one another.

For example:

The boundary between needlepoint striae and the

surrounding glass phase is clearly distinct;

The boundary between radiating and flowing mottles is clearly distinct;

The boundary between textured bubbles and the surrounding glass phase is clearly distinct.

Note: For a more detailed description of The Ceramic Trace Laws, please refer to *Survey of Ceramics Trace Model Study*.

第三节 陶瓷迹型出现位置的合理性与变化的同步性

一、陶瓷迹型出现位置的合理性

陶瓷迹型出现位置的合理性关注的是陶瓷迹型出现的位置是否符合陶瓷迹型风化的原理及规律。

以元青花上的迹型为例：

（一）CO型坑点斑出现在釉表面凸起处

元青花瓷器上的CO型坑点斑通常都出现在釉表面凸起处，釉表面其他地方通常光滑洁净。

（二）针眼斑在沙滩斑上的分布

元青花瓷器上的针眼斑在沙滩斑上的分布有一定规律，一般来说，在沙滩斑中心部分针眼斑以磨砂针眼斑形式出现，在沙滩斑与玻璃相过渡的地方，针眼斑通常以雾状针眼斑形式出现。

二、陶瓷迹型变化的同步性

陶瓷迹型变化的同步性关注的是同一件器物上的各迹型风化强度是否同步。

（一）晶相与玻璃相的同步性

通常来说，同一件器物上的晶相与玻璃相的风化强度具有同步性，当一件器物上的玻璃相有一定风化强度，其晶相应表现出更高的风化强度。

（二）同一迹型单项的同步性

对于同一迹型单项而言，其二维成像与三维成像的风化强度应该是同步的。

Section 3:

Ceramic Trace Location Rationality and Change Congruency

1. Ceramic Trace Location Rationality

Ceramic Trace Location Rationality focuses on whether or not the locations where ceramic traces appear fit the principles and laws of the weathered ceramic traces.

The following examples of YUB traces illustrate this principle:

A. CO Type Pit Mottles Present on Areas of Raised Glaze

CO type pit mottles usually present on areas of raised glaze, the surrounding glaze level remains smooth and clean.

B. Needlepoint Mottling on Flowing Mottle

The distribution of needlepoint mottling on flowing mottle has regularity. The center of beach mottles while usually presents with frosted needlepoint mottling, and the borders between the beach mottle and glass phase usually present with foggy needlepoint mottling.

2. Ceramic Trace Change Congruency

The concept of Ceramic Trace Change Congruency refers to whether or not there is a congruency in trace weathering severity according to their respective weathering resistance.

A. Congruency between Crystallization Phase and Glass Phase

Usually, the weathering severity of crystallization phase and glass phase on the same piece of ceramic should be congruent. This is to say that if a piece's glass phase displays a certain weathering severity, the adjacent crystallization should even more so display such weathering severity.

B. Congruency of a Single Trace

For a single trace, its two and three-dimensional appearances of weathering severity should be congruent.

第八章

元青花迹型标准图谱模型建构

阅读提示：

本章展示了元青花迹型标准图谱模型的部分图片，阐述了在建构元青花标准图谱模型时其标本的选择标准及来源，并论述了元青花标准图谱模型的可靠性及自证性。

主要论述问题：

1. 选择建构元青花标准图谱模型的标本有哪些标准？
2. 元青花标准图谱模型有什么重要特征？

Chapter 8

Yuan Underglaze Blue Standard Trace Atlas Model Construction

Text Note:

This chapter introduces a portion of images that compose the YUB Standard Trace Atlas Model, elaborates on the selection and origin of these images, and expounds upon the reliability and self-evidence of this model.

第一节
标本选择与来源

一、标本选择

元青花标本的真实可靠性，决定了元青花迹型标准图谱模型的真实可靠性。

元青花标本选取正确与否，决定了比对鉴定的结论准确与否。因此，为了确保标本的真实性、可靠性和代表性，在元青花标本选取的过程中，对其来源需考虑如下因素：

（一）元青花生产基地

（二）元青花贸易中转站

（三）元青花流向目的地

（四）有明确100年以上传世时间的元青花

（五）有明确的发掘时间、发掘地点及年代依据

二、标本来源

目前，建构元青花迹型标准图谱模型的标本来源于以下四个单位：

（一）景德镇陶瓷考古研究所

他们的标本是元青花生产基地的代表。

出土地点：江西省景德镇市珠山区

出土时间：1985年

样本数量：瓷片共15件

（二）内蒙古包头博物馆

他们的标本是元青花内陆贸易中转站及目的地的代表。

出土地点：内蒙古自治区包头市燕家梁

出土时间：2006年

样本数量：瓷片与整器共13件

（三）泰国曼谷大学东南亚陶瓷博物馆

他们的标本是元青花海上贸易目的地的代表。

出土地点：泰国清迈地区

出土时间：1975年

样本数量：整器共39件

（四）印度尼西亚国立博物馆

他们的标本是元青花海上贸易目的地的代表。

出土地点：印度尼西亚马鲁古群岛、巴厘岛及哈马里拉岛

出土时间：1890—1959年

样本数量：整器共6件

三、研究合作单位

除了用于建构元青花迹型标准图谱模型的标本以外，本书所展示的其他元青花标本分别来自国内外七家博物馆、研究单位及私人收藏，它们分别是：

（一）中国科学院高能物理研究所

（二）台湾鸿禧美术馆

（三）金乐轩

（四）广东省文物鉴定站

（五）广州东方博物馆

（六）美国波士顿艺术博物馆

（七）美国旧金山亚洲艺术博物馆

除了景德镇、包头、泰国、印尼的研究单位与博物馆提供的元青花标本有明确的发掘时间、发掘地点及年代依据以外，其余单位提供的研究标本均没有明确的发掘时间及地点。但经过迹型比对分析后，发现这些单位收藏的元青花瓷器及残片都与来自景德镇、包头、泰国、印尼的标本迹型高度相似，本质充分吻合，可以说明它们均为元代的青花瓷器。

Section 1:

Selection and Origin of the Samples

1. Sample Selection

The veracity and reliability of samples establishes the veracity and reliability of the YUB Standard Trace Atlas Model.

The genuineness of the samples decides the accuracy of conclusions in comparative authentication. Because of this, in order to guarantee the veracity, reliability, and representativeness of these samples, the following key factors must be considered during the process of sample selection:

A. YUB Production Area

B. YUB Trade Hubs

C. YUB Target Markets

D. YUB of clear provenance of 100 years or more

E. Clear Excavation Record (Location, Date, Age Foundation)

2. Sample Origins

Presently, the origin of samples used in the construction of the YUB Standard Trace Atlas Model includes four locations:

A. Jingdezhen Ceramic Archeology Research Institute

The samples represent the production location of YUB.

Excavation Location: Jiangxi Province, Jingdezhen City, Zhushan District

Excavation Time: 1985

Number of Samples: 15 YUB Shards

B. Inner Mongolia Baotou Museum

The samples represent the continental trade hub as well as target market of YUB.

Excavation Location: Inner Mongolia, Baotou City, Yanjialiang

Excavation Time: 2006

Number of Samples: 13 YUB Wares and Shards

C. Bangkok University, Southeast Asian Ceramics Museum

The samples represent a maritime trade route and target market of YUB.

Excavation Location: Thailand, Chiangmai and surrounding areas

Excavation Time: 1975

Number of Samples: 39 YUB Wares

D. National Museum of Indonesia

The samples represent a maritime trade route and target market of YUB

Excavation Location: Indonesia: Maluku islands (Moluccas), Bali, and Halmahera

Excavation Time: 1890~1959

Number of Samples: 6 YUB Wares

3. Research Partner Organizations

Other sample images listed in the book come from seven International and Domestic Museums, Research Institutions, and Private Collections, they are:

1. Institute of High Energy Physics -- Chinese Academy of Science
2. The Chang Foundation, Taiwan

3. Jinlexuan Collection
4. Guangdong Provincial Cultural Relic Authentication Station
5. Guangzhou Oriental Museum
6. Museum of Fine Art, Boston U.S.A.
7. Asian Arts Museum of San Francisco U.S.A

Aside from the above listed YUB samples from Jingdezhen, Inner Mongolia, Thailand, and Indonesia, which have clear excavation record, the samples offered by other institutions are not of clear excavation date or location. However, through comparative analysis, confirmation that all the wares and shards were of Yuan Dynasty date was attained.

第二节
元青花迹型标准图谱模型

一、元青花迹型标准图谱模型说明

（一）元青花迹型标准图谱模型的可靠性

元青花迹型标准图谱模型选取了景德镇、内蒙古、泰国及印尼出土的元青花标本，这批标本有明确的发掘时间、发掘地点及年代依据。所以，在这些标本迹型图片中提炼出来的元青花迹型标准图谱模型，可靠性是毋庸置疑的。

（二）元青花迹型标准图谱模型的自证性

由于标本均有可靠的发掘时间、发掘地点及年代依据，在此基础上提炼出来的元青花迹型标准图谱模型具有自证性。标本的迹型图片就是证据，在此基础上建构的元青花迹型标准图谱模型是元青花比对鉴定的客观物证系统。

Section 2:

Yuan Underglaze Blue Standard Trace Atlas Model

1. YUB Standard Trace Atlas Model Explanation

A. Reliability of the YUB Standard Trace Atlas Model

The YUB Standard Trace Atlas Model is composed of excavated samples from Jingdezhen, Inner Mongolia, Thailand, and Indonesia; which all have clear excavation date, excavation location, and age foundation. As such, the trace atlas model founded on the extraction of these trace sample images leaves no uncertainty.

B. Self-Evidence of the YUB Standard Trace Atlas Model

As the samples are all of established excavation record, there is a self-evidence nature to the trace atlas model built on their foundation. The YUB Standard Trace Atlas Model, constructed with these sample images, is the objective material evidence system for YUB Trace Model Material Evidence Authentication.

二、元青花迹型标准图谱模型展示
2. YUB Standard Trace Atlas Model

流淌斑
Flowing Mottles

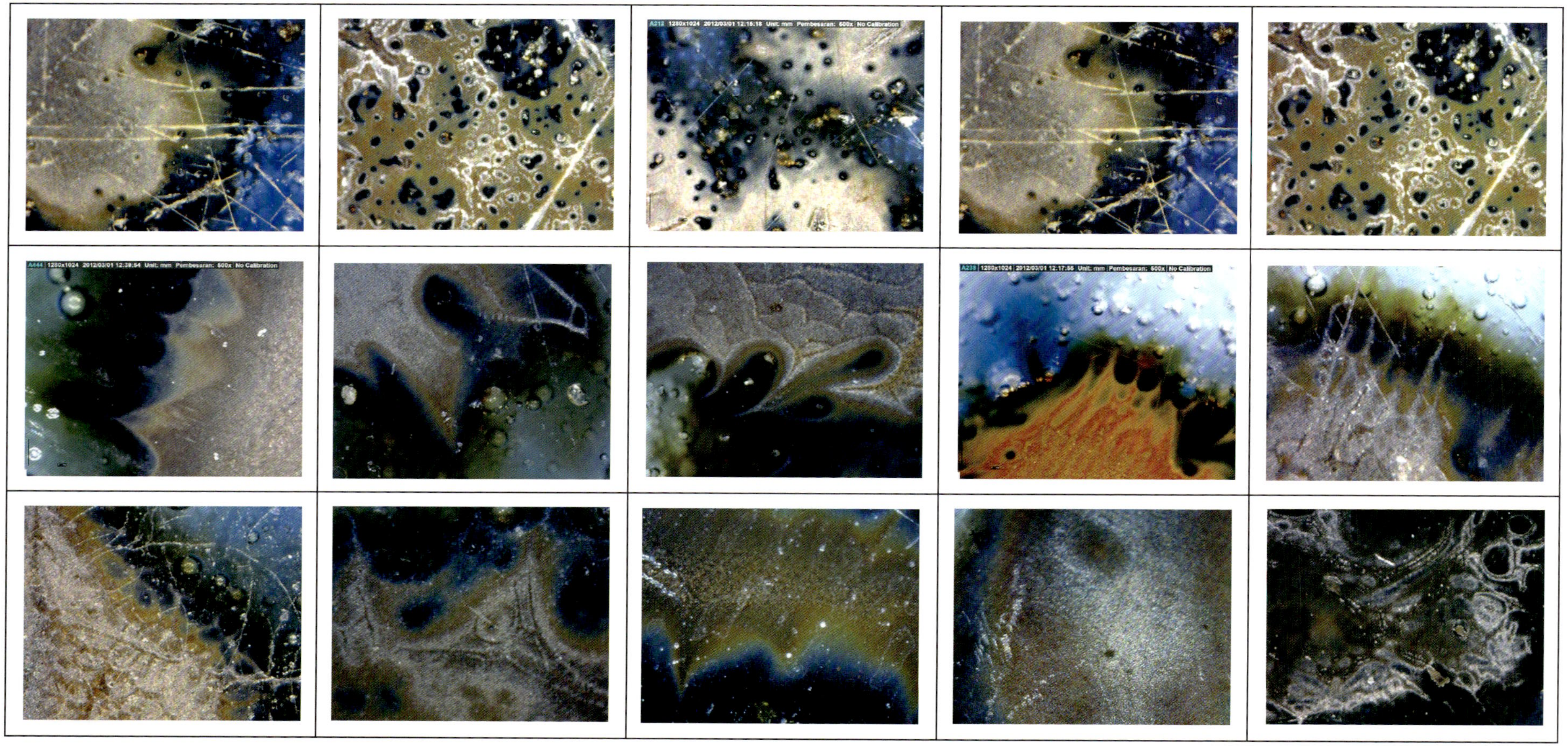

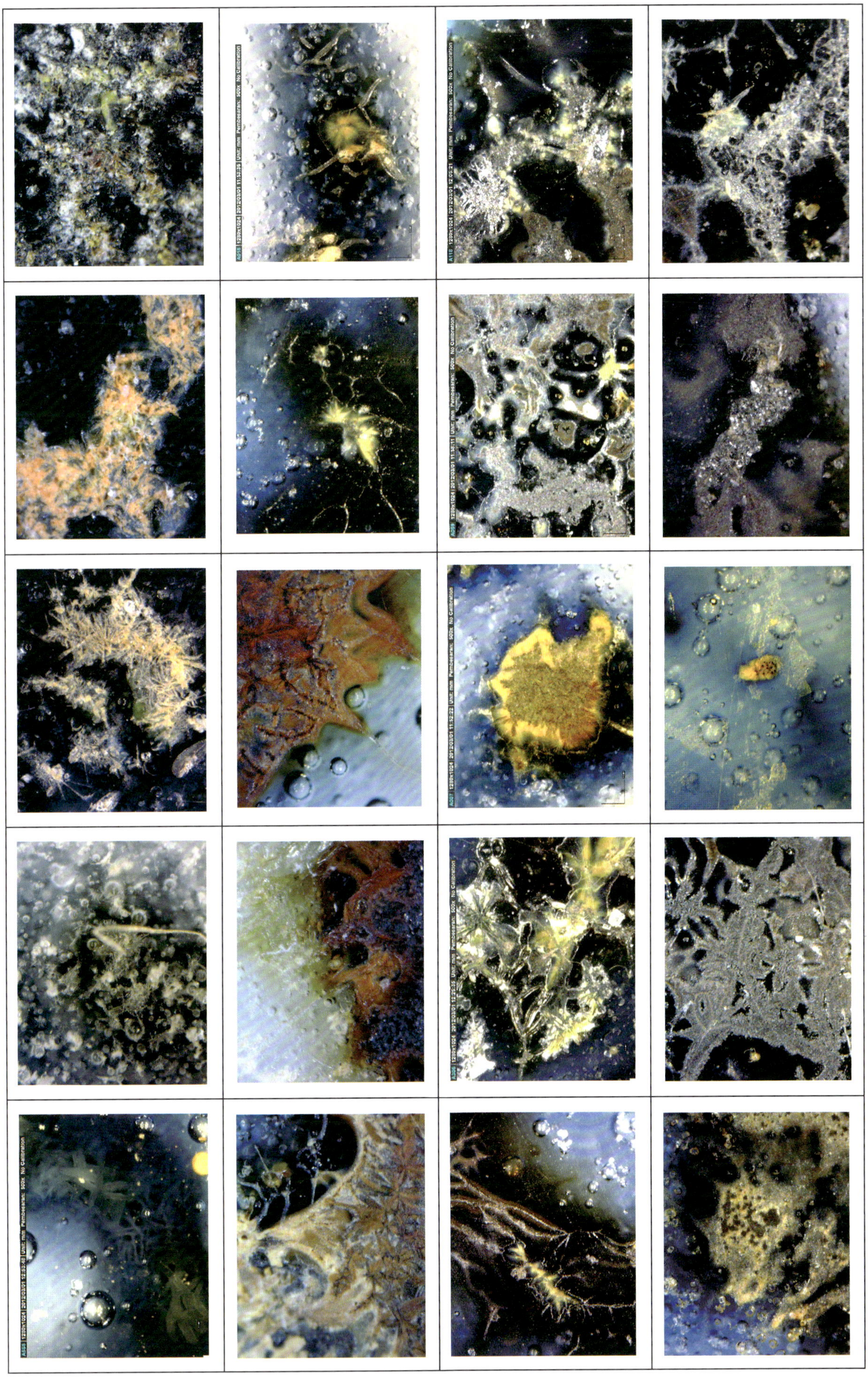

放射斑
Radiating Mottles

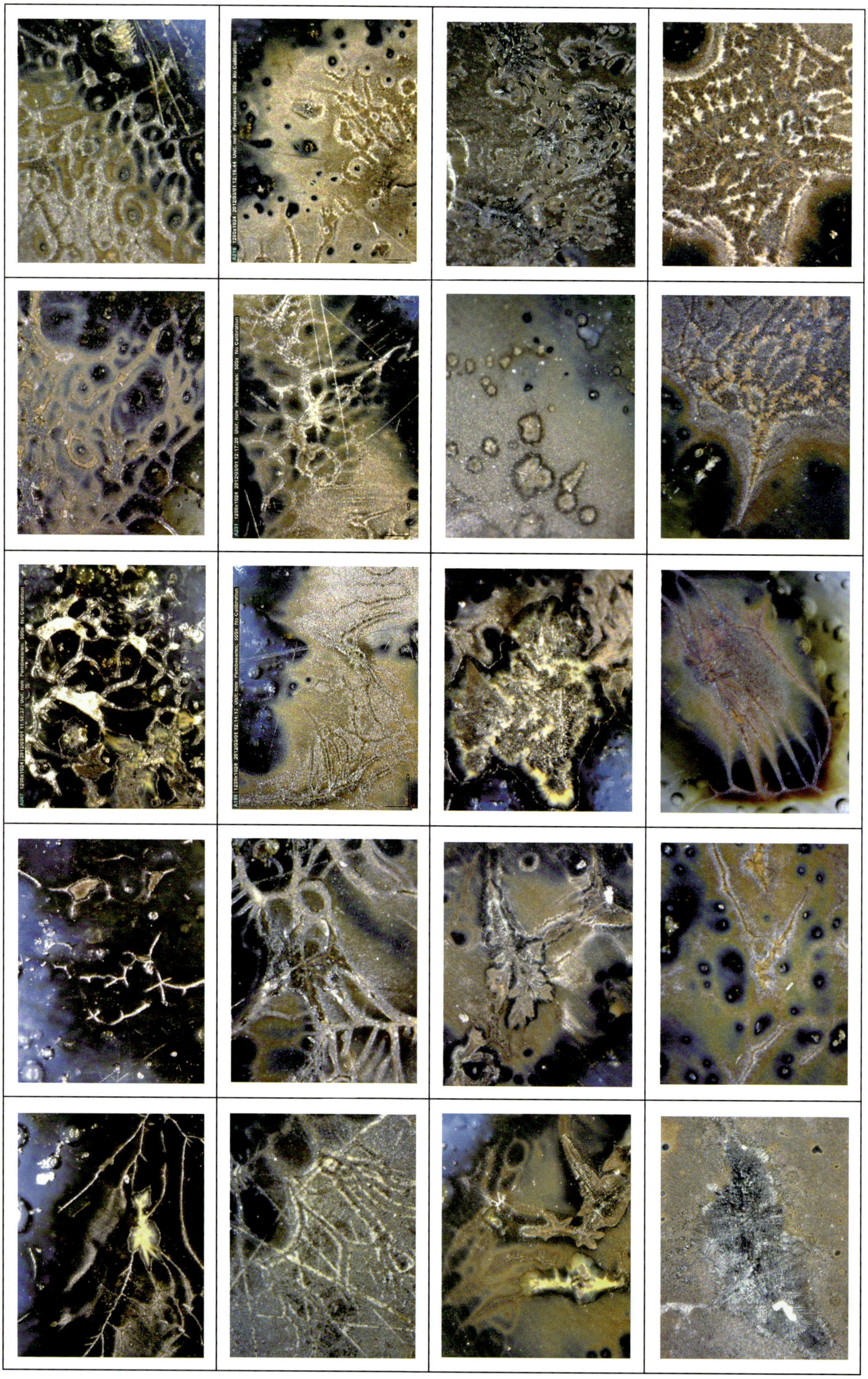

混合斑块及纹路
Mixed Mottles and Striae

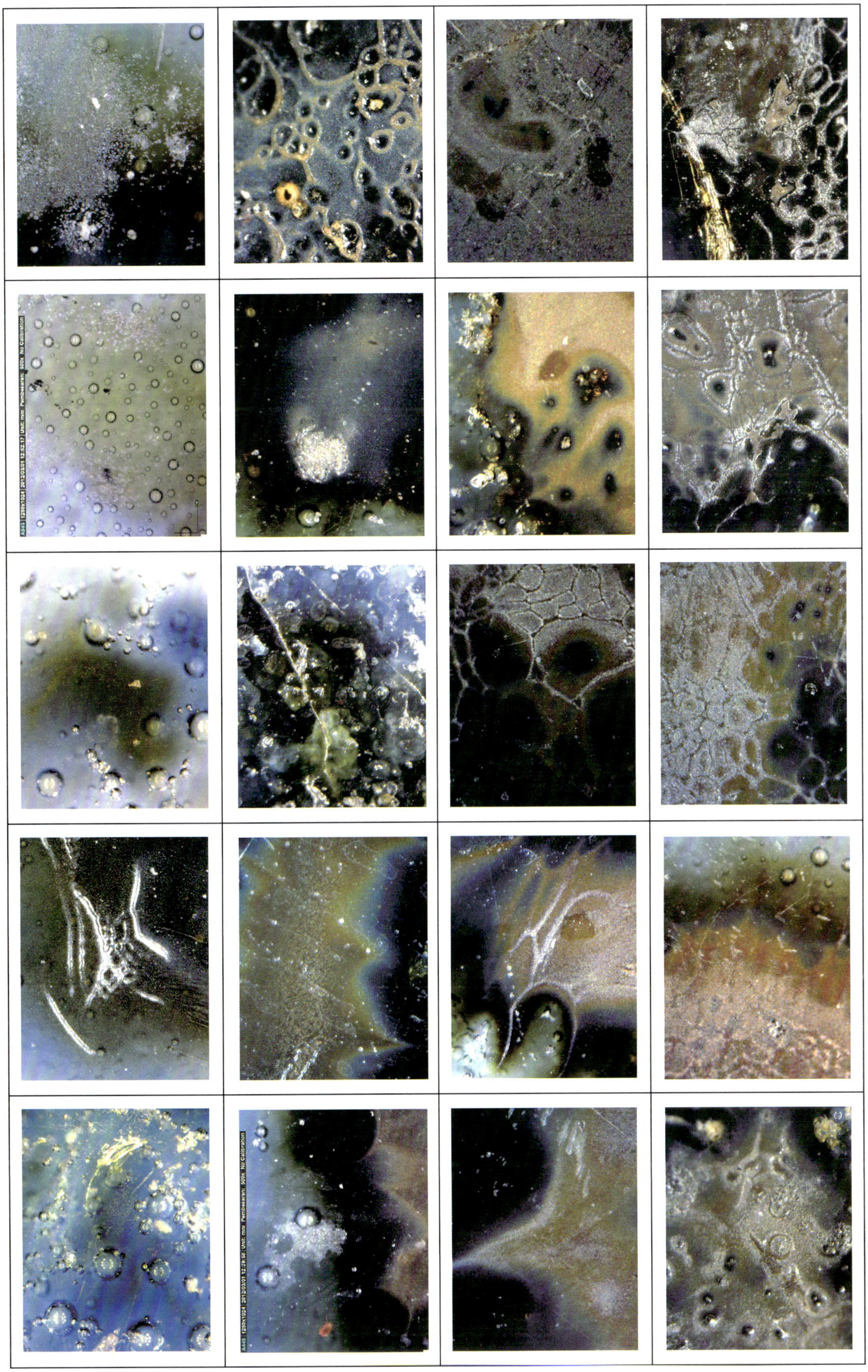

针眼斑
Needlepoint Mottles

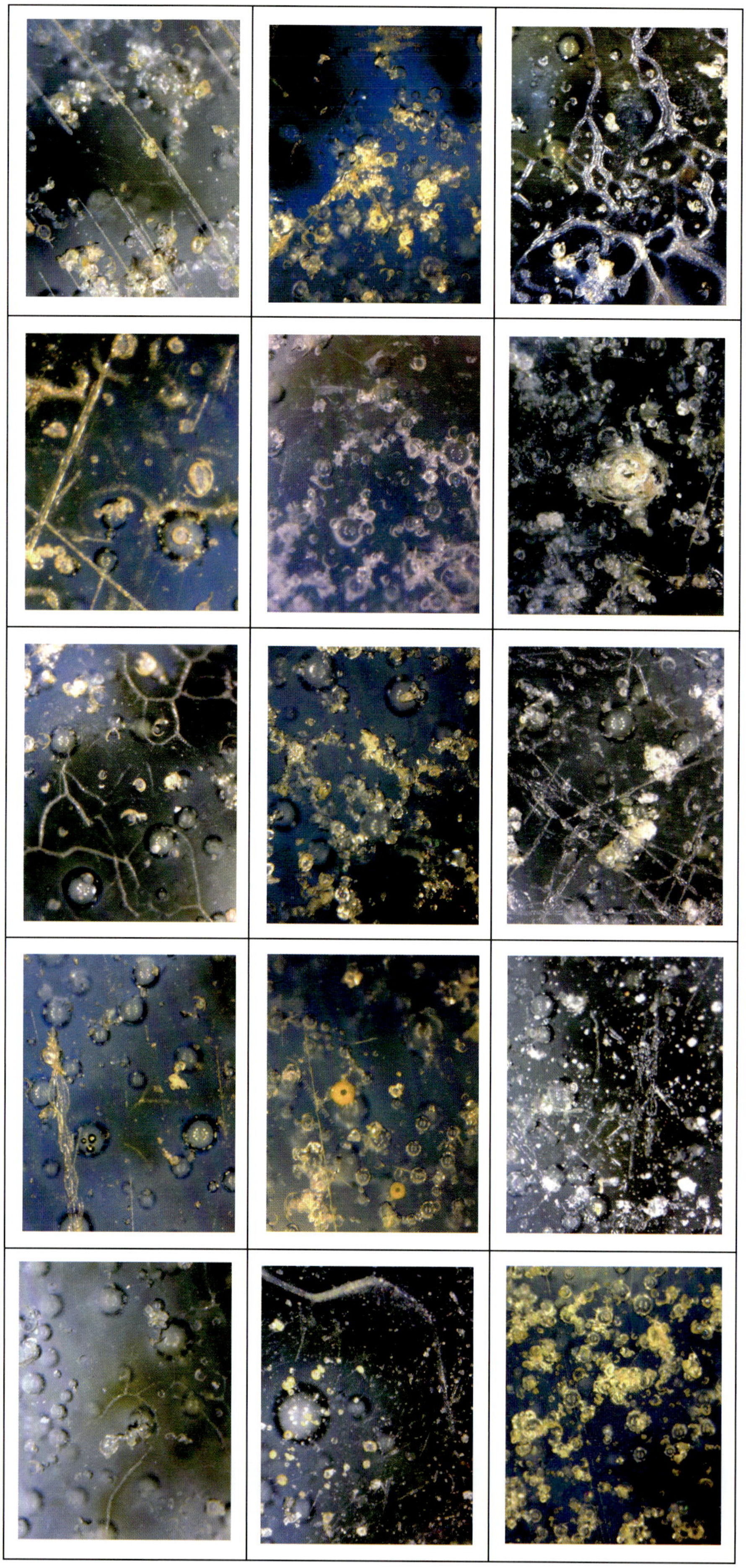

坑点斑
Pit Mottles

（续表）
（Continued）

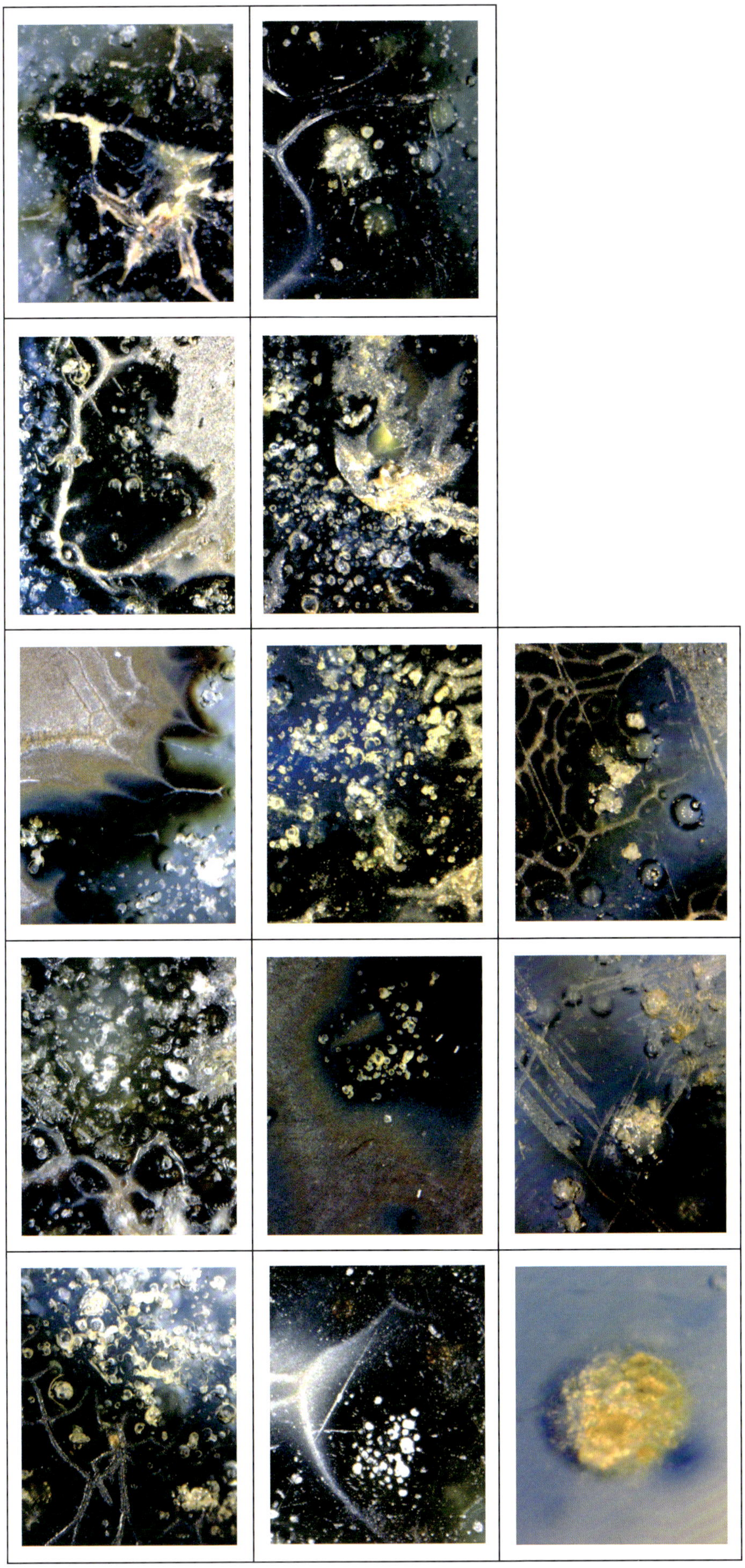

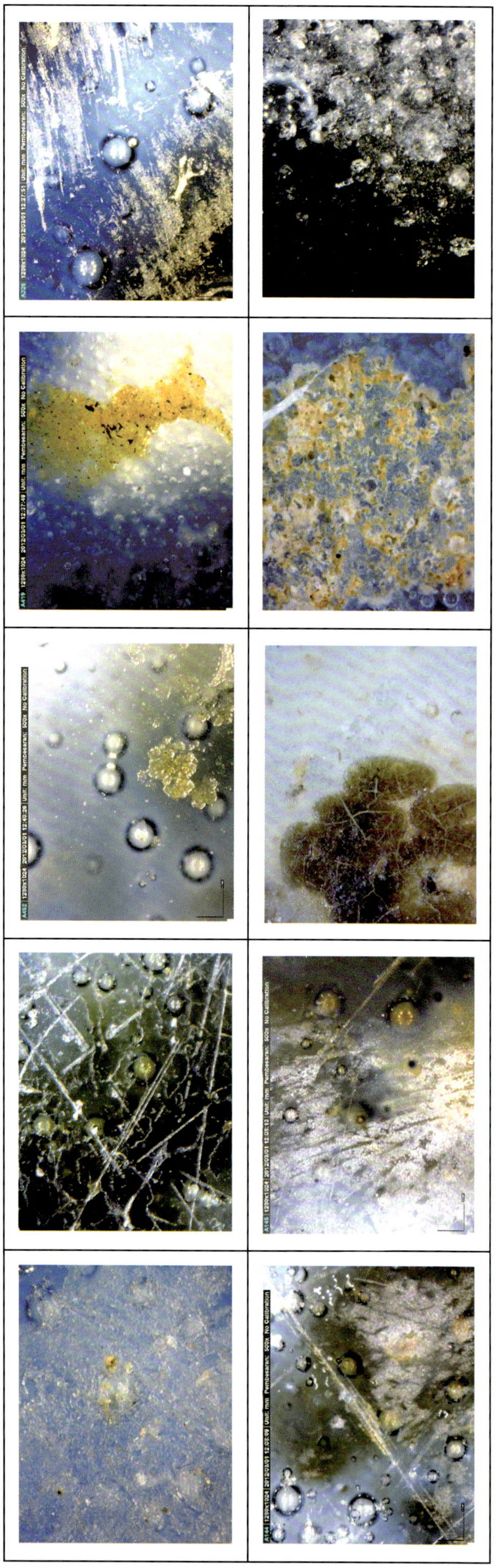

物盖斑
Overlay Mottles

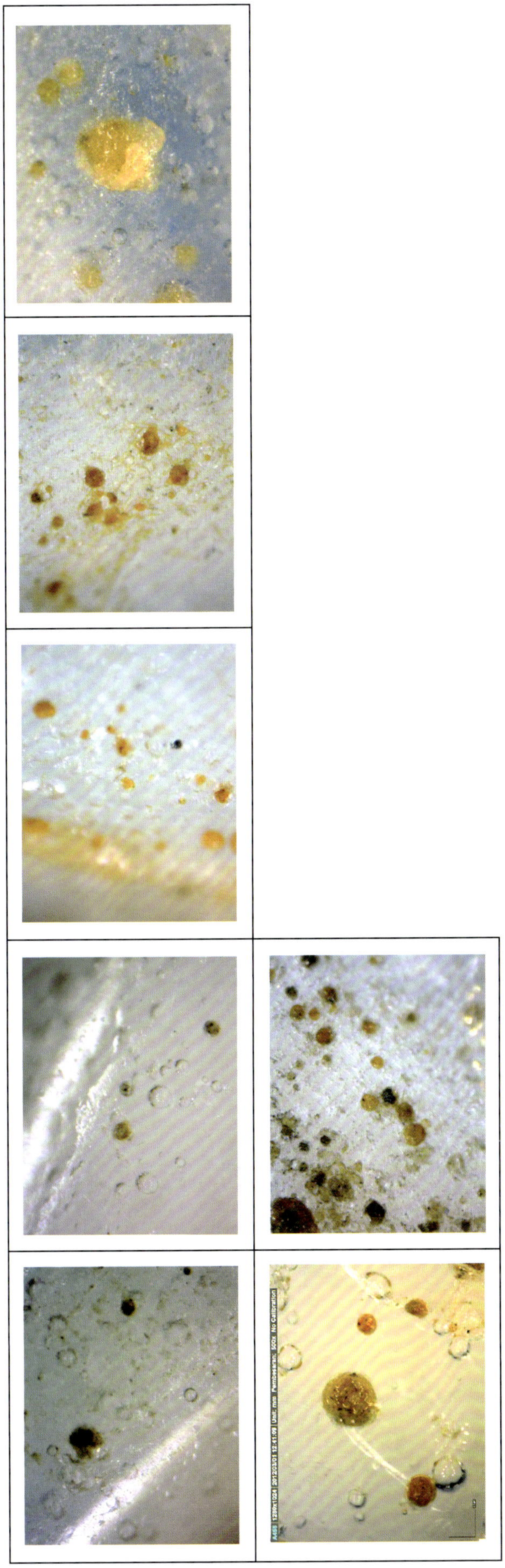

泡根斑
Bubble Roots

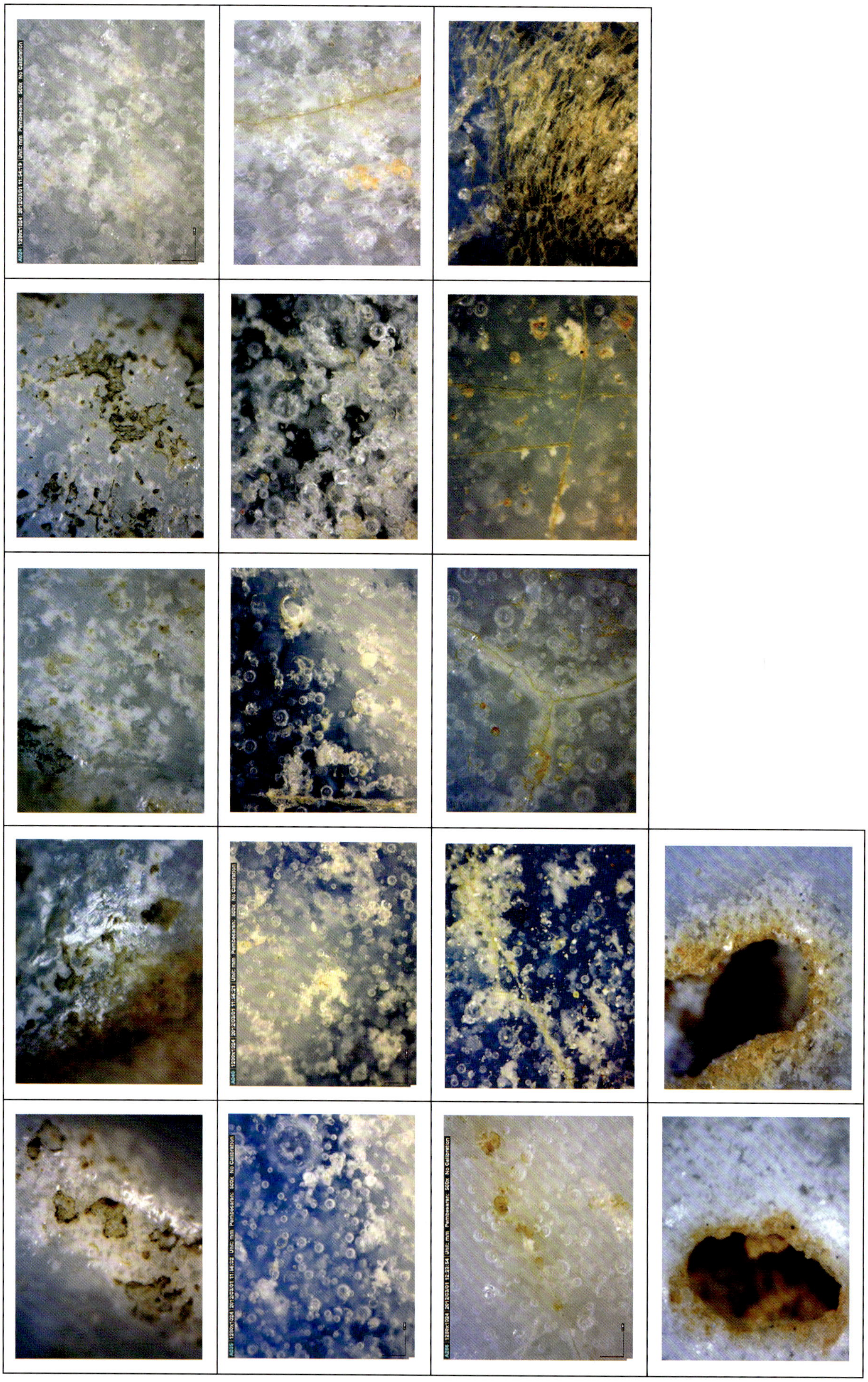

絮状斑
Floccus Mottles

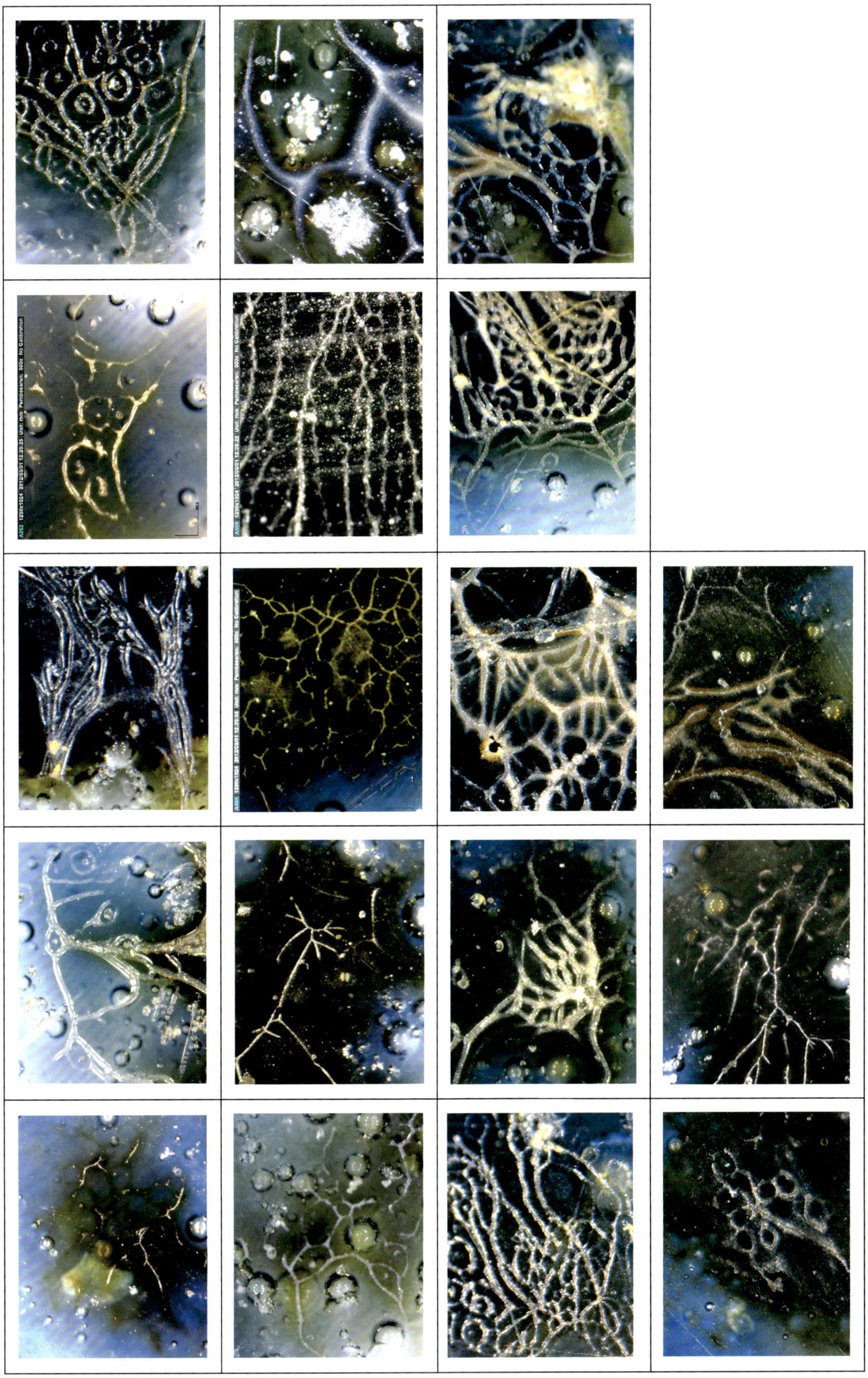

流淌纹
Flowing Striae

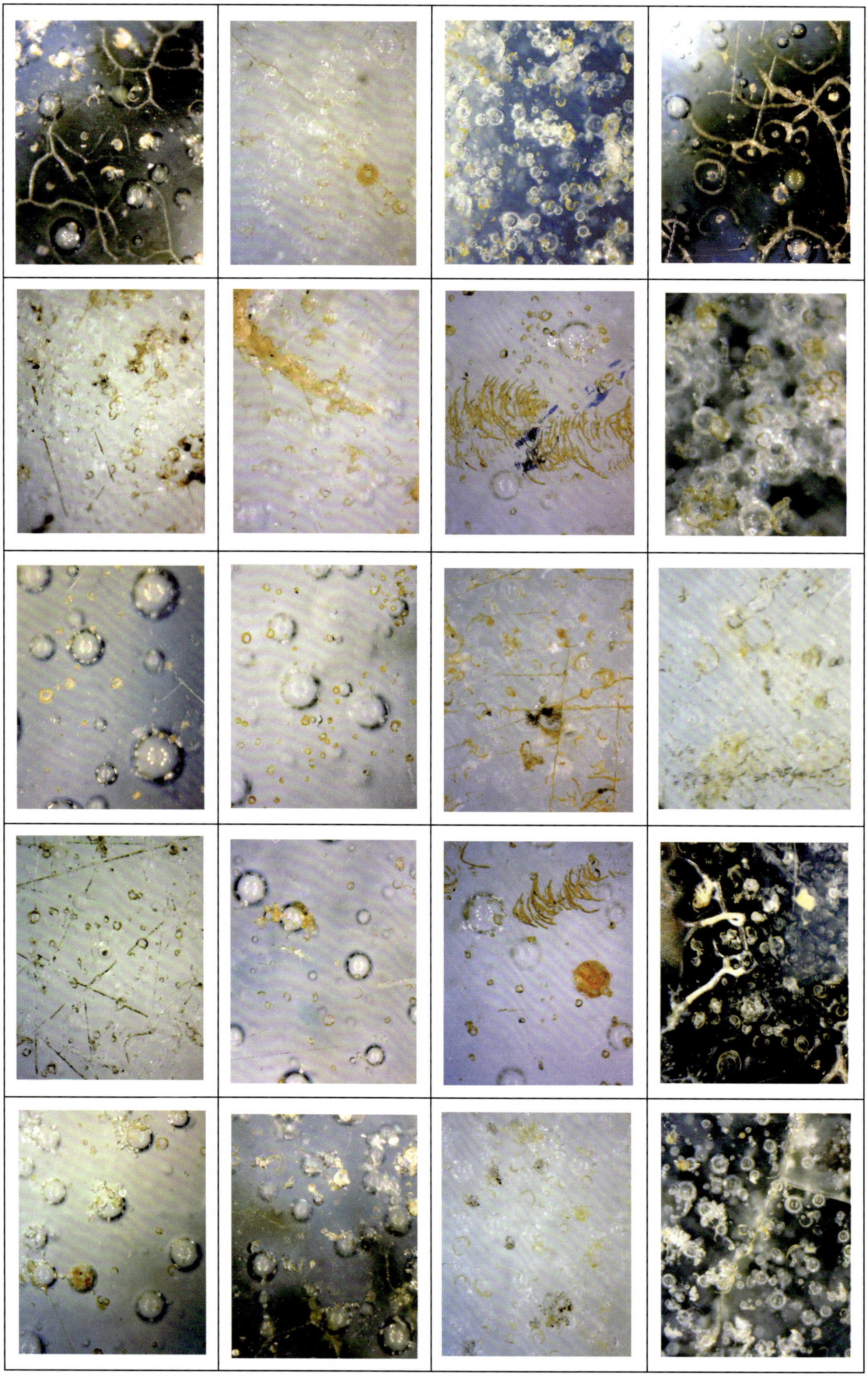

C形、O形纹
C and O Shaped Striae

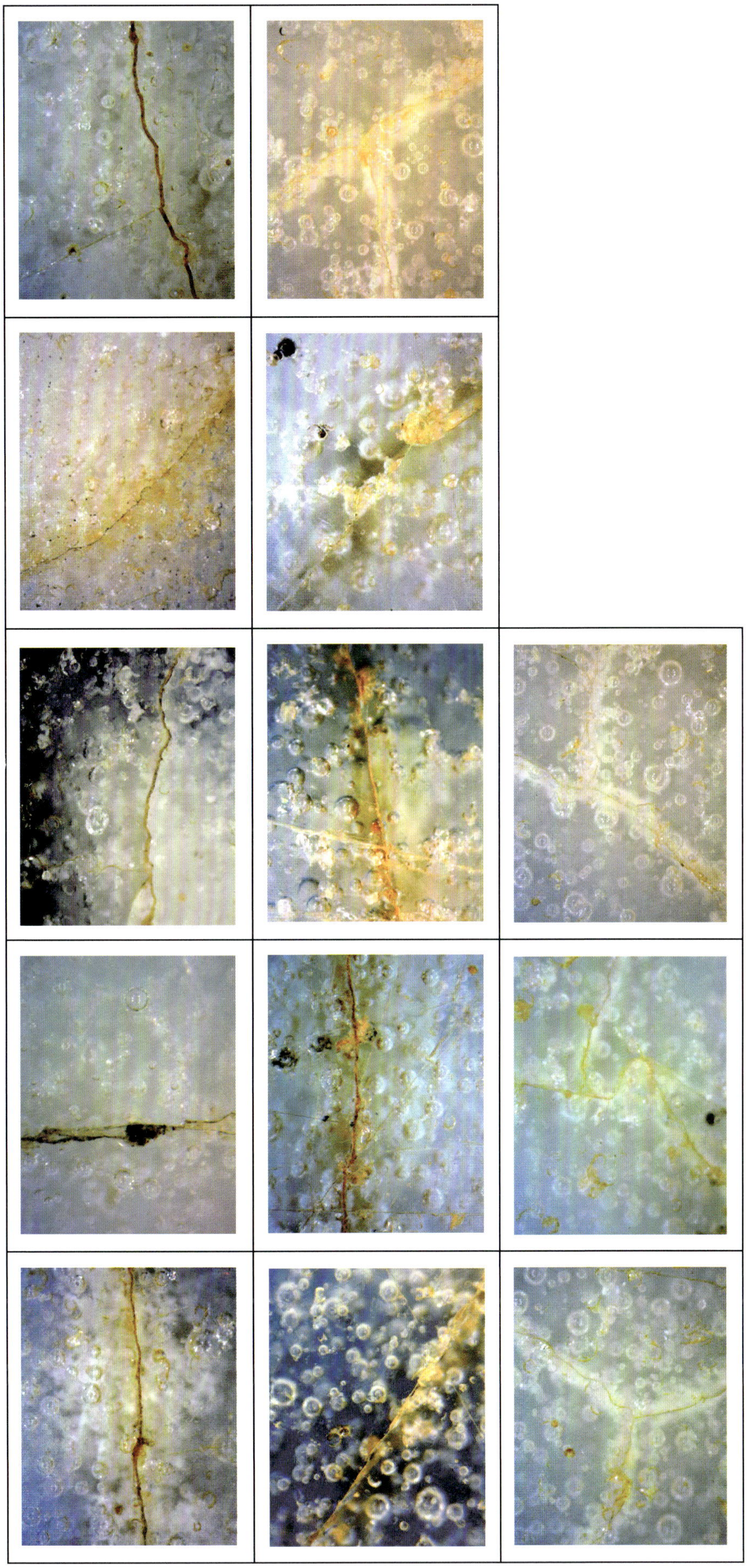

釉裂纹
Glaze Cracks

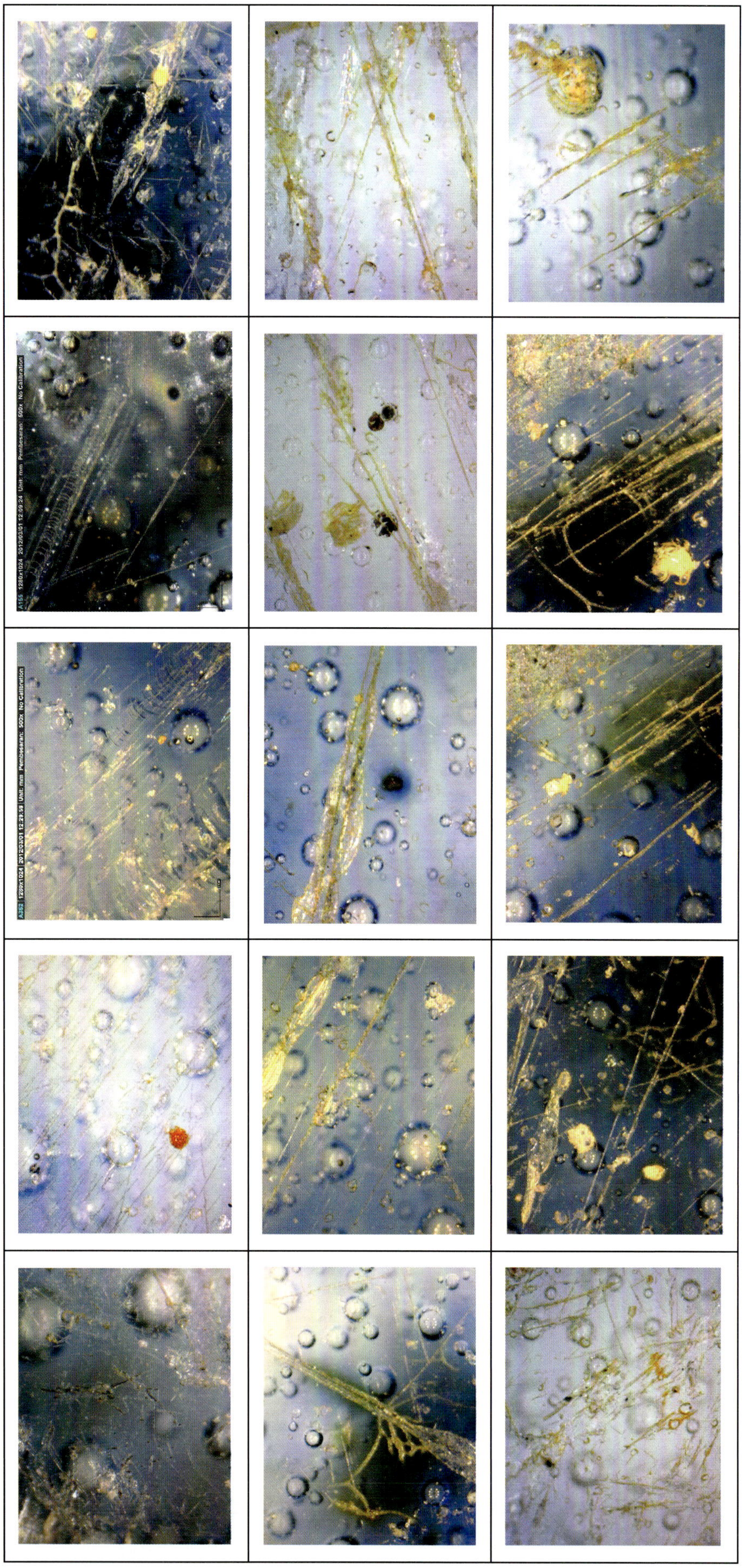

划痕 Scratches

（续表）
（Continued）

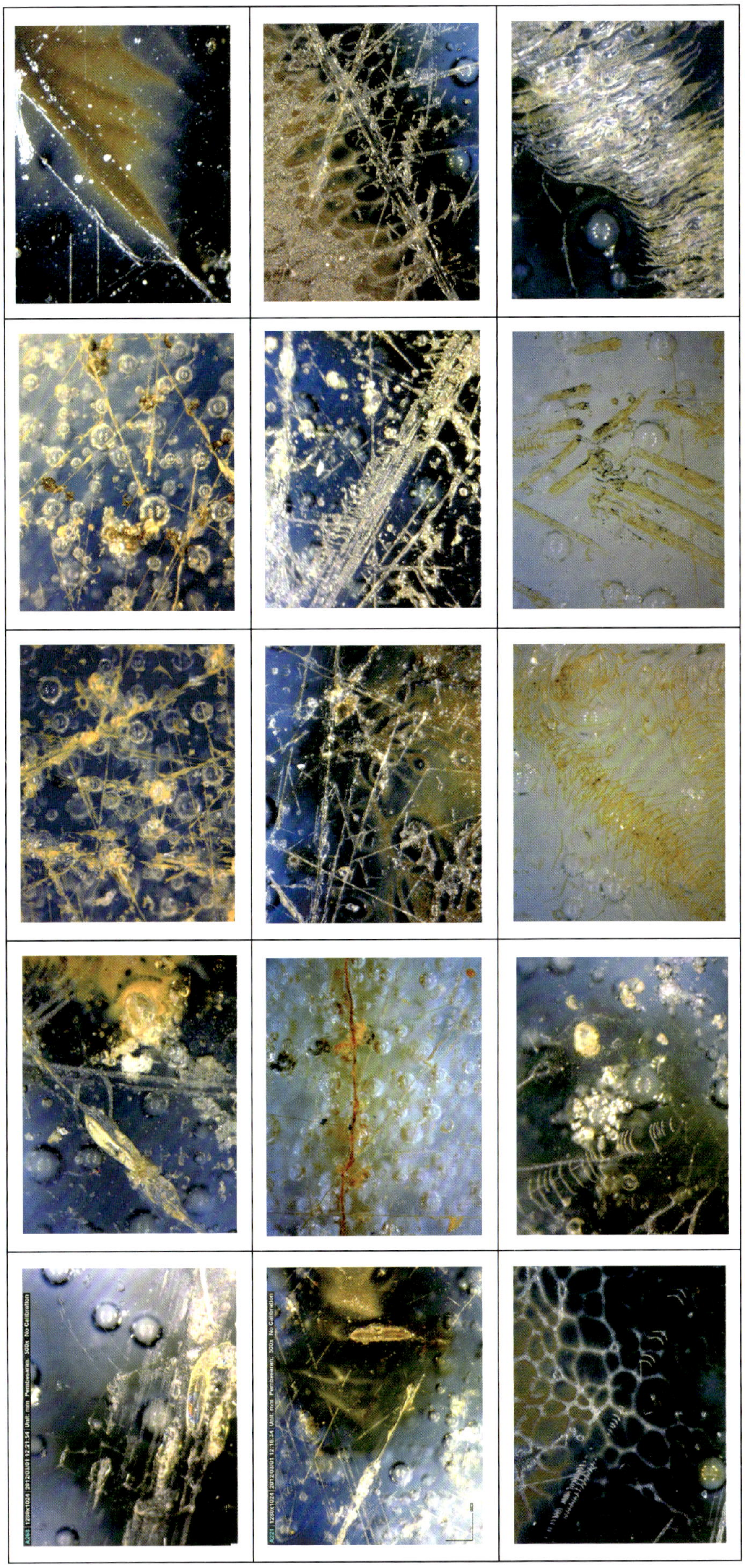

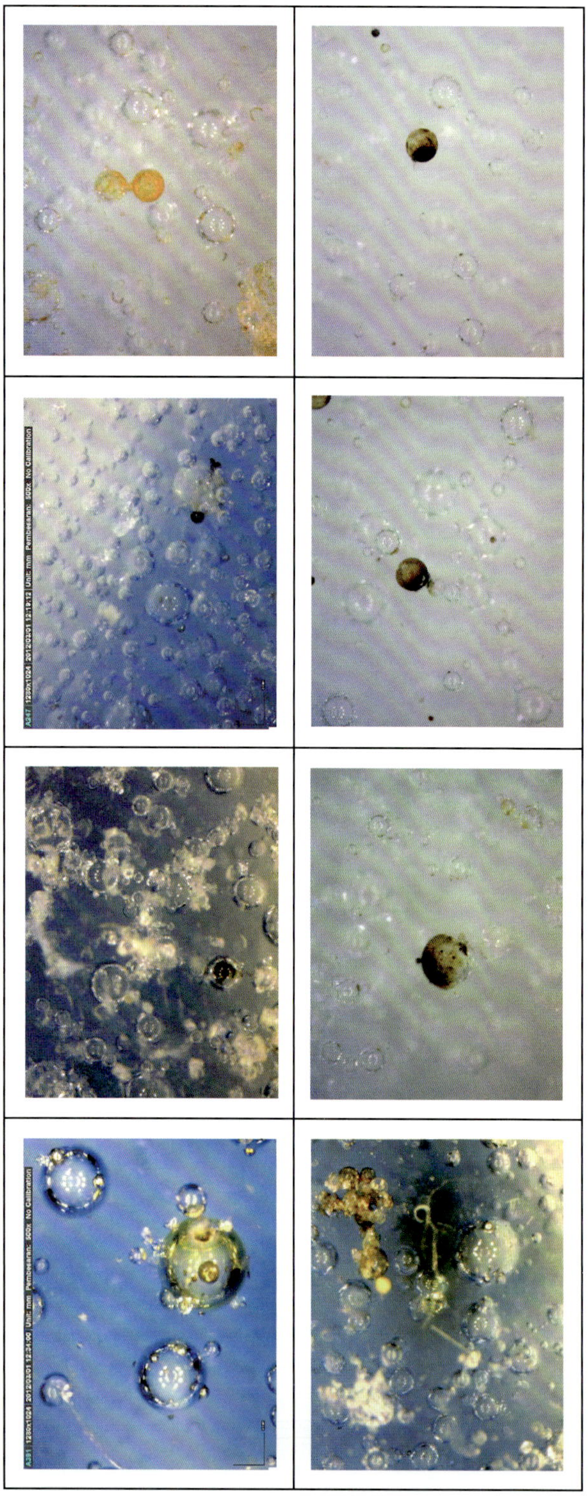

色变泡
Color Change Bubbles

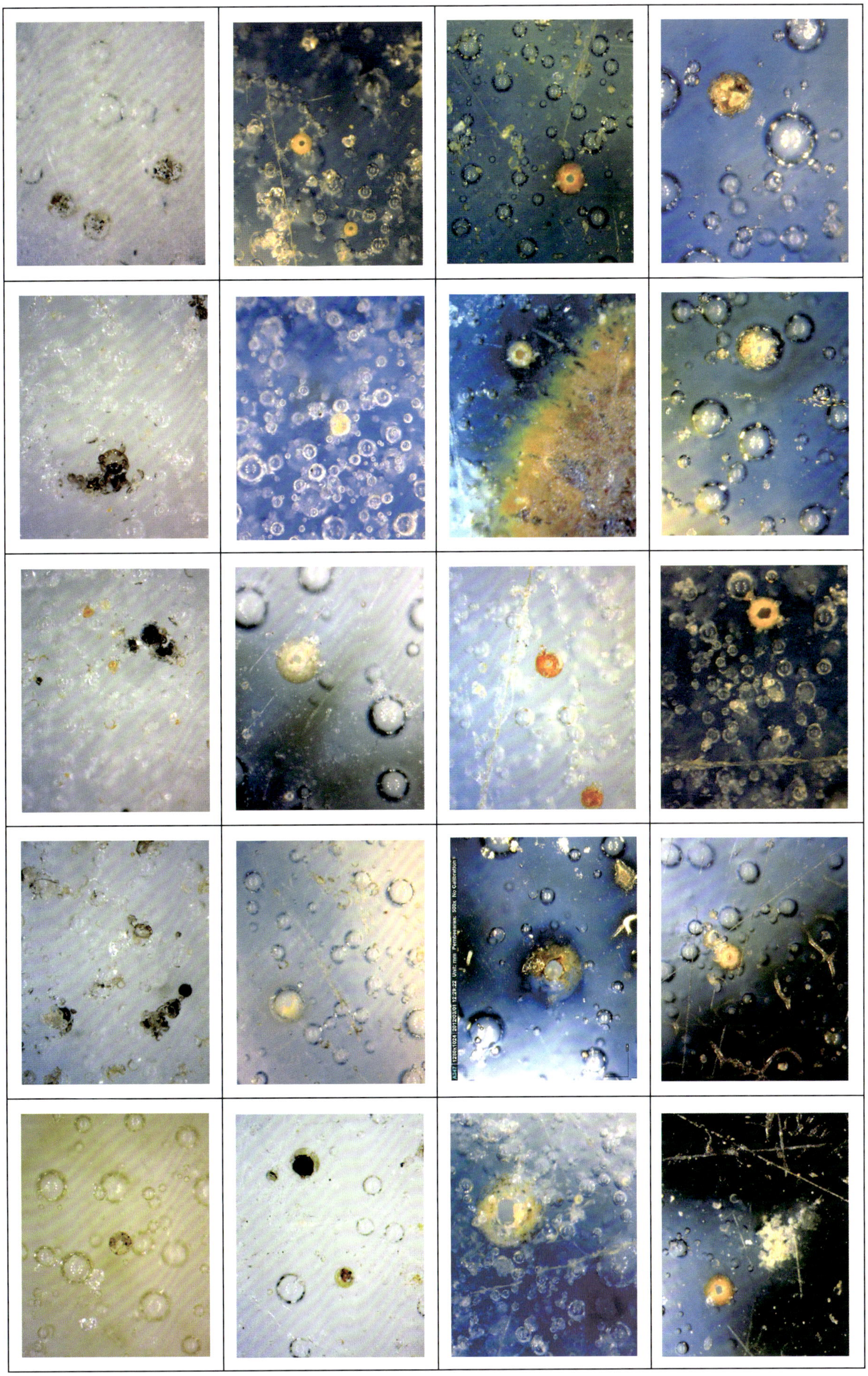

壁变泡
Textured Bubbles

（续表）
（Continued）

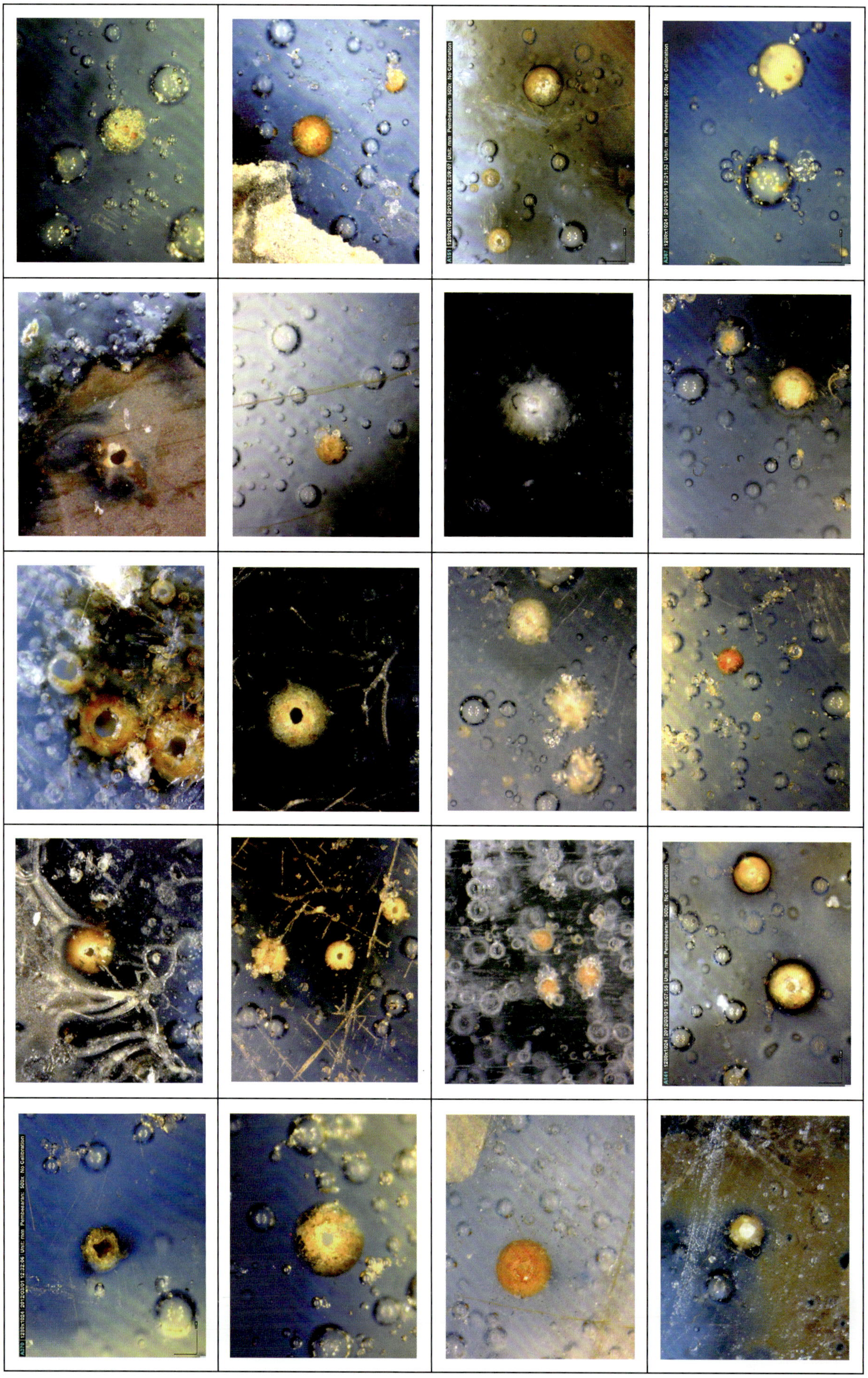

玻璃相与气相
Glass Phase and Gas Phase

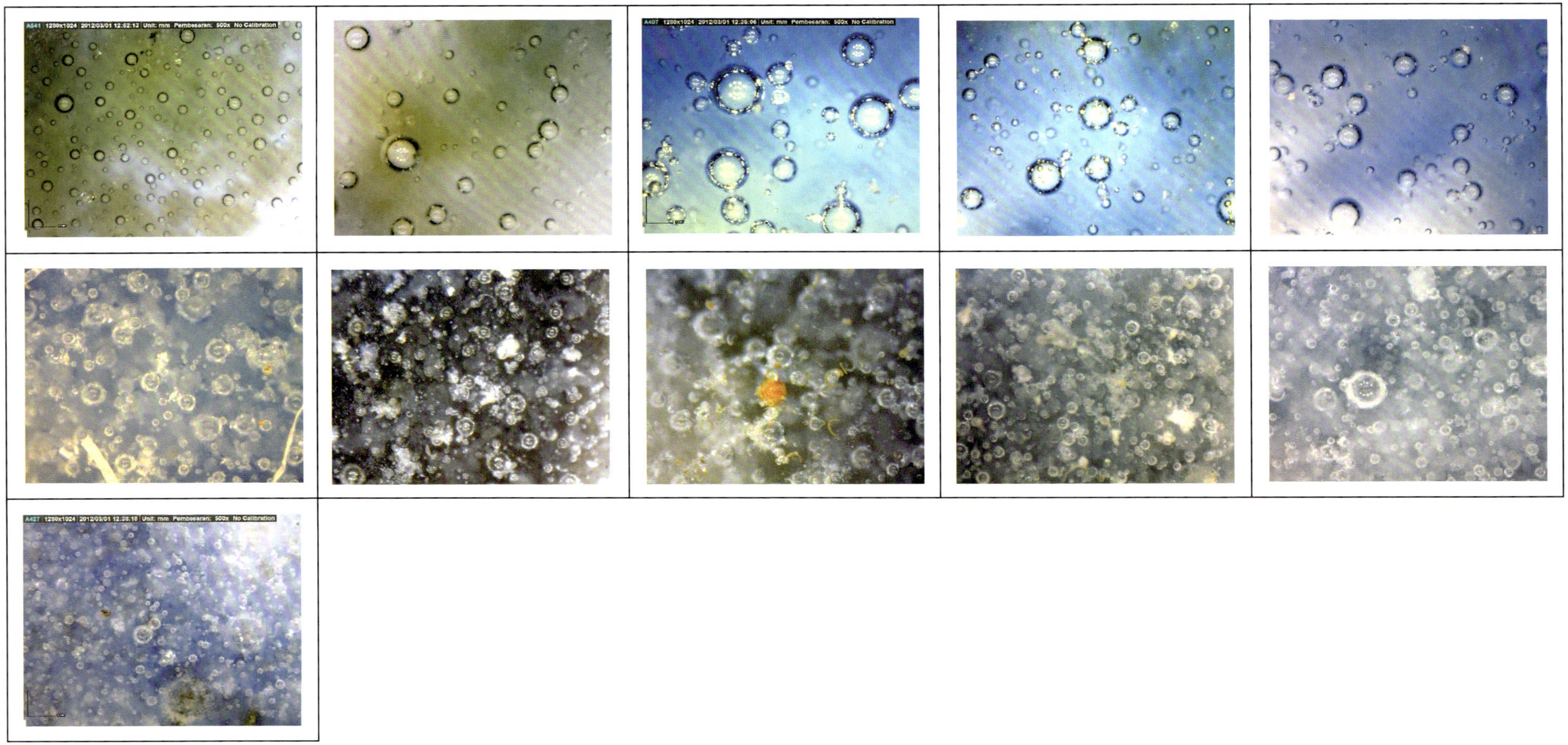

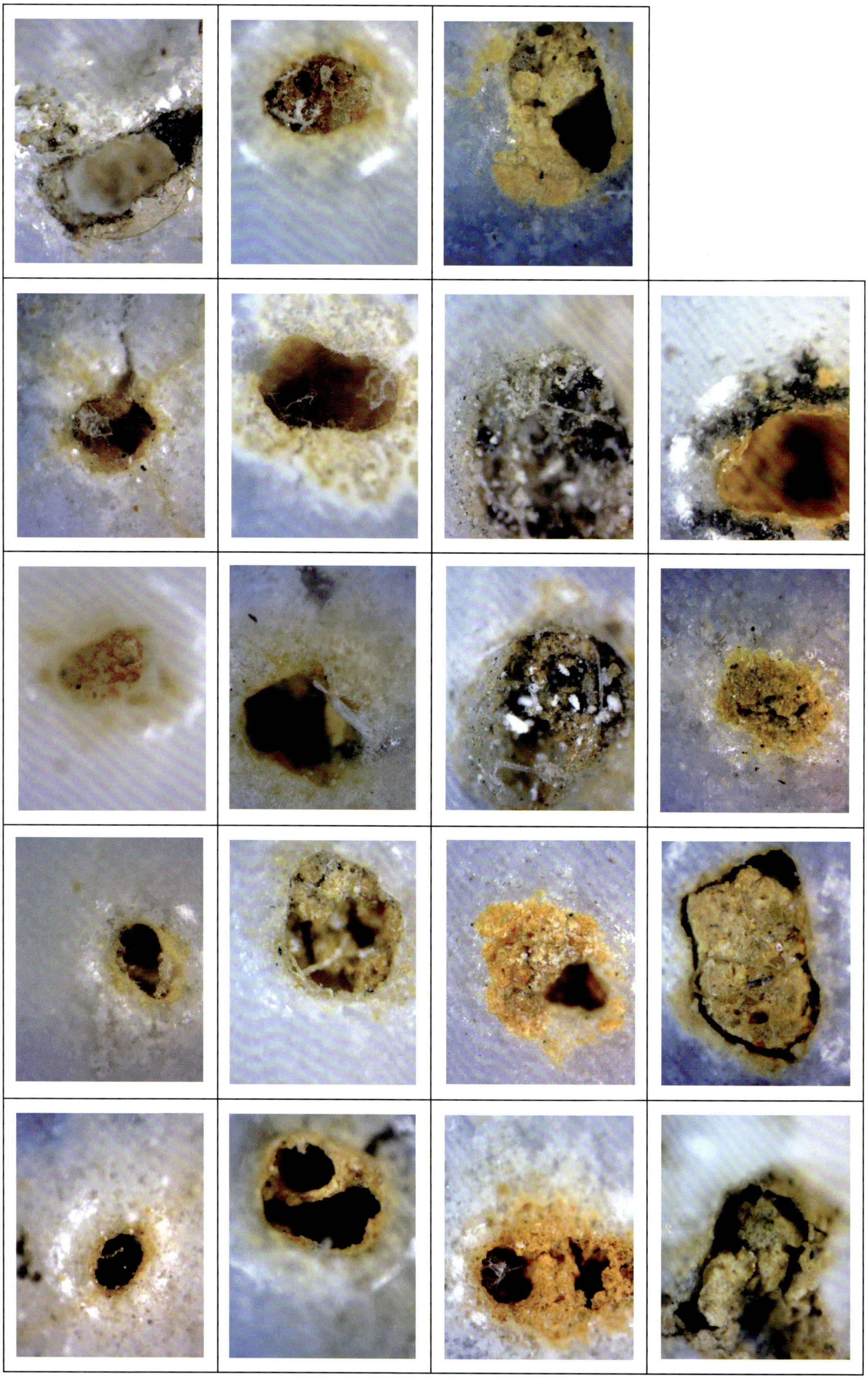

鬃眼 Bristle Pits

二维及三维成像对应图
Corresponding Two and Three-dimensional Images

流淌斑
Flowing Mottles

二维 Two-dimensional	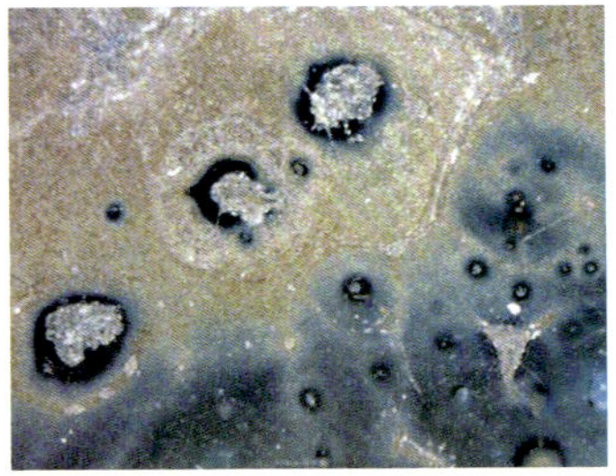	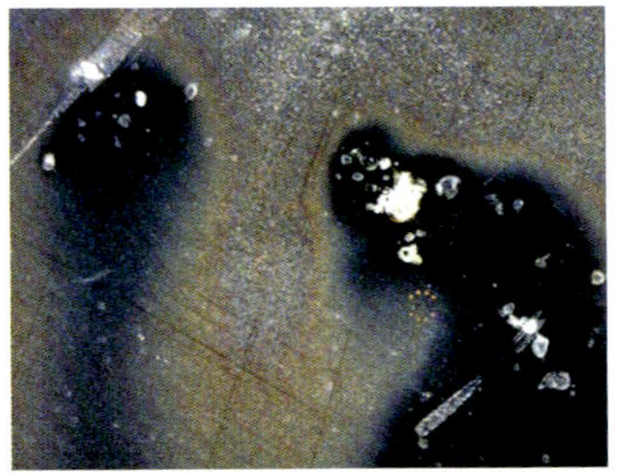		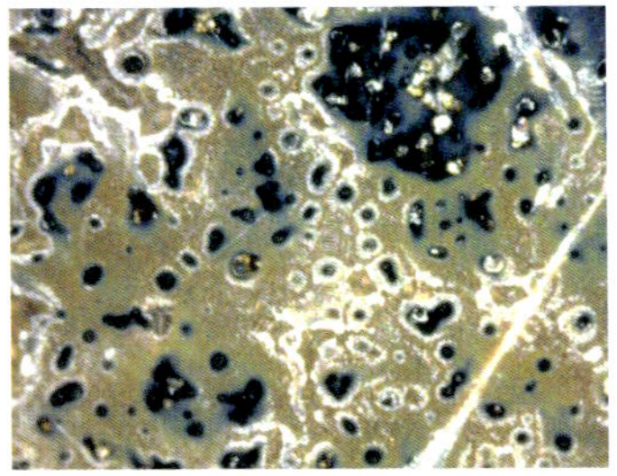
三维 Three-dimensional	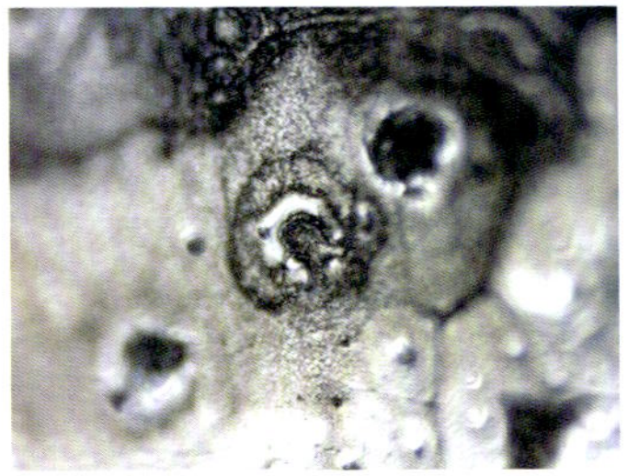	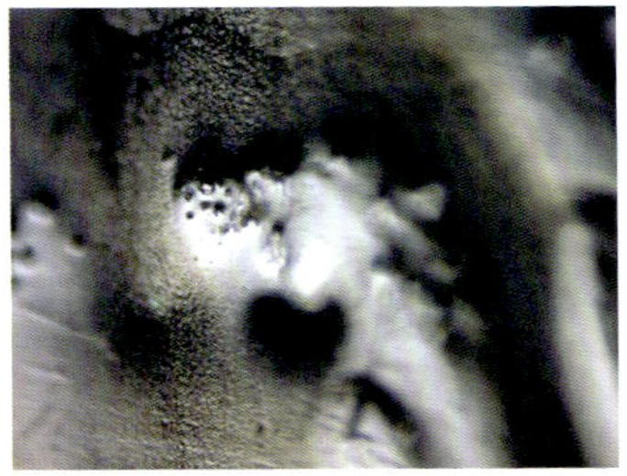	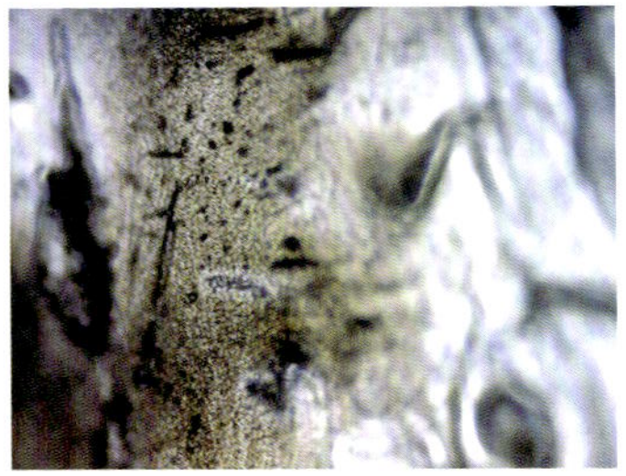	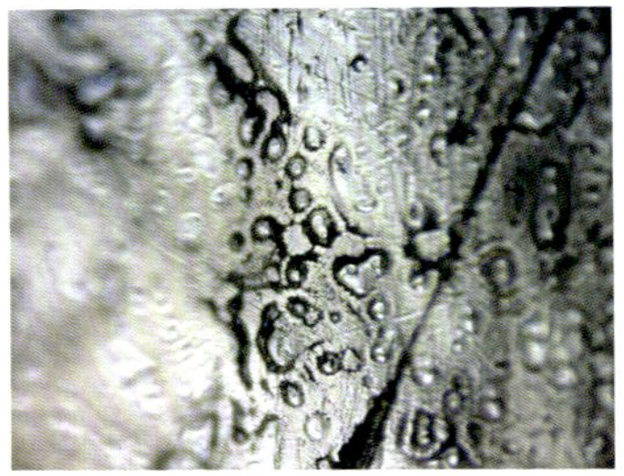

放射斑
Radiating Mottles

二维 Two-dimensional		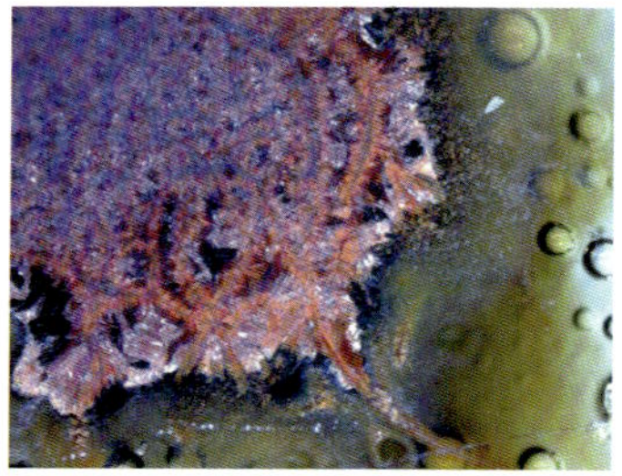	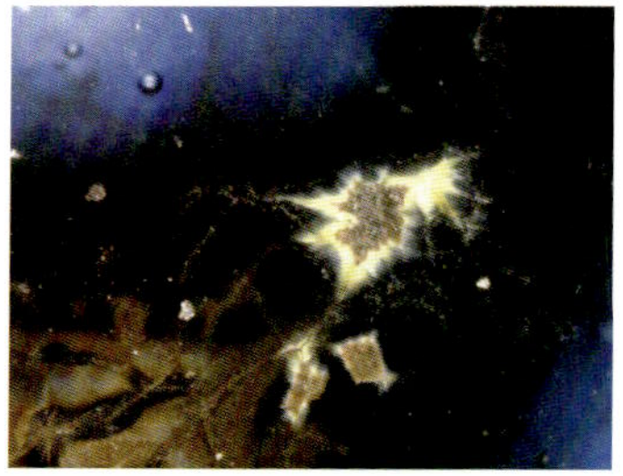	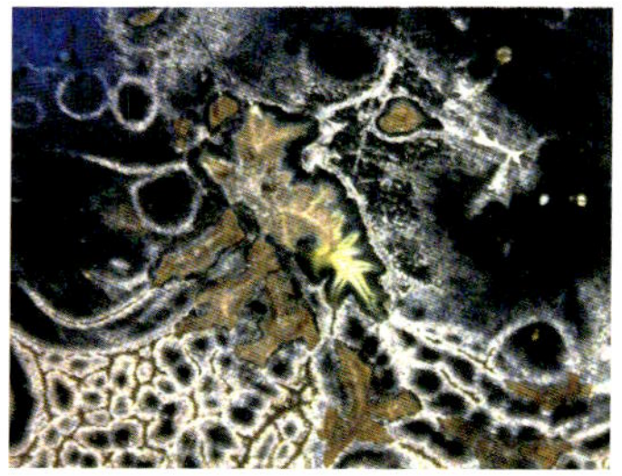
三维 Three-dimensional	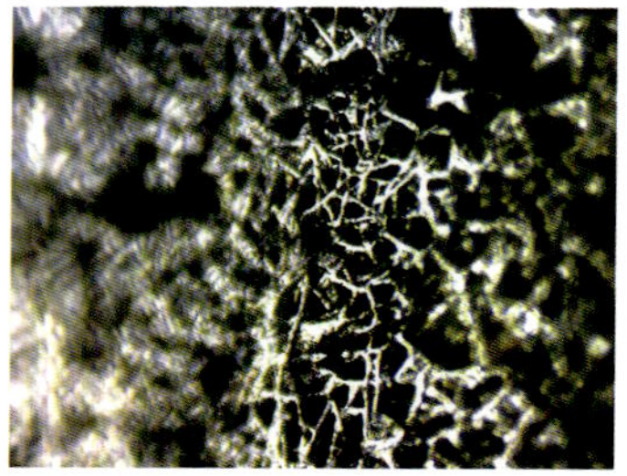	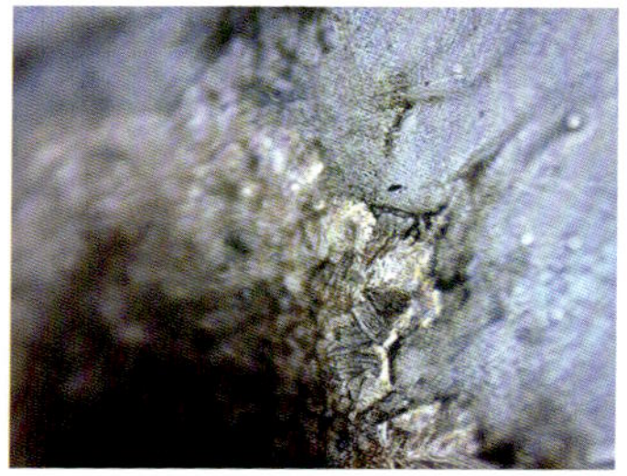	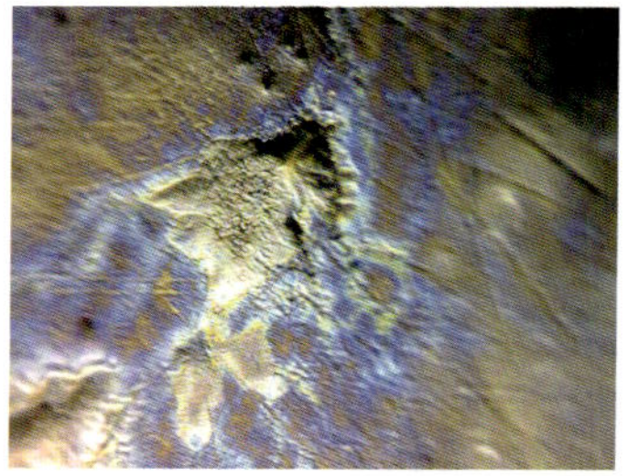	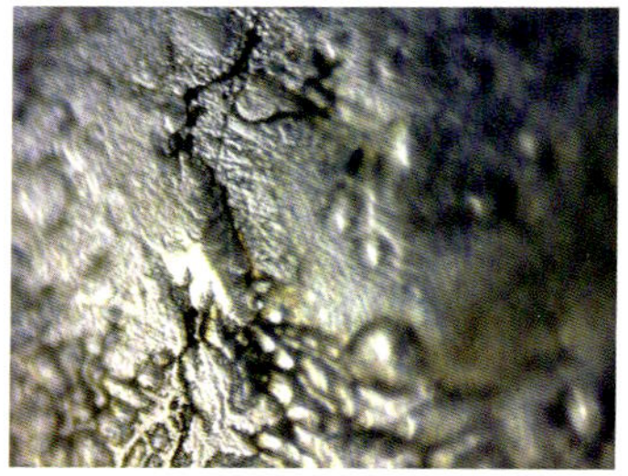
二维 Two-dimensional	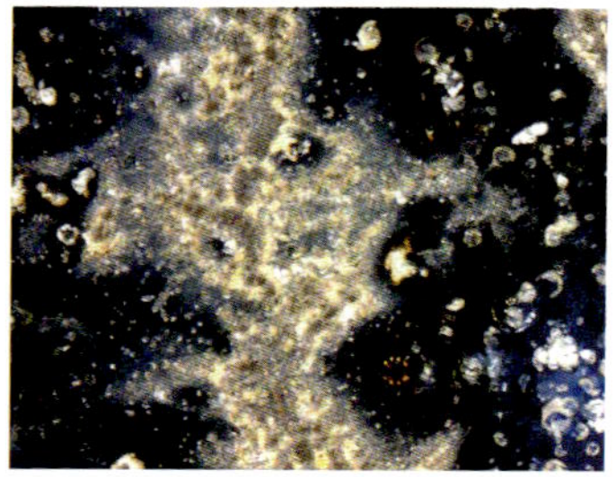	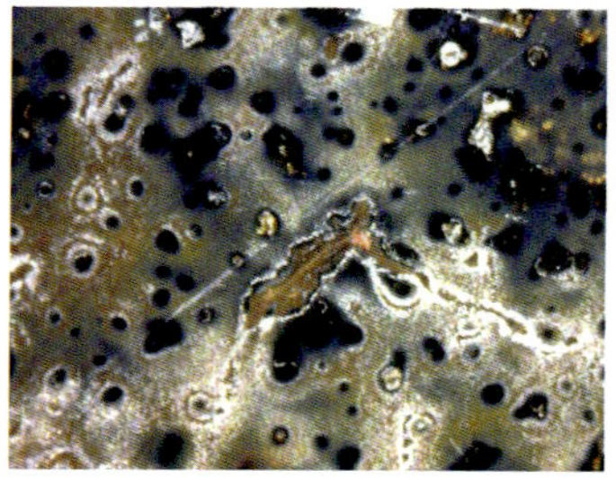		
三维 Three-dimensional		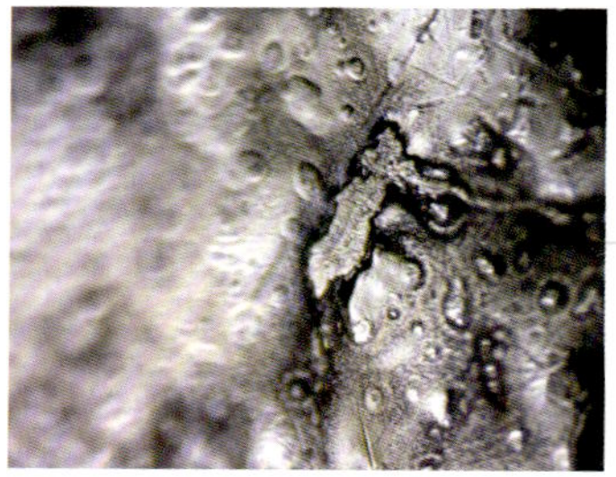	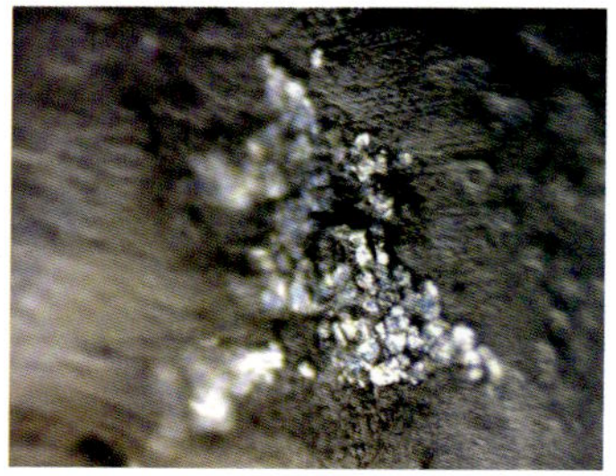	

针眼斑
Needlepoint Mottles

二维 Two-dimensional		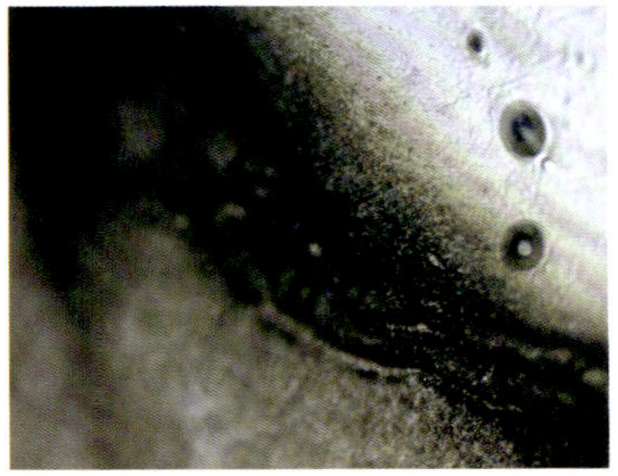	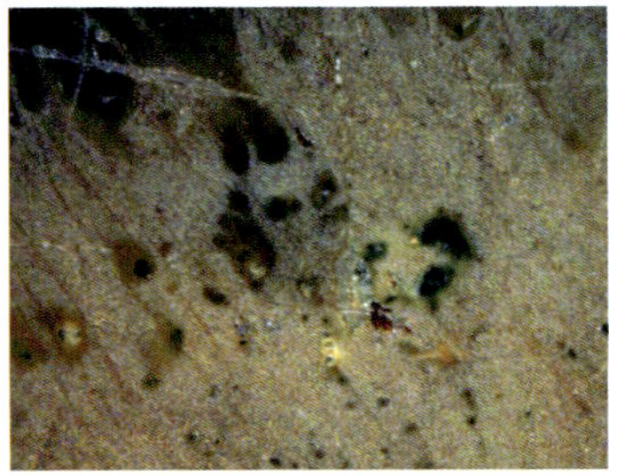	
三维 Three-dimensional	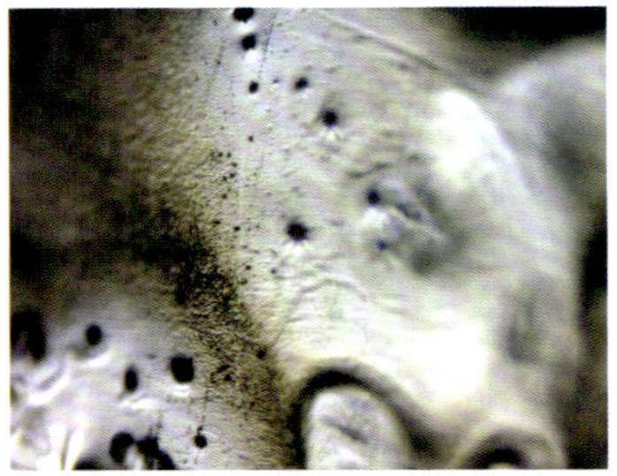	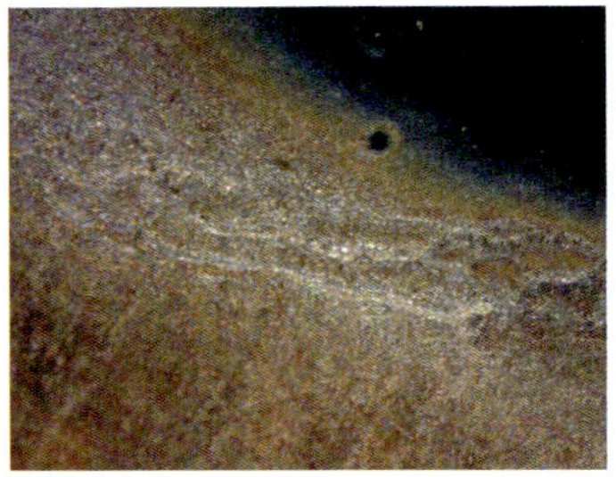	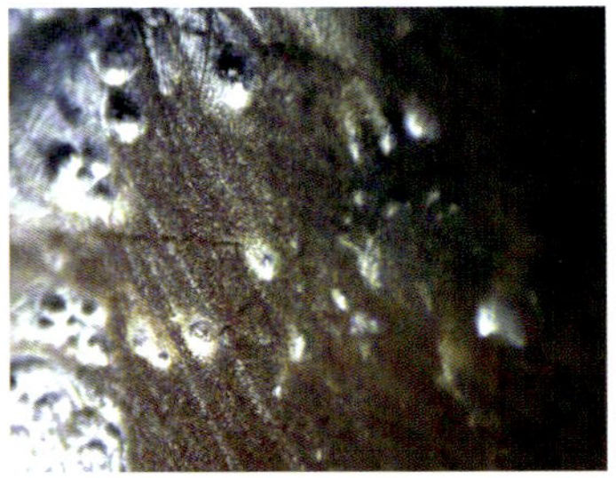	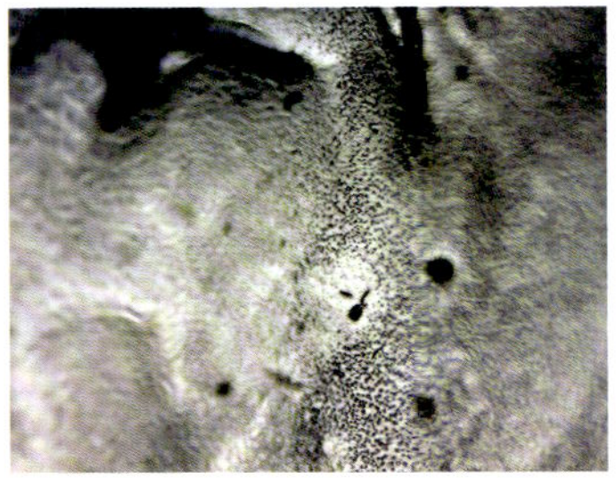

坑点斑
Pit Mottles

二维 Two-dimensional	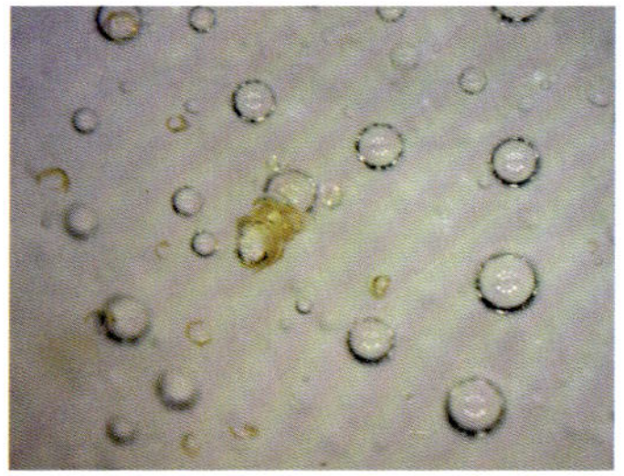	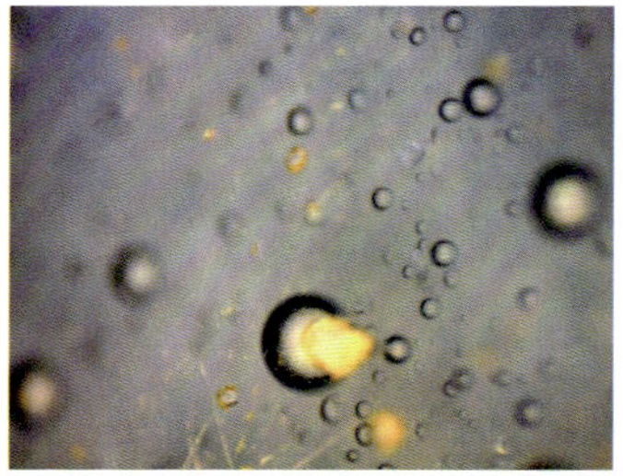	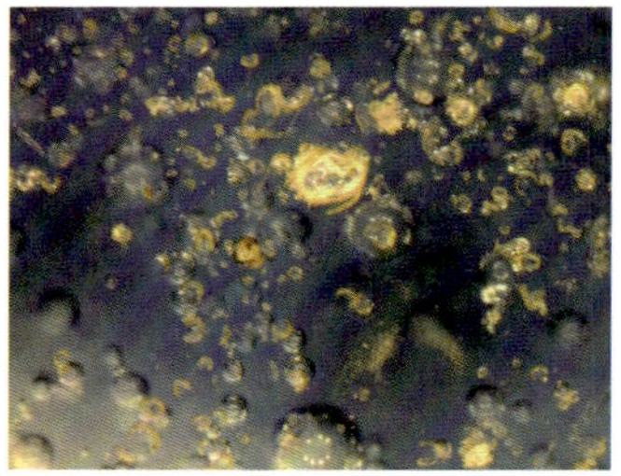	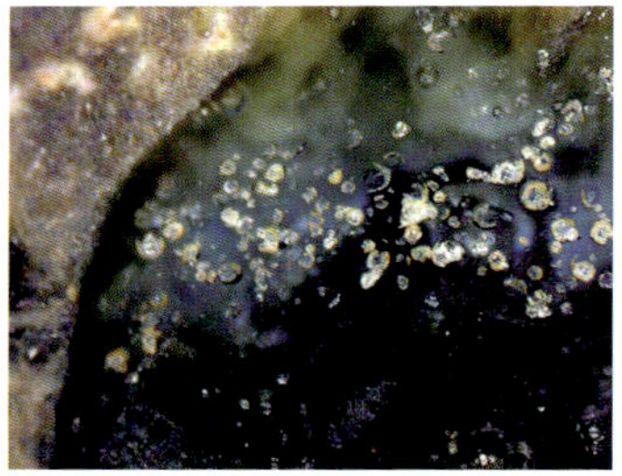
三维 Three-dimensional	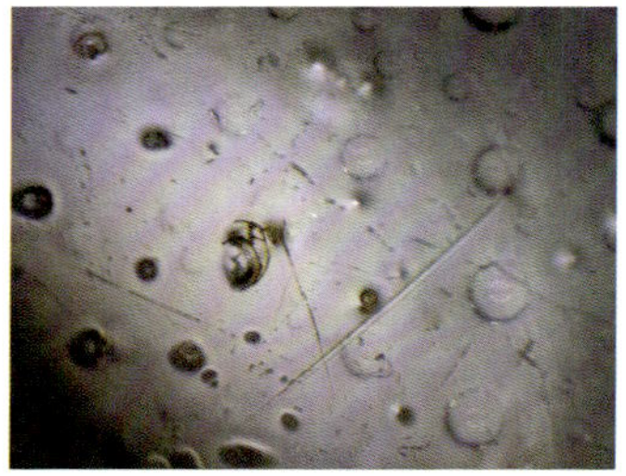	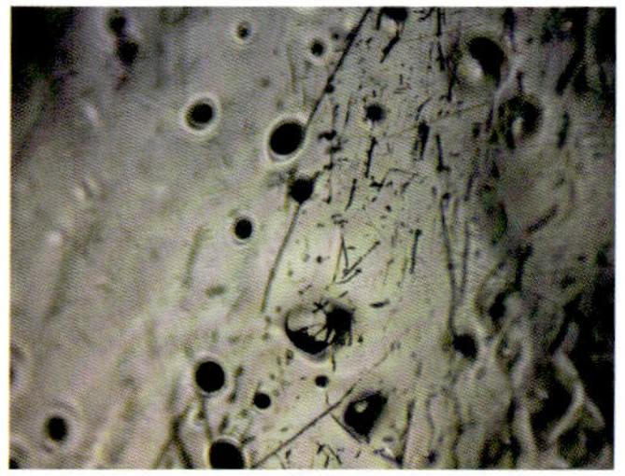	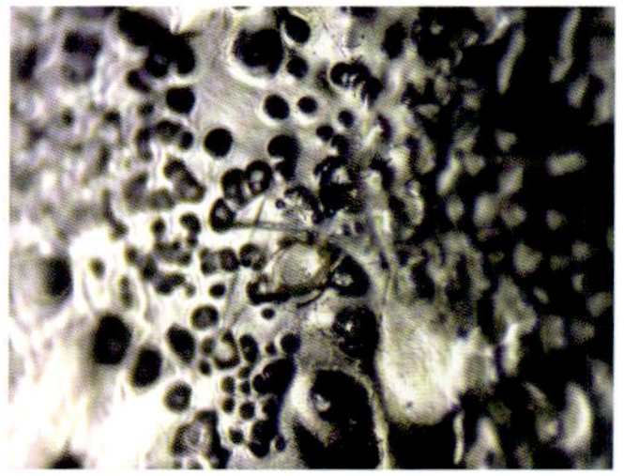	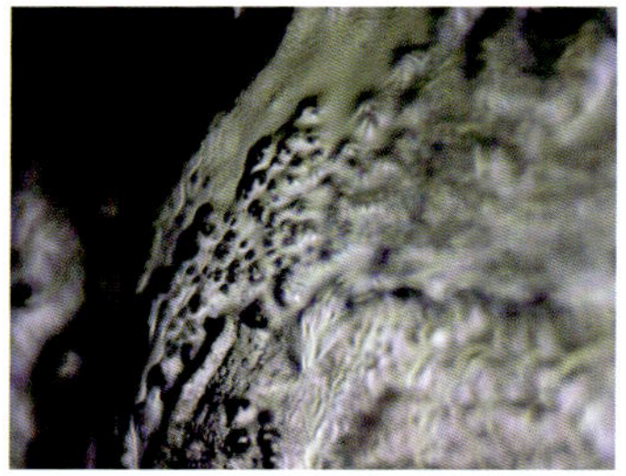
二维 Two-dimensional	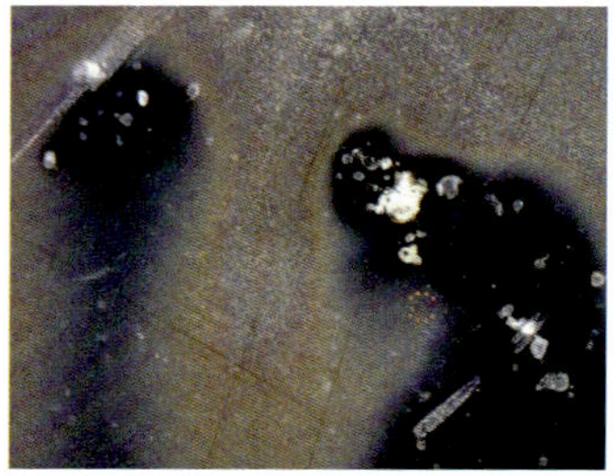			
三维 Three-dimensional	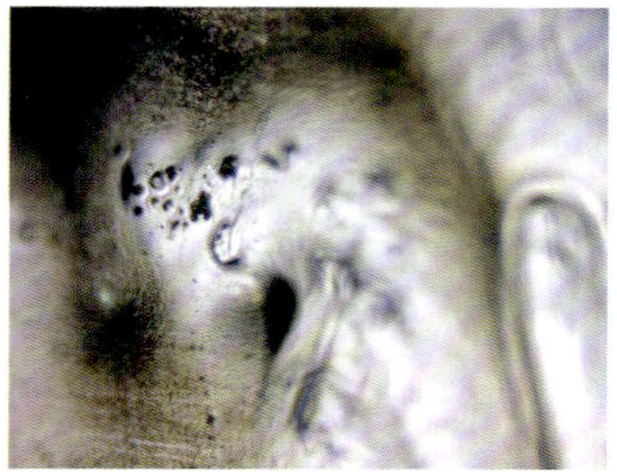			

流淌纹
Flowing Striae

二维 Two-dimensional			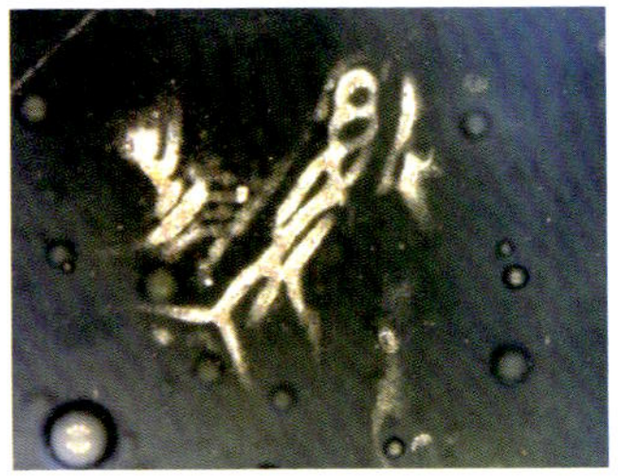	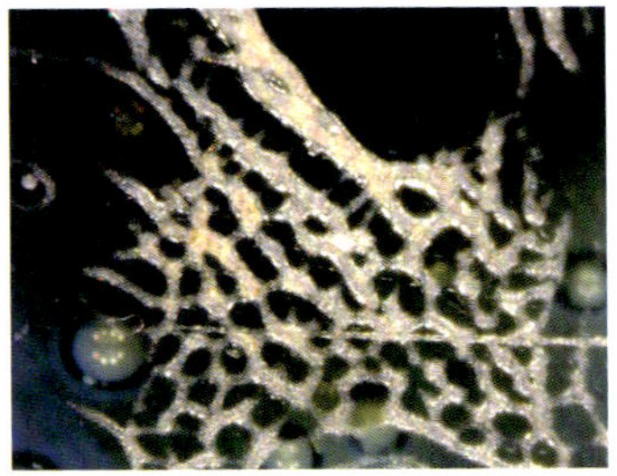
三维 Three-dimensional		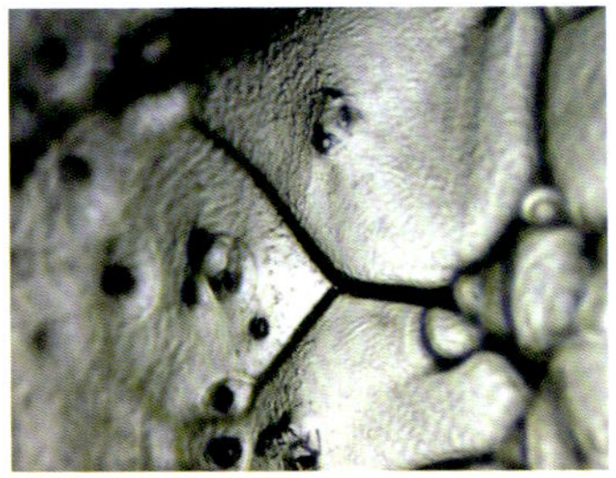	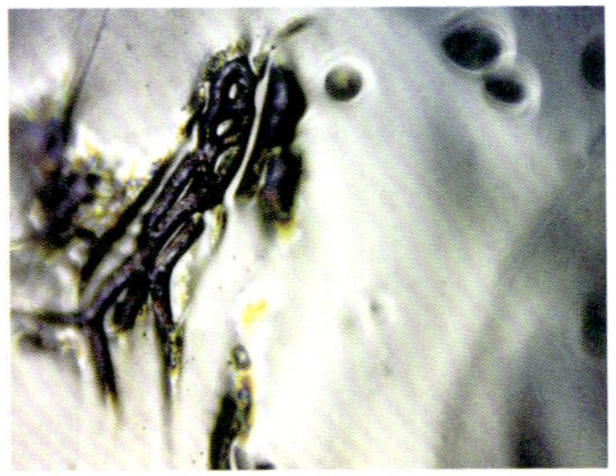	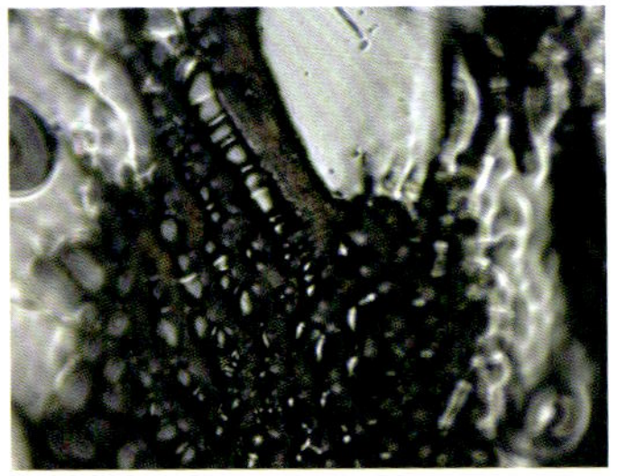
二维 Two-dimensional		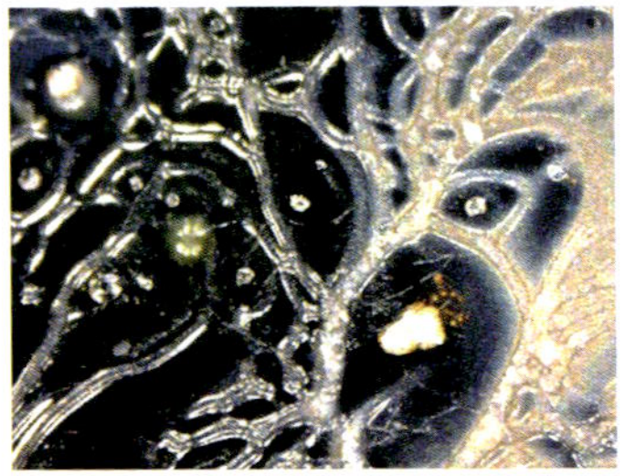		
三维 Three-dimensional	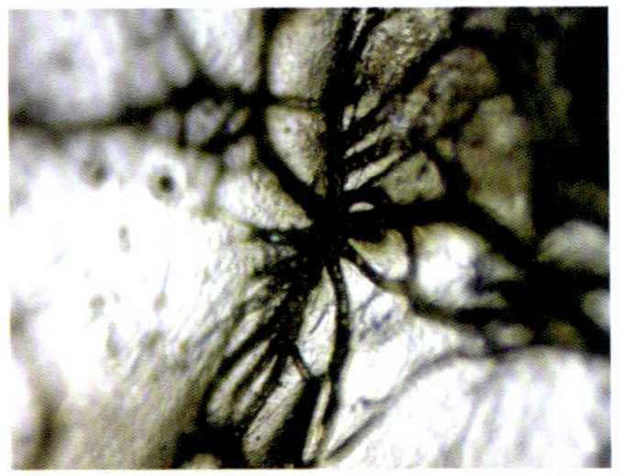			

（续表）

（Continued）

二维 Two-dimensional	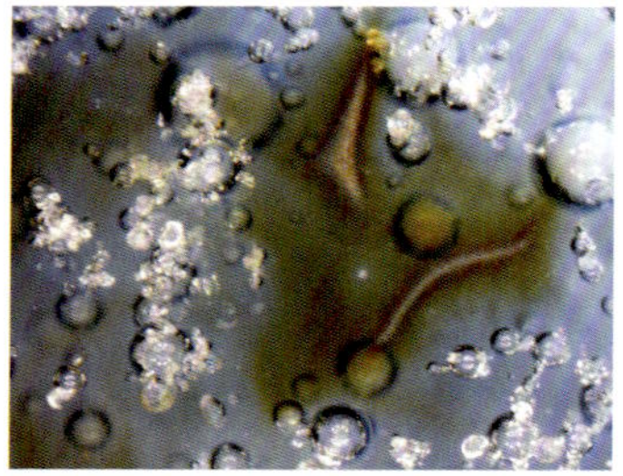		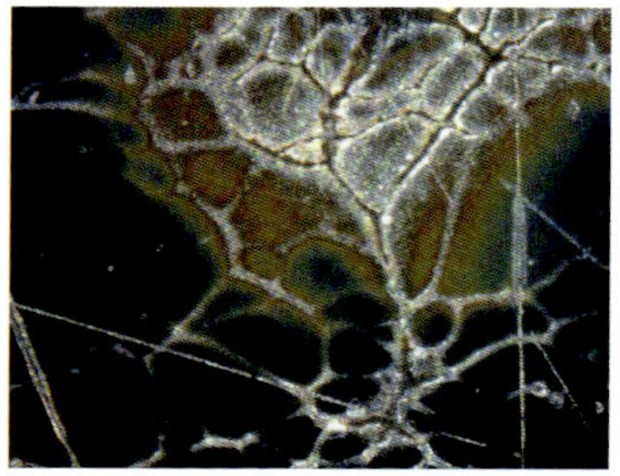	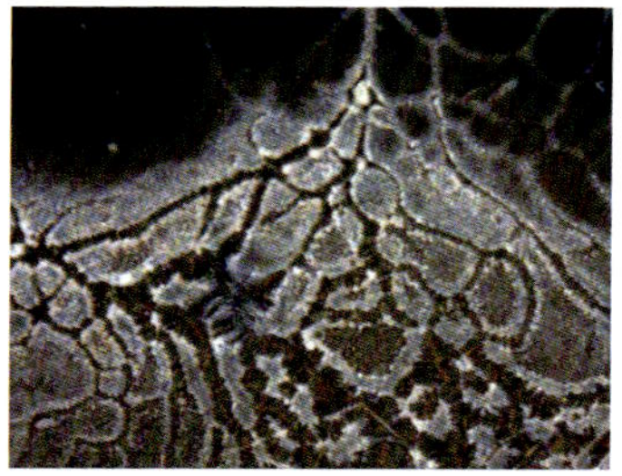
三维 Three-dimensional	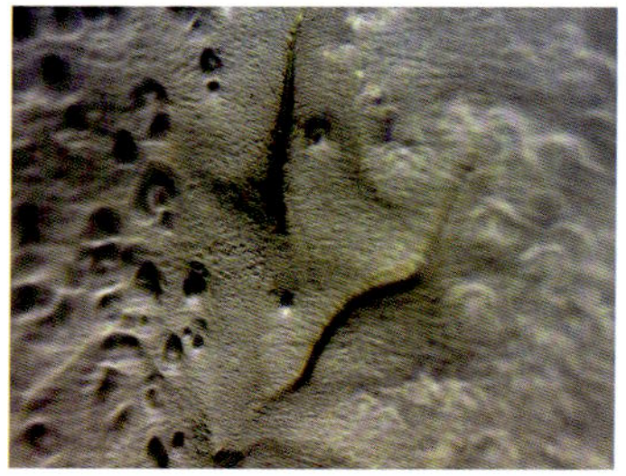	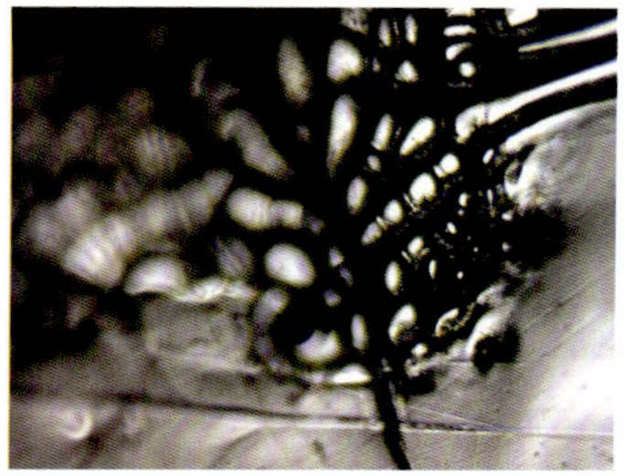	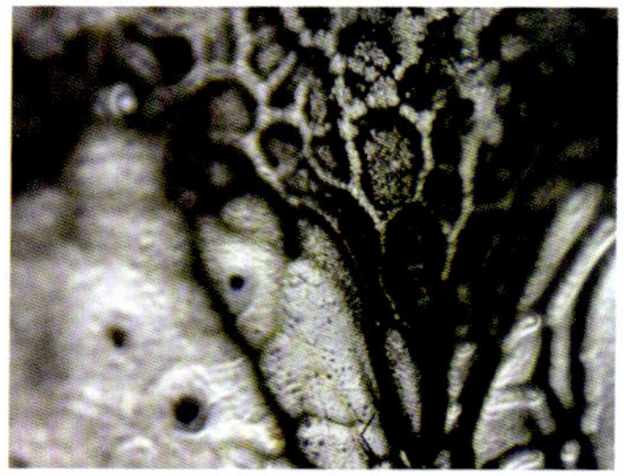	

划痕
Scratches

二维 Two-dimensional		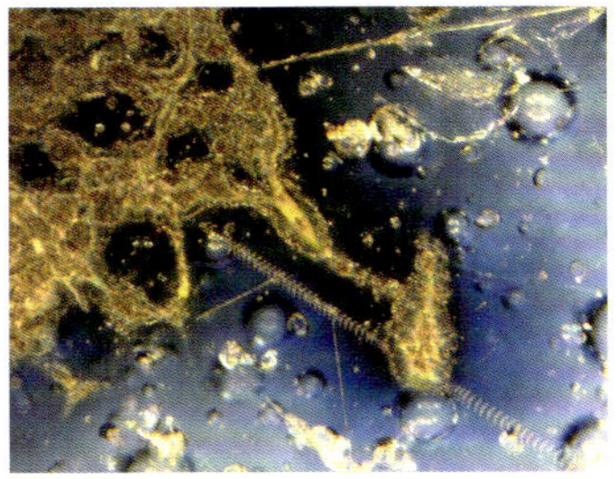	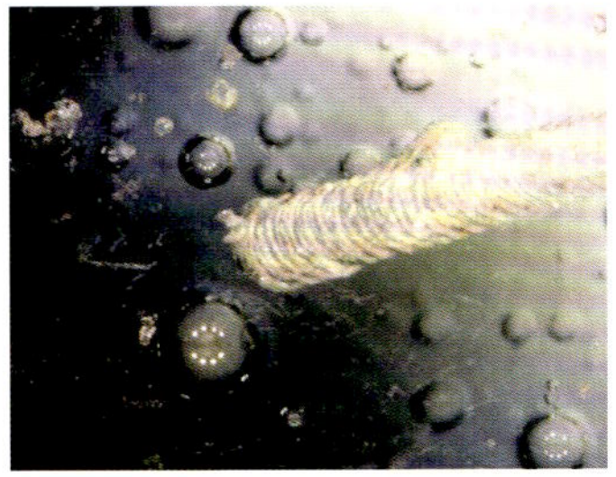	
三维 Three-dimensional	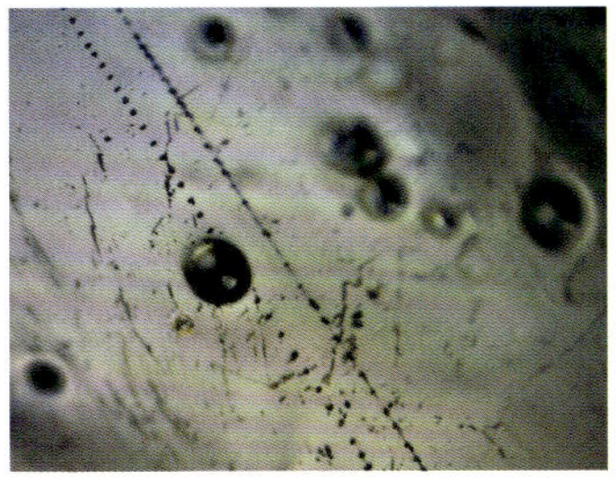	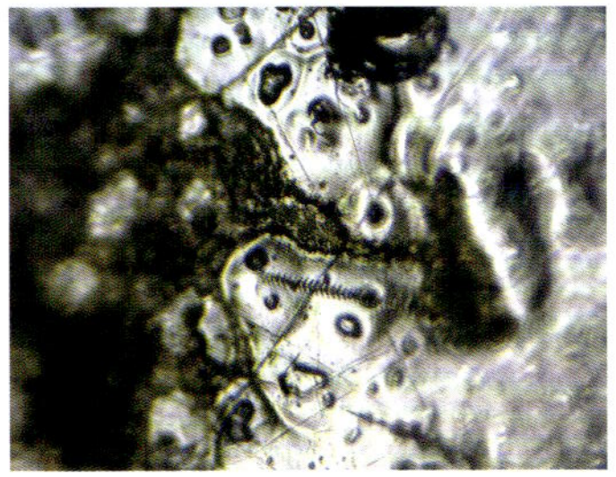	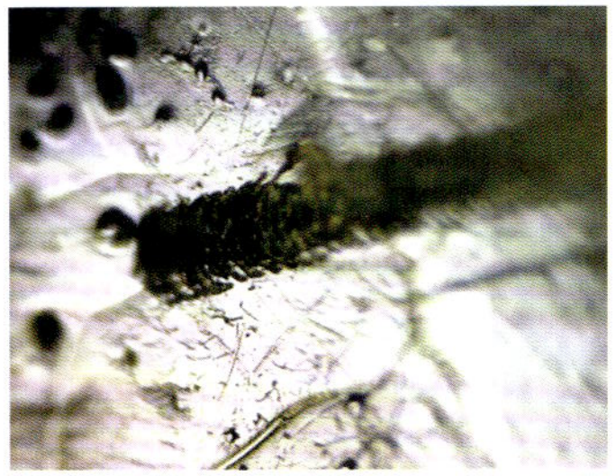	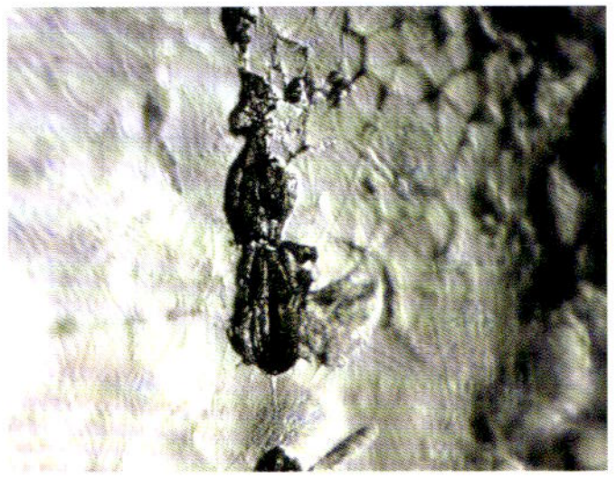
二维 Two-dimensional				
三维 Three-dimensional	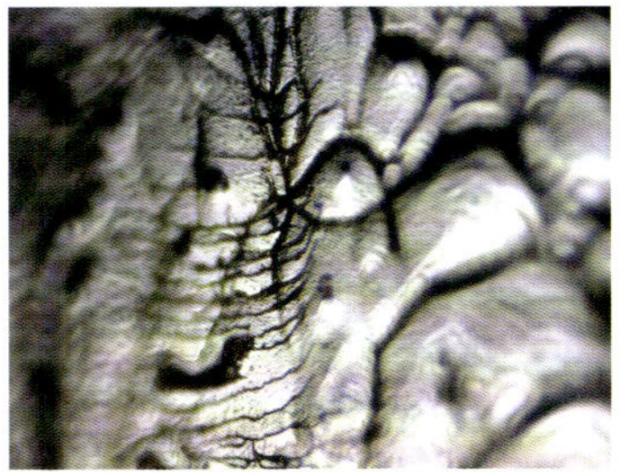			

色变泡
Color Change Bubbles

二维 Two-dimensional	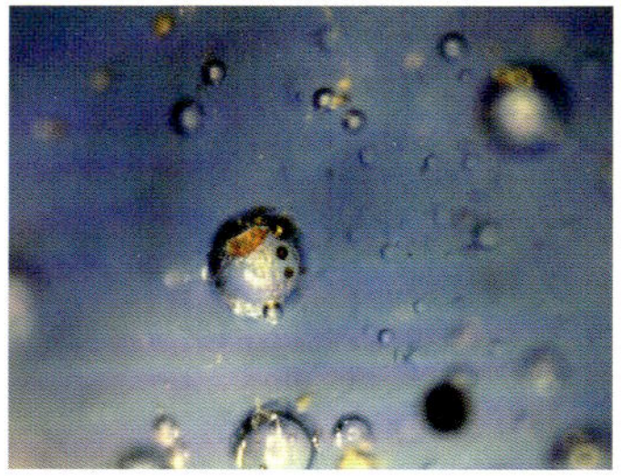	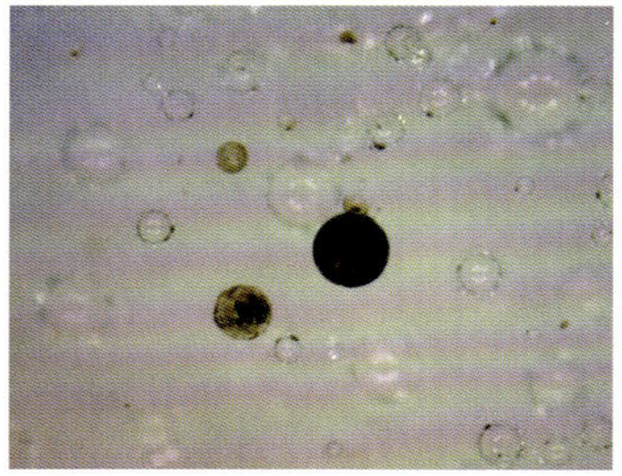	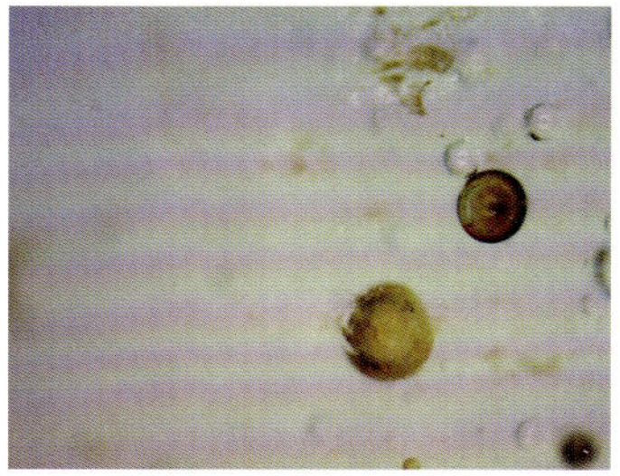	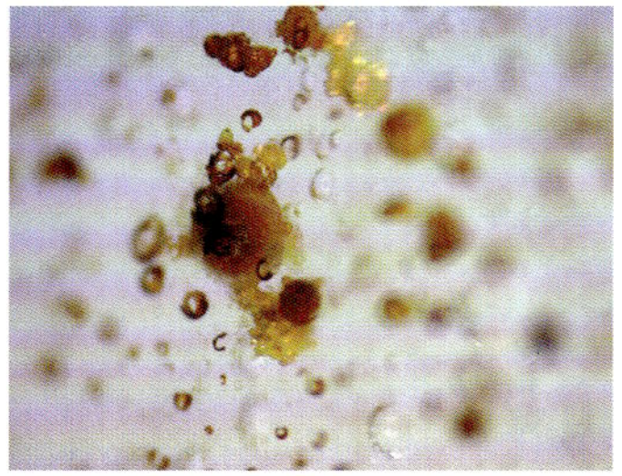
三维 Three-dimensional	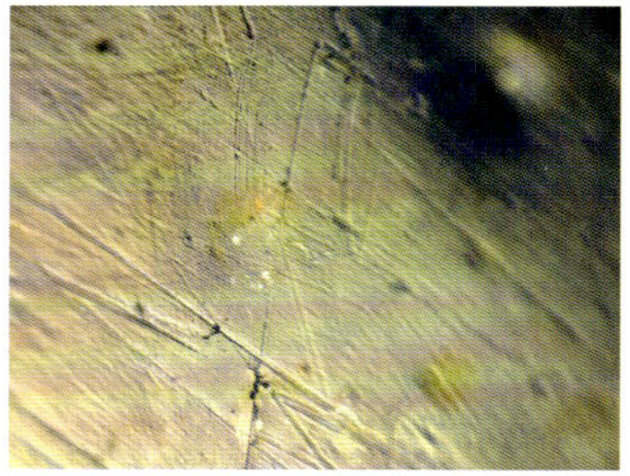	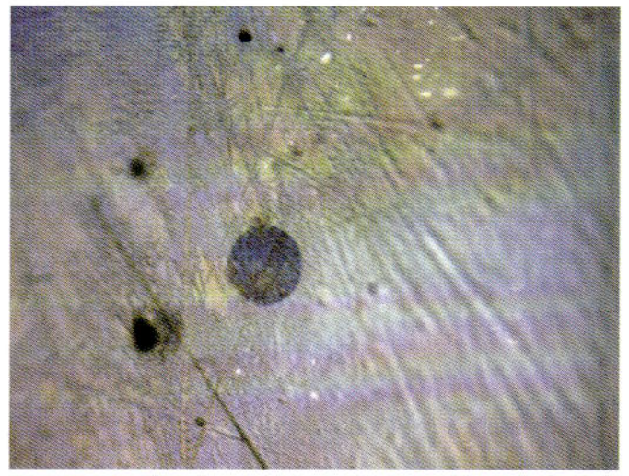	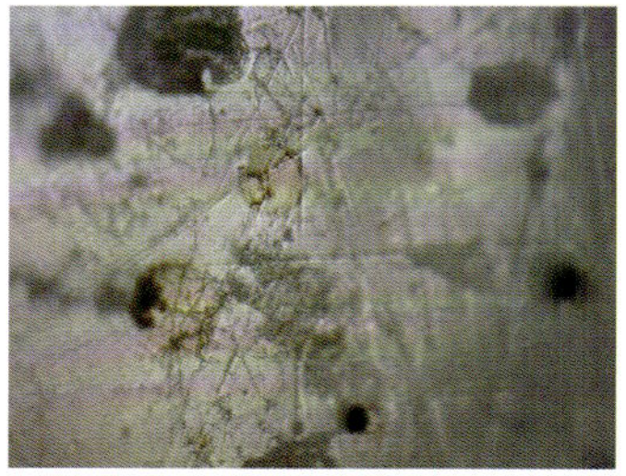	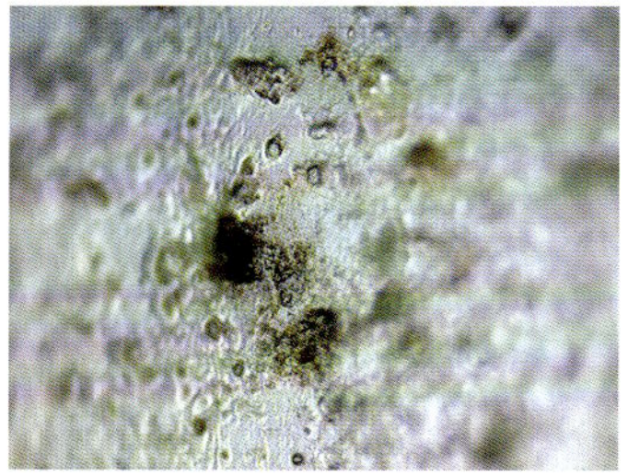

壁变泡
Textured Bubbles

二维 Two-dimensional		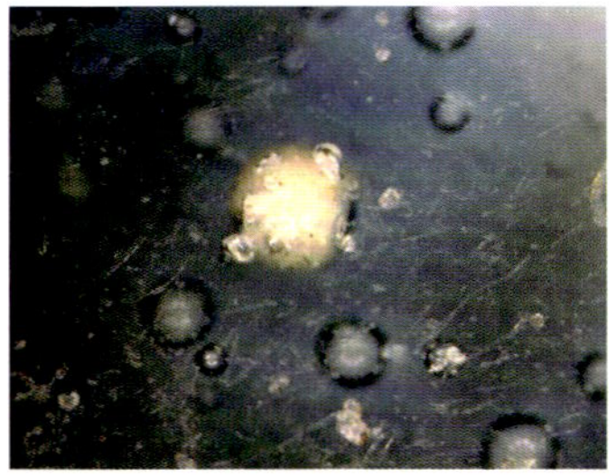	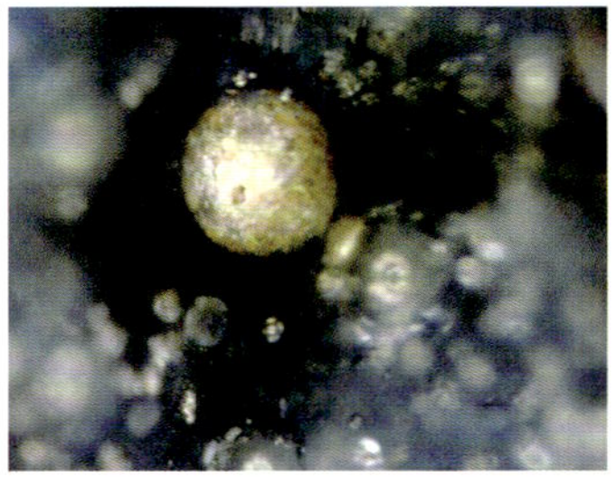	
三维 Three-dimensional		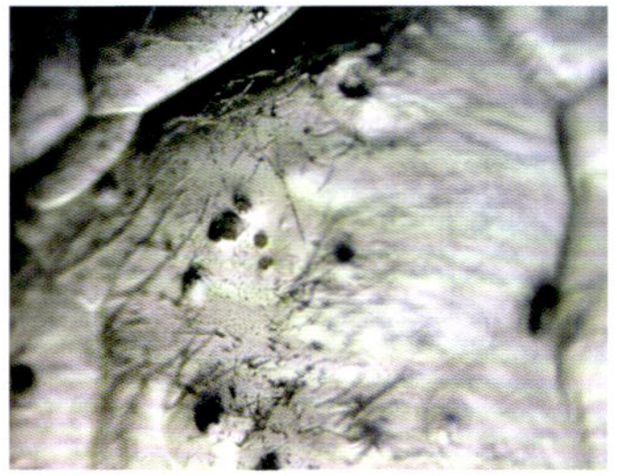	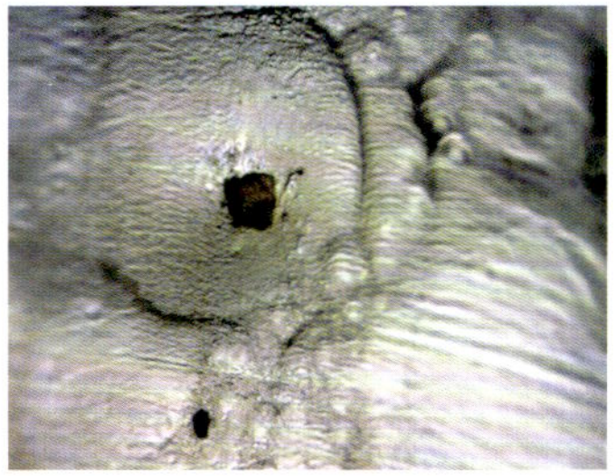	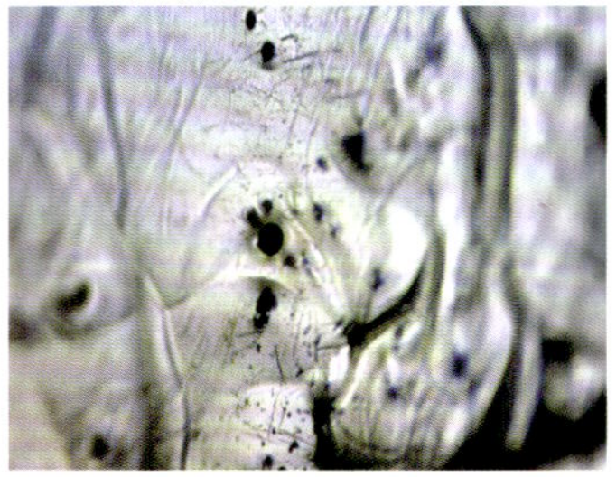
二维 Two-dimensional	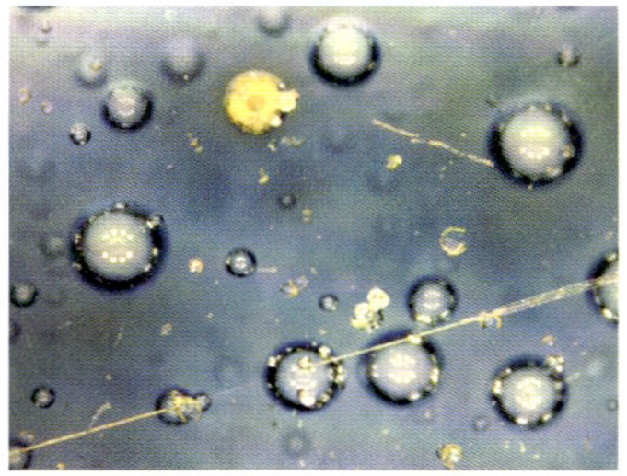	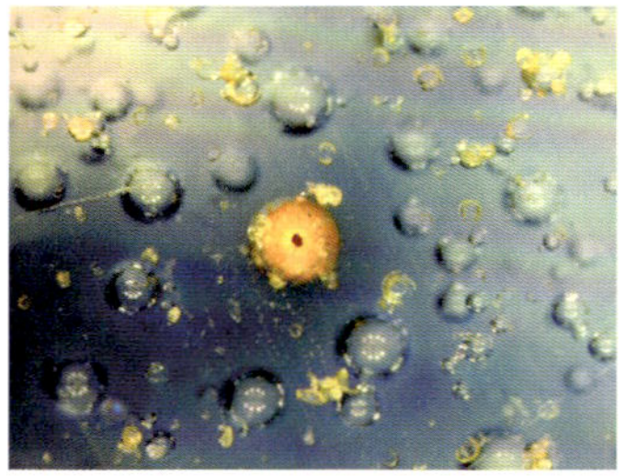		
三维 Three-dimensional	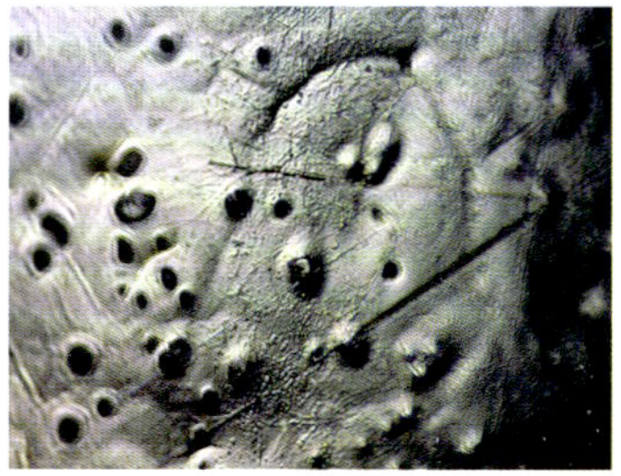	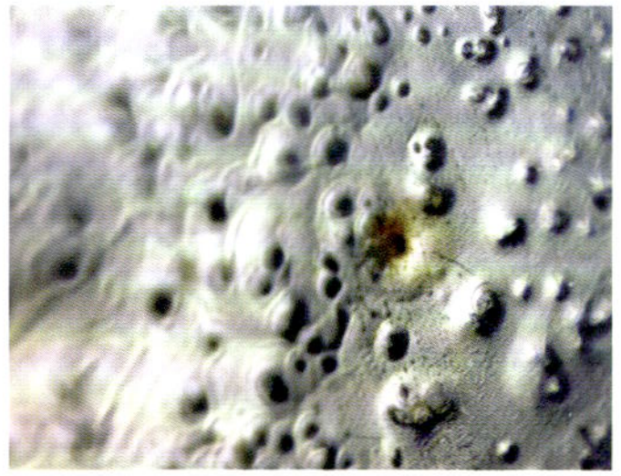		

第九章

元青花迹型真品与赝品比对分析

阅读提示：

本章将元青花真品与赝品上的四大迹型类别（斑块、纹路、气泡及鬃眼）分类进行深入的比对描述及分析。

主要论述问题：

1. 元青花真品与赝品上的各斑块种类有什么区别？
2. 元青花真品与赝品上的各纹路种类有什么区别？
3. 元青花真品与赝品上的各气泡种类有什么区别？
4. 元青花真品与赝品上的鬃眼有什么区别？

Chapter 9

Genuine and Forged Yuan Underglaze Blue Trace Comparative Analysis

Text Note:

This chapter enters into the deep comparative description and analysis of the four trace categories (Mottles, Striae, Bubbles, and Bristle Pits) of genuine and forged YUB.

科学研究的目的是对自然现象进行探索。研究取得的成果能提高人们对自然现象及规律的认识，具有认识论的意义。

文物保护的目的就是传承中华民族的文化。传承文化首先要识真驱假，文物以真为贵，只有真，才有传承的必要，才能彰显民族文化的价值与特色。

文物鉴定识真驱假，于过去而言，是使真正的民族文化得以传承；于未来而言，既是对子孙后代负责，又是对国家与民族负责。

文物鉴定识真驱假，有利于倡导社会诚信、维护市场公平、繁荣文化市场，使民族文化发扬光大。

当代陶瓷造假技术已经可以蒙骗不少眼学专家。当代假鉴、乱鉴藏品，也蒙骗了不少藏家。

如果我们再用肉眼与高仿技术抗衡，那无疑是螳臂当车，心有余而力不足。所以，必须借助科学仪器，延伸我们的观测器官，这样才能有效识破陶瓷迹型假象，提高陶瓷鉴定水平。

陶瓷生产出来以后，就会产生风化现象。长期的自然风化，会在陶瓷表面留下痕迹。古陶瓷上存在着的这些风化迹型，正等待我们去观察和发现。从来不缺少迹型物证，缺的是判别迹型真假的眼力，就像从来不缺少演员，缺的是舞台。

利用科学仪器观察陶瓷迹型，识破人为做旧迹型的假象，是一门慢工出细活的学问。研究者必须坚持不懈、扎扎实实地去观察大量的真品标本上的迹型，才能领悟到“真迹与假迹”的微妙区别，才能从相似的真假迹型中辨识出它们的“不似”之处。

“真迹与假迹”在500倍显微成像下，至今尚存真假难辨的情况。研究者要继续深入研究，在这些真假难辨的迹型中找出差异，有效地识真驱假。

本章比对分析时选用的真品元青花均为已被证实的元代青花瓷器，赝品均为研究团队定制的高仿元青花。

The purpose of Scientific Research is the exploration of Natural Phenomenon. The fruits of research elevate our understanding of natural phenomenon and laws, and are meaningful to the theory of knowledge.

The goal of relic conservation is the preservation of [Chinese] culture, but in order to preserve culture we must ensure the authenticity of such relics. Only when relics are authentic are they worth conservation, and only then is there a clearer depiction of a culture's value and characteristics.

Cultural relic authentication is the preservation of a people's culture, and carries a responsibility to our future generations, our country, and our people.

Cultural relic authentication can initiate society's trust, ensure market equality, proliferate the cultural market, and carry forward national culture.

Currently, forgery techniques and false authentication have pulled the wool over the eyes of many experienced professionals and collectors.

If we continue forward with using the naked eye to contend with forgery technology, even though there may be a will, there is no capacity to keep up. Thus, we must draw support from scientific instruments to enhance our observation ability, and effectively cut through the false appearance of ceramic traces and elevate our authentication standard.

From the firing of ceramics onwards, the weathering phenomenon takes place. A long period of weathering leaves traces on the surface of ceramics. The traces left on the face of antique ceramics are just waiting for our observation and discovery. Similar to the saying "there is never a lack of actors, just a lack of stages"; ceramics have never lacked material evidence, there has only been a lack of vision to differentiate true and false ceramic traces.

The use of scientific instruments cuts through the false trace appearances of man-made forgeries. However, it is a slow work of systematic learning that yields fine results. The microscopic observation of ceramic traces is a laborious project that requires unending patience and determination to observe huge amounts of authentic samples in order to discover the fine dissimilarities between genuine and forged traces. Only then are we able to decipher the seemingly indistinguishable, and separate real from fake.

Under the current limitation of 500X magnification observation, difficulty still presents when distinguishing real and fake traces. Researchers must relentlessly continue to deepen research, and dig out the differences in these seemingly indistinguishable traces, and bring forth effective authentication means.

The genuine samples used in this chapter for comparative analysis are all YUB of known authenticity, and the forgeries are high–end fakes purchased by the research team for the purpose of research.

第一节
元青花斑块真品与赝品比对

一、流淌斑

（一）火焰形沙滩斑

火焰形沙滩斑斑块尾部呈火焰形，是元青花瓷器上一种典型迹型。赝品上少见火焰形沙滩斑。

1. 真品二维特征

见图9-1-1。

（1）沙滩斑上的雾状针眼斑与磨砂针眼斑关系分明，层次清晰。

（2）沙滩斑与玻璃相界线分明，图片整体干净清晰。

2. 赝品二维特征

见图9-1-2。（该器物釉表面曾被腐蚀剂腐蚀）

（1）沙滩斑上雾状针眼斑与磨砂针眼斑二者关系模糊。

（2）沙滩斑与玻璃相界线不分明，图片整体涂污模糊。

（二）荷叶形沙滩斑

荷叶形沙滩斑是元青花瓷器上较火焰形更常见的沙滩斑。

1. 真品二维特征

见图9-1-3、图9-1-5。

（1）沙滩斑上的雾状针眼斑与磨砂针眼斑关系分明，层次清晰。

（2）沙滩斑上的玻璃相圆孔清晰独立，与周围沙滩斑界线分明，彼此有明显的颜色差异。

（3）沙滩斑整体与周围玻璃相界线分明。

2. 真品三维特征

（1）沙滩斑下凹，整体显得细腻平滑。

（2）玻璃相圆孔凸起，表面光滑洁净。

（3）沙滩斑与玻璃相圆孔有高度差，界线分明。

（4）沙滩斑上的磨砂针眼斑呈密集点状凹坑。

见图9-1-3、图9-1-4，二者为同一器物同一位置图片，图9-1-3为二维图片，图9-1-4为三维图片。

见图9-1-5、图9-1-6，二者为同一器物同一位置图片，图9-1-5为二维图片，图9-1-6为三维图片。

图9-1-4及图9-1-6中，箭头A及箭头B所指的玻璃相与周围沙滩斑相比呈凸起状，周围沙滩斑下凹，二者有明显高度差，界线分明。

图9-1-4及图9-1-6中，玻璃相圆孔表面光滑洁净，与周围沙滩斑界线分明。

沙滩斑上的磨砂针眼斑呈密集点状凹坑，斑块整体显得细腻平滑（见图9-1-6）。

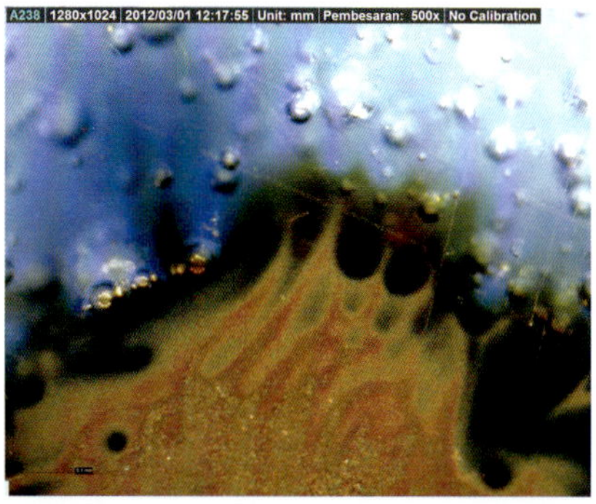

图9-1-1

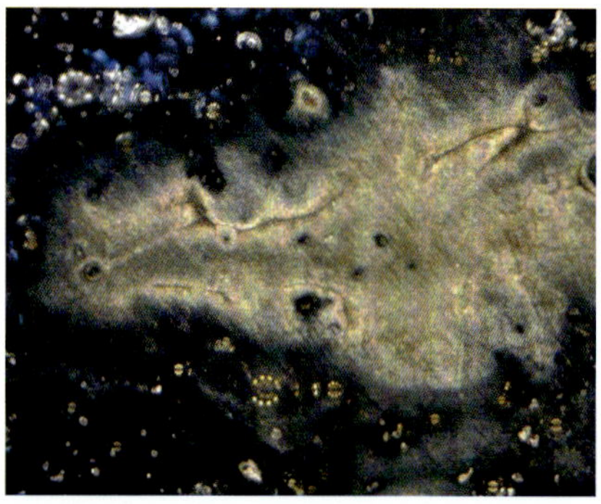
图9-1-2

Section 1:
Genuine and Forged Yuan Underglaze Blue Mottle Comparison

1. Flowing Mottle

A. Flame Shaped Beach Mottle

Flame shaped beach mottles refer to the typical YUB trace type of beach mottles with flame-like edges. The occurrence of this trace type on forged articles is extremely rare.

I. Two-Dimensional Characteristics of Genuine Article

See picture 9-1-1.

a. Clearly defined relationship between the foggy and frosted needlepoint mottling on the beach mottle, clear gradation.

b. Clear delineation between the beach mottle and surrounding glass phase, the image as a whole is clean and clear.

II. Two-Dimensional Characteristics of Forged Article

See picture 9-1-2 (this piece has undergone treatment with aging reagent).

a. Muddled relationship between the foggy and frosted needlepoint mottling on the beach mottle.

b. No clear delineation between the beach mottle and surrounding glass phase, the image as a whole is muddled.

B. Lotus Leaf Shaped Beach Mottle

Lotus leaf shaped beach mottles refer to the typical YUB trace type of beach mottles which occur more commonly than flame shaped.

I. Two-Dimensional Characteristics of Genuine Article

See pictures 9-1-3 and 9-1-5.

a. Clearly defined relationship between the foggy and frosted needlepoint mottling on the beach mottle, clear gradation.

b. Clear independence of the glass phase openings on the beach mottle, retaining clear delineation with said mottle, and clear color difference between the two.

c. Clear delineation between the beach mottle and surrounding glass phase.

II. Three-Dimensional Characteristics of Genuine Article

a. The beach mottle is slightly concave, as a whole appears fine and even.

b. The glass phase openings are convex, surface smooth and clean.

c. Topographical discrepancy between the beach mottle and glass phase.

d. Frosted needlepoint mottling appears as densely distributed pin points.

See pictures 9-1-3 and 9-1-4, where 9-1-3 is the two-dimensional and 9-1-4 is the three-dimensional view of the same location.

See pictures 9-1-5 and 9-1-6, where 9-1-5 is the two-dimensional and 9-1-6 is the three-dimensional view of the same location.

The glass phase indicated by Arrows A and B in pictures 9-1-4 and 9-1-6 respectively, are convex in shape, raising up above the surrounding, slightly concave, beach mottle. There is a clear topographical discrepancy and delineation between the two.

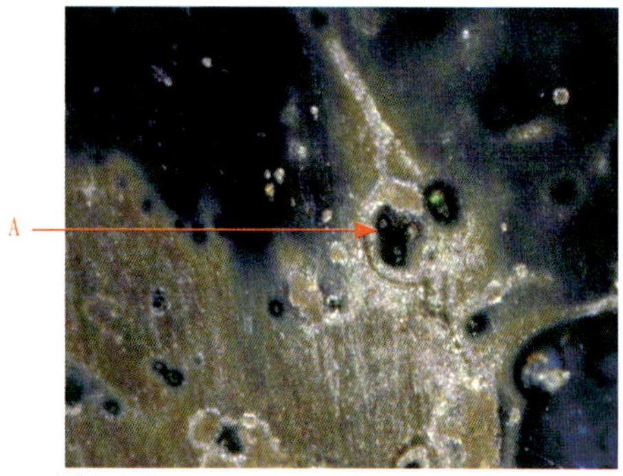

图9-1-3

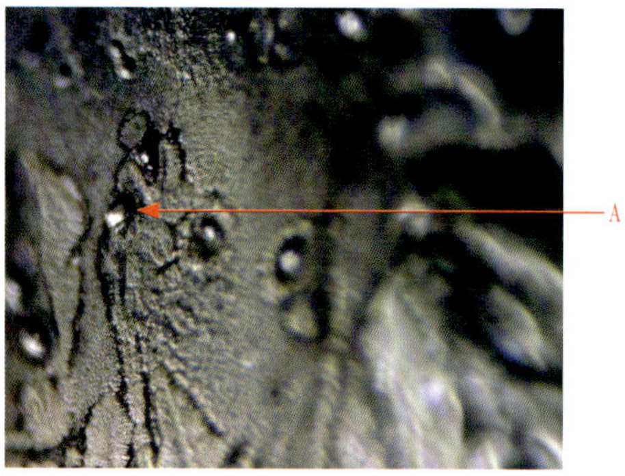

图9-1-4

图9-1-5

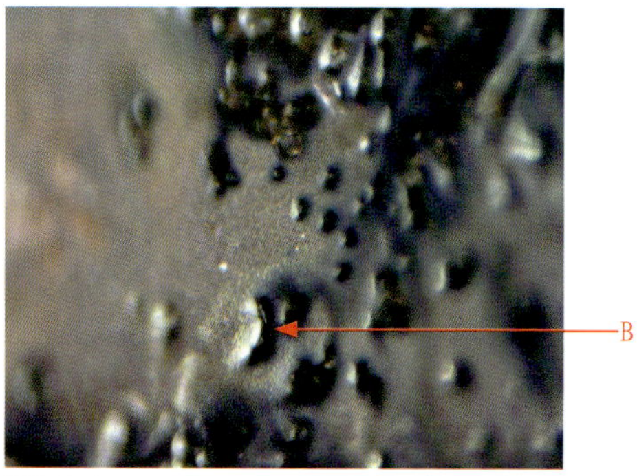

图9-1-6

3. 赝品二维特征

见图9-1-7、图9-1-9。

（1）沙滩斑上的针眼斑形貌一致，没有雾状或磨砂状之分（见图9-1-7）。

（2）沙滩斑上的雾状针眼斑没有明显的浓淡过渡，磨砂针眼斑分布均匀，没有边界感（见图9-1-9）。

（3）沙滩斑没有明显色阶变化。

（4）玻璃相圆孔模糊不清。

（5）沙滩斑与玻璃相界线模糊不清。

4. 赝品三维特征

见图9-1-8、图9-1-10。

（1）沙滩斑上没有明显的点状凹坑（见图9-1-8）。

（2）玻璃相圆孔表面粗糙（见图9-1-10）。

（3）沙滩斑与玻璃相之间没有明显高度差。

（4）沙滩斑与玻璃相界线不清。

见图9-1-7、图9-1-8，二者为同一器物同一位置图片，图9-1-7为二维图片，图9-1-8为三维图片。（该器物釉表面未被腐蚀剂腐

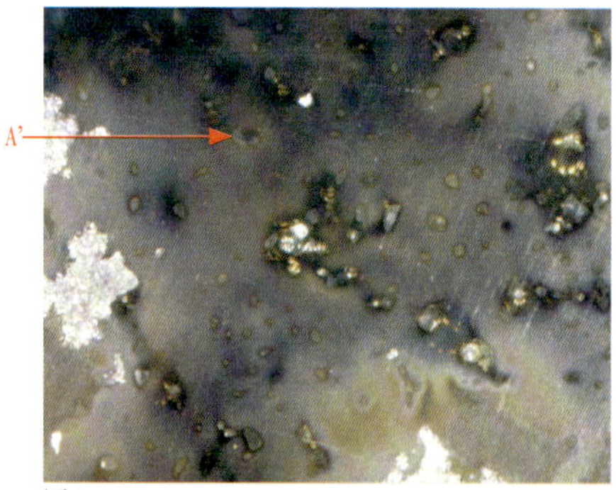

图9-1-7

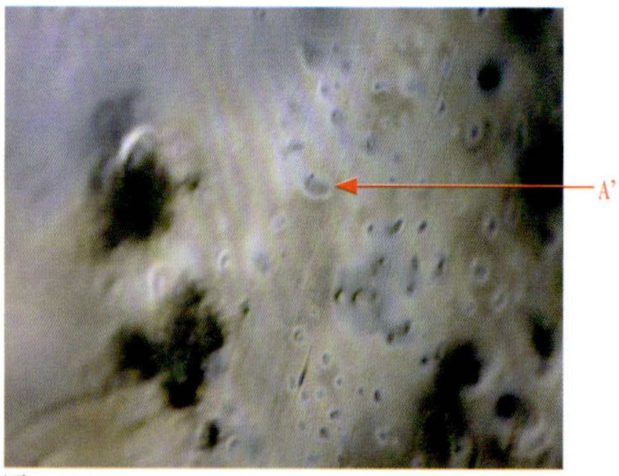

图9-1-8

The glass phase openings in pictures 9-1-4 and 9-1-6 are smooth and clean and clearly delineated from the surrounding beach mottle.

The frosted needlepoint mottling appears as densely distributed pin points, and the mottle as a whole appears fine and even (see picture 9-1-6).

III. Two-Dimensional Characteristics of Forged Article

See pictures 9-1-7 and 9-1-9.

a. The needlepoint mottling on the beach mottle is uniform, no delineation between foggy and frosted (see picture 9-1-7).

b. No clear density gradation in the foggy needlepoint mottling, and the frosted needlepoint mottling is evenly distributed without any sense of borders (see picture 9-1-9).

c. The mottle as a whole lacks color spectrum.

d. Glass phase openings muddled.

e. Delineation between glass phase and beach mottle muddled.

IV. Three-Dimensional Characteristics of Forged Article

See pictures 9-1-8 and 9-1-10.

a. No clear pin points on the beach mottle (see picture 9-1-8).

b. Coarse surface on the glass phase openings (see picture 9-1-10).

c. No clear topographical discrepancy between the glass phase and beach mottle.

d. Boundary between the glass phase and beach mottle unclear.

See pictures 9-1-7 and 9-1-8, where 9-1-7 is the two-dimensional and 9-1-8 is the three-dimensional view of the same location (this piece has not undergone treatment with aging reagent).

See pictures 9-1-9 and 9-1-10, where 9-1-9 is the two-dimensional and 9-1-10 is the three-dimensional view of the same location (this piece has undergone treatment with aging reagent).

The shape of the glass phase opening indicated by Arrow A' in picture 9-1-8 can faintly be seen. There is a lack of topographical discrepancy with the surrounding beach mottle, and its borders are unclear.

The glaze surface in picture 9-1-8 as a whole is relatively smooth, this means that the weathering severity of both the glass phase and beach mottle are relatively low.

There is no clear topographical discrepancy between the glass phase and beach mottle in picture 9-1-10. Areas of frosted needlepoint mottling, although presenting with color variation, do not have noticeable pin points, and the glaze surface as a whole is smooth (see Arrow B').

2. Radiating Mottle

A. Yellow Series Radiating Mottle

I. Two-Dimensional Characteristics of Genuine Article

See pictures 9-1-11 and 9-1-12.

a. Radiating mottle is independent and clear with evident radiating property.

b. Some mottles present with a lined border, which as a whole are very fine and reserved. Very few present as thick, but still retain an overall reserved feel. The borders retain a distance from the edge of the radiating mottle.

c. Glass phase is viewable between the mottle and its border, and the glass phase inside and outside the border is clean and clear.

d. Needlepoint striae can extend out from the mottle border, and the striae are clear and independent.

e. The surroundings can present with relatively delineated frosted needlepoint mottles (see picture 9-1-11).

f. The outlying glass phase is clean and clear with the possible appearance of CO striae and pit mottles; they retain independence and clear delineation (see picture 9-1-12).

II. Three-Dimensional Characteristics of Genuine Article

a. Portions of radiating mottle surfaces are smooth and fine.

b. Portions of radiating mottle surfaces have a radiating

蚀）

见图9-1-9、图9-1-10，二者为同一器物同一位置图片，图9-1-9为二维图片，图9-1-10为三维图片。（该器物釉表面曾被腐蚀剂腐蚀）

图9-1-8中的玻璃相圆孔隐约可见其轮廓，与周围沙滩斑没有明显高度差，界线也不明显（见箭头A’所指处）。图9-1-8中釉表面整体光滑，无明显点状凹坑，说明沙滩斑与玻璃相二者的风化强度都较低。

图9-1-10中的玻璃相与周围沙滩斑无明显高度差，沙滩斑上的磨砂针眼斑所在处虽有颜色变化但不见点状凹坑，釉表面整体较光滑（见箭头B’所指处）。

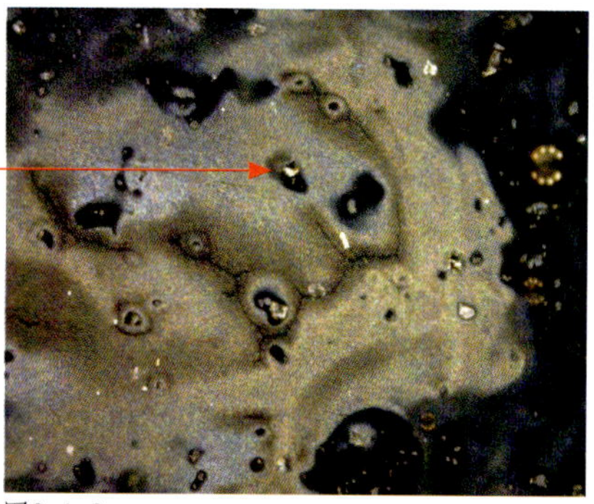

图9-1-9

图9-1-10

二、放射斑

（一）黄色系放射斑

1. 真品二维特征

见图9-1-11、图9-1-12。

（1）放射斑独立清晰，有明显放射感。

（2）有时放射斑边沿有一条包边。包边整体纤细、精致，少量的稍粗，但总体都是清晰的，与放射斑轮廓保持一致。

（3）放射斑与包边之间可见玻璃相，包边内外的玻璃相干净清晰。

（4）放射斑边沿有时会延展出针眼型阴纹，纹路清晰独立。

（5）放射斑周围分布有边界感较强的磨砂针眼斑（见图9-1-11）。

（6）放射斑周围的玻璃相干净清晰，可见C形纹及坑点斑等迹型零星分布，彼此独立，界线分明（见图9-1-12）。

2. 真品三维特征

（1）部分放射斑表面光滑细腻。

（2）部分放射斑表面有放射纹路，但还是比较平滑细腻。

（3）放射斑一般都高于周围釉表面，与之界线分明。

（4）放射斑周围分布有褐色系放射斑及清晰独立的流淌纹等迹型，彼此界线分明。

见图9-1-13、图9-1-14，二者为同一器物同一位置图片，图9-1-13为二维图片，图9-1-14为三维图片。

见图9-1-15、图9-1-16，二者为同一器物同一位置图片，图

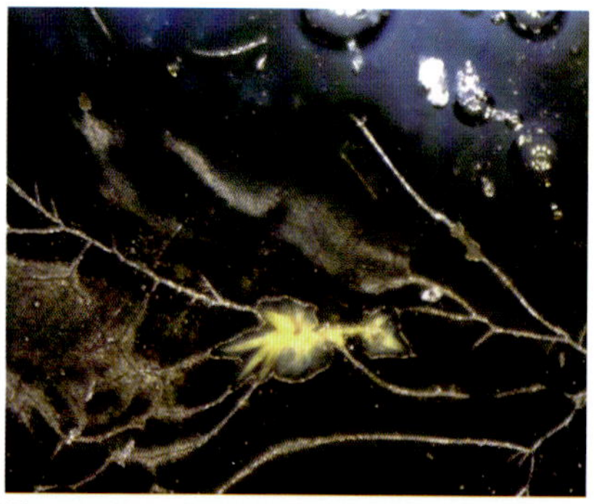
图9-1-11

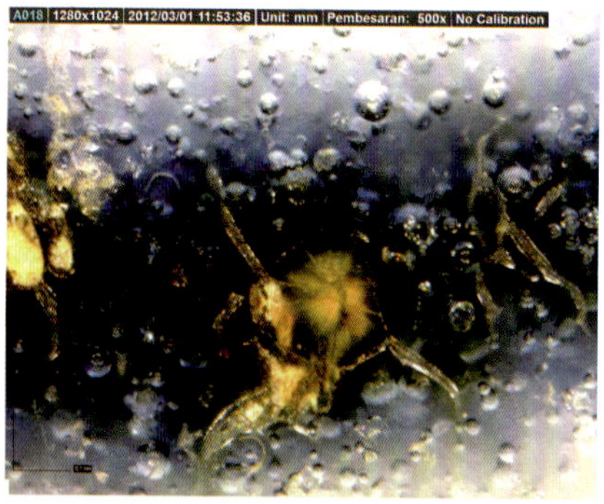

图9-1-12

feel, but retain a relatively smooth and fine property.

c. Radiating mottles, in general, are higher than the surrounding glaze surface, and have a clear delineation.

d. Mottle surroundings can present with brown series mottles, independent flowing striae, and so forth trace types; delineation is retained.

See pictures 9-1-13 and 9-1-14, where 9-1-13 is the two-dimensional and 9-1-14 is the three-dimensional view of the same location.

See pictures 9-1-15 and 9-1-16, where 9-1-15 is the two-dimensional and 9-1-16 is the three-dimensional view of the same location.

Radiating Mottle A in picture 9-1-13 and Mottle B in picture 9-1-15 both present within the glaze level. Mottle A has a fine and smooth surface, while the surface of Mottle B presents with radiating striae, but retains a relatively smooth nature.

Mottle A is surrounded by brown series mottles as well as depressed and raised striae. The brown mottle has a fine, densely striated surface, appearing relatively even. The needlepoint striae are concave. The raised striae are elevated above the surrounding mottle. The traces retain independent delineation and clear borders (see picture 9-1-14).

The needlepoint striae radiating out from Mottle B are concave with needlepoint-mottled centers; they have clear delineation from Mottle B (see picture 9-1-16).

III. Two-Dimensional Characteristics of Forged Article

a. The mottle is rough and muddled, and the needlepoint mottling is unclear, lacking gradation. As a whole, the color is uniform, lacking color variation (see picture 9-1-17 Arrow A').

b. The mottle border is grainy (see picture 9-1-19 Arrow B').

c. The glass phase surrounding the mottle has a wildly sporadic disbursement of pit mottles that lack depth variety. The glass phase is coarse and muddled (see pictures 9-1-17 and 9-1-19).

IV. Three-Dimensional Characteristics of Forged Article

1. Mottle surface is coarse and muddled.

2. The glass phase surrounding the mottle is also grossly muddled with severe damage.

See pictures 9-1-17 and 9-1-18, where 9-1-17 is the two-dimensional and 9-1-18 is the three-dimensional view of the same location (this piece has undergone treatment with aging reagent).

See pictures 9-1-19 and 9-1-20, where 9-1-19 is the two-dimensional and 9-1-20 is the three-dimensional view of the same location (this piece has undergone treatment with aging reagent).

Radiating Mottle A' has a surface that is coarse and muddled; as well as blurred and unclear (see picture 9-1-18).

The glass phase surrounding radiating Mottle A' and B' have pitting with wildly sporadic distribution that lack independent delineation (see pictures 9-1-18 and 9-1-20).

B. Brown Series Radiating Mottle

I. Two-Dimensional Characteristics of Genuine Article

a. Brown series radiating mottles can occur over glass phase as well as over beach mottles (see pictures 9-1-21 and 9-2-23).

b. On mottles that lack lined borders, the surrounding glass phase is clean and clear (see picture 9-1-21).

c. On mottles that have borders, the borders have clear independence. The mottle is contained within a beach mottle, and a small portion of glass phase is visible around its edge. Clear delineation with the surrounding beach mottle is retained (see picture 9-1-23 Arrow B).

d. The foggy needlepoint-mottling border of the beach mottle has a density gradation; and the relatively delineated frosted needlepoint mottling lacks gradation with some areas densely and some sparsely distributed (see picture 9-1-23).

II. Three-Dimensional Characteristics of Genuine Article

a. The mottle is clearly depicted, its surface finely striated, but appears smooth.

b. The mottle has a convex shape, and is clearly higher than the surrounding glass phase.

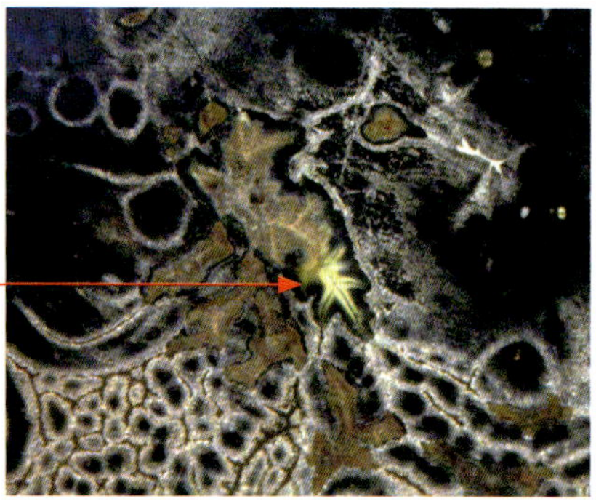

图9-1-13

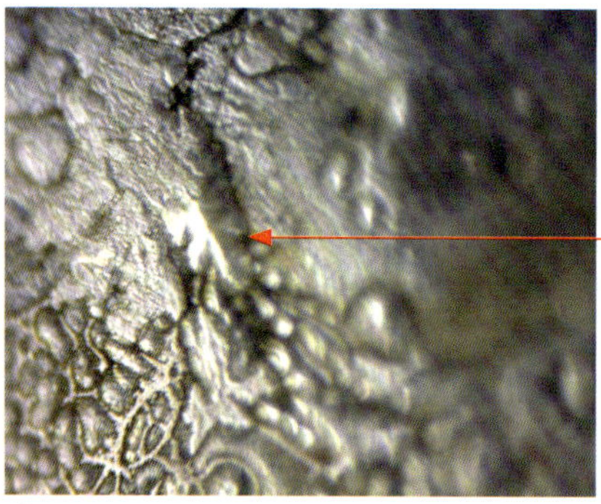

图9-1-14

9-1-15为二维图片，图9-1-16为三维图片。

图9-1-13中的黄色系放射斑A及图9-1-15中的黄色系放射斑B均位于釉层中，形状清晰可见，放射斑A表面光滑细腻，放射斑B表面有细微纹路，但还是显得较平滑细腻。

放射斑A周围分布有褐色系放射斑及阴纹、阳纹等其他迹型种类。褐色系放射斑表面有细密纹路，显得较平滑；针眼型阴纹明显凹陷，阳纹凸起。迹型种类之间彼此独立，界线分明（见图9-1-14）。

放射斑B周围分布有针眼型阴纹，呈凹陷状，内可见针眼斑，纹路清晰，与放射斑B界线分明（见图9-1-16）。

图9-1-15

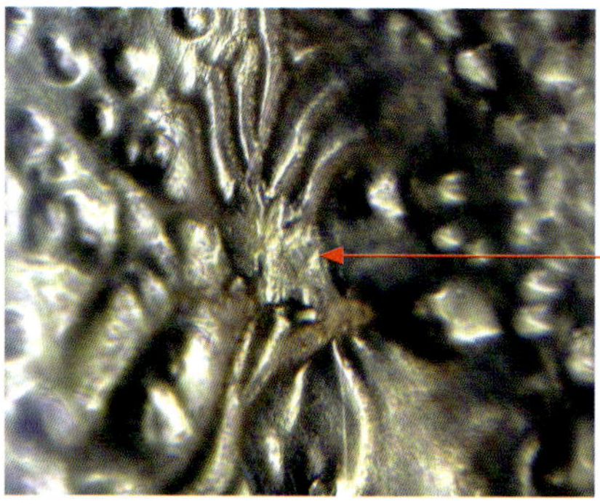

图9-1-16

3. 赝品二维特征

（1）放射斑形貌粗糙模糊，针眼斑不清晰，没有层次变化。整体颜色一致，缺乏颜色变化（见图9-1-17箭头A’所指处）。

（2）放射斑外围的包边粗粝（见图9-1-19箭头B’所指处）。

（3）放射斑周围的玻璃相上杂乱无序地分布着坑点斑，深浅一致，玻璃相显得涂污模糊（见图9-1-17、图9-1-19）。

4. 赝品三维特征

（1）放射斑表面粗糙涂污。

（2）放射斑周围釉表面涂污，破坏严重。

见图9-1-17、图9-1-18，二者为同一器物同一位置图片，图9-1-17为二维图片，图9-1-18为三维图片。（该器物釉表面曾被腐蚀剂腐蚀）

见图9-1-19、图9-1-20，二者为同一器物同一位置图片，图9-1-19为二维图片，图9-1-20为三维图片。（该器物釉表面曾被腐蚀剂腐蚀）

放射斑A’表面粗糙涂污，模糊不清（见图9-1-18）。

放射斑A’与放射斑B’周围玻璃相上的坑点斑呈杂乱无序的凹坑，分布无规律可循，凹坑之间界线不清（见图9-1-18、图9-1-20）。

c. Mottle is clearly delineated from the surrounding glass phase.

d. The surrounding glass phase is smooth and clean.

e. On the beach mottle surrounding the radiating mottle, clearly visible pin points of frosted needlepoint mottling present.

See pictures 9-1-21 and 9-1-22, where 9-1-21 is the two-dimensional and 9-1-22 is the three-dimensional view of the same location.

See pictures 9-1-23 and 9-1-24, where 9-1-23 is the two-dimensional and 9-1-24 is the three-dimensional view of the same location.

Radiating Mottle A in picture 9-1-21 is clearly depicted and the surface has finely dense striation, but is smooth as a whole. The surface is convexly raised higher than the surrounding glaze surface, and has clear delineation from the surrounding glass phase that is smooth and clean (see picture 9-1-22).

Radiating Mottle B is clearly depicted with a convex shape that is noticeably higher than the surrounding beach mottle, the two retaining mutual delineation. The encompassing beach mottle has clearly visible frosted needlepoint mottle pin points (see picture 9-1-24).

III. Two-Dimensional Characteristics of Forged Article

a. The mottle appears muddled and is not clearly delineated from the surrounding glass phase (see picture 9-1-25 Arrow A').

b. The border of the mottle is grainy, and the glass phase between the mottle and the border is unclear (see picture 9-1-27 Arrow B').

c. The surrounding glass phase has a dense, wildly sporadic distribution of needlepoint mottling and pitting. It is unclear, lacks gradation, and is coarsely muddled as a whole (see pictures 9-1-25 and 9-1-27).

d. Needlepoint striae present around the mottle, but the borders are muddled and unclear (see picture 9-1-27).

IV. Three-Dimensional Characteristics of Forged Article

a. The surface of the mottle is coarse and muddled, and generally unclear.

b. The glass phase surrounding the mottle is also grossly muddled.

c. A mottle that is surrounded by depressed striae of a certain depth and width may not present with any visible striae or relatively thin striae in the two-dimensional view, which shows a lack of congruency.

See pictures 9-1-25 and 9-1-26, where 9-1-25 is the two-dimensional and 9-1-26 is the three-dimensional view of the same location (this piece has undergone treatment with aging reagent).

See pictures 9-1-27 and 9-1-28, where 9-1-27 is the two-dimensional and 9-1-28 is the three-dimensional view of the same location (this piece has undergone treatment with aging reagent).

Mottle A' has a surface that is coarsely muddled and unclear. The glass phase located above the mottle is grossly muddled. To the bottom right of the mottle (indicated by Arrow B') is depressed striae of a certain depth and width (see picture 9-1-26) that do not show up clearly as empty or needlepoint striae in the two-dimensional view (see picture 9-1-25), which shows a lack of congruency.

Mottle C' has a surface that is coarsely muddled and unclear. The mottle is surrounded by depressed striae of a certain depth and width (see picture 9-1-28) that only present as very faint striae in the two-dimensional view (see see picture 9-1-27 Arrow D'), which shows a lack of congruency. The surrounding glass phase is coarsely muddled.

C. Yellow and Brown Series Radiating Mottle Combination

I. Two-Dimensional Characteristics of Genuine Article

see picture 9-1-29.

a. The yellow series mottle is positioned within the glaze level, and as such the weathering severity is relatively low, and can retain its inherent properties (see Arrow A).

b. Brown series mottles occur at the surface of the glaze and are clearly depicted. Foggy needlepoint mottling is distributed evenly across the mottle surface, but does not

图9-1-17

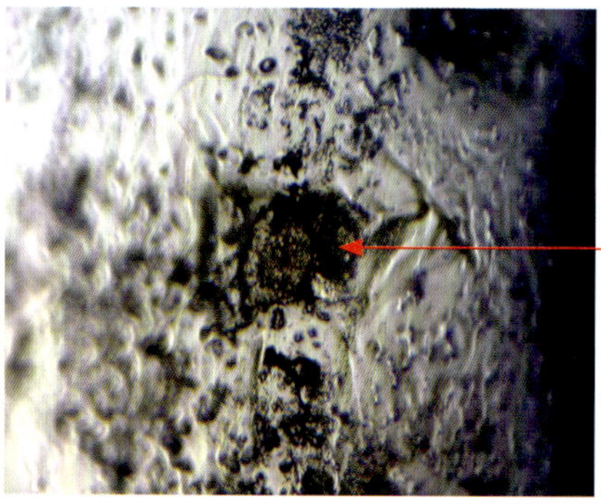

图9-1-18

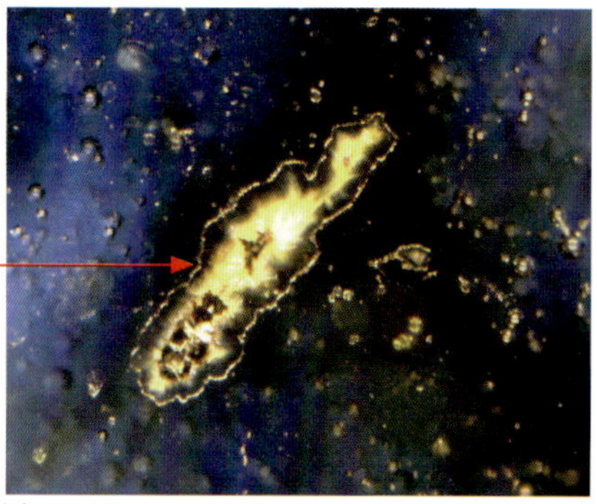

图9-1-19

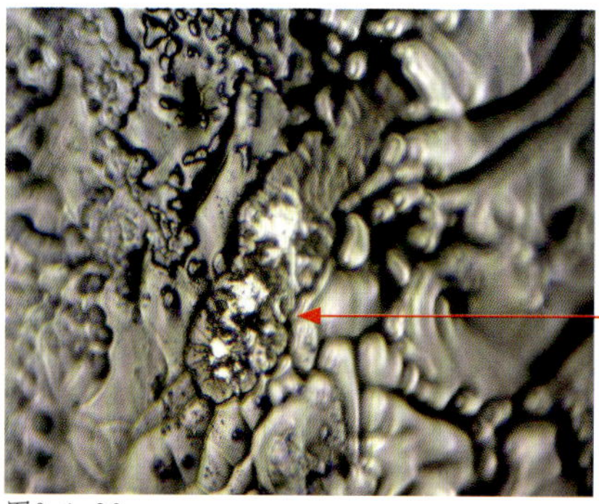

图9-1-20

（二）褐色系放射斑

1. 真品二维特征

（1）褐色系放射斑可以出现在玻璃相上，也可出现在沙滩斑上（见图9-1-21、图9-1-23）。

（2）有时褐色系放射斑没有包边，周围玻璃相干净清晰（见图9-1-21）。

（3）有时褐色系放射斑边沿有包边，清晰独立。放射斑位于沙滩斑中间，与包边之间可见玻璃相，与沙滩斑界线分明（见图9-1-23箭头B所指处）。

（4）沙滩斑边沿分布有由浓到淡过渡的雾状针眼斑，中心有边界感较强的磨砂针眼斑，没有浓淡过渡，有的地方分布密集，有的地方几乎没有。二者皆清晰（见图9-1-23）。

2. 真品三维特征

（1）褐色系放射斑成像清晰，表面有细密纹路，但总体显得平滑。

（2）褐色系放射斑呈凸起状，明显高于釉表面。

（3）褐色系放射斑与周围玻璃相界线分明。

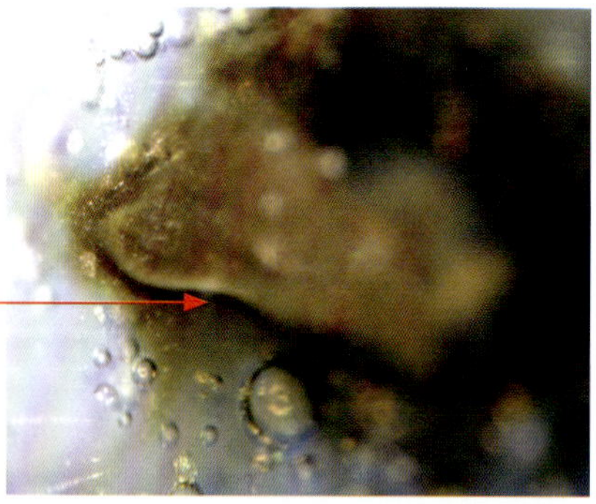

图9-1-21

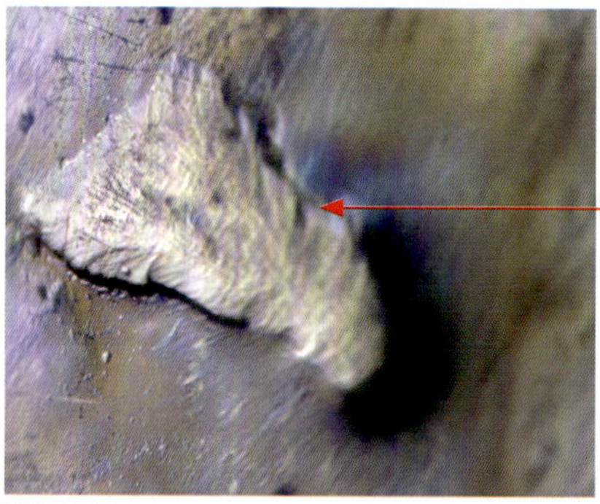

图9-1-22

extend past the boundaries of the mottle (see Arrow B).

c. Needlepoint mottling and flowing striae can present outside the mottle, clearly depicted, mutually independent and clearly delineated.

II. Three-Dimensional Characteristics of Genuine Article

a. The surface above the yellow series mottle is glossy.

b. The surface of the brown series mottle can be densely striated, but retains a general smoothness.

c. The mottle is surrounded by clear independent flowing striae; they are mutually delineated.

See pictures 9-1-29 and 9-1-30, where 9-1-29 is the two-dimensional and 9-1-30 is the three-dimensional view of the same location.

Yellow Series Mottle A is clearly depicted as located within the glaze level, and as such it receives relatively high protection from the glaze and has lower weathering severity; its surface is glossy and smooth. Brown Series Mottle B is located at the surface of the glaze, and as such receives relatively low glaze protection and relatively high weathering severity; thus its surface is densely striated. The two are mutually delineated. Mottles A and B are surrounded by depressed and raised striae as well as other traces. The depressed striae are concave, the raised are convex, and are delineated from the radiating mottle (see picture 9-1-30).

III. Two-Dimensional Characteristics of Forged Article

see picture 9-1-31.

a. The yellow series mottle is within the glaze level, retaining yellow coloration (see Arrow A').

b. The brown series mottle is located at the glaze surface and its surface presents with frosted needlepoint mottling; as a whole the mottle appears blurry (see Arrow B').

c. The surrounding glass phase is covered with wildly sporadic pitting.

IV. Three-Dimensional Characteristics of Forged Article

a. The surface of the yellow series mottle presents with fish scale or muscle tissue-like striation.

b. The surface of the brown series mottle also presents with fish scale or muscle tissue-like striation, and the surface is coarsely muddled.

See pictures 9-1-31 and 9-1-32, where 9-1-31 is the two-dimensional and 9-1-32 is the three-dimensional view of the same location (this piece has undergone treatment with aging reagent).

Yellow Series Mottle A' and Brown Series Mottle B' both have muscle tissue-like striation, with the striation on Mottle B' presenting more poignantly; its appearance, as a whole, is unreservedly muddled (see picture 9-1-32).

3. Needlepoint Mottles

A. Needlepoint Mottling on Flowing Mottle

I. Two-Dimensional Characteristics of Genuine Article

See pictures 9-1-33 and 9-1-35.

a. Towards the center of a beach mottle, the frosted needlepoint mottling has a strong border.

b. At the edges of the beach mottle, the foggy needlepoint mottling is the most common, with a density gradation presenting.

c. Different types of needlepoint mottling on flowing mottles can present with different density distribution. They give the mottle a layered effect as well as color variation; the mottle as a whole is clean and fine.

II. Three-Dimensional Characteristics of Genuine Article

a. Foggy needlepoint mottling presents with even gradation.

b. In areas of sparse foggy needlepoint mottling, the characteristics are not highly visible; areas of denser distribution resemble very fine sand.

c. Frosted needlepoint mottling has dark coloration and presents as pin points.

d. The needlepoint mottling follows the general shape

（4）褐色系放射斑周围玻璃相光滑洁净。

（5）褐色系放射斑邻近的沙滩斑上可见磨砂针眼斑形成的点状凹坑。

见图9-1-21、图9-1-22，二者为同一器物同一位置图片，图9-1-21为二维图片，图9-1-22为三维图片。

见图9-1-23、图9-1-24，二者为同一器物同一位置图片，图9-1-23为二维图片，图9-1-24为三维图片。

褐色系放射斑A成像清晰，表面有细密纹路，但总体显得平滑，斑块凸起，明显高于釉表面，与周围玻璃相界线分明。周围玻璃相光滑洁净（见图9-1-22）。

褐色系放射斑B成像清晰，呈凸起状，明显高于周围沙滩斑，二者之间界线分明。放射斑邻近的沙滩斑上可见磨砂针眼斑形成的点状凹坑（见图9-1-24）。

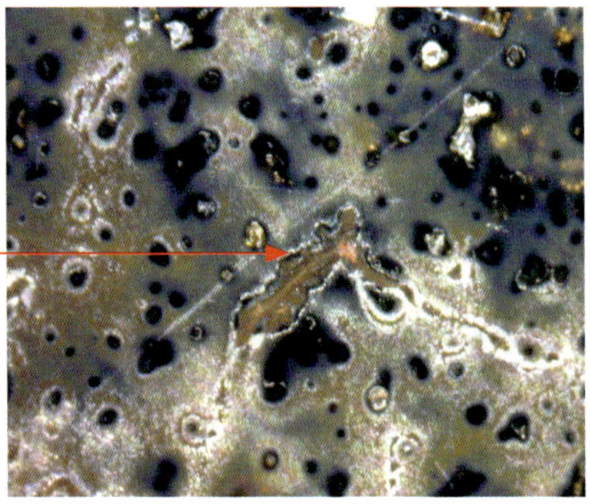

图9-1-23

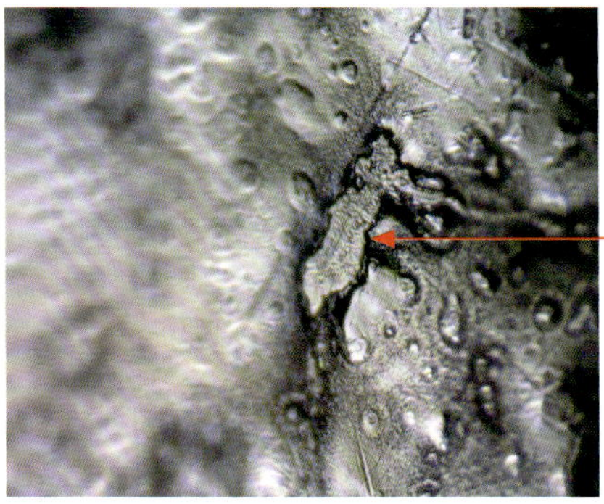

图9-1-24

3. 赝品二维特征

（1）褐色系放射斑形貌模糊，与周围玻璃相界线不清（见图9-1-25箭头A'所指处）。

（2）褐色系放射斑外围的包边粗粝，包边与放射斑之间的玻璃相模糊不清（见图9-1-27箭头B'所指处）。

（3）放射斑周围的玻璃相上，针眼斑和坑点斑杂乱无序地密集分布，不清晰，无层次感，整体显得涂污模糊（见图9-1-25、图9-1-27）。

（4）放射斑周围隐约可见针眼型阴纹，纹路轮廓模糊不清（见图9-1-27）。

4. 赝品三维特征

（1）放射斑表面粗糙涂污，模糊不清。

（2）放射斑周围的玻璃相粗糙涂污。

（3）放射斑周围有流淌纹形成的有一定深度和宽度的凹槽，但在该位置的二维成像图中却不见流淌纹或者纹路较细，缺乏陶瓷迹型变化的同步性。

见图9-1-25、图9-1-26，二者为同一器物同一位置图片，图9-1-25为二维图片，图9-1-26为三维图片。（该器物釉表面曾被腐蚀剂腐蚀）

见图9-1-27、图9-1-28，二者为同一器物同一位置图片，图9-1-27为二维图片，图9-1-28为三维图片。（该器物釉表面曾被腐蚀剂腐蚀）

放射斑A'表面粗糙涂污，模

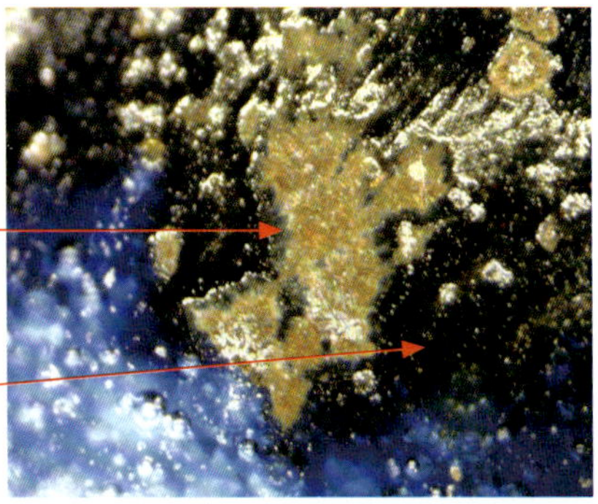

图9-1-25

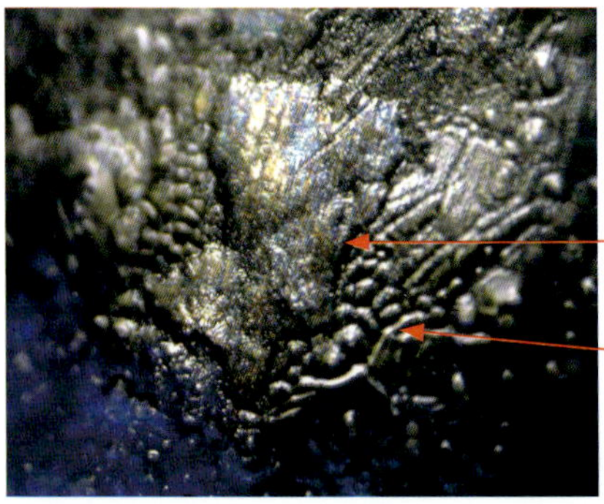

图9-1-26

of the underlying flowing mottle, and has distinctive borders.

e. The mottle has color variation, and as a whole is clean and fine.

See pictures 9-1-33 and 9-1-34, where 9-1-33 is the two-dimensional and 9-1-34 is the three-dimensional view of the same location.

See pictures 9-1-35 and 9-1-36, where 9-1-35 is the two-dimensional and 9-1-36 is the three-dimensional view of the same location.

The foggy needlepoint mottling in picture 9-1-34 and 9-1-36 have even gradation. Areas of sparse distribution are not highly visible; the glaze level is relatively clean and smooth (see Arrows A and D). Areas of denser distribution appear as evenly distributed, fine sand (see Arrows B and E).

Arrow C in 9-1-34 and Arrow F in 9-1-36 are frosted needlepoint mottling with a darker and denser distribution of pitting than that of the foggy variety, appearing more topographical and deeper in general.

The needlepoint mottling follows the shape of the underlying flowing mottle with relatively clear boundaries and are not sporadically dispersed. The beach mottle as a whole is clean and fine (see pictures 9-1-34 and 9-1-36).

The distribution regularity of the needlepoint mottling offers a layering effect to the beach mottle that appears as a color spectrum across the mottle (see picture 9-1-36).

III. Two-Dimensional Characteristics of Forged Article

a. No clear density gradation of foggy needlepoint mottling (see pictures 9-1-37 and 9-1-39).

b. Mottling occurs sporadically, and does not follow the general shape of the underlying beach mottle. On the edges of the beach mottle, in areas of foggy mottling, frosted mottling also presents; its distribution is disorderly, lacking a clear boundary and rational placement (see picture 9-1-39 Arrow C').

IV. Three-Dimensional Characteristics of Forged Article

a. New glaze without human forced aging is glossy and clean as a whole, needlepoint mottling is absent and beach mottles lack layering (see picture 9-1-38).

b. On glaze that has undergone human forced aging, needlepoint mottling appears as a blackened powdery material deposited on the glaze surface, it lacks topographical distinction (see picture 9-1-40).

c. Frosted needlepoint mottling occurs sporadically and not necessarily within the constraints of the underlying beach mottle; it lacks regularity and boundaries (see picture 9-1-40).

d. The mottle as a whole is coarsely muddled (see picture 9-1-40).

See pictures 9-1-37 and 9-1-38, where 9-1-37 is the two-dimensional and 9-1-38 is the three-dimensional view of the same location (this piece has not undergone treatment with aging reagent).

See pictures 9-1-39 and 9-1-40, where 9-1-39 is the two-dimensional and 9-1-40 is the three-dimensional view of the same location (this piece has undergone treatment with aging reagent).

Aside from slight color disparity in picture 9-1-38, the boundary of the mottle is nearly indistinguishable; the glaze is glossy and clean. Needlepoint mottling is not visible, and the mottle as a whole lacks layering.

The foggy needlepoint mottling in picture 9-1-40 is not clearly visible, the glaze is relatively glossy (see Arrow B'). The frosted mottling indicated by Arrow C' does not resemble the independent pitting seen on genuine articles, but rather looks like black powder sporadically dispersed on the glaze surface lacking topographical distinction. The frosted mottling does not follow the general shape of the underlying beach mottle. It is irregular, lacks clearly defined boundaries, and causes the mottle to be coarsely muddled as a whole.

B. Needlepoint mottling on Radiating Mottle

I. Two-Dimensional Characteristics of Genuine Article

a. Frosted needlepoint mottling does not exceed the boundary of the underlying mottle (see picture 9-1-41).

b. The peripheral radiating mottle is within the glaze level, and retains yellow coloration (see picture 9-1-41 Arrow A and picture 9-1-42 Arrow C).

糊不清。放射斑上方的玻璃相粗糙涂污。放射斑右下方箭头B’所指处有流淌纹形成的有一定深度和宽度的凹槽（见图9-1-26），但在该位置的二维成像图片中却不见流淌纹（见图9-1-25），缺乏陶瓷迹型变化的同步性。

放射斑C’表面粗糙涂污，模糊不清。放射斑周围有流淌纹形成的有一定深度和宽度的凹槽（见图9-1-28），但在该位置的二维成像图片中的流淌纹却很细，而且模糊不清（见图9-1-27箭头D’所指处），缺乏陶瓷迹型变化的同步性。周围玻璃相粗糙涂污。

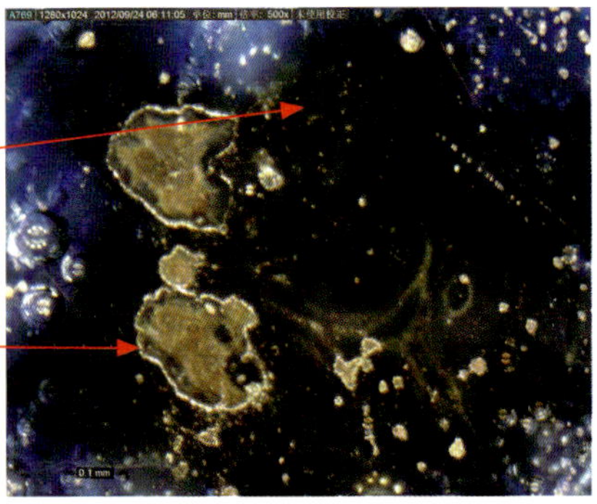

图9-1-27

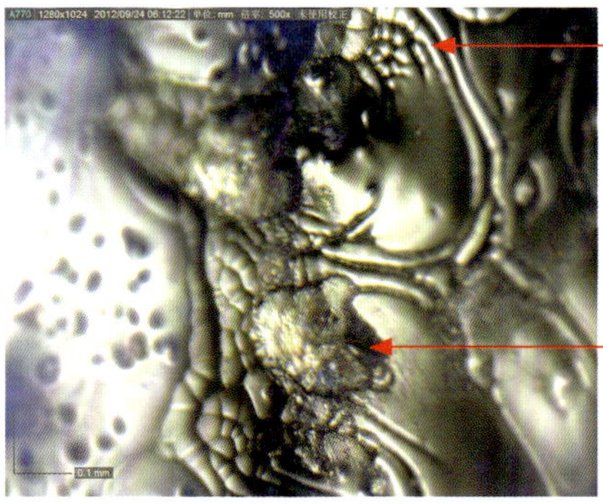

图9-1-28

（三）黄色系与褐色系放射斑组合

1. 真品二维特征

见图9-1-29。

（1）黄色系放射斑处于釉层中，成像清晰，风化作用不明显，保持原态（见箭头A所指处）。

（2）褐色系放射斑处于釉表面，成像清晰，放射斑上可见白色雾状针眼斑分布，但不超过放射斑的范围（见箭头B所指处）。

（3）放射斑周围分布有流淌纹及针眼斑，成像清晰，彼此独立，界线分明。

2. 真品三维特征

（1）黄色系放射斑表面光滑细腻。

（2）褐色系放射斑表面有细密纹路，但总体显得较平滑。

（3）放射斑周围分布有清晰独立的流淌纹，彼此界线分明。

见图9-1-29、图9-1-30，二者为同一器物同一位置图片，图9-1-29为二维图片，图9-1-30为三维图片。

黄色系放射斑A位于釉层中，形状清晰可见，因为受釉层保护程度较好，风化强度低，表面光滑细腻。褐色系放射斑B位于釉表面，受釉层保护程度较差，风化强度高，表面有细密纹路，二者界线分明。放射斑A与B周围分布有清晰独立的阴纹、阳纹等其他迹型种类，阴纹凹陷，阳纹凸起，与放射斑界线分明（见图9-1-30）。

3. 赝品二维特征

见图9-1-31。

（1）黄色系放射斑处于釉层中，呈黄色（见箭头A’所指处）。

（2）褐色系放射斑处于釉表面，斑块上可见白色磨砂针眼斑，整体显得混沌（见箭头B’所指处）。

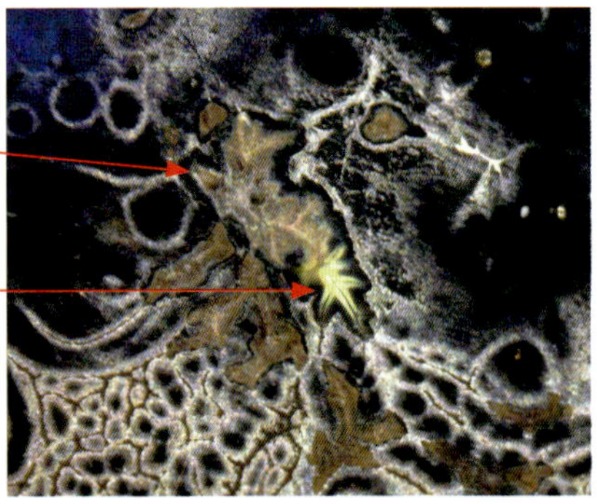

图9-1-29

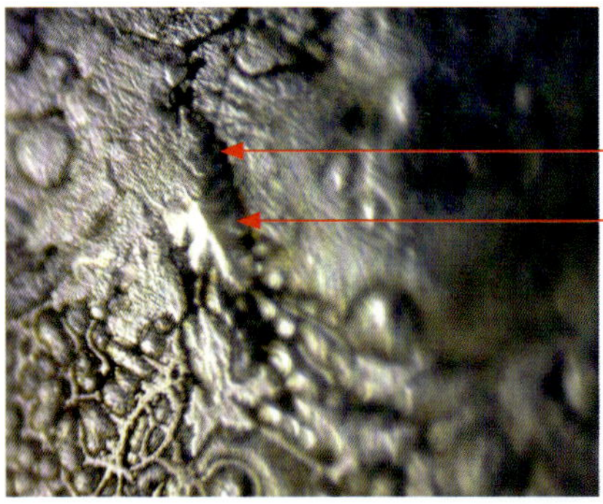

图9-1-30

c. The border of the mottle is fine and reserved (see picture 9-1-41 Arrow B and picture 9-1-42 Arrow D).

d. The mottle as a whole is refined and reserved, with a color spectrum (see pictures 9-1-41 and 9-1-42).

e. The glass phase surrounding the mottle is clean and clear (see pictures 9-1-41 and 9-1-42).

II. Two-Dimensional Characteristics of Forged Article

See pictures 9-1-43 and 9-1-44 (this piece has undergone treatment with aging reagent).

a. Frosted needlepoint mottling more evident on the black series radiating mottle (see Arrows A' and E').

b. Mottle within the glaze level is yellow (see Arrow B'); mottle on the glaze surface is brown (see Arrow F').

c. The radiating mottle border is coarse and fuzzy (see Arrows C' and G').

d. Needlepoint mottling extends beyond the boundaries of the radiating mottle; the surrounding glass phase also presenting with sporadic distribution which shows a lack of rational placement (see Arrows D' and H').

e. The glass phase has sporadic distribution of CO striae, needlepoint mottles and pitting, the mottle in general is coarsely muddled, lacking color spectrum and layer gradation.

C. Needlepoint mottling on Glass Phase

I. Two-Dimensional Characteristics of Genuine Article

See picture 9-1-45.

a. Grainy needlepoint mottling with sparsely distributed granule-like pits that are clear and independent.

b. The mottling and surrounding glass phase are mutually delineated.

c. The glass phase surrounding is clean and clear.

II. Two-Dimensional Characteristics of Forged Article

See picture 9-1-46 (this piece has undergone treatment with aging reagent).

a. Needlepoint mottling sporadic without any observable regularity.

b. The needlepoint mottles are muddled with no clear delineation from the surrounding glass phase.

c. The glass phase as a whole is coarsely muddled.

4. Pit Mottles

A. CO Type Pit Mottles

I. Two-Dimensional Characteristics of Genuine Article

a. CO type pit mottles have alternating size and depth (see pictures 9-1-47—9-1-50).

b. A unit image can present with CO type pit mottles as well as CO striae. The striae assume yellow coloration while the pits are white; they are independent and mutually delineated (see picture 9-1-47).

c. A unit image can present with CO type pit mottles, CO striae, and CO pit groups. They have sparse distribution, and are independent and mutually delineated (see pictures 9-1-47 and 9-1-48).

d. CO type pits retain clear delineation from the surrounding traces such as flowing mottles, flowing striae and the glass phase (see pictures 9-1-47 and 9-1-48).

e. The glass phase surrounding the pits is clean and clear (see pictures 9-1-47 and 9-1-48).

f. It is possible for floccus mottling to present in association with CO type pitting (see picture 9-1-49).

II. Three-Dimensional Characteristics of Genuine Article

a. CO type pitting generally occurs in areas and raised glaze surface.

b. Only finely reserved CO striae or mottles are present on the glaze surface, they are clear and independent.

c. The surface area of visible CO striae and mottle is much smaller than that of the two-dimensionally visible mottle; they are mutually delineated.

See pictures 9-1-50 and 9-1-51, where 9-1-50 is the two-dimensional and 9-1-51 is the three-dimensional view of the

（3）周围玻璃相上杂乱无序地分布有坑点斑。

4. 赝品三维特征

（1）黄色系放射斑所在的釉表面有鱼翅状的放射纹路。

（2）釉上的褐色系放射斑的表面有鱼翅状的放射纹路，表面显得粗糙涂污。

见图9-1-31、图9-1-32，二者为同一器物同一位置图片，图9-1-31为二维图片，图9-1-32为三维图片。（该器物釉表面曾被腐蚀剂腐蚀）

黄色系放射斑A'和褐色系放射斑B'都有鱼翅状的放射纹路，放射斑B'上的鱼翅状纹路更明显，整体显得粗糙涂污且具扩张性（见图9-1-32）。

图9-1-31

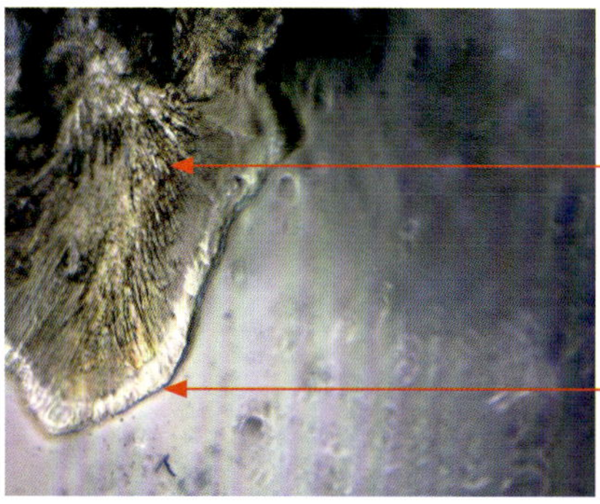

图9-1-32

三、针眼斑

（一）流淌斑上的针眼斑

1. 真品二维特征

见图9-1-33、图9-1-35。

（1）在沙滩斑中心部位，针眼斑以磨砂形式分布，有较强的边界感。

（2）在沙滩斑边沿部位，针眼斑大多以雾状形式分布，有从浓到淡的均匀过渡。

（3）不同形式的针眼斑在沙滩斑上疏密不一的分布，使沙滩斑有层次感，也有色阶变化，整体显得精致、细腻。

2. 真品三维特征

（1）雾状针眼斑表现出均匀的过渡。

（2）雾状针眼斑分布稀疏处特征不明显，雾状针眼斑分布密集的地方如同均匀铺展的细沙。

（3）磨砂针眼斑表现为深色点状凹坑。

（4）针眼斑的分布随着沙滩斑的轮廓走势，有较整齐的边界。

（5）沙滩斑有色阶变化，整体显得精致、细腻。

见图9-1-33、图9-1-34，二者为同一器物同一位置图片，图9-1-33为二维图片，图9-1-34为三维图片。

见图9-1-35、图9-1-36，二者为同一器物同一位置图片，图9-1-35为二维图片，图9-1-36为三维图片。

雾状针眼斑在图9-1-34及图9-1-36中均表现出均匀的过渡：雾状针眼斑分布稀疏处的特征不明显，釉表面显得较光滑洁净（见箭

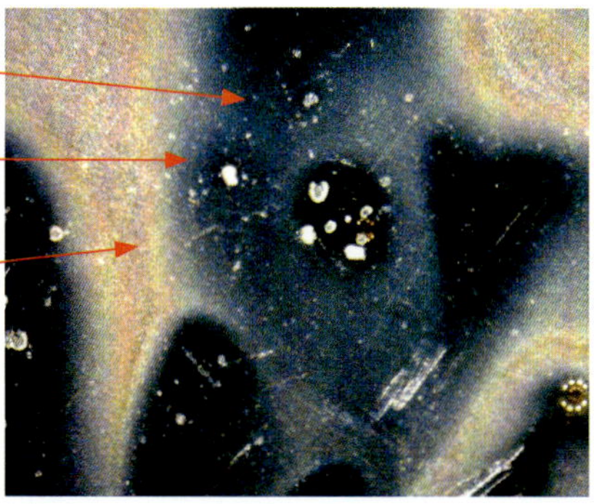

图9-1-33

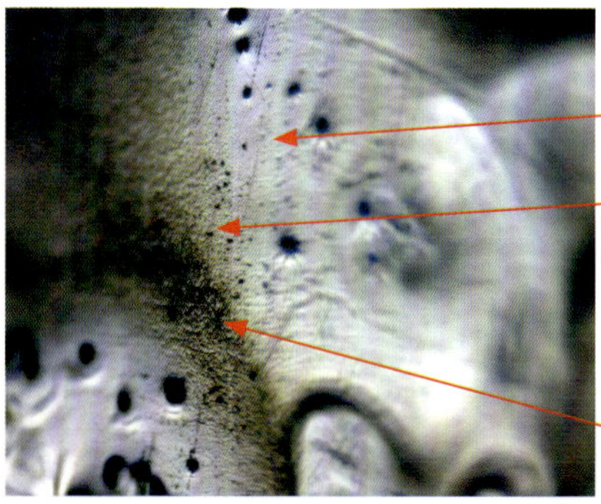

图9-1-34

same location.

The CO type pit mottles indicated by Arrow A in picture 9-1-50 are clearly visible on areas of raised glaze in picture 9-1-51. The pit indicated by Arrow A presents on the peak of a small mound on the glaze surface; non-raised areas of the glaze remain clean and smooth.

Pit Mottle B in picture 9-1-50 is located on an area that is not clearly raised in picture 9-1-51, a small pronged C shaped striation is visible. The surface area of Mottle B in picture 9-1-51 is smaller than its two-dimensional counterpart.

See pictures 9-1-52 and 9-1-53, where 9-1-52 is the two-dimensional and 9-1-53 is the three-dimensional view of the same location.

The pit indicated in picture 9-1-52 presents as a finely reserved C striation on the surface of the glaze in picture 9-1-53. Additionally, two small dark pits, smaller than that of picture 9-1-52, are visible on the glaze surface (see Arrow C). This indicates that part of the mottle is present within the glaze level. The C shaped striation has clear delineation from the surrounding glass phase.

Aside from the CO type pit mottle, the glass has fine scratches and needlepoint type pit mottles distributed across the surface, which are all mutually delineated and clear. Aside from these traces, the glaze surface is clean and smooth (see picture 9-1-53).

See pictures 9-1-54 and 9-1-55, where 9-1-54 is the two-dimensional and 9-1-55 is the three-dimensional view of the same location.

The CO type pit mottles in picture 9-1-54 are clearly visible on areas of raised glaze in picture 9-1-55. The pit mottles present on the peaks of small mounds across the glaze surface; non-raised areas of the glaze remain clean and smooth.

The surface area of the pit indicated by Arrow D in picture 9-1-54 appears smaller in picture 9-1-55. This indicates that part of the pit is present within the glaze level. Pit Mottle D and the other surrounding traces have mutual delineation, and the surrounding glaze is clean and smooth.

III. Two-Dimensional Characteristics of Forged Article

See pictures 9-1-56 and 9-1-57 (this piece has undergone treatment with aging reagent).

a. CO type pit mottles are sporadic and muddled with coloration uniform to that of the CO striae; additionally, the size and depths of the pits lack variation.

b. CO type pit mottles, CO striae, needlepoint mottles and other traces are densely distributed across the glaze surface and there is no clear delineation between them.

c. The image as a whole is coarsely muddled.

IV. Three-Dimensional Characteristics of Forged Article

a. In general the glaze surface does not have CO striae, or the CO shape is unclear.

b. The three-dimensionally observable CO type pit mottle surface area is the same or larger than the two-dimensional view.

c. The entire glaze surface has dense and sporadic distribution of pitting and scratches, the surface as a whole is coarsely muddled.

See pictures 9-1-58 and 9-1-59, where 9-1-58 is the two-dimensional and 9-1-59 is the three-dimensional view of the same location (this piece has undergone treatment with aging reagent).

The CO type pit mottles in picture 9-1-58 are blotched on areas of raised glaze in picture 9-1-59. The pit mottles present on the peaks of small mounds across the glaze surface; non-raised areas of the glaze are somewhat smooth.

The pit indicated by Arrow A' in picture 9-1-58 presents as a blotch on the surface of the glaze in picture 9-1-59. The blotch is not fine or reserved and its surface area is larger than that of the pit mottle in picture 9-1-58, there is no evident C or O striation.

See pictures 9-1-60 and 9-1-61, where 9-1-60 is the two-dimensional and 9-1-61 is the three-dimensional view of the same location (this piece has undergone treatment with aging reagent).

Mottle B' in picture 9-1-60 presents faintly as an O striation in 9-1-61, but the surrounding glaze surface has become indistinguishable, there is a sporadic distribution of pits and scratches, and its general appearance is coarse and muddled from severe damage.

头A、箭头D所指处）；雾状针眼斑分布更密集的地方如同均匀铺展的细沙（见箭头B、箭头E所指处）。

图9-1-34中箭头C及图9-1-36中箭头F所指的磨砂针眼斑是分布较雾状针眼斑更加密集的深色点状凹坑，立体感较强，斑块整体呈现的颜色较雾状针眼斑更深。

针眼斑在沙滩斑上整体的分布基本随着沙滩斑的轮廓走势，有较整齐的边界，而不是杂乱无章地分布。沙滩斑整体显得精致、细腻（见图9-1-34、图9-1-36）。

针眼斑有规律地分布也使沙滩斑从右至左产生色阶变化，富有层次感（见图9-1-36）。

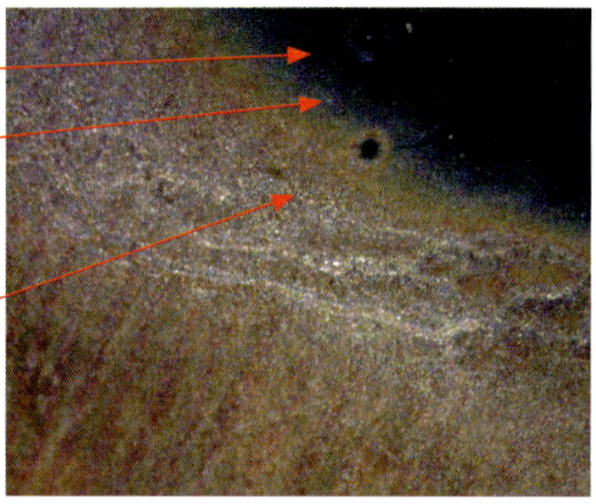

图9-1-35

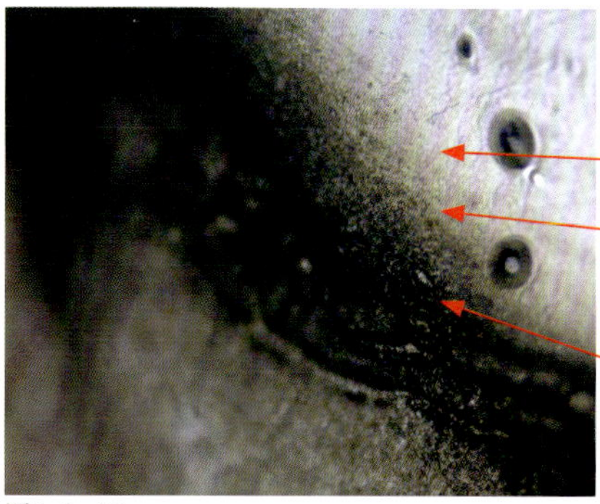

图9-1-36

3. 赝品二维特征

（1）雾状针眼斑由浓到淡的过渡都不明显（见图9-1-37、图9-1-39）。

（2）针眼斑分布没有规律，并非按照沙滩斑的轮廓走势。在沙滩斑边沿的雾状针眼斑所在处也出现磨砂针眼斑，磨砂针眼斑分布凌乱，边界不整齐，缺乏陶瓷迹型出现位置的合理性（见图9-1-39箭头C'所指处）。

4. 赝品三维特征

（1）未经人为做旧的赝品瓷器釉表面整体光滑洁净，不见针眼斑，沙滩斑缺乏层次感（见图9-1-38）。

（2）经过人为做旧的磨砂针眼斑表现为黑色的粉末状物质，散落堆积在釉表面，缺乏立体感（见图9-1-40）。

（3）磨砂针眼斑在沙滩斑上整体的分布并未随着沙滩斑的轮廓走势，没有规律，没有整齐的边界（见图9-1-40）。

（4）沙滩斑整体显得粗糙涂污（见图9-1-40）。

见图9-1-37、图9-1-38，二者为同一器物同一位置图片，图9-1-37为二维图片，图9-1-38为三维图片。（该器物釉表面未经过腐蚀剂腐蚀）

见图9-1-39、图9-1-40，二者为同一器物同一位置图片，图9-1-39为二维图片，图9-1-40为三维图片。（该器物釉表面曾被腐蚀剂腐蚀）

图9-1-38中除了一些颜色变化，基本看不出沙滩斑的轮廓，釉表面整体光滑洁净，不见针眼斑，沙滩斑缺乏层次感。

图9-1-40中雾状针眼斑的特

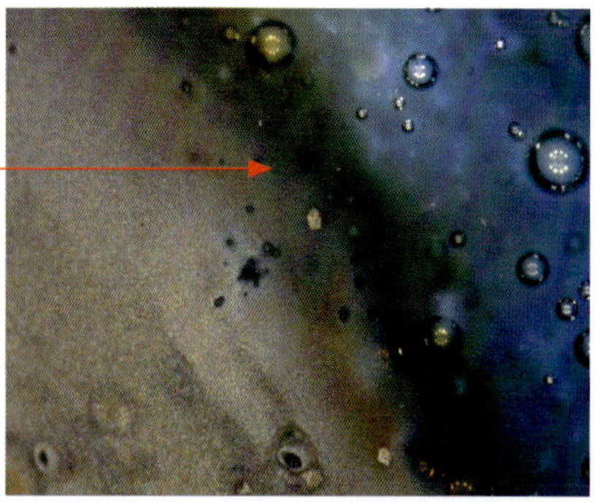

图9-1-37

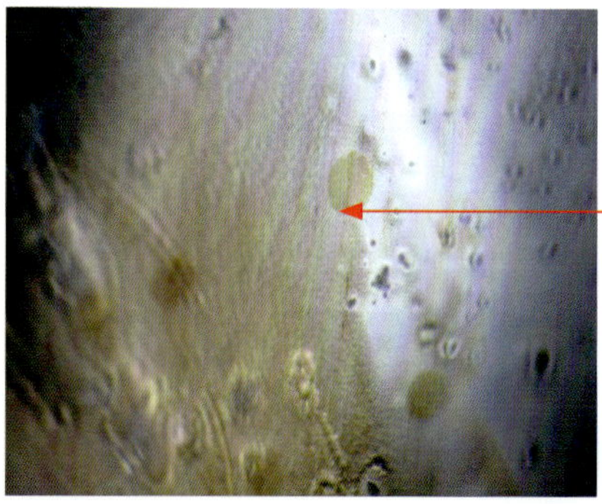

图9-1-38

B. Needlepoint Type Pit Mottle

I. Two-Dimensional Characteristics of Genuine Article

See picture 9-1-62.

a. The mottle appears white; its edge has a fine lined border.

b. Scratches appear in the same unit image, but they are mutually delineated and have clear borders.

c. The surrounding glass phase is clean and clear.

II. Three-Dimensional Characteristics of Genuine Article

a. Pit mottles have a concave shape that is clear and independent. The two and three-dimensional surface areas are the same.

b. Pit mottles can occur in association with other traces, but they retain clear delineation.

c. The pit mottles retain delineation from the surrounding glass phase with clear borders.

d. The surrounding glass phase is clean and smooth.

See pictures 9-1-62 and 9-1-63, where 9-1-62 is the two-dimensional and 9-1-63 is the three-dimensional view of the same location.

The light colored pit mottle in picture 9-1-62 is clearly visible as darker coloration in picture 9-1-63. Mottle A is a concave pit on the surface of the glaze; its two and three-dimensional surface areas are the same. It has clear delineation from the surrounding glass phase, which is clean and smooth.

III. Two-Dimensional Characteristics of Forged Article

See picture 9-1-64.

a. Needlepoint pit mottles are abundant with irregular appearances and sporadic distribution.

b. The image as a whole is coarsely muddled.

IV. Three-Dimensional Characteristics of Forged Article

a. Pit mottles have concave shape, two and three-dimensional surface areas are similar.

b. The surrounding glass phase is coarsely muddled as a whole.

See pictures 9-1-64 and 9-1-65, where 9-1-64 is the two-dimensional and 9-1-65 is the three-dimensional view of the same location (this piece has undergone treatment with aging reagent).

The pit mottles indicated by Arrow A' in picture 9-1-64 are visible as glaze pits in picture 9-1-65. They are concave pits on the surface of the glaze; their two and three-dimensional surface areas are the same. The glass phase has sporadically scattered pits of alternating sizes and irregular distribution; its general appearance is coarsely muddled.

5. Floccus Mottles

A. Two-Dimensional Characteristics of Genuine Article

See pictures 9-1-66 and 9-1-67.

I. Floccus mottling usually occurs in areas of structural instability or damage on the glaze surface and disperse down into the glaze level.

II. The center of the mottle is non-transparent and milky white, and the edges feather out like goose down.

B. Three-Dimensional Characteristics of Genuine Article

I. Floccus mottling is not visible on the surface of the glaze, only the entry point on the glaze surface is (i.e. pitting, crack, etc.) The three-dimensional surface area of the entry point is much smaller than the underlying flaw and floccus mottles observable with two-dimensional imaging.

II. The glass phase surrounding the entry point remains clean and smooth, without any other visible surface flaws.

See pictures 9-1-68 and 9-1-69, where 9-1-68 is the two-dimensional and 9-1-69 is the three-dimensional view of the same location.

The floccus mottle indicated by Arrow A in picture 9-1-68 is not visible in picture 9-1-69. The glaze surface only presents with a few pit mottles, and is generally smooth, making it clear that the floccus mottling is within the glaze level.

The floccus mottling indicated by Arrow B is not visible

征不明显，釉表面较光滑洁净（见箭头B’所指处）；箭头C’所指的磨砂针眼斑不像真品呈现独立点状凹坑，而是黑色的粉末状物质，散落堆积在釉表面，缺乏立体感。磨砂针眼斑在沙滩斑上整体的分布也未随着沙滩斑的轮廓走势，没有规律，没有整齐的边界。沙滩斑整体显得粗糙涂污。

（二）放射斑上的针眼斑

1. 真品二维特征

（1）磨砂针眼斑的分布不超出放射斑的范围。（见图9-1-41）

（2）放射斑边沿部位的釉下放射斑呈黄色。（见图9-1-41箭头A及图9-1-42箭头C所指处）

（3）放射斑的包边纤细收敛（见图9-1-41箭头B及图9-1-42箭头D所指处）。

（4）放射斑整体细腻精致，具有色阶变化（见图9-1-41、图9-1-42）。

（5）放射斑周围的玻璃相干净清晰（见图9-1-41、图9-1-42）。

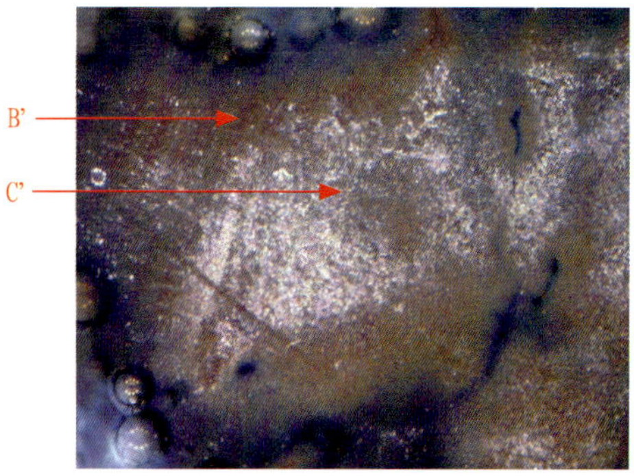

图9-1-39

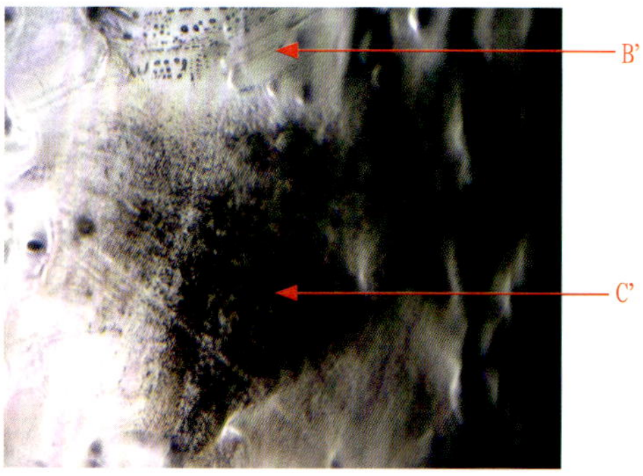

图9-1-40

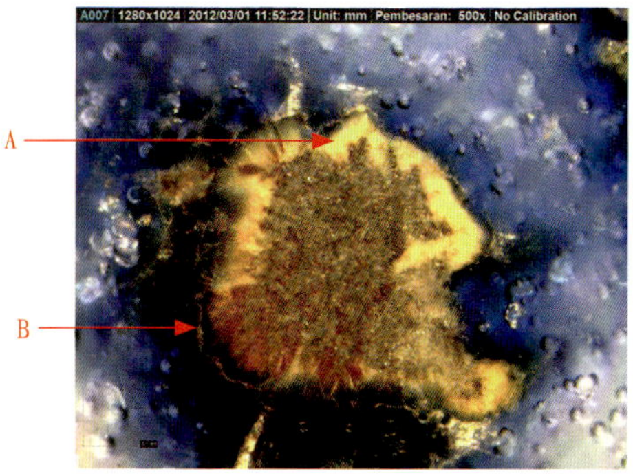

图9-1-41

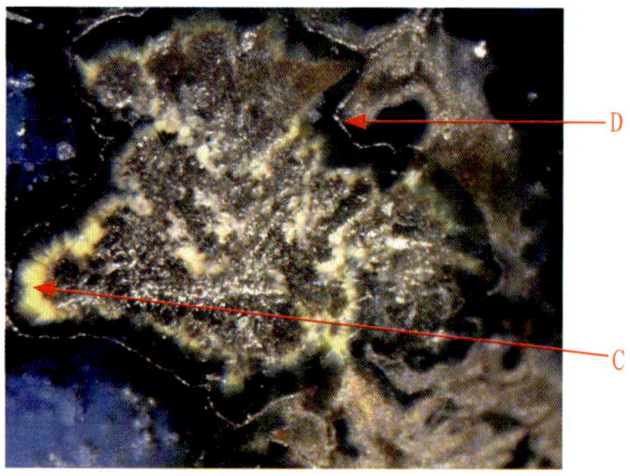

图9-1-42

2. 赝品二维特征

见图9-1-43、图9-1-44。（该器物釉表面曾被腐蚀剂腐蚀）

（1）磨砂针眼斑在黑色系放射斑上较明显。（见箭头A’及箭头E’所指处）

（2）釉下放射斑呈黄色；（见箭头B’所指处）釉上放射斑呈褐色。（见箭头F’所指处）

（3）放射斑的包边粗糙，有毛边。（见箭头C’及箭头G’所指处）

（4）针眼斑超出放射斑范围，在邻近的玻璃相上也有分布，而且无规律可循，缺乏陶瓷迹型出现位置的合理性。（见箭头D’及箭头H’所指处）

（5）周围玻璃相上杂乱无章地分布有许多CO纹、针眼斑及坑点斑，斑块整体显得涂污模糊，缺乏颜色和层次变化。

（三）玻璃相上的针眼斑

1. 真品二维特征

见图9-1-45。

（1）颗粒针眼斑呈颗粒状，针眼之间清晰独立，分布疏朗。

（2）针眼斑与其周围的玻璃相界线分明。

（3）针眼斑周围的玻璃相干净清晰。

2. 赝品二维特征

见图9-1-46。（该器物釉表面曾被腐蚀剂腐蚀）

（1）针眼斑到处都是，分布无规律可循。

（2）针眼斑形貌模糊，与周围玻璃相界线不分明。

(3) 图片整体显得粗糙、涂污。

in picture 9-1-69, and the glaze retains its glossiness, making it clear that the floccus mottling is within the glaze level.

Mottle C is most likely the entry point through which the floccus mottle dispersed into the glaze level (see picture 9-1-69).

C. Two-Dimensional Characteristics of Forged Article

See pictures 9-1-70 and 9-1-71 (this piece has undergone treatment with aging reagent).

a. The "floccus mottles" are white clusters.

b. The edges are definite without fuzziness, and do not extend in all directions.

D. Three-Dimensional Characteristics of Forged Article

I. Corrosion blotches present on the glaze surface, the surface area is the same as the two-dimensional image.

II. The surface of the blotches is coarse without clear borders or delineation with the surrounding glass phase.

III. The surrounding glaze surface is muddled.

See pictures 9-1-72 and 9-1-73, where 9-1-72 is the two-dimensional and 9-1-73 is the three-dimensional view of the same location (this piece has undergone treatment with aging reagent).

The two and three-dimensional surface areas of the "floccus mottle" indicated by Arrow A' are the same. The mottle's surface is coarse, lacking defined borders or clear delineation with the surrounding glass phase. The glaze surface in general is muddled. Thus they are not genuine floccus mottles.

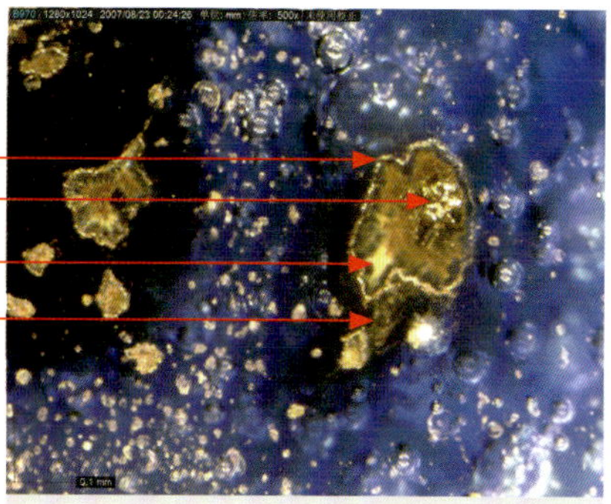

图9-1-43

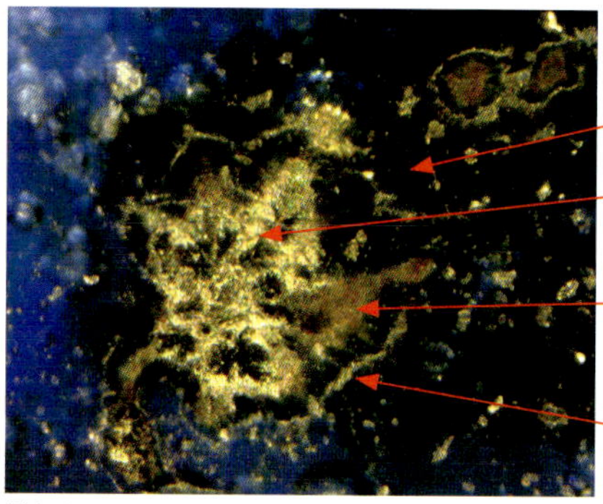

图9-1-44

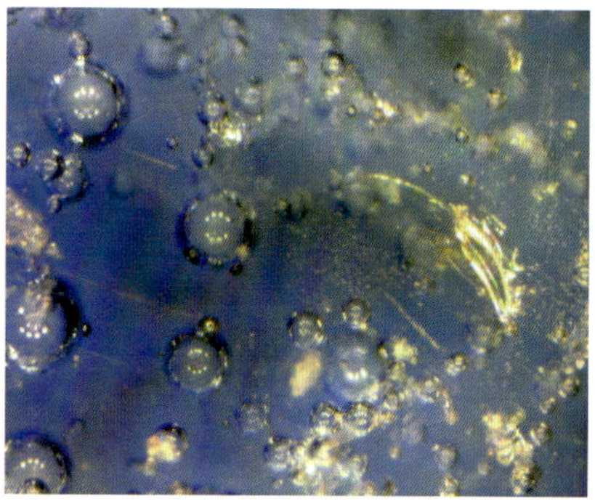
图9-1-45

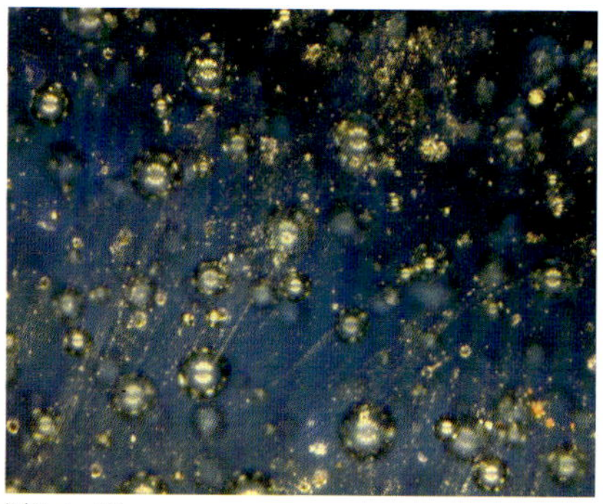
图9-1-46

四、坑点斑

（一）CO型坑点斑

1. 真品二维特征

（1）单位图片中CO型坑点斑与CO纹伴生，CO纹呈黄色，坑点斑呈白色，二者都独立清晰，彼此界线分明（见图9-1-47）。

（2）单位图片中CO型坑点斑与CO纹、连环坑点斑群同时存在，分布疏朗，独立清晰，彼此界线分明（见图9-1-47、图9-1-48）。

（3）CO型坑点斑与周围玻璃相以及沙滩斑、流淌纹等其他迹型种类界线分明（见图9-1-47、图9-1-48）。

（4）CO型坑点斑周围玻璃相干净清晰（见图9-1-47、图9-1-48）。

（5）CO型坑点斑所在处的釉层中存在絮状斑（见图9-1-49）。

（6）坑点斑有大小及深浅的差异（见图9-1-47—图9-1-50）。

2. 真品三维特征

（1）CO型坑点斑大都分布在釉表面凸起处。

（2）釉表面只见纤细收敛的C形纹或O形纹，清晰独立。

（3）釉表面只见纤细收敛的C形纹或O形纹以及面积小于坑点斑二维成像面积的风化斑块，彼此界线分明。

见图9-1-50、图9-1-51，二者为同一器物同一位置图片，图9-1-50为二维图片，图9-1-51为三维图片。

图9-1-50中的CO型坑点斑在图9-1-51中都随机分布在釉表面凸起处（见箭头A所指处）。二维成像的CO型坑点斑，与三维成像中一个个凸起的“小山包”一一对应，釉表面没有凸起的地方光滑洁净。

图9-1-50中箭头B所指的CO型坑点斑在图9-1-51中所在处凸起不明显，可见一条末端有分叉的C形纹。坑点斑B的三维成像面积要小于二维。

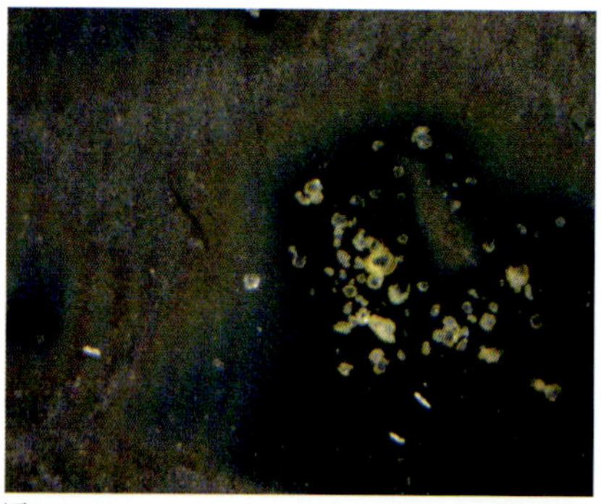
图9-1-47

图9-1-48

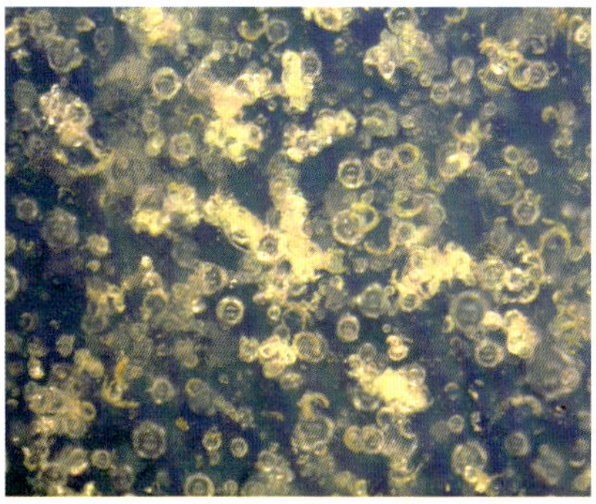

图9-1-49

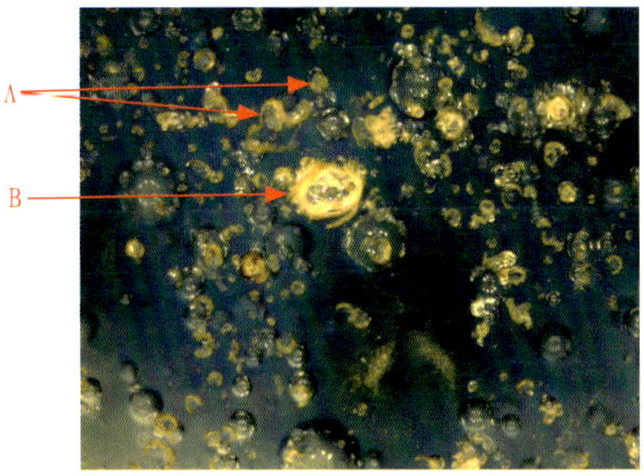

图9-1-50

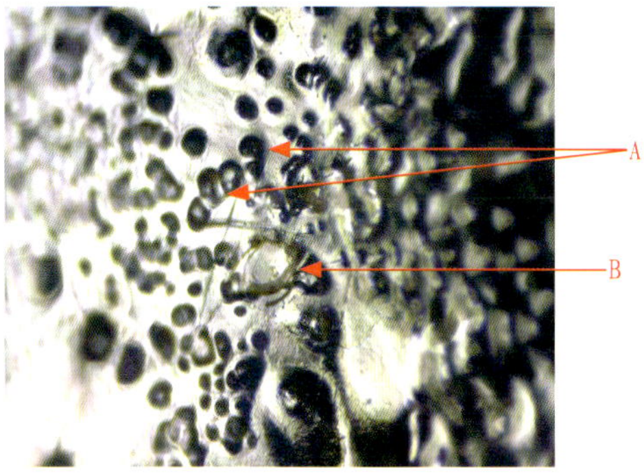

图9-1-51

见图9-1-52、图9-1-53，二者为同一器物同一位置图片，图9-1-52为二维图片，图9-1-53为三维图片。

图9-1-52中的CO型坑点斑在图9-1-53中只见C形纹，纹路收敛清晰，同时还有两处面积小于图9-1-52中CO型坑点斑的深色斑块（见箭头C所指处），说明CO型坑点斑部分存在于釉层中。C形纹、深色斑块与玻璃相界线清晰。

周围玻璃相上除CO型坑点斑外还有各自独立清晰的划痕及针眼型坑点斑，彼此界线清晰，玻璃相其余地方光滑洁净（见图9-1-53）。

见图9-1-54、图9-1-55，二者为同一器物同一位置图片，图9-1-54为二维图片，图9-1-55为三维图片。

在图9-1-54、图9-1-55中，CO型坑点斑都分布在釉表面凸起处。二维成像的CO型坑点斑，与三维成像中一个个凸起的“小山包”一一对应，釉表面没有凸起的地方光滑洁净。

CO型坑点斑在图9-1-55中的三维成像明显比图9-1-54中的二维成像面积要小，说明坑点斑部分存在于釉层中（见箭头D所指处）。坑点斑D与其他邻近的坑点斑及玻璃相之间界线分明，周围玻璃相光滑洁净。

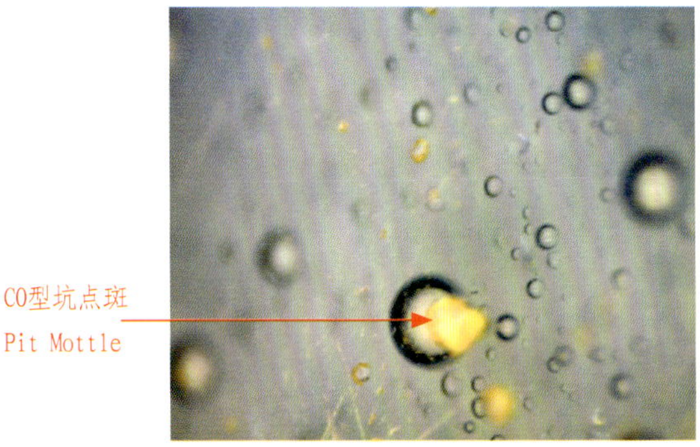

图9-1-52

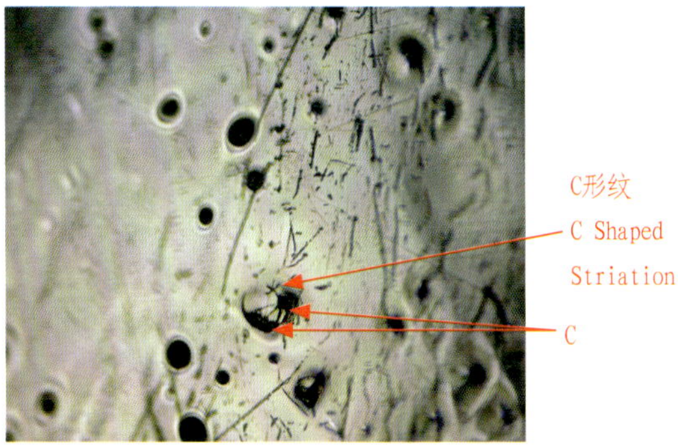

图9-1-53

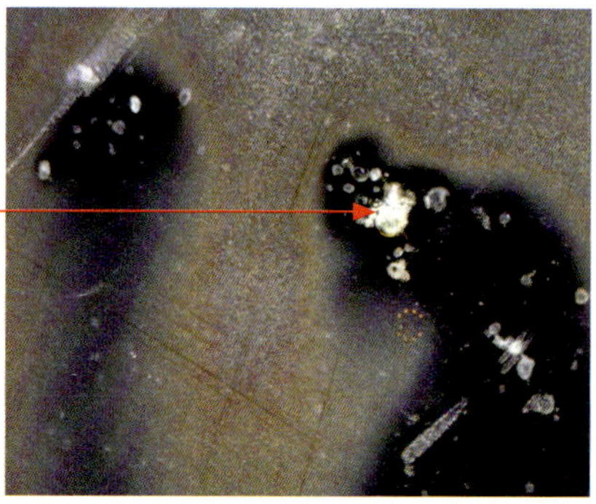

图9-1-54

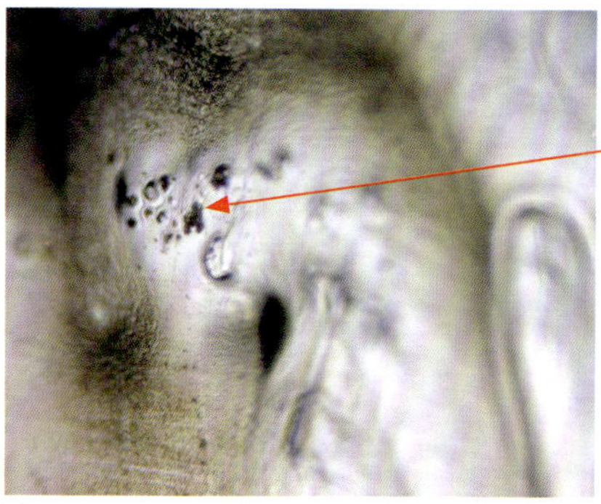

图9-1-55

3. 赝品二维特征

见图9-1-56、图9-1-57。（该器物釉表面曾被腐蚀剂腐蚀）

（1）CO型坑点斑形貌杂乱、混沌、模糊不清，颜色与CO纹一致，大小及深浅差异不大。

（2）CO型坑点斑、CO纹、针眼斑等迹型种类分布密集，彼此界线不分明，与周围的玻璃相界线也不清晰。

（3）图片整体凌乱涂污。

4. 赝品三维特征

（1）一般釉表面不见CO纹或CO纹不清晰。

（2）CO型坑点斑三维成像的面积大于二维。

（3）周围釉表面杂乱无章地分布着坑点斑、划痕，整体显得粗糙混沌。

见图9-1-58、图9-1-59，二者为同一器物同一位置图片，图9-1-58为二维图片，图9-1-59为三维图片。（该器物釉表面曾被腐蚀剂腐蚀）

图9-1-58中的CO型坑点斑在图9-1-59中都分布在釉表面凸起处。二维成像的CO型坑点斑，与三维成像中一个个凸起的“小山包”一一对应，釉表面没有凸起的地方比较光滑洁净。

图9-1-58中箭头A’所指的两

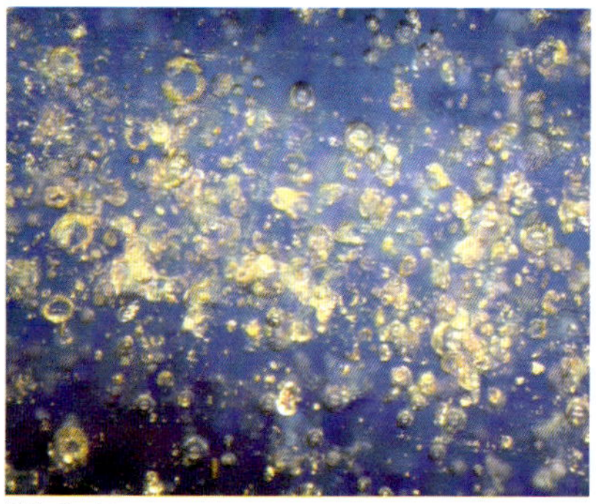
图9-1-56

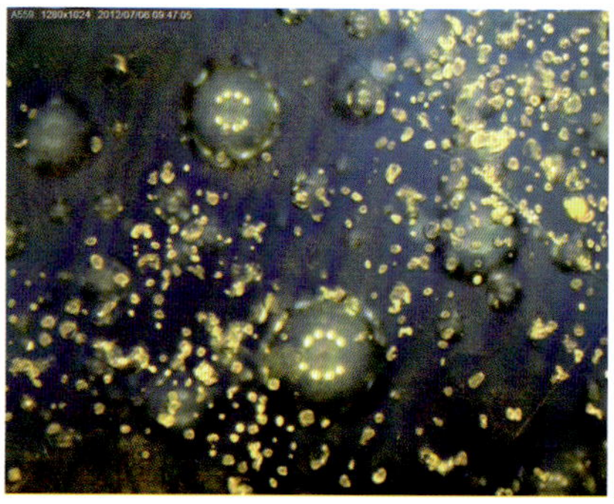
图9-1-57

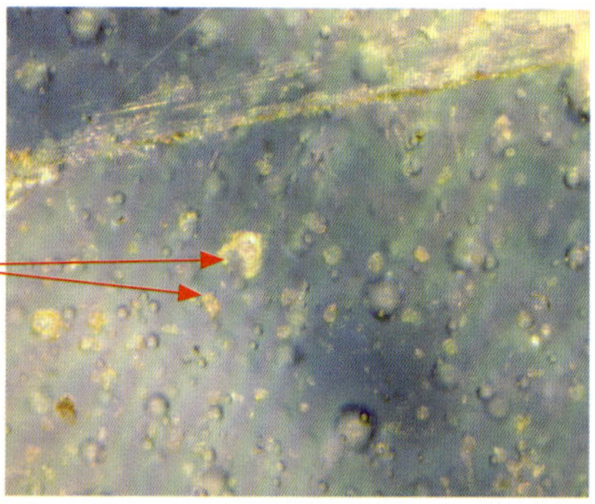

图9-1-58

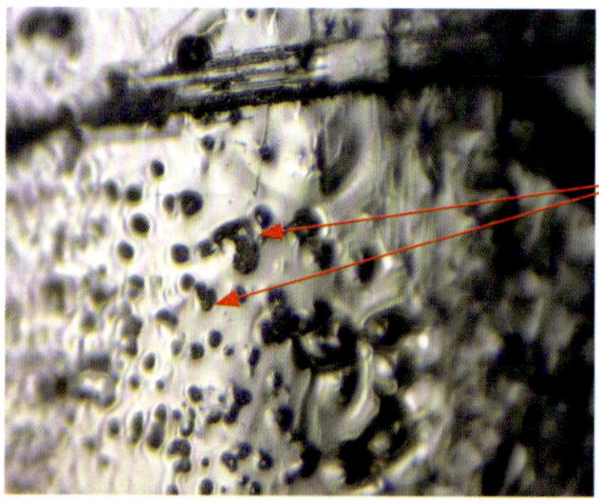

图9-1-59

个CO型坑点斑在图9-1-59中的三维成像的面积均大于二维，不见CO纹轮廓。

见图9-1-60、图9-1-61，二者为同一器物同一位置图片，图9-1-60为二维图片，图9-1-61为三维图片。（该器物釉表面曾被腐蚀剂腐蚀）

图9-1-60中的CO型坑点斑B’在图9-1-61中隐约可见O形纹轮廓。周围釉表面杂乱无章地分布着坑点斑、划痕，破坏严重，整体显得粗糙混沌。

（二）针眼型坑点斑

1. 真品二维特征

见图9-1-62。

（1）针眼型坑点斑呈白色，外沿有纤细的包边。

（2）单位图片中还有少数划痕存在，但都各自独立清晰，界线分明。

（3）周围玻璃相干净清晰。

2. 真品三维特征

（1）针眼型坑点斑呈凹陷状，清晰独立，三维成像面积与二维相当。

（2）针眼型坑点斑与附近其他迹型种类界线分明。

（3）针眼型坑点斑与周围玻璃相界线分明。

（4）针眼型坑点斑周围玻璃相光滑洁净。

见图9-1-62、图9-1-63，二者为同一器物同一位置图片，图9-1-62为二维图片，图9-1-63为三维图片。

图9-1-62中白色的针眼型坑点斑在图9-1-63中呈深色，成像清晰。坑点斑为釉表面上一凹坑，三维成像面积与二维相当，与周围玻璃相界线分明。周围玻璃相光滑洁净（箭头A所指处）。

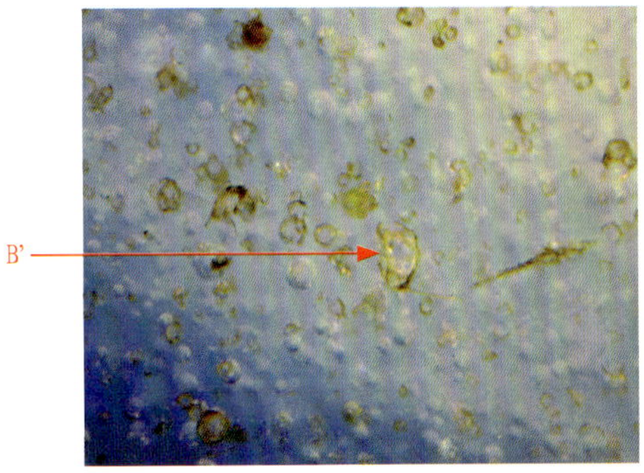

图9-1-60

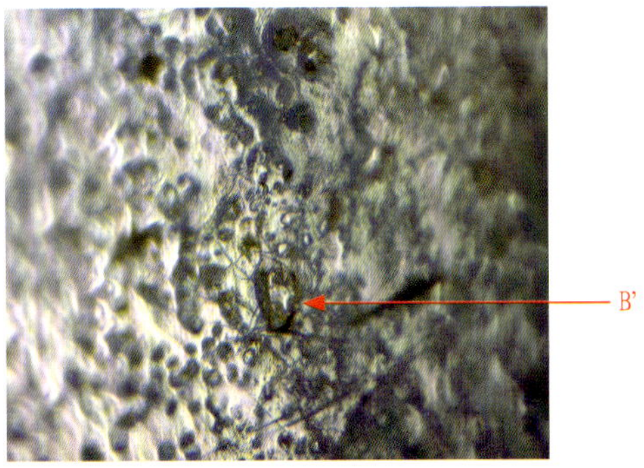

图9-1-61

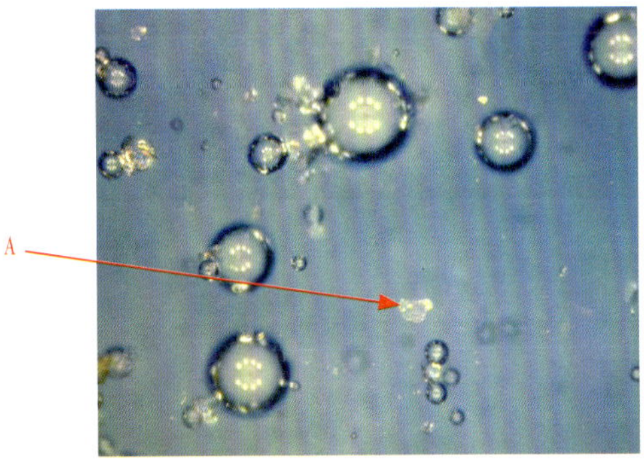

图9-1-62

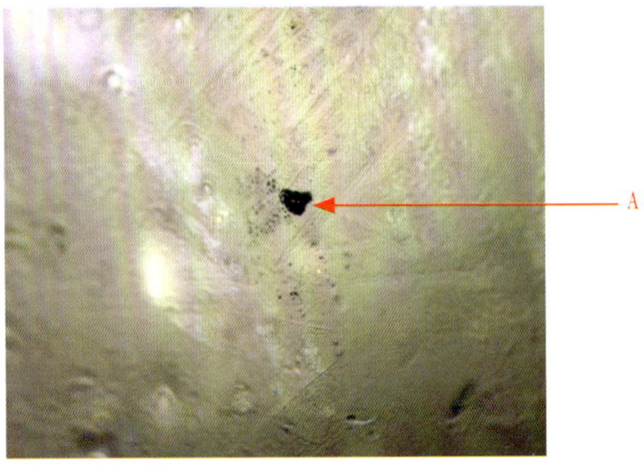

图9-1-63

3. 赝品二维特征

见图9-1-64。

（1）针眼型坑点斑数量较多，形貌大小不一，分布杂乱无章。

（2）图片整体凌乱涂污。

4. 赝品三维特征

（1）针眼型坑点斑表现为凹坑，三维成像面积与二维相当。

（2）周围玻璃相整体显得粗糙涂污。

见图9-1-64、图9-1-65，二者为同一器物同一位置图片，图9-1-64为二维图片，图9-1-65为三维图片。（该器物釉表面曾被腐蚀剂腐蚀）

图9-1-64中箭头A’所指的两处针眼型坑点斑在图9-1-65中表现为两处凹坑，三维成像面积与二维相当。周围玻璃相上有大小不一、杂乱无章的凹坑，玻璃相整体显得粗糙涂污。

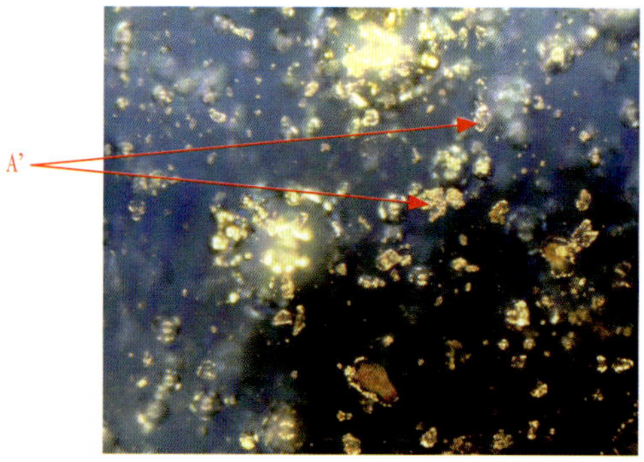

图9-1-64

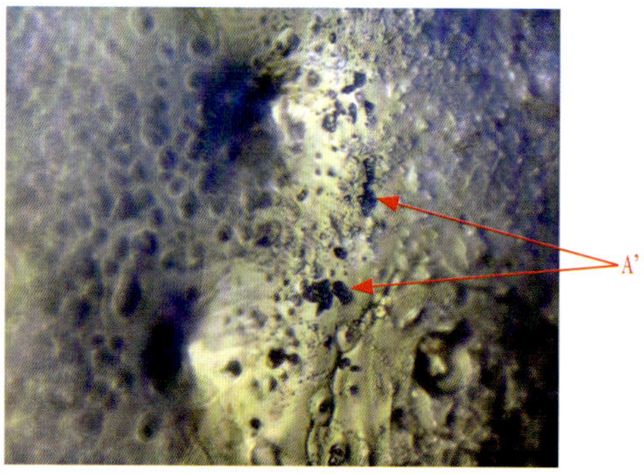

图9-1-65

五、絮状斑

1. 真品二维特征

见图9-1-66、图9-1-67。

（1）絮状斑一般在釉层组织结构稳定性较差处或破损处出现，由釉损处呈梯度向周边的釉下扩散。

（2）絮状斑中心色白如牛奶，不透明；斑块边沿呈绒状，半透明，有向四周漫延的趋势。

2. 真品三维特征

（1）絮状斑在釉表面不可见，釉表面釉损处（如坑点斑、釉裂纹）的三维面积远远小于釉损处与絮状斑二维成像面积的总和。

（2）釉表面釉损处以外的地方光滑洁净，无其他明显的大面积损伤。

见图9-1-68、图9-1-69，二者为同一器物同一位置图片，图9-1-68为二维图片，图9-1-69为三维图片。

图9-1-68中箭头A所指的絮状斑在图9-1-69中却不可见，釉表面只见零星几处坑点斑，总体较光滑，说明絮状斑存在于釉层中。

图9-1-68中箭头B所指的絮状斑在图9-1-69中不可见，釉表面光滑洁净，说明絮状斑存在于釉层中。

箭头C所指的坑点斑属于釉表面破损处，应该是絮状斑形成的通道（见图9-1-69）。

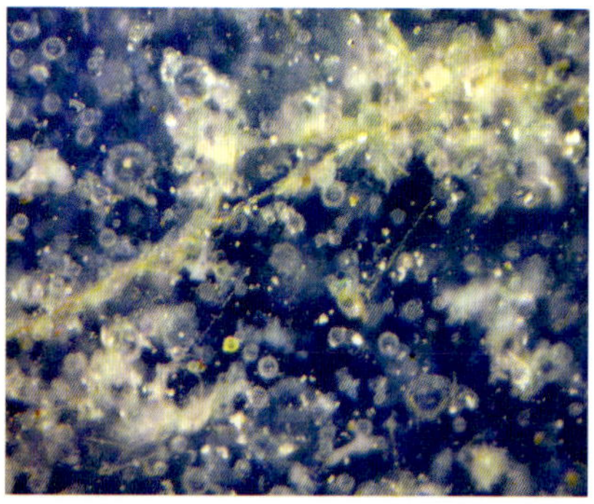
图9-1-66

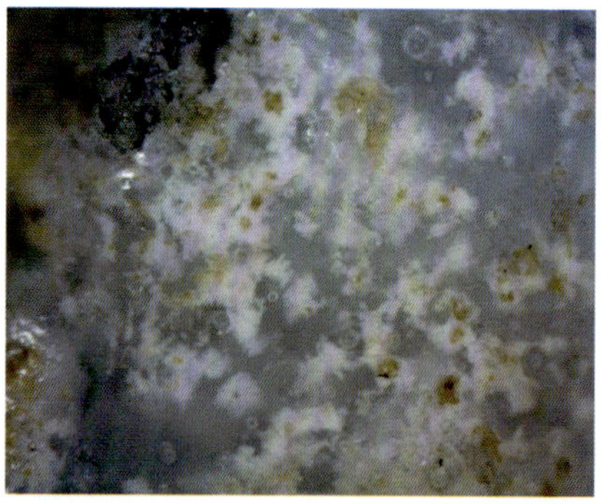
图9-1-67

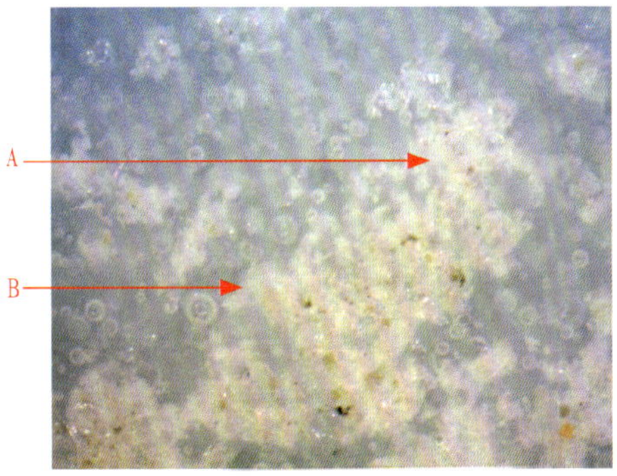

图9-1-68

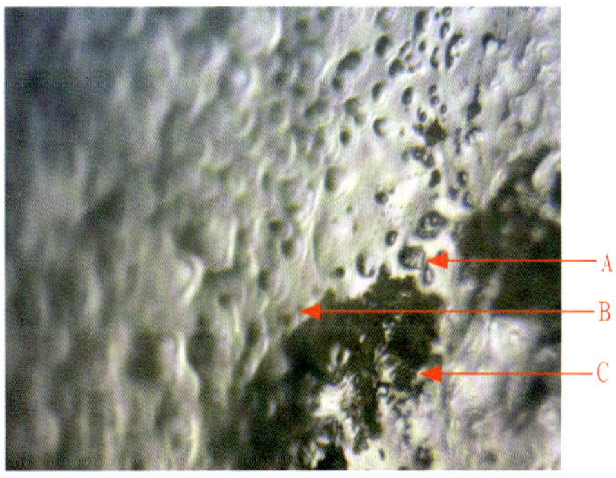

图9-1-69

3. 赝品二维特征

见图9-1-70、图9-1-71。（该器物釉表面曾被腐蚀剂腐蚀）

（1）絮状斑呈白色，团状。

（2）斑块边沿收敛，没有毛边，也没有向四周漫延的趋势。

4. 赝品三维特征

（1）釉表面存在腐蚀斑块，三维成像面积与二维相当。

（2）腐蚀斑块表面粗糙，与玻璃相界线不分明。

（3）周围釉表面粗糙涂污。

见图9-1-72、图9-1-73，二者为同一器物同一位置图片，图9-1-72为二维图片，图9-1-73为三维图片。（该器物釉表面曾被腐蚀剂腐蚀）

图9-1-72中箭头A'所指的絮状斑的二维成像面积与图9-1-73中的三维相当，斑块表面粗糙，与玻璃相界线不分明。周围玻璃相粗糙涂污。斑块A'并非真正的絮状斑。

图9-1-70

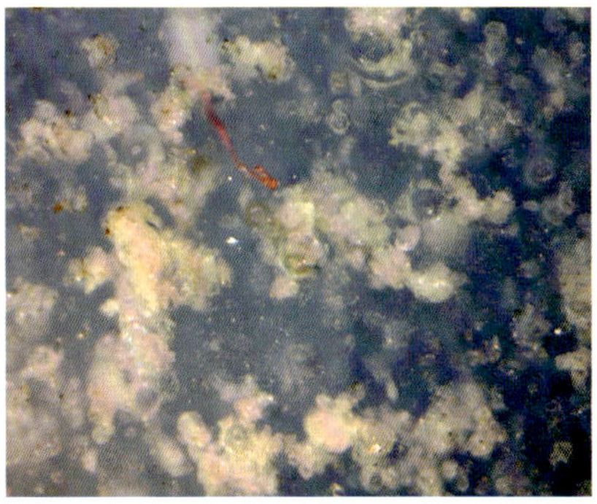
图9-1-71

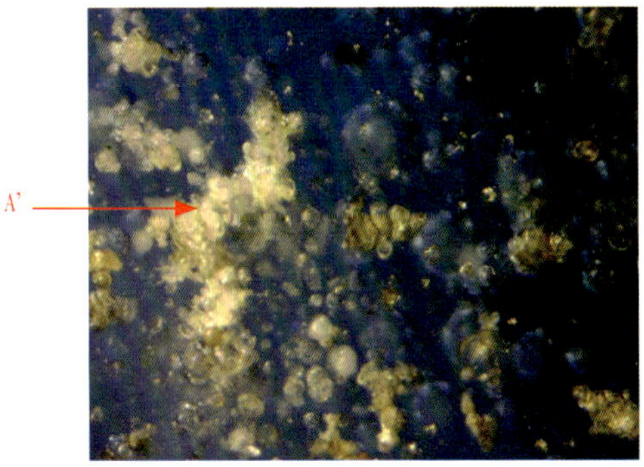

图9-1-72

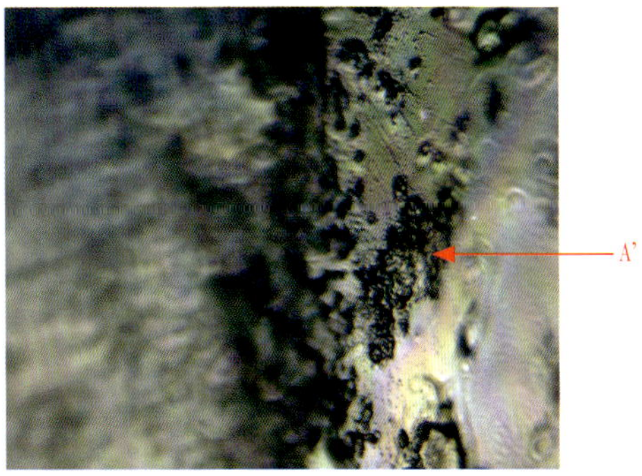

图9-1-73

第二节
元青花纹路真品与赝品比对

一、流淌纹

（一）中空型阴纹

1. 真品二维特征

见图9-2-1。

（1）呈网状分布的中空型阴纹清晰独立，纹路间彼此界线清晰。

（2）中空型阴纹内部未完全被针眼斑覆盖，与边界之间留有一定的空间。

（3）中空型阴纹周围的玻璃相干净清晰。

2. 真品三维特征

（1）中空型阴纹剖面一般都呈“W”形。

（2）纹路脊部反光的部分较光滑，不反光处有风化物质堆积。

（3）纹路与周围玻璃相界线分明。

（4）周围玻璃相光滑洁净。

见图9-2-1、图9-2-2，二者为同一器物同一位置图片，图9-2-1为二维图片，图9-2-2为三维图片。

中空型阴纹的凹槽有一定深度及宽度，纹路脊部凸起，脊部反光的部分较光滑，不反光处有风化物质堆积。玻璃相被纹路以网状形式切割，一块块玻璃相凸起，像蒸笼里的窝头。纹路与周围玻璃相界线分明。周围玻璃相光滑洁净（见图9-2-2）。

图9-2-1

图9-2-2

3. 赝品二维特征

见图9-2-3。

（1）中空型阴纹模糊不清，彼此之间界线不分明。

（2）纹路之间的玻璃相被针眼斑覆盖，模糊不清。

4. 赝品三维特征

（1）中空型阴纹的凹槽较浅。

（2）纹路脊部光滑洁净，无风化物质覆盖。

见图9-2-3、图9-2-4，二者为同一器物同一位置图片，图9-2-3为二维图片，图9-2-4为三维图片。（该器物釉表面未被腐蚀剂腐蚀）

图9-2-3中的中空型阴纹在图9-2-4中的凹槽较浅，纹路脊部光滑洁净，无风化物质覆盖。

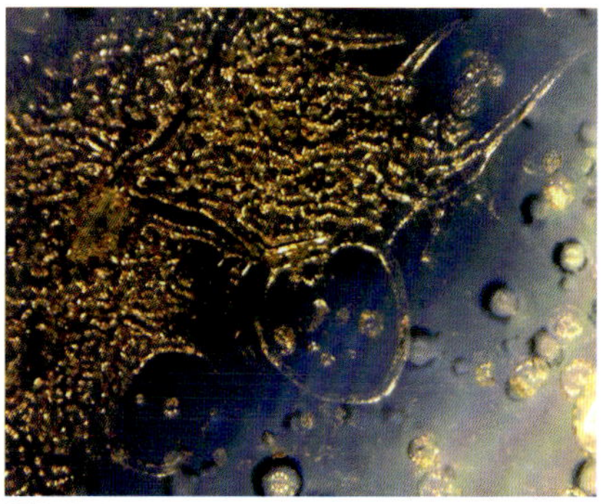
图9-2-3

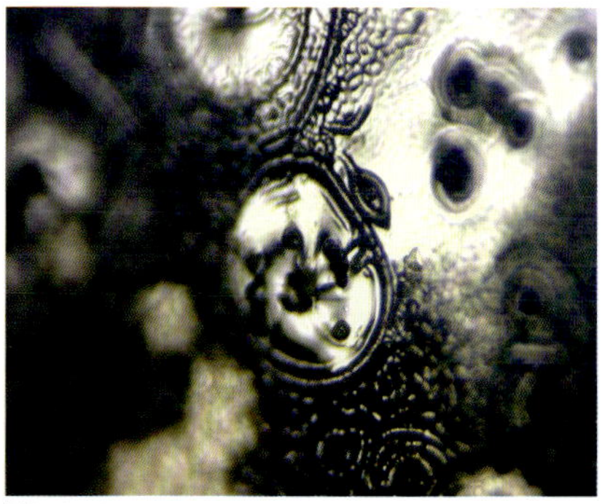
图9-2-4

Section 2:

Genuine and Forged Yuan Underglaze Blue Striae Comparison

1. Flowing Striae

A. Empty Striae

I. Two-Dimensional Characteristics of Genuine Article

See picture 9-2-1.

a. Striae assume a webbed network, but are independent and mutually delineated with clearly defined borders.

b. The interiors of the striae are not completely covered by needlepoint mottling, with a certain 'empty' space between their borders.

c. The surrounding glass phase is clean and clear.

II. Three-Dimensional Characteristics of Genuine Article

a. The cross section of the striation is a "W" shape.

b. The convex center of the striae is relatively glossy, portions that are not reflective have been covered by weathering deposits.

c. The borders between the striae and surrounding glaze are clear.

d. The surrounding glaze surface is clean and clear.

See pictures 9-2-1 and 9-2-2, where 9-2-1 is the two-dimensional and 9-2-2 is the three-dimensional view of the same location.

The empty striae have general concavity with certain depths and widths, with the center of the striae having convexity giving the striae approximate "W" shaped cross sections. Reflective areas are glossy, and non-reflective areas have weathering deposits. The glaze surface has become dissected by the striae network and rises up in a series of mounds, similar to rows of hot buns on a baking tray. The borders between the striae and surrounding glaze surface are clearly defined, and the glaze surface is clean and smooth (see picture 9-2-2).

III. Two-Dimensional Characteristics of Forged Article

See picture 9-2-3.

a. The striae are muddled and not clearly defined, lacking clear delineation from the surrounding glass phase.

b. The glass phase within the striae network has become covered with needlepoint mottling and is generally muddled.

IV. Three-Dimensional Characteristics of Forged Article

a. The concavity of the striae is relatively shallow.

b. The convex centers are clean and smooth, no weathering deposits present.

See pictures 9-2-3 and 9-2-4, where 9-2-3 is the two-dimensional and 9-2-4 is the three-dimensional view of the same location (this piece has not undergone treatment with aging reagent).

The striae have a general, but very shallow concavity. The convex center of the striae is completely glossy, and lacks weathering deposit covering.

B. Needlepoint Striae

I. Thin Needlepoint Striae

a. Two-Dimensional Characteristics of Genuine Article

See picture 9-2-5.

(a) The striae present as thin lines; fine and reserved,

（二）针眼型阴纹

1. 较细针眼型阴纹

（1）真品二维特征

见图9-2-5。

A. 针眼型阴纹形如细线，清晰收敛，紧致无毛边。

B. 针眼型阴纹与周围玻璃相界线清晰分明。

C. 针眼型阴纹周围的玻璃相上分布少数坑点斑，但玻璃相整体还是显得干净清晰。

（2）真品三维特征

A. 针眼型阴纹剖面呈“U”形。

B. 纹路呈凹陷状，边沿圆滑。

C. 针眼型阴纹与周围玻璃相界线清晰分明。

D. 纹路周围的玻璃相上有坑点斑零星分布，彼此独立。

E. 周围玻璃相光滑洁净。

见图9-2-5、图9-2-6，二者为同一器物同一位置图片，图9-2-5为二维图片，图9-2-6为三维图片。

图9-2-5箭头A所指的针眼型阴纹在图9-2-6中呈凹陷状，进入釉层一定深度，清晰收敛，边沿圆滑。与周围玻璃相界线分明，周围的玻璃相上可见零星坑点斑。阴纹与坑点斑彼此独立。周围玻璃相光滑洁净。

（3）赝品二维特征

见图9-2-7。

A. 针眼型阴纹模糊，有毛边。

B. 针眼型阴纹与周围玻璃相界线模糊。

C. 纹路周围的玻璃相上杂乱无序地分布着针眼斑及坑点斑，整体显得涂污模糊。

（4）赝品三维特征

A. 针眼型阴纹的凹槽很细很浅，有毛边，表面粗糙。

B. 各迹型种类间界线模糊不清。

C. 周围玻璃相也比较涂污。

见图9-2-7、图9-2-8，二者为同一器物同一位置图片，图9-2-7为二维图片，图9-2-8为三维图片。（该器物釉表面曾被腐蚀剂腐蚀）

图9-2-7中的纹路在图9-2-8中凹槽显得很细很浅，表面粗糙，有毛边（见箭头A’所指处）。各迹型种类间界线模糊不清。纹路周围的玻璃相也比较粗糙涂污。

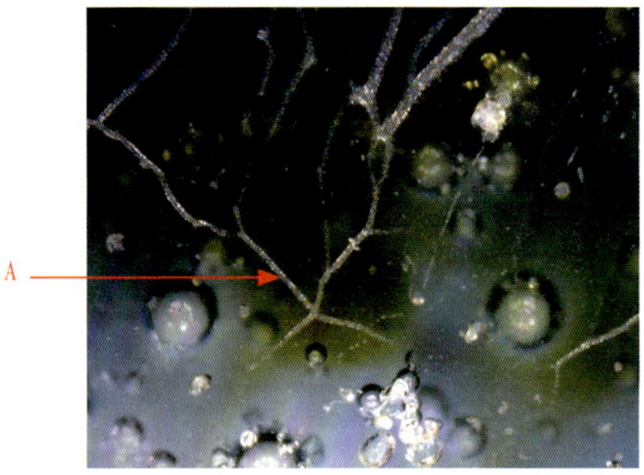

图9-2-5

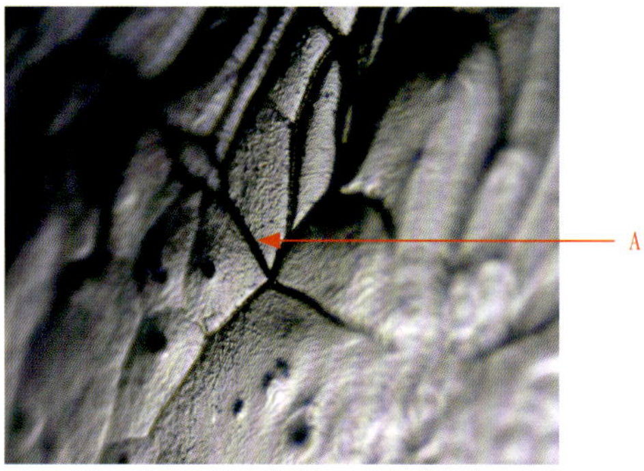

图9-2-6

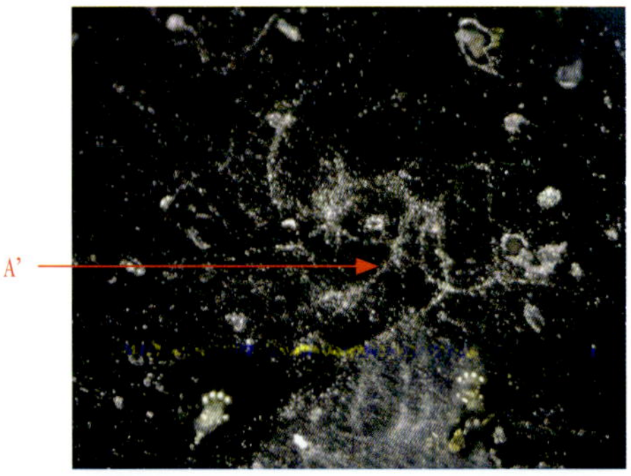

图9-2-7

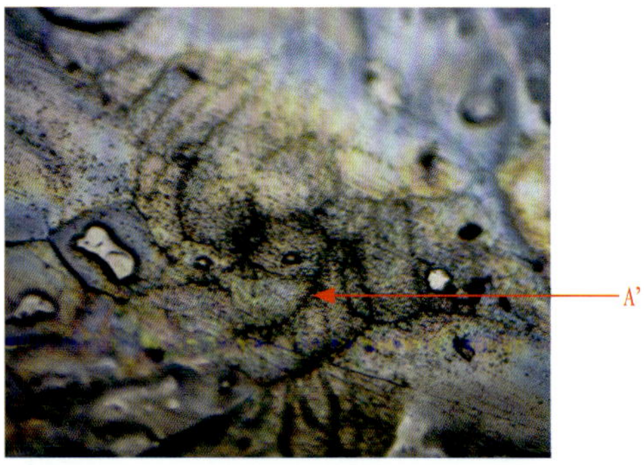

图9-2-8

without fuzzy edges.

(b) There is clear delineation with the surrounding glass phase.

(c) The surrounding glass phase can present with a small amount of pit mottles, but generally retains a clean and clear appearance.

b. Three-Dimensional Characteristics of Genuine Article

(a) The striae have an approximate "U" shaped cross section.

(b) They have a general concavity with rounded edges.

(c) They are clearly delineated from the surrounding glaze surface.

(d) Some clearly independent and finely distributed pitting presents on the surrounding glass phase.

(e) The surrounding glaze surface, as a whole, is clean and smooth.

See pictures 9-2-5 and 9-2-6, where 9-2-5 is the two-dimensional and 9-2-6 is the three-dimensional view of the same location.

Striation A extends a certain depth into the glaze level and has a general concave "U" shape. It is reserved and clear, and its edges are rounded. It retains clear delineation from the surrounding glaze surface, which presents with a misting of fine and independently distributed pits, but has an overall clean and smooth nature.

c. Two-Dimensional Characteristics of Forged Article

See picture 9-2-8.

(a) Striae are muddled with fuzzy edges.

(b) The borders between the striae and glass phase have become blurred.

(c) The glaze surface surrounding the striae has become littered with a sporadic and irregular distribution of pitting, its general appearance muddled.

d. Three-Dimensional Characteristics of Forged Article

(a) The striae have a very shallow concavity, its surface coarse and edges fuzzy.

(b) There is no clear delineation between traces.

(c) The glaze surface, in general, is coarsely muddled.

See pictures 9-2-7 and 9-2-8, where 9-2-7 is the two-dimensional and 9-2-8 is the three-dimensional view of the same location (this piece has undergone treatment with aging reagent).

The striation indicated by Arrow A' is shallow with a coarse surface and fuzzy edges. There is no clear inter-trace delineation and their borders are unclear. The glaze surface is coarsely muddled.

II. Thick Needlepoint Striae

a. Two-Dimensional Characteristics of Genuine Article

See picture 9-2-9.

(a) Striae have a certain width to them and are filled with frosted needlepoint mottling and can present with white and tangerine coloration.

(b) The striae are clearly delineated from the surrounding glass phase.

(c) The glass phase is clean and clear.

b. Three-Dimensional Characteristics of Genuine Article

(a) The striae have an approximate "U" shaped cross section.

(f) The striae have a concave shape with rounded edges.

(b) The relatively broad striae can present with internal granulation and color spectrum.

(c) The striae retain clear delineation from the surrounding glaze surface.

(d) The glaze surface is clean and smooth.

See pictures 9-2-9 and 9-2-10, where 9-2-9 is the two-dimensional and 9-2-10 is the three-dimensional view of the same location.

The striation in picture 9-2-9 appears concave in picture 9-2-10 and has a clear height discrepancy with the surrounding glaze. There is clear granulated material within the striae interior that presents with a purple and dark brown color variation (see Arrow A).

2. 较粗针眼型阴纹

（1）真品二维特征

见图9-2-9。

A. 针眼型阴纹都有一定宽度，纹路内部被磨砂针眼斑不均匀地覆盖，有白色及橘黄色的色阶变化。

B. 纹路与周围玻璃相界线分明。

C. 周围玻璃相干净清晰。

（2）真品三维特征

A. 针眼型阴纹剖面是“U”形。

B. 纹路呈凹陷状，边沿圆滑。

C. 纹路较宽的可见内部颗粒物质，有色阶变化。

D. 纹路与周围玻璃相界线分明。

E. 周围玻璃相光滑洁净。

见图9-2-9、图9-2-10，二者为同一器物同一位置图片，图9-2-9为二维图片，图9-2-10为三维图片。

图9-2-9中箭头A所指的纹路在图9-2-10中呈凹陷状，与周围玻璃相有明显高度差。纹路凹槽内有明显颗粒物质分布，并有紫蓝色及深褐色的色阶变化。

图9-2-9中箭头B所指的纹路在图9-2-10中呈凹陷状，与周围玻璃相有明显高度差。纹路凹槽内有明显颗粒物质分布，并有紫蓝色及白色的色阶变化。

纹路A及纹路B边沿都较圆滑，与周围玻璃相界线分明，周围玻璃相光滑洁净（见图9-2-10）。

（3）赝品二维特征

见图9-2-11。

A. 针眼型阴纹有一定宽度，但纹路模糊、有毛边。

B. 各迹型种类间界线模糊不清。

C. 周围玻璃相上分布有针眼斑、坑点斑，玻璃相也混沌模糊。

（4）赝品三维特征

A. 针眼型阴纹有一定宽度，但与周围玻璃相几乎在同一平面，凹槽很浅。

B. 纹路的凹槽内粗糙涂污。

C. 周围玻璃相上有许多坑点斑，形貌一致。

见图9-2-11、图9-2-12，二者为同一器物同一位置图片，图9-2-11为二维图片，图9-2-12为三维图片。（该器物釉表面曾被腐蚀剂腐蚀）

图9-2-11中的针眼型阴纹在图9-2-12中有一定宽度，但与周围玻璃相几乎在同一平面，凹槽很浅，凹槽内粗糙涂污（见箭头A’所指处）。

周围玻璃相上有许多坑点斑，形貌一致（见图9-2-12箭头B’所指处）。

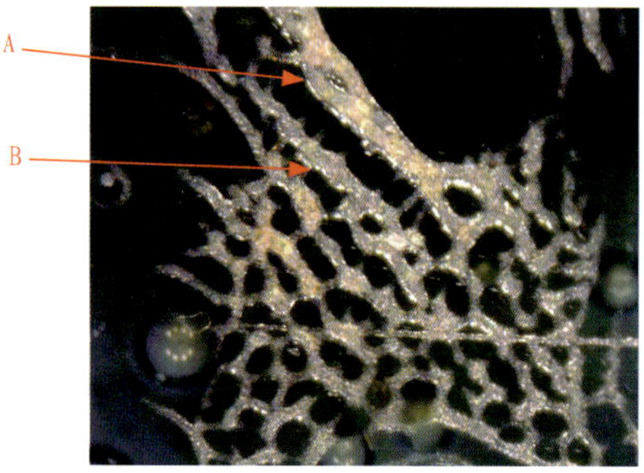

图9-2-9

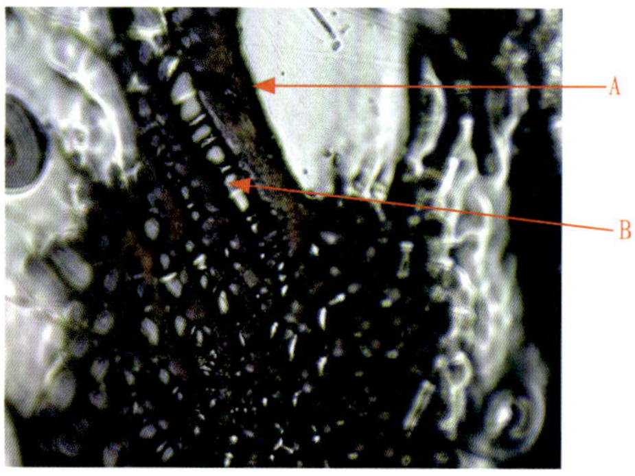

图9-2-10

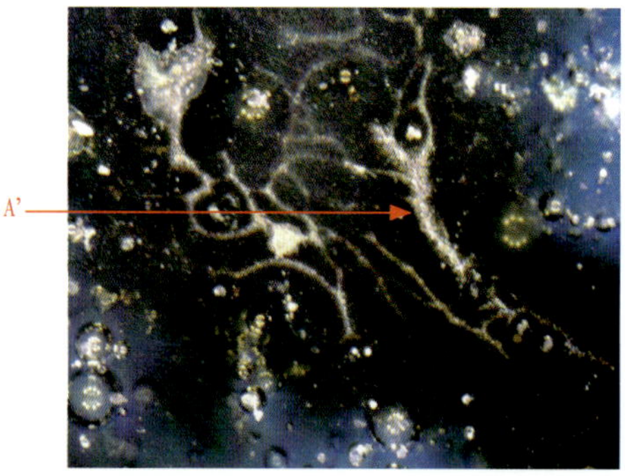

图9-2-11

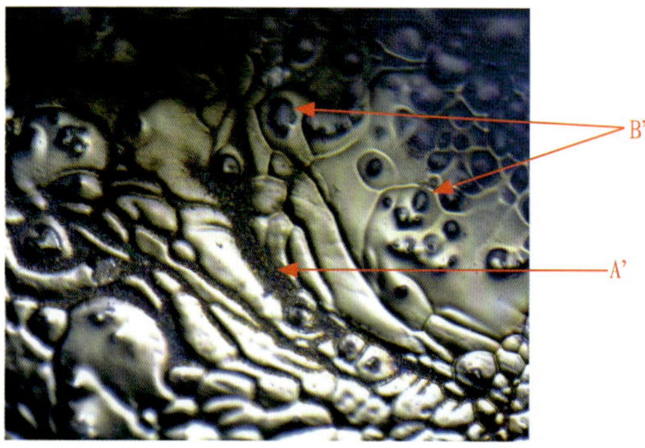

图9-2-12

Striation B in picture 9-2-9 appears concave in picture 9-2-10 and has a clear height discrepancy with the surrounding glaze. There is clear granulated material within the striation interior that presents with a purple and white color variation.

The edges of striae A and B are rounded, clearly delineated from the surrounding glaze surface, and the glaze surface is clean and clear.

c. Two-Dimensional Characteristics of Forged Article

See picture 9-2-11.

(a) The striae have a certain width, but are muddled and have fuzzy edges.

(b) There is no clear delineation between the traces present.

(c) The surrounding glass phase is filled with needlepoint mottles and pitting, and the general appearance is muddled.

d. Three-Dimensional Characteristics of Forged Article

(a) The striae have a certain width, but are almost entirely level with the surrounding glaze surface, with no height discrepancy noticeable.

(b) The striae interior is coarse and muddled.

(c) The surrounding glaze surface is filled with pit mottles, their appearances are all similar.

See pictures 9-2-11 and 9-2-12, where 9-2-11 is the two-dimensional and 9-2-12 is the three-dimensional view of the same location (this piece has undergone treatment with aging reagent).

The striation indicated by Arrow A' in picture 9-2-11 with a certain width, appears in picture 9-2-12, but lacks any real depth. It is essentially level with the surrounding glaze surface, and its contents are coarse.

The surrounding glaze surface is filled with pit mottles, their appearances all similar (see Arrows B').

A. Raised Striae

I. Two-Dimensional Characteristics of Genuine Article

See pictures 9-2-13 and 9-2-15.

a. The raised striae are brown in color, and some wider striae present with saw-like edges.

b. The edges of the beach mottle have foggy needlepoint mottling with an even density gradation.

c. The center of the surrounding beach mottle has frosted needlepoint mottling with relatively clear borders.

II. Three-Dimensional Characteristics of Genuine Article

a. Striae edges have saw-like borders and the surface is relatively glossy.

b. Raised striae are relatively higher than the surrounding beach mottle.

c. Striae borders are clearly delineated from the surrounding beach mottle.

d. The frosted needlepoint mottling surrounding the striae have dark coloration and present as pin points.

See pictures 9-2-13 and 9-2-14, where 9-2-13 is the two-dimensional and 9-2-14 is the three-dimensional view of the same location.

See pictures 9-2-15 and 9-2-16, where 9-2-15 is the two-dimensional and 9-2-16 is the three-dimensional view of the same location.

Striation A is clearly depicted in picture 9-2-14. It has a convex shape that is higher than the surrounding beach mottle with a smooth surface and saw-like border, delineating it from the surrounding needlepoint mottling. The frosted needlepoint mottling indicated by Arrow B appears clearly as dark pin points.

Striation C is clearly depicted with a raised shaped higher than the surrounding beach mottle. Its surface is somewhat glossy, its edges saw-like, and it has clear delineation from the surrounding needlepoint mottling. The needlepoint mottling indicated by Arrow D presents with dark coloration and a general concave shape (see picture 9-2-16).

III. Two-Dimensional Characteristics of Forged Article

See pictures 9-2-17 and 9-2-19.

a. Striae edges not clearly defined amongst the beach mottle.

（三）阳纹

1. 真品二维特征

见图9-2-13、9-2-15。

（1）阳纹呈褐色，部分较粗的纹路有明显锯齿状边沿。

（2）周围沙滩斑的边沿部位分布有雾状针眼斑，有从浓到淡的均匀过渡。

（3）周围沙滩斑的中心部位有磨砂针眼斑，有较强的边界感。

2. 真品三维特征

（1）阳纹边沿呈锯齿状，纹路表面较光滑。

（2）阳纹凸起，高出周围沙滩斑。

（3）阳纹与周围沙滩斑界线分明。

（4）周围沙滩斑上的磨砂针眼斑呈深色点状凹坑。

见图9-2-13、图9-2-14，二者为同一器物同一位置图片，图9-2-13为二维图片，图9-2-14为三维图片。

见图9-2-15、图9-2-16，二者为同一器物同一位置图片，图9-2-15为二维图片，图9-2-16为三维图片。

图9-2-13中的阳纹A在图9-2-14中成像清晰，纹路凸起，高于周围沙滩斑，纹路表面光滑，边沿呈轻微锯齿状，与周围针眼斑界线分明。图9-2-13中箭头B所指处的磨砂针眼斑在图9-2-14中呈深色点状凹坑，成像清晰。

图9-2-15中的阳纹C在图9-2-16中成像清晰，纹路凸起，高于周围沙滩斑，纹路表面光滑，边沿呈明显锯齿状，与周围针眼斑界线分明。图9-2-15中箭头D所指处的磨砂针眼斑在图9-2-16中呈深色点状凹坑，成像清晰。

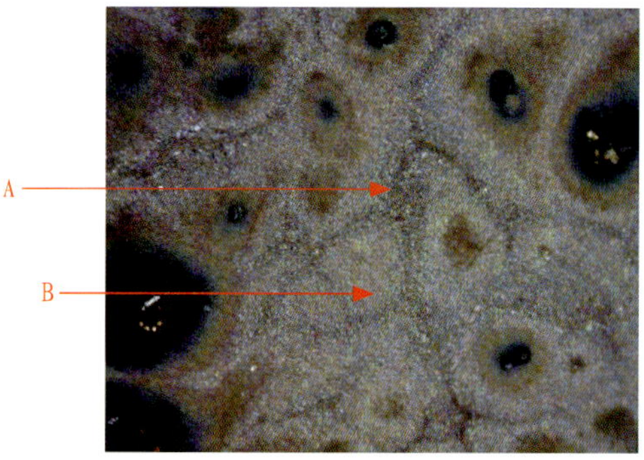

图9-2-13

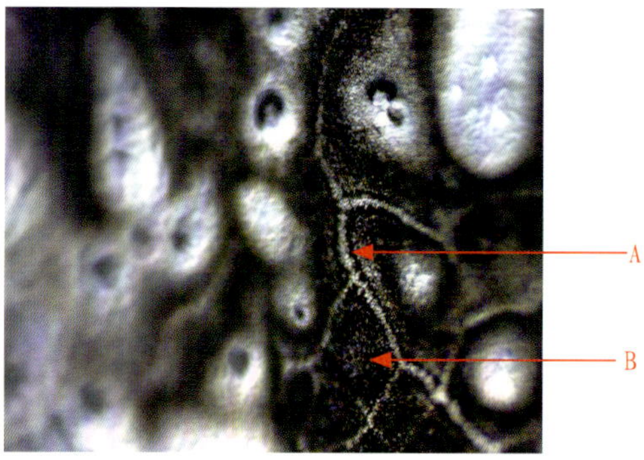

图9-2-14

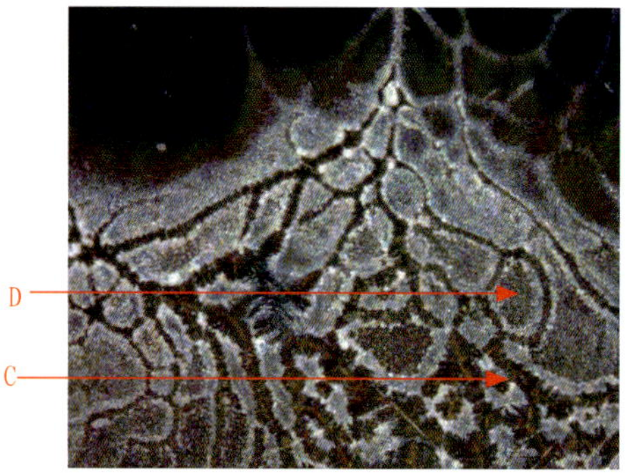

图9-2-15

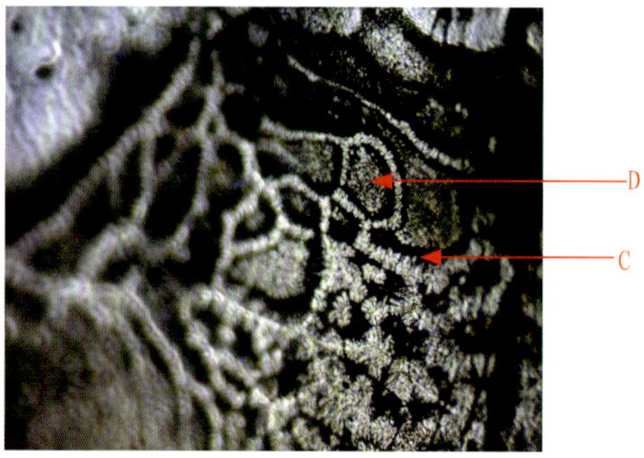

图9-2-16

b. No clear borders with the frosted needlepoint mottling.

c. No clear delineation between separate traces.

d. The needlepoint mottling and pitting surrounding the striae are sporadic and generally muddled (see picture 9-2-19).

IV. Three-Dimensional Characteristics of Forged Article

a. At times the striae border is not clear, and separation from beach mottle is not evident.

b. Striae and surrounding beach mottle are essentially on the same plane, lacking height differentiation.

c. Beach mottles without man-made aging are glossy and smooth; they lack the fine dark colored pin points of frosted needlepoint mottling.

d. Aged beach mottles present as coarse and muddled, lacking clearly defined pitting of frosted needlepoint mottling.

See pictures 9-2-17 and 9-2-18, where 9-2-17 is the two-dimensional and 9-2-18 is the three-dimensional view of the same location (this piece has not undergone treatment with aging reagent).

See pictures 9-2-19 and 9-2-20, where 9-2-19 is the two-dimensional and 9-2-20 is the three-dimensional view of the same location (this piece has undergone treatment with aging reagent).

The striation indicated by Arrow A' is fairly visible in picture 9-2-17, but its edges are not clearly defined. It is on an even plane with the surrounding beach mottle, lacking height differentiation. The beach mottle is relatively glossy, it lacks frosted needlepoint mottling, which means the beach mottle has relatively low weathering severity.

The striation indicated by Arrow B' is visible in picture 9-2-20, but its borders are muddled and it exists on an even plane with the surrounding beach mottle, lacking clear height discrepancy. The beach mottle's frosted needlepoint mottling is coarse and muddled; there is no evident independent pin points clearly presenting.

2. C and O Shaped Striae

A. Two-Dimensional Characteristics of Genuine Article

I. CO striae present clearly with width variation, it is common to see two converging or nearly touching C striae, with a forked tip (see picture 9-2-23).

II. Striae can present with a color spectrum, and color disparity between different striae (see pictures 9-2-21 and 9-2-22).

III. CO striae can present with associated floccus mottling (see picture 9-2-24).

IV. Striae retain clear delineation with surrounding glass phase (see pictures 9-2-21—9-2-24).

V. The surrounding glass phase is clean and clear (see pictures 9-2-21—9-2-24).

B. Three-Dimensional Characteristics of Genuine Article

I. Visible striae are fine and reserved, clearly independent.

II. Clear delineation between the striae and surrounding glaze surface.

III. Surrounding glaze surface is clean and smooth.

See pictures 9-2-25 and 9-2-26, where 9-2-25 is the two-dimensional and 9-2-26 is the three-dimensional view of the same location.

The C striation in picture 9-2-25 presents clearly as a dark thin line, more reserved in picture 9-2-26. The mottle indicated by Arrow A is only visible as a fine forked striation in picture 9-2-26. The glaze surface surrounding the striation is smooth and clean and also presents with clearly independent scratches and needlepoint type pits, and it is clearly delineated from the striation.

C. Two-Dimensional Characteristics of Forged Article

See pictures 9-2-27 and 9-2-28 (these pieces have undergone treatment with aging reagents).

I. CO striae are uniform, lacking clear width discrepancy.

II. The coloration is uniform, and lacks color spectrum or disparity.

III. No clear delineation with the surrounding glass phase.

3. 赝品二维特征

（1）阳纹在沙滩斑上轮廓不清晰（见图9-2-17、图9-2-19）。

（2）沙滩斑上的磨砂针眼斑没有明显边界感（见图9-2-17、图9-2-19）。

（3）图片中各迹型种类之间界线不分明（见图9-2-17、图9-2-19）。

（4）阳纹周围的针眼斑、坑点斑分布凌乱，整体显得涂污模糊（见图9-2-19）。

4. 赝品三维特征

（1）有时阳纹的轮廓不清晰，与沙滩斑界线不分明。

（2）阳纹与周围沙滩斑几乎处于同一平面，没有明显高度差。

（3）未被腐蚀剂腐蚀过的沙滩斑光滑洁净，不见磨砂针眼斑形成的清晰独立的点状凹坑。

（4）被腐蚀剂腐蚀过的沙滩斑粗糙涂污，不见磨砂针眼斑形成的清晰独立的点状凹坑。

见图9-2-17、图9-2-18，二者为同一器物同一位置图片，图9-2-17为二维图片，图9-2-18为三维图片。（该器物釉表面未被腐蚀剂腐蚀）

见图9-2-19、图9-2-20，二者为同一器物同一位置图片，图9-2-19为二维图片，图9-2-20为三维图片。（该器物釉表面曾被腐蚀剂腐蚀）

图9-2-17中的阳纹A’在图9-2-18中可见轮廓，与周围沙滩斑几乎处于同一平面，没有明显高度差。周围沙滩斑光滑洁净，不见磨砂针眼斑形成的清晰独立的点状凹坑，可见沙滩斑风化强度较低。

图9-2-19中的阳纹B’在图9-2-20中的轮廓不清晰，与周围沙滩斑几乎处于同一平面，没有明显高度差。沙滩斑整体粗糙涂污，不见磨砂针眼斑形成的清晰独立的点状凹坑。

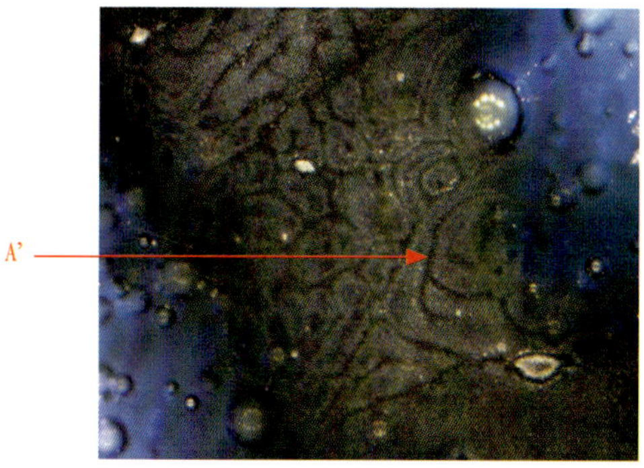

图9-2-17

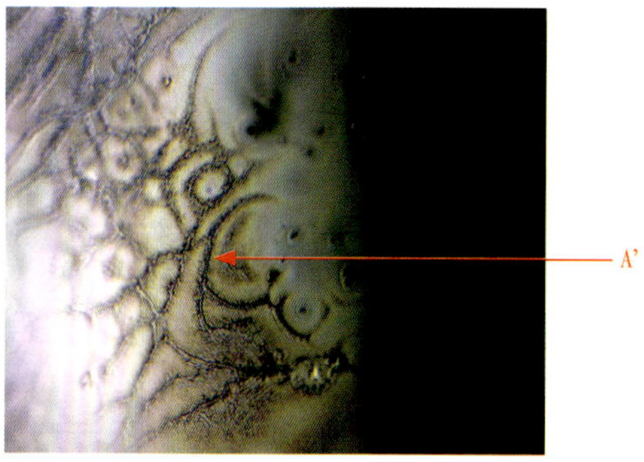

图9-2-18

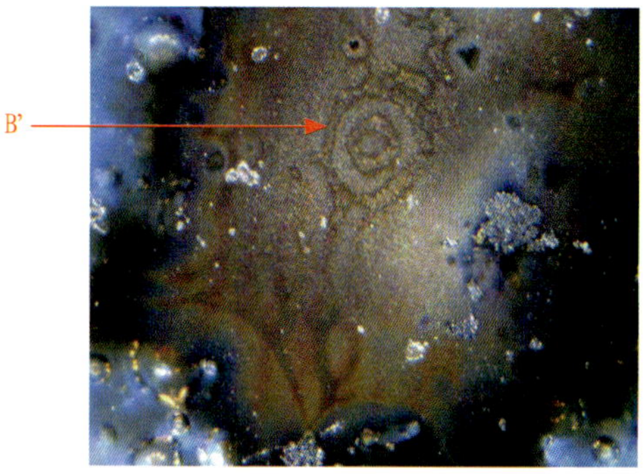

图9-2-19

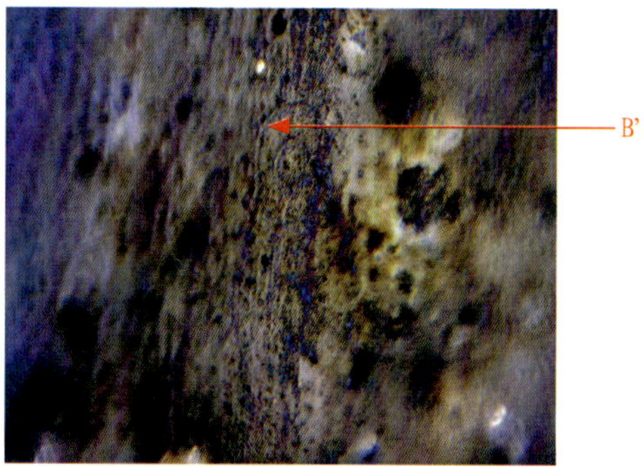

图9-2-20

IV. The surrounding glass phase has become pitted and is generally muddled.

V. No floccus mottling occurring in association with CO striae.

D. Three-Dimensional Characteristics of Forged Article

I. The three-dimensional appearance is thicker than that of the two dimensional.

II. Surrounding glaze surface is severely damaged, it has sporadic covering of irregular pitting, appearance muddled.

See pictures 9-2-29 and 9-2-30, where 9-2-29 is the two-dimensional and 9-2-30 is the three-dimensional view of the same location (this piece has undergone treatment with aging reagent).

The three-dimensional view of Striation A' is much thicker than the two-dimensional view. The surrounding glaze surface is severely damaged, it is muddled with sporadically dispersed pitting.

3. Scratches

A. Two-Dimensional Characteristics of Genuine Article

See picture 9-2-31.

I. Scratch has irregular shape, with needlepoint mottling presenting internally, but not extending past the scratch borders.

II. The scratches are clearly delineated from the surrounding glass phase.

III. The glass phase is clean and clear.

B. Three-Dimensional Characteristics of Genuine Article

I. The scratch has a depressed shape, its interior uneven and coarse. Internal pitting is fine and densely distributed, and the edges of the scratch are rounded and smooth.

II. The scratch retains clear delineation from the surrounding glaze surface.

III. The surrounding glaze surface is smooth and clean.

See pictures 9-2-31 and 9-2-32, where 9-2-31 is the two-dimensional and 9-2-32 is the three-dimensional view of the same location.

Scratch A presents as a clear depression in the glaze surface with an interior that is uneven and coarse. There is a fine, dense distribution of pitting within the scratch, and its edges are smooth and round. The scratch is clearly delineated from the surrounding glaze surface, which is smooth and clean.

C. Two-Dimensional Characteristics of Forged Article

See pictures 9-2-33 and 9-2-34 (this piece has undergone treatment with aging reagent).

I. Coloration uniform without evident needlepoint mottling.

II. There are also CO striae and occurring in association with the scratches, but the glass phase is generally muddled and unclear (see picture 9-2-34).

D. Three-Dimensional Characteristics of Forged Article

I. The scratch is coarse and muddled; edges are not rounded but diffused.

II. The three-dimensional image of the scratch is larger than the two-dimensional.

III. The surrounding glaze surface is sporadically littered with pitting, and the general appearance is muddled.

See pictures 9-2-35 and 9-2-36, where 9-2-35 is the two-dimensional and 9-2-36 is the three-dimensional view of the same location (this piece has undergone treatment with aging reagent).

Scratch A' appears as a depression in the glaze surface and its three-dimensional appearance is larger than two-dimensional.

Scratch A' is coarse with jagged an unrounded edge that has a diffused feel. There is no clear delineation with the surrounding glaze level, which has become littered with sporadic pitting and generally appears muddled and unclean (see picture 9-2-36).

二、C形纹、O形纹

1. 真品二维特征

（1）C形纹、O形纹（以下简称CO纹）纹路清晰，有粗细变化，常见有两条紧挨或距离较近的C形纹，如同分杈的枝丫（见图9-2-23）。

（2）有的在同一个纹路上有色阶变化，邻近的CO纹有色差（见图9-2-21、图9-2-22）。

（3）有时CO纹下会出现絮状斑（见图9-2-24）。

（4）CO纹与玻璃相界线分明（见图9-2-21—图9-2-24）。

（5）周围的玻璃相干净清晰（见图9-2-21—图9-2-24）。

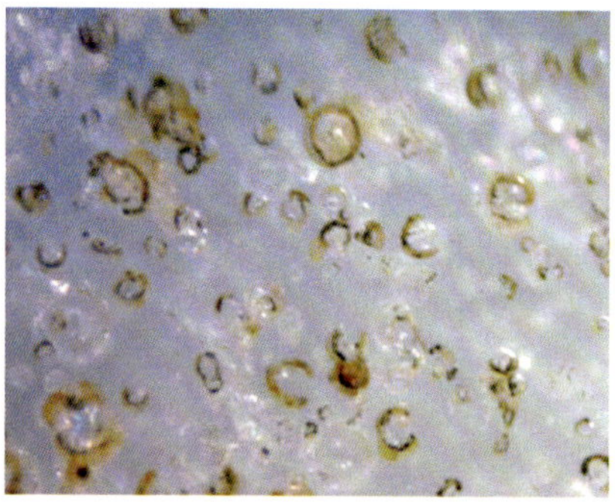
图9-2-21

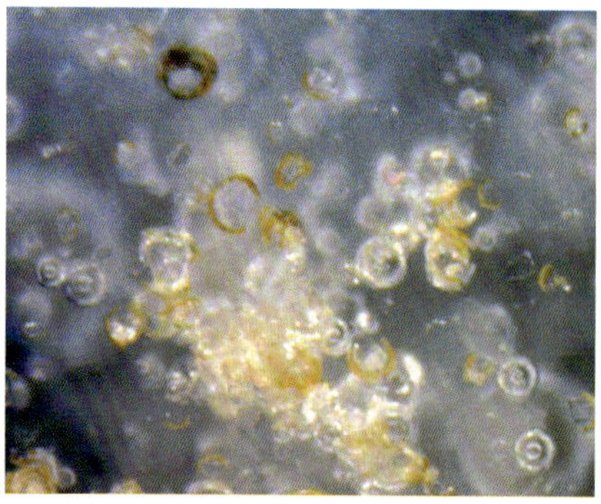
图9-2-22

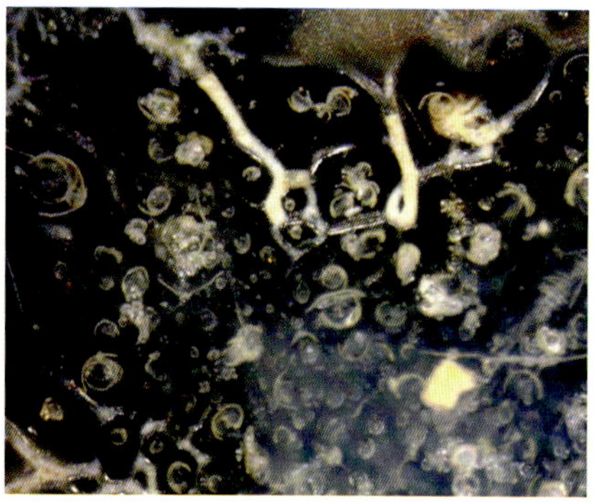
图9-2-23

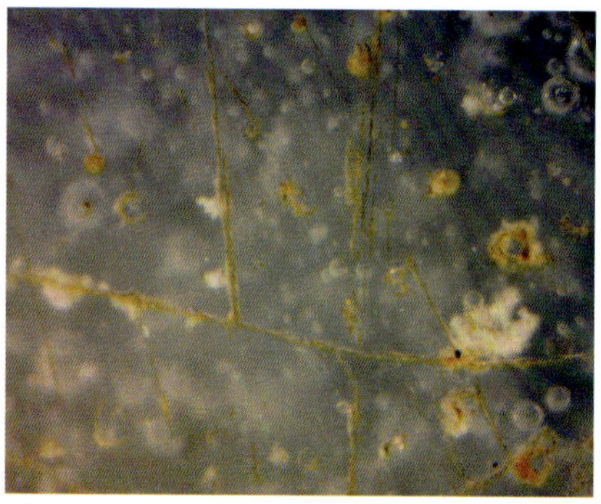
图9-2-24

2. 真品三维特征

（1）CO纹纤细收敛，清晰独立。

（2）CO纹与周围玻璃相界线分明。

（3）周围玻璃相光滑洁净。

图9-2-25中的C形纹在图9-2-26中颜色显得更深，但纹路比图9-2-25中的更细更收敛。图9-2-25中箭头A所指的斑块在图9-2-26中呈两条纤细的分叉纹路，纹路与周围玻璃相界线清晰，周围玻璃相上除C形纹外还有各自独立清晰的划痕及针眼型坑点斑，彼此界线分明。玻璃相其余地方光滑洁净。

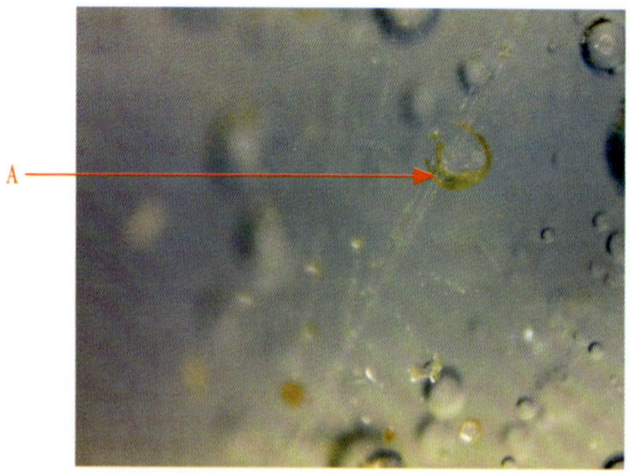

图9-2-25

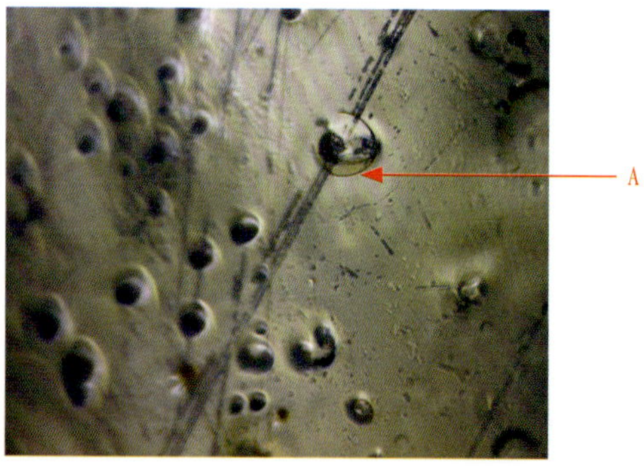

图9-2-26

3. 赝品二维特征

见图9-2-27、图9-2-28。（该器物釉表面曾被腐蚀剂腐蚀）

（1）CO纹形貌一致，粗细变化不明显。

（2）CO纹颜色单一，没有色阶或色差变化。

（3）CO纹与玻璃相界线不清晰。

（4）周围玻璃相也被针眼斑覆盖，浑浊模糊。

（5）CO纹所在处的釉层中不见絮状斑。

4. 赝品三维特征

（1）CO纹纹路的三维成像要比二维成像粗。

（2）周围釉表面杂乱无章地分布着坑点斑，破坏较严重，显得粗糙涂污。

见图9-2-29、图9-2-30，二者为同一器物同一位置图片，图9-2-29为二维图片，图9-2-30为三维图片。（该器物釉表面曾被腐蚀剂腐蚀）

图9-2-29中箭头A’所指的CO纹，在图9-2-30中的三维成像的纹路比二维成像要粗，周围釉表面杂乱无章地分布着坑点斑，破坏较严重，整体显得粗糙涂污。

图9-2-27

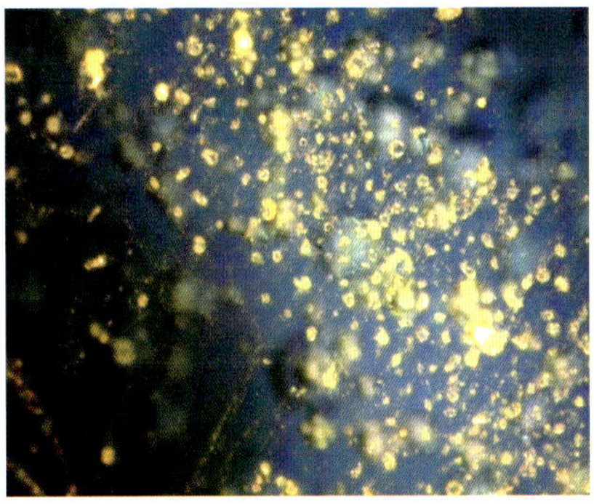

图9-2-28

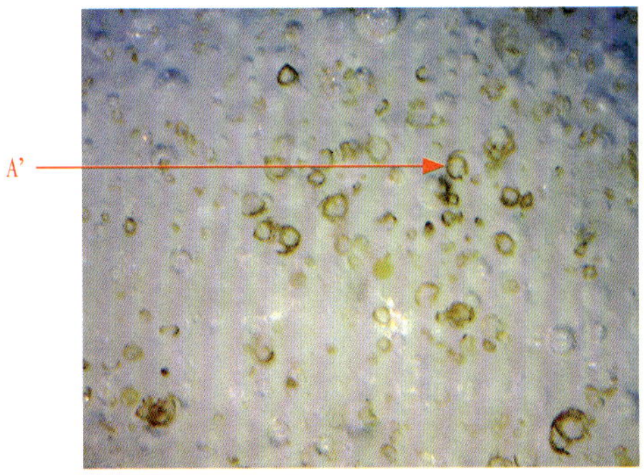

图9-2-29

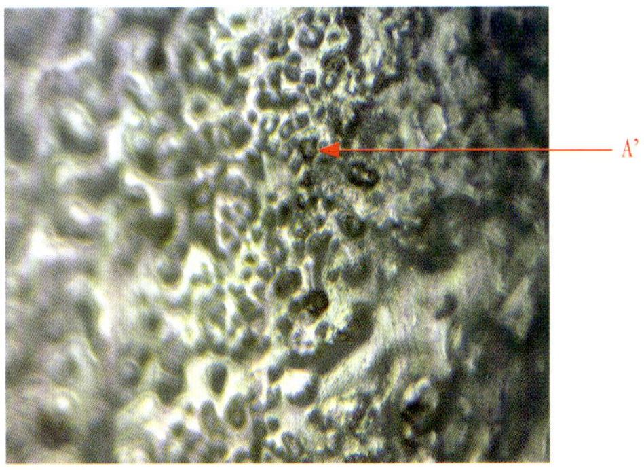

图9-2-30

三、划痕

1. 真品二维特征

见图9-2-31。

（1）划痕呈不规则形状，上面有磨砂针眼斑，针眼斑不超出划痕范围。

（2）划痕与周围玻璃相界线分明。

（3）周围玻璃相干净清晰。

2. 真品三维特征

（1）划痕呈凹坑状，内部粗糙不平，内部的坑点细小且分布密集，凹坑边沿圆滑。

（2）划痕与周围玻璃相界线分明。

（3）周围玻璃相光滑洁净。

见图9-2-31、图9-2-32，二者为同一器物同一位置图片，图9-2-31为二维图片，图9-2-32为三维图片。

图9-2-31中的划痕A在图9-2-32中呈凹坑状，内部粗糙不平，内部的坑点细小且分布密集，凹坑边沿圆滑，与周围玻璃相界线分明。周围玻璃相光滑洁净。

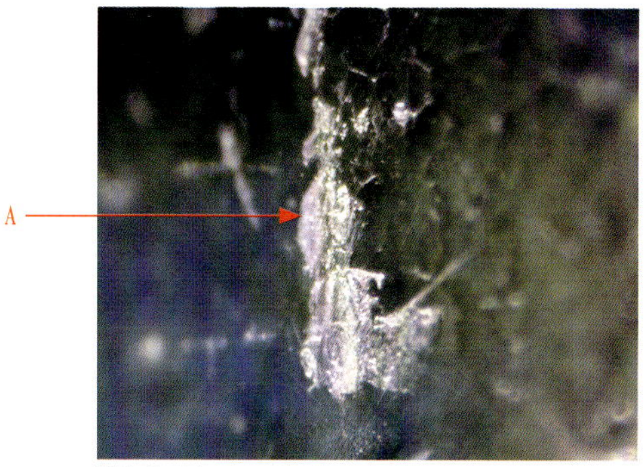

图9-2-31

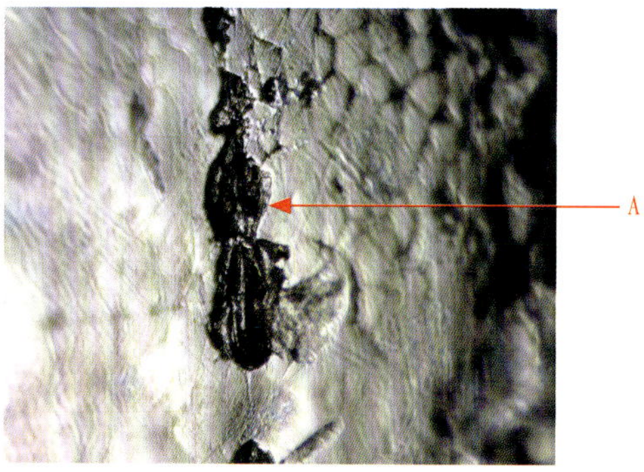

图9-2-32

3. 赝品二维特征

见图9-2-33、图9-2-34。（该器物釉表面曾被腐蚀剂腐蚀）

（1）赝品上的划痕颜色一致，划痕上针眼斑不明显。

（2）玻璃相上除划痕以外还有CO纹及坑点斑存在，但彼此界线模糊，整体显得混乱涂污（见图9-2-34）。

4. 赝品三维特征

（1）划痕粗糙生硬，边沿不圆滑，有毛刺感，具有扩张性。

（2）划痕的三维成像面积比二维要大。

（3）周围玻璃相上杂乱无章地分布有坑点斑，整体显得粗糙涂污。

见图9-2-35、图9-2-36，二者为同一器物同一位置图片，图9-2-35为二维图片，图9-2-36为三维图片。（该器物釉表面曾被腐蚀剂腐蚀）

图9-2-35中的划痕A’在图9-2-36中呈长形凹坑，三维成像面积比二维要大，凹坑内有颜色变化，但大部分还保持无色。

划痕A’粗糙生硬，边沿不圆滑，有毛刺感，具有扩张性。玻璃相上其他地方杂乱无章地分布有坑点斑，整体显得粗糙涂污（见图9-2-36）。

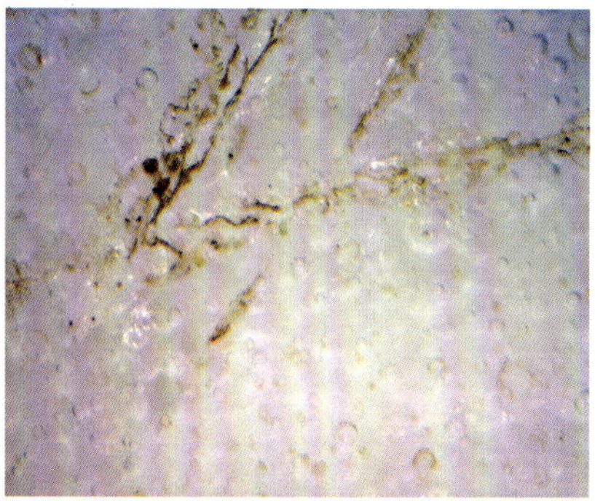

图9-2-33

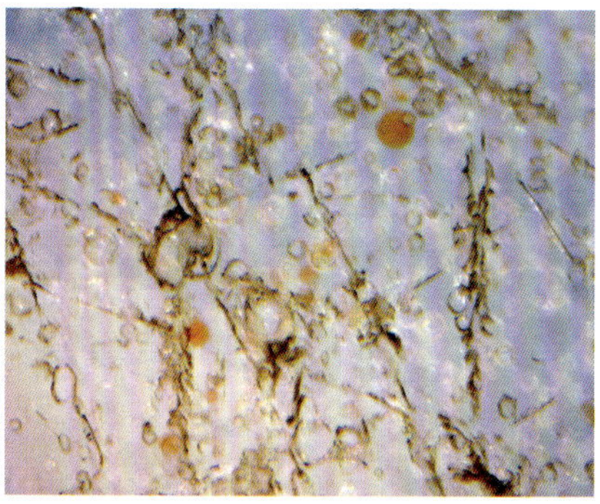

图9-2-34

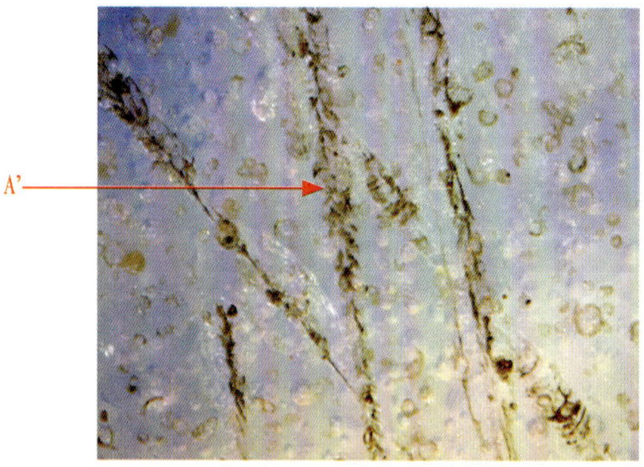

图9-2-35

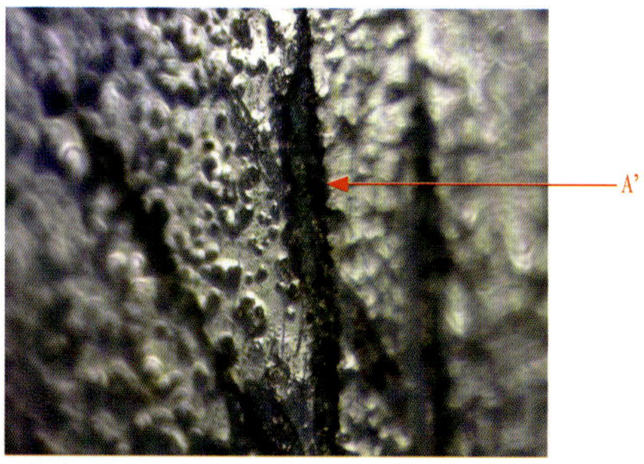

图9-2-36

第三节
元青花气泡真品与赝品比对

一、色变泡

（一）真品二维特征

见图9-3-1、图9-3-2。

1. 单位图片中有色变泡群，包括全变泡和局变泡。

2. 单项色变泡中有色阶变化。

3. 泡与泡之间有色差变化。

4. 色变泡与周围玻璃相界线分明。

5. 周围玻璃相干净清晰。

（二）真品三维特征

1. 气泡所在处釉表面可见通道。

2. 通道清晰独立，面积远远小于气泡面积。

3. 通道周围的釉表面保持光滑洁净。

见图9-3-3、图9-3-4，二者为同一器物同一位置图片，图9-3-3为二维图片，图9-3-4为三维图片。

图9-3-3中的气泡A在图9-3-4中隐约可见轮廓，釉表面无明显划痕或损伤，但有一处颜色较深，应该是外界连接气泡内的通道所在处。周围釉表面光滑洁净。

见图9-3-5、图9-3-6，二者为同一器物同一位置图片，图9-3-5为二维图片，图9-3-6为三维图片。

图9-3-5中的气泡B在图9-3-6中隐约可见轮廓，所在处釉表面存在许多划痕，它们应该是外界连接气泡内的通道。除有划痕存在以外，釉表面保持光滑洁净。

图9-3-1

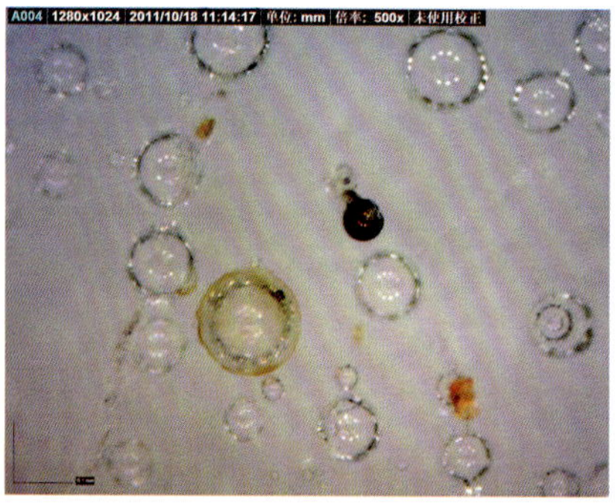

图9-3-2

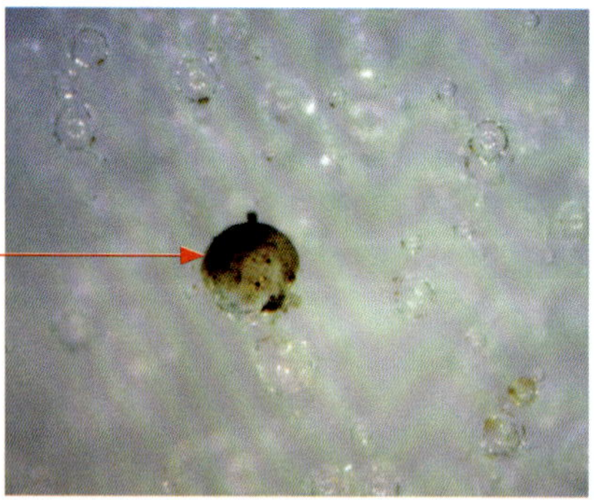

图9-3-3

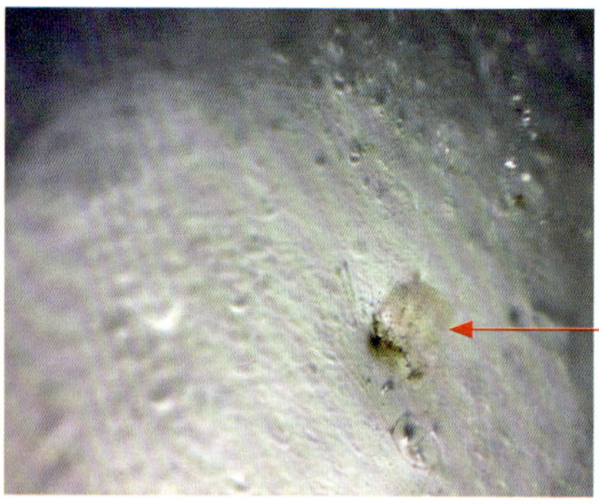

图9-3-4

Section 3:
Genuine and Forged Yuan Underglaze Blue Bubble Comparison

1. Color Change Bubbles

A. Two-Dimensional Characteristics of Genuine Article

See pictures 9-3-1 and 9-3-2.

I. A unit image can present with color change bubble groups; with semi and fully changed bubbles both present.

II. A single color change bubble can present with color spectrum.

III. There is color disparity amongst bubbles.

IV. The color change bubbles retain clear delineation from the surrounding glass phase.

V. The surrounding glass phase is clean and clear.

B. Three-Dimensional Characteristics of Genuine Article

I. Clearly visible coloration channel presents on the glaze surface near the color change bubble.

II. The coloration channel is clearly independent, and much smaller than the underlying bubble.

III. The glaze surface surrounding the channel is smooth and clean.

See pictures 9-3-3 and 9-3-4, where 9-3-3 is the two-dimensional and 9-3-4 is the three-dimensional view of the same location.

Bubble A is faintly visible in picture 9-3-4. There are no evident scratches or damage on the glaze surface, but one point is darker than the rest, which is most likely the coloration channel. The surrounding glaze surface retains a smooth and clean nature.

See pictures 9-3-5 and 9-3-6, where 9-3-5 is the two-dimensional and 9-3-6 is the three-dimensional view of the same location.

Bubble B is faintly visible in picture 9-3-6. The glaze surface has multiple scratches, any of which can act as the coloration channel. Aside from the scratches, the glaze surface is smooth and clean.

C. Two-Dimensional Characteristics of Forged Article

The coloration of bubbles on forged article is essentially uniform, lacking color disparity (see pictures 9-3-7 and 9-3-8, the piece has undergone treatment with aging reagent).

D. Three-Dimensional Characteristics of Forged Article

I. The glaze surface is littered with relatively large and diffused corrosion mottles.

II. The surrounding glaze surface has a sporadic dispersion of pitting, and the general appearance is muddled.

See pictures 9-3-9 and 9-3-10, where 9-3-9 is the two-dimensional and 9-3-10 is the three-dimensional view of the same location (this piece has undergone treatment with aging reagent).

Bubble A' is faintly visible in picture 9-3-10 but is overlaid with a coarsely diffused corrosion mottle. The surrounding glaze surface is densely covered in sporadic pitting with uniform appearances (see Arrow B' in picture 9-3-10).

See pictures 9-3-11 and 9-3-12, where 9-3-11 is the two-dimensional and 9-3-12 is the three-dimensional view of the same location (this piece has undergone treatment with aging

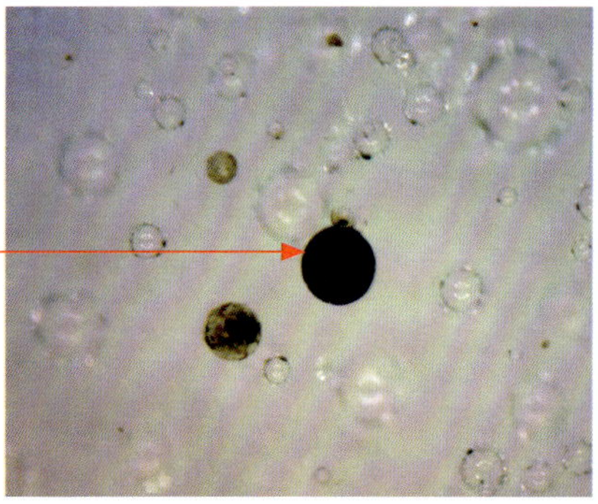

图9-3-5

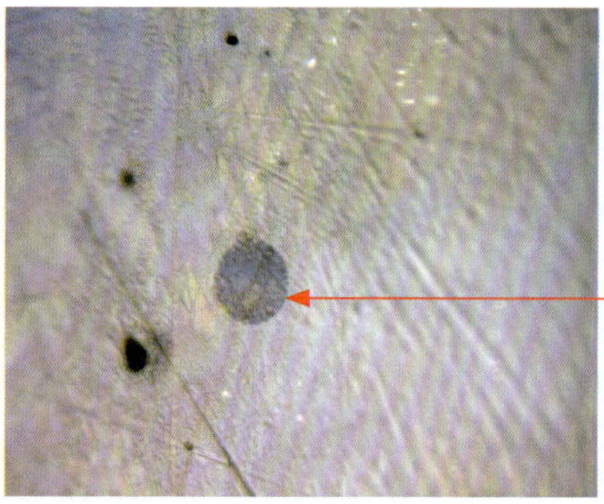

图9-3-6

（三）赝品二维特征

赝品整个器物上的气泡颜色一致，没有色差变化。（见图9-3-7、图9-3-8，该器物釉表面曾被腐蚀剂腐蚀）

（四）赝品三维特征

1. 气泡所在处的釉表面可见面积较大的粗糙的腐蚀斑块，具有扩张性。

2. 周围釉表面有坑点斑密集分布，整体显得混沌涂污。

见图9-3-9、图9-3-10，二者为同一器物同一位置图片，图9-3-9为二维图片，图9-3-10为三维图片。（该器物釉表面曾被腐蚀剂腐蚀）

图9-3-9中的气泡A’在图9-3-10中隐约可见轮廓，其所在处釉表面一大部分已被破坏，显得粗糙，具有扩张性。周围釉表面可见坑点斑密集分布，形貌一致（见图9-3-10箭头B所指处）。

见图9-3-11、图9-3-12，二者为同一器物同一位置图片，图9-3-11为二维图片，图9-3-12为三维图片。（该器物釉表面曾被腐蚀剂腐蚀）

图9-3-11中的气泡C’在图9-3-12中隐约可见轮廓，其所在处釉表面可见一处腐蚀斑块，显得粗糙，具有扩张性。周围釉表面凸起处均可见腐蚀斑块存在，表现一致（见图9-3-12箭头D所指处）。

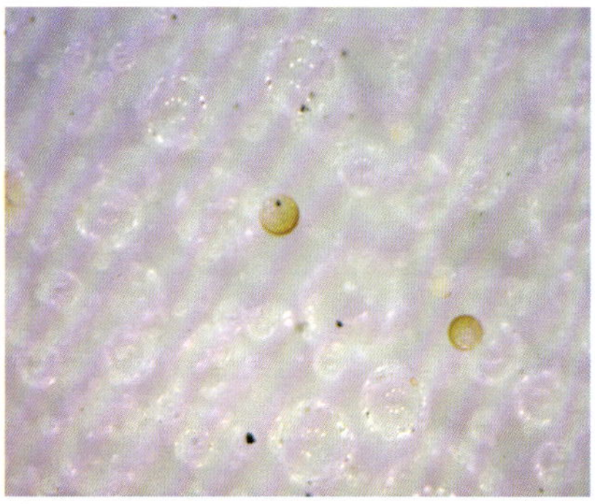
图9-3-7

图9-3-8

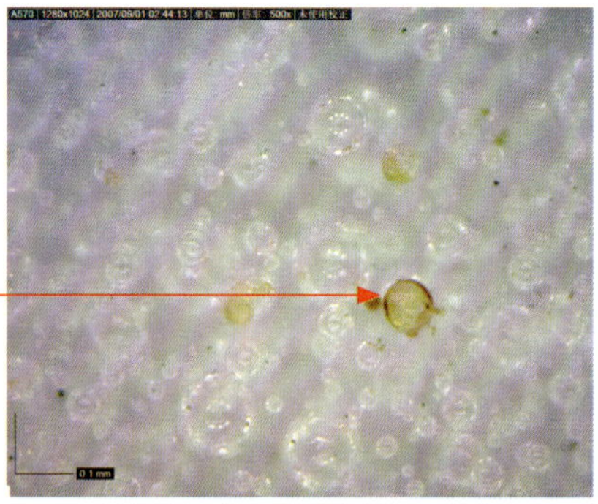

图9-3-9

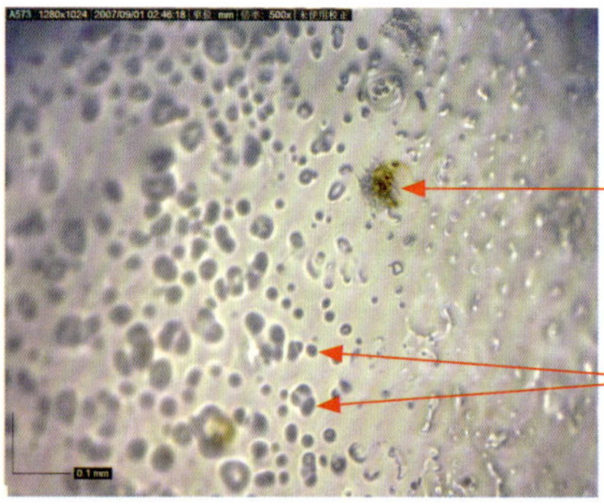

图9-3-10

reagent).

Bubble C' is faintly visible in picture 9-3-12 and is overlaid with a coarsely diffused corrosion mottle. All areas of raised humps on the surrounding glaze surface present with corrosion mottles with uniform appearances (sec Arrow D' in picture 9-3-12).

2. Textured Bubbles

A. Unbroken Mouth Textured Bubbles

I. Two-Dimensional Characteristics of Genuine Article

a. The bubble interior presents with foggy, frosted, and grainy needlepoint mottling.

b. Foggy needlepoint mottling is fine and evenly distributed (see picture 9-3-13).

c. Grainy needlepoint mottling occurs with a yellow and white color spectrum (see picture 9-3-15).

d. The bubble retains clear delineation from the surrounding glass phase (see pictures 9-3-13 and 9-3-15).

e. The surrounding glass phase is clean and clear (see pictures 9-3-13 and 9-3-15).

II. Three-Dimensional Characteristics of Genuine Article

a. A channel is clearly visible on the glaze surface in the vicinity of the bubble.

b. The channel is clearly independent, its surface area is much smaller than the underlying bubble.

c. The surrounding glaze surface is smooth and clean.

See pictures 9-3-13 and 9-3-14, where 9-3-13 is the two-dimensional and 9-3-14 is the three-dimensional view of the same location.

Bubble A is not clearly visible, but is located under the red ring in picture 9-3-14. Scratch B is clearly visible on the glossy and clean glaze surface, and is most likely the channel connecting the external environment and the bubble interior.

See pictures 9-3-15 and 9-3-16 where 9-3-15 is the two-dimensional and 9-3-16 is the three-dimensional view of the same location.

Bubble C is not clearly visible, but is located under the red ring in picture 9-3-16. Mottle D is not visible in picture 9-3-16, while mottle E presents on the glaze surface.

Because of this, we know that mottle D is present on the interior of Bubble C, and is an internal weathering mottle. The mottle indicated by Arrow E is on the glaze surface, resulting from surface weathering, and it is most likely the channel between the bubble interior and the external environment.

III. Two-Dimensional Characteristics of Forged Article

See pictures 9-3-17 and 9-3-19.

a. The materials on the bubble interior are blurry and muddled.

b. No clear delineation with the surrounding glass phase.

c. Surrounding glass phase littered with sporadically distributed pitting, its general appearance muddled.

IV. Three-Dimensional Characteristics of Forged Article

a. The glaze surface above said bubble has become grossly damaged and presents with coarse and diffused corrosion mottles.

b. The corrosion mottle has a surface area larger than the underlying bubble, indicating that the bubble is a faux textured bubble.

c. The surrounding glaze level is littered with sporadically distributed pitting, giving it a generally muddled appearance.

See pictures 9-3-17 and 9-3-18, where 9-3-17 is the two-dimensional and 9-3-19 is the three-dimensional view of the same location (this piece has undergone treatment with aging reagent).

Bubble A' is not visible in picture 9-3-18 and as such is indicated with a red circle. The overlying glaze surface has become damaged, and the coarsely diffused corrosion mottle extends beyond the edge of the underlying bubble. The glaze surface has sporadic pitting and is generally muddled.

See pictures 9-3-19 and 9-3-20, where 9-3-19 is the two-

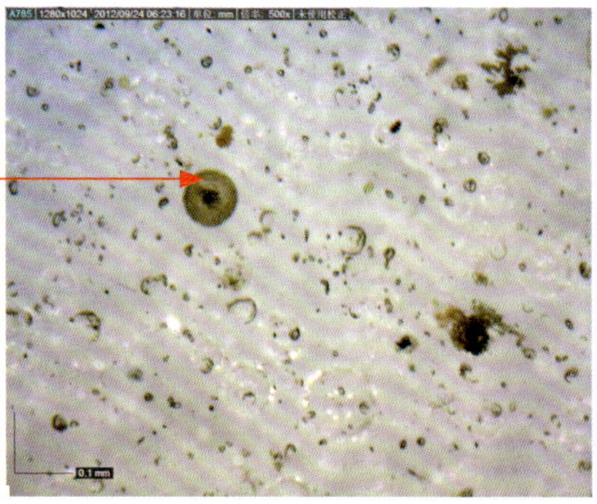

图9-3-11

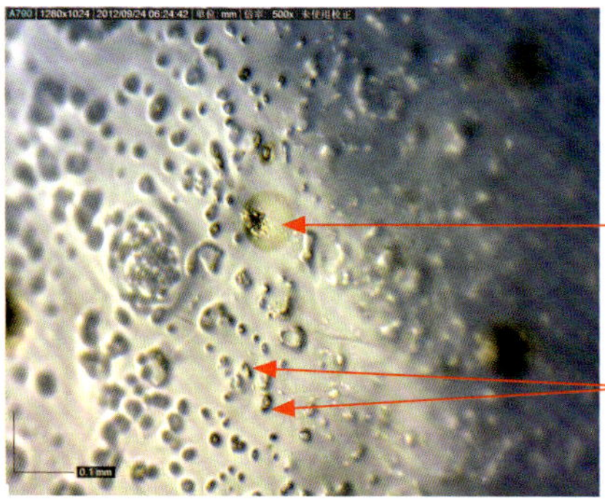

图9-3-12

二、壁变泡

（一）非破口壁变泡

1. 真品二维特征

（1）非破口壁变泡内壁的风化以雾状针眼斑、磨砂针眼斑或颗粒针眼斑等形式呈现。

（2）雾状针眼斑分布细腻均匀（见图9-3-13）。

（3）颗粒针眼斑有黄色及白色的色阶变化（见图9-3-15）。

（4）壁变泡与周围玻璃相界线分明（见图9-3-13、图9-3-15）。

（5）周围玻璃相干净清晰（见图9-3-13、图9-3-15）。

2. 真品三维特征

（1）气泡所在处釉表面可见通道。

（2）通道清晰独立，面积远远小于气泡面积。

（3）通道周围的釉表面保持光滑洁净。

见图9-3-13、图9-3-14，二者为同一器物同一位置图片，图9-3-13为二维图片，图9-3-14为三维图片。

图9-3-13中的气泡A，在图9-3-14中位于红圈釉下处，不可见。图9-3-14中的划痕B在光滑洁净的釉表面清晰可见，应该是外界连接气泡内的通道。周围釉表面保持光滑洁净。

见图9-3-15、图9-3-16，二者为同一器物同一位置图片，图9-3-15为二维图片，图9-3-16为三

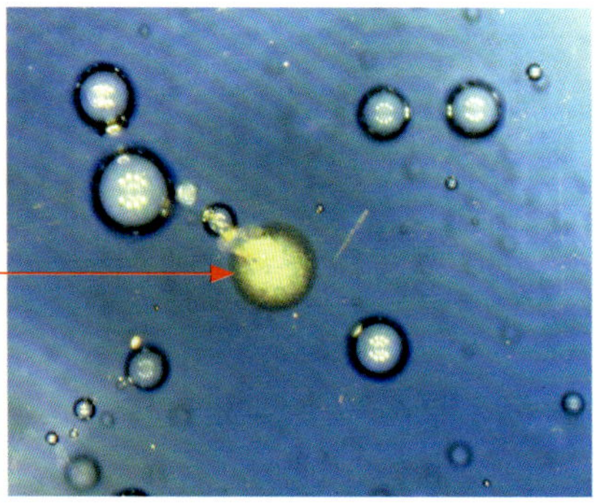

图9-3-13

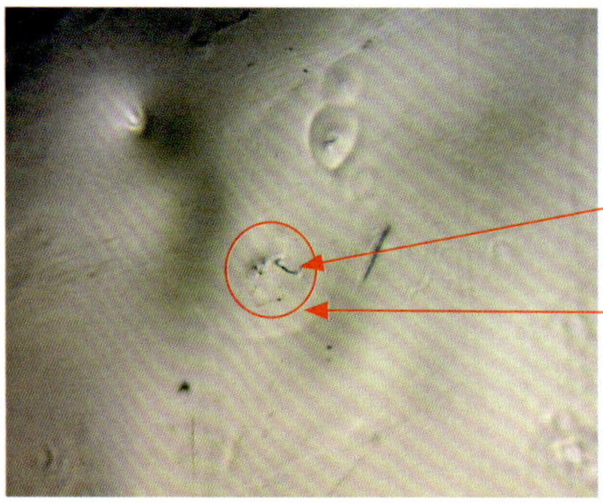

图9-3-14

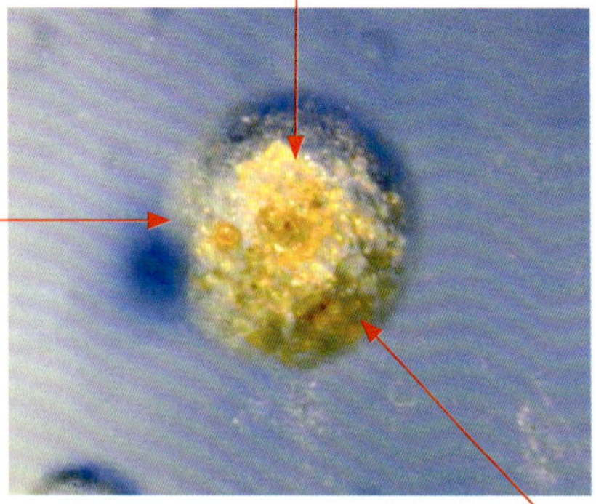

图9-3-15*

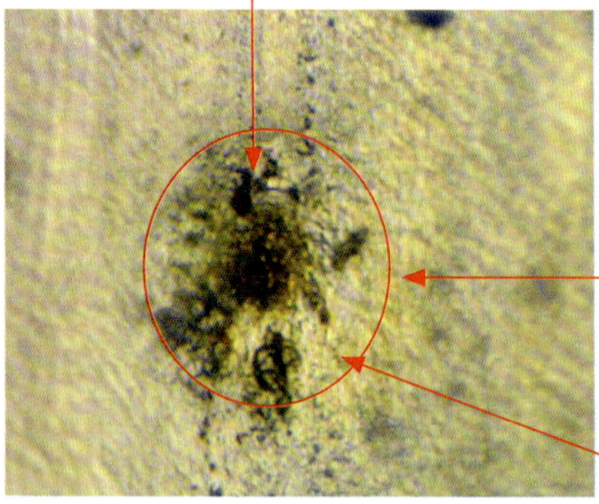

图9-3-16*

*图片经过裁剪放大处理。

*Picture cropped and enlarged to show detail.

dimensional and 9-3-20 is the three-dimensional view of the same location (this piece has undergone treatment with aging reagent).

Bubble B' is not visible in picture 9-3-20 and as such is indicate with a red circle. The overlying glaze surface has become damaged, and the coarsely diffused corrosion mottle is larger than the underlying bubble. This is a faux textured bubble. The glaze surface surrounding the bubble is generally muddled with sporadic pitting.

B. Broken Mouth Textured Bubbles

I. Two-Dimensional Characteristics of Genuine Article

a. The mouth of the bubble is rounded with smooth edges (see pictures 9-3-21 and 9-3-23).

b. The bubble interior presents with frosted and grainy needlepoint mottling, but retains an overall fine and reserved quality (see pictures 9-3-21 and 9-3-23).

c. At times foreign material present beneath the bubble opening (see picture 9-3-21).

d. Some bubbles present with internal color spectrum (see pictures 9-3-21 and 9-3-23).

e. Broken mouth bubbles can occur in association with CO type pit mottles, which are clearly delineated and independent, and can present with color disparity (see picture 9-3-23).

f. The bubble retains clear delineation from the surrounding glass phase (see pictures 9-3-21 and 9-3-23).

g. The glass phase is clean and clear (see pictures 9-3-21 and 9-3-23).

II. Three-Dimensional Characteristics of Genuine Article

a. The bubble mouth is rounded and smooth.

b. It is possible for the surrounding glaze surface to present with channels other than the broken mouth.

c. The channel is clearly independent, its area is smaller than the underlying bubble.

d. The glaze surface surrounding the bubble opening remains smooth and clean.

See pictures 9-3-21 and 9-3-22, where 9-3-21 is the two-dimensional and 9-3-22 is the three-dimensional view of the same location.

Bubble A is not visible in picture 9-3-22 and as such is indicated with a red circle. The mouth of Bubble A is clearly depicted with rounded smooth edges. The surrounding glaze surface presents with a pit mottle (see Arrow B) and some scratches (see Arrow C) that are mutually delineated. Aside from these, the glaze surface is smooth and clean. The pit mottle, scratches and mouth opening can all act as channels between the bubble and the external environment.

See pictures 9-3-23 and 9-3-24, where 9-3-23 is the two-dimensional and 9-3-24 is the three-dimensional view of the same location.

Bubble D is not visible in picture 9-3-24 and as such is indicated with a red circle. The mouth of Bubble D is clearly depicted with rounded smooth edges.

The area immediately surrounding the bubble mouth presents with a small number of CO type pit mottles (see Arrow E) that are clear and independent with mutual delineation; aside from these, the glaze surface is smooth and clean. This goes to show that the majority of the weathering occurs on the bubble interior. The CO type pit mottles as well as the bubble mouth can act as channels between the bubble interior and the external environment.

III. Two-Dimensional Characteristics of Forged Article

See picture 9-3-25.

a. The interior nature of the bubble has unclear depiction.

b. The bubble and surrounding glass phase are not clearly delineated.

c. The surrounding glass phase is littered with pitting, and is generally muddled.

IV. Three-Dimensional Characteristics of Forged Article

a. The surrounding glaze surface presents with corrosion mottles with surface areas larger than the underlying

维图片。

图9-3-15中的气泡C在图9-3-16中位于红圈釉下处，不可见。图9-3-15中箭头D所指的斑块，在图9-3-16中却消失了。图9-3-15中箭头E所指斑块，在图9-3-16中也可见。

由此可推断，箭头D所指斑块不在釉表面，而在气泡C内壁，是内壁风化形成的斑块；箭头E所指斑块处于釉表面，是釉表面风化形成的斑块，也应是外界连接气泡内的通道所在处。

3. 赝品二维特征

见图9-3-17、图9-3-19。

（1）赝品上的非破口壁变泡内壁的物质成像模糊。

（2）壁变泡与周围玻璃相界线不分明。

（3）周围玻璃相上分布有坑点斑，整体显得涂污模糊。

4. 赝品三维特征

（1）有的壁变泡所在处的釉表面一大部分已被破坏，显得粗糙，具有扩张性。

（2）有的壁变泡所在处的釉表面存在腐蚀斑块，斑块最大直径甚至超过气泡最大直径，所谓的非破口壁变泡实际是假象壁变泡。

（3）周围玻璃相上分布有坑点斑，整体显得粗糙模糊。

见图9-3-17、图9-3-18，二者为同一器物同一位置图片，图9-3-17为二维图片，图9-3-18为三维图片。（该器物釉表面曾被腐蚀剂腐蚀）

图9-3-17的气泡A’在图9-3-18中位于红圈釉下处，其所在处釉表面一大部分已被破坏，显得粗糙，具有扩张性，周围玻璃相上分布有坑点斑，整体显得粗糙模糊。

见图9-3-19、图9-3-20，二者为同一器物同一位置图片，图9-3-19为二维图片，图9-3-20为三维图片。（该器物釉表面曾被腐蚀剂腐蚀）

图9-3-19中的气泡B’在图9-3-20中位于红圈釉下处，其所在处釉表面已被破坏，显得粗糙，腐蚀斑块的最大直径甚至超过气泡最大直径，具有扩张性，所谓的非破口壁变泡实际是假象壁变泡。周围玻璃相上分布有坑点斑，整体显得粗糙模糊。

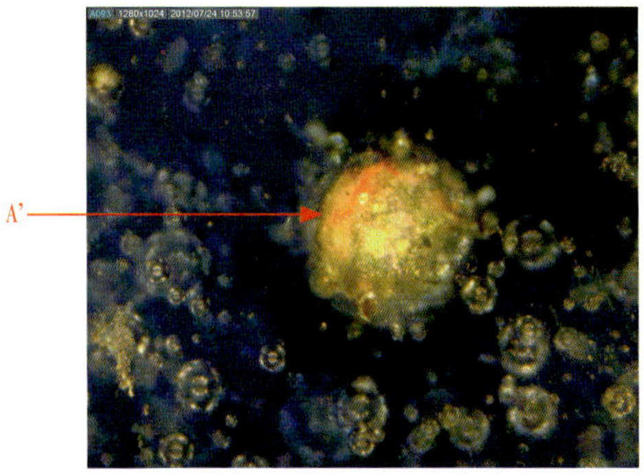

图9-3-17

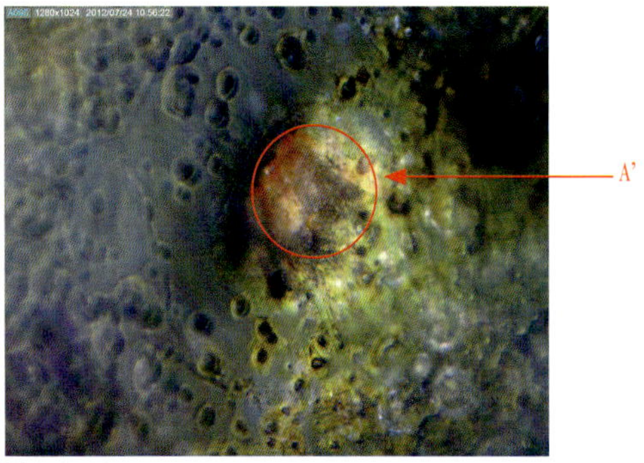

图9-3-18

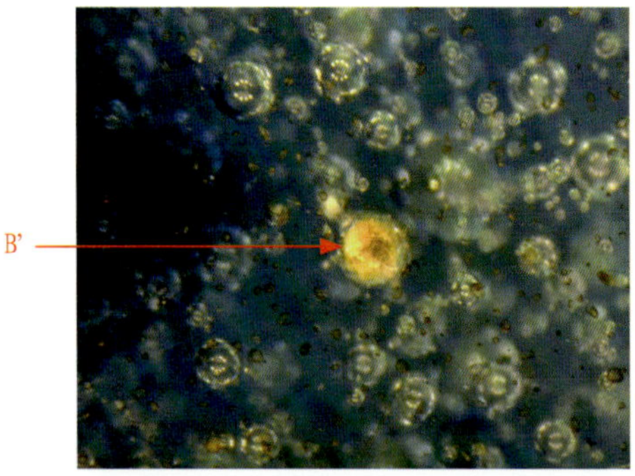

图9-3-19

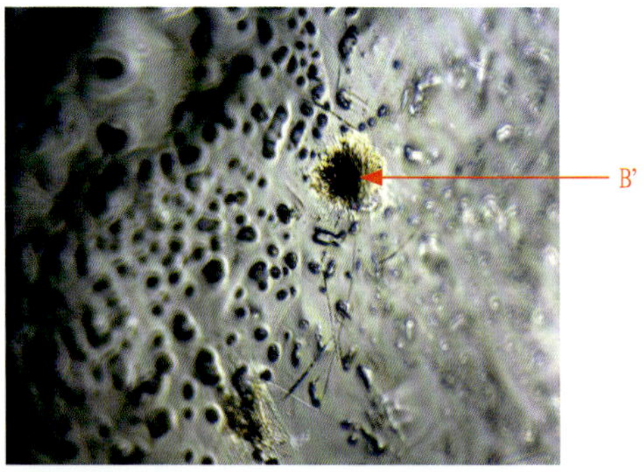

图9-3-20

bubble, indicating that this is a faux broken mouth bubble.

b. The surrounding glaze surface has sporadic distribution of pitting, giving it a general muddled appearance.

See pictures 9-3-25 and 9-3-26, whcrc 9-3-25 is the two-dimensional and 9-3-26 is the three-dimensional view of the same location (this piece has undergone treatment with aging reagent).

Bubble A' is not visible in picture 9-3-26 and as such is indicated with a red circle. The mouth of Bubble A' is clearly depicted, but has rough jagged edges. The glaze surface has coarsely diffused corrosion mottles, one of which completely covers the underlying bubble and extends beyond its surface area. This is a broken mouth bubble with faux texture. The surrounding glaze surface is generally pitted and muddled.

（二）破口壁变泡

1. 真品二维特征

（1）气泡破口呈较规整的圆形，边沿圆滑（见图9-3-21、图9-3-23）。

（2）破口壁变泡内壁的针眼斑包括磨砂型及颗粒型等，气泡整体显得精致、细腻（见图9-3-21、图9-3-23）。

（3）有时破口下方可见物质存在（见图9-3-21）。

（4）有的气泡内壁有色阶变化（见图9-3-21、图9-3-23）。

（5）有时破口壁变泡所在处及邻近的釉表面存在CO型坑点斑（如箭头E所指处）。坑点斑与壁变泡有时有色差变化，各自独立清晰，界线分明（见图9-3-23）。

（6）破口壁变泡与周围玻璃相界线分明（见图9-3-21、图9-3-23）。

（7）周围玻璃相干净清晰（见图9-3-21、图9-3-23）。

2. 真品三维特征

（1）气泡破口边沿圆滑。

（2）气泡所在处釉表面可见除破口以外的通道。

（3）通道清晰独立，面积小于气泡面积。

（4）通道周围的釉表面保持光滑洁净。

见图9-3-21、图9-3-22，二者为同一器物同一位置图片，图9-3-21为二维图片，图9-3-22为三维图片。

图9-3-21中的气泡A在图9-3-22中位于红圈釉下处，不可见。气泡A的破口在图9-3-22中清晰可见，破口圆滑。破口周围有一处坑点斑（见箭头B所指处）和几处划痕（见箭头C所指处），清晰独立。除此以外釉表面光滑洁净。这说明图9-3-21中气泡A的风化斑块大部分都处于气泡内壁。坑点斑、划痕及破口都可以是外界连接气泡内的通道所在处。

见图9-3-23、图9-3-24，二者为同一器物同一位置图片，图9-3-23为二维图片，图9-3-24为三维图片。

图9-3-23中的气泡D在图9-3-24中位于红圈釉下处，不可见。气泡D的破口在图9-3-24中清晰可见，破口圆滑。破口周围有几处颜色较深的CO型坑点斑（如箭头E所指处），坑点斑彼此独立清晰，界线分明，除此以外釉表面较光滑洁净。这说明气泡D的风化斑块大部分都处于气泡内壁，破口周围的CO型坑点斑很有可能是除破口以外外界连接气泡内的其他通道。

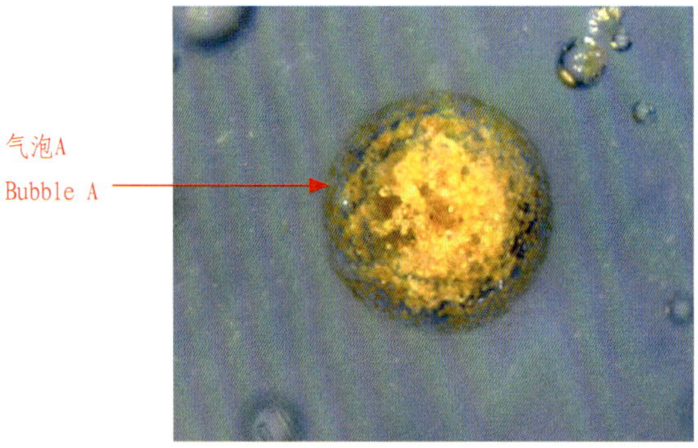

图9-3-21

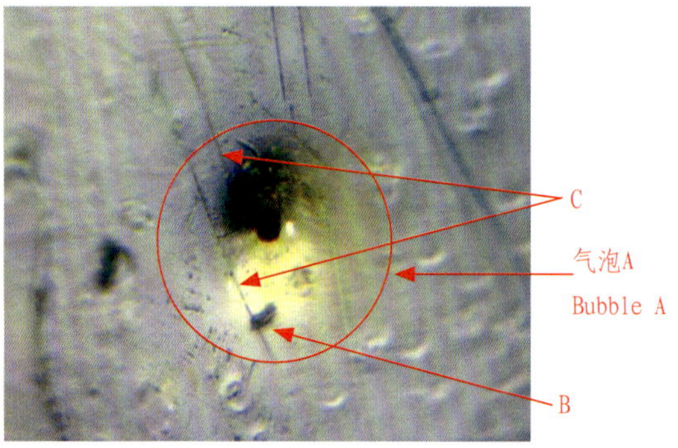

图9-3-22

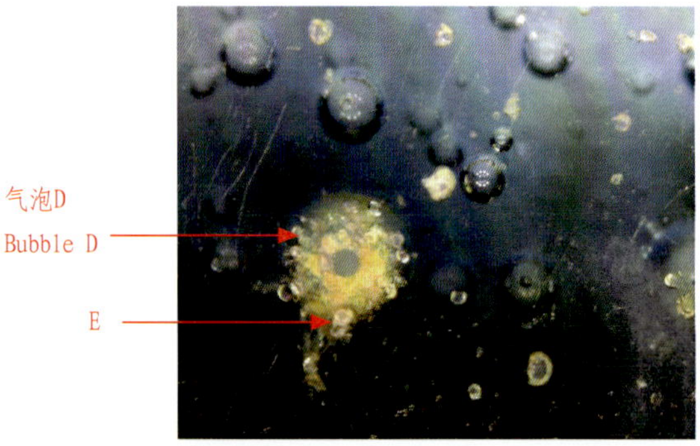

图9-3-23

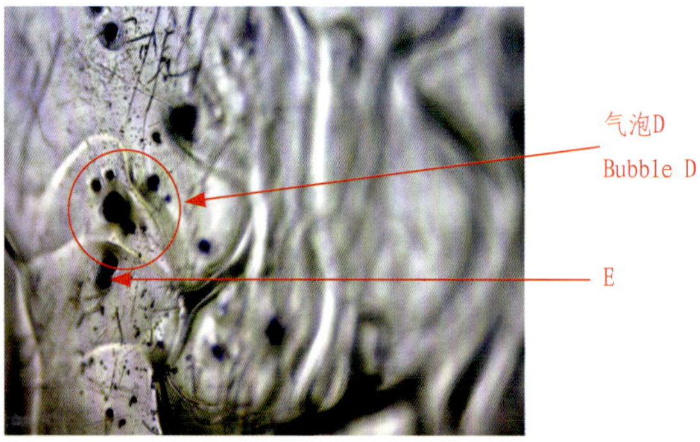

图9-3-24

3. 赝品二维特征

见图9-3-25。

（1）破口壁变泡泡壁内物质成像模糊。

（2）破口壁变泡与周围玻璃相界线不分明。

（3）周围玻璃相上分布有针眼斑和坑点斑，整体显得涂污模糊。

4. 赝品三维特征

（1）有的破口壁变泡所在处的釉表面存在腐蚀斑块，斑块最大直径甚至超过气泡最大直径，所谓的破口壁变泡实际是破口假象壁变泡。

（2）周围玻璃相上分布有坑点斑，整体显得粗糙模糊。

见图9-3-25、图9-3-26，二者为同一器物同一位置图片，图9-3-25为二维图片，图9-3-26为三维图片。（该器物釉表面曾被腐蚀剂腐蚀）

图9-3-25中的破口壁变泡A′在图9-3-26中，其所在处釉表面已被破坏，显得粗糙，腐蚀斑块的最大直径甚至超过气泡最大直径，具有扩张性，所谓的破口壁变泡实际是破口假象壁变泡。周围玻璃相上分布有坑点斑，整体显得粗糙模糊。

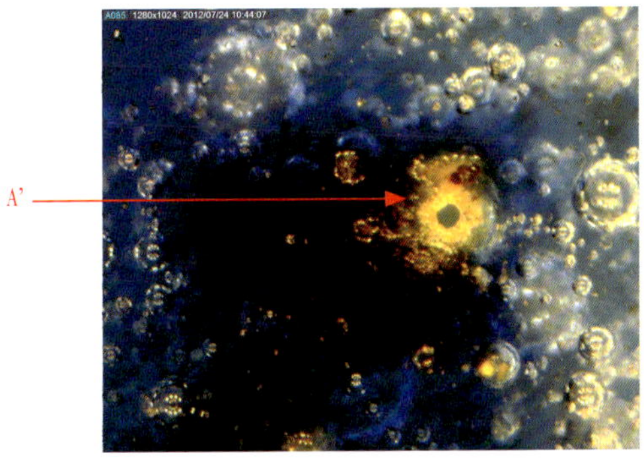

图9-3-25

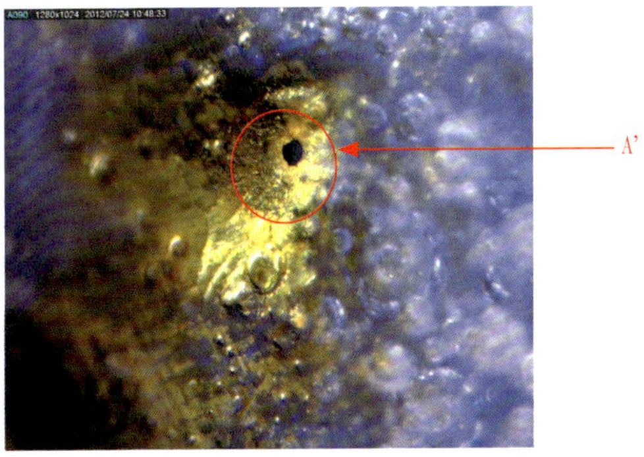

图9-3-26

第四节
元青花鬃眼真品与赝品比对

一、真品二维特征

（一）鬃眼内部及口部周围的釉表面存在颗粒物质（见图9-4-1、图9-4-3、图9-4-6）。

（二）鬃眼内部及口部周围的釉表面存在纤丝，纤丝有颜色变化（见图9-4-2、图9-4-3）。

（三）鬃眼内部及口部周围的釉表面会有颜色变化（见图9-4-2、图9-4-4、图9-4-5、图9-4-7）。

（四）部分鬃眼口部周围釉下出现絮状斑或色变泡（见图9-4-5、图9-4-6）。

二、赝品二维特征

见图9-4-8—图9-4-13。

（一）鬃眼内部沉积堆积物很少。

（二）鬃眼内部及口部周围大部分都未变色，少见色阶变化。

（三）鬃眼内部及口部周围出现的纤丝通常也表现为一种颜色。

（四）鬃眼口部周围的釉表面反光。

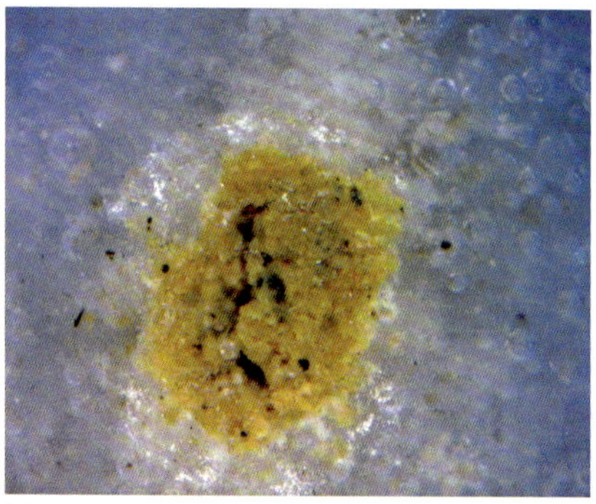
图9-4-1

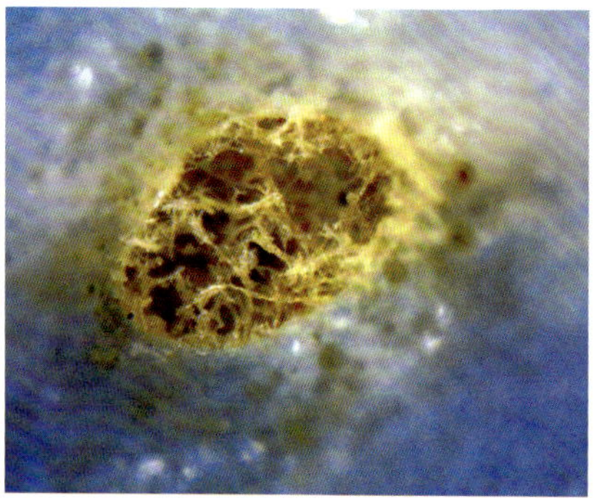
图9-4-2

图9-4-3

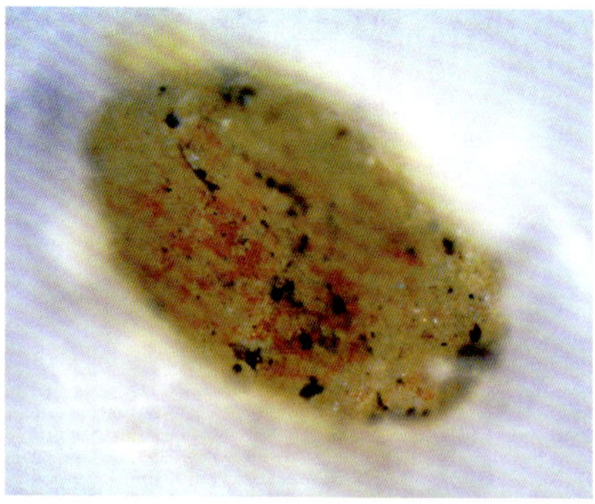
图9-4-4

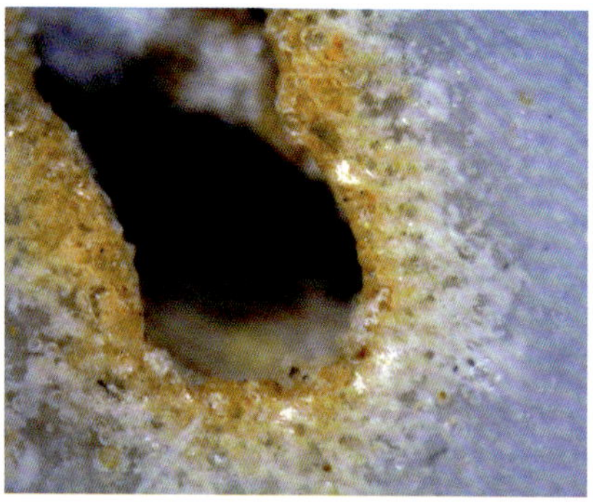
图9-4-5

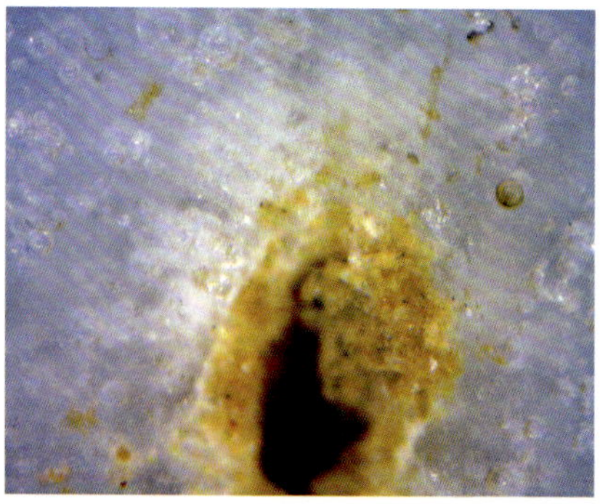
图9-4-6

Section 4:
Genuine and Forged Yuan Underglaze Blue Bristle Pit Comparison

1. Two-Dimensional Characteristics of Genuine Article

A. The pit interior and mouth surroundings can present with granulated materials (see pictures 9-4-1, 9-4-3, 9-4-6).

B. The pit interior and mouth surroundings can present with filaments of varying widths, lengths, and coloration (see pictures 9-4-2 and 9-4-3).

C. The pit interior and mouth surroundings can present with color change (see pictures 9-4-2, 9-4-4, 9-4-5 and 9-4-7).

D. Some pits present with colored bubbles or floccus mottling in the glaze level surrounding the pit mouth (see pictures 9-4-5 and 9-4-6).

2. Two-Dimensional Characteristics of Forged Article

See pictures 9-4-8—9-4-13.

A. Relatively few material deposits within the pit interior.

B. The pit interior and mouth surroundings present without coloration or limited color change.

C. The pit interior and mouth surroundings can present with filaments, but coloration is uniform.

D. The trumpet shaped mouth surrounding the pit has high glossy reflectivity.

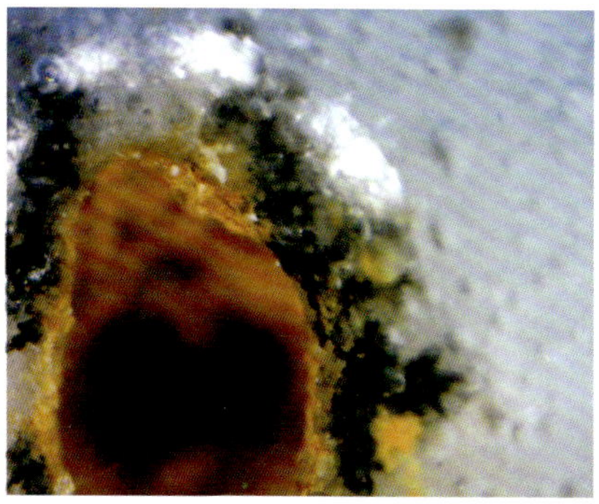
图9-4-7

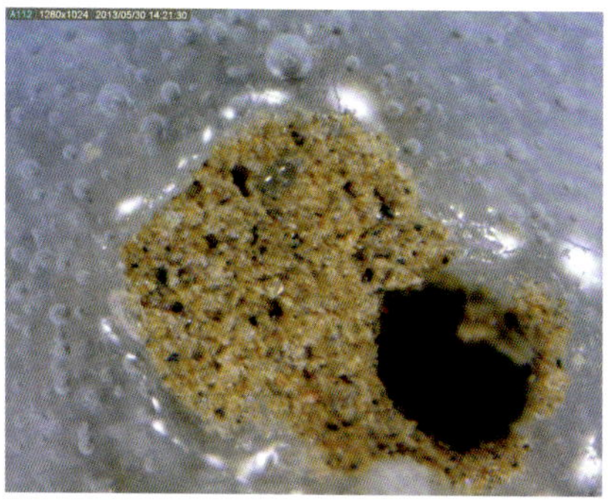
图9-4-8

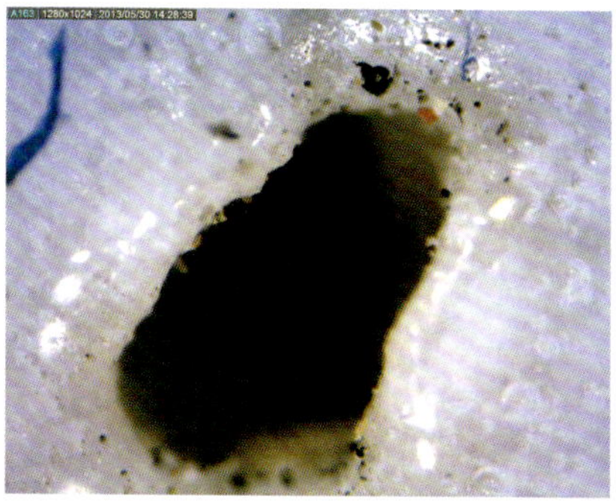
图9-4-9

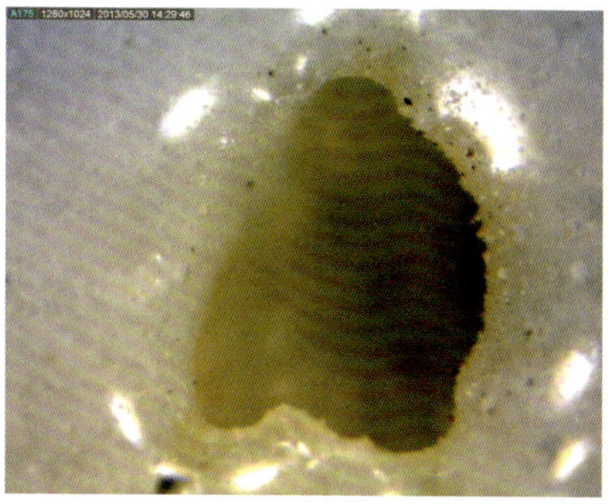
图9-4-10

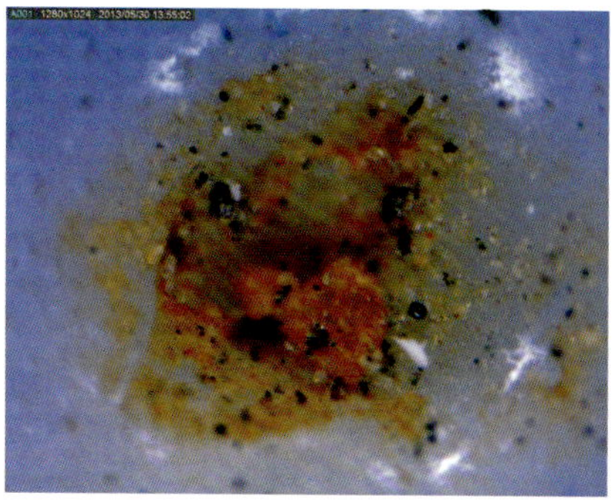
图9-4-11

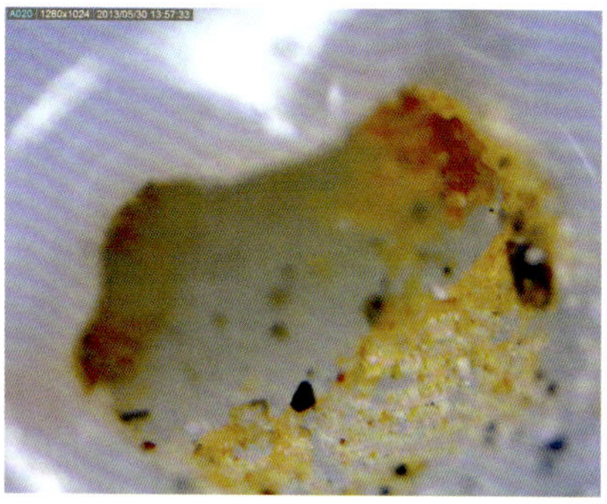
图9-4-12

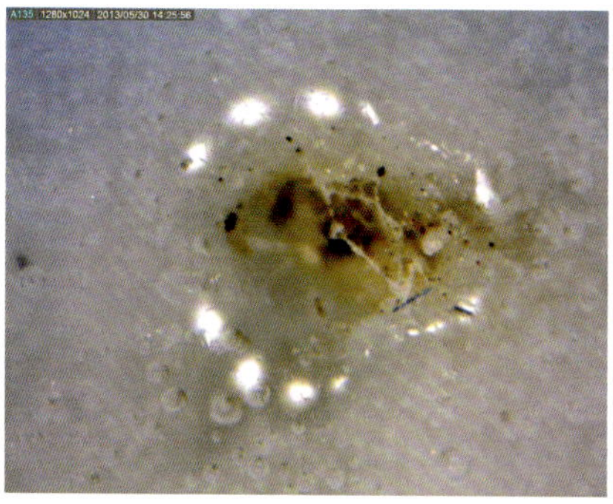
图9-4-13

第十章

元青花迹型物证鉴定方法与操作

阅读提示：

本章主要阐述了元青花迹型物证鉴定的方法要点和鉴定操作程序，并展示元青花鉴定操作案例。

主要论述问题：

1. 元青花迹型物证鉴定主要包括哪两部分？
2. 论证元青花迹型本质充分吻合的要素有哪几点？
3. 为什么说已鉴定合格的元青花分值的高低与其真实性是没有关系的？

Chapter 10

Trace Model Material Evidence Authentication of Yuan Underglaze Blue: Methodology and Operation

Text Note:

This chapter describes the key operation points of the YUB Trace Model Material Evidence Authentication method as well as offers an operational authentication case study in the form of a YUB Authentication Report.

第一节 元青花迹型物证鉴定方法

鉴定陶瓷的传统方法主要是眼学目鉴，包括用肉眼看器形、看胎质、看纹饰、看款识、看底足。

相对于眼学的“五看”，元青花迹型物证鉴定在此基础上，更强调利用显微镜观察瓷器迹型的“五看”：看斑块、看气泡、看纹路、看鬃眼、看玻璃相。此“五看”就是：

1. 通过观察、比对和分析被鉴定器物的迹型与图谱的迹型，发现二者迹型之间的高度相似性；

2. 在被鉴定器物迹型与图谱迹型高度相似的基础上，深入论证迹型的本质吻合。

这两个部分具有内在联系和因果关系。迹型比对是元青花迹型物证鉴定的前提，而迹型本质论证则是鉴定的核心。

这种迹型物证鉴定方法能够减少非客观因素对鉴定的影响，让鉴定结果更加准确、真实。熟练掌握方法并且正确操作，可以大大提升鉴定的准确率。

一、迹型物证鉴定特征

从陶瓷鉴定发展的历史来看，鉴定过程中往往会运用到比对的方法。眼学鉴定如此，迹型鉴定同样如此。但眼学鉴定的比对与迹型鉴定的比对，比对的对象和使用的标准都截然不同。

眼学鉴定的比对对象是陶瓷外观的各个特征，使用的鉴定标准是鉴定者记忆表象中标准器外观的各个特征。

迹型物证鉴定比对的对象是陶瓷釉层的显微迹型，使用的鉴定标准是标准图谱模型中的迹型图片，这些图片就是物证系统。总的来说，迹型物证鉴定主要有三个特性：

（一）标准可靠性

作为迹型物证鉴定比对时使用的标准，元青花迹型标准图谱模型是可靠的。

元青花迹型标准图谱模型是观察研究一定量的有明确发掘时间、发掘地点、年代依据及有明确传世记载的元青花标本后，按其迹型现象提炼概括出来的物证系统。

可靠的标本来源是建构元青花迹型标准图谱模型的基础和前提。

（二）证据现实性

眼学鉴定都是听鉴定结论，且不说每位专家的表述有差异，听者的理解能力也不尽相同，所以才有“百闻不如一见”的说法。

陶瓷迹型鉴定是看得见的鉴定，是阳光下的鉴定。阳光是鉴定者与被鉴定者之间的信息透明与对等，不存在神秘与“忽悠”，阳光是鉴定的新理念，是增加鉴定说服力的正能量。

陶瓷迹型比对过程就是观察过程，就是寻找、提取物证的过程。所以，迹型的物证鉴定更强调眼见为实。鉴定时所使用的元青花迹型标准图谱模型是现实可见的，而不是眼学鉴定中储存在鉴定者头脑中的表象记忆。

迹型鉴定比对时，标准图谱模型中的元青花迹型图片会与被鉴定器物的迹型图片同时被展示出来，二者之间的共同点及差异一目了然。

这种现实中可观察到的物证证据，更具说服力。

（三）比对客观性

眼学鉴定比对是依据鉴定者记忆中的表象进行判断，这个表象记忆的准确性是存在偏差的。眼学鉴定比对的判断过程还会受到诸多因素的影响与制约，如鉴定者的学识水平、身体状况、外部环境，甚至道德品质等等。而迹型鉴定比对是根据现实中可视的标准图谱模型，即物证要素来进行比对判断，这就减少了许多人为因素的干扰，具有不以人的意志为转移的客观属性。

陶瓷迹型就是客观实在的物证，迹型鉴定将过去主观经验的

Section 1:
Yuan Underglaze Blue Trace Model Material Evidence Authentication Method

Traditional ceramic authentication is mainly centered on experience-based naked-eye appraisal methods. It utilizes the naked-eye check of the shape, clay, decoration, marking, and base.

In contrast to the "Five Checks" of naked-eye appraisal, Trace Model Material Evidence Authentication of YUB builds on this foundation and emphasizes comprehensive microscopic observation, bringing about a new "Five Checks": Mottles, Bubbles, Striae, Bristle Pits, and Glass Phase. These "Five Checks" mean:

1. Through observation, comparison, and analysis of the traces of the authenticated item and Standard Trace Atlas Model, we can determine the degree of their similarities.

2. On the foundation of their similarities, we can deeply expound upon the nature of these traces.

These two parts have an inherent connection as well as a cause and effect relationship. Trace comparison is the premise of Trace Model Material Evidence Authentication and nature of trace proofs are the authentication core.

This type of Trace Model Material Evidence Authentication method can decrease the impact of non-objective factors, and allow for higher accuracy and veracity in authentication. Proper grasp of these methods, and precise operation, will greatly increase the accuracy of authentication.

1. Trace Model Material Evidence Authentication Characteristics

Looking at a history of its development, the ceramic authentication process has almost always relied on the use of comparison methods; experience-based authentication and Trace Model Material Evidence Authentication alike. However, the objective and standard used in these two types of comparative authentication are not the same.

Experience-based authentication uses all of the externally observable properties for comparison, and the standard used is the memory that the authenticator has of externally observable properties of sample pieces they have observed.

Trace Model Material Evidence Authentication uses ceramic glaze level traces for comparison, and the standard used is the trace images from the Trace Atlas Model, which represent the material evidence system. Generally speaking, Trace Model Material Evidence Authentication has three main characteristics:

A. Sample Reliability

As the standard for Trace Model Material Evidence Authentication—the YUB Standard Trace Atlas Model is reliable.

The YUB Standard Trace Atlas Model is the material evidence system that represents the series of trace appearances extracted and condensed from the observation of YUB samples of known excavation date, location, period proof, and provenance.

The reliable source of samples is the foundation and premise of the YUB Standard Trace Atlas Model construction.

B. Evidence Transparency

Experience-based authentication offers authentication results orally, and due to the discrepancies in expert explanation and differences in the listeners' ability to understand what is being said, there is an absence of tangible proof.

"A picture is worth a thousand words."

人证，改进为科学客观的物证，这种比对手段和比对过程，更加强调实事求是，降低主观因素的影响。因此也更具公正性。

二、迹型比对

在元青花迹型物证比对鉴定中，应该如何把握比对的高度相似性？究竟有多么相似，才能通过迹型比对这一关？我们要关注两点：

（一）器物的整体迹型现象

要判断一件元青花的整体迹型现象是否具备元代青花瓷的普遍性特征，要求综合观察器物的先天性迹型及后天性迹型。

先天性迹型包括流淌斑、放射斑、团状斑、流淌纹及鬃眼等。后天性迹型包括针眼斑、坑点斑、泡根斑、絮状斑、CO纹、划痕、色变泡、壁变泡及鬃眼风化的多样性等（见表10-1-1）。

鉴定时首先要了解一件元青花上一共包含了哪些迹型种类，这些迹型种类是否是那个时代迹型普遍应有的。例如，在清代的瓷器上通常是找不到絮状斑的，所以絮状斑就不属于清代的普遍性迹型种类。

（二）迹型的具体特征

在掌握了一件元青花的普遍性迹型特征后，我们需要观察比对每一个迹型种类的具体特征。比对时需要重点观察比较的一系列迹型特征，请参考表10-1-1。

比如火焰形沙滩斑，它属于元青花上的先天性迹型，能在一定程度上反映当时的用材，如青料及釉料的含量比例和属性等。我们要抓住火焰形沙滩斑的本质属性，关注沙滩斑是否具有“火焰形”特征，也就是是否具有流淌延展的特征。沙滩斑是三簇火苗还是五簇火苗都不重要，不要去追求“火苗”的绝对相似，因为世界上不可能找到一模一样的“火苗”。

同时，还要关注火焰形沙滩斑上其他后天性迹型的表现，如火焰形沙滩斑上针眼斑的表现特征是否与图谱相符等等（见表10-1-1）。

三、迹型本质论证

元青花迹型物证鉴定除了迹型比对之外，还需要对迹型形成本质进行逻辑论证。

迹型形成本质论证实质就是对迹型比对的结果进行论述及分析。通过观察比对被鉴定器物的迹型与标准图谱模型的迹型，将最终结果的本质吻合程度用逻辑方式阐明。

可以说，任何证据都难以起到百分之百的证明作用。亲子鉴定比对DNA也不可能达到100％吻合，只能是高度相似。同样，在元青花迹型物证鉴定中，迹型现象也没有绝对完全的相似，只有本质的充分吻合。在迹型高度相似的基础上，论证迹型形成本质充分吻合需要包含如下几个因素：

（一）被鉴定器物迹型现象是否与图谱一样反映了当时的制瓷用材及烧制工艺；

（二）被鉴定器物上后天性迹型的多样性；

（三）被鉴定器物上迹型的变化是否具有同步性；

（四）被鉴定器物上迹型出现的位置是否具有合理性；

（五）被鉴定器物迹型现象是否具有量变特征；

（六）被鉴定器物迹型现象是否能够反映时间过程性原理；

（七）被鉴定器物迹型现象是否体现了迹型形成与发展的诸规律。

以上七点是被鉴定器物迹型本质吻合的充分理由。迹型高度相似仅仅是迹型本质吻合的理由之一，即迹型表现特征的静态理由，还要综合论证与迹型本质吻合的其他因素，即能反映迹型形成过程特征的动态理由，这样，鉴定才能得到最终的充分物证证明，才能切实显示迹型物证的“鹰眼”作用。比如，某件元青花上的火焰形沙滩斑的先天形貌与后天针眼斑的特征都与图谱吻合，且能够反映陶瓷迹型的量变原理、时间过程性原理和迹型形成与发展的诸规律，那么我们就可以推断被鉴定器物上的火焰形沙滩斑与图谱高度相似，并具有迹型的本质吻合性。具备了迹型高度相似及本质吻合的充分理由，就可以对被鉴定器物做出实然性判断，是就是，不是就不是。

Using the YUB Standard Trace Atlas Model in YUB authentication offers observable proof and transparent results. Transparency in authentication breaks down the barriers between the expert and the audience, and brings to light all that is being seen in authentication.

This comparative authentication is the process of observing and searching for material evidence. Thus, Trace Model Material Evidence Authentication emphasizes what is actually observable, and does not rely on the memory of images left in the mind of the authenticator.

While carrying out Trace Model Material Evidence Authentication, the images of the YUB Standard Trace Atlas Model and images of the piece being authenticated are available for side-by-side comparison; their similarities and differences tangibly observable.

This type of observable objective material evidence is conclusive.

C. Comparison Objectivity

As experience-based authentication relies on the memory of the authenticator to offer proof, the accuracy of these memories presents with bias. Additionally, the process of authentication meets with other key influences and restrictions of the authenticator, i.e. their ability, their health, external factors, moral character, and so forth. Trace Model Material Evidence Authentication, on the other hand, utilizes the material evidence of the Trace Atlas Model, limiting the disturbance of human factors, and increasing the objectivity of authentication.

Ceramic traces are objective material evidence, and Trace Model Authentication is the progression from subjective experience-driven human witness towards more scientific, objective, and concrete material evidence. This type of comparative technique and comparison process places more emphasis on resolute truth and decreases the impact of subjective factors. Because of this, it is characteristically less biased.

2. Trace Comparison

During the process of Trace Model Material Evidence Authentication of YUB, how can we grasp the degree of similarity in comparison? Just how similar do traces need to be to pass the test of trace comparison? To answer this we need to focus on two points:

A. Holistic Trace Appearance

In order to determine whether a YUB piece's holistic trace appearance is or is not consistent with the Typical YUB Trace Characteristics, we must comprehensively observe a piece's innate and acquired traces.

Innate traces include flowing mottles, radiating mottles, blotch mottles, flowing striae, and bristle pits. Acquired traces include needlepoint mottles, pit mottles, bubble roots, floccus mottles, CO striae, scrapes, color change bubbles, textured bubbles, and multiplicity of bristle pit weathering (see table 10-1-1).

Thus when authenticating, we first need to discover what trace categories are included on the piece, and understand if these are the Typical Trace Types of the said period. For example, floccus mottling is not known to occur on Qing Dynasty porcelain, thus floccus mottling is not a Typical Trace Type of Qing Dynasty porcelain.

B. Specific Trace Characteristics

After grasping a piece's typical trace characteristics, we must observe and compare each of the specific trace characteristics. During comparison we must emphasize the comparative observation of the series of trace characteristics listed in table 10-1-1.

Using flame shaped beach mottles as an example: Belonging to the YUB innate trace category, they can, to some extent, reflect the materials used during the day, i.e. the composition and nature of the dye and glaze. We must grasp the nature of flame shaped beach mottles, and focus on whether the beach mottles have the "flame shape" characteristics, specifically is it or is it not characteristically flowing. Whether the flames are three-pronged or five-pronged is not important; we do not need to find the exact same flame shape, as no two flames are the same.

At the same time, we must pay attention to the acquired traces that present on the flame shaped beach mottle, i.e. whether the needlepoint mottling characteristics are typical (matching the atlas model), and so forth (see table 10-1-1).

3. Nature of Trace Proofs

Aside from Trace Comparison, Trace Model Material Evidence Authentication of YUB must carry out logical proofs as to the nature of the traces.

Essentially, Nature of Trace Proofs are the discussion and analysis of the results of Trace Comparison. Through the comparative observation of the authenticated piece's traces and those of the Trace Atlas Model, we must use logic to clearly explain the degree of similarity between the natures of the resultant traces.

We can say that any form of evidence has difficulty in reaching a one hundred percent match. Even DNA testing cannot reach a one hundred percent match, but can only attain a high degree of certainty. Similarly, trace appearances cannot be identical; they can only have a fully matched nature. On the foundation of high similarity, to prove the fully matched trace nature, the following criteria must be met:

1. The traces reflect the same materials and techniques as the Trace Atlas Model;
2. The acquired traces present with multiplicity;
3. The trace changes occur with proper congruency;
4. The traces present in rational locations;
5. The traces have quantitative change characteristics;
6. The traces reflect the passage of time principle;
7. The traces embody the Ceramic Trace Laws.

The above-listed criteria are the Nature of Trace Grounds for Full Match. The high similarity of trace appearances is only one portion of the grounds for full trace nature match. It is the static grounds of the trace's appearance characteristics, thus we must further comprehensively prove the other factors in play for a trace nature match. In this way we can reflect the dynamic grounds of the trace's formation process. Only then can we reach a final material evidence based conclusion and act as the "Hawkeye" authority in authentication.

For example: If a certain piece of YUB has innately formed flame shaped mottles and acquired needlepoint mottling that match the Trace Atlas Model, and can reflect the quantitative change and passage of time principles as well as the laws that govern trace formation and change; then we can assert that the beach mottles on this piece have both a high similarity to the Trace Atlas Model and have a matching trace nature. Through using high trace similarity and fully matching nature criteria, we can offer resolute decisions about the authenticity of the piece in question: Either it is or it is not authentic.

表 10-1-1

反映元青花材料、工艺的迹型特征			反映量变原理的迹型特征		反映时间过程性原理的迹型特征		反映迹型出现位置合理性的迹型特征		反映迹型变化同步性的迹型特征	
先天迹型种类			二维成像	三维成像	二维成像	三维成像	二维成像	三维成像	二维成像	三维成像
流淌斑	沙滩斑	火焰形及荷叶形	有色阶变化	颜色有由浅至深的变化		沙滩斑呈凹陷状，与玻璃相圆孔有明显高度差				
			沙滩斑上的玻璃相圆孔干净清晰，与沙滩斑界线分明	沙滩斑上的玻璃相圆孔光滑洁净，与沙滩斑界线分明						
			周围玻璃相干净清晰	周围玻璃相光滑洁净						
			与周围其他迹型各自独立清晰，界线分明							
放射斑	白色系									
	红色系		形貌轮廓清晰，有清晰的色阶变化（橘红、橘黄等等）	形貌轮廓清晰						
			周围玻璃相干净清晰	周围玻璃相光滑洁净						
			与周围其他迹型各自独立清晰，界线分明							
	黄色系		形貌轮廓清晰	所在处的釉表面光滑洁净						
			放射斑与其表面的分相（黑色系放射斑）各自独立清晰，界线分明	放射斑位于釉下，其所在釉表面光滑洁净，其表面的分相（黑色系放射斑）独立清晰						
			外围有精致细腻的包边	放射斑与周围釉表面有高度差						
			包边内外的玻璃相干净清晰	包边内外的玻璃相光滑洁净						
			周围玻璃相干净清晰	周围玻璃相光滑洁净						
			与周围其他迹型各自独立清晰，界线分明							

（续表）

反映元青花材料、工艺的迹型特征		反映量变原理的迹型特征		反映时间过程性原理的迹型特征		反映迹型出现位置合理性的迹型特征		反映迹型变化同步性的迹型特征	
先天迹型种类		二维成像	三维成像	二维成像	三维成像	二维成像	三维成像	二维成像	三维成像
放射斑	褐色系	形貌轮廓清晰	有的表面较粗糙；有的表面有细密纹路，但总体还是比较平滑细腻						
		外围有精致细腻的包边	与周围釉表面有高度差						
		包边内外的玻璃相干净清晰	包边内外的玻璃相光滑洁净						
		周围玻璃相干净清晰	周围玻璃相光滑洁净						
		与周围其他迹型各自独立清晰，界线分明							
		放射斑与其表面的分相（黑色系放射斑）各自独立清晰，界线分明	放射斑位于釉表面，其表面的分相（黑色系放射斑）独立清晰						
	黑色系	形貌轮廓清晰	位于釉层中的放射斑所在釉表面光滑洁净						
			位于釉表面的放射斑形貌轮廓清晰						

（续表）

反映元青花材料、工艺的迹型特征			反映量变原理的迹型特征		反映时间过程性原理的迹型特征		反映迹型出现位置合理性的迹型特征		反映迹型变化同步性的迹型特征	
先天迹型种类			二维成像	三维成像	二维成像	三维成像	二维成像	三维成像	二维成像	三维成像
流淌纹	阴纹	中空型	纹路边线清晰精致	W形纹路凹槽较浅者脊部洁净，呈哑光						
			纹路内部清晰可见一条或多条连续或错综的细线	W形纹路凹槽较深者，脊部反光部分断续						
			与周围玻璃相界线分明							
			与周围其他迹型各自独立，界线分明							
		针眼型	U形纹路内针眼斑密实，无虚空，有时可见白色、橘黄色等的色阶变化	纹路凹槽内可见颗粒风化物质，有时可见白色、紫色及橘黄色的色阶变化		U形纹路有一定宽度和深度			U形纹路内针眼斑密实，无虚空	U形纹路有一定宽度和深度，有时纹路内可见风化物及色阶变化
			U形纹路与周围玻璃相界线分明，周围玻璃相干净清晰	U形纹路边沿圆滑，与周围玻璃相界线分明，周围玻璃相光滑洁净						
			U形纹路与周围的沙滩斑界线分明，沙滩斑有量变特征			U形阴纹在沙滩斑上呈凹陷状，与沙滩斑有高度差				
			V形纹路内针眼斑有时漫延到周围玻璃相上，浓淡过渡均匀	针眼斑三维成像面积小于二维面积						
			纹路与周围其他迹型各自独立，界线分明							

（续表）

反映元青花材料、工艺的迹型特征		反映量变原理的迹型特征		反映时间过程性原理的迹型特征		反映迹型出现位置合理性的迹型特征		反映迹型变化同步性的迹型特征	
先天迹型种类		二维成像	三维成像	二维成像	三维成像	二维成像	三维成像	二维成像	三维成像
流淌纹	阳纹	粗的纹路边沿呈锯齿状	粗的纹路边沿呈锯齿状，光滑有细密纹路						
流淌纹	阳纹	纹路与沙滩斑上的针眼斑界线分明			纹路凸起，高出周围沙滩斑				
流淌纹	阳纹		纹路周围沙滩斑上的磨砂针眼斑呈独立点状凹坑						
玻璃相	玻璃相清晰透澈								
玻璃相	有雾状斑块，清浊相间								
独立大气泡	三两出现								
气泡大小比例	气泡大小比例较悬殊								
气泡分布	分布疏朗，偶有较密集								
鬃眼		口部周围有颜色变化		周围釉下有絮状斑					
鬃眼		口部周围呈炭黑色		周围釉下有色变或壁变泡					
鬃眼		口部有纤丝或颗粒物质		内部的团簇颗粒物大于口部最大直径					
鬃眼		内部有针眼斑		内部沉积多种物质					
鬃眼		内部有颜色变化							
鬃眼		口部及内部纤丝有色阶变化							
鬃眼		口部及内部纤丝有粗有细，错综交杂							
鬃眼		周围玻璃相呈哑光，反光较弱							

（续表）

后天风化迹型			反映量变原理的迹型特征		反映时间过程性原理的迹型特征		反映迹型出现位置合理性的迹型特征		反映迹型变化同步性的迹型特征	
迹型种类			二维成像	三维成像	二维成像	三维成像	二维成像	三维成像	二维成像	三维成像
针眼斑	在流淌斑上	雾状针眼斑	由浓到淡，过渡均匀细腻				通常出现在沙滩斑与玻璃相交界处		由浓到淡，过渡均匀细腻	
		磨砂针眼斑	有的地方密集，有的地方稀疏，有明显边界感	呈独立点状凹坑密集分布，有明显边界感			一般出现在沙滩斑中部		有的地方密集，有的地方稀疏，有明显边界感	呈独立点状凹坑，密集分布，有明显边界感
		颗粒针眼斑	针眼独立，针眼之间可见底板，彼此界线分明	呈独立点状凹坑，针眼之间可见底板，彼此界线分明					针眼独立，针眼之间可见底板，彼此界线分明	呈独立点状凹坑，针眼之间可见底板，彼此界线分明
	在放射斑上	磨砂针眼斑	分布于放射斑形貌范围内，有明显边界感	呈独立点状凹坑密集分布，有明显边界感			一般出现在釉表面放射斑形貌范围内			
	在玻璃相上	颗粒针眼斑	独立清晰，与玻璃相界线分明				有时在蓝色青花纹饰处或碘酒斑处出现，一般不超出其范围			
			有纤细包边							
坑点斑	CO型坑点斑		与周围玻璃相界线分明		有C形、O形纹伴生	釉表面只可见清晰纤细的C形或O形纹		CO型坑点斑通常都出现在釉表面凸起处		
			与周围的其他迹型各自独立清晰，界线分明		大小不一、深浅不一的坑点斑或坑点斑群	除CO纹以外，还可见面积比CO型坑点斑二维成像面积要小的斑块		釉表面其余地方光滑洁净		
			周围玻璃相干净清晰	周围玻璃相光滑洁净		釉表面只可见面积比坑点斑或坑点斑群二维成像面积要小的风化斑块				
					单位图片中CO纹、CO型坑点斑及坑点斑群同时存在，彼此界线分明					
					与色变泡或壁变泡伴生	见色变泡及壁变泡部分				

（续表）

后天风化迹型		反映量变原理的迹型特征		反映时间过程性原理的迹型特征		反映迹型出现位置合理性的迹型特征		反映迹型变化同步性的迹型特征	
迹型种类		二维成像	三维成像	二维成像	三维成像	二维成像	三维成像	二维成像	三维成像
坑点斑	CO型坑点斑			坑点斑所在处釉下有絮状斑	釉表面通常只见坑点斑，坑点斑有量变特征，不见絮状斑				
	针眼型坑点斑	有纤细包边，内可见独立针眼斑	独立凹坑，面积小于或等于二维面积						
		有纤细包边，不可见针眼斑							
		实心不透影，不见包边							
		与周围玻璃相界线分明	与周围玻璃相界线分明						
		与周围其他迹型各自独立清晰，界线分明							
		周围玻璃相干净清晰	周围玻璃相光滑洁净						

（续表）

后天风化迹型		反映量变原理的迹型特征		反映时间过程性原理的迹型特征		反映迹型出现位置合理性的迹型特征		反映迹型变化同步性的迹型特征	
迹型种类		二维成像	三维成像	二维成像	三维成像	二维成像	三维成像	二维成像	三维成像
坑点斑	外伤型坑点斑	有色阶变化		可见针眼斑及沉积物					
		内有针眼斑	呈独立凹坑，边沿圆滑			针眼斑不超过坑点斑范围			
	浸水型坑点斑	有的形貌为上下各一半圆弧	呈独立近圆凹坑，边沿圆滑						
		有的坑点斑内可见磨砂针眼斑	呈独立凹坑，边沿圆滑，坑点斑内凹凸不平			磨砂针眼斑不超过坑点斑范围			
		与周围玻璃相界线分明	与周围玻璃相界线分明						
		与周围其他迹型各自独立，界线分明	与周围其他迹型各自独立，界线分明						
		周围玻璃相干净清晰	周围玻璃相光滑洁净						
泡根斑		同一泡根斑内有色阶变化		面积较大的泡根斑可见多种沉积物					
		单位图片中邻近的多个泡根斑之间有色差变化							
		与周围玻璃相界线分明	与周围玻璃相界线分明						
		与周围其他迹型各自独立清晰，界线分明	与周围其他迹型各自独立清晰，界线分明						
絮状斑			釉损处以外的地方光滑洁净，无其他明显大面积损伤	斑块中心色白如牛奶，不透明；斑块边沿呈绒状，半透明，有向四周漫延的趋势	釉表面通常只见釉损处，釉损处有量变特征，不见絮状斑				
				在破损处（如坑点斑、釉裂纹等）周围釉下，絮状斑呈梯度扩散状					

（续表）

后天风化迹型	反映量变原理的迹型特征		反映时间过程性原理的迹型特征		反映迹型出现位置合理性的迹型特征		反映迹型变化同步性的迹型特征	
迹型种类	二维成像	三维成像	二维成像	三维成像	二维成像	三维成像	二维成像	三维成像
CO纹	单位图片内的CO纹粗细及大小都不一致，彼此清晰独立		有C形、O形纹伴生（见CO型坑点斑部分）	见CO型坑点斑部分				
	CO纹纤细		与色变泡或壁变泡伴生	见色变泡及壁变泡部分				
	C形纹有清晰分叉	C形纹精致收敛，分叉清晰	周围釉下有絮状斑	釉表面通常只见CO纹，CO纹有量变特征，不见絮状斑				
	单项C形或O形纹上有色阶变化							
	单位图片中多个CO纹有色差变化							
	与周围玻璃相界线分明							
	与周围其他迹型各自独立，界线分明							
	周围玻璃相干净清晰	周围玻璃相光滑洁净						
釉裂纹	釉裂纹本身及其周边釉下颜色与周围色变泡及壁变泡有差异	釉裂纹周围釉表面光滑洁净	釉裂纹周围釉下出现絮状斑	釉表面只见釉裂纹，不见絮状斑				
	釉裂纹本身及其周边釉下未变色或变色不明显，但釉裂纹周边出现零星色变泡或壁变泡	釉裂纹周围釉表面光滑洁净						

（续表）

后天风化迹型	反映量变原理的迹型特征		反映时间过程性原理的迹型特征		反映迹型出现位置合理性的迹型特征		反映迹型变化同步性的迹型特征	
迹型种类	二维成像	三维成像	二维成像	三维成像	二维成像	三维成像	二维成像	三维成像
划痕	单位图片内：形貌方向不一致，粗细长短不一致，有交叉	划痕边沿圆滑，与玻璃相界线分明，面积小于或等于二维面积	划痕所在处釉下有絮状斑	釉表面只见划痕，不见絮状斑				
	有“牛毛纹”划痕	划痕边沿圆滑，面积小于或等于二维面积	划痕内部有针眼斑	划痕内部粗糙				
	有“蜈蚣”划痕	“蜈蚣”的“足”清晰可见，彼此独立，面积小于或等于二维面积	划痕有部分与沙滩斑重叠，被沙滩斑上的针眼斑覆盖					
	单项划痕上有色阶变化							
	单位图片中各个划痕有色差变化							
	与周围玻璃相界线分明							
	与周围其他迹型各自独立，界线分明							
	周围玻璃相干净清晰	周围玻璃相光滑洁净						

（续表）

后天风化迹型			反映量变原理的迹型特征		反映时间过程性原理的迹型特征		反映迹型出现位置合理性的迹型特征		反映迹型变化同步性的迹型特征	
迹型种类			二维成像	三维成像	二维成像	三维成像	二维成像	三维成像	二维成像	三维成像
气泡	色变泡		单项色变泡中有色阶变化	色变泡所在处釉表面通道不明显						
			单位图片中多个色变泡有色差变化	色变泡所在处釉表面有一个或多个明显通道，通道收敛，清晰独立，且与周围迹型界线分明						
			色变泡上可明显观察到颜色较深的色块（即通道所在处）							
			周围玻璃相干净清晰	周围玻璃相光滑洁净						
	壁变泡	雾状非破口壁变泡	雾状针眼斑均匀细腻	气泡所在处釉表面通道不明显						
			单项壁变泡中有色阶变化	气泡所在处釉表面有一个或多个明显通道，通道收敛，清晰独立，且与周围迹型界线分明						
			单位图片中多个壁变泡有色差变化							
			周围玻璃相干净清晰	周围玻璃相光滑洁净						
		磨砂非破口壁变泡	单项壁变泡中有色阶变化	气泡所在处釉表面通道不明显						
				气泡所在处釉表面有颜色变化，是由釉层中透出来的。颜色与壁变泡二维成像颜色相近，但显得更淡。颜色变化面积小于气泡最大直径						
			单位图片中多个壁变泡有色差变化							
			气泡内的物质有堆积感，有时斑块之间可见玻璃相	气泡釉表面有一个或多个明显通道，通道收敛，清晰独立，且与周围迹型界线分明						
			周围玻璃相干净清晰	周围玻璃相光滑洁净						

（续表）

后天风化迹型			反映量变原理的迹型特征		反映时间过程性原理的迹型特征		反映迹型出现位置合理性的迹型特征		反映迹型变化同步性的迹型特征	
迹型种类			二维成像	三维成像	二维成像	三维成像	二维成像	三维成像	二维成像	三维成像
气泡	壁变泡	颗粒非破口壁变泡	单项壁变泡中有色阶变化	气泡所在处釉表面通道不明显						
			单位图片中多个壁变泡有色差变化	气泡所在处釉表面有颜色变化，是由釉层中透出来的。颜色与壁变泡二维成像颜色相近，但显得更淡。颜色变化面积小于气泡最大直径						
			气泡内风化颗粒不在同一平面上							
			气泡内物质有堆积感，有时斑块之间可见玻璃相	气泡所在处釉表面有一个或多个明显通道，通道收敛，清晰独立，且与周围迹型界线分明						
		破口壁变泡	破口圆滑，接近正圆	气泡所在处釉表面除破口外无其他明显通道，破口清晰独立，与周围迹型界线分明						
			破口下方可见块状物质存在							
			气泡内壁风化情况可参考非破口壁变泡情况	气泡所在处釉表面除破口外还可见其余通道，但彼此各自独立分明，与周围迹型界线分明						
			周围玻璃相干净清晰	周围玻璃相光滑洁净						

Table 10-1-1

Reflects YUB Materials and Techniques			Reflects Quantitative Change Principle		Reflects Passage of Time Principle		Reflects Trace Location Rationality		Reflects Trace Change Congruency	
Innate Trace Category			2D Image	3D Image	2D Image	3D Image	2D Image	3D Image	2D Image	3D Image
Flowing Mottles	Beach Mottles	Flame Shape & Lotus Leaf Shape	Color Spectrum	Light to dark color gradation		Beach mottle is depressed, clear height discrepancy with glaze openings				
			Glaze openings on the beach mottle are clean and clear, delineated from surrounding beach mottle							
			Surrounding glass phase is clean and clear	Surrounding glaze surface is smooth and clean						
			Mutually independent from surrounding traces, clearly delineated							
Radiating Mottles	White Series									
	Red Series		Clearly visible boundary, clear color spectrum	Clearly defined border						
			Surrounding glass phase is clean and clear	Surrounding glaze surface is smooth and clean						
			Mutually independent from surrounding traces, clearly delineated							
	Yellow Series		Clearly visible boundary	Surrounding glaze surface is smooth and clean						
			Mottle and other split phases mutually independent, clearly delineated	Mottle is below the glaze suface, which is smooth and clean, surface split phases are clearly independent						
			Surrounded by a fine lined border	Mottle has height discrepency with surrounding glaze surface						
			Glass phase within and outside the border is clear and clean	Glaze surface within and outside the border is smooth and clean						
			Surrounding glass phase is clean and clear	Surrounding glaze surface is smooth and clean						
			Mutually independent from surrounding traces, clearly delineated							

(Continued)

Reflects YUB Materials and Techniques		Reflects Quantitative Change Principle		Reflects Passage of Time Principle		Reflects Trace Location Rationality		Reflects Trace Change Congruency	
Innate Trace Category		2D Image	3D Image	2D Image	3D Image	2D Image	3D Image	2D Image	3D Image
Radiating Mottles	Brown Series	Clearly visible boundary	Some surfaces are grainy; some striated, but generally smooth and refined						
		Surrounded by a fine lined border	Mottle has height discrepency with surrounding glaze surface						
		Glass phase within and outside the border is clear and clean	Glaze surface within and outside the border is smooth and clean						
		Surrounding glass phase is clean and clear	Surrounding glaze surface is smooth and clean						
		Mutually independent from surrounding traces, clearly delineated							
		Mottle and other split phases mutually independent, clearly delineated	Mottle is on the glaze surface, other split phases mutually independent, clearly delineated						
	Black Series	Clearly visible boundary	Presenting within the glaze level, the glaze surface is smooth and clean						
			Presenting on the glaze surface with clearly visible boundary						

(Continued)

Reflects YUB Materials and Techniques			Reflects Quantitative Change Principle		Reflects Passage of Time Principle		Reflects Trace Location Rationality		Reflects Trace Change Congruency	
Innate Trace Category			2D Image	3D Image	2D Image	3D Image	2D Image	3D Image	2D Image	3D Image
Flowing Striae	Depressed Striae	Empty Striae	Striae border clear and refined	Shallow W shaped striae interior is clean and matte						
			Striae interior has clear single or multi-line, continuous or intermittent fine line	Deep W shaped striae interior is intermittently reflective						
			Surrounding glass phase is clean and clear	Surrounding glaze surface is smooth and clean						
			Mutually independent from surrounding traces, clearly delineated							
		Needlepoint Striae	Densly filled needlepoint mottling in U shaped striae interior, with white or orange color spectrum	U shaped striae is coarse, interior presents with grainy materials with white, purple, and orange spectrum		U shaped striae have a certain depth and width			Densly filled needlepoint mottling in U shaped striae interior	U shaped striae have a certain depth and width, interior presents with weathering materials and color spectrum
			U shaped striae clearly delineated from surrounding glass phase, which is clear and clean	U shaped striae edges are rounded, clearly delineated from surrounding glaze surface, which is smooth and clean						
			U shaped striae clearly delineated from surrounding beach mottle; the beach mottle has quantitative change characteristics			U shaped striae are depressed into beach mottle and have a clear height discrepancy				
			V shaped striae needlepoint mottling has gradual dispersion onto the surrouding glass phase, the gradation is gradual	3D needlepoint mottling smaller than or the same as 2D image						
			Mutually independent from surrounding traces, clearly delineated							

(Continued)

<table>
<tr><th colspan="2">Reflects YUB Materials and Techniques</th><th colspan="2">Reflects Quantitative Change Principle</th><th colspan="2">Reflects Passage of Time Principle</th><th colspan="2">Reflects Trace Location Rationality</th><th colspan="2">Reflects Trace Change Congruency</th></tr>
<tr><th colspan="2">Innate Trace Category</th><th>2D Image</th><th>3D Image</th><th>2D Image</th><th>3D Image</th><th>2D Image</th><th>3D Image</th><th>2D Image</th><th>3D Image</th></tr>
<tr><td rowspan="3">Flowing Striae</td><td rowspan="3">Rasied Striae</td><td>Thick striae present with saw-like border</td><td>Thick striae present with saw-like border, smooth with striated surface</td><td></td><td></td><td colspan="2" rowspan="3"></td><td colspan="2" rowspan="3"></td></tr>
<tr><td>Striae clearly delineated from needlepoint mottling on the beach mottle</td><td>Striae and surrounding beach mottle clearly delineated</td><td></td><td>Striae higher than surrounding beach mottle</td></tr>
<tr><td></td><td>Frosted needlepoint mottling presents as independent pin points on the beach mottle surrounding the striae</td><td colspan="2"></td></tr>
<tr><td rowspan="2">Glass Phase</td><td>Glass phase is clean and clear</td><td colspan="2" rowspan="5"></td><td colspan="2" rowspan="2"></td><td colspan="2" rowspan="2"></td><td colspan="2" rowspan="2"></td></tr>
<tr><td>Intermittent clear and foggy patches</td></tr>
<tr><td>Independent Large Bubbles</td><td>Appear sparsely but in groups of two or three</td><td colspan="2"></td><td colspan="2"></td><td colspan="2"></td></tr>
<tr><td>Bubble Size Disparity</td><td>Bubble size relatively disparate</td><td colspan="2"></td><td colspan="2"></td><td colspan="2"></td></tr>
<tr><td>Bubble Dispursement</td><td>Sparse dispursement, rarely relatively dense</td><td colspan="2"></td><td colspan="2"></td><td colspan="2"></td></tr>
</table>

(Continued)

Reflects YUB Materials and Techniques	Reflects Quantitative Change Principle		Reflects Passage of Time Principle		Reflects Trace Location Rationality		Reflects Trace Change Congruency	
Innate Trace Category	2D Image	3D Image	2D Image	3D Image	2D Image	3D Image	2D Image	3D Image
Bristle Pits	Color changed around mouth		Associated under the glaze floccus mottles					
	Charcoal black around mouth		Associated under the glaze color change or textured bubbles					
	Mouth presents with filaments or granulated materials		Internal material granules larger than the pit mouth					
	Internal needlepoint mottling		Multiple types of internal deposits					
	Internal coloration							
	Filaments have color spectrum							
	Filaments have girth disparity, multi-directional							
	Surrounding glass phase is matted with relatively low refelctivity							

(Continued)

Acquired Traces			Reflects Quantitative Change Principle		Reflects Passage of Time Principle		Reflects Trace Location Rationality		Reflects Trace Change Congruency	
Trace Categories			2D Image	3D Image	2D Image	3D Image	2D Image	3D Image	2D Image	3D Image
Needlepoint Mottles	On Flowing Mottles	Foggy	Density disparity, even and fine				Presents at the border of beach mottle and glass phase		Density disparity, even and fine	
		Frosted	Some places dense, some places sparse, strong border feel	Dense independent pin point distribution, clearly defined border			Presents within the center of the beach mottle		Some places dense, some places sparse, strong border feel	Dense independent pin point distribution, clearly defined border
		Grainy	Independent grains, glass phase presents between grains, mutually delineated	Independent pits, glaze surface presents between pits, mutually delineated					Independent grains, glass phase present between grains, mutually delineated	Independent pits, glaze surface presents between pits, mutually delineated
	On Radiating Mottles	Frosted	Dispersed within radiating mottle border, strong border feel	Independent pin points, strong border feel			Presents within the radiating mottle that are on the glaze surface			
	On Glass Phase	Grainy	Clearly independent, delineated from surrounding glass phase				Presents on blue dye area or ioding mottle, does not exceed the border			
			Fine borders							

(Continued)

Acquired Traces		Reflects Quantitative Change Principle		Reflects Passage of Time Principle		Reflects Trace Location Rationality		Reflects Trace Change Congruency	
Trace Categories		2D Image	3D Image	2D Image	3D Image	2D Image	3D Image	2D Image	3D Image
Pit Mottles	CO Type Pit Mottles	Clearly delineated from the glass phase	Clearly delineated from the glaze surface	In association with CO striae	Fine CO stirae clearly visble on the glaze surface		Present on areas of raised glaze		
		Mutually independent from surrounding traces, clearly delineated		Size and depth disparate pit mottles or pit mottle group	Aside from CO striae, pits with smaller area than 2D image visible		Surrounding glaze level smooth and clean		
		Surrounding glass phase is clean and clear	Surrounding glaze surface is smooth and clean		Visible weathered mottles with smaller area than 2D image				
				Clearly delineated CO stirae, CO pits, and pit groups within a unit image					
				In association with color change or textured bubbles	See color change and textured bubbles				
				In assosiction with under the glaze floccus mottle	Pit has quantitative change characteristics, floccus mottle not visible				

(Continued)

Acquired Traces		Reflects Quantitative Change Principle		Reflects Passage of Time Principle		Reflects Trace Location Rationality		Reflects Trace Change Congruency	
Trace Categories		2D Image	3D Image	2D Image	3D Image	2D Image	3D Image	2D Image	3D Image
Pit Mottles	Needlepoint Type Pit Mottles	Has fine lined border, interior has independent needlepoint mottles	Independent pits, size smaller or the same as 2D image						
		Has fine lined border, Interior without needlepoint mottles							
		Completely filled and not transparent, no border							
		Clearly delineated from the glass phase	Clearly delineated from the glaze surface						
		Mutually independent from surrounding traces, clearly delineated							
		Surrounding glass phase is clean and clear	Surrounding glaze surface is smooth and clean						

(Continued)

Acquired Traces		Reflects Quantitative Change Principle		Reflects Passage of Time Principle		Reflects Trace Location Rationality		Reflects Trace Change Congruency	
Trace Categories		2D Image	3D Image	2D Image	3D Image	2D Image	3D Image	2D Image	3D Image
Pit Mottles	Damage Type Pit Mottles	Color Spectrum		Visible needlepoint mottling and material deposits					
	Underwater Type Pit Mottles	Presents with disconnected semi-circles	Independent half sphere pits, smooth edges						
		Some have frosted needlepoint mottling within the pit mottle	Independent pits with coarse interior and rounded edges			Needlepoint mottling does not exceed boundary of pit mottle			
		Clearly delineated from the glass phase	Clearly delineated from the glaze surface						
		Mutually independent from surrounding traces, clearly delineated							
		Surrounding glass phase is clean and clear	Surrounding glaze surface is smooth and clean						

(Continued)

Acquired Traces	Reflects Quantitative Change Principle		Reflects Passage of Time Principle		Reflects Trace Location Rationality		Reflects Trace Change Congruency	
Trace Categories	2D Image	3D Image	2D Image	3D Image	2D Image	3D Image	2D Image	3D Image
Bubble Roots	Color spectrum within single root		Larger roots present with multiple deposits and color spectrum					
	Bubble root color disparity within a unit image							
	Clearly delineated from the glass phase	Clearly delineated from the glaze surface						
	Mutually independent from surrounding traces, clearly delineated	Mutually independent from surrounding traces, clearly delineated						
Floccus Mottles		Area surrounding glaze flaw smooth and clean, no other large glaze flaws	The center of the mottle is non-transparent and milky white, and the edges feather out like goose down	Only glaze flaw visible on the glaze surface and has quantitative change characteristics, floccus mottle not visible				
			Floccus mottle disperses out and into the glaze level surrounding the glaze flaw (i.e. pits, cracks)					

(Continued)

Acquired Traces	Reflects Quantitative Change Principle		Reflects Passage of Time Principle		Reflects Trace Location Rationality		Reflects Trace Change Congruency	
Trace Categories	2D Image	3D Image	2D Image	3D Image	2D Image	3D Image	2D Image	3D Image
CO Striae	Clearly delineated CO stirae with width and size disparity within a unit image		In association with CO style pits (See CO Type Pit section)	See CO Type Pit section				
	CO Striae thin and refined	CO Striae thin and refined	In association with color change or textured bubbles	See color change and textured bubbles				
	C striae have clear split ends	C striation is reserved, split clear	In association with under the glaze floccus mottling	CO striae presents with quantitative change characteristics, floccus mottle not visible				
	Color spectrum on a single C or O striation							
	Color dispraity within unit image							
	Clearly delineated from the glass phase	Clearly delineated from the glaze surface						
	Mutually independent from surrounding traces, clearly delineated							
	Surrounding glass phase is clean and clear	Surrounding glaze surface is smooth and clean						

(Continued)

Acquired Traces	Reflects Quantitative Change Principle		Reflects Passage of Time Principle		Reflects Trace Location Rationality		Reflects Trace Change Congruency	
Trace Categories	2D Image	3D Image	2D Image	3D Image	2D Image	3D Image	2D Image	3D Image
Glaze Cracks	Coloration of glaze crack and associated color change or textured bubbles is disparate	Surrounding glaze surface is smooth and clean	In association with under the glaze floccus mottling	Only crack visible, floccus mottle not visible				
	Coloration of glaze crack and associated color change under the glaze is not present, but surrounding color change or textured bubbles are present	Surrounding glaze surface is smooth and clean						
Scratches	Direction width and length disparity, intersecting scratches within unit image	Scratch edge is rounded and smooth, clearly delineated from surrounding glaze surface, area smaller or same as 2D image	In association with under the glaze floccus mottling	Only scratch visible, floccus mottle not visible				
	"Ox Hair" Scratches present	Scratch edge is rounded and smooth, area smaller or same as 2D image	Scratch interior has needlepoint mottling	Scratch interior coarse				
	"Centipede" Scratches present	"Centipede" feet are visible, clearly independent, area smaller or same as 2D image	In areas of scratches intersecting beach mottle, beach mottle covers over scratch					
	Color spectrum within a single scratch							
	Color dispraity within unit image							

(Continued)

Acquired Traces	Reflects Quantitative Change Principle		Reflects Passage of Time Principle		Reflects Trace Location Rationality		Reflects Trace Change Congruency	
Trace Categories	2D Image	3D Image	2D Image	3D Image	2D Image	3D Image	2D Image	3D Image
Scratches	Clearly delineated from the glass phase	Clearly delineated from the glaze surface						
	Mutually independent from surrounding traces, clearly delineated							
	Surrounding glass phase is clean and clear	Surrounding glaze surface is smooth and clean						

(Continued)

Acquired Traces		Reflects Quantitative Change Principle		Reflects Passage of Time Principle		Reflects Trace Location Rationality		Reflects Trace Change Congruency	
Trace Categories		2D Image	3D Image	2D Image	3D Image	2D Image	3D Image	2D Image	3D Image
Air Bubbles	Color Change Bubbles	Color spectrum within a single bubble	Coloration channel not clear						
		Color disparity amongst bubbles within unit image	One or several clear channels which are reserved, clearly independent from the surrounding glaze surface						
		Clearly observable areas of darker coloration (Coloration channel)							
		Surrounding glass phase is clean and clear	Surrounding glaze surface is smooth and clean						

(Continued)

Acquired Traces			Reflects Quantitative Change Principle		Reflects Passage of Time Principle		Reflects Trace Location Rationality		Reflects Trace Change Congruency	
Trace Categories			2D Image	3D Image	2D Image	3D Image	2D Image	3D Image	2D Image	3D Image
Air Bubbles	Textured Bubbles	Foggy Unbroken Mouth Textured Bubbles	Needlepoint mottling evenly distributed and fine	Coloration channel not clear						
			Color spectrum within a single bubble	One or several clear channels which are reserved, clearly independent from the surrounding glaze surface						
			Color disparity amongst bubbles within unit image							
			Surrounding glass phase is clean and clear	Surrounding glaze surface is smooth and clean						
		Frosted Unbroken Mouth Textured Bubbles	Color spectrum within a single bubble	Coloration channel not clear						
				Coloration present is from within bubble, similar to 2D image, but lighter. Coloration area smaller than bubble area.						
			Color disparity amongst bubbles within unit image							
			Bubble interior has deposited materials, some have color spectrum, glass phase visible at some points	One or several clear channels which are reserved, clearly independent, and delineated from the surrounding traces						
			Surrounding glass phase is clean and clear	Surrounding glaze surface is smooth and clean						

(Continued)

Acquired Traces			Reflects Quantitative Change Principle		Reflects Passage of Time Principle		Reflects Trace Location Rationality		Reflects Trace Change Congruency	
Trace Categories			2D Image	3D Image	2D Image	3D Image	2D Image	3D Image	2D Image	3D Image
Air Bubbles	Textured Bubbles	Grainy Unbroken Mouth Textured Bubbles	Color spectrum within a single bubble	Coloration channel not clear						
			Color disparity amongst bubbles within unit image	Coloration present is from within bubble, similar to 2D image, but lighter. Coloration area smaller than bubble area.						
			Weathered granules within the bubble occur at different levels	One or several clear channels which are reserved, clearly independent, and delineated from the surrounding glaze surface						
			Bubble interior has deposited materials, some have color spectrum, glass phase visible at some points							

(Continued)

Acquired Traces			Reflects Quantitative Change Principle		Reflects Passage of Time Principle		Reflects Trace Location Rationality		Reflects Trace Change Congruency	
Trace Categories			2D Image	3D Image	2D Image	3D Image	2D Image	3D Image	2D Image	3D Image
Air Bubbles	Textured Bubbles	Broken Mouth Textured Bubbles	Mouth is smooth, almost a perfect circle	No visible channels aside from the bubble mouth, mouth is clearly independent and delineated from surrounding traces						
			Material deposits visible beneath bubble mouth							
			For internal weathering characteristics see Unbroken Mouth Textured Bubbles	Visible channels aside from the bubble mouth present, but they are mutually independent and delineated from surrounding traces						
			Surrounding glass phase is clean and clear	Surrounding glaze surface is smooth and clean						

第二节
元青花迹型物证鉴定操作

一、迹型观察记录

（一）全面扫描记录

在获取被鉴定器物迹型图片时，无论是整器或残片，都要求对其整个面积进行全方位扫描式观察记录。

从口沿、器身至器底，不要遗漏，同时要做好观察不同部位的标记记录。被鉴定陶瓷，只要观察工具能够做到，都要进行观察。所以，鉴定观察的过程是全向扫描，尽量做到无死角的观察记录。

全向扫描法就是利用500倍的数码显微镜，快速对被鉴定器物按由上至下、由里至外的顺序全面扫视，拍摄记录器物上各种迹型种类（斑块、纹路、气泡、鬃眼等）的图片。全面扫描记录后，能够让我们大致了解器物的整体迹型现象是否具备元代青花瓷的普遍性，做到心中有数。

（二）重点记录

重点记录就是对一些典型迹型进一步归类遴选，建构被鉴定器物的显微图谱模型，以便接下来与元青花标准图谱模型进行比对。

在对被鉴定器物全向扫描记录的基础上，对某些需要更仔细、深入观察比较的迹型种类，可以重点记录，就是拍摄记录多张该迹型种类不同位置、不同表现的二维成像及三维成像图片，以获取翔实的数据和迹型特征。同时也要留意该迹型出现的位置与其各迹型特征之间的联系。

二、迹型形成本质论证

在完成迹型比对后，还要完成迹型本质的逻辑论证。论证时可从以下七个方面行论证：

（一）被鉴定器物迹型现象是否与图谱一样反映了当时的制瓷用材及烧制工艺；

（二）被鉴定器物上后天性迹型的多样性；

（三）被鉴定器物上迹型的变化是否具有同步性；

（四）被鉴定器物上迹型出现的位置是否具有合理性；

（五）被鉴定器物迹型现象是否具有量变特征；

（六）被鉴定器物迹型现象是否能够反映时间过程性原理；

（七）被鉴定器物迹型现象是否体现了迹型形成与发展的诸规律。

Section 2:
Yuan Underglaze Blue Trace Model Material Evidence Authentication Operation

1. Trace Recording Process

A. Comprehensive Scanning

Regardless of whether it is a complete ware or just a shard, a full-scan observation record of the entire piece needs to be completed when collecting images for authentication.

We need comprehensive scanning from the mouth, to the body, and down to the foot; meanwhile taking observation recordings in the process. Simply put, any portion of the piece that is technically practical to do so, should undergo observation. As such, the authentication observation utilizes a holistic scanning technique in order to offer a complete observation record.

Currently, comprehensive scanning utilizes a 500X magnification digital microscope to effectively scan a ware from top to bottom, inside to outside, in a pre-determined flow, whilst taking image recordings of each type of trace (mottles, striae, bubbles, bristle pits, and so forth) on the piece. After comprehensive scanning and image recording, we can have a better, more general understanding as to whether or not the piece in question is in accordance with the typical characteristics of a YUB ware.

B. Emphasized Recording

Emphasized recording is essentially a more specific image taking process, with certain typical traces as the focus in order to construct a Trace Atlas Model for the piece in question that can be later compared against the YUB Standard Trace Atlas Model.

On the foundation of the comprehensive scan record, we can further develop imaging for trace categories that need specific attention or deeper observation (i.e. taking several images at different locations of a single trace type). This also includes two and three-dimensional corresponding imaging in order to offer more robust proof of the characteristics of a certain trace category.

At the same time, special attention can be paid to the location of traces and the inter-trace relationships.

2. Nature of Trace Proofs

After completing the Trace Comparison phase, it is time to move on to the Nature of Trace Proofs. Proofs need to be carried out from the following seven perspectives:

1. Do the traces reflect the same materials and techniques as the YUB Standard Trace Atlas Model?
2. Do the acquired traces present with multiplicity?
3. Do the trace changes occur with proper congruency?
4. Do the traces present in rational locations?
5. Do the traces have quantitative change characteristics?
6. Do the traces reflect the passage of time principle?
7. Do the traces embody the Ceramic Trace Laws?

三、元青花迹型分值统计

（一）元青花迹型分值设定

见表10-2-1。

表10-2-1

序号	迹型形成本质充分吻合理由	满分分值
1	符合元青花的用材及烧制工艺	10分
2	符合陶瓷迹型量变原理	20分
3	符合陶瓷迹型时间过程性原理	20分
4	具备元青花迹型普遍性特征及多样性特征	45分
5	具备陶瓷迹型出现位置的合理性特征（或迹型变化的同步性特征）	5分

（二）元青花迹型分值统计说明

1. 元青花的用材及烧制工艺

流淌斑、放射斑、团状斑、流淌纹、气泡大小及分布及玻璃相等先天性迹型现象，能够反映青花瓷器的原材料及烧制工艺。（具体迹型表现特征请参考表10-1-1。）

用以绘制元青花纹饰的青料与元青花上的流淌斑、放射斑、团状斑、流淌纹等迹型都有密切联系。

青料来自于钴土矿。钴土矿是长时间自然形成的，自然界钴土矿的化学成分并非是简单的混合。钴土矿各组分有部分会形成固溶体，在微观结构上如结点的形状及大小可能随成分的变化而改变，出现类质同象现象。同时，钴土矿中各组分的分布也不均匀。所以，用某个时代独特的钴土矿制成的青料绘制青花纹饰，在瓷器制成后，每一种钴土矿所表现出的迹型是独特的。元青花所用的钴土矿到现在已难以找到或已开采殆尽，所以它们表现出的迹型是难以复制的。

现代仿制的青料配方只是简单地将青料各组分混合，即使仿制做到了成分、含量相同，也难以完全还原元代时钴土矿的结构，因此现代配制青料所形成的迹型特征，仍会与真品迹型有差异。

如，被检器物上的先天性迹型与元青花迹型标准图谱高度相似，且本质吻合，即可获得迹型材料分值满分10分。

2. 陶瓷迹型量变原理

反映陶瓷迹型量变原理的迹型特征请参考表10-1-1。

在综合观察分析整件被检测器物上的所有迹型特征后，如该器物的综合迹型现象能够充分反映陶瓷量变原理，即可获得迹型量变分值满分20分。

3. 陶瓷迹型时间过程性原理

反映陶瓷迹型时间过程性原理的迹型特征请参考表10-1-1。

在综合观察分析整件被检测器物上的所有迹型特征后，如该器物的综合迹型现象能够充分反映陶瓷时间过程性原理，即可获得迹型时间过程性分值满分20分。

4. 元青花迹型普遍性特征及多样性特征

元青花的后天性迹型总共有九种：针眼斑、坑点斑、泡根斑、絮状斑、CO纹、划痕、色变泡、壁变泡和多样性鬃眼。它们在标准图谱中的特征可参考表10-1-1。

每一种与元青花迹型标准图谱高度相似且本质吻合的后天性迹型均可获5分，如九种迹型都达标，则可获得迹型风化强度多样性分值满分45分。

5. 陶瓷迹型出现位置的合理性特征（迹型变化的同步性特征）

反映迹型出现位置合理性的迹型特征请参考表10-1-1。

反映迹型变化同步性的迹型特征请参考10-1-1。

在综合观察分析整件被检测器物上的所有迹型特征后，如该器物的综合迹型现象具有迹型出现位置的合理性或迹型变化的同步性，即可获得迹型合理性分值满分5分。

6. 小结

综上所述，被检测器物满分可获得100分，合格分数为70分。分值累积达到70分者，就可判定它为真品。在分数合格的器物中，并不是分数越高，真实性也越高，这里

3. YUB Trace Point System

A. YUB Trace Point Settings

See Table 10-2-1.

Table 10-2-1

Criteria	Nature of Trace Grounds for Full Match	Available
1	Matches YUB Materials and Techniques	10 Points
2	Matches Ceramic Trace Model Quantitative Change Principle	20 Points
3	Matches Ceramic Trace Model Passage of Time Principle	20 Points
4	Matches YUB Typical Characteristics and Multiplicity Characteristics	45 Points
5	Matches Ceramics Trace Location Rationality (or Proper Congruency)	5 Points

B. YUB Trace Grounds for Full Score Explanation

I. YUB Materials and Techniques

Flowing mottles, radiating mottles, blotch mottles, flowing striae, bubble size and distribution, glass phase, and so forth innate characteristics can reflect the materials and techniques used on YUB (for specific trace appearance characteristics see Table 10-1-1).

The dye used in applying the underglaze blue decoration has a direct impact on the formation of traces like flowing mottles, radiating mottles, blotch mottles and flowing striae.

The dye comes from Cobalt ores which are the product of years of natural formation processes. As such, natural cobalt ores do not have simple chemical compositions. Certain parts of each component of the ore can form solid solutions, creating changes to the molecular crystal structures within the compound. Additionally, the distribution of components throughout the ore is also irregular. Thus, the traces created during the firing of ceramic dyes from different periods throughout history obtain distinctive characteristics. Due to the differences in Cobalt ore compositions, the trace characteristics that each ore present have discrepancies. The exact ore used during the Yuan Dynasty is now unfeasibly found and mine deposits have been exhausted, thus their trace characteristics are extremely difficult to recreate.

Modern day forgeries are only able to recreate the basic chemical composition of the dyes in simplistic mixtures of the present components, and are unable to reduce the dyes back to the structure of Yuan Dynasty Cobalt ores. Thus, there are inherent differences in the trace characteristics of genuine pieces.

If the piece in question has the prescribed innate traces highly similar and with matching nature to those found on the YUB Standard Trace Atlas Model, 10 Points can be awarded.

II. Ceramic Trace Model Quantitative Change Principle

For the traces that reflect the quantitative change principle, please see Table 10-1-1.

After the comprehensive observation and analysis of all the trace characteristics on the entire piece have been completed, if the trace characteristics are able to fully reflect the quantitative change principle, the piece can be awarded 20 points.

III. Ceramic Trace Model Passage of Time Principle

For the traces that reflect the passage of time principle, please see Table 10-1-1.

After the comprehensive observation and analysis of all the trace characteristics on the entire piece have been completed, if the trace characteristics are found to fully reflect the passage of time principle, the piece can be awarded 20 points.

IV. YUB Typical Characteristics and Multiplicity Characteristics

There are a total of nine YUB acquired trace types: Needlepoint mottling, pit mottles, bubble roots, floccus mottles, CO striae, scratches, color change bubbles, textured bubbles, and bristle pits with multiplicity characteristics. For

的分值与其后天性迹型的多样性有关，后天性迹型种类越多，说明该器物风化强度越高，这与其所处的不同环境有关。

四、元青花迹型标准图谱模型的局限性

目前建构的元青花迹型标准图谱模型只能作为鉴定一部分元青花的比对标准，有一定局限性。

根据史料及文献的记载，元代时的景德镇地区是青花瓷器烧制的主要地区，但目前研究团队采集到的有明确发掘时间、地点和年代依据的标本，都未能证明它们出产的窑口。其中在景德镇市珠山区出土的元青花标本，我们只能推断它们很有可能是景德镇地区的窑口烧制的。而其余三个国家及地区出土的元青花标本，由于其迹型特征与形成本质都与景德镇市珠山区的标本迹型高度吻合，加上文献与史料的记载，我们推测它们很有可能都产自元代景德镇地区的窑口。

有的器物在反映用材及烧制工艺的迹型特征上与标准图谱不相似，但其后天性风化迹型却能够反映陶瓷迹型的基本原理和诸规律，这需要另一套物证系统去提供证明，目前这一套标准图谱模型尚不能证明这类器物的真实性。

五、总结

在实际鉴定操作时，绝不能因观察到少量与图谱相似的迹型就匆忙下“真品”的结论，一定要综合分析器物整体迹型现象和迹型之间的关系，根据瓷器迹型各方面的特征表现做出判断，这样才能减少失误，提高鉴定的准确率。

元青花迹型物证鉴定方法，是在传统眼学鉴定的基础上发展而来的。传统的眼学鉴定，是人本身对物的认识，而迹型的物证鉴定，是人借助科学仪器对物的认识。科学仪器延伸了人类的观察器官，提高了人类的认识能力，使得人们对元青花的鉴定从感性认识上升到了理性认识，从认识的低级阶段走向了认识的高级阶段，这也是社会与科技进步使然。

迹型物证方法比经验人证方法要进步，这是不容置疑的，但这仅仅说明迹型物证的方法对事物的认识更接近真实的判断，决不是说这种方法已经绝对证明了真实。任何证明都不可能做到百分之百。所以，我们决不能用形而上学的眼光将迹型物证鉴定的方法绝对化。

新的陶瓷迹型物证鉴定方法，是在眼学鉴定基础上的发展与优化。但是，科学的研究探索是无止境的，我们深信这种建立在学科基础上的迹型物证鉴定方法能够在未来陶瓷科学鉴定的路上走得更远！

their standard characteristics within the YUB Standard Trace Atlas Model please refer to table 10-1-1.

Each type that has a high similarity and matched nature with the YUB Standard Trace Atlas Model can earn 5 points, for a total composite score of 45 points.

V. Ceramics Trace Location Rationality (Proper Congruency)

For location rationality characteristics of the YUB Standard Trace Atlas Model Please refer to table 10-1-1.

For congruency characteristics of the YUB Standard Trace Atlas Model Please refer to table 10-1-1.

If traces occur with location rationality or with the proper trace congruency, 5 points can be awarded.

VI. Summary

The total available score for any authenticated piece is 100, with a score of 70 considered passing. Pieces that have achieved a score of 70 or above are deemed as authentic. This is not to say that for passing pieces that the higher the score, the more 'real' a piece is. This score is related to the multiplicity of the acquired traces of a piece, which is directly connected to its post-firing environment and the weathering severity it incurred.

4. YUB Standard Trace Atlas Model Limitations

Currently the YUB standard Trace Atlas Model can only be used in the comparative authentication of a certain number of YUB, and as such is inherently limited.

According to historical records, the Jingdezhen area during the Yuan Dynasty was the main production site for YUB. However, all the samples collected by our research team, with known excavation record and age, or of concrete provenance are yet to have their kiln origin proven. Amongst these samples, there were shards excavated in Zhushan District in Jingdezhen. We can assume that they are very likely to have come from kilns around the Jingdezhen area. However, for the rest of the samples from the three other countries and areas, due to the similarity of the characteristics and nature of their traces, we can only deduce that they were made in kilns in the Jingdezhen area during the Yuan Dynasty.

When innate traces show a piece's materials and techniques do not match the YUB Standard Trace Atlas Model, but the piece's acquired traces still do in fact reflect the Principles of Ceramics Trace Model Study and Ceramic Trace Laws, another material-evidence system to prove their authenticity is needed, this model is not suitable for authenticating such pieces.

5. Summary

During the process of testing this authentication method, it was found impractical to only include small amounts of atlas model-like images in order to hastily assign the conclusion "Authentic". It is imperative to comprehensively analyze the holistic trace characteristics and inter-trace relationships, in order to decrease error and improve authentication accuracy.

Trace Model Material Evidence Authentication of YUB has been developed on the foundation laid by experience-based authentication. Traditional experience-based authentication utilizes our own understanding of objects, while Trace Model Material Evidence Authentication utilizes the help of scientific instruments. Instruments that help to broaden our observation and heighten our understanding. This marks our movement from perceptual knowledge to conceptual knowledge in ceramic authentication, and a shift from low to high understanding, and is the result of societal and technological advancement.

Trace Model Material Evidence Authentication is an advancement on experience-based authentication. Though undeniable, this only highlights that material evidence-based authentication is getting closer to certainty; it does not mean that we have reached full assurance. No proof is able to attain 100% certainty, and as such we must be careful not to haplessly rest on our laurels in Trace Model Material Evidence Authentication.

Trace Model Material Evidence Authentication is the development and optimization based on the foundation of naked-eye authentication. However, scientific research is never ending, and we strongly believe that this new material evidence authentication method, rooted within science, can continue to develop and improve for many years to come.

附：青花天鹅莲池纹匜迹型物证鉴定报告

一、送检器物基本情况

（一） 送检器物名称：青花天鹅莲池纹匜。

（二） 送检器物尺寸：通高约4.7cm，底径约5.5cm，流长约2.5cm。

（三） 送检器物实图：

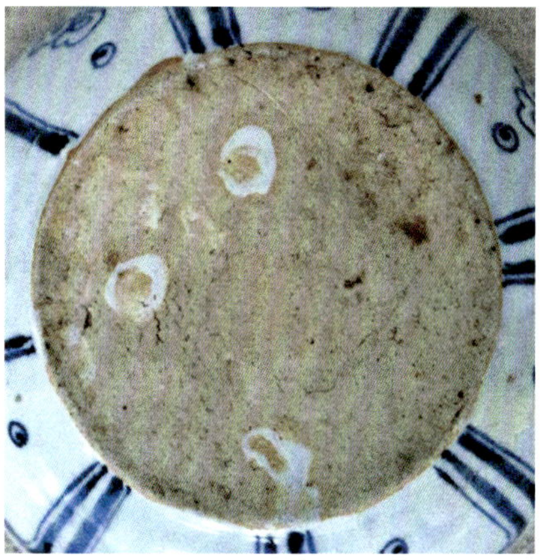

二、鉴定性质

迹型物证鉴定。

三、鉴定条件

（一）鉴定工具：500倍数码光学显微镜和其他辅助工具。

（二）鉴定指标：送检器物的斑块、纹路、气泡、鬃眼等迹型类别。

四、鉴定方法

（一）送检器物迹型现象与标准图谱模型比对

（二）送检器物迹型形成本质论证

五、鉴定操作流程

（一）送检器物全方位扫描检测
（二）送检器物重点区域检测
（三）送检器物迹型二维成像记录
（四）送检器物迹型三维成像记录

六、送检器物迹型与元青花迹型标准图谱模型比对

（一）流淌斑比对

送检器物流淌斑二维成像

检图1

标准图谱模型流淌斑二维成像

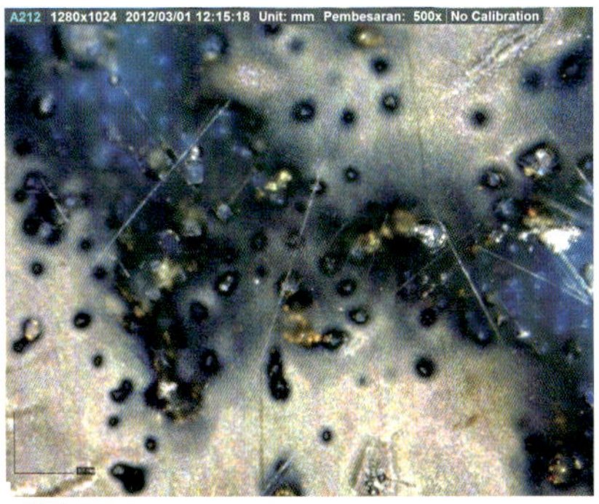

标图1

送检器物流淌斑三维成像

检图2

标准图谱模型流淌斑三维成像

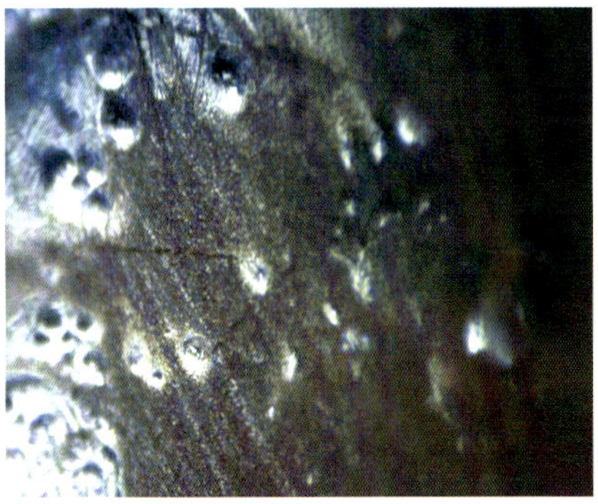

标图2

◆ 二维特征

见检图1。

1）送检器物的沙滩斑大部分属于荷叶形沙滩斑，斑块独立清晰。
2）沙滩斑中间不规则地分布有玻璃相圆孔，圆孔清晰独立，与周围沙滩斑界线分明。
3）沙滩斑周围玻璃相干净清晰，可见针眼斑和坑点斑随机零星分布。

◆ 三维特征

见检图2。

1）沙滩斑风化成凹陷的“洼地”，低于周围玻璃相。
2）玻璃相圆孔凸起，高于周围沙滩斑，圆孔表面光滑洁净，与周围沙滩斑界线分明。

◆ 迹型本质论证

1）送检器物上沙滩斑的表现特征与元青花迹型标准图谱模型上沙滩斑的表现特征高度相似，说明送检器物的用材及烧制工艺与元青花瓷器标本相符。
2）沙滩斑与玻璃相圆孔清晰的界线体现了陶瓷迹型的分明性规律。
3）沙滩斑与周围玻璃相的明显高度差体现了陶瓷迹型的层次性规律，符合陶瓷迹型的时间过程性原理。
4）沙滩斑周围玻璃相干净清晰，不见人为做旧的涂污痕迹。

（二）放射斑比对

1. 红色系放射斑

送检器物红色系放射斑二维成像

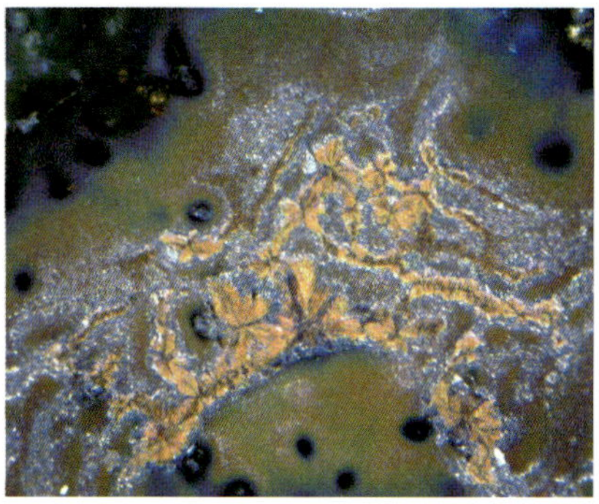

检图3

标准图谱模型红色系放射斑二维成像

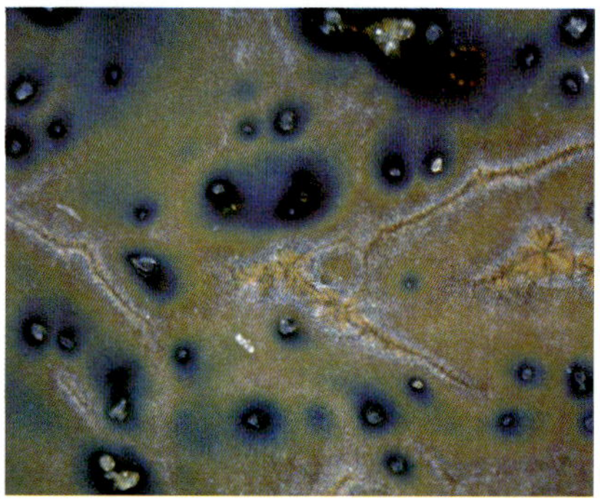

标图3

送检器物红色系放射斑三维成像

检图4

标准图谱模型红色系放射斑三维成像

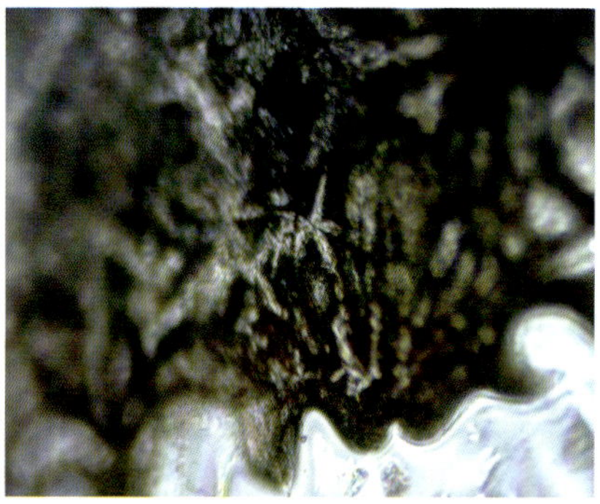

标图4

◆ 二维特征

见检图3。
1）红色系放射斑呈枫叶形状，颜色为橘黄色。
2）红色系放射斑与周围沙滩斑界线分明。

◆ 三维特征

见检图4。

1）红色系放射斑形状轮廓清晰可见。

2）红色系放射斑高于周围沙滩斑，二者界线分明。

◆ 迹型本质论证

1）送检器物的红色系放射斑与元青花迹型标准图谱模型上红色系放射斑的表现特征高度相似，说明送检器物的用材及烧制工艺与元青花瓷器标本相符。

2）红色系放射斑与沙滩斑清晰的界线体现了陶瓷迹型的分明性规律。

2. 黄色系及褐色系放射斑

送检器物黄色系及褐色系放射斑二维成像

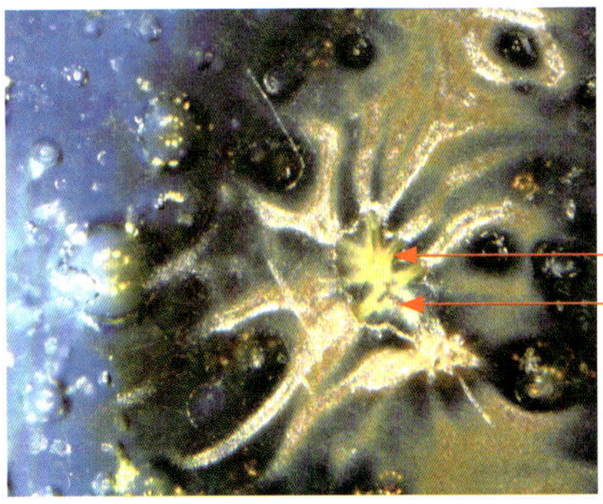

检图5

标准图谱模型黄色系及褐色系放射斑二维成像

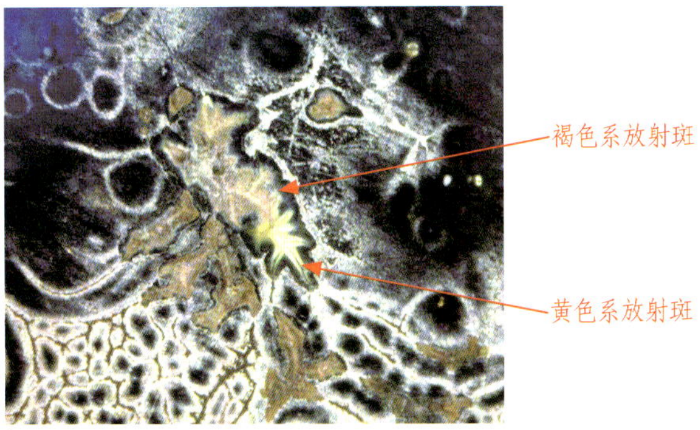

标图5

送检器物黄色系及褐色系放射斑三维成像

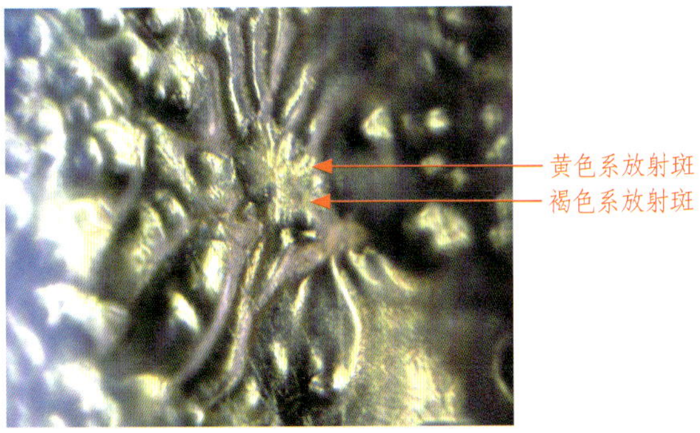

检图6

标准图谱模型黄色系及褐色系放射斑三维成像

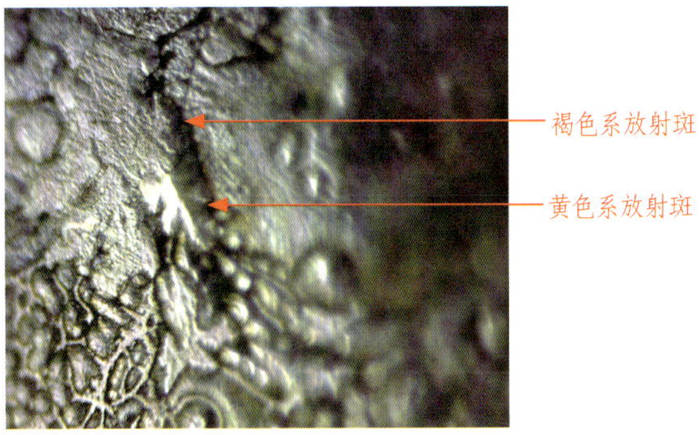

标图6

◆ 二维特征

见检图5。

1）黄色系放射斑呈不规则形状，颜色为鲜黄色。

2）褐色系放射斑呈不规则形状，颜色为咖啡色。

3）两种色系的放射斑均与周围迹型界线分明。

◆ 三维特征

见检图6。

1）黄色系放射斑位于釉层中，放射斑形状轮廓清晰可见，由于受釉层保护程度较高，所在釉表面较光滑，反光，且隐隐透着放射斑的黄色。
2）褐色系放射斑位于釉表面，受釉层保护程度较低，表面有细密纹路。

◆ 迹型本质论证

1）送检器物上黄色系及褐色系放射斑的表现特征与元青花迹型标准图谱模型上黄色系及褐色系放射斑的表现特征高度相似，说明送检器物的用材及烧制工艺与元青花瓷器标本相符。
2）黄色系及褐色系放射斑与周围迹型清晰的界线体现了陶瓷迹型的分明性规律。
3）黄色系与褐色系放射斑的三维成像特征具有量变特征，符合陶瓷迹型的量变原理。

（三）针眼斑比对

1. 雾状针眼斑

送检器物雾状针眼斑二维成像

检图7

标准图谱模型雾状针眼斑二维成像

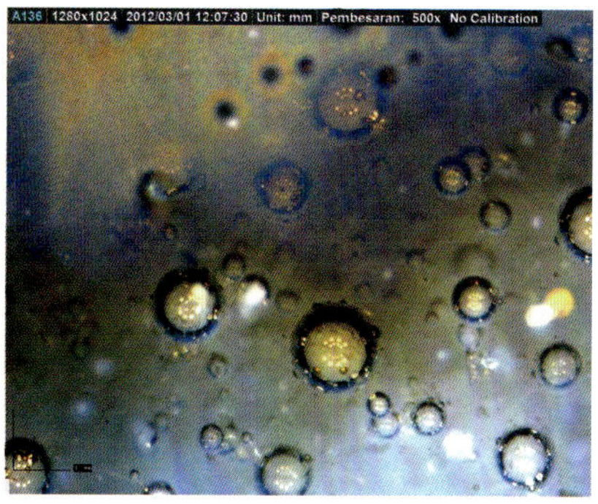

标图7

2. 磨砂针眼斑

送检器物磨砂针眼斑二维成像

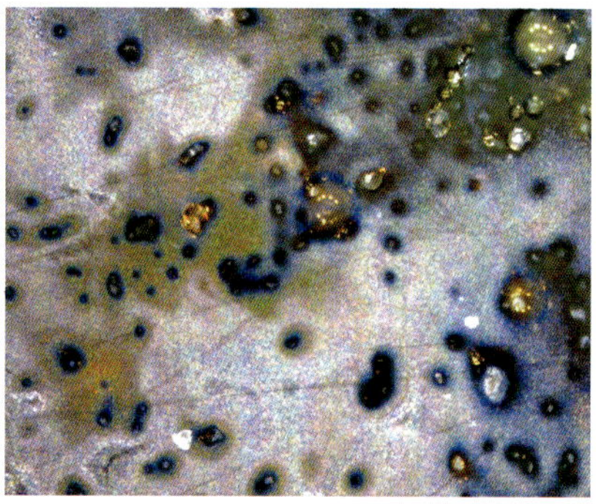

检图8

标准图谱模型磨砂针眼斑二维成像

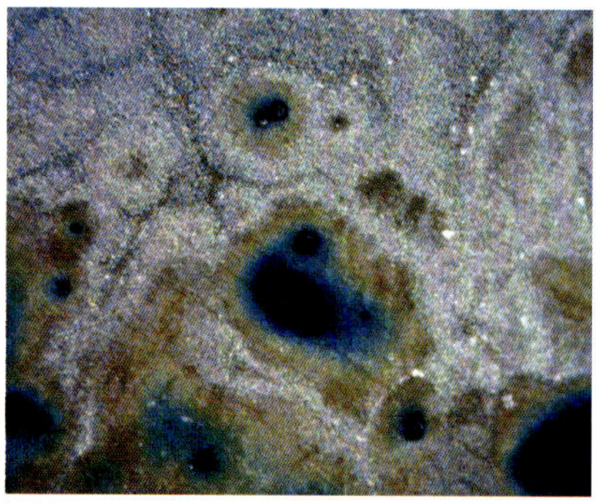

标图8

送检器物磨砂针眼斑三维成像

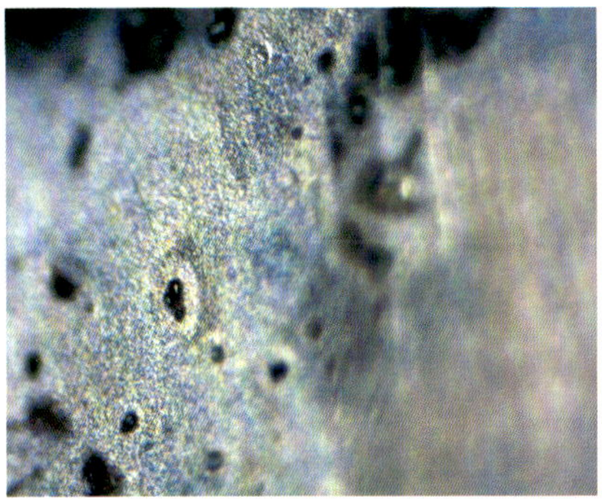

检图9

标准图谱模型磨砂针眼斑三维成像

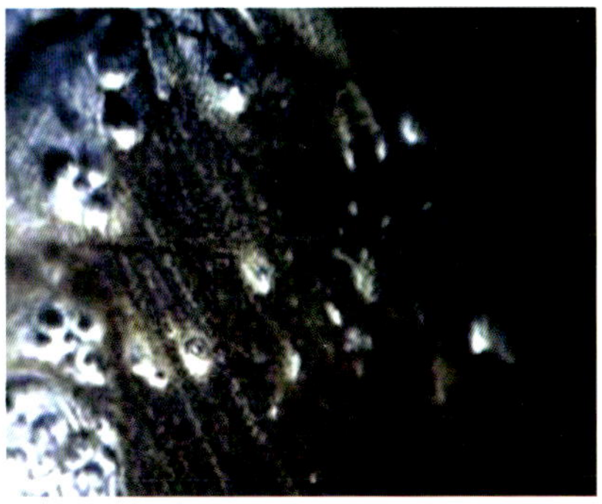

标图9

◆ 二维特征

1）沙滩斑边沿分布有雾状针眼斑，中心有磨砂针眼斑，二者皆清晰（见检图7）。
2）雾状针眼斑呈现由浓到淡的、均匀细腻的过渡（见检图7）。
3）磨砂针眼斑有明显的边界感，没有浓淡过渡，分布不均匀，分布稀疏处可见褐色沙滩斑（见检图8）。
4）有时针眼斑这种分布规律使沙滩斑产生三到四种明显的颜色变化：深褐色、深青色、浅褐色、白色（见检图7、检图8）。

◆ 三维特征

见检图9。
1）雾状针眼斑分布稀疏处三维成像特征不明显，与周围玻璃相过渡均匀。
2）磨砂针眼斑成像清晰，呈独立点状凹坑。

◆ 迹型本质论证

1）送检器物上针眼斑的表现特征与元青花迹型标准图谱模型上针眼斑的表现特征高度相似。
2）针眼斑的分布规律及表现特征是由于流淌斑受釉层保护的程度不一，导致各处风化强度有差异，这是陶瓷迹型层次性规律的体现。
3）针眼斑的分布及不同的表现形式使流淌斑产生色阶变化，体现了陶瓷迹型的色差规律。
4）针眼斑的分布规律及表现特征符合陶瓷迹型的量变原理，也具有迹型出现位置的合理性及迹型变化的同步性。

（四）坑点斑比对

1. CO型坑点斑

送检器物CO型坑点斑二维成像

标准图谱模型CO型坑点斑二维成像

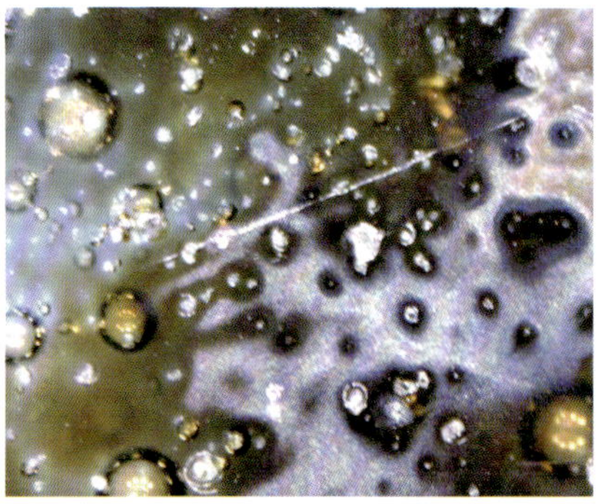
检图10

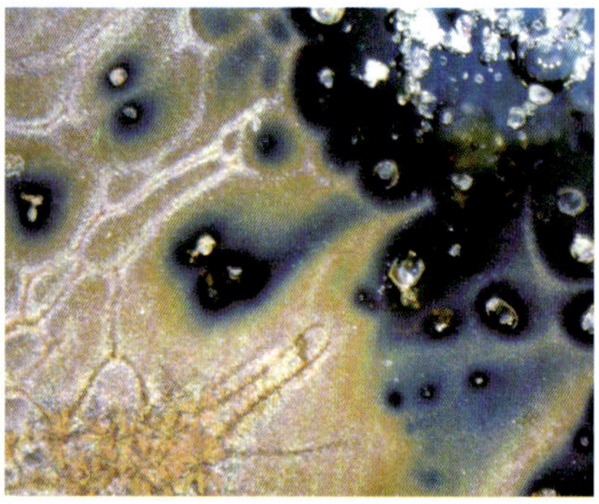
标图10

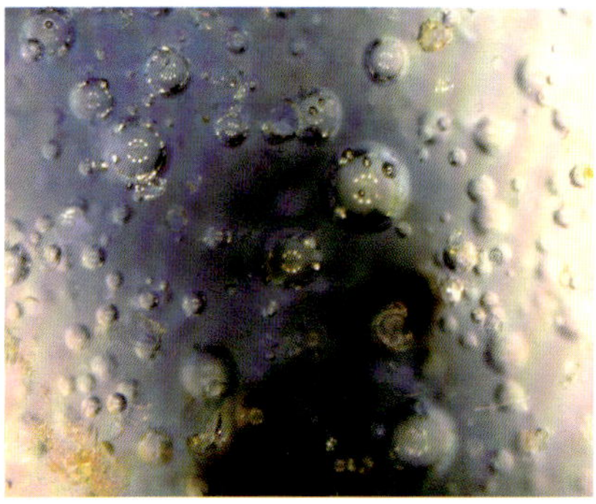
检图11

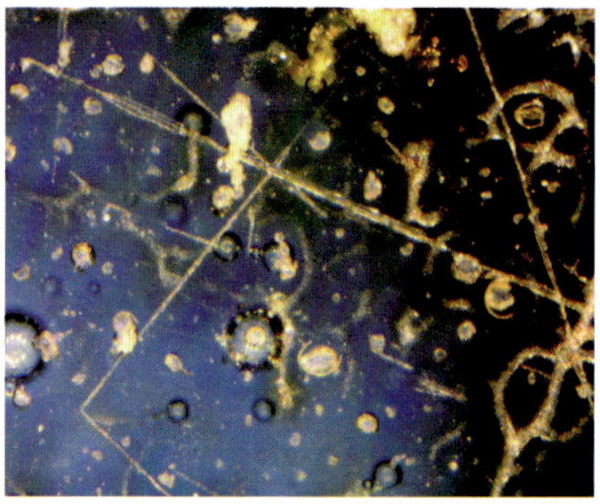
标图11

送检器物CO型坑点斑三维成像

标准图谱模型CO型坑点斑三维成像

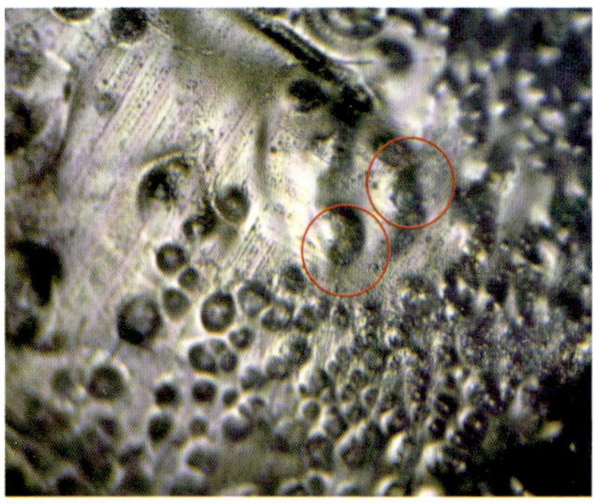
检图12

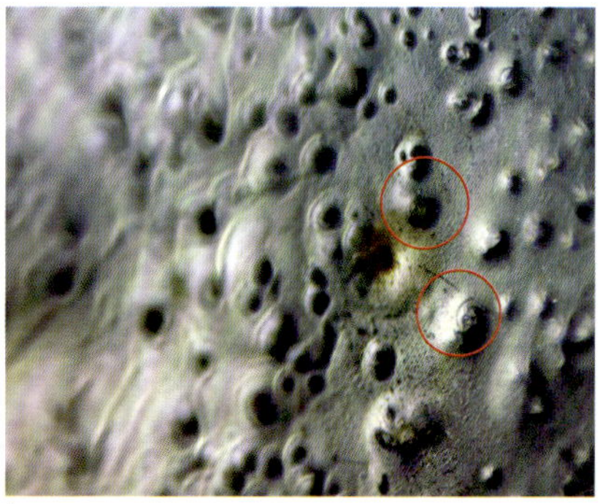
标图12

◆ 二维特征

见检图10、检图11。

1）CO型坑点斑大小不一，各个坑点斑之间距离不等。

2）CO型坑点斑独立清晰，与周围玻璃相界线分明。

3）可见坑点斑与CO纹伴生的现象：一是坑点斑与CO纹紧挨或邻近，二者界线清晰分明；二是坑点斑与CO纹重叠。

◆ 三维特征

见检图12。

1）CO型坑点斑大部分出现在釉表面凸起处。

2）CO型坑点斑所在处的釉表面只见纤细的C形纹，不见坑点斑，这是因为CO型坑点斑是C形纹纵向往釉层中发展的结果，坑点斑深入釉层，三维成像无法全面观察到深入釉层的坑点斑。

◆ 迹型本质论证

1）送检器物上CO型坑点斑的表现特征与元青花迹型标准图谱模型上CO型坑点斑的表现特征高度相似。

2）CO型坑点斑与CO纹半生的现象体现了从C形、O形纹发展成的坑点斑的时间过程，符合陶瓷迹型的时间过程性原理。

3）CO型坑点斑的表现特征符合陶瓷迹型的量变原理。

4）从存在于釉表面的C形、O形纹发展到深入釉层中的坑点斑，体现了陶瓷迹型的层次性规律。

5）CO型坑点斑具有迹型出现位置的合理性。

2. 针眼型坑点斑

送检器物针眼型坑点斑二维成像

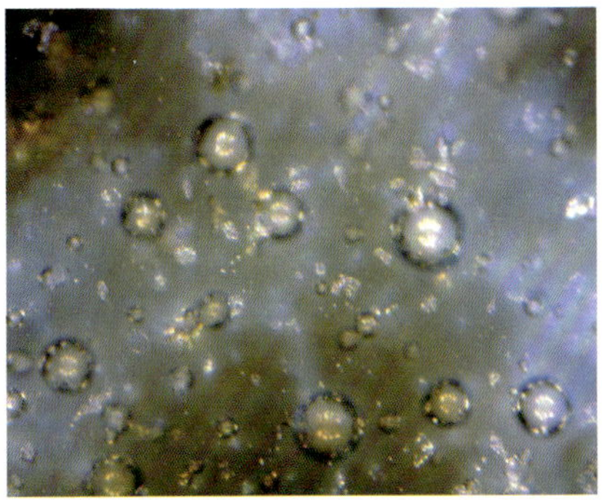

检图13

标准图谱模型针眼型坑点斑二维成像

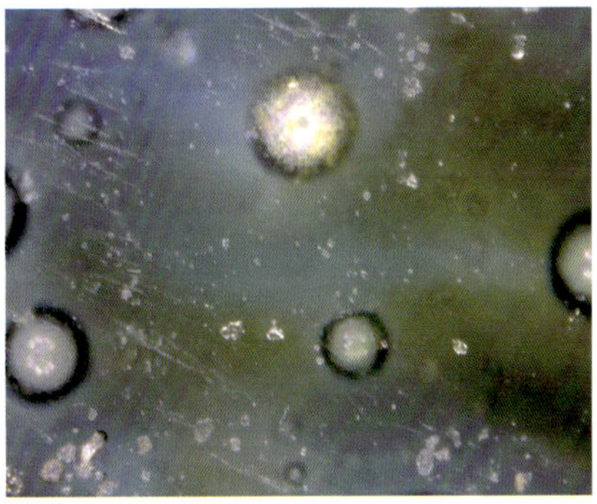

标图13

◆ 二维特征

见检图13。

1）针眼型坑点斑清晰独立，形状各异，大小不一。

2）针眼型坑点斑外沿有纤细的包边，斑内还可见针眼斑分布。

3）针眼型坑点斑与周围玻璃相界线分明。

◆ 迹型本质论证

1）送检器物上针眼型坑点斑的表现特征与元青花迹型标准图谱模型上针眼型坑点斑的表现特征高度相似。

2）针眼型坑点斑外沿清晰纤细的包边及斑内的针眼斑符合陶瓷迹型的量变原理。

（五）流淌纹比对

送检器物流淌纹二维成像

标准图谱模型流淌纹二维成像

检图14

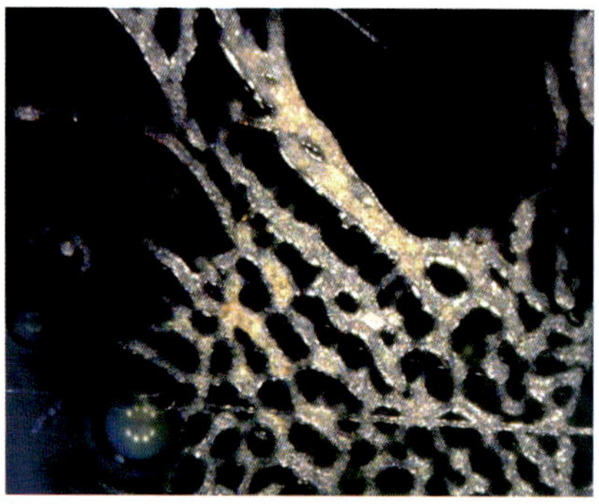

标图14

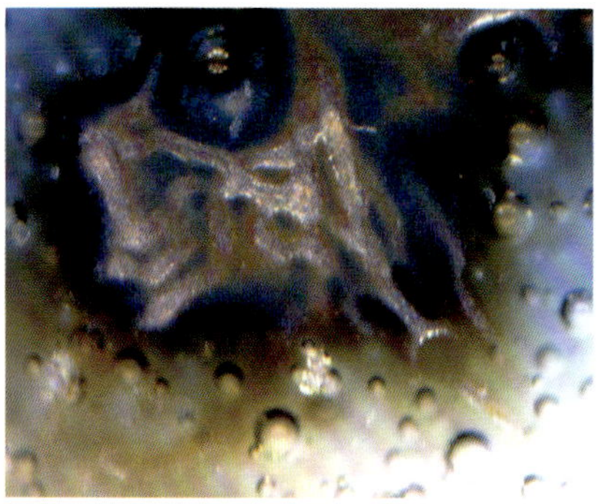

检图15

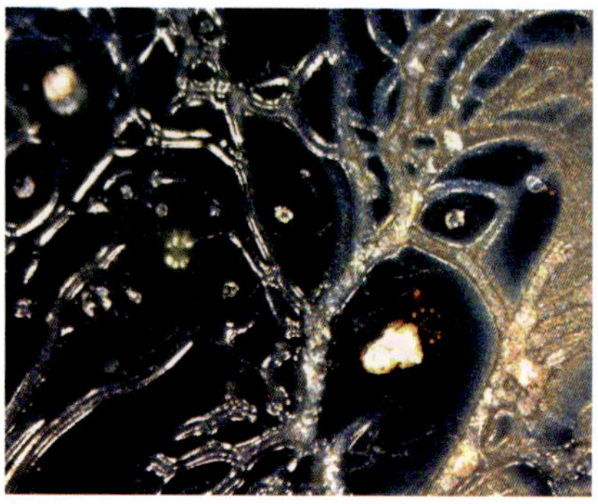

标图15

送检器物流淌纹三维成像

标准图谱模型流淌纹三维成像

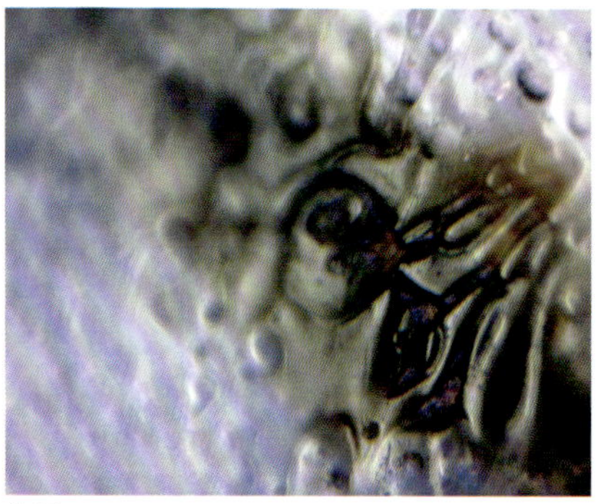

检图16

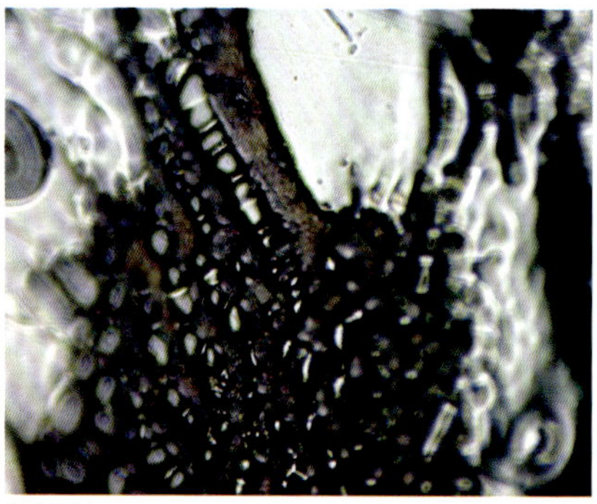

标图16

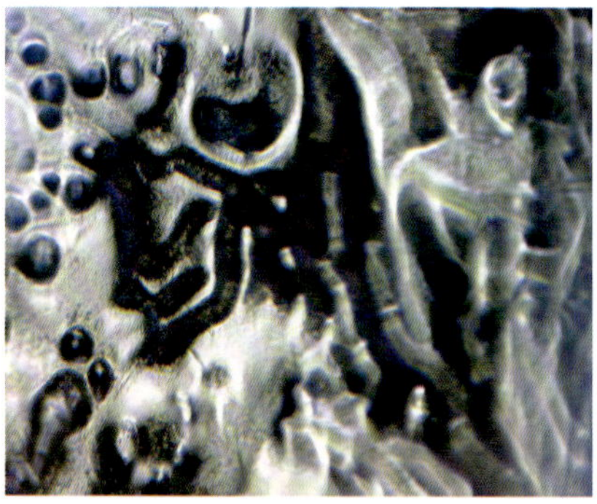

检图17

标图17

◆ 二维特征

1）送检器物上的流淌纹大部分属于针眼型流淌纹（见检图14、检图15）。
2）纹路有白色及橘黄色等颜色变化，有的纹路的橘黄色部分上还可见白色针眼斑（见检图14）。
3）针眼斑不超出纹路的两条边界，纹路与周围玻璃相界线清晰（见检图14）。

◆ 三维特征

见检图16、检图17。
1）纹路剖面呈“U”形，纹路凹槽较深较宽，纹路与周围玻璃相有明显高度差。
2）纹路边缘干净圆滑，与周边的玻璃相界线分明。
3）纹路内部有深紫色及橘黄色等颜色变化。

◆ 迹型本质论证

1）送检器物上流淌纹的表现特征与元青花迹型标准图谱模型上流淌纹的表现特征高度相似，说明送检器物的用材及烧制工艺与元青花瓷器标本相符。
2）流淌纹具备量变特征，符合陶瓷迹型的量变原理。
3）流淌纹上的色阶变化体现了陶瓷迹型的色差规律。
4）流淌纹与周围玻璃相的明显高度差体现了陶瓷迹型的层次性规律，也符合陶瓷迹型的时间过程性原理。
5）流淌纹二维与三维成像特征具有迹型变化的同步性。

（六）CO纹比对

送检器物CO纹二维成像

标准图谱模型CO纹二维成像

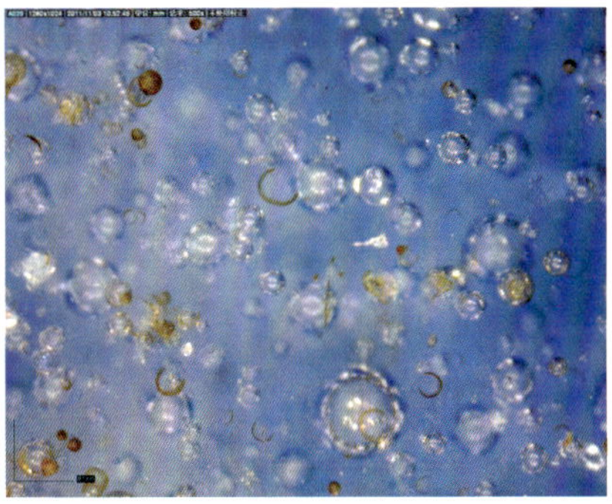
检图18

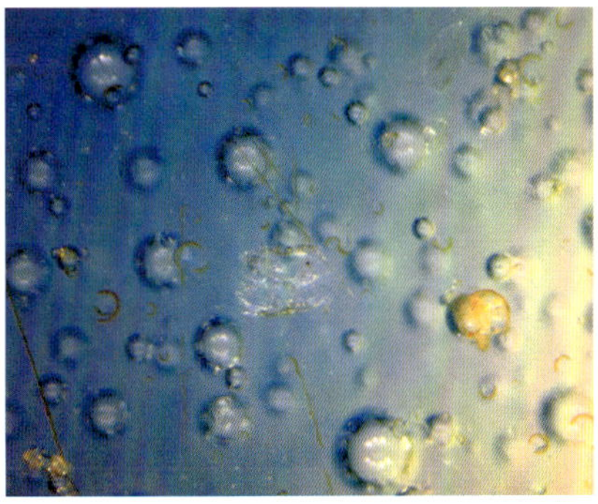
标图18

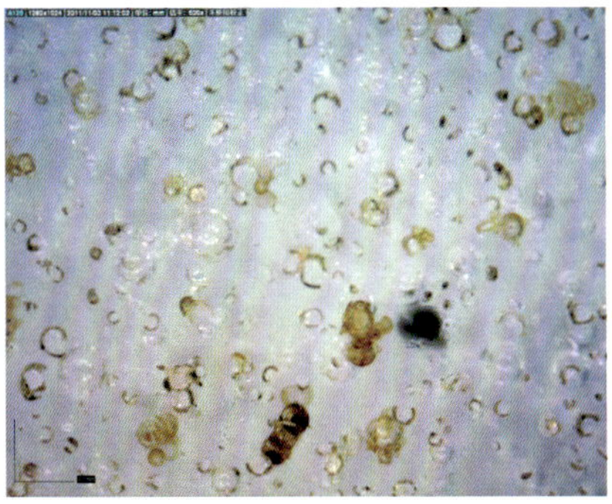
检图19

标图19

送检器物CO纹三维成像　　标准图谱模型CO纹三维成像

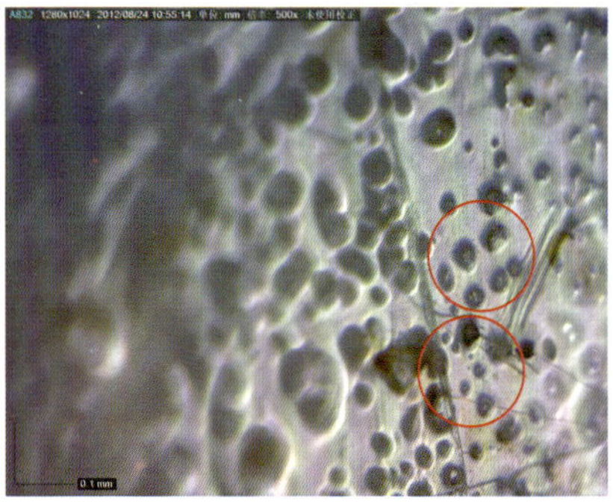
检图20

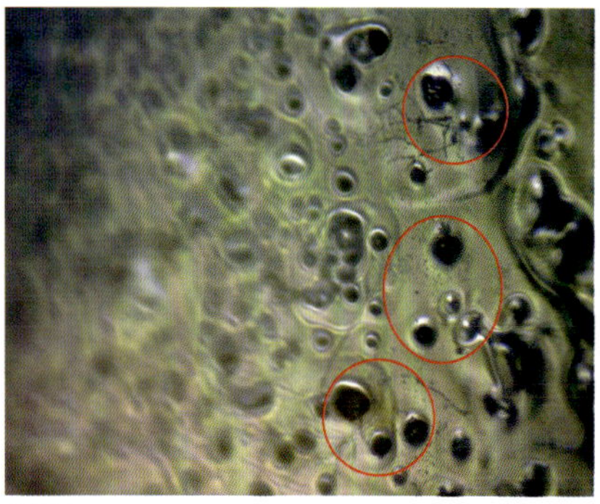
标图20

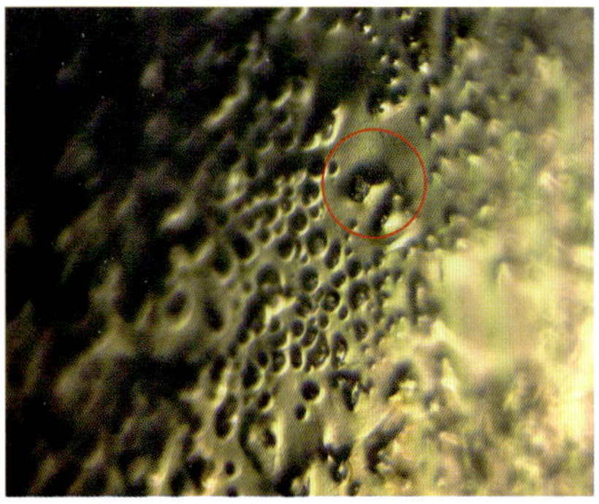
检图21

标图21

◆ 二维特征

1）CO纹大小参差，粗细不一，距离不等（见检图18、检图19）。
2）单项C形纹或O形纹有色阶变化（见检图19）。
3）单位图片中的CO纹有色差变化（见检图19）。
4）CO纹与周围玻璃相界线清晰（见检图18、检图19）。
5）单位图片中CO纹邻近出现色变泡、划痕等多个迹型，并且彼此界线分明（见检图18、检图19）。

◆ 三维特征

见检图20、检图21。
1）CO纹出现的位置在釉表面凸起处。
2）CO纹呈黄色或褐色，纹路清晰收敛，纹路与周围玻璃相界线清晰。

◆ 迹型本质论证

1）送检器物上CO纹的表现特征与元青花标准图谱模型上CO纹的表现特征高度相似。
2）单位图片中CO纹之间的色差变化及单项CO纹上的色阶变化体现了陶瓷迹型的色差规律。
3）CO纹与周围玻璃相清晰的界线体现了陶瓷迹型的分明性规律。
4）CO纹的颜色及清晰收敛的纹路具有量变特征，符合陶瓷迹型的量变原理。
5）CO纹与色变泡伴生的现象符合陶瓷迹型时间过程性原理。
6）单位图片中除CO纹以外有多种迹型独立共存，体现了陶瓷迹型风化强度的多样性。

（七）划痕比对

送检器物划痕二维成像　　标准图谱模型划痕二维成像

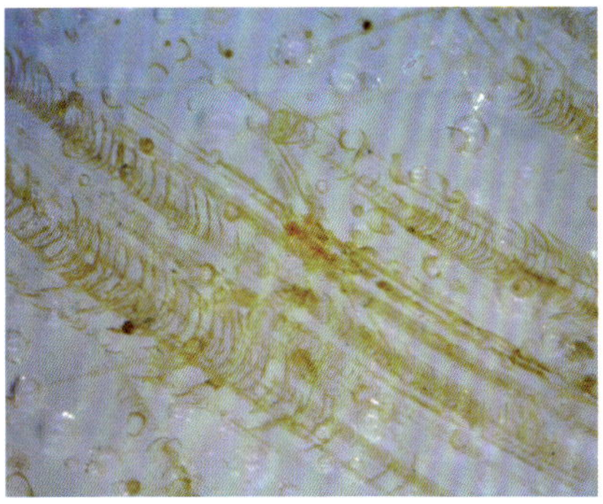
检图22

标图22

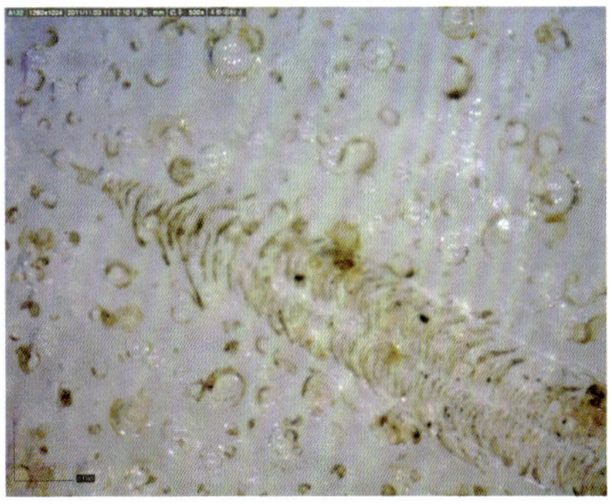
检图23

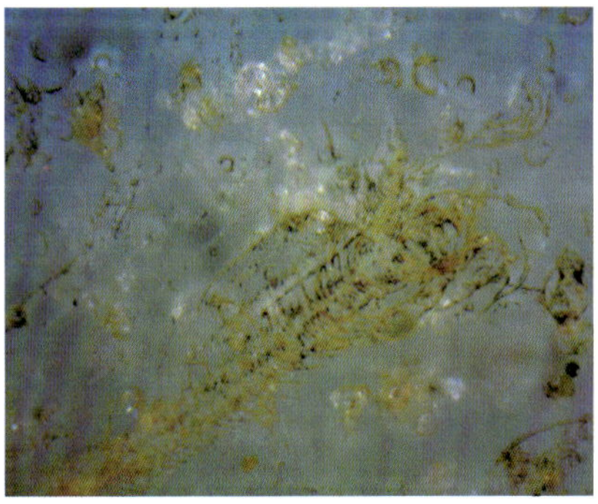
标图23

送检器物划痕三维成像　　标准图谱模型划痕三维成像

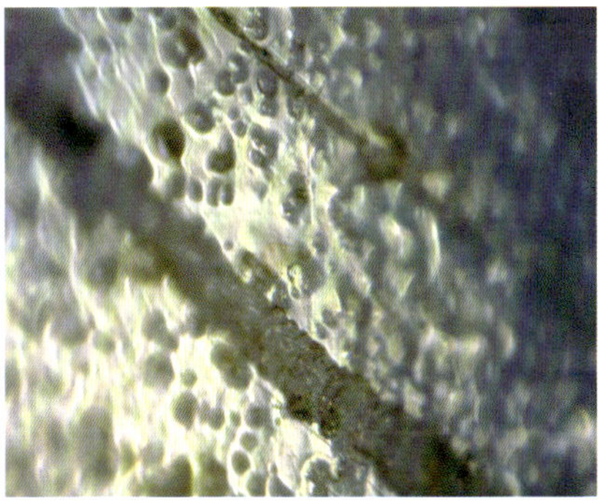
检图24

标图24

检图25

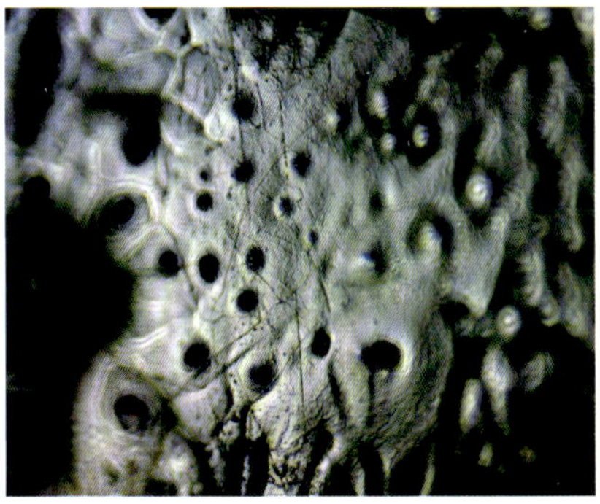
标图25

◆ 二维特征

1）单位图片中的划痕具有粗细、方向、长短的变化（见检图22、检图23）。
2）单位图片中的划痕具有直线、曲线及蜈蚣形等多种形状（见检图22、检图23）。
3）单项划痕有色阶变化（见检图23）。

◆ 三维特征

1）蜈蚣形划痕三维成像呈凹陷状，划痕内有色阶变化，与周围玻璃相界线分明（见检图24）。
2）直线划痕边沿圆滑，与周围玻璃相界线分明（见检图25）。

◆ 迹型本质论证

1）送检器物上划痕的表现特征与元青花迹型标准图谱模型上划痕的表现特征高度相似。
2）划痕的分布及不同的表现特征体现了陶瓷迹型的随机性规律。
3）单项划痕上的色阶变化体现了陶瓷迹型的色差规律。
4）划痕与周围玻璃相清晰的界线体现了陶瓷迹型的分明性规律。
5）划痕边沿圆滑，符合陶瓷迹型的量变原理。

（八）色变泡比对

送检器物色变泡二维成像

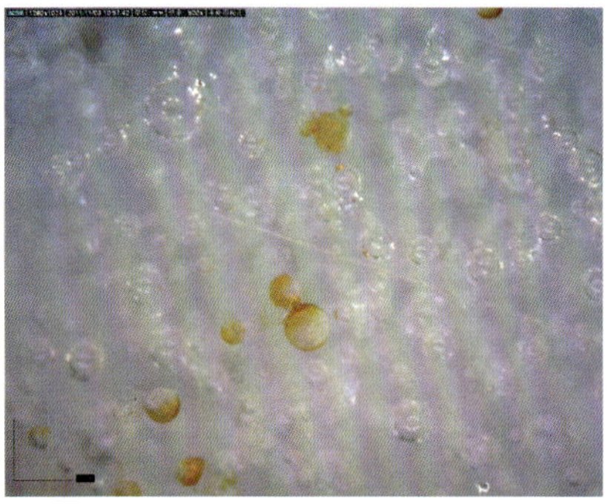
检图26

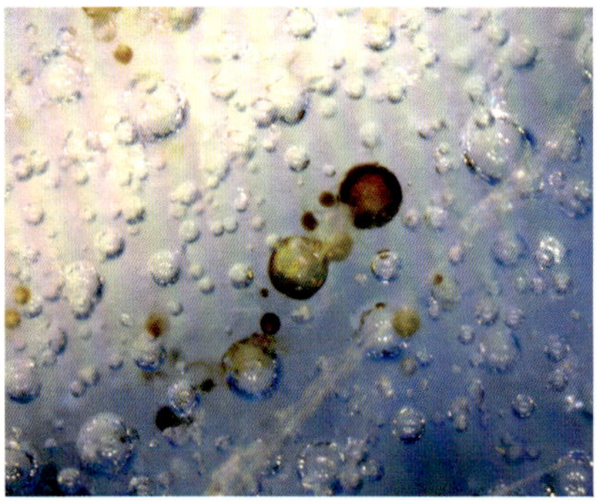
检图27

标准图谱模型色变泡二维成像

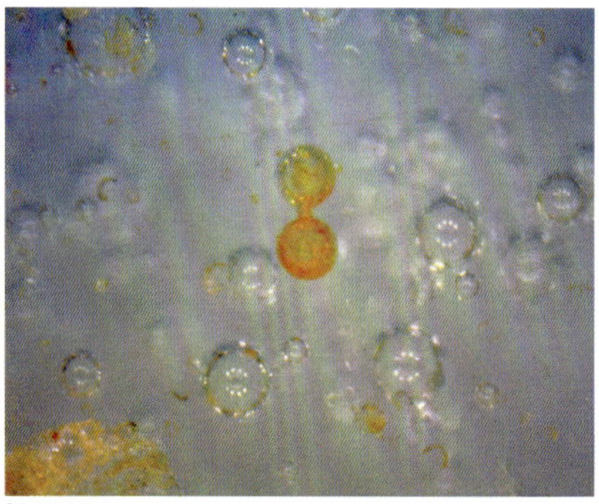
标图26

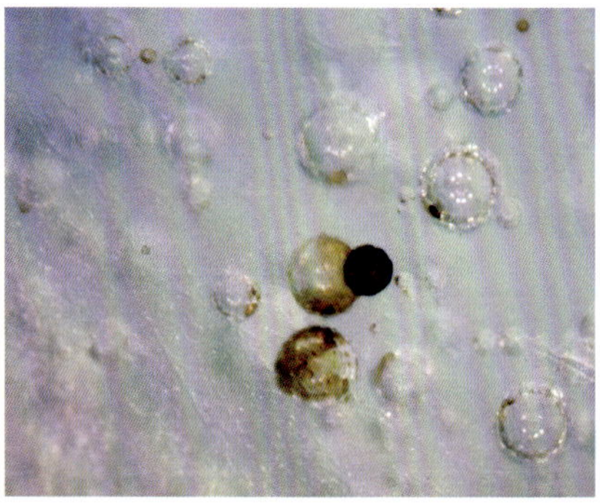
标图27

送检器物色变泡三维成像　　**标准图谱模型色变泡三维成像**

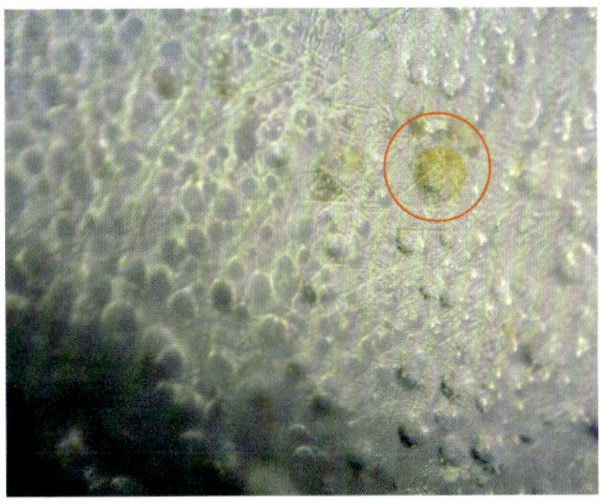
检图28

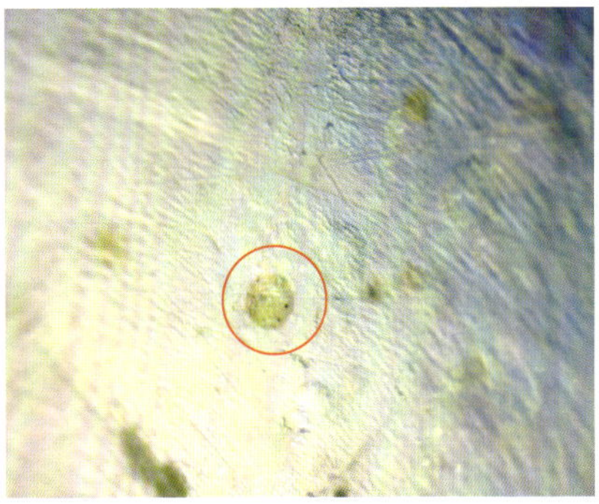
标图28

检图29

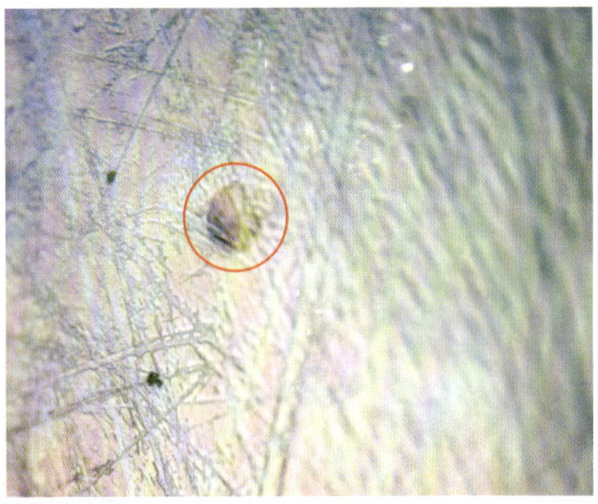
标图29

◆ 二维特征

1）单位图片中局变泡与全变泡同时存在（见检图27）。
2）单项气泡中有色阶变化（见检图27）。
3）单位图片中不同色变泡之间有色差变化（见检图27）。
4）气泡内有独立的具有颜色差异的色块（见检图27）。
5）色变泡与周围玻璃相界线分明（见检图26、检图27）。

◆ 三维特征

1）有的色变泡所在釉表面只见色变泡淡淡的轮廓，釉表面比较光滑洁净，说明釉表面通往气泡的通道细微，用500倍显微镜难以观察到（见检图28）。
2）有的色变泡所在釉表面有较多微小划痕。划痕属于釉表面的结构缺陷，它们也可能是外界连接气泡内的通道，外界物质通过釉表面的通道进入釉层中的气泡内，使气泡变色，形成色变泡（见检图29）。

◆ 迹型本质论证

1）送检器物上色变泡的表现特征与元青花迹型标准图谱模型上色变泡的表现特征高度相似。
2）单位图片中色变泡之间的色差变化及单项色变泡中的色阶变化体现了陶瓷迹型的色差规律。
3）色变泡上颜色较深的色块通常是通道所在处，一般是颜色最早变化和颜色较深的地方。随着风化继续，颜色变化逐渐向四周扩散，这是量变的特征，符合陶瓷迹型的量变原理。

（九）壁变泡比对

1. 非破口壁变泡

送检器物非破口壁变泡二维成像

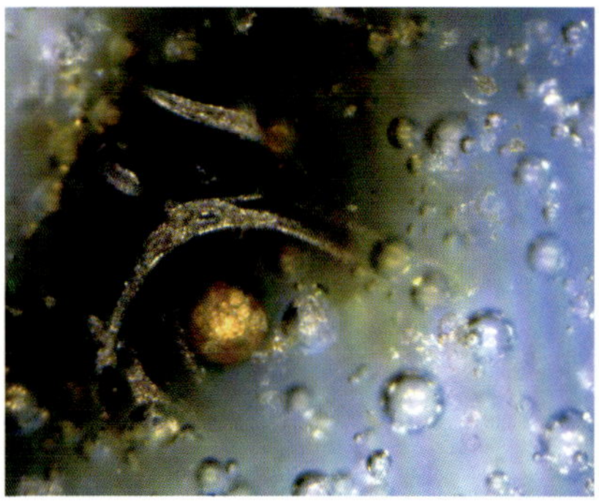
检图30

标准图谱模型非破口壁变泡二维成像

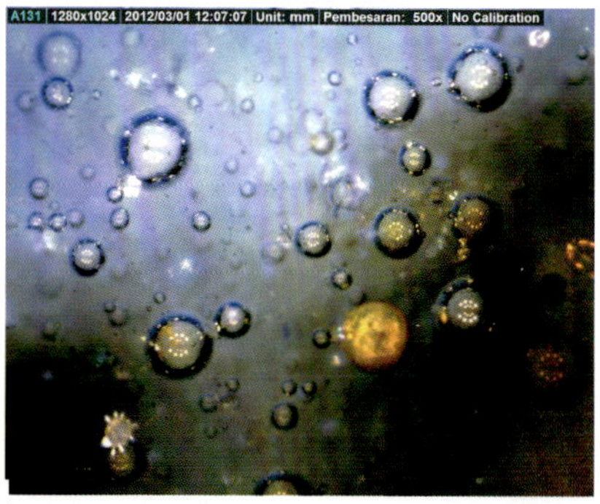

标图30

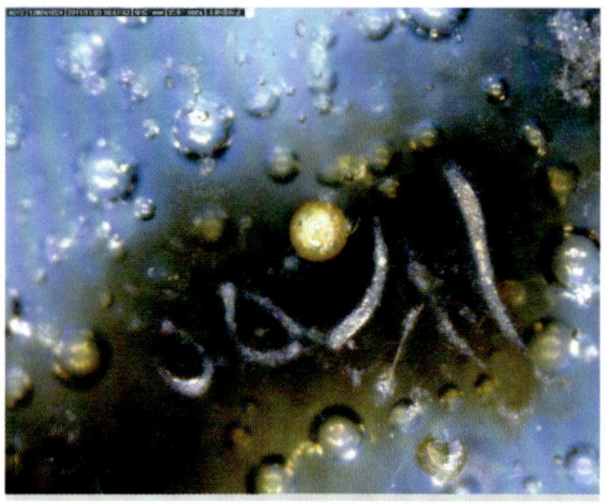
检图31

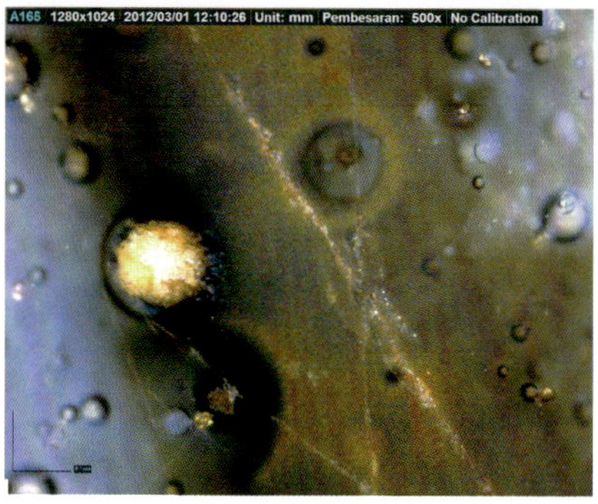

标图31

送检器物非破口壁变泡三维成像

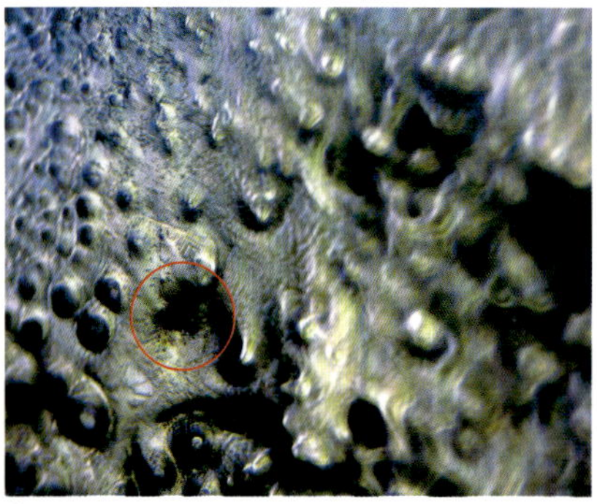
检图32

标准图谱模型非破口壁变泡三维成像

标图32

◆ 二维特征

1）送检器物上的非破口壁变泡大部分为磨砂针眼型（见检图30、检图31）。

2）非破口壁变泡内质地显得较均匀，单项气泡内有明显色阶变化（见检图30、检图31）。

3）非破口壁变泡内壁的风化堆积有差异，有的壁变泡内壁风化物堆积较少，密集程度较低，还可见玻璃相（见检图30）；有的壁变泡内壁风化物堆积较多，密集程度较高，不可见玻璃相（见检图31）。

◆ 三维特征

见检图32。

1）非破口壁变泡周边玻璃相除划痕以外，比较光滑洁净。

2）非破口壁变泡在釉表面三维可视面积小于二维可视面积。

◆ 迹型本质论证

1）送检器物上非破口壁变泡的表现特征与元青花迹型标准图谱模型上非破口壁变泡的表现特征高度相似。

2）非破口壁变泡上的色阶变化体现了陶瓷迹型的色差规律。

3）非破口壁变泡的三维特征属于量变的特征，符合陶瓷迹型的量变原理。

2. 破口壁变泡

送检器物破口壁变泡二维成像

检图33

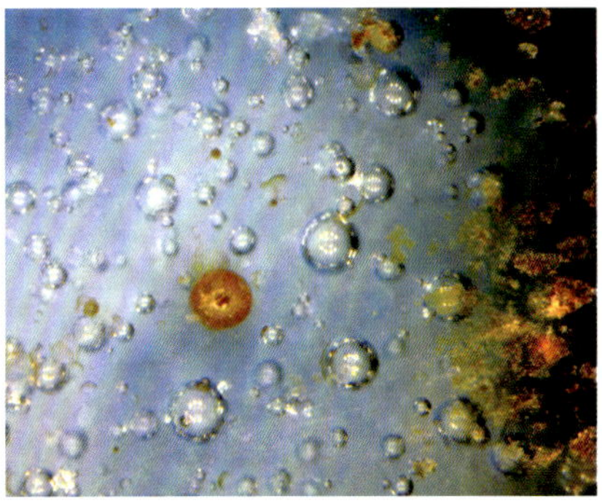

检图34

标准图谱模型破口壁变泡二维成像

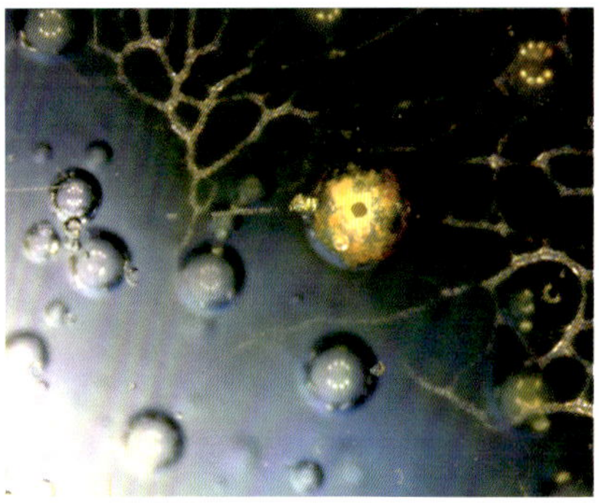

标图33

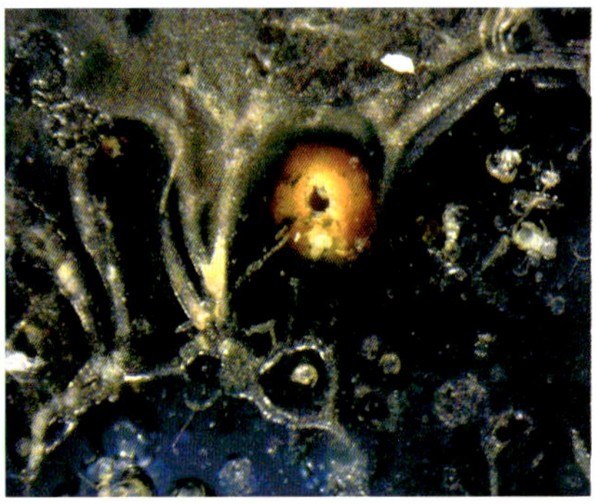

标图34

送检器物破口壁变泡三维成像

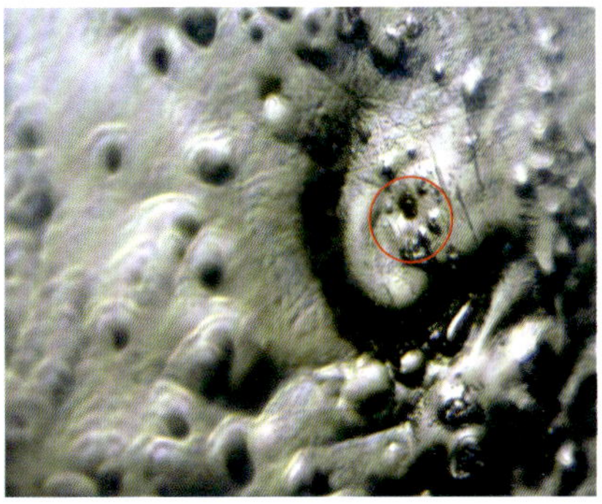

检图35

标准图谱模型破口壁变泡三维成像

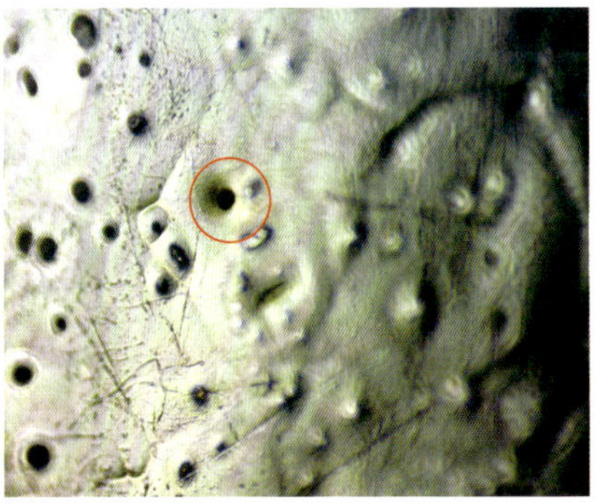

标图35

◆ 二维特征

1）送检器物的破口壁变泡包括磨砂针眼型（见检图33），以及颗粒针眼型（见检图34）。

2）磨砂针眼型壁变泡破口呈不规则形状，破口下方有物质存在。泡壁内质地显得较均匀，单项壁变泡内有明显色阶变化（见检图33）。

3）颗粒针眼型壁变内壁的风化物堆积较少，密集程度较低，还可见玻璃相，单项壁变泡内有明显色阶变化（见检图34）。

◆ 三维特征

见检图35。

1）破口壁变泡三维成像只见破口，清晰独立，不见壁变泡轮廓，说明壁变泡的风化斑块处于气泡内壁。

2）破口壁变泡破口圆滑，破口周围釉表面有几处凸起的地方，除此以外釉表面较干净。

3）凸起处属于釉层分相，组织结构稳定性差，它们很有可能是外界连接气泡内的通道，外界物质通过釉表面的通道进入釉层中的气泡内，使气泡内壁发生质地变化，失去透影性，形成壁变泡，除此以外，破口也可以是通道之一。

◆ 迹型本质论证

1）送检器物上破口壁变泡的表现特征与元青花迹型标准图谱模型上破口壁变泡的表现特征高度相似。

2）破口壁变泡上的色阶变化体现了陶瓷迹型的色差规律。

3）釉表面清晰独立的壁变泡破口体现了陶瓷迹型的分明性规律。

4）破口壁变泡圆滑的破口及其他三维成像特征都属于量变特征，符合陶瓷迹型的量变原理。

（十）玻璃相与气相综合现象比对

送检器物玻璃相与气相二维成像

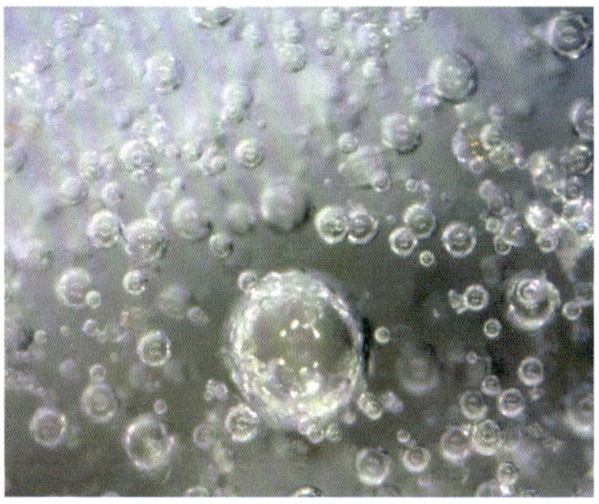

检图36

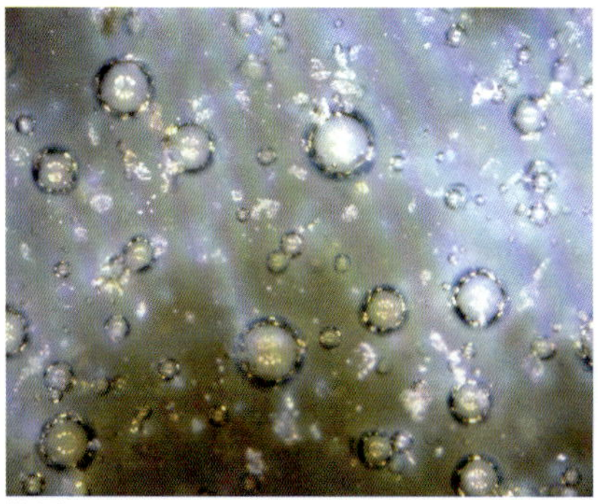

检图37

标准图谱模型玻璃相与气相二维成像

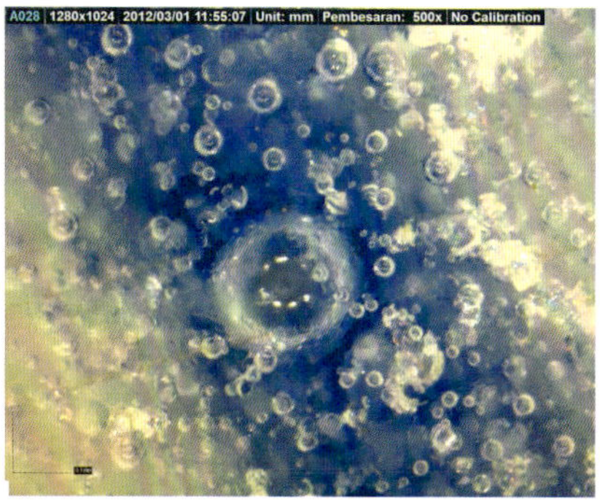

标图36

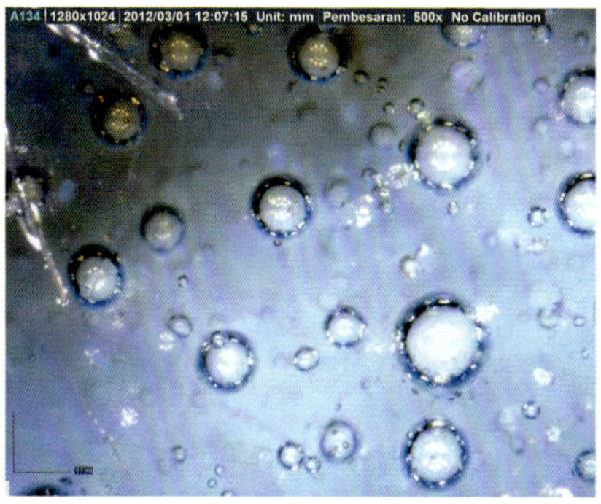

标图37

◆ 二维特征

1）送检器物玻璃相总体显得清澈干净，为清晰型玻璃相（见检图36、见检图37）。
2）气泡分布较疏朗，单位图片中大小气泡之间比例较悬殊（见检图37）。
3）单位图片里可发现个别独立大气泡（见检图36）。

◆ 迹型本质论证

送检器物上玻璃相与气相的综合表现特征与元青花标准图谱模型上玻璃相与气相的综合表现特征高度相似，说明送检器物的用料及烧造工艺与元青花瓷器标本相符。

（十一）鬃眼比对

送检器物鬃眼二维成像

标准图谱模型鬃眼二维成像

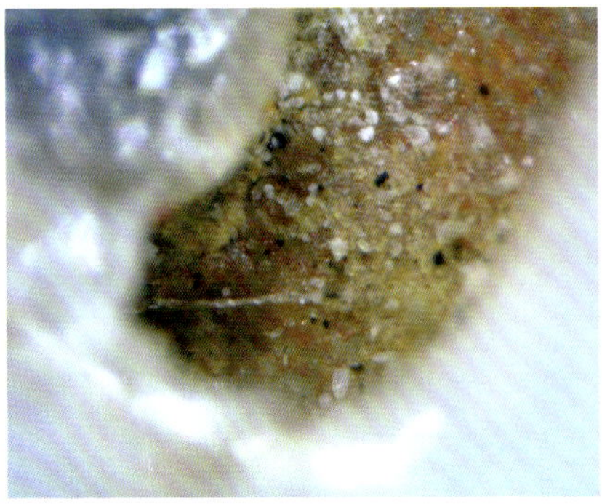
检图38

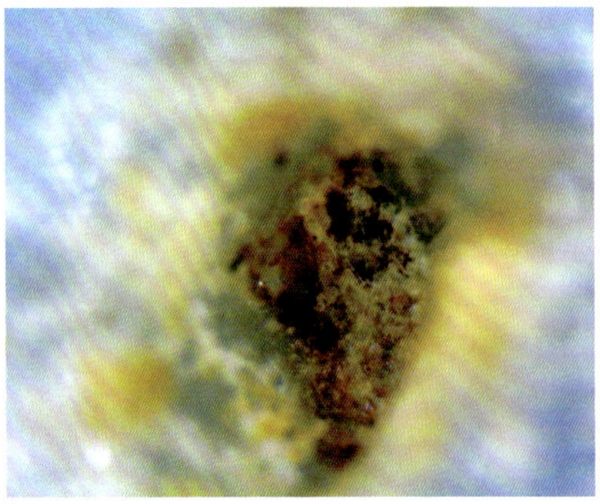
标图38

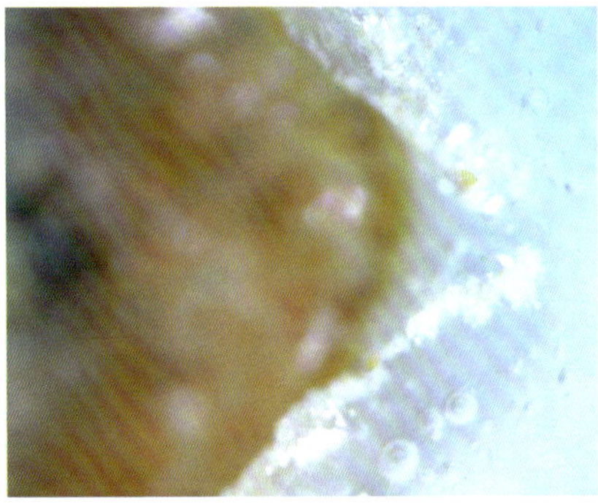
检图39

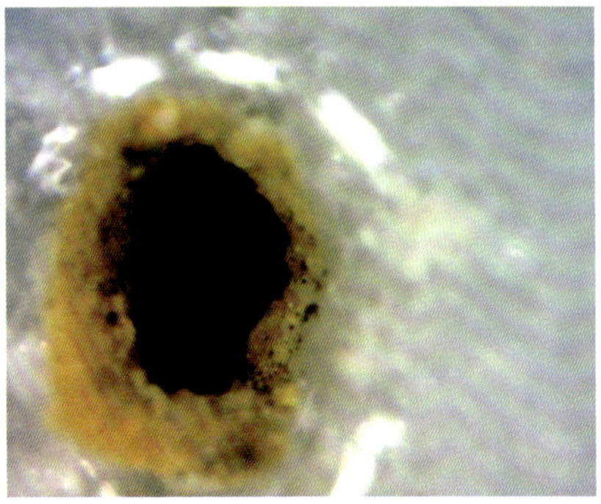
标图39

◆ 二维特征

1）鬃眼口沿圆滑（见检图38、检图39）。
2）鬃眼内部可见颜色变化，也有纤丝及其他物质沉积（见检图38）。
3）鬃眼口部周围釉下出现絮状斑（见检图39）。

◆ 迹型本质论证

1）送检器物上鬃眼的表现特征与元青花迹型标准图谱模型上鬃眼的表现特征高度相似。
2）鬃眼圆滑的口沿属于量变特征，符合陶瓷迹型的量变原理。

3）鬃眼口部周围釉下出现絮状斑体现了陶瓷迹型的层次性规律，符合陶瓷迹型的时间过程性原理。
4）鬃眼内部的颜色变化、口沿及内部的纤丝及风化沉积物体现了陶瓷迹型风化强度的多样性。

七、迹型现象比对结果综述

◆ 经显微仪器检测发现，送检器物共有流淌斑、放射斑、针眼斑、坑点斑、絮状斑、流淌纹、CO纹、划痕、色变泡、壁变泡、鬃眼等十一种迹型，其中后天性迹型达八种（包括针眼斑、坑点斑、絮状斑、CO纹、划痕、色变泡、壁变泡及多样性鬃眼）。
◆ 经与元青花迹型标准图谱模型比对后发现，送检器物在能够反映元青花用材、烧制工艺、量变原理、时间过程性原理及其他陶瓷迹型规律的重要迹型上，不管是二维还是三维成像，都与元青花迹型标准图谱模型高度相似，具备元青花迹型的普遍性特征。除此之外，送检器物上后天性风化迹型的种类数量体现了迹型的多样性，迹型出现的位置及表现特征也与图谱迹型一样，具有迹型出现位置的合理性及迹型变化的同步性。因此从迹型现象表现特征和迹型形成原理及规律来看，送检器物的迹型特征与元青花迹型标准图谱模型高度相似且充分吻合。

八、送检器物迹型分值评定及鉴定结论

（一）送检器物存在与元青花迹型标准图谱模型高度相似的，可证明其用材及烧制工艺的迹型，说明送检器物的用材及烧制工艺与元青花瓷器标本相符，因此送检器物可获得迹型材料分值满分10分；
（二）送检器物存在符合陶瓷迹型量变原理的迹型，因此送检器物可获得迹型量变分值满分20分；
（三）送检器物存在符合陶瓷迹型时间过程性原理的迹型，因此送检器物可获得迹型时间过程性分值满分20分；
（四）送检器物上的后天性迹型总数达到八种，体现了陶瓷迹型风化强度的多样性，因此送检器物获得迹型风化强度多样性分值满分45分中的40分；
（五）送检器物上迹型的存在位置与表现特征与元青花迹型标准图谱模型一样，具有陶瓷迹型存在位置的合理性及迹型变化的同步性，因此送检器物可获得迹型合理性分值满分5分。
（六）经过与元青花迹型标准图谱模型的比对以及对送检器物迹型形成的本质论证，送检器物的显微迹型可得95分，因此鉴定该送检器物为元代青花瓷真品。

Underglaze Blue Yi with Swan in Lotus Pond Pattern: Trace Model Material Evidence Authentication Report

1. General Information of Test Piece

A. Name: Underglaze Blue Yi (Pouring Vessel) with Swan in Lotus Pond Pattern

B. Measurements: Height ~ 4.7 cm; Base Width ~ 5.5 cm; Spout Length ~ 2.5 cm

C. Whole Piece Image:

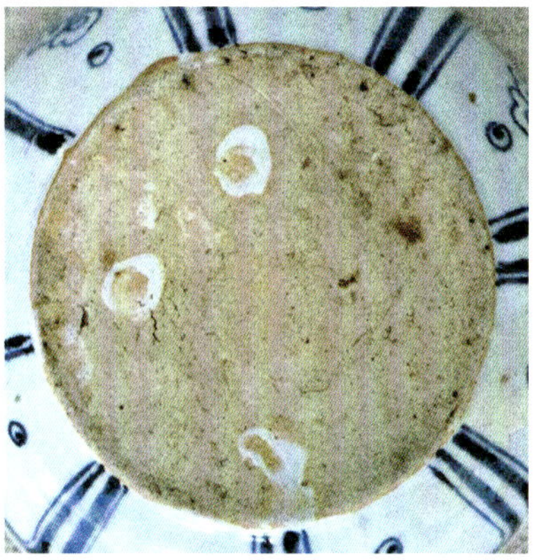

2. Authentication Method: Trace Model Material Evidence Authentication

3. Authentication Requirements:

A. Authentication Equipment: Digital 500X Magnification Optical Microscope and associated tools.

B. Authentication Focus: Mottles, Striae, Bubbles, Bristle Pits and so forth Trace Categories.

4. Authentication Method:

A. Trace comparison with the YUB Standard Trace Atlas Model

B. Trace Nature Proofs

5. Authentication Operating Procedure

A. Holistic Scan and Sampling

B. Focus Area Sampling

C. Two-Dimensional Record Taking

D. Three-Dimensional Record Taking

6. Trace Comparison with the Yuan Underglaze Blue Standard Trace Atlas Model (YUBSTAM)

A. Flowing Mottle Comparison

Two-Dimensional Sample Flowing Mottle Image

Sample Image 1

Two-Dimensional YUBSTAM Flowing Mottle Image

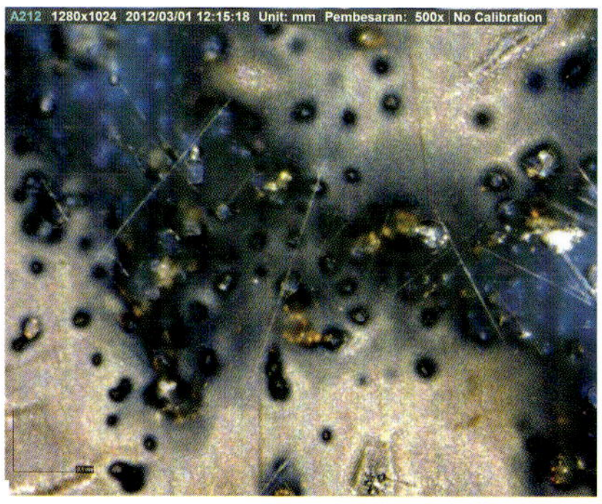

YUBSTAM Image 1

Three-Dimensional Sample Flowing Mottle Image

Sample Image 2

Three-Dimensional YUBSTAM Flowing Mottle Image

YUBSTAM Image 2

◆ Two-Dimensional Characteristics

See Sample Image 1.

1) Majority of the piece's beach mottles are lotus leaf shaped, they are clearly delineated.

2) There is a random distribution of glass phase openings on the beach mottle, they are clearly independent and delineated from the surrounding beach mottle.

3) The glass phase surrounding the beach mottle is clean and clear with sparsely distributed needlepoint mottling and pit mottles.

◆ Three-Dimensional Characteristics

See Sample Image 2.

1) The weathered surface of the beach mottle is clearly concave, and lower than the surrounding glass phase.

2) Glass phase openings are raised bumps higher than the beach mottle; they are smooth and clean and clearly delineated from the beach mottle.

◆ Trace Nature Proofs

1) The characteristics of the test piece's beach mottles and those of the YUB Standard Trace Atlas Model are highly similar; this indicates that the materials and techniques used in the firing of the test piece are consistent with YUB samples.

2) The clear delineation between the beach mottle and the glass phase openings embodies the Ceramic Trace Law of Distinction.

3) The height discrepancy between the beach mottle and surrounding glaze surface embodies the Ceramic Trace Law of Gradation, and is in accordance with the Passage of Time Principle.

4) The glass phase surrounding the beach mottle is clean and clear, there are no muddled signs of man-made aging.

B. Radiating Mottle Comparison

I. Red Series Radiating Mottle

Two-Dimensional Sample Radiating Mottle Image

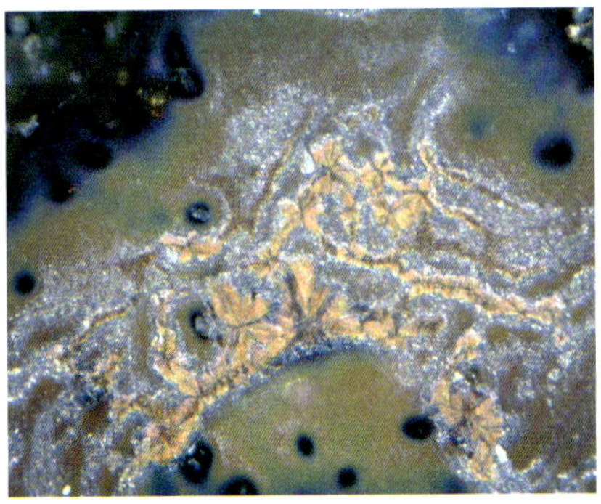

Sample Image 3

Two-Dimensional YUBSTAM Radiating Mottle Image

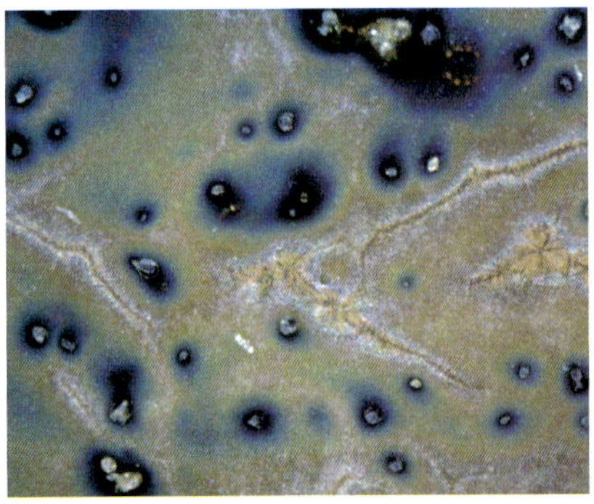

YUBSTAM Image 3

Three-Dimensional Sample Radiating Mottle Image

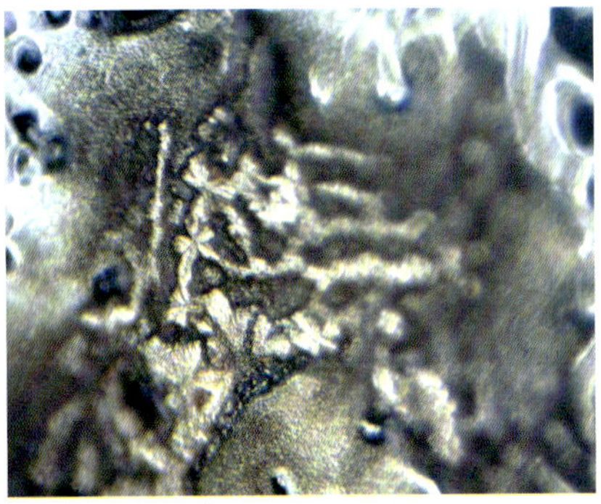

Sample Image 4

Three-Dimensional YUBSTAM Radiating Mottle Image

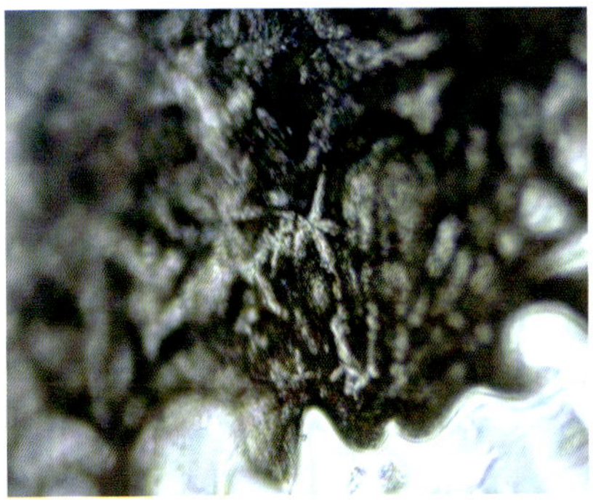

YUBSTAM Image 4

◆ Two-Dimensional Characteristics

See Sample Image 3.

1) Mottle assumes a maple leaf shape, and has a dark tangerine coloration.

2) Mottle is clearly delineated from the surrounding beach mottle.

◆ Three-Dimensional Characteristics

See Sample Image 4.

1) The boundary of the radiating mottle is clearly visible.

2) The radiating mottle is higher than the surrounding beach mottle, and they are clearly delineated.

◆ Trace Nature Proofs

1) The characteristics of the test piece's red series radiating mottles and those of the YUB Standard Trace Atlas Model are highly similar; this indicates that the materials and techniques used in the firing of the test piece are consistent with YUB samples.

2) The clear delineation between the beach mottle and the red series radiating mottle embodies the Ceramic Trace Law of Distinction.

II. Yellow and Brown Series Radiating Mottle

Two-Dimensional Sample Radiating Mottle Image

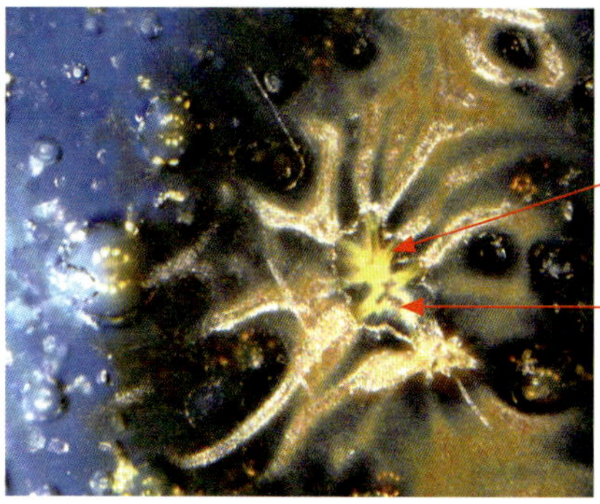

Sample Image 5

Two-Dimensional YUBSTAM Radiating Mottle Image

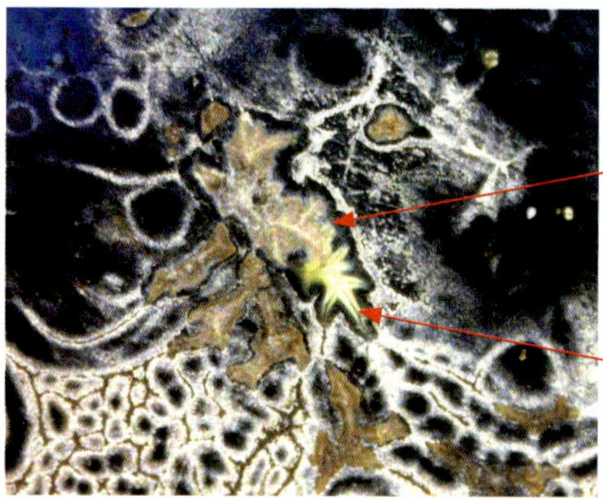

YUBSTAM Image 5

Three-Dimensional Sample Radiating Mottle Image

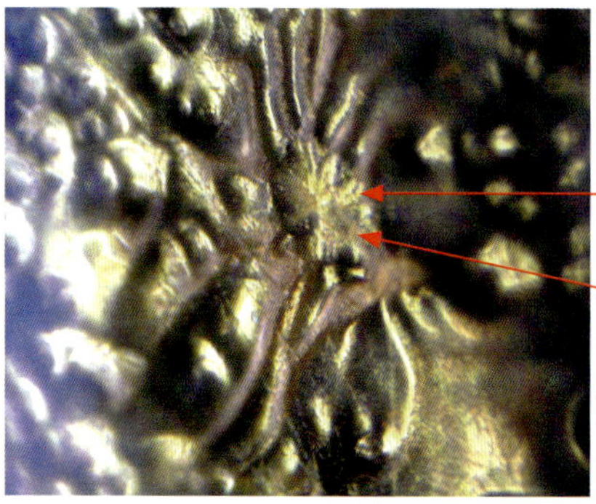

Sample Image 6

Three-Dimensional YUBSTAM Radiating Mottle Image

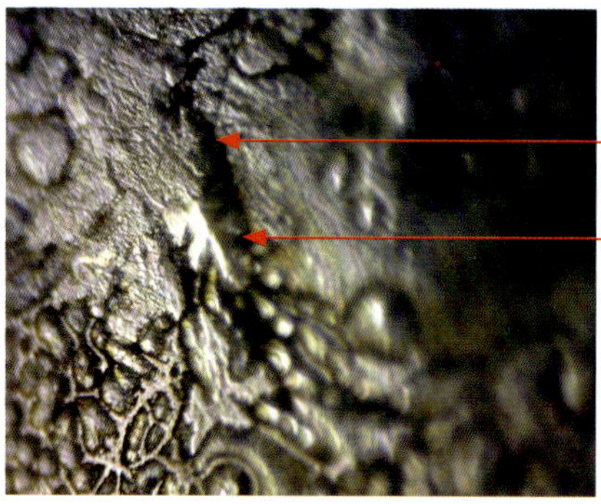

YUBSTAM Image 6

◆ Two-Dimensional Characteristics

See Sample Image 5.

1) Yellow series mottles are irregularly shaped and have bright yellow coloration.

2) Brown series mottles are also irregularly shaped and have a coffee coloration.

3) Both color series mottles have clear delineation from the surrounding traces.

◆ Three-Dimensional Characteristics

See Sample Image 6.

1) The yellow series mottle is present within the glaze level, and the radiating border is clearly visible. Due to its relatively high glaze protection, its surface is smooth and clean with a slightly reflective quality and faint yellow coloration.

2) The brown series mottle presents at the glaze surface, and as such receives relatively low glaze protection. Its surface is finely striated.

◆ Trace Nature Proofs

1) The characteristics of the test piece's yellow and brown series radiating mottles and those of the YUB Standard Trace Atlas Model are highly similar; this indicates that the materials and techniques used in the firing of the test piece are consistent with YUB samples.

2) The clear delineation between the glass phase and the yellow and brown series radiating mottle embodies the Ceramic Trace Law of Distinction.

3) The three-dimensional images of the yellow and brown series mottles show quantitative change characteristics, and are in accordance with the Quantitative Change Principle.

C. Needlepoint Mottle Comparison

I. Foggy Needlepoint Mottle

Two-Dimensional Sample Foggy Needlepoint Mottle Image

Sample Image 7

Two-Dimensional YUBSTAM Foggy Needlepoint Mottle Image

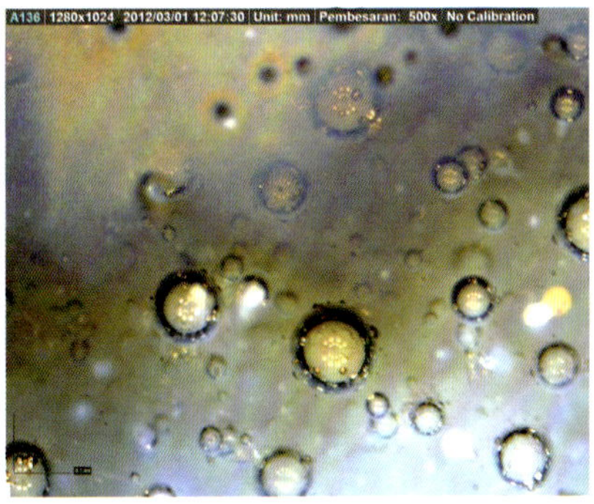

YUBSTAM Image 7

II. Frosted Needlepoint Mottle

Two-Dimensional Sample Frosted Needlepoint Mottle Image

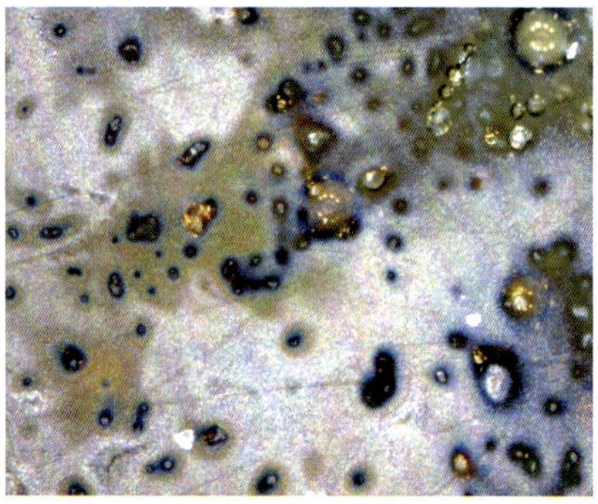

Sample Image 8

Two-Dimensional YUBSTAM Frosted Needlepoint Mottle Image

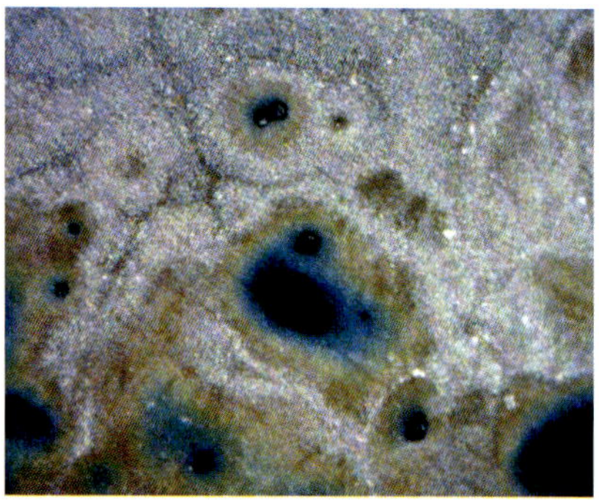

YUBSTAM Image 8

Three-Dimensional Sample Frosted Needlepoint Mottle Image

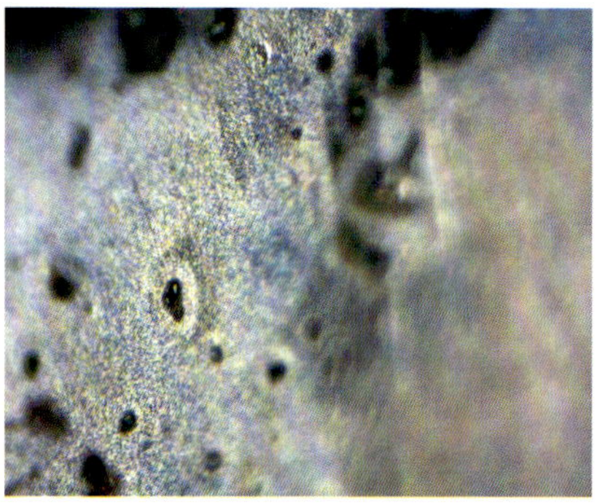

Sample Image 9

Three-Dimensional YUBSTAM Frosted Needlepoint Mottle Image

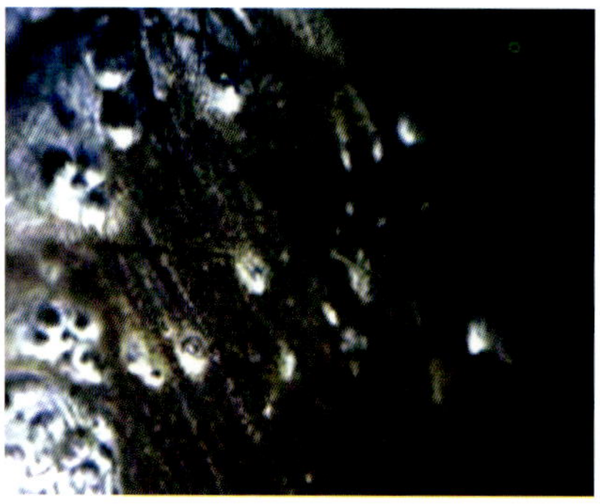

YUBSTAM Image 9

◆ Two-Dimensional Characteristics

1) Foggy needlepoint mottling on the edges, and frosted needlepoint mottling in the center of the beach mottle. All are clearly depicted (see Sample Image 7).

2) Foggy needlepoint mottling has density disparity, with an even and fine density gradation (see Sample Image 7).

3) Frosted needlepoint mottling has strong border feel without density gradation. The distribution is uneven, and in areas of sparse distribution, the brown beach mottle is visible (see Sample Image 8).

4) Needlepoint mottling with such distribution gives the beach mottles a 3-4 layer color spectrum: Dark brown, dark blue, light brown, white (see Sample Image 7 & 8).

◆ Three-Dimensional Characteristics

1) Foggy needlepoint mottling is not visible in areas of sparsest distribution, and has an even transition to the glaze surface (see Sample Image 9).

2) Frosted needlepoint mottling is clearly depicted as independent pin points (see Sample Image 9).

◆ Trace Nature Proofs

1) The characteristics of the test piece's needlepoint mottling and that of the YUB Standard Trace Atlas Model are highly similar.

2) The irregular distribution and variable appearance of needlepoint mottling is due to the differences in glaze protection of flowing mottles, which leads to discrepancies in weathering severity. This embodies the Ceramic Trace Law of Gradation.

3) The distribution and appearance of needlepoint mottling gives the underlying flowing mottle color spectrum, which embodies the Ceramic Trace Law of Chromatic Aberration.

4) The irregular distribution and appearance of the needlepoint mottling is in accordance with the Quantitative Change Principle, and present within location rationality and have trace congruency.

D. Pit Mottle Comparison

I. CO Type Pit Mottle

Two-Dimensional Sample CO Type Pit Mottle Image

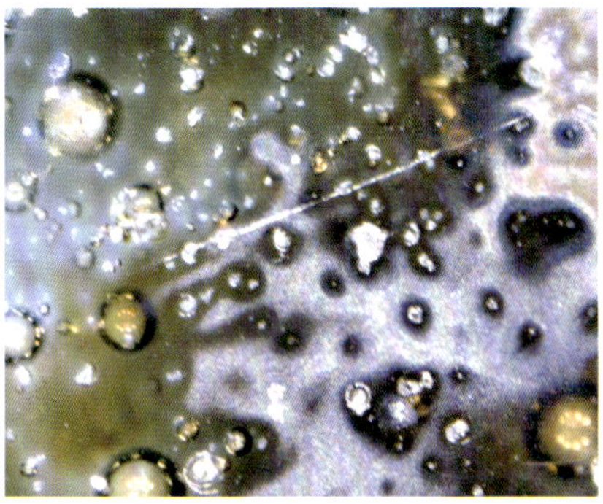

Sample Image 10

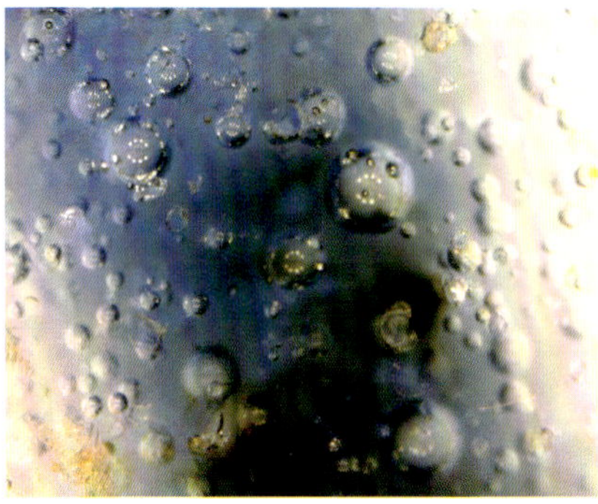

Sample Image 11

Two-Dimensional YUBSTAM CO Type Pit Mottle Image

YUBSTAM Image 10

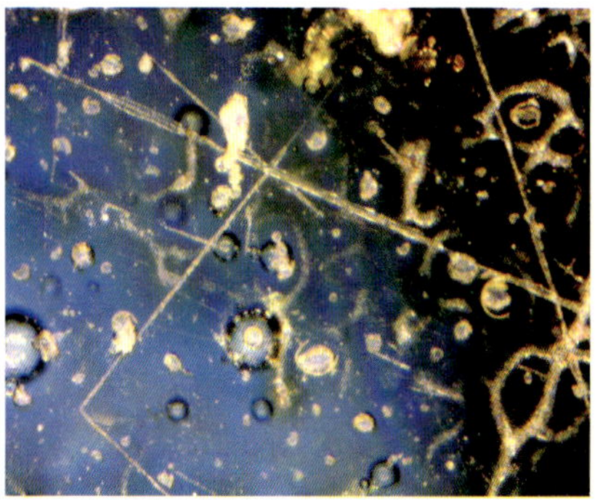

YUBSTAM Image 11

Three-Dimensional Sample CO Type Pit Mottle Image

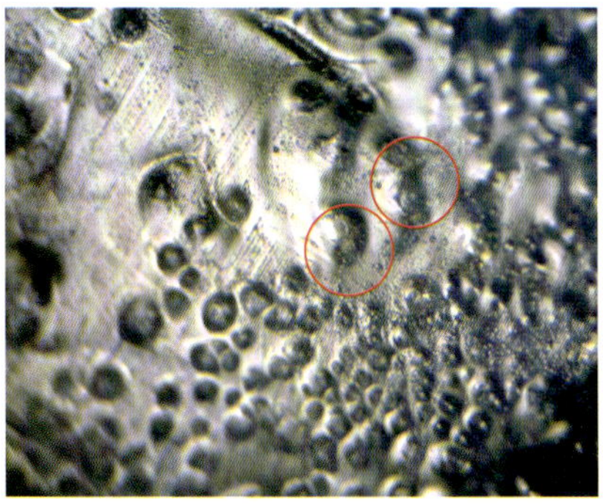

Sample Image 12

Three-Dimensional YUBSTAM CO Type Pit Mottle Image

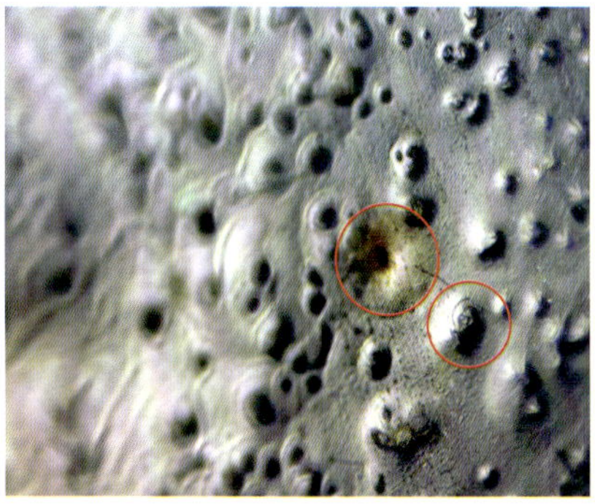

YUBSTAM Image 12

◆ Two-Dimensional Characteristics

See Sample Image 10 & 11.

1) Pits are size disparate, with varied inter-pit distances.

2) Pits are clearly independent, retaining delineation from the surrounding glass phase.

3) Present in association with CO striae in two forms: One being in close proximity, but retaining clear delineation; the other is overlapping.

◆ Three-Dimensional Characteristics

See Sample Image 12.

1) Majority of CO type pits occur on areas of raised glaze.

2) At the point of the pit, only a small C striation is visible. This is because the pit is the development of a C striation and extends down into the glaze level, and three-dimensional imaging does not allow for its observation.

◆ Trace Nature Proofs

1) The characteristics of the test piece's CO type pit mottles and those of the YUB Standard Trace Atlas Model are highly similar.

2) The occurrence in association with CO striae suggests that these pits are developed from C and O shaped striae over a passage of time; this is in accordance with the Passage of Time Principle.

3) The CO striae on the glaze surface and CO type pit mottles developed within the glaze level are consistent with the Ceramic Trace Law of Gradation.

4) CO type pit mottle characteristics are in accordance with the Quantitative Change Principle.

5) CO type pit mottles occur in the rational locations.

II. Needlepoint Type Pit Mottle

Two-Dimensional Sample Needlepoint Type Pit Mottle Image

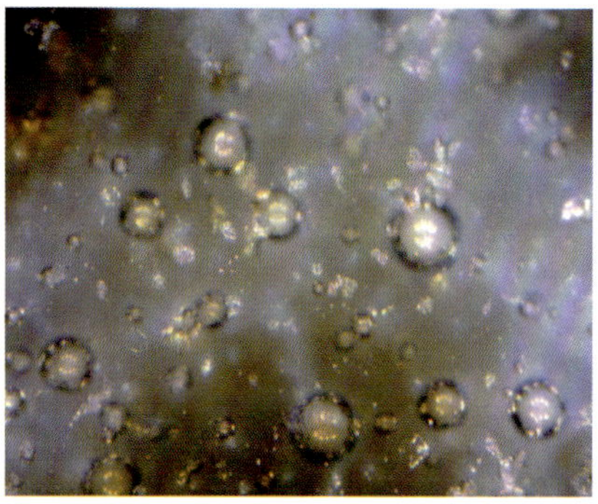

Sample Image 13

Two-Dimensional YUBSTAM Needlepoint Type Pit Mottle Image

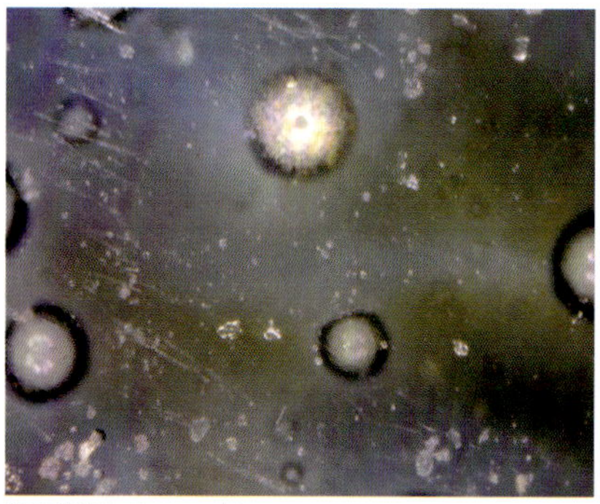

YUBSTAM Image 13

◆ Two-Dimensional Characteristics

See Sample Image 13.

1) Pits are independent and clear, shapes and sizes disparate.

2) Some pits have a fine border with needlepoint mottling on the interior.

3) Clearly delineated from the surrounding glass phase.

◆ Trace Nature Proofs

1) The characteristics of the test piece's needlepoint type pit mottles and those of the YUB Standard Trace Atlas Model are highly similar.

2) The fine borders and internal needlepoint mottling are in accordance with the Quantitative Change Principle.

E. Flowing Striae Comparison

Two-Dimensional Sample Flowing Striae Image

Sample Image 14

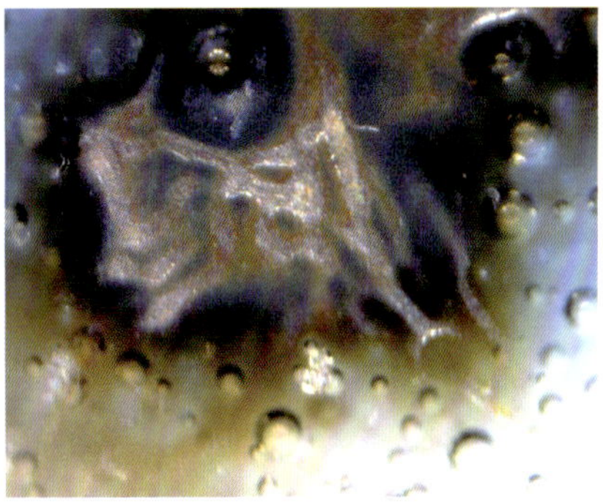

Sample Image 15

Two-Dimensional YUBSTAM Flowing Striae Image

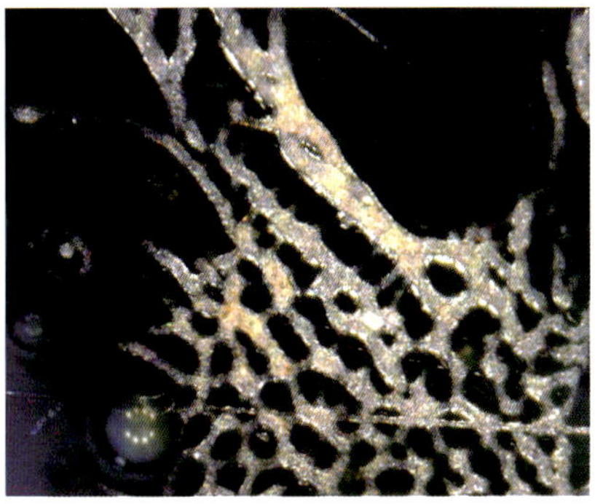

YUBSTAM Image 14

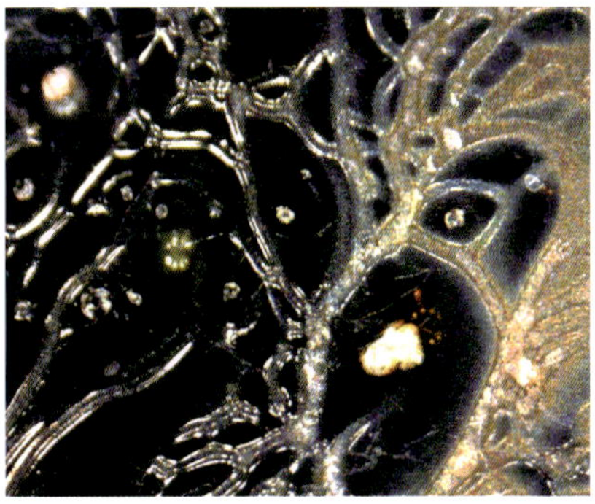

YUBSTAM Image 15

Three-Dimensional Sample Flowing Striae Image

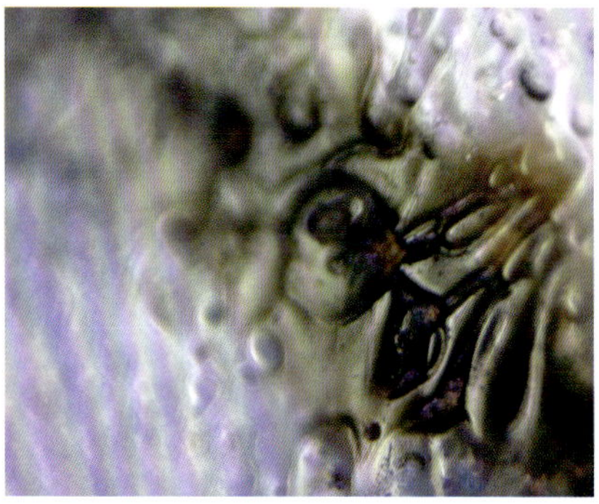

Sample Image 16

Sample Image 17

Three-Dimensional YUBSTAM Flowing Striae Image

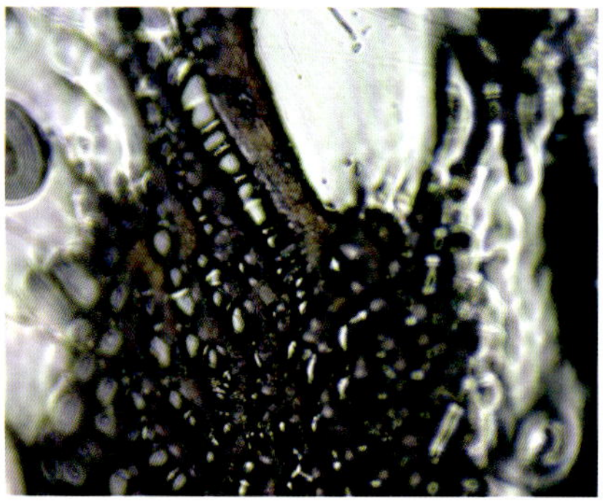

YUBSTAM Image 16

YUBSTAM Image 17

◆ Two-Dimensional Characteristics

1) Striae are needlepoint striae (see Sample Image 14 & 15).

2) White to orange color spectrum within a single striation, with orange coloration presenting along with white needlepoint mottling (see Sample Image 14).

3) Needlepoint mottling does not extend beyond the border of the striae, and the striae have clear delineation from the surrounding glass phase (see Sample Image 14).

◆ Three-Dimensional Characteristics

See Sample Image 16 & 17.

1) Striae have a "U" shaped cross-section, and the striae centers are deep and wide with clear height discrepancy from the surrounding glaze surface.

2) The edges of the striae are rounded, clean and smooth and have a clear delineation from the surrounding glaze surface.

3) The striae interior present with a dark purple to orange color spectrum.

◆ Trace Nature Proofs

1) The characteristics of the test piece's flowing striae and those of the YUB Standard Trace Atlas Model are highly similar; this indicates that the materials and techniques used in the firing of the test piece are consistent with YUB samples.

2) The flowing striae have characteristics that are in accordance with the Quantitative Change Principle.

3) The color spectrum of the striae embodies the Ceramic Law of Chromatic Aberration.

4) The height discrepancy between the striae and the surrounding glaze surface embodies the Ceramic Law of Gradation and is in

accordance with the Passage of Time Principle.

5) The two and three-dimensional characteristics of the striae have trace change congruency.

F. CO Striae Comparison

Two-Dimensional Sample CO Striae Image

Two-Dimensional YUBSTAM CO Striae Image

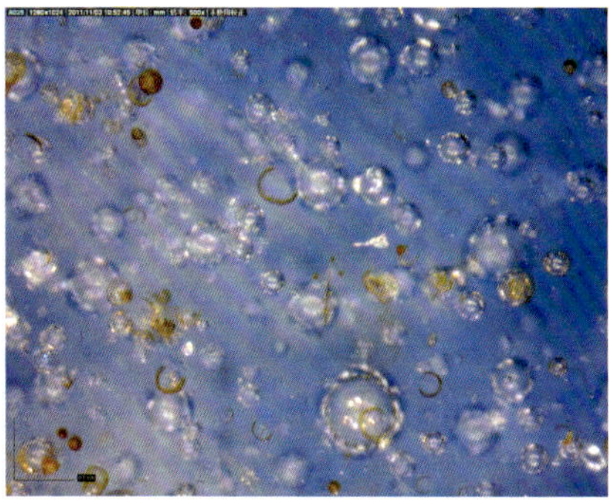

Sample Image 18

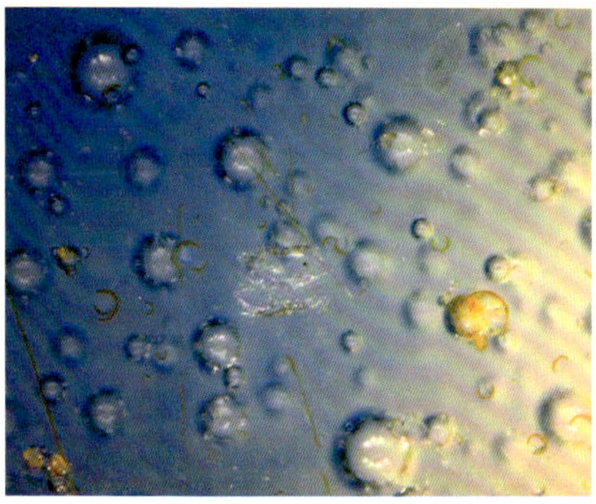

YUBSTAM Image 18

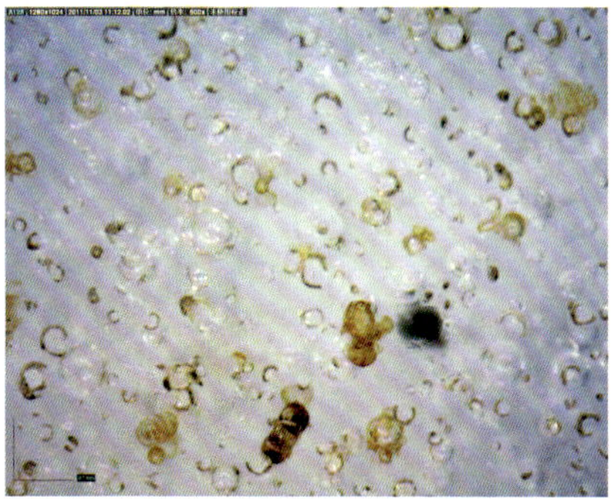

Sample Image 19

YUBSTAM Image 19

Three-Dimensional Sample CO Striae Image

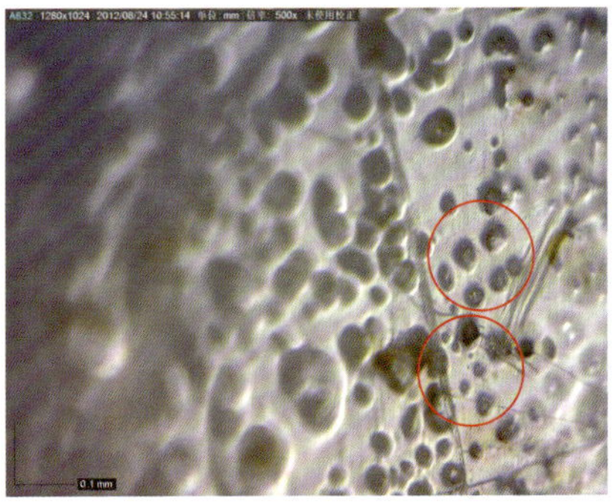
Sample Image 20

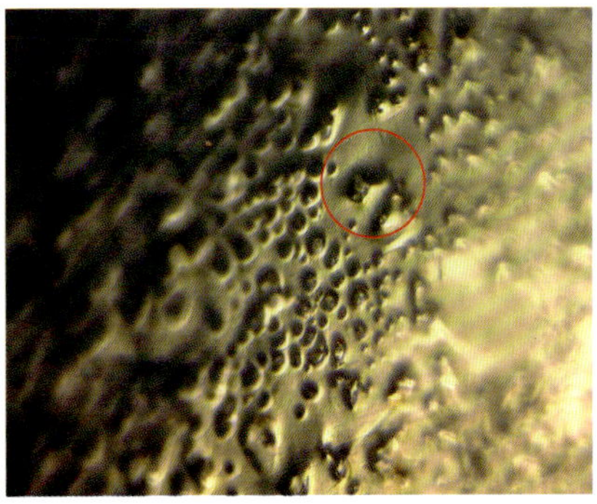
Sample Image 21

Three-Dimensional YUBSTAM CO Striae Image

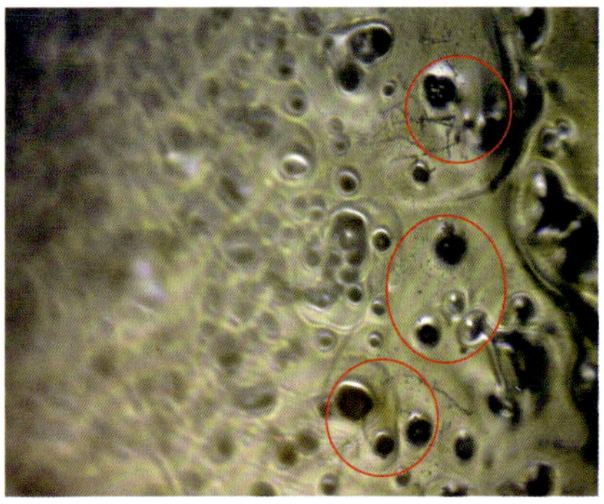
YUBSTAM Image 20

YUBSTAM Image 21

◆ Two-Dimensional Characteristics

1) Size, thickness, and inter-striae distance are disparate (see Sample Image 18 & 19).

2) Single C or O striation present with color spectrum (see Sample Image 19).

3) Color disparity within unit image (see Sample Image 19).

4) Striae retain clear delineation from the surrounding glass phase (see Sample Image 18 & 19).

5) Multiple traces (color change bubbles, scratches, etc.) within unit image in close proximity to CO striae, all retaining mutual delineation (see Sample Image 18 & 19).

◆ Three-Dimensional Characteristics

See Sample Image 20 & 21.

1) Striae occur primarily on areas of raised glaze.

2) Striae is yellow or brown as well as fine and reserved. Striae are clearly delineated from the surrounding glaze surface.

◆ Trace Nature Proofs

1) The characteristics of the test piece's CO striae and those of the YUB Standard Trace Atlas Model are highly similar.

2) Color spectrum within a single striation and color disparity within a unit image embodies the Ceramic trace Law of Chromatic Aberration.

3) Clear delineation from the surrounding glass phase embodies the Ceramic Trace Law of Distinction.

4) The fine reserved shape and coloration of the striae are both characteristic of quantitative change and as such the striae are in accordance with the Quantitative Change Principle.

5) CO striae occur in association with color change bubbles which is in accordance with the Passage of Time Principle.

6) Within a unit image, aside from the CO striae, there are multiple independent trace types also presenting. This occurrence indicates the multiplicity of the ceramic trace weathering severity.

G. Scratch Comparison

Two-Dimensional Sample Scratch Image

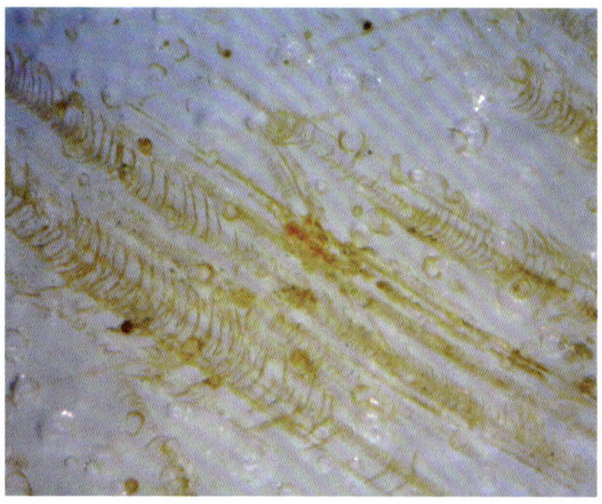

Sample Image 22

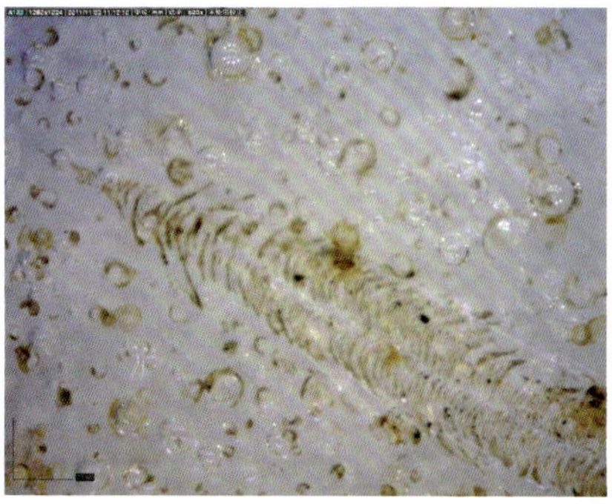

Sample Image 23

Two-Dimensional YUBSTAM Scratch Image

YUBSTAM Image 22

YUBSTAM Image 23

Three-Dimensional Sample Scratch Image

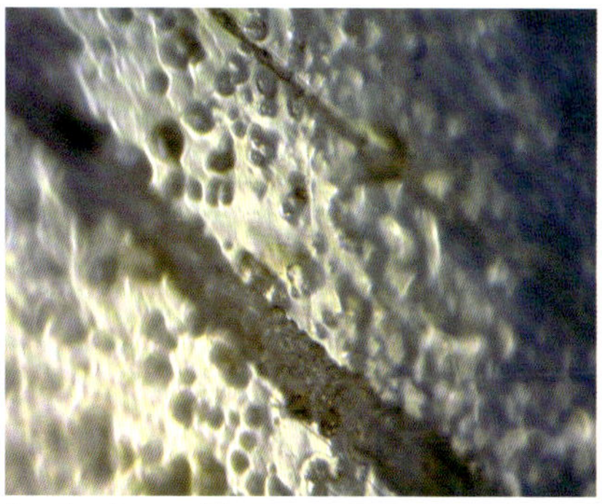

Sample Image 24

Sample Image 25

Three-Dimensional YUBSTAM Scratch Image

YUBSTAM Image 24

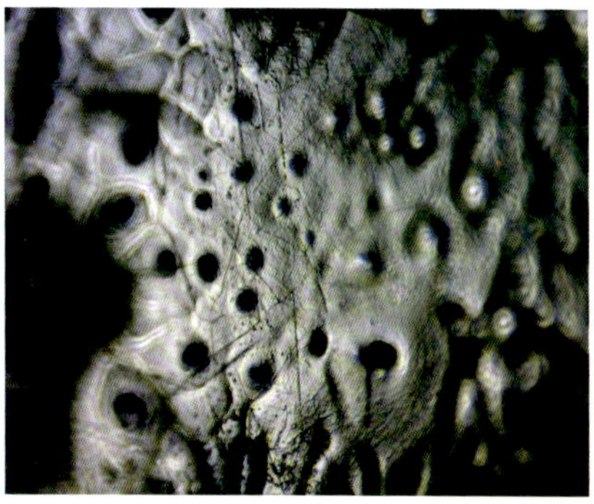

YUBSTAM Image 25

◆ Two-Dimensional Characteristics

1) Scratches within a unit image are direction, width, and length disparate (see Sample Image 22 & 23).

2) Within one unit image, straight, curved, and "centipede" scratches occur in conjunction (see Sample Image 22 & 23).

3) A single scratch occurs with color spectrum (see Sample Image 23).

◆ Three-Dimensional Characteristics

1) The "centipede" scratch is concave with internal color spectrum, its "feet" are visible and it is clearly delineated from the surrounding glaze surface (see Sample Image 24).

2) Straight scratches have smooth rounded edges, and are clearly delineated form the surrounding glaze surface (see Sample Image 25).

◆ Trace Nature Proofs

1) The characteristics of the test piece's scratches and those of the YUB Standard Trace Atlas Model are highly similar.

2) The abundance of scratch appearances embodies the Ceramic Trace Law of Randomness.

3) Color spectrum within a single scratch embodies the Ceramic Trace Law of Chromatic Aberration.

4) The clear delineation between the scratches and surrounding glass phase embodies the Ceramic Trace Law of Distinction.

5) The rounded smooth edges of the scratches are in accordance with the Quantitative Change Principle.

H. Color Change Bubble Comparison

Two-Dimensional Sample Color Change Bubble Image

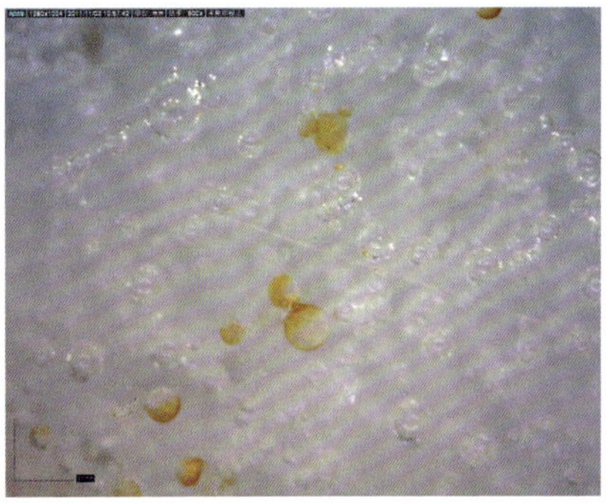

Sample Image 26

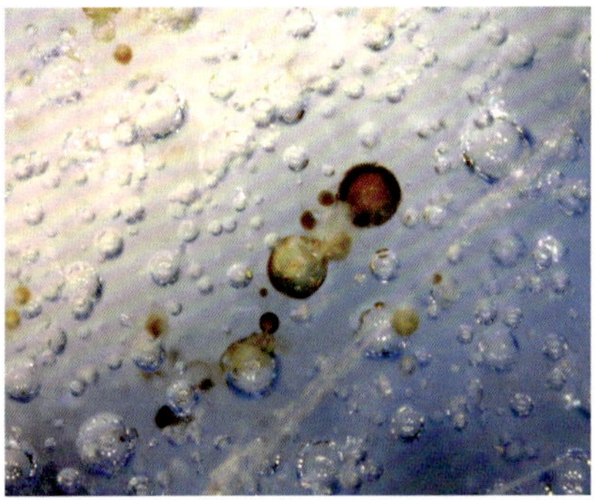

Sample Image 27

Two-Dimensional YUBSTAM Color Change Bubble Image

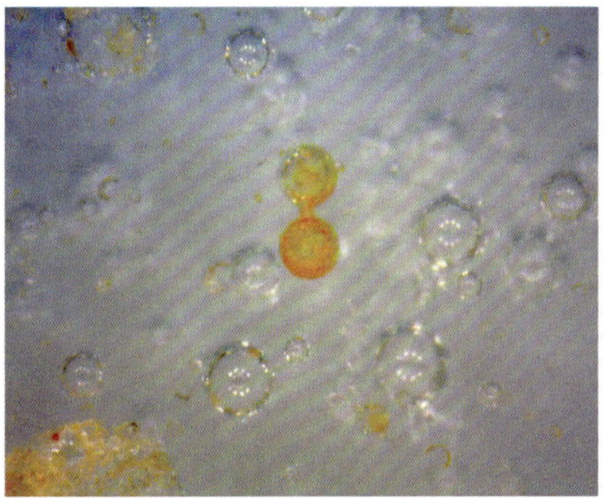

YUBSTAM Image 26

YUBSTAM Image 27

Three-Dimensional Sample Color Change Bubble Image

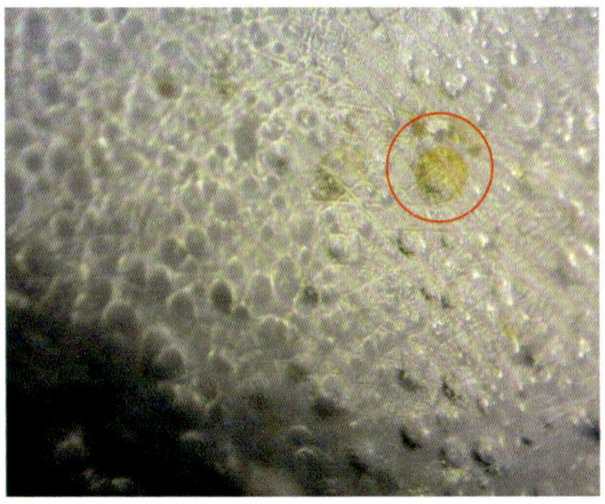
Sample Image 28

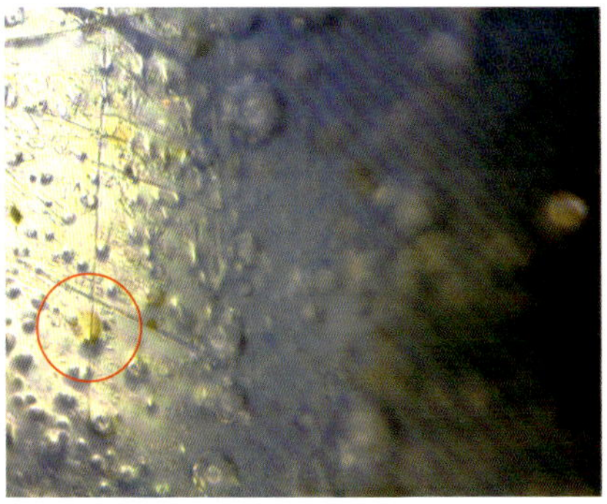
Sample Image 29

Three-Dimensional YUBSTAM Color Change Bubble Image

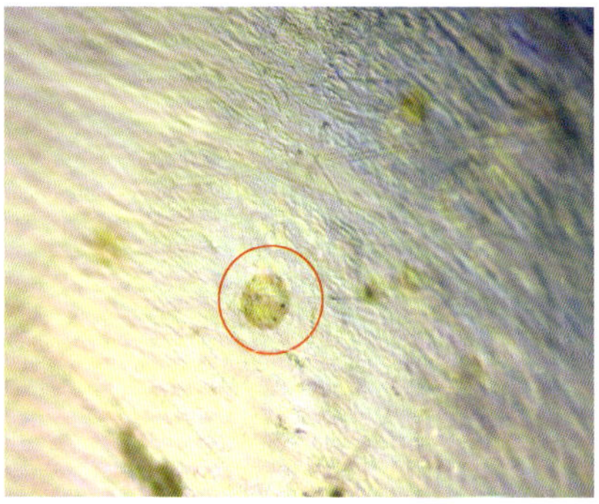
YUBSTAM Image 28

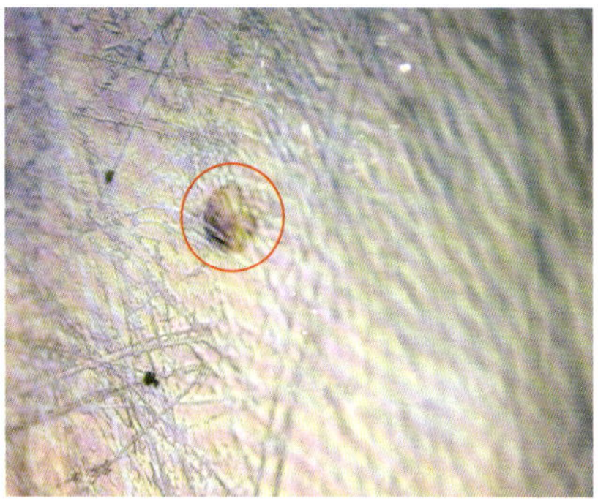
YUBSTAM Image 29

◆ Two-Dimensional Characteristics

1) Appearance of semi and fully-changed bubbles within a unit image (see Sample Image 27).
2) Color spectrum within a bubble (see Sample Image 27).
3) Color disparity between bubbles within one unit image (see Sample Image 27).
4) Bubble occurs with a single spot of coloration (see Sample Image 27).
5) Color change bubbles retain clear delineation from the surrounding glass phase (see Sample Image 26 & 27).

◆ Three-Dimensional Characteristics

1) The glaze surface above the color change bubble presents with a faint outline of the underlying bubble, but retains smooth clarity. This indicates that the coloration channels are acutely minute and not observable with a 500X magnification microscope (see Sample Image 28).
2) Some bubbles present with overlying glaze scratches. These scratches are considered glaze flaws, and are likely the coloration channels between the external environment and the bubble interior allowing foreign materials to pass into the bubble and cause coloration (see Sample Image 29).

◆ Trace Nature Proofs

1) The characteristics of the test piece's color change bubbles and those of the YUB Standard Trace Atlas Model are highly similar.
2) Color spectrum and color disparity both embody the Ceramic Trace Law of Chromatic Aberration.
3) The areas of darker coloration within a bubble are the areas of coloration channel where weathering first takes place and slowly

disperses throughout the bubble. This is a sign of quantitative change, which is in accordance with the Quantitative Change Principle.

I. Unbroken Mouth Textured Bubble Comparison

Two-Dimensional Sample Unbroken Mouth Textured Bubble Image

Two-Dimensional YUBSTAM Unbroken Mouth Textured Bubble Image

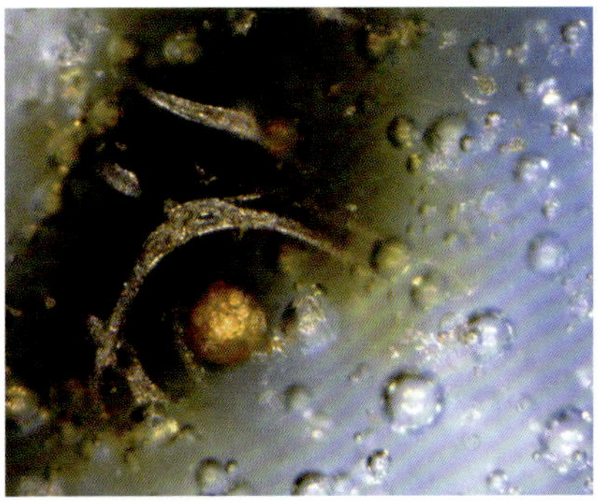

Sample Image 30

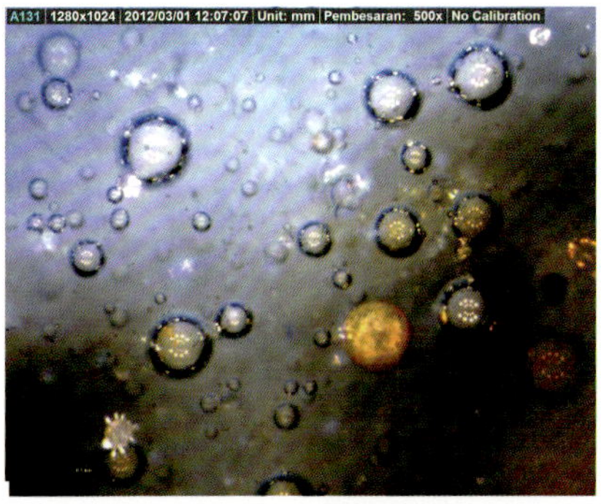

Standard Image 30

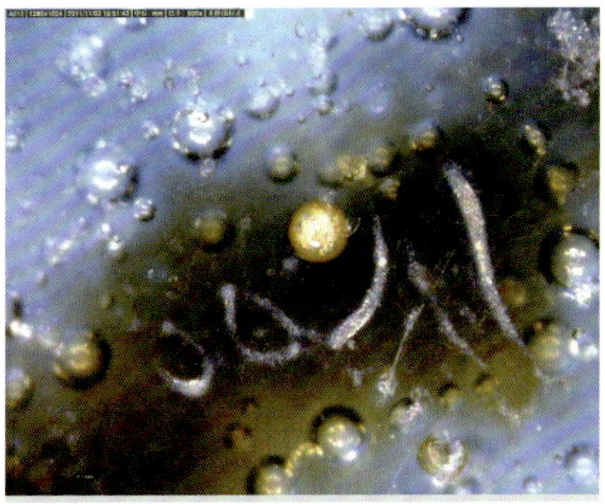

Sample Image 31

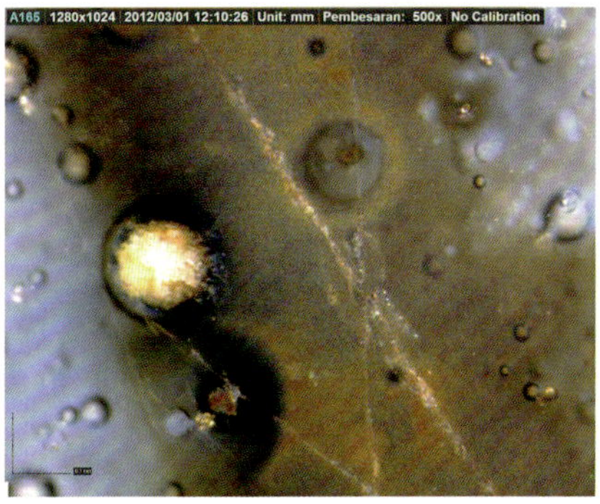

YUBSTAM Image 31

Three-Dimensional Sample Unbroken Mouth Textured Bubble Image

Three-Dimensional YUBSTAM Unbroken Mouth Textured Bubble Image

Sample Image 32

YUBSTAM Image 32

◆ Two-Dimensional Characteristics

1) Majority of the unbroken mouth textured bubbles on the test piece are frosted needlepoint bubbles (see Sample Image 30 & 31).

2) The internal materials are evenly distributed, and a single bubble presents with color spectrum (see Sample Image 30 & 31).

3) The interior weathering deposits are disparate. Some bubbles present with relatively less deposits and low density distribution, with the glass phase still visible in areas (see Sample Image 30); while others have high amounts of deposits and dense distribution in which the glass phase is no longer visible (see Sample Image 31).

◆ Three-Dimensional Characteristics

1) Aside from the few scratches, the glaze surface surrounding the bubble is smooth and clean (see Sample Image 32).

2) The area of the bubble visible through three-dimensional imaging is smaller than that of two-dimensional imaging (see Sample Image 32).

◆ Trace Nature Proofs

1) The characteristics of the test piece's unbroken mouth textured bubbles and those of the YUB Standard Trace Atlas Model are highly similar.

2) The color spectrum presenting in the bubble embodies the Ceramic Trace Law of Chromatic Aberration.

3) The three-dimensional characteristics of the textured bubbles are in accordance with the Quantitative Change Principle.

J. Broken Mouth Textured Bubble Comparison

Two-Dimensional Sample Broken Mouth Textured Bubble Image

Two-Dimensional YUBSTAM Broken Mouth Textured Bubble Image

Sample Image 33

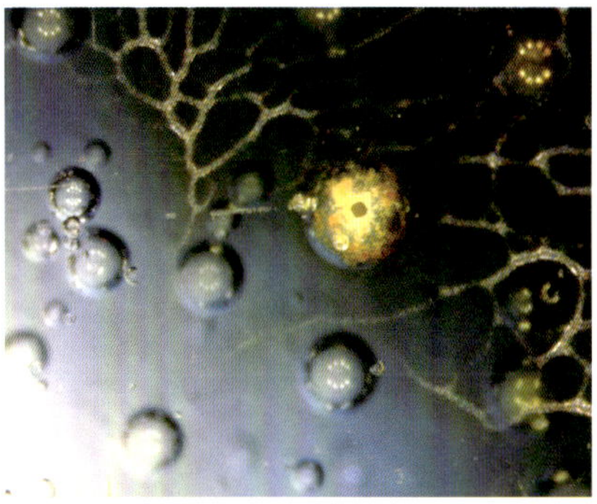

YUBSTAM Image 33

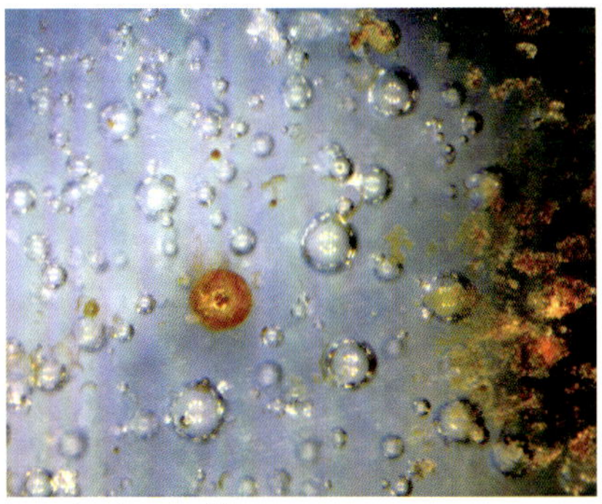

Sample Image 34

YUBSTAM Image 34

Three-Dimensional Sample Broken Mouth Textured Bubble Image

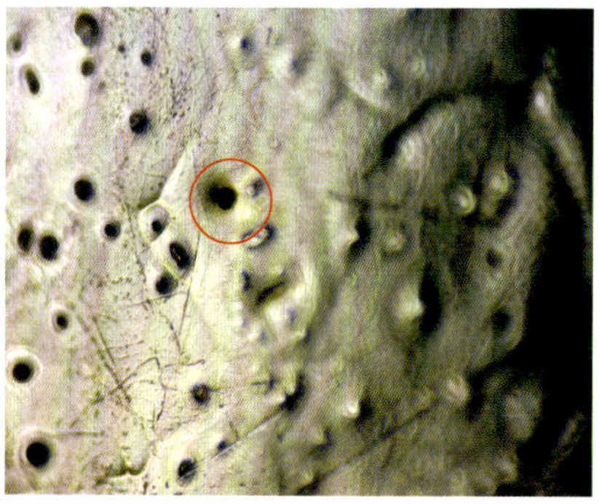

Sample Image 35

Three-Dimensional YUBSTAM Broken Mouth Textured Bubble Image

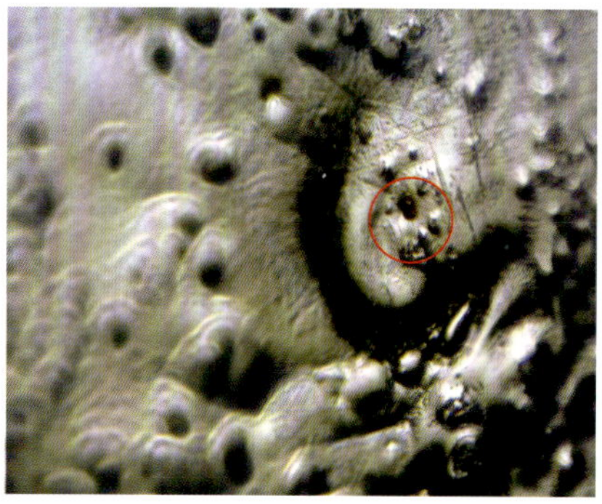

YUBSTAM Image 35

◆ Two-Dimensional Characteristics

1) Broken Mouth Bubbles include frosted needlepoint type (see Sample Image 33); and grainy needlepoint type (see Sample Image34).

2) The mouth of the frosted variety is irregularly shaped, and materials are visible below the mouth. The interior deposits are relatively evenly distributed and have color spectrum (see Sample Image 33).

3) The grainy variety deposits are relatively sparse and less densely distributed with glass phase visible between deposits and a single bubble presenting with color spectrum (see Sample Image 34).

◆ Three-Dimensional Characteristics

See Sample Image 35.

1) Only the bubble mouth is visible, clear and independent; the bubble form is not visible, which indicates that the weathering is all present within the interior of the bubble.

2) The mouth is rounded and smooth, and aside from a few bumps, the glaze surface is smooth and clean.

3) The bumps are areas of spilt phase and lower structural stability that can act as channels between the bubble and the external environment allowing for the bubble to weather and become textured. Additionally, the bubble mouth can also act as a weathering channel.

◆ Trace Nature Proofs

1) The characteristics of the test piece's broken mouth textured bubbles and those of the YUB Standard Trace Atlas Model are highly similar.

2) The color spectrum within the bubble embodies the Ceramic Trace Law of Chromatic Aberration.

3) The clearly delineated bubble mouth on the smooth clean glaze surface embodies the Ceramic Trace Law of Distinction.

4) The rounded smooth bubble mouth and its three-dimensional characteristics are all in accordance with the Quantitative Change Principle.

K. Comprehensive Glass and Gas Phase Appearance Comparison

Two-Dimensional Sample Glass and Gas Phase Appearance

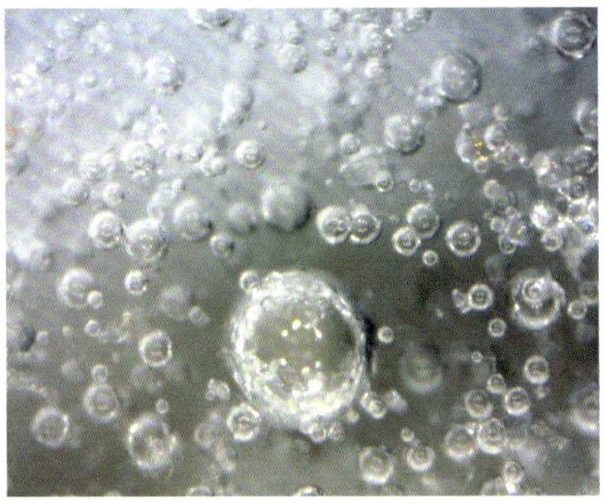

Sample Image 36

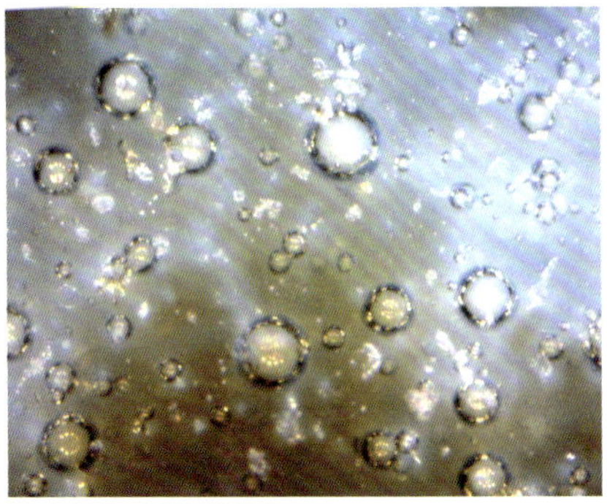

Sample Image 37

Two-Dimensional YUBSTAM Glass and Gas Phase Appearance

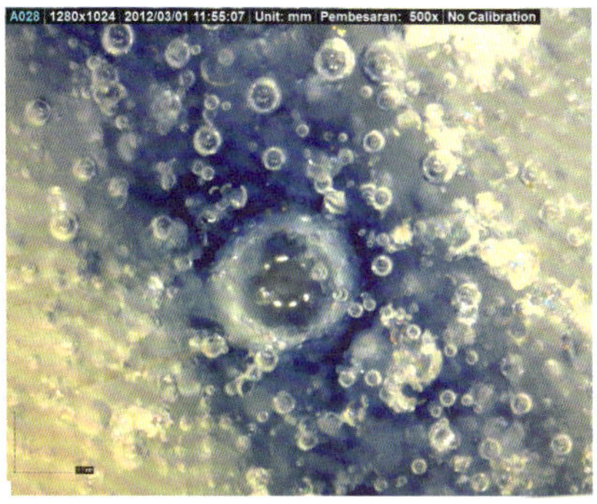

YUBSTAM Image 36

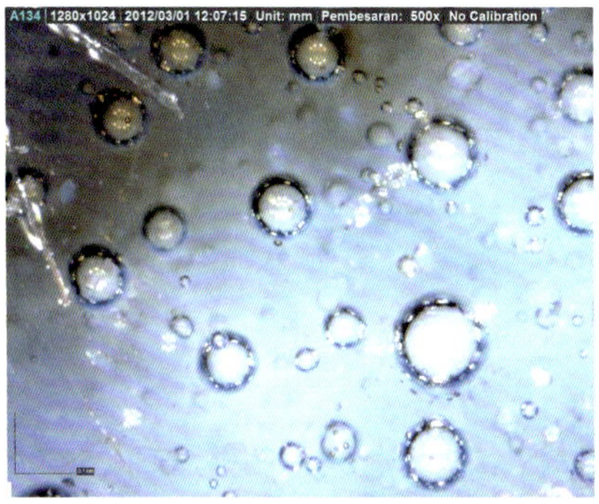

YUBSTAM Image 37

◆ Two-Dimensional Characteristics

1) The glass phase is pristinely clean, and is a clear type glass phase (see Sample Image 36 & 37).

2) Bubbles have relatively sparse distribution, and the size of bubbles within a unit image is widely disparate (see Sample Image 37).

3) A unit image can present with a single independent large bubble (see Sample Image 36).

◆ Trace Nature Proofs

The characteristics of the test piece's glass phase and bubble distribution and those of the YUB Standard Trace Atlas Model are highly similar; this indicates that the materials and techniques used in the firing of the test piece are consistent with YUB samples.

L. Bristle Pit Comparison

Two-Dimensional Sample Bristle Pit Image

Sample Image 38

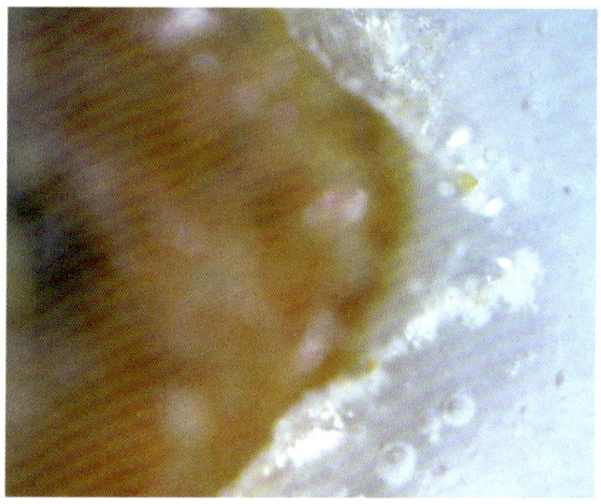

Sample Image 39

Two-Dimensional YUBSTAM Bristle Pit Image

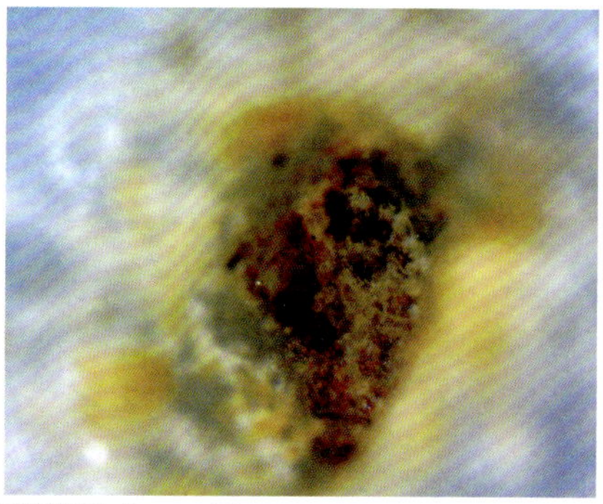

YUBSTAM Image 38

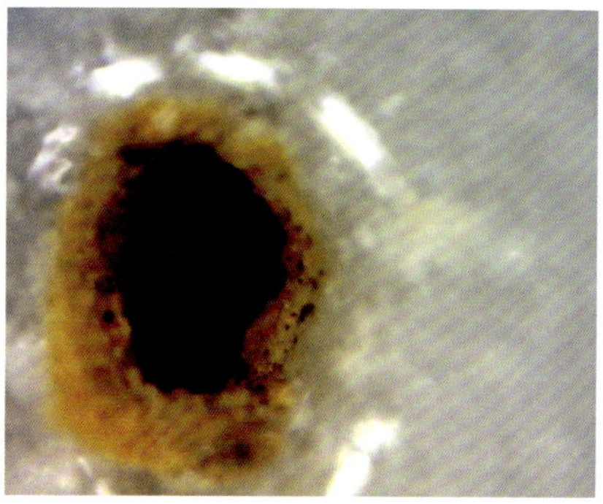

YUBSTAM Image 39

◆ Two-Dimensional Characteristics

1) Pit mouth is rounded and smooth (see Sample Image 38 & 39).

2) Pit interior has color spectrum as well as filaments and material deposits (see Sample Image 38).

3) Floccus mottling presents beneath the glaze surface surrounding the pit mouth (see Sample Image 39).

◆ Trace Nature Proofs

1) The characteristics of the test piece's bristle pits and those of the YUB Standard Trace Atlas Model are highly similar.

2) The rounded smooth mouth of the bristle pit is in accordance with the Quantitative Change Principle.

3) The floccus mottling beneath the glaze surface surrounding the bristle pit mouth embodies the Ceramic Trace Law of Gradation and is in accordance with the Passage of Time Principle.

4) The coloration as well as filaments and material deposits on the pit mouth and within the pit interior are all indicative of ceramic trace weathering multiplicity.

7. Trace Appearance Comparison Comprehensive Results

By using microscopic observation it has been found that the tested piece has eleven traces: flowing mottles, radiating mottles, needlepoint mottles, pit mottles, floccus mottles, flowing striae, CO striae, scratches, color change bubbles, textured bubbles, and bristle pits; of which eight are acquired traces (including needlepoint mottles, pit mottles, floccus mottles, CO striae, scratches, color change bubbles, textured bubbles, and bristle pits with trace multiplicity).

After comparison with the YUB Standard Trace Atlas Model it has been found that the piece's primary traces display material and firing technique characteristics consistent with YUB samples. This is in accordance with Quantitative Change and Passage of Time Principles, and embodies the Ceramic Trace Laws. Regardless of two or three-dimensional, images are all highly similar to the YUB Standard Trace Atlas Model, and have typical characteristics of YUB. Aside from this, the acquired trace quantity displays trace change multiplicity. Additionally, the trace locations are consistent with those of the YUB Standard Trace Atlas Model, and as such the locations of traces have rationality and traces occur with congruency. Therefore, from a trace appearance characteristics and trace nature principles and laws perspective, the tested piece and the YUB Standard Trace Atlas Model are highly similar and a sufficient match.

8. Trace Valuation and Authentication Result

A. The characteristics of the test piece and those of the YUB Standard Trace Atlas Model are highly similar; this indicates that the materials and techniques used in the firing of the test piece are consistent with YUB samples, and as such the piece receives full points for Matching YUB Materials and Techniques: 10 Points.

B. The traces of the tested piece are in accordance with the Quantitative Change Principle, and as such receives full points for Matching The Ceramic Trace Model Quantitative Change Principle: 20 Points.

C. The traces of the tested piece are in accordance with the Passage of Time Principle, and as such receives full points for Matching The Ceramic Trace Model Passage of Time Principle: 20 Points.

D. The number of acquired trace types on the test piece was 8, and as such it is in accordance with trace multiplicity, it receives 40 of the 45 available points for Matching YUB Typical Characteristics and Multiplicity Characteristics: 40 Points.

E. The locations of traces on the test piece are consistent with those of the YUB Standard Trace Atlas Model, and as such Matches Ceramics Trace Location Rationality. In addition, traces also have Proper Congruency, and as such the piece receives full points for this category: 5 Points.

F. After conducting Trace Comparison with the YUB Standard Trace Atlas Model, and Nature of Trace Proofs on the test piece; the test piece's traces received a score of 95 Points, and as such this piece has been proven to be a genuine article of Yuan Dynasty Underglaze Blue Porcelain.

参考文献
References

[1]. 龚轼. 陶歌[M]. http://wenku.baidu.com/view/0ea4848702d276a200292e9b.html.

[2]. 叶喆民. 中国陶瓷史[M]. 北京：三联书店,2006.

[3]. 冯先铭. 中国陶瓷[M]. 上海：上海古籍出版社,2006.

[4]. 李辉柄. 青花瓷器鉴定[M]. 北京：紫禁城出版社,2012.

[5].百度百科 http://baike.baidu.com/view/33124.htm.

[6]. 张志刚,郭演仪,陈尧成. 唐代青花瓷器研讨[J]. 景德镇陶瓷学院学报,1989(2)：65-72.

[7]. 张志刚,罗宗真,郭演仪,陈尧成. 扬州唐城出土青花瓷的测定极其重要意义[J]. 中国陶瓷,1984(3)：56-59.

[8]. 赵青云,张学. 中国唐青花瓷研究[M]. 合肥：黄山书社,2011.

[9]. 吴仁敬,辛安潮. 中国陶瓷史[M]. 上海：上海书店,1937.

[10]. 夏鼐. 巴黎伦敦展出的新中国出土文物巡礼[J]. 考古,1973(3)：170-177.

[11]. 罗学正. 青花瓷产生与发展规律探讨[J]. 江西文物,1990(2)：11-16.

[12]. 陈雨前,朱浙安. 宋代景德镇青白瓷"尚玉"审美意蕴研究[J]. 中国陶瓷,2006,42(12)：58-62.

[13]. 同[12].

[14]. 陶宗仪. 南村辍耕录[M]. 北京：中华书局,2004.

[15]. 宋濂. 元史[M]. 北京：中华书局,1976.

[16]. 同[15].

[17]. 同[14].

[18]. 刘新园. 元代窑事小考（一）[J]. 景德镇陶瓷学院学报,1981,2(1)：67-78.

[19]. 徐玉玲,程红璞,李丽艳. 从元代青花的审美特征看青花瓷的发展趋势[J]. 中国陶瓷,2010,46(2)：71-74.

[20]. 袁南征. 再谈元青花[J]. 2012上海元代青花瓷器国际学术研讨会论文稿（一）,2012：123-126.

[21]. 陈克伦. 元青花研究中的几个问题[J]. 2012上海元代青花瓷器国际学术研讨会论文稿（一）,2012：1-9.

[22]. 黄云鹏. 黄窑说瓷[M]. 南昌：江西美术出版社,2009.

[23]. 柯玫瑰. 伊朗和印尼留存的元青花[J]. 2012上海元代青花瓷器国际学术研讨会论文稿（二）,2012：487-491.

[24]. 陈尧成,郭演仪,陈虹. 中国元代青花钴料来源探讨[J]. 中国陶瓷,1993(5)：57-62.

[25]. 同[20].

[26]. 刘新园,白焜. 高岭土史考——兼论瓷石、高岭与景德镇十至十九世纪的制瓷业. 景德镇陶瓷网. http://www.cnjdz.net/new/ceramics/taoci/2003/0314204343.htm.

[27]. 同[20].

[28]. 同[18].

[29]. 同[18].

[30]. 蔡路武,熊樱菲. 湖北元青花的新发现及相关问题探讨[J]. 2012上海元代青花瓷器国际学术研讨会论文稿（二）,2012：379-393.

[31]. 同[18].

[32]. 汪庆正. 元青花及明洪武瓷议[J]. 景德镇陶瓷,1983(1)：34-36.

[33]. 黄薇,黄清华. 元青花瓷器早期类型的新发现——从实证角度论元青花瓷器的起源[J]. 2012上海元代青花瓷器国际学术研讨会论文稿（二）,2012：394-406.

[34]. 同[21].

[35]. 同[33].

[36]. 同[33].

[37]. 同[18].

[38]. 同[32].

[39]. 张浦生,霍华. 横空出世的元末明初人物图青花瓷[J]. 2012上海元代青花瓷器国际学术研讨会论文稿（一）,2012：41-53.
[40]. 同[39].
[41]. 周丽丽. 关于元青花戏曲人物故事图瓷器性质的认识[J]. 2012上海元代青花瓷器国际学术研讨会论文稿（一）,2012：81-106.
[42]. 徐松. 宋会要辑稿[M]. 北京：中华书局, 1957.
[43]. 陈垣. 沈刻元典章校补[M]. 北京：北京大学研究所国学门, 1931.
[44]. 同[21].
[45]. 上海博物馆. 幽蓝神采元代青花瓷器特集[M]. 上海：上海书画出版社,2012.
[46]. 同[45].
[47]. 蒋祁. 陶记 [M].
[48]. 同[18].
[49]. 同[45].
[50]. 刘兴. 江苏丹徒元代窖藏瓷[J]. 文物,1982(2)：27-29.
[51]. 肖梦龙. 江苏金坛元代青花云龙罐窖藏[J]. 文物,1980(1)：61-64,104.
[52]. 陈世华. 句容出土元代青花瓷器[J]. 东南文化,1991(3)：229-230.
[53]. 介绍一件元青花盖罐[J]. 文物,1991(7)：53,107.
[54]. 南京南郊明墓清理简报[J]. 南方文物,1997(1)：29-32.
[55]. 南京江宁县明沐晟墓清理简报[J]. 考古,1960(9)：12,45-49.
[56]. 南京中华门外明墓清理简报[J]. 考古,1962(9)：7-8,30-38
[57]. 南京明汪兴祖墓清理简报[J]. 考古,1972(4)：24,32-34,71-72.
[58]. 河北省博物馆. 保定市发现一批元代瓷器[J]. 文物,1965(2)：19-20,24,60-62.
[59]. 河北省文物研究所. 河北定兴元代窖藏文物[J]. 文物,1986(1)：91-93,97,106.
[60]. 中国科学院考古研究所,北京市文物管理处,元大都考古队. 元大都的勘查和发掘[J].考古,1972(1)：20-29,73-75.
[61]. 冯先铭. 我国陶瓷发展中的几个问题——从中国出土文物展览陶瓷展品谈起[J]. 文物,1973(7)：16,22-31,89-90.
[62]. 林西县文物管理所. 内蒙古林西县元代瓷器窖藏[J]. 文物,2001(8)：3,74-78,85.
[63]. 唐汉三,李福臣,张松柏.内蒙古赤峰大营子元代瓷器窖藏[J]. 文物,1984(5)：91-95.
[64]. 李彩萍. 呼和浩特东郊保合少出土窖藏金元瓷器[J]. 内蒙古文物考古,1994(1)：92-96.
[65]. 王霞，元代集宁路古城遗址出土瓷器解读[J].北方文物，2008（3）：56-58.
[66]. 新疆博物馆. 新疆伊犁地区霍城县出土的元青花瓷等文物[J]. 文物,1979(8)：28-33.
[67]. 刘裕黑,熊琳. 江西高安县发现元青花、釉里红等瓷器窖藏[J]. 文物,1982(4)：60-71,104-105.
[68]. 萍乡市博物馆. 萍乡市发现元代青花瓷器等窖藏文物[J]. 江西历史文物,1986(1)：49-51,153-154.
[69]. 江西波阳县出土的元代瓷器[J]. 文物,1976(11)：89-90,104.
[70]. 上饶市出土两件元代青花玉壶春瓶[J]. 江西文物,1990(2)：122-123,127.
[71]. 江西九江发现元代青花瓷器[J]. 文物,1992(6)：96-97,109.
[72]. 叶涵鋆,夏跃南,胡承恩.歙县出土两批窖藏元瓷珍品[J]. 文物,1988(5)：87-90,107.
[73]. 蚌埠市博物展览馆. 明汤和墓清理简报[J]. 文物,1977(2)：38-42,101.
[74]. 桑坚信. 杭州市发现的元代瓷器窖藏[J]. 文物,1989(11)：23-29,105.
[75]. 景竹友. 三台出土元代窖藏[J]. 四川文物,1993(6)：64-67.
[76]. 同[61].
[77]. 谢明良. 元代青花瓷备忘录[J]. 2012上海元代青花瓷器国际学术研讨会论文稿（一）,2012：23-28.
[78]. 同[41].
[79]. 同[23].
[80]. 同[21].
[81]. 同[21].

[82]. 庄良有. 菲律宾与印尼的元青花瓷[J]. 2012上海元代青花瓷器国际学术研讨会论文稿（二）,2012：478-486.
[83]. 同[82].
[84]. 同[82].
[85]. 同[82].
[86]. 同[82].
[87]. 南京市文物保管委员会. 南京江宁县明沐晟墓清理简报[J]. 考古,1962(9)：31-36.
[88]. Photograph © [2013] Museum of Fine Arts, Boston. Meiping-shaped vase with blueand-white decoration of Daoist immortals Chinese, Yuan dynasty, mid-14th century Porcelain, Jingdezhen ware Overall：42.4cm (16 11/16in.) Other (diameter of foot)：13cm (5 1/8 in.) Museum of Fine Arts, Boston Harriet Otis Cruft Fund and Seth Kettell Sweetser Fund 24.113
[89]. 冯先铭. 中国古陶瓷图典[M]. 北京：文物出版社,1998.
[90]. 同[45].
[91]. 许之衡. 饮流斋说瓷[M]. 济南：山东画报出版社,2010：13.
[92]. 同[88].
[93]. 同[45].
[94]. 同[89].
[95]. 任志录. 玉壶春瓶略论[J]. 故宫学刊, 2009(5)：754-799.
[96]. 同[89].
[97]. 同[89].
[98]. 同[45].
[99]. 同[45].
[100]. 陈定荣. 元代青花瓷造型装饰溯源[J]. 江西文物, 1990(2)：32-39.
[101]. 孟夏, 肖福科. 论元青花的基本特征及其造物思想[J]. 陶瓷科学与技术, 2008(3)：72-74.
[102]. 同[45].
[103]. 同[45].
[104]. 叶佩兰. 元代瓷器[M]. 北京：九州图书出版社, 1998.
[105]. 同[45].
[106]. 刘新园. 元青花特异纹饰和将作院所属浮梁磁局与画局[J]. 景德镇陶瓷学院学报, 1982(3)：9-20.
[107]. 同[106].
[108]. 斐光辉. 至正型青花瓷[M]. 福州：福建美术出版社, 2004.
[109]. 彭涛. 细分“至正型”元青花的尝试[J]. 2012上海元代青花瓷器国际学术研讨会论文稿（一）,2012：41-53.
[110]. 同[21].
[111]. 周丽丽. 瓷器宗教纹样、吉祥图案综述[J]. 上海博物馆集刊, 1996(00)：120-143.
[112]. 同[111].
[113]. 同[89].
[114]. 孙瀛洲. 陶瓷研究与鉴定[M]. 北京：紫禁城出版社, 2008.
[115]. 林业强. 元青花龙纹考：以至正瓶为中心 [J]. 2012上海元代青花瓷器国际学术研讨会论文稿（二）,2012：127-144.
[116]. 同[114].
[117]. 同[108].
[118]. 同[89].
[119]. 同[114].
[120]. 周高亮, 栾兆鹏. 元青花纹饰题材初探[J]. 中原文物, 2012(4)：83-87.
[121]. 同[106].
[122]. 同[106].
[123]. 同[114].
[124]. 刘毅. 元青花人物图案分析[J]. 2012上海元代青花瓷器国际学术研讨会论文稿（二）,2012：222-225.
[125]. 同[45].
[126]. 同[124].
[127]. 同[124].
[128]. 同[111].
[129]. 马希桂. 中国元青花[M]. 上海：上海古籍出版社, 1999.
[130]. 同[106].
[131]. 同[129].
[132]. 同[111].
[133]. 黄云鹏. 元青花的装饰特色[J]. 江西文物, 1990(2)：29-31.
[134]. 陆军,于昕. 浅谈水墨画在青花中的应用[J]. 景德镇陶瓷, 2010(04)：15-17.
[135]. 熊炜. 论中国画笔法[J]. 江苏教育学院学报, 2009,25(4)：76-78.
[136]. 朱裕平. 青花瓷的绘画笔法[J]. 上海工艺美术, 2002(1)：41-42.
[137]. 徐铮铮. 元代青花瓷器绘

画风格及其形成原因[D]. 重庆：重庆大学美术系，2006.
[138]. 同[137].
[139]. 同[137].
[140]. 同[21].
[141]. 李家治，陈显求，张福康，郭演仪,陈士萍. 中国古代陶瓷科学技术成就[M]. 上海：上海科学技术出版社，1985.
[142]. 同[141].
[143]. 陈尧成，郭演仪，陈虹. 中国元代青花钴料来源探讨[J]. 中国陶瓷，1993(5)：57-62.
[144]. 同[141].
[145]. 同[141].
[146]. 张福康. 中国古陶瓷的科学[M]. 上海：上海人民美术出版社,2000.
[147]. 冯先铭，安志敏，安金槐，朱伯谦，汪庆正. 中国陶瓷史[M]. 北京：文物出版社，1982.
[148]. 李家治. 中国科学技术史（陶瓷卷）[M]. 北京：科学出版社，1998.
[149]. 同[141].
[150]. 陈尧成，张志刚，郭演仪. 历代青花瓷器和青花色料的研究[J]. 硅酸盐学报,1978,6(4)：225-241. http：//www.cnki.net/KCMS/detail/detail.aspx?QueryID=40&CurRec=1&recid=&filename=GXYB197804000&dbname=CJFD1979&dbcode=CJFQ&pr=&urlid=&yx=.
[151]. 同[141].
[152]. 同[148].
[153]. 陈治戈，蒋孝锋，鲁虹. 服装设计的计算机方法[M]. 南京：江苏科学技术出版社，2005.
[154]. 同[153].
[155]. 同[106].
[156]. Canby, S.R. 2009, Shah ‘Abbas The Remaking of Iran, The British Museum Press, London.
[157]. 吴隽，李家治. 景德镇历代青花瓷胎釉化学组成的多元统计分析[J]. 陶瓷学报，1997,18(3)：130-135.
[158]. 同[26].
[159]. 同[106].
[160]. 同[146].
[161]. 同[89].
[162]. 同[89].
[163]. 同[22].
[164]. 同[22].
[165]. 同[22].
[166]. 同[22].
[167]. 同[22].
[168]. 同[22].
[169]. 同[22].
[170]. 同[22].
[171]. 同[89].
[172]. 同[22].
[173]. 同[22].
[174]. 同[22].
[175]. 同[22].
[176]. 同[22].
[177]. 同[22].
[178]. 同[22].
[179]. 同[22].
[180]. 同[22].
[181]. 同[22].
[182]. 同[22].
[183]. 同[22].
[184]. 同[22].
[185]. 同[22].
[186]. 陈正兰，叶福华. 元青花瓷鉴赏[J]. 景德镇陶瓷，2013(1)：134.
[187]. 同[89].
[188]. 同[89].
[189]. 同[89].
[190]. 同[22].
[191]. 李家驹. 陶瓷工艺学[M]. 北京：中国工业出版社，2010.
[192]. 同[191].
[193]. 同[191].
[194]. 同[191].
[195]. 陈尧成，张志刚，郭演仪. 中国古代陶瓷科学技术成就[M]. 上海：上海科学技术出版社，1985.
[196]. 郭演仪，陈尧成. 元大都发掘的青花和影青瓷[J]. 考古，1982(1)：101.
[197]. 同[146].
[198]. 罗宏杰，李家治，高力明. 中国古瓷中钙系釉类型划分标准及其在瓷釉研究中的应用[J]. 硅酸盐通报,1995(2)：50-53. http：//www.cnki.net/KCMS/detail/detail.aspx?QueryID=44&CurRec=1&recid=&filename=GSYT199502010&dbname=CJFD1995&dbcode=CJFQ&pr=&urlid=&yx=.
[199]. 田英良，孙诗兵. 新编陶瓷工艺学[M]. 北京：中国轻工业出版社,2009.
[200]. 李丽霞，贾茹. 硅酸盐物理化学[M]. 天津：天津大学出版社,2010.

[201]. 曹志峰, 赵志强. 重火石光学玻璃化学稳定性的研究[J]. 长春光学精密机械学院学报, 1987,31(2): 59-65.http://www.cnki.net/KCMS/detail/detail.aspx?QueryID=64&CurRec=1&recid=&filename=CGJM198702010&dbname=CJFD1987&dbcode=CJFQ&pr=&urlid=&yx=.
[202]. 赵彦钊, 殷海荣. 玻璃工艺学[M]. 北京: 化学工业出版社,2006.
[203]. 冯明良. 玻璃表面之组成, 结构与特性[J]. 玻璃, 1986(2): 39-42. http://www.cnki.net/KCMS/detail/detail.aspx?QueryID=20&CurRec=1&recid=&filename=BLZZ198602011&dbname=CJFD1986&dbcode=CJFQ&pr=&urlid=&yx=.
[204]. 王承遇, 陶瑛. 玻璃的表面结构和性质[J]. 硅酸盐通报,1982(1): 24-34. http://www.cnki.net/KCMS/detail/detail.aspx?QueryID=24&CurRec=1&recid=&filename=GSYT198201007&dbname=CJFD1982&dbcode=CJFQ&pr=&urlid=&yx=.
[205]. 同[191].
[206]. 同[191].
[207]. http://www.flickr.com/photos/nasacommons/7544559478/sizes/l/in/photostream/.
[208]. http://www.cnsa.gov.cn/n1081/n7619/n7905/45514.html.
[209]. 张金升, 张银燕, 王美婷, 许凤秀. 陶瓷材料显微结构与性能[M]. 北京: 化学工业出版社,2007.
[210]. 同[191].
[211]. 吴隽, 李家治, 郭景坤.景德镇青花瓷彩上斑点显微结构的研究[J]. 无机材料学报, 1999(1): 143-149.
[212]. 王承遇, 陶瑛. 硅酸盐玻璃的风化[J]. 硅酸盐学报,2003,31(1): 78-85.http://www.cnki.net/KCMS/detail/detail.aspx?QueryID=28&CurRec=1&recid=&filename=GXYB200301016&dbname=CJFD2003&dbcode=CJFQ&pr=&urlid=&yx=.
[213]. 同[202].
[214]. 杭州南宋官窑博物馆. 南宋官窑文集[M]. 北京: 文物出版社,2004.
[215]. 同[212].
[216]. 同[214].
[217]. 戴树桂. 环境化学[M]. 北京: 高等教育出版社,2006.
[218]. 同[217].
[219]. 同[217].
[220]. 马燕如. 我国水下考古发掘陶瓷器的脱盐保护初探[J]. 博物馆研究, 2007,97(1): 85-89. http://www.cnki.net/KCMS/detail/detail.aspx?QueryID=36&CurRec=1&recid=&filename=BWYJ200701019&dbname=CJFD2007&dbcode=CJFQ&pr=&urlid=&yx=.
[221]. 同[150].
[222]. 吴隽. 古陶瓷科技研究与鉴定[M]. 北京: 科学出版社,2009.
[223]. 同[26].
[224]. 同[212].